SO-EDH-042

Free Methodist Church
2746 Ocean Beach Hwy.
Longview, WA 98632

ASBURY
BIBLE
COMMENTARY

ASBURY BIBLE COMMENTARY

Eugene E. Carpenter
General Editor
Old Testament Section and General Articles

Wayne McCown
General Editor
New Testament Section

ZondervanPublishingHouse
Academic and Professional Books
Grand Rapids, Michigan
A Division of HarperCollinsPublishers

Asbury Bible Commentary
Copyright © 1992 by The Zondervan Corporation

Requests for information should be addressed to:
Zondervan Publishing House
Academic and Professional Books
Grand Rapids, Michigan 49530

Library of Congress Cataloging-in-Publication Data

Asbury Bible commentary / Eugene E. Carpenter and Wayne McCown,
    general editors.
        p.   cm.
    Includes bibliographical references.
    ISBN 0-310-39640-9
    1. Bible—Commentaries. 2. Bible—Theology. I. Carpenter.
Eugene E., 1943- . II. McCown, Wayne.
BS491.2.A72 1992
220.7—dc20   90-47578
                                                        CIP

Jacket design by Kurt Dietsch
Jacket photo by The Crosiers

Printed in the United States of America

92 93 94 95 96 / DH / 10 9 8 7 6 5 4 3 2 1

This edition is printed on acid-free paper and meets the American National Standards Institute Z39.48
standard.

CONTENTS

PART III: THE NEW TESTAMENT

CONTRIBUTORS

BILL T. ARNOLD
  Associate Professor of Old
    Testament and Semitic
    Languages, Ashland
    Theological Seminary,
    Ashland, Ohio

DAVID R. BAUER
  Associate Professor of Biblical
    Studies, Asbury Theological
    Seminary, Wilmore, Kentucky

ROBERT D. BRANSON
  Professor of Biblical Studies,
    Warner Southern College,
    Lake Wales, Florida

TERRY L. BRENSINGER
  Associate Professor of Biblical
    Studies, Messiah College,
    Grantham, Pennsylvania

K E BROWER
  Dean and Lecturer in New
    Testament, Nazarene
    Theological College,
    Manchester, England

WAYNE E. CALDWELL
  General Editor, The Wesleyan
    Church, Indianapolis, Indiana

WILLIAM R. CANNON
  A Bishop of the United Methodist
    Church (ret.), Atlanta,
    Georgia

EUGENE E. CARPENTER
  Director of Graduate Studies and
    Professor of Old Testament
    and Biblical Languages, Bethel
    College, Mishawaka, Indiana

ANTHONY CASURELLA
  Professor of New Testament,
    Western Evangelical Seminary,
    Portland, Oregon

MILO L. CHAPMAN
  President Emeritus, Warner Pacific
    College, Portland, Oregon

JOSEPH E. COLESON
  Professor of Hebrew Scriptures,
    Roberts Wesleyan College,
    Rochester, New York

OWEN P. DICKENS
  Associate Professor of Religion,
    Asbury College, Wilmore,
    Kentucky

JOSEPH R. DONGELL
  Assistant Professor of Biblical
    Studies, Asbury Theological
    Seminary, Wilmore, Kentucky

H. RAY DUNNING
  Professor of Theology, Trevecca
    Nazarene College, Nashville,
    Tennessee

JOEL B. GREEN
  Academic Dean and Associate
    Professor of New Testament,
    New College Berkeley,
    Berkeley, California

VICTOR P. HAMILTON
  Professor of Religion, Asbury
    College, Wilmore, Kentucky

VERN A. HANNAH
  Dean of Academics, Canadian
    Nazarene College, Winnipeg,
    Manitoba

JOEL H. HUNT
  Assistant Professor of Old
    Testament Studies, C. P.
    Haggard School of Theology,
    Azusa Pacific University,
    Azusa, California

DAN G. JOHNSON
Senior Minister, Indian River City United Methodist Church, Titusville, Florida

DAVID W. KENDALL
Senior Pastor, First Free Methodist Church, McPherson, Kansas

DENNIS F. KINLAW
Chancellor, Asbury College, Wilmore, Kentucky

GEORGE KUFELDT
Professor Emeritus of Old Testament, School of Theology, Anderson University, Anderson, Indiana

GEORGE HERBERT LIVINGSTON
Professor Emeritus of Old Testament, Asbury Theological Seminary, Wilmore, Kentucky

GEORGE LYONS
Professor of Biblical Literature, Northwest Nazarene College, Nampa, Idaho

WAYNE MCCOWN
Senior Vice President and Provost, Roberts Wesleyan College, Rochester, New York

ALAN J. MEENAN
Senior Pastor, First Presbyterian Church, Amarillo, Texas

ROY F. MELEUGIN
Gould and Marie Cloud Professor of Religion, Austin College, Sherman, Texas

M. ROBERT MULHOLLAND, JR.
Vice President and Professor of New Testament, Asbury Theological Seminary, Wilmore, Kentucky

E. HERBERT NYGREN
Professor Emeritus of Religion and Philosophy, Taylor University, Upland, Indiana

JOHN N. OSWALT
Professor of Old Testament and Semitic Languages, Asbury Theological Seminary, Wilmore, Kentucky

CARL SCHULTZ
Professor of Old Testament and Chair, Division of Religion and Philosophy, Houghton College, Houghton, New York

LANE SCOTT
Professor of Theology and Ethics, C. P. Haggard School of Theology, Azusa Pacific University, Azusa, California

R. LARRY SHELTON
Pastor, Eastside Four Square Church, Kirkland, Washington

FRANK ANTHONY SPINA
Professor of Old Testament, The School of Religion, Seattle Pacific University, Seattle, Washington

JOHN STANLEY
Associate Professor of Bible, Warner Pacific College, Portland, Oregon

LAWSON G. STONE
Associate Professor of Old Testament, Asbury Theological Seminary, Wilmore, Kentucky

DAVID L. THOMPSON
F. M. and Ada Thompson Professor of Biblical Studies, Asbury Theological Seminary, Wilmore, Kentucky

DONALD A. D. THORSEN
Associate Professor of Theology, C. P. Haggard School of Theology, Azusa Pacific University, Azusa, California

WESLEY E. VANDERHOOF
Professor of Biblical Literature and
Religion, Dean of
Undergraduate Curriculum
and Registrar, Roberts
Wesleyan College, Rochester,
New York

ALEXANDER VARUGHESE
Professor of Religion, Mount
Vernon Nazarene College,
Mount Vernon, Ohio

WILLIAM H. VERMILLION
Pastor, Oregon City Evangelical
Church, Oregon City, Oregon

ARTHUR W. WAINWRIGHT
Professor of New Testament,
Candler School of Theology,
Emory University, Atlanta,
Georgia

JOHN R. WALTERS
Collection Development Librarian
and Assistant Professor of
New Testament, Asbury
Theological Seminary,
Wilmore, Kentucky

JOSEPH S. WANG
Professor of New Testament,
Asbury Theological Seminary,
Wilmore, Kentucky

LAURENCE W. WOOD
Frank Paul Morris Professor of
Systematic Theology, Asbury
Theological Seminary,
Wilmore, Kentucky

JAMES D. YODER
Professor Emeritus of New
Testament Language and
Literature, Evangelical School
of Theology, Myerstown,
Pennsylvania

ABBREVIATIONS

WORKS CITED

AB	*Anchor Bible, The*
ANET	*Ancient Near Eastern Texts*
ASV	*American Standard Version*
BBC	*Beacon Bible Commentary*
BE	*Bible Expositor, The*
BI	*Biblical Illustrator*
BSC	*Bible Student's Commentary*
BNTC	*Black's New Testament Commentaries*
CBC	*Cambridge Bible Commentary*
CBQ	*Catholic Biblical Quarterly*
DSBS	*Daily Study Bible Series, The*
DV	*Douay Version*
EBC	*Expositor's Bible Commentary, The*
HBC	*Harper's Bible Commentary*
HBD	*Harper's Bible Dictionary*
HCS	*Hermeneia Commentary Series*
HE	*Ecclesiastical History, Eusebius*
HNTC	*Harper's New Testament Commentaries*
IB	*Interpreter's Bible, The*
IBC	*International Bible Commentary, The*
ICC	*International Critical Commentary*
IDB	*Interpreter's Dictionary of the Bible*
IDBS	*Interpreter's Dictionary of the Bible Supplement*
IOT	*Introduction to the Old Testament, R. K. Harrison*
ISBC	*International Standard Bible Commentary*
ITC	*International Theological Commentary*
JB	*Jerusalem Bible*
JBL	*Journal of Biblical Literature*
JPS	*Jewish Publication Society*
KJV	*King James Version*
LBC	*Layman's Bible Commentary*
LXX	*Septuagint, The*
MT	*Masoretic Text*

MNTC	*Moffatt New Testament Commentary, The*
NASB	*New American Standard Bible*
NBC	*New Bible Commentary, The*
NBD	*New Bible Dictionary, The*
NCBC	*New Century Bible Commentary*
NEB	*New English Bible*
NEBC	*New English Bible Commentaries*
NIC	*New International Commentary*
NICNT	*New International Commentary on the New Testament*
NICOT	*New International Commentary on the Old Testament*
NIDBA	*The New International Dictionary of Biblical Archaeology*
NIGTC	*New International Greek Testament Commentary*
NIV	*New International Version*
NKJV	*New King James Version*
OTL	*Old Testament Library*
OTMS	*Old Testament Message Series*
PC	*Pulpit Commentaries*
RSV	*Revised Standard Version*
SBLDS	*Society of Biblical Literature Dissertation Series*
SPCK	*Society for the Propagation of Christian Knowledge*
TB	*Tyndale Bulletin*
TBC	*Torch Bible Commentaries*
TNTC	*Tyndale New Testament Commentaries*
TOTC	*Tyndale Old Testament Commentaries*
UBS	*United Bible Societies*
WBC	*Wesleyan Bible Commentary, The*
WdBC	*Word Biblical Commentary*
Wycliffe	*Wycliffe Bible Commentary, The*
ZPEB	*Zondervan Pictorial Encyclopedia of the Bible, The*

OLD TESTAMENT

Ge	Genesis

Ex	Exodus	Php	Philippians
Lev	Leviticus	Col	Colossians
Nu	Numbers	1Th	1 Thessalonians
Dt	Deuteronomy	2Th	2 Thessalonians
Jos	Joshua	1Ti	1 Timothy
Jdg	Judges	2Ti	2 Timothy
Ru	Ruth	Tit	Titus
1Sa	1 Samuel	Phm	Philemon
2Sa	2 Samuel	Heb	Hebrews
1Ki	1 Kings	Jas	James
2Ki	2 Kings	1Pe	1 Peter
1Ch	1 Chronicles	2Pe	2 Peter
2Ch	2 Chronicles	1Jn	1 John
Ezr	Ezra	2Jn	2 John
Ne	Nehemiah	3Jn	3 John
Est	Esther	Jude	Jude
Job	Job	Rev	Revelation
Ps(s)	Psalm(s)		
Pr	Proverbs		

APOCRYPHA

Ecc	Ecclesiastes	1Es	1 Esdras
SS	Song of Songs	2Es	2 Esdras
Isa	Isaiah	Tb	Tobit
Jer	Jeremiah	Jth	Judith
La	Lamentations	RE	The Rest of Esther
Eze	Ezekiel	WS	The Wisdom of Solomon
Da	Daniel	Eccus	Ecclesiasticus
Hos	Hosea	Bar	Baruch
Joel	Joel	STHC	The Song of the Three Holy Children
Am	Amos		
Ob	Obadiah	Sus	Susanna
Jnh	Jonah	Bel	Bel and the Dragon
Mic	Micah	PrM	Prayer of Manasses
Na	Nahum	1Mc	1 Maccabees
Hab	Habakkuk	2Mc	2 Maccabees
Zep	Zephaniah		
Hag	Haggai		

PSEUDEPIGRAPHA

Zec	Zechariah	AM	Assumption of Moses
Mal	Malachi	2Ba	Syriac Apocalypse of Baruch
		3Ba	Greek Apocalypse of Baruch

NEW TESTAMENT

Mt	Matthew	1En	Ethiopic Book of Enoch
Mk	Mark	2En	Slavonic Book of Enoch
Lk	Luke	3En	Hebrew Book of Enoch
Jn	John	4Ezr	4 Ezra
Ac	Acts	JA	Joseph and Asenath
Ro	Romans	Jub	Book of Jubilees
1Co	1 Corinthians	Aris	Letter of Aristeas
2Co	2 Corinthians	Adam	Life of Adam and Eve
Gal	Galatians	LP	Life of the Prophets
Eph	Ephesians	MA Isa	Martyrdom and Ascension of Isaiah

3Mc	3 Maccabees	TBen	Testament of Benjamin
4Mc	4 Maccabees	TDan	Testament of Dan
OS	Odes of Solomon	TGad	Testament of Gad
PJ	Paralipomena of Jeremiah	TJob	Testament of Job
PA	Pirke Aboth	TJos	Testament of Joseph
Ps 151	Psalm 151	TLevi	Testament of Levi
PS	Psalms of Solomon	TNaph	Testament of Naphtali
Sib	Sibylline Oracles	TPat	Testament of the Twelve Patriarchs
Ahi	Story of Ahikar		
TAb	Testament of Abraham	ZF	Zadokite Fragments
TAd	Testament of Adam		

PART I

General Articles

GENERAL INTRODUCTION

William R. Cannon

The Bible is the single source of the faith and morals set forth in the Christian religion. Though biblical teaching and practices may be amplified by tradition and explicated and even justified by various systems of philosophy, their basic conceptions and original models are provided by God in sacred Scripture so that the Bible is the sole foundation on which both Christian theology and ethics are built. The doctrines of the Christian church were propounded by councils and theologians subsequent to the completion of the Bible and are developments from principles contained therein. But these doctrines in no way contradict the Scripture or infringe upon and contravene its divine oracles and commandments and its blessed promises, which give life and hope to all who believe. Rather, they are like flowers that spring from biblical seeds. The germinal ideas for all Christian doctrines are in the Bible. Thus the teaching of the church, as affirmed by the Second Vatican Council, "is not above the word of God, but serves it, teaching only what has been handed on, listening to it devoutly, guarding it scrupulously, and explaining it faithfully by divine commission and with the help of the Holy Spirit; it draws from the deposit of faith everything it presents for belief as divinely revealed."[1]

The Bible is the revelation of God to people. If we believe that there is a God who created us and endowed us with minds capable of acquiring and dispensing knowledge, of adjusting ourselves to God's creation and to a degree controlling and improving the conditions under which we live, then it is only reasonable to assume that God can communicate with us and disclose to us who he is, what he expects of us, and in turn what we can expect of him. "It would be absurd," writes Richard Watson, the first and some would claim the greatest Methodist theologian after Wesley, "to think that he who has given us the power of communicating ideas to each other should have no means of communicating with us immediately from himself."[2] There are three distinct means of communication from God to us displayed in the Bible.

The first of these is that of action, the mighty deeds of God in history, which Holy Scripture is careful to record, for example, the call of Abraham, the blessing of Jacob, the plight of the Israelites in Egypt, the Passover and deliverance of God's people from bondage, the wilderness sojourn, the rise and fall of a nation and its restitution—all from the pages of the Old Testament. God's action reaches its climax as it is narrated in the Gospels through the birth, ministry, death, and resurrection of Jesus. The Acts of the Apostles describes Pentecost, the organization of the church, and the missionary expansion of Christianity. This is plain history. But the events of that history could not have occurred without divine intervention. It is the history of God in action among and in behalf of his people.

The second means of communication that God employs is that of speech. God spoke directly to Moses in the burning bush on Mount Horeb, and he continued to have conversation with him throughout the remainder of Moses' career as the leader of God's people. The prophets introduced their oracles with "Thus saith the Lord." And every word Jesus ever spoke fell from the lips of the Incarnate God.

The third means of communication from God to us, as seen in the Bible, is through the experience of saints and heroes, their reflections on their relationships with God and their admonitions and counsel to us, for example, the Psalms, the Wisdom literature of the Old Testament, the apocalyptic writings, and the Epistles.

Revelation is not human discovery. God does not yield himself to the probing ingenuity of human beings. To discover something one must be superior to and more intelligent than the thing he discovers. The scientist can discover the secrets of nature because he has a mind that nature does not possess. God is uncreated, while we are creatures, and he belongs to a higher order of life than we do. If we are to know anything about him, he must disclose himself to us. And this he has done in the Bible.

The disclosure of God is to human beings. The mighty acts of God had to have witnesses. The words God spoke were to particular persons who had to give God their attention, had to understand what he said, remember his directives, and transmit them to his people. To be sure, the Bible is the disclosure of the character, the mind, the purpose, and the will of God. Revelation is a divine act in which God takes the initiative. But if God is the subject and provides the sustance of his disclosure, the object of what he says and does is some person, that is, a prophet, a seer, an apostle, perhaps a priest, or even a king. This person must be able to apprehend God's message to him. He must be able to comprehend in terms of his own understanding the revelation, or disclosure, God gives to him.

This means that God, on his part, adjusts himself to the person with whom he communicates, while the person who receives the communication does so in terms that he understands and that have relevance to the times and situation in which he lives. The Bible is a glorious display of God's gracious adaptation of himself to all sorts and conditions of people in all ages of history and in the various stages of human development. It is likewise the inspiring record of people's receiving and apperceiving God's disclosure of himself to them under most untoward conditions and often in times most primitive and even barbaric. In the childhood of the race, God dealt with simple and childlike people in ways comparable to theirs so that Adam heard his voice as he walked in the garden in the cool of the evening.

Therefore, the geography, the cosmology, and the scientific information that the Bible provides is inadequate and out of date; only an ignoramus would assume otherwise. It did not lie within the scope of divine providence to provide general knowledge through revelation. In ordinary affairs God left people to fend for themselves. In making his will and purpose known to them, God came down to their level, knowing that it was impossible for them to rise up to his. " 'For my thoughts are not your thoughts, neither are your ways my ways,' declares the Lord" (Isa 55:8).

The correlative of revelation is inspiration, which may be thought of as the human means of receiving the divine disclosure in whatever form that disclosure takes, and more especially in translating it into writing and thereby preserving it for the use of posterity. The person to whom the revelation was given was not always the one who wrote about it, and there was often a long lapse of time between the divine disclosure and the written account of it. For example, the book of Genesis, which gives us the account of the flood and the narrative of the patriarchs, has to have been written hundreds of years aftr these events took place. And even the four Gospels are not contemporary with the life of Jesus, which they portray. In order, therefore, to guarantee the validity of the written accounts of his revelations, God had to inspire the biblical writers by endowing them with his Spirit so that what they wrote would be faithful and true.

The old theory of verbal inspiration is that God used the sacred writers as his secretaries to whom he dictated the Holy Scriptures word by word so that they are altogether without error. This presumably was the view of the early church. Saint Augustine puts it succinctly: "Since they wrote the things which he showed and uttered to them, it cannot be pretended that He is not the writer. . . ."[3] But to hold to this view, the Patristic writers had to resort to what appears to us a farfetched and imaginary method of interpretation, namely, the allegorical, in which the divine writers say one thing but mean another. Origen, for example, thought the first chapter of Genesis, taken at face value, was absurd. It is impossible, he said, for the first, second, and third days of creation to have existed with a morning and evening and yet without sun, moon, and stars. The first day did not even have a sky above it. He could not imagine God planting a vineyard as a farmer would do.[4] To him all this is written figuratively to lay bare some mystical meaning. Augustine follows suit, saying that Eden signifies the church: its four rivers, the Gospels; its fruit trees, the saints; and the tree of life, Jesus Christ.[5] By this method one can read into the Bible anything one wants to put there. Indeed, any form of biblical literalism suffers great intellectual strains when the contents of the Bible are minutely scrutinized and subjected to a comparison with what science has discovered and with a contemporary understanding of the world and its history. If God had dictated it, he certainly would have known as much and more than we do, and the style and content of his book would be of the same quality and character throughout.

This is not the case. The Bible is a library of sixty-six books written over a period of many centuries and displaying the styles and talents of many different authors. God took what he had and used those who were willing to be used, with their limitations and deficiencies, to his own appointed ends. The purpose of the Bible is simply to present God's plan of salvation, and those who wrote it were inspired by the Holy Spirit to convey to humankind the story of redemption, and in this regard their work is perfect and without fault or blemish. "I want to know one thing," writes John Wesley, "the way to heaven—how to land safe on that happy shore. God himself has condescended to teach the way; for this very end he came from heaven. He hath written it down in a book. O, give me that book! At any price give me the Book of God! I have it. Here is knowledge enough for me."[6] Rather than speak of the inerrancy of Scripture or verbal inspiration, it is much better to speak of the indefectibility of the Bible or its infallibility, the breathing of the Holy Spirit on its authors to assure their accuracy in presenting God's plan of salvation in its perfection.

The zenith of the Bible is Jesus Christ. The Old Testament is preparation for his coming. The Gospels are the good news of the salvation that is given through his life, death, and resurrection. The Acts of the Apostles describes his church—the New Israel abrogating and superseding the Old. The Epistles are explanations of his person and ministry, and the Revelation is a vision of his kingdom. The Bible ends with Jesus, and revelation ceases; for when that which is perfect is come, nothing more can be said.

This commentary is a careful exegesis of the entire Bible, explaining its contents, book by book, in terms of the intentions of the authors who composed it and addressed it to the peoples of their own time. At the same time, it is an inspiring exposition of the Bible's message for us and the peoples of all times. For in these writings of human beings, we find the eternal Word of God, which is the means of our salvation.

We should, affirms Pope Pius XII, "feel filial gratitide towards God who has sent us these books—as the letters of a Father to his own children."[7]

NOTES

[1]Walter M. Abbott and Joseph Gallagher, eds., "Dogmatic Constitution on Divine Revelation" in *The Documents of Vatican II* 2.10 (New York: American Press, 1966), 118.

[2]Richard Watson, *Theological Institutes.* (New York: Carlton and Phillips, 1856), 1:71.

[3]Augustine, *De Consensus Evangel,* 1.

[4]Origen, *De Principis* 4.1.16.

[5]Augustine, *The City of God* 13.21.3.

[6]Albert C. Outler, ed., *Sermons I,* Vol. 1 of *The Works of John Wesley* (Nashville: Abingdon, 1984), 105.

[7]Pope Pius XII, *Encyclical Divino Afflante Spiritu* (1943), quoted by Jean Levie, *The Bible, Word of God in Words of Man,* S. H. Treman, trans. (London: Geoffrey Chapman, 1961), 153.

NATURE, CHARACTER, AND ORIGIN OF SCRIPTURE

R. Larry Shelton

The Wesleyan understanding of Scripture grows out of the classical Reformation tradition that sees the Bible as the primary authority for the church. John Wesley's "man of one book" testimonial is reminiscent of the *sola scriptura* watchword of the Reformers. He views the Bible as *the* key to understanding God's word of salvation for the community of faith. Wesleyans have always attempted to integrate their understanding of Scripture into theological thought and spiritual life. Wesley used Scripture, reason, tradition, and experience as the foundations of authority for the church and the individual believer. In so doing, he exhibited a creative and balanced approach *toward understanding and interpreting God's Word* for his people. Rather than developing a dogmatic, rationalistic system of doctrines and creeds, Wesleyans have sought to integrate the content of Scripture with life in a way that some have termed "practical divinity."[1]

The issue of the authority and inspiration of Scripture is of foundational importance for Wesleyans, as for all Christians. On the issues of the authority and inspiration of Scripture, John Wesley rests firmly within the mainstream of orthodox Protestant theology. There are areas in which he is innovative, such as his integration of Scripture, reason, and experience. Yet his emphasis on the role of the Holy Spirit in the inspiration and authority of Scripture grows out of standard Protestant roots.

According to Wesley, the Holy Spirit operates through the Scriptures in three fundamental ways: First, in inspiring the development and writing of Scripture; second, in the authentication of the authority of Scripture in the church (the internal testimony of the Holy Spirit); third, in the interpretation of Scripture by the believer. To appreciate Wesley's position more fully on the authority of Scripture, a brief historical survey of the church's understanding of the authority of Scripture will be helpful.[2]

AUTHORITY OF SCRIPTURE

Since apostolic times, the church has wrestled with the certainty of God's communication on the basic issues of salvation. A dual threat, of persecution from without and heresy from within, held much of the early church's attention. It needed an authoritative and fixed point of reference for its teachings and life. Jesus and the apostles viewed the Jewish Scriptures as authoritative foundations for their teachings. The early church, in turn, viewed the teachings of Jesus and the apostles as authoritative. What were the Christians in the post-apostolic age to use as their basis for theological authority?

In the second and third centuries, theologians and apologists such as Justin Martyr, Irenaeus, Tertullian, and Cyprian began to address this problem. They did so by emphasizing the role of the bishops and the "rule of faith" of the church as the standards of orthodox theological authority. They taught that the appointment of bishops was a divine act. The role of a bishop was to preserve the apostolic teachings and to maintain the "rule of faith," which was the sum of the essential Christian teachings. Irenaeus saw the bishops as preserving the same faith as that of the apostles. Their work was, in this sense, apostolic. Additionally, Irenaeus taught that the existence of the church was the result of the work of the Holy Spirit. He reasoned that since the Holy Spirit created the church, the Spirit used the church as the conduit for revelation.

A dual basis of authority thus developed in the first several centuries of Christianity: the written deposit of the Scriptures and apostolic writings and the traditions of the church's teachings as maintained by the bishops in the rule of faith. These two streams worked together. They did not come into conflict with one another in the early church. According to Tertullian, the teaching of the apostles, delivered both orally and in writing, is the doctrinal tradition of the church. The church in turn preserves and interprets the apostolic teaching, both in the Scriptures and in the rule of faith of the church. As heretics became increasingly adept at interpreting the written Scriptures to support their teachings, the church began to strengthen its position as well. The Fathers maintained that the church was the only possessor of the Scriptures. They also maintained that it was the sole context in which the Scriptures could be interpreted with the assistance of the Holy Spirit.

Augustine contributed to this trend in the late fourth and early fifth centuries by stressing that the church holds the key to the meaning of the Bible and is the most reliable interpreter of Scripture. For Augustine, it is Christ who illumines the Scriptures through the same Spirit who inspired them. But the Spirit works only *within the church* where heretics have no access to either the Scriptures or the Spirit. In the fifth century, Vincent of Lerins summarized and standardized this doctrine. In his "Vincentian Canon" he stated categorically that the church is the only authoritative interpreter of Scripture. This standard-setting document stated that those teachings are orthodox that are believed *"always, everywhere, and by all."* Scripture was still considered authoritative, but it now shared this authority with the teachings and interpretations of the church.[3]

Throughout most of the Middle Ages (sixth through fifteenth centuries), the authority of the Scriptures remained linked to the authority of the church. But the church's interpretations of Scripture became increasingly problematic due to its habit of using the allegorical methods employed by Origen and the School of Alexandria, beginning in the third century. Throughout the Middle Ages, the grammatical/historical meaning of the text of Scripture was at the mercy of these innovative allegorical interpretations. Martin Luther later called some of these fanciful renderings "mere jugglery" and "monkey tricks."

In the late Middle Ages, scholars such as Thomas Aquinas and Hugh and Andrew of St. Victor began to question the extensive use of allegorical interpretation. Renewed emphasis on the *literal sense* of Scripture and the role of the mind of the human author in the process of inspiration by the Holy Spirit resulted in a new interest in the grammatical/historical sense of the text and an interest in biblical languages. In the fourteenth century, the Franciscan Nicolas of Lyra taught that the literal message of Scripture was the *basis* for all other meanings. He noted that God was the "principal author" of Scripture, and insisted that the meaning of Scripture rested upon the words of the inspired writers. This is in strong contrast to the medieval practice of allegorizing the meanings of the text so that only the authoritative teachers of the church could unravel their secret meanings, a practice that had submerged the meaning and authority of Scripture beneath stifling traditions. Nicolas thus led the way in breaking down the tyranny of the church's authoritative tradition and bad methodology.[4]

With the dawning of the Protestant Reformation, a new and fresh role developed for Scripture in the church. Martin Luther's emphasis on *sola scriptura*, "Scripture alone," became the watchword of the Reformation. Not only did he assert that the Scripture was authoritative, but he denied the authority of the pope and the traditions and interpretations of the church. The Roman Catholic Church viewed the authority of Scripture as resting on that of the church. Luther pointed out that the Bible derives its authority *from itself*, as *inspired* by the Holy Spirit. He said, "No believing Christian can be forced to recognize any authority beyond the sacred Scripture, which is exclusively invested with divine right, unless, indeed, there comes a new and attested revelation."[5] He thus sought to return to the apostolic teachings, which he believed had been silenced by the church's role as the final doctrinal authority.

For Luther, the authority of Scripture rests on several issues: its inspired character, its reliability for salvation, and the internal testimony of the Holy Spirit. First, Luther viewed the Bible as authoritative because he believed it to be inspired by the Holy Spirit. He wrote very little concerning the nature of inspiration, but he was clear in asserting that the Scriptures are not a dictated collection of supernatural syllables. Some writers received historical materials by research, while the Holy Spirit superintended their arrangement and interpretation of details. Luther believed that inspiration involves an objective quality that includes both phraseology and diction. Yet it is the subject matter of Scripture, Christ, to which the Spirit witnesses in the Word. Scripture mediates the living Word by the operation of the Holy Spirit and thus becomes the *medium of salvation*. The inspiredness of the Scriptures lies, then, in their ability, through the Spirit, to produce in the believer all that is needed for salvation. It is because the Spirit makes *Christ present* through the Scriptures that they have redemptive effectiveness.[6]

This leads to the reliability of Scripture, which is Luther's second basis for authority. The Scriptures are reliable because they produce in the reader the conviction that they proclaim the love of God and his power to save.[7] Through personal spiritual struggle, Luther found in the Bible a God who saves. It is precisely this saving role that proved to him that Scripture is a divine Word. Its character as the Word of God becomes evident through its function as a saving Word. Scripture's authority thus consists in its ability to do the work of salvation through the Spirit in the hearts of those who hear it.

Finally, the internal testimony of the Holy Spirit affirms the Bible's inspiration and thus its authority. Luther believed that the inspired character of a book could be evaluated only on internal criteria. For him, the primary internal criterion is the Holy Spirit's witness in the church to the reality of Christ crucified. This internal witness of the Holy Spirit (*testimonium Spiritus Sancti internum*) attests the Scripture as the genuine Word of God.[8] It is Jesus Christ working in and through Scripture who is the infallible Word of God. The Scripture is authoritative because it faithfully reveals Christ through the human instrumentality of the biblical writers, whose inspiration comes from the Spirit. Ultimately, then, it is the content of Scripture, not its form or written style, that is authoritative.

Luther believed that the inner testimony of the Spirit witnesses to Christ and establishes Scripture as inspired and authoritative. He believed we would certainly err by thinking that *mere* human reason could perceive the authority of God's Word. As the Holy Spirit penetrates our hearts, the Bible becomes not simply God's Word, but God's Word "for me." It is the saving activity that the Spirit effects through Scripture that verifies its authority. Authority is thus a functional element that relates to both the *character* of Scripture itself and to the *effect* it produces in the believer through the Spirit.[9]

The other major Reformers, John Calvin and Huldrych Zwingli, also founded their understanding of the authority and inspiration of Scripture on the reliability of Scripture and the internal testimony of the Holy Spirit. Zwingli, the leader of the Reformation in Zurich, emphasized that Scripture is the Word of God because it brings to pass precisely what it declares. For example, prophecies found in Scripture are fulfilled and salvation that is promised comes to pass. Additionally, the Holy Spirit directs and applies the content of Scripture to the reader.[10] Thus, the reliability of Scripture and the internal testimony of the Holy Spirit are the foundational principles in Zwingli's doctrine of the authority of Scripture.

John Calvin also based his view of the authority of Scripture on its reliability and the internal testimony of the Spirit. He reacted negatively to the Roman Catholic assertion that the certainty of faith comes through the infallible church. Likewise, he rejected the rationalistic view that the certainty needed for faith comes through reason, and he dismissed the view of the Enthusiasts who said faith can be verified by direct revelation to their spirits. For Calvin, Scripture is self-authenticating. God uses Scripture to communicate his purpose of salvation. Since Scripture reliably brings people to faith as the internal testimony of the Spirit *(testimonium Spiritus Sancti internum)* verifies its authenticity, it is inspired by God and thus authoritative.[11] This classical Reformed position is summarized eloquently in the Westminster Confession of 1647:

> We may be moved and induced by the testimony of the Church to a high and reverent esteem of the Holy Scripture, and the heavenliness of the matter, the efficacy of the doctrine, the majesty of the style, the consent of all the parts, the scope of the whole (which is to give all glory to God), the full discovery it makes of the only way of man's salvation, the many other incomparable excellences, and the entire perfection thereof, are arguments whereby it doth abundantly evidence to be the Word of God; yet, notwithstanding, our full persuasion as assurance of the infallible truth and divine authority thereof, is from the inward work of the Holy Spirit, bearing witness by and with the Word in our hearts.[12]

John Wesley held this Reformation view of scriptural authority. He believed the purpose of Scripture is *to communicate the way of salvation*. His well-known "man of one book" statement indicates his is a functional view of Scripture:

> I want to know one thing—the way to heaven; how to land safe on that happy shore. God Himself has condescended to teach the way; for this very end He came from heaven. He hath written it down in a book. O give me that book! . . . let me be *homo unius libri* (a man of one book). In His presence I open, I read His book; for this end, to find the way to heaven."[13]

He felt the intention of Scripture was to provide information and inspiration for salvation and the Christian life. In his view, Scripture functions sacramentally as a "means of grace." By this he means that it is one of "the ordinary channels whereby He might convey to men, preventing, or sanctifying grace." These means of grace are prayer, searching the Scriptures, and the Lord's Supper.[14] The goal of these means is salvation and the power behind them is God himself. Wesley says in this regard: ". . . the whole value of the means depends on their actual subservience to the end of religion; that consequently all these means, when separate from the end, are less than nothing, and vanity; that if they do not actually conduce to the knowledge and love of God they are not acceptable in His sight. . . ."[15]

When Scripture, as a means of grace, is used in a way that is subservient to God's saving purposes, its purpose is fulfilled. Thus, there is no inherent spiritual virtue in the text of Scripture. Only as it functions through the power of the Holy Spirit can it bring to the reader the saving merits of Jesus Christ. Clearly, Wesley believes the authority of Scripture to be grounded on the work of Christ. He says, "Scripture is thus a means to this end, that the man of God may be perfect, thoroughly furnished to all good works."[16] He notes further:

> We know that there is no inherent power in the words that are spoken in prayer, in the letter of Scripture read, the sound thereof heard, or the bread and wine received in the Lord's Supper; but that it is God alone who is the giver of every good gift, the author of all grace; that the whole power is of him, whereby through any of these [means] there is any blessing conveyed to our soul.[17]

So, according to Wesley, the primary basis for the authority of Scripture is twofold: its *reliability* for communicating salvation and the *internal witness* of the Holy Spirit. In both instances the critical factor is the work of the Holy Spirit. Like Luther and Calvin, he relates the authority of Scripture to the living witness of God's Spirit. Wesley thus stands in the mainstream of the classical Protestant view of the authority of Scripture. The Christian experiences the living witness of the Holy Spirit who brings the gospel to the heart through the means of Scripture.[18]

Ray Dunning has made a perceptive analysis of the Wesleyan position on the authority of Scripture. He points out that some Wesleyans do attempt to base the authority of Scripture on the *nature* or *form* of the original autographs of the Bible. According to this rational, deductive approach, the authority of Scripture rests on the conviction that the original copies of the text were preserved from error by the Holy Spirit and are thus divine in character. This argues for their authenticity and authority.

Citing A. M. Hills and H. Orton Wiley, both major Wesleyan holiness theologians, Dunning argues that the literal accuracy of Scripture defended by rational arguments is not the *major concern* for Wesleyans. What Wesleyans consider important is the doctrine of *prevenient grace* as the Holy Spirit witnesses to the authenticity of the written Word through which God speaks.[19] The only authority that makes any difference in the reading of Scripture is the authority given via the moral conviction that God is speaking. Because Scripture has shown itself to be a reliable vehicle through which the Holy Spirit conveys the knowledge of the saving work of Christ, it witnesses to the church of its own authority by the internal testimony of the Holy Spirit. By observing that Scripture functions as an effective and reliable means of grace that bears the content of God's message, the church recognizes through the Spirit's witness (*testimonium*) that it is, indeed, the authentic Word of God, and thus authoritative.

INSPIRATION OF SCRIPTURE

Scripture is authoritative because it is reliable. The reliability of Scripture, as well as the internal testimony of the Spirit, comes from its inspiredness. It is the inspiration of Scripture by the Holy Spirit that makes it effective in working salvation through the Spirit's witness.

Inspiration in the Text

The inspiredness of Scripture is axiomatic among evangelical Wesleyans. As Dunning points out, opinions about the mode and extent of inspiration vary according to the weight given to the divine and human elements involved in the development of the biblical books.[20]

The primary biblical passages that deal with the phenomenon of inspiration are 2Ti 3:16–17 and 2Pe 1:20–21. These passages refer, however, to the OT, which was the only authoritative Scripture in existence at the time the NT books were being written. The word *theopneustos* occurs in the former passage to convey the inspired character of Scripture and translates, "inspired" or "God-breathed." Since the term does not occur elsewhere in the Bible, it is difficult to determine the exact nuance that the writer intended to convey. Classical Greek usage of the term is not helpful either, since the concept of inspiration in that context often connotes the ecstatic seizure in which a prophet spoke words in a frenzied state that came directly from a divine source. Such a usage seems more in tune with the mantic "channeling" process associated with spirit-possession in the occult experiences. This is not the intention in the Timothy passage. As Dunning has stated, 2Ti 3:16 deals more with the *use of Scripture* than with the method of its production.[21] The *hina* clause in 2Ti 3:17 indicates purpose. The passage indicates that inspired Scripture has the purpose or use of equipping the believer for "every good work." In this light, both function and origin have a relationship to inspiredness. It is "profitable" for teaching, reproof, correction, and instruction in righteousness as a result of its being given by "inspiration of God." The common denominator in the relationship between the production and fulfillment of Scripture is the Holy Spirit. The inspiredness of Scripture is, thus, evidenced by its redemptive effect in the lives of believers.

In his *Explanatory Notes Upon the New Testament* Wesley says, regarding 2Ti 3:16:

> The Spirit of God not only once inspired those who wrote it, but continually inspires, supernaturally assists those that read it with earnest prayer. Hence it is so profitable for doctrine, for reproof or conviction of them that are in error or sin, for the correction or amendment of whatever is amiss, and for instructing or training up the children of God in all righteousness.[22]

Here, Wesley and Dunning agree that the Spirit operates not only in the production, but in the *preservation* and *interpretation* of Scripture. Questions surrounding the meaning of inspiration do not get answered by merely accepting the inspiration of Scripture as fact. As William Abraham notes, before the term "inspire" can be applied to describe God's activity in relation to Scripture, on must first observe what the term means in everyday contexts. To do this, Abraham draws the analogy between the way in which a good teacher can motivate and direct his/her students to learn most effectively and the way the Holy Spirit interacts with the personalities and natural abilities of human agents. He notes that "inspiring" involves more than just speaking or performing other isolated functions related to the transmission of information. On the contrary, the routine activity of the teacher's example is also part of the inspiration process—i.e., supervision, teaching, lecturing, discussing, publishing. Thus, inspiration is not simply the dictation of facts to be transcribed by the students, but it is an *entire relationship* in which the student functions to accomplish the goals of learning.[23] Inspiration is not just the dictation and transcription of information. It also involves the nurturing and guiding in a process that engages the mind and will of the learner as well as the motivation and superintendence of the teacher. Biblical writers, then, "spoke from God" as they were "borne along" by the Holy Spirit (2Pe 1:20–21). Inspiration involves at least five variables: the relationship between the prophet and God, the setting or context, the perception of spiritual need in the community, the trustworthy communication of truth by the prophet, and the prophet's illumination by the Holy Spirit.

This broader understanding of inspiration is described by both I. Howard Marshall and J. I. Packer as a "concursive" action of the Spirit of God. The analogy of the process of God's creation and providence in the universe is helpful here. On one level were natural phenomena that can be explained scientifically in terms of cause and effect. On another level were supernatural events that must be understood *theologically*. The creation event can therefore be seen from two angles, with complementary interpretations—the natural and the supernatural.

In a similar way the composition of the Bible involved various natural oral and literary processes such as collection of information from witnesses, composition of letters directed to specific situations, writing of prophetic messages, and gathering of various documents. Simultaneously, the same Spirit who participated in Creation also took part in the process of the production of the Scriptures. The result of this process is that the Bible is the work of God and human authors. From this perspective the Spirit has worked "concursively" with the human processes. Such a view is complementary to both the divine and human factors in the development of the Bible. In this view the human authors are more than stenographers and the Spirit is more than merely an observer of the process.

This idea of a mutual undertaking also deals satisfactorily with the varied character of the diverse material in the books of the Bible. God and humans share in the whole process of composition.[24] The relationship between human authors and the Holy Spirit provides a context in which their research, interpretation, and writing result in a product that has its origin in God as well as in the life of the community of faith.

In the end, as I. Howard Marshall shows, the acceptance of the divine inspiration of Scripture is a matter of faith. If the authoritative guide for our faith is Jesus Christ, then we will share his attitude toward the OT Scriptures. His teachings, and those of the apostles and prophets, should be accepted as inspired based on faith generated by the Holy Spirit. As the Westminster Confession states, ". . . our full persuasion and assurance of the infallible truth, and divine authority thereof, is from the inward work of the Holy Spirit, bearing witness by and with the word in our hearts."[25]

Theories of Inspiration

Among Protestant evangelicals, theories of inspiration have developed that involve both deductive and inductive methodologies. Trembath examines several examples of each approach, concluding that deductivists begin with a particular doctrine of God and man that requires that all communication from God must be inerrant in its form. Inspiration, then, must be understood by examining the form of the Bible itself. Inductivists, on the other hand, evaluate inspiration by examining the effect it brings to the believing community. The effect they look for is the experience of salvation.[26] "Inspired" texts are, simply speaking, those through which the Spirit works to communicate faith and salvation.

According to Trembath's evaluation of the deductivist theories of inspiration, they base their arguments on an a priori presupposition that there is a direct *cause and effect* relationship between the character of God and the truthfulness of the Bible. They assume a basic theological claim about the meaning of inspiration and then attempt to deduce from this assumption what the Scripture must be. Norman Geisler illustrates the argument for this position:

(1) Whatever God utters is errorless (inerrant).
(2) The Words of the Bible are God's utterances.
(3) Therefore, the words of the Bible are errorless (inerrant).[27]

When inspiration begins with such an understanding of the doctrine of God, it tends to be thought of as a passive process in which human beings are either vehicles for divine communication or passive receivers.[28] In this view the process of inspiration is not concursive.

Randall Basinger and David Basinger challenge this method by contending that such an approach implies a dictation theory of inspiration and is inconsistent with a theology of free will. They note that if a concursive approach to inspiration is accepted, free human activity by the writers must also be accepted. These free human activities cannot be totally controlled by God without violating human freedom. If God creates free moral creatures, then he cannot totally control the words that they write and, therefore, he cannot guarantee inerrancy of the biblical text. In short, the Basingers are arguing that God cannot perfectly control the biblical writers without removing their freedom.[29]

Deductive theories of inspiration attempt to base their arguments for biblical inspiration on externals—categories of "objective" data—that carry considerable sway despite the faith experience of the reader. Inductive theories attempt the opposite. A. H. Strong, for example, asserts that God's work of inspiration is discerned in part when persons are inspired to faith through the Bible. He shows that inspiration is a part of the character of the Bible because of its effects in bringing people to faith.

This contrasts sharply with the deductive approach of B. B. Warfield and others who locate inspiration in the "divine status" of the biblical words themselves. Strong also reasons that an individual will accept or reject the authority of Scripture in direct symmetry with whether one accepts or rejects its message. He defines inspiration in this way:

> "Inspiration is that influence of the Spirit of God upon the minds of the Scripture writers which made their writings the record of a progressive divine revelation, sufficient, when taken together and interpreted by the same Spirit who inspired them, to lead every honest inquirer to Christ and to salvation."[30]

This emphasis on the role of the Holy Spirit in both the writing and reading of Scripture is consistent with John Wesley's view of the Bible as a means of grace. This view agrees with the concursive concept of the Spirit's role in inspiration as defined above. Furthermore, Strong's emphasis on the role of Scripture in leading readers to Christ is in line with Wesley's functional view of Scripture's authority and redemptive purpose.

Given the Wesleyan emphasis on the experiential work of the Holy Spirit in the life of the church, as well as the necessity of free will, a concursive or dynamic understanding of inspiration seems more consistent with a Wesleyan theological point of view. Wesley's emphasis on the saving function of Scripture (reliability) and the internal testimony of the Spirit place him firmly in the orthodox Patristic and Reformation traditions. His use of reason is always in relationship to tradition and experience in the context of Scripture. Thus, his theological position on salvation, the inspiration of Scripture, and the pragmatic role of experience is incompatible with the rationalistic/deductive systems of establishing theological authority and biblical inspiration. A Wesleyan view of inspiration should reflect a cooperative, redemptive, interpersonal process that is validated by an existential spiritual encounter with the Holy Spirit. Experiential and observable redemptive effects of the Scripture, which function as a means of grace to believers, attest to the reality of the spiritual encounter.[31]

SPECIAL REVELATION

To love and serve God, one must first know him. John Wesley believed that the general knowledge of God's existence, the "light which lights every man," was known in some measure in the creation and in the conscience of persons. His comment on Jn 1:9 expresses this view: "By what is vulgarly termed natural conscience, pointing out at least the general lines of good and evil. And this light, if man did not hinder, would shine more and more to the perfect day."[32]

Although this general revelation of God is valuable, it does not give specific knowledge of the way of salvation. This general knowledge must be supplemented by the special revelation by which God discloses his nature and purpose for humanity. Wesley writes:

We had, by nature, no knowledge of God, no acquaintance with Him. It is true, as soon as we came to the use of reason, we learned "the invisible things of God, even His eternal power and Godhead, from the things that are made." From the things that are seen we inferred the existence of an eternal, powerful Being, that is not seen. But still, although we acknowledge His being, we had no acquaintance with Him. As we know there is an Emperor of China, whom yet we do not know; so we knew there was a King of all the earth, yet we knew Him not. Indeed we could not by any of our natural faculties. By none of these could we attain the knowledge of God. We could no more perceive Him by our natural understanding, than we could see Him with our eyes. For "no one knoweth the Father but the Son, and he to whom the Son willeth to reveal Him. And no one knoweth the Son, but the Father, and he to whom the Father revealeth Him."[33]

From this passage it is safe to conclude that Wesley believed in the *necessity of special revelation* by God himself so that humanity could know him in a saving way. Building upon this, Dunning points out that the Christian faith is a response to God's self-disclosure. The OT, through the history of Israel, is in one sense a preliminary self-disclosure, while the complete and final self-revelation is in the person and work of Jesus of Nazareth. To respond to this revelation of God's character and saving purpose is to act in faith. The result of this response is the gift of salvation. This is the objective of the self-disclosure of God.[34]

For three major reasons God must make himself known by his own initiative:

(1) the transcendence of God—the corresponding finitude of man
(2) the personal nature of God
(3) the fallenness of humanity—the resultant lack of ability to discern him[35]

Furthermore, the purpose and context of God's self-disclosure is salvation. God makes himself known in order to save. Since humanity is fallen, the ability to perceive the personal character of God is affected. Therefore, God must directly bridge the gap between his existence and humanity's blindness. This he does by revealing his own loving and saving nature.

How this divine revelation occurs is another issue of concern. Abraham notes that theologians have usually blurred the distinction between inspiration and revelation, or divine speaking. This has led to the mislabeling of inspired Scripture as revelation. When this misidentification occurs, the formation of Scripture appears to involve the direct intervention of God in a way that minimizes human participation in the process.

This confusion of inspiration with divine speaking also limits revelation to words or propositions. One problem with this is that revelation occurs through many kinds of events and activities. In John 21, the despondent disciples are confronted with the risen Christ. Yet it was not until they followed his directions and caught fish that they recognized him. They immediately perceived who he was because of the meaning the event carried for them (Jn 21:7). Jesus did not tell them verbally who he was, but revealed himself through his act. It was the context in which the event of catching fish occurred that established this event as revelation. As Abraham says, "Revealing is an activity that is accomplished in, with, and through other acts and activities."[36] Inspiration, on the other hand, is the process in which human beings and the Holy Spirit work together to provide the interpretation of revelation that forms the sacred writings.

Revelation involves divine speaking as well as divine acting. Information about the nature of God and his purposes is necessary in order to interpret what he is doing or has done. Without divine speaking, we have no knowledge of the character or performance of God. His promise to forgive sins cannot be known without his making known the information that enables us to respond to him in order to be forgiven. The same holds true for all his promises and all his commands. This does not mean, however, that divine speaking must be couched as propositions of written or oral communication.

Some philosophers have objected to the idea of God's speaking on the grounds that he is a spirit and therefore does not have vocal cords. Abraham notes that it is logically meaningful to think of a personal being communicating information without the use of physical means such as vocal cords. The concept of telepathy affirms the communication of impressions from one mind to another without the normally recognized oral or written means. He sees telepathy, in this sense, as analogous to divine speaking.[37] From this position it is not necessary to limit the concept of divine speaking to those forms of communication that involve dictated or written proposition, or audible, verbal communication.

Special revelation does not exclude divine speaking, as neo-orthodox or liberal theology often concludes, neither is it exclusively propositional as fundamentalism insists. Revelation and inspiration are *distinct* but *related* aspects of God's process of communication. Revelation occurs through various means and in various contexts such as visions, dreams, the urim and thummim, theophanies, angels, divine speaking, historical events, and the incarnation of Jesus Christ. The writer of Hebrews expressed it as follows: "In the past God spoke to our forefathers through the prophets at many times and in various ways, but in these last days he has spoken to us by his Son" (1:1–2, NASB). The Bible is the means by which the revelation of God, in redemptive acts and words, is interpreted and recorded by the inspired writers. The truths of revelation impact the readers of Scripture who are prepared by the Holy Spirit to understand the divine message revealed by God. As Horne explains it, "Revelation has to do with *what* is communicated; inspiration with *how* it is communicated; illumination with *why* it is communicated" (emphasis mine).[38]

Thus, the purpose of God's revelation in creation, history, and the conscience of humanity is to bring us to himself. God has revealed his character and saving love through the special revelation of divine acts and words in history, and ultimately through Jesus Christ. The writers of

Scripture have reported and interpreted these words and events with the full cooperation and inspiration of the Holy Spirit. The result is an inspired account that communicates to us the character and saving work of God in a way that is completely trustworthy and reliable to bring us to salvation. The Holy Spirit applies this Scripture to our hearts in a way that enables us to respond in faith to God's salvation message. This is the purpose for which Scripture was written (Jn 20:30, 31; 2Ti 3:16).

CANON OF SCRIPTURE

The term "canon" comes from a Greek word that meant "straight rod" or "ruler." It developed a metaphorical connotation used by the church Fathers to refer to the norm of church doctrine—the "rule of faith" or "rule of truth." Initially, the term referred to a collection of holy Scriptures near the end of the fourth century. It continued in common usage from that time in Christian terminology to describe a list of books, and gradually came to designate a normative collection of writings.[39] Thus, through a complex process of development, the list of Scriptures that the church considers inspired came to be called "the canon." This is the collection of writings that the church regards as authoritative for the Christian faith and life.[40]

Which writings should be considered canonical and how did the church come to that position? Historically, the church since the fourth century has accepted the sixty-six books of the Old and New Testaments as the authoritative canonical books. The books known as the Apocrypha were added by Jerome and others to the Latin Bible to be used for purposes of devotion and edification. Though not originally intended for consideration on a par with the canonical OT books, popular usage in the Middle Ages didn't distinguish between the canonical and extra-canonical books of devotion.[41]

The process of determining which writings to include in the canonical collection proved to be an enormous task. Both the Jewish and Christian canons developed over many centuries as a result of specific historical situations. In Israel, the principle of canonical authority was established with the giving of the law through Moses (Ex 24). Other authoritative utterances, documents, and collections developed as Israel journeyed through enslavement and liberation in the exilic and post-exilic periods. The saving actions and revelations of God were interpreted, recorded, and collected. The testimonies of faith and the prophetic critiques and values became a collection of written documents that eventually attained a threefold division into Law, Prophets, and Writings. The process of formal canonical collection seems to have begun in seventh-century Judah during the reign of Josiah (622–609 B.C.). The rediscovery of the book of law led Josiah to acknowledge the written law of Yahweh as the highest authority over Israel.[42]

Development and definition of the OT canon accelerated during the Babylonian Exile (586–539 B.C.). As Israel's religious system dissociated from the temple in Jerusalem, her theologicans worked to reshape its identity to fit their faith to new surroundings. They became a people of the book, for the canon was indestructible, flexible, and portable. After the Exile, the word of God became increasingly identified with the written Scriptures. The concept of inspiration began to be understood not only as a gift bestowed upon the living prophets, but as an attribute of the sacred writings as well. Following the Exile, prophetic activity decreased and dynamic element of inspiration became more closely associated with the books that mediated God's word to his people.[43]

Several hundred years later, two major developments forced Jewish theologians back, firmly, into being a people of the book. Christianity was on the increase, with its new interpretations of the Jewish scripture, and the destruction of the temple in Jerusalem in A.D. 70 left them few alternatives. The Jews focused again on the Scriptures for their identity, unity, and security. Their religious leaders emigrated to the coastal city of Jamnia and worked to define ways the Jewish faith could survive with the loss of its religious institutions. By A.D. 90, they had reached a consensus on the content of the thirty-nine books of the OT canon, which is nearly identical with what Jesus and the apostles had accepted as "the Scriptures."[44]

The NT canon is the result of a long process in which the books that the church came to regard as authoritative and inspired were selected from a large number of writings circulating among the churches. Through this process the "authoritative tradition was collected, ordered, and transmitted in such a way as to enable it to function as sacred Scripture for a community of faith and practice."[45]

This selection process involved the comparison of Christian writings with the accepted norm of apostolic teaching, the "rule of faith." The motivation in the church to collect the most useful of these writings for study and teaching was strong. It was fueled further by a need to clarify the authority and extent of the writings to protect them from misuse by the heretics. Most notable among these early heretics was Marcion (ca. A.D. 140), who wished to limit authority to an edited version of Luke and ten of Paul's epistles.

The process of identifying the canon of Scripture began with an informal identification of those writings that were most edifying to the church. Gradually, more specific criteria were applied, and by A.D. 200 twenty-one of the NT books found acceptance in the canon by general consensus of the church. Evaluation of inspiration and authority involved grouping the books into three categories: (1) *homologoumena*, or universally accepted works; (2) *antilegomena*, or books accepted by some and disputed by others; and (3) *notha*, or documents that were clearly not of canonical status. During the fourth century, Jerome and Augustine acknowledged the twenty-seven books of the canon, and their opinions were validated by decisions rendered at the Councils of Hippo (A.D. 393) and Carthage (A.D. 397).[46] They used several criteria to discern which books were authoritative and inspired. F. F. Bruce lists the following as tests of canonicity and authority:

(1) Apostolic authority that reflects either apostolic authorship or influence;
(2) Antiquity and orthodoxy that indicate content based on an apostolic foundation;
(3) Catholicity, or universal recognition and use in the church. Some early church leaders saw inspiration by the Holy Spirit also as a test of canonicity.[47]

While not all the books that now make up the NT can be ascribed to an author who was an apostle, the church did insist on establishing apostolic authority or validation for the writings that were accepted as canonical. Apostolic influence upon such writers as Mark and Luke gave weight to their authenticity and acceptance. The relationship of James and Jude to the holy family may have given their writings a preferred place. Also, if a certain writing was the work of an apostle or associate, then it would likely be viewed as belonging to the apostolic age. Thus, antiquity became a corollary criterion for canonical inclusion. At this time, it was established that the doctrine in any writing that was considered orthodox must be consistent with the teachings of the apostles, as summed up in the rule of faith. This insistence on antiquity was to prevent Gnostic or other heresies from finding expression in writings endorsed by the church for devotional and doctrinal use. Furthermore, works used among many churches received greater respect than those used only in local areas. This catholicity of usage enhanced the church's conviction that a work should be included in the canon.[48]

In this process, clearly the church did not commission or authorize the writing of a book of Scripture. It recognized and acknowledged the inspired character of those writings that were in conformity with the above characteristics. As these writings continued to be used by the Holy Spirit to edify and enrich the life of the church, the church recognized them as canonical and inspired.[49] Indeed, one group of evangelical scholars sees an inseparable connection between inspiration and canonicity; they cannot be separated. The ultimate basis for canonicity is simply this: if the writing is inspired (God-breathed) it is canonical. If it is not inspired, it is not canonical.[50]

Others see canonicity as involving the form and function of the writings in the life of the church. Canon is thus not just a list, but the shape of the way the sacred writings work in the life of the church. James Sanders and Brevard Childs have interpreted the concept of canon on two major bases: They are interested not only in the processes of collecting the Scriptures, but also the shape and form of the interpretation and use of the Scriptures in the church. Canon thus becomes a hermeneutical concept that interprets Scripture both in its historical context and as it continues to function in the community of faith.[51]

Thus, the NT canon is a list of twenty-seven books that the church came to view as expressing its definitive and normative testimony of the Christian faith and life. These books were the expression of the apostolic witness of God's redemptive revelation as it culminated in Jesus Christ and was universally taught throughout the Christian church. They were discerned by the church to embody the fullest expression of the Christian faith as interpreted by the writers under the inspiration of the Holy Spirit.

CONCLUSION

The canonical Scripture is thus considered by the Christian church to be the authoritative interpretation of God's revelation to Israel and the church. The divine revelation in the form of word and act is communicated and interpreted to the community of faith through the Holy Spirit's activity. As this inspired understanding of God's communication is proclaimed in oral and written form, the Holy Spirit works concursively with the prophets and writers to enable them to express accurately and authoritatively the content and significance of God's saving message. The written result of this process takes the form of Scripture. The internal testimony of the Holy Spirit enables the church to perceive the authentic inspired message of God through these writings. It is this communication that enables God's purposes of salvation to be realized in his people. In short, Scripture is considered authoritative and canonical because through it the inspired writers, working concursively with the Holy Spirit, are able to communicate reliably a spiritually valid interpretation of God's revelations in history.

To those who are receptive to the Spirit's testimony, which is God's saving work revealed in Jesus Christ, Scripture functions as a means of grace that transforms and saves those who believe and obey its message. The Wesleyan understanding of the authority of Scripture is based on a commitment to its saving function as a means of grace and on its inspired character, which is revealed by the witness of the Spirit. This basis of authority in the function of Scripture is consistent with the Wesleyan emphasis on the redemptively effective work of the Holy Spirit at every point in the faith and life of the Christian and the church.

NOTES

[1]Thomas Langford, *Practical Divinity* (Nashville: Abingdon, 1983).

[2]R. Larry Shelton, "John Wesley's Approach to Scripture in Historical Perspective," *Wesleyan Theological Journal*, 18:1 (Spring 1981), 23–50.

[3]For a more thorough discussion of the development of the authority of the church in relation to Scripture, see R. Larry Shelton, "Martin Luther's Concept of Biblical Interpretation in Historical Perspective" (Th.D. Diss., Fuller Theological Seminary, 1974), chap. 1. Also, see Ellen Flessemanvan Leer, *Tradition and Scripture in the Early Church* (Assen, Netherlands: van Gorcum, 1954). See also

Herbert T. Mayer, "Scripture, Tradition, and Authority in the Life of the Early Church," *Concordia Theological Monthly*, vol. 38 (1967).

[4]Beryl Smalley, *The Study of the Bible in the Middle Ages* (Oxford: Basil Blackwell, 1952), 88–120; see also, Shelton, Ibid., chap. 2. Also, note F. W. Farrar, *History of Interpretation* (New York: Dutton, 1886), 276ff.

[5]Martin Luther, *D. Martin Luthers Werke*, ed. J.F.K. Knaake, vol. 2 (Weimar: Hermann Nachfolger, 1966–71), 279.

[6]Herman Sasse, "Luther and the Word of God," *Accents in Luther's Theology*, ed. Heino O. Kadai (St. Louis: Concordia, 1967), 84. See also, Regin Prenter, *Spiritus Creator* (Philadelphia: Fortress, 1953), 107. H. H. Kramm, *The Theology of Martin Luther* (London: James Clarke, 1947), 116.

[7]Albert Peel, "The Bible and the People: Protestant Views of the Authority of the Bible," *The Interpretation of the Bible*, ed. C. W. Dugmore (London: Society for Promoting Christian Knowledge, 1946), 68. See also, Shelton, op. cit., "John Wesley's Approach to Scripture," 32 and notes.

[8]Paul Althaus, *The Theology of Martin Luther*, trans. Robert C. Schultz (Philadelphia: Fortress, 1966), 75.

[9]Jack Rogers and Donald McKim, *The Authority and Inspiration of the Bible* (San Francisco: Harper & Row, 1979), 79; see also Shelton, "John Wesley's Approach to Scripture," 32. For a more specific treatment of the role of the Holy Spirit in the theology of the Reformers, including the Spirit's role in Scripture, see R. Larry Shelton, "The Holy Spirit in the Theology of the Reformers," *The Spirit and the New Age*, eds. R. Larry Shelton and Alex R. G. Deasley, (Anderson, Ind.: Warner, 1986), 168–76.

[10]Huldrych Zwingli, "Of the Clarity and Certainty or Power of the Word of God," *Library of Christian Classics*, vol. 24, ed. Geoffrey Bromiley (Philadelphia: Westminster, 1953), 82. Also, see R. Larry Shelton, "The Emphasis of the Zurich Reformers on the Subjective Work of the Holy Spirit in the Interpreter." *The Asbury Seminarian*, 29:3 (July 1974), 18–33.

[11]John Calvin, *Institutes of the Christian Religion*, in John T. McNeill (ed.), and F.L. Battles (trans.), *Library of Christian Classics*, Vol. 30 (Philadelphia: Westminster, 1967), I, vii, 3; I, vii, 1–5. See also, Rogers and McKim, *The Authority and Inspiration of the Bible*, 103–14. On the concept of the *testimonium Spiritus Sancti internum*, see Bernard Ramm, *The Witness of the Spirit* (Grand Rapids: Eerdmans, 1960).

[12]Philip Schaff, ed., *The Creeds of Christendom*, vol. 3 (Grand Rapids: Baker, 1966), 603.

[13]John Wesley, *The Works of John Wesley*, 14 vols. (Grand Rapids: Baker, 1978 reprint), 5:3. See Shelton, op. cit., "John Wesley's Approach to Scripture," 39 and notes.

[14]John Wesley, "The Means of Grace," *The Works of John Wesley*, Sermons I, ed. Albert C. Outler (Nashville: Abingdon, 1984), 381.

[15]Ibid.

[16]Wesley, "The Means of Grace," (Baker), 279.

[17]Wesley, "The Means of Grace," (Abingdon), 382.

[18]See Shelton, "John Wesley's Approach to Scripture," 37.

[19]H. Ray Dunning, *Grace, Faith, and Holiness*, (Kansas City: Beacon Hill, 1988), 58–65.

[20]Ibid., 67.

[21]Ibid., 66.

[22]John Wesley, *Explanatory Notes Upon the New Testament* (London: Epworth Press, 1966), 794.

[23]William J. Abraham, *The Divine Inspiration of Holy Scripture*, (New York: Oxford Univ. Press, 1981), 63–64. Abraham notes that "inspiration will result in a reliable account of God's saving acts." Unlike a human teacher who is fallible and may inspire truth or falsehood, God as the agent of inspiration is omniscient and infallible by definition. "Therefore what he inspires will bear significant marks of truth and reliability . . . this has obvious consequences for the content of the Bible as inspired by God." See p. 68.

[24]I. Howard Marshall, *Biblical Inspiration* (Grand Rapids: Eerdmans, 1982), 40–45.

[25]Ibid., 46; Schaff, *The Creeds of Christendom*, 603.

[26]Kern Robert Trembath, *Evangelical Theories of Biblical Inspiration* (New York: Oxford Univ. Press, 1987), 45, 70, 71. Trembath sees examples of the deductivists as Charles Hodge, B. B. Warfield, John Warwick Montgomery, and E. J. Carnell. The inductivist examples are Augustus H. Strong, Bernard Ramm, and William J. Abraham.

[27]Norman Geisler, *A General Introduction to the Bible* (Chicago: Moody, 1968), 53.

[28]Trembath, *Evangelical Theories of Biblical Inspiration*, 8ff.; Abraham, *The Divine Inspiration of Holy Scripture*, 11–12. Trembath also analyzes the inductive approaches of Bernard Ramm and William Abraham, both of whom emphasize that the inspiration of Scripture from its effects in the redeemed life of the community. Ramm extensively develops the classical issue of the internal testimony of the Holy Spirit in two books: *The Witness of the Spirit*, (Grand Rapids: Eerdmans, 1959); and in *Special Revelation and the Word of God*, (Grand Rapids: Eerdmans, 1961).

[29]Randall Basinger and David Basinger, "Inerrancy, Dictation and the Free Will Defence," *The Evangelical Quarterly*, 55 (1983): 177–80.

[30]A. H. Strong, *Systematic Theology*, (Old Tappan, N.J.: Revell, 1907), 196ff.

[31]It should be noted that a view of inspiration such as has been described does not preclude the validity and contribution of historical and critical studies of Scripture. Indeed, when the presuppositions of the practitioners of critical methodologies are not antisupernaturalistic, these methods contribute essential foundations for understanding Scripture. See William Abraham, *Divine Revelation and the Limits of Historical Criticism*, (New York: Oxford Univ. Press, 1982); Robert W. Lyon, "Evangelicals and Critical Historical Method," *Interpreting God's Word for Today*, vol. 2, Wesleyan Theological Perspectives series, eds. Wayne McCown and James Earl Massey (Anderson, Ind.: Warner, 1982).

[32]Wesley, *Explanatory Notes*, 303.

[33]John Wesley, *Wesley's Standard Sermons*, ed. Edward H. Sugden (London: Epworth, 1961), 2:215.

[34]Dunning, *Grace, Faith, and Holiness*, 97.

[35]Ibid., 98. Dunning devotes two chapters to an extensive study of the philosophical and theological background and implications of the doctrine of revelation.

[36]William Abraham, *Divine Revelation*, 11. Abraham deals extensively with the distinction between inspiration and divine speaking. He takes issue with a number of scholars who do tend to identify Scripture with divine speaking and who thus erase the distinction between inspiration, which involves the participation of humans, and revelation, which humans receive but in which they do not participate except to record or interpret their perception of the revelation.

[37]Abraham, *Divine Revelation*, 22.

[38]C. M. Horne, "Revelation," *The Zondervan Pictorial Encyclopedia of the Bible*, vol. 5, ed. Merrill C. Tenney (Grand Rapids: Zondervan, 1976), 89. Horne distinguishes between revelation and inspiration, but then falls back into the merging of the two concepts by noting that the Bible is the product of revelation. He says that the interpretation of revelation, which is involved in inspiration, is also revelation so that the Bible is revelation in word. This places the inspired prophets and apostles in the role of the recorders of the divine interpretation of revelation and is inconsistent with a concursive view of inspiration.

[39]Brevard S. Childs, *Introduction to the Old Testament as Scripture* (Philadelphia: Fortress, 1979), 49f.

[40]William Sanford LaSor, David A. Hubbard, and Frederic Wm. Bush, *Old Testament Survey* (Grand Rapids: Eerdmans, 1982), 18.

[41]F. F. Bruce, *The Canon of Scripture*, (Downer's Grove, Ill.: InterVarsity, 1988), 98f.; see also, R. Laird Harris, *Inspiration and Canonicity of the Bible* (Grand Rapids: Zondervan, 1971), 131f.

[42]Robert Gnuse, *The Authority of the Bible* (New York: Paulist, 1985), 105; LaSor, Hubbard, and Bush, *Old Testament Survey*, 18ff. The development of the OT canon is discussed thoroughly in the above works by Childs, Hubbard, LaSor, and Bush. Also, see G. W. Anderson, "Canonical and Non-Canonical," *The Cambridge History of the Bible*, vol. 1, eds. P. R. Ackroyd and C.F. Evans (Cambridge: Cambridge Univ. Press, 1980).

[43]Gnuse, *The Authority of the Bible*, 106f.

[44]Lee Martin McDonald, *The Formation of the Christian Biblical Canon*, (Nashville: Abingdon, 1988), 60ff.; LaSor, Hubbard, Bush, *Old Testament Survey*, 22.

[45]Childs, *The New Testament As Canon*, (Philadelphia: Fortress, 1984), 25.

[46]Glenn Barker, William Lane, and Ramsey Michaels, *The New Testament Speaks* (New York: Harper & Row, 1969), 28.

[47]F. F. Bruce, *The Canon of Scripture*, (Downer's Grove, Ill.: InterVarsity, 1988), 255–69.

[48]Ibid., 260–62.

[49]Barker, Lane, and Michaels, *The New Testament Speaks*, 30–31.

[50]LaSor, Hubbard, Bush, *Old Testament Survey*, 25.

[51]James A. Sanders, *Torah and Canon*, (Philadelphia: Fortress, 1972); Childs, *The New Testament As Canon*; also, see Frank A. Spina, "Canonical Criticism: Childs Versus Sanders," *Interpreting God's Word for Today*, vol. 2, Wesleyan Theological Perspectives, eds. Wayne McCown and James E. Massey (Anderson, Ind.: Warner, 1982), 165–94.

THE PLACE AND FUNCTIONS OF SCRIPTURE

Donald A. D. Thorsen

INTRODUCTION

Since the inception of the Wesleyan tradition, Scripture has remained the primary source of religious authority. The functions of Scripture have varied, ranging from the theological to the devotional. But the place of Scripture has remained *central* to Wesleyans, and the variety of functions of Scripture has remained *vital* it its *beliefs* and *practices*.

In this essay we will delineate the place and functions of Scripture as they have been evident throughout the Wesleyan tradition, beginning with John Wesley. Although the Wesleyan tradition includes more than the theology of Wesley himself, his legacy provides the stimulus from which the tradition developed. We will begin by examining the place of Scripture in relationship to other sources of religious authority in the theology of Wesley and the Wesleyan tradition as a whole. We will continue by examining the functions of Scripture. Generally speaking, the functions of Scripture include the establishment of right *beliefs* (orthodoxy), a right *heart* (orthokardia), and right *actions* (orthopraxis).[1]

PLACE OF SCRIPTURE

John Wesley

John Wesley considered himself to be in the Reformation tradition of *sola scriptura* (Scripture alone), and he liked to refer to himself as *homo unius libri* (a man of one book).[2] For Wesley, Scripture represented the "words of the Spirit of God," the "rule of faith" and "of right and wrong," and the "inviolable Word of God."[3] There was no question that Scripture represented the primary source of religious authority.

In affirming *sola scriptura*, Wesley never intended *solus* (alone) to mean exclusive religious authority.[4] Wesley considered Scripture primary, but he recognized that other factors played *complementary* roles in matters of faith and practice. In particular, Wesley referred to *tradition*, *reason*, and *experience* as inextricably bound up with Scripture in our understanding of true Christianity.

Some may question whether tradition, reason, and experience represent genuine sources of religious authority. But for Wesley, with his Anglican background, there was no question about including tradition and reason. To these he added experience as complementary to the primary authority of Scripture, particularly in confirming, illuminating, and applying the truths of Scripture. Wesley did not intend to be innovative; he intended only to make explicit that which had always occurred in theology. Yet his inclusion of experience represents a unique contribution to the development of theological method in church history.

According to Wesley, tradition represented the one source of religion other than Scripture that added substantively to Christianity. Scripture represents the primary substance of Christian belief and practice; tradition, reason, and experience represent complementary—albeit secondary—resources in the interpretation of Scripture. Yet tradition gives to us the canon of Scripture. It also gives to us the creeds and the earliest teachings of Christian antiquity, which provide the standards of orthodoxy.

With regard to reason, Wesley argued for the reasonableness of Christianity, for example, in *An Earnest Appeal to Men of Reason and Religion.* The idea of the reasonableness of Christianity was widely accepted in eighteenth-century Britain due in large part to the writings of John Locke. Wesley did not advocate a rationalistic or scholastic understanding of religion. On the contrary, reason represented an intellectual activity for reflecting upon the truths of Scripture, organizing those truths, and applying them.[5] Certainly reason possessed limitations, but Wesley had no qualms about affirming the interdependent relationship between reason and a right interpretation of Scripture.

Wesley considered experience an essential factor in conceptualizing theology as well as in living out the Christian life. According to Wesley, experience *does not* supply the substance of Christian truth, but it serves to clarify and enhance that which Scripture teaches. He believed that Christianity involved more than "formal" or "rational religion"; it also involved the heartfelt witness of the Holy Spirit with our own spirits that we are children of God.[6] This experiential dimension is crucial for personal faith as well as the establishment of individual beliefs. Experience, for example, may serve as a corrective to deficient interpretations of Scripture.[7] Like reason, experience as a source of religious authority has limitations. Wesley was well aware of how deceptive our experiences in life may be.[8] But he was convinced that there is an undeniable link between the truths of Scripture and our experience of them, and that the linkage should be recognized and developed theologically.

In summary, Wesley affirmed the primary authority of Scripture while at the same time affirming the genuine—albeit secondary—religious authority of tradition, reason, and experience. He saw the four sources of religious authority as complementary and interdependent. As a shorthand reference to Scripture, tradition, reason and experience, some Wesley scholars refer to the "Wesleyan quadrilateral."[9] The term was *not* used by Wesley, and it should not be conceived as a geometric figure with equilateral sides and relations. Instead the quadrilateral should be conceived as a heuristic metaphor for studying the dynamic way in which

Wesley understood the primacy of scriptural authority in concert with tradition, reason, and experience.

Wesleyan Tradition

Wesley's strong insistence upon the primacy of scriptural authority had a lasting effect upon the religious tradition developed from his teaching. In both Britain and the United States, which were the initial spawning grounds of Methodism, the priority of Scripture continued as a fundamental aspect of belief and practice. The primacy of scriptural authority may be seen in a number of ways in the development of the movement. First, early Methodists continued Wesley's claim that all standards of doctrine were based upon Scripture. No standards were considered valid if separable from Scripture. Second, some standards were established that sought to assist Methodism in clarifying the accountability of that religious community to Scripture.[10] With regard to the latter, Nathaniel Burwash summarizes the standards of doctrine provided by Wesley:

> I. The Standard of Preaching—the fifty-two sermons embraced in the four volumes
>
> II. The Standard of Interpretation—Wesley's *Explanatory Notes Upon the New Testament*
>
> III. The Standard of Unity with the Sister Churches of the Reformation—the Twenty-five Articles of Religion (adapted from the Anglican Thirty-nine Articles)[11]

These standards of doctrine all attempted to develop accountability to Scripture. Of these standards, Edward Sugden comments that the *Sermons* and *Notes* were particularly important to the early Methodist preachers in sermon preparation because they considered sound biblical preaching central to Methodist worship.[12]

Wesley's interpretation of Scripture in the *Sermons* and the *Notes* reflects his high regard for the trustworthiness of the text, particularly the Greek text. But Wesley was not a slavish literalist. His alterations of the King James Version, his treatment of technical problems in Scripture, and generally his appeal to tradition, reason, and experience in the interpretation of Scripture reveal his openness to critical scholarship.[13] This concern for the study of Scripture and its proper interpretation has persisted throughout the Wesleyan tradition. Thomas Oden notes that Wesley's "own pattern of openness was followed largely by Methodist biblical interpreters that came after him."[14] For example, the biblical scholar Adam Clarke (1760–1832) followed in Wesley's tradition of affirming the necessity and authority of Scripture, bringing critical concerns to the study and application of Scripture.[15]

In the field of theology, Richard Watson (1781–1833) and William Pope (1822–1903) first outlined and defended the theology of the Wesleyan tradition and its distinctive Arminian emphases. For the most part, Wesley scholars have not considered it important to write systematic theologies *per se*, but they have been careful to articulate their beliefs in light of critical scholarship. In *Theological Institutes*, Watson was faithful to the evangelical heritage of Wesley, distinguishing it from Calvinistic views of predestination, which limit the atonement of Jesus Christ. Watson affirmed the infallibility of Scripture, and studied it in light of the exegetical contributions of Protestant scholarship.[16] In *Compendium of Christian Theology*, Pope argued that Methodist theology conformed to scriptural, catholic, and orthodox beliefs of church history, and that its Arminian emphases varied only from the extreme forms of Calvinism.[17]

As Methodism developed, at least two basic positions emerged in the Wesleyan tradition with respect to Scripture: evangelicals and liberals. On the one hand, evangelicals continued to believe, as Wesley had believed, that Scripture is the primary revelation of God and that standards of doctrine should conform to it and to the orthodox creeds of the Christian antiquity. Evangelicals minimized the authority of tradition, reason, and experience, and focused primarily on Scripture. Most evangelical Wesleyans avoided the fundamentalist doctrine of inerrancy, but the leaven had an effect upon some of their views.[18] Liberals, on the other hand, wished "to maximize intellectual freedom to explore and develop various new theological positions more amenable to emergent culture."[19] Those denominations, for example, whose mergers formed the United Methodist Church, experienced far greater influence from liberals than other Wesleyan branches. In 1972, the United Methodist Church added a statement on "Our Theological Task" in its *Book of Discipline*, which embraces the principle of doctrinal pluralism.[20] The diversity stems from various opinions concerning the relative authority of Scripture, tradition, reason, and experience.

Although two basic positions on Scripture can be discerned in the Wesleyan tradition, many individuals, groups, and denominations consider themselves somewhere between the two. Most continue to recognize the primary authority of Scripture, though there is also recognition that the interpretation of primacy varies. Certainly the religious authority explicitly attributed to tradition, reason, and experience represents a distinctive characteristic of historic Wesleyanism. The inclusion of experience reflects both a strength and weakness of the tradition. The strength lies in the sophistication and vitality that the Wesleyan tradition brings to its understanding of Scripture; the weakness lies in the capriciousness and lack of accountability to Scripture that may occur.

FUNCTIONS OF SCRIPTURE

Right Belief

Wesley regarded himself and the Methodist movement to be within the mainstream of Christian beliefs derived from Scripture and classical orthodoxy. In a somewhat biased account, Wesley traced the lineage of

Methodism through the "religion of the Church of England" and "the primitive church" to the "religion of the Bible" and that which Wesley called "old religion."[21] This "old religion" predated Scripture, and it consisted of "no other than love: the love of God and of all humankind."[22]

At the start of the Methodist revival, Wesley did not articulate a confession of right beliefs. He did not see the need because he considered Methodism to be firmly within the orthodox succession of the Church of England. Wesley's earliest doctrinal publication was entitled *The Doctrine of Salvation, Faith and Good Works*, which he extracted from the *Homilies* of the Church of England.[23] As the Methodist movement grew, however, a growing need arose for Wesley to address specific questions raised in the context of the ministry. Wesley met with the Methodist preachers at annual conferences, where question of doctrine and polity were decided and then published in the *Minutes*. Wesley designated these *Minutes* "our doctrines" long before other standards of doctrine were established.[24]

Standards of Doctrine. In time, Wesley recognized the need for more formal standards of doctrine. In 1746, he published the first of four volumes of *Sermons*, which came to serve as the foremost standard of doctrine in Methodism. Anglicanism had a long tradition of setting forth distinctive doctrinal positions in the form of sermons. To Wesley sermons were not inferior to other modes of theological writing. On the contrary, he intended to write *ad poplum* (to the bulk of humanity), designing "plain truth for plain people," and abstaining "from all nice and philosophical speculations."[25] For this reason, Albert Outler describes Wesley as "a *folk-theologian*: an eclectic who had mastered the secret of plastic synthesis, simple profundity, and common touch."[26]

One of the most distinctive ways in which Wesley communicated Christian beliefs in a practical way was through hymns. Both John and Charles Wesley made use of popular British tunes in order to communicate scriptural truths to people, utilizing the evangelistic, instructional, and devotional dimensions of hymnody. Charles was prolific in his musical creativity, writing more than 6500 hymns. John also wrote hymns, but was most influential in publishing *A Collection of Hymns of the Use of the People Called Methodists*. The *Collection of Hymns* was so filled with scriptural, experimental (experiential), and practical theology that John claimed, "In what other publication of the kind have you so distinct and full an account of scriptural Christianity?"[27]

Although Wesley may have been practical in his approach to theology, his theology was not inferior in quality. Wesley never intended to write a systematic theology, so readers of his writings should not evaluate him by such standards. Rather than being concerned with the formulation of a system of beliefs, Wesley was concerned about the way in which people approached theological issues *and* how they lived in response to those decisions. Again, Wesley resembled the Anglican tradition in which he was raised. Anglicans distrusted theological systems, and consequently focused more upon the methodology one followed in reaching theological decisions than upon reaching any finality in systematic content. Paul More suggests, "What we have to look for in the ecclesiastical literature of England is not so much finality as direction."[28] Thus, the spirit of Anglicanism and Wesley's theology reflects more of a methodology than a system of belief.

Theological Method. The methodology Wesley inherited was distinct from that of Continental Protestantism. Anglicans conceived of themselves as within the mainstream of Reformation theology, but as incorporating tradition and reason into their theological method. They fancied themselves to be a *via media* between the ecclesiastical authoritarianism of the Roman Catholic Church and tendencies toward the exclusivistic authority of *sola scriptura*. By introducing reason as a mediating source of religious authority, Anglicans believed they would find the right balance theologically between the truths of Scripture and the exegetical contributions of church history. Henry McAdoo explains, "If the distinctiveness of Anglicanism lies not in a theology but a theological method, the distinctiveness of the method lies in the conjunction of these elements [Scripture, tradition, and reason] in one theological instrument."[29]

Just as Wesley accepted the orthodoxy of the Church of England, he accepted the theological method consisting of Scripture, tradition, and reason. The addition of *experience* was not an attempt at innovation but at clarifying that which he perceived to take place in all theological processes. In so doing, Wesley affirmed and enhanced the *via media*, producing a more inclusive and integrative approach to dealing with both the doctrinal and practical issues that arose in the context of the Methodist movement.

The methodology Wesley employed was largely inductive in character. He let Scripture speak for itself. Yet his induction extended beyond the study of Scripture. Wesley argued that theological decisions should draw inductively upon exegetical data found in the annals of orthodox church history, that all relevant data should be critically and logically integrated into one's beliefs, and that experience reveals essential insights into the confirmation, illumination, and application of biblical truths. Wesley's references to Christianity as "experimental religion" relates to his inductive approach to Scripture and theology.[30] The experimental dimension primarily referred to the felt experience of God's Holy Spirit in the life of the believer, but it also referred to the fact that the investigation of relevant data for theology extended beyond an inductive study of Scripture to life itself. One could constructively investigate tradition, reason, and experience in complementing one's interpretation of Scripture. Wesley felt compelled to do so in order to develop a sufficiently integrative understanding of Christian faith and practice. It was an understanding that Wesley considered representative—consciously or unconsciously—of all Christians who preceded him.

Although he was more concerned about method than finality in how one considered theological issues, he provided more than the *Minutes* and *Sermons* as standards of doctrine. Eventually, Wesley formulated the

Twenty-five Articles as the doctrinal summary of the early Methodists. The Articles were not in themselves unique, being an edited form of the Thirty-nine Articles of the Church of England. Wesley thus affirmed the great classical doctrines of church history and the greater Protestant Reformation. These doctrines include orthodox positions on God, the Trinity, Jesus Christ, the Incarnation, the Atonement, the Holy Spirit, and the church. The standards of doctrine distinctive of Methodism, however, continue to reside in the *Minutes, Standard Sermons*, and *Notes*. In particular, Wesley considered it incumbent upon Methodists to revive from Scripture several crucial doctrines that had been neglected or ignored in Christendom. Those doctrines included salvation by faith, with an Arminian concern for the universal scope of the gospel (Mk 1:15; Jn 3:16); assurance of salvation, with an emphasis upon the inner witness of the Holy Spirit (Ro 8:16); and entire sanctification, with an *unremitting belief* in the power of God to perfect one's intentions to love God and one's neighbor (Mt 5:48).

After Wesley, the Methodists largely affirmed those standards of doctrine established by him. As the nineteenth century progressed, both British and American Methodist churches placed more emphasis upon the Articles than upon the other historic standards of doctrine. Oden notes that the Methodist churches continued to affirm "established standards of doctrine" derived from Wesley, but that the more convenient and catholic articulation of doctrinal articles won precedence in church disciplines.[31] This trend was also characteristic of splinter groups from Methodism, such as the black and Holiness churches, which developed their constitutional articles of religion based upon the Twenty-five Articles. The result was that Scripture maintained its place of primacy, while tradition, reason, and experience became less important in the articulation of theological method.

During the twentieth century, little changed in Wesleyan denominations concerning the affirmation of Scripture, articles of religion reflective of the Twenty-five Articles, and other "established standards of doctrine." The most notable exception pertains to the statement on doctrinal pluralism that emerged in the United Methodist Church. The statement has been widely praised and condemned in terms of its continuity with the spirit of Wesleyanism. Those who praise it maintain that United Methodism has recaptured many of the catholic elements in Wesley, while those who condemn it maintain that pluralism is an affront to scriptural authority and an accommodation to culture.

Catholic Spirit. Since the time of Wesley, a "catholic spirit" has characterized the tradition. Wesley first referred to the "catholic spirit" as universal love toward others—an obvious outgrowth of Jesus' command to love.[32] Such love extended beyond love for God and neighbor to include, more specifically, toleration toward differences in theological opinion. Wesley made a distinction between "essentials" of Christian belief and "opinions."[33] He held to a minimum those doctrines that are essential to scriptural Christianity; most are a matter of opinion. Opinions, however, should not preclude fellowship and cooperation, particularly in the ministry. Wesley's spirit was one of openness rather than antagonism toward other Christians, Protestants and Catholics alike. A unity of doctrinal opinions was less important to Wesley than a clear conscience with regard to a unity of love. This unity of love provided the foundation for ecumenical concerns unique to his era. Wesley did not naïvely expect ecclesiastical barriers to disappear, but he did expect that Christians could avoid contention on the one hand and "provoke one to another to love and good works" on the other.[34]

In the twentieth century, Wesleyan denominations have been involved with a variety of ecumenical activities both among themselves and with other traditions. To begin with, a number of mergers have occurred among Methodist-related denominations. For example, several denominations merged to form The Methodist Church in 1939, which experienced further mergers in 1968 to form the United Methodist Church. Among evangelical denominations, the Wesleyan Church merger also occurred in 1968.

With regard to ecumenical relations outside the Wesleyan tradition, the United Methodist Church has led the way in ecumenical dialogue. Methodist leaders such as Bishop G. Bromley Oxnam (1891–1963) and Frank M. North (1850–1935) served important roles in establishing the National Council of Churches, and John R. Mott (1865–1955) helped to form the World Council of Churches. Among evangelical Wesleyans, Holiness denominations served as charter members of the National Association of Evangelicals. Bishop Leslie R. Marston (1894–1979), a Free Methodist, served as the second president of the organization. Evangelical Wesleyans also became involved with the World Evangelical Fellowship. Dialogue and cooperation between liberal and evangelical Wesleyans occurs primarily within the World Methodist Council. However, cooperation at the Council-sponsored conferences seems less effective than in other ecumenical associations.

Right Heart

From the outset of the Methodist revival, Wesley emphasized that his ministry was concerned for heartfelt faith in the life of Christian believers. Wesley himself had had a heartwarming experience at a religious meeting on Aldersgate Street in 1738. After hearing Martin Luther's "Preface to the Epistle to the Romans," Wesley claimed to sense an assurance, reminiscent of Romans 8:2. God "had taken away *my* sins, even *mine*, and saved *me* from the law of sin and death."[35] Wesley scholars debate the actual significance of the Aldersgate event. However, despite debate, Wesley thereafter emphasized the experiential dimension intrinsic to Christian faith and practice.

In theology Wesley was concerned also about incorporating the experiential dimension into matters of Christian faith and practice. Wesley often liked to refer to true Christianity as "heart-religion." In the Preface to the *Sermons*, Wesley equated true religion with that which is both scriptural *and* experimental in nature. We have already seen that in using the term *experimental*, Wesley referred primarily to the heartfelt element of faith. According to Wesley, faith involved more than the intellect or intellectually affirmed beliefs. Faith involved trust, reminiscent of Luther's evangelical concerns, yet it was faith that was sensed in the lie of a believer *and* practically lived out in works of love. Wesley's emphases upon the felt assurance of salvation and the expectation of divine empowerment for a lifestyle of love distinguished him from Luther and the other Reformers. In explication of what he meant by true, scriptural, experimental religion, he commented:

> . . . herein is more especially my desire, first, to guard those who are just setting their faces toward heaven (and who, having little acquaintance with the things of God, and the more liable to be turned out of the way) from formality, from mere outside religion, which has almost driven heart-religion out of the world; and secondly, to warn those who know the religion of the heart, the faith which worketh by love, lest at any time they make void the law through faith, and so fall back into the snare of the devil.[36]

The *Collection of Hymns* represents an excellent example of how Wesley, borrowing a line from one of Charles' hymns, sought to "Unite the pair so long disjoined, Knowledge and vital piety."[37] John Wesley considered the hymnbook "a little body of experimental and practical divinity," and he recommended it for worship "as a means of raising or quickening the spirit of devotion, or confirming his faith, of enlivening his hope, and of kindling or increasing his love to God and man."[38] We see how important it was to conceive of religion as a matter of the heart and of love, which is the goal of scriptural religion. Mildred Wynkoop rightly characterizes Wesley as advocating biblically based beliefs that result in a theology of love.[39]

Religious Affections. Religion was to be a matter of the heart, which included love and other religious affections. The most common meaning of "affections" as found in Wesley's writings pertains to "the general orientation of the person."[40] This orientation includes the emotions. So it was important to Wesley that theology understand the causes, nature, and importance of felt experience within believing individuals in order to establish a holistic vision of Christian life and theology.

Wesley believed that right beliefs alone were insufficient, both for the biblical authors and also for contemporary Christians. In the Preface to his *Explanatory Notes Upon the New Testament*, Wesley said that "An exact knowledge of the truth was accompanied, in the inspired writers, with an exactly regular series of arguments, a precise expression of their meaning and a genuine vigor of suitable affections."[41] These affections were critical to the inspiration of the Scriptures, so the Scriptures become critical to developing similar affections. In order to understand and apply Scripture in the best way possible, he argued that "we should observe the emphasis which lies on every word—the holy affections expressed thereby, and the tempers shown by every writer."[42] He found it lamentable that such holy affections were regarded so little by Christians.

In the interpretation of Scripture, Wesley provided numerous hermeneutical steps a believer should follow to understand and apply Scripture correctly. To begin with, one should begin the study of Scripture within the context of prayer. In addition, one should frequently pause to reflect upon the state of one's present life in relationship to that which is read. These devotional steps and others served to hold in balance the critical study of Scripture and its spiritual and social relevance.[43]

The development of right affections as well as sensitivity to the witness and guidance of the Holy Spirit do not occur without some preparation or training on the part of believers. Wesley's Arminianism affirmed the synergistic cooperation between God's call and people's response in effecting full salvation. That salvation includes the believer's justification and sanctification. With regard to justification, Wesley expected a decisive and conscious conversion on the part of believers. However, justification involved more than the imputation of righteousness. It also involved the *impartation* of righteousness in the new birth (1Pe 1:3). Christians had the privilege of sensing in their own spirits, through the witness of the Holy Spirit, that they had become children of God (Ro 8:16).[44] The new birth ushers in the possibility of living a Christlike life, wholly motivated by love. This possibility pertains to sanctification—"loving the Lord their God with all their heart, and their neighbour as themselves; and the being purified from pride, anger, and evil desire, by a 'faith of the operation of God.'"[45]

Wesley believed that a relative degree of Christian perfection was attainable in this life because Scripture talks about becoming perfect (Mt 5:48), loving God with all one's heart, soul, mind and strength (Mt 22:37–40; Mk 12:28–30), perfecting holiness (2Co 7:1), crucifying the sinful nature (Gal 5:24), becoming blameless (1Th 5:23), and going on to maturity, which means perfection (Heb 6:1). Wesley did not advocate absolute or Adamic perfection. But he concluded that we need to develop a significant understanding of Christian perfection—in terms of the perfecting of love—that makes sense of scriptural teachings and our experience of the power of God to transform the lives of believers. Christian perfection was conceived of in terms of love because only "love is productive of all right affections."[46]

Means of Grace. The development of love in the renewal of the image of God, which Wesley strove to engender in the lives of Christians, involved human as well as divine participation. Wesley believed that God's grace represented the beginning, continuation, and end of all aspects of salvation, but that grace did not preclude responsibility on the part of individuals. Once people responded to God in faith, growth was to be sought "with all diligence, in the way which [God] hath ordained."[47]

Wesley emphasized the means of grace as the ordinary way in which to encourage worship and effect growth.

He distinguished between instituted means of grace and prudential means of grace. The instituted means of grace include those channels found in Scripture, specifically instituted by Jesus Christ, through which God conveys blessings to humans. The channels include the following:

> . . . prayer, whether in secret or with the great congregation; searching the Scripture (which implies reading, hearing, and meditating thereon) and receiving the Lord's Supper, eating bread and drinking wine in remembrance of him; and these we believe to be ordained of God as the ordinary channels of conveying his grace to the souls of men.[48]

The list is not exhaustive because Wesley also considered such activities as fasting and the assembling of believers in small groups for fellowship, nurture, and witness to be indispensable emphases in the early church.[49] His own emphasis upon small groups was influenced through formative contacts in his early life with the pietistic theology and worship practices of the Moravians. He incorporated small-group dynamics into the Methodist revival, and then improved upon them by establishing a highly efficient organization of societies, classes, and bands. New converts were enfolded into small groups as quickly as possible, and, in fact, most worship, evangelism, social service, and Christian nurture occurred within the dynamic of small groups.

The prudential means of grace included the rules for giving structure to the Christian life, particularly as implemented in small groups. These rules were based upon principles found in Scripture and could vary, depending upon changing circumstances of an individual or society. This is why they were considered prudent for growth in grace. They promoted prayer; the hearing, reading, and meditation upon Scripture; and so on. Wesley considered the rules to be essential for establishing spiritual discipline in the lives of believers and in providing guidelines to which individuals must submit in order to maintain good standing in the Methodist movement. As a result, the Methodist societies, classes, and bands involved a high degree of religious zeal and accountability. But another result was a high degree of success in evangelism, Christian nurture, church renewal, and social service.

Great Awakenings. The Great Awakening is usually identified with the several religious revivals that occurred in the United States during the eighteenth and nineteenth centuries. Methodism in the United States both contributed to and benefited from these events. Although they were not exclusively Methodist awakenings, the term aptly symbolizes the spirit of Wesley's ministry and the theology of the Wesleyan tradition in England, the United States, and around the world.

In the United States under the episcopal leadership of Francis Asbury (1745–1816), itinerant preachers, known as circuit riders, spread the gospel by horseback across the growing nation. Once people became

Methodists, they were enfolded into weekly class meetings for "fellowship in Christian experience."[50] Emphasis upon personal conversion, inner assurance of salvation, and holy living continued as primary themes, and revivalism became the dominant means for effecting the ministry.

As Methodism grew to become the largest Protestant denomination in the United States by 1840, some of the distinctive characteristics of Methodism began to wane. Emphases upon revivalism and small groups diminished as did emphasis upon such doctrines as sanctification. With regard to the latter, the Holiness movement emerged within Methodism during the middle of the nineteenth century as a part of the Higher Christian Life Movement.

The Holiness movement emphasized two crisis moments in the lives of believers: conversion and entire sanctification. Entire sanctification signifies that transformation, subsequent to conversion, when the total consecration of the believer is met by the gracious empowerment of God to live lives characterized by full intention to love God and one's neighbor. Entire sanctification was thought to come, like conversion, in an instant by grace through faith. This emphasis had been present in Wesley, but the Holiness movement emphasized the *crisis* dimension to the extent that it tended to neglect the *progressive* aspect of sanctification present before and after any such crisis moments. Melvin Dieter suggests that Holiness proponents such as Phoebe Palmer (1807–1874) "centered more on the significance of the experience of the critical moment than on the nature of the ongoing relationship" with God.[51] As such, the Holiness movement shifted away from the balance Wesley had maintained in his interpretation of Scripture.

The movement did, however, preserve Wesley's emphasis upon right affections characteristic of the original Methodist movement. Holiness in fact came to symbolize the essence of Wesleyanism. With its emphasis upon the wholeness of the Christian experience, as characterized by holy living, the movement sought to revive the holistic vision of Christianity put forth by Wesley. For example, Palmer was one of the most effective Holiness revivalists, traveling across the United States to promote evangelism and holiness in churches and camp meetings. Non-Methodists supported holiness teachings on Christian perfection through the ministries and writings of such people as Charles Finney (1792–1875) and Asa Mahan (1799–1889), who became representative of the Oberlin perfectionist teaching.

Palmer also revived the importance of small groups, for example, as found in her Tuesday Meetings for the Promotion of Holiness. These meetings were held weekly in New York City, which influenced Christians inside and outside Methodism. Today the mandatory discipline of small groups has largely disappeared from the Wesleyan tradition, though evangelical churches and para-church groups still encourage their formation. Interestingly, modern proponents of church growth appeal to the small group dynamics of Pietism and Wesleyanism as models of success on which to develop contemporary strategies for growth.

The Holiness movement produced a wealth of practical theology, including published sermons, devotional literature, magazines, tracts, and hymnody. This practical theology served to put into the hands of common and often poor people easily accessible guides to Scripture that were of evangelistic, instructional, and devotional use. The pervasiveness of such literature reinforced the American camp meeting revivals and the Sunday school movement of the late nineteenth century. Today, emphasis upon hymnody and worship within the Wesleyan tradition may still be found, as for example in the theology of such Methodists as Geoffrey Wainright, whose book *Doxology: The Praise of God in Worship, Doctrine and Life: A Systematic Theology* (Oxford Univ. Press) presents theology within the context of *doxa* (giving glory).

Protests against the lack of holiness preaching within Methodist churches in the United States resulted in the secession of such denominations as the Wesleyan Methodist Church in 1843 and the Free Methodist Church in 1860, the first self-styled Holiness denominations. Within mainline Methodism, however, the influence of the Holiness movement formally took hold in the National Campmeeting Association for the Promotion of Holiness, which was organized in 1867. This organization later became the National Holiness Association, which promoted holiness through publications and missions as well as camp meetings, and is now known as the Christian Holiness Association. Eighteen denominations and nearly fifty colleges and theological seminaries comprise the Association.

In Britain, holiness emphases were imported from the United States through the meetings held by the husband and wife team of Robert Pearsall Smith (1827–1899) and Hannah Whitall Smith (1832–1911), whose devotional writings are still popular today. Their influence, along with that of William Boardman (1810–1886), contributed to the emergence of the Keswick Convention in 1876, which became part of the Higher Christian Life Movement in Britain. The Keswick Convention does not involve a doctrinal system; it is a "Convention for the Promotion of Practical Holiness," through week-long conventions or meetings with emphases upon sin, God's provision, consecration, being filled with the Holy Spirit, and service.[52] Although Keswick theology reflects mainstream Protestantism, its emphasis upon the development of holy living through spiritual disciplines reflects its holiness origins in Methodism; however, it differs from the American Holiness movement in its understanding of the nature of sanctification. Keswick teaching gained influence in the United States near the end of the nineteenth century through the ministry and organizations established by such people as Dwight L. Moody (1837–1899).

In Keswick teaching and that of the Holiness movement, the experience of sanctification often became identified with Holy Spirit baptism. This language originated with John Fletcher (1729–1785),

Wesley's chosen successor, rather than Wesley himself. But Wesley did not oppose Fletcher's Pentecostal and dispensational hermeneutic to his biblical interpretation of Christian perfection.[53] In this respect, Fletcher emphasized the promise to every believer of the Holy Spirit's full blessing. Fletcher's writings became influential in the United States, where more editions of his writings were published than those of Wesley.

Holy Spirit-baptism language eventually became incorporated into the Pentecostal movement in the United States. Some Pentecostals argued for sanctification as a second definite work of grace prior to baptism in the Holy Spirit, which represented a third definite work of grace and was confirmed by the gift of tongues. Other Pentecostals, influenced by Baptist and Reformed backgrounds, considered conversion the only prerequisite for baptism in the Holy Spirit.[54] Within the Holiness tradition, no consensus has been reached concerning the proper interpretation and role of Holy Spirit baptism. However, in the broad Wesleyan movement within contemporary Methodist, Holiness, and Pentecostal churches, Dieter observes that all basically find their understanding of "full salvation" in the succinct questions and responses outlined by Wesley in his *Plain Account of Christian Perfection*:

Q. What is Christian Perfection?

A. The loving God with our heart, mind, soul, and strength. . . .

Q. Can any mistake flow from pure love?

A. I answer, (1) Many mistakes may consist with pure love. (2) Some may accidentally flow from it; I mean love itself may incline us to mistake. . . .

Q. How shall we avoid setting perfection too high or too low?

A. By keeping to the Bible, and setting it just as high as the Scripture does. It is nothing higher and nothing lower than this . . . love governing the heart and life, running through all our tempers, words, and actions. . . . [Christian] perfection . . . is purity of intention, dedicating all the life to God.[55]

Right Action

Wesley was active throughout his life in advocating actions commensurate with a Christian life of love for one's neighbor as well as for God. Acts of love were varied, ranging from evangelical ministries to social activism. Wesley considered a *biblically based* ministry to be inextricably bound up with the complex needs of society, and he did his best to balance evangelical and social concerns.

The broad Wesleyan movement following Wesley also manifested a noteworthy tradition of social as well as spiritual concern and activism. The balance found in Wesley, however, was not always characteristic of the various branches of Methodism. Sometimes denominations shifted, emphasizing the social to the neglect of the spiritual, or emphasizing the spiritual to the neglect of the social. But overall Wesleyans have been on the forefront of evangelical *and* social ministries.

Social Holiness. Wesley exhibited a marvelous balance between the need for right actions on both a private and public level. Holiness, for example, was seen neither as a purely private dimension of Christianity nor as a purely public dimension. Holiness, almost by definition, was something that affected the whole of one's life. Since people are spiritual as well as social beings, holiness should relate to all areas of life.[56]

With regard to people's spiritual needs, Wesley sought to proclaim the gospel message and to nurture those who believe. In order to accomplish this ministry, Wesley began with Scripture, yet was willing to entertain that which could be distilled from tradition, reason, and experience. Thus, Wesley experimented with the unorthodox practices of preaching out-doors, establishing extended intra-church meetings, singing hymns to popular tunes, appointing lay preachers, and eventually ordaining them for the "effective work of the ministry." The societies, classes, and bands were, as Colin Williams describes them, "important experiments . . . essential to translate faith into forms of discipline, in order to relate the faith to the common concerns of daily life and to provide for the mutual growth of the members."[57] They also served as the training centers for those outside established programs in the Church of England who were interested in pursuing missions work, particularly in the American colonies. Methodist missionaries were officially sent from Britain to the American colonies in 1769.

Wesley is well known for his emphasis upon salvation, holiness, and other aspects of the spiritual life, but his care for people extended beyond their spiritual well being. Considering his time and place in history, Wesley was in the forefront of helping alleviate the social needs of eighteenth-century Britain. His care for souls extended to the whole person, especially recognizing the importance of caring for the poor, the uneducated, the sick, or those who—for various reasons—were dispossessed by society, for example, slaves and prisoners. Wesley especially sought care for the poor. It was toward them that he directed his primary evangelistic thrusts and his social concern. For example, he provided basic medical care and wrote simple medical manuals to aid those who could not afford professional care.[58] He also established an orphanage and what came to be known as "The Poor House" for those, especially widows, who could not care for themselves. Wesley took it upon himself to educate those who otherwise did not have the means to be educated, and eventually established Kingswood School to service a larger number of children. He even made it possible for people to receive money who had immediate needs for small loans by creating a benevolent loan fund.[59]

Wesley's concern for the poor extended beyond actual acts of goodwill toward the poor. He wrote sermons—all *biblically* based—for the purpose of instructing Methodists on how to handle their money. In addition to giving to the ministry, Methodists were exhorted to give to the needs of the poor—those whom Outler describes as "Wesley's self-chosen constituency: 'Christ's poor.' "[60] In *The Use of Money*, Wesley exhorted Christians to *gain* all they can, *save* all they can, and *give* all they can.[61] He soon discovered that his Methodist followers were good at the first two principles, but ignored the third principle against surplus accumulation. He regarded surplus accumulation to be the leading sin prohibiting effective Christian praxis.[62]

Most Wesley scholars recognize that his teachings on social holiness and social responsibility concentrate on the renewal of society rather than on its transformation. Wesley did, however, exhibit characteristics of realized eschatology, that is, belief in the biblical promises of kingdom renewal for the present. Williams argues that Wesley's emphasis upon the new way of life available to Christians, the inward dynamic of religion, and the possibility of social renewal point to a belief that far-reaching renewal would result from the life of his societies.[63]

Wesley lived in an era that did not possess the same social consciousness shared by modern Christians. So we must not expect from Wesley the kind of theological sophistication and praxis held by Christians today. But in his religious and economic radicalism, he laid the conceptual groundwork for later involvements by Methodists, for example, in the growth of the British Liberal Party, the rise of socialism, and activism on behalf of industrial laborers. In the words of Vivian Green, Wesley's "Religious radicalism had acted as a midwife to political reform."[64] Thus, we are not surprised when Williams finds in Wesley's abolitionist support of Wilberforce, a belief "that God appoints times (*kairoi*) when an attack on great social evils can succeed, but that for their success the complete obedience of his followers and the leaders he has appointed is required."[65]

Way of Being. Wesley saw the necessity of balancing right actions along with right beliefs and a right heart. Although he considered right beliefs essential to Christianity, his ministry focused more upon the need for a right heart and right actions. From his perspective, the essence of biblical Christianity reflected more of a way of being than a way of believing. That way of being included more than the state of one's heart; it also included actions that emanated from the character one develops in the context of a personal relationship with God. Thus, it became important to Wesley to determine those biblical principles that guide us toward determining right actions.

Wesley not only considered it important to determine what those principles are, he considered it vital to inculcate them in the lives of the Methodists. In 1739, soon after his experience at Aldersgate, he responded to requests of some of his followers to organize small groups in which prayer might occur and Scripture be studied in an atmosphere of accountability. The initial intentions of the people who came to Wesley were simply to avoid sin and seek salvation. Wesley responded by forming small groups for those with "a desire to flee from the wrath to come, to be saved from their sins," which constituted the only prerequisite for membership.[66] But Wesley did not settle for ministering for these spiritual goals alone. He instituted *The Rules of the United Societies* to provide disciplines for developing whole people—whole Christians—in relationship to themselves individually, to their accountability group, and to others, including the church and society.

Simply stated, the rules consist of doing no harm, doing good, and attending upon all the ordinances of God.[67] The ordinances of God, of course, are derived from Scripture. They largely include the instituted means of grace described earlier: the public worship of God; ministry of the Word, either read or expounded; the Supper of the Lord; private prayer; searching the Scriptures; and fasting, or abstinence. The rules themselves constitute the prudential means of grace critical to the organization and function of the societies, classes, and bands.

Doing no harm included such traditional acts as not taking the name of God in vain. But it also included prohibitions reflective of a concern for problems that affected society. For example, the rules prohibit the buying and selling of uncustomed goods, the giving or taking of things on usury, and laying up treasures upon earth. We have already seen that Wesley considered the accumulation of wealth to be one of the greatest threats to the well-being of individual Christians as well as of society.

Doing good involved the longstanding Christian concern for sins of omission as well as those of commission. As Christians had opportunity and as far as it was possible, Wesley expected that good works should be performed that ministered to the whole person. He urged doing good

> to their bodies, of the ability which God giveth, by giving food to the hungry, by clothing the naked, by visiting or helping them that are sick, or in prison; to their souls by instructing, reproving, or exhorting all they have any intercourse with; trampling under foot that enthusiastic doctrine of devils, that we are not to do good unless "our heart be free to it". . . .[68]

In and of themselves, these rules appear unremarkable. When seen in the context of Wesley's small-group organization and his personal social ministry and published exhortations, we discover a *holistic* and *visionary* activism. Even H. Richard Niebuhr recognized that the sanctification and perfection emphases of Wesley and the Wesleyan tradition represent one of the great church historical proponents of both individual *and* socio-cultural transformation.[69]

Revivalism and the Social Gospel. In the century following Wesley, Methodism continued a strong emphasis upon the well-being of individuals through its emphasis upon revivalism and a concomitant concern for holiness and Christian nurture. We have already seen how the Wesleyan tradition, especially in its Holiness, camp meeting, and Keswick branches, promoted optimism in the spiritual transformation of individuals. These emphases continued to be promoted through revivals, camp meetings, missions, and so on.

Following the biblical injunction to make disciples throughout the world, Methodists were actively involved worldwide in planting churches, schools, and medical facilities. The Methodist Episcopal Church in the United States organized its own mission board as early as 1833. Other Wesleyan denominations established theirs, bringing the same zeal for revival and holy living to mission work. Methodist missionaries of note include William Taylor (1821–1902), who established missions on six continents; E. Stanley Jones (1884–1973), who was an innovator in employing methods of evangelism appropriate to a particular culture; and J. Waskom Pickett (1890–1981), whose missions writings inspired leaders in the contemporary Church Growth Movement.

A prominent sense of social consciousness and activism toward service for and the transformation of culture has historically characterized the Wesleyan tradition. These emphases began with Wesley, but his followers broadened them, becoming more inclusive in their ministry to persons around the world and to the need for social and political involvement in changing unjust social structures. One of the early examples of social concern in the United States may be found in the Wesleyan Methodist Church, which in 1843 argued for abolition as a reason for forming a new denomination. Similarly, the Free Methodist Church argued for abolition in 1860. Both representative of the Holiness movement, these churches advocated other traditional Wesleyan concerns, for example, the need for simple lifestyle and social concern on behalf of the poor. They also advocated greater participation of women in ministry, allowing women to preach and teach. Timothy Smith, author of *Revivalism and Social Reform*, argues that the origins of social Christianity in the United States rest in large measure upon the mid-century revivalists, particularly those who advocated perfection in the Wesleyan tradition.

The best example of social concern among evangelical Wesleyans in the nineteenth century may be found in the formation of the Salvation Army. William Booth (1829–1912), who grew up in British Methodism, founded the Salvation Army in London during the 1860s to minister through evangelism, social work, and rescue homes. During the latter decades of the century, the work of the Army spread to the United States and around the world. The movement continues as a symbol of dedicated concern for the social as well as spiritual well-being of people. Among evangelicals Wesleyans, the Salvation Army is the most prominent social-activist group.

The Methodist Episcopal Church in the United States acted significantly in line with its heritage of social service. In the 1880s, the northern bishops addressed the problems of workers during the labor crises. In 1908, that church adopted a Social Creed, under the editorial direction of Harry F. Ward (1873–1966), which formally addressed critical problems of industrial laborers. Frank North took the Social Creed to the Federal Council of the Churches of Christ in America, a forerunner of the National Council of Churches, where it was widely adopted by other

Protestant denominations. The Social Creed was later modified in 1912 to include other social concerns, and it is regarded as a classic statement of the goals of the social gospel.[70]

At the turn of the twentieth century, the term *social gospel* gained prominence as a description of the effort to relate biblical and theological insights to the problems of society. However, the social gospel increasingly became identified with liberal Christianity, both outside and inside the Wesleyan tradition. Members of the Methodist Episcopal Church, both northern and southern, became concerned with greater social relevance in the communication and application of the gospel.

After World War I, the optimism of the social gospel movement began to wane. However, the influence continued to persist among denominations influenced by liberal concerns. In recent decades, evangelically influenced denominations have become more socially aware and active through the National Association of Evangelicals and the World Evangelical Fellowship. Both evangelical and liberal Wesleyans have had difficulty trying to maintain the balance between spiritual and social concerns found in the theology and ministry of Wesley. But, overall, the Wesleyan tradition has been more conscious and active than most denominations in holding these tensions in balance.

CONCLUSION

Throughout the whole of the Wesleyan tradition, Scripture has maintained its primary role in the reflection upon and in the formulation of right *doctrines*, right *hearts*, and right *actions*. The primacy of Scripture, however, has not precluded the integration of insights from tradition, reason, and experience as genuine, albeit secondary, sources of religious authority. The result has been a tradition that creatively holds in tension elements of Christianity often left in isolation. These are some of the elements that Wesleyanism seeks to hold in balance: primacy of scriptural authority and the complementary authorities of tradition, reason, and experience; standards of doctrine and doctrinal toleration, reflective of Wesley's emphasis upon a catholic spirit; formal characteristics of religion and a religion of the heart; and evangelical and social concern for the well-being of all people. These elements represent only a few of the ways in which Wesleyans affirm the place and function of Scripture, but they represent distinctive aspects of the tradition.

NOTES

[1]Gregory S. Clapper suggests *orthokardia* as complementary to the categories of orthodoxy and *orthopraxis* in studying the theology of John Wesley. We consider the three categories helpful to the study of Wesleyanism as a whole. See Gregory S. Clapper, *John Wesley on Religious Affections* (Metuchen, N.J.: Scarecrow Press, 1989), 154–56, 171–73.

[2]For example, see Preface, §5, "Sermons on Several Occasions," *Works* (Bicentennial ed.), 1:105.

[3]"The Circumcision of the Heart" (1733, sermon 17), §2, *Works* (Bicentennial ed.), 1:402;"On Faith, Heb. 11:6" (1788, sermon 106), I.8, *Works* (Bicentennial ed.), 3:496; "The Witness of Our Own Spirit" (1746, sermon 12), §6, *Works* (Bicentennial ed.), 1:302–3); and "Seek First the Kingdom" (1725, sermon 134), [§10], *Works* (Bicentennial ed.), 4:220).

[4]See also Albert C. Outler, ed., *John Wesley* (New York: Oxford University Press, 1980), 28, n101.

[5]See Laurence W. Wood, "Wesley's Epistemology," *Wesleyan Theological Journal*, 10.1 (1975): 52. See also "The Case of Reason Impartially Considered" (1781, sermon 70), §§1–6, II.10, *Works* (Bicentennial ed.), 2:587–89, 599–600.

[6]See "The Witness of the Spirit, I" (1746, sermon 10), "The Witness of the Spirit, II" (1767, sermon 11), and "The Witness of Our Own Spirit" (1746, sermon 12) in *Works* (Bicentennial ed.), 1:267–313.

[7]See also Harald Lindström, *Wesley and Sanctification* (1980; reprint, Grand Rapids: Zondervan, 1983), 139.

[8]See "The Nature of Enthusiasm" (1750, sermon 37), *Works* (Bicentennial ed.), 2:44–60.

[9]Albert C. Outler coined the term "Wesleyan quadrilateral." See "The Wesleyan Quadrilateral in John Wesley," *Wesleyan Theological Journal* 20.1 (1985): 7–18.

[10]See Thomas C. Oden, *Doctrinal Standards in the Wesleyan Tradition* (Grand Rapids: Zondervan, 1988), 21.

[11]Nathaniel Burwash, ed., *Wesley's Doctrinal Standards* (Toronto: William Briggs, 1881), xi.

[12]See Edward H. Sugden, Introduction, *John Wesley's Fifty-Three Sermons*, ed., Edward H Sugden (Nashville: Abingdon, 1983), 4–5.

[13]See also George C. Cell, *John Wesley's New Testament Compared with the Authorized Version* (Chicago: Winston, 1938); Oden, *Doctrinal Standards* 82–84; Robin Scroggs, "John Wesley as Biblical Scholar," *Journal of Bible and Religion*, 28.4 (October, 1969): 415–22; R. Larry Shelton, "John Wesley's Approach to Scripture in Historical Perspective," *Wesleyan Theological Journal*, 16.1 (1981): 23–50; and Colin Williams, *John Wesley's Theology Today* (New York: Abingdon, 1960), 23–28.

[14]Oden, *Doctrinal Standards*, 83.

[15]See Adam Clarke, General Preface, *Commentary on the Holy Bible: One-Volume Edition* (Grand Rapids: Baker, 1967), 8–10, and *Christian Theology* (New York: G. Lane & P.P. Standford, 1842), 47–63.

[16]See Richard Watson, *Theological Institutes* (New York: B. Waugh and T. Mason, 1833), 56–70, 510–44.

[17]See William Pope, *A Compendium of Christian Theology* (2d ed.; New York: Phillips & Hunt, 1881), 1:20–21.

[18]See William J. Abraham, *The Coming Great Revival: Recovering the Full Evangelical Tradition* (San Francisco: Harper & Row, 1984), 102–8.

[19]Oden, *Doctrinal Standards*, 108–9.

[20]See *The Book of Discipline of the United Methodist Church 1972* (Nashville: United Methodist Publishing House, 1972), 68–82.

[21]See "On Laying the Foundation of the New Chapel" (1777, sermon 112), II.3, *Works* (Bicentennial ed.), 3:585–86.

[22]"An Earnest Appeal," §2, *Works* (Oxford ed.), 11:45, quoted by Wesley in "On Laying the Foundation of the New Chapel" (1777, sermon 112), II.1 *Works* (Bicentennial ed.), 3:585.

[23]See "The Doctrine of Salvation, Faith and Good Works," *John Wesley*, ed., Albert C. Outler (New York: Oxford Univ. Press, 1964), 123–33.

[24]Oden, *Doctrinal Standards*, 25.

[25]Introduction, 2–3, "Sermons on Several Occasions," *Works* (Bicentennial ed.), 1:103–4.

[26]Outler, *John Wesley*, 119.

[27]Preface, §5, "A Collection of Hymns for the Use of the People Called Methodists," *Works* (Bicentennial ed.), 7:74.

[28]Paul E. More, introductory essay, *Anglicanism*, ed. Paul E. More and Frank L. Cross (Milwaukee: Morehouse-Gorham, 1935), xx.

[29]McAdoo, *Spirit of Anglicanism*, vi.

[30]For example, see Preface, §6, "Sermons on Several Occasions," *Works* (Bicentennial ed.), 1:106.

[31]See Oden, *Doctrinal Standards*, 65–66.

[32]See "Catholic Spirit" (1750, sermon 39), *Works* (Bicentennial ed.), 2:94.

[33]For example, see "Catholic Spirit," (1750, sermon 39), I.1–6, *Works* (Bicentennial ed.), 2:82–85; "On Patience" (1784, sermon 83), §11, *Works* (Bicentennial ed.), 3:177; and "On God's Vineyard" (1787, sermon 107), IV.4, V.7, *Works* (Bicentennial ed.), 3:514, 517.

[34]"A Letter to a Roman Catholic," §16, *Works* (Jackson ed.), 10:85.

[35]*Journal*, §14, *Works* (Bicentennial ed.), 18:250, 24 May 1738.

[36]Preface, §6, *Works* (Bicentennial ed.), 1:106.

[37]Charles Wesley, "A Collection of Hymns for the Use of the People Called Methodists," (hymn 461), 1.5, *Works* (Bicentennial ed.), 7:644.

[38]Preface, §4, 8, "A Collection of Hymns for the Use of the People Called Methodists," *Works* (Bicentennial ed.), 7:74, 75.

[39]See Mildred Bangs Wynkoop, *A Theology of Love: The Dynamic of Wesleyanism* (Kansas City: Beacon Hill Press, 1972), 9–11.

[40]Gregory S. Clapper, *John Wesley on Religious Affections: His Views on Experience and Emotion and Their Role in the Christian Life and Theology* (Metuchen, N.J.: Scarecrow Press, 1989), 51.

[41]Preface, §11, *Explanatory Notes Upon the New Testament* (1755 reprint; London: Epworth Press, 1976), 9.

[42]Preface, §12, *Explanatory Notes Upon the New Testament*, 10.

[43]See Preface, *Explanatory Notes Upon the Old Testament*, 3 vols. (1765 reprint; Salem, Ohio: Schmul, 1975), 1. Cf. summaries of Wesley's scriptural hermeneutics in William M. Arnett, "John Wesley—Man of One Book" (Diss., Drew University, 1954), 89–96; and Outler, introduction, *Works* (Bicentennial ed.), 1:58–59.

[44]See "The Witness of the Spirit, I" (1746, sermon 10), "The Witness of the Spirit, II" (1767, sermon 11), and "The Witness of Our Own Spirit" (1746, sermon 12), *Works* (Bicentennial ed.), 1:267–313.

45"The Means of Grace," (1746, sermon 16), [I].2, *Works* (Bicentennial ed.), 1:378.

46"To Dr. Conyers Middleton," VI.I.6, *Letters* (Telford ed.), 2:377, 24 January 1749.

47"A Plain Account of Christian Perfection," §19, *Works* (Jackson ed.), 11:403.

48"The Means of Grace," (1746, sermon 16), II.1, *Works* (Bicentennial ed.), 1:381.

49Williams, *John Wesley's Theology Today*, 135.

50*The Oxford Dictionary of the Christian Church*, eds., F. L. Cross and E. A. Livingstone (1958; rev. ed., Oxford: Oxford University Press, 1983), 909.

51Melvin E. Dieter, "The Wesleyan Perspective," *Five Views on Sanctification*, ed., Melvin E. Dieter, et al. (Grand Rapids: Zondervan, 1987), 41.

52See Steven Barabas, *So Great Salvation* (London: Marshall, Morgan & Scott; Grand Rapids: Eerdmans, 1952), 21, 108.

53See Dieter, "The Wesleyan View," *Five Views of Sanctification*, 43–46.

54See Donald Dayton, *The Theological Roots of Pentecostalism* (Grand Rapids: Zondervan, 1987).

55Dieter, "The Wesleyan Perspective," *Five Views of Sanctification*, 45–46, quoting Wesley, "Plain Account of Christian Perfection," §§19, 27, *Works* (Jackson ed.), 11:394, 397, 444.

56In this section, I draw upon my work in *The Wesleyan Quadrilateral*, (Grand Rapids, Zondervan, 1990), 93–95.

57Williams, *John Wesley's Theology Today*, 140.

58For example, Wesley published *Primitive Physic[k], Or an Easy and Natural Method of Curing Most Diseases* (1747; London: Epworth Press, 1960), which was reprinted twenty-one times during his lifetime.

59For an account of these social services, see "A Plain Account of the People Called Methodists," XII–XV, *Works* (Jackson ed.), 8:263–68.

60Outler, introductory comment, "The Use of Money" (1760, sermon 50), *Works* (Bicentennial ed.), 2:263.

61"The Use of Money," (1760, sermon 50), *Works* (Bicentennial ed.), 2:263–380.

62See Outler's comments in the introductory comment to "The Danger of Riches" (1781, sermon 87), *Works* (Bicentennial ed.), 3:227.

63See Williams, *John Wesley's Theology Today*, 194–98; cf. 179–82.

64Vivian H. H. Green, *John Wesley* (London: Nelson, 1964), 158.

65Williams, *John Wesley's Theology Today*, 197n13.

66"The Nature, Design, and General Rules of the United Societies," §4, *Works* (Jackson ed.), 8:270.

67See Ibid., 269–71.

68Ibid., 270–71.

69See H. Richard Niebuhr, *Christ and Culture* (New York: Harper & Row, 1951), 218–19.

70Stephen C. Mott, "Social Creed of the Churches," *Dictionary of Christianity in America*, eds., Daniel G. Reid, et. al. (Downers Grove, Ill.: InterVarsity, 1990), 1101.

THE BIBLE AND TRUTH

Laurence W. Wood

Since the Enlightenment, we require that truth be based on a critical evaluation of the facts of experience. The motto of the Enlightenment was: "Dare to think for oneself!" This meant a rejection of blind submission to tradition and authority. This new demand for individual freedom to think critically for oneself without coercion and interference revolutionized the face of Western society. It particularly called into question the uncritical, believing attitude of traditional Christians that the Bible is the ultimate written revelation of God.

This does not mean that critical thinking is hostile toward Christian belief. In fact, scholars of the Enlightenment era have shown that critical thinking emerged out of the concerns of Christian theology with its commitment to the nature of truth. The rise of modern philosophy and the development of the natural sciences, sociology, psychology, and historical criticism are rooted in the concerns of Christian theology.[1]

An internationally known theologian/philosopher insists that the demand of the Enlightenment for individual freedom to think critically for oneself is the mature result of Christian faith itself. The truth concerning the revelation of God is not best preserved through suppressing critical questions. He concludes that there is no need to protect the Bible from critical examination because the divine revelation is capable of meeting the test of a matured and thoughtful mind. Otherwise, if belief is compelled by mere authoritarian claims, faith easily degenerates into blind gullibility and self-delusion, as Feuerbach and Freud have charged.[2]

The question that Enlightenment thinking reformulated in particular was epistemological. Epistemology is a branch of philosophy that seeks to determine the nature and limits of knowledge. Of course, the question "What can we know?" has been a central issue since the earliest days of ancient Greek philosophy. But in the modern world this question took precedence over the question "What is reality?"

THE SYNTHESIS OF GREEK PHILOSOPHY AND BIBLICAL REVELATION

Pre-Enlightenment thinking had largely emphasized the nature of what-is-real in itself antecedent to the mind's knowledge of it. This branch of philosophy is called ontology. This type of philosophical inquiry had begun with the earliest Greek philosophers and resulted in the development of ontological categories classically formulated by Plato and Aristotle.

Even the creeds of the church and the development of Christian theology adapted these Greek categories for expressing the message of the Bible.

The Early Christian Apologists. The earliest Christian intellectuals in the second century A.D. where called apologists (*apologia*, "a defense") because they felt the need to defend the Bible. These men had been converted from paganism, had already been trained in philosophy, and had read widely in the worldly wisdom of their day. Their intent was to show that the biblical faith was based on thoughtful consideration of the facts and that its truth could be readily embraced by any educated citizen of the Roman Empire.

Their success in showing that the Bible is intellectually respectable enhanced the missionary expansion of the church, for historians have shown that the greatest threat to the spread of the Christian gospel in its earliest days was not the mystery religions with the barbaric idea of the dying and rising of gods. Though the masses of people were not well educated and were easily swayed by mythological folklore, the faith of the earliest Christians simply did not fit into this irrational network of beliefs. The appeal of these believers to historical facts as a basis for their faith put their beliefs altogether outside the framework of myth. That was not the case with popular religions that were embraced by their pagan neighbors throughout the Roman Empire.

The Threat of Stoicism to Christian Faith. The real threat to the Christian missionary expansion came from the Stoics.[3] These intellectuals developed a philosophy of religious consolation in a world troubled with political upheaval, personal tragedy, and family disintegration. Borrowing elements from the thinking of Plato and Aristotle, they espoused a rational view of the universe that offered the worshiper a pantheistic union with God and a fellowship of universal brotherhood. The pursuit of God and the pursuit of Truth were one and the same goal. Salvation was for the few, not the masses, since the intellectual cultivation of one's mind was the only adequate preparation for enjoying oneness with God.

Stoicism specifically rejected the traditional folklore of popular religion. Stoicism's appeal lay in the ability of its ideas to explain the meaning of life and its therapeutic effect to calm one's panic-stricken feelings of dread.

Stoicism's religious philosophy was in direct conflict with the claims of the newly emerging Christian faith. Unlike the abstract and impersonal God of Stoicism, Christian believers claimed that God was personal, infinite in goodness, wisdom, and power, and was the Creator and Sustainer of the universe. They further claimed that access to this personal God was mediated through his incarnation in one Jesus of Nazareth, without whom it was impossible to have personal and intimate fellowship with God.

Salvation was also dependent, not only upon the historical appearance of God in Jesus Christ, but upon his personally chosen witnesses. Unlike Stoicism, which limited salvation to the intellectual elite, Christian faith offered universal salvation to all peoples of the world of whatever rank or education. Good news, not simply good views, was the decisive difference between Stoicism and Christianity. Both claimed that salvation was the result of knowing the Truth, but the gospel of Jesus Christ is the Truth. Truth is not merely a beautiful system of ideas that one intellectually embraces, but Truth is the announcement of a personal God whose Son has brought light and life to all who will embrace his personhood. God's truth was historically and factually made known in his created world, unlike the popular, mythical religions whose stories were in no way interested in dependence upon facts and documented events of history. Thanks in large part to writings of early Christian apologists and our early church Fathers, along with the martyrs who laid down their lives for the sake of the truth of the gospel, the missionary expansion related in the book of Acts continued until the Roman Empire and the entire Western world had largely embraced Christianity, even if some of it was an aberration. For Christian faith had proved itself intellectually superior to the religious philosophy of Stoicism, and it was felt to be emotionally more satisfying than the ecstatic popular religions of the ancient world.

Christianizing Greek/Roman Thought. The conversion of the Roman Empire and the Western world was, of course, not an easy process. Many skirmishes with paganism continued, and some unfortunate elements of the popular religions made their way into the Christianized world. Also, some negative elements of pagan philosophy were appropriated by the church. On the other hand, many positive elements of philosophical traditions that the church adapted from the classical world helped to make explicit the essence of the gospel.

The development of Christian doctrine was generally successful in synthesizing the message of the gospel with the philosophy of Plato and Aristotle. In fact, the early Christian thinkers were able to use the categories of Plato and Aristotle (and Stoicism) to say things that Greek and Roman philosophers were unable to say because they lacked the biblical revelation. Based on the concept of general revelation, Christian faith acknowledges that a measure of God's truth is accessible to all people. For example, Greek thinkers developed a system of logic and philosophy that made it possible to construct a rational view of the world, and these categories were foundational for the church in developing our system of beliefs. In this way, the church used Greek categories to say things that Greeks themselves were unable to say.

For example, Plato developed a view of the supersensible level of reality—that there is a realm of reality that transcends the five senses. This intangible world is not subject to the decay and flux of the temporal world. Augustine borrowed this platonic category to explain the meaning of spiritual realities. To be sure, Plato did not understand the Christian meaning of the supernatural world—that God created the world out of nothing and that he is totally different in his essence from the natural world. In adapting Plato's concept of the supersensible world, Augustine was able to explain the Christian doctrine of God and creation, which was totally unknown to Plato himself.

THE DE-CONVERSION OF THE CHRISTIAN SYNTHESIS

The shift away from ontology. This conversion process of developing a Christian worldview took time to effect, but no sooner had it seemingly been accomplished than a *de-conversion process* began in the sixteenth century. Here we enter the modern period with its secularization process. The focus of attention is no longer on the objective meaning of the world, but on its subjectivizing interpretation. Not God, but Man!

For most philosophers, this subjectivizing of truth resulted in a general consensus of opinion that has been dominant over the last two centuries—that ontology (the idea of a universal and normative truth binding for all people) is not a possibility.

With the rise of modern philosophy and the emergence of Enlightenment thinking, the subjective emphasis on autonomous, critical reasoning replaced the more objective focus of the ontological thinking of the premodern world. Not a synthetic worldview, but an exact analysis of things based on a critical evaluation of the facts of human experience became the focus of philosophy. This humanistic narrowing down of the criterion of truth pushed the question of ontology into the background.

In the natural sciences, A. N. Whitehead sought to reinstate the ontological question. He charged that the scientific movement, which began in 1600 has been anti-intellectual because it assumed that knowledge was simply restricted to an interpretation of brute facts, and it too quickly rejected the need to gain a larger perspective of the whole picture of reality. He believed this anti-intellectualism was an overreaction to the ontological/speculative systems of medieval thought.

Whitehead said that modern science "has never cared to justify its faith or to explain its meaning." This elimination of the ontological question from science resulted in "scientific materialism," and this view assumes that there is an irreducible brute fact that can be known independently of any value, meaning, or purpose. Whitehead called this fact/value dichotomy naïve because it fails to see that its own assumption of a value-free fact is a value itself imposed on the fact.[4] Yet this fact/value dichotomy is the most prominent feature of the post-Enlightenment era. It is called "positivism" because it presupposes that "facts" are simply posited (or given) in a literal and straightforward way without the need for interpretation. Facts allegedly can be known independently of any presuppositions.

The beginning of the fact/value split in Descartes. Since the beginning of philosophical reflection with the ancient Greeks, there has always been an awareness of the distinction between sensibility and intellect, between experience and thought, between the rational and the empirical, between appearance (facts) and reality (what something is in its very essence). But at the beginning of modern philosophy (1600 A.D.), Descartes radicalized the *distinction* between appearance and reality into a *dualism.*

In the early part of his educational training under Jesuit teachers, Descartes complained in his *Discourse on Method* of an overwhelming sense of personal doubt about religious beliefs. He felt the need to develop a system of reason that would lead to absolute certainty about ultimate truth independent of the Bible and church authority. This absolute certainty was based on the autonomous, subjective thinking of the individual alone. This shift toward subjectivity accelerated the move toward the de-conversion of the Christian synthesis.

Descartes' basic principle for developing this system of reason was the method of doubt. Never accept anything as true that is not self-evident to the subjective, autonomous thinking of the individual. What is accepted as true must present itself to the mind *clearly* and *distinctly*. Out of this method of suspicion and distrust one supposedly would be led to the discovery of truth.

An obvious implication of this rationalism is its *antihistorical* attitude. More specifically, if the criterion of truth is absolute clarity and absolute precision, then history is downgraded to nothing more than varying degrees of unreliable reports. This of course had negative implications for acceptance of the history of the Bible.

THE RISE OF THE MODERN HISTORICAL CONSCIOUSNESS

The beginning of modern biblical criticism. One of Descartes' followers was Baruch Spinoza (1632–1677), who became the father of modern biblical criticism. In his *Theologico-Political Treatise*, written in 1670, Spinoza divided truth into two parts—self-evident knowledge and experiential knowledge. A philosopher through rational reflection can know absolute truth through a logical arrangement of ideas in a coherent fashion. This truth is clear, distinct, and self-evident. On the other hand, experiential knowledge is a lesser form of knowledge since it depends upon the historically conditioning factors of our bodily sense and private experiences.

Spinoza believed religion was for the majority of people, while philosophy was for the educated. He concluded that the Bible is for the masses of people because it uses historical experiences, allegories, legends, and parables to teach piety and morality. However, he taught that the Bible cannot serve as a criterion of truth because it is based on the particularities of history; only philosophy can provide one with absolute truth because it alone uses reason to establish the meaning of the universe. At best, the Bible illustrates these eternal truths of reason.

Spinoza's concern to discover universal truth motivated him to examine the Bible in a critical way. He was offended by its claim to contain special revelations of truth that could not be known by the sheer light of reason alone. Out of his concern to demonstrate clearly and distinctly what is infallible truth, he provided a systematic and objective foundation for biblical criticism. Ironically, the negative attitude toward historical knowledge, which the rationalism of Descartes implied, became a basis for developing the historical-critical method. For Spinoza, even though clear, distinct, and self-evident truths were limited to logical reasoning, this demand for mathematical precision provided a basis for recognizing the need to determine as precisely as possible what the facts of history are.

Lessing's broad ditch between history and faith. The emergence of historical criticism came to be known as the "rise of the modern historical consciousness." A key person who gave further precise formulation to the theological problem emerging from this dualism of reasoned knowledge and experiential knowledge was Ephraim Lessing (1729–1781). He stated the problem in terms of the contrast between faith and history. The truths of faith provided certainty just as mathematical axioms are certain, but the truths of history are problematic because they are tinged with the question of whether certain events actually happened.

Since the resurrection of Jesus cannot be proved clearly, distinctly, and self-evidently, as can mathematical axioms and other universal truths of reason, the Resurrection supposedly could not serve as the basis of the certainty of faith. For the proof of faith is self-authenticating, but historical facts are established only with varying degrees of probability. One cannot jump from probability to certainty. Lessing said, "Accidental truths of history can never become the proof of necessary truths of reason." He added that to jump from the level of historical probability to the level of certainty of truth about God is impossible to do with intellectual integrity. He called this gap between faith and history an "ugly, broad ditch which I cannot get across, however often and however earnestly I have tried to make the leap."[5]

Kierkegaard's Leap of Faith. Søren Kierkegaard (1813–1855) suggested a way to resolve this gap between faith and history precisely in terms of a leap of faith. Christian faith has its sole condition in the initiative of God. God confronts us through the witness of the Bible and creates the possibility of our believing in the resurrected Jesus as Savior and Lord.

Faith has a historical basis, but the certainty of faith is not based on reason's attempt to prove the facts of divine revelation in history. These facts are acknowledged to be true only because of faith's encounter with the God of the Bible. Any attempt to prove historically the fact of Jesus' divine sonship or his resurrection from the dead is a futile human effort to do what only God can do! Actually, the attempt to prove historically or rationally the existence of God and his revelation in history is works-righteousness. It is a subtle kind of self-salvation by proving for ourselves that God can be believed.

Only by a leap of the will does faith come into being, and this leap can occur only in the moment of God's self-introduction. It is not a blind leap. One does not simply decide to jump. Rather, this leap is a response to God's appeal to us in the moment of his calling us through the witness of Scripture.

Kierkegaard defines faith and truth in the same terms. No mortal can ascertain objective truth. Only God knows the truth of what-is and as it actually is. Truth is always subjective for us. That is, "An objective uncertainty held fast in an appropriation-process of the most passionate inwardness is the truth."[6] Truth is a *choice* rather than a mere intellectual insight into the actual nature of things.

For Kierkegaard there are emotional and intellectual dimensions of knowing, but the primary way of knowing is volitional. Likewise, faith is the attitude of trusting in the facts of the biblical revelation even though objectively these facts cannot be shown to be clear, distinct, and self-evident. We believe the Bible to be true precisely because we cannot rationally prove them to be true. If we could prove them to be true, we would not need a relationship with God to establish them as true for us.

This means that faith would no longer be necessary because we would have proved for ourselves the truth of God. So the relationship between faith and history is a paradox. It is not a logical contradiction as such, but a truth that transcends the ability of reason to analyze and explain according to the rules of its own finite logic.[7]

Kierkegaard's solution to this problem of faith and history was supplied in large part from his theology of Lutheran pietism, which emphasized the personal and subjective dimensions of faith. But he was a creative "defender" of Christian faith who was to become a powerful resource for new insights for addressing the problem of faith and history as it was further developed in the next century.

The philosophical source of Kierkegaard's creative synthesis of faith and history is derived from the critical philosophy of Immanuel Kant, who was the philosopher of the Enlightenment (see especially Kierkegaard, *Philosophical Fragments* and *A Concluding Unscientific Postscript*). Incidentally, Kant's rationalism was in an important sense a secularizing of the mystical elements of his pietistic upbringing. Both rationalism and pietism stress an individualistic and intuitive knowledge of truth. This compatibility between pietism and rationalism is often overlooked. This is why Tillich says "rationalism is the daughter of mysticism."[8]

Kant's divorce between faith and a knowledge of history. Kant (1724–1804) denied the possibility of knowing anything beyond our five senses. We know only appearances. Our five senses filter out the reality behind appearances. This means that what-is-real-in-itself undergoes a transformation in the process of being received by the senses. This was a total subjectivizing of truth! What really lies outside and beyond our sense impressions is an unknown X.

Kant did believe on the basis of practical reason that there was a larger dimension to reality than our natural sense experience. This larger dimension included the reality of God, the immortal self, and freedom; but these are only ideas and rational inferences. They are logical hunches (an "as if" they are true and real, though we cannot know for sure).

This divorce between faith and knowledge, between appearance and reality was basic to Kierkegaard's idea of the leap of faith. Kant said that objective truth in itself is beyond the pale of human reason to know, and Kierkegaard agreed with him. However, Kierkegaard was not a deist like Kant. Kierkegaard insisted that we could still experience the transcendent God through the leap of faith. This leap was for him a real appropriation (and not a mere hunch or inference) of the reality of God because of God's self-introduction to the believer in the moment of faith.

Kant's theory of knowledge became the presupposition of much of subsequent philosophies of history—that whatever meaning and value lie in the objects of our knowledge are the result of the activity of our own personal mind and not the inherent characteristics of reality itself.[9]

Troeltsch's incorporation of Kant's dualism into the historical-critical method. Kant's influence is especially seen in the philosophy of Ernst Troeltsch (1865–1923). His writings in historiography are the classical formulation of the problem of faith and history. All attempted solutions to this problem in contemporary theology begin with his description of the problem.

He believes the rise of the modern historical consciousness now makes it impossible for a thoughtful person to believe in any form of traditional Christianity. Historical criticism has brought about the "conclusive dissolution" of the traditional historical picture of Jesus. The idea that any one event such as the life and death of Jesus could have absolute significance for the whole history of humankind is impossible, he concludes. Historical relativism makes such a view impossible.[10]

Troeltsch defined three basic principles of the historical-critical method.[11] First, there is the principle of historical criticism itself. This means the critic has to cope with judgments of varying degrees of probability in regard to the events contained in the tradition. That is, all historical knowledge is reduced to the level of finite happenings. History, by Troeltsch's definition, eliminates any act of a transcendent God. Second, there is the principle of analogy. This principle serves as the very basis of criticism regarding the probability of past events. Through the comparison of what is reported in the historical documents to what we observe in our ordinary daily experiences, we judge the probability of events. Troeltsch writes: "On the analogy of events known to us we seek by conjecture and sympathetic understanding to explain and reconstruct the past."[12] This principle of analogy restricts the possibility of an event to what we have observed, known, and experienced.

Third, there is the principle of correlation. This means that there is a naturalistic cause-effect relationship among all events. No changes can occur at any point without preliminary and subsequent alterations in the historical process so that all events stand necessarily in an unending correlative relationship. He writes: "The sole task of history in its specifically theoretical aspect is to explain every movement, process, state, and nexus of things by reference to the web of its causal relations. That is, in a word, the whole function of purely scientific investigation."[13] This effectively eliminates the possibility of God acting in a decisively and purposive manner in a historical revelation.

Troeltsch contends that these self-evident principles affected theology at first only reservedly, then more energetically, then ultimately they completely uprooted the historical claims of traditional theology. He says the historical method, like leaven, bursts the hitherto existing form of theological methods and produces a radical transformation both in theology and church history.[14]

THE PROBLEM OF FAITH AND HISTORY: THEOLOGICAL ALTERNATIVES

Barth's theology of the Word of God. Certainly the most brilliant attempt to come to terms with Troeltsch's philosophy of history was Karl Barth's. In his *Church Dogmatics*, Barth embraced orthodox theology. He affirmed all the essentials of classical Christianity and gave them an explanation and defense superior to anything known before in the history of theology.

Yet his epistemology still suffered from the positivistic assumption that fact and value could be split into two entirely separate components. The action of God in history is not capable of being verified; only in the moment of faith do we know that these historical events occurred, and only in faith do we know what interpretation (a subjective value) ought to be given to these events (an objective fact).

Now God's Word (unverifiable value) comes through the words of the Bible (a record of objective fact), but the words of the Bible are not the same as the Word of God. God's Word is God himself! To call the Bible the Word of God would then mean that the Bible is God and that would be idolatry! So the decisive component of revelation is not a historical event, but the Word of revelation.

Barth says frankly that revelation "has nothing to do with the general problem of historical understanding."[15] This means revelation is not a part of the ordinary sphere of history as we naturally know it.

This is crucial to Barth's theology of the Word of God. For he wants to guard against the idea of revelation being something one could "have." Revelation is always a matter of God's free grace. Revelation is not available to us through human effort or human reason. God is known only because he makes himself known. So the basic meaning of revelation is not defined as historical information or doctrines about God; rather revelation is God's introduction of himself to us. It is the "moment" of the pure presence of God without any other specific content. This is why Barth says that revelation is not a concern of critical history.

This dualism of revelation and history means that historical criticism cannot at all distort or destroy God's Word in Scripture. Historical criticism can make judgments about what is factual or mythical in Scripture. Barth frankly says the Bible is full of errors of fact.[16] While the Bible can be assessed according to the principles of historical criticism, the Word of God in the Bible cannot be critically evaluated. For God speaks through these fallible Scriptures and lets himself be known. The only proof of the truthfulness of the Bible is God's personal authentication of it in faith. And so in faith Barth affirms all the major doctrines of traditional Christianity, such as the virgin birth of Jesus Christ, his incarnation, and resurrection.

Barth turns Troeltsch's historiography upside down and rejects it as having any relevance to the meaning of the truth of revelation in Scripture. The historical critical method is important for those who have an academic interest in the history of the Bible. Otherwise, critical history and faith are totally divorced.[17] Barth concludes that "there are no [historical or critical] problems in the axiomatic *Deus dixit* [God said]."[18]

Wolfhart Pannenberg disagrees. He thinks that Barth's reduction of the concept of the Word of God to mean only divine encounter is dangerously close to the ancient heresy condemned in the NT—docetism or gnosticism.[19] Gnosticism assumed that only the privileged few could achieve a secret and private revelation of God and that it was not open to historical observation or proof.

Bultmann's existentialist alternative. In spite of Barth's brilliant exposition of Christian theology and largely orthodox defense of it, his dualism of faith and critical history softened and weakened the historical core of biblical revelation. Consequently, the existentialist theology of Rudolf Bultmann, a NT scholar who was formerly aligned with Barth in their earlier professional career, was often more widely accepted in academic theological circles than Barth's extreme and one-sided definition of revelation.

Bultmann's main response to Barth was that if revelation is independent of historical criticism, why claim that revelation has a historical point of reference at all![20] And if the historical question is strictly an academic consideration, why not reinterpret the phrase "faith in Jesus Christ" in a symbolic way?

This is indeed what Bultmann did. "Faith in Christ" is a symbolic expression for experiencing a more authentic understanding of the meaning of existence! In this way, one can effectively use the terms and ideas of the existentialist philosophy of Martin Heidegger to reformulate Christian belief, and the traditional doctrines about other worlds and supernatural events can be dropped altogether!

Bultmann's philosophical split between fact and value propelled him to make a real divorce between faith and historical events. For Barth, the divorce between faith and history was only epistemological. For Bultmann, it was actual and real (ontological). The truth of Christian faith was reduced to psychological insight about the possibilities of personal existence. This made historical events as well as historical criticism irrelevant to faith.[21]

But a question must be addressed to Bultmann and the existentialists in general. Is it really possible to talk about the meaning of personal existence in isolation from the history of revelation? Such a relational theology is inadequate if it eliminates the ontological reality of God's personal being and his power to act in real history.

Gerhard von Rad shows the decisive importance of Israel's experience with a personal God as forming the basis of their understanding of history. He writes: "There are only two peoples in antiquity who really wrote history—the Greeks and, long before them, the Israelites."[22] Von Rad also shows that it was Israel's experience of God in history that gave rise to the true meaning of personal existence:

> Here alone, in his encounter with God, does mankind become great and interesting, breaking through the enigma of his humanity to discover all the inherent potentialities of his self-conscious existence. He becomes, in the final analysis, a man taken over by God, one who must surrender to God all his rights over his own history and who by the very fact of so doing is led to new and unsuspected horizons of freedom.[23]

Psychoanalysts have been especially interested in the origin of the idea of the personal. Erich Fromm is representative of those who seek to explain the origin and development of personhood. He says the "seeds" of the meaning of personhood "are to be found in the history of monotheistic religion." He writes:

> The development of the human race as far as we have any knowledge of it can be characterized as the emergence of man from nature. . . . He finds his security by going back, or holding on to these primary bonds. He still feels identified with the world of animals and trees, and tries to find unity by remaining one with the natural world.[24]

Fromm shows that Abraham's awareness of God's transcendence over nature made him aware of his own difference from nature, and from this awareness emerged the feeling of moral responsibility as a person in relationship to God. Fromm frankly acknowledges that belief in God was a necessary stage in human development.[25]

This does not mean, of course, that no degree of personal awareness was to be found among the ancient people. Of course they possessed a sense of individuality, but it was marked by fear and a desire to be joined to mother nature through mythical rituals.

The experience of history and the personal are interrelated and both emerged out of God's disclosure of himself as transcendent. This point is conceded by the Marxist Czech philosopher Vitezslav Gardavasky, who says: "Not merely the Book of Genesis but the Old Testament as a whole contains something which is exceedingly important for the whole of European thought in particular . . . this is the first appearance of the idea of transcendence, of a step beyond all that has so far been achieved." He goes on to say that "the dream of a personal identity in the midst of Time begins to show itself here for the first time."[26]

The modern understanding of person thus focuses on the rational component of *self*-awareness and individual freedom to stand outside the relativities of nature. Human beings are not bound to their natural environment through their instinctual makeup as animals are. We are able to exercise a measure of control over our environment through our capacity for rationality.

The concept of personhood came to an explicit stage of development for the first time during the early Christian centuries when theology was attempting to explain the relationship between God and Jesus. E.L. Mascall writes:

> The concept of personality is not, of course, confined to Christianity or even to the Judeaeo-Christian revelation, but it is very significant that it was only when it centered into theology, through the controversies in the early church about the nature of God, that its full content and implications became manifest. . . . The idea of personality was present in Greek thought only in embryo, and to this day it is practically absent from Hinduism and Buddhism."[27]

The relational categories of Bultmann's existentialist theology cannot deal adequately with the meaning of revelation. For the emergence of the meaning of the personal arose first out of the human awareness of God's real personal existence. To drop this ontological dimension of God's personal intelligence and his capacity to act decisively in history (as Bultmann does) is to erode the very basis of a relational interpretation of Christian theology.

Bultmann and the secular psychoanalytic tradition in general represent a departure from the father of the existentialist movement himself, Kierkegaard, who has plainly shown that the meaning and discovery of *personal* existence is impossible without having first been known and loved by a transcendent God whose essence is other than the world.

Pannenberg's concept of truth as personal/historical. Pannenberg argues that a critical-historical study of the Bible requires us to believe that God is a personal, self-conscious, and intelligent being whose power to make himself known and to be seen is his power to act. This means that theological knowledge is historical knowledge, and historical knowledge is derived through the historical-critical method.

Because God is a real individual who is free to act, Pannenberg makes historical events the primary feature of revelation. The interpretation ("the Word") is the secondary component of revelation, and it must emerge out of a natural consequence of understanding the meaning of the events of revelation. So the Word of God is not a superimposed interpretation on the facts of biblical history; rather, the function of the Word is to report what God has really done in history. He thus rejects a fact/value divorce between faith and history.

The knowledge (rational insight) that faith presupposes is a knowledge of history that is intelligible to the human mind. To put the knowledge of revelation over against ordinary knowledge "is [to be] in danger of distorting the historical revelation into a gnostic knowledge of secrets."[28] Pannenberg develops a theology of reason integrated with faith, which proposes that God has made himself known within the context of our ordinary processes of thought. Based on Paul's comments that the Resurrection "was not done in a corner" (Ac 26:26) and on his appeal to "the open statement of truth" (2Co 4:2), Pannenberg says: "The historical revelation is open to anyone who has eyes to see." He polemicizes a strong methodically objective approach in this way: "Nothing must mute the fact that all truth lies right before the eyes, and that its appropriation is a natural consequence of the facts."[29]

This means a knowledge of revelation is a knowledge of history, of what factually has happened in the space-time spectrum. What cannot be known in the Bible by means of the historical-critical method cannot be true for Christian faith. And of course, the key historical event that the historical-critical method (properly understood) has demonstrated with the highest degree of probability is the resurrection of Jesus of Nazareth. Pannenberg's painstaking, comprehensive, and scholarly investigation into the historical probabilities of this central event of the Bible is compelling and convincing. Unlike any other contemporary theologian, Pannenberg has clearly forced the issue that either Christian theology must affirm the historical fact of Jesus' resurrection (including the empty tomb), or Christian theology has no redeeming message to give to our broken and meaningless world.[30]

He insists that "Christian faith must not be equated with a merely subjective conviction that would allegedly compensate for the uncertainty of our historical knowledge about Jesus."[31] This would turn faith into superstition. The task of the theologian is to assess critically the truth of Christian faith. To define faith as a "fortress into which Christianity could retreat from the attacks of scientific knowledge . . . can only lead to destroying any consciousness of the truth of the Christian faith." He goes on to say: "Faith can breathe freely only when it can be certain, even in the field of scientific research, that its foundation is true."[32]

Pannenberg's difference from the majority of contemporary theologians has been his rejection of the Enlightenment's dualism of faith and knowledge, value and fact, appearance and reality, the subjective and the objective. His quarrel is not with the Enlightenment's insistence on critical reason, but with its unwarranted assumptions about the impossibility of obtaining a knowledge of a historical revelation. He particularly refutes Troeltsch's analysis that the historical critical method is essentially hostile toward believing in the reliability of the Bible as a historical record. Many, if not most, contemporary theologians follow Kant's dualistic epistemology in which history is split between the sacred and the profane. Pannenberg rejects this dualism and insists that God works in the ordinary world of observable history.

> Such a splitting up of historical consciousness into a detection of facts
> and an evaluation of them (or into history as known and history as

experienced) is intolerable to Christian faith, not only because the message of the resurrection of Jesus and of God's revelation in him necessarily becomes merely subjective interpretation, but also because it is the reflection of an outmoded and questionable historical method. It is based on the futile aim of the positivist historians to ascertain bare facts without meaning in history.[33]

Pannenberg insists on the original unity of fact and meaning, event and interpretation. Every event imposes its own meaning to each inquirer. To be sure, not every event possesses equal clarity, but its clarity will be disclosed in proportion to the knowledge of its "context of occurrence and tradition in which it took place and through which it is connected with the present and its historical interest."[34]

This is a realist theory of perception—that there is a reality antecedent to the mind and that the mind can know it really and truly. It is a "realist" theory because it claims we can know things truly, but it is also realistic because no one can really live without believing this. Even the skeptic David Hume admitted that the practical demands of our human nature require us to act as if we do in fact know things as they really are.[35]

This is an assumption that cannot be proved, of course, as it is with the case of all assumptions. And it is specifically a refutation of the Kantian theory of perception—that we can know only the impersonal brute "facts" of our five senses and that any "interpretation" that we give to these "facts" are biased and represent our personal set of subjective values. This positivistic assumption implies that there is no reality beyond our own five senses except for the mere inferences (values) we wish to make about these facts. These inferences allegedly are private and have no universal or normative authority beyond the person who holds them.

According to those theologians (as Bultmann) who hold to a Kantian dichotomy of fact and interpretation, history is the realm of finitude only. And finitude is supposedly governed by the impersonal, mechanistic law of cause and effect. History thus eliminates the realm of freedom and transcendence altogether. At best, God is an unprovable (and thus an impersonal and abstract) value. And human freedom is something we "feel" and imagine ourselves to possess.

This modern split between the personal and the historical, between value and fact, between the subjective and the objective, between interpretation and event is the false presupposition that is destructive to Christian faith rather than the historical critical method being the danger. Pannenberg's scholarship is committed to the overthrow of this depersonalizing and dehumanizing Kantian dichotomy and its false connection with the historical critical method.

It would not be accurate in the strict sense of the word to say that Pannenberg is trying to prove faith. Pannenberg is willing to subsume knowledge under the category of faith in the Reformers' terminology. Faith, in this respect, includes *notitia*, *assensus*, and *fiducia* (knowledge, agreement, and trust). Pannenberg further points out the relationship of faith and knowledge when he writes: "One cannot really know of *God's revelation* in Jesus Christ without believing. But faith does not take the place of knowledge."[36] Thus, faith has its sole condition in the work of God and is not the accomplishment of man, though at the same time Pannenberg contends that the knowledge that faith presupposes must be open to critical historical research. Therefore, it is trust in Jesus that creates fellowship with God and not theoretical knowledge. He writes:

> He who believes in Jesus has salvation in Jesus whom he trusts, without regard to the question how it stands with historical and theological knowledge of Jesus. The presupposition is, of course, that fellowship with Jesus really mediates and assures salvation. The research and knowledge of theology, or at least of the theoretical disciplines of theology, deal with the truth of this presupposition of faith. Such knowledge is thus not a condition for participating in salvation, but rather it assures faith about its basis. It thereby enables faith to resist the gnawing doubt that it has no basis beyond itself and that it merely satisfies a subjective need through fictions, and thus is only accomplishing self-redemption through self-deception.[37]

Since the only means of ascertaining the revelation of God in Jesus of Nazareth is through the historical method, Pannenberg cannot subscribe to any form of an authoritarian "word of God" theology as in Barth and Bultmann. This only suppresses critical rationality and compels one to believe. Until the Enlightenment, the Bible had been more or less identified as the authoritarian Word of God because it was supernaturally inspired. In Neoorthodoxy (Barth), the Word of God was no longer identified with the Bible, but with divine encounter. In existentialist theology (Bultmann), the Word of God was identified with kerygmatic proclamation (the proclaiming of Jesus Christ as a symbol of human self-understanding).

Pannenberg says Barth's and Bultmann's shift away from the orthodox concept of revelation nevertheless left intact the idea of authoritarianism. "But for men who live in the sphere in which the Enlightenment has become effective, authoritarian claims are no longer acceptable."[38] Pannenberg in this way is seeking to point out the inadequacy of all authoritarian theologies, which in essence would exempt the truth-claim of Christian faith from critical rationality.

If Pannenberg so strongly insists that the revelatory events are open for anyone who has eyes to see and that the interpretation of these events is self-evident to historical reason, why is there no general consensus of opinion concerning the revelation of God in Jesus of Nazareth? Pannenberg's answer is found in Paul's statement (2Co 4:4) that "the god of this world has blinded the minds of the unbelievers."[39]

If this is so, then historical reason can hardly qualify as the sole means of ascertaining the proper interpretation of revelatory events. Instead, one must rely also upon the Holy Spirit, "who will guide you into all the truth"

(Jn 16:13). This is not to introduce the Holy Spirit as a stopgap for ignorance, but a fundamental biblical recognition that our powers of reason also come under the curse of the Fall. The work of the Holy Spirit is to convict and convince persons of the truth (Jn 16:8). Without the work of the Spirit no one can even claim that Jesus is Lord (1Co 12:3).

In agreement with Pannenberg, this spiritual intuition is not an irrational act of faith. Rather, through the work of the Spirit, who is also the Spirit of Truth, our minds are able to see. This is so because the Spirit "regenerates" the capacity of the mind to know what morally and spiritually it had been inhibited from knowing, just as the Spirit "regenerates" our hearts and makes it possible for us really to love others unselfishly and to embrace them in friendship.

This is not to say that faith is a substitute for knowledge. But it is to say that a knowledge of the truth is dependent upon a relationship with God. For a relationship with God regenerates and restores our cognitive (knowing), affective (feeling), and volitional (willing) abilities. Of course, that relationship does not increase our so-called "I.Q.," but it does help to clear away the prejudices and moral distortions that obscure the proper functioning of our intelligence.

We are assuming here that the Fall (Ge 3) distorts our capacity to know as well as our capacity to love. We are also assuming the need of divine grace to deliver the mind (as well as the heart) from its distractions and inhibitions so that it can think clearly and truly. This is not simply a Calvinist doctrine, which is carried to any extreme in some instances by Calvinist theologians. It is also a basic premise of the Catholic tradition. Contemporary neo-Thomist scholars in the Catholic tradition have been calling attention to the widespread Protestant misunderstanding of natural theology in this regard.[40] On the other hand, many in the Protestant tradition reject any type of rational proofs because of their extremely negative view of the fallenness and depravity of the mind to know the truth of God. The consequence of this excessive skepticism is that faith is made a substitute for knowledge.

Pannenberg makes a helpful distinction between the logic and psychology of faith. Psychologically, we enter the dimension of faith before we come to understand the logic of what we believe. Logically, we spend the rest of our lives trying to understand with our minds the truths of faith.[41]

This interaction between the logic and psychology of faith shows that there is a reciprocal connection between believing and understanding. We cannot truly understand without believing. For example, the resurrection of Jesus cannot be seen through the "eyes of the old aeon," Pannenberg says.[42] This means that only believers know Jesus was raised from the dead. Trust in Jesus is initiated by Jesus, not by the historical method, Pannenberg says. But the logic of faith's claim that Jesus was raised from the dead depends upon the historical-critical method. Yet unless the historical method has been informed by the faith of the new reality in

Christ, then the critical historian will misunderstand the historical data concerning Jesus' resurrection.

It is misleading when Pannenberg insists that the historical-critical method is the only means for determining the truth of the Bible. In fact, Pannenberg's reformulation of the historical-critical method actually provides a basis for seeing that the concept of biblical inspiration is also a necessary aspect of the biblical revelation.

Cullmann's integration of historical criticism and biblical inspiration. Oscar Cullmann, a highly respected (now retired) NT scholar from the University of Basel, Switzerland, has shown that historical criticism necessarily leads one to affirm the inspiration of the Scriptures. Cullmann devoted much of his writings to showing that NT form-critical methodology does not in itself prejudice the case against the historical reliability of the Bible. He thus engaged in dialogue with Bultmann's opposite form-critical assumption that the NT is largely mythological. This assumption is not derived from form criticism but from his existentialist philosophy.[43]

Cullmann showed that simply because many events in the Scriptures are not capable of being historically tested does not necessarily require that a critical thinker label them as mere myth. These "historically uncontrollable events" are labeled "historicized myths" by Cullmann because they are so intertwined with "historically controllable events." He points out that it is impossible at times to differentiate the historically controllable from the uncontrollable elements.

In this respect, Cullmann chooses to speak of events, such as, the Creation, the Fall, the Virgin Birth, the Second Coming, etc., as historicized myths, but *not* mere myths. These divine events are real events in space/time, but they do not come under the control of the critical historian except indirectly. These historicized myths, Cullmann says, "really *happen*" and "must not be conceived as metaphysical and nontemporary"; rather, they are "included in the *temporal* process."[44]

The distinction Cullmann is making between "history" and "myth" corresponds to the traditional distinction between what is naturally and what is supernaturally known. Historicized myths are divine, temporal events that cannot be historically determined. They are "myths" only in this limited sense of not coming under direct historical control.

Cullmann agrees with Pannenberg about the importance of historical criticism for those whose thinking has been marked by the Enlightenment.[45] Cullmann shows that the Bible invites this kind of critical evaluation.

> Just as *eyewitnessing* is a fundamental accompaniment to a witness of faith for the apostle, and one cannot be thought of without the other (εἶδεν καὶ ἐπίστευσεν ["he saw and believed," RSV], Jn 20:8), in the same way, research on the narrated events with any available means precedes faith in the interpretation of the events for the exegete.[46]

Does this mean that the critical exegete must take a neutral or negative attitude about the so-called "historicized myths" in the Bible? Do the reported events need to be demythologized as Bultmann says? Cullmann points out that what does fall under the category of being historically controllable indirectly confirms those parts, such as the Creation, the Eschaton, etc., which are not under historical control. Especially the witness of the prophets and the apostles is a key to faith because they stand in close proximity to revelatory events. This leads Cullmann to say: "It must be noted that the apostle's eyewitness is more important than that of all the other biblical witnesses because it relates to the decisive event and in this way indirectly *guarantees the revelations of all the previous witnesses.*"[47]

What Cullmann is pointing out here is that the knowledge upon which faith has its point of departure does not always qualify as historically controllable knowledge. Though faith is rooted in historical events, these events do no always qualify as being historically demonstrable. It is the witness of the prophets and the apostles that creates faith and not what can be merely demonstrated historically. Thus faith includes the credibility of the witnesses of divine revelation, who themselves stand in a relationship to the witness of their predecessors, which culminates in the final witness of the apostles to Jesus Christ.

This chain of witnesses to divine revelation, which culminates in the witness of the apostles, is the basis for Cullmann's statement that their witness "indirectly *guarantees the revelations of all the previous witnesses.*" He writes:

> Faith is therefore also a faith in the witnesses, or rather in their function in salvation history. Faith intrudes upon us as we hear the witness, although we see the human weakness and imperfection of the witnesses themselves. *We* cannot be eyewitnesses any more. But to be *witnesses* ourselves we must believe in their witness. This looks like dead "faith in authority." But the biblical witnesses, the prophets and apostles, are so closely bound up with the salvation history revealed to them that their witness as such can become an object of a true and living faith in their mission[,] the basis of which lies in the mission of the bearer of revelation, Christ. We have seen that the biblical witnesses too believe in the witness of their predecessors, so that the new facts and their interpretation are connected with the salvation history of the past. We find ourselves in this same situation, but now vis-à-vis the *whole* salvation history of the Bible.[48]

Through a form-critical analysis that is thorough and persuasive, Cullmann has demonstrated that the NT speaks of the tradition of the apostles in a definitive way. He shows that Christ, exalted to the right hand of God, is considered by the NT writers to be the "direct author of the tradition of the apostles, because he himself is at work in the apostolic transmission of his words and deeds."[49]

Among numerous texts to support this conclusion is an analysis of Jn 16:13 and 14:27. These passages report that the Holy Spirit would give to the apostles the teachings of the historical Jesus and bring to their remembrance the things that they had been taught. So far as the New Testament is concerned, its truth concerning the revelation of God in history is reliable and trustworthy because of the unique relationship between the apostles and the earthly Jesus and the outpouring of the Spirit of Christ at Pentecost, who spoke through them the living Word of God.

In this way, Cullmann has shown that there is no difference between the apostolic witness and revelation. In this sense, the Scriptures are not a dead letter but a living word because the Holy Spirit inspired the historical records and likewise confronts the reader with Jesus Christ directly through these records.[50]

One of the theologically reasoned conclusions of Pannenberg is that Jesus' resurrection from the dead confirms his claim to be one with God. If Easter is the proof of Jesus' claim to be God, then Cullmann has shown that Pentecost is the confirmation of Jesus' claim that the Holy Spirit would inspire them to be faithful witnesses of his reality and authenticate its truth in the minds and hearts of those who read and hear its testimony.

So the doctrine of biblical inspiration is not so easily dismissed as Pannenberg thinks. It was not developed out of an authoritarian attitude. It is not the result of a deductive logical system of thought. The truth of Scripture of course does not stand on the basis of the idea of its inspiration. That is, it is not the doctrine of inspiration that guarantees the truthfulness of the Scriptures. The truth of Scripture rests on the historical factuality of Jesus' life, death, resurrection, and the outpouring of his Holy Spirit. And it is out of these facts that we come to recognize the nature of biblical inspiration; namely, that the earthly Jesus promised that his Spirit would come and teach them and remind them of things they had learned from him and that they would be guided into the truth by his superintending presence.

He further promised that the truth of what they reported would be authenticated by the same Holy Spirit. So it is not gnostic to believe that the whole of Scripture is inspired by God. It is derived from a proper understanding of the biblical texts themselves, which can be brought under historical control.

Just as there are good historical foundations for believing in the resurrection of Jesus from the dead, so there are good historical foundations for believing in the divine inspiration of the Bible itself. Furthermore, this recognition of the divine inspiration of the Bible imposes certain restraints on the conclusions of the historical critical method itself. An ongoing dialogue continues between historical criticism and faith. Faith needs historical criticism to help it understand the objective foundations for itself, but historical criticism also cannot ignore the Spirit as the ultimate source of the biblical teachings. Theology and historical criticism must therefore be mutually interrelated and complement each other rather than compete with each other. Frankly, this means that the truths of Scripture cannot be subordinated and upstaged by historical criticism for the simple reason that historical criticism itself points faith in this direction to affirm the Bible's inspiration. This interdependence of faith and the historical critical method is the basis, then, for Cullmann's statement that the NT texts themselves invite critical historical inquiry.

CONCLUDING COMMENTS

The significance of Pannenberg and Cullmann is in their showing that the Enlightenment's emphasis on critical thinking is not unspiritual and antithetical to faith. The problem with the philosophy of the Enlightenment was that it was not critical enough, for it failed to be self-critical and to recognize its own naturalistic presuppositions.

Faith and knowledge, while distinct, are inseparable. To know the truth in any field of knowledge requires the personal interest of the scholar in his subject along with a critical awareness of his assumptions (beliefs). This is no less true for the critical historian who seeks to examine the historicity of Jesus' resurrection from the dead. Pannenberg writes:

> Anyone who will not trust himself to the God revealed in Jesus' resurrection will also obscure for himself any recognition of the history which reveals God, even if he once possessed it. For no one could clearly recognize God's divinity and love and yet persist in refusing to trust him. And so in fact only believers hold fast to the recognition of God's revelation in Jesus' resurrection.[51]

Intellectual insight and trust are mutually related. Only from the standpoint of the faith of those who participate in the New Creation can we have the eyes to see and the mind to know the truth of the gospel of Jesus Christ. And only from the standpoint of the mind's insight that Jesus is Lord can we come to believe in him.

The synthesis of critical thinking of the Enlightenment and the development of a systematic/ontological worldview typical of the classical creeds of the church is biblically and theologically necessary if we wish to make the biblical revelation intelligible today. For if we are to speak of truth in reference to the Bible, we are not permitted to redefine the contents of the Bible in a gnostic manner as if its truth were a blind affirmation inaccessible to rational reflection. And if the content of the Bible is available for rational interpretation, then its truth can be framed into an intelligible worldview. In this way, both the epistemological emphasis of the Enlightenment and the ontological emphasis of the pre-modern world can be brought together for the development and deepening of our faith and understanding of God's revelation.

NOTES

[1]Ernst Cassirer, *The Philosophy of the Enlightenment*, trans. Fritz C. A. Koelln and James P. Pettegrove (Princeton: Princeton Univ. Press, 1951), 182–96.

[2]Wolfhart Pannenberg, "Response to the Discussion," in *Theology as History*, eds. James Robinson and John B. Cobb, Jr. (New York: Harper and Row, 1967), 229.

[3]Paul Tillich, *The Courage To Be* (New Haven: Yale Univ. Press, 1952), 9–10.

[4]A. N. Whitehead, *Science and the Modern World* (New York: Macmillan, 1954), 12, 23–24.

[5]See *Lessing's Theological Writings*, trans. Henry Chadwick (London: Adam and Charles Black, 1956), 55.

[6]Søren Kierkegaard, *Concluding Unscientific Postscript*, trans. David F. Swanson and Walter Lowrie (Princeton: Princeton Univ. Press, 1941), 182.

[7]Ibid., 504.

[8]Paul Tillich, *A History of Christian Thought* (New York: Simon and Schuster, 1968), 315.

[9]See Maurice Mandelbaum, *The Problem of Historical Knowledge* (New York: Liveright, 1938), 205.

[10]See Ernst Troeltsch, *Die Bedeutung der Geschichtlichkeit Jesu für den Glauben* (Tübingen: Mohr, 1911), 1–2, 15.

[11]See Troeltsch "Über historische und dogmatische Methode in der Theologie," *Gesammelte Schriften* (Tübingen: Mohr, 1913), 2:731–38.

[12]Troeltsch, "Historiography," *Encyclopedia of Religion and Ethics*, ed. James Hastings (1913), 6:718.

[13]Ibid.

[14]See Troeltsch's *Gesammelte Schriften*, II:730.

[15]Karl Barth, *Church Dogmatics*, trans. G. T. Thomson (Edinburgh: T. and T. Clark, 1963), I:1:168.

[16]Ibid., I:2:531.

[17]Ibid., I:2:56–57.

[18]Ibid., I:2:57.

[19]Wolfhart Pannenberg, *Revelation as History*, trans. David Granskou and Edward Quinn (London: Sheed and Ward, 1969), 135.

[20]Rudolf Bultmann, *Essays: Philosophical and Theological*, trans. James C. G. Grieg (London: SCM, 1955), 261.

[21]See Bultmann's essay, "New Testament and Mythology," in *Kerygma and Myth*, ed. Hans Werner Bartsch (New York: Harper and Row), 1961).

[22]Gerhard von Rad, *The Problem of the Hexateuch and Other Essays*, trans. E. Dickens (New York: McGraw-Hill, 1966), 167.

[23]Ibid., 153.

[24]Erich Fromm, *The Art of Loving* (New York: Harper and Row, 1956), 53–54.

[25]Ibid., 53–69.

[26]Vitězslav Gardavasky, *God Is Not Yet Dead*, trans. Vivenne Menkes (Baltimore: Penquin, 1973), 28.

[27]E. L. Mascall, *The Importance of Being Human* (New York: Columbia Univ. Press, 1958), 39.

[28]Pannenberg, *Revelation as History*, 135.

[29]Ibid., 136–37.

[30]Wolfhart Pannenberg, *Jesus: God and Man*, trans. Lewis L. Wilkins and Duane A. Priebe (Philadelphia: Westminster, 1968), 53–114.

[31]Pannenberg, *Theology as History*, 131.

[32]Ibid.

[33]Ibid., 126.

[34]Wolfhart Pannenberg, *Basic Questions in Theology: Collected Essays* (Philadelphia: Westminster, 1983), 1:127.

[35]David Hume, *An Inquiry Concerning Human Understanding* (Indianapolis: Bobbs-Merrill, 1955), 194.

[36]Pannenberg, *Theology as History*, 128.

[37]Ibid., 269.

[38]Ibid., 226.

[39]Pannenberg, *Revelation as History*, 136.

[40]E. L. Mascall, *He Who Is* (Hamden, Conn.: Archon, reprint 1970), 25.

[41]Pannenberg, *Theology as History*, 269.

[42]Pannenberg, *Jesus: God and Man*, 99.

[43]Oscar Cullmann, *Salvation in History* (Geneva, Ala.: Allenson, 1967), 49.

[44]Ibid., 143.

[45]Ibid., 57.

[46]Ibid., 73.

[47]Ibid., 296.

[48]Ibid., 323.

[49]Oscar Cullmann, *The Early Church*, ed. A. J. B. Higgins; trans. Stanley Goodman and A. J. B. Higgins (London: SCM, 1966), 59.

[50]Ibid., 81.

[51]Wolfhart Pannenberg, *Faith and Reality* (Philadelphia: Westminster, 1977), 66–67.

THE BIBLE AND THEOLOGY

Dennis F. Kinlaw

A discussion of how John Wesley did theology should begin by asking whether he actually merits that attention. A consideration of the present state of theological discourse and the marginal role that Wesley plays in that discussion makes the question inescapable. Yet interest in Wesley as a theologian will not go away. And in recent dialogue, both in evangelical and conciliar circles, his work has drawn renewed attention.

Few would question Wesley's importance as an evangelist, a revivalist, a social reformer, and an organizer. But was he a serious theologian? Does his method of doing theology interest us? Few of the accepted authorities on the history of Christian thought consider him that important. Not many, however, would now agree with Edward Caldwell Moore, the Parkman Professor of Theology at Harvard and Adolf Harnack's first American pupil, who wrote in 1912:

> Methodism of the earlier age had as good as no intellectual relations whatsoever . . . This evangelical movement in the Church of England manifested deep religious feeling, it put forth zealous philanthropic effort, it had among its representatives men and women of great beauty of personal character and piety. Yet it was completely cut off from any living relation to the thought of the age. There was among its representatives no spirit of theological inquiry.[1]

The prevailing tendency has been to see Wesley as unoriginal and marginal. I challenge that assumption. For obvious reasons he has largely been ignored as a theologian. If we examine his writings, we will find a theological mind of excellent quality and a way of doing theology that can be helpful for us today.

It has been easy for scholars to ignore Wesley as a theologian because of the style and format of his work and because he preached to a non-scholarly audience.

First, a consideration of the form of his work. Nowhere in his writings did he make any serious attempt to present a systematic theology. A survey of his output will reveal that in this corpus a substantive treatment of almost every subject a systematician addresses can be found. But he never tried to pull it all together. One looks in vain for anything like Calvin's *Institutes*, Melanchthons' *Loci Communes*, or Aquinas' *Summa Theologica*. His approach to the most serious theological questions was occasional and particular. Yet the subjects specifically addressed by him cover a veritable catalogue of responses to major theological questions. His sermons, tracts, pamphlets, treatises, letters, and hymns cover all significant subjects. But the form of address was not that employed by the systematician.

On occasion he did write in a careful and extensive manner on the weighty matters. An example of this is found in his "An Earnest Appeal to Men of Reason and Religion" (1743) and "A Farther Appeal to Men of Reason and Religion" (1745). These articles fill 245 pages in the Jackson edition of Wesley's works (8:280; in the Oxford/Abingdon edition, Vol. 11). Albert Outler considered this the most important single essay left to the church by Wesley. In this work he indicates both his concern to see England revived and his confidence in the fitness of the Methodist message to produce such revival. Outler describes its treatment of Methodist doctrine as "the plain, old doctrines of the Henrician reformers, the ancient Fathers, and the apostles."[2]

Of similar size is his "The Doctrine of Original Sin according to Scripture, Reason, and Experience." This fills 273 pages in the Jackson edition (Vol. 9). It is a significant work that presents the classical orthodoxy of the early Fathers and the most widely accepted tradition of the church through the centuries, particularly as he learned it from Anglican tradition.

Similar comments can be made about his "A Plain Account of Christian Perfection" (Vol. 11, Jackson edition). In this, Wesley addressed the most controversial part of his theology. His position in this work brought him into sharp conflict with many of his peers, and many regarded him as outside the pale of orthodoxy.

The reality, however, is that Wesley was picking up and developing a legitimate theme found both in the Scriptures and in the tradition of the church. John L. Peters claims that Wesley's theology here represents a hope found in writers as diverse and as scattered through the history of the church as Clement of Alexandria, Macarius the Egyptian, Augustine, Tauler, à Kempis, François de Sales, Juan de Castaniza, Madame Guyon, Molinas, Fénelon, the Cambridge Platonists, Pascal, Jeremy Taylor, and William Law.[3]

It is rather difficult to write this off as a Wesleyan idiosyncrasy. Any serious look at the hymnody of the church will reveal that here Wesley was addressing the deep cry of many Christians. His knowledge of Scripture, Christian literature, and experience was extensive. He would not drop his concern for this aspiration of grace.

Wesley had a sophisticated knowledge of biblical and Christian thought. He had wrestled his way through Christian faith with its presuppositions and implications, and had brought into an integrated whole his own intellectual response to them. But he seems never to have felt the need to put it in writing.

A second reason why Wesley may have been overlooked as a serious theologian is his style. He did not write primarily for academics and erudite persons. He wrote mostly to common people. If he had to choose between the rich and the poor, the educated or the uneducated, the noble or the commoner, his preference was always the poor, the uneducated, and the commoner. In 1757 he wrote to a friend, "I love the poor; in many of them I find pure, genuine grace unmixed with paint, folly, and affectation."[4] The common folks were his people and when he wrote, he wrote primarily for them. This affected his style. But his purpose and goals included everyone.

It was not that he did not have the intellectual gifts or the philosophical and theological training needed to address these subjects as a scholar. His education and natural gifts made him a master of the classics as well as Scripture. He was at home in the history of philosophy and that of Christian theology. More than 1400 different authors are referred to in his works and some 3000 different items ranging from pamphlets to twelve-volume sets are mentioned. In the sermons alone are more than 2500 quotations and allusions to source materials that are readily identifiable. But when he quotes, whether from the classics, the Scriptures, or the Fathers, he does so "carelessly from memory (who was there to check his texts?) and yet rarely off target."[5]

A third factor that has contributed to the neglect of Wesley by the systematicians and historians of Christian thought is more subtle. It may be that it is the best indicator of his genius. I speak of his openness, the way he viewed the working of God's Spirit of grace in human history and how he felt we should respond to that working past and present. Here is the best opportunity to see the creativity with which he believed theology should be done.

A central aspect of his thought here is classically expressed in what is known as the Vincentian Canon: *What has been believed everywhere, always and by all.*[6]

The best test of orthodoxy in Vincent's opinion was whether a dogma has been "believed everywhere, always, and by all."

The assumption is that God in no age leaves himself without a witness, that if one will look far enough and hard enough the true seeker will find *in any age* those whose faith is continuous with that of the prophets and apostles, a faith that has been maintained in an unbroken line by the Spirit of God from Abraham's day to one's own. Wesley believed in that royal line of faith and passionately wanted to stand as close to the center of it as he could. Therefore, his work reflects a profound interest in continuity with Christians in all ages and in true catholicity. His concern is diachronic and synchronic. He had little interest in special pleading or idiosyncratic particularities. He wanted to know what the Spirit was saying to the world and to the church. He believed in the unity of God's truth and that what God was saying in one day and place would be consonant with what he was saying on everyday and in every place. Wesley felt that the more we could know of the working and the speaking of the Spirit diachronically through history and synchronically now currently, the more confident we could be of our understanding of God's Word for our particular day and place.

Wesley did not feel that all of the Spirit's speaking and working was of equal value. Some was normative and some illustrative and confirmatory. The normative part is that which is found in the Old and New Testaments. The Bible is the special gift to the church from the Spirit of God. It was inspired by him and is the standard by which everything else is to be measured. Here Wesley was completely one with the Reformers. *Sola Scriptura* was as much an item of faith for him as it was for Calvin and Luther.

The practical seriousness with which Wesley took the claims of Scripture is revealed in "A Short History of the People Called Methodists," published in 1781, in which Wesley tells how Methodism got its name.

In November 1729, Wesley and three other students at Oxford began to meet regularly to read their Greek New Testaments. Over the next six years other students joined them. The discipline of their lives caused them to be pejoratively tagged "Methodists." But from their perspective one thing alone bound them together: ". . . it being their one desire and design to be downright Bible Christians, taking the Bible, as interpreted by the primitive Church and our own for their whole and sole rule."[7]

In 1738, Wesley, just returned from Georgia, found himself in a similar group, all of whom were "resolved to be Bible Christians at all events; and, wherever they were, to preach with all their might plain, old, Bible Christianity."[8]

In 1766 he looked back across more than a third of a century and said that it was in 1729 that he "began not only to read, but to study, the Bible as the one, the only standard of truth and the only model of pure religion."[9]

In 1746 Wesley published the sermons that he had been preaching over the previous decade. In the Preface to those sermons he opened his heart in a revealing passage:

> I am a spirit come from God and returning to God; just hovering over the great gulf, till a few moments hence I am no more seen—I drop into an unchangeable eternity! I want to know one thing, the way to heaven—how to land safe on that happy shore. God himself has condescended to teach the way: for this very end he came from heaven. He hath written it down in a book. O give me that book! At any price, give me the Book of God! I have it. Here is knowledge enough for me. Let me be *homo unius libri* [a man of one book].[10]

For Wesley the Bible was God's Word, the special work of the Spirit who had inspired it. As such it was completely normative for Wesley. God had given it for that purpose. The extent to which he believed this is revealed in a letter to Thomas Whitehead about possible revelations from the Spirit apart from Scripture.

> The Scriptures are the touchstone whereby Christians examine all, real or supposed, revelations. In all cases they appeal "to the law and to the testimony," and try every spirit thereby.

. . . though the Spirit is our principal leader, yet He is not our rule at all;
the Scriptures are the rule whereby He leads us into all truth.[11]

The Scriptures were God's infallible guide in all things eternal, the
ultimate test of all in faith or practice, the gift of the Spirit to the church.

A second gift of the Spirit to the seeking heart was found for Wesley in
the historical witness of the church. He believed that God's Spirit was at
work in every age, that everywhere there was a recognizable consistency in
the way the Spirit worked, and that the history of the church illustrates and
confirms that normative witness given in Scripture.

In his "A Short History of the People Called Methodists," he speaks of
his discipleship group: ". . . it being their desire to be downright Bible
Christians; taking the Bible, *as interpreted* by the primitive church and our
own, for their whole and sole rule."[12]

Early Methodists felt the need for the help that *the primitive church* and
their own could give them to protect them from any private interpretations
of Scripture. Wesley had no interest in individual and idiosyncratic
interpretations. He wanted to be a part of that common faith believed
"everywhere, always and by all." In fact, he wanted to be as close to the
center of that as he could get. So a knowledge of what the Spirit had done
or was doing anywhere, evaluated against the Scriptures, could serve as a
primary help in enabling him to break out of the limitations inherent
within his own private understanding and experience.

In this Wesley was very much an Anglican. He was part of a
theological tradition that included Thomas Cranmer, Richard Hooker,
Lancelot Andrewes, Jeremy Taylor, and others who had guided the
English church into that "middle way" between Rome and European
Protestantism. They recognized the supreme authority of the Scriptures,
but knew the value of the work of the Spirit in the life of the church
through the centuries in enabling true seekers after God to understand
more fully the truths revealed in Scripture.

Richard Hooker (1554–1600) was easily the most influential of these,
recognized as the greatest of Anglican theological writers. The reality,
though, is that he never fully outlined a theological system. Primarily he
gave a method of doing theology. A key element in this was proper
consideration of the teaching and practice of the "primitive" church, the
undivided church of the first five centuries. There Hooker and Anglicanism
found a guide second only in importance to the Scriptures.

Lancelot Andrewes (1555–1626) expressed this in his famous five
finger exercise: "One canon, two testaments, three creeds [Apostles',
Nicene, and Athanasian], four [ecumenical] councils, five centuries, and
the series of Fathers in that period."[13]

In other words, the basic character of historic orthodoxy had been
established in the first 500 years of the church. Wesley and his friends were
not about to deprive themselves of any enlightenment to be found in the
Spirit's working in those early centuries. In this they found themselves

identifying with Eastern Orthodoxy and with Roman Catholicism as well as with their own Church of England. However, their commitment to *Sola Scriptura*, a perspective shared by the primitive church and their own, forced them to dissociate themselves from many of the traditions that developed later, which they found incompatible with Scripture and with the faith and practice of the primitive church.

Here we find Wesley's position differing a bit from many European Reformers. Their break with tradition was more radical than his. In their revolt against Rome, the Reformers found far less in the church of the Middle Ages with which they could identify. The result was an effort on their part at repristination, which is not so characteristic of Wesley.

Perhaps the point at which this is most obvious is in Wesley's work on Christian perfection. Grateful for the Reformed emphasis on justification by faith, Wesley found himself unwilling to divorce this from biblical teaching on the necessity of personal holiness. He was concerned not only for God's work *for* us, but also for God's work *in* us. He believed the Scriptures promised a *real* change as well as a *relative* change in the coming of grace to the human heart. In this he found himself at one with an emphasis found in the literature of the medieval church. This is why George Croft Cell can speak of Wesley's theology as a "necessary synthesis of the Protestant ethic of grace with the Catholic ethic of holiness."[14]

Here we get what is perhaps the best indication of how Wesley did theology. From his reading of Scripture, years before he came to understand the Reformed doctrine of justification by faith, Wesley was convinced that the Scriptures taught the necessity of holiness of heart. When he came to personal justifying faith, he found great freedom. But the biblical demand for holiness continued to haunt him. With his brother Charles and his colleagues he conducted a study of Scripture, the witness of the church through the centuries, and the working of grace within their hearts and the hearts of those to whom they ministered. The account of this is contained in his "A Plain Account of Christian Perfection, As Believed and Taught by the Reverend Mr. John Wesley, from the year 1725 to the year 1777." It is a remarkable story of how a group of seekers after God submitted to the Scriptures, learned from the witness of the church and from their peers, and then gave more definitive explication of Christian perfection as presented in Scripture than had previously been done.

This illustrates for us Wesley's method and philosophy. The fact that he believed the canon was closed did not preclude his confidence that more could be learned about the work of God and his Spirit. There was an *openness* in Wesley that permitted him to explore further implications of "the faith once delivered." He was convinced that new insights would not contradict central convictions of orthodoxy but that they would amplify our understanding of the grace given in Christ. Thus he explored possibilities of grace that Luther and Calvin would have declared beyond the concern of the orthodox.

In all that has been said here, it is obvious that Wesley was a traditional Anglican in both his theology and in how he theologized. On one occasion William Laud, seventeenth-century archbishop of Canterbury and a major force in the development of Anglicanism, was challenged by a Jesuit on his view of authority and the reasons for his view that Scripture was to be accepted as authoritative. His response identifies the major elements in Anglican theology. There are four:

> First, there is "the testimony and witness of the Church, and her tradition."
>
> Second, there is "the testimony which the Scripture gives to itself."
>
> Third, there is "the inward testimony which by its nature is subjective, so that hence can be drawn no proof to others."
>
> Fourth, there is "natural reason."[15]

Wesley would have placed these elements in a different order, but the basic factors in his theological method were remarkably Anglican. Scripture, reason, tradition, and experience were the essential ingredients.

In recent years Wesleyan scholars have seen in all of this what is identified as the "Wesleyan quadrilateral." They usually identify experience as the unique element that Wesley introduced. But the quotation from William Laud indicates that Wesley was not the first to introduce personal experience and the subjective into theological debate. Yet experience was a crucial concern to Wesley. This was for him a third gift from the Spirit, a personal and immediate authentication that moved Christian truth from information about God and faith in the Gospel to an existential personal apprehension of that truth for oneself. He had no question about the intellectual importance of dogma. But he believed that the rationale needed a pneumatological confirmation and that such pneumatological confirmation was the privilege of every believer. Thus truth could and should involve both intellection and personal experience.

Perhaps the best illustration of this is Wesley's own experience of the biblical truth that sinners are justified by faith alone and that it can happen in an instant. A careful reading of Wesley's *Journal* for the early months of 1738 will reveal the step-by-step progress of the work of the Spirit in his heart and mind as he submitted himself to the Scriptures and exposed himself to the witness of Peter Böhler and his friends. The result was that an intellectual concession became a life-transforming passion. A. Skevington Wood explains it:

> Words were translated into realities, and the doctrine came alive for him. The cardinal tenet of the Protestant Reformation, which is the root of all truly Christian belief, now not only seized his mind but touched his heart. The kindling was to be felt throughout the land as a consequence. It was indeed a strange warmth, as Wesley so accurately analyzed it, for he was not a man given to emotional impressions. That this should

happen to him of all people was sufficient to attest it as a work of supernatural grace.[16]

When Wesley included experience as an appropriate element in doing theology, he was not speaking of human experience *per se*. He was speaking of human experience that was the result of the operation of the Spirit of grace in one's life. That subjective work, he believed, was consonant with, and in its own way, authenticated existentially the more objective work of the Spirit present in Scripture and found in the best of the spiritual life of the church.

This means that Wesley's interest was primarily soteriological. The Bible was not given only for cognitive purposes. He was never content with just a rational orthodoxy. He was an evangelist first, last, and always. He wanted to see truth translated into life. So good theology should change more than one's thought. It should transform one's life and destiny.

A fourth element in Wesley's understanding of how the Spirit works in the believer and in the church was his understanding of the role of human reason.

Here again Wesley was obviously debtor to his Anglican heritage in which human reason, along with Scripture and tradition, played a crucial role. He believed that human rationality was part of the image of God imparted to humankind at the Creation. It was a key factor in human superiority to the rest of the creation. Therefore human reason was to be respected and used.

This was a crucial corollary of his doctrine of creation. Wesley was a monotheist. He believed that there was one God and one alone from whose hand all that exists came, that God is a God of truth, eternal truth. As there is a unity in the universe there is also a unity in truth. There is an internal consistency, an inner coherence in truth as there is in nature. Therefore, wherever one finds truth, that truth is consistent with all truth since it all comes from a single Source, and that Source preserves his own integrity. The truth found in tradition is consonant with that revealed in Scripture. And truth found in human experience is consonant with that found in Scripture and tradition. Human reason is God's special gift to his creature to detect, pursue, test, and systematize that truth.

In Wesley's "An Earnest Appeal to Men of Reason and Religion," he speaks of this. His question is: "What do you mean by *reason*?" His answer is as follows:

> I suppose you mean the eternal reason, or the nature of things; the nature of God, and the nature of man, with the relations necessarily subsisting between them. Why, this is the very religion we preach; a religion evidently founded on, and every way agreeable to, eternal reason, to the essential nature of things. Its foundation stands on the nature of God and the nature of man, together with their mutual relations.[17]

Human reason is a reflection of divine reason. It was a gift from the Creator to the creature, put within him to enable him to perceive, understand, and interpret the nature and significance of reality as it relates to eternal truth. Thus, it is God's greatest natural gift to enable us to grasp the truth that comes to us in Scripture, history, and human experience.

Wesley recognized the greatness of this divine gift, though he realized that it had its limitations. These were at least twofold: human reason is finite, and human reason is fallen.

Wesley concurred with Job (11:7) that human beings by searching cannot fathom the mysteries of God nor find out his limits. He is infinite and we are finite. He is eternal and we are creatures of time. Therefore, it is appropriate that our searchings and our findings should be marked by humility and a profound sense of awe.

But our problems are more than just our finitude. We are fallen. Equipment that was perfect when it came from the hand of the Creator has been damaged. Our sin has left its scars. Luther said that in the Fall man became *incurvatus in se*, "bent in upon himself." Reason given originally to know and glorify the Creator has now become subject to the self-interest of the creature who is "curved in upon himself." The result is a state of blindness, what Wesley would identify as "nature's night." Note his brother's hymn:

> Long my imprisoned spirit lay,
> Fast bound in sin and nature's night;
>   Thine eye diffused a quickening ray;
> I woke, the dungeon flamed with light;
>   My chains fell off, my heart was free,
> I rose, went forth, and followed Thee.

So a tool given to apprehend truth degenerated into an instrument used to justify our own rationalizations and self-interest.

But there is help. The same Spirit who spoke in Scripture and history can quicken the human spirit and release it so that its reason can be free to perceive and follow the truth of God. Here again we do not understand Wesley if we miss the pneumatological and the soteriological notes.

Thus, we see the basic elements to which Wesley turned to do theology. In recent years, as note above, these have been referred to as "the Wesleyan Quadrilateral."[18] We must be careful not to think of these as equal. The priority is with the Scriptures. They alone are infallible. They alone are the norm. Then tradition, experience, and reason become priceless instruments to pursue eternal truth.

Two further notes must be sounded if we are to understand better the way Wesley did theology. Wesley believed in "prevenient grace" and was open to the Spirit that works in that grace. He believed firmly in man's fallenness as did Calvin and Luther. He accepted without question Paul's teaching that we are dead in our trespasses and sins. We are incapable in ourselves of any movement toward God. But our hope is not in an eternal decree. A quickening Spirit is at work in every person. This is the basis of the biblical "whosoever will." That Spirit will sometime, somewhere quicken every person to respond to grace. The quickening does not save. It simply brings a ray of light into our darkness and so touches our spirits that we are able to pursue that light. This is the prevenient grace of God. It has cognitive as well as soteriological implications. Thus, the central key to theological understanding is pneumatological. The rational element is subordinate to this.

The second note in Wesley is his openness to God's Spirit. He believed that the canon was closed. We do not wait for further revelation similar to that found in Scripture. In that sense revelation is complete. But our understanding of that revelation is another matter. Wesley demonstrated this in his willingness, with his colleagues, to define further their understanding of Christian perfection. This may be one reason that he felt no great urgency to produce "the complete systematic." One has the feeling that he neither felt it was possible nor particularly relevant. What we do know is that his handling of Scripture, reason, tradition, and experience was the means whereby millions came to a remarkably full and creative understanding of human possibilities in grace and enlarged understanding of the ethical implications of the gospel. It is time for the church at large, that "holy catholic church," to look more carefully at one whom theologians have tended to ignore.

NOTES

[1]E. C. Moore, *An Outline of the History of Christian Thought Since Kant* (New York: Charles Scribner's Sons, 1912), 194.

[2]Albert C. Outler, *The Wesleyan Theological Heritage*, ed. Thomas C. Oden and Leicester Longden (Grand Rapids: Zondervan, 1991), 49.

[3]John L. Peters, *Christian Perfection and American Methodism* (Grand Rapids: Zondervan, 1985), 20.

[4]John Wesley, *The Works of John Wesley* (1872; reprint, Grand Rapids: Zondervan, 1958), 12:200.

[5]Outler, *Wesleyan Theological Heritage*, 113.

[6]Vincent of Lérins, *Commonitoria*, 2:1; *Fathers of the Church*, 7:270.

[7]Wesley, *Works*, 8:348.

[8]Ibid., 349.

[9]Ibid., 11:367.

[10]John Wesley, *Wesley's Standard Sermons*, ed. E. H. Sugden (1921; reprint, Grand Rapids: Zondervan, 1986), 1:31–32.

[11]John Wesley, *The Letters of the Rev. John Wesley, A. M.*, ed. John Telford (London: Epworth, 1931), 2:117.

[12]Wesley, *Works*, 8:348.

[13]Lancelot Andrewes, *Opuscula* (Oxford: Library of Anglo Catholic Theology, 1841–63), 91.

[14]G. C. Cell, *The Rediscovery of John Wesley* (New York: Henry Holt, 1935), 361.

[15]H. R. McAdoo, *The Spirit of Anglicanism* (London: Adam & Charles Black, 1965), 341.

[16]A. Skevington Wood, *The Burning Heart: John Wesley, Evangelist* (Grand Rapids: Eerdmans, 1967), 67.

[17]Wesley, *Works*, 8:12.

[18]Donald A. D. Thorsen, *The Wesleyan Quadrilateral* (Grand Rapids: Zondervan, 1990).

THE BIBLE AND LITERATURE

Joseph R. Dongell

INTRODUCTION

For generations readers have recognized and commented upon various literary features of the Bible. Whether one holds the Gospel of Luke as the most beautiful book ever written, cherishes suspense and imagery in the stories of OT heroes, or declares Paul's description of love (1Co 13) to be most sublime, one has engaged to some degree in literary criticism. It is but a small step from such appreciation to a more systematic exploration of the literary character of biblical texts with an eye not only toward great enjoyment in reading, but toward greater understanding as well.

Most literary phenomena appear more frequently in some genres, less frequently in others. Archaic English verb forms, for example, will be found more often in prayers, homilies, and traditional ceremonies than in doctors' prescriptions, weather bulletins, and political commentaries. Various literary features in the Bible, then, are usefully organized and treated according to the genres in which they most typically appear.

Of course the genres themselves deserve careful treatment in any discussion of literary matters. Simply put, a literary genre is defined as a group of texts with several features in common with each other. It is a sensitivity to genre that prompts a bookstore manager to devote separate sections of the store to science fiction, romance, and mystery. But the "several features" held in common by the texts within a genre can be identified more specifically. In generic analysis, texts are grouped together that show some commonality in form, social setting, and intention.[1]

The importance of addressing the literary genre of biblical texts arises from the fact that God's truth has come to expression in the language and literature of particular human societies. The Scripture is, therefore, both linguistically and historically conditioned, requiring that interpretation be carried out within these parameters. On the one hand, the linguistic character of the Bible requires that we read its texts in the light of the societal constraints and expectations brought into play simply by the use of language. Languages are, after all, not the private possessions of individuals, but consist of complex social agreements shared by many persons about how their language ought to work. Were these conventions to be dissolved, individuals would become linguistically isolated and communication would be impossible. On the other hand, the historical nature of the Bible and the languages it employs requires that we read texts in the light of their placement in the evolution and devolution of human languages and their conventions. As anyone who compares Shakespearean English with modern English may suspect, languages, like people, horses, and trees develop, mature, grow old, and die.

The particular conventions that make communication in any language possible include not only vocabulary and syntax but also genre. As soon as readers or listeners encounter discourse, they begin classifying, whether consciously or unconsciously, that discourse according to genres known to them. In our own language and culture such initial formulas as "Once upon a time," "Ladies and gentlemen," "Dearly beloved," and "Whereas. . . Be it resolved" generate powerful expectations in our minds about what forms and structures will follow, what typical social setting is assumed, and what sorts of intention might lie behind the discourse. Such expectations are a major constituent meaning, allowing us to make sense of what we encounter. When our generic expectations regarding form, function, or setting are not fulfilled, we may be embarrassed, amused, or confused. For example, a declamation of praise offered at the birthday celebration of an octogenarian may too nearly approach the genre of a "eulogy for the deceased" to please the family. Or a suitor, hoping to improve his chances through humor, may use the parliamentary formula "Whereas. . . , be it resolved. . ." to propose marriage to his companion. How often have friendships been damaged when the hearer has categorized a remark wrongly as "serious statement" rather than as "joke"! Far from being a pointless exercise, then, generic classification bears a heavy load in the task of accurate interpretation, since genre conveys meaning just as certainly as do words and syntax.

For generations biblical scholars have sought to identify and classify biblical literature according to its type, or genre. In so doing, they stand in some continuity with the interests of ancient literary theorists such as Aristotle, who considered Lyric, Epic, and Drama as the fundamental categories into which all literature could be grouped. Even in typical university curricula today, these same categories are often expressed as poetry, novels, and drama, with such subgroupings or overlappings as tragedy, comedy, satire, biography, and essay.[2] But as generic theory has been pursued with greater rigor, and the biblical genres have been subjected to closer analysis in the last century, generic analysis has developed into a technical discipline. Several of its more important conclusions, assumptions, and weaknesses are described in greater detail below.[3]

First, though the Bible now stands as a written document, much of its material initially arose as speech. This is due not only to the largely oral nature of ancient societies, but also the preference of certain discourse genres for spoken communication. Prophetic warnings and encouragements, for example, were likely reduced to writing only after their initial oral delivery before a live audience (cf. Jos 36:4, 32). It is more appropriate, then, to have in mind the great variety of nonliterary social and religious settings (*Sitze im Leben*) in ancient society as the womb that gave birth to many genres, than to have in mind as the source the individual genius of the professional scribe. In any case, a genre has been adequately described when the setting in which it first arose has been identified.

Second, genres, as certainly as languages and societies, change and develop over time. At its inception, a genre might be compact and concise. But as its use increases and the uses to which it is put are broadened, the same genre may become complex and overloaded until it fades away entirely or is transformed into something qualitatively different. Or a single genre may be merged with several other genres to form a hybrid, or mixed genre. In theory, at least, it should be possible to construct a relative dating of texts sharing the same genre by plotting the evolution of their generic forms. Such a project is complicated, however, by several of the following points.

Third, generic definition must admit a degree of fluidity. Not only do mixed genres muddy the waters of analysis, but speakers and writers are constantly adapting genres to address more effectively the immediate needs of their particular situations.[4] The differences between two texts of the same genre, then, may flow less from the larger evolution of the genre than from the specific historical contexts in which they were formed. The peculiar creativity of one prophet may not affect later prophets employing the same genre. It follows that not all texts "fit" into single generic categories, and that generic evolution can be plotted only with great reserve.[5]

Fourth, some genres are susceptible of more precise structural description than others. As will be noted below, Psalms identified as Thanksgiving Psalms contain distinct and predictable components, whereas Royal Psalms share little more than a royal theme. Such unevenness in generic definition and description is especially obvious when texts are grouped together, for example, solely according to their content or to their supposed lack of historicity. In such cases generic definitions are doubtful, and conclusions founded upon them should be viewed with suspicion.

Fifth, genres may vary in size, from a few words or phrases to huge complexes of material that span a group of biblical books. A letter, for example, may be as brief as 2 John or as extensive as Romans. Additionally, genres may be a host to or hosted by other genres. The short letter from the apostles and elders at Jerusalem (Ac 15:23−29) is hosted within the ancient historiography of Luke−Acts, while a Pauline letter typically hosts within it other genres: e.g., hymn (Phm 2:6−11), allegory (Gal 4:21−31), code of household ethics (Col 3:18−4:1). Therefore, the distinction sometimes made between literary forms (smaller, hosted units) and literary genres (larger, hosting units), while useful at times, admits many exceptions.

Sixth, though literary theory typically defines a genre as a group of texts sharing certain characteristics, a number of texts seem to be unique, the single example of a type of literature. Whether such a text is the only survivor among many members of its class, or the only text of that sort ever produced, one can immediately detect the inappropriateness of speaking "typically" about any one of its features. But inasmuch as one can describe its structure, purpose, and setting, we consider it appropriate to include such texts in this discussion of biblical literature.

Seventh, whatever the history of a genre, whether it arose in oral or written mode, and whether it arose in the royal court, the temple, the family, or the market place, the biblical materials now stand within finished literary compositions that supply (or imply) distinctive literary and historical contexts. However deeply the interpreter may probe the layers of redaction or the evolution of genres, the task of interpreting Scripture requires attention, finally, to the shape and function of any given biblical text as a finished literary component within a finished literary whole.

Generic analysis, then, presents itself as a necessary endeavor though fraught with complexity and ambiguity. The brief survey below will set forth only the more important biblical genres along with prominent literary characteristics noteworthy for each. More comprehensive treatments of biblical genres and their literary features can be located in the resources cited in the following discussion.

GENRES OF OT LITERATURE

The Literature of the Pentateuch

The traditional partitioning of the Hebrew Bible into the Torah, the Prophets, and the Writings suggests that the first books of Scripture (the Pentateuch) constitute a unity, though it is not immediately obvious what sort of unity this might be. After all, the story of Israel's formation and journeying is brought to some resolution only with Joshua's conquest of the land (Jos 1–24). Furthermore, the Pentateuch comprehends such diverse materials as creation accounts, genealogies, family stories, travel narratives, and a host of regulations both cultic and civil, which at first glance rule out literary unity. Yet thematic and stylistic signals sufficiently set the Pentateuch off as an intentionally purposeful whole.[6] It is useful, then, to characterize the Pentateuch as *Torah*, as a unique amalgam of story and commandment that circumscribes the nature of God's people by setting forth their founding history and their codes of conduct.[7]

The broad categories of story and law that encompass most material within the Torah can be further subdivided, though not always with great confidence.[8] The lengthiest genre of story, the *saga*, narrates past events in a long, episodic format. Many diverse materials may be hosted by the saga as it plays out its various themes. In the absence of more specific structural differentiation, subgenres must be defined in light of content: Primeval sagas concern themselves with the origin of the world (e.g., Ge 1–11). Family sagas attend to the experiences of a family and its patriarch, especially in the events of conception, birth, journey, danger, marriage, and death (e.g., Abraham, Ge 12–25). In heroic sagas, the family is of less importance, as the virtues and significance of the individual command great attention (e.g., Moses, Ex 1–Dt 34).

The genres of Tale, Novella, and Legend, despite the common association of these labels with fiction, must be defined primarily according to their structure. The *Tale* comprises a single scene in which a small cast of characters moves in simple fashion from some tension to its resolution (e.g., Sarah in trouble, Ge 12:9–13:1). The *Novella* is far more complex than the tale, though shorter than the saga. Its complexity is discerned in its capacity for larger casts, multiple subplots within the main movement from problem to resolution, and artful characterization (e.g., the story of Joseph, Ge 37–47). The *Legend* has less interest in plot than do saga, tale, and novella, for it underscores more the virtue of a hero than the resolution of a problem (e.g., Abraham's offering of Isaac, Ge 22).

Also meriting attention is the *Myth*, a genre well attested in the ancient Near East. Such texts typically recount fantastic battles between the gods, the supernatural deeds of mighty heroes, accounts of creation, and accounts of a cosmic flood. More significantly, these myths employ a distinctive view of time and space. Past, present, and future, though not homogeneously merged, are fundamentally identical to each other, since nothing genuinely new can arise within them. Similarly, separate spaces may be considered to be essentially identical. It is important to note, however, that the OT does not contain materials that neatly match these characteristics. The biblical narration of creation and flood, while displaying several remarkable similarities with such pagan mythic texts as *Enuma Elish*, reject mythical perceptions of time and space, place the events of Creation and Flood within the continuum of Israel's history, and expound the unique transcendence of God over all creation.[9]

The genres described above arose no doubt in a variety of settings (family, court, cult, or other societal institutions) and for a variety of purposes (entertainment, instruction, legitimation) that are quite beyond our ability to recover with confidence. But whatever their pre-literary history, the genres expressing these biblical materials now serve the controlling purposes of the Pentateuch and its component books. An adequate interpretation of any individual narrative must therefore account for its role within the unifying themes and larger sweep of the Pentateuchal narrative.

Mention of unity and purpose leads us naturally to consider the artistry of biblical narrative. Contrary to the expectations of many modern readers, even the simplist biblical narratives give evidence of the skillful manipulation of vocabulary and syntax. The narrator may speak volumes by saying nothing, or may pack powerful emotions into the briefest lines. A lifetime of bitter disappointment is viewed through the lens of Rachel's cry: "Give me sons; if not, I shall die!" (Ge 30:1).[10] Readers will spot gaps in stories, at seemingly crucial points, which in the hands of the narrator create suspense, curiosity, and surprise.[11] Dramatic irony, occasioned when the reader knows more than a character knows, illumines dialogue brilliantly by revealing hidden meanings otherwise inaccessible. Plays on words, the careful repetition of key terms, and judicious control of the rate of new information demonstrate yet in other ways the artistry of biblical narrative and the promise of reward for the close reader.

The character of the Pentateuch comes to still fuller light when narrative material shares center stage with legal materials.[12] But the subdivision of these materials into distinct literary genres, and exploration into the origins and history of such genres have not yielded convincing results. Provisionally, we may say that several distinct linguistic patterns may be isolated. *Casuistic Law* sets forth conditions, often with lengthy elaboration or in series, under which a penalty should be enforced (e.g., "When fire breaks out and catches in thorns so that the stacked grain or standing grain or the field is consumed, he that kindled the fire shall make full restitution," Ex 22:6). *Apodictic Law* issues a simple command, whether positive or negative (e.g., "You shall have no other gods before me," Ex 20:3). A *Capital Crime* and its penalty may be coupled in a brief formula employing the Hebrew participle and infinitive absolute (e.g., "Whoever strikes a man so that he dies shall be put to death," Ex 21:12). Finally, the *Curse* formula sets forth a threat of punishment and the behavior that would prompt it (e.g., "Cursed be he who misleads a blind man on the road," Dt 27:18). It is worth noting how frequently no justification is provided for these directives, and how little suggestion there is of a pre-Sinai legal history. Apparently, the presentation of Israelite law in the Pentateuch stresses the *comprehensive newness* of Israel's *situation* through the Mosaic covenant at Sinai, and her pledge of unswerving obedience to God.[13]

Mention of the Mosaic covenant brings into view the last legal genre to be considered. Throughout the ancient Near East, *Covenants* (i.e., legal/religious treaties) were used to create, formalize, and sustain relationships between various parties (e.g., the Hittite king Hattusilis III and Ramses II of Egypt). Although certain differences may be noted between particular conventual forms, an impressive uniformity in them over nearly two millennia points to a covenant tradition common throughout the ancient Near East. Typical components of the covenant are a) the preamble [in which the king is introduced], b) the historical prologue [wherein the past relationship is narrated], c) the stipulations [which describe obligations incumbent upon both parties], d) the deposit and public reading [wherein provisions are made for storage and periodic public reading of the covenant], e) the witnesses [in which the gods of both states are listed, under the assumption that they will punish violators of the covenant], and f) blessings and curses [wherein the benefits or catastrophes are listed that will attend those who hold or break the covenant].[14]

Though various covenants are mentioned or described in the OT (Ge 21:27; 31:44–46; Jos 9:6–16; 24:1–27), most prominent is the Mosaic covenant that bound Israel to Yahweh as a chosen people (Ex 24:1–11).

Its similarity to the Hittite Suzerainty treaties, which follow the treaty elements listed above, is especially palpable in Deuteronomy. Though the book presents itself more as an exhortation than a covenant, much of it can be correlated with the standard components of the Suzerainty treaty.[15] Like a powerful king, God has sovereignly laid down all of the stipulations by which Israel, the subject people, must abide. Her continued obedience assures her of continued protection and blessing under her king, while disobedience places her in jeopardy.

Historical Literature

The connected narrative of Israel's story extends beyond the Pentateuch narrative of Israel's history from the conquest of Canaan to Judah's fall at the hands of the Chaldeans. This complex of material (Jos–2Ki) shows evidence of literary and theological unity, in that it consistently links the vicissitudes of Israel's history to the measure of her obedience to the Mosaic covenant. From this vantage point, the whole story can be reduced to the dictum that faithfulness brings life and prosperity to the nation, while disobedience brings national disaster.[16]

A unified work of such magnitude as the Deuteronomistic History[17] and Chronicles may be termed a *History*, a genre that may have arisen in or around the royal court among scribes who would have had access to court records and other related sources. The Bible's historical narratives will not conform to certain modern expectations that historiography be dispassionate and "objective." The biblical writers wrote, rather, with intense desire to affect the behaviors and values of their readers. Its treatment of various periods in Israel's history and her kings is not so uniform and proportional as some might prefer. The twelve-year reign of Omri is dispensed with in eight verses (1Ki 16:21–28), while the twenty-two year reign of his son Ahab swells to six chapters that contain an assortment of related stories. Little light is shed in the economic, social, and political concerns that are the focus of modern historiography. Instead, the biblical writers were consumed with the question of Israel's relationship to God. In short, biblical history selects and arranges its material according to its own viewpoint in the service of its own ends.

Among the larger components of histories are *Accounts*, which employ a rather simple, straightforward style in narrating or explaining thematically related events (e.g., 1Ki 6:1–7:51; Solomon constructs the temple).[18] Shorter still are *Reports*, which narrate a single incident without attention to plot or character development (e.g., 1Ki 5:1–12; Solomon and Hiram make a treaty). The *Notice* is indistinguishable from a single statement (e.g., 1Ki 3:1; Solomon's marriage alliance). All readers are familiar with the *List*, which may present with or without ordering a collection of items (1Ch 2:1–3:24, genealogy; 2Sa 23:24–39, soldier; 1Ki 4:2–19, officials). The original settings and purposes of these genres may have varied widely.

By means of the *Theological Summary*, a narrator interprets various persons or events theologically (e.g., Jdg 2:11–3:6, evaluating the period of the judges).[19] A more formulaic summary found throughout the book of Kings is the *Regnal Résumé*, which appears in both introductory and concluding formats. In the former may appear a) the king's name and date of accession, b) the king's age at accession, c) the length of reign, d) the name of the king's mother, e) a theological evaluation. "In the twelfth year of Joram son of Ahab king of Israel, Ahaziah son of Jehoram king of Judah began to reign. Ahaziah was twenty-two years old when he became king, and he reigned in Jerusalem one year. His mother's name was Athaliah, a granddaughter of Omri king of Israel. He walked in the ways of Ahab and did evil in the eyes of the Lord, as the house of Ahab had done, for he was related by marriage to Ahab's family" (2Ki 8:25–27). In the concluding formula may appear a) reference to other sources of information regarding the king's reign, b) the king's death and burial, c) succession. It is hardly possible to overestimate the value of such summaries for tracking the historian's theological evaluation of the parts and whole of Israel's history from the divine point of view.[20]

Distinguishable from the histories (e.g., Deuteronomistic, and the Chronicles) are Nehemiah and Ezra. Though the first-person perspective of the latter would at first blush suggest biography, their greater focus upon the nation and its struggles than upon the person of the narrator argues for their generic classification as *Memoir*.[21]

Literary features identified in the Pentateuchal narratives (i.e., skillful plot development, characterization, use of irony, repetition of key terms or motifs, etc.) pertain as well to narratives with Israel's history. And the artistry of the history narratives pertain to the Pentateuchal narrative materials.

Prophetic Literature

The largest genre within prophetic literature, the *Prophetic Book*, begins with a superscription that may identify the prophet, his ancestry, his place of origin, the kings during whose reigns he prophesied, and a general indication of the content of the prophecy, e.g., the introductory lines of the book of Amos: "The words of Amos, one of the shepherds of Tekoa— what he saw concerning Israel two years before the earthquake, when Uzziah was king of Judah and Jerobam son of Jehoash was king of Israel" (1:1). But the body of a prophetic book follows no normal pattern, sometimes appearing as a collection of diverse (though thematically related) materials.[22]

Among the more prominent genres of prophetic literature is the *Announcement of Disaster*,[23] in which the prophet speaks as God's messenger of forthcoming judgment. Typically presented are: a) the commissioning of the prophet for announcing the disaster; b) an accusation, including the reasons for judgment; c) a prediction of the judgment; and d) a concluding generalization. We see this in Jeremiah 29:30–32.

> Then the word of the Lord came to Jeremiah: "Send this message to all the exiles: 'This is what the Lord says about Shemaiah the Nehelamite: Because Shemaiah has prophesied to you, even though I did not send him, and has led you to believe a lie, this is what the Lord says: I will surely punish Shemaiah the Nehelamite and his descendants. He will have no one left among this people, nor will he see the good things I will do for my people, declares the Lord, because he has preached rebellion against me.'"

See also Ezr 17:11–21. Announcements made to nations are less rigid in form and more expansive in their accusation than announcements of disaster made to individuals.

Though the *Announcement of Salvation*, which foretells God's beneficial intervention, may follow the same general format as the announcement of disaster, reasons for God's action are frequently omitted.

> "This is what the Lord Almighty, the God of Israel, says: 'I will break the yoke of the king of Babylon. Within two years I will bring back to this place all the articles of the Lord's house that Nebuchadnezzar king of Babylon removed from here and took to Babylon. I will also bring back to this place Jehoiachin son of Jehoiakim king of Judah and all the other exiles for Judah who went to Babylon,' declares the Lord, 'for I will break the yoke of the king of Babylon'" (Jer 28:2–4).

By the *Oracle of Salvation* the prophet speaks God's word of encouragement. In it, a) God's gracious dealings from the past are recounted; b) the prophet exhorts, "Fear not!"; c) the results of God's actions are depicted; and d) God's motivation for saving is explored. "But now, this is what the Lord says—he who created you, O Jacob, he who formed you, O Israel: 'Fear not, for I have redeemed you; I have called you by name; you are mine. When you pass through the waters I will be with you; and when you pass through the rivers, they will not sweep over you. . . .'" (Isa 43:1–2; see 41:8–13).

Another format in which the prophet declares God's anger is the *Woe*. After the interjection "Woe!" comes the identification of those subject to punishment, a description of their offensive behavior, and an announcement of the punishment due them. "Woe to you who are complacent in Zion, and to you who feel secure on Mount Samaria, you notable men of the foremost nation, to whom the people of Israel come!" (Am 6:1; see also 2–7).

Disputes between God and Israel may take the form of a *Rîb*, or a complaint lodged against the violator of a treaty. Accordingly, a) an introduction provides background, b) witnesses are questioned and accusations made, c) the prosecutor extols the faithfulness of God and the unfaithfulness of Israel, d) appeasement by cultic means is deemed useless, and e) guilt and destruction are announced. "Stand up, plead your case before the mountains. . . . Hear, O mountains, the Lord's accusation. . . . I brought you up out of Egypt and redeemed you from the land of slavery. . . . Will the Lord be pleased with thousands of rams. . . ? Therefore I will give you over to ruin and your people to derision; you will bear the scorn of nations" (from Mic 6; see also Isa 1 and Jer 2).

Or the prophet may issue a *Summons to Repentance*. After the messenger formula ("Thus says the Lord"), the wayward are directly admonished to repent. Motivation for repentance is then supplied by promise and/or threat. "This is what the Lord says to the house of Israel: 'Seek me and live; do not seek Bethel, do not go to Gilgal, do not journey to Beersheba. For Gilgal will surely go into exile, and Bethel will be reduced to nothing'" (Am 5:4–5; see also 5:6–7, and 5:14–15).

In the *Vision Report*, a prophet recounts viewing such things as forthcoming events or symbolic objects (e.g., the basket of fruit, Am 8:1–3). After declaring that a vision had occurred and describing what had been seen, the prophet concludes with its explanation. "This is what the Sovereign Lord showed me: a basket of ripe fruit. 'What do you see, Amos?' he asked. 'A basket of ripe fruit,' I answered. Then the Lord said to me, 'The time is ripe for my people Israel; I will spare them no longer'" (Am 8:1–2). As one variety of vision report, the *Call Narrative* describes one's entry into prophetic service. Its components may include the initial encounter between God and a man, his divine commission to be a prophet, his objections (real or implied) to the commission, divine reassurance, and a confirming sign (Isa 6; Jer 1:4–19; Ezr 1–3).

The caveats set forth in the introduction above should be borne in mind especially with prophetic literature. Each of these genres rarely occurs in the pattern described, with variation outscoring regularity. The original social settings of these genres is impossible to fix with certainty, though the *Rîb* would seem at home in the (international) law court and the Oracle of Salvation may well have originated as the priestly response to an individual lament. Furthermore, the identification of genres within the prophetic books does not, in our view, immediately settle questions regarding the literary unity and authorship of prophetic books.

The language of the prophets is, on the whole, best characterized as poetic. While our treatment of larger poetic structures will be delayed until the following section, some accounting of the intricacies of poetic technique is appropriate here. Alliteration, the recurrence of similar sounds at the beginnings of successive words or syllables, may be detected in Isa 1:18–20, where a recurring "k" sound attracts the reader's attention. Assonance, the recurrence of similar sounds in accented vowels, appears in Isa 53:4–7, where fifteen occurrences of the "u" sound intensify the atmosphere of grief and sorrow. Paronomasia, the play between similarly sounding words, is employed in Isa 5:7 where "justice" and "bloodshed" appear in adjacent lines, as do "righteousness" and "cry." With onomatopoeia, the sounds of words approximate the realities they describe. In Isa 42:14 the recurring "p" and guttural sounds bring to mind the distressed breathing of a woman in labor.[24] All of these techniques, which are of course nearly impossible to reproduce in English translation, invigorate the linguistic medium, excite the imagination, and thereby increase the impact of the prophetic message.

Poetic Literature

It is commonly estimated that poetry comprises one third of the OT. Though it is found in the Pentateuch, Historical Books, and extensively in the Prophets, and therefore is not limited to one portion of the Canon, poetry is especially at home in the Psalms and Wisdom Literature.

In this century, the Psalms have become a focus of intense generic study. Certain groupings of psalms (e.g., Wisdom Psalms, Torah Psalms, Songs of Trust, Royal [Messianic?] Psalms, Festival Psalms, Liturgies) are defined solely by their content, employing no regular structure. But much clearer patterns are discernible with others.[25] *Laments* (e.g., Pss 3, 5, 7, 9–10, 14, 22, 25, 26) typically include: a) an address to God; b) a complaint in which the trouble is identified (whether sin, sickness, or national crisis); c) a confession of trust in God; d) a petition for salvation, often with motives suggested for God's saving action; e) words of assurance that salvation will come; and f) a vow to praise God publicly for salvation.

Thanksgivings (e.g., Pss 34, 92, 116, 118, 138) characteristically embrace a) a statement of intent to praise and thank God; b) a description of an earlier distress; c) a remembrance of the cry for help; d) a recounting of the deliverance; e) a conclusion. Within the conclusion may be found prayers for future help, expressions of faith, blessings, exhortations, and repeated declarations of God's faithfulness.

Hymns of Praise (e.g., Pss 100, 104, 114, 148) may focus upon God's power and grace in creating the world, in calling and redeeming Israel, or in overseeing the course of history. Commonly, these psalms employ a) an invocation, in which various audiences are called to worship God; b) a body, in which various reasons [often introduced by "who" or "for"] for praising God are stated and elaborated upon; and c) a conclusion, which may resume the original exhortation to praise God.

Though particular occasions or general circumstances may be proposed for the origin of these psalms and their genres, it is important to bear in mind that they now stand together as a collection that no doubt served the needs of Israel as a worshiping community of faith. Several levels of reading, then, are possible for most psalms, in addition to an overtly Christian reading evidenced throughout the NT and early Christian interpretation.

In Wisdom literature, especially Proverbs, other distinctive genres can be isolated.[26] The *Observational Sayings*, usually consisting of one or two lines, describe the way things are in the world and among people. These sayings appear content to record an observation without clearly proposing or implying to the listener a course of action to be taken. "A cheerful look brings joy to the heart, and good news gives health to the bones" (Pr 15:30). On the other hand, *Wisdom Sayings* strive to press home a lesson or value, and expect to affect the behavior of the hearer accordingly. "The

Lord is far from the wicked but he hears the prayer of the righteous" (Pr 15:29). One subcategory of Wisdom Saying is the *"Better" Saying*, which contrasts two situations, preferring one to the other. "Better a little with the fear of the Lord than great wealth with turmoil" (Pr 15:16). Both Wisdom and Observational Sayings may be cast as *Numerical Sayings*, which list items sharing a crucial feature. "There are three things that are too amazing for me, four that I do not understand: the way of an eagle in the sky, the way of a snake on a rock, the way of a ship on the high seas, and the way of a man with a maiden" (Pr 30:18–19). Instruction for right living may also take the form of direct address. Positive instructions, or *Commands*, prescribe behaviors to be adopted. "Drink water from your own cistern, running water from your own well" (Pr 5:15). Negative instructions, or *Prohibitions*, forbid other behaviors. "Do not eat the food of a stingy man, do not crave his delicacies" (Pr 23:6). Both Commands and Prohibitions are often accompanied by supporting reasons.

Hebrew poetry, especially prevalent in Psalms and Proverbs, consists not of rhymes and precise syllabic counts but of balanced thoughts.[27] In *Synonymous Parallelism*, two (or three) lines share nearly identical content.

> The heavens declare the glory of God [a];
>   the skies proclaim the work of his hands [a'].
> Day after day they pour forth speech [b];
>   night after night they display knowledge [b'].
> There is no speech or language [c]
>   where their voice is not heard [c'].
> Their voice goes out into all the earth [d],
>   their words to the ends of the world [d'].
>   (Ps 19:1–4)

In *Antithetic Parallelism*, two lines set forth a contrast.

> A cheerful heart is good medicine,
>   but a crushed spirit dries up the bones.
>   (Pr 17:22)

In *Synthetic Parallelism*, the second line advances the thought of the first line, often bringing it to completion.

> The law of the Lord is perfect,
>   reviving the soul.
>   (Ps 19:7)

In *Climactic Parallelism*, the second line echoes the beginning of the first line, but supplies its own conclusion.

> Ascribe to the Lord, O mighty ones,
>   ascribe to the Lord glory and strength.
>   (Ps 29:1)

But each sort of parallelism, it must be noted, is capable of wide variation. The second line may omit elements clearly implied from the first line, and may compensate for the loss by adding an element that has no parallel in the first line.

> Let them give thanks to the Lord for his unfailing love,
> and his wonderful deeds for men.
>
> (Ps 107:21)

More complex arrangements result when lines already joined together in parallelism are grouped in a larger parallelism with other line clusters.

More ambiguous is the metrical character of Hebrew poetry. Of several competing theories, most convincing is that which analyses poetic lines by the number of stressed syllables, largely disregarding unstressed syllables. Accordingly, the parallelisms described above are frequently cast in a $3+3$ metrical pattern, though variations abound (e.g., $2+2$; $4+4$; $2+2+2$; $4+3$). One meter, the $3+2$, has been dubbed the Qinah ("lament"), because of its use in the book of Lamentations and similar materials. The halting shortness of the second line enhances the sense of despair otherwise communicated by the poet.

In the hands of the poet, such matters as parallelism, word play, meter, and the like are hardly a detachable cloak merely enhancing the "basic content" of a passage. They contribute meanings of their own, and permit the poet to speak the language of deep emotion that has gripped so many through the centuries.

THE GENRES OF NT LITERATURE

The Gospels

A moment's reflection will confirm that the Gospels cannot be classified as biographies, at least according our modern expectations of what biographies should be. After all, almost nothing can be found in the Gospels about Jesus' childhood or development toward adulthood. No probing analysis of the inner workings of his mind is attempted, nor is there any tracing of his road to self-understanding. What materials have been assembled in the Gospels focus almost exclusively on the last year(s) of Jesus' life, with even these materials disproportionately weighted toward his final week.

But if modern generic expectations are ruled out of order in Gospel analysis, prospects for classifying the Gospels according to ancient literary genres are not much brighter. It can safely be declared that there are no other ancient documents "just like" the canonical Gospels. As is commonly believed today, the Gospels are *sui generis* (i.e., of their own kind), a new literary genre arising out of a new religious movement.[28]

Yet positing the uniqueness of the Gospels so strongly is misleading. Gospels manifest general structural similarity with *ancient tragedy* in their common movement from initial tension, through rising tension, to climax, resolution, and epilogue. Points of contact can also be drawn to *ancient comedy*, in the sudden reversal from near disaster to final triumph (e.g., crucifixion and resurrection). More importantly, it is unreasonable to demand that documents grouped together under a single generic designation mirror each other so precisely as some would demand. In fact, ancient biographies appear to be a sufficiently diverse genre as to allow the Gospels to be classified among them, albeit as a unique subgrouping approaching the aretalogy (a narrative of the miraculous deeds of a hero, cf. Philostratus' *Life of Apollonius of Tyana*).[29]

Whatever one's conclusions may be regarding Gospel genre, the *composite* nature of each Gospel shines through. The story of Jesus is comprised of distinct narrative units that have themselves invited generic classification. In reading the Gospels one will encounter parables, exorcism stories, miracle stories, controversy stories, wisdom sayings, warnings, prophecies, apocalyptic discourses, rulings, sermons, and simple historical narratives, along with many other genres often mixed in ways that defy straightforward classification. At the very least, the interpreter can gain insight by classifying a given text generically for the purposes of comparing it with similar texts.

The composite character of the Gospels has been fully appreciated by source critics (who explore for literary sources behind each Gospel) and form critics (who isolate and trace units of tradition back to their oral forms). Their work tended to shatter the Gospels into a thousand pieces that were then employed to reconstruct the history of Gospel tradition from its various phases of literary (written) expression, through the oral tradition of the primitive church, and on to Jesus insofar as that was deemed possible. Little interest was reserved for the evangelists themselves, who were viewed as mere compilers of various traditions that, through subtraction, addition, and modification, had lost much of their historical value.

But by the middle of the twentieth century, redaction criticism had begun to refocus attention on the evangelists, who were seen in truer light as creative authors and reflective theologians. Under the assumption that each evangelist had artfully woven materials together to achieve particular ends, it was but a short step to a more genuinely "literary" criticism that entertained works as coherent wholes. Accordingly, two diverse approaches to the Gospels have fallen into disrepute. On the one hand, as already indicated, it is no longer possible to hammer out issues of source and form criticism and suppose that one has "interpreted" a Gospel. For not until one has begun looking *at* a Gospel, not simply *through* it, will that Gospel itself come into direct view. On the other hand, the practice of producing Gospel harmonies is shown to be of dubious value. The blending of separate narratives into a single all-encompassing narrative wipes out the distinctive approach of each, and creates a fifth Gospel that supplants the other four.

The literary reading sensitive to the uniqueness of each Gospel, then, will approach the Gospels as *coherent, relatively self-contained wholes*.[30] The contrast between the story's beginning and end will be carefully explored.

Close attention will be paid to ways in which the plot is developed from initial conflict, through heightened tension, to final resolution. Plot movement will be tracked by noting such devices as causation, foreshadowing, flashbacks, repetition, and prophecy-fulfillment. An author's use of symbols will be traced. The role of characters within the development of the plot will be examined, along with observing which characters undergo change or show complexity. Characters that are aligned with the "correct point of view" in the story will be distinguished from the ambiguous or those set in opposition.

A literary reading will also attend to the selection, ordering, and arrangement of materials. Has one story been inserted within another to enhance their effect (cf. Mk 5:21–24)? Have stories been arranged in parallel or chiastic patterns to highlight their similarities (cf. Mk 2:1–3:6)? Has a recurrence of similar incidents created strong expectation or emphasis (cf. Mk 8:27–10:52)? What are the proportions between different kinds of material, and between different portions of the narrative? Why has a given story been placed here and not elsewhere? What has been omitted from the narrative that might, according to our expectations, have been included? Other standard agenda of literary analysis, such as the use of irony and figures of speech, will be pursed as well. Though definitive answers to these questions may not always be found, such probing characterizes the sort of reading that will bring many rewards.

Historiography

In discussions of NT genres, the Acts of the Apostles is commonly set apart from the Gospels and classified as "history," since it narrates a series of events extending beyond the terminus of the ministry of Jesus in the Gospels.

Yet such a viewpoint must be refined in two ways. First, as has been established for decades, Acts must be seen as one part of a larger literary whole of Luke-Acts. And, as has become increasingly apparent, Luke and Acts are bound together not only externally by the preface of Acts (1:1–5), which recalls the Gospel, but by stylistic, thematic, and theological commonalities running through their length. Even the Lukan infancy narrative (1:4–2:52), which has often been considered a late addition to the Gospel, manifests clear organic connection to the whole. The two volumes must be considered together, then, when the question of literary genre is raised.[31]

A second point of refinement concerns the classification of Luke-Acts as historiography. On the one hand, such a classification is well justified in light of the writings of the work of such ancient historians as Herodotus, Thucydides, Polybius, and Josephus. Impressive similarities between their work and Luke-Acts are their multivolume formats and their use of prefaces. Luke 1:1–4 is a shining example of a historiographical preface that suggests the importance and scope of the work, the qualifications and intentions of the writer, and the role of predecessors. The whole preface is carefully arranged in a chiastic pattern, making it one of the most literarily sophisticated passages in the NT.

But on the other hand, presumptions about the nature of ancient historiography should be scrutinized. In one widespread modern caricature of history writing, the historian proceeds in strictly chronological order, mapping out in a precise and vigorously objective fashion some course of events. Coverage of the target events is relatively complete and evenly proportioned. The historian's motives arise largely from his status as a professional whose guild is committed to the accurate recording of human history for the general benefit of future generations.

However, little modern historiography conforms to such a caricature, even less does ancient historiography. In the case of Luke-Acts, the narrator writes without apology *as an advocate* of the Christian gospel, as one seeking to *persuade* and *instruct* his readers. Most certainly, these goals were not pursued less with a view toward the general well-being of future generations, than with a view to immediate difficulties pressing upon particular Christian communities. Furthermore, the order (cf. Lk 1:3 "an orderly account" [$\kappa\alpha\theta\varepsilon\xi\hat{\eta}s$]) with which he narrates events is chronological in its broad strokes, but not minutely so. For example, Jesus' visit to Nazareth has been transposed from a later position (as in Mk 6:1–6) to an initial, keynote position for Jesus' public ministry (Lk 4:16–30), while the so-called Travel Narrative (Lk 9:51–19:44) defies all attempts at chronological and geographical plotting. The order by which the narrator arranges material is that order that best serves the *rhetorical purposes* toward which the whole work has been aimed.

Examination of Acts reveals that the writer makes no claim to a comprehensive and proportional history of the early church. Early on, the story grows progressively restrictive, until at its midpoint, a single character (Paul) becomes its exclusive focus. The radical selectivity of the narrator surely serves his immediate theological purposes. Finally, the narrator must be acknowledged to be more than a matter-of-fact chronicler. The creation and maintenance of suspense, use of irony, recurring themes and patterns, as well as stylistically distinct prefaces all point to a literarily sensitive writer.

One of the strongest links between Luke-Acts and ancient historiography is found in their common interest in the speeches of major characters. Even a cursory look at Acts reveals their importance, not only by their bulk but by their strategic functions. But do these speeches represent the exact words of the speakers as preserved in oral and written sources? While it is impossible to answer with certainty, the practices of ancient historians are suggestive. It was not uncommon for the gist of a speech to be acquired by the historian, and later (during the literary composition of the narrative) filled out according to what was known about the speaker and what would be appropriate to the setting in which the speech was delivered. The *essential content* of the speech could be attributed to the speaker, while the *style* and *phraseology* could be attributed to the writer.[32] If such were the compositional history of various speeches in Luke-Acts, some differences between, for example, Paul's speeches (in Acts) and his communication with churches (in the epistles) could be accounted for without great difficulty. As this example demonstrates, awareness of the literary genre of Luke-Acts, and the accompanying awareness of its literary relatives, can help the reader determine more readily the nature and intent of NT historiography.

Letters[33]

Ancient letters served as communication between parties separated by some distance, and attended a wide variety of purposes. For centuries, NT letters were compared with those composed by classical authors and found to be wanting in literary quality. Around the turn of the last century, with the vast discoveries of Egyptian papyri recording quite mundane matters in a simple style, Deissmann advanced the romantic view that the NT letters were best placed among these epistolary papyri as examples of informal, artless, private Hellenistic letters. But in truth, the somewhat public character of NT letters and their occasional literary flourishes suggest that they be placed somewhere between the formal literary productions of the learned on the one hand, and common everyday correspondence on the other.

Some insight can be gained by viewing NT letters according to a taxonomy of epistolary types proposed by Quintilian, the ancient rhetorician. His scheme classified Hellenistic letters largely by their purpose and content. Viewed through this lens, Galatians and part of 2 Corinthians approximate letters of Rebuke; 1 Thessalonians approaches a letter of Consolation; Philemon and part of Philippians correspond with letters of Recommendation; and Romans can be viewed as a Protreptic letter (one calling readers to a certain lifestyle).[34] But such singular categories cannot account sufficiently for the complexity of purpose in a writer like Paul since in nearly every letter of his may be found passages of praise, admonition, exhortation, recommendation, advice, gratitude, and instruction. The surest conclusion to be drawn from exploring these ancient epistolary types affirms the multiplicity of purpose and variety of content typically present in NT letters.

More fruitful still is examination of letter form. Standard features of a Hellenistic letter were the *Introduction* (including the identification of sender and receiver; the salutation; a healthwish often taking the form of a prayer; and occasionally a notice that the writer held the reader in his memory), the *Body* (in which the main concern of the letter was broached), and the *Closing* (including final greetings to the reader, greetings to third parties, perhaps a closing prayer sentence, and occasionally the date). It is not certain that the letters of Hebrews, James, Peter, Jude, and John are in fact "real" letters. The absence of certain letter features (e.g., final greeting in James, initial greeting in Hebrews) supports the view that several are homilies or testaments merely cast in letter form. But the Pauline letters do not suffer from these uncertainties, and are well illumined by comparison with standard Hellenistic letter form.

In the letter *Opening*, Paul is never content merely to identify himself and his readers. In most cases, his apostolic status is affirmed at the outset, establishing not only his authority as an ambassador of Christ but signaling his intention that the letter itself mediate his authoritative presence to the community gathered to read it (see 1Co 5:3–4). His readers are not simply identified by name, but are described in theologically significant ways (e.g., as saints [Php 1:1]; faithful brethren [Col 1:2]; the sanctified [1Co 1:2]; and the called [Ro 1:6]). Furthermore, every Pauline salutation grants God's grace and peace to the readers. It is possible that such a greeting intentionally merges both Greek and Jewish forms of address (*chairein* and *shalom*, respectively) to signal the universal unifying power of the gospel.

Attracting most attention has been the Pauline *Thanksgiving*, which is more extensive than the short, formulaic Hellenistic thanksgiving to the gods for protection from danger. Instead of thanking God for protection, Paul thanks God for the readers' commendable growth in the faith, places them within the larger progress of the gospel throughout the world, and prays for their continued spiritual development. Readers not only are inclined toward the writer by his praise and prayer for them, but acquire a sense of identity within the worldwide Christian movement. Furthermore, the Pauline Thanksgiving anticipates themes that will be treated later in the body of the letter. Paul's praise of the Corinthians for their fullness of spiritual gifts, for example, adumbrates later directives regarding the same matter (1Co 12–14). Finally, whether explicitly by reference to the approaching day of Christ (e.g., 1Co 1:8; Php 1:6; 1Th 1:10; 2Th 1:6–12), or implicitly by his praise of their spiritual successes, Paul is already in his Thanksgiving about the business of shaping the behavior of his readers.

The beginning of the *Body* may be signaled by such openings as the Disclosure formula (e.g., "I want you to know/not be ignorant that. . . [Ro 1:13; Php 1:12], the Appeal formula ("I appeal to you. . ." 1Co 1:10), or the Amazement formula ("I am astonished that. . ." Gal 1:6). But beyond the initial formulae, little standard structure can be detected.[35] The body may be composed of a series of relatively independent discussions (e.g., 1Co), or may weave through an intricately connected argument (e.g., Ro, Gal). Occasionally, large divisions can be detected that correspond on the one hand with foundational theological argument (often termed the "indicative"), and on the other hand with specific behavior instructions for the readers (often termed the "imperative"). Both in Ephesians and Romans, for example, Paul moves from a depiction of God's gracious salvation to exhortations for living a life commensurate with that salvation (Ro 1–11, 12–16; Eph 1–3, 4–6). It is theologically significant that the command to satisfy the ethical demands of the gospel is in these cases preceded by an elaborate presentation of the grounds for that obedience.

Paul's *Closings* differ from the brief formulaic closure of Hellenistic letters. In the place of a simple wish for good health may appear a request for prayer (e.g., Ro 15:30–33; Eph 6:18–20; Col 4:2–4; 1Th 5:25), greetings (e.g., Ro 16:2–18; 1Co 16:19–20; 2Co 13:11–13; Col 4:10–15) a closing grace (e.g., 1Co 16:23–24; Gal 6:18; Php 4:23), and a doxology (Ro 16:25–27). In almost every case, Paul's intense feelings, whether of warmth (1Co 16:24; 2Co 13:12–13) or warning (1Co 16:22; Gal 6:17), come to final expression.

Analysis of NT letters in light of ancient rhetoric has proved provocative, if not always determinative. Since they seek to persuade readers to take a (future) course of action, most letters should be classified as deliberative speech. Portions of Romans, Galatians,[36] and 2 Thessalonians correspond in varying degrees to standard components of persuasive speech: the proemium (the case is stated and the hearer's sympathy is gained); the narratio (the background of the case is presented); the probatio (the case is argued); the confutatio (the opponents arguments are neutralized); the conclusio (the matter is concluded and settled). Yet argumentative style, even more clearly than argumentive structure is employed by Paul in Romans. In a style known as the diatribe, Paul battles vociferously against hypothetical opponents who offer objections to Paul's claims. The objections Paul places in the mouths of these opponents are turned by him both to strengthen and extend his claims.[37]

But in all efforts to analyze the features and components of these letters in the light of Hellenistic rhetoric and epistolary form, their *occasional* nature must not be obscured. With few exceptions, these letters have been written to specific congregations to address particular problems. Conversely, they have not been composed as abstract theological treatises to serve the general doctrinal inquiries of a timeless audience. It is the circumstance of the modern reader who overhears (one side of) an ancient conversation between a congregation and its spiritual leader, which creates both the difficulty and delight of encountering the epistles.

Apocalyptic Literature

The book of Revelation strikes most readers as patently different from all other NT books. Isolated passages in other books (e.g., Mk 13 and its parallels; 2Th 2) may bear some resemblance to it, but its nearest biblical relatives would appear to be the OT books of Daniel and Zechariah. Beyond the boundaries of the Canon, however, can be found numerous documents sufficiently similar to Revelation and Daniel to be classified along with them in the single generic category of Apocalypse. Among the more significant of these extrabiblical apocalypses are 1, 2, and 3 Enoch; 4 Ezra; 2 and 3 Baruch; and the Apocalypse of Zephaniah. The nature of the biblical apocalypses will come more sharply into focus when characteristics of this larger group of apocalypses are brought to light.[38]

Apocalypses typically were written pseudonomously, under the names of illustrious heros of the past such as Enoch, Abraham, Isaiah, or Ezra. Motives for pseudonymity may have varied from a desire to add an authoritative ring to what was written to a desire to protect the writer from possible reprisals. But whatever the motive, the writer was now able, by assuming the vantage point of the ancient hero, to cast known past events in the form of unfulfilled prophecy. In 1 En 83–90, for example, Enoch relates to his son Methuselah his visions of the forthcoming events from the flood to the Maccabean revolt. Such pseudoprophecy often divided the course of history into distinct ages that led to the cataclysmic end of all history, often with intense interest in the punishment of the wicked.

The means by which God would reveal such secrets of the future to the seer varies widely in apocalyptic literature. Sometimes a dream or vision provides the open window of revelation, while on other occasions the seer might be transported to supernatural regions for a much more direct encounter. Not uncommonly does an angelic guide accompany the seer, interpreting perplexing scenes and answering his questions. Yet it seems likely that most visions and supernatural journeys do not report actual experiences, but are the products of fertile imagination taking form in standard literary dream or vision genres to promote the particular concerns of the author.

Another prominent characteristic of apocalyptic literature is its love of images, symbols, and symbolic numbers. Fire, ice, smoke, light, darkness, precious stones, wind, the sea, clouds, mountains, trees, and countless other "props" laden with symbolic meaning form the surrealistic landscape of the narrative [cf. 1 En]. Grotesque monsters, angels (both fallen and righteous), animals of all sorts, and wretched sinners in the throes of their punishment take leading roles in the unfolding dramas. Colors (e.g., white, red, black) paint the scene with added significance. Items appear not in simple pluralities but in suggestive 3's, 7's, 12's, and the like.

The similarities between the book of Revelation and the larger grouping of apocalyptic literature as described above are apparent and should not be discounted. Though the genre of apocalypse can be defined only in generalities and with many exceptions, Revelation's place within the genre is secure. But salient differences should be noted between this canonical apocalypse and its non-canonical cousins. Revelation is not pseudepigraphical; it is not cast as divine revelation to an ancient hero, and it does not review a long sweep of known history in the guise of prophecy. Furthermore, while some apocalyptic literature can be read as explorations of the curious into the esoteric, Revelation from beginning to end presses hard the ethical demands laid upon those who wish to be faithful to God in the midst of fiery trials. Furthermore, the secrets it exposes are not reserved for an inner circle of wise men, but demand complete and accurate promulgation to the addressed churches (22:16–19).[39]

The structure of Revelation reveals a far more complex and confusing pattern than is found in other apocalypses. After an initial collection of seven letters to churches in Asia Minor, the focus shifts to the visionary realm for the bulk of the book, until a final postscript. When postscript (1:4–8) and prescript (22:10–21) are examined, Revelation appears to have been cast as a letter (again, unlike other apocalypses), though without standard letter components described above.[40] The structure of the bulk of the book, in its labyrinthine progression of ordered scenes, is not easily understood, enhancing the mystery and awe so powerfully presented in language and symbol.

Insofar as the churches to whom the book is addressed were to find encouragement and illumination in what they read, we may conclude that its symbolism should be interpreted within the parameters of the ancient setting in which it was written. Anachronistic adaptations of ancient symbols to modern realities cut the linkage between the book and its originally intended readers, while leading to arbitrary and erratic interpretation. On the other hand, an exclusively futurist reading of the whole fails to account for the immediately pastoral concern of the writer. A healthy reading strategy that violates neither the nature of the genre nor a high view of inspiration would seek to discover the relevance of Revelation for its original readers.

NOTES

[1]Cf. with "structure, function, and attitude" according to Charles H. Talbert, *What is a Gospel?: The Genre of the Canonical Gospels* (Philadelphia: Fortress, 1977), 6.

[2]M. H. Abrams, *A Glossary of Literary Terms*, 5th ed. (Fort Worth: Holt, Rinehart & Winston, 1988), 72–74.

[3]Cf. Gene M. Tucker, *Form Criticism of the Old Testament*, Guides to Biblical Scholarship (Philadelphia: Fortress, 1971), 1–9.

[4]James Muilenburg, "Form Criticism and Beyond," *JBL* 88 (March 1969): 1–18.

[5]See Tremper Longman III, *Literary Approaches to Biblical Interpretation*, vol. 3 of Foundations of Contemporary Interpretation (Grand Rapids: Zondervan, 1987), 78–80.

[6]Brevard S. Childs, *Introduction to the Old Testament as Scripture* (Philadelphia: Fortress, 1979), 128–31.

[7]George W. Coats, *Genesis*, Forms of the Old Testament Literature Series, vol. 1 (Grand Rapids: Eerdmans, 1983), 24.

[8]For the following treatment of narrative genres, we are dependent largely upon Coats, *Genesis*, 5–10.

[9]Brevard S. Childs, *Myth and Reality in the Old Testament* (Naperville, Ill.: Alec R. Allenson, 1960), 72–93.

[10]Robert Alter, *The Art of Biblical Narrative* (New York: Basic Books, 1981), 178–89.

[11]Longman, *Literary Approaches to Biblical Interpretation*, 97.

[12]"Large collections of law: Covenant Code" Ex 20:22–23:33; Deut. Code: Dt 12–26; Holiness Code: Lev 17–26; Priestly Code: Ex 25:31, 3:29–Lev 16; Decalogue: Ex 20:2–7; Dt 5:6–21.

[13]Brevard S. Childs, *Old Testament Theology in a Canonical Context* (Philadelphia: Fortress, 1985), 55.

[14]George Herbert Livingston, *The Pentateuch in Its Cultural Environment* (Grand Rapids: Baker, 1974), 153–56.

[15]Typical outlines: Craigie: Preamble (Dt 1:1–5); Historical Prologue (1:6–4:49); General Stipulations (5–11); Specific Stipulations (12–26); Blessings and Cursings (27–28); Witnesses (30:19, 31:19; 32:1–43); McCarthy: Introduction (Dt 4:41–11:32); Stipulations (Dt 12:1–26:15); Blessing and Curse (26:16–28:68). Peter C. Craigie, *The Book of Deuteronomy*, The New International Commentary on the Old Testament (Grand Rapids: Eerdmans, 1976), 20–24; Dennis J. McCarthy, *Treaty and Covenant*, Analecta Biblica 21a (Rome: Biblical Institute Press, 1978), 157–87.

[16]Martin Noth, *The Deuteronomistic History*, Journal for the Study of the Old Testament Supplement Series no. 15 (Sheffield: JSOT Press, 1981), 89–99.

[17]Not all of Noth's proposal need be accepted to recognize the cohesiveness of Joshua–2 Kings.

[18]Our discussion of these genres is largely dependent upon Burke O. Long, *I Kings*, Forms of the Old Testament Literature Series, vol. 9 (Grand Rapids: Eerdmans, 1984), 4–8; 262–263.

[19]David E. Aune, *The New Testament in Its Literary Environment*, Library of Early Christianity (Philadelphia: Westminster, 1987), 102.

[20]Long, *I Kings*, 259. Judean kings more regularly follow the pattern.

[21]Ibid., 8.

[22]Ronald M. Hals, *Ezekiel*, The Forms of the Old Testament Literature XIX (Grand Rapids: Eerdmans, 1989), 352–53.

[23]Our discussion of prophetic genres is largely dependent upon W. Eugene March, "Prophecy," in *Old Testament Form Criticism*, ed. John Hayes (San Antonio, Tex.: Trinity University Press, 1974), 141–78. See also Claus Westermann, *Basic Form of Prophetic Speech*, trans. Hugh Clayton White (Philadelphia: Westminster, 1967), 90–204.

[24]Norman K. Gottwatt, "Hebrew Poetry," in *Interpreter's Dictionary of the Bible*, ed. George Buttrick (Nashville: Abingdon, 1962) 3:829–38.

[25]Our discussion here follows Erhard S. Gerstenberger, *Psalms: Part I*, Forms of the Old Testament Literature XIV (Grand Rapids: Eerdmans, 1988), 2–21; Hans-Joachim Draus, *Psalms 1–59: A Commentary*, trans. Hilton C. Oswald (Minneapolis: Augsburg, 1988), 38–43; Bernhard W. Anderson, *Out of the Depths: The Psalms Speak for Us Today*, rev. ed. (Philadelphia: Fortress, 1983), passim.

[26]Roland E. Murphy, *Wisdom Literature: Job, Proverbs, Ruth, Canticles, Ecclesiastes, Esther*, The Forms of the Old Testament Literature XIII (Grand Rapids: Eerdmans, 1981), 172–85.

[27]Kraus, *Psalms*, 32–38.

[28]Werner Georg Kümmel, *Introduction to the New Testament*, rev. ed., trans. Howard Clark Kee (Nashville: Abingdon, 1975), 37.

[29]Aune, *The New Testament in Its Literary Environment*, 46–49.

[30]For a useful summary of the literary reading of a Gospel, see Davie Rhoads and Donald Michie, *Mark as Story: An Introduction to the Narrative of a Gospel*

(Philadelphia: Fortress, 1982). See also Leland Ryken, *How to Read the Bible as Literature* (Grand Rapids: Zondervan, 1984), 33–86; 131–38.

[31]Aune, *The New Testament in Its Literary Environment*, 77–80.

[32]Ibid., 91–93; 124–28.

[33]See William G. Doty, *Letters in Primitive Christianity*, Guides to Biblical Scholarship (Philadelphia: Fortress, 1973); Ryken, *How to Read the Bible as Literature*, 155–58. Aune, *The New Testament in Its Literary Environment*, 158–225.

[34]Cf. Aune, *The New Testament in Its Literary Environment*, 161–69; 204–212.

[35]John Lee White, *The Body of the Greek Letter: A Study of the Letter-Body in the Non-Literary Papyri and in Paul the Apostle*, SBL Dissertation Series 2 (Missoula, Mont.: Society of Biblical Literature, 1972).

[36]Hans Dieter Betz, *Galatians: A Commentary on Paul's Letter to the Churches in Galatia*, Hermeneia (Philadelphia: Fortress, 1979), 14–25.

[37]Aune, *The New Testament in Its Literary Environment*, 198–202.

[38]John J. Collins, *Daniel*, The Forms of the Old Testament Literature XX (Grand Rapids: Eerdmans, 1984), 2–5.

[39]The differences between Revelation and other apocalyptic literature prompts Koester to go so far as to consider it "a critical discussion of already existing apocalyptic views and speculations." Helmut Koester, *History and Literature of Early Christianity*, Introduction to the New Testament vol. 2 (New York: Walter de Gruyter, 1982), 248.

[40]Aune, *The New Testament in Its Literary Environment*, 240–43.

INTRODUCTION TO THE OLD TESTAMENT

Eugene E. Carpenter

NAME, MEANING, SIGNIFICANCE

The word "testament," as in OT or NT, is a translation of the Latin word *testamentum*, which in turn was a translation of the biblical idea of "covenant." As many have noted, it is an inadequate translation of the biblical term used for covenant *diathēkē*. The Latin word *testamentum* indicates "a last will and testament," and English "testament" follows suit. But the Old and New Testaments should be named the Old and New "Covenants." This terminology would indicate a dynamic living relationship/agreement between God and his people—not a "last will and testament" by God to his people.

The Septuagint (LXX) (see below, Ancient Versions, pp. 121ff.), a Greek translation of the Hebrew Bible, used the Greek term, *diathēkē* to translate the Hebrew *bᵉrît*, "covenant," rather than *sunthēkē*. This latter Greek term indicated a covenant between equals; the former referred to a covenant or testament between unequals. To the biblical writer, the parties in the covenant between Israel and God were not equal. And, just as importantly, the word *diathēkē*, though it could mean *testament* as in "last will and testament," could also mean covenant. It is unfortunate that English translators have used *testament*, for, as far as English is concerned, "covenant" is much more suitable than *testament* for translating *diathēkē*. This Greek term catches well the meaning of the Hebrew, which implied the "cutting of a covenant" between the relevant parties.

So "testament" is not a helpful English translation to the extent that it misses the biblical sense of a living "covenant" between two persons or parties. Moreover, calling the Hebrew Scriptures the "Old" Testament is open to abuse, since there are several key covenants in the OT, such as the Abrahamic Covenant, Sinai Covenant (the one most referred to), Davidic Covenant, Palestinian Covenant, and the New Covenant (Jer 31:31–34). In an essential way many would hold that all the these "old" covenants are still vital and being realized to some extent. Jesus came not to destroy the law, but to "fulfill" the law; and, in the case of the New Covenant of Jeremiah, he came to institute that covenant (Mk 12:24; Mt 26:28; Lk 22:20; 1Co 11:23–25). Hence, Jeremiah's New Covenant is a reaffirmation and realization of the "Old" Covenant in Christ through/by the Holy Spirit, while in reality the whole old covenant (entire corpus of Scripture) is an announcement and preparation for the New Covenant.

The writings we call the Old Covenant comprise over three-fourths of the Christian Bible. The early church fathers, Tertullian (A.D. 160–230) and Origen (c. A.D. 185–254), were the first to designate the collected writings of the Jewish Scriptures taken over by the church as the "Old Testament." (Tertullian used the word *instrumentum*, not *testamentum*.)

In the NT, Paul refers to the reading of the "old covenant" (2Co 3:14, *palaias diathēkēs*) as equal to "when Moses is read" (2Co 3:15). The writer of Hebrews speaks of the Mosaic Covenant as "that first covenant" (8:7) and the New Covenant in Christ as a "second covenant" (8:7), but then also describes the first covenant as having grown old (8:13, *pepalaiōken tēn prōtēn*; cf. 9:15). It is clear that the entire Old Covenant as we understand it is not referred to in these passages. It is unfortunate that the entire corpus of texts comprising our present Old Covenant came to be called "the Old Testament [Covenant]"; since it contains, among many things, the announcement promising the "New Testament [Covenant]" as well (e.g., Jer 31:31–34; Heb 8:7–13), which was to complete, actualize, and expand the heart of the covenants in the OT itself, but, at the same time, tie the two covenants together organically. Jesus came not to abolish the essential religious, moral, and ethical content and heart of the Mosaic Covenant, but to bring its lofty, moral, spiritual, and ethical goals representing the will of the covenant God, Yahweh, to realization (Mt 5:17).

It was the nature and character of the ancient Hebrew Scriptures, which are identical to the Protestant form of the OT canon, that caused them to become an integral part of the Christian Bible. The early Christians appealed to the Hebrew Scriptures to explain what had happened, was happening, and would happen among them; they also used it to buttress and establish their own faith. They were convinced that the man Jesus was none other than the Messiah (Messiah, OT = Christ, NT) of the ancient Hebrew Scriptures. They believed that the kingdom of God depicted in them was dawning in Jesus' life, words, and actions, and in and among those disciples and followers he was calling and gathering around him. The new "people of God" were the product of the New Covenant now realized, but also a *continuation* of the "people of God" depicted in the Old Covenant (Ro 2:28–29), which was now seeing its true fruition and completion in the New Covenant.

Both A. M. Hunter and F. F. Bruce (Bruce, *Books and Parchments*, 73–75) note at least three themes that tie the Old and New Covenants together: (1) God coming as Savior, bringer of salvation, ultimately through Christ; (2) redeemed community of God's people (*ekklēsia* used in both LXX and NT for this group), the elect people of God, (3) God's free electing love bestowed upon all who exercise faith in him. And finally, it can be said with certainty, that neither covenant is sufficiently comprehended without the other. The Old Covenant is the launching pad for the ongoing fulfillment found within its own pages and in the New Covenant itself.

CANON, CONTENT, COMPOSITION

To speak of the OT "canon" means to refer to those books recognized and approved as the official, authoritative, and received sacred books used by the church for determining faith and practice. This is a simple fact; but there are issues and questions that arise because of the several major Christian groups, each of which recognize a different list of sacred books, although most of the books in their respective canons are common among these groups. The Protestant list of OT books considered canonical is thirty-nine, while the Roman Catholic (forty-six), and Jewish (twenty-four) differ in number, classification, or arrangement.[1]

Hebrew Bible (24)	English Bible (39)	English Bible (46)
Jewish	Protestant	Roman Catholic
TORAH	LAW	LAW
Genesis	Genesis	Genesis
Exodus	Exodus	Exodus
Leviticus	Leviticus	Leviticus
Numbers	Numbers	Numbers
Deuteronomy	Deuteronomy	Deuteronomy
PROPHETS	HISTORY	HISTORY
Former Prophets	Joshua	Josue (Joshua)
Joshua	Judges	Judges
Judges	Ruth	Ruth
1–2 Samuel	1 Samuel	1 Kings (1 Samuel)
1–2 Kings	2 Samuel	2 Kings (2 Samuel)
Latter Prophets	1 Kings	3 Kings (1 Kings)
Isaiah	2 Kings	4 Kings (2 Kings)
Jeremiah	1 Chronicles	1 Paralipomenon (1 Ch)
Ezekiel	2 Chronicles	2 Paralipomenon (2 Ch)
The Twelve	Ezra	Esdras-Nehemias (Ezr-Ne)
Hosea	Nehemiah	Tobias (Tobit)
Joel	Esther	Judith
Amos		Esther
Obadiah	POETRY	
Jonah	Job	POETRY AND WISDOM
Micah	Psalms	Job
Nahum	Proverbs	Psalms
Habakkuk	Ecclesiastes	Proverbs
Zephaniah	Song of Solomon	Ecclesiastes
Haggai		Canticle of Canticles
Zechariah	MAJOR PROPHETS	Wisdom of Solomon
Malachi	Isaiah	Ecclesiasticus (Sirach)
	Jeremiah	
WRITINGS	Lamentations	PROPHETS
'Emeth	Ezekiel	Isaias (Isaiah)
(Truth)	Daniel	Jeremias (Jeremiah)
Psalms		Lamentations
Proverbs		Baruch
Job	MINOR PROPHETS	Ezechiel (Ezekiel)
Megilloth	Hosea	Daniel
Song of Solomon	Joel	Joel
	Obadiah	

Hebrew Bible (24)	English Bible (39)	English Bible (46)
Jewish	Protestant	Roman Catholic
Ruth	Jonah	Amos
Lamentations	Micah	Abdias (Obadiah)
Ecclesiastes	Nahum	Jonas (Jonah)
Esther	Habakkuk	Micheas (Micah)
Daniel	Zephaniah	Nahum
Ezra-Nehemiah	Haggai	Habacuc (Habakkuk)
1–2 Chronicles	Zechariah	Sophonias (Zephaniah)
	Malachi	Aggeus (Haggai)
		Zecharias (Zechariah)
		Malachias (Malachi)
		1 Machabees (1 Maccabees)
		2 Machabees (2 Maccabees)

NOTE: Confusion arises because of the different nomenclature used to refer to the various extant bodies of literature recognized in some way by the various bodies of the church. For example:

Protestant Terminology	Roman Catholic Terminology
Canonical* (39 books)	Proto-Canonical*
Apocryphal (11 books)	Deuterocanonical*
Pseudepigraphal (60 +)	Apocryphal

The establishment of these differing canons can be explained to a large extent by the historical fortunes of the groups involved and the history of the books and documents included in the canon of each group. However, the basis for all of the Christian "canons" is the Palestinian Hebrew canon as listed above, consisting of twenty-four books arranged in three major divisions.

The twenty-four books that make up the Hebrew Bible represent only a portion of the literary output of ancient Israel. The books included in the canon were recognized by A.D. 90 at the latest, but probably much earlier. R. T. Beckwith argues for the closing of the threefold organization of the Jewish canon by 164 B.C. (*Mikra*, 58), and the practical use of this canon earlier. Debates about the canonicity of Ezekiel, Esther, Proverbs, Ecclesiastes, and Song of Solomon did continue after 164 B.C. and even c. A.D. 90. However, it seems that there was a functioning Hebrew Canon well before A.D. 90, and the books under discussion c. A.D. 90 were *already* in the standard list of canonical books.

These twenty-four books were believed to have been inspired by God; therefore, they possessed a *normative* character and acknowledged *authority* for the Jewish, and later, the Christian community, serving as the guideline for faith and practice. The fundamental features of these sacred writings were put forth in the ancient traditions: God did indeed inspire them and their "self-authenticating" nature, demonstrating and convincing persons and communities in various ways of their divine authority and truth. These

---

*Used to form faith and doctrine

sacred documents had not been declared authoritative by virtue of having been included in a recognized canon of books, but were included in the list because of their self-demonstrated authority. Authority preceded canonicity.

As the above chart shows, the Hebrew canon was divided into three major divisions: (1) The *Torah* (Law) Genesis–Deuteronomy; (2) the *Prophets* (former and latter): (a) Joshua–2 Kings, excluding Ruth, (b) Isaiah–Ezekiel, plus twelve minor prophets; (3) the *Writings*, remaining books. This threefold division of the canon originated in ancient times, but details of the process are now lost to us. It was originally argued that the three divisions were recognized one at a time in chronological sequence: (1) Torah, fifth century B.C.; (2) Prophets, third century B.C.; (3) Writings (hagiographa, "holy writings," including Daniel, Chronicles, and other disputed books), A.D. 90, at the Council of Jamnia. Beckwith has effectively challenged this position and argued cogently for a recognition of the threefold organization of the Hebrew Scriptures by 164 B.C., when Judas Maccabaeus gathered the holy writings (1Mc 1:56–57; 2Mc 2:14–15). Judas supposedly would have found ready at hand the recognized books; hence, even then the canon was "closed." At any rate, it seems certain that the threefold division of the Hebrew canon was established by 132 B.C. when it is clearly mentioned in the prologue to the book of Ecclesiasticus, a book included among the apocrypha (see "Apocrypha and Pseudepigrapha," pp. 141ff.).

The Christian church became the heir to the Hebrew Scriptures and was born with a canon in its hands. The Hebrew canon was given the stamp of approval by our Lord, all three divisions of it being alluded to in Luke 24:44, where Psalms stands for the entire division of the Writings. Some scholars argue for an expanded Alexandrian OT canon (*Mikra*, 81), including the books commonly known as the Apocrypha, which are in the Roman Catholic canon listed above. But there is no evidence that the Jews attached divine authority to these books. Some Christians include them among the Old Testament Scriptures, but the Roman church did not canonize them until A.D. 1546 at the Council of Trent. Jews did not canonize them.

The apocryphal books became an issue and part of the Christian canon because of the church's use of the Septuagint (LXX), a translation of the Hebrew Palestinian canon. The Hebrew Palestinian canon had never included these extra apocryphal books, and neither Philo, the Jew, (c. 20 B.C.–A.D. 45) nor Josephus (A.D. 90) regarded the Apocrypha as canonical.

For fifteen centuries the church's "functional canon" included the apocryphal books, although they were not considered inspired and authoritative by many. During the renaissance and reformation era, the Protestant Reformation adopted only the recognized Jewish canon as Old Testament canon. At the Council of Trent in 1546 the Roman Catholic Church affirmed a broader canon of forty-six books including the Apocrypha, as listed in the chart. (See note at bottom of chart.) This historical fact is evidenced in modern English Bibles that print the Apocrypha as a separate section or in a separate volume of the Bible (e.g., *Oxford Annotated Bible; RSV Apocrypha;* or the *New English Bible With Apocrypha*).

David Hubbard observes in *Old Testament Survey,* "The Christian Church was born with a canon in its hands. The apostolic community never knew what it was not to have authoritative writings" (p. 17). The OT did comprise a body of *authoritative* writings for Jesus and the church. Jesus (Mt 1:22; 4:1–1; Jn 5:39), Paul (Ro 1–2; 1Co 1; Gal 3:8, 22; 4:30 [indeed, the entirety of Galatians]; 2Ti 3:16), Hebrews, James, John, Revelation, all show utter dependence upon the OT Hebrew canon as holy Scripture, quoting it hundreds of times to clinch their arguments and as God's revealed source of truth. The Apocrypha is not cited in this way.

The Old Testament was considered *revelatory* by both the OT writers (Da 2:27–28, 9:22; Am 3:7; Ex 25:9), and NT writers (2Pe 1:21; Heb 4:12–13; 2Ti 3:15). As revelation, it is both active, informing us about that which God alone can make known to us, and passive, itself being the result of God's act of revealing. The OT "uncovers or lays bare" God's character, nature, wisdom, and love, otherwise unavailable to human beings (*gālāh; apokaluptō*). And the OT is God's *progressive* revelation, for he did not reveal all of himself or his intentions at one time to the human race (Heb 1:1–3). The greatest revelations are two: that God is both Creator and Redeemer, working redemptively through time and history to save the human race from destruction; and that the OT is inspired and trustworthy in that it is "God breathed" (2Ti 3:16). The OT ultimately has God as its author through his agency of divinity, the Holy Spirit, and his agents of humanity, individual human beings.

The recognition of a canon of authoritative OT Scripture was affirmed by the church Fathers many times: Melito of Sardis (A.D. 170; all but Esther), Epiphanius in Cyprus (late fourth century; all included), Origen (A.D. 185–254), Athanasius (A.D. 367, letter), Jerome (A.D. 347–420) and others. All of these record the books of the Palestinian Hebrew canon as authoritative, excluding the apocryphal books but indicating that they are considered by some to be beneficial reading.

ANCIENT VERSIONS

Although we do not have the original manuscripts that comprised the books of the OT, we do have copies of those books in their original languages. In addition, we have many translations from Hebrew or Aramaic of those ancient manuscripts into various other languages. These extant ancient Hebrew/Aramaic documents are of inestimable value for establishing the best possible reading(s) of the sacred text(s) that have come down to us. It will be possible to note only the most important ancient versions.

Aramaic Targums (Bruce, 123; targum means "translation") are primary Aramaic translations based on the Hebrew text. They arose after the Exile (586–538 B.C.) because many of the Jews had lost the ability to read or speak their mother tongue. Beginning in the time of Ezra–Nehemiah, when the Hebrew text was read, an Aramaic translation, or paraphrase, was produced for the hearers. No more than one verse of the Pentateuch nor more than three verses of the Prophets could be translated and commented upon at one time. These oral interpretations were simple, but grew to become significant so that they were eventually recorded in writing, thus giving rise to the Aramaic Targums. These targums were read regularly in the synagogues. The translations and paraphrases themselves also became arcane and difficult to understand. The surviving targums come from Palestine or Babylon.

There are targums for nearly every part of the OT. The official targum for the Pentateuch is called the Targum of Onkelos; it arose in Babylonia in the second–third century A.D. The official Babylonian targum of the prophets, both former and latter, is the Targum of Jonathan ben Uzziel. The targums for the third part of the Hebrew Bible, the Writings, are diverse. Other targums arose, such as the Targum of Pseudo Jonathan covering the Pentateuch, a Palestinian targum on the Torah, and targums on the Hagiographa, or Writings, of the Hebrew Bible. Targums are also evidenced in the Qumran documents, such as the Targum of Job and one on Leviticus. While most biblical books have a targum for them, Ezra, Nehemiah, and Daniel do not. These targums have proved to be helpful in testing the reliability of the Masoretic text and in indicating the state of Hebrew texts used in the late B.C. and early A.D. era.

The Septuagint, meaning seventy (LXX), is an ancient Greek translation of Hebrew and Aramaic manuscripts produced sometime c. 285–246 B.C. in Alexandria, Egypt, supposedly at the order of Ptolemy Philadelphus. The tradition concerning this translation is found in the Letter of Aristeas. Supposedly, seventy-two Jews were chosen and sent to Alexandria from Jerusalem to translate the Torah (Ge–Dt) into Greek. They completed their task in seventy-two days! Various versions of this story exist. Much of modern scholarship believes that this translation took place over a long period of time and culminated not long before the Christian era.

For some unknown reason, the resulting ancient version was called the Septuagint. Possibly it was given this name in memory of the seventy sons of Israel who went to Egypt (Ex 1:1–7) or in recognition of the seventy elders who accompanied Moses up mount Sinai (Ex 24). The Prophets and the Writings were translated after the Pentateuch, but opinions vary as to when they were completed. Probably they were completed by the time of Jesus ben Sirach, late in the second century B.C.

However, the LXX was the Hebrew Scriptures, plus much more. The Apocrypha (see "Apocrypha and Pseudepigrapha," pp. 141ff.) were included. The Pentateuch was well translated, the Prophets and Writings were a free rendering of the Hebrew text and simply inaccurate in some places. Passages are transposed from their original placement in the

Hebrew manuscripts. Jeremiah is much shorter in the LXX, an additional psalm is added to the Psalter, and Job is much shorter than in the Hebrew Masoretic text. It appears that a good bit of this is because of the fluidity of the Hebrew manuscripts available at this time, although this is a moot issue. The LXX was largely preserved by the Christian church; the Jews rejected it fully by A.D. 100, using their own Hebrew canon that did not include the Apocrypha. However, most of the OT quotes in the NT are from the LXX version rather than the Hebrew manuscripts known to us now (Ellis, Longennecker).

The LXX was first printed in the Complutensian Polyglot Bible of 1522. The most used edition of the LXX in the twentieth century was completed by Afred Rahlfs, Würtemburg Bible Society, 1935.

Various revisions and rival versions to the LXX were produced. Rival versions included the excessively literal translation of Aquila (A.D. 30); the relatively free, but well done and reworked Greek version by Theodotian (A.D. 190), based on an earlier pre-Christian Greek translation. Theodotian's Daniel quickly replaced a corrupted LXX translation of Daniel in the church. Symmachus, A.D. 170, produced another version in which he tried to be accurate, but produced a Greek idiomatic (a modern day "dynamic equivalency" product) version.

Origen (A.D. 185–254) attempted a revision of the LXX itself. His Hexapla (sixfold) was completed in A.D. 245; it was the OT in six parallel columns. This work ran to seven thousand pages and included: (1) Hebrew text, (2) Hebrew text in Greek letters, (3) Aquila's Greek version, (4) Symmachus' Greek version, (5) Origen's revised LXX, (6) Theodotian's Greek version. Origen's goal was to bring the LXX, column five, into conformity, as much as possible, with the Hebrew text of column one. Hesychius for Alexandria and Lucian of Antioch produced later recensions of the LXX.

The language of the LXX greatly influenced the language of the NT and has been beneficial, as well as troublesome, throughout the centuries of Bible translation. It does preserve a translation of the OT from a Hebrew text that was over one thousand years older than our extant manuscripts representing the Masoretic text. But, as noted earlier, the quality of the Greek of the translation is poor at times. The LXX also has pride of place for being the OT text used most by the early Christians. The Greek of the LXX illuminates the semantic range of NT Greek words. It was a missionary tool used by God to spread his gospel throughout the Mediterranean world.

However, it was the *Latin Bible*, Jerome's Vulgate (popular, common), that powerfully influenced the church for over a thousand years. Two centuries after Christianity moved into the Roman world, Latin translations became necessary. Many, some unworthy, secondary Latin translations were produced based on the Greek LXX or other extant Greek texts. Thus, old Latin secondary translations of the OT abounded in Jerome's day; and at the request of Damascus (Roman bishop, A.D. 366–

84), Jerome undertook a new standard edition of the Latin Bible. Using the Hebrew text, He completed his translation in A.D. 405, having lived in Bethlehem since c. A.D. 386 in order to perfect his Hebrew. He did not translate the Apocrypha and held a low view of them (*Mikra*, 81f.). However, not until the ninth century was the supremacy of his new translation fully recognized. The fortunes of Jerome's work varied through the centuries. Its use in textual criticism and reconstruction is minimal, but its influence upon the thinking and language of Christians in Europe and the West generally has been enormous. Many other versions of the OT were produced; English versions alone would require a book to list them and their histories.

LANGUAGE, TEXTS, LITERATURE

The OT was first written in Hebrew and Aramaic. Nearly all of the OT is in Hebrew; Aramaic is found only in the following passages: Ge 31:47; Ezr 4:8–6:18, 7:12–26; Jer 10:11; Da 2:4b–7:28. Hebrew and Aramaic are not Indo-European languages. The following chart gives an idea of the place of Aramaic and Hebrew among the Semitic family of languages.

GROUP I East Semitic*	GROUP II Northwest Semitic	GROUP III South Semitic
Babylonian	Hebrew	Arabic
Akkadian	Ugaritic	Ethiopic
Assyrian	Moabite	(Old South Arabic?)
	Eblaite	
	Phoenician	
	Aramaic	
	Amorite	

Hebrew

Hebrew was the tongue of ancient Israelites and the written language in which the inspired writers penned the OT. In Isa 19:18 it is called "the language (lip) of Canaan"; in several places it is designated as "Judean," "language of the Jews," (2Ki 18:26; Isa 36:11, 13; 2Ch 32:18; Ne 13:24).

Hebrew Alphabet

As indicated above, Hebrew is a part of the Semitic family of languages. It is especially close to Phoenician, Moabite, Edomite, Amorite, Eblaite, Aramaic, and Ugaritic. Ugaritic has contributed important insights to a better understanding of biblical Hebrew in vocabulary, morphology, orthography, syntax, and poetics. The earliest Hebrew manuscripts were written in an ancient Canaanite script, an angular script,

---

*Semitic is an adjective derived from "Shem," Noah's son.

that was replaced by the well-known square Aramaic script c. 200 B.C. Most manuscripts of the Hebrew Bible are in the latter script.

Hebrew was originally written without vowels; only consonants were written. In the Dead Sea Scrolls, the Hebrew and Aramaic is without vowels. The vowel points found printed in our Hebrew Bibles were not established until the ninth century A.D. The original pronunciation of ancient biblical Hebrew is unknown.

Hebrew was written using twenty-two letters from right to left. This was common among the North Semitic languages. Psalm 119 is illustrative, for it has twenty-two sections. Each section has eight verses, all beginning with the same letter of the alphabet. The twenty-two sections run through the Hebrew alphabet consecutively.

The use of Hebrew as a common spoken language declined after the Jews returned from the Exile (538 B.C.), but continued to hold first place as Israel's "sacred tongue." Use of Hebrew revived during the Maccabean Era (164 B.C.–63 B.C.). Aramaic replaced Hebrew as the vernacular.

Numerous features of biblical Hebrew still remain unclear or only partially understood, the Hebrew "verbal system" being the most notorious example. The meaning of about two thousand Hebrew biblical words still are not certainly understood. Nevertheless, herculean accomplishments have been made in gaining a better understanding of this human language in which God chose to reveal himself and his counsel. And a much-needed intermediate Hebrew grammar has now been published by Waltke and O'Connor (*An Introduction to Biblical Hebrew Syntax*, 1990).

Aramaic

Aramaic evidently originated among the Arameans in northern Syria. These people may have been part of the ancestry of Abraham (Ge 28:2–5; Dt 20:5). After a long history, Aramaic became widely spoken and understood under the Assyrians, during the eighth century B.C., after the Arameans were conquered. This situation is well illustrated in 2 Ki 18:17–37 (Isa 36:2–22) in 701 B.C. This *lingua franca* of the Near East endured from the eighth to fourth centuries B.C., when Alexander the Great overturned the Persian Empire (331 B.C.), even continuing in various dialects into the NT era, until the Arab conquests of the seventh century. The Aramaic used in the biblical sections listed above came to be called "biblical Aramaic," but was later discovered to be a form of the "official" Aramaic (*Reichsaramäisch*) used in the Near East during the late Assyrian, Babylonian, and Persian Empires. The letter in Ezra (4:8–6:18; 7:12–26) may faithfully represent genuine documents from the officials of the Persian Empire. Several dialects of Aramaic are still spoken in a few areas of the Levant and in Iraq, Persia, and Syria.

Arguments concerning the nature of the Aramaic used in the book of Daniel have often been used to date the book; but, although still helpful to some extent, the Aramaic of Daniel allows a broad provenance for the completion of the book. Ne 8:8ff. may indicate that an Aramaic targum (oral paraphrase; *mᵉp̄ōrāš* = Aram. *mep̄āros*) of the biblical text, which was read in Hebrew, was presented to the people. If so, this is the earliest instance of this that we have.

From 1893–1908 a large collection of Aramaic documents was found in Upper Egypt that indicated the fortunes and vicissitudes of a small Jewish colony located in Syene and on a small island called Elephantine. The documents present nearly a century of correspondence in the fifth century B.C., during which Persia was the dominant world power. The Aramaic of these documents helps us to understand the development of the Aramaic language; the contents reveal remarkable facts about conditions in this ancient Jewish community "in exile" and the policies of both Jewish authorities in the homeland and the Persian authorities toward this Jewish colony, which desired to preserve/rebuild a temple for worship outside of Jerusalem in Elephantine. The temple was destroyed soon after 400 B.C. Further finds of documents written in Aramaic have continued among the Dead Sea Scrolls.

Masoretic Text

Modern Hebrew texts resulted from centuries of copying and preserving ancient Hebrew sacred documents. Unfortunately, the older copies were always discarded. Scribes who copied the worn-out manuscripts destroyed the old documents because of the confidence they had in the veracity and adequacy of the new ones. Until 1947, when the Dead Sea Scrolls (DSS) were discovered, the extant Hebrew manuscripts dated no earlier than A.D. 900, with the exception of the Nash Papyrus dated in the first century B.C., which contained little more than the Ten Commandments. Among the manuscripts of the DSS were manuscripts dating before 100 B.C., so that the oldest known Hebrew manuscripts were pushed back by a thousand years.

Perhaps even to this day the most significant find for OT studies was a complete scroll of the Hebrew text of Isaiah (1QIsaᵃ), which is to be dated to the second century B.C. The Jewish community where these were found was in an area northwest of the Dead Sea, known as Qumran (possibly Essenes or closely related to them). The community existed from c. 130 B.C.–A.D. 70, when Jerusalem fell to the Romans. All of the OT books except Esther are represented in these finds.

By the end of the first century A.D. a standard consonantal Hebrew text emerged. This traditional text was safeguarded in various ways by Masoretes, who had produced it (*masorah* = tradition). These workers were indeed "tradition keepers." They surrounded the text with notes called "masora" but did not touch the consonantal text itself. Elaborate safeguards had previously been set up, and continued to be set up, to maintain the integrity of each copy. By A.D. 900, vowel points were added to this "Masoretic" text. Other markings indicated punctuation, variant readings, and *kᵉtîḇ* / *qērē* readings. The verse divisions of the Masoretic text go back to very early dates in the Christian era. The Masortic text contains 23,100 verses. The chapter divisions were much later (c. A.D. 1244).

Because of the work of the Masoretes, our modern Hebrew text is called the Masoretic text. The Masoretes lived in Tiberias and Babylonia, and introduced all of these various signs to the heretofore consonantal texts, fixing, to a great extent, the pronunciation and meaning of the text. The masora they supplied helped to interpret and explain the text and any changes they had made. Two masoretic families from the Tiberian textual studies school, Ben Asher and Ben Naphtali, specialized in preserving the best possible text. The Ben Asher text has been accorded preference over the Ben Naphtali text and was the basis for *Biblia Hebraica*, (BH3) 3d ed. (Stuttgart, 1937).

The most influential early printed Hebrew Bible was Daniel Bromberg's Bible published in Venice, 1410–1417. In 1937, Rudolf Kittel published the third edition of his *Biblia Hebraica*. This edition became internationally accepted and was based mainly on the Leningrad Codex (c. A.D. 1000–1026) with reference to the codex of the Pentateuch in the British Museum and the Cairo codex of the prophets (late ninth century A.D.). The most recent edition of the Hebrew Bible is the *Biblia Hebraica Stuttgartensia*, edited by K. Ellinger and W. Rudolph (1977). It is close to BH3, but provides a better critical textual apparatus, better editions of the masora *parva* and *magna*, and greater fidelity to the Leningrad Codex (L). Other editions of the Hebrew text are, however, under preparation and Snaith's edition produced in 1958 by the British and Foreign Bible Society is still helpful; he tried carefully to reproduce the Ben Asher text.

Samaritan Pentateuch

The Samaritan Pentateuch is not a version but a rival Hebrew text type to the Masoretic text (A.D. 90). It is an independent witness to Hebrew text types. In the fifth century B.C. the Samaritans adopted and adapted the Pentateuch alone as their sacred Scriptures. Since there were some changes in the extant Hebrew manuscripts during the later centuries, the Samaritan Pentateuch is an important tool for doing textual criticism, which tries to ascertain the probable original readings of the Masoretic text. It differs from the received Masoretic text in mostly minor ways. At times it agrees with the Septuagint, at times with the Masoretic text, at times with the manuscripts among the DSS.

The diligent study of the Dead Sea Scrolls has supported Kahle's view that the Samaritan Pentateuch represents a "popular revision of an older text in which antiquated forms and constructions, not familiar to people of later times, were replaced by forms and constructions easier to be understood, difficulties were removed, parallel passages were inserted" (*Cairo Geniza*, 1st ed., 147ff.). The DSS have shown that before the Masoretic text was standardized (A.D. 90) several Hebrew text types were being used at Qumran. Some Hebrew texts from Qumran are similar to the "popular" text type of the Samaritan Pentateuch; so it seems that the

Samaritan Pentateuch may be a popular Palestinian Hebrew text edited by the Samaritans themselves.

The Samaritan Pentateuch varies from the Masoretic text nearly six thousand times. But these variances are nearly all minor. In two thousand of these cases it agrees with the Septuagint (LXX). A couple of these variations are especially revealing about the differences between the Jews and Samaritans. Mt. Gerazim is emphasized in the Samaritan Pentateuch (cf. Dt 12:5; cf. 11:29). Mt. Gerazim replaces Mt. Ebal in Dt 27:4–8, and inserts a tendential passage right after the Ten Commandments in Ex 20:2–17 and Dt 5:6–21, which emphasizes Mt. Gerazim again.

The Samaritan Pentateuch was first acquired and published by European scholars in the seventeenth century. In 1632 it was published in the Paris Polyglot Bible. A. von Gall provided the standard printed edition of the Samaritan Pentateuch in 1914–18, Giessen, Germany. It was reprinted in 1963 in Berlin.

Literature

Anyone who undertakes to read or study the OT will discover an amazing, delightful, but at times bewildering array of all kinds of literary materials and genres in its pages (see "The Bible and Literature," pp. 93ff.). Legal material, wisdom material, poetry, prose, apocalyptic, proverbs, didactic, parabolic and prophetic materials, history, lawsuit patterns, eulogies, laments, psalms, riddles, torah, genealogies, short stories, oracles, woes, myths, epic—these are all terms that must be used to describe the broad sweep of literature found in the OT. And the way these various genres and styles of writing are combined is unique in the literature of the world. This multiplicity of languages, theology, history, and literary forms is matched by the stentorian voice it gives to the unified story of the mighty acts and words of God in time and eternity. Any interpretative approach to the OT must deal with this complex reality of language and style used to *communicate* the *content* of the text if the veracity and integrity of the message are to be discerned.

BACKGROUND OF THE OLD TESTAMENT: PEOPLES, KINGDOMS, CULTURES, CHRONOLOGY, GEOGRAPHY

The Middle East provided the setting for the events recorded in the OT. Specifically, Mesopotamia, Egypt, and Syria-Palestine constitute the core of "the Bible world." All of this area that lies along the Tigres and Euphrates rivers in Mesopotamia up to the Persian Gulf, and the tillable land bordering the Syrian desert, plus the coastal land of the eastern Mediterranean is known as the Fertile Crescent. J. H. Breasted gave it the name and it has stuck. The southwestern tip of this "crescent" extends through Palestine, and arable land continues all the way into the Nile valley in Egypt. Here was the cradle of civilization and the scene of God's memorable activities in time and history as recorded in the OT.

Before Abraham appeared on the scene (Ge 11–12), civilizations had risen and fallen. By 3000 B.C. or before full-fledged writing systems had appeared, complex communities and large temple areas had developed. Abraham himself has been dated around 2000 B.C. (suggestions vary from 2400 B.C.–1500 B.C.), so complex civilizations had been in existence for a thousand years. Before he came on the scene, the biblical story had already begun in a world that had witnessed the rise and fall of many human kingdoms. However, it has proved almost impossible to identify much of the early persons, places, or events recorded in Ge 1–11. Many of the persons and places in Ge 14 still elude us.

Mesopotamia (literally, "between the rivers") was one of the earliest cradles of civilization. It is a fertile area, and the Tigres and Euphrates rivers mothered civilizations in this very area. The great cities of ancient Mesopotamia grew and spread along the rivers. Cities such as Ur, Nippur, Babylon, Assur, and Nineveh sprang up. These cities developed into powerful city-states. The city-states of Assur and Babylon eventually spawned the Assyrian and Babylonian kingdoms, which played such important parts in biblical history.

The languages of the kingdoms of Assyria and Babylon was *Akkadian.* The *Neo-Assyrian Empire* flowered and ruled the area from 911 B.C. to 609 B.C., using the Assyrian language, a subdivision of Akkadian, and a powerful military machine to accomplish its purposes. The Neo-Assyrian Empire was the greatest period of Assyrian domination and that phase of Assyria's history that directly touched Israel. In 722 B.C. Assyria, under King Shalmaneser V, carried Israel, the northern kingdom, into captivity and transplanted foreigners into the land. But soon thereafter the empire deteriorated. The capital, Nineveh, fell to the Babylonians by 612 B.C. The last vestiges of the military might of Assyria fell in 609 (2Ki 23:29–30), after holding out at Haran for some years. The Babylonians (Chaldeans) absorbed the Assyrian land to a great extent. Isaiah spent much of his time resisting the advances of the arrogant Assyrian kings.

The empire of Babylon had ancient roots; it developed and ruled from 2217 B.C. to 1595 B.C., when the Hittite king, Murshili I, sacked the great city. The *Neo-Babylonian Empire* came to power for a relatively short time (747 B.C. to 538 B.C.).

Under the Old Babylonian Empire, legal, cultural, and social developments touched the Israelites. Most important was King Hammurabi's Law Code (1792–1750 B.C.), which can be compared with great benefit to Moses' laws given in the OT.

But it is the later Neo-Babylonian Empire that affects Israel's history and thinking most profoundly. Merodach-Baladan II (721–710; 703 B.C.) sent envoys to Jerusalem, who were received by Hezekiah (Isa 39). Subsequently, Isaiah issued a prophecy of doom and exile and punishment for this unwise action by Hezekiah (2Ki 20; Isa 39). The Babylonian king, Nebuchadnezzar II (605–562 B.C.), captured Jerusalem and exiled Judah in 586/7 B.C., exiling even the remnant of Israel later (2Ki 24:10–25:21). Babylon suffers the infamy of being assigned the greatest oracles of doom given by Jeremiah (Jer 50–51), and became a symbol of those who oppose God and his people (Rev 18).

Egypt was known as "the gift of the Nile" and played a large part in the formative period of Israel's history. Northern and southern Egypt were united early in the third millennium B.C. and great pharaohs ruled the land. The Egyptian civilization developed to a high level by the middle of the third millennium and continued largely unchanged for three thousand years. Only in 331 B.C. did Alexander the Great change the face of ancient Egypt, in fact the face of the Middle East.

The early pharaohs especially were believed to be gods or divine beings in human form. The culture was relatively stable, and the status quo was constantly sought in Egypt. Times of great upheaval are recorded, however. The ancient Hebrews and the later Israelites had close contact with this civilization. Israel was held captive by Egypt for 400 years during the New Kingdom (c. 1550–1100 B.C.), until, under Moses, the Lord liberated them. The Exodus took place during the second half of the second millennium B.C. under Pharaoh Rameses II (c. 1290 B.C.). After Israel's deliverance from Egypt, the kingdom played a declining part in Israel's history and development, but was always there—often as a temptation to Israel to trust in the horses of Egypt for safety and security rather than the Lord (Isa 21:1–3).

A knowledge of Egyptian language, culture, politics, military might, and economics helps one to understand the OT, especially from 2000 B.C. to 164 B.C.

Syria-Palestine is the focal point for the major events and issues of the OT story. It did not mother, so far as we know, a bona fide super empire, such as Mesopotamia or Egypt did; but it did foster powerful city-states, such as Jericho and Ebla, with which Israel had to interact at her own peril. And this area, both in ancient times and today, served as a buffer zone between super powers or as a prize to be fought over by these same powers. Many important trade and travel routes passed through the area and these resulted in great wealth for inhabitants of the land.

The most seductive feature of this area for the Israelites was the corrupt, polytheistic fertility religions of its inhabitants. Vivid descriptions of this area and its religious disarray are contained in documents from ancient Ugarit (c. fourteenth century B.C.) and the Tell-el-Amarna tablets (early fourteenth century B.C.). Israel was commanded by God to conquer the land and destroy its inhabitants and their religious practices because of their utter corruption and the danger it held for the Israelites.

Syria-Palestine was sifted and tossed by the super powers, first Egypt, then the Hittite kingdom, the Assyrian kingdom, the Babylonian kingdom (old and new), the Persian Empire, the Grecian Empire, and finally Rome. But the central theological fact about Palestine proper is that is was, and is still, to nurture Israel as God's people. It is described as a land "flowing with milk and honey" (Ex 3:8), and it was and remains Israel's homeland.

Persia was a vast empire (Est 1:1), extending from India westward to

Greece and the upper Nile region. Cyrus the Great (Isa 44:8; 45:1), anointed by Israel's God, consolidated the power of Persia through his victories over Medea (559 B.C.) and Babylon (538 B.C.). The empire lasted until it was conquered by Alexander the Great in 331 B.C.

The influence upon and relation of Persia to ancient Israel is discussed fully by Edwin M. Yamauchi in his recent book, *Persia and the Bible* (Baker, 1990). The major theological and historical event that brings Israel and Persia together in the Bible is the edict of Cyrus (538 B.C.; Ezr 1:1–4) which permitted the Jews to return to their homeland to rebuild their temple and city and to reestablish the worship of their God. Cyrus' decree was lost but later recovered by Darius I and put into effect again (Ezr 5:1–6:15).

The reign of Darius I (522–436 B.C.) is the political setting for the completion of the second temple (520–516 B.C.) and the post-exilic prophets Haggai and Zechariah (cf. Ezr 5:1–3). Other Persian monarchs are mentioned in Ezra-Nehemiah, Esther, Daniel, and Zechariah. A striking fact about this great empire is that Israel's God is expressly stated to have chosen its greatest monarch, Cyrus, to do his bidding on behalf of the people of Israel. The books of Esther, Zechariah, Haggai, and Ezra-Nehemiah relate events concerning Israel during the regency of Persia. The Elephantine Papyri from Egypt record events occurring in a Jewish colony under the hegemony of Persia during the fifth century B.C. These documents from southern Egypt are in Aramaic and shed light on events in the city of Jerusalem as well as the life and worship of this small group of Jews.

Greece. In 331 at Gaugamala in Persia, however, the Grecian Empire established itself in the Middle East through its leader Alexander the Great, when he conquered Persia. Greek religion, culture, politics, architecture, and philosophy subsequently forced itself not only upon the Jews in Palestine and elsewhere but upon the entire region all the way to India. Greece is mentioned clearly in only two OT books, Daniel and Zechariah, but is prominent in several apocryphal books.

Alexander died in Babylon in 323 B.C. At that time his empire broke up into four separate political areas. The territory inherited by his general Seleucus I in the north and the territory inherited by Ptolemy (Lagi) in the south became the most important political and religious influences upon the Jews until the coming of Pompey of Rome in 63 B.C. The Ptolemies in Egypt ruled the areas of Palestine and Phoenicia until defeated by the Seleucids in 198 B.C. at Panium by Antiochus III. According to ancient tradition, it was during the time of the Ptolemies that the Greek translation of the Hebrew Scriptures took place (see above, Ancient Versions). Parts of the books of Daniel and Zechariah have these events and persons in mind.

These centuries of Israelite history were not lived out in a vacuum. Rather, Israel was often plunged into life and death struggles among themselves and against these pagan powers, which God used more than once to punish his apostate people (Isa 1:2). But neighboring nations overstepped their roles and received judgment at the hands of God as well.

Chronology. Because of the nature of biblical accounts up until the six books of Samuel, Kings, and Chronicles, scant knowledge of the early period makes it difficult to ascertain the chronology of the OT. Chronologies that scholars have constructed differ with one another in important areas. But it is helpful to have a general timeline in mind when reading and studying the OT. Below are several suggested chronologies, which should be regularly consulted when reading or studying OT materials. Also refer to John Bright's "Chronological Charts" I–VIII, pp. 415–73, in *A History of Israel*, 3d edition, and note the excellent article on chronology in *Westminster Bible Atlas*, pp. 9–16.

Geography. Even an elementary grasp of the geography of Palestine is helpful for understanding certain parts of the OT. In fact, the correct interpretation of certain written texts depends upon a knowledge of the layout of the land.

In the OT, the land of Palestine is called the "land of Canaan" (Lev 25:38) and the "land of promise" (Ge 13:14–17) that was sworn to Abraham and his descendants. After Israel was given the land as an inheritance, it became known as "the land of Israel" (Dt 1:8), but was still ultimately God's land (2Ch 7:20). OT Palestine extended from Dan to Beersheba (Jdg 20:1 etc.) in its north–south axis, and was bounded on the west by the Great Sea (Mediterranean) and on the east by the Jordan Valley. During the time of the Judges and later, Israel included territory east of the Jordan, termed Transjordan. But even under David and Solomon, Israel did not possess all of the area promised to Abraham (Nu 34:1–12). The geographical location of the land was strategic, forming as it did a land bridge that connected many nations, empires, and three continents (Europe, Asia, Africa).

The north–south features of the land are easily recognized and helpful to the student of the OT. These major features are the coastal plain running along the edge of the Mediterranean, the lowlands (shephelah) east of the sea, then the central mountains lying west of the Jordan valley. At the northern edge of the coastal plain, Mt. Carmel juts out into the Mediterranean Sea, which in ancient times provided a spectacular theatre for Elijah's defeat of the prophets of Baal (1Ki 18:18–46). Moving east, the next prominent geographical feature of Palestine is the Jordan rift area. The Jordan River runs southward, fed by its upper tributaries and the Sea of Galilee. It follows a meandering path for about two hundred miles and empties its salt-laden waters into the Dead Sea, the lowest body of water in the world (1,290 ft. below sea level). Waters do not flow out of the Dead Sea. Eastward across the Jordan River lies the Transjordanean Plateau.

The major areas in Palestine were northern Israel which encompassed Galilee (the northernmost part of the country) and Samaria, and southern Israel, Judah, and the Negeb, a high steppe area south of Beersheba, which received little rainfall. Farther south lies the Sinai Peninsula; northeast and southeast are the sprawling Syrian and Arabian deserts.

Israel inhabited the central mountain ranges for the most part, and were called a "people of the hills" in the OT (1Ki 20:28). The Palestinian area has two seasons, rainy (December–March) and dry (May–September). Sometimes rains fell both earlier and later than usual, and the OT refers to these as "early" and "latter" rains (cf. Jer 3:3, 5:24; Joel 2:23). The rainfall, however, occurs on the western slopes of the central mountain ranges and the western side of the Transjordanean Plateau. The eastern parts of these two geographical features are arid. They yield little produce or vegetation of any kind. The disunity of Israel is sometimes considered a result of her broken, fragmented geographical features, but Israel's God and Israel's revealed religion from Yahweh would have been enough to overcome this natural barrier to unity. Isaiah did not attribute the nation's failures to geographical barriers, but to Israel's refusal to pay attention to Yahweh's guidance (Isa 47:18–19).

ARCHAEOLOGY

Archaeology is approaching a systematic science and discipline of recovering the past by finding and examining ancient sites. These sites are then carefully sifted through in order to uncover buildings, written documents, artifacts, and natural features that may shed light upon any particular period in the past. But archaeology is also an art, often depending upon the gifts and abilities of specific individuals who must make judgments, often based on little evidence.

Archaeology has been used as one way into the world of the Bible, into the ancient cultural, historical, political, economic, sociological, and linguistic settings when the events, peoples, places, and writings (at least the early sources, both oral and written) first appeared.

"Biblical archaeology" is not a special kind of archaeology, but merely refers to the exploration and examination of artifacts that touch upon the biblical world (today, especially, Israel, Iran, Lebanon, Turkey, Iraq, Syria, Palestine, Jordan, Saudi Arabia, Egypt, and the Sinai Peninsula). Peter Craigie defines biblical archaeology as "an approach by the student of the Old Testament to the findings of Middle Eastern archaeology in order to discover what light may be shed on the biblical text" (p. 81).

Many scholars and archaeologists no longer use the term, and since c. 1970 archaeology has taken on a much more cosmopolitan character and approach to making use of its data. Specialists from many fields are employed to obtain the broadest picture of the archaeological data possible. This is sometimes called "new archaeology," and involves many specialists from various disciplines. A new "secularization" of archaeology has occurred during the past thirty years, as it has been necessary for archaeologists to appeal to government and other public agencies in order to obtain funds to continue the increasingly expensive process of modern archaeological procedures.

The scientific axioms, postulates, and practices of modern archaeology are relatively recent. Only at the end of the nineteenth century were these procedures created and adapted. And these tedious procedures were applied rigorously only well into the twentieth century. Two major processes were established: *stratigraphy* and *topographical analysis*. The first, stratigraphy, entails the careful identification and classification of the different levels encountered in a dig. The second, sometimes ceramic typology, entails the careful recording and description in an orderly scientific fashion of objects found in the various strata. Improved methods of dating the various layers and artifacts have been developed during the past two decades. Additional help is gained in dating items and layers by comparing objects found in one location with those from another.

Archaeology gives us another "window" besides the various written texts of the OT and of the ancient world through which to observe the various facets of the world of the Bible. The discovery of ancient Ras esh Shamra on the coast of modern Syria and the Ugaritic clay tablets discovered there in 1928–29, the discovery of ancient Ebla at modern Tell Mardik (begun in 1964) and finding of the Dead Sea Scrolls (1947–) are perhaps the best known "finds" that have benefited from the latest archaeological methods. These finds, each in its own way, have enhanced our understanding and illumination of many different areas of OT study: culture, history, linguistics, philology, epigraphy, religion studies, sociological issues, political systems, military issues, ancient warfare, temples, cities, and more.

It is important to remember that archaeology does not "prove" the *theological* message of the Bible, though it certainly can in some sense support certain aspects and features and claims of the biblical text. Archaeology does help establish that the OT scriptures are from a time when and a place where real people, real cultures, real languages were involved. God is a God who speaks and acts in history as well as in his own unique sphere of existence. Further, archaeology serves to control theories that are formed without a proper reference to facts that can be known about a particular era or location. On the other hand, archaeological "truth" is itself often incomplete and, to a large extent, always subjective. Written documents take pride of place among the artifacts discovered. But probably no more than three percent of over five thousand sites located and surveyed in Palestine alone have been systematically and scientifically examined. Much remains to be done.[2]

THEOLOGY OF THE OLD TESTAMENT

OT theology (see "The Bible and Theology," pp. 82ff.) is an important part of understanding the OT, and in some form has always been studied and practiced in the church and the academy. However, not until the eighteenth century did the discipline of biblical theology became a separate concern of study apart from systematic theology or dogmatic theology.

Biblical theology examines and presents the *origin* and *development* of the OT writings in order to give an adequate presentation of the *teachings* and *beliefs* contained in the sacred documents. Biblical theology is differentiated from dogmatic theology in methodology, content, and purpose. Approaches to OT theology vary. Some try to describe the theology solely on the basis of the sacred documents, a *descriptive* approach, while others try to establish the message of the text as a normative guide for the Christian church today, a *prescriptive* approach. Conservative Wesleyan Arminians have subscribed largely to the second approach.

Whatever approach is used, interpreters should describe as well as possible what their methodologies and presuppositions are for carrying out their work. Then careful textual, linguistic, literary, historical, semantic, and philosophical exegesis must establish the basic foundational themes and aspects of any OT theology. Currently, a multifaceted and interdisciplinary approach is being developed. Anthropology, sociology, psychology, poetics, and linguistics, in addition to various new perspectives, such as feminist, Third World (liberation) viewpoints are offering helpful insights to mine the riches of these ancient revelational documents. The unity of the OT writings, their literary genre and character, the more important theological themes that run through large sections of the materials, poetics, and literary criticism are employed to help correct the atomistic approaches and results obtained in the first half of the twentieth century. Paul D. Hanson observes,

> The rich diversity of traditions found in the Old Testament does not yield a chaotic theological picture, but one which is both dynamic and unified. The reason is that this approach goes beyond analysis of individual periods or traditions to grasp the overall development of biblical theology, by paying attention to all levels of tradition and all periods. The unifying factor is the divine-human relationship, which is traced throughout the span of biblical history, guided by the belief that God is true to God's purpose for creation and humanity and that a trustworthy human witness to that purpose is found in the confessions of God's people that arose over the centuries (*HBD*, 1062; cf. Goldingay, *Theological Diversity*, 181–99).

Soulen (*Handbook*, 32) observes that biblical theology was marked by the following concerns, which apply to OT biblical theology:

(1) An opposition to the influence of philosophy and philosophical theology
(2) An opposition to the presumed tendency of dogmatic theology
(3) An emphasis upon Hebrew thought in contradistinction to Greek thought
(4) An emphasis upon the unity of the Bible
(5) An approach to biblical language which concentrated on word studies

(6) An emphasis upon the distinctiveness of the Bible vis a vis its environment
(7) An emphasis on divine revelation in history
(8) The interrelationship of biblical study and theological concern

Scholars have tried to locate the "centers" or "themes" of the OT that are vital for the production of an OT theology. Many centers have been proffered during the past two hundred years (Hasel, *Basic Issues*, 1981). In the twentieth century, the most comprehensive unifying synchronic approach using a center was Walter Eichrodt's attempt to establish *the covenant* as the central focus of OT theology. His herculean effort was seminal, but was also highly critiqued. G. von Rad took a different diachronic approach and centered upon the multiplicity of themes and the development of these themes within the OT itself, refusing to assert a "center" of the OT. Recently, the central themes or guiding principles of an OT theology have been argued as "creation" and "redemption" (salvation theology) (cf. Goldingay, *Theological Diversity*, 167–239). Other central themes of OT theology have been suggested: the people of God, community, the kingdom of God, Yahweh as Lord, the holiness of God, Deuteronomy, God, etc.

Ironically, as a result of all this, a great appreciation has arisen for the *diversity* of OT theology without, however, giving up the attempt to find a *unifying* concept(s). It seems that a major component of an OT theology will be God's formation, preservation, and redemption of "his own unique people" (Ex 19:5–6), among whom he dwells (Ex 25:8), making them distinct because of his presence (Ex 33:15). Various covenants must be taken into account in God's formation of his people and his enthronement among them: Noahic, Abrahamic, Sinaic, Davidic, Palestinian, and Jeremiah's New Covenant. All of this eventually works out, according to a diverse but ultimately unifying process, to the realization of the kingdom of God (Bright, *Kingdom*).

BIBLICAL CRITICISM AND STUDY
OF THE OLD TESTAMENT

To read and study the OT critically means to do so with a keen discerning judgment. The application of various skills, techniques, knowledge, wisdom, and art to the corpus of OT texts being examined is necessary. Many kinds of biblical research and criticism have been developed since the beginning of the Reformation (A.D. 1517). During only the past thirty years interdisciplinary skills, models, and techniques have become a vital part of the process of criticism, as well as the traditional grammatical–historical and critical approaches to interpretation.

The proper goal of all criticism is to discover the meaning and significance of the OT canonical texts for the purpose of providing authoritative and normative guidance for the people of God in the world today. *Textual criticism* attempts to establish the original wording of the biblical text and, also, as a result of this, to establish the possible formation and transmission of the text. Every autograph (original manuscript) of every OT book is lost; therefore, the goal of textual criticism is to recover the best "critical text" possible. Most modern translations are based on these resultant eclectic Hebrew and Aramaic critical texts (see Language, Texts, Literature above).

Ancient texts, such as the OT, were copied by hand and human errors resulted. Many kinds of copying errors have been categorized and classified; the textual expert is aware of all of these. Textual criticism per se is also called "lower criticism" because it is literally foundational for all of the other kinds of criticism employed.

The sources available for doing OT textual criticism are scant in comparison to the many manuscripts and other resources available for establishing a critical NT text (see Languages, Texts, Literature above). Briefly, the sources used are, in general, (1) the Hebrew Masoretic Text from c. the tenth century A.D.; (2) the Greek OT in its Septuagintal form; (3) other ancient versions/recensions of the Septuagint; (4) Aramaic Targums; (5) the Samaritan Pentateuch, an ancient Hebrew text itself; and (6) other ancient witnesses of the ancient Hebrew OT text (e.g., Dead Sea Scrolls, etc.). A standard work in this field is *The Text of the Old Testament: An Introduction to the Biblia Hebraica* by Ernst Wuthwein, Eng. trans. by Escoll F. Rhodes (Eerdmans, 1979).

Historical Criticism attempts to establish the historical milieu of a document. This involves many things and various disciplines are employed, such as linguistics, sociology, anthropology, and comparative studies of various kinds. Certainly it is important to establish the time, place, events, persons, general milieu, and sources. All of this is necessary in order to help the reader understand the literary document. Sometimes historical reasoning has been used in a negative way to argue that humankind's contemporary experience of reality should be the plumbline to establish the meanings and significance of ancient texts, even though these ancient texts recognized a worldview different from that of the modern world. Clearly, this does not allow the manifold witness of the OT to challenge us seriously or to speak to our contemporary worldviews. The OT claims to be a unique record to God's words and acts toward his people. Properly controlled historical criticism has revealed a vast panorama of the environment and world of the OT (e.g., Bright, *History*).

Literary Criticism (see "The Bible and Literature," pp. 93ff.) in biblical studies originally, and hence traditionally, referred to the same studies also designated as "source criticism." According to this discipline many OT scholars held that the Pentateuch was composed of four major documents (J, E, D, P) stemming from different times, places, and persons (or groups) and vastly different in style, meaning, and purpose. This was an unfortunate and inaccurate use of the term *literary criticism*. This particular view of the composition of the Pentateuch is still held by many OT historical–critical scholars today. But it has undergone major changes during the twentieth century and, in effect, the whole edifice is being seriously challenged at the end of the twentieth century. The original form and presuppositions of the four-document theory have changed radically, and other viable positions are being put forth. Some positions are modified documentary positions; some are radical challenges to the traditionally accepted critical position. However, conservative scholars have resisted, and continue to resist, any form of this theory that reduces the veracity, authority, inspiration, or revelatory character of the OT writings (see Canon, Content, Composition, pp. 118ff.).

"Literary Criticism" today is understood to mean the application to the OT of the canons of literary criticism used to investigate literature of any kind. Poetics, the study of the use of language and style to obtain meaning, has helped to reestablish the unity, the beauty, the integrity, the quality, and the meaning and significance of OT literature. Many subcategories of literary criticism exist: rhetorical criticism, an examination, through the use of language and literary stylistics, of how the author(s) has (have) established his/her meaning; redaction criticism, an examination of a literary document to discover how the author has formed and linked his materials together (edited them), to establish their meaning and significance; linguistics, the formal scientific study of human language, involves the application of some aspects of modern linguistics to the task of biblical exegesis to discover meaning; *structuralism* is an attempt to discover underlying deep patterns (conventions) of universal meaning and significance in the biblical texts; reader response criticism is a focus on the perspective of the readers and how they create meaning/significance from the text. A new approach seems to come to light nearly each year.

Form Criticism (Hermann Gunkel) originally sought to establish fixed literary patterns (usually small sections) and then to use these patterns to go behind the present text to help establish the meaning/significance of the literary pattern in its current context. Often the final goal was not reached or could not be because, according to this approach, no larger literary context existed within which to interpret the smaller forms. And, many times scholars tended to stress the meaning/significance of a reestablished "original" text rather than the extant text under consideration.

The meaning of "form criticism" has proved to be fluid, and today it tends to fall together with literary criticism, using genres as the interpretational units. An attempt has been made to subsume the more recent literary approaches under the general rubrics of form criticism. The study of the OT using form criticism revealed the marvelous multiplicity of literary styles, forms, and methods in the OT, but tended to atomize the text into isolated units rather than to develop the possible unity of the text.

Canon criticism is relatively new in biblical criticism, but already at least two major different functions and definitions of it are discernible. Brevard Childs works with the final canon of books delivered to the church as sacred Scripture, which are thus normative to some extent for discovering

God's word to his people. He stresses *the final form* of biblical documents as *the form* to be vigorously analyzed and studied in order to perceive keys to actualizing the sacred text for our day. Another approach that has similarities is fostered by James Sanders, who stresses the authority of the various canonical stages of a historical document as well as its final shape. Thus the *diachronic process of canonization* itself and insights/helps gained from studying it are on a par with any reading of the final form of the text received by the church.

As a result of these approaches, great emphasis has been put on the need to study the various OT documents as wholes and to study them in relationship to the final contours of the canonical shape of the entire OT/NT itself. However, Sanders' appreciation of the various historical stages of documents as they moved to their final form does give us an added depth dimension for appreciation of the theology of the final form of the text and how it got to be what it is.

No single approach listed above is sufficient of itself to exhaust the task of hermeneutics in interpreting the OT. Many methods and many perspectives must be used, but they must, to have integrity, allow the OT Scriptures to exhibit their true character along with their original genius and inspiration.

BIBLIOGRAPHY

Achtemeier, Paul J. *Harper's Bible Dictionary*. San Francisco: Harper & Row, 1985.

Bright, John. *A History of Israel*. Philadelphia: Westminster, 1981.

Bruce, F. F. *The Books and the Parchments*, rev. ed. Old Tappen, N.J.: Revell, 1984.

————. *The Canon of Scripture*. Downers Grove, Ill.: InterVarsity, 1988.

von Campenhausen, Hans. *The Formation of the Hebrew Bible*, trans. J. A. Coker. Philadelphia: Fortress, 1972.

Charlesworth, James H., ed. *The Old Testament Pseudepigrapha*, 2 vols. Garden City, N.Y.: Doubleday, 1983, 1985.

Cotterell, Peter and Max Turner. *Linguistics and Biblical Interpretation*. Downers Grove, Ill.: InterVarsity, 1989.

Craigie, Peter C. *The Old Testament*. Nashville: Abingdon, 1986.

Eichrodt, Walter. *Theology of the Old Testament*. 2 vols., trans. J. A. Baker. Philadelphia: Westminster, 1961–1966.

Friedman, Richard Elliott. *Who Wrote the Bible?* New York: Summit, 1987.

Goldingay, John. *Approaches to Old Testament Interpretation*. Updated. Downers Grove, Ill.: InterVarsity, 1990.

————. *Theological Diversity and the Authority of the Old Testament*. Grand Rapids: Eerdmans, 1987.

Hasel, Gerhard. *Old Testament Theology: Basic Issues in the Current Debate*. Grand Rapids: Eerdmans, 1975.

Kaiser, Walter C., Jr. *Toward an Old Testament Theology*. Grand Rapids: Zondervan, 1978.

LaSor, William Sanford, D. A. Hubbard, F. W. Bush. *Old Testament Survey*. Grand Rapids: Eerdmans, 1982.

Longman, Tremper III. *Literary Approaches to Biblical Interpretation*. Grand Rapids: Zondervan, 1987.

Mulder, Martin Jay, ed. *Mikra: Text, Translation, Reading and Interpretation of the Hebrew Bible in Ancient Judaism and Early Christianity*. Philadelphia: Fortress, 1988.

von Rad, Gerhard. *Old Testament Theology*. 2 vols., trans. D. M. G. Stalker. Edinburgh, Oliver and Boyd, 1965.

Reventlow, H. Graf. *Problems of Old Testament Theology in the Twentieth Century*. Philadelphia: Fortress, 1985.

Shanks, Hershel and Dan P. Cole, eds. *Archaeology and the Bible: Early Israel*, vol. 1. Washington, D.C.: Biblical Archaeology Society, 1990.

Shanks, Hershel. *Ancient Israel*. Englewood Cliffs, N.J.: Prentice-Hall, 1988.

Soulen, Richard N. *Handbook of Biblical Criticism*, 2d ed. Atlanta: John Knox Press, 1981.

Thomas, D. Winton. *Documents from Old Testament Times*. New York: Harper & Row, 1958.

Waltke, Bruce K. and M. O'Connor. *An Introduction to Biblical Hebrew Syntax*. Winona Lake, Ind.: Eisenbrauns, 1990.

Walton, John H. *Ancient Israelite Literature in Its Cultural Context*. Grand Rapids: Zondervan, 1989.

Wright, G. Ernest and Floyd V. Filson. *The Westminster Historical Atlas to the Bible*, rev. ed. Philadelphia: Westminster, 1956.

Wurthwein, Ernst. *The Text of the Old Testament: An Introduction to Biblia Hebraica*, trans. E. F. Rhodes. Grand Rapids: Eerdmans, 1979.

NOTES

[1]The Ethiopian Canon consists of 81 books, including Jubilees and 1 Enoch. The Greek Orthodox differs slightly from the Catholic Canon; it adds 1 Esdras, Prayer of Manasseh, 3 and 4 Maccabees, and Psalm 51. (See also "Apocrypha and Pseudepigrapha," pp. 141ff.)

[2]For a succinct summary of great archaeological discoveries relating to the Bible, see *The Wesley Bible* (Nashville: Thomas Nelson, 1990), 1980–2000. See *The NIV Study Bible* (Grand Rapids: Zondervan, 1985) for a list of ancient texts relating to the OT.

APOCRYPHA AND PSEUDEPIGRAPHA

Eugene E. Carpenter

The two collections of literature known as the Apocrypha and the Pseudepigrapha respectively are considered uninspired and nonauthoritative by Protestants. They have never been regarded as part of the official Hebrew canon (*Mikra*, 81–84). The church father Jerome held that the church could read them for "example of life and instruction of manners," but added that the church does not "apply them to establish any doctrine" (Beckwith, in Mulder's *Mikra*, 343). However, this massive body of heterogenous Jewish/Christian literature has great value for various reasons, some of which will be noted below.

APOCRYPHA

Fifteen books are traditionally included among the Apocrypha:

2 Ezra (= 1 Esdras; c. 120 B.C.)
Tobit (c. 200 B.C.)
Judith (c. 150 B.C.)
Additions to Esther (c. 140 B.C.)
Wisdom of Solomon (c. 30 B.C.)
Sirach (c. 132 B.C.)
1 Baruch (c. 150–50 B.C.)
Bel and the Dragon (c. 100 B.C.)
1 Maccabees (c. 110 B.C.)
2 Maccabees (c. 110–70 B.C.)
Prayer of Manasseh (second–first century B.C.)
Letter of Jeremiah (c. 300–100 B.C.)
Prayer of Azariah with the Song of the Three Young Men
　　　(c. second–first century B.C.)
Susanna (second–first century B.C.)
4 Ezra (= 2 Esdras: c. A.D. 100)

James H. Charlesworth notes that the Prayer of Manasseh and 4 Ezra are more properly pseudepigrapha (Charlesworth, 2:xxvii). The dates of these books range from 200 B.C. to A.D. 90.

HISTORY AND EVALUATION

These Apocryphal books were never included in the Palestinian Jewish canon. Since the eighteenth century some scholars have argued that their presence in the Christian canon for many centuries can be traced to an expanded Jewish/Alexandrian canon that was subsequently adopted by Christians. This hypothesis was built upon the presence of various (not all) Apocryphal books in several LXX manuscripts of the OT (Vaticanus, Sinaiticus, Alexandrinus). But for cogent reasons this theory is no longer tenable.

In addition, it is now known that some assumptions that might seem to support an expanded Alexandrian canon are not well founded. It is, for instance, now known that Hellenistic Judaism was not independent of Palestinian Judaism and would not have arrogantly formed its own canon. And it is known that most of the Apocryphal books were not composed in Greek in Egypt, as was supposed in the past, but are translations of Palestinian originals, which were written in Aramaic or Hebrew.

Also, 1 Maccabees 4:46; 9:27; 14:41 explicitly assert that the spirit of prophecy had ceased in that day. Beckwith (*Mulder's Mikra*, 83) notes, as does Philo, that the famous prologue of Ecclesiasticus, which was written in Egypt, refers to the three divisions of the Hebrew canon (Law, Prophets, Writings). But there is no evidence that any of the Apocrypha had a place among the three divisions of the Hebrew canon. Philo never once quotes a book of the Apocrypha as Scripture.

So it is clear that nearly all the evidence points to the fact that the Apocrypha were never part of the Hebrew canon. It is equally clear that Jesus and his disciples did not receive these books as canonical. While OT history from Abraham culminates in Christ, the intertestamental period covered by the Apocryphal books is disregarded by the historical summaries in the sermons of the book of Acts. Bruce Metzger observes that recognition of the difference between noncanonical and canonical books can be reached by a careful examination of them. He says, "When one compares the books of the Apocrypha with the books of the Old Testament, the impartial reader must conclude that, as a whole, the true greatness of the canonical books is clearly apparent" (Metzger, *Apocrypha*, 172).

Nevertheless, some Apocryphal books did get into the Christian canon and were uncritically considered canonical throughout the Middle Ages. Jerome (fourth century A.D.) began a translation of the OT into Latin (see "Introduction to the OT," pp. 116ff.) from available LXX texts. But he decided to translate into Latin from Hebrew and to limit his translation (Vulgate) to the Jewish canon. He did not include the Apocryphal books and did not use them to establish doctrine. Eventually, however, they were included, but Jerome's position toward them never changed.

During the time of the Reformation (sixteenth century), doctrinal disputes raised the issue of the canonical status of the Apocryphal books. The Roman Catholic Church used 2 Maccabees 12:43–45 to bolster the idea of purgatory and of masses for the dead. Job 12:9, Ecclesiasticus 3:30, and 2 Esdra 2:33 support the notion that good deeds earn merit. Therefore, Luther placed them at the end of the OT section in his German Bible (1539). As others had, he termed them "Apocrypha," not to be read as Holy Scripture, but as literature that could be read beneficially. The Westminster Confession of Faith (1646–48) designated the Apocrypha as merely secular literature. The Anglican Church accepted the Apocrypha for instruction in life, but not for the purpose of doctrinal formation.

The Roman Catholic Church, in response, declared the entire Vulgate canonical, which lacked only 1 and 2 Esdras and the Prayer of Manasseh. These three books were included as an addendum in some later Roman Catholic editions of the Bible. Today the Apocrypha is commonly termed deuterocanonical by the Roman Catholic Church.

Interestingly, the Orthodox Church considers the Roman Catholic deuterocanonical (Apocryphal) books as orthodox, plus 3 and 4 Maccabees, Psalm 151, 1 Esdras, and the Prayer of Manasseh. In an effort to create a truly ecumenical version, editors of *Oxford Annotated Bible* (RSV, 1977 edition) included the entire Apocrypha.

There is, however, as Luther stated, much profit from reading the Apocrypha. These books give invaluable historical and cultural background information. John Bunyan, in a famous narrative, tells how, while he was incarcerated, God spoke to him from Ecclesiasticus 2:1, a passage he had stored away in his memory. But this experience is more indicative of the manifold ways God can teach truth and comfort his people than of how an Apocryphal book can be elevated to the level of inspired Scripture. A humorous anecdote about how 2 Esdras 6:42ff. inspired Christopher Columbus to search for new lands illustrates the ingenuity of the human mind more than it establishes grounds for adding the book to the sacred canon.

Above all, these books help us to understand Judaism during the Second Temple period (515 B.C.–A.D. 70). Theology, angelology, demonology, history, politics, religious development, the use and interpretation of the OT canonical scriptures (see Mulder, 379–420) are all pieces the Apocrypha contributes to the puzzle of the intertestamental period. This material also provides background essential to an understanding of the development of various sects we read about in the NT. Information on the Pharisees, Sadducees, Zealots, Essenes, the Hasidim, and Greek philosophy and religion is also in the Apocrypha.

PSEUDEPIGRAPHA

In 1985, Doubleday published the second volume of *The Old Testament Pseudepigrapha*, edited by James H. Charlesworth. Fifty-two documents plus supplements (some sixty-five in all) are included in this monumental work on the OT pseudepigrapha.

Charlesworth offers the following careful definition of "pseudepigrapha": (1) a Jewish or Christian writing (sole exception of Ahiqar, an Assyrian work that helps us to understand early Jewish thought), (2) writings that are attributed to famous figures of Israel's past, (3) writings that claim to contain God's word or message, (4) writings that frequently build upon ideas and narratives present in the Old

Testament, (5) writings composed during the period 200 B.C. to A.D. 200 or that preserve Jewish traditions from that period. It is clear that the term "pseudepigrapha" is now a catchall term and, since it is well established internationally, is the accepted nomenclature for this collection of literature. Its literal meaning of "false superscriptions" is true of only some of the documents.

As might be expected, there is some fluidity in the number of books included among this literature. Ewert (p. 80) notes that about eighteen documents make up the "standard list" of pseudepigrapha. However, since this list of eighteen was created, others have come to light. For instance, some have been found among the Dead Sea Scrolls. It will be convenient to list the fifty-two documents Charlesworth edits according to his classifications. These books were never serious contenders for canonicity in mainline Christianity even though at least two of them are quoted in the NT (Jude 14–15 = 1 Enoch 1:9; and Jude 9 is from the Assumption of Moses). However, the Ethiopian canon contains Jubilees and 1 Enoch among its eighty-one canonical writings (Cowley, 318–23). Most books of the pseudepigrapha have been preserved for us in the Oriental churches such as the Ethiopic, Coptic, and Syriac.

1. APOCALYPTIC LITERATURE AND RELATED WORKS

1 Enoch (Ethiopic Apocalypse of Enoch)
2 Enoch (Slavonic Apocalypse of Enoch)
3 Enoch (Hebrew Apocalypse of Enoch)
Sibylline Oracles
Treatise of Shem
Apocryphon of Ezekiel
Apocalypse of Zephaniah
4 Ezra
Greek Apocalypse of Ezra
Vision of Ezra
Questions of Ezra
Revelation of Ezra
Apocalypse of Sedrach
2 Baruch (Syriac Apocalypse of Baruch)
3 Baruch (Greek Apocalypse of Baruch)
Apocalypse of Abraham
Apocalypse of Adam
Apocalypse of Elijah
Apocalypse of Daniel

2. TESTAMENTS

Testaments of the Twelve Patriarchs
Testament of Job
Testaments of the Three Patriarchs
Testament of Abraham

Testament of Isaac
Testament of Jacob
Testament of Moses
Testament of Solomon
Testament of Adam

3. EXPANSIONS OF THE OLD TESTAMENT AND OTHER LEGENDS

The Letter of Aristeas
Jubilees
Martyrdom and Ascension of Isaiah
Joseph and Asenath
Life of Adam and Eve
Pseudo-Philo
Lives of the Prophets
Ladder of Jacob
4 Baruch
Jannes and Jambres
History of the Rechabites
Eldad and Modad
History of Joseph

4. WISDOM AND PHILOSOPHICAL LITERATURE

Ahiqar
3 Maccabees
4 Maccabees
Pseudo-Phocylides
The Sentences of the Syriac Menander

5. PRAYERS, PSALMS, AND ODES

More Psalms of David
Prayer of Manasseh
Psalms of Solomon
Hellenistic Synagogal Prayers
Prayer of Joseph
Prayer of Jacob
Odes of Solomon

The other thirteen pseudepigraphal works discussed by Charlesworth need not concern us here. They are bits and pieces of lost works known only from quotations or allusions in the works of the church historian Eusebius (fourth century A.D.) and ultimately by Alexander Polyhistor (first century A.D.).

The mere evidence of so much literary activity from this era is astounding. More astonishing is the fact that the OT inspired and influenced nearly all of this literature to some extent. The ancient traditions of the Jews continued to inform and mold their thinking and aspirations regardless of those to whom they were subservient.

Perhaps more important is the background—social, political, cultural, and religious—that this extracanonical material provides to help us interpret the canonical materials of both the OT and the NT. Many significant theological issues are highlighted in this literature. Major issues are the concept/meaning of sin and death, the origins and power of death, the problem of theodicy (God's rule in a fallen world), his transcendence, the progress/lack of progress in history, the Messiah, the messianic kingdom, resurrection, eternal life, the Son of Man, the end of the world, the fate of the ungodly, heaven, hades, hell, paradise, angelology, and demonology. All of these issues and more are touched upon significantly. The materials themselves, often of a composite nature, raise the issues of syncretism and authorship of ancient documents.

The literature offers an array of apocalyptic materials that may include one canonical book, Daniel, and that enables scholars to investigate the literary, social, and religious phenomena of apocalyptic genre. Apocalyptic materials, concepts, and ideas are scattered throughout this literature (e.g., 1 Enoch, Testaments of the Twelve Patriarchs, 4 Ezra, Sibylline Oracles, Assumption of Moses, etc.). Not only do these books help us to understand Daniel better, but we can also better grasp the use of literary conventions in apocalyptic writings. Mark 13, 2 Thessalonians 2, and Revelation are all more easily understood because of information gleaned from the study of these books. No apocryphal or pseudepigraphal material is given the veneration and respect attributed to Daniel by NT writers. The unique qualities of the canonical apocalypse of Daniel is clearly evident in comparison to its pedestrian imitators.

Chapter 14 of 4 Ezra (= 2 Esdras) records a tantalizing legend of Ezra's supposed restoration of all of the ancient sacred writings of the Jews after they had been destroyed. In forty days and nights, Ezra, through the Holy Spirit (14:22), and five scribes (14:29, 37) reproduce ninety-four books of the sacred writings. The twenty-four canonical books were made available to the public (14:45). The seventy other books were given only to the wise, "for in them is the spring of understanding, the fountain of wisdom, and the river of knowledge" (14:47). The seventy books reserved only for "the wise" are possibly to be equated in concept with the noncanonical books that later churchmen and scholars eventually labeled apocryphal or pseudepigraphal. "Seventy" in this context of forty days could mean merely all other religious books outside of the twenty-four accepted canonical Jewish books. While 4 Ezra 14 records a legend of dubious historical accuracy, the chapter probably reflects an important aspect of canonical versus extracanonical literature for the Jewish community in that day (c. A.D. 90), after the fall of Jerusalem to the Romans when apocalyptic "deliverance" was largely held in abeyance.

BIBLIOGRAPHY

Achtemeier, Paul J. *Harper's Bible Dictionary*. San Francisco: Harper & Row, 1985.

Beckwith, Roger. *The Old Testament Canon of the New Testament Church*. Grand Rapids: Eerdmans, 1985.

Cate, Robert L. *A History of the Bible Lands in the Intertestamental Period*. Nashville: Broadman, 1988.

Charlesworth, James H., ed. *The Old Testament Pseudepigrapha*, 2 vols. Garden City, N.Y.: Doubleday, 1983, 1985.

Cowley, R. W. "The Biblical Canon of the Ethiopian Church Today," *Ostkirchliche Studien* 23 (1974), 318–23.

Ewert, David. *A General Introduction to the Bible*. Grand Rapids: Zondervan, 1983.

Fritsch, C. T. "Pseudepigrapha." *Interpreter's Dictionary of the Bible*. Vol. 3. Nashville: Abingdon, 1962, 962ff.

Harris, R. Laird. *Inspiration and Canonicity of the Bible*. Grand Rapids: Zondervan, 1979.

Kraft, Robert A. and George E. Nickelsburg. *Early Judaism and Its Modern Interpreters*. Philadelphia: Fortress, 1986.

Metzger, B. M. *An Introduction to the Apocrypha*. New York: Oxford, 1957.

Mulder, Martin Jan, ed. *Mikra: Test, Translation, Reading and Interpretation of the Hebrew Bible in Ancient Judaism and Early Christianity*. Philadelphia: Fortress, 1988.

Patten, Priscilla and Rebecca Patten. *Before the Times*. San Francisco: Strawberry Hill Press, 1980.

Rost, Leonard. Trans. David E. Green. *Judaism Outside the Hebrew Canon*. Nashville: Abingdon, 1971, 1976.

Russell, D. S. *Between the Testaments*, 3d ed. Philadelphia: Fortress, 1965.

_____. *The Method & Message of Jewish Apocalyptic*. Philadelphia: Westminster, 1964.

Soulen, Richard N. *Handbook of Biblical Criticism*, 2d ed. Atlanta: John Knox, 1981.

A Concordance to the Apocryphal Deuterocanonical Books of the Revised Standard Version. Centre Informatique et Bible—Bible Data Bank. Grand Rapids: Eerdmans, 1983.

INTRODUCTION TO THE NEW TESTAMENT FROM A WESLEYAN PERSPECTIVE

Wayne McCown

This essay attempts a brief overview of the NT as viewed from three perspectives: literary, historical, and theological. Thereafter, a Wesleyan perspective of the NT will be delineated, with special attention to the doctrinal and devotional interests of the movement.

At the outset, it must be acknowledged that there is considerable diversity of opinion among contemporary evangelical Wesleyans with regard to many of the matters to be treated. On the other hand, a conscious effort has been made to represent the moderate mainstream of the movement.

While John Wesley and his followers have always given attention to both testaments, the primacy belongs to the NT. It is viewed as the fulfillment of the OT, and the OT is interpreted by the light of the NT. In this respect, the contemporary Wesleyan movement stands in the mainstream of Christian tradition.

The same is generally true in regard to the use of the Bible in Wesleyan churches. Typical of the Protestant tradition, preaching from the Bible is the central act of worship, and study of the Bible is the norm for instructional curricula. Further, evangelical Wesleyans share strong convictions about the authority of Scripture (holding it to be the Word of God) and its role in modern life.

On the other hand, evangelical Wesleyans do not come from the same mold as other modern evangelical Protestants. (Some evangelicals often do not understand this fact: Wesleyans sometimes feel quite uncomfortable when lumped together with them.) Contemporary evangelical Wesleyans are distinguished by several historical realities: (1) Their rootage is in Anglicanism; (2) they are Arminian in theology; (3) they belong to the Methodist movement; (4) they were more influenced by the holiness revivals of the nineteenth century than by the debate between Fundamentalism and Liberalism; (5) many of the denominations within Wesleyanism were born out of those revivals and/or the social struggles of that era. In addition to these influences, it is a fact that contemporary evangelical Wesleyans are also *Wesleyan* (not Reformed, Baptist, Pentecostal, or Independent).

Thus, while they stand in the mainstream of Christianity and share much common ground with other evangelicals, contemporary Wesleyans do represent a distinctive way of viewing, studying, and using the Bible. Ways in which the Wesleyan way is distinctive will be described in the final section of this essay.

THE LANGUAGE AND LITERATURE
OF THE NEW TESTAMENT

The NT is a relatively short book, yet, rightly called, it is not a book at all but a collection of twenty-seven "books." Actually, most of these books are letters; the remainder (the Gospels, Acts, and Revelation) consists of materials representing three differing genres. (These twenty-seven books, individually read, are brief, some shorter than a page.)

While some of the NT is easy to read, the contemporary reader finds much of it difficult to interpret. That is a consequence of several possible factors: (1) Originally written in another language (see below), these documents have to be translated into English for most readers; (2) all of them were written in the first century and must be interpreted against the context of that period (see below); (3) the shorter the writing, the less opportunity the reader has to "get on board" (i.e., the context for interpreting the contents is foreshortened); (4) most of the documents were written to address specific situations about which we have little information (thus, the original audience could understand them more easily than we); (5) the subject matter, in a number of instances, is of a difficult nature for some modern readers (e.g., theological argumentation).

None of the NT was written for the sake of producing a body of Christian "literature" as such. The letters are probably all genuine, written to address real situations, to meet specific needs. Similarly, the motive that gave rise to the other writings is utilitarian: The purpose was to serve the practical needs of the church as those were coming to the fore in the latter half of the century. The authors were not writers by profession, but church leaders, evangelists, and teachers who used writing as a tool in their missionary work.

Thus the NT, which contains some of the world's finest literature (e.g., Jesus' parables) was not written with that lofty end in view. Rather, the NT illustrates the truth of Longinus' dictum that "sublimity is the echo of the greatness of the soul." Its greatness inheres in its contents, not its form.

Further, the NT was not written and arranged to accord with some grand design (except insofar as that exists in the mind of God). Rather, the several letters and various materials having been collected, a kind of natural sequence emerged:

Gospels
Acts
Pauline letters
Non-Pauline letters
Revelation

The Pauline corpus, whose thirteen letters comprise nearly half of the NT, reflects the following principles for arrangement:

1. The letters are ordered by length, not date, the longest (Romans) first and the shortest (Philemon) last.

2. A "second" letter to the same addressee, however, is attached to the "first."

3. The Pastoral Letters (1 and 2 Timothy, Titus) are put at the end of the corpus, reflecting recognition of their distinction as letters addressed to individual persons and not churches.

4. Hebrews is then appended, showing the uncertainty of the early church regarding its authorship.

The first two of these principles also dictated the order of the non-Pauline letters. These letters, along with Hebrews, which today is regarded as non-Pauline, are typically labeled the "Catholic Epistles" or "General Letters." This title refers to the fact that several of the major letters (e.g., James, 1 Peter, 1 John) were written for a general or broadly designated or unidentified audience. On the other hand, two of the letters in this group are addressed to a specific person or church: 3 John is sent "to my dear friend Gaius" and recipients of 2 John are "the chosen lady and her children." This latter is generally interpreted as metaphorical, referring to a specific congregation. By attachment to 1 John, however, these two are included among the General Letters. By contrast, two of Paul's letters that were written for a wider audience are grouped with the Pauline corpus and not with the general letters; these are Galatians, which was sent "to the churches in Galatia," and Ephesians, which went "to the saints." The added words *in Ephesus* are spurious, not being found in several important early manuscripts.

Contemporary scholars customarily classify Paul's letters as follows:

Early Letters (Galatians, 1 Thessalonians, 2 Thessalonians)
Major Letters (1 Corinthians, 2 Corinthians, Romans)
Prison Letters (Colossians, Philemon, Ephesians, Philippians)
Pastoral Letters (1 Timothy, 2 Timothy, Titus)

(Note: This listing presumes the authenticity of the Pastoral Letters, and the so-called "South Galatian theory" with a corresponding early dating of Galatians.)

The four gospels naturally fall into two subgroups: the Synoptics and John. the word *synoptic* denotes a common point of view. Matthew, Mark, and Luke parallel one another at many points because they share the same material. John, which presumably was written much later, takes an independent approach. The order of the four in the NT apparently reflects the chronology of their origins as understood by the early church. Modern scholarship, for the most part, assigns priority to Mark.

In sum, while it may reflect some logic, the present order of NT books is an afterthought. The arrangement may be providential, but it is not inspired. On the other hand, it is instructional.

Internally, the literary forms deployed in the NT are ordinary enough. The letter, of course, was and is a common form of communication. Further, most of the epistles use the elements standard in first-century letters. For example, the opening typically includes (1) introduction of writer, (2) identification of addressees, and (3) a formal greeting.

In the NT, however, certain literary forms are highly refined. For example, as did the rabbis, so Jesus also used stories to teach spiritual truths. Storytelling, of course, is as old as history and a common means of human discourse. But some persons are better storytellers than others; no one, admittedly, was ever better than the Master Teacher. So well did Jesus use this ordinary device that merely to mention "parables" brings his name to mind.

In terms of the broader category of literary genre, Acts reflects the use of forms common to ancient historiography, and Revelation reflects the apocalyptic literature of early Judeo-Christian tradition. As noted above, the letters of the NT reflect the epistolary genre of their day.

Gospel, however, is a new form. Unique to the NT, it appears to rise from the nature of the materials and their use in the early church. On the other hand, as a literary form, *gospel* is not highly sophisticated or complex: The words and works of Jesus are simply told, using a general chronological frameword and highlighting certain events such as his passion and death.

Ordinary but transformed: that summarized not only the literature but also the language of the NT.

The original Greek of these writings is not, for the most part, the literary Greek of the period. It represents, rather, the ordinary vocabulary and form of the language as used in everyday conversation. Scholars call it *koine*, i.e., common Greek.

It should be noted that our understanding of the language of the NT changed considerably in the last century. Previously, it was thought, because NT Greek is somewhat different from so-called *classical* Greek, that biblical discourse was of a "higher" species than ordinary discourse. Due in large part to new archeological finds, we now know it differs from literary Greek because it reflects a "lower" form of the language, as used in everyday spoken communication.

In short, the extraordinary beauty and power of the NT does not inhere in its language or literature, which are commonplace. In this respect, the written Word mirrors the Word incarnate: "He had no beauty or majesty to attract us to him" (Isa 53:2). It is to this One that the NT, the written Word, bears witness; and it does not eclipse him with a beauty all its own. Instead, consistent with the revelation of the Word "made flesh," so it appears, once again, that God has used the simple things of this world to confound the wise. To him be glory forever and ever! Amen.

THE HISTORICAL CONTEXT OF THE NEW TESTAMENT

The era that constitutes the NT period can be simply delineated: The dates of the events recorded and the writings preserved are roughly consonant with the beginning and end of the first century A.D. According to a commonly accepted chronology, Jesus' birth occurred in 4 B.C. and Revelation was written in A.D. 96.

The historical data, however, are not evenly spread. The gospels report little (almost nothing) during the thirty years following Jesus' birth and the beginning of his ministry. Their narrative focuses on the time of his ministry, death, and resurrection (A.D. 27–30). Acts covers the next three crucial decades (A.D. 30–62?) although not in an even manner. Paul's letters overlap the latter part of Acts (A.D. 49–62), except for the Pastoral Letters, which presumably postdate Acts (A.D. 64–66?). It is not known when the gospels were written nor the dates of the remainder of the NT. Most of them probably were written between A.D. 50 and 70, although various scholars argue for earlier dates (e.g., for Matthew) as well as later (e.g., for Hebrews). Since exact dating, however, is impossible, we are uncertain of our knowledge during the thirty years A.D. 66–96. So the historical information given us by the NT illumines primarily the forty years A.D. 27–66, stretching out to both ends of the first century.

This was a time in the history of the biblical world that was extraordinarily complex. Three major forces were at work, contributing to and shaping the world into which Jesus came and in which the NT was written: Greek culture, the Roman Empire, and Jewish religion.

Greek culture

Greek culture was introduced throughout the world of the New Testament by Alexander the Great during the intertestamental period. A young military genius, Alexander conquered the entire Persian Empire and more through a series of brilliant campaigns (334–323 B.C.) Asia Minor came under his dominion in 334–333 B.C., Syro-Palestine in 332 B.C., and Egypt in 332–331 B.C. Alexander's vision included not only the conquest of the world but the propagation of Greek culture, i.e., the hellenization of all peoples.

Upon his death at the age of thirty-two, his kingdom was divided among three of his generals. Initially, Palestine fell under the rule of the Ptolemies of Egypt (323–198 B.C.); subsequently, the Seleucids of Antioch got the upper hand in the region and ruled briefly (198–164 B.C.). The important point here is that the population of the area was subject to direct Greek rule for more than 150 years.

During that time, the Greek language was imposed on the Jewish nation and became, furthermore, the *lingua franca* of the entire NT world. Thus, the NT was written in Greek, though Jesus, Paul, James, Peter, and John all doubtless spoke Aramaic and read Hebrew as well.

Another significant event, reflecting the influence of Greek culture on the Jews, was the translation of the OT from Hebrew into Greek. The dating of this translation, known as the Septuagint and designated LXX, is uncertain; it may have been done over an extended period (350–200 B.C.). The LXX became popular among the Jews dispersed throughout Egypt, Asia Minor, and even Palestine. The mother tongue of the Jews in those places was Greek. Moreover, the LXX is the Bible version that the NT authors quoted most often.

Finally, it is to be noted that the introduction of Greek culture gave rise to diverse and often conflicting responses on the part of the Jews. Moreover, the degree of assimilation by this alien culture varied widely in different regions (e.g., in Alexandria versus Jerusalem). Thus, this period is fraught with considerable tension and strife within the Jewish community, as some strove to preserve their biblical culture against the powerful influence of the Greek culture.

The Roman Empire

A bloody revolt in Judea brought relative independence to that region for a century (164–63 B.C.), until which time the Jewish government became so weakened by corruption and internecine strife that the Romans stepped in and annexed the area. Thus, all of the NT world came under the dominion of the Roman Empire. Greece and Asia Minor had already been brought under Roman rule during the previous century.

Romans rulers play a significant role in the historical narrative of the NT. They are directly associated with such significant events as Jesus' birth and his crucifixion, the death of James, Paul's arrest and his appeal to Rome.

Two other key influences attributable to the Roman Empire may be mentioned. (1) The legacy of Herod the Great, who ruled Judea and Galilee 37 B.C.–A.D. 4, cannot be overlooked. To him are attributed many building projects, such as the city of Caesarea and most especially the Second Temple. This was the temple of Jesus' day, subsequently destroyed by the Romans in A.D. 70. (2) The spread of Christianity in the first century presumes the *Pax Romana* and the Roman system of major highways, with the corresponding freedom of citizens like Paul to travel from one region to another within the bounds of the empire.

It must be acknowledged that Rome also represented a threat, first to Judaism and later to Christianity within the first century. (The former is illustrated by the Roman destruction of Jerusalem in A.D. 70; the latter is portrayed dramatically in the final book of the NT.) Thus, the Roman Empire left its mark on the NT in more ways than one.

Jewish Religion

The Jewish religion represents another major influence. By the time of the NT, the differing responses to the influences of Greek culture and the Roman Empire had crystallized (in Judea) into three quasi-political "parties." The role that the Pharisees, Sadducees, and Herodians play, especially in the Gospels, is evident, as is that of the ruling body of the Jews, the Sanhedrin.

Other factions and population subgroups that are more in the background also play roles in the NT story: Zealots, Samaritans, Galileans, Hellenists, tax collectors, God-fearers, and, by way of counterpoint, the Gentiles.

Moreover, the NT is saturated with references to the Jewish religion, in terms of particulars such as the temple and synagogue; rabbis and priests; laws, feasts, and rites such as almsgiving, prayer, and fasting. The fact is that the NT is steeped in Judaism.

Among the more prominent influences of the Jewish religion, the following merit special attention: (1) the Jewishness of Jesus; (2) the use of the Hebrew Scriptures, i.e., the OT; and (3) as a countepoint, the breakthrough of Christianity into the gentile world.

The Jewishness of Jesus is easily assumed; its significance is also too quickly dismissed. The fact is that the Word became flesh as a Jew; moreover, Jesus lived his entire life among the Jews and directed his ministry primarily to them (not exclusively, however, because he also had contact with Samaritans and Gentiles). He was called rabbi, and observed the religious customs of the Jews: circumcision, *bar mitzvah* at age twelve, weekly synagogue worship, Scripture reading, prayer, the Jewish feasts (in Jerusalem), worship in the temple, etc.

In addition and most important, Jesus spoke of himself and was perceived by his followers in Jewish categories. He called himself the Son of Man. Demons (in the presence of witnesses) and a Roman soldier (at the Crucifixion) declared Jesus to be the Son of God. His disciples confessed him as Messiah. And the charge nailed to his cross read, "The King of the Jews." The writers of the NT refer to him hundreds of times as the Christ, i.e., Messiah. Throughout the NT the significance of his person and work are interpreted in the light of the Hebrew Scriptures.

Indeed, on other matters as well, the OT is the primary sourcebook for the NT authors. Few citations are attributable to other sources, but hundreds of their quotations come from the OT. In addition, the writers make numerous allusions and indirect references to the OT. The NT is saturated with OT vocabulary, concepts, and themes. So dependent is it that the NT cannot be properly interpreted apart from the OT. From the Christian perspective, the two books are one: The OT is the foundation and the NT is the fulfillment.

As a counterpoint, the breakthrough of Christianity into the gentile world constitutes a development of significant proportions. But is was not without struggle, as Acts shows us. The central motif of that story, moreover, carries through the NT and beyond. Indeed, the nature of the relationship between Judaism and Christianity is still fundamentally unresolved. But this much is clear: Early in its history (by the middle of the first century), Christianity, due in part to external forces, began to break the shackles of Judaism and move more freely into the gentile world. By the end of the NT era, Christianity, which was born in the womb of Judaism, had established itself as an independent religion.

In summary, the NT era was a historical period rich in diversity. Major contributors were Greek culture, the Roman Empire, and Jewish religion. Each of these left its mark on the writings of the NT and, in turn, the Christian church.

One other feature of the century, shared by Roman, Greek, and Jew, deserves special notice: Like the twentieth century, this was an era of great spiritual hunger.

Among the Jews, this hunger was manifest in the Qumran community; the Dead Sea Scrolls reflect a prayerful expectancy for the coming of a Teacher of Righteousness. Similarly, the "pious poor" in the Christian narratives of the Gospels exhibit a longing for God's deliverance. Zechariah, Simeon, and Anna all prophesied the salvation of God. Anna spoke to "all who were looking forward to the redemption of Israel (Lk 2:38); God revealed to Simeon "that he would not die before he had seen the Lord's Christ" (Lk 2:26).

There was also a great deal of genuine spiritual hunger in the Greco-Roman world, as illustrated in the stories of the Ethiopian eunuch (Ac 8) and Cornelius the centurian (Ac 10). It is also evidenced in the number of "God-fearers" attending Jewish synagogues throughout the empire, many of whom responded readily to the Gospel and thereby formed the nucleus of the churches planted through the missionary activities of Paul and others.

Spiritual hunger fueled the rapid growth of the Christian church (beginning at Pentecost) and its spread throughout Judea (see Ac 21:20), Samaria (Ac 8.4–25; 9:31) and "to the ends of the earth" (Ac 1:8; see Ro 15:23–24) in the first century and beyond. The reception of the Gospel by so many who represented diverse ethnic backgrounds and every social class was due in part to widespread spiritual need. So, too, today salvation comes not so much to the high and mighty as to those upon whom God's favor rests, "those who hunger and thirst for righteousness" (Mt 5:6).

THE THEOLOGICAL CONTENT OF THE NEW TESTAMENT

The NT itself is not a theological treatise. Yet it is a significant theological sourcebook. This significance derives from two factors: (1) the nature of the Bible, which recounts God's revelation in human history, and (2) the importance of the NT as the norm for Christian faith and practice. The NT bears witness to Jesus Christ, the revelation of God in human flesh, born to save all humankind; in addition, it is in the NT that we have reliable data for a theology deriving from Jesus and interpreting his significance.

Parts of the NT are more theological than others. (Perhaps at this point is should be recalled that the NT represents a collection of disparate materials that contain personal exchanges and historical narratives as well as sermon briefs and theological arguments.) Yet all of it is set within a theological framework: the NT is the story of Jesus Christ and the witness of the early church to the significance for all the world of his person and work. Thus, even the narrative parts serve a theological purpose. That purpose is aptly described in John 20:31: "These are written that you may believe that Jesus is the Christ, the Son of God, and that by believing you may have life in his name."

The NT stands in a stream called revelatory or redemptive history. It is known in scholarly circles as *Heilsgeschichte*, "the history of salvation." This history has its origins in the OT. The NT declaration of Jesus as "the Christ, the Son of God" (Mk 1:1), i.e., the Messiah, shows its linkage to the OT as well as its sense of both historical and soteriological fulfillment.

NT theology is not a system of ideas or doctrines. It is, rather, the description and interpretation of God's saving activity in biblical history, which finds its fulfillment in the Messiah who gave his life for our redemption.

"Redemption is the divine activity whose objective is the deliverance of men, both as individuals and as a society, from their sinful predicament and their restoration to a position of fellowship and favor with God."[1] The point is that "God so loved the world that he gave his one and only Son, that whoever believes in him shall not perish but have eternal life. For God did not send his son into the world to condemn the world, but to save the world through him" (Jn 3:16–17).

Everything else in NT theology flows from that fact and the acknowledgment of its significance. "The Gospels record the words and works of Jesus; the Acts relates the establishment and extension of the movement set up by Jesus' ministry; the epistles explicate further the meaning of Jesus' redemptive mission; and the Revelation outlines the consummation of the redemptive work of Christ for the world and human history."[2]

The earliest confessions of faith centered on Jesus: "Jesus is Lord" (Ro 10:9; cf. 1Co 12:3); "Jesus is the Son of God" (1Jn 4:15; cf. Heb 4:14). A fundamental creed, predating Paul, declared "that Christ died for our sins according to the Scriptures, that he was buried, that he was raised on the third day according to the Scriptures, and that he appeared to Peter, and then to the Twelve" (1Co 15:3–5).

Some of the most essential elements of NT theology are represented in this early creedal formulation. First, the theology of the NT is consistently Christocentric. Second, it accords with "the Scriptures," i.e., the OT. Third, it is based on historical events, most notably Jesus' death and resurrection. Fourth, it consists of affirming ("on the third day") and interpreting ("for our sins") the meaning of these events. Such are the quintessential characteristics of "doing" NT theology today as well.

There have been in the twentieth century numerous outstanding studies of NT theology that have contributed significantly to our understanding of both its form and content. First to be mentioned are those exploring salvation history. They have illumined the relations between God and his people: history and revelation, salvation, and eschatology; the OT and the NT.

A second area that has been thoroughly researched is the Christology of the NT. Several scholars have studied the titles ascribed to Jesus, investigating their origins in the OT, their use throughout religious history, and the meaning and significance that they carry in the NT. The Christology of the gospel writers has also been examined. Their selection, ordering, and interpretation of materials influence our knowledge and understanding of Jesus. So their own perceptions of his words and work are critically important. Other scholars have focused on the theology of Jesus himself insofar as that can be ascertained from sayings attributed to him. Another approach has been the study of individual NT authors and/or books. In particular, the Christology of earliest Christian communities and of Paul have been fruitful areas of investigation. The "hymns" of the NT church (e.g., Php 2:6–11; Col 1:15–20) have also been thoroughly mined for their Christology.

A third area receiving major attention has been the teaching(s) of the NT concerning humankind. One scholar (Bultmann) organized his entire treatment of Paul's theology under two heads: "Man prior to the revelation of faith" and "Man under faith." While this approach must be, and has been, criticized as off-center, it contributed significantly to our understanding of such topics as humankind in relation to flesh, sin, and the world; God's righteousness and reconciliation; grace and faith; freedom from sin; and walking in the Spirit. Other studies have also helped us to understand these important matters, extending the investigation to other NT materials.

Word studies represent a fourth area in which significant contributions have been made in this century. A massive ten-volume work, translated from German into English, *The Theological Dictionary of the NT (TDNT)* epitomized the tremendous effort modern scholars have invested in understanding the NT on its own terms. In this work, thousands of Greek word families are investigated against the background of their usage in the Hebrew Scriptures as well as in extrabiblical sources; then their usage and meaning in the NT are described in some detail. Still a monumental scholarly resource, the *TDNT* has been replaced in evangelical circles with the *Dictionary of NT Theology*. This three-volume work is more accessible; its entries are in English, though the language underlying word studies is Greek.

These major works by no means exhaust the list of available resources that have been published in this century. Warner Press has published essays by evangelical Wesleyans on the following topics: salvation, the Bible, Christian ethics, the church, the Holy Spirit, and last things. The general title of this five-volume work is *Wesleyan Theological Perspectives*.

For the following reasons, the continuing study of NT theology is vital to the health of the modern church: (1) Bible study brings believers into direct, personal contact with the documents essential to formation of their faith; (2) the study of NT theology helps to develop perspective and balance with respect to that which is most important to Christian faith as viewed by the NT; (3) inevitably, an infusion of NT theology enriches the vocabulary of faith and broadens the categories of contemporary Christians; (4) Bible study is invigorating as it brings new vitality and freshness to the church.

Wesleyans have benefitted immeasurably from their continuing study of the Bible (as part of the tradition of Wesleyanism). Contemporary Wesleyans have also been immensely helped by scholarly contributions to NT theology in this century. However, in both areas rich treasures remain to be mined.

A WESLEYAN PERSPECTIVE ON THE NEW TESTAMENT

Evangelical Wesleyans use the NT as their primary theological sourcebook. They regard its teachings as normative for both doctrine and life. Most declare that anything not found in the Bible nor that can be proved by it can be required as an article of belief or as necessary to salvation.

Thus, Wesleyans take the Bible seriously. They are concerned, when doing theology, that resulting views are "biblical"; those that are not are subject to challenge. References to specific supporting texts are commonplace and considered important in theological argumentation. Indeed, when engaged in a reexamination of major tenets, biblical studies of the topic are *de rigueur*. Church doctrine must be based upon the Holy Scriptures, and documentation of NT support is especially important.

Evangelical Wesleyans, however, are inclined to examine such support in relation to the total biblical context. They are not so focused on the fine grammatical detail of Scripture as are their evangelical peers. Rather, their approach to reading the Bible is more holistic.

One consequence is that evangelical Wesleyans have had little involvement in the "battle for the Bible." The doctrine of inerrancy is not really that crucial to their interests. Like their forefather, John Wesley, they affirm the truthfulness of the Bible's teachings (God, creation, humankind, etc.). But particular details may be disputed at no threat to their faith; thus, they rarely become defensive respecting the interpretation of a single text.

Wesleyans look to the Scriptures to inform them on matters of Christian doctrine and the holy life. Other matters, such as historical details, are subservient to these major interests. Their focus reflects their understanding of God's primary purpose for revealing himself to us.

Throughout its history, beginning with the Wesleys, the theological interests of the movement have been dominated by the Gospel: God's salvation in Christ. Correspondingly, in the areas of Christology and soteriology, Wesleyan theology is comparatively well developed. Other areas, such as eschatology, garner much less attention. The same profile is reflected in their theological use of the NT.

Evangelical Wesleyans accept at face value and without qualification what the Scriptures declare concerning Jesus Christ. They believe implicitly the Christological affirmations of the traditional creeds: Being God, he became man and lived a sinless life in this world; having offered his life for our atonement, he was raised from death and exalted to God's right hand where he sits enthroned as Lord. One day he will come again to take his own to be with him, and then with the Father will judge all humankind. In brief, Jesus Christ is our Savior and Lord of all.

Wesleyans accept the NT's interpretation of these events on the basis of the OT Scriptures. They view them as the fulfillment of God's saving purpose in history. Wesleyans take seriously the biblical claim that "God was in Christ, reconciling the world to himself" (2Co 5:19). Further, all the NT is interpreted in the light of that theological affirmation.

Accordingly, evangelical Wesleyans are especially drawn to three "moments" in the history of Jesus: (1) the Incarnation; (2) the Cross; and (3) the Resurrection.

The Incarnation symbolized the fact that "*God* was in Christ." In accord with the orthodox creeds, evangelical Wesleyans believe that Jesus was conceived by the Holy Spirit and born of the Virign Mary, joining the deity of God and the humanity of man: Jesus was God in human flesh, truly and fully both God and man.

Further, they declare that he came to save us. Following the NT writers, they attribute saving significance to Jesus' death. His death is regarded as a vicarious sacrifice: Jesus suffered, was crucified, died, and was buried *for us*. His blood is regarded as an atoning sacrifice, poured out for the forgiveness of sins—not ours only but for the sins of the whole world.

The Resurrection is accepted as historical fact. Just as Jesus physically died so he was physically raised from death. To this fact is attributed great theological significance. In the first place, it is symbolic of Christ's victory over Satan, sin, and death. Second, it is the surety of our own resurrection to eternal life. Third, it is the basis of his exaltation to God's right hand.

All the rest of history is viewed in the light of this fact: Jesus is our exalted Lord! He intercedes for us. He pours out his Spirit upon us. He empowers us for witness to the world. One day all his enemies will be brought into complete subjection. One day he will return to judge all people. One day every tongue will confess that he is Lord, to the glory of God the Father.

Wesleyan theology is Christocentric. All other matters of doctrine pale by comparison, excepting one that is closely related to the first: God's salvation in Christ. Indeed, Wesleyans are distinguished for their attention to soteriology; moreover, the witness of the NT has been especially important in their study of this doctrine.

Wesleyan soteriology has a comprehensive character. For example, while the Protestant doctrine of justification receives due attention, it represents for Wesleyans only one aspect of God's saving work. Thus, it is arrayed alongside other biblical terms such as reconciliation, regeneration, and adoption: Wesleyans take all of these together to achieve a view of the complete picture. Consequently, "justification" does not occupy the same place of prominence that it does in Reformed theology.

Wesleyan studies of NT soteriology highlight as real the personal experience of divine forgiveness, cleansing, and empowerment, which results in a new life and relationship with God through Jesus Christ. Taking the NT at face value, Wesleyans believe that God can and does actually impart new life so that in Christ we have in fact a new spiritual nature imbued with faith, hope, and love.

This transforming experience of salvation happens in a moment, but God's work in the believer continues throughout life. God uses the crises in spiritual experience *and* the process of growth to accomplish his work in us. This is an area to which Wesleyans have devoted a great deal of study under the subject of sanctification.

Holiness before God and love for neighbor represent the epitome of God's work in the believer, according to the Wesleyan interpretation of Scripture. Contemporary scholarship has contributed significantly to our understanding of holiness. Not only has the subject been examined historically, theologically, and experientially, it has been thoroughly studied biblically. Admittedly, there has resulted in recent decades some shifts of emphasis within Wesleyanism regarding the doctrine and its treatment. But these shifts have also resulted in a more holistic approach to the NT.

Holiness is part of the warp and woof of the Scriptures; to preach the Bible (especially the NT) is to preach holiness whether or not that particular terminology is used. Increasingly, Wesleyan preachers are less concerned about preserving the shibboleths of the doctrine and are devoting more energy to applying the biblical message to needs of their parishioners.

That is the heart and burden of the Wesleyan gospel. It is a Christ-centered message that borrows heavily from the language of the NT, accepting at face value its declarations concerning Jesus. In looking to Jesus, the focal matter of interest is his saving work for and in the believer. The proclamation of that saving Gospel and its continuing application is what energized the movement called Wesleyan.

Wesleyans have a practical bent. They are not so interested in theology for theology's sake. They want to know the benefits of the doctrine, how it applies, how it works out in real life. Reflecting the influence of Pietism on Wesley, they are as concerned with devotion as with theology. That is certainly true in their reading and use of the NT.

John Wesley advocated reading both the OT and the NT daily. His instructions are devotional in nature: Begin and end with prayer, read with the single purpose of knowing God's will, examine yourself "with both heart and life being scrutinized" by the light given, apply what is learned immediately (from the Preface to Wesley's *Explanatory Notes Upon the OT*).

Clearly, for Wesley Bible study was more than a scholarly exercise; it was a devotional one.

Wesley never wrote a systematic theology. He was not a theologian in that sense; rather, he was a field evangelist, a circuit-riding preacher, a busy church administrator. While he read widely, Wesley found in the Bible his daily spiritual nourishment. It was the source of his own personal vigor and virtue and the source of the hundreds of sermons he preached as well as of his theology. His theology issued from a life of devotion and ministry. Like the theology of the NT, Wesley's is embedded in his letters, sermons, notes on the Bible, and tracts.

Several corollaries flow from this heritage: (1) Wesleyans do not read the NT through the grid of a particular systematization of theology; they simply read it for what it is, a collection of early Christian documents. (2) Wesleyans have a certain affinity for working through such documents (letters, tracts, etc.), searching for theological and practical guidance. (3) Like Wesley, his followers tend to be practical people, deeply involved in the work of ministry. (4) Contemporary Wesleyans continue to look to the Scriptures for spiritual sustenance, sermon ideas, and instruction for daily life. The devotional tradition is alive and well in the Wesleyan movement.

The dominant hermeneutic in the movement is called the inductive method. Its primary feature is direct, personal study of the English Bible. The process begins by observation, discovering what is in the text itself. The use of outside tools or references is interdicted. Observations are recorded both in the text and alongside it. These collected data, then, become the basis for interpretation, which in turn forms the basis for application. The process is not considered to be sound or complete without working through each of these steps.

Obviously, this is a straightforward, if rigorous, process. It is not peculiarly "Wesleyan"; many other contemporary groups committed to serious Bible study also deploy the same or similar method. But it is this approach to the Bible that forms the basis of much of Wesleyan life today.

Because of their interest in the practical issues of living as Christians in the world, Wesleyans have a high appreciation for the exhortatory materials of the NT. Thus, while Paul is highly valued for his doctrinal treatment of sin and sanctification, James's letter is not regarded as a "strawy epistle," as Martin Luther held, but is esteemed for its teachings on faith and works, etc. The applied ethical teachings of the NT epistles are accorded as much attention as the doctrinal sections.

Like their peers, contemporary Wesleyans do not draw heavily on such brief letters as 2 and 3 John, 2 Peter, and Jude. By comparison, however, their attitudes toward and handling of the NT are more balanced. Hebrews, 1 and 2 Peter, and James are accorded as much respect as Paul's writings; and none of the gospels is more favored than another, while the interest in Revelation is not disproportionate to the rest of the NT.

Contemporary Wesleyans do bring to their reading of the NT a special interest in soteriology and a certain understanding of Christian experience. They also bring a devotional desire for spiritual nourishment and a volitional determination to apply God's Word to the issues of life.

Since the time of Wesley, those issues have always been viewed as embracing social concerns as well as personal ethics. The resurgence of Wesleyan involvement in social redemption reflects the heritage in justice and mercy as modeled by the movement's founder in the eighteenth century. For evangelical Wesleyans, at stake is not the question of either/or. The Wesleyan ideal is a proper balance between the two: personal salvation hand in hand with social redemption.

Therefore, the Wesleyan appropriation of the NT is driven by its sense of mission. That mission derives from its understanding of the NT. Its central message constitutes the Wesleyan gospel; the NT functions as the guiding norm for the members and ministries of the movement. Both its theological study and its devotional life have a common source, and that source is the Bible. As Wesley claimed to be "a man of one book," so his spiritual heirs are "people of the Book." They understand that Book, though written by human authors in the languages and literary forms of their times, to be an inspired and trustworthy record of God's revelation. Further, they believe God continues, by his Holy Spirit, to speak through this Word to each generation and culture, including our own. As believers, they are committed to proclaiming the central message of the Bible, God's salvation in Christ, to all the world. And that witness, they are convinced, must be attested not only in word but in deed. So by lives of holiness and through works of love as well as in the preaching of the Gospel, they declare, "The Word became flesh and lived for a while among us" (Jn 1:14). That is the Wesleyan way, and it reflects our way of understanding the NT.

NOTES

[1]George E. Ladd, *A Theology of the New Testament* (Grand Rapids: Eerdmans, 1974), 26.
[2]Ibid., 28.

PART II

The Old Testament

GENESIS
Alan Meenan

INTRODUCTION

Genesis is about beginnings: creation, the origin of species, the inception of man, the birth of nations, and the dawn of salvation history. In the content it expresses, Genesis is unique among biblical books yet is an integral part of the entire Christian canon in the foundational function it provides.

Genesis derived its name from the Greek translators who attempted to define the content of the book from the frequent use of the Hebrew word *toledoth,* most commonly translated "generations." The ancient Hebrews simply took the first word of the book to designate the title of the book. Hence it was called *bereshith,* or "In the beginning." Either way, whether by using *toledoth* or *bereshith,* the book is well named. It is a book of cosmological, national, and theological beginnings, setting the stage for the continuing drama of God's dealing with humankind and, in particular, his dealing with the people of Israel. It thereby introduces us to the earliest ancestors of the nation and their emergence from the ancient Near Eastern milieu in which they originated to become the forefathers of a chosen race.

Genesis makes clear the fact that the Israelites were not a different race of people per se, but simply a chosen race based on a spiritual distinctiveness as opposed to an a priori national consciousness or physical uniqueness. They continued to be related to the peoples and tribes of nations that surrounded them. It is through the stories of the Israelite patriarchs described in ch. 12 and following that the consciousness is born of a people with a special mission and destiny in the world.

Genesis, therefore, is primarily theological history. It depicts the unfolding saga of a God who makes and keeps covenants with the progenitors of a nation. Israel's theological distinctiveness, then, is closely allied with the concept of covenant. When that is lost, there is nothing. When that is retained, Israel's uniqueness as a chosen race remains.

I. STRUCTURE

Genesis has a clearly defined structural framework delineated by the repeated occurrence of the word *toledoth,* "the generations of." This genealogical formula serves to introduce both genealogical and narrative sections of the book. In a sense, it functions either as a divider within the book, as is the case with genealogical lists 5:1; 10:1; 11:10; 25:12; and 36:1, or as a superscription to the narrative material that follows 6:9; 11:27; 25:19; and 37:2.

In every case *toledoth* is followed by the genitive of the progenitor (Skinner, 41) but as such emphasizes the progeny. Thus each *toledoth* summarizes what precedes and introduces what follows. In 2:4 the writer relates the beginning of human history to cosmic history and thereby introduces the Adam narrative. Ch. 5 concludes the story of Adam by listing his progeny, and it paves the way for the Noah narrative, which is introduced by the *toledoth* of 6:9. Similarly, ch. 10 and 11:10–26 summarize the progeny of Noah and set the scene for the story of Abraham, which is introduced by the *toledoth* of 11:27. So, too, Abraham's progeny through Ishmael is summarized in 25:12, while the Jacob narrative is introduced in 25:19. In turn, Isaac's progeny through Esau is summarized in 36:1, 9 and allows the *toledoth* of 37:2 to introduce the Joseph narrative.

It is possible to conclude from these observations of the occurrence of *toledoth* that in instances in which the formula is followed by a genealogy (5:1; 10:1; 11:10; 25:12; 36:1, 9), the emphasis is simply on the dimension of human history and is tangential to the major thrust of the book. It is offered, I suspect, for the sake of some kind of completeness, since it enables Israel to determine its relationships with its surrounding nations. That is particularly true in the genealogical lists of ch. 10, which hint at the basis of world population, and in 25:12–18 and ch. 36, which trace the progeny of Ishmael and Esau respectively. The genealogical lists of ch. 5 and 11:10–26 are simply concerned to fill in detail of the lineage from Adam to Noah and from Noah to Terah, Abraham's father.

The writer's obvious emphasis is on the Hebrew patriarchs and Israelite roots. That is the reason why the largest body of Genesis material (chs. 12–50) is concerned with a mere four generations of one family, specifically the Hebrew patriarchs and God's dealing with them. Contrast that with the many generations, personalities, and cosmic concerns of the first eleven chapters. It is the reason why the progeny of Ishmael is summarily dismissed in seven brief verses. Such disproportionate selectivity betrays the bias and intent of the writer. Genesis is not a book whose primary function is to trace the origin and hence the meaning of life in human historical terms. However, in the more significant use of *toledoth* in introducing narrative passages (2:4; 6:9; 11:27; 25:19; 37:2), the book functions at a theological dimension that transcends human relationships. It is the characters introduced by *toledoth*—Adam, Noah, Abraham, Jacob, and Joseph—who are the bearers of the revelation of God. Their history is a story of man's relationship with God—a theological history.

The function of the *toledoth* formulae, then, is to structure the book of Genesis into a unified composition, summarizing each major narrative section of the book and connecting it with the one that follows. In their highly organized use, they betray a major concern "to describe both creation and world history in the light of the divine will for a chosen people" (Childs, 149).

II. AUTHORSHIP

Genesis has been considered from time immemorial to be an integral part of the first five books of the OT, commonly referred to as the Pentateuch. Traditionally, both Jews and Christians have ascribed authorship of the Pentateuch to Moses. He is the central figure in the books. Unlike his contemporaries, Moses was well educated, having been reared as the son of Pharaoh's daughter. Several references in the Pentateuch itself indicate that Moses was responsible for certain writings (Ex 17:14; 24:4–8; 34:27; Nu 33:1–2; Dt 31:9, 22, 24) not to mention the various allusions to Mosaic authorship throughout the remaining Scripture in both the OT and NT. However, specific biblical evidence for the pen of Moses is lacking in Genesis. Events related in the book occurred, of course, prior to the life of Moses and undoubtedly existed in some written or oral form prior to the events of the Exodus. Whether or not Moses utilized these ancient sources must remain inconclusive and beyond the scope of this commentary.

With the rise of higher criticism in the late eighteenth century, doubt was raised on Mosaic authorship of the Pentateuch and, in particular, of Genesis. The theorists postulate the existence of various sources within the text "distinguished from one another by their use of divine names, by peculiarities of style, and by perceptible differences of representation" (Skinner, xliv). Two of the major sources, the Yahwistic (J) and Elohistic (E) "documents" were combined into a composite narrative and later joined to the Priestly source by a postexilic editor to form the book in its present state.

While much of the linguistic criteria used by literacy critics must be considered suspect in determining the extent and nature of ancient sources, there does appear to be strong evidence in the narrative of the existence of composite material. A feature known as "doublets," in which two stories resemble one another, may, on occasion, reflect one particular event from two sources and with disparate perceptions. The most familiar instances cited as doublets are the encounters of Abraham and Isaac with Abimelech at Gerar (Ge 20, 26; cf. also 12:10ff.). Arguments regarding the authorship of Genesis may always remain speculative. Kidner (*Genesis,* 16ff.) has taken the source critics to task, while others within the literacy criticism camp have challenged the established consensus (e.g., John Van Seters, *Abraham in History and Tradition,* 1975; and Rolf Rendtorff, "Die Überlieferungs-geschichtliche Problem des Pentateuch," 1977). The way beyond the dilemma may consist in a recognition of the essential unity of the book and its message, within its canonical context. (For summary and possibilities see Eugene Carpenter, "The Pentateuch." ISBE, vol. 3. Grand Rapids: Eerdmans, 1985.) That Genesis exhibits an easily recognizable unity is beyond dispute despite the nature of its composition (cf. Skinner, lxv). That unity is enhanced, as we have previously noted, by the use of the *toledoth* formula by a redactor to provide the final canonical shape of the book.

III. CANONICAL SHAPE

From the outset, the focus of Genesis is on God and his dealings with humankind. The opening chapters relate the story of a God who creates. The emphasis is primarily on the Creator rather than his creation per se. Man himself is perceived in terms of the *imago dei*. The ensuing chapters depict a God who judges his creation. In the Abraham narrative, God is the Covenant Maker, the One who initiates interpersonal relationship with humanity. The story of Jacob emphasizes that aspect of God that transforms human life, while the Joseph narrative stresses God's providential sustaining power. In each instance, by reversing the causal nexus, one comes to an understanding of the nature of God through an appraisal of his acts. One must first ask what God has done (his *heilsgeschichte*) before one can determine what he is like.

The foundation for *heilsgeschichte* (salvation history) is encountered initially in creation. The ultimate good portrayed in the opening chapters of the book provides the ideal situation to which salvation history must return if it would have any meaning. As such, the canonical shape of the book indicates God's redemptive plan for the whole of his creation and that, ultimately, any adequate definition of redemption must take all of creation into account. Israel, therefore, cannot be considered, on this basis, as the sole object of salvation history (which might arguably be the case had Genesis begun at ch. 12 without reference to primeval history). Rather, within the framework of the book, Israel is given a crucial role in affecting God's reconciliation for all nations.

The opening chapters also serve to set forth the need for a salvation history at all. Having already depicted an ideal state, sin and judgment (or the curse) can be more readily understood in relative terms. Genesis begins with a perfect order and moves to a degenerate order. It is important to comprehend the problem posed in the early sections of the book if one is ever to come to grips with the solution to the problem in terms of covenant. An antidote has no particular meaning apart from a diagnosis of the disease. It is this study of the disease that occupies the attention of the first eleven chapters.

Genesis' primeval history, having related the inauguration of sin into the created order, then enumerates a history of increasing alienation from God. Beginning with the Fall, the problem of sin is generalized and expanded to reach its climax at the Tower of Babel. Sin has finally taken on cosmic proportions, and any solution must inevitably involve the entire universe.

As God calls the world into being in the primeval history of chs. 1–11, so during the patriarchal history, chs. 12–50, he calls a special people into existence. It is through this latter call that the divine purpose of salvation history will be accomplished. At the heart of God's call to the patriarchs lies a promise of divine blessing most often portrayed in terms of posterity and land. These promises represent the essence of the covenant relationship that God establishes with Israel. It is the motif of covenant that gives insight into the patriarchal age of the final thirty-nine chapters of the book.

In the light of the universalizing of sin portrayed in the first eleven chapters and the subsequent picture of a degenerate world it depicts, God acts to inaugurate the process of salvation history to bring an ultimate solution to the problem of sin and to restore the ideal of the original creation. God's call to Abraham, Isaac, Jacob, and Joseph takes the form of a command coupled with a promise. As each patriarch responds by obedience to the command, he is rewarded with the realization of the divine blessing. Two things should be noticed about God's promise and its consequent realization. First, the "theology of call" perceptible in (though not exclusive to) the patriarchal history is clearly contrasted to the "theology of the serpent" described in (though not exclusive to) the primeval history. Simply put, the serpent revealed untruth regarding God by bringing into question God's veracity and loving concern ("Did God really say," 3:1ff.). The human reaction was distrust of God, which led to disobedience (eating the forbidden fruit) and which, in turn, resulted in the divine curse (3:14–19). By contrast, in the "theology of the call," God reveals the truth about himself. It is the truth concerning his veracity and loving concern, integral to the covenant which he establishes with Israel's ancestry. The human response, in this instance, is displayed as trust—trust in a God who is able to stand behind his promises—and obedience to his commands. Such obedience elicits the divine favor and the tangible realization of the promised blessings.

Second, the promises are not always fully realized within the life span of a particular patriarch. Ge 15:13 specifically assigns the fulfillment of the promise of the land to a point beyond the Exodus. As such, the promises to the patriarchs and their realization function within a larger canonical framework stretching from Abraham to Joshua. The stories of the patriarchs are told, within the structure of the canon, with this eschatological dimension. The schema of promise-fulfillment extends beyond the bounds of Genesis itself, beyond the patriarchal age to the distant future. This is nowhere more clearly seen than in the final verses of the book. Joseph is dying. In his last spoken legacy to his progeny, he rehearses the truth about God: his veracity and loving concern. God will be true to his promises, he declares in 50:24. Then, as a reinforcing instruction to his brothers, Joseph asked that his bones be carried up from Egypt and buried in the land God had promised. For more than four hundred years Joseph's dead bones would remind Israel of a living theology that would encourage them to continue to hope in the eventual fulfillment of the promise.

Genesis will end where it began with an unapologetic focus of God. As creation declares the nature of God, so the story of re-creation, or salvation history, continues to define his character. In that regard, Genesis points beyond primeval and patriarchal histories to the reality of God whose creative acts are not confined to any specific era and who himself transcends history. A. W. Tozer may well have been describing Joseph's death when he penned, "When a man of God dies, nothing of God dies."

IV. OUTLINE

COMMENTARY

I. PRIMEVAL HISTORY (1:11–11:26)

A. Creation (1:1–2:25)

The emphasis of the entire book of Genesis is unmistakably upon God—a God who brings the world into being, acts sovereignly over his creation, enters into covenant relationship with it, transforms it, and maintains it. It represents a story of a relationship between the Creator and his creation. That relationship forms the basis of all of history in general and of salvation history in particular. God created the world teleologically. That is, there was a divine purpose for creation. Creation belonged to its Creator, and he had a revealed purpose for it.

The opening section of Genesis, perhaps the best-known portion of the Scripture, clearly establishes the God of the Bible as the God of creation. He calls the world into being and, in accordance with his will, he desires harmony with his creation (cf. Eph 1:10). The narrative of the first eleven chapters, however, demonstrates that the world God created is unresponsive to his call. God's will is distorted by the serpent and blatantly disobeyed by humankind. The result is the total disintegration of the harmonious, ideal state envisaged by the Creator.

Genesis' primeval history poses the problem that underlies the dilemma of relationship between Creator and creation, which spans both the OT and NT and is not ultimately resolved until the kingdom of God is realized eschatologically in the final scenes of the book of Revelation: "The kingdom of the world has become the kingdom of our Lord and of his Christ, and he will reign for ever and ever" (11:15).

1. The origin of the universe (1:1–2:3)

God occupies center stage in this chapter. Thirty-four times, in as many verses, the word *God* is paired with an action verb. The writer is more concerned with the "who" of creation than with the process or "how" of creation. The brevity of the chapter further underscores the scant regard the author demonstrates in the process of creation per se. Sun, moon, sky, and sea are summarily dismissed in a few brief sentences despite modern human fascination with the creative process. As such, the primary purpose of the narrative is to elicit praise of the Creator. In that sense, ch. 1 must be considered a liturgical hymn.

The idea of a liturgical hymn is enhanced by the symmetrical form of the chapter. Each new creation event is announced by the formula **and God said, "Let there be"** or something similar. Each creation is confirmed (**and it was so** or "God made/created/did it"). Each time but one the creation period is validated: **And God saw that it was good.** Finally, each Creation period is concluded with the words: **And there was evening and there was morning.** The structure of ch. 1 implies a creedal confession in the God who creates rather than a scientific dissertation about the origin of the world. The Bible is mute regarding the various scientific theories on how the world came into being, apart from affirming God's sovereign, creative role in it.

In the beginning God created can also be translated as a temporal clause: "When God began to create." In this latter way creation may be understood as an ongoing process. Either interpretation is feasible. The crucial verb, of course, is **created** (Heb. *bará*). It means "to cut" or "carve" or "shape" something. As such, contrary to some, *bará* does not necessarily connote the idea of creation *ex nihilo*. It may well express the concept of using material like a sculptor. This idea is borne out in v.2, which does not indicate that God began with nothing, but that there was an existing chaos. In this regard, v.2 begins with chaotic matter. Vv.3ff. portray the shaping of matter into an orderly universe. The Creator is One who brings order out of chaos not only in the natural world but, by implication, over personal history as well.

The opening chapter of the book communicates much about the character of the Creator God it introduces. From his creative acts, one can deduce the nature of his being. Because the world did not come into existence by accident, but reflects order and design, one can postulate a Deity who designs teleologically. The universe is an expression of his will. The immensity of creation affords a conception of the innate power of the Creator. He exercises sovereignty over all that he has made. Indeed, the means by which creation was brought into being was effortless. God characteristically spoke the world into being (vv.3, 5, 6, 8, 9, 10, 11, 14, 20, 22, 24, 26, 28, 29; cf. Jn 1:1–3). The designation for **God** (Heb. *Elohim*) itself connotes the idea of strength. *El* is the strongest One. By combining these two perceptions of the God of Genesis, both his purpose and power, one recognizes a Deity who has the ability to fulfill his original purpose for creation and redeem an unresponsive world. The kind of God who can create is the kind of God who can re-create.

From the beginning, God is encountered as One who is separate from his creation. He himself is uncreated. His existence is apparent. He is as real as his creation. As he calls it into existence, he calls it to harmonious responsiveness and obedience. As he has committed himself to his creation, so creation is invited to commit itself to its Creator, who has demonstrated himself trustworthy. Creation cannot exist apart from its Creator. It is inextricably bound to him. He, by contrast, is transcendent and not bound by the nature he controls. He creates freely and for the aesthetic delight of both Creator and creature (cf. Job 38:7; Ps 19:1).

The climax of the passage is the creation of humankind **in our image"** (v.26). That is, humankind is to exercise dominion over creation (v. 26). In so doing, humans partake of the nature or image of God by virtue of the fact that such exercise should demonstrate rationality, purpose, and authority. The text culminates in 2:1–3 with the reference to the seventh day. The process of creation having ended, God **rested** (Heb. *sabat,* from which we derive the word "Sabbath"). It represents a day of celebration that comes from achievement and models for us a Sabbath or rest that comes from a satisfying conclusion to a job well done and the recognition that all of life is God's gift.

2. The origin of man (2:4–25)

Ch. 2 focuses on the climax of God's creation and in so doing draws an important distinction between himself and his creation. *Elohim* is the Author of the entire universe, including man and, therefore, has authority over all. Man, by contrast, is earth-bound and geocentric (v.7). He derives authority on the basis of God's gift (1:29–30). As the climax of creation, man exercises dominion over creation and, in so doing, reflects an attribute of godlike-ness. Rather than being a separate and parallel story of creation, ch. 2 functions in such a way as to set forth the ideal situation in which the drama of man will take place.

The scene is defined (vv.8–17) as **Eden** (Heb. "pleasure"). Its location is specified (vv.10–14). Its nature is variously described. While every tree is pleasant to the sight and good for food (v.9), two trees are distinguished. The trees disclose the nature of God's grace to the man whom he has created. The **tree of life** encapsulates the mystery of life. It represents the source of life to which man must have access and on which he must depend. God has provided this external source. Its presence symbolizes life that is both immortal and pleasurable. Divorced from this source of eternal existence, man's life will no longer possess the qualities of godlike transcendence. In Rev 2:7, the tree of life refers to fellowship with God.

The **tree of the knowledge of good and evil** (v.17) makes responsible human existence possible. Like the tree of life, there is nothing of intrinsic distinctiveness with the tree of knowledge. It is chosen simply to give definition to God's command. When man knows the command of God, he knows what is good. The negation of the command is evil. By obeying the command of God and not eating of this tree, man demonstrates his compliance with the purpose of God. Since good and evil are relative terms, evil is perceived by the author as violating God's design. Creation was intended to be theocentric. Only thus can harmonious existence be perpetuated. The tree of knowledge, then, highlights a created order that is maintained by obedience to the Creator. That was the only knowledge necessary for man: to acquiesce to the will of God and

continue to experience harmony with the rest of creation as well as with God or participate in disobedience, which will bring chaos to the created order. The loss of man's innocence results not from his knowledge of these alternatives but from his conscious decision to defy God's command. One is guilty on the basis of what one does rather than what one knows.

Vv.16 and 17 articulate the dilemma of ch. 2. How shall man respond to the Creator? Will he recognize the Creator's sovereign right over his creation? How will the human interact with the rest of the created order? Will he use it for God's glory or for his own satisfaction? What will become of man himself? Will he become self-destructive? But before the drama unfolds with answers to these questions, the emergence of woman is related in 2:18–25. Man is no longer alone. A human community now exists in Eden to further the ideal of creation's harmonious coexistence. The man and the woman are of the same nature (vv.22, 23) and are brought into being in true partnership (vv.18, 20), bound together in an intense love (v.24) that allows them freely to be themselves (cf. v.25).

B. Sin Enters the Created Order (3:1–6:8)

1. The fall of man (3:1–24)

A new character is introduced into the narrative in the form of a serpent. How one interprets the serpent is immaterial to the intent of the plot. The character of the serpent is clear enough. It is intrinsic to neither God nor man but exits apart from each, possessing an inimitable craftiness (3:1a). The introduction of the serpent brings into focus again the problem posed in 2:16–17. In the ensuing dialogue with the woman, the Creator's authority is maliciously challenged, realities are distorted, and God himself is misrepresented. By appealing to the unreasonableness of God's command, the serpent sets itself over against God. God is no longer depicted as benevolent, desiring the harmonious well-being of his creation. He is defined by the serpent as selfishly malevolent, with only his own best interests at stake.

In undermining the correlation between God's commands and man's own best interest, the serpent portrays a false view of sin as something beneficial to man. In so doing the serpent creates for man a false view of man by promising him elevation to the level of deity (vv.4–5): **You will be like God.** The temptation posed is great. Man becomes suspicious of God. He is no longer to be trusted. Sin is no longer considered destructive. Man's own interests are best served by self-determination.

Man chooses the path of the serpent and thereby usurps the divine prerogatives and becomes his own authority. Distrust leads to disobedience. Eve succumbs to the persuasion of the Tempter (v.6). Sin quickly spreads to Adam and results in shame (v.7). They are ill at ease together. The disintegration of harmony within creation has begun. The serpent's promise of their eyes being opened (v.5) comes true but in a distorted and pathetic manner (v.7).

With renewed encounter with God and, feeling the guilt of their crime, Adam and Eve hide. Edenic Paradise is transformed into a courtroom. The accused attempt to rationalize their participation in the crime (vv.12–13). The pathetic nature of their defense is exposed. Sentence is decreed by the Judge (vv.14–19). A curse is placed sequentially upon the serpent in its

creatureliness, upon the woman in her childbirth, and upon man in his labors.

With respect to the demonic force God promises the ultimate subjugation of the serpent by the seed of the woman. It is the good news that the damage caused by the serpent is only temporary. The curse is extended beyond Adam and Eve's experience of toil, pain, and death to a cosmic judgment as well; for the earth itself is called to yield thorns and thistles. Redemption, if it is to occur, will necessarily have to include the entire cosmos and not merely man. All this is a result of man's distrust of the Creator.

Perhaps the most remarkable thing about God's sentence is that it is shot through with evidence of his grace toward his creation. Not only is that loving-kindness perceived explicitly (cf. v.21), but there is a hint of a plan to redeem his creation (v.15). God will not give up on his world. This grace is also apparent in the mitigation of the punishment. The guilty pair, deserving death (cf. 2:17), are not only spared, but protected. They are given, again, the gift of life, albeit outside of Paradise and removed from the Tree (or Source) of Life (vv.22–24). The way back to God is deliberately more difficult and prefigures the elaborately designed systems to make atonement possible in the OT. The **cherubim** as guardians of Paradise (v.24) are elsewhere depicted as guardians of the Holy of Holies and the ark it contained (Ex 36:35; 37:7–9). Only when Christ died are those guardians "set aside"; the veil embroidered with the cherubim is torn, and the way to God is reopened (Mt 27:51).

2. The spread of sin (4:1–16)

The fall of humankind witnesses the enlargement of sin in terms of its occurrence and intensity. Ch. 4 relates the first murder and its consequences.

The logic of alienation from God is alienation from one's fellows. Cain, whose name is derived from the Hebrew *qânâh* meaning "to get" (v.1), is brought into confrontation with his younger brother Abel (Heb. "vapour," "nothingness"). For whatever reason, Abel's offering was accepted by YHWH, whereas Cain's was not. The predicament thus presented is a common one. Life deals its bitter blows. How will Cain deal with it? Presumably the older brother bore some culpability in the rejection of his offering (cf. v.7a). The dilemma to do good or evil is dramatically portrayed in the warning Cain receives from God (v.7). Sin aggressively stalks its prey like a wild animal, eager to destroy the harmony of the created order (cf. 1Pe 5:8). Whereas the serpent illustrated the subtle craftiness of sin, evil is here depicted as powerful and destructive. Yet, nevertheless, it is a force that can be mastered (v.7b), though, alas, not on this occasion by Cain.

The latter half of the narrative concerns Cain's punishment and has similarities with the judgment of 3:9ff. With inquiry (vv.9–10), judgment (v.11), and sentence (v.12) culminating in banishment (v.16), Cain is condemned to be a fugitive away from the presence of God yet incomprehensibly marked and protected by the God whom he has offended. Cain has not only been guilty of murder but of lying and insolence to God (v.9). He has abrogated his responsibility toward his brother (v.9b). By repeating the term **brother** three times (vv.9, 10, 11), God asserts the responsible nature of our existence within the created order. Murder, then, is not only an attack against God's sovereignty over creation in that all life belongs to him, but a strike against the harmony intended between creatures.

3. The descendants of Cain (4:17–24)

The path of disobedience continues to be traced through the line of Cain and particularly in the song of Lamech (vv.23–24), where man now asserts the right to take vengeance and hence further challenges the rule of God. Creation is set on a course of disintegration through the family of Cain evident in an explosion of sin.

4. The birth of Seth (4:25–26)

Ch. 4 ends with a ray of hope for an alternative outcome to the story of humankind. Adam and Eve give birth to another son, Seth, to replace the murdered Abel. The tragic path exposed by Cain and his progeny is not the final word. The family of Adam has produced two divergent streams juxtaposed with each other, one working against God's design for creation, the other affirming man's dependence on the Creator (v.26). While Cain's line is described only as far as Lamech, it is the progeny of Seth that will occupy our attention in subsequent chapters.

5. The ten patriarchs from Adam to Noah (5:1–32)

By bringing the unhappy story of humanity's increasing alienation from God to a close, ch. 5 serves to introduce the narrative of Noah by means of genealogy. The Adam story has been concluded. Adam's line of descent through Seth is now of principle concern to the sacred historian.

The genealogy comprises ten generations, tracing the drama of humankind from the Creation to the Flood. A second extended genealogy of ten generations occurs in 11:10–29, outlining the period from the Flood to Abraham. These are not exhaustive lists, but by selecting ten, the narrative suggests the completion of a historical era. Similarly, the seven generations of Cain (4:16–22) and the three periods of fourteen generations each in Mt 1 (despite the fact that kings Ahaziah, Joash, and Amaziah are omitted to achieve the fourteen generations in the second period) are examples of selective genealogies that imply the completion of eras.

Though the text appears to indicate a view that life prior to the Flood was quantitatively longer, the lack of precise information inherent in these genealogies may reflect a less than accurate accounting of years. If one compares the ancient Summarian King List, one discovers a list of Mesopotamian kings that omits certain names while attributing the years of their reigns to predecessors. That may well be the case here. In the midst of the chapter's rehearsal of the life and death of the patriarchs, one man's life stands out as qualitatively distinct. Enoch is described twice as one who **walked with God** (vv.22, 24). It is language that indicates intimacy, integrity, and obedience. As a result of such piety, Enoch is taken into the presence of God, presumably without experiencing death. The chapter ends with an account of the birth of Noah. It is upon him that the future redemption of creation will depend. Through Noah the hope born with Seth continues to shine.

6. The wickedness of the people of the earth (6:1–8)

The extent of man's depravity reaches its climax in this passage. The line of Cain holds no promise for humankind and there is a breakdown in the line of Seth (if we understand "the sons of God" [bᵉnê 'ĕlôhîm] in v.2 as Sethites). God pronounces judgment upon the entire human race (v.3). The context suggests that 120 years will pass before judgment will be executed. There will still be opportunity for man to repent and affirm God's design for creation. During this probationary period, God's purpose for creation is at stake. God's intent has been thwarted. If creation cannot recover and become willingly subject to its Creator, God will take severe measures to eradicate his creation (v.7).

The spread and intensifying of sin depicted in earlier chapters reaches its peak in ch. 6 with the intermarriage of the **sons of God** with **the daughters of men.** Though the sons of God may refer to heavenly beings, it is more likely to mean Seth's progeny, which the context of 4:25–26 might imply (cf. Dt 14:1; Hos 1:10). The interpretation of **Nephilim** determines, in large part, one's understanding of the sons of God. Nephilim need not mean giants, but may simply be synonymous with "mighty men" or "overlords" (v.4; cf. 10:8). The reason, then, that God is so troubled with his creation is that even the redemptive line of Seth (the sons of God) has not lived up to its potential. By blatant disregard of God's will for creation's well-being, the Sethites promote their own interest (v.2). God is grieved by the unresponsiveness of his creation to his will, and in v.6 we gain insight into his heartache.

To this point in the narrative of Genesis, sin is merely perceived in its universalizing tendencies. Now we confront, in a vivid manner, the effect that such sin has on the Creator. God is not One who is detached from his creation; he is One who has emotionally invested in it. He enters into the world's pain and brokenness. And in that anguish, God resolves to begin again. Noah becomes the means of that new possibility (v.8) and, again, the light of hope is not extinguished.

C. Judgment on Sin (6:9–9:17)

1. The Flood (6:9–8:19)

The toledothic formula (**This is the account of. . .**") in v.9 introduces a new section to the book. Just as 2:4 inaugurated the story of Adam, so 6:9 begins the story of Noah with a brief synopsis of his character. In contrast to Noah's righteousness, the world is thrice condemned as corrupt (vv.11–12) and twice cited as filled with violence (vv. 11, 13)! So God declares his intent to destroy his creation by means of a cosmic flood (6:13, 17; 7:4, 23). By so doing, the contagious spread of sin seen in earlier chapters will be halted, if only temporarily.

Despite the seeming wrath of God's plan, the divine mercy is clearly seen in the instructions given to Noah, which will enable the family of Noah to survive the Flood (6:18). Provision is also made for the continuity of the animal world. Two of every species are to be included in the ark that Noah is commissioned to build (vv.19ff.). Lovely is the description of obedience that was the hallmark of Noah's life: **Noah did everything just as God commanded him** (v.22). Noah would not merely survive the flood, but he would carry the promise of a new humanity into a new age.

The Deluge occurs as it was predicted. It is not within the scope of this commentary to express an opinion regarding the natural or historical features of the Flood. This is evidently a historical recollection of a fact rooted in history. God executes judgment on a recalcitrant creation (7:4, 6, 10ff.). This harsh indictment upon the world (6:7, 13, 17; 7:4, 23) betrays, not a God acting vindictively, but One who grieves over his creation (6:6). At the moment of judgment, Noah and his family are ushered into the ark. One

senses the compassion and mercy of God in the acknowledgment that **the LORD shut him in** (7:16). While he is decisive in destroying the world, God is also careful to ensure the salvation of righteous Noah. God has not given up on creation.

The new beginning is stated succinctly: **But God remembered Noah** (8:1). It portrays a faithful and loving God who does not forget his people in their distress (cf. Ex 2:24). It is this remembering that enables the possibility of a new creation. Noah "steps into a virgin world washed clean by judgment" (Kidner, 92).

2. The covenant of the rainbow (8:20–9:17)

The first event that occurs in this new creation is an act of worship (8:20). God is given his rightful place. In response to Noah's devotion, God resolves to remain with his creation despite humankind's propensity to sin (v.21). His sustaining the world (cf. Col 1:17) is totally an act of grace. Notice the similarities of the "two" creations. The image of God remains (9:6; cf. 1:27), as does the mandate to be fruitful and multiply (9:1; cf. 1:28).

To guarantee God's resolve never again (thrice repeated, 8:21; 9:11, 15) to destroy the earth, God establishes a covenant with Noah. It is a unilateral covenant of grace embracing every living creature in its generous scope (9:10, 12). God's **never again** is symbolized in the choice of the rainbow as a perpetual sign that he will never forget his promise (vv.13–17).

D. Sin Continues Unabated (9:18–11:26)

1. Noah's blessings and curses (9:18–29)

It is not long before the new world of Noah experiences again the effect of sin. The particular nature of the sin here is unclear. The incident described is surely a euphemism for some sexual indiscretion. The point of the story is simply to compare the faithfulness of Shem and Japheth with the dishonor of Ham and leads into a curse on Canaan (vv.25–27). It is probable that etiological purposes are at work here, and the references to Noah's sons suggest future conflict between Israel anticipated in Shem and the Canaanites.

2. The Table of Nations descended from Noah (10:1–32)

The family of nations is represented here for three possible reasons: to satisfy human interest, to illustrate the interrelatedness of human clans and their place in the economy of one Creator, and to demonstrate the fulfillment of the mandate given to Noah: "Be fruitful and increase in number and fill the earth" (9:1, 7). The families of Japheth and Ham are dealt with first with the effect of clearing the field for the family of Shem, which will occupy most of our attention in subsequent chapters. The family of Japheth is handled summarily (vv.2–5). They are described as coastal peoples. Ham receives the major attention (vv.6–20) with particular interest given to Nimrod (vv.8–12) and Canaan (vv.15–19). Nimrod's story of earthly success is tarnished somewhat with the references to Babel and Assyria while the cursed Canaan will eventually suffer dispossession of its land by Israel.

The family of Shem will now become the main concern of the OT and, presumably, the specific line of Eber (vv.21, 25ff.), source of the word "Hebrew." More detailed attention is given to the descendants of Shem in 11:10–30.

3. The confusion of the languages at Babel (11:1–9)

Primeval history reaches its apex of mayhem in the episode of Babel. The story gives an explanation for the diversity of languages and for the spread of peoples over the whole earth. In the latter sense it relates to the preceding chapter. The project is grandiose, capturing the feeling of pride and self-sufficiency. As such, it represents humanity in conflict with God, not only in terms of independence from God, but possibly resistance to the idea of populating the whole earth (v.4, cf. 1:28; 9:1, 7). At any rate, God's decisive statement, **Come, let us** (v.7) stands in stark contrast to the ineffectual **Come, let's** of the people (vv.3–4). The solution to the language confusion will await the birth of the church when the effects of Babel will be reversed (Ac 2:5–11).

4. The descendants of Shem (11:10–26)

The final section in Genesis' primeval history is a singular *toledoth* pointing to Israel. Ch. 10 depicts the spread of humankind through the earth while this passage particularizes the story to one specific line. Genesis is now ready to recount its patriarchal history. The sin of Adam has universalized, and humankind is impotent to retard its devastation. The Creator must become the Redeemer. The line of Shem, then, must be understood as the hope of the *whole* world.

A symbolic ten generations from Shem to Abraham neatly matches the ten generations from Adam to Noah (5:1–32). The number suggests completeness. God's choice of this one line does not betray any special merit on the part of the family of Shem (cf. Dt 7:6–7). It is not even conclusive that he was firstborn of Noah's sons. Though, in any case, God set aside the laws of primogeniture in the cases of Jacob (25:23) and Ephraim (48:19–20). Indeed, the choice was rather strange in view of God's mandate to populate the earth, for the end of the *toledoth* announces that Sarah is barren (11:30)! That is where the hopeless conclusion of primeval history takes us. That is where patriarchal history must begin.

II. PATRIARCHAL HISTORY (11:27–50:26)

A. Abraham (11:27–25:18)

1. Abram's call to obedience (11:27–14:24)

Essential to our understanding of the patriarchal narratives is their connection with primeval history. The latter culminates with the widespread universalizing of sin in the created order. The problem of sin's magnitude is posed in such a way as to threaten the "good" of God's creation. The patriarchal history represents a possible solution to the dilemma. The God who calls the world into existence now calls a community into being. Is the Creator able to be a Redeemer? The future destiny of all humankind is wrapped up in the future of a particular people. As the primeval saga leads to despair, so the patriarchal stories evoke hope.

The call of God to Abram (12:1) can be properly understood in this context. It is a command directed to a situation of hopelessness to which Abram responds by obedience. The succession of clauses relating God's call and Abram's response gives rise to a consideration of the nature of a God who can elicit such obedience. He is a God who initiates relationships with humankind and exercises authority over them. He alone will determine human destinies. Obviously Abram perceives this God who utters

the call as One able to stand behind the promises of vv.2–3, for the patriarch embraces the call and believes the promise (v.4).

The theology of the call (12:1–4) stands in contrast to the theology of the serpent (3:1–13). Whereas the latter questioned the veracity of God and elicited distrust and disobedience, which lead to the curse (vv.14–19), so now the call reveals the truth about God, which prompts trust and obedience and which, in turn, leads to blessing. The cycle of sin's dominance is now broken, and the potential for re-creation realized.

Significantly, Abram is depicted both in his fidelity (12:1–9; 13:1–18) and infidelity (12:10–20). The struggle to trust is never easy. Intrinsic to the call and standing sentinel over it is the faithfulness of a God who will not allow the promise to be placed in jeopardy. Faced with impending crises, Abram responds first in a cowardly, underhanded way (12:10–20), taking matters into his own hands even at the risk of sacrificing his wife. In the second instance (13:1–18), he acts to the contrary and trusts God to the point that he is prepared to risk the promise itself! As a result, the covenant is not only kept intact, but it is reiterated with greater magnitude than before (13:14–17).

Ch. 14 recounts the first recorded war in Scripture. The significance of its occurrence rests in the fact of Lot's involvement (v.12) and, as a result, Abram's intervention. Abram's victory is credited to **God Most High** (vv.19, 20) by Melchizedek, king of Salem (Jerusalem), who greets Abram with a blessing. The enigma of Melchizedek's role was somewhat mitigated by David in Ps 110, when he sat on Melchizedek's throne and sang of a greater than Melchizedek who would one day occupy the throne of Zion. The greatest interest in Melchizedek is expressed in Heb 5–7, where Jesus Christ is depicted as a type of Melchizedek. Here in Genesis the "king of righteousness" (Heb 7:2) receives only scant mention.

2. God's commitment to the covenant (15:1–18:15)

a. The covenant dramatized (15:1–21)

The divine revelation of 15:1–5 grows out of chs. 13 and 14. Abram had shown himself to be faithful to the promise of God in his dealings with Lot. Now God, in a crucial dramatization, binds himself to the Abramic covenant. **Do not be afraid, Abram. I am your shield, your very great reward** (v.1) is a declaration of God's protection. The reward Abram is promised (v.1) stands in contrast to the spoil he refused in 14:22–24. The covenant takes the form of a promise of an heir and of innumerable descendants. The reference to a **reward** (v.1) also represents a promise of land (vv.18–21). But while the earnest of land is conceivable for Abram, the patriarch challenges the promise of an heir (vv.2–3). Abram has no son and recognizes the utter impossibility of childbearing in old age (cf. Ro 4:18–25). Can God be trusted not only to indicate his loving concern for the patriarch but to demonstrate his ability to transform a situation of hopelessness into the realization of the promise?

In response to Abram's challenge, God simply reiterates the promise (v.5). On this occasion Abram accepts the word of God as trustworthy. He believes God to be God (v.6)! Such faith in the God of promise is commended as the right thing. Ro 4:18ff. makes clear that Abram's faith is in the One who speaks to humankind's barren

and helpless condition and thereby affords a genuine genesis. Again, God's reassuring word and Abram's ready obedience are paratactically juxtaposed. We are not told what transpired between vv.2 and 6 that prompted Abram to ready obedience. His response is without explanation. It is simply stated that he believed God. That belief brings him into right relationship with God.

Still Abram seeks reassurance (v.8). Faith never exists in a vacuum. So God graciously and dramatically binds himself to this righteous one and thereby illustrates his commitment to the covenant promises he has made (vv.9–21). The rather strange perspective of this particular covenant lies in the fact that it is God who unilaterally binds himself to the promise. Nowhere is Abram asked to walk through the body parts of the beasts. This is an act of God's sovereign grace and demands nothing more of Abram than his trust. And, as if to prepare him for experiences when such trust may not be easy and to alert Abram to the fact that the realization of the promise will not be realized immediately, God rehearses a short synopsis of Israel's future (vv.13–16). But even though the promise will tarry, Abram is encouraged to wait. Its advent is certain (cf. Hab 2:3).

b. The birth of Ishmael (16:1–16)

The following episodes (16:1–18:15) underline God's commitment to the covenant despite any distrust on Abram's part. God alone stands behind the promise, and Abram's failure to trust God will not reflect negatively on God's veracity. ("Let God be true, and every man a liar," Ro 3:4.) By the end of ch. 18, Abram is still without an heir, and ch. 16 tells of Abram's taking matters into his own hands. Having experienced God's great promise and responding to it in faith, Abram functions in a way that will help the process along. Abram has failed to understand God as One who creates *ex nihilo* and effects redemption in situations of barrenness. Nevertheless, Ishmael participates in the Abramic blessing (16:10) but, in conflict with his kinsmen, will not enjoy the blessing of land.

c. Abram becomes Abraham (17:1–27)

The covenant established, there follows a fuller description of what is involved in this special relationship that God has initiated. The covenant marks the birth of a salvation history that is symbolized both in the change of Abram's name (hence a change in his status) and the visible sign of belonging to God (circumcision). The covenant is more than an agreement between two consenting parties; it becomes the very fiber of the community's life. The life of faith must be marked by complete allegiance to the all-powerful God (v.1). Unfortunately, Abraham does not comprehend the full extent of newness inherent in the promise and scorns the idea of another heir apart from Ishmael (v.17). While Ishmael will be blessed (v.20), the promise must be extended through the child of God's grace.

d. The promise of Isaac (18:1–15)

The theme of incredulity is extended to Sarah who views with derision the promise of a son in her old age (v.12). There is nothing new in the message brought by the divine visitants to Abraham, but Sarah must now be brought into partnership in the faith venture. Reason argues against the promise. Faith confronts the heart of the issue: **Is anything too hard for the LORD?** (v.14). That is the fundamental question now imposed upon the community of faith. The answer to it will determine the future and the very existence of the community.

3. Abraham's failure: Covenant in jeopardy (18:16–21:34)

a. The destruction of Sodom and Gomorrah (18:16–19:38)

An important aspect of the covenant is God's remembering. In the Flood narrative, creation is saved because God remembers Noah (8:1). Israel is rescued in Egypt because God remembers the patriarchal covenant (Ex 2:24). In the present text, Lot and his family are saved because God remembers Abraham (19:29). God responds to Abraham's intercession for Lot and demonstrates his grace by showing kindness to Lot for Abraham's sake.

Abraham's special relationship to God is articulated in 18:16–33 as Abraham intercedes for Sodom. V.19 implies a particular friendship and the esteem in which God holds Abraham. That such an esteem is mutual is evidenced in the patriarchal prayer, which exhibits Abraham's faith in the justice of God (v.25), reverence and humility in his manner of address (v.27), and love for the inhabitants of the city. By contrast, Lot, who is probably a man of distinction in Sodom (19:1), is influentially impotent to dissuade Sodom from continuing in sin (18:20). In an attempt to show hospitality to God's messengers, Lot succeeded only in placing his own daughters at risk. This further enraged the citizenry, and Lot had to be rescued by those whom he had sought to protect (19:4–11)! Lot was not able to carry any weight even with his own family members (v.14). His own indecision contributed to the final disintegration of his family (vv.16–20).

Clearly, Lot is rescued not because of any virtue in him, but solely because of God's love for Abraham. As such, the story serves to highlight an alternative view of God as One who shows patient mercy and grace to a reluctant convert within the broader context of One who punishes sin and destroys the children of disobedience. God is depicted as One who is not indifferent either to sin itself or to means whereby humankind can be rescued from its consequences.

The horrifying narrative closes with Abraham overlooking the quiet devastation of Sodom and Gomorrah (19:27–29). God's judgment is vividly portrayed. It is an image Abraham is not likely to forget. Lot has fled to Zoar, and fear is his constant companion (v.30). His end is one of ignominy, and his legacy is Moab and Ammon (vv.31–38).

b. Abraham's sin at Gerar (20:1–18)

Despite the ominous example of disobedience in the previous chapter, Abraham lapses back into faithlessness and, just before the birth of the child of promise, the covenant is once more placed in jeopardy. Only divine intervention extricates the patriarch from the entanglements of his scheming. God prevents Abimelech from touching Sarah (v.6), appears in a dream to the king to disclose the truth about the situation (vv.3–7), and hears the prayer of Abraham for Abimelech's healing (vv.7, 17).

Ironically Abraham's lack of faith is juxtaposed to Abimelech's faith. The man outside the covenant promise demonstrates faith to the man of faith who exhibits none! God must stand as sole guarantor of the covenant. Abraham's failure is a result of a wrong perception of the situation (v.11), fear (v.11b), the casuistry of a half-truth

(v.12), and expediency (v.13). And, as his righteous action led to the saving of another in the previous chapter, so here his faithlessness jeopardizes the life of another (v.3). One individual's acts often profoundly affect many.

c. The birth of Isaac (21:1–34)

God's promise initially articulated in 12:2 finally reaches its fulfillment in the birth of a son. The promise has defied reason, and from the barrenness of Sarah's womb, as from one who is "as good as dead" (Ro 4:19; Heb 11:12), the child of the promise appears. Isaac is born entirely by the grace of the God who "calls things that are not as though they were" (Ro 4:17). For Abraham and Sarah, there was no basis for hope within themselves. But by reliance upon God, the question posed in 18:14 finds its affirmation. So the God who spoke into the chaos and molded creation from it and breathed the breath of life into Adam's lifeless form is the same God who speaks a word of promise to the barren womb of Sarah and brings to it fertility. The same God would one day speak into the cavernous tombs of Lazarus and Jesus and give life to the dead!

Inevitable conflict arises between the child of the promise and the child of expediency (vv.8–21). Yet, while one is undeniably chosen to perpetuate the promise (v.12), both are loved and cared for by God. This is clearly seen in the crisis faced by Hagar and Ishmael, where God redresses a situation of hopelessness; once again, in the midst of death (v.16), God extends his grace in abundant provision (v.19) and blessing (vv.18 20). Ishmael means "God hears."

Ch. 21 concludes with a pact between Abraham and Abimelech in which, contrary to the previous chapter, Abraham deals with candor and clarity. The basis of the relationship between these two is now established on mutual loyalty and cemented in the form of a covenant (vv.27, 32). It remains to be seen whether Abraham is really now living by faith.

4. Abraham's success: The test of obedience (22:1-24)

The seriousness of faith is nowhere more clearly highlighted than in the narrative of Abraham's offering Isaac to God. This is no play acting but a genuine struggle that brings the patriarch to the pinnacle of his walk with God. God genuinely must know the extent of Abraham's trust in the call. Abraham's response to God's voice is immediate (vv.1-3). They have a history with one another, and though the command to sacrifice Isaac is absurdly incomprehensible, Abraham demonstrates faith in God's dependability. This is a God whom he can trust though he may not understand. We are assured in Heb 11:17-19 that Abraham is convinced that God can "raise the dead" and so will give Isaac back from death.

The enigmatic summons to kill Isaac threatens the promise. Abraham will be left bereft of progeny and a future hope. It is a negation of all that has been accomplished in the miracle birth of the son. It is a return to hopelessness. The significant difference this time from other occasions in which the promise was placed in jeopardy lies in the fact that it is the Promise-Giver, not the promise-bearer who is the responsible party. And since the Promise-Giver stands as sole guarantor of the promise (15:1-21), a threat to the promise is a threat to the veracity of God. Abraham must rely a priori on the Promise-Giver, otherwise the promise is of no intrinsic value.

The issue at stake supersedes the concept of promise per se and focuses on a God who demands unequivocal trust and allegiance. It is a message of timeless character particularly appropriate at times when the church is inclined to accommodate her standards to the world and compromise faith to something much less demanding. Abraham's obedience illustrates the serious nature of faith and encourages the community to allow God to be fully God.

The narrative concludes with an affirmation of God as Provider (v.14). In the appearance of the ram (v.13), God shows grace and sets the entire story in the context of providential care. In response to Abraham's obedience, God once more reiterates the divine obligations of the covenant (vv.16-18). The promise is still very much alive.

5. The future of the covenant assured (23:1-25:18)

The Abraham narrative has run its course. Through trials and tribulations the promise has remained intact. Chapter 22 took us to the climax of the patriarch's relationship with God. It is now time for the promise to be passed on to subsequent generations.

a. The death of Sarah (23:1-20)

In the midst of the section on Abraham and Sarah, the writer to the Hebrews (11:8-19) makes it clear that "all these people were still living by faith when they died"; and though they "admitted that they were aliens and strangers," they were nonetheless "longing for a better country." In such a summary, the importance of the present chapter is perceived. The investment in the piece of land to bury Sarah is an investment in the promise. It is a last witness to God's promise of this land for Abraham and Sarah's progeny.

And as in keeping with Joseph's last wish (50:25), Sarah's tomb bears witness to a living hope.

b. A bride for Isaac (24:1–67)

In Abraham's old age (v.1) it is imperative that a wife be found for Isaac if the promise is to be perpetuated. As before, God intervenes providentially (though hidden) to ensure success. The emphasis is not so much placed upon the leading of God per se as it is upon the willingness of those who put themselves at his disposal and discover his guidance in retrospect. The aged patriarch displays a profound faith in the covenant God (v.7). The promise cannot be invalidated or modified by generations yet unborn.

The actors in this drama are engagingly colorful: Abraham, characterizing the defiant faith of a seasoned man of God; the old servant exhibiting devotion to his master and determined to execute his vow with prudence and faith; the lovely Rebekah, impulsive and adventurous; and Laban, already showing aspects of the conniving intrigue that will later mark his encounters with Jacob. The story, not without humor, is eloquently told in such a way that God is nowhere visible but everywhere perceived. Issuing from his solemn vow with Abraham, the old servant asks for God's guidance (vv.12–14) and is immediately (v.15) rewarded handsomely. Rebekah is more than a man could possibly hope for, combining as she does beauty, purity, gracious hospitality, and good family credentials. It is scarcely conceivable that he could have doubted for a moment that this was the girl for whom he had prayed (v.21).

Laban is portrayed as a religious man whose language betrays knowledge of Abraham's God (vv.31, 50). Familiar as we are with Laban from the Jacob narrative, it is certain in showing deference to Abraham's servant that Laban noticed the ring, the bracelets, and the camels. Perhaps he is motivated by more than piety both in welcoming the stranger into his home (vv.31–33) and in supporting Rebekah in her resolve to accompany him (vv.50–51). As the deal is struck, God is acknowledged as having been at work in the sequence of events (vv.27, 48, 56). Lovely is the resolve of Rebekah (v.58). She is asked to leave the familiarity and security of home to traverse difficult and potentially dangerous terrain to love a man whom she has never set eyes upon (cf. 1Pe 1:8). Rebekah's simple, laconic response (v.58) embodies the life of faith and results in blessing (v.60), undeserved love (v.67), and the perpetuity of the promise. God has faithfully brought matters committed to him to a happy end.

c. The death of Abraham (25:1–18)

With the death of Abraham, the promise passes to Isaac. Abraham dies a friend of God, having been the recipient of God's goodness and blessing throughout a long, full, and fruitful life (vv.7–8). He is buried with Sarah, testifying, as we have observed before, to the fidelity of the God of the covenant. He dies in the confidence that all has been done to ensure the transmission of the promise.

Both Isaac and Ishmael are present for the burial ceremony (cf. 35:29). While the special election of Isaac is acknowledged, it is clear that Abraham cared for and loved each of his sons (including those mentioned in v.2; cf. v.6). Significantly, the narrative ends with a rehearsal of Ishmael's descendants (vv.12–18). Though not the benefactor of the promise itself, Ishmael's future is also blessed by God. However, for the continuance of the special promise of salvation history, we must look elsewhere. Isaac and his family have become the repository of the promise, and it is to their continuing story that we now must turn.

B. Jacob (25:19-37:2)

1. Jacob's deceitful character (25:19-27:45)

One of the great scandals of the book of Genesis is God's choice of Jacob as a bearer of the promise. This schemer is trouble from his very inception and epitomizes the sinful condition of fallen nature described earlier in the primeval history (vv.1-11). Jacob poses a problem for the perpetuity of the promise. One is forced to ask whether this is the best with which God has to work. Can the covenant survive the self-seeking interest of Jacob? Will God continue to stand as a sole guarantor of the promise committed to Abraham?

The opening section of the Jacob narrative illustrates the need for some kind of transformation in the life of this patriarch if the promise is to have any impact on the promise-bearer. Jacob's actions betray a return to the defective theology of the serpent first seen in ch. 3 (see "Canonical Shape" in the introduction). By taking things into their own hands, neither Jacob nor Rebekah places any dependence on the promise. Such disbelief in the God of the covenant invariably leads to distrust and inevitable disobedience. Jacob resorts to "playing God." Jacob is an offense to sensitive minds. Yet in God's choice of Jacob as a bearer of the promise and the eventual transformation of his name and character (32:22-32), one sees the earnestness of hope for us all. It is God's strange strategy to choose "the lowly things of this world and the despised things—and the things that

are not—to nullify the things that are, so that no one may boast before him" (1Co 1:28-29).

a. Jacob cheats his brother Esau (25:19-34)

Thematically important is the fact that Jacob (as well as Esau) is born out of barrenness (v.21; cf. 11:30). If the promise is to pass on to the next generation, it must come (as it did the first time) through the power and grace of God. The promise depends on the Promise-Giver. However, the gift is given in conflict (vv.22-23). Jacob's character is immediately apparent. His name confirms the initial impression. The word *Jacob* is a wrestling term for one who wrestles with another man to take his place. Jacob's whole life will be marked by such conflict. That conflict permeates the entire family (vv.27-28) and disrupts the established law of primogeniture.

The contrast between the sins is nowhere more clearly seen than in the exchange between them in the matter of food and birthright (vv.29-34). Esau too readily sacrifices the promise for the more immediate satisfaction of temporal needs (cf. Heb 12:16-17). He sells out too cheaply. Jacob, on the other hand, is cognizant of a future safeguarded by privilege and shrewdly schemes to secure it. The wordplay on **red, stew,** and **Edom** (v.30), each containing the same Hebrew letters, implies an association of ideas. Esau and the Edomites are destined for pottage while Jacob and the Israelites are destined for birthright (cf. Brueggemann, 218).

b. Isaac moves to Gerar (26:1-35)

Most of what we know about Isaac is couched either in terms of his relationship with Abraham (chs. 21-25) or in terms of his relationship with his son Jacob (chs. 25–35). His identity is largely wrapped up in theirs. This chapter appears, by contrast, to give us particular insight into the character of Isaac himself. However, the variety of stories featured are similar to those encountered previously (12:10–13:2; 20:1–21:34) and are here placed together in such a way as to highlight the benefits of the promise and to create a context in which one might better understand the rationale for Jacob's struggle to be the next promise-bearer. That is to say that while the material of ch. 26 may originate from distinct and separate Abraham or Isaac traditions, the chapter now functions teleologically within the canonical framework of the Jacob tradition.

The Abrahamic covenant is renewed with Isaac in the now familiar call to obedience (v.3a) and the promise of blessing (vv.3b–4). Isaac's response of obedience (v.6) is reminiscent of his father's faith and distinguishes him as a true heir of the promise. The fact that he so quickly places the covenant in jeopardy (vv.7–11), like his father before him, should not be surprising. The pretense of calling Rebekah his sister for fear of being killed himself reflects similar passages in the Abraham tradition (12:10–20; 20:1–18, though those are supposed in 26:1), as is the dispute over water rights (26:18–22; cf. 21:25), the greeting of Abimelech (26:22; cf. 21:22), and the covenant agreement at Beersheba with Abimelech and Phicol (v.28; cf. 21:31–32). The details differ somewhat in each telling, with the deliberate result of depicting Isaac as a man of esteem in Gerar and Beersheba who enjoys great prosperity (vv.12–14), the obvious favor of God (v.28), good fortune (vv.32–33), a measure of piety (v.25), and respect among the surrounding nations (vv.26–31). We can be confident that such tangible benefits associated with the promise-bearer could not have escaped the notice of the younger son.

c. Jacob deceives Isaac (27:1–45)

It is apparent from the previous chapter that Jacob coveted the promise because he perceived that it brought with it substantial material blessings. That the birthright/blessing addressed the temporal matters of prosperity, wealth, political preeminence, and protection is clearly evident (vv.28–29). Prompted by what he would derive from the promise, Jacob's unholy motive (selfishness) spawns unholy means (deceit) to obtain a holy result (the blessing). Jacob has not yet encountered God. Bethel (28:10–22) and Penuel (32:22–32) lie before him.

All four actors in the drama carry some degree of culpability and, as such, each shares in the tragedy. Esau's indifference to the birthright (25:32) causes him to be deprived of the blessing, with resulting heartache (27:34) and hatred for his brother (v.41). Isaac, presumably with prior knowledge of God's election of Jacob (25:23), yet governed by his palate, shows partiality to Esau (v.28). He is depicted as a pathetic old man, impotent to help his anguished son (27:37). Jacob, now the promise-bearer, is condemned to the life of a fugitive (vv.43–45) because of his deceit. The blessing has become a burden. Finally it should be noted that Rebekah, co-conspirator with Jacob, never sees her son again. All are punished. Yet even in the midst of despair, the fugitive son of the promise finds himself seeking refuge and a wife among the very kinsmen to whom Abraham had turned when he sought to safeguard the covenant (24:3–4). The blessing continues secure. And Esau, while not chosen to carry the blessing, is not left without hope (27:40). God will not only be the God of Israel, but of all the nations.

2. Jacob's sojourn in Paddan Aram (27:46–31:55)

a. The journey to Haran (27:46–28:22)

Rebekah, at the risk of losing her son, secures a future for him through clever diplomacy. She appeals to the dangers in syncretism (27:46) and thereby succeeds in prompting Isaac to send Jacob to the land of his own kinsfolk. So the next phase of Jacob's life begins as he journeys to the plain of Aram in northwestern Mesopotamia.

The significance of the journey to Haran is marked by a surprise theophany. God reveals himself to the deceitful fugitive. There is no word of reproach for Jacob. God simply takes the initiative in extending grace to this schemer. Jacob's dream conveys the presence of God both visually (28:12) and audibly (vv.13–15). The stairway signifies uninterrupted fellowship between God and humankind. The messengers inform God on matters of human need. But it is God's speech that is most crucial. It is an unqualified promise of constancy and commitment to Jacob. God meets Jacob in his solitary barrenness and assures him of his place in the covenant, allotting him land and progeny (similar, as one would expect, to the covenants of Abraham and Isaac). But this covenant contains the particular promises to Jacob of God's presence and protection and of Jacob's safe return (v.15).

The theophany leads Jacob to acknowledge the reality of the divine encounter and to make an appropriate response. Jacob elects to trust this God of Abraham and Isaac. He becomes Jacob's God (28:21). Bethel is legitimized as a cultic center (v.19), and Jacob, who has come a considerable distance in his understanding of God, makes a conditional vow (vv.20–21). He still has a way to go.

b. Jacob's wives and children (29:1–30:24)

Nestled between the accounts of the two theophanies (28:10–22; 32:22–32) is the fascinating Laban material. The transformation of the character of Jacob is yet incomplete though it has begun. Jacob is still the deceiver, but in Laban he has met his match. For twenty years (31:41) Jacob will be exploited by his uncle in much the way he exploited his own father and brother. Laban's duplicity is portrayed in the marriage arrangements made with Jacob (29:15–25). Such trickery results in serious contention between the two competitive sisters who have now become Jacob's wives. The family strife Jacob experienced as a youth has followed him to Haran. Favoritism in each instance (25:28; 29:30) brought destructive elements in its wake. Jacob's sons are born in envy, rivalry, and dispute.

The plot intensifies when it becomes apparent that the younger sister, Rachel, beloved of Jacob, is barren (29:31). Like Sarah (11:30) and Rebekah (25:21) before her, Rachel's barrenness will testify that the future belongs to God who gives life to the dead and calls into existence things that do not exist (Ro 4:17). And because of God's faithfulness to the promise, this family has a future and a hope. Rachel's barrenness provides the motif of all that transpires. It represents the pathos in which Leah names her sons (29:32–35). It evokes bitter feelings between the sisters (30:1). It is the cause of angry words between Jacob and Rachel

(30:1–2). It is the motive for presenting the maids as surrogate mothers (vv.3–13). It explains the enigmatic recourse to the mandrakes (vv.14–17).

Throughout the narrative God is depicted as One concerned for the dispossessed. It is because Leah is unloved that God blesses her (29:31), while the favored Rachel is barren. Life and death, birth and barrenness belong to God. God retains the last word in the situation. Jacob's deceptions catch up on him, and the despised Leah becomes the mother of six Israelite tribes including the priestly and kingly tribes of Levi and Judah. God will not be manipulated either by threat (30:1) or mandrake (v.14). It is in the act of remembering Rachel (v.22) that God and God alone grants her fertility. The future is in his hands.

c. Jacob's crisis with Laban (30:25–31:55)

Jacob's crisis with Laban in these verses brings into focus God's faithfulness to his promise of 28:13–15 and completes the period of Jacob's exile in Paddan Aram. He left home as an empty-handed fugitive and now returns a wealthy man. All that he possesses has been given to him by God. Jacob's recognition of God's protection and provision marks a new fidelity for the patriarch, which has resulted from God's revelation of himself (28:10–22). The effects of the theophany at Bethel are everywhere apparent. Jacob's plan to return home after the birth of Joseph (30:25) is a response to the vow he made to God (28:15, 21). The acknowledgment of God's presence (31:5) is reminiscent of the stairway (28:12) and the promise accompanying it (v.15). So, too, is the reference to the angelic message in a dream (31:11; cf. 28:12). The mention of the God of Bethel (v.13) makes explicit the con-

nection between the covenant promise and its fulfillment in the Laban encounter (31:42).

The success of Jacob's exile in Paddan Aram is due to God's watching over the promise. Jacob owes everything to God. And in keeping with the intent of the covenant, others share in the blessing specifically given to the elect (30:27; cf. 28:14b; Nu 10:29). So it is not surprising that Laban wants Jacob to stay. But the God who has prospered Jacob is now calling him to return home (31:3). In the process of departure and the conniving of Laban, Jacob (30:31–43) and even Rachel (31:19–35) epitomize the extent of deception within this family. The incidents of the speckled lambs and the household deities are humorously related and illustrate the depths of folly to which deception will lead. Jacob must yet learn that it is God who will rescue him from the anger of Laban (v.24) and enable their parting to be somewhat amicable (vv.44–55).

3. Jacob's transformation (32:1–32)

The theophanies of chs. 28 and 32 are of historical interest for the nation. They explain why Bethel is an important religious shrine and how the nation got its name, Israel. However, the position of this theophany is particularly interesting. It is sandwiched between Jacob's preparations for encountering Esau (32:3–21) and the actual meeting itself (33:1–17). Evidently, the unexpected meeting with the night stranger (32:22–32) provides insight into the meeting with Esau. The perceived enemy seems not so much to be the brother as it is the stranger with whom Jacob must struggle. He must first be reconciled with the divine visitant before he can seek reconciliation with Esau.

Jacob's primary concern is with the brother he has previously wronged (27:1–41). So he does everything conceivable to ensure a peaceful reunion. He first sends messengers to announce his arrival and to begin possible negotiation for safe passage (32:3–5). Esau's only response to the messengers is an ominous approach with four hundred men. Jacob, seized with fear, plans ways to minimize his losses in battle (32:7–8; 33:1–3). He prays (32:9–12). In the prayer Jacob reminds God of the promises God made earlier (28:13–15) and appeals to his faithfulness (32:10), which the patriarch has already experienced in the Laban crisis. He asserts that the idea to return home was God's (v.9). Recognizing that he deserves no special favors, he nevertheless pleads for mercy. Jacob is here placing his hope in God to deliver him. It is in that state of despair that God will once more demonstrate his grace to Jacob. God will stand again as guarantor of the promise.

On the day before the encounter, as an act of appeasement, Jacob sends generous presents ahead for Esau (32:13–21). Later he will show extreme deference to his brother as they approach one another (33:3). It is in the context of this impending meeting with Esau that the enigmatic encounter with the stranger occurs. This One, not Esau, is the real challenge before him. The most plausible identity of the stranger is God himself, and the canonical placement of the passage suggests that Jacob has to reckon with God, not Esau. That is the a priori relationship with which he must deal.

This conflict brings to a head Jacob's lifetime of conflict (with Esau, Isaac, Laban, Leah, and Rachel). Can it be, perhaps, that all these conflicts really represented manifestations of this one? All this time can Jacob have been struggling against God? Finally, Jacob is to become a conqueror in a profoundly spiritual sense. He finds victory in spiritual surrender. Such surrender always involves a struggle. In this case it lasts all night (32:24), and it comes amid weeping and prayer (Hos 12:4). Jacob craves a blessing no matter what it costs him—and there is a cost. The patriarch sustains physical injury and limps away from the experience. However, the blessing that the struggle brings is presented in Jacob's name and, by implication, transformed character. Jacob is forced to confess his old character by divulging his old name, "supplanter." He becomes **Israel,** which may mean "God rules" (after von Rad). The father of the tribes of Israel prevails by submitting himself to God. That is the only kind of victory man has with God. When day breaks, the stranger is gone. Jacob is gone. Only Israel is left. The transformation of the patriarch is complete. He is ready to meet Esau. Peniel will forever serve to remind us of a God who transforms the lives of men and women.

4. Jacob's return to Canaan (33:1–37:2)

a. Jacob's crisis with Esau (33:1–17)

Now a broken (albeit victorious) man, Jacob recognizes the truth about God as One on whom he must rely. His focus has to shift from looking at himself to gazing upon God. What Jacob experiences at Penuel is not an ontological change but a change of relationship. Jacob is now Israel. With the new status he is afforded, the past mistakes are forgiven and the future gleams with opportunity. We shall see later that the transformation was not absolute. But it is, nonetheless, out of this new-found confidence in God that reconciliation with Esau takes place.

The meeting between the two brothers is full of pathos. Jacob's attempts to gain favor from Esau are seen in his excessive deference and showering of gifts on his brother (indicative, no doubt, of the weight upon Jacob's conscience). But it is the sheer grace of Esau's response that is most striking in the narrative (vv.4, 9). It is as if Esau, like the nocturnal combatant, sets past sins aside and freely offers Jacob forgiveness and restitution. In this context, the use of the word *face* (v.10) is significant. Jacob had dreaded seeing Esau's face (32:20). Unexpectedly, he had seen God's face (v.30) and received pardon and renewal. Now, he declares, seeing Esau's face is like seeing God's face, presumably because of the similarity of experience.

b. Events in Canaan (33:18–35:29)

The effects of a life of deceit are sure to be seen in such a person's offspring. This is certainly true for Jacob in the saga of Shechem. The patriarch arrives in the city and settles there. He builds an altar and calls it **El Elohe Israel** (33:20), recalling his vow of 28:20–21. The period of exile is now over. The new problem is how Israel, the promise-bearer, will live out the affirmation of the altar name in the new situation of accommodation to non-Israelite groups in Canaan.

Dinah's **disgrace** and Shechem's subsequent desire to marry her (34:3–4) highlights the problems of both sexual violation and syncretism. Jacob and his sons are understandably upset by Shechem's action. Their retaliatory response, however, is entirely disproportionate to the offense. Their deception is clearly seen in their abuse of circumcision. Intended as a symbol of faith, it

is now employed as a means of exploitation and massacre. The question of syncretism is addressed by Hamor, whose conciliatory attitude encourages cooperation between the Israelites and their neighbors (vv.8–12, 18–24). The sons of Jacob are not interested in cooperating with the inhabitants of Shechem. They are simply making use of religious scruple to exact vengeance. While the uniqueness of the nation is preserved, one must deplore the deceitful, murderous way in which the matter was handled. Only Jacob expresses his disdain of their actions and the potential consequences (v.30). Simeon and Levi are without remorse (v.31). The danger of syncretism has been inappropriately addressed. It will remain a problem for a considerable time to come.

The Jacob narrative moves to its close with Jacob journeying south to Bethel, Bethlehem, and Hebron to be reunited with Esau at his father Isaac's deathbed (35:29). Bethel, the first stop on the journey, provides an opportunity for the purification desperately needed after the atrocity of Shechem (vv.2–4) and for a chance to remember the covenant (vv.9–12). The account of three deaths underscores a tradition moving to its close. Rachel's beloved nurse is buried at Bethel (v.8), Rachel herself dies on the way to Bethlehem while giving birth to Benjamin (vv.16–20), and Isaac is entombed at Hebron (vv.27–29). The story of Jacob is told. Benjamin brings to completion the family of the promise. From now on the number twelve will symbolize the whole. Jacob moves off center stage, and the drama of salvation history moves on to the next generation. They are not a promising lot (34:25–31; 35:22). Fortunately, the future of the promise remains dependent on the

Promise-Giver, not the promise-bearers.

The *toledoth* of ch. 36 brings the Jacob narrative to an end by rehearsing the descendants of Esau. Jacob's family may continue as the promise-bearers, but Esau's descendants are not rendered illegitimate because of that. As in the case of Isaac and Ishmael, the heir of God's choice may be the recipient of the covenant promises, but the non-elected son is also loved and blessed. God is not the God of Israel only, but of the whole world. Esau and Jacob part as friends, and that brotherhood, living on in their progeny in the nations of Edom and Israel, is never forgotten (cf. Dt 23:7).

C. Joseph (37:2–50:26)

The story of Joseph represents an important bridge between the renowned patriarchal trilogy (Abraham, Isaac, and Jacob) and Israel's bondage in Egypt. The promise motif, which has run consistently through the earlier narratives, is eclipsed in the bondage of the land of the pharaohs. The Exodus is the inevitable consequence of the promise. The Joseph narrative explains how the family of Jacob came to be in Egypt. These last fourteen chapters also serve to describe Joseph's ascendancy over Reuben, Jacob's firstborn and to show how Joseph achieved his unusual position in Egypt, and how the ancestors of the nation were rescued from the great famine. It is a human-interest story out of which has emerged a theology of providential provision. God continues to stand watch over the promise.

1. The consequences of Joseph's prophetic dreams (37:2–41:57)

a. Joseph's brothers (37:1–38:30)

The theme of the Joseph narrative is announced from the beginning and is inherent in the elements of the dream. Joseph is introduced abruptly as one favored by his father (37:3) and chosen by God. The perpetuity of the promise will depend on him even though all the sons of Jacob share in the promise-bearing. This is, supremely, a story of divine providence.

Jacob learned nothing from his parents' inappropriate favoritisms (25:28). His special affection for Joseph, symbolized in the gift of the ostentatious coat (37:3), prompts intense bitterness among the brothers (vv.4, 11). Joseph's dreams only further exacerbate the problem (vv.5, 8). But the dream now sets the agenda for all that follows. The dream becomes inextricably bound up with the promise to the patriarchs. Ironically, those who bear the promise jeopardize the dream by plotting to kill the dreamer (vv.18–20). The dreamer is perceived to be a threat. Murder is one obvious solution to the problem. So the conspiracy is concocted. But God, in his hiddenness, is guarding the dream and, by implication, the dreamer as well.

It is fascinating to note that the events of Joseph's imprisonment and potential demise transpire at Dothan, the very place where Elisha the prophet would visibly experience God's protection in the form of fiery chariots (2Ki 6:13–17). Now, God's provision has a different course to run, though it is no less preserving. Deception follows deception as the story unravels from Reuben's attempt to rescue Joseph to the libelous announcement to Jacob (37:32). It is not surprising to find such deception in a family where the father modeled duplicity.

The story of Judah's lineage (38:1–30) interrupts the flow of the Joseph narrative. It may have functioned originally as a separate tradition, but in its present canonical setting it forms a striking contrast between the piety of Joseph, particularly in regard to his refusal to be seduced by Potiphar's wife (39:7–8), and the immorality of Judah, who actively seeks the companionship of one whom he suspects of cultic harlotry (38:15–16). Joseph obviously does stand out as righteous in his generation. Judah's family evidences grave wickedness, illicit sex, and self-centered deception, all of which evoke God's displeasure (38:7, 10, et. al.). Yet even in the heinous sin of Judah's clan, the family continues to be bearers of the promise; and from the struggle in Tamar's womb (39:27–30) will issue, one day, One who will redeem Israel (Mt 1:3).

b. Imprisonment (39:1–40:23)

Clearly, as the Joseph saga is taken up once more, the central character is perceived as one on whom the blessing of God rests (39:2–3, 5, 21, 23). Such an observation is important in light of the events that now occur in Joseph's life. In a context of seductive temptation, deception, slander, and injustice, Joseph emerges unscathed. His faith, prudence, and integrity remain intact. The dream/blessings will not be placed in jeopardy because of a fling of passion. The significance of the statement **The LORD was with Joseph** (vv.2–3, 21, 23) is evidenced in the hidden but proactive manner of God's protective care of his servant. Joseph's success (v.2) is due to God as are the blessings Joseph imparts to those with whom he has dealings though they may be outside the covenant—Potiphar (v.5), the cupbearer (40:6–8), Pharaoh (41:16), and ultimately Egypt itself (v.57). More subtly one may recognize God's hidden providence in Joseph's imprisonment (39:20). He could have reasonably expected death for his alleged rape of Potiphar's wife. Whether the

captain of the guard mitigated his sentence because of past service or possible misgivings concerning the accuracy of the charges or because God influenced Potiphar's thinking, one can be sure that God was providentially preserving Joseph and safeguarding the dream.

Joseph's imprisonment does not distract from the ultimate realization of the dream. God prospers his servant even in such dire straits (39:21–23). Indeed, the fate of the cupbearer and the baker during the prison episode are secondary to the fate of Joseph himself. Their dreams are simply tools that connect the reader with the larger dream of Joseph. It is that dream that most concerns the narrator, for in Joseph's dream lies the future of God's promise to Israel. Interestingly, in this context dreams and their interpretations represent the activity of God, not of Joseph per se (40:8; 41:25). Joseph was given special ability to interpret the dreams of both the prisoners (40:20–22) and Pharaoh (41:54). Others are unsuccessful in explaining the mystery of the dreams (v.8). These revelations of God lie outside the epistemology of Egypt, indeed of any except God's chosen servant. Yet, even in his chosenness, Joseph acknowledges his own utilitarian role in the dreams (40:8, 41:16) and pleads with the cupbearer to remember him when the cupbearer is restored to his position (v.14). However, the cupbearer forgets Joseph (v.23). It is certain that God does not.

c. Promotion (41:1–57)

The ways of God now stand juxtaposed to the ways of the world (v.32). The mighty Egyptian empire stands helpless before the revelation of God. Yet to perpetuate the covenant made with the patriarchs, the one who is blessed becomes a blessing (cf. 12:3).

Egypt will be spared the famine because the sons of Israel must survive the drought if the promise is to remain intact. Joseph will act as the connecting link between the two. To accomplish this, Joseph is first empowered by God and then empowered by Pharaoh. Following the interpretation of Pharaoh's dream (vv.25–32), Joseph proposes an ambitious survival plan (vv.33–36). The effect of the proposal is to catapult Joseph to a position of prominence, second only to that of Pharaoh himself (v.43), and to rescue Egypt from starvation (vv.55–57). God grants Joseph the gift of interpretation to discern the future of events while Pharaoh acclaims him vizier (vv.40–41), grants him the insignia of office (v.42), provides him a royal name (v.45), and legitimizes his office by marriage (v.45). Such good fortune is reflected in the naming of his sons (vv.50–52) and is attributed to God.

2. God's providence acknowledged (42:1—47:31)

a. Joseph's brothers come to Egypt (42:1—44:34)

Twenty-two years have passed since Joseph's brothers sold him to the Ishmaelite caravan (37:25ff. cf. 37:2; 41:46; 45:6). The intervening narrative has followed the changing fortunes of Jacob's treasured son. Now the scene is set for the reunion of Joseph with his family. The exciting account that follows shows intense, dramatic effect with lots of intrigue and suspense. The effects of the famine have been widespread, causing the sons of Israel to journey to Egypt to obtain food for the family (42:2). In Egypt they are recognized by their brother, and their homage to him (v.6) is a reminder of Joseph's dreams, which prompted so much of the action recorded in these chapters in the first place (37:5–11). The dream has reached its fulfillment. Joseph is able to save his family from starvation, as he has saved Egypt. The promise continues to be secure.

The drama here is full of pathos. Joseph, now governor of Egypt, exploits the situation to the full. The brothers, fearful and naïve, show genuine signs that they have changed drastically since the time Joseph was with them. Jacob, now old and never having fully resolved his grief, closely clutches Benjamin, his youngest son, by Rachel. One suspects that Jacob knew the character of his sons and their hatred for Joseph well enough that he felt sure they were somehow implicated in the crime against the treasured son. This would explain his reticence to give up Benjamin.

Joseph provides an exceptionally fine character study. On the surface he appears ruthless and vindictive (42:7). Underneath, however, he displays tender affection (v.24), genuine compassion (v.25; 43:27), overwhelming kindness (43:16), and an eagerness to embrace his brother (vv.29–30)— traits one has come to expect of this man. The brothers, by contrast, are plagued by the guilt of the crime they committed long before against their brother (42:21–22) and the deception of their father that followed. Like Jacob in his meeting with Esau (33:3), whom he had previously wronged, so these sons of Jacob do excessive obeisance to Joseph (42:6; 43:28; 44:14), unwittingly fulfilling the latter's prophetic dreams of his youth (37:5–11).

The manner in which Joseph is able to ensure seeing his younger brother is clever. But the thought of allowing Benjamin to journey to Egypt with his brothers strikes dread in the heart of his father. The crisis is reached when the family again runs out of provisions

(43:1–2). Jacob succumbs to the plea of Judah (vv.8–9) and gives permission for Benjamin to go. The craftiness of Jacob is once more depicted in the list of appeasements he suggests to accompany the caravan (vv.11–12; cf. 32:13–21). Finally he invokes the mercy of El Shaddai to grant them favor with the Egyptian governor (43:14). That trust has not disappointed him in the past; it will not in the future.

The drama is heightened in the masterminded strategy employed by Joseph to expose the true character of the brothers. They are presented an opportunity to betray Benjamin as they once had Joseph, and the stakes are raised from the mere twenty shekels of silver (37:28) to the price of their own liberty (44:10, 17). The suspense reaches its climax as Judah steps forward to make his moving petition (vv.18–34). The twenty-two years of guilt and deception have wrought their ills. This is a time for a new beginning as Judah pleads not for mercy but to suffer on his brother Benjamin's behalf (v.33).

b. Joseph reveals himself to his brothers (45:1–28)

Judah's moving appeal (44:18–34) evokes Joseph's self-disclosure and brings the Joseph narrative to a dramatic and emotional climax (vv.2–3). Presumably the brothers knew him as Zaphenath-Paneah (41:45). Now they know him as Joseph (vv.3–4). Cognizant of their guilty fear (42:21; 45:3), Joseph does not exact revenge but extends grace to them (vv.5ff.). Joseph's gracious action results from God's prior grace proffered to him. He is able to identify the hand of God in the powerful theological statement of God's providence in vv.4–5: **You sold [me] . . . God sent me.** Four times

Joseph makes the affirmation of God's sovereign control in the events of human history (vv.5, 7, 8, 9). The implications for one's understanding of divine providence are significant. First, one may observe that God seeks to influence for good humankind's attitudes and actions even when they are evil. He does not promote the evil itself but may influence the expression of it so that a better thing will occur. The changing attitudes of the brothers (37:18–28), for example, may be indicative of the action of God in minimizing the fate of Joseph. Second, it is apparent that God influences the attitudes and actions even of people of unfaith. Examples clearly include Potiphar, Pharaoh, and the cupbearer. Third, we may notice that God acts ex post facto. Even after persons have resisted his influence, God builds on the evil to accomplish ultimate good. This is obviously the case in many instances in the life of Joseph. God builds on the worst scenario to effect eventual redemption. This is how we must understand the Cross. In this way human freedom to do evil is neither overwhelmed by nor able to withstand the ultimate success of God's sovereignty.

The chosen family, once facing the abyss of starvation and hopelessness, is now provided with the abundance of the best of the land (vv.18, 20). God has intervened again to change the fortunes of Israel and to prosper the covenant he made with the patriarchs. The call to the life of faith was heard in the barrenness of the wombs of Sarah, Rebekah, and Rachel. It is now heard in the barrenness of the land (45:11). The continuity of the chosen community carries within it the concept of the God who alone preserves the patriarchal promise.

c. Jacob journeys to Egypt (46:1–47:31)

The invitation to journey to Egypt marks a crucial point in the unfolding drama of God's dealings with his people. It is the precursor to the story of bondage and deliverance to be related in the book of Exodus when Israel recognizes itself not only as called but also as a redeemed community. The decision to venture south from Hebron is a serious matter. This may be why Jacob pauses at Beersheba and seeks the favor of the God of his father, Isaac (46:1). Implicitly he may be wanting reassurance that his leaving will not place the promise in jeopardy. Such reassurance is given in the renewal of the covenant with the added provision that it will be in Egypt that Israel will become a numerous people (46:3). The promise of a return to Canaan is reiterated (cf. 15:13–16). They will go down a small number (46:8–27) and will return an exceedingly great multitude (Dt 10:22).

In Egypt, Joseph continues to acquit himself with diligence and foresight (47:13–26). He blesses Egypt. Similarly, in his meeting with Pharaoh, Jacob blesses the empire (vv.7, 10). Egypt is spared and thereby blessed because of the family of promise. It is one of the benefits of the covenant. The blessing is not restricted to Israel, but through them others, too, will enjoy the fruit of the blessing. Rather than the journey to Egypt placing the promise in jeopardy, it is the means whereby the promise is released to the world. But Jacob himself is not at home in Egypt (cf. Jn 17:16). He is still on the journey. As a primary bearer of the promise, he must pass on a sense of the blessing's perpetuity. The covenant does not belong to Egypt but to the land promised to Abraham, Isaac, and Jacob. At the end of this patriarch's life,

the transmission of the promise is of critical importance. So the father of the nation forces Joseph to swear that he will bury Jacob with his fathers in Hebron (47:29–30). The promise remains intact.

3. The covenantal blessing carried forward (48:1–50:26)

a. Jacob blesses the sons of Joseph (48:1–22)

In the course of his precarious life, Jacob found that the promise of God never failed. He had learned to trust. It is now time for the promise to be passed on to succeeding generations. They, too, must learn to trust the promise. Jacob is now ill (v.1). There remains one final task for him to perform. It is the one item that is cited in Heb 11:21 to epitomize Jacob's faith pilgrimage. Joseph and his two sons are summoned to Jacob's deathbed, where the patriarch blesses Ephraim and Manasseh (vv.8–20) by calling on the God who had protected him (v.15) and redeemed him (v.16, possibly a reference to Penuel).

In claiming the two grandsons as his own (48:5) and blessing them, Jacob binds Ephraim and Manasseh to the promise. It cannot pass without notice that the primary blessing is given to the younger boy (v.14) despite Joseph's protests (vv.17–18). It is a gentle reminder of a similar occasion in Jacob's youth when the claims of primogeniture were upset. In both instances, the younger brother is placed before the older (v.20; cf. 27:36). This time, however, Ephraim does not secure the greater blessing through devious, underhanded cunning. He receives it with quiet resignation. How much different Jacob's life would have been had that been the case in his own youth.

b. Jacob bestows blessings on his own sons (49:1–28)

The blessing of the two sons of Joseph would surely be out of place if there were no blessings given to Jacob's other sons. So this penultimate chapter of Genesis provides closure to the transmission of the promise and leads into the death of the patriarch. In this proleptic address to his sons a connection is made with the previous chapter. Ephraim has been given the primary blessing before both Joseph's firstborn (48:20) and even Jacob's firstborn, who has forfeited primacy in the tribes (vv.3–4). The blessings on the sons generally relate to their settlement in the land promised to the patriarchs, and, in this sense, the narrative brings completion to the promise motif, which has run through most of the book. The promise given to Abraham, Isaac, and Jacob will find its eventual fulfillment in the settlement of the tribes. Yet even in the fulfillment there is born a new promise of One who will rule the nations (v.10). The community is called to journey constantly onward.

c. Death and burial of Jacob (49:29–50:14)

It is said that Tertullian once observed of the Christian community, "Our people die well!" If there is an art to dying well, then Jacob certainly possessed it. His is the death of one confident in the promise. His final charge to his sons is that he be buried in the land of the promise with his fathers Abraham and Isaac (49:29). It is a vivid lesson for his children, whom he has sought to bind to the promise. Egypt can never be their home. They must remain children of the promise, and the realization of the promise will come only in their return home. The sons of the patriarch are true to their word. Jacob is buried in Hebron. He is given the burial rites of an Egyptian (50:2–3) and is attended with great honor (vv.7–9). But he does not die an Egyptian. He dies embracing the promise of a future hope for his people.

d. Joseph's dream for the future (50:15–26)

The narrative now hastens to a conclusion, but what a magnificent conclusion it is! It is not really the end. Indeed, it is another beginning, truly a new genesis. What is going to happen now that Jacob is dead? Joseph's brothers have their ideas (v.15). They are not yet rid of their guilt (vv.16–17). Joseph is not interested in the question of culpability; for him the dream has come true. Joseph reassures his brothers (v.21). God had providentially used their evil designs to work a plan of redemption: **You intended to harm me, but God intended it for good** (v.20). God's plans cannot be thwarted ultimately. His plans are for humankind's *good*. Such a God is worthy of trust.

Joseph's own commitment to the promise is beautifully portrayed in his death scene (vv.24–26). This is the articulated apex of his faith (Heb 11:22). He acknowledges God's immortality: **I am about to die. But God . . .** affirms God's fidelity (v.24b) and expresses the certain hope of God's visitation (v.25). His bones symbolize his faith (v.26), and the Hebrews' care for them for four hundred years as the wish of a dying man. Through times of bondage and oppression they would be a reminder of the promise. While it was spoken of another, Heb 11:4 can readily apply to Joseph: "By faith he still speaks, even though he is dead." His dead bones speak of a living theology and the future of the promise.

BIBLIOGRAPHY

Aalders, G. Charles. *Genesis*. BSC. Vols. 1–2. Grand Rapids: Zondervan, 1981.

Brueggemann, Walter. *Genesis*. Interpretation. Atlanta: John Knox, 1982.

Childs, Brevard S. *Introduction to the Old Testament as Scripture*. Philadelphia: Fortress, 1979.

Delitzsch, Franz. *A New Commentary on Genesis*. 2 vols. Edinburgh: T. & T. Clark, 1897.

Driver, Samuel Rolles. *The Book of Genesis*. Westminster Commentaries. London: Methuen, 1905.

Kidner, Derek. *Genesis*. TOTC. Downers Grove, Ill.: InterVarsity Press, 1967.

Rad, Gerhard von. *Genesis*. OTL. Philadelphia: Westminster, 1961.

Skinner, John A. *A Critical and Exegetical Commentary on the Book of Genesis*. ICC. Edinburgh: T. & T. Clark, 1910.

Wood, Leon J. *Genesis*. BSC. Grand Rapids: Zondervan, 1975.

EXODUS
John N. Oswalt

INTRODUCTION

The book of Exodus, along with its predecessor, Genesis, is fundamental to the formation of biblical theology. Here much of the nature and character of God, as well as that of humanity is displayed. But the special contribution of Exodus is to the theology of salvation. Here we learn of the need for salvation, its nature, its means, and its intended outcome. A proper understanding of the book's teachings on these matters will go far toward explaining NT truth, while an improper understanding has again and again provided fertile soil for heresy.

I. AUTHOR, DATE, AND COMPOSITION

Jewish tradition has held that Exodus was one of the five books of the Law (Lat. *Pentateuch*) that Moses wrote at the command of God. Internal evidence does not contradict this position. Although the book never says explicitly that Moses was its author, it does include materials that must have come from Moses himself, such as private conversations between himself and God. Furthermore, no other author is indicated.

At the same time, it must be said that along with the other books of the Pentateuch, Exodus does not betray that unity of style and development that we usually associate with a single author. This factor along with other apparent difficulties has lead many OT scholars to suppose that all five of the books had a complex compositional history, coming into their final form only sometime after the Jews' return from Babylonian exile in 539 B.C.

Conservative scholars have pointed out that these theories are based on negative assumptions concerning the possibility of divine revelation and about the historical worth of the text. In contrast, they have argued that we should not evaluate ancient literature according to the standards that are current today and have pointed out the various ways in which discoveries about the ancient Near East have supported biblical statements. Conservatives have recognized, however, that it is no disservice to the plain claims of the text to see Moses as editor rather than as author. As an editor, he may have written significant portions of the final copy (cf. Dt 31:9) and may also have used the work of other individuals, whether earlier than he or contemporary with him, to round out the whole (cf. Nu 21:14). If this is so, it solves many of the so-called problems.

In any case, it is clear that the reader is meant to read Exodus as the report of those events that were formative to Israel's existence as a nation. But it is also clear that Exodus is not to be read alone. At the outset it is to be read in the light of Genesis. Exodus begins with a reference to those who went down to Egypt with Jacob (1:1), and it is built around the implicit question of whether God is able to keep the promises of land, progeny, and name, which God had made to Abraham in the former book (e.g., 12:1–3).

By the same token, Exodus gives rise to questions that can be answered only by the succeeding book, Leviticus. As Exodus closes, it gives in great detail the structure of the worship center, the tabernacle, where God will be present in the midst of his people. But beyond generalities, Exodus does not spell out how God will meet with them nor what the implications of his presence are for them. Those issues, and others like them, are dealt with in detail in Leviticus.

Thus it is apparent that while Exodus is a unit in itself, dealing with the deliverance from Egypt and what that means, it is not intended to be read as a solitary unit. It is a part of a larger compositional whole. Modern scholarship would have us believe that this work was the result of centuries of all-but-unconscious community shaping, with certain unknown individuals giving direction from time to time. It takes much less credulity to believe that the work is that of a single great intellect working under the inspiration of God.

II. BACKGROUND

Since Exodus does not report the name of the pharaoh of the Exodus nor give any other information concerning date, it is not possible to date the Exodus with certainty. Using biblical figures and working backward from the date of Solomon's death (the first biblical event that can be tied into our dating system—ca. 930 B.C.), a date of 1440 B.C. was arrived at. However, archaeologists in the earlier part of this century argued that evidence supported a later date—ca. 1290. Recently several parts of that evidence have been challenged so that the whole issue is undergoing rethinking at this time. Many of a more conservative bent are returning to the earlier date, while a more radical position increasingly doubts there was an exodus at all. Such a conclusion asks us to believe that the great edifice of Hebrew faith was built upon a wholly imaginary foundation.

One of the interpretive controversies regarding the Exodus concerns the number of people involved. Ex 12:37, in agreement with Nu 1:46, asserts that there were about 600,000 fighting men, which would factor out to a total group of about 2.5 million people. Without discounting the miracles of food and water, the logistics of transporting this number of people and the indications that the entire populations of Egypt and Canaan were not this large at this time suggest that these numbers are not intended to be taken literally. Several tentative explanations have been offered, but none has gained universal acceptance. In any case, it is plain that a very large number of people was involved and that we need more information about the use of numbers in ancient times.

In recent years it has been recognized that the biblical covenant shares certain similarities in structure with one type of ancient Near Eastern treaty. This treaty was between a great king and a subject people. Several features of this treaty form made it useful for what God was seeking to teach Israel.

It begins with a historical prologue explaining what has happened to cause this king and this people to enter into a covenant; it is because of what God has done in coming to us in our time and space that relationship with him is possible. The king commits himself to protect and care for this people in recognition of their dependence on him; God, unlike the idols, binds himself to his people. The people are to abide by the king's demands in view of, and in support of, their relationship with the king; obedience does not produce relationship with God, it is in response to, and maintenance of, an already existing relationship. The treaties almost always demand recognition of one king alone; there is only one God for Israel. The treaties are sealed with the most solemn blessings and curses; to live in obedient relation to God is life and health, to refuse to do so is destruction.

Thus it appears that, at God's direction, Moses took the general form of these political treaties and adapted it to the uniquely religious purposes of God.

III. PURPOSE

The popular title of the book: Exodus, is that assigned to it in the Septuagint, the Greek translation of late pre-Christian times. In Greek the word means "the way out." At first glance, the reader may think this refers to the way out of Egyptian bondage. But if that were the case, the book should end at ch. 15 with the great song of praise after the crossing of the Red Sea. The fact that the book does not end there but continues with the giving of the law and the building of the tabernacle provides a clue that the author does not consider the physical bondage in Egypt to be the Israelites' most critical problem. Even in the story of the Israelites' deliverance, the recurring phrase "You [or they] shall know that I am the LORD" suggests that the primary problem was theological. To be sure, the Hebrews did need deliverance from bondage; their cries of distress had been heard by a compassionate God. But more than that, they needed to know God. Had their sole need been for deliverance, one climactic act would have sufficed. Instead, there were ten plagues, which in fact constituted a demonstration of God's absolute superiority over all other powers. Thus physical deliverance is not an end but a means to an end. Nor was that end merely theological understanding; it was the experiencing of God as vitally present among them. As Exodus shows us, it was necessary that the people experience his delivering power (chs. 1–18), enter into a binding covenant with him (chs. 19–24), and give themselves in glad service to him (chs. 25–40), in order to experience his presence (40:35–38).

IV. OUTLINE

I. Deliverance (1:1–18:27)
    A. In Egypt (1:1–13:16)
        1. Preparation (1:1–6:27)
            a. Need for deliverance (1:1–22)
            b. Preparation of a deliverer (2:1–25)
            c. Call of the deliverer (3:1–4:28)
            d. Offer of deliverance (4:29–6:27)
        2. Plagues (6:28–13:16)
            a. Initial plagues (6:28–10:29)
            b. Climactic plague and its results (11:1–13:16)
    B. To Sinai (13:17–18:27)
        1. Red Sea crossing (13:17–15:21)
        2. Red Sea to Sinai (15:22–18:27)
II. Revelation (19:1–40:38)
    A. The Covenant (19:1–24:18)
        1. Preparation (19:1–25)
        2. Presentation (20:1–23:33)
        3. Sealing (24:1–11)
    B. The Tabernacle (24:12–40:38)
        1. Instructions (25:1–31:18)
        2. The golden calf (32:1–34:35)
        3. Construction (35:1–40:38)

COMMENTARY

I. DELIVERANCE (1:1–18:27)

The first main division of the book details how God brought his people out of Egypt (1:1–13:16) and to the foot of Sinai (13:17–18:27). It demonstrates his faithfulness, his incomparable power, and his providential care; and it shows how human deliverance is dependent upon divine self-revelation.

A. In Egypt (1:1–13:16)

The actual deliverance involves two aspects: preparation (1:1–6:27) and plagues (6:28–13:16). The preparation section functions to bring the

crucial question "Who is the Lord?" into sharp focus, while the plagues demonstrate in an incontrovertible way that the Lord of the universe is none other than the God of Abraham, Isaac, and Jacob.

1. Preparation (1:1–6:27)

Preparation for deliverance involves a delineation of the need for deliverance (1:1–22), an explanation of the preparation (2:1–25) and call (3:1–4:28) of a deliverer, and the initial offer of deliverance (4:29–6:27). As these themes are developed it is made clearer and clearer that the deepest problem of Moses and the people is that they do not know God.

a. Need for deliverance (1:1–22)

This chapter sets the stage for what is to follow. It tells who needs deliverance (vv.1–7), why (vv.8–10), and from what specific oppression (vv.11–22). As the chapter proceeds, it becomes clear that nothing less than their obliteration as a people is threatened.

Assuming the reader's knowledge of the book of Genesis, Exodus begins with a simple recapping of the names of the persons involved in the entry into Egypt. But this recapping makes a significant point in the light of Genesis. God's promises of family and name to Abraham (Ge 12:3), Isaac (Ge 26:4–5), and Jacob (Ge 28:13–15) have so far been fulfilled that now seventy persons are involved. God is faithful. Moreover, that faithfulness continued into the next generations so that the Israelites multiplied and expanded at an unusual rate (vv.6–7).

This pharaoh (vv.8–10) was probably the new kingdom monarch Thutmose III, if we accept the early date of the Exodus (see the introduction). The Egyptians' anxieties concerning this large Semitic population would have been heightened because Semitic peoples had controlled the entire Nile Delta area during the period known as the Second Intermediate as late as one hundred years prior to this. Pithom and Rameses (v.11) have been identified with the sites of Tell el-Maskhuta and Tell el-Ratabah in the Delta area. Archaeologists have reported that it is possible to detect a shift from mud bricks with straw to ones without straw in succeeding levels of these cities (see 5:6–19).

The first intimation of conflict between the Lord, the true God, and Pharaoh, who believed himself to be God, appears in vv.15–22. The Lord has promised that Israel will be a great nation, a source of blessing to all humanity (Ge 12:3); Pharaoh proposes to destroy them as a people by killing all the male babies. Who will triumph? Thus we see that while the need for deliverance is indeed a human problem, it is also a divine one: can God keep his promises of blessing?

There is no reason to think that the two women mentioned in v.15 were the only midwives for the Hebrews. They are simply representative of the entire group. The response of these women is indicative of the ultimate outcome of the contest: powerful as Pharaoh is, if a conflict arises between obeying him and obeying God, there really is no contest. To "fear God" is to live in obedience to him because we have an accurate understanding of his power and righteousness.

b. Preparation of a Deliverer (2:1–25)

Two elements in the deliverer's preparation are stressed: his miraculous preservation (vv.1–10), and his initial failure (vv.11–25). God's means of preparation are beautifully ironic: the very person who had decreed the destruction of the people of God would become the grandfather of their deliverer; the resources of the oppressing power would be used to raise and train the one who would break that power. How characteristic of God's grace it is that not only is Jochebed's (6:20) baby given back to her, but she is paid to do what she would gladly have done for nothing (v.9). The name *Moses* also has an Egyptian etymology that means "given birth."

Here (vv.11–25) Moses seeks to deliver his people in his own strength without incurring any responsibility (v.12). This is not God's way. Not only does it fail to reveal God, which is essential to any genuine salvation, it also relies solely on destruction of the human oppressor through human ability. Thus Moses' effort is a classic example of human effort to do God's work, which the Greek text speaks of as "the flesh" (Jn 6:63; Ro 8:5, NIV "sinful nature"; 2Co 1:12, NIV "worldly").

At least Moses could deliver some shepherdesses from their marauding cohorts (vv.16–20). Perhaps he believed this would be the extent of his future labors. **Midian** proper is located east of the Sinai peninsula on the western edge of the Arabian peninsula. Evidently at this time its territory also extended into Sinai (3:1).

The account of preparation closes by identifying the true source of hope for all the oppressed of earth (vv.24–25). It is not in a failed man, but in a God who hears and sees, who remembers his commitments and is moved by a caring heart (see also 3:7–9).

c. Call of the deliverer (3:1–4:28)

Here is a classic in world literature as it describes every person's attempt to evade responsibility and avoid the imperative of service to God. Moses focuses on his inadequacy, but God, by focusing upon his own adequacy, shows Moses that this is not the issue.

The encounter takes place at **Horeb,** another name for Mount Sinai (3:12). This mountain was associated with God's self-revelation to Elijah (1Ki 19:8), and Habakkuk (Hab 3:3, there called Mount Paran). Here the revelation occurs through **the angel of the LORD,** who is not merely a messenger, but God himself in visible form (vv.2, 4). The burning bush is symbolic of God's holiness, which sets its vessel

alight but does not consume it. That holiness is further emphasized by the command for Moses to remove his **sandals,** which were defiled because of their contact with ordinary soil.

In vv.6–9 God shows how he is the God of the past, present, and future. He is the One who made gracious promises in the past, who is now moved by his people's need, and who will bring them into a glorious future.

Moses' protest that he is not worthy is met by God's promise that he will be with him (3:11–12). Likewise, his claim not to know God well enough (v. 13) is met by God's promise to reveal his timeless reality (I AM) as the God of the past (v.16), the present, and the future (vv.18–22).

The first request that Moses was to make (3:18) of the Egyptians underlines that God's purpose for the Hebrews was not merely to set them free, but to make them his people in worship. Nevertheless, it was implicit in such a request that the slaves would not be returning, and God knows it will be rejected (v.19). This initial mention of Pharaoh's hard-heartedness shows that he was not predestined apart from his own free choice. See below on 4:21 for further discussion. Ultimately, the oppressors would provide the materials for the later offerings given to build the tabernacle (vv.21–22; see 35:22–24).

Moses' third objection (4:1–9) is that he has no means of compelling attention. God's response is to demonstrate his power. It seems likely that the two signs were deliberately chosen to show God's power over evil (vv.3–4) and sin (vv.6–7). Turning the Nile to blood (v.9) would demonstrate power over the source of Egypt's national life.

Moses' final objection (4:10–12) betrays a certain desperation. God has demolished the other arguments by simple reference to his own character and power. Moses does not deny these but asserts that he is unable to declare them. God insists that since he is the Creator, Moses' mouth poses no problem for him.

The real reason behind Moses' objections now appears. He does not want to do what God wants. But God leaves him no way out by revealing that Aaron is already coming and can serve as Moses' spokesman. Moses must either disobey or go. His request to his father-in-law for permission to return to Egypt is not yet a glad acceptance of a commission, as seen by the following incident (4:24–26) and by his questions in 6:12. Nevertheless, Moses was obeying. While attitude is important and must finally be brought into line, action is even more important.

The mention of hardening Pharaoh's heart (4:21) requires careful thought. Clearly Pharaoh is not someone who would like to obey God but cannot because of God's predetermined will. Rather, he is a proud, determined tyrant who believes he is God and intends to do as he pleases (see 3:19; 7:22; 8:15). God did not harden Pharaoh's heart against his will. Probably the phrase is intended to convey that although Pharaoh may believe his hardness is entirely of his own momentary choice, it is really the result of proud willfulness, which has left him unable to do other than the sum of all those other choices. God has made the world that way, and in that limited sense our choices are determined.

Scholars disagree about the meaning of the mysterious event narrated in 4:24–26, but the most probable hypothesis is that Moses, who is going to call his people to covenant faithfulness, thought so little of the covenant that he had not circumcised his own son (see Ge 17:9–14 for the origins of the

practice). It is evident that Moses and Zipporah had previously discussed whether or not to perform the rites since she immediately diagnosed the problem and took the appropriate action. We may be grateful to God that he does not normally require such rigid obedience. Nevertheless, at certain key points in salvation history, he has shown us the extreme danger of taking him lightly (see also Lev 10:1–3; Jos 7:14–26; 2Sa 6:6–7; Ac 5:1–11).

d. Offer of deliverance (4:29–6:27)

Moses and Aaron's initial announcement (4:29–31) met with a good deal of acceptance. The prospect of a magical release without cost or difficulty always meets with such approval. However, God's activity is never without cost and difficulty, as it was not here. It is in the context of this difficulty that the underlying issue of the book emerges: Who is Yahweh? (5:2) What is his power? Can he be trusted? The real problem of the people was their ignorance of God. Until they came to know him, mere physical deliverance could only lead to a different kind of bondage.

Since Pharaoh was considered God incarnate by the Egyptians, there was no reason why he should obey some unknown god of the Semites. Since he could not accept the reality of Yahweh's revelation, he had to imagine some other reason for the Hebrews' request. Surely they had too much time on their hands (5:8). Let them spend that time gathering the straw used to bind the mud bricks together while drying.

God's offer of deliverance made the situation worse, not better. This is often true in life: to begin to follow God is to attract the attention and the wrath of God's enemies. V.23 brings to a sharp focus the questions that emerged about God's nature and character.

In 6:1–12 we see how the crisis, which now existed as a result of Pharaoh's recalcitrance and the dramatically worsened situation, provided a setting for the needed demonstration of God's character.

The precise meaning of 6:2–3 is uncertain since the name (here appearing as *the LORD*) certainly does appear in the Abraham, Isaac, and Jacob narratives. Either of two solutions is possible. Perhaps Moses in transcribing those narratives has inserted the name in those places where the personal, covenant-keeping nature of God had appeared (e.g., note where "Lord" appears in Ge 22). The other possibility is that while the patriarchs knew and used the title "the Lord," they had never known the character (name) of God as would these Israelites.

God's larger purpose in the Exodus is explained here (6:6–8). Political freedom is not an end, but a means whereby the people might know God and enter into a living relation with him. Likewise, deliverance from guilt and condemnation is also a means to those same ends. To **know** God (v.7) is to learn his character by intimate personal experience. The importance of this concept is revealed in its occurring eleven times in chs. 6–14. "**Faltering lips**" (6:12, 30) speaks of Moses' continuing sense of inadequacy, either physically or spiritually.

It is not clear why Moses and Aaron's family tree is included at this point (6:13–27). Perhaps it serves to remind the reader that Moses and Aaron were not just anyone, but full-blooded members of the Levitic clan whom God had chosen to be his particular ministers. This interpretation is favored by the genealogy's being bracketed before and after by Moses' protest about faltering

(uncircumcised) lips. Although only three generations are cited between Jacob and Moses, at least 407 years elapsed between the birth of Levi and the death of Amram (based on 12:40).

2. Plagues (6:28–13:16)

The plagues are not so much designed to procure the Israelites' freedom as they are designed to reveal God (7:5). Thus they constitute an attack upon the Egyptians' gods. From the Nile to life itself, God shows that all the powers the Egyptians worshiped were in his hands.

a. Initial plagues
(6:28–10:29)

The recalcitrance of Pharaoh is a given right from the start (7:4, 13). He does not wish to accept the evidence of the miracle and seeks satisfactory reasons to support his unfaith: sorcery and trickery. The Bible does not explain how the sorcerers were able to duplicate the miracle and the first two plagues (7:22; 8:7). They may have used sleight of hand or demonic power. In any case, their best efforts ultimately failed (see 8:18–19).

The first plague (7:14–22) struck at the Nile, upon whose life-giving waters Egypt was, and is, completely dependent. Thus God was shown to be superior to the Nile goddess (v.17). Some have asserted that the phenomenon was actually a sudden surge of red clay-laden water from a tributary far upstream. However, this explanation is called into question both by the miraculous timing and the extent, affecting even water in jars.

The second plague (8:1–15) reveals God's power over the amphibian and reptilian world. The Egyptians gave special reverence to animals that could live in two different environments. They did this because they were eager to be able to live in the environment of the underworld after death. But God shows that these beasts and their representative gods have no special power at all. Although the magicians also produced frogs, it is still to Moses and Aaron that Pharaoh looks for relief (8:8). Perhaps he finally has an inkling that he is dealing with a divine power beyond the reach of magic.

The third and fourth plagues, gnats and flies (8:16–30), represent God's power over the insect world. Again, the Egyptians revered insects because of their apparent ability to thrive in filth and even bring life out of it. These powers would be of special importance to those who sought to live through the corruption of death. But God shows that the powers of the insect gods belong to him. Another sign of the supernatural, besides timing and extent (see on 7:19), is selectivity (8:22–23). While natural causation is by no means entirely excluded from miraculous events (thus it would be natural for swarms of insects to follow upon the decay of millions of dead frogs), it is the work of the supernatural to cause the event to occur in one locality and not in another. In a profound illustration of human nature Pharaoh first attempts to bargain with God for his obedience but in the end refuses to keep his side of the bargain (8:25–32).

The fifth and sixth plagues (9:1–12) especially affected livestock. Here again is a contest between the Lord and the Egyptian gods. The great gods were symbolized by sacred animals such as the bull, the ram, and the he-goat. God shows that these gods are as helpless before him as are their human ministers (v.11).

The seventh and eighth plagues (9:13–10:18) primarily affected vegetation. Egypt's wealth and culture rested upon a superabundance of grain, which the irrigated Nile Valley produced. Thus one of the greatest gods was Osiris who symbolized the plants that died each fall and rose to new life in the spring. His idol's complexion was green to reinforce this connection. But even great Osiris is subject to the God of the Hebrews. What vegetation the hail did not destroy (9:31–32) the locusts did (10:5–6, 15).

In a forceful statement to Pharaoh, God underlines the purpose of the plagues (9:15–16). If destruction was God's purpose, he could have done that long since. Rather, using the Egyptian gods and Pharaoh himself as foils, God intends to reveal himself to the world. See also 12:12.

Because of the desert on the west, rainstorms are uncommon in Egypt. Thus it would be frightening enough that this great storm should occur at all. But that it should begin and end precisely on Moses' cue (vv.23, 33) would make it frankly terrifying.

Finally, Pharaoh admits that there is some other standard than his own to which he is accountable (9:27). But intellectual assent does not guarantee surrender of the will (v.35). In this regard, it is important to notice the interchange between 9:34–35 and 10:1. From the perspective of his own responsibility, Pharaoh hardened his own heart. But from the perspective of God's purposes this act was entirely within a plan.

Pharaoh's words in v.10 are ironic. He says something like, "The Lord really will be with you if I ever let you go on those terms." Faced with incontrovertible proof of his helplessness before God, Pharaoh still tries to dictate terms (10:11). Pride would rather see everything around it **ruined** (v.7) than admit anything superior to itself. Finally Pharaoh is forced to recognize

the Lord's existence even if he will not
acknowledge him (**"the LORD your
God,"** v.17). See the discussion on
9:27.

The ninth plague (10:21–29) was an
attack on the sun god himself, Egypt's
highest god, Amon-Re. By showing his
control over the sun, God demonstrated that no Egyptian idol could
stand before him. Still Pharaoh tried to
save some scrap of his pride by bargain-
ing with the Lord (10:24).

b. Climactic plague and its results (11:1–13:16)

The tenth plague (11:1–9) attacks
the very heart of Egyptian faith, which
was in life itself. The Egyptians were
obsessed with keeping the good life of
Egypt intact right into the next world.
Thus, though the gods, who were after
all but representations, might fail, still,
if life and the life force continue, then
their faith could survive. When the
Lord shows that even the continuation
of life itself (as symbolized in the
firstborn) is within his control, there is
nothing left but to admit defeat.
Though Pharaoh may never see Moses
again (10:29), Pharaoh's officials will;
and far from loftily permitting the
Israelites to leave, those officials will
beg them to go (11:8).

Ex 12:1–13:16 deals with the implications of the tenth plague. This plague
was significant not only because it
finally prompted the Egyptians to let
the Israelites go (12:31–42), but because it revealed the fundamentally
spiritual nature of salvation. Passover
(12:1–30) and the consecration of the
firstborn (13:1–16) are both recogni-
tions that the real enemy of Israel and
the Hebrew race is death and that God
has conquered it.

The special nature of the tenth
plague is indicated by the fact that it is
the only one against which the Israelites had to take action so that they
would be protected from it. Not merely
the oppressors are under the curse; the
oppressed are as well. There is nothing
about being oppressed that automatically exempts the victims. Thus Passover teaches that the real enemy is
death. This is confirmed in Passover's
fulfillment in the Last Supper (Lk
22:7–30). Jesus openly refers the symbolism to himself and what he would
do for the world on the next day.

The first month (12:2) of the agricultural calendar was the month of
Nisan, extending from about March 15
until about April 15 of the modern
calendar. About this time pagans celebrated the rebirth of the mythical vegetation gods. The Israelites celebrated
God's actual conquest of death in the
real world of time and space. This
victory is not something to be remembered in morbid privacy; rather, it
should be shared with others in joy.
Later Judaism decreed that no fewer
than ten could share the Passover meal.
Judaism has also invested every element
of the meal with meaningful symbolism. So the bitter herbs are taken to
symbolize the bitterness of oppression,
the leaven sin, and so forth. But the
only element that the Exodus text
explicitly interprets is that of the lamb's
blood. It is this factor that turns away
the death angel (v.13; see also v.23).
The meal is to be eaten in readiness for
the journey because those who have
experienced God's deliverance from
death need to be prepared to act on all
that that deliverance may portend
(12:11).

Passover was a one-day festival celebrated on Nisan 14. The Feast of
Unleavened Bread continued for one
week after that until the twenty-first
day (v.18). Probably this feast originally commemorated the fact that bread
prepared and kept in readiness for a

journey such as the Hebrews were about to make could have no yeast in it for fear of spoilage. Another explanation is given in 12:39: they did not even have time to let bread rise. When God acts, we must be ready to move. **"Cut off from the community"** (12:19) emphasizes again (see on 4:24–26) that it is God who determines the terms of our reconciliation. A casual and half-hearted approach to these terms can only indicate an unwillingness to submit to him. Moses' careful communication of God's commands (12:21–28), emphasizing their continuing nature and their teaching function, illustrates the same point.

The information about the death of Pharaoh's firstborn in 12:29 might be assumed to be helpful in identifying the Pharaoh of the Exodus. Unfortunately, several of the pharaohs between 1500 and 1200 B.C. were succeeded by someone other than their firstborn son.

The second result of the tenth plague, expulsion, is discussed in 12:31–42. **"Bless me"** (12:32): Now Pharaoh knows that far from being God Incarnate of the whole world, he cannot even guarantee the prosperity of his own soul and body; they are in the hands of the Hebrew God. This is a direct fulfillment of God's prophecy in 8:10 and 9:14. Another fulfillment occurs in vv.35–36 where 3:21–22 are reprised. Pharaoh has no choice but to obey.

The Hebrews seem to have traveled southeast from the Delta area where they lived. See 13:17–18 and 14:3. On the numbers involved in the Exodus, see the introduction. The Greek translation of the OT, the Septuagint, has 12:40 reading that it was 430 years from Abram's entry into Canaan until the Exodus. This would shorten the Egyptian sojourn to something like 220 years. This reading is supported by

the ancient Samaritan version of the Pentateuch and is followed by the NT (Gal 3:17).

The further ordinances concerning Passover seem strange at this point (12:43–49) until we consider what appears to be the author's purpose in this: exodus—freedom from bondage—is misunderstood unless it is seen, both before and after, as having its meaning in the greater deliverance—from death. The particular content of these ordinances is to restrict participation in the Passover to those who are wholeheartedly participating in the covenant of Abraham as symbolized by circumcision.

A third result of the tenth plague was the sanctifying of the firstborn (13:1–2, 11–16). Because God had graciously spared them, all firstborn, human and animal, were his. Thus they had to be sacrificed or bought back.

If Passover was more associated with deliverance from death, then Unleavened Bread focused more on deliverance from oppression (13:8–9). Perhaps this explains the apparent discrepancy with 12:2 over the date of the celebration. **Abib** (13:4) is the second month of the agricultural calendar, evidently the actual month in which the Hebrews left Egypt (see also Ex 23:15; 34:18; Dt 16:1). Leviticus commands that the combined feasts of Passover and Unleavened Bread be kept in the first month (23:5), as does Ex 12:2ff. Apparently, for a time at least, the Hebrews kept Abib as the first month of their calendar. Later confusion arose, and the Judeans seem to have celebrated in Nisan, the first month, and the Israelites in Abib, the second month. This may explain Hezekiah's actions in 2Ch 30.

Obedience (13:9) is an outward sign of inner adherence. It is not a substitute, but it is an important sign. And it is an irreplaceable teaching device for the young (vv.8, 14).

B. To Sinai (13:17–18:27)

Although the people of Israel now knew the power of God and his supremacy over all gods, they did not yet know his care for them in a direct experiential way. The experiences described in this segment of the book could leave them in no doubt of his providential care. He provided victory over enemies (14:29–31; 17:8–15), water (15:22–27; 17:1–7), food (16:1–36), and indirectly, social organization (18:13–27).

1. Red Sea Crossing (13:17–15:21)

As pointed out earlier, God's purpose in the Exodus was not merely to get the people out of Egypt and into Canaan. That purpose could have been accomplished much more expeditiously than it was. Rather, his purpose was to enter into a vital relationship with them. For that purpose they needed to know and trust him. For that to take place the long way through the wilderness with all its attendant hazards was necessary before they faced the wars of conquest in the Promised Land (13:17–18).

Red Sea (v.18) is actually "Reed Sea," an apparent reference to the shallow waters at the northern end of the Gulf of Suez. The precise locations of the sites mentioned on the journey toward the sea (13:20–14:2) are uncertain. But it seems apparent that they were generally southeast of the Nile Delta so that the wilderness between the Nile valley and the Gulf of Suez was on their west and the Gulf was on the east (14:2). **The pillar of cloud** and **fire** (13:21) was a visual symbol of God's guiding and protecting presence.

The Egyptians had mastered the use

of the horse and light chariot at this time and had turned it into a fearsome weapon (14:7). Perhaps it was confidence in this that led them to change **their minds** (v.5). This statement is another indication that a simplistic view of God's hardening the heart (v.4) is unwarranted. See above on 4:21.

In 14:11–12 is the first occurrence of what was to become a familiar refrain. Although the Hebrews knew something of God's power, they were not convinced of his care. Similarly many today would rather live in bondage to sin because they are afraid to trust God. Nevertheless, Moses had come to the place (contra 5:22–23) where he believed implicitly in God's intention and ability to deliver. God will **gain glory** through his creatures either by our submitting to him and being delivered or by our refusing to submit and being crushed (14:17–18).

It is not necessary, to be faithful to the biblical account, to believe that the water of the Reed Sea was hundreds of feet deep, as it would be in the Red Sea proper (see above on 13:17–18) or even in the southern end of the Gulf of Suez. Water ten feet deep would be just as effective a barrier. Nevertheless, it is plain that the Hebrews did not escape the Egyptian army by running through a swamp, as some antisupernaturalists today would maintain. Although natural means (**a strong east wind**) were employed, the result, in timing, manner, and extent, was supernatural. To deny this claim of the Israelites is to believe that their entire faith is rooted in a fiction.

"Made ... wheels ... come off" (14:25) is literally "turned aside the wheels." The verb translated "turn aside" can also mean "take away," thus the NIV translation; however, the ancient versions' use of words like "jammed" (see NIV note) suggests that what may have been meant was that the chariot wheels would not run straight and bogged down in the sand of the seabed. The nervousness of the Egyptians is easily understandable in light of their recent experiences with the Lord. Apparently the Egyptians had almost crossed the seabed but in their confusion had turned back just when the waters came together again.

The Song of the Sea (15:1–21). An experience of the delivering power of God is frequently cause for song. The high emotions of joy and gratitude find particular expression in poetry and melody. The great burden of the first three verses is personal. The first person pronoun occurs eight times. God, who has been abstract and impersonal, has acted personally for them. The Maker of the universe is indeed their personal God. This kind of knowledge of God is the particular distinction of biblical religion. For a similar expression see Isa 12:1–3.

The second stanza of the song (15:4–10) emphasizes the contrast between the might of the Egyptians and the might of God. The second person pronoun is prominent; God is the dominant reality. As he promised, they now know him to be Lord. The boast of earth's mighty is nothing in contrast with the mere breath of God's **nostrils** (vv.8–10).

The third stanza (vv.11–19) contrasts God and the gods. As God's unique character has been shown through delivering his people, so it will be seen in his triumph over the nations (**Philistia, Edom, Moab,** and **Canaan**) as he leads the Israelites into their inheritance. Here we see the fulfillment of 8:10 and similar statements: there is none like God. **"Your unfailing love"** (15:13) refers to the central character of the biblical God. The Hebrew word being translated is *ḥesed,* which no single English word can adequately translate. Besides this phrase, words like "mercy," "grace," "kindness," and "lovingkindness" are used. The basic thought is the undeserved, passionate loyalty of a superior to an inferior. Moses is confident that God will continue the unmerited favor he has already shown.

While the men were celebrating with Moses, the women, led by Miriam, were rejoicing with a similar song, of which we have probably only the main theme preserved (15:20–21).

2. From the Red Sea to Sinai (15:22–18:27)

The story of the wilderness wanderings is one of the people's continued inability to trust and of God's continued providence. This theme appears here immediately after the great song of praise. The word *grumbled* (KJV "murmured" (15:24) will occur again and again throughout the remainder of the Pentateuch. It is the opposite of faith, trust, and acceptance. Nevertheless, God leads to the antidote to the bitter waters and mildly encourages them to believe. Concerning **"any of the diseases"** (v.26), some believe that the function of the ceremonial and dietary laws was to preserve health. Thus if the Hebrews followed the law, they would be more healthy. But it is also possible that the plagues are referred to here. In that case the sense is merely that obedience to God's commands will mean the Hebrews need not fear the kind of destruction visited upon the Egyptians. In 15:27 we see God's generosity following testing. No certain identification has been made of the places mentioned here. The traditional location is on the southwestern side of the Sinai Peninsula.

The Israelites seemed unable to transfer knowledge gained in one area to another. That God had provided water is quickly forgotten when food becomes a problem (16:1–36). After forty-three days (**fifteenth day,** 16:1) on the way, all of their own food would have been exhausted. Perhaps they had had to travel this slowly to allow flocks and herds to forage. At any rate, they were now at a place where they were forced to trust God. That was a fearsome prospect: better to satisfy the flesh in slavery then be dependent on the provision of a loving God (16:3).

The giving of the **manna** became both an opportunity to train the Israelites in obedience ("**I will test them,**" 16:4) and to teach them theological truth (vv.6–8). Just as deliverance from bondage was not the ultimate need of the Israelites in Egypt, so here the ultimate need is not supply of temporal necessities. What the Israelites need to know most is the providential love and mercy of God.

"**The Glory of the LORD**" (16:10): The Hebrew word for "glory," *kabod,* has the connotations of weightiness, significance, and reality. Thus this glory is not merely a bright evanescence, but something that conveys visually the unshakable reality of God. See also 34:29–35; 40:34; 2Ch 7:1; Jn 1:14. Discussions of the means God may have used to perform this miracle are unprofitable. The point is that God provided for his people at the very moment when he said he would and in ways it was clear nature could not. "**What is it?**" (16:15): The Hebrew for this question is *man-na,* which, in a touch of humor, provides the biblical name of the food (v.31).

The people's response to the commands concerning the manna (16:19–30) provides a graphic illustration of the perverseness of human nature when it comes to provision for our own needs. What God commands not to do,

we do (v.27). Of special prominence are commands relating to the Sabbath. The daily business of procuring one's living is not to be practiced on the seventh day. This is another way in which God reminds us that we are not the ultimate providers of our needs. The manna becomes the first of several visible reminders of God's faithfulness in the past (16:32–34, see also Nu 17:10; Jos 4:20–24). V.34 reports how the command of v.33 was eventually fulfilled after the construction of the tabernacle (see Heb 9:4).

Again the people do not trust God for water when it is not immediately available (17:1–7). **Horeb** (17:6) probably refers to the general territory rather than the mountain itself (see on 3:1, 12), since they had not yet reached the mountain (19:2). To test God in this way (17:7) is to act out of unbelief, demanding that he prove himself true (see Dt 6:16; Lk 4:12). On the other hand, God invites those whose faith is small to put him to the test (Mal 3:10) and let him prove his trustworthiness.

God was preparing a people through whom the Savior of the world could come. Amalekite attempts to destroy Israel put them in a deadly position (17:8–16; see Dt 25:17–19). A similar judgment was pronounced upon Edom for a similar sin (Ob 8–10; Mal 1:2–4). The dependence of victory on the raised staff showed that God, not Israel, was the source of Israel's military victories. See 1Sa 15 for the final development of this episode.

Ex 18:1–12 provides the first biblical instance of someone's coming to belief through the testimony of another. Jethro is called a **priest** (18:1). If he was a priest of the Lord, it was with a limited understanding of him, as v.11 indicates. Apparently Moses had sent Zipporah and their two sons back from Egypt during the height of the danger in Egypt. Now Jethro brings them to Moses and has an opportunity to hear Moses' testimony about God's self-revelation in delivering and caring for Israel. The result is Jethro's affirmation "**Now I know**" (v.11). Although he had not seen what God had done, he was able to recognize the obvious implications from Moses' report: there is none like the Lord. Jethro's actions (v.12) show that he was not merely giving intellectual assent to God's transcendance, but was acting upon that awareness by submitting himself to this transcendant One. To know God rightly is to experience the true end of salvation.

Like every great man, Moses was tempted to take too much upon himself. Perhaps he felt every decision must come straight from God through himself (vv.15–16). This would have been the Egyptian pattern. Jethro graciously (vv.19, 23) suggests a better way in which the administration of the nation can be decentralized. It is to Moses' credit that he sees the wisdom of this suggestion and implements it at once (vv.24–25).

II. REVELATION (19:1–40:38)

With ch. 19 the second main section of the book begins. In the first section it was shown that the self-revealing acts of God are the means of salvation. In this section it is explained that the goal of salvation is obedience and worship. Why does God deliver? So that his people may know and share his character (19:1–24:18) and so that they may constantly experience his presence in joyous service (25:1–40:38).

A. The Covenant (19:1–24:18)

In 19:1–24:18 God invites his delivered people to enter into a covenant relation with him. This covenant is grounded upon who God is and what

he has done for Israel. In recognition of these, Israel agrees to act and live in certain ways that are themselves a further manifestation of God's nature. Thus the covenant serves two purposes: it is a vehicle of committed relationship between God and humanity, but it is also a device within which people learn what God is like by trying to do what he wants. 19:1–25 constitutes the preparation for the covenant, while 20:1–23:33 is the presentation of the covenant. 24:1–18 reports the ceremonies that seal participation in the covenant. For a discussion of the ancient Near Eastern background to the covenant, see the introduction.

1. Preparation (19:1–25)

The preparation for the covenant is in three parts: the first is remainder and promise (vv.3–8); the second is action (vv.10–15); the third is visual and auditory (vv.16–25). It can hardly be accidental that these correspond with the commonly recognized human faculties: cognitive, volitional, and affective. On every level God was seeking to bring the people to the place where they would commit themselves to him without hesitation. The effectiveness of this preparation can be seen in the response recorded in ch. 24.

God reminds the people of their experience of the consequences of disobedience ("**what I did to Egypt**") and obedience ("**how I carried you**"), and offers them a special relationship to himself in which they will function as his specially chosen priests (vv.3–8). The clear implication is that the nation is to function as mediators between God and the world. The initial response, as one might expect, is positive.

Those who make a verbal commitment need to confirm that commitment with some form of action (vv.10–15). Three kinds of activity are enjoined here: washing (v.10), establishing of limits (vv.12–13), and sexual abstinence (v.15). All are associated with ritual purification. These actions conveyed the sense that an extraordinarily solemn moment was upon them. They also expressed a preliminary kind of obedience. Having obeyed in these matters, they would be more likely to obey in others later.

Preparations for the covenant were capped with a series of visual and auditory effects (vv.16–19). These combined to produce a sense of awe and wonder in the people. Whatever else they might think about the covenant that God was about to offer them, they were not likely to dismiss it as something trivial and ordinary. Later Moses would remind the people that no one else had ever heard the audible voice of God (Dt 4:33, 36). This covenant was unique.

God's final preparation was to underline to Moses his deadly nature for any humans who are not especially prepared to meet him (vv.20–24). Not even the ordinary priests could survive. Casual familiarity with the Most High is a dangerous thing (see 2Sa 6:6–7).

2. Presentation (20:1–23:33)

The presentation of the covenant has four parts: (1) the prologue (20:1–2); (2) a summary of the requirements for the people (20:3–17); (3) expanded requirements for the people (20:22–23:19); (4) God's commitment (23:20–33). Parts 2 and 3 encompass what we know as "the law." Here we see the law in its correct context. Obedience to it is a response to God's grace shown through his past deliverance and his future promises.

The first two verses of ch. 20 form a prologue. The reason for this covenant's being offered is stated succinctly. God, who had become their God by

virtue of what he had done for them in Egypt, offers it. Covenant-keeping is not a means of entering a relationship with God. Rather, it is the way an already existing relationship—one created solely by God's gracious intervention in their history—is lived out.

Ex 20:3–17 summarizes in ten absolute commands what God expects of his people. Nothing of this sort appears in the law codes of other ancient Near Eastern peoples. This is not surprising since those societies were all polytheistic, and polytheism is of necessity relativistic. But where only one God exists, his will is absolute. It may be asked why this summary statement is couched in such largely negative terms. Surely it is because norms that are stated positively leave us in doubt about limits. While "You shall not commit adultery" does not tell me how to cherish my spouse, it leaves no doubt whatsoever about what I *cannot* do and still cherish my spouse. The importance of these commands can hardly be overstated. If indeed their Author is the Author of all existence, as the Bible maintains, then this cursory expression of his expectations for his covenant people is also an expression of the norms of human life.

The first commandment calls for exclusive worship of God. Interestingly, this statement does not require God's people to deny the existence of other deities, but rather to *act* as if they did not exist. At the outset, God is less concerned about what we think than what we do. Ultimately, the two must coincide (Dt 4:35, 39–40), but at the outset obedience comes first (Jn 7:17). So long as polytheism exists, ethical relativism and magical manipulation of divine power cannot be escaped.

The second commandment speaks to God's transcendence. As with monotheism, this doctrine is fundamental to any concept of ethical absolutes and to religion based on trust and commitment rather than manipulation. God is not a part of this world and cannot be represented by, or manipulated by, anything in it. To attempt to do so is inevitably to localize him and, ultimately, to divide him. The introduction of idolatry has long-term consequences, which our children and grandchildren will feel. This should not be surprising, since this is a world of cause and effect (see below on 34:6–7).

The third commandment speaks of making God appear insignificant through casual use (**"misuse,"** lit. "use in an empty way" 20:7) of God's name. The most immediate reference here is to invoking God's name while swearing to do something that the swearer knows is either impossible or unlikely. By using God's name in that way we make the Lord of the universe appear faithless, or, worse, worthless. See also Jas 5:12.

The fourth command (20:8–11) is one of the two commands stated positively. Also, it is the only one of the laws relating to worship and ceremony that makes its way into the Ten Commandments. The rationale given for the Sabbath is rest. The day is to be kept holy, that is, different from all other days in which ordinary work is undertaken. But **"holy"** also means given over to the Lord and thus reflecting his nature. Dt 5:15 adds a further rationale: God has delivered his people from slave labor; the Sabbath is a day to rejoice in that freedom from work.

The command regarding parents is the second positive command. No nation that forgets its debt to those who have gone before can endure. Self-centered arrogance that cuts its ties to previous benefactors will break the threads of continuity and development upon which any civilization depends. But more specifically, no nation can

endure in which the family structure is not consciously upheld. To refuse to honor one's parents, however fallible they may be or have been, destroys the sense of identity and place upon which healthy personhood depends.

The use of the word *murder* (20:13 NIV) is accurate, for this command does not in itself prohibit warfare or capital punishment. It does prohibit the killing of one individual by another for some self-serving reason such as rage or aggression. It speaks of the value of each individual's life.

The seventh commandment summarizes the whole sexual ethic by focusing on the breach of marital fidelity. Adultery is thus seen as the most serious sexual sin. All the others are bad, but this one caps them all. Why? Because it is a breach of covenant. It suggests that a person's sexuality is his or hers to use as he or she wishes regardless of how it affects others. Adultery is also wrong because it suggests that sex can be legitimately expressed outside the bonds of heterosexual covenant.

Stealing (20:15) suggests that I can get something for nothing. Thus it contravenes God's world of responsibility and discipline. It also denies dependence on God for one's needs. Finally, this prohibition points to the value of personal property.

The command concerning false testimony helps us to see the focus of the previous three commands. It is not so much that the acts of lying or thievery or sexual infidelity or murder are forbidden in themselves as it is that these ways of treating others are forbidden: do not take somebody's property, or spouse, or life, or reputation. Thus the Jews could say that these commands are fulfilled in the single command "Love your neighbor" (Mk 12:31; Gal 5:14).

The final commandment (20:17) brings the whole series around full

circle. It is the human lust for acquisi-
tions, especially acquisition at the expense of another, that is at the heart of
idolatrous religion (Isa 57:17; Col
3:5). God is reduced to gods—a device
for getting what we want. Our parents,
our spouse, and our neighbor become
merely aids or hindrances to that lust to
possess. To all of this the Creator
pronounces a thunderous "No!"

Ex 20:18–21 recaps the motivational value of the awesome signs. See the
comment on 19:16–24.

In the expanded stipulations of the
covenant (20:22–23:19), the Israelites
were given concrete examples of how
the preceding terse, absolute principles
would function in everyday life. They
are stated in the "if—then" form common to law codes of that time. Some of
the laws show great similarity to earlier
laws from both Babylon and Sumer.
This is not to say that they were copied
from those cultures, but that they were
a part of the common culture of the
day. It is evident that God uses whatever he can from a given setting,
purifying it as necessary, to convey his
truth to that setting. But by placing
these laws in the context of the covenant and the Ten Commandments, he
shows that ethical behavior is not merely a matter of social pragmatism, as it
appears to be in Babylon and Sumer,
but is a means of response to a consistent, purposeful Creator whose own
character is ethical and who has already
graciously delivered.

The first laws relate to the worship of
God (20:22–26). Probably the prohibition against dressed stone altars was
another attempt to distinguish Hebrew
worship from that of their idolatrous
neighbors. See below on 34:17–26.

God's concern for the helpless follows immediately upon his concern for
proper worship (21:1–11). Slavery is
not forbidden, as that would leave the

destitute with no means of survival. But
the institution is strictly regulated, with
clear provisions against the creation of
a permanent underclass. Servitude for
life was possible only through the
servant's own choice. A woman born
into poverty had almost no chance of a
normal marriage. As unideal as concu-
binage was, it was preferable to the
alternative: prostitution. Given these
realities, the laws seek to ensure that
the concubine will be treated as a
person of worth, not as an expendable
sex device (21:7–11).

The next group of laws relate to
personal injury (21:12–32). The basic
principles are equality (vv.23–25) and
responsibility. If a person injured another, whether intentionally (v.14) or
as a result of failure to take reasonable
precautions (v.29), that person would
experience the same results or their
equivalent. While there is some differentiation in punishment when injuries
occur across class lines (vv.26, 27, 32),
these are much less pronounced than in
other law codes where, for instance, a
slave's striking a noble was cause for
death.

The person who committed manslaughter (21:12–13) was permitted to
escape vengeance by living in special
protected cities ("**A place I will designate**"; see Nu 35:6; Dt 4:41–43;
19:2–10.) But the murderer had no
such escape. See Dt 19:11–13; 1Ki
2:28–34.

21:15, 17 illustrate the vital importance of the family, especially in that
society. See also above on 20:12.

"**Punished**" (21:20) is literally "suffer vengeance," if not death itself,
something judged equal to the crime.
"No serious injury" (vv.22–25) is ambiguous because it is not specified
whether the reference is to the mother
or the child. Many commentators conclude that it refers to the mother, the

child necessarily having died as a result of the premature birth. Others argue that both mother and child are included, "no injury" implying that the child was close enough to term to survive. It is impossible to ascertain which is correct. Freedom for the slave (vv.26–27) would be of more benefit to him or her than the enforcement of a like punishment on the master. Since the owner of the animal is not directly responsible for the death, redemption is possible (v.30).

Ex 21:33–22:15 lists laws relating to property loss. In other cultures thievery was usually punishable by death. Here multiple restitution is the key (22:1). Property does not equal life in value. This law probably provides the basis for Zacchaeus' action in Lk 19:8. Ex 22:2–4 gives some qualifications to this concept. If a householder kills a thief in an act of stealing, he is held to be justified; but if he kills the thief at a later time (**"after sunrise,"** the next day) he is a murderer.

Since it was common for parcels of land to be small and odd-shaped without clear definition of boundaries, statements such as those found in 22:5–6 were necessary. In complex cases where there is no clear responsibility for theft or loss, an ajudication was required with single restitution for a judgment of negligence and double for malfeasance (22:7–15).

Miscellaneous laws relating to social and religious righteousness (22:16–23:9). The apparently indiscriminate mixing of ceremonial and social laws is a testimony to Israel's wholistic view of obedience to God. While there was no penalty for premarital sex per se, it was insisted that a marriage result. The **bride price** (22:16) was a sum of money paid by the groom to the father of the bride. Other laws forbade certain practices associated with the corrupt Canaanite religion (22:18–20). Magic was an attempt to manipulate divine power through rituals apart from commitment, trust, or ethical behavior. As such, it was diametrically opposite of biblical faith. Bestiality (v.19) was one way of expressing the conviction that gods, animals, and humans are all part of one universal system.

All persons are recipients of God's grace. No one has a right to take advantage of another's misfortune (22:21–27; see Am 2:7–8, where oppression mixed with incest and ritual prostitution is presented as a particularly vile example of Israel's apostasy).

The first part of v.29 is obscure. A literal rendering is "do not defer your excess and your juice." In view of the remainder of the verse, it probably refers to the offering of firstfruits (see below on 23:16). **Firstborn** sons could not be sacrificed (as firstborn animals had to be). They had to be redeemed on the eighth day after birth (v.30; 13:15; see also Lk 2:23).

The first three verses of ch. 23 provide three pointed examples of what it means not to bear false witness either for or against another. The next six verses prohibit taking advantage of another's misfortune, not even an enemy's (vv.4–5).

The final group of stipulations has to do with religious observances (23:10–19). The sabbath principle extended to the land (23:10–11). Not only does this have social value for the poor, but it also allows the land to recover some of its fertility (see Leviticus 25:1–7). Furthermore, it provides relief for the workers, both human and animal. At the heart of all the Hebrew worship was the recognition of God alone. Practically speaking, other gods did not exist for the Hebrews (see also 20:23; 22:20; and the comment on 20:3).

The last laws form a preliminary

introduction to the three annual pilgrimage feasts held in April, June, and September. For fuller treatments see Lev 23 and Dt 16. The Feast of Unleavened Bread (23:15) was a weeklong festival celebrated during the seven days immediately after Passover about April 1 (see Ex 12:17–20). At about this same time pagans would be celebrating the rising of the vegetation god from the dead. The Israelites were to remember God's gracious acts in history on their behalf. The Feast of Harvest (23:16) was held seven weeks after the end of the Feast of Unleavened Bread. This was about the first of June at the end of the wheat harvest. This was a feast of thanksgiving to God and a dedication of the tithe to him. It is also called the Feast of Weeks and the Feast of Pentecost. The Feast of Ingathering came at the end of the grape harvest, the final harvest of the year, about September 25. It is also called the Feast of Tabernacles or Booths (see Lev 23:33–43). **Yeast** was symbolic of sin (23:18). There is some reason to believe cooking a kid in its mother's milk was a Canaanite magic ritual supposed to ensure the mother's continued fertility (23:19).

The stipulations section of the covenant closes with God's commitment to his people (23:20–33). In response to their continued covenant obedience, he would wipe out their enemies (vv.22–23, 27–28) and give them long, abundant lives (vv.25–26), establishing them within spacious borders (v.31). The only obstacles to this promise of blessing would be rebellion against God and the worship of the gods of their defeated enemies (vv.24, 32–33). Biblical religion is not compatible with any religion that sees the divine as part of this world. One of the reasons for worshiping the pagan gods was their supposed ability to provide these bless-

ings. But God is the only one who can truly provide them. See also Hos 2:5–8. The conquest would be progressive according to God's plan (vv.27–30), although not nearly so progressive as the Hebrews' disobedience made it eventually become. The borders described here (v.31) were attained in Solomon's time.

3. Sealing (24:1–11)

The sealing of the covenant was marked by two events: the first was a symbolic act in which the two parties accepted the terms of the covenant and invoked a curse on themselves should they break it (vv.3–8). The second was a covenant meal in which the two parties, or their representatives, celebrated the new relationship (vv.1–2, 9–11).

God's preparation (ch. 19) had achieved its desired effect. The people may have little understood the seriousness of their commitment, but they made it. The twelve stones were historical markers bearing witness to what would take place here (see also Jos 4:20–24). **Fellowship offerings** (24:5, called "peace offerings" in KJV) were a thank offering given in recognition of God's gracious reconciliation (Lev 3:1–17). The significance of the blood ceremony (24:6–8) is that the people (half of the blood) and God (half of the blood) invoked upon themselves a death like that of the sacrificial animals if they broke the covenant (see Jer 34:18–19 for a similar rite).

Two aspects of the description of the covenant meal are significant. Like Isa 6:1, where only the train of God's robe is describable, here only the pavement beneath his feet is described (24:10). Human language is not adequate to describe the ineffable. Second, **God did not raise his hand** (24:11). The covenant blessings meant that God's holiness would not destroy his people. But not even Moses could look directly into God's face (33:20).

B. The Tabernacle (24:12–40:38)

To this point God had given the covenant in an oral form and Moses had recorded it (24:4). Now God would give a miraculously written copy of the Ten Commandments (24:12; 31:18) as well as instructions for the tabernacle. It was probably at this same time that Moses received the further amplification of the covenant stipulations recorded in Leviticus. This final subdivision of the book has to do with the realization of God's ultimate purpose in the Exodus: his taking up residence among his people. He delivers and calls to obedience, all to the end that we may experience the fullness of his presence. The material is divided into three parts: the instructions (25:1–31:18), the golden calf episode (32:1–34:35), and the report of the building of the tabernacle (35:1–40:38). The third section is in most places a word-for-word duplication of the first. This duplication shows some of the significance God attached to the realization of his desire to be present among his people. It also speaks of the importance of satisfying our needs in God's ways, not ours, if those needs are to be truly satisfied.

1. Instructions (25:1–31:18)

God's plans for his residence among his people take into account a number of factors relating to our human condition. We need some tangible means of recognizing and celebrating God's presence; we need beauty and majesty; we need a sense of dignity and worth that genuine involvement in a great undertaking can bring; we need to feel that each one's gifts and abilities have significance. In wonderful ways the taber-

nacle and its equipment served these purposes while also providing a valuable teaching aid for the whole theology of salvation. The instructions generally move from the interior outward to the court and end with such miscellaneous items as anointing oil and incense. Two exceptions are the incense altar and the basin, which are described with the miscellaneous items. (In the description of construction, they appear in the more expected order: 37:25–29; 38:8.)

First, is a description of the voluntary manner (25:2) and the richness and variety (vv.3–7) of the offerings to be accepted for the work (see also 35:4–29). Immediately following come instructions for the ark (25:10–22). This box would sit in the innermost room of the tabernacle, in the place where the idol would stand in a pagan temple. But it was not a representation of God. Rather, it served to remind the Israelites of their covenant with the transcendent God who had redeemed them in a historic event and had committed himself to them.

The ark and most of the other wood parts of the tabernacle were made of **acacia** (25:10), a hard, orange-brown wood still found in the Sinai Desert and excellent for cabinetry. In it was **the Testimony** (v.16), the two tablets of the law that testified to the commitment made to the covenant by both parties. On its top was the **atonement cover**. The Hebrew word *kipporet* may mean simply "cover" or "lid," but the verb "to cover" is also used with a theological meaning: to atone for (cover up) sin. And since this was the place blood was sprinkled in atonement for the sins of the nation on the Day of Atonement (Lev 16:14), this translation is probably correct. Since no complete description of the **cherubim** (25:19) is given, we do not know what they looked like, except that they had wings (v.20). God is not the ark nor in it nor even on it. He is other than anything earthly. But because of his covenant, he will manifest himself in connection with the ark (v.22).

The table (25:23–30) held the bread of the Presence. These twelve loaves of bread were not for the purpose of feeding God, as in pagan temples, but rather represented God's caring for his people's need (Lev 24:9). Thus there was a loaf for each tribe.

The lampstand (25:31–40) was shaped like an almond tree with six branches and one central stem. The lamps were probably flat bowls with four slots molded into turned-in rims. The bowls would be kept filled with olive oil (27:20), and trimmed wicks would be laid in the slots. The seven lamps would then be suspended from the stem and branches of the stand.

The portable structure that housed the ark, the table, and the lampstand is described in ch. 26. The innermost component was made of gold-sheathed **frames** standing on end. They were probably joined by some sort of tongue and groove arrangement (v.17). The resulting walls were made rigid by special corner frames (vv.23–25) and by **crossbars** joining the frames through rings at their centers and perhaps at top and bottom (vv.26–28). The frames rested upon silver bases (vv.19, 21, 25). The resulting walls formed three sides of a rectangle. They were covered on the outside by linen curtains joined together with **loops** and **clasps** (vv.1–6). The ceiling was formed by curtains of goat hair similarly joined. These ceiling curtains hung down a short distance over the side walls and their linen coverings (vv.7–13). The whole structure was then protected by two leather covers, one of ram skin and the other of another skin,

whose origin is uncertain (NIV **"sea cows"**). The fourth or east side of the rectangle was covered by a beautifully woven drapery suspended from five posts (vv.36–37). The interior was divided into two spaces by a similar drape (vv.31–35).

In front of the tabernacle proper stood the altar (27:1–8). It was hollow (v.8) with a grate inside it (v.4). The horns (v.2) were probably vertical projections that helped to keep the wood and sacrifices from falling off. Stone altars with such projections have been recovered in Israel.

The tabernacle was to stand in a courtyard 150 feet long and 75 feet wide (27:18). The courtyard was formed by linen curtains suspended from bronze pillars banded with silver (vv.9–10). On the east side was a gateway drape made similar to the entry and interior veils in the tabernacle (vv.16–17).

Ch. 28 describes the priestly garments. As with the tabernacle and court, the dominant color is white, the universal symbol of purity, but such rich colors as gold, blue, purple, and red were also prominent. The **ephod** (28:4) was a kind of decorative vest or apron worn under the breastpiece (vv.26–28). Not only did the high priest carry the names of the twelve tribes on his shoulders (v.12), but over his heart (v.29). Thus his function as mediator and representative was doubly reinforced. The term **"breastpiece for making decisions"** (v.15) probably derives from the fact that the Urim and Thummim, used to discern God's will, were kept in the breastpiece (v.30; Nu. 27:21). **The robe of the ephod** (28:31) was probably a garment worn under the ephod. **Pomegranates** (v.33) were a fruit frequently associated with fertility and life in the ancient Near East. The priest could not enter God's presence unannounced and unprepared because he might die (v.35). **"As on a seal"** (v.36) may indicate an older, more decorative style of writing. **"Holy to the LORD"** reminds the reader of two things: whatever is set apart to God, like the priest here, is expected to share his character; and that character is markedly distinct from all others. Since the priest is holy to God, two things ensue: faulty offerings made unintentionally are sanctified by the priest's offering them; the responsibility for any intentionally faulty offerings will rest upon the priest. Since the robes were open at the bottom, it was possible that the genitalia of the priests might be exposed to anyone standing below them. The prescribed **undergarments** (v.42) would prevent that.

The detail and length of the commands for the ceremony of priestly ordination (29:1–46) underline how seriously the OT takes the holiness of God. That holiness, the essential difference between God and fallen humans, will destroy any who come into his presence without having dealt with their own condition according to God's prescriptions. In three places in this ceremony (vv.10, 15, 19) the necessity of substitutionary atonement is emphasized by the priests' laying their hands on the sacrificial animal's head. It dies in their place. Furthermore, the prominence of blood must not be overlooked (vv.12, 16, 20–21). Sin is not atoned for by mere offerings. There is no atonement without bloodshed. By itself, the smell of burning flesh is hardly **pleasing** (v.18). But the aroma of burning sacrifice is pleasing to God because it represents reconciliation between himself and his people.

Throughout the OT the **anointing oil** (29:21) signifies the presence of the Spirit of God in that person's life. The **wave offering** (v.24) is a gift of grati-

tude to God. Certain portions of the **fellowship offerings** (those given by the Hebrews to express gratitude, vv.26–28) were to be given to the priests for their support (see Lev 7:28–36). **Seven days** (v.30) probably refers to the period of consecration. The garments were also worn during holy days.

That which is **sacred** (29:31) must not be put to some other use than God directs, nor is it allowed to come into contact with what is not sacred. Since sin is not only a matter of choice, but also a matter of association, the altar needs to be atoned for (vv.35–37). Thus all spiritual contamination was removed from it. In pagan worship this contamination would come from the presence of evil gods, but the OT so deflates the demonic realm that consecration has nothing to do with driving out demons.

God's purpose in the Exodus deliverance is made explicit in 29:42–46: He brought them out so that he might dwell among them and be God among them. This is his same purpose in salvation from sin: the indwelling presence of the Holy Spirit.

The final section of the tabernacle instructions (30:1–31:18) seems to deal with matters that are deemed somewhat miscellaneous: the incense altar (30:1–10), the tabernacle offering (vv.11–16), the basin (vv.17–21), the anointing oil (vv.22–33), the incense (vv.34–38), the inspired craftsmen (31:1–11), and the Sabbath (vv.12–18).

The significance of the regular offering of incense (30:8) is not specified. It was, and is, a common element in many religions, the smoke and odor lending an aura of awe and mystery to the ceremonies (see Isa 6:4). In Lk (1:10) and Rev (8:3–4) incense is particularly associated with prayer (see also Ps 141:2).

Although the function of the ritual described in 30:11–16 was to provide money for the maintenance of the tabernacle, the concept behind it expresses God's ownership of the people. No king or ruler could count them as though they were his own. Although the text does not specify it, this may have been David's sin in the matter of the census reported in 2Sa 24. "Cross over" (v.14) probably refers to the act of crossing over a line for the purposes of counting. Ex 30:15 establishes that the worth of a person's life has no relation to one's wealth or capacity for contribution.

The **hands** and **feet** (30:19) are those parts of the body in most direct contact with the world and thus most likely to be defiled. Especially in more primitive cultures, cleansing from actual physical defilement could be necessary. But even there the symbolic reference to spiritual defilement would be understood.

Both the rich contents and unique function of the **anointing oil** (30:22–33) are another expression of the extreme worth and value of God. The contents are both rare and extremely valuable; the oil is used for worship and nothing else. Since no other persons or objects could have this particular oil upon them, it made apparent the unique functions and relationships to God of those persons and objects.

Just as the anointing oil, the incense was to be made from particularly precious materials and was reserved for tabernacle use only. Merely casual or self-serving uses were forbidden (v.38).

The craftsmen who were to do the work were chosen and empowered by God (31:1–11). It is especially important to notice the reference to Spirit-filling (v.3). This is the first occurrence

in the Bible of this phraseology (although the concept appears in different words in Ge 41:38). This expression is used to describe a person who is divinely enabled to transcend limited human ability in a given area, whether it be technical skill, as here, or wisdom (Ge 41:38), or leadership (Jdg 6:34), or moral life (Isa 32:15–17). This concept would eventually provide a fundamental expression of the believer's life with God (Nu 11:29–30; Mt 3:11; Jn 14:15–17; Ac 1:8). Here it also serves to guard against a false dichotomy, that since the priests are specially set apart for God's service, they are the only ones to whom God relates and through whom he works. Every person can be filled with the Spirit of God to fulfill his or her particular calling.

As the Sabbath is the only ceremonial observance mentioned in the Ten Commandments, it is the only one mentioned here in connection with the tabernacle instructions (31:12–17). Surely this is not accidental but speaks to the special significance of this observance. Refusal to work on one day in seven represented not only the Israelite's commitment to godlikeness (v.17) and a commitment to be a marked people (v.13), but also a recognition that it was not their work but God's providence that provided their needs (16:21–26). To **know that** God is **the Lord** (31:13) it is necessary not only to experience his power (chs. 6–14) and providence (chs. 16–18), but also to live in a state of covenant obedience with him (chs. 20–40). That truth is expressed here in the specifics of Sabbath obedience. The harshness of the punishment for Sabbath-breaking (v.14) reflects the extreme importance of the lessons being taught here. How shall we find peace with a holy God? By establishing our way and asking God to conform to it? That is no more possible than is our redefining the laws of physical science to our liking. Yet human sinfulness continues to insist upon its own way. Somehow the Hebrews had to recognize that it was God's way or no way. For another illustration of this same point, see Lev 10:1–3 and Nu 15:32–36.

2. The Golden Calf (32:1–34:35)

At the same time God was giving Moses instructions for meeting the people's need for a tangible center for worship and guidance (see above on 25:1ff.), the people despaired of having that need met by God and insisted that Aaron meet it for them. The results were both tragic and predictable. Whenever humans insist on meeting their own needs, deification of creation follows. And close behind that comes misuse of resources and the uninhibited expression of sexuality as the worship of the life force. In many ways this brief and poignant story teaches us the heart of the biblical drama as clearly as any other portion of Scripture. Serving God is not merely a matter of making a decision. Nor are God's options merely to bless or to curse. Somehow a faithful God must find ways to continue on with a people whose performance again and again falls short of their best intentions. He must do so until they can finally realize that the cure for their sinfulness lies beyond themselves.

"**Make us gods**" (32:1): The same Hebrew word can mean "God," "god," or "gods." Here it is probably used to mean "a god" in the sense of "an idol." Instead of voluntary and varying contributions (see 25:2; 35:21–29), the people are required to bring a gift, and one kind only (vv.2–3). "**Calf**" (32:4) is almost certainly a pejorative diminutive, much as a prejudiced person might call an adult of another race "boy." The idol was probably of a full-grown bull,

similar to idols the Israelites had known in Egypt. The bull idol represented life, fertility, and power. The biblical writer mockingly calls it a calf. "**These are your gods**" probably indicates that Aaron and the people did not recognize any essential problem in what they were doing. If Moses, wherever he was, was worshiping the invisible Yahweh, they were merely worshiping the visible one (so also v.5). They did not recognize that to make an idol of God was to undermine every truth about God that he was trying to teach them. The Hebrew word for "revelry" (v.6) has a wide range of meaning from simple play to sexual activity (Ge 26:8). In view of the sexual orgies regularly associated with bull worship, that connotation is surely intended here.

God's response to this flagrant breach of the covenant was perfectly just. The people had sworn on pain of death to keep the covenant. Now they have broken it and deserve to die. They are no longer God's people (32:7). Nevertheless, there are undertones here that suggest something else is going on. Has God really forgotten his promise to Abraham (v.13; see 2:24)? Would he so easily shift the promise to Moses (v.10)? Why is he so easily moved by Moses' appeal (v.14)? One suspects that we have here not a revelation of an arbitrariness in God so much as a test of Moses. Will Moses reject this fallible people and accept the honor lightly dangled before him, or will he care more for the honor of God than about his own? If this interpretation is correct, Moses passes the test with flying colors.

As passionate as Moses was for the honor of God, he is equally towering in his rage over the people's foolishness (32:19–20). He symbolizes the brokenness of the covenant by hurling the divinely inscribed tablets (31:18) to the ground, and he forces the people to defile the pulverized idol by passing it through their own digestive tracts. If no one else understands, he at least does: idolatry cannot coexist with the truth that God is not part of this world. And if that understanding is lost, all the rest of biblical faith is as well. That faith is uniquely dependent on the truth that God transcends this world.

Ex 32:24 is one of the great expressions of the human tendency to excuse ourselves and deny personal responsibility. The results of Aaron's inability to stand up to the people in their demand for a god to manipulate are threefold: brother set against brother (vv.25–29), a plague (v.35), and the distance of God (33:3). God had planned for brother to serve brother, for health and abundance, and for his presence in their midst, but all that is jeopardized by the people's efforts to achieve these things for themselves (see on 32:1).

The most serious problem is the distance of God. Moses' concern is seen in his attempt to maneuver God into an "or else" situation (32:31–32). God, in effect, tells him to calm down (v.33). But Moses' statement is a final rejection of any offer to make a nation for himself (see v.10). God's words and actions in response (vv.33–35) show that he will forgive the Israelites as a people and continue his election of them, but that individual Israelites will still experience the temporal results of their actions. He goes on to say (33:1–3) that he will keep his promise to give the people the land of Canaan but that he himself cannot go with them because of their stubborn (**stiff-necked**) tendency to disobedience. People with that attitude cannot survive in the presence of a holy God. The people's shocked response is to take off the **ornaments,** which probably symbolize their pride (v.6).

One of the results of the golden calf incident was a new level of intimacy between Moses' and God (33:7–34:35). The central issue is whether God will go with the people to the Promised Land. Moses argues that without God's presence for himself personally and with the people as a whole, the whole enterprise is pointless. This underlines what the entire book of Exodus and, indeed, the whole process of salvation, is about: experiencing God's presence (see on 24:12–40:38). The upshot of these encounters is that Moses himself becomes a symbol of God's presence through the radiance of his face (34:29–30).

The tabernacle was also called the Tent of Meeting (40:2), and some believe that 33:7–11 is a reference to the tabernacle, here placed out of chronological order for reasons of topical coverage (Moses' meetings with God). But that does not seem correct since this tent is pitched outside the camp (v.7) and the tabernacle was set up in the center of the camp (Nu 2:2). Thus it appears that this tent was a temporary measure until the tabernacle was completed.

"Face to face" (33:11), literally "mouth to mouth," is an expression of extreme intimacy but also of directness in communication. If Moses is to lead God's people, then he must have an intimate knowledge of God and his ways (v.13). It is the experience and evidence of the presence of God (v.16) that distinguishes biblical religion from all others. This is summed up in the word *glory:* the awesome reality of God. See above on 16:10. God will reveal his character (**name**) to Moses and give him a glimpse of his actual being (33:19–23). But mortality and corruption cannot survive a direct and unmediated experience of immortality and perfection. In Christian tradition the cleft rock is seen as a symbol of Christ, through whose protection we sinners can come into the presence of God and live.

God's response to Moses' plea is to reaffirm the covenant (34:1–28). In many ways this is a brief reenactment of chs. 19–24. God manifests himself (vv.5–7), offers his presence and protection (v.10), stipulates what the people's side of the agreement will entail (vv.11–26), and directs that the covenant be put in writing (vv.27–28). Interestingly, this promulgation of the covenant is one-sided. God merely states that he is willing to go on with the previous relationship even though it has been technically dissolved by disobedience. The stipulations deal specifically with two aspects: the response of the people to idol worshipers (vv.11–16) and true worship (vv.17–26). This is as might be expected in view of the recent bout with idolatry.

Compassion is not the dissolution of moral cause and effect (34:6–7). Unless there are real consequences for guilt, there is no such thing as mercy. However, it should not be thought that God arbitrarily punishes the descendants of sinners. This statement means that a person's actions have long-term consequences because God has made the world that way. God's mercy is in his limiting the deadly effects of sin to three or four generations. The effects of righteousness he extends to a thousand generations (see Dt 7:9).

Ex 34:11–17 provides a theological explanation for the destruction of the peoples who lived in the land of Canaan. Any attempt to coexist with them would result in an acceptance of their false religions. While many falsehoods can coexist together, the truth cannot coexist with any of them. Jealousy (34:14) has an unsavory connotation in English. It is petty and posses-

sive. That is not the case in Hebrew. It is the same word as is sometimes translated "zeal." So it was because Jesus was jealous for the house of God that he drove out the money changers (Jn 2:17). God's jealousy is on our behalf, not his.

In view of the preceding verses, it is likely that the stipulations for worship here (34:18–26) are specifically designed to set the Hebrew worship apart from the pagan worship practices of the Canaanites. Of special prominence are the three pilgrim feasts (vv.23–24): Unleavened Bread (and Passover, v.18, 25); Weeks (or Firstfruits, vv.22, 26); and Ingathering (v.22). **At the turn of the year** (v.22): This feast occurred in September. The civil year began in the autumn, as the Jewish New Year still does. See above on 23:14–19 for a further discussion of the feasts.

3. Construction (35:1–40:38)

This final section of the book contains the joyous report of how the tabernacle was constructed in express obedience to the commands of God. God's way of supplying our needs is better than our own. That this report begins with yet another rehearsal of the sabbath regulations further emphasizes the importance of these commands over against the other statutes on worship (see also 20:8–11; 23:10–12; 31:12–17).

The first large segment of this section (35:4–36:7) describes the collection of materials and appointment of workers for the construction. The stress is on the fact that there was something: time, talent, or material, that every person could contribute. See also 25:1–7. Thus the whole community was involved in the work. Contrast these factors with the construction of the golden calf (cf. 32:2–4). Furthermore, the participation was voluntary, not coerced (see 35:5, 21, 22, 29; 36:3). Those who have experienced the electing (ch. 19) and forgiving (ch. 34) grace of God do not need coercion to give. In fact, they may need to be restrained (36:5–7).

Between 35:30 and 39:30 the report is in largely the same words as are contained in the instructions (25:10–30:21). For comment on these, see the discussion on the corresponding elements there. On the Spirit-empowered leaders (35:30–36:1), see 31:1–11. On the tabernacle (36:8–38), see 26:1–37. On the ark (37:1–9), see 25:10–22. On the table (37:10–16), see 25:23–30. On the lampstand (37:17–24), see 25:31–40. On the altar of incense (37:25–29), see 30:1–10. On the altar of burnt offering (38:1–7), see 27:1–8. On the bronze basin (38:8), see 30:17–21. On the courtyard (38:9–20), see 27:9–19. At the end of these descriptions is a list of the total amounts of the metals used in the construction (38:21–31).

For a discussion of the priestly garments described in 39:1–31, see above on 28:1–43.

The final report of the building appears in 39:32–43. Everything had been done exactly according to God's requirements. The result is blessing (v.43). What is being emphasized here is that covenant obedience brings blessing, whereas covenant breaking results in curse (32:10).

The climax of the book appears in ch. 40. These events are what the entire book has been leading up to, what all the previous experiences have been in aid of. The Hebrew people were delivered from bondage and brought into a covenant of obedience, all in order that they might experience the presence of God in their midst. As in the case of the tabernacle specifications, the extreme importance of obedience is emphasized by duplication: vv.1–15 give God's commands for setting up the tabernacle, then vv.16–33 report in an almost word-for-word fashion how Moses set up the tabernacle according to God's command. Now the **glory** can come down from the mountain and live in the very midst of the people (40:34–38). But even this is not the fulfillment of God's dearest desire. One day the Glory would tabernacle in human flesh (Jn 1:14), so that in the end he might dwell in all flesh (Jn 17:5, 22, 24; 2Co 3:18).

BIBLIOGRAPHY

Cassuto, Umberto. *A Commentary on the Book of Exodus*. Reprint. Jerusalem: Magnes, 1983.

Childs, Brevard. *The Book of Exodus*. OTL. Philadelphia: Westminster, 1974.

Cole, R. Alan. *Exodus*. TOTC. Grand Rapids: Eerdmans, 1973.

Cox, Leo G. "The Book of Exodus." BBC. Edited by A. F. Harper. Kansas City: Beacon Hill, 1969, 1:169–316.

Haines, Lee. *Exodus*. WBC. Edited by C. W. Carter. Grand Rapids: Eerdmans, 1967. 1:159–290.

LEVITICUS
John E. Hartley
Lane Scott

INTRODUCTION

I. TITLE AND PLACE IN THE CANON

The Jewish title for Leviticus is *wayyiqrā*, "And He Called," the first words of the book. The English title is derived from the name the book bears in the Latin Vulgate, *Leviticus*, "pertaining to the Levites."

The historical perspective apparently determined placement of the book in the Canon. In the words of Brevard S. Childs,

> . . . the book of Leviticus has been given a definite historical setting as instructions to Moses in the context of the Sinai covenant. Even elements of the narrative are continued from the previous book (Lev. 8–9 joins Ex. 29). The final chapters look forward to the imminent entrance into the promised land and connect smoothly with the book of Numbers (p. 157).

Theological considerations are also important in the placing of Leviticus immediately after Exodus. In the latter book God establishes the Sinai covenant with Israel and directs Moses in the building of the tabernacle. Leviticus gives instructions for worship at the tabernacle and for holy living before God. Basic theological themes introduced in Exodus, such as God's holy presence and human sinfulness, are central to Leviticus, where regulations are given in order that a sinful people may worship the holy God.

II. AUTHOR AND DATE

Leviticus does not name its author, and there is no command in the text for Moses to write down what God said to him. But it may well be that Moses did put in writing what God revealed and that that material was the primary source for Leviticus. The issues of author and date are best studied from the standpoint of belief in the Canon as Scripture, that is, the completed texts. In the authors' opinion, Leviticus was compiled and edited into its final shape by the exilic and postexilic scribes who endeavored to preserve for posterity the received Mosaic tradition.

III. CONTENT AND STRUCTURE

Leviticus is part of the material Yahweh revealed to Moses at Sinai concerning the establishment of the cult as the official place of worship. Thus it fits into the broader corpus of Ex 25:1–Nu 10:10. Nevertheless, in the Canon Leviticus has been set apart as its own book. It has a formal heading in 1:1–2. This heading does triple duty. It introduces the whole book as well as the sacrificial legislation (chs. 1–7) and the first unit (chs. 1–3). This heading ties specifically into Ex 40, for Moses hears Yahweh speaking from the Tent of Meeting, which has just been set up and filled with Yahweh's glory (Ex 40:16–38). The end of the book is marked by a summary formula at 26:46, which concludes the last section and the book as a whole and possibly chs. 17–26. With the inclusion of ch. 27, a final summary statement came at v.34.

The material in Leviticus has been assembled around topics: sacrificial regulations (chs. 1–7), putting the sanctuary into operation (chs. 8–10), laws on ritual purity (chs. 11–15), laws on holy living (chs. 17–26). At the center of the collection is the regulation for the Day of Atonement (ch. 16). The Day of Atonement removed the people's sins and cleansed the sanctuary. This day ensured that an atoned-for people could continue to worship Yahweh at a newly cleansed sanctuary.

Another important part of the structure of Leviticus is the blessings and curses in ch. 26. Blessings and curses are an integral part of the covenant. In this light, in addition to being the conclusion to Leviticus, ch. 26 stands as part of the larger complex from Ex 25:1–Lev 26:46. This genre clearly informs us that all of Leviticus is to be understood as having its authority and meaning within the context of the Sinaic covenant.

The content of Leviticus is almost entirely laws from God concerning sacrifices, worship, and holy living. The book has only four narrative passages: the ordination of Aaron and his sons and the offering of the first sacrifices (chs. 8–9), the punishment of Nadab and Abihu (10:1–7), the ritual error of Eleazar and Ithamar (10:16–20), and the punishment of a blasphemer (24:10–16, 23). God had called Israel to become "a kingdom of priests and a holy nation" (at Mount Sinai, Ex 19:6), and the punishment of a blasphemer (24:10–16, 23). God had called Israel to become "a kingdom of priests and a holy nation" (at Mount Sinai, Ex 19:6). Leviticus presents laws for sacrifice and worship by which a sinful people might approach the holy God and find forgiveness in order to become a holy people. These laws are for the laity who are to take an active part in the various rituals. In neighboring societies official religious activity was relegated to the priests, who developed such highly technical rituals that they alone were able to participate in the cultus. But the delivery of God's regulations to all of Israel about sacrifice and worship effectively halted tendencies toward an elite and autocratic priesthood.

Chs. 17–26 contain laws for holy living. Central to the regulations in this section is the command from God, "Be holy because I, the LORD your God, am holy" (19:2). Israel is to live according to the revealed character of God (cf. Mt 5:48). A holy life is expressed in generosity, mercy, and love toward others. The people are to love their neighbors as themselves (19:18). And they are to love the foreigner who lives among them (v.34). The seeds are sown here to reach the high standard that Jesus set forth to love one's enemies (Mt 5:44). The people are to show mercy to the poor by not stripping their fields and by allowing the poor to glean there (19:9–10). In concern for others, landowners are to pay their hired workers speedily (v.13). A life of love is built on the plank of justice. Merchants are to have just weights and measures (vv.35–36). The people are to decide matters of dispute justly without deference to the rich or the poor (v.15). The union of justice and love leads to fidelity in sexual relationships. This rules out adultery, incest, homosexuality, and bestiality (chs. 18, 20).

To facilitate holy living, God sets aside days and seasons for worship (chs. 23, 25). These times of worship are for the people to commune with their God. By being in his presence, God sanctifies them, making their hearts holy. Worship is a transforming experience. Sanctification also takes place in obeying the laws God has given. Israel is to be a holy people. The people reach this goal by conforming to both the cultic and the moral law. The practice of fidelity in both spheres contributes to the development of personal integrity. These two ways of responding to God should not be separated as we moderns tend to do.

IV. NEW TESTAMENT USAGE

The book of Leviticus is a key to understanding the death of Jesus. He died as the perfect sacrifice to atone for all sins of all people. His death fulfilled all the sacrificial order and he was the ultimate Day of Atonement (cf. Heb 9–10). Since his sacrifice was once for all time, no more sacrifices are needed.

The cultic laws inform Christians of the character of Yahweh's holiness. It is important to understand the principles underlying these laws so that Christians may see how they are to live among and yet be distinct from their neighbors. For example, the laws against offering children to Molech may address the contemporary issue of abortion. On the other hand, the fact that Jesus did away with the laws of ritual purity is evidence of the glorious freedom we have in the redemptive work of Jesus.

The moral laws speak loudly to Christians, for they are grounded in the revelation of Yahweh's character. Jesus took up the commandment to love one's neighbor as oneself (19:18) and declared it to be the second greatest commandment (Mt 22:39; Mk 12:31; Lk 10:27). Other laws like not reaping up to the border of one's field nor gathering the gleanings (19:9) have to be transposed in order to be applied to contemporary culture. But the principle of not hoarding all that one makes for oneself and sharing one's abundance with the poor and unfortunate is clear. These moral laws offer numerous examples and illustrations of how to apply the great law of love in everyday situations.

The parenthetic material inspires Christians as it motivated the Israelites to be careful to keep the Word of God. These exhortations carry the promise of life, i.e., a blessed, peaceful, long life in the land of promise (18:5). Jesus promises that those who believe in him have eternal life (Jn 6:47). This parenthetic material, on the other hand, solemnly warns of devastating punishment to those who do not keep Yahweh's statutes (18:24–30). So, too, Jesus warns of eternal punishment to all those who fail to trust in him (cf. Mt 25:41–46). As the song says, "Trust and obey, for there is no other way to be happy in Jesus."

V. OUTLINE

A. Regulations for Sacrificing Animals and Treatment of the Blood (17:1–16)
 1. The place for sacrifice (17:1–9)
 2. Prohibitions on eating blood (17:10–16)
B. Laws Governing Sexual Behavior (18:1–30)
 1. Admonition to keep Yahweh's commandments (18:1–5)
 2. Laws forbidding incest (18:6–18)
 3. Laws forbidding defiling sexual practices (18:19–23)
 4. Exhortation (18:24–30)
C. Laws for Holy Living (19:1–37)
 1. Faithfulness in worship (19:1–8)
 2. Conduct of interpersonal relationships through love and respect (19:9–37)
 3. The practice of justice in court and business dealings (19:15–16, 35–36)
D. Punishments for Sacrifice to Molech, Sorcery, and Sexual Offenses (20:1–27)
 1. Punishments for sacrifice to Molech and sorcery (20:1–6)
 2. A call to consecration (20:7–8)
 3. Laws carrying the death penalty (20:9–16)
 4. Laws carrying the punishment of being cut off from the people (20:17–18)
 5. Laws carrying the punishment of childlessness (20:19–21)
 6. Final call to holy living (20:22–26)
 7. Prohibition against sorcery (20:27)
E. Laws for the Priests (21:1–24)
 1. Regulations for priests (21:1–9)
 2. Regulations for the high priest (21:10–15)
 3. Imperfections that disqualify one from serving as a priest (21:16–24)
F. Laws Governing the Eating of Sacred Food and Presenting Unacceptable Sacrifices (22:1–33)
 1. Conditions that keep priests from eating sacred food (22:1–9)
 2. A priest's family and sacred food (22:10–16)
 3. The offering of unacceptable sacrifices (22:17–33)
G. Israel's Sacred Festivals (23:1–44)
 1. The Sabbath (23:1–3)
 2. Passover (23:4–8)
 3. Firstfruits (23:9–14)
 4. Feast of Weeks (23:15–22)
 5. Feast of Trumpets (23:23–25)
 6. Day of Atonement (23:26–32)

COMMENTARY

I. INTRODUCTION (1:1–2)

The opening words, **"The Lord called to Moses and spoke to him from the Tent of Meeting,"** indicate that Leviticus is a continuation of the history of God's revelation to Israel recorded in the book of Exodus. Exodus concludes with the building and furnishing of the tabernacle (40:1–38). Now God speaks to Moses and gives him instructions for the sacrifices that are to be offered at the tabernacle.

II. REGULATIONS FOR THE SACRIFICES (1:3–7:38)

This section contains regulations for the various types of sacrifices that the Israelites were to make. For background on the history and development of the text in this and following sections of Leviticus, the reader should consult the appropriate commentaries and dictionaries.

In 1:3 through 6:7 regulations for five types of offerings are given. An appendix follows in 6:8 through 7:38 that presents further instructions for the various sacrifices. The listing of regulations for each of the offerings is introduced by the authoritative words, **"The Lord said to Moses, 'Say to the Israelites'"** (cf. 1:1–2; 4:1–2; 5:14; 6:1, 8–9, 24–25; 7:22–23, 28–29). A brief explanation of the instructions for the five offerings and of major items in the appendix will provide the background for an explanation of the major theological themes in these sections.

A. The Burnt Offering (1:3–17)

The burnt offering is considered first among the various sacrifices. Through the burnt offering, atonement was made for basic human sinfulness. In accordance with the type of animal offered, regulations for three different rituals are given. There is a ritual for herd animal (vv.3–9), one for animals from the flock (vv.10–13), and still another for birds (vv.14–17). While there is some difference in detail, the basic aspects of the rituals are the same. Seven steps are prescribed:

1. Presentation of the animal (vv.3, 10, 14): The animal from the herd was to be a bull; that from the flock, a sheep or goat; and the bird, a dove or pigeon. The offerings from the herd and flock were to be males without defect. The requirement that an animal be male is explained by the higher value that Hebrew society accorded males in general; that it be without defect reflects the central concern of the sacrificial system as a whole, God's holiness. The only appropriate offering for the holy God of Israel is a valuable and flawless one. But some people were too poor to offer cattle, sheep, or goats, thus the provision for the sacrifice of doves or pigeons.

2. Laying a hand on the sacrificial animal's head (v.4): The full meaning of this gesture is difficult to determine, but it is clear that the animal comes from the one making the offering. It may be assumed that at this point the offerer made a confession of sin.

3. Slaughter of the animal (vv.5, 11, 15): The offered animal was to be slaughtered at the entrance to the Tent of Meeting; in the oldest times the offerer slew the animal. Regulations

also mention that the animal is to be killed before the Lord, i.e., in God's presence.

4. Dashing of blood on the altar (vv.5, 11, 15): The priests were instructed to drain the slaughtered animal's blood and dash it against the altar. The blood is represented as the means of atonement for sin (cf. 17:11).

5. Cutting up of the offering (vv.6, 12, 17): The slaughtered animal was cut into pieces so that it could be arranged on the altar.

6. Washing the intestines and legs (vv.9, 13): Dirt and feces had to be removed lest they defile the altar. For this reason the regulations required careful washing of the innards.

7. Burning the animal (vv.9, 13, 17): The priest burned all the parts that were arranged on the altar. As it burned, the aroma pleased God, moving him to show mercy to the supplicant.

B. The Grain Offering (2:1–16)

As the name implies, this offering was made with raw grain or of baked dough derived from refined grain or meal. The grain offering was a gift to God, a memorial to God's constant grace. Most often it accompanied burnt or peace offerings. The passage presenting the grain offering is divided into three brief sections: (1) the basic regulations, including the ritual for the offering (vv.1–3), (2) additional regulations for baked grain offerings (vv.4–10), and (3) miscellaneous regulations (vv.11–16).

1. The grain offering was to be prepared according to specified regulations and presented to the priest, who burned it on the altar. Thus offered, the grain is described as a memorial, **an aroma pleasing to the LORD** (v.2). Implicit in the term **memorial** is the idea that the offerer remembers God's

constant grace in providing one's daily food.

2. In addition to raw grain, baked loaves or cakes of finest flour could be given as a grain offering. Specific directions for baking are given. The most likely reason that the use of yeast and honey are forbidden is because both are subject to fermentation.

3. Among miscellaneous regulations is the instruction to use salt as a seasoning for the grain offering (v.13). The term **salt of the covenant** used here emphasizes the binding character of God's covenant with his people. Jesus may have had the concept of the salt of the covenant in mind when he said to his followers, "You are the salt of the earth" (Mt 5:13).

C. The Peace Offering (3:1–17)

The Hebrew term for the sacrifice is *zebah shelāmîm*. The basic idea in the word *shelāmîm*, from which the name of the offering is derived, is "prosperous, well-being." The condition of blessedness that the term describes comes to the individual through his or her covenant relationship with God. The purpose of this offering was to give God praise for some specific blessing, to fulfill a vow, or simply to express one's love for God (cf. 7:11–18; 22:18–21). The peace offering took the form of a festive meal with the offerer's family, the priest, and invited guests participating.

Regulations for the peace offering are divided into three sections: (1) the offering of cattle (vv.1–5), (2) an offering from the flock (vv.6–16), and (3) an appendix that forbids the eating of fat or blood (v.17).

D. The Sin Offering (4:1–5:13)

The Hebrew term for the sin offering, (*hattā't*), is derived from the root (*hātā'*), which means "fail, sin." The

purpose of the sin offering was to expiate the unintentional sin of the offerer. There is no provision in the sacrificial system for the atonement of sins committed knowingly (cf. Nu 15:30–31).

The regulation for a sin offering is divided as follows: (1) introduction (4:1–2), (2) ritual for purification of an anointed priest who sins unintentionally (vv.3–12), (3) for the whole community (vv.13–21), (4) for a leader (vv.22–26), (5) for an individual (vv.27–35), (6) four cases requiring a sin offering (5:1–6), (7) alternative sin offerings (vv.7–13).

Rituals for the sin offering are almost identical to those of the burnt offering. In cases of the offering of the anointed priest and the congregation, blood is sprinkled before the veil as well as dabbed on the horns of the altar and against the altar. The special handling of the blood is to expiate a specific sin. The ritual achieves expiation, but God in his sovereign freedom pronounces that **"he will be forgiven."** The one major difference is that only the fat tissues are burned on the altar; the remainder of the animal is burned outside the camp (4:8–12).

E. The Guilt Offering (5:14–6:7)

The guilt offering provided a means of expiating sins that were breaches of faith against God. Where property was involved, the person had to compensate for the loss and add 20 percent. Also a person who felt guilty about violating sacred law, though he or she was unaware of any actual wrong doing, could remove the guilt by this offering.

Regulations for the guilt offering are structured according to the two cases involved: (1) ritual concerning breaches of faith in matters of worship (5:14–16), (2) ritual concerning unwilling violations of God's commands (vv.17–19), and (3) miscellaneous situations requiring a guilt offering (6:1–7).

The four basic theological themes found in the regulations for the various sacrifices are the holiness of God, human sinfulness, the divine provision for atonement, and gratitude to God for his blessings. Each of these themes will be considered in turn.

God's holiness is reflected throughout the instructions for making the offerings. Sacrificial animals are to be flawless (1:3, 10: 3:1, 6; 4:3, 23, 28, 32; 5:15, 18; 6:6) in accordance with the pure character of God to whom they are offered. The instruction to remove all dirt and feces by washing the innards (1:9, 13) is clearly associated with the divine purity. And in addition to these specific regulations, the detailed instructions for making the offerings and the great care required in preparing them make it clear that the offerer is approaching the holy God of Israel.

A second theme found in the regulations, one that stands in stark contrast to God's holiness, is the sinfulness of human beings. One of the reasons for the institution of the offerings is for the expiation of the Israelites' sins (1:4). That the death of an animal is required for the expiation of sin clearly teaches that the penalty for sin is death. Too, the requirement that a sin offering will be made for unwilling and unintentional sins shows that all sin is destructive of a relationship with God and needs cleansing.

The third theme central to this section is the divine provision for atonement. The laying of one's hands on the head of the sacrificial animal signifies that the penalty for sin is death and that the animal's death is necessary for the atonement of sin (1:4). Moreover, the dashing of the slaughtered animal's blood against the altar signifies that the animal's life has been poured out to God (v.5). The burnt offering (vv.2–17) shows that the offerer is sinful in the whole of his/her being and that God makes a total claim on his/her life. To live in fellowship with God, sinful persons must make expiation for sin regularly. Provision was made through the sacrifices for Israelites frequently to experience the removal of sin. These offerings foreshadow the atonement that Christ made in his death. In the words of the book of Hebrews, "We have been made holy through the sacrifice of the body of Jesus Christ once for all" (10:10).

The fourth theme found in these chapters is that of expressing gratitude to God. This theme is seen especially in the regulations for the grain offering (2:1–16) and the peace offering (3:1–17). The grain offering is burned as a memorial; the offerer wishes God to remember him in light of the covenant. In the act of remembering, the offerer expresses gratitude to God. The peace offering is a ritual provision for praising God. Praise might be rendered for some specific blessing or simply be offered spontaneously to God.

F. Further Regulations for the Sacrifices (6:8–7:38)

Regulations for the five offerings are followed by a group of additional instructions for the various sacrifices. The primary concerns in this section are the requirement to keep the altar fire continually burning, distribution of the unburned animal parts, and the prohibition of the eating of the blood and fat. The structure of this appendix is as follows: (1) additional instructions for the burnt offering (6:8–13), (2) for the grain offering (vv.14–23), (3) for the sin offering (vv.24–30), (4) for the guilt offering (7:1–10), (5) for the peace offering (vv.11–21), (6) prohibition against eating fat and blood (vv.22–27), and (7) distribution of animal parts to the priests (vv.28–38).

Two key themes are presented in this material. First is the requirement that priests are to have a share in the portions of sacrifice that are not consumed on the altar. Faithful service is rewarded with worthy benefits. This theme is carried forward in the NT as the church is instructed to support its ministers (1Co 9:7–14).

A second theme concerns the sacredness of the various offerings. The sacrifices are God-appointed means for the expression of thanksgiving to God, renewal of the covenant, the expiation of sin, and the reception of God's blessing. As God-appointed rituals where the divine presence is experienced, the offerings are holy. The NT applies this message to Christian worship, especially to the celebration of the Eucharist (cf. 1Co 11:27–34).

III. ORDINATION OF PRIESTS AND INITIATION OF SACRIFICES (8:1–10:20)

Chs. 8–10 constitute the second major section of Leviticus. Regulations for the sacrifices having been presented in the previous chapters, the present material describes the inauguration of the offerings. Because a priesthood was required for the making of sacrifices, the ordination of Aaron and his sons is first recorded; then these chapters describe making the first offerings on the new altar.

A. Ordination of Aaron and His Sons as Priests (8:1–36)

The great significance of the occasion is underscored by the gathering of the entire Israelite community to witness the ordination of Aaron and his sons (v.3). Throughout this section, Moses'

obedience to God is stressed (see 8:4, 5, 9, 13, 17, 21, 29, 34, 36; 9:6, 7, 10; 10:15). Obedience to God's commands is required if divine forgiveness is to be received and God's glorious presence is to be experienced. In Wesleyan thought, obedience to God is a necessary prerequisite if one is to walk in the fullness of God's grace.

With the whole nation assembled at the Tent of Meeting, Moses presents (*hiqrîb*) Aaron and his two sons to God. *Hiqrîb* is the word commonly used in OT texts for presentation of an offering. Its use in 8:6 signifies that the priests are presented to God and are thereby wholly sanctified for his service at the altar. Paul exhorts believers to present themselves to God as living sacrifices (Ro 12:1). John Wesley understands both testaments as teaching the necessity of full consecration.

Having presented Aaron and his sons to God, Moses washes and clothes them. Washing rendered the priests ritually clean for the ordination ceremony. Aaron is clothed according to the instructions God had given Moses in Ex 28:3–5. The special garments are clearly intended to exalt God's holiness and majesty.

Next, Moses anoints the tabernacle. By this anointing, the tent and all its furnishings are consecrated. Any person or object that is sanctified is set apart to God and made holy. It is this basic conception of holiness that John Wesley applies to believers who would become entirely sanctified.

Finally, Moses offers the sacrifice that God had commanded for the ordination ceremony (vv.14–30). In the course of the ritual Moses takes some of the slaughtered ram's blood and places it on the lobe of Aaron's right ear, on the thumb of his right hand, and on the big toe of his right foot (v.23). These actions symbolize the consecration of the priests' hearing from God, the work (of their hands) for God, and their walk with God. Through these offerings, Aaron and his sons are sanctified for priestly service in the tabernacle.

B. Offering of the First Sacrifices (9:1-24)

Aaron and his sons stayed for seven days at the entrance to the Tent of Meeting in the presence of God as they had been instructed (8:35-36). Now on the eighth day they offer to God the first sacrifices on behalf of the people. In keeping with his role as God's spokesman, Moses promises the people that God will appear to them that day (v.4).

The public offerings are described in vv.7-21. Aaron and his sons present a sin offering, a burnt offering, and two peace offerings. The opening sentence (v.7) makes clear that the sacrifices are to make atonement for the people. The priests present the offerings as they are instructed, and Aaron concludes the ceremony by lifting his hands and blessing the people (v.22).

At this point, Moses and Aaron go into the Tent of Meeting where they enter God's presence. Having been blessed by God, they return outside and bless the people as they come out of the tabernacle (v.23). At the moment, the glory of God appears to all the people. Fire from the presence of God consumes what is left of the sacrifices Aaron had offered. Spontaneously, the people shout for joy and fall prostrate before God.

The central lesson here is that God forgives his people who make offerings in the way he instructs. In the NT, atonement for sin has been accomplished through the death of Jesus. A clear explanation of this basic biblical truth can be found in John Wesley's sermon "Salvation by Faith."

C. Death of Aaron's Sons (10:1-20)

The material in 10:1-20 records two violations of God's instructions for the offerings. The first (vv.1-7), which appears more serious, results in the death of Nadab and Abihu. These two sons of Aaron offer unauthorized fire at the altar. As a consequence, fire roars out from God's presence and kills them. Scholars are divided in their interpretation of the priests' action and of the significance of this incident. Moved by the excitement of God's appearing, Nadab and Abihu were apparently attempting to incorporate some pagan ritual into the divinely sanctioned worship of God. Also, it appears that their motive was to promote themselves and their families over Aaron as high priest.

Here is an abiding lesson. God will indeed bless us with his power and presence if we seek him in faith according to the ways he instructs us. On the other hand, his judgment will certainly fall on those like Nadab and Abihu who attempt to manipulate and display God's power and presence.

The second incident (vv.16-20) involves Aaron's failure to eat the priests' portion of the sin offering. Moses becomes angry when he discovers that Aaron and his two remaining sons have not followed the regulations for the sacrifice. But Moses accepts Aaron's explanation that eating the offering on the day that such tragic events have occurred would be displeasing to God. This incident shows that the priests had some freedom to adapt regulations for the sacrifices if the revisions were in keeping with God's will.

These two incidents become the occasion for further instructions for priestly service (vv.8-15). Especially noteworthy is the prohibition against drinking alcohol while on duty in the Tent of Meeting. One whose senses are confused by drink might accidently transgress the sacred regulations. Drunkenness is condemned throughout the Bible.

Also, it should be noted that the priests are exhorted to distinguish between the holy and the profane and between the ritually clean and the ritually unclean. Moreover, they are to teach the people about these important matters. Priests were to render judgments on questions. Under the new covenant, God appoints pastors and teachers whose responsibility is that of teaching his people the things of Christ.

IV. REGULATIONS FOR TREATMENT OF CLEAN AND UNCLEAN (11:1–15:33)

In this, the third major section of Leviticus, the writer presents regulations concerning ritual purity regarding: (1) meat (ch. 11), (2) childbirth (ch. 12), (3) grievous skin diseases and mildew on garments and walls (chs. 13–14), and (4) discharges from the genitals (ch. 15). This material is integrally related to both the previous sections on sacrifices and the priesthood and the following section, which presents laws for holy living. The connection with the previous section is evidenced in the requirements that atonement for uncleanness be made (14:19–32) and that the priests implement the various regulations for ritual purity (10:10–11). The close tie with the following section on holy living (chs. 17–26) is evident in the exhortation to follow the dietary regulations as an expression of consecration to God (11:44–45). This exhortation is based on the declaration "I am the LORD your God," which is repeated throughout chs. 17–26.

Standing between these two sets of regulations are instructions for the Day

of Atonement (ch. 16). This arrangement is clearly intentional on the part of the author of Leviticus. The regulations on uncleanness preceding ch. 16 clarify the key purpose of the Day of Atonement, that is, the purification of the tabernacle from the uncleanness of the people (16:16, 19, 33). Through the ritual on that most important day, Israel became a cleansed and forgiven people. As such, they were motivated to serve God with their whole beings. Consecration in daily living is essential for a vital relationship with God. Thus regulations for holy living (chs. 17–26) aptly follow the ritual for the Day of Atonement.

A. Clean and Unclean Animals (11:1–47)

This speech is structured as follows: (1) introduction (vv.1–2a), (2) list of clean and unclean animals (vv.2b–23), (3) instructions on uncleanness due to contact with unclean animals (vv.24–40), and (4) exhortation to holiness (vv.41–45).

1. The introduction differs from preceding ones in that Aaron is included with Moses in God's address. The inclusion of Aaron here is in keeping with the role of the priests in instructing the people on ritual points (cf. 10:10–11).

2. Animals are classified in vv.2b–23 as those that are clean and may be eaten and those that are unclean and forbidden as food. Four categories distinguish life spheres of the respective animals: (1) animals living on land (vv.2b–8), (2) fish living in water (vv.9–12), (3) birds that fly in the air (vv.13–19), and (4) insects that inhabit land and air (vv.20–23). The author cites a principle as the basis for cleanness or uncleanness in each case except with regard to birds. Land animals that are clean are those with a

completely divided hoof and that chew the cud. Fish are clean if they have fins and scales, and clean insects are those that have jointed legs for hopping on the ground. Land animals, fish, and insects lacking the cited characteristics are unclean and forbidden as food. While no principle is given for distinguishing clean and unclean birds, it may be noted that the list of twenty birds forbidden as food (vv.13b–19) is primarily composed of birds of prey and feeders on carrion.

3. Lev 11:24–40 gives instructions concerning uncleanness due to contact with unclean animals. As a parallel to the previous list the author treats first uncleanness from contact with large land animals (vv.26–28). The next unit lists a group of unclean varmints and lizards and defines uncleanness through contact with their carcasses (vv.29–38). Uncleanness occurs through direct contact with a carcass or through contact with an object that the unclean animal has touched.

4. In vv.41–45 the writer presents a prohibition against eating any kind of crawling animal and an exhortation to be holy by avoiding contact with unclean animals. The command **"I am the LORD your God, consecrate yourselves and be holy, because I am holy"** (v.44) is the key to the interpretation of the entire section in that it sets forth the fundamental purpose for regulations on ritual purity. These regulations are given for the practice of obeying the holy God at every meal.

B. Cleanness and Uncleanness in Giving Birth (12:1–8)

This regulation treats the birth of a son (vv.2–4), the birth of a daughter (v.5), and sacrifices for purification after childbirth (vv.6–8).

1. On giving birth to a son a woman becomes unclean for seven days (v.2).

Seven is a significant number because it symbolizes perfection. Uncleanness is due to the secretion of blood that occurs with childbirth, not giving birth itself (cf. vv.4, 5, 7). Bodily secretions in general cause a person to be unclean, but the issue of blood is especially offensive. After seven days the woman is technically clean, but she is required to avoid contact with anything sacred for thirty-three more days.

2. The birth of a daughter (v.5) renders a woman unclean for fourteen days, and she is required to separate herself for sixty days. The reason for the differences between the regulations on the birth of a son or daughter are not given, but the longer periods of time for a girl may be that a girl becomes unclean through menses.

3. Sacrifices for purification are to be offered after childbirth (vv.6–8). The new mother is required to present a sacrificial offering at the conclusion of her time of purification (vv.6–8). She is to present a lamb for a burnt offering (cf. ch. 1) and a pigeon or dove for the sin offering (cf. chs. 4–5). It is important to note that a sin offering rather than a guilt offering is required of the mother. This indicates that what is at issue is not a specific act of sin but uncleanness that requires expiation before that mother may enter the sanctuary. Also noteworthy in this text is the fact that women, as well as men, are required to present sacrifices at the sanctuary.

C. Skin Diseases and Grievous Growths (13:1–14:57)

This lengthy regulation treats procedures for distinguishing grievous skin diseases from abrasions of the skin, determining the existence of spreading mildew in houses and garments, quarantine of persons afflicted with skin disease and objects spotted with mildew, and the purification of such persons and objects. A central role is assigned to the priests in all of these procedures. The regulation is divided into four subunits: (1) regulations concerning skin diseases (13:1–46), (2) regulations concerning mildew (vv.47–59), (3) procedures for purification of persons with skin diseases (14:1–32), and (4) procedures for purification from mildew (vv.33–57).

1. Regulations concerning skin diseases (13:1–46)

Unfortunately a great deal of confusion regarding these verses results from the translation in standard English versions of the Hebrew word ṣāra'aṯ as leprosy. The Hebrew term is a general term denoting various skin diseases like psoriasis and fungal infections. The word *leprosy* is used today to refer to a specific illness know technically as Hansen's disease.

Seven cases of skin disease are presented: (1) lesions of the skin (vv.2–8), (2) lacerated tissue (vv.9–17), (3) change in a healed boil (vv.18–23), (4) an infected burn (vv.24–28), (5) a lesion in the beard or hair (vv.29–37), (6) white spots covering the body (vv.38–39), and (7) a sore on a bald head (vv.40–44). In each case symptoms are described and procedures given the priests for determining whether a condition is indeed a skin disease. If symptoms are clear, the priest immediately pronounces the person clean or unclean. But if the symptoms do not provide for a clear prognosis, the priest is to order a quarantine of seven days followed by reexamination. If the second examination is still inconclusive, another period of quarantine is required. As soon as clear evidence is available to the priest, he is to make a definitive pronouncement.

It is important to note that the role of the priest in these regulations is not that of a physician. Rather his assignment is the protection of the sanctuary from any and all types of uncleanness.

Following the seven cases is instruction for excluding unclean persons from the community (vv.45–46). Those pronounced unclean because of skin disease are to dress in mourning. Also they are to cry "unclean, unclean" (cf. La 4:15) on the approach of other persons to warn them of the danger of becoming unclean through contact with the diseased. Afflicted persons are to live outside the city for the rest of their lives or until such time as they are healed.

2. Regulations concerning mildew (13:47–59)

This regulation presents directions for handling mold, mildew, and other fungi in wool, linen, or leather garments. Such growths develop in clothing that has not been recently washed and has been stored in a warm, damp place. The regulation is similar to that for handling a person inflected with skin disease. The infected garment is shown to the priest, who examines and isolates the material for seven days. If the priest determines, on reexamination after seven days, that the growth has spread, he identifies it as mildew and burns the garment. But if the growth has not changed, the material is washed and isolated for seven more days. If on the second examination the growth has not faded, the garment is declared unclean and burned. But if the growth has faded, it is cut out of the garment. Should the mildew return at a later time, the material must be burned. A garment that appears to be without mildew after the first washing must be rewashed. If it appears normal, it is pronounced clean.

3. Cleansing from skin diseases (14:1–32)

This section presents required procedures for the reinstatement into the covenant community of a person who has been excluded because of a skin disease. The priest is to determine by examination if a person has recovered and to pronounce him/her clean in the case of recovery. However, it is only after the person has passed through an elaborate ritual of restoration that the priest pronounces the victim clean. Readmission to the covenant community of such a person is a significant event for the excluded individual who has been considered as good as dead. All four basic sacrifices are offered in the ritual, indicating that the recovered person has full access to the altar once again.

The beginning ritual involves two birds (vv.4–7). One bird is killed and its blood mixed with fresh water in a clay pot. The death of this bird symbolizes the awful destiny of the person afflicted with a grievous skin disease. The priest then sprinkles the recovered person seven times with the blood of the dead bird and pronounces him/her clean. The second bird, having been dipped in the same blood, is released to the open fields. The parallel with the release of the scapegoat on the Day of Atonement (16:21–22) suggests that the released bird carries away the impurity of the once-diseased person. Next the recovered person is to wash his/her clothes, shave his/her hair, and bathe (vv.8–9). This washing symbolizes the total removal of impurity.

On the eighth day the recovered person is to offer a series of sacrifices. The word *present* in v.11 is not the normal term used for presenting a sacrifice. Rather it is the term used of a person making a significant decision about one's status as he/she stands at the entrance to the Tent of Meeting. The moment of regaining access to Yahweh at the sanctuary would certainly have been overpowering!

The priest presents a guilt offering on behalf of the healed individual (cf. 5:14–6:7). Why is a guilt offering required in this instance? A possible explanation is suggested in other OT literature. The grievous skin disease mars a person who is created in God's image (Ge 1:27) and keeps him from direct access to God at his sanctuary. An offering that expiates the transgressions of that which is holy (cf. 5:15–16) is required for full restoration of one who has been healed of a grievous skin disease.

The anointing with oil of the recovered person is rich with symbolic meaning (vv.15–18). It signifies that Yahweh will abundantly bless the individual who is now fully reconciled with the community.

Next the priest makes the sin offering for the healed individual. Through this sacrifice the recovered person is completely cleansed from all impurity. He may now enter God's presence with full confidence.

Special provision is made for the poor who have recovered from a grievous skin disease (vv.21–22). The poor individual may substitute two doves or pigeons for the sin and burnt offerings. However, no substitute is permitted for the guilt offering.

4. Cleansing from mildew (14:33–54)

In the event a person discovers the presence of mildew on the walls of his house, he is to tell the priest, who will conduct an inspection. If the priest confirms the finding of mildew, he closes the house for seven days. On reexamination, if he finds that the spot of mildew has spread, he orders the infected area to be removed and the walls scraped. The residue is taken outside the town, and the house is replastered. After this, if the mildew reappears, the house is to be torn down. Anyone who enters an unclean house becomes unclean himself and must wash his clothes (vv.46–47).

But if upon reexamination of a quarantined house the priest finds the mildew gone, he is to pronounce the house clean. Then offerings similar to the initial offerings presented by an individual who has recovered from a grievous skin disease are made (vv.49–53).

D. Unclean Discharges (15:1–33)

In this speech any discharge, regular or irregular, from one's genitals renders a person unclean. The material is presented in an inverse pattern. The law treats abnormal discharges from a male's genitals (vv.2–15), then normal discharges (vv.16–18) followed by normal discharges from a female's genitals (vv.19–24), and then abnormal discharges (vv.25–30). This law treats both sexes on a common basis. Both sexes were made unclean by a woman's monthly period, which, due solely to it nature, was longer. No reason is given as to why such discharges were classified as unclean. Ancient people usually labeled emissions from the body as taboo, especially abnormal ones. Sexual discharges are tied to the wonder and mystery of life. In addition, these laws prohibited sexual activity from taking place as a part of Israelite worship. This fact is in stark contrast to the fertility rites that were common to the cults of Israel's neighbors.

According to the law (v.24), a man who contacts a woman's menses becomes unclean for seven days. But in 20:18 such an act carried the heavy penalty of one's being cut off from the community. In this light this law may be interpreted to mean that a man unknowingly contacts her menses at the beginning of her period. In that case, since it happened accidentally, he becomes unclean for the same length of time as the woman.

Abnormal discharges make a person unclean for as long as the discharge lasts. Anything or any person that comes close to the area of the discharge becomes secondarily unclean. This includes a bed or anything on which the person with the discharge sits. Then any person who uses one of these objects made unclean also becomes unclean. A person made unclean secondarily becomes clean by washing his/her clothes, bathing in water, and waiting until evening. A man who has an emission of semen follows the same procedure. In these cases the uncleanness is mild. It is up to each person to comply with the law without any involvement of a priest. The only danger is entering the area of the sanctuary while ritually unclean.

A male or female with an abnormal discharge can be reinstated into community life after full recovery from the defilement. Because one's illness is out of the ordinary, sacrifices are required. After recovering, one has to wait seven days to be sure recovery is complete. That person washes his/her clothes and bathes in water. On the eighth day one brings two doves or two young pigeons, the least expensive sacrifice, to the priest at the Tent of Meeting. He/she offers one as a burnt offering (cf. ch. 1) and one as a sin offering (cf. chs. 4–5). Then the person is fully reinstated in the community.

Jesus does away with these laws on impurity from sexual discharges. He dramatically demonstrates his power over such abnormal discharges by healing the woman who had a flow of blood for twelve years (Mk 5:25–34). Although she touches him, she does not incur his wrath for making him unclean, but she experiences his redemptive grace in healing power. While the NT is not concerned with impurity from sexual discharges, it calls every believer to conduct oneself in complete moral purity in sexual relationships (cf. 1Co 6:12–20; Heb 13:4; 1Pe 3:2–7).

V. THE DAY OF ATONEMENT (16:1–34)

A. Priestly Preparations (16:1–5)

Once a year, on the tenth day of the seventh month, Israel celebrates the Day of Atonement. On this day the high priest, a son of Aaron, goes into the very Holy of Holies to put blood on the mercy seat to make atonement for all the sins of the priests and the people. At the start of this day instead of his regal clothes, the high priest wears the pure, sacred linen garments like those worn by the regular priests. These garments represent purity and humility. Before putting them on he has to bathe his entire body, symbolic of complete removal of that which is earthly.

B. Instructions for Sin Offerings (16:6–19)

1. Selection of the goats (16:6–10)

The high priest has to present a bull for his own sin offering. The people have to provide two goats. Lots are cast over the goats. One goat is to be offered as the people's sin offering. The other goat is to be offered to Azazel. The precise meaning of Azazel is not known. It could be a name for the goat, i.e., the scapegoat or the name of a demon or the name of a wilderness location to which the goat departs. The parallel language, **"for the LORD"** and "for Azazel" (NIV **"for the scapegoat"**), favors the view that it is the name of a demon to which the goat is sent. Some object that the Scriptures would not prescribe a sacrifice to a demon. But there is no hint of this goat's being a sacrifice. This goat is not ritually slain, there are no rites with its blood, and it is not burned on an altar. Rather, it carries the sins of the congregation to Azazel and leaves them at their source. This ritual has atoning merit, for by returning sins to their source, the power of these sins over the congregation is completely broken. Similarly, Jesus, who was made sin for us (2Co 5:21), descended into hell after his death in order to leave sins there at their source and break the power of sin in the lives of all who believe on him.

2. The offerings for Aaron and the people (16:11–19)

Aaron first offers the sin offering for himself. He takes the blood of that offering into the Holy of Holies and sprinkles its blood over the mercy seat and before it. This expiates his own sins and those of his household. He comes out of the Holy Place. Next he offers the goat for the people's sin offering. He returns into the Holy of Holies and sprinkles the blood on the mercy seat. This action cleanses the Holy of Holies from the uncleanness of the people. No other person may be in the Holy Place at this time, for that person would contaminate the Holy Place and render these rites ineffectual. Then the high priest takes some of the blood of both animals and puts it on the horns of the altar to cleanse the altar. Some take this to be the altar of incense, while others take it to be the main altar before the Tent of Meeting. The latter is preferred, for nothing is said about the other furniture in the Holy Place.

C. Ritual for the Scapegoat (16:20–22)

The ritual of releasing the goat for Azazel takes place at this point. A person appointed to the task leads the goat out into the wilderness, making sure that this animal ladened with the sins will not return to the camp and defile it. This action removed the people's sins to their source, breaking the power of these sins over the people. Later the goat is led out of the city and cast over a cliff, plunging to its death.

D. Ritual for the Whole Burnt Offering (16:23–28)

Now the high priest puts off the linen garments, bathes himself, and puts on his regular regal clothing. He then offers his own whole burnt offering and the people's whole burnt offerings. These sacrifices also have atoning merit. Coming at this place, these sacrifices represent a praise offering to the Lord.

E. Instruction for the Annual Celebration of the Day of Atonement (16:29–34)

These words establish the Day of Atonement as an annual festival in Israel's calendar. They require that the people completely fast, abstaining from food, drink, sexual activity, and all earthly joys for this entire day. On this day the sins of all the people as a unit are forgiven. In addition, all the furniture for the sanctuary and the sanctuary itself are atoned. Every sin pollutes. This pollution is drawn to the sanctuary and the horns of the altar. The higher the official who sins, the further into the sanctuary the pollution penetrates. If this pollution is not removed, the efficaciousness of the altar, the mercy seat, and the sanctuary itself is lost. Or to state it positively, the blood rites recharge the sanctuary, keeping it

as a place where the congregation can meet God.

VI. INSTRUCTIONS FOR HOLY LIVING (17:1–26:46)

This section of Leviticus presents instructions for living a holy life before God. It includes requirements for making sacrifices, regulations concerning the conduct of priests, instructions on Israel's sacred festivals and the Sabbath Year and Year of Jubilee, and laws concerning many aspects of daily life. In addition, one finds here exhortations to live consecrated lives. Enforcing the laws and exhortations is a final chapter in which God promises to bless Israel if they live faithfully before him but curse them if they are disobedient.

A. Regulations for Sacrificing Animals and Treatment of the Blood (17:1–16)

1. The place for sacrifice (17:1–9)

These laws require that every domesticated animal—namely cattle, sheep, and goats (cf. 1:2)—be offered on the altar before the Tent of Meeting. If a person does not follow this procedure, that person will be guilty of shedding blood and be subject to the penalty of being cut off from the people of God. The fact that these penalties are so severe indicates the heavy value the OT places on all life. The purpose of this law was to put an end to the practice of making sacrifices in the open field. This practice was dangerous, for the people not only made sacrifices to God, they also directed their sacrifices to satyrs, i.e., goat demons, which they believed inhabited these open lands. By placating these field demons with their slaughtering, which they considered to be a sacrifice, the popular belief was that they could avoid those forces such as blight, mildew, and locust, that diminished greatly the yield of a field or even wiped out the entire harvest. Yahweh does not permit worship or acknowledgment of any other deities. That is why the transgression of this standard carried the heavy "cut off" penalty.

A major problem with interpreting this law is that it conflicts with the law in Dt 12:20–27, which permits the slaughter of domesticated animals at one's home. Conservatives reconcile these laws by understanding this law in Leviticus to apply only to the wilderness period, being set aside by the new law in Deuteronomy for the time of occupying the land. The major problem with this interpretation is that v.7b says that this law is an eternal statute. Other scholars, for the most part, find the setting for this law to be the small community of Jews gathered about Jerusalem in the early days after the return from Babylonian captivity. In their opinion the priestly leaders of this community put away the law found in Deuteronomy. This position does not seem realistic, for it does not seem likely that the priests of this small community would formulate laws that would place a great hardship on Jews scattered throughout the land of Israel and the diaspora, and undermine support from the very people who would form the nucleus of a Jewish community in Israel. In light of the great obstacles to these two positions, a third alternative is proposed. This position follows the understanding of the term for "slaughter" by Jewish scholars like Akiba, Siphra, and Levine. They take this word to refer to ritual slaughter, not slaughter in general. This prohibition, then, forbids the making of peace offerings in an open field away from an official altar where no official priest would be present to manipulate the blood properly. In this light there is no tension between the laws in this chapter in Leviticus and those in Dt 12.

2. Prohibitions on eating blood (17:10–16)

No blood may be eaten, either directly or in meat. The essential and the theological reason for this standard is given in v.11. This verse is important, for it is the only word in the sacrificial legislation that gives any indication of why blood has the power to expiate sins. The primary reason rests in God's design; God has given it this power. The essential reason is that blood carries the life force of a person. Ancient Hebrews placed the locus of a person's life in the breath and in the blood. People die when they stop breathing; so, too, their life flows from them as they lose their blood. Of these two loci of life, blood, of course, is the more tangible. So the blood used in the sacrificial rituals represents the life of the slain animal. God accepts this blood in place of the person who has forfeited his life by sinning. Blood also serves to cleanse the altar from the pollution caused by that person's sins. Blood has the power solely because of God's mercy in providing his people a way to remove their sins so that they may continue to worship him.

This categorical law against eating blood means that the blood of a clean wild animal has to be drained and covered before an Israelite can eat the meat of game. Meat from an animal found dead, whether it died as a result of mauling by another animal or naturally, can be eaten. But the person, whether an Israelite or a resident alien, who eats that meat becomes ritually unclean and must wash his clothes and wait until evening before becoming clean again.

B. Laws Governing Sexual Behavior (18:1–30)

The regulations in this section forbid the practice of incest. When Leviticus was written, large extended families formed the core of Israelite society. The laws presented here forbid sexual intercourse with any family member except one's spouse. The chapter is divided into four basic units: (1) admonition to keep Yahweh's commandments (vv.1–5), (2) laws forbidding incest (vv.6–18), (3) laws forbidding defiling sexual practices (vv.19–23), and (4) exhortation (vv.24–30).

1. Admonition to keep Yahweh's commandments (18:1–5)

The Israelites are exhorted to avoid the immoral sexual practices of the Egyptians and the Canaanites. Their motive for living pure lives sexually is their relationship with the Lord their God. The formula **"I am the LORD your God"** (v.2) is written as a preamble to the laws on holy living, and its use here corresponds with its function at the head of the Decalogue (Ex 20:2). This formula serves to remind the Israelites that their existence as a holy nation rests on Yahweh's self-revelation as their holy God.

2. Laws forbidding incest (18:6–18)

The opening prohibition, **"No one is to approach any close relative to have sexual relations"** (v.6), governs the list of regulations that follow. The use of **"close relative"** is intended to cover both blood relatives and relatives by marriage.

Underlying these laws on sexual relationship is the biblical conception of sexual intercourse, which establishes a one-flesh unity between the man and woman who engage in it (cf. Ge 2:24; 1Co 6:16). D. S. Bailey, in *The Mystery of Love and Marriage,* describes the one-flesh unity as an enduring union of the two persons in their whole beings. Therefore, any other union with a member of one's family is forbidden.

3. Laws forbidding defiling sexual practices (18:19–23)

In addition to the prohibition against sexual intercourse with relatives, a number of other sexual practices are forbidden. One must not have intercourse with a neighbor's wife (v.20). Adultery is condemned throughout the Bible (cf. Ex 20:14, 17). Parents are not to offer their children to Molech (v.21). The exact nature of this sacrifice is not known, but most scholars believe that children were burnt on a special brazier as a sacrifice to the god Molech. The text states that it profanes God's name. To profane is to debase that which is holy. God has given his name to the Israelites to be carried through their offspring, and they must not tarnish his reputation through false worship that destroys human life. Homosexuality is strictly forbidden (v.22). Such conduct is detestable, an activity that God abhors. Bestiality is forbidden for both sexes (v.23). The Hebrew word for sexual intercourse used in the case of a woman is the same word used in 19:19 for breeding animals. Its use in this text shows how degrading bestiality is.

4. Exhortation (18:24–30)

The chapter closes with the admonition for the Israelites to keep God's laws and not become defiled like the neighboring societies. If Israel keeps God's commandments, God will cause their land to prosper, but if they are disobedient, he will punish them by expelling them from the land.

C. Laws for Holy Living (19:1–37)

The material in ch. 19 is a series of laws pertaining to holy living in the manifold aspects of daily life. The various laws can be grouped under three main topics: (1) faithfulness in worship (vv.3–8, 12, 19, 20–22, 27–28, 30–31), (2) conduct of interpersonal relationships through love and respect (vv.11, 13–14, 17–18, 20, 29, 32–34), and (3) the practice of justice at court and in business dealings (vv.15–16, 35–36).

Controlling this group of laws is the thesis presented in the opening verses: Israel is to be holy because God is holy (v.2). All the laws that follow reflect God's will that Israel conduct every aspect of daily life in conformity with God's holy character.

1. Faithfulness in worship

Holiness in worship is characterized by single-minded devotion to God. The Israelites are not to turn to other gods or to make graven images (v.4). Moreover, they are to follow the regulations for worship (vv.5–8) that God has prescribed. The natural order, created by God, reflects his holiness. The Israelites are not to confuse God's ordering of nature by sowing a field with different kinds of seeds, making cloth out of different kinds of material, or mating different kinds of animals (v.19). Neither are they to mar the bodies God has given them by tatooing or cutting themselves (vv.27–28).

2. Conduct of interpersonal relationships through love and respect

An integral relationship exists between love and holiness. Holiness transforms self-centered tendencies in human love into dynamic caring for the well-being of others. Israelites are commanded to love their neighbors as themselves (v.18). They are not to oppress one another; the rich are to have compassion for their employees (v.13). Handicapped persons are to be treated with respect (v.14). Special provisions are to be extended to the poor. Farmers are to leave the corners of their fields and the gleaning from the harvest for the poor to gather (vv.9–10). God's people must respect the elderly (v.32). Aliens living among the Israelites are to be treated the same as native-born persons. Indeed, God commands that the alien be loved as oneself (v.34).

3. The practice of justice in court and business dealings (vv.15–16, 35–36)

Justice is to be practiced in an evenhanded way. Here is one of the few texts in Scripture where partiality is prohibited concerning the poor as well as the rich (v.15). Spreading slander is also prohibited as a miscarriage of justice. The use of honest scales and weights in commercial transactions is commanded (vv.35–36).

These moral rules make specific the nature of holy living. Each in its own way shows the concrete meaning of living according to God's love and justice. The Wesleyan doctrine of Christian holiness has frequently appealed to biblical laws in order to demonstrate the true character of Christian perfection. (See John Wesley's sermons on the Sermon on the Mount.)

D. Punishments for Sacrifice to Molech, Sorcery, and Sexual Offenses (20:1–27)

Ch. 20 prescribes punishments for a series of unlawful activities. Breaking the first laws listed (vv.2–16) results in the death penalty. Not quite so severe, the punishment for breaking the second set of laws is to be cut off from the people (vv.17–18). The penalty attached to the last set of laws is childlessness (vv.20–21). Along with the listing of punishments, the chapter contains parenthetic passages (vv.7–8, 22–26). The concluding verse (v.27) repeats the law prohibiting the practice of sorcery and prescribes the death penalty for a medium or spiritist.

1. Punishments for sacrifice to Molech and sorcery (20:1–6)

The law against offering children to Molech carries the death penalty (cf. 18:21). The severity of the punishment derives from the nature of the sin: it defiles the sanctuary (cf. 16:33) and profanes God's holy name. Likewise, the person who communicates with departed spirits and ghosts prostitutes himself and is to be put to death (cf. 20:27).

2. A call to consecration (20:7–8)

The listing of laws and punishments is interrupted with the reminder that it is God himself who makes one holy. Emphasis on holy living is always in danger of lapsing into legalism. No better prevention for this illness is available than the constant reminder that holiness derives from God himself and not from law-keeping as an end in itself.

3. Laws carrying the death penalty (20:9–16)

Those who curse their fathers or mothers are to be put to death. To curse means to pronounce an oath against a person, imploring the powers of nature to inflict on that person (in this case, a parent) the harm envisioned in the curse. Such a curse is the highest form of rebellion against one's parents. The death penalty is also prescribed for breaking the laws against adultery

(v.10), incest (vv.11–12), homosexuality (v.13), marrying both a woman and her daughter (v.14), and bestiality (vv.15–16).

4. Laws carrying the punishment of being cut off from the people (20:17–18)

A man who marries his sister commits a disgraceful act. Since a brother is charged with guarding his sister's honor, he is held responsible for initiating the marriage and must bear his iniquity. But the text implies that the sister is also guilty, and both the man and the woman are to be cut off from the people. The taboo against touching blood explains why sexual relations are forbidden during a woman's monthly period (v.18).

5. Laws carrying the punishment of childlessness (20:19–21)

Marriage to an aunt or a brother's wife is forbidden. Such unions fall under the curse of childlessness. This is a severe penalty, for it means the end of both family lines.

6. Final call to holy living (20:22–26)

In this passage Israel is called to live differently from her neighbors, for God's people are to live according to God's laws. The goal for all Israel does is to be God's glory: **"You are to be holy to me, because I, the LORD, am holy"** (v.26a).

7. Death penalty for sorcery (20:27)

The seriousness of the offenses committed by mediums and spiritists is indicated by the repetition of the law forbidding sorcery and prescription of the death penalty for such actions.

E. Laws for the Priests (21:1–24)

Chs. 21 and 22 contain instructions for the priests, especially the conditions under which they may minister. The latter part of ch. 22 presents regulations for the wholeness of animals used as sacrifices.

1. Regulations for priests (21:1–9)

Priests are forbidden to officiate while they are ceremonially impure. Since contact with a corpse renders a priest unclean, he is not to participate in funerals except for his immediate family, including an unmarried sister who is dependent on him (v.3). Customs associated with mourning such as shaving one's head or beard or cutting the body (v.5) are forbidden to a priest. In addition, priests are not to defile themselves by marriage to women who have been made impure through prostitution. Divorced women are also forbidden as wives for the priests (v.7). These regulations concerning priestly marriage are based on the sanctity of sex taught throughout the Scripture (cf. Ge 2:24). In a word, priests are to do all they can to lead holy lives, for they present the offerings to God, who is holy (v.8).

2. Regulations for the high priest (21:10–15)

Even stricter regulations are required of the high priest. He is forbidden mourning altogether, even for his immediate family, save possibly his wife. Outward signs of mourning such as tearing one's clothes (v.10) are not to be practiced by the high priest. Like the priests, he is forbidden marriage to a prostitute or a divorcée, but for him marriage to a widow is also prohibited. He must marry a virgin from among the Israelites (v.14).

3. Imperfections that disqualify one from serving as a priest (21:16–24)

The descendants of Aaron are set apart for priestly service. But those with a bodily defect are not to conduct a sacrifice, though by virtue of their birth they may eat the food allotted the priests (v.22). The disqualification of persons with bodily defects is based on the concept of wholeness as a witness to holiness.

F. Laws Governing the Eating of Sacred Food and Presenting Unacceptable Sacrifices (22:1–33)

1. Conditions that keep priests from eating sacred food (22:1–9)

In the preceding passage the prohibition of priestly service by those with physical defects is permanent, but it does not stop them from sharing in food from the sacrifices. In this paragraph conditions of uncleanness cited keep a priest from partaking of the sacred food so long as the unclean conditions last. See the notes on chs. 11, 13, and 15 for explanation of the uncleannesses specified here. The overriding purpose for these regulations is to guard against mishandling or treating lightly the sacred offerings and thereby showing disrespect for God's holy name (v.2).

2. A priest's family and sacred food (22:10–16)

A priest's family is permitted to eat the sacred food, but outsiders who are guests or hired workers in his house may not partake. Slaves are considered members of the household and may eat. The daughter of a priest who marries a layman ceases to be a member of the priest's household, but she may return and partake of sacred food if she is widowed or divorced and has no child. A widow with children is supported by the dead husband's family. A person who mistakenly eats sacred food is to make restitution according to the requirements of the guilt offering given in 5:14–19. The passage concludes with the admonition for the priests not to permit the desecration of the sacred food (vv.15–16).

3. The offering of unacceptable sacrifices (22:17–33)

The main point is the prohibition against offering defective animals in the sacrifices. Specifically named as unacceptable are animals that are blind or injured and those with warts or sores (v.22). Castrated animals are also unfit for sacrifice (v.24). The reason that a sacrificial animal is to be whole is that it is an offering to the holy God, and only a valuable and flawless one is appropriate as an offering to him.

G. Israel's Sacred Festivals (23:1–44)

Ch. 23 contains regulations for observing the sacred festivals. **Feasts of the LORD** are assemblies established for the observance of some special phase of Israel's life before God. A brief regulation concerning Sabbath observance is given first, and there follows instructions for celebrating the Passover (vv.4–8), Firstfruits (vv.9–14), Feast of Weeks (vv.15–22), Feast of Trumpets (vv.23–25), Day of Atonement (vv.26–32), and Feast of Tabernacles (vv.33–44).

1. The Sabbath (23:1–3)

The term **"sabbath of rest"** comes from the word *shābat,* which means "to rest, to cease" (cf. Ge 2:2–3 and Ex 20:8–11 for background on the divine institution of the Sabbath). Here Sabbath observance is to include a sacred assembly. Since it would have been impossible for all of the Israelites to attend a weekly gathering at the temple, this assembly must refer to a community gathering. The Christian Sabbath assembly was transferred to Sunday during the first century, most

likely because that was the day Christ rose (cf. 1Co 16:2).

2. Passover (23:4–8)

Ex 12 gives a detailed account of the observance of the Feast of Passover and the Feast of Unleavened Bread. The first month (v.5) was Abib, called Nisan in a later time (cf. Ne 2:1; Est 3:7). It corresponds with the latter part of March and the first part of April. Observance of Passover is to begin at sundown on the fourteenth of that month. The Feast of Unleavened Bread begins on the fifteenth day. Basic activities include the eating of unleavened bread for seven days, holding sacred assemblies on the first and seventh days when no regular work may be performed, and the presentation of offerings during each of the seven days (cf. Nu 28:16–25).

3. Firstfruits (23:9–14)

This festival is intended as a perpetual occasion for Israel to remember that God gave her as an inheritance a land "flowing with milk and honey" (cf. Dt 26:1–11). At the beginning of the annual harvest, a sheaf of the first grain gathered is to be brought to the priest, who elevates the sheaf before the Lord (v.11). The priest's elevating the sheaf toward God symbolized the dedication of the harvest to the Lord and reception of it again from God. On the same day a peace offering is to be made to God (see notes on 3:1–17).

4. Feast of Weeks (23:15–22)

This festival marks the close of wheat harvest and the beginning of barley harvest and is to be observed fifty days after Firstfruits. Later the name would be changed to Pentecost in keeping with the fiftieth day (after Firstfruits) on which the festival was held. Two loaves made from the new grain and baked with yeast are to be offered to the Lord. In addition a burnt offering, a sin offering, and peace offerings are to be made. On the day that the Feast of Weeks is observed, a sacred assembly is to be held and no regular work is to be done.

5. Feast of Trumpets (23:23–25)

The first day of the seventh month is designated as a day of rest and a time for sacred assembly commemorated with the blowing of trumpets, probably rams' horns. On this occasion a burnt offering is to be presented. These observances set apart the entire seventh month as a high time before God; it was the seventh month when Israel received forgiveness for her sin.

6. Day of Atonement (23:26–32)

The tenth day of the seventh month is set apart as the Day of Atonement. See the notes on ch. 16 for a discussion of the regulations for this festival.

7. Feast of Tabernacles (23:33–44)

This festival begins on the fifteenth day of the seventh month and lasts for seven days (v.34). It is a pilgrimage festival, one in which all males from across Israel are to appear. The designation "Feast of Booths" or "Feast of Tabernacles" comes from the requirement that all Israelites live in booths made of tree branches for the seven days of the festival (v.42). The Feast of Tabernacles is to be observed with sacrifices offered on each of the seven days and by assemblies on the first and last days. This festival is intended to remind the Israelites of God's graciousness in sustaining them when they lived in booths in the wilderness after their deliverance from Egypt.

H. Rules Concerning Oil and Bread at the Tabernacle (24:1–9)

This law establishes the providing of oil for the lamp in the Holy Place and bread for the table of the Presence. The lamps had to be trimmed daily, and the bread of the Presence was changed weekly. The oil was to be of the highest quality; such oil gives a bright light and produces less smoke. In ancient times the lamp burned all night. Later some of the lamps were kept lighted at all times (Josephus, *Antiquities* 3.8.3). The bread was made of fine flour. The amount of flour stated here would produce very large loaves. Some suggest that the loaves were stacked into two columns of six loaves each. When the bread was replaced, the priests ate the old bread, symbolizing that all twelve tribes were in fellowship with Yahweh about the table.

I. Punishment of a Blasphemer and Miscellaneous Laws (24:10–23)

1. The case of blasphemy (24:10–14)

A half-breed, his mother being an Israelite and his father an Egyptian, left his dwelling, possibly outside the camp, entered the area where the Israelites lived, and got into a quarrel with an Israelite. During the quarrel, the half-breed used God's name in a blasphemous manner. What he actually said is, unfortunately, not stated. Did he curse the Israelite, using God's name, or did he utter a worthless curse or did he say God's personal name in anger? The use of two words for cursing strongly suggests that the half-breed uttered God's personal name in a spiteful way. The hearers knew he had broken the third commandment. However, they did not know the penalty since this person was a half-breed. They took him to Moses who, in turn, waited for a word of judgment from Yahweh. The penalty for this person was death by stoning outside the camp and with all the congregation participating. Those who heard the curse were to lay their hands on the half-breed's head as a witness that he was indeed guilty. In taking a person's life, the responsibility fell to the whole congregation, not just a few.

2. Miscellaneous laws (24:15–23)

Attached to this report are some laws. If a person **curses his God** or gods, he is guilty in relationship to that god. But a person who curses the name of Yahweh shall be under the death penalty. This is true for an Israelite and for a foreigner. Murder carries the death penalty (cf. Ex 21:12–14). Other kinds of injuries and losses are to be decided on the principle of an eye for an eye and a life for a life. This principle is called *lex talionis*. Scholars used to blush before this standard. But the study of Near Eastern law has reversed their concern. In some old law codes like Ur-nammu, personal injury carried the penalty of a fine. Injuries against the god or his king, however, had severer penalties. With the introduction of *lex talionis* in law codes such as Hammurabi's the worth of persons was elevated. Injury to a person became a criminal offense. Furthermore, it needs to be emphasized that *lex talionis* was a guide for establishing equivalences in deciding cases. It was not carried out literally. On the other hand, adequate compensation for a loss was to be set by the court; on the other hand, the courts were not to require excessive compensation. In no case is one able to compensate for the talking of a human life.

J. The Sabbatical Year and the Year of Jubilee (25:1–55)

Ch. 25 sets forth regulations for the sabbatical year and the Year of Jubilee. The chapter is divided into the follow-ing sections: (1) regulations for the sabbatical year (vv.1–7), (2) com-mandments for the observance of the Year of Jubilee (vv.8–12), (3) instruc-tions on the effect of the Year of Jubilee on property (vv.13–34), and (4) effect of the Jubilee on persons (vv.35–55).

1. Regulations for the sabbatical year (25:1–7)

After entering the Promised Land the Israelites are to plant and harvest crops for six years and then give the land a sabbath (rest) during the seventh year (vv.3–4). Whatever grows on its own during that year is not to be harvested by the landowner exclusively for himself; the produce is to be avail-able to everyone in his household, for his livestock, and even for the wild animals in the area (vv.6–7). While it is true that the practice of allowing the land to lie fallow every seventh year replenishes the soil, the primary reason for this agricultural sabbatical is recog-nition that the earth is the Lord's; it is a **sabbath to the LORD** (v.4).

2. Commandments for the observance of the Year of Jubilee (25:8–12)

The fiftieth year after Israel's occupa-tion of the land is to be observed as the Year of Jubilee. The word *jubilee* comes from the Hebrew *yôḇēl*, meaning "ram's horn," which is blown as a trumpet. The blowing of the trumpet on the Day of Atonement during the forty-ninth year is to signal the beginning of the Year of Jubilee. Scholars are uncertain whether this meant that the jubilee was to begin immediately with the blowing of the trumpet or six months later when the fiftieth year started. The main pro-visions of this special year are: (1) all leases are to expire and everyone is to return to his family property (vv.10, 13) and (2) all slaves are to be freed (v.10). The theological principle on which these provisions are based is given in v.23: **"The land is mine and you are but aliens and my tenants."**

3. Instructions on the effect of the Year of Jubilee on property (25:13–34)

If an Israelite falls into poverty, he may lease, but not sell, his patrimony. The price of a lease is to be calculated in reference to the coming Year of Jubilee. The greater the time before the next Year of Jubilee, the greater the lease price that might be charged for the land (vv.14–17). The general admonition is to be fair in setting lease prices (v.14).

Provision is made for the redemption of property that has been sold. Should poverty force a person to sell his land, a kinsman-redeemer can purchase the land and restore it to the original owner (v.25). But if he has no relative to redeem his land and has prospered sufficiently on his own, an Israelite may buy back his former land (vv.26–27). If he remains in poverty, the person will return to his property during the Year of Jubilee (v.28). This provision for the reclamation at any time of land sold on lease discouraged the accumulation of land into large estates. Its purpose was to guarantee inheritance of the land to each successive generation of a family. This law is built on the premise that God is the real owner of the land.

Special provision is made for urban property. A person has the right to redeem a house in a city within a year of its sale. If he does not redeem it by the end of the year, it becomes the permanent property of the purchaser and is not to be returned during the Jubilee Year. But houses in the rural areas may be redeemed like the land (vv.29–31).

An exception to this provision for the redemption of houses in the cities is the case of the Levites. They always have the right to redeem their houses wherever they may be. This exemption does not mean that the Levites are privileged, but because they do not own their own land, they must be allowed to redeem the property that is theirs, namely, houses (vv.32–34).

4. Effect of the Year of Jubilee on debtors (25:35–55)

Israelites are prohibited from charging interest on loans made to the poor among them or making a profit on the sale of goods to the unfortunate. Rather, Israelites are to lend a hand to those who are unable to support themselves. The compelling reason for extending aid to the poor is God's graciousness shown to Israel when he brought the people out of Egypt and gave them the land of Canaan (v.38).

Israelites are forbidden to make slaves of their fellow countrymen. Provision is made here for poor people to sell themselves into servitude, but they are to be treated as hired hands and not as slaves. The reason is that the Israelites are God's servants; therefore they may not be enslaved (v.42). Those who are sold as hired servants are to be liberated in the Year of Jubilee (cf. Dt 15:12–18).

While fellow Israelites may not be enslaved, foreigners may be bought as slaves. Also, aliens living among the Israelites may be placed in slavery (vv.44–46).

There is provision for the redemption of an Israelite who has sold himself to an alien living among Israelites. Such a hired Israelite servant may repurchase his freedom if he is able, or his freedom may be repurchased at any time by his kinsman. The repurchase price depends on the number of years to the next jubilee, when he will become free automatically (vv.47–55). These laws regarding Israelite slaves are based on the fact that all Israelites are God's servants whom he has redeemed from Egyptian bondage.

K. Blessings and Curses (26:1–46)

The material in ch. 26 serves as a conclusion to the laws for holy living (chs. 17–26). To encourage obedience to these laws, God promised to reward the faithful and to punish the disobedient. The chapter is divided into five sections: (1) commandments from the Decalogue restated (vv.1–2), (2) blessings of obedience (vv.3–13), (3) punishments for disobedience (vv.14–39), (4) promise of forgiveness upon repentance (vv.40–45), and (5) summary statement (v.46).

1. Commandments from the Decalogue restated (26:1–2)

The chapter opens with a restatement of two of the first four commandments from the Decalogue. Idolatry proved to be a persistent problem as the Israelites frequently turned to the worship of pagan gods of Canaan. Sabbath keeping demonstrates faithfulness to God, and because the Sabbath occurs weekly, it serves as a constant means of spiritual renewal for the faithful.

2. Blessings of obedience (26:3–13)

The Israelites are promised prosperity, peace, and security if they obey God's commands (vv.3–8). In addition, God promises to keep his covenant, originally made with Abraham, and to increase their numbers greatly (v.9). Above all, God promises to make his dwelling among them, to walk among them and be their God, and to own them as his people (vv.11–13). These promises are enduring; they are

God's promises in Christ for his people in all times.

3. Punishments for disobedience (26:14–39)

The passage describes five periods of punishment, each increasingly more severe than the preceding one, that God will inflict on the Israelites if they refuse to obey him. The words **"I will punish you for your sins seven times over,"** which appear in the opening to the description of the second period of punishment (v.18) and are repeated in vv.21, 24, and 28, virtually underscore the intensification of the punishments (e.g., Am 4:6–11; Isa 9:8–10:4). The climax is seen in the desolation of the land and the exile of its people.

Severe punishments will come upon the Israelites if they disobey God's laws for holy living. The punishments are the opposite of promised rewards for obedience. The punishments are a warning of God's rejection unless the people repent. The five punishments increase in severity as God's effort to move his people to repentance increases. God will cut off his people but only after great efforts of forewarning. In the place of prosperity God will cause the soil to be infertile, and it will yield no crops (v.20). Instead of peace, terror will reign in Israel as enemies plunder and enslave the people (vv.17, 25, 33, 36–39). Rather than enjoy security, the people will be attacked by disease (v.16), famine (v.26), wild animals (v.22), and enemy nations (v.17). And rather than enjoy God's presence among them as their gracious Deliverer, they will experience his anger (v.17).

4. Promise of preservation upon repentance (26:40–45)

In spite of such disobedience on the part of Israel and such severe punishment from God, forgiveness is promised if the Israelites repent. It is significant that God promises to remember his covenant, for it is through his covenant that God has demonstrated his everlasting faithfulness toward his people. By remembering, God is promising to preserve the identity of the remnant as Israel, his people, whether they live in a foreign land or in the Promised Land.

5. Summary statement (26:46)

In summarizing the passage on blessings and curses, the author emphasizes the divine source of the decrees, laws, and regulations.

VII. GIFTS, VOWS, AND TITHES (27:1-34)

A. Redemption of Persons Pledged to God (27:1-8)

As a sign of devotion to Yahweh, a person may make a vow of himself or of a child. Since human sacrifice was banned in Israel, the vow was to be fulfilled by the payment of a sum. The price varied according to age and gender: from one month to five years, a male—five shekels, a female—three shekels; from five to twenty years, a male—twenty shekels, a female—ten shekels; from twenty to sixty years, a male—fifty shekels, a female—thirty shekels; over sixty years, a male—fifteen shekels, a female—ten shekels. It is possible that these values were set on the basis of what a person would fetch in the slave market. The price then seems to be determined according to a person's strength, not on the inherent worth of a person. To get some feel for the cost, it has been postulated that a person could earn a shekel a month.

B. Redemption of Property Pledged to God (27:9-34)

A person could pledge to God a member of his flock or a piece of property. A pledged animal becomes holy. But the person may not make a substitution for the object vowed. But if the vowed animal was unclean, the person could reclaim it by paying its worth plus 20 percent. A house or field may be dedicated to Yahweh, and it may be reclaimed the same way. Apparently an owner continued to work a dedicated field, and the yield became the sanctuary's. There are some exceptions to these laws. Firstborn animals could not be vowed because they automatically belonged to Yahweh. Anything devoted (i.e., placed under the heaviest vow) could not be reclaimed. All tithes automatically belonged to Yahweh. Tithes of produce but not of animals could be reclaimed by paying their value plus 20 percent.

These laws established guidelines for gifts. They provided for the conversion of some gifts into currency in order that the sanctuary might have funds for operation.

All vows were voluntary. The Scripture sternly warns, nevertheless, that it is far better not to vow than to vow and not pay (Dt 23:21-23; Ecc 5:4-5).

BIBLIOGRAPHY

Childs, B. S. *Old Testament Theology in a Canonical Context.* Philadelphia: Fortress, 1986.

Gnuse, R. *You Shall Not Steal: Community and Property in Biblical Tradition.* Maryknoll, N.Y.: Orbis, 1985.

Gray, G. B. *Sacrifice in the Old Testament.* Oxford: Clarendon, 1975.

Harrison, R. K. *Leviticus.* TOTC. Downers Grove, Ill.: InterVarsity Press, 1980.

———— . *Introduction to the Old Testament.* Grand Rapids: Eerdmans, 1969.

Hartley, J. E. *Leviticus.* WBC. Vol. 4. Waco: Word, 1991.

Levine, B. A. *Leviticus.* The JPS Torah Commentary. Philadelphia: The Jewish Publication Society, 1989.

Milgrom, J. *Cult and Conscience: The "Asham" and the Priestly Doctrine of Repentance.* Leiden: Brill, 1976.

Neufeld, E. *Ancient Hebrew Marriage Laws with Special Reference to General Semitic Laws and Customs.* London: Green, 1944.

Noordtzij, A. *Leviticus.* BSC. Translated by R. Tostman. Grand Rapids: Zondervan, 1982.

Porter, J. R. *Leviticus.* CBC. Cambridge: Cambridge University Press, 1976.

———— . *The Extended Family in the Old Testament.* London: Edutext Publications, 1967.

Vaux, R. de. *Ancient Israel.* 2 vols. New York: McGraw-Hill, 1965.

———— . *Studies in Old Testament Sacrifice.* Cardiff: University of Wales, 1964.

Wenham, G. C. *The Book of Leviticus.* NICOT. Vol. 3. Grand Rapids: Eerdmans, 1979.

NUMBERS
Victor P. Hamilton

INTRODUCTION

I. TITLE

The English title "Numbers" is carried over from the Septuagint's *Arithmoi* and the Vulgate's *Numeri*. This might suggest, mistakenly, that Numbers focuses on statistics as much as on anything. This is hardly the case. In point of fact, only five out of thirty-six chapters (chs. 1–4, 26) are "numbers" chapters, centering as they do on censuses. The remainder have nothing to do with numbers at all. And while these censuses are indeed critical to an understanding of the book's structure and theology, they comprise approximately only one-seventh of the book.

The Hebrew title "In the Wilderness" is taken from the fifth Hebrew word of 1:1. All action in Numbers took place in the wilderness, either at Sinai (1:1–10:10) or beyond Sinai (10:11–36:13), but never beyond the wilderness. The wilderness is a place of transition, somewhat bleak and threatening, a territory between promise and fulfillment. It is through this wilderness that God's people must pursue a geographical itinerary, but more importantly a spiritual pilgrimage. Thus "wilderness" functions at both literal and metaphorical levels.

II. CONTENT

Several chronological markers throughout Numbers help us to determine the time period covered by the biblical data: (I use the scheme day/month/year).

Ex 40:17	Nu 1:1	7:1	10:11	33:38	Dt 1:3
1/1/2	1/2/2	[1/1/2]	20/2/2	1/5/40	1/11/40
(tabernacle erected)			(leave Sinai)	(Aaron dies)	

Some observations emerge from this. First, 1:1–10:10 covers only twenty days, 10:11–33:38 covers thirty-eight-plus years, and the last few chapters cover six months. Two brief sections (chronologically) bracket a much greater middle unit. Second, the material in 7:1ff., although placed after the material of 1:1ff., actually antedates it, showing that at least here strict chronological sequence was not paramount.

Scholars have long debated the best way to outline Numbers to capture most effectively the essence of the book's contents. There have been almost as many proposed outlines as authors. I would suggest the most faithful approach (following Olson) is to divide Numbers into two generations. The census of the first generation appears in 1:1–46. The material in 1:47–25:18 tells the wilderness history of that first generation before it left Sinai (1:46–10:10) and after it left Sinai (10:11–25:18). Almost all of the material in 1:46–10:10 is last-minute directions to Israel about organization of the camp, plus various laws and regulations to be observed. It is in the second part, 10:11–25:18, that the first generation proves itself to be unfaithful followers of God. There is sin after sin, problem after problem, crisis after crisis. As a result, this first generation is condemned to die in the wilderness.

Then we find a census of the second generation, 26:1–65. The material in 27:1–36:13 provides the reader with a bit of its beginnings. It is a unit that begins (27:1–11) and ends (36:1–13) with the second-generation daughters of the first-generation Zelophehad. In both instances they act magnanimously, and so we start to reflect on the possibility that this new generation might not repeat the sins of their fathers. Still, we are not certain. At least her beginning is propitious. There is nothing ugly or vicious or disappointing as there was with the first generation. Numbers has taken us through the death of the old (1:1–25:18) and introduced us to the birth of the new (26:1–36:13).

III. AUTHORSHIP

Like most of the books of the OT canon, Numbers is, technically speaking, anonymous. The ancients, unlike we moderns, did not feel the need to identify "authors" for their compositions. In fact, it may be debated whether or not our concept of author was even shared in literary circles of the Bronze and Iron ages.

Traditionally the book of Numbers, as is the case for most of the Pentateuch, is assigned to Moses. And, indeed, there is at least one explicit reference to his writing activities in Numbers (see 33:2). There is greater use of the phrase "and the LORD spoke to Moses" in Numbers than in any other Torah book. It occurs at the head of most of the chapters and frequently in the body of the chapter. To be sure, this in itself does not prove Mosaic authorship, but it does make clear that the author(s)/editor(s) intended the audience to read and interpret the bulk of Numbers as a product of revelation revealed by God to Moses for/about Israel. And who is better qualified to write about that revelation than its recipient?

There are many scholars who understand the references to Moses in the Pentateuch to be theological and ideological rather than historical. For them, Numbers was written in phases over several centuries. The earliest part would be several poetic sections of Numbers (10:35; 21:14–15, 17–

18, 27–30; 23:7–10, 18–24; 24:3–9, 15–24). Second would be stories composed around the time of David/Solomon to Elijah, attributed to the Yahwist (J) and the Elohist (E). This would include the likes of 10:29–12:16 and 20:14–25:5. Then several centuries later, around Ezekiel and Ezra's time (i.e., late exilic and postexilic) some priestly writers took this small core of ancient poetry and early narrative and substantially added to that their own elaborate fabric of codes, rituals, and narratives. Of course, the conservative is uncomfortable with this proposal in that such a position radically minimizes, if not eliminates, the historical value of the book's contents.

IV. THEOLOGY

One reason why many commentators have been hesitant to speak about an overarching theology in Numbers is the presence in Numbers of genres of literature that are not only radically distinct, but often ones that seem at first sight to be arranged almost haphazardly.

There are indeed many different types of material in Numbers: statistical information (chs. 1–4, 26); legal matter (5:11–31; 27:1–11; 36:1–13); travelogues (33:1–49); items dealing with worship and the cult (5:1–10; 6:1–21; 7:1–9:14; 15; 18; 19; 28–29); ancient poems (scattered throughout chs. 21 and 22–24); and of course a good amount of narrative (chs. 11–14; 16; 20–21; 25; 31–32).

I would suggest that all of these disparate materials revolve around the theme of holiness; specifically, the holiness mandated of a community as it prepares to break camp (1:1–10:10), and the holiness expected of that community as it heads toward the full geographical and spiritual fulfillment of God's will for its future (10:11–36:13). Childs (p. 199) comments, "In spite of its diversity of subject matter and complex literary development, the book of Numbers maintains a unified sacerdotal interpretation of God's will for his people which is set forth in a sharp contrast between the holy and the profane."

The "holy" is, of course, the blessing presence of God (6:22–27) in the midst of his people as they change from campers to marchers, and his expectation that those whom he blesses will live distinct, separated lives. There are, however, innumerable instances cited in Numbers which would, if allowed to happen, call into question that uniqueness.

On one hand, 1:10–10:10 deals with potential threats to that holiness: uncleanness, deliberate sin, infidelity, violation of a vow, and presumptuous observance of sacred festivals.

Numbers 11:1–25:18, on the other hand, describe actual threats to that holiness. For the most part, the greatest threat lies within the sphere of relationships within the community. There are a number of narratives here (chs. 11–14, 16) that detail a murmuring, back-stabbing, strife-fomenting group of malcontents. Is this the way God's redeemed and set-apart people are to live? How can the Lord bless, keep, and make his face shine on such troublemakers? He cannot, for the sacred character of the community is impugned when the fabric of that community is torn by dissension and nit-picking. It compels God to move from blessing to judgment. He turns the spell of Balaam into a blessing, but he does not do the same with Israel's penchant for divisiveness or her lapse into sexual debauchery.

In some instances God may have to give up on an entire generation (and even its leaders, viz., Moses and Aaron) and regroup with a second generation. But for this new generation the standard of holiness is not diminished. They too live under the possibility of blessing or judgment. They too must choose between cleanness and defilement, between holy living and autonomy. God is committed transgenerationally both to the perpetuation of Israel's existence and to the nonnegotiable standard of holiness by which any generation of his followers must live.

V. INFLUENCE ON WESLEYAN THOUGHT

One possible contribution to Wesleyan thought is a survey of the Hebrew root q-d-sh ("to be holy") and a host of other words derived from it, plus two other Hebrew verbs ṭ-m-'/ṭ-h-r, ("to be unclean/to be clean"). But especially for the former, the returns are meager. The verb appears but eleven times in Numbers (i.e., less than once every three chapters). The word qodesh is used 57 times (exceeded only by Exodus [70 times] and Leviticus [92 times] and equaled by Ezekiel). In most instances it translates as "the sanctuary" (i.e., the Holy Place). Qadosh ("holy") is used in connection with the Nazirite (6:5, 8) and three times in the Korah episode (16:3, 5, 17).

The Hebrew words for "to be clean/unclean" appear most often in Exodus–Numbers. Of 212 uses of tahor ("to be clean") in the OT, 93 are in Leviticus–Numbers (= 43.7 percent). Of 283 uses of tme' ("to be unclean") in the OT, 182 are in Leviticus–Numbers (= 64.3 percent). But again, it is not a simple matter to move from Numbers' concern about (physical) purity to Wesleyan concern about moral purity.

It may be that a more promising approach could be discovered by pursuing the thematic lines of Numbers rather than by tracing vocabulary distribution. It is clear that a major concern of Numbers is the formation of a community of believers on the march in whose presence God is pleased to dwell. Every law that is given, every precept that is mandated, emphasizes the nature of separation to God. All of the narratives in Numbers powerfully illustrate what happens to holy people whenever they live in unholy ways.

Wesley's well-known statement is apropos: "Christian religion is essentially a social religion, and . . . to turn it into a solitary religion is indeed to destroy it." And again, "The Gospel of Christianity knows of no religion, but social religion, no holiness, but social holiness." Numbers testifies to the challenge of social holiness, not only to love God whom one cannot see, but to love others whom one can see.

VI. OUTLINE

I. Preparing To Leave Sinai (1:1–10:10)
  A. First Census of the Twelve Tribes (1:1–54)
  B. Arrangement of the Tribes (2:1–34)
  C. Census of All Levites (3:1–51)
  D. Census of Adult Levites (4:1–49)
  E. God's Will for His People: Camp Purity (5:1–31)
  F. The Nazirite Vow (6:1–27)
  G. Gifts for Tabernacle Usage (7:1–89)
  H. Ordination Service of the Levites (8:1–26)
  I. Passover and the Cloud (9:1–23)
  J. Two Silver Trumpets (10:1–10)

II. From Sinai to Kadesh (10:11–25:18)
  A. Departure From Sinai (10:11–36)
  B. Complaint and Rebellion (11:1–35
  C. Family Opposition (12:1–16)
  D. A Spy Story (13:1–14:45)
  E. Cultic Information for Future Generations (15:1–41)
  F. The Sin of Korah, Dathan, and Abiram (16:1–50)
  G. Aaron's Budding Rod (17:1–12)
  H. Priests and Levites: Privileges and Duties (18:1–32)
  I. Cleansing for Contamination (19:1–22)
  J. Judgment on Moses and Aaron (20:1–29)
  K. Victory, Rebellion, Victory (21:1–35)
  L. Balak and Balaam Versus Israel (22:1–24:25)
  M. Moabite Woman and Hebrew Men (25:1–18)

III. Second Generation of Israelites (26:1–36:13)
  A. Second census (26:1–65)
  B. Questions About Inheritance and Succession (27:1–23)
  C. Public Offerings (28:1–29:40)
  D. Vows (30:1–16)
  E. Holy War Against the Midianites (31:1–54)
  F. A Request to Settle East of the Jordan (32:1–42)
  G. Wilderness Itinerary (33:1–56)
  H. Boundaries of the Promised Land (34:1–29)
  I. Levitical Cities and Cities of Refuge (35:1–33)
  J. Integrity of Tribal Lands (36:1–13)

COMMENTARY

I. PREPARING TO LEAVE SINAI (1:1–10:10)

A. First Census of the Twelve Tribes (1:1–54)

Twice God instructed Moses to take a census. The first was of the first generation, those who came out of Egypt (1:1–46). The second will be of the second generation, those who will actually enter the Promised Land (26:1–65). After opening directives (vv.1–3), Moses is assigned a representative from each tribe, except that of Levi, to assist in the project (vv.4–16). The census included "males twenty years old and above" from the twelve tribes (vv.17–46) but exempted the Levites (vv.47–54). The totals were as follows (with six tribes supplying 50,000 and six tribes less than 50,000):

50,000+

Simeon:	59,300
Judah:	74,600
Issachar:	54,400
Zebulon:	57,400
Dan:	62,700
Naphtali:	53,400

-50,000

Reuben:	46,500
Gad:	46,650
Ephraim:	40,500
Manasseh:	32,200
Benjamin:	35,400
Asher:	41,500

Total: 603,550 (v.46)

This census was God's idea (v.2), not Moses'. But the responsibility for expediting the census was Moses' (and Aaron's). God did not volunteer information to Moses vis-a-vis the number of recruits available and qualified to bear arms. God was commander. Moses was executor. The purpose of the census was to determine the size of Israel's potential army (**all the men in Israel twenty years old or more who are able to serve in the army,** v.3). God will give Canaan to his people as he promised, but Israel will not inherit the land without confronting militarily the indigenous occupants.

The size of available soldier power was admittedly staggering. Add women and children, and Israel's population topped the two million mark, a whopping increase from the meager "seventy" of Ge 46:8–27 and Ex 1:1–5.

A number of modern scholars (e.g., Mendenhall, Gottwald) have attempted to reduce substantially the numbers in the census by redefining the meaning of the Hebrew word 'eleph ("thousand") or 'alaphim ("thousands"). Mendenhall, for example, understood the Hebrew word originally to have designated the military unit of the tribe. Thus, according to this reading, Reuben contributed not 46,500 soldiers, but rather 500 soldiers from a total of forty-six military units. The overall total, by this reckoning, is in the range of 5,000–6,000, not half a million plus.

To be sure, the high numbers must be understood as a fulfillment of God's repeated promises to Israel's founding fathers to make their descendants numerous and prosperous (Ge 12:2–3; 13:16; 15:5; 17:2; 22:17; et al.). On the other hand, impressive statistics as these were an enticement to substitute manpower for Godpower. Gideon's 32,000 and 10,000 were "too many" for Yahweh in liberating his people from the Midianites; instead 300

Figure 1. Arrangement of the tribes

sufficed (Jdg 7). Counting noses must never become a surrogate for counting on God.

An ominous note appears in vv.47–54, a section that briefly notes the threefold responsibility of the Levites vis-à-vis the tabernacle: dismantling, porterage, and reassembly. Any outsider (v.51), i.e., any non-Levite, anybody from one of the lay tribes who attempts to overstep his limits and usurp Levitical responsibilities, shall die. (The word is concealed in the NIV). Israel must not be careless in preparing for the enemy (vv.1–46), but neither should she be indifferent or casual when it comes to entering into the presence of the Holy One (vv.47–54).

B. Arrangement of the Tribes (2:1–34)

Nothing was haphazard or ad hoc in Numbers. The order of positioning the tribes around the Tent of Meeting was a product of divine revelation as much as was the Decalogue. There was no first-come-first-served basis for choice sites (see fig. 1).

So then, Numbers has begun with two sections addressed to the lay tribes. In both cases Israel obeyed the divine revelation explicitly (1:54; 2:34). One

may count on God's favor when his people so respond to his directives.

Probably more critical than the arrangement of the tribes around the Tent of Meeting was the placement of God's dwelling in the middle of the camp as the tribes marched to Zion. This was not to protect the shrine or shield it from damage. Israel's God is not in need of our protection, as if he needs to be concealed from the action. No, the point made was that God's presence must be central among his own. If we make it marginal or inconsequential, we doom ourselves to a life of frustration and failure.

C. Census of All Levites (3:1–51)

The focus now shifts from the numbers in the lay tribes to the numbers in the tribe of Levi. This census was to be exhaustive, including all Levites from a **month old** (v.15). The grand total came to 22,000 (v.39), which was about 2.7 percent of the total laymen in the camp.

The actual census (vv.14–39) is bracketed by information about the Levites' relationship to the priests (vv.1–10) and to laypersons (vv.40–51). In the former section, the Levites are designated as subordinate to the priests and are to assist them. In the latter section, the text states that the Levites are to replace permanently the lay Israelites in the tabernacle (see also vv.7–8, 11–13; 8:14–19).

The Gershonite Levites are to camp on the west side of the tabernacle (v.23), the Kohathites on the south side (v.29), and the Merarites on the north side (v.35). I would suggest that what Nu 3 envisions is a Levitic encampment functioning for the laity as a protective cordon around the sacred tabernacle area. As such, Nu 3 provides amplification on the general statement of 1:53, that the Levites are **to set up their tents around the tabernacle of the Testimony so that wrath will not fall on the Israelite community.**

This interpretation is lost by the NIV's mistranslation of verses like 7 and 8: [The Levites] are to *perform duties* for [Aaron]. . . . They are to *take care of* all the furnishings (italics mine). The Hebrew expression is better translated, "They shall *perform guard duty* for him; they shall *guard* all the furnishings." Once again a red flag is waved. The Holy One dwells in the middle of his people. They are, however, to know their limitations, part of which is keeping their distance and knowing their role.

D. Census of Adult Levites (4:1–49)

In this second census of Levites, only physically qualified males were reckoned. This is made clear by the sevenfold statement that the census was limited to those falling within the age range of thirty to fifty (vv.3, 23, 30, 35, 39, 43, 47). The reason for this restriction was that these Levites would be involved in heavy, physical labor, i.e., dismantling, carrying, and reassembling the tent—hardly a job for an infant or elderly Levite.

Each of the subtribes of Levites had different responsibilities when it was time to break camp and move on. The Kohathites transported the **most holy things** (vv.4–18). The Gershonites were responsible for carrying the curtains (vv.21–28). The Merarites carried the framework of the tent— poles, ropes, crossbars, etc. (vv.29– 33). A later reference informs us that the Gershonites and Merarites used wagons in expediting their responsibilities (7:6–8), while the Kohathites carried their assigned objects on their own shoulders (7:9).

Clearly the Kohathites had the weightiest assignment—the transportation of the **most holy things** (v.4). For this reason certain cautions were directed to them but not to their colleagues. First, even before the Kohathites were to commence their work, the priests entered and covered the sacred objects (vv.5–14). Second, if the Kohathites touched any of the sacred things (v.15b), or even looked at them (v.20), they would die.

Once again a solemn note is sounded. It was imperative that everybody in the camp know his ministry and limitations. A holy God will have it no other way. It was equally imperative that everybody respect the presence of the Divine Majesty.

E. God's Will for His People: Camp Purity (5:1–31)

Numbers now shifts its focus from census lists to regulations that were to govern individual's relationships to each other. But the overarching concern was still the same—purity in the camp and conformity to the divine will—as that in chs. 1–4.

Three different cases are delineated. The first involved the expulsion from the camp of any person who, for any reason, was unclean (vv.1–4). It is imperative that we not equate uncleanness with sinfulness. For example, to be the victim of some ravaging skin disease does not automatically mean that the diseased person is a sinner. In the OT uncleanness is a physical concern, a situation that has the potential to contaminate the dwelling place of God. Viewing uncleanness in moral categories is more an emphasis of the NT, but one that is without meaning without the OT's earlier concerns.

The second case involved a situation where one person stole from another, i.e., one believer from another believer (vv.5–10). In the case of such a trespass, the offending culprit confessed his sin first, then made full restitution plus 20 percent. This recalls exactly the counsel given by Jesus (Mt 5:23), i.e., making things right with people precedes making things right with God. The point in the whole section is, of course, that God's people cannot possibly be a match for the enemy when their own relationships with one another have soured.

The third case concerned (1) the husband whose wife was guilty of adultery, but for which the husband lacked proof, and (2) the husband who suspected his wife of infidelity (vv.11–31). Thus, not only actual sin must be dealt with (vv.5–10), but possible sin as well. In such an instance the wife was subjected to an annoying but not life-threatening ordeal to determine guilt or innocence. (By the way, there was no corresponding law that addressed the concerns of the suspicious wife.) Adultery in the OT was not only a sin, a violation of moral law, but an act that contaminated and unleashed impurity in God's camp. As such it was an aberration that must be confronted quickly and thoroughly.

F. The Nazirite Vow (6:1–27)

Except for vv.22–27, which feature the blessing of Aaron in prayer for the Israelites, ch. 6 focuses on the office of the Nazirite, one of the few positions in the OT open to male and female. The word *Nazirite* comes from a Hebrew verb which means "to dedicate or separate oneself."

The law stated that a person who volunteered for such an office vowed that he/she, while in that office, would abstain from: (1) drinking intoxicants, (2) cutting his/her hair, and (3) touching a corpse (vv.3–8). Subsequent verses prescribe the ritual to be followed when the Nazirite period is terminated unexpectedly (vv.9–12) or as originally planned (vv.13–21). The major difference between the two rituals was that in the former the Nazirite presented a guilt offering (v.12), while in the second he presented a fellowship/peace offering (vv.14, 17, 18), thus indicating the serious nature of a premature end to the vow one made to God.

Clearly, ch. 6 emphasizes what the Nazirite must not do and the ritual for his desanctification from the holy office. Nothing is really said about what he was to do, how he was to spend his days while under the vow, or the nature of his ministry. Once again Numbers shows its concern for obedience and the perpetuation of holiness in God's camp. Anything that threatens to tear this fabric must be dealt with.

Aaron's prayer (vv.22–27) is perhaps unexpected at this point—after census lists (chs. 1–4), regulations for camp cleansing (ch. 5), and the Nazirite vow (6:1–21). Does its placement here suggest that God desires to give Israel not only directives and laws, but blessing and his presence as well? Might it suggest that where there is obedient and holy living (1:1–6:21), the result is the presence of a blessing God (vv.22–27)?

G. Gifts for Tabernacle Usage (7:1–89)

According to Nu 7, Israel's twelve tribal leaders jointly contributed gifts to the completed and consecrated tabernacle consisting of six covered carts and twelve oxen for the Gershonite and Merarite Levites to haul the dismantled tabernacle (vv.1–8). (The Kohathites, however, were to carry the holy things of the Tabernacle on their shoulders, not on carts—v.9.)

Then, individually and spread over twelve days, each leader contributed to the anointed altar the identical gift, as follows: one silver plate and one silver bowl, each filled with fine flour and oil for cereal offerings; one gold ladle filled with incense; and twenty-one sacrificial animals for the burnt/sin/fellowship offerings (vv.10–83).

Finally, the contribution of each leader is duly recorded, and the totals for each gift are provided (vv.84–88), followed by a brief reference to Moses standing once again in God's presence (v.89).

Clearly, chronological concerns have been subordinated to thematic and theological concerns in the book of Numbers. Most, if not all, of the material in Nu 7 (the longest chapter in the Pentateuch) could have been distributed throughout Ex 40—Nu 6. For example, data about the twelve gifts of sacrificial animals might have been squeezed into Lev 1–7, or the gifts of draught carts for two branches of the Levites could have as reasonably appeared back in ch. 4.

Chs. 5–8 focus on the responsibility of the laity, from Nazirites to husbands/wives to tribal leaders. One of those responsibilities included the generous provision of offerings to the sanctuary priests to be used in public worship whenever needed. Liberality was the order of the day. There was no room for penny-pinching scrooges.

H. Ordination Service of the Levites (8:1–26)

After an introductory section containing instructions to Aaron on how to arrange the lamps on the lampstand (vv.1–4), the remainder of the chapter describes the dedication of the Levites (vv.5–22) and the age of their retirement from the Levitical work force (vv.23–26).

First, the Levites were purified (vv.5–7). Then the Israelites placed their hands on the Levites' heads (v.10), after which Aaron presented them to the Lord as a wave offering (vv.11, 13, 15, 21), which must be some kind of a lifting ceremonial. Of interest here is that these two rites (hand imposition and waving) are elsewhere used exclusively for animal offerings but never with humans. The Levites were exceptions to this because they were literally sacrifices brought by the Israelites (see esp. v.11). Obviously the Levites were not offered up on any altar. In essence, however, the Levites became ransom for Israel, the means of her atonement (v.19).

These rituals completed, the Levites were now permitted to begin the **work** of the Lord at the Tent of Meeting. **Work** is a key word in this chapter, appearing in vv.11, 15, 19, 22, 24–26. In each case the work referred to must be specifically the moving of the tabernacle, the one time where Levites handled holy things, and thus the need for purification.

Ch. 8 is an appropriate conclusion to the Levitic prescriptions spread over chs. 3–8: (1) ch. 3, completion of the census of Levites and their guard duty responsibilities around the tabernacle;

(2) ch. 4, partial census for mature Levites and their responsibilities for removal labor; (3) ch. 7, work tools for the Levites; (4) ch. 8, work force of Levites inducted; (5) 8:23–26, Levites retire from work force but continue with guard duties.

I. Passover and the Cloud (9:1–23)

The first fourteen verses of the chapter perpetuate the emphasis of vv.1–8, that Israel (priest, Levite, or laity) do nothing that would offend the presence of a holy God in their midst and bring upon herself divine wrath. The concern here is proper observance of Passover. Two points are emphasized. First, an individual is to observe Passover one month later than usual if either (1) he was unclean or (2) on a distant journey. A person was not free to ignore these restrictions, either by participating in the first-month Passover or by putting Passover observance on hold, something to be done when it is convenient and schedules permit. The second main point is that all other individuals must observe Passover at the decreed time. The consequences for violation were considerable (v.13).

The second half of the chapter is anticipatory, looking forward to the day when Israel will leave Sinai and continue her trek to the land of promise (vv.15–23). When the camp was at a resting place, the **cloud** covered the entire tabernacle (v.15). When the camp was on the march, however, the fire cloud rose and was suspended over the parts of the dismantled tabernacle. The rising of the cloud signaled Israel to move on. The descent of the cloud signaled the people to stop and camp.

The critical issue here is that God directed the march, both its moves and stops, as much as he directed Passover observance. In vv.18–23 the key phrase **at the Lord's/his command** appears seven times. God did not delegate this responsibility to any person. He reserved that privilege for himself.

J. Two Silver Trumpets (10:1–10)

The final piece of information given to Israel before departure from Sinai concerned two silver trumpets to be sounded by the priests, both to call the community to worship and to announce that it was time to break camp and move on to a new location. As such the use of the trumpets would be restricted, at least partially, to the wilderness sojournings. However, their use as a prelude to battle (v.9) guaranteed their use even after Israel enters into its **own land**. It was not enough that the rising cloud signal advancement. To the divine work the human response was added. The sound of the trumpet that went out to the community of faith perhaps portends the sound of the loud trumpet that will one day summon believers into the heavenly tabernacle (Mt 24:31; 1Co 15:52).

II. FROM SINAI TO KADESH (10:11–25:18)

A. The Departure From Sinai (10:11–36)

Mountains are not for living on but for visiting. The old gospel song "I'm Living on a Mountain" is appealing but not biblical.

In this chapter we have geographical information (from the wilderness of Sinai to the wilderness of Paran, v.12) and data about the order of march (vv.14–28, picking up on ch. 2). We also read that Moses insisted that a relative of his by marriage, Hobab, accompany the march (vv.29–32).

But most important of all is the emphasis on the presence of God with his people, underscored by repeated references to the cloud (vv.11, 12, 34).

In fact, this section is ringed by that theme. Thus 10:11–36 highlights the cloud of 9:15–23 rather than the trumpets of 10:1–10. That God is with his people led Moses to prayer and worship (vv.35, 36).

B. Complaint and Rebellion (11:1–35)

The change in atmosphere between the end of ch. 10 and the beginning of ch. 11 is as great as the difference between day and night. Everything in 1:1–10:36 paints a positive picture of the relationship between God and his people. On the other hand, most of the material in 11:1ff. is replete with accounts of rebellions by Israel followed by divine judgment. The shattering abruptness in the break of the narrative flow between 10:36 and 11:1 matches the shattering abruptness of the break in the relationship between God and Israel.

Two incidents are highlighted in ch. 11. In the first (vv.1–3) the people **complained about their hardships**. The divine response was to send a consuming fire on the outskirts of the camp; hence the name for this site, Taberah, i.e., "Burning." The second account (vv.4–35) recalls the craving both of the rabble (i.e., non-Israelites) and of the Israelites for more variety in the food. The wailing of the people even got to Moses (vv.10–15). God sent the people bountiful amounts of quail, but while the **meat was still between their teeth** (v.33), he sent a devastating plague among them as well. This site was given the symbolic name Kibroth-Hattaavah, i.e., "Graves of Craving."

One wonders why the people escaped judgment when earlier they committed exactly the same sin of murmuring and wanting to go back to Egypt (see Ex 16). On that occasion God gave them manna but no plague. Here he gave them quail plus a plague. The answer may lie in the fact that Ex 16 describes a pre-Sinai, precovenant sin (for which the consequences are lesser). Nu 11 describes a post-Sinai, postcovenant sin (for which the consequences are greater).

C. Family Opposition (12:1–16)

Moses was to learn that a man's foes may be of his own household. His sister Miriam and brother Aaron took him to task both because of Moses' choice of wife (why they waited until this point to vent their displeasure is not clear) and because it appeared to them that Moses was suggesting that he was God's vicar, that God would speak only to Moses and only through Moses.

Thus the voice of protest and complaint continues in this section of Numbers—the people against the march (11:1–3), the rabble against the food (vv.4–35), Moses against his role (vv.10–15), and now siblings against Moses. (And that atmosphere will perpetuate itself in the narrative of chs. 13–14.)

God's response, for he cannot allow nit-picking and backbiting to go unchallenged, was to strike Miriam with leprosy. The reason Aaron was not similarly punished is because of either a minor role he may have played or, more likely, because leprosy would have disqualified him from the priesthood.

Happily, God defended Moses (vv.6–8) rather than Moses defending Moses. What Moses did do was to intercede for the healing of his sister (v.13). Noteworthy is the absence of any attempt on Moses' part to defend either his marriage or his unique role. Moses is a humble person (v.3), one who feels no need always to get in the last word or engage in shouting matches with character assassins.

D. A Spy Story (13:1–14:45)

God did not inform the people of the nature of the land of Canaan—its attractions and challenges. Instead, he mandated Moses to send out twelve spies (one from each tribe) to explore the land and report back to the larger assembly. Their discoveries and the report of them were a mixed blessing: **The land is fertile, but its occupants are terrifyingly large. Therefore, let us return to Egypt** (my paraphrase). Only Caleb (and later, Joshua) dissented from the majority view. He granted the truth of all that his colleagues said about Canaan but then counseled an advance to the land for God had promised it to Israel.

The spies' lack of faith quickly spread to the entire assembly (ch. 14). Those who rejected God and his promises greatly outnumbered those who believed God and his promises. The consequences of that negative mindset were disastrous. The spies met immediate death (v.37). The remainder of the congregation would perish and not enter the Promised Land (vv.29–30). Their children, however, would be granted that privilege (v.31) but only because of the intercession of Moses (vv.13–20). Once again, Moses was not expected to bring Israel to repentance so that she might merit divine forgiveness; instead, he interceded for Israel so that God would annul his decree to wipe out Israel completely (see Ex 32:11–14, 31–32; 33:12–16; 34:9; Nu 11:2; 12:11–13).

So, then, God wrote off this first generation, vestiges of which continued through ch. 25. If the land was ever to be possessed, it would be due to the second generation (chs. 26–36). All of the promises made to the first genera-

tion are now shifted to the second. Even the first generation's admission of guilt (14:40) did not negate their eventual demise. Only Caleb and Joshua would be holdovers, Noahlike, from their generation.

E. Cultic Information for Future Generations (15:1–41)

Five different concerns are addressed in this chapter: (1) supplementary data about the burnt, grain, and fellowship offerings (vv.1–16); (2) the offering of firstfruits (vv.17–21); and (3) the contrast between unintentional sin (vv.22–29) and defiant sin (vv.30–31); (4) an instance of the death penalty for Sabbath violation (vv.32–36); and (5) wearing tassels on one's clothing (vv.37–41).

What is of interest is that here one discovers unexpectedly a conglomeration of legal material sandwiched between the spy story of chs. 13–14 and the account in ch. 16 about rebellion against Moses by Korah, Dathan, and Abiram. What, if anything, is the relationship of ch. 15 to its immediate context? Most commentators suggest no relationship at all, which, I suggest, is incorrect.

To begin with, note that vv.1–21 deal with sacrifices that are voluntary and given to God in gratitude and praise. One finds little of either praise or gratitude in chs. 13, 14, and 16. Unintentional sin (vv.22–29) is contrasted with defiant sin (vv.30–31). The sin of the spies (ch. 13), the people (ch. 14), and Korah (ch. 16) was defiant sin. For these there was no sacrificial provision. Only the prayers of Moses saved the perpetrators (14:13–19; 16:22). God wants his people to be **consecrated** (v.40), but no holiness is exemplified in chs. 13, 14, and 16.

Most evident is the focus of this chapter on the future, evidenced by expressions like **after you enter the land** (v.2; cf. v.18), and **the generations to come** (vv.14, 15, 21, 23, 38). Yet in the previous chapter God had said that this first generation would, under no circumstances, enter the land. Ch. 15 is a word to the second generation of divine promise ("I will bring you into the land"), and of divine expectation ("You shall be my holy people").

F. The Sin of Korah, Dathan, and Abiram (16:1–50)

Three individuals led a revolt against Moses: Korah from the Kohathite branch of the tribe of Levi, and Dathan and Abiram from the tribe of Reuben. Why Levites (a clerical tribe) and Reubenites (a lay tribe) united in this protest is unclear. One recalls from ch. 2 that both the Reubenites and Kohathite Levites were to march on the south side of the tabernacle. Perhaps their proximity to each other led to their feeding each other's discontent.

What was their complaint? It was rooted in their perception that Moses and Aaron claimed a monopoly on holiness and accordingly **set [themselves] above the LORD's assembly** (v.3). Once again Moses felt no need to defend himself but rather turned the matter over to God for adjudication. Thus he made a proposal to Korah and the Levites (vv.5–11) and to Korah himself (vv.16–17) by which the matter would be settled. The end of the showdown was that Moses' detractors died either by being buried alive (v.33), by fire (v.35), or by plague (v.49).

The complaint of Dathan and Abiram, who represented the political faction, was Moses' ineffective leadership (vv.13–14). Korah's complaint about the need to democratize holiness in the camp was a smokescreen for what really bothered him. It is clear from vv.10 and 40 that he was dissatisfied with the limitations imposed on him as a Levite and as a result aspired to become a priest, and take the censer, the fire, and the incense, and stand before the Lord. Thus the real issue was not a religious one per se, but one of personal power and pride. In addition, Moses/Aaron and Korah were first cousins (see Ex 6:16ff.). Perhaps that proximity but lack of power also goaded Korah into revolt.

G. Aaron's Budding Rod (17:1–12)

The previous chapter made the point emphatically that Aaron's priestly ministry was not something he stumbled into or manipulated his way into, but rather something for which he was chosen by God. This chapter continues and affirms that divine election.

A representative from each tribe presents a staff to Moses on which he writes the name of that representative. Then the staffs are placed in front of the ark. The one God chooses will sprout. In this way God will, Moses hopes, stop his people's grumbling (v.5).

It was Aaron's staff that sprouted, budded, blossomed, and bore almonds (v.8). That staff was then placed permanently in front of the ark as a warning to Israel.

As a result, the laypeople panicked and refused to have anything to do with the tabernacle (vv.12–13), a classic case of overreaction. How can there be vital worship of God if God's house is viewed as a lion's den that devours those who ever enter it? Ch. 18 will address this phobia.

H. Priests and Levites: Privileges and Duties (18:1–32)

Three concerns emerge in this chapter, and all are a perpetuation of the

Korah rebellion of ch. 16. The first (vv.1–7) focuses on the guard duties of the priests and Levites when it comes to keeping unauthorized people distant from inner and outer areas of the tabernacle.

The second section (vv.8–20) outlines the offerings or gifts (from sacrifices, firstfruits of harvest, firstborn animals) that were given to the priests. Third (vv.21–32), a tithe is presented to the Levites (vv.21–24) in lieu of a Levitical inheritance and as a compensation for their labors around the tabernacle. In turn, the Levites give a tithe of their tithe to Aaron (vv.25–30). In sum, the last two-thirds of the chapter announce, "Make sure you pay your preacher, and preacher, make sure you tithe." Note how often **holy** or **most holy** occurs in vv.8–32 (8, 9, 10, 17, 29, 32). It is the sanctity of tithing, not its legality, that is emphasized.

There is one novel element in the chapter, and that is in response to the panic the laity had developed vis-à-vis the tabernacle (17:12–13). Assurance is given to the laity that from now on priests and Levites alone will **bear the responsibility for offenses against the sanctuary/priesthood** (vv.1 [twice], 23). From this point on God's wrath will be directed vicariously to the Levite, or priest, who is negligent in his tabernacle duties.

I. Cleansing for Contamination (19:1–22)

Prescribed in ch. 19 is the ritual to be followed when one has become impure because of physical contact with something deceased (vv.11–16, 18, 22). Note the frequent use of **touch** in these eight verses.

In such instances a red heifer (or cow) was slaughtered outside the camp in the presence of a supervising priest, and its blood was sprinkled in the direction of the tabernacle (vv.3–4). Then the heifer was totally incinerated while the priest watched (v.5). The red hide of the heifer symbolically added to the quantity of blood, as did the red **cedar wood** and **scarlet wool** (v.6). Thereafter the ashes of the heifer were stored outside the city (v.9), ready to be mixed with water and sprinkled on anyone who had become ritually impure due to corpse contamination (vv.17–19). The whole ritual is described as a **purification from sin** (v.9). The NIV translation may be improved by reading v.9b as "purification from contamination."

Why discuss such a ritual at this point in Numbers? To begin with, this ritual addresses the needs of an individual who had become impure by touching something that was dead. One recalls that there had been many instances of death in the preceding three chapters: Korah and his coinsurrectionists (16:35); the 14,700 plague casualties (16:49); the fear of death (17:1–13); death for encroachment (18:3, 7, 22); and death for failure to tithe (18:32). It is appropriate to follow this with a ritual involving contact with the deceased.

Second, note the pattern in which instances of divine judgment in the present (chs. 11–14) are followed by a chapter involving cultic regulations for the second generation and beyond (15:15, 21, 23). Again, chs. 16–18 are concerned with divine judgment in the present or immediate future. Ch. 19, on the other hand, sets forth a cultic ritual for the future—it is to be a **lasting ordinance** (vv.10, 21).

J. Judgment on Moses and Aaron (20:1–9)

There is little in this chapter that inspires hope in Israel's future. The sin of Moses and Aaron meant that Moses would be denied the privilege of leading Israel into Canaan (vv.2–13), and Aaron would die in the wilderness (vv.22–29). Between the death notice of Miriam and the proleptic announcement of Moses' death, and the death of Aaron, is the account of Edom's stubborn refusal to allow Israel passageway through her territory (vv.14–21). Thus two major problems asserted themselves. How would Israel ever make it to Canaan with hurdles like recalcitrant Edomites in the way, and an indispensable leader like Moses out of the way?

It is ironic that a ceremony dealing with provision of "the *water* of cleansing" (19:20, italics mine) is now followed by an account of Moses and Aaron producing *water* from a rock. Again it is ironic that the event that met the real physical needs of the people (**there was no water**) was the same event that led to Aaron's death and Moses' demise. Thus mercy and judgment operated concurrently.

Told by God to **speak** to the rock (v.8), Moses instead **struck the rock twice** (v.11), after giving the grumbling Israelites a tongue lashing (v.10b; see Ps. 106:33b). In his words to Moses (v.12) the Lord did not repeat Moses' actual actions but rebuked him because he did not **trust in [him]** and **honor [him] as holy**. As a result, Aaron and Moses will be denied leadership of the community (v.12b). Their mutual lack of trust undercut God's mercy to Israel. Stubborn Edomites can be handled diplomatically, but unfaithful leadership is another matter. Moses opened this chapter by burying his sister and concluded it by burying his brother. Between, he buried his own destiny.

K. Victory, Rebellion, Victory (21:1–35)

The morbid atmosphere of ch. 20 gives way to a more optimistic atmosphere in ch. 21. There the rebellion of Moses and Aaron (vv.1–13, 22–29) ringed an account of confrontation with the enemy (vv.14–21). Here the account of Israel's victory over the Canaanite king of Arad (vv.1–3) and over Sihon and Og (vv.10–35) encloses the narration of another rebellion by Israel (vv.4–9). This is the first time a positive note has been struck since 10:11 (since leaving Sinai).

There are two distinct patterns within these stories of murmuring (cf. 20:1–13 with 21:4–9). In the first there is an initial need (20:2) followed by a complaint (v.3), then by Moses' intercession (v.6), which results in God's meeting the need by miraculous provision (20:11). In the second there is an initial complaint (21:4b–5) followed by God's anger and punishment (v.6), then by Moses' intercession (v.7), and finally by a reprieve of the punishment (v.9). In the first pattern there is a genuine need ("there was no water," 20:2). In the second there is no genuine need (**the people grew impatient,** 21:4).

The people's confession, **We sinned** (v.7) and their request for the Lord to remove the venomous snakes recalls similar talk by Pharaoh to Moses about the plagues (Ex 8:8; 9:27–28). God's provision of a bronze snake as therapy for the condemned was a type of another provision of God for the eternally condemned (Jn 3:14–15).

The largest portion of this chapter covers Israel's defeat of Sihon, king of the Amorites, and of Og, king of Bashan (vv.10–35). Of interest is the total absence of Moses from the confrontation of vv.21–31. This story is adjacent to the incident at the rock for which Moses is to be punished. The silence about Moses' role in 21:21ff. may be a reflection of that episode. Moses will, accordingly, have only a minimal role to play in leading Israel any further to Canaan.

L. Balak and Balaam Versus Israel (22:1–24:25)

Earlier when Israel was anticipating a move into alien territory, it was she who lived in terror of non-Israelites (chs. 13–14). Now the tables are reversed, and the Moabites are **filled with dread** (22:2) because of the approaching Israelites. To remove that threat, King Balak, in his naïveté, hired a distant magician (Balaam) to pronounce a curse on these invaders, which is similar to an American president employing a preacher to put a hex on the Soviet Union.

In some ways Balaam is both appealing and stupid. He initially turned down the offer, not because the price was too low, but because God, Yahweh of Israel, told him not to accept (22:12, 13, 18). Only when the Lord gave him a green light (v.20), did he proceed.

It is ironic that although a seer, Balaam was not so perceptive as the donkey on which he rode. The donkey could see the angel of the Lord but Balaam could not. Here God performed two miracles. He opened the donkey's mouth (22:28) (thus showing that the donkey owed her powers of speech and sight not to any convention of talking animals), and, second, he opened Balaam's eyes (v.31). Two parts of Balaam's body were touched supernaturally. Here it was his eyes. Later it would be his mouth (23:5, 16). It is intriguing to note that when the donkey did speak, Balaam registered no surprise but engaged her in dialogue (22:28–30)!

When Balak and Balaam finally met, Balak was, understandably, anxious to get on with the proceedings. Accordingly, he prefaced Balaam's anticipated curse with proper ritual (22:40; 23:14, 30). As a matter of fact, Balak built no less than twenty-one altars throughout this fiasco (23:1, 14, 29) at Balaam's request.

Then came the shock! Each time Balaam opened his mouth to curse Israel, he blessed her. Actually, in this narrative Balaam has assumed the role of the donkey. Donkeys are supposed to bray, not talk. Balaam was hired to curse, not bless. Both creatures stepped out of their normal role—by God's good grace.

Balaam's words about Israel are found in four oracles: (1) 23:7–10; (2) 23:18–24; (3) 24:3–9; (4) 24:15–19. A few isolated and brief oracles follow in 24:20–24. Each oracle speaks in grandiose fashion of Israel and her future, using vivid metaphors and similes. In the first, Israel is spread out like dust (23:10). In the second and third, she is like a crouching lion (23:24; 24:9). The fourth focuses on an individual who will rise like a star out of Israel (24:17). This was more than Balak could tolerate, so he and Balaam parted ways silently (v.25).

There should be no problem in relating this unit to Numbers. For one thing, the prophecies of Balaam affirmed that God's unequivocal commitment to his people will continue well into the future, even beyond this first generation whose death in the wilderness has already been announced. Nothing or no one is able to hinder God from doing that. An omnipotent God and not a human manipulator is the determiner of history.

On the other hand, the narrative functions as a condemnation of God's people, at least indirectly. The donkey does God's will. Balaam, albeit unintentionally, does God's will. But what of Israel? Balaam and his donkey are more appealing than the nation. Placing the Balaam story beside the various stories recorded in chs. 11–21 leads to the conclusion that Israel's real enemy is Israel. God can change a hireling's words of curse into blessing, but he cannot change a community's words of backbiting, criticism, and faultfinding into doxology. God's people need not fear the hex of a religious magician or the threats and taunts of a Moabite king. But whenever they degenerate into a community ruled by a quarrelsome, self-serving, and envious spirit, there is cause for grave concern. Unholiness, not magic, is Israel's undoing.

M. Moabite Women and Hebrew Men (25:1–18)

Encamped in Shittim, east of the Jordan and almost directly across the river from Jericho, Israel's men managed to find time to indulge their sexual passion with the local women of Moab. On the verge of Israel's entering the land and thus realizing the fulfillment of God's promises to the fathers, there was excitement and stimulation in the air. But it was excitement engendered by Moabite maidens and not by the mighty workings of God. And the sin was not merely of a sexual nature (v.1). It also included apostasy (vv.2–3).

Interestingly, Nu 31:16 informs the reader that the impetus behind the scheme of the Moabite seductresses was none other than Balaam of chs. 22–24. Balaam was prepared to share his services either for a fee (chs. 22–24) or gratuitously (ch. 25). He was the kind of person who refused to quit. His malice having been stymied in one instance, he soon stumbled upon another opportunity to express it. Where the potency of spell failed, possibly the potency of seduction would succeed.

So brazen was the sin of the people that one of them was bold enough even to engage in sexual intercourse **at the entrance to the Tent of Meeting** (v.6). Phinehas the priest, grandson of Aaron, was the person most outraged by this overt blasphemy. On earlier occasions it had been Moses who made atonement for sinful Israel (Ex 32:30), but here Moses stood in the shadow of his grandnephew (v.13). Moses talked (v.5), but Phinehas acted (vv.7–8). Phinehas **was zealous for the honor of his God** (v.13).

Again Numbers makes the point that God's people need not fear the external enemy. Neither hex nor invasion may overcome them. The real threats to their well-being and destiny were within and were of a seductive nature.

III. SECOND GENERATION OF ISRAELITES (26:1–36:13)

A. Second Census (26:1–65)

There were two censuses of the lay tribes in Numbers, one in ch. 1 and this one in ch. 26. In both instances notations about the Levites follow the census (1:47–53; 26:57–62). Furthermore, both censuses came on the heels of a recent event that is introduced with an "after . . ." clause (. . . **after the Israelites came out of Egypt** [1:1]; **after the plague** [26:1]. And last, both censuses were limited to **men in Israel twenty years old or more** (1:3; 26:4), those who **were able to serve in the army** (1:3; 26:2).

Alongside of the parallels between the two, one must also discern the differences. There are at least three. In the first place, the census of Nu 26 went beyond giving totals for tribes to include the emergence of subclans within each tribe (e.g., **through Hanoch, the Hanochite clan; through Pallu, the Palluite clan** [26:5]). This extra information served as a vivid reminder of the promise by God of swift multiplication of his people and of blessing on them.

Secondly, this second census is dotted throughout with brief flashbacks to earlier episodes in Numbers, and without exception it recalls negative events. Note first the replacement of Moses and Aaron (1:3) with **Moses and Eleazar son of Aaron** (26:1). The absence of Aaron thrusts one back to 20:22–29. Again, vv.8–10 recall the disastrous coup attempt led by Korah, Dathan, and Abiram (ch. 16) when numbering the Reubenites. The last few verses of the chapter, especially v.65, recall the unfaithful spies of chs. 13–14 and the unbelief they engendered among the people. These rewindings of the tape in this census were not merely for sake of recollection. They were loud and clear messages for the second generation. Her future is not guaranteed unconditionally. She may have as much of the grace of God as she desires, but she is not offered immunity from judgment.

Thirdly, vv.63–65 make it very clear that not one person of that first generation who exited from Egypt is included in this new census. Those in this census are born post-Exodus or post-Sinai (excluding Caleb and Joshua). Thus, one comes to the end of this chapter with a bit of excitement and a bit of apprehension. Here is a fresh start, a new beginning. But will this second generation rise above the temptations ahead? Or will they lower themselves to the level of the preceding generation?

B. Questions About Inheritance and Succession (27:1–23)

Two issues emerge on the heels of the second census, and both deal with the relationship of the second to the first generation. In the first issue (vv.1–11), the focus is on the concern of the five daughters of the deceased Zelophehad. There were no sons to inherit his property. Since property is to be willed to one's sons (Dt 21:15–17), what was to be done when there were no sons? This story provides an illustration of a legislative procedure by which a new law may be enacted in a case of novel circumstances (for other examples see Lev 24:10–16 and Nu 15:32–36). In this case the new law allowed inheritance to pass to daughters (v.8), to brothers of the deceased (v.9), to uncles of the deceased (v.10), or to the nearest living relative (v.11).

One admires these five daughters, both for their aggressiveness and their faith. They did not take their plight passively as something over which they had no control. They approached the entrance to the Tent of Meeting (vv.1–2) for a different reason than did Zimri and Cozbi (25:6). There was no alert Phinehas needed on this occasion to spear the trespassers. The daughters also were part of the second generation and thus recipients of God's promises. They will not be judged for their father's sin (v.3). Those promises enabled them to see beyond the tragedy of the past, the uncertainty of the present, and into the hope of the future.

The second issue focuses on Moses' successor (vv.12–23). He does have sons, unlike Zelophehad, but there is no indication that the mantle of leadership is to be placed on either of them. Moses, with a limited future for himself (vv.12–14), sees a bright future for the second generation. But it is imperative that that generation be provided with the best leadership possible. Otherwise, they will be **like sheep without a shepherd** (v.17; cf. Mt 9:36). Joshua is the one divinely chosen. Why? What are his qualifications?

Joshua did have a sense of involvement with Israel's history and he had been discipled by Moses, but these were not the criteria for his being chosen to lead the Israelites. Rather it was the presence of the Holy Spirit (v.18) in his life, a fact no less true for Moses himself (11:17). Moses was elated at the choice and even exceeded God's command to lay his **hand** on Joshua (v.18) by laying both **hands** on him (v.23).

C. Public Offerings (28:1–29:40)

Nu 28–29 constitutes a code of sacrifices for the various sacred occasions of the year. There was to be at least one sacrifice every day of the year. That in itself serves as an indication of how critical a role sacrifice played in community worship in the OT.

In all, offerings for eight separate occasions are listed, according to the frequency of that occasion. These are (1) the daily offerings (28:2–8), (2) weekly Sabbath offerings (vv.9–10), (3) monthly offerings (vv.11–15), (4) Passover offering and Unleavened Bread offering (vv.16–25), (5) Feast of Weeks offering (vv.26–31), (6) Feast of Trumpets offering (29:1–6), (7) Day of Atonement offering (vv.7–11), and (8) Feast of Tabernacles offering (vv.12–38). Of course numbers 4–8 are once-yearly offerings. Thus the offerings ranged from daily, to weekly, to monthly, to annual.

If one sets out in tabular form all the requirements of this cultic calendar, it will appear as shown as in figure 2.

In addition to burnt and sin offerings, two other offerings are also prescribed—the drink and grain offerings. The first two are of animals. The third is of wine. The fourth is of flour mixed with olive oil. Absent from this list is any reference to either the peace offering or the guilt offering. This may be because these two offerings were voluntary and thus were not a part of the prescribed order of public ritual (see my discussion at 7:1–89).

Several facts emerge from these two chapters. First, these were directives not for private worship but for communal worship. There is no concept here of "only God and me." Second, these were commands, not suggestions. For that reason, of the forty verses in this chapter, thirty-eight constitute a divine speech. There is an introductory verse (v.1), and one final verse indicating that Moses transmitted God's speech (v.40).

Third, the number of animals offered as burnt offerings (1,243) outnumbered those offered as sin offerings (30) in approximately a 40:1 ratio. The burnt offering was not primarily expiatory in purpose; rather, it was a spontaneous expression of praise and gratitude. It is clear from these lists that in public worship praise outdistanced contrition.

Fourth, far and away the most frequently offered animal was the lamb. Think of the impact on the community beholding every single day the offering of a lamb. Certainly the groundwork is laid here for John the Baptist's "Behold the Lamb of God" (Jn 1:29 KJV).

Last, the immediately preceding chapters had established policies for Israel to follow once she is settled in Palestine. The second generation will persist (ch. 26). Nobody will be denied an inheritance (27:1–11). Joshua will follow Moses (vv.12–23). And here Israel's life is to be permeated by public worship. But such worship must be neither purely formal nor primarily aesthetic nor cerebral. At the heart of worship is offering.

D. Vows (30:1–16)

Vow (Heb. *neder*) is a term that applied both to the original pronouncement of a vow as well as to its subsequent fulfillment and payment. What ch. 30 affirms is that any vow taken in God's name is irrevocable. For that

Occasion	Frequency per year	Type of Offering			
		Burnt			Sin
		Young Bulls	Rams	Male Lambs	Goats
1. Daily					
morning	365			1(365)	
evening	365			1(365)	
2. Sabbath	52			2(104)	
3. Monthly	12	2(24)	1(12)	7(84)	1(12)
4. Passover/ Unleavened Bread	7	2(14)	1(7)	7(49)	1(7)
5. Weeks	1	2	1	7	1
6. Trumpets	1	1	1	7	1
7. Day of Atonement	1	1	1	7	1
8. Tabernacles	1				
Day one		13	2	14	1
Day two		12	2	14	1
Day three		11	2	14	1
Day four		10	2	14	1
Day five		9	2	14	1
Day six		8	2	14	1
Day seven		7	2	14	1
Day eight		1	1	7	1
Annual totals (1,273)		113	37	1093	30

Figure 2. Cultic calendar

reason Ecc 5:4–5 cautions restraint in making vows to God. It is better not to make a vow in the first place than to make one and then try to back out of fulfilling it.

Interestingly, only one verse (v.2) discusses vows offered by a man, while thirteen verses elaborate on vows made by a woman (vv.3–15). In this second and larger grouping, one discovers that (1) a girl's vow may be nullified by her father (vv.3–5) or by her fiance (vv.6–8), (2) that the vow of widows and divorcees is binding (v.9), and that (3) a wife's vow may be nullified by her husband (vv.10–15). The catch was that the father/husband had to act immediately if the daughter's/wife's vow was to be voided (vv.5, 8, 12, 14).

To illustrate how this policy would

work, one would assume that if a woman took a special vow, say, to be a Nazirite (i.e., a vow of separation, Nu 6), the husband/father could veto such a decision if action was taken promptly.

Here, then, is an instance of a law addressing family relationships. Family issues have popped up now and then in Numbers. Recall the jealous husband (5:5–31), or Aaron and Miriam disputing with Moses (ch. 12), or the brotherless daughters of Zelophehad (27:1–11; 36). And while the law clearly subordinated the daughter to the father and the wife to the husband, the real onus for implementing these regulations fell squarely on the male. He must truly be an effective leader of his household. There was no room for the sluggish, wishy-washy, ineffective father or husband. Through these laws and narratives that focus on some aspect of marital/family relationships, possibly the point was made that national faith would truly exist only as it was fed by family faith.

E. Holy War Against the Midianites (31:1–54)

Moses received a general directive from God to **take vengeance** on the Midianites (v.1). This repeats God's command to Moses to "treat the Midianites as enemies, and kill them, because they treated you as enemies. . ." (25:17–18). To expedite that order, Moses sent 12,000 soldiers along with Phinehas the priest into battle. This was the second generation's first encounter with an enemy, and they anticipated an even more potent enemy ahead, the Canaanites.

Interestingly, little of the chapter describes the actual combat, only six verses (vv.7–12) out of fifty-four. Vv.1–6 are preparatory, and vv.13–54 are the sequel. The sequel comprises the lengthiest segment of the chapter and the one that interests us.

Four items emerge in this sequel. First, Moses was displeased that the soldiers had allowed the real villains of the Midianites to live, i.e., their seducing women (vv.13–18). Second, strict purification procedures were implemented both for the soldiers who fought and for the objects that were captured (cleansing by fire and water) (vv.19–24). Third, the war spoils (captives and beasts) were to be divided equally among the soldiery and among the general citizenry. The soldiers presented .02 percent of their share (1/50) to the Levites (vv.25–47). Fourth, an offering of golden jewelry was given to the Lord as a memorial (vv.48–53).

So the real areas itemized in this holy war event were (1) total obedience to God's will and no second-guessing or editing of that will, (2) cleansing and purification over against defilement, (3) tithing and support of those in positions of religious leadership, and (4) the need for God's people to be continually generous with their possessions and their need to be constantly reminded of that.

F. A Request to Settle East of the Jordan (32:1–42)

Somewhat unexpectedly, representatives of two tribes of Israel (Reuben/Gad) and of the half-tribe of Manasseh approached Moses with a double request: (1) to be settled east of the Jordan (vv.1–5a) and (2) not to be made to cross the Jordan (v.5b).

Moses responded angrily (vv.6–15), but primarily to the first request rather than to the second. Moses, furthermore, justified his position by invoking the spy story of Nu 13–14. The behavior of these would-be Transjordanians, he claims, was like that of the ten spies whose negativism discouraged the people. Here one people about to enter the land became two groups with different territorial intentions. It is interesting that Moses did not ever consult Yahweh about the Transjordanians' request as he did, say, with the concern of Zelophehad's daughters (ch. 26). The reason is likely his conviction that the daughters were venting a legitimate concern, while the request of these tribes was illegitimate.

The two-and-a-half tribes then offer a compromise (vv.16–19). If they are allowed to make temporary provision for their property and dependents, they will accompany the other tribes across the Jordan. Then once they are settled, they themselves will return to Transjordan to claim their inheritance. Thus, the first request is nonnegotiable; the second may be surrendered.

Moses agreed to this proposal (vv.20–24) and left such instructions with Joshua (vv.28–30). Jos 22 records the implementation of this agenda. Bracketing Moses' directive to Joshua was a pledge of faithfulness by the Transjordanians (vv.25–27, 31–32). The incident concludes with Moses (not God!) giving this territory to the Transjordanians (vv.33–42). Thus potential friction between reluctant bargainers and a reluctant giver was avoided.

Had Moses chosen to be obstinate or the Transjordanians to be uncompromising, an explosion would have occurred. How a community handles and resolves conflict is a clear indication of its spiritual mettle. There are three ways in which conflict may be dealt with: (1) avoidance ("We have no problems"); (2) conquest ("There's not enough room for both of us"); (3) procedural resolution (reconciliation/compromise). Where the third method is pursued, unity (even if shaky) will prevail.

G. Wilderness Itinerary (33:1–56)

Most of this chapter (vv.1–49) is a stage-by-stage description of Israel's itinerary from the departure from Egypt to the plains of Moab. Some forty sites are mentioned, and about forty years of history are summarized via geography. It is told in the third person plural rather than the first person plural, as if Moses were distancing himself from the group about whom he is writing.

Everything surrounding ch. 33 is oriented to the future and the second generation (e.g., the Transjordanian settlement [ch. 32]), and the boundaries of the Promised Land not yet reached [ch. 34]). Here is one chapter devoted exclusively to the past with the appearance of a travelogue or a geographical diary.

There is a playoff within this chapter between the "they" of the past (vv.1–49) and the "you" of the present and future (vv.50–56). If vv.1–49 are annalistic, vv.50–56 are exhortational. Moses changes roles from historian to preacher. Compromise worked well in ch. 32, but there is no room for compromise in 33:50–56. Internal differences need to be ironed out, but the inhabitants of Canaan need to be expelled and their icons destroyed. The God who guided the first generation will guide the second generation, too, but this was not intended to encourage complacency among the people.

The numerous sites listed *ad seriatim* indirectly make the point that Israel did not make her way through the wilderness haphazardly. The successful, albeit detoured, journey from Rameses to the plains of Moab is scarcely a delightful serendipity. It testifies to God's specific leadership of his people.

Several of the names recall a place at which God did something sensational (Rameses, Marah, Kibroth Hattaavah, the Desert of Sinai, etc.). Others are but atlas entries. The twelve sites in vv.18b–30a are unknown. Alush, Rithmah, and Rissah are not memorable, but God was there, too, leading and directing his own.

H. Boundaries of the Promised Land (34:1–29)

If God's leadership of his people in the past had a geographical specificity to it (ch. 33), so does his leadership of his people in the future (ch. 34). Although not even there yet, the Israelites were given exact boundaries for their future home. It is God who delegated the territory and set southern/western/northern/eastern boundaries. Since Moses had never been there himself, and lacking an atlas, much of this data would presumably be meaningless to Moses. What would an individual who had spent most of forty years in Midian and another forty years in the desert understand by geographical minutiae like **run a line from Hazar Eanan to Shepham** (v.10), or **from Mount Hor to Lebo Hamath** (v.8)?

The southern boundary is in the wilderness of Zin (v.3), while the northern boundary extends to **Lebo Hamath** or **to the entrance of Hamath** (v.8). The land will also extend from the eastern border at the Jordan River (v.12) to the Great Sea (i.e., the Mediterranean) on the west (v.6). At no time in her history did Israel ever occupy all of this area. The closest she came was during the reign of David. What God promised was never totally appropriated.

In addition to boundary data, God instructed Moses to appoint twelve tribal leaders whom God himself had chosen and who would be responsible to oversee future divisions of the land among the tribes (vv.16–29). Three

such lists of leaders of the twelve tribes appear in Numbers: those in this chapter, the lists of twelve census supervisors in 1:5–16, and the twelve spies listed in 13:4–15. Each list appears at a significant point in Numbers: (1) the organization and inauguration of the march of Israel toward Canaan; (2) decisive rebellion in the desert, which led to the death of the first generation; and (3) the future allocation of the land to the second generation. Both Joshua and Caleb appeared in lists 2 and 3. Survivors from the first generation, they would function as models of faith to the younger generation.

I. Levitical Cities and Cities of Refuge (35:1–33)

The boundaries of the Promised Land having been outlined (ch. 34), it was appropriate to add data about where the Levites were to settle (35:1–8). Had the Levites been a monastic order, such information would not have been necessary. But they were a tribe of families, and as such they were in need of real estate on which to build houses, and land on which to graze their beasts.

To meet that need, forty-eight cities (not identified in Nu 35, but see Jos 21 for the names) were assigned to the Levites. Each city was to have pastureland that formed a square of 3,000 feet per side and whose perimeter was 1,500 feet in every direction from the town wall. Altogether, these allotments would represent fifteen square miles, or about .1 percent of the land of Canaan.

Six of these forty-eight towns were designated additionally as **cities of refuge** (vv.9–33). Three were to be located on the west side of the Jordan and three on the east side (a seemingly odd division, given the much higher population of Cisjordanians over Transjordanians. Why not four and two or five and one?).

The purpose of these cities was to provide a haven from the **avenger of blood** (v.19) for the person guilty of accidental homicide (the only crime for which the OT provides asylum). In societies lacking a strong central authority, the defense of private property and life was the task of the family of the victim (i.e., the avenger of blood). The purpose of the cities of refuge was to control blood revenge by making it possible for public justice to intervene between the slayer and the avenger of blood.

Again, the emphasis in both sections (chs. 1–8 and chs. 9–33) is on the need of the people of God to run their in-house affairs in a God-glorifying way, both by providing for the needy and by protecting the deserving.

J. Integrity of Tribal Lands (36:1–13)

Ch. 36, again involving the daughters of the deceased Zelophehad, takes the reader back to ch. 27. There the problem was whether the sonless father's name should be preserved by granting land inheritance to daughters. The answer was yes. Here the male members of the tribe of Manasseh raised a problem about the ruling made in ch. 27. In view of the concept of fixed tribal division, what would happen to their inheritance should these women marry outside their tribe? God acknowledged the force of this concern

and as a result mandated that propertied women were bound by law to marry within their tribe. Each of the late Zelophehad's five daughters abided by this decree (vv.10–12).

At least four theological issues emerge from this legal case. First, indirectly God renewed his promise of the gift of land to Israel, thus a legal decision on the issue of land inheritance. Second, all tribes were included in this promise, and no one tribe was to benefit from circumstances that threatened to deprive another tribe from its land inheritance. Third, not all the issues facing God's people may be solved simply by appealing to God's past word at Sinai. In both chs. 27 and 36 God was sought out for a fresh word.

Fourth is the refreshing emphasis on the obedience of the five daughters. They are one of the few models in Numbers of compliance with God's word, especially when laid alongside the likes of the rabble (ch. 11); Miriam and Aaron (ch. 12); the spies (chs. 13–14); the Sabbath-breaker (ch. 15); Korah, Dathan, and Abiram (ch. 16); Moses and Aaron (ch. 20); and the Israelite men (ch. 25). The accounts of Zelophehad's daughters in chs. 27 and 36 form an inclusio for the events and organization of the second generation whose appearance is emphasized in the genealogy of ch. 26. If they are typical of the second generation, the future of God's people is guaranteed.

BIBLIOGRAPHY

Budd, P. J. *Numbers.* WdBC. Vol. 5. Waco: Word, 1984.

Childs, B. S. *Introduction to the Old Testament as Scripture.* Philadelphia: Fortress, 1979.

Hamilton, V. P. *Handbook on the Pentateuch.* Grand Rapids: Baker, 1982.

Mann, T. W. *The Book of the Torah. The Narrative Integrity of the Pentateuch.*
    Atlanta: John Knox, 1988.
Milgrom, J. *Numbers.* The JPS Torah Commentary. Philadelphia: The Jewish
    Publication Society, 1989.
Noth, M. *Numbers, A Commentary.* OTL. Philadelphia: Westminster, 1969.
Olson, D. T. *The Death of the Old and the Birth of the New.* Literary and
    Theological Framework of the Book of Numbers. Chico, Calif.: Scholars,
    1984.
Sturdy, J. *Numbers* CBC. Cambridge: University Press, 1976.
Vaulx, J. de. *Les Nombres* (Sources Bibliques) Paris: J. Gabalda, 1952.
Wenham, G. J. *Numbers:* An Introduction and Commentary. TOTC. Downers
    Grove, Ill.: InterVarsity, 1981.

DEUTERONOMY
Eugene E. Carpenter

INTRODUCTION

I. TITLE, CONTENT, AND CANONICAL PLACEMENT

The first two words in the Hebrew text of Deuteronomy, *'elleh haddᵉbārîm*, comprised the title that the Jews most commonly used for this book. The Hebrew means "these are the words." The title was sometimes given in a shortened form as simply *dᵉbārîm* ("words"). These are the words given to Israel by Yahweh through Moses: "They are not just idle words for you—they are your life" (32:47). And even Jesus chose to live by them: "It is written: 'Man does not live on bread alone, but on every word that comes from the mouth of God'" (Mt 4:4; Dt 8:3). All of humankind made in the image of God (Ge 1:26–28) and specifically the nation of Israel potentially recreated in his image at Sinai (Ex 20–24), were to obey and heed the words of Yahweh. Thereby they reflected him (cf. Ge 2:15–17; Dt 26:18).

Another title used by the Jews when referring to Deuteronomy was "the book of exhortations" (*sēpₑer tôkāḥôt*), which emphasizes the mode of delivery of "these words" rather than the words themselves. The exhortatory nature of this book is central to the spirit of the book and a significant dimension of its meaning. Deuteronomy is a convincing example of a holistic appeal to the emotions and the mind.

The name Deuteronomy is an English rendering of the Latin Vulgate's title *Deuteronomium*, "second law." The Vulgate took the title from the Greek translation of the Hebrew phrase meaning "a copy of this law" (Dt 17:18). Rather than a second law, Deuteronomy represents the law of Sinai (Horeb in Deuteronomy). It is an exposition of that covenant in a new literary, theological, and historical setting. The literary nature of the book is difficult to define. The various names that have been used to designate it make this evident. However, the general character and purpose of the book is clear.

An idea of its character can be gained by analyzing the major speech segments delivered by Moses. After a brief introduction (1:1–5) that sets the theological, literary, and historical context, the first exhortatory address of Moses sets forth God's requirements in order for Israel to take the land and to become God's people. Moses' second address (4:44–28:68) declares even more earnestly the theological basis needed for Israel to become God's people. Interestingly, John Wesley (*Notes*) calls the speech in ch. 4 a "pathetic exhortation to obedience." This speech includes the basic covenant stipulations (the "Shema," 6:4–9; the "Ten Words," 5:6–21) and leads into the specific covenant stipulations in 12–26. The concluding covenant rituals and a review of the covenant theology consummate this address in 27:1–28:68. Moses' third address (29:1–30:20) begins and ends with his charge to Israel to keep the covenant. His closing words (31:1–33:29) depict Israel's future rebellion but also express his final blessings upon the people he loves. An account of the death of Moses and a eulogy conclude the book. Deuteronomy is sometimes called "the last will and testament of Moses" because of these final chapters.

Deuteronomy is a finished literary document. Many references in it refer to events of the past: Sinai (Horeb), the Exodus, the wilderness wanderings, the fathers, the golden calf, and others. But clear implications about the future are here as well: a rebellion of Israel, the reality of exile, a return from exile, the taking of the land, a circumcised heart, and covenant blessings. A call to commitment in the present appears regularly. Deuteronomy gathers up all of these features in an effective literary-theological style that makes the book a dynamic transition piece. It moves the reader and the theme from the Pentateuch (Genesis–Numbers) into the historical books (Joshua–2 Kings).

But it is, nevertheless, not a mere transition piece. It elucidates everything that has occurred before so that Israel may understand and respond correctly to the great words/deeds that God has wrought on its behalf. It also projects the significance of those words/deeds for the history of God's people. The future of Israel hinges upon her choice of two ways: *the way of faith and love*, followed by blessings; or *the way of disbelief and enmity*, followed by curses (cf. Ge 2:17; Dt 28:2, 15). The free choice of Israel to serve Yahweh is a central tenet in Deuteronomy. Wesleyans have understood this moral choice of a free will, made possible by grace, as the entrance into fellowship with God. However, although the book indicates that even if the covenant curses are realized because of Israel's unbelief, it also asserts that the future can be altered by Israel's repentance and Yahweh's forgiveness and mercy. These factors enhance and enlarge the seemingly simple black/white character often asserted of the theology.

Israel's history as recorded in Joshua through 2 Kings follows the pattern of the covenant stipulations in Deuteronomy: obedience = blessing; disobedience = cursings, as recorded in the covenant in Moab (chs. 29–30). Ample illustrations of repentance, mercy, forgiveness, and renewal punctuate the narrative. Deuteronomy sets the plumbline by which the writers of the history evaluate the nation of Israel, the chosen people of God.

Hence, Deuteronomy is a pivotal document in the OT. It ties together the Pentateuch and the later history of Israel, furnishing the ethical-religious guidelines by which God's people were to live or perish. Their welfare was not dependent upon whether they were in the Promised Land. It depended upon their obedience of faith toward Yahweh. God would come to them even in a strange land; "if from there you seek the Lord your God, you will find him if you look for him with all your heart and with all your soul" (4:29; cf. Jer 29:13)). Yahweh's appeal through Moses was not merely for Israel to obey some external code; it was essentially an impassioned plea for his people to love him with all their heart, all their soul, and all their might (6:4–9; cf. Mt 22:37; Mk 12:29–30; Lk 10:27).

II. STRUCTURE, MEANING, AND SIGNIFICANCE OF DEUTERONOMY

The research of literary critics into the form and structure of biblical books during the past thirty years has been fruitful for the study of Deuteronomy. Many ancient covenants have been unearthed and examined in detail. The basic structure of these covenants (called "suzerain-vassal treaties") is reflected to some degree in the design of Deuteronomy. However, the book is more than a suzerain-vassal treaty; it seeks above all to establish relationships based on an appeal to love, not on the power politics of the ancient Near East. Thus it is a relational document more than a legal document.

At least four major areas of concern are fused here: (1) the theological, (2) the literary, (3) the historical, and (4) the canonical.

A. Theological

The biblical writers first and foremost reported the activity of Yahweh in human history and in divine history. Their uniqueness lies in this role as Israel's historians and theologians. Deuteronomy is thoroughly theological. Through Moses, the mediator of the covenant, Yahweh offers his kingdom to the people of Israel. The heart of Moses' message is "Seek first the kingdom of Yahweh and his righteousness and all these other things will be added unto you." This points clearly to the message that the new covenant Mediator, Jesus Christ, would later deliver to the Jews of his day. In and through Moses, the kingdom of Yahweh comes to the people of Israel; the kingdom becomes a potential reality. God encounters his people in his words/deeds.

One of the theological burdens of Deuteronomy, then, is to present to Israel the essence of the kingdom in God's covenant words which reflect his loving, gracious, merciful character. They call Israel to commitment to him. The literary structure, the historical narrative, and the selection of words are geared to achieve this theological impact upon Israel and all subsequent readers of the book.

The "people of God" is a major theological theme here. Yahweh calls Israel to be his unique ethical-religious nation. They can be that people if they follow the covenant that Yahweh is offering to them. Faithfulness to the covenant will enable them to rise to that ethical-religious imitation of God for which humankind was created. They are Yahweh's people by *choosing* his covenant; they are not his by necessity or by their own nature. Wesleyan scholarship affirms this vital relational truth. The purpose of Yahweh's covenant was to create a holy fellowship. The Israelites' obedience to the demands of the covenant was an expression of loving fellowship between God and his people (5:10; 7:9; 10:12; 11:1, 13, 22; 13:3; 19:9; 30:16, 20). This was the chief command and goal of the Mosaic covenant (6:4–9).

After a comprehensive review of the last one hundred years of research into the significance of covenant for OT theology, Ernest W. Nicholson observed:

> The concept of a covenant between Yahweh and Israel is, in terms of "cash value," the concept that religion is based, not on natural or ontological equivalence between the divine realm and the human, but on *choice*: God's choice of his people and their "choice" of him, that is, their free decision to be obedient and faithful to him. Thus understood, "covenant" is the central expression of the distinctive faith of Israel as "the people of Yahweh," the children of God by adoption and free decision rather than by nature or necessity (pp. 215–16).

Martin Noth has helped us realize that the key to understanding law in OT theology is that law is meaningful only within covenant. Yahweh's gracious covenant relationship with Israel was established before he gave the law. A clear understanding of the theology of covenant in Deuteronomy begins with recognizing that the covenant exists because Yahweh loves Israel and has freely chosen her (4:37; 7:6–8). He desires, therefore, that his people imitate him by loving and choosing him. So Israel is not ultimately defined by law, but by her free choice of Yahweh out of a motive of love. Nor did Israel's possession of the land ultimately define the nation either, for they are declared to be Yahweh's people before they conquer the land. (For further discussion of covenant and the people of God in OT theology see Goldingay, 44–96; 134–66.)

The OT and the NT covenants have the same goal, although only the new covenant fully realizes that goal. But the difference between the two is described already in the old covenant: only under the new covenant could God's people realize the experience of the circumcised heart, which was the true essence of the old covenant (10:16; 30:6). In the new covenant, God's desire under the old covenant (5:29) became a reality (30:6; Jer 31:31–34; cf. Dt 5:29). Both covenants demand entrance into God's kingdom through loving God supremely and loving people selflessly. Other major theological motifs will be noted below and in the commentary.

B. Literary

Deuteronomy is given to us in a language, style, and literary form that conveys its message with persuasion and power. God aided the inspired writers as they chose the best literary style and form for his purpose. He aided in the use of the appropriate poetics to drive home his theological-historical messages (cf. Sternberg, *Poetics,* 1986).

The word most descriptive of the book is found in 1:5. *Deuteronomy is torah.* Torah includes story, history, teaching, instruction, law, Yahweh's words. Torah is both theological and historical, both relational and legal, both prophecy and history. These elements are fused in Deuteronomy so closely that they are inseparable. The book must be read as one dynamic, living message. It is not primarily legal material, but *haggadah* (story) with law imbedded in it. God incarnates himself in it among his people.

C. Historical

Deuteronomy has been described by Gerhard von Rad, the greatest OT theologian of this century, as having an "atmosphere of the timeless." Indeed, the message of Deuteronomy intersects people of all cultures and ages. It is intimately and effectively addressed to the past, present, and future. Its central message breaks cultural barriers. The incarnational nature of Deuteronomy—i.e., the fact that God speaks within the narrative to a culturally bound people—is precisely the element that makes it timeless and able to speak to all times and cultures. Thus the "atmosphere of the historical and the cultural" is evident in Deuteronomy.

In biblical thought, history cannot be separated from theology nor, therefore, from ethics. From the creation, history is conceived as the interaction between God's word and his created order. The historical and theological combine to present an authoritative and normative guide—to Israel then and to God's people for all future time.

D. Canonical

The canonical aspect of Deuteronomy refers to the unique way in which the book has come to us in the form in which we now have it. The canonical concern indicates the book's placement and function in the Pentateuch and the following history of Israel. This commentary will deal with the final canonical shape of Deuteronomy and with its present placement within the Scriptures of the OT.

III. AUTHORSHIP, COMPOSITION, DATE

The date, composition, and authorship of Deuteronomy have been moot issues for over a hundred years. The best approach must involve a consideration of critical data and appropriate presuppositions about the text *as Scripture.*

Deuteronomy seems to have reached substantially its present form during the middle to late period of the United Monarchy, with some later editing. The book reports the words of Moses in a dynamic way that preserves their significance for the Israelite community at that time and for subsequent communities of God's people (cf. Craigie, 29, n. 31).

IV. NEW TESTAMENT USAGE OF THE OLD TESTAMENT

It is important to note the impact of Deuteronomy on the NT. The *United Bible Society's Greek New Testament* lists 195 citations or quotations from Deuteronomy in the NT. This number is exceeded only by quotes or citations from Psalms, Isaiah, Genesis, and Exodus, in that order. Deuteronomy is quoted often in writings of Qumran and in the other Jewish literature of the intertestamental period (c. 350–0 B.C.) The first great commandment given by Jesus comes from Dt 6:5, which calls for a relationship of love to Yahweh. Three times Jesus quotes Deuteronomy when resisting the Devil (Mt 4:1–11; Dt 6:13, 16; 8:3). By doing so, Jesus may be affirming Deuteronomy as the word of God par excellence in the OT and still perfectly valid under the new covenant. He and Moses agreed that God's foremost command is to "seek first God's [Yahweh's] kingdom and his righteousness, and all these things will be given to you as well." Israel did not do so; but the perfect Son of God, the Head of the second Israel, did. Thus he inherited the kingdom and was the first to enter that land and its blessings, but only, like Moses, after absorbing the curses of the covenant on behalf of others (cf. 1:37; 3:26; 32:51).

V. OUTLINE

The following outline traces the unfolding of Deuteronomy as the exhortation and plea of Moses to all Israel to do the whole Torah of Yahweh.

   I. Introduction: Theological, Literary, and Historical (1:1–5)

  II. Moses' First Exhortatory Address (1:6–4:43)
      A. Distrust in Yahweh—Failure To Take the Land
         (1:6–46)
      B. Israel Begins to Possess the Land (2:1–3:22)
      C. Yahweh Lets Moses See the Land (3:23–29)
      D. Moses Charges Israel to Take the Land (4:1–40)
      E. Moses Appoints Cities of Refuge East of the Jordan
         (4:41–43)

 III. Moses' Second Exhortatory Address (4:44–28:68)
      A. Stipulations, Decrees, and Laws, East of the Jordan
         (4:44–49)
      B. Summons to Commitment to the Covenant Established
         at Horeb (5:1–11:32)
      C. Summons to Commitment to the Covenant Established
         at Horeb: Represented and Expanded in Moab
         (12:1–26:19)
         1. Purity and unity of Israel's worship (12:1–13:18)
         2. Purity/holiness of Yahweh's people (14:1–21)
         3. Economics of Yahweh's people (14:22–15:23)
         4. The religious year of Yahweh's people (16:1–17)
         5. Leaders of God's people (16:18–18:22)

COMMENTARY

I. INTRODUCTION: THEOLOGICAL, LITERARY, AND HISTORICAL (1:1–5)

This commentary deals with the key theological themes and motifs of Deuteronomy. For background information about the cities and geographical locations mentioned in these verses, see the standard introductions, dictionaries, and encyclopedias (e.g., IOT, NBC, HBD, NLBC). Key Hebrew words and phrases in the Hebrew text will be discussed only when they help our understanding of the theological message.

Much of Deuteronomy was first delivered orally and then put into writing. Its skillful poetics and documentary structure indicate this dual origin. Its admonitory and sermonic material is especially geared to encourage and persuade its readers to complete commitment to the Lord and his proffered covenant.

In the book's brief introduction the words **"all that the LORD had commanded [Moses]"** indicate that this is the major theme. In about eighty words the author sets the scene for Moses' speeches of **all that the LORD [Yahweh] had commanded him concerning** Israel.

There is no more powerful concept in the OT than Yahweh's word. In Genesis his word calls forth the creation. In both Ex 20:1–17 and Dt 5:6–21 the Ten Commandments of Yahweh outline the ethical-religious order for Israel in which she was to live. The words of Yahweh are literally Israel's life (32:47): not merely her physical, material life; but above all, her ethical-religious life (6:25).

The words Moses delivers are the words spoken to all Israel in Moab. Priests, Levites, kings, judges, elders, and leaders are all considered to be brothers of the one nation, the people of God. The writer stresses that these words were delivered in the region east of the Jordan. Israel, therefore, knew them and committed herself to them before crossing the Jordan. She bound herself ethically-religiously to do them.

As Moses delivers and explains the words of God, he includes a historical review so that Israel might learn from the theological and historical lessons of the past. His words about the past enlighten Israel's present and also her future.

II. MOSES' FIRST EXHORTATORY ADDRESS (1:6–4:43)

The passage 1:6–4:43 contains what some consider to be the first introduction to the laws that are to follow in chs. 12–26. According to this view, chs. 5–11 then serve as a second introduction to chs. 12–26. However, these two sections are better viewed as consecutive sections, the second one developing more fully certain key issues in the first. That is, in a crescendo of exhortation to all Israel, chs. 5–11 continue and develop certain issues briefly mentioned in 1:6–4:43.

The history of Israel that is narrated in 1:6–4:43 portrays Israel as a people of incorrigible unbelief in the face of Yahweh's persistent covenant faithfulness (2:7, 24–25, 29; 3:21; 4:29–31). Deuteronomy 1:6–46 is the classic example of Israel's pattern of failure. The Lord's discipline is recalled in 2:1, 14–15 and 8:5 as he tried to encourage and lead Israel to faith and action. On the other hand, 2:2–3:11 records Israel's success when the people followed Yahweh in faith. The result was the conquering and inheritance of the Transjordanian territory as Yahweh began (2:25) to give the land to Israel. Our author presents this narrative as a prelude to the anticipated possession of all the land west of the Jordan.

Ch. 4 sets forth the ethical-religious requirements for future possession of the land that Yahweh was giving to Israel (4:1–4). It begins to emphasize the necessity for Israelites to fulfill their divine vocational call, evidenced by the giving of God's unique Torah (4:5–8) and his historical interventions on their behalf (4:32–34). Their uniqueness and their righteousness depended on their faithfulness to the Lord (4:4, 9; 6:25), to their living wholly unto him. Without living according to his ethical-religious model, Israel could accomplish nothing. But Israel could find God even in a strange land if the people met the stated condition for this gracious restoration: "You will find him if you look for him with all your heart and with all your soul" (4:29).

A. Distrust in Yahweh—Failure to Take the Land (1:6–46)

This section dramatically presents Israel as a model of an unbelieving, rebellious people. The form of the chapter reflects the major concern of the text. For example, some corresponding parallels are:

A. Go in and possess the land (vv.6–8).

B. Triumphs and multiplication of Israel (vv.9–12).

C. Wise leaders chosen (vv.13–18).

D. Go up and possess the land (vv.19–21a).

E. Do not fear the peoples (v.21b).

F. Request for spies (vv.22–24).

G. Good report of spies (v.25).

H. But you were not willing; you rebelled; unbelief (vv.26, cf. 32) is the central issue.

-G'. Evil report of spies (v.28).

-F'. Rejection of spies (v.28).

-E'. Fear of the people expressed (v.28).

-D'. Land is given to others (vv.34–40).

-C'. The leaders' foolish choice (v.41).

-B'. Defeats and decrease of Israel (vv.42–44).

-A'. Do not go in and possess the land (v.42).

The structure clearly shows that the central theme of the passage is in vv.26, 32: **"You rebelled. You did not trust."**

Bad faith clearly produced corrupt theology in Israel, illustrated by the people's grotesque charge against Yahweh in v.27: **"The LORD hates us; so he brought us out of Egypt to deliver us into the hands of the Amorites to destroy us."** V.28 completes this hideous distortion of Yahweh's true motive for bringing his people out: the Israelites are afraid of the people, cannot conquer them, and are discouraged. The direct speech emphasizes that these words are of major importance.

Israel charged Yahweh falsely. They not only forgot his deeds and words (1:29ff.), more seriously they misinterpreted them. Even after repentance (1:41), they do not perceive things correctly; they insist upon being hotheaded and stiff-necked despite Yahweh's warning. The result of this failure of faith was forty years of discipline in the desert (2:1, 14–15). Only those who did not take part in the rebellion and distrust of Yahweh could then enter the land (2:14–15; 4:4).

The shocking irony of Israel's failure strikes home when vv.27–28 are analyzed: they are nothing less than the complete reversal of Yahweh's stated purposes for choosing Israel. The issue is clear in 4:37–38. He does not hate Israel (1:27), he loves them and their

forefathers (4:37). He did not bring Israel out of Egypt to give them over to the Amorites (1:27); he brought them out to give the Amorites into their hands (4:38). The people in the land are not too strong for Israel (1:28); the Lord will drive them out (4:38). Israel should not lose heart (1:28), but should take heart (4:34). Their brothers are not against them (1:28), for God has chosen them all for the same purpose (3:18–20; 4:38). Israel should not grumble (1:27); rather, Yahweh is to be her praise (10:21) and things will go well (4:40). Israel could not "know" Yahweh and his way unless they would trust him. To know God and to interpret his deeds/words correctly on their behalf required obedience to the Lord.

B. Israel Begins to Possess the Land (2:1–3:22)

Dt 2:1–3:22 develops a success model of Israel. Israel's obedience to Yahweh is affirmed several times. They are commanded not to touch the lands that Yahweh had given to the descendants of Esau (2:8), Moabites (v.9), and Ammonites (v.19). They carefully obey (vv.8, 37 and implied in the other cases) and do not encroach upon these peoples' lands but pay for food and water (vv.6, 28). The men of the rebellious generation have died by the Lord's judgment (vv.14–15), and Israel is now open to a new beginning.

A new generation might produce a successful model for the future. This is Yahweh's hope and appeal (4:1, 4, 14, 20, 38). This time Israel follows the Lord's commands in every way (2:32–35; 3:6–7). Joshua is assured that the same success can accompany his leadership (3:22). In all of this, it is evident that Yahweh is giving the land; Israel is not taking it by force (2:5, 25, 31, 36; 3:3, 18, 20), a fact they acknowledge.

The writer makes it clear that Israel's inheritance of the land is not unique. The Lord drove out the previous inhabitants for the descendants of Esau and for the Ammonites just as he had done for the Israelites (2:5, 9, 12, 19, 21; cf. Am 9:7). Israel received its land in order to be the unique ethical-religious people of Yahweh through trusting him and by observing his great Torah. This relationship depends on more than mere possession of land. The land does not uniquely define them so much as do Yahweh's **righteous decrees and laws** (4:5–8). A true Israelite was one who had Yahweh's righteous decrees and laws on his heart, one who had made a willing commitment to love and obey God (cf. Ro 2:25–29). A specter of warning, however, haunts 2:1–3:11. Yahweh, the owner of all the land, repeatedly has caused various peoples to be dispossessed. In turn, he has caused nations to take possession of the land. The land is Yahweh's. Israel can forfeit the land and be dispossessed.

The total destruction (*ḥerem*) of the conquered territory and its inhabitants was enjoined upon Israel by Yahweh (2:34; 3:6, where *naḥᵃrēm* is used). *Ḥerem* is a technical term used to describe something given over to Yahweh for total destruction, immediately or in the near future. If Israel kept any of the things devoted to destruction before the Lord, they themselves would be **set apart for destruction** (7:25–26; *ḥerem* is used).

The taking of the land was not based on any capricious partiality of Yahweh for Israel per se. Only since he had chosen them and as they responded to him were they special. The solidarity of Israel was vitally important; all Israelites were one. Those who had received their inheritance in the Transjordanian region (Reubenites, Gadites, and one-

half of the tribe of Manasseh) were to affirm this solidarity by helping other tribes take the land that Yahweh was giving to them (3:18–22). The possibility of an early division in Israel's unique community would be lessened if this process was followed. The western tribes could not claim that others were disheartening them, since the Transjordanian tribes would help them conquer their territory. Future references of Moses to all of Israel entering the land refers also to the Transjordanian group, for in fact all Israel went over to possess the land.

C. Yahweh Lets Moses See the Land (3:23–29)

Dt 3:23–29 is touching but tragic. Moses takes on truly heroic proportions in this graphic depiction of his vain pleadings for grace from Yahweh so that he might enter the land. He is denied and even rebuked (v.26); he accepts the Lord's sovereign decision. His character here is exemplary, for Moses does not ask for redress, even though Yahweh is angry with him because of the people who provoked him. Moses is not accustomed to Yahweh's rejection of his pleadings (9:19–20, 25–29). He is, however, assured that the land will be taken by Joshua. But the warning in the passage is to Israel. If Moses is kept from the land because of a sin that Israel provoked in him, how much more should Israel be denied entrance. And how can Israel remain in the land?

D. Moses Charges Israel to Take the Land (4:1–40)

In ch. 4 Moses addresses all of Israel, now about to enter the land to take possession (vv.1–4). In contrast to the model of failure in ch. 1, Moses is urgent in his instructions to Israel about how to possess the land, to keep it, and to return to Yahweh when failure occurs.

The third point is notable, for it demonstrates the breadth of the "deuteronomistic theology" in Deuteronomy. It is far more than obedience = blessing; disobedience = cursing. More importantly it involves repentance upon failure and a new restoration to Yahweh, even in a strange land. This restoration is envisioned as a reality that will occur when the "heart religion" of this book is realized: when **"you seek the LORD your God, you will find him if you look for him with all your heart and with all your soul"** (v.29). This verse anticipates the Shema (6:4–9) and indicates the motivation for keeping the decrees, laws, commandments, and stipulations of the covenant (cf. 5:29).

The character of God is ultimately the foundation of the covenant; he determines the true deuteronomistic theology (v.31). He is merciful, he is faithful to his covenant, and he will not abandon or destroy his people. He will not forget his covenant when they break the covenant, if they will turn and seek him (v.29). He will never break his covenantal oath (v.31). These verses emphasize that Israel forgets but Yahweh does not; his people abandon him, but he does not forsake them. He is merciful, and they should be. They should imitate him. The remaining theological basis that Moses presents for Israel's future success can be noted only summarily as follows:

1. Israel's covenant faith must result in the keeping/doing of the commands that God is giving them (vv.1–4, 6, 12–14). The concrete life of faith for Israel finds adequate expression only in their careful observance of the Torah. By obedience their ethical-religious calling is fulfilled. Israel's Torah was

unique; its source was Yahweh (vv.6–8).

2. Upon entering the land, Israel must be careful to reject idolatry and all false gods. The basis for Israel's faith was laid in the "Ten Words" all Israel heard at Horeb (4:12; 5:4, 22–27). Vv.15–26, 35–36, and 39–40 deal solemnly with the threat that idolatry poses for Israel when they enter Canaan. Loving Yahweh, the supreme goal of the covenant, is not possible if idolatry interferes; therefore the first two commandments must be carefully followed. The polytheism of Canaan and the idolatry of those nations could pose an insurmountable obstacle to Israel's fulfillment of her covenant with Yahweh.

3. Israel must remember her unique creation by Yahweh (vv.32–34). Israel was literally created out of nothing (a clear parallel to original creation in Ge 1) and taken from Egypt to be God's own people. Yahweh's past deeds and words proved that there is no God but Yahweh. Thus, Israel, out of a heart of gratitude, should follow the requirement named in the first commandment (vv.35–36, 39–40).

4. Israel must remember the true purposes and motivation of Yahweh and not distort his character and goals (vv.37–40; cf. 1:27–28) as they did earlier.

E. Moses Appoints Cities of Refuge East of the Jordan (4:41–43)

The appointment of the cities of refuge in 4:41–43 is appropriately placed here. All Israel will cross the Jordan to take Canaan. But a system of social order and justice is instituted for those who would remain in the land east of the Jordan.

III. MOSES' SECOND EXHORTATORY ADDRESS (4:44–28:68)

Dt 4:44–28:68 is the central section of the book both in theology and position. Dividing the material into five sections helps discover its meaning and significance. The various sections will be discussed according to the outline, III.A–E.

Ch. 4 introduced the "Ten Commandments" (v.13) and indicated the necessity of Israel's observance of the first two commandments. According to Moses (5:22–32; Ex 19:1–20:20), all Israel heard the Ten Commandments given. Ch. 5 stresses these Ten Words, and ch. 6 emphasizes the need for Israel to obey them out of supreme love for Yahweh (6:4–9 et al.). The Shema in 6:4–9 is the key to the theology of the book. Israel's love for Yahweh involved an internal attitude toward him. Obedience to the commandments flowed from this motive. Wesley realized the importance of the Shema for a true religion of the heart (*Notes,* 604). Wesleyans have largely concurred with his evaluation. Chs. 6–11 exhort Israel to trust, love, and cling to Yahweh who has freely chosen them because of his love (7:6–8; Wesley, *Notes,* 607; Clarke, *Commentary,* 211) for them and their ancestors. Ch. 11 closes this section by echoing the Shema twice (vv.1, 22) and by encouraging Israel to keep the religious, ethical, and civil laws. The emphasis is on the proper motivation for doing so. This obedience of love will make them holy unto Yahweh.

Israel's holiness cannot be separated from Yahweh's social, ethical, and religious instructions. Israel's holiness was an individual holiness but also a corporate, social holiness. Their holiness was permeated and kept alive by love. Wesley later defined this concept and experience as the essence of true holiness.

Clarke asserted that few parts of Scripture "can be read with greater profit by the genuine Christian than the Book of Deuteronomy" (Clarke, 204).

For more on 11:29 and the covenant ceremony to be completed at Mount Ebal and Mount Gerazim, cf. 11:29–30; 27:1–26.

The presentation of the laws in chs. 12–26 follows closely the order of the Ten Words and also the order of the two Great Commandments. Chs. 27–28 close off 5:1–28:68 and echo chs. 1–4. Once again these last two chapters represent the options that Israel has and the results that follow.

A. Stipulations, Decrees, and Laws East of the Jordan (4:44–49)

The brief introduction in vv.44–49 goes with the following material in chs. 5ff. The Torah (1:5) that Moses began to expound is further explained and preached (4:44). It consists, as already noted earlier, of the stipulations (*'ēdôt*), decrees (*huqqîm*), and laws (*mišpaṭim*) spoken to Israel by Moses when they left Egypt (4:45). There is no other law in heaven or under the earth for which to search.

B. Summons to the Commitment to the Covenant Established at Horeb (5:1–11:32)

The Ten Commandments were mentioned in 4:13. There they are also called his covenant. Moses now updates that experience. Those hearing him are responsible. The contemporary charge to the current generation is Moses' burden (5:3).

For a detailed discussion of some of the technical issues involved in the text of the Ten Words, see the standard commentaries. These Ten Words are the basis for the instruction following in chs. 12–26. Note the personal, comprehensive, incarnational, and affective dimension of these instructions from Yahweh. One did not enter the covenant by merely obeying them, but by faith and trust in Yahweh's goodness (7:8), because of which it was to one's benefit to keep the instructions from the sovereign Lord (4:5–8).

Yahweh gave instructions on how Israel was to live after he had graciously chosen them, loved them, and delivered them; they owed their deliverance and salvation to him (5:6). Grace was extended before the Torah was given. Exodus preceded Sinai. A new heart would one day be given to Israel (30:6ff.) so that she could keep the Torah. In the meantime, the grace of forgiveness was available if the Torah was broken (4:31). Yahweh, merciful and gracious, would not reject a repentant heart. He delivered his people and pleaded with them to follow him. He brought them out: first the love/choice, then the Exodus, then Sinai, then forgiveness, then restoration.

God's mercy is never ending, but his just dealing with sin corresponds to the offense. The third commandment (5:11) is best understood in its ancient Near Eastern setting where the name of a person or a god was intimately related to the character of that being. To misuse Yahweh's name was to abuse and scorn Yahweh's character. No Israelite was to bear (claim) Yahweh's name and live in disobedience to his Torah, for that would bring reproach upon the Lord. The reason given for keeping the fourth word of Yahweh in 5:15 stresses the humanitarian concerns of Deuteronomy (cf. Ex 20:8). An emphasis on humaneness and brotherhood runs through the book. The reason for Sabbath observance illustrates the reason why Israel should care for slaves: Israel had been in slavery, but Yahweh had delivered them. The fifth commandment continues to illus-trate the high regard for persons that permeates Deuteronomy. The second great commandment is assumed and illustrated throughout this book. The length of life in the land is an ethical-religious issue (5:16). Respect for one's parents results in Yahweh's blessing. The tenth word for Israel is a clear example that the Mosaic covenant was a spiritual, affective, "heart" religion to its core. The terms *covet* (*ṭaḥmōd*) and *desire* (*tiṯ'awweh*) (v.21) are the same words used of Eve when she failed the test in the Garden (Ge 3:6). In 5:29 Yahweh cries, **"Oh, that their hearts would be inclined to fear me and keep all my commands always, so that it might go well with them and their children forever!"**

The phrase **"it might go well"** is used here to describe what Israel will receive if she is righteous: trusting Yahweh and keeping his instructions (6:25). *Ṭôb,* "good," is also the word used seven times in Ge 1 to describe the original creation. It indicates that the creation enjoyed a perfect state of health and order. This was God's goal also for Israel. Israel maintained no idol of Yahweh in the Holy of Holies as other nations did. The Ten Commandments located in the mercy seat (ark) directed Israel to love both God and humankind.

The people of Israel bound themselves to the implications of the Ten Words (for the significance of a covenant relationship, see Nicholson's introduction and comments) and to other words of the Torah that Moses received alone (5:23–27). Before the Torah is expounded in chs. 12–26, Moses once again grounds the Torah in the love of God and in the ethical-religious essence of the Torah (5:32–33).

Dt 6:4–9 contains the Shema Jesus quoted when he gave what he called the Great Commandment: **"Love the**

Lord your God with all your heart and with all your soul and with all your strength." There is no question about what the center of the theology of Deuteronomy is: supreme love for Yahweh. Everything else in the Law and the Prophets is a footnote (Mt 22:37; Lk 10:27). Moses' appeal in Deuteronomy is to the heart of Israel. He implores the circumcision of their hearts unto Yahweh and the keeping of the Torah. If Moses could reach Israel's heart, the obedience of faith would follow. The second Great Commandment is implied throughout the book. It is stated explicitly in Lev 19:18. The exhortation to faith in 6:4, followed by a command to love, is found ten times and only in Deuteronomy.

Dt 6:4 may mean: The Lord God (1) is one Lord—not many, or (2) the Lord is one—a unity. He is not composed of a number of petty deities, each reflecting a dimension or attribute of Yahweh himself. This teaching guarded against both polytheism and the worship of multiple manifestations of Yahweh.

Four other major points are dealt with in this chapter. Israel must not forget Yahweh (v.12) after being blessed in the land; they must fear him (vv.2, 13) in order to take the land and remain in the land. They must also preserve traditions for their children (v.20–25). By diligent observance of the whole law, they would be a righteous people. The faithful observance of the Ten Words depended on Israel's love for Yahweh (5:29; 6:4–9).

In ch. 7 Israel is a "treasured possession" (v.6, 'am segullâ[h]) by virtue of being chosen and loved by Yahweh (4:37). He expects reciprocal love from them (v.9). The essence of Yahweh's character is holy love (v.6). Yahweh chose Israel because he loved them (7:7–8). They were to be holy (qâdôš)

unto him in position (v.6) and character (vv.1–5). In keeping the Torah (vv.12–16), forgiveness and grace assured Israel of restoration if and when they turned away.

To break away from their earlier model of failure (1:6–46), Israel is exhorted to remember (7:18) and not to fear the **"peoples you now fear"** (vv.18–21). Yahweh will conquer them methodically and orderly **"little by little"** (v.22).

The nations posed the threat of Israel's apostasy upon their entering the land (vv.4, 16, 25). Israel is commanded, on the basis of Yahweh's evaluation, to wipe out the inhabitants of Canaan. Apostasy would have totally negated Israel's calling. But Israel could be destroyed, too (v.26), if they become like the inhabitants of the land (vv.25–26). The people are utterly to abhor the Canaanite religion. But the Torah provided for repentance and restoration if apostasy occurred.

Several remarkable assertions are found in 8:1–19. Many of them indicate Yahweh's concern with Israel's attitudes (vv.2, 5, 17). The forty years of wandering in the desert tested the people to determine what was in their hearts, for the source of keeping the Torah lay in the condition of the heart of Israel (v.2). Another purpose of their wandering was that they might know (not "to teach" as in NIV, but hôdî'akâ) that humankind lives on the word of God (v.3).

The gift of the land is one of Yahweh's blessings for a faithful people. But the land can be her most subtle and enticing enemy. The terms **"remember"** and **"forget"** are used five times in these few verses (8:2, 11, 14, 18–19) to indicate Israel's failure to trust Yahweh (vv.19–20). If Israel forgets the benefits of Yahweh, they will be destroyed.

The tendency of Israel to abuse Yahweh's blessing of prosperity in the land involves smugness and self-centeredness. Their inner attitude is the source of the problem: "You will say in your heart, my strength and the might of my hand have produced this wealth and power for me" (8:17, my trans.). Yahweh blesses them; he is faithful to the ancestors of his people (v.18).

The worldview of Deuteronomy is holistic. It includes all of the various perspectives of life. The glue that holds it together is the ethical-religious texture of reality. If that texture is missing or corrupted, meaninglessness and chaos ensues. In Yahweh Israel had the source of their religion and ethics. That religion and those ethics could create a nation and a people "wherein righteousness" would dwell. Jesus knew that humankind ultimately lives by the Word of God; therein lay his own hope (cf. 8:3, 10).

The direct quote of the people of Israel in 9:4 reveals the central problem in this section: Israel's false assumption (as in 8:17 also) that God was giving the land to them because of their own righteousness, a thought conjured up in their hearts. In fact the people are not righteous except as God makes them righteous. But Yahweh will keep them as his people since he will forgive their sins if they keep the covenant instructions of repentance when they sin (4:29).

Israel is depicted in these verses as a stiff-necked and rebellious people from the day they left Egypt (9:7, 13, 22, 24). They ultimately need to be converted (30:6). Through Moses' repeated intercessions on behalf of the people, they are restored several times (vv.25–29).

This passage has a more powerful theme than failure and hopelessness running through it: the faithfulness of Yahweh to the ancestors (v.27), the willingness of the Lord to listen to his faithful servant Moses (v.20), his unwillingness to put a blot on his own character (v.28), and his unwillingness to forsake his people though they were stubborn (vv.13–14) and could have been replaced. Except for Moses' faithful intercessions and, above all, Yahweh's willingness to remain among his people, the apple of his eye (32:10), Israel would have been cast off (Wesley, *Notes*, 586). Moses simply reports, **"The LORD listened to me at this time also. It was not his will to destroy you. 'Go', the LORD said to me, and lead the people on their way, so that they may enter and possess the land that I swore to their fathers to give them'"** (10:10b–11). Yahweh exhorts them to circumcise their hearts (10:16).

What if the system that is supposed to provide mediation and justice (*mispat*), the priesthood, is itself corrupt? There is no hope. Thus the gravity of Aaron's sin, thus the recording of Moses' words, **"but at that time I prayed for Aaron too"** (9:20). The restoration of the covenant and the rewriting of the Ten Words and their placement in the ark show Yahweh once again sealing his love for the ancestors and their rebellious offspring.

A note of despair, puzzlement, and confusion permeates this section. It causes original hearers and subsequent readers to wonder how, being a rebellious and stiff-necked people, they can stand before the Lord. The answer comes at once in 10:12–13: **"And now, O Israel, what does the LORD your God ask of you but to fear the LORD your God, to walk in all his ways, to love him, to serve the LORD your God with all your heart and with all your soul, and to observe the LORD's commands and decrees that I** am giving you today for your own **good?"** (cf. Mic 6:8). These verses ask for love and obedience for Israel's own benefit.

The literary quality of Deuteronomy is evident in these strategically placed passages. Much of 7:7–8 is summarized in 10:14–15. Yahweh's hortatory wish for his people in 5:29 becomes an imperative in 10:16; this verse also contains the solution to the problems detailed in 9:1–10:11. Israel, knowing that they were freely chosen (v.15) are to be like their God. They are to love aliens among them because Yahweh loves aliens. They were aliens once themselves; a bond of common humanity enlightens Israel's ethics.

Ch. 11 is a work of art both theologically and structurally. It is an exhortatory summary of 5:1–11:32. It closes the section (chs. 5–11) containing the Ten Words and the legal foundation of Israel's Torah and opens the following hortatory section before ch. 12. It introduces the superstructure of the decrees, laws, commandments, stipulations, in short, Torah, that follow in chs. 12–26. Significantly, a repetition of the Shema is imbedded in vv.13, 18–20. It emphasizes the two choices before Israel and recalls Jos 24:15 (also Dt 28; 30:19–20). The stress on the need for the present generation to choose is emphasized (Clarke, 213). A vital part of the worship of the people of God in any era must be the reclaiming of the past in a new dynamic way that informs and molds the future. The people of Israel were to bind themselves to the covenant. The chapter appropriately begins, **"Love the LORD ... remember"** (vv.1–2). Remember, for by remembering you will see how Yahweh has loved you.

C. Summons to Commitment to the Covenant Established at Horeb: Represented and Expanded in Moab (chs. 12–26)

The instructions contained in chs. 12–26 are part of a covenant of grace based on love. The covenant was created by Yahweh's choice. His people entered into it also by choice. These laws were given to help a relationship mature and grow, a relationship established by Yahweh.

The doing or not doing of the covenant laws per se did not guarantee Israel's place as the covenant people; the mystery of that privilege was *trust in* and *love for* the merciful, loving Lord of the covenant. Continuing in the covenant required an ongoing expression of faith in Yahweh.

To be Yahweh's special people, Israel had to be different—holy—by being like him in motive (loving and choosing) and action. They were to use the good gift of his grace, the Torah, to help them reflect his character. Children of Yahweh were able to remain a part of Yahweh's people if they exercised a proper attitude toward him. If, upon sinning, they repented and called on Yahweh according to the stipulations of the covenant, they remained within the covenant community.

The specific commands of Yahweh were his gift to Israel, his unique people, holy unto him. These "words" instructed Israel to live out in a visible, concrete, social-cultural setting a life that reflected who they were. Without the Torah they did not know how to be a community of his people. By keeping the instructions in Dt 12–26, Israel pursued an ethical-religious life unparalleled by any other people. That life was to be a challenge to neighboring nations to reject their corrupt ethical-religious practices and to adopt the attitudes and lifestyle of Yahweh's people. Thus the goal of the legal sections in Deuteronomy, as McConville has noted, is to "inculcate a spirit of law-observance rather than to promulgate law *per se*" (p. 154).

Many parallels can be drawn between these laws and other law codes discovered in the ancient Near East. But their theology and their special perspective lie in their reflection of the *will* of Yahweh. He was not like other gods.

After laying the foundation for these laws, the Shema (6:4–9) and the Ten Commandments (5:6–21), the writer now instructs Israel to be his special people and a holy nation by presenting them with a specific lifestyle to pursue. They must do more than "believe," they must pursue a certain "way of Yahweh" (*derek Yhwh*), entered willingly on the basis of love.

About 50 percent of the laws in the Book of the Covenant in Ex 20:21–23:33 are paralleled in Dt 12–26. They often differ slightly in their Deuteronomistic setting. The reasons are important: theological reasons in Deuteronomy (McConville), historical development (Thompson, von Rad), and ethical concerns are involved. The changes in the laws in Deuteronomy reflect theological more than historical concerns and developments that may have occurred after the giving of the Book of the Covenant (Ex 20:22–23:33). Deuteronomy weaves theological concerns together with humanitarian issues (Dt 5:15; 15:12–18). For instance, the reason for Sabbath observance in Dt 5:12 is a humanitarian concern for slaves; it is a more purely theological issue in Ex 20:8. The same law that deals with the release of a male Hebrew slave in Ex 21:2–6, in Dt 15:12 also mentions the release of a female slave. However, the major purpose of the Torah is to help Israel love Yahweh by trusting/obeying him and to inculcate care for/love among the chosen people. The following comments are concerned primarily with how the laws in chs. 12–26 help Israel to love God and one another, to be a kingdom of priests and a holy people (Ex 6:7; 19:5–6; Dt 7:6; 26:16–18).

1. Purity and unity of Israel's worship (12:1–13:18)

The major emphasis in Dt 12 has been debated by scholars, Wesleyan and Reformed, Catholic and Protestant. Some claim that ch. 12 emphasizes the unity of Israel's worship, and others assert that it emphasizes the purity of its worship. In fact, the chapter deals with these as inseparable issues of importance for God's people: purity and unity in Israel's worship of Yahweh is required. Ch. 12 sets the stage, the tone, and the perspective for all the instructions for God's people that follow. It elaborates what Israel must do/be in worship and in life to be holy before God. The chapter is an elaboration of Dt 7:6—**"For you are a people holy to the LORD your God. The LORD your God has chosen you out of all the peoples on the face of the earth to be his people, his treasured possession."** The nation's worship must be according to his place, his time, his instructions (chs. 12, 16), and directed solely to him.

Israel must not worship as neighboring nations worshiped their gods (12:4, 31); therefore total separation from surrounding religious practices is demanded (12:1–4). Israel must worship at God's chosen place, among their tribes. This requirement runs through chs. 12–26. Both Yahweh's choice and his place are emphasized.

Dt 13:1–18 is more concerned with the contamination of Israel's religion by Canaanite practices and theology and with the purity and holiness of Israel's worship. Israel must cling to Yahweh according to the Shema (6:4–9), which is alluded to and partially repeated in 13:3. The call of the Shema is clearly echoed: **"To find out whether you love him with all your heart and with all your soul."**

The places from which corruption and impurity and resultant apostasy may spring are dealt with in a systematic fashion in ch. 13. The writer cites the prophet, the family, and the city as sources of faithlessness. Even the prophet, however, cannot overrule the Torah's demand for Israel to love and serve Yahweh exclusively. No future revelation of any prophet could ever overrule the essence of the Torah: supreme love for Yahweh and a life of faith demonstrated through obedience. Those engaged in rebellious practices are placed under the death sentence (13:5, 9, 15). Ch. 12 rules out any external corruption of Israel's holiness unto Yahweh (7:6), and ch. 13 deals with internal corruption.

2. Purity/holiness of Yahweh's people (14:1–21)

Dt 14:1–21 demonstrates how the structure of the material helps to communicate its theological message. Vv.2 and 21 include a reference to Israel's call to be a holy people, repeating 7:6. Vv.2 and 21 frame the food laws, indicating that these instructions have ethical-religious purposes. Even Israel's food laws were to show that they were Yahweh's people. Adherence to these laws would show Israel's separation to Yahweh.

Any other benefits Israel may have received from her prescribed food laws were secondary to the theological purpose they served—to set off Israel as Yahweh's people. It was a religious witness through the visible medium of culture. All of Yahweh's creation is good (cf. Ge 1 where it is called "good" seven times). Some of these foods had pagan religious connections. Faithfulness in this matter would witness to other peoples about Israel's God through Israel's faithfulness and love for him. The call for an inclusive concern for Yahweh is equally important for God's people today.

The final editor of these laws impresses his theological concern upon the reader. Holiness unto Yahweh, unity of purpose, procedure, and place in Israel's worship are based on the supreme love of Israel for God. The essence of obedience was not to be lost in some legalism of *ex opere operato* ("merely by doing it, it is effective") or *do ut des* ("I give in order that you will give"). Israel's obedience was to be motivated by love. The presentation of Israel's laws is so laced with motivational clauses urging holiness and love unto Yahweh that the clauses form an intrinsic part of those laws.

3. Economics of Yahweh's people (14:22–15:23)

This section is tied together in various ways by the writer, reflecting a supreme concern for the care and maintenance of various classes of people in Israel. Economics was subordinate to concern for persons in the community. Shalom (peace) and righteousness were to characterize them. Social holiness was to characterize all relationships.

Dt 14:22–29 instructs Israel about the tithe and emphasizes the importance of the issue with an emphatic verbal construction ('assēr tᵉ 'assēr, v.22). Setting aside the tithe was not an option in Israel; it was needed to care for the Levites, the aliens (gērîm), the fatherless, and the widows. No better evangelistic witness based on the lifestyle of the community was ever devised. The regular yearly tithe (cf. Lev

27:30–33; Nu 18:21–32) was to be used to rejoice in fellowship before Yahweh at the place the Lord had chosen (cf. 2Co 9:7).

The instructions in 14:22–29 are framed by the inclusio in v.23, **"so that you may learn to revere the LORD your God always,"** and in v.29. The giving of the tithe is worth a double reward in these verses, one internal (fear of Yahweh) and the other external (increase of crops/produce).

In 15:1–11 the Lord sets out a plan for preserving the community in which the concept of an ethical and religiously based care of one another would never perish. Persons were favored over financial aggrandizement. In these eleven verses, "brother" (*'ah*) occurs six times and "neighbor" is mentioned (*rē[a]'*) once. "Bless" occurs three times (vv.4, 6, 10). These key terms are important. They contain theological teaching of the Torah. Yahweh will bless Israel if they keep his commandments (vv.5–6); and he will bless them if they care for the poor (vv.7, 10).

The striking thing about this is that God blesses those who love (obey) him and who love one another—the two great commandments lifted up by Jesus and the apostles. A failure in either arena negates the integrity of the other.

Dt 15:7, 10 contains the Hebrew word for heart (cf. NIV), and in each case the attitude of the heart is potentially distorted (e.g., v.10—*w*lō' *yēra*' *l*bāb*ekâ*). In an emphatic Hebrew construction the Israelite is commanded to be "openhanded" to his brother (vv.8, 11) True heart religion results when persons live according to the moral order placed before them by Yahweh's Torah.

The next section (15:12–18) concerns the release of Hebrew slaves who have served their masters seven years. According to the extent to which Yah-

weh has blessed the master, the master is to bless the slaves with provisions when they leave. The ethical basis for this care was their enslavement in Egypt and the Lord's rescue (v.15). Israel is to be like God, to imitate him in every aspect of life. Israel was to be to Yahweh like the slaves who chose to stay with their masters (v.16). The people were to serve their master willingly because they loved him; they were love slaves to him forever. They were to choose Yahweh on the *basis of love*.

Only the best is to be offered to God (15:21). Israel is to love Yahweh with all the heart, soul, and strength. There is to be perfect love for Yahweh. Vv.19–23 serve as an inclusio for the entire section since it deals with both a yearly event and fellowship and praise before Yahweh as did 14:22–27.

4. The Religious year of Yahweh's people (16:1–17)

This section describes the three major festivals of the year for Israel: Passover, Feast of Weeks, and Feast of Tabernacles. These feasts and festivals had theological implications and punctuated Israel's secular year with "sacred time." Israel's time was Yahweh's time.

The significance of the Passover as recounted here lay in Israel's need always to **"remember the time of [their] departure from Egypt."** The ceremony was to be held in the sacred space, the place Yahweh would choose to cause his Name to dwell (v.5), a directive given for each festival (vv.5, 11, 15). So the people of God dedicated sacred (hallowed) time and sacred space to Yahweh for the purpose of remembering and renewing who they were.

The Feast of Weeks was held at the beginning of the wheat harvest seven weeks after the standing grain began to be harvested (cf. Ex 23:16; 34:22; Lev

23:15–21; Nu 28:26–31). The purpose was to promote social solidarity within the community and rejoicing and praise before Yahweh. His blessings were to be kept in perspective by Israel, as the people remembered that they had been slaves in Egypt and had been unable to enjoy the blessings of Yahweh there (v.12).

The Feast of Tabernacles was celebrated for seven days (cf. Ex 23:16; 34:22; Lev 23:34). The Israelites were to be joyful and celebrate (vv.14–15), and no one was to appear without something for the Lord. It cost a person to serve Yahweh (v.16).

In these festivals Israel renewed her commitment to Yahweh and recognized his sovereignty over all of life. The celebrations functioned also as an evangel to other nations, a witness before them, of what Yahweh had done for Israel and their reciprocal response of love to him. (For more technical descriptions of the details of the feast see NBC or HBD.) Peter mentions that one of God's purposes in calling out a people (1Pe 2:9) is that they "may declare the praises of him who called [them] out of darkness into his wonderful light."

5. Leaders of God's people (16:18–18:22)

This section describes the character, election procedures, and responsibilities of Yahweh's leaders for his holy people. The major concern of all of this material is that the Torah be observed. The literary structure of this section indicates its major concerns. The first and final paragraphs deal with the classes of leading spokesmen for Yahweh's functioning righteous community (16:18–20; 18:14–22). Things **detestable** to Yahweh are listed in 16:21–17:7; 18:9–13; matters pertaining to priests and Levites are set

forth in 17:8–13; 18:1–8. Finally, at the center lies the section on the king (17:14–20). The king of Israel is important for our writer. He sets the pattern, the model, for the nation. The Torah should be incarnate in him.

The king is to be chosen by Yahweh, not Israel. He must come **"from among your own brothers"**; he cannot be a foreigner (*nakrî*). And he is to submit to the teachings of the Torah. He is to study it **"all the days of his life."** As a result, he will **"not consider himself better than his brothers and turn from the law to the right or to the left"** (17:20). A more revolutionary conception of kingship in the ancient Near East could not be imagined. No king in Israel ever measured up to the standard—until Jesus Christ, who was God's incarnation of the Torah in its fullness.

6. Social shalom of God's people (19:1–21:23)

Ch. 19 describes cities of refuge set aside in the land west of the Jordan (cf. 4:41–43) after Yahweh has given them the land. Amidst a chapter dealing with murder, manslaughter, and false witnesses, the writer reminds Israel that Yahweh gives success because Israel is keeping the Torah **"to love the LORD [their] God and to walk always in his ways"** (vv.8–9). V.10 gives the motive clause for Israel's assigning and operating the cities of refuge in the land: so that innocent blood will not be shed and so that Israel will not be guilty of bloodshed. According to the theology of Deuteronomy, the presence of either of these crimes would result in a curse falling on the land and Israel.

The fact that Israel could add three more cities in the land to the three previously set aside shows that the Torah of Israel foresaw changing circumstances and made allowance for that in principle.

7. Military conduct/theology of God's people (20:1–20)

As Yahweh's holy people, Israel must conduct warfare in a way pleasing to him. Holy warfare by Israel is described in this chapter as warfare in which only the will of Yahweh is to be done in the war.

The taking of Canaan from its inhabitants was not to be a land grab by a group of land-hungry descendants of Abraham, Isaac, and Jacob. Yahweh was giving it to Israel to fulfill his promises to the patriarchs. This holy war had a theological purpose. It was the fulfilling of Yahweh's promises, which involved establishment of an ethical-religious community of God's people in the land and judgment of the Canaanites through Israel. War from this perspective by God's people is not possible today. Nor are God's people commanded to destroy their political, military, or religious enemies, but to love them. Because Yahweh conducted this war as a warrior (Ex 15:3, 7; see Lind) the biblical writer approves of it. God himself was involved with his people in the war to conquer Canaan.

God ordered the *herem*, the complete destruction of cities, to avoid the corruption of his people (vv.16–18). This provision was necessary for two reasons. First, the Canaanites were not going to change for the better, for Yahweh had allowed their cup of iniquity to become full (Ge 15:16). Later, because of its ethical-religious corruption under wicked kings, Israel would be treated no differently. When its cup of iniquity was full, God cast Israel out of the land to be punished by Assyrians and Babylonians. Second, Israel was especially vulnerable at the early stages of her history, and the importance of

impressing the people with the grave consequences of ethical-religious corruption in the land of the Amorites needed to be made. God's stringent procedures against Ananias and Sapphira at the outset of the new covenant people (Acts 5:1–11) closely parallels the principle of Dt 20. Because distant cities did not pose the threat of immediate ethical-religious contamination, they were not placed under the *herem* for complete destruction. Israel's conduct of war had to be carried out within the parameters of holy war prescribed by Yahweh and Yahweh alone.

The radical inclusiveness of Israel's call to be Yahweh's holy people becomes clear as more and more areas and dimensions of Israel's life are placed within the perspective of 7:6. **"For you are a people holy to the LORD your God. The LORD your God has chosen you out of all the peoples on the face of the earth to be his people, his treasured possession."**

But did Israel fulfill her calling? The writer says that the people had not and would not, but at the same time he urges them to circumcise their hearts to love God (10:16). Moses predicts the future apostasy of Israel. He also describes the future circumcision of their hearts so that they will love God supremely (30:6). But even that seems conditional upon Israel's willing obedience to the Lord (v.10).

True Jews, according to Deuteronomy, are those whose hearts Yahweh has circumcised and upon which he has inscribed the ethical-religious code of the Torah (see also Jer 31:31–34; Ro 2:25–29).

8. Removal of blood guilt from Yahweh's people (21:1–9)

These verses give Israel instructions on what to do about an unsolved murder. The purpose of the ritual procedures is to absolve the "blood guilt" or community guilt of the nation. The blood of an innocent victim cried out for justice from the ground (Ge 4:10) and brought covenant curses upon the people of Israel if not atoned for (v.8). Israel's land was to remain clean, a place wherein righteousness and justice were normative. If the land became corrupt, Yahweh would cast them out of it.

9. Justice, holiness, love, mercy: Character of God's society (21:1–25:19)

This long section contains miscellaneous laws. Some of them are easily understood; others are not clear with respect to their original significance in the cultural or legal sense of that time. For a discussion of the textual issues and the fine legal problems raised by a few of these commandments, consult detailed studies and commentaries.

All of these instructions aim to fulfill Dt 7:6. This occurs when Israel loves Yahweh wholeheartedly and when those who make up his unique community love each other as they love themselves. In other words, Jesus' "most important word" from Deuteronomy was the essence of the Law and the Prophets (Mt 22:37–40).

Look at the specific reasons, goals, purposes, and motives embedded in the legal materials. Israel should obey these laws so that Yahweh may bless them (22:7; 24:19) and so that the land will not be defiled (21:23; 23:14; 24:4). The death penalty was demanded so that Israel would remain holy to Yahweh by purging the evil from among them (21:21; 22:21, 24; 24:7). These instructions also provide for Israel to express humane concern and love for both people and creatures (21:14, 17; 22:1–3, 6–7, 16, 19, 29–30; 23:15,

20; 24:5–7, 10–15, 17–22; 25:1–10). Israel is to detest what Yahweh detests (22:5; 23:18; 24:4; 25:16) and thereby be holy unto him. Israel is not to confuse the natural order of things that God created and approves of (22:9–11). The holy purpose of these miscellaneous ethical, religious, and civil laws is clear: they all hang on the "great commandment" to love God and neighbor. By this they would be God's holy people.

10. The thanksgiving celebration of God's people in the land (26:1–15)

Just before the conclusion to the body of Torah (instruction) in 12:1–26:15, a cultic ritual of celebration is described, which Israel is to observe after settlement in Canaan and enjoyment of its produce and Yahweh's blessing. In essence, the ritual instructs the Israelite to assert, "I am not self-made. From sure destruction and a pointless existence, Yahweh has made me one of his people." At the place chosen by Yahweh, the Israelite will confess, "I am in the promised land of inheritance today. My father was a *perishing* (cf. NIV; Heb. *'arammî 'ōbēd 'ābî*) wanderer. Yahweh rescued us from Egypt and gave us this land. Now in gratitude I am joyfully giving back to him the best of the produce of the land" (vv.3–11). If Israel is faithful to keep that ritual and to affirm its reality, the people will remain in the land.

11. Yahweh, your God: You, his people, follow his decrees/laws (26:16–19)

This short conclusion to chs. 12–26 could not be more fitting. As indicated earlier, it looks back to 7:6 (cf. 14:2, 21, et al.). The foundation for keeping the Torah of Yahweh is a love for Yahweh that issues in obedience

(26:16–17). Ex 6:7 has declared God's purpose in liberating Israel from Egypt: "I will take you as my own people, and I will be your God." Ex 19:6 has asserted, "You shall be for me a kingdom of priests and a holy nation." Lev 20:26 had repeated, "You are to be holy to me because I, the LORD, am holy, and I have set you apart from the nations to be my own." Dt 26:16–19 records the time when Israel, in Moab, becomes Yahweh's people, his treasured possession: **"You will be a people holy to the LORD your God, as he promised."**

Yet one wonders whether Israel has "circumcised its heart" (10:16) that Yahweh might put his Torah into their inner constitution (5:29). If so, the destiny of God's people is awesome: **"He will set you in praise, fame and honor high above all the nations he has made"** (26:19). Isaiah caught the possibilities implied in the declarations of Deuteronomy (Isa 48:17–19).

D. Covenant Ritual of Commitment Upon Entering the Land (27:1–26)

Ch. 27 describes two things that were important for Israel's formal entrance into the land that Yahweh was giving them. First, the words of this Torah, which Moses had delivered and expounded to them, were to be written down (v.3). Certainly this included the Ten Words and the instructions for Israel contained in chs. 12–26. So ch. 27 appropriately records the inscription of the covenant stipulations. But the readers and the hearers of the Torah were to understand these covenant stipulations within the framework of love and holiness that the writer had carefully woven into the various individual commands. To fail to do so would be to remove the heart and soul of the Torah itself and turn it into a mere legal document based on do's and don'ts, within the context of power politics of the ancient Near Eastern suzerain and his vassals.

The Hebrew construction in v.8 uses the word *bā'(')ēr* found in Dt 1:5. There it was noted that the word describes what Moses was doing as he re-presented in Moab the covenant he received at Horeb. In any case, the repetition of the word in 27:8 describing the writing of the law **"on these stones"** seems to assert that the hortatory sections, the motive clauses, added to the Torah by Moses were the exposition and were to be recorded on the plastered stones. The motive clauses were originally in the laws when Moses spoke them, and the Hebrew may indicate that they were put on the plastered stones in Moab. So Israel was to read the Torah in the spirit of these hortatory aspects; they should not have misused it by making it only a legalistic code. It was never that.

Moses, the priests, and the Levites were to declare: **"You have now become the people of the LORD your God. Obey the LORD"** (vv.9–10). The curses listed in vv.15–26 are representative of various laws given to Israel in the earlier parts of the book.

E. Recounting the Blessings/Cursings of the Covenant (28:1–68)

In vv.1–14 the covenant blessings are recounted, and in vv.15–68 a repetition of the curses is set forth— the two ways open to Israel (30:19). The extent of the blessings/cursings reaches to the total life experience of Israel before Yahweh (vv.3–6; 16–19). If Israel keeps faith with Yahweh **"The LORD will make [the nation] the head, not the tail"** (v.13). If Israel breaks faith with Yahweh, **"The alien

... will be the head, but [Israel] will be the tail" (28:43–44).

To be Yahweh's unique ethical-religious people, Israel had to be different in a visible, cultural way, as well as in the heart. Only then could the nations "see" (*weraʾû*, v.10) that they were different and reflected the character of their God by being called by his name. The Hebrew of v.11 contains an interesting and powerful wordplay. The Hebrew reads: *wehôtîrkâ yhwh leṭôbâh*. The verb, which can be translated literally as "and Yahweh will cast unto you," is the verb from which the noun Torah is formed. Its use suggests that if Israel keeps the Torah (instruction, teaching; that which is cast, thrown), the Lord will "torah" unto them goodness and prosperity. Yahweh will cast goodness (*ṭôb*) to Israel because she lives "holy" within the moral order of righteousness offered to her in the Torah, God's gift to Israel for life, not death (32:47).

Many of the prophets refer to this section when they indict Israel for breaking Yahweh's covenant and failing to keep faith with him. Their cursings are not amorphous and pulled from the air. They draw upon the specific curses mentioned in these words. The greatest irony would be that Israel should experience a reversal of the Exodus, a return to Egypt (v.68).

IV. MOSES' THIRD EXHORTATORY ADDRESS (29:1–30:20)

Ch. 11 describes a covenant ritual of commitment to be performed by Israel in the land of Canaan after crossing the Jordan. The covenant renewal described here is one Israel is going "to enter" (lit. "to go over into the covenant") so that Yahweh may confirm that Israel is his people and he is their God. Israel is to guard its heart so that

it will not turn from Yahweh (v.18 [Heb. v.17], *lebab pōneh*). But the foreboding message of this passage is found in v.4 (Heb. v.3). For there it is asserted that Yahweh has not yet "**to this day**" given his people a heart to know (comprehend), eyes to see, and ears to hear.

The true essence of the Torah still escapes them. But the implication is that in doing it they shall know it. The sequence of several "heart" passages in Deuteronomy (4:29; 5:29; 10:12, 16; 30:2, 6, 10) adds a major motif in the book. Israel's self-inflicted blindness should not, however, be used to cloud the proper appeal and significance of Yahweh's Torah so perfectly stated in 6:4–9 and 10:12–13. Any future failure of Israel will be because Israel forsakes Yahweh's covenant (29:24–25). This clearly implies and emphasizes an improper heart attitude and not the mere breaking of a specific decree of Yahweh. Any persistent future failure of Israel will be a failure of the heart. The final verse indicates that it was not necessary for Israel to know additional secret counsels of Yahweh in order to be his people. The public Torah was enough.

Ch. 30 continues the thought of the future apostasy and exile of Israel. The return and acceptance of Israel are based on the circumcision of the heart that Yahweh himself will accomplish (v.6). "**Heart**" is used six times in this chapter (vv.1, 2, 6, 10, 14, 17). Each time its use is significant. The amazing work of God in circumcising the heart (v.6) is predicted upon Israel's turning its own heart (v.1) and returning to him (*wešabtâ ʿad yhwh*, v.2) with the whole heart. Yahweh will then circumcise the heart, making possible Israel's love of the Lord with all the heart and soul. Then Yahweh will bless his people (v.9) as he blessed their fathers, "**if**

[they] obey the LORD [their] God and keep his commands and decrees that are written in this Book of the Law and turn to the LORD [their] God with all [their] heart and with all [their] soul" (v.10). No biblical concept teaches the love of God without the concomitant expression of obedience to his words. So Jesus could say that he came to fulfill the law, not to destroy it.

The ability to choose Yahweh's way is made possible because of God's grace, the gift of the Torah to Israel. In words the people can adopt and comprehend, the Torah is now completed and sufficient (30:11–14). They are in her **mouth** and in her **heart**. She can, if she will, do them (v.14). For Paul's reference to this passage, see Ro 10:6ff. A true Jew was one who obeyed because he loved with all of his heart (vv.17–18). His life lay in loving Yahweh from his heart (vv.6, 19–20). By choosing to be holy unto Yahweh, Israel would **live** (vv.19–20). A choice for Yahweh and his holy way is **life**.

A comparison of 4:25–31 with 30:1–20 reveals many parallel concerns. Chs. 4 and 30 bracket the central chapters of the book. Both talk about covenant curses, exile, a converted ("turned") heart, the future days, the call of "heaven and earth as witnesses" (4:26; 30:19), and more. The structure of the book itself, especially the bracketing of the central chapters by these parallel sections, witnesses to the primary concern of the writer. He encloses the book with the call that **"if from there you seek the LORD your God, you will find him if you look for him with all your heart and with all your soul"** (4:29; cf. 30:2)—no matter where you are (4:29), even in the most distant place (30:4).

V. MOSES' CLOSING EXHORTATORY WORDS AND ACTS (31:1–33:29)

Deuteronomy is more than a covenant/treatise, both in form and content. Chs. 31–34 could be termed the last will and testament of Moses. But that is not sufficient even for these chapters. They also do more than record the transfer of leadership of Israel from Moses to Joshua. They are concerned with more than Moses' death. They are chapters whose major concern is still the people of Yahweh and their destiny and the faithfulness of Yahweh to his people. In this sense Deuteronomy reminds one of part of a national epic of Yahweh's people, an epic in which Moses plays a major part as a hero but in which Yahweh himself is the supreme Defender, Teacher, and Savior of his chosen people.

The section from 31:1 through 32:47 has three major concerns. First, Moses encourages both Israel and his successor, Joshua, to be courageous and take the land that Yahweh is giving (31:3–8). Yahweh would never forsake Israel.

Second, Moses establishes "this Book of the Law" (31:26) and rehearses Israel's relationship with God ("Moses' Song," 32:1–43) as witnesses for Yahweh against Israel whenever the people rebel in the future (32:15–18; 26–29; esp. vv.16, 19). And Israel will rebel despite Moses' instructions to read the law (hattôrâh hazzōʾt, 31:9–12) during the Feast of Tabernacles every seven years, the year of release. He could have chosen no better time for the renewal of this Torah, for the year of release (15:1–11) provided for a new start toward social righteousness and holiness.

Third, this section develops the motif of Israel's future rebellion against Yahweh. Israel's true internal, spiritual condition is heartbreaking (31:27). They will forsake the Lord; he will not forsake them. Israel remains rebellious and stiff-necked.

It is through the words of "this Torah" that the prophets will remind the nation of the curse that follows disobedience (Dt 11:26–27; Lev 26:14ff.). But these very words also will call her to repentance and circumcision of heart (30:1–10). At the center of the covenant is a merciful God who is more interested in dispensing mercy than wreaking vengeance and is determined to love his rebellious people rather than hate them. He will deal, however, with those who abuse and destroy his people:

> Sing in jubilation concerning his
>   people, O nations.
> Indeed, he will avenge the blood of
>   his servants.
> He will turn in vengeance upon their
>   adversaries;
> Indeed, he will atone for his land, his
>   people. (32:43, my trans.)

Moses' song was not only written down the day he composed it, it was also disseminated orally among the people. It was not to remain hidden on a parchment in a darkened royal chamber. It was to be in the hearts and minds of the people.

The words announcing the death of Moses on Mount Nebo recall 3:23–29. It was because of Israel that Yahweh was angry with Moses. And it was because of the provocation of the people that Moses was unfaithful toward Yahweh and thereby did not sanctify Yahweh among them. Yet Israel would enter the land; Moses would not. The people would occupy the land; Moses could only see it (32:52), although he had endured agony and pain on their behalf. In the ancient world, however, it was understood that the greater

always blessed the lesser. Moses, after being denied entrance into the land, blesses Israel (33:1ff.), for he was truly **the man of God** (*'îš hā'ĕlōhîm*).

After blessing the various tribes, Moses concludes with a blessing for all Israel:

> Blessed are you, O Israel!
>   Who is like you,
>   a people saved by the Lord?
> He is your shield and helper
>   and your glorious sword.
> Your enemies will cower before you,
>   and you will trample down their
>   high places. (33:29)

Much attention is often given to the fact that in chs. 27–28 the curses recounted outnumber the blessings. But after the dismal picture of Israel's breaking the covenant and forsaking of Yahweh (31:16, 20), the book concludes with Moses' final blessing upon Israel. The nation is divinely favored as God's people, for he will not forsake or abandon them. In the end they are **"a people saved by the LORD"** (*'am nôšā' bayhwh*, 33:29).

VI. DEATH AND EULOGY OF MOSES; JOSHUA'S SUCCESS (34:1–12)

Moses finally climbs the mountain and views the land from a strategic point. Jericho, which lay opposite him, would become a witness to Israel and all Canaan to what Yahweh could do for his people if they wholly followed Joshua and the Torah of Moses. So Moses not only saw the land, he saw the city that would soon be given to Israel by Yahweh, opening up the potential subjugation of all the land at one stroke. Not even a mighty fortified city could stop them if they followed Yahweh (Jos 5:13–6:27). V.4 is the only direct speech in ch. 34. It records the fulfillment of a major theme in the book: the faithfulness of Yahweh to keep his promises to the fathers and to his servant Moses.

Moses, the heir, died, and Israel wept. A magnificent eulogy of Moses closes the book, for Moses was the prototype of all prophets. No one like him appeared again—not until the One greater than Moses came (Heb 3:1ff.). Jesus, because of his perfect obedience to the Father in love, entered the inheritance promised to the descendants of Abraham, Isaac, Jacob, and Moses (Heb. vv.3–10).

BIBLIOGRAPHY

Books

Clarke, Adam. *Commentary on the Holy Bible*. Kansas City: Beacon Hill, 1972.

Clements, R. E. *God's Chosen People*. London: SCM Press, 1968.

Craigie, Peter. *The Book of Deuteronomy*. Grand Rapids: Eerdmans, 1976.

Fretheim, Terence E. *Deuteronomic History*. Nashville: Abingdon, 1983.

Goldingay, John. *Theological Diversity and the Authority of the Old Testament.*Grand Rapids: Eerdmans, 1987.

Kline, Meredith. *The Structure of Biblical Authority*. Grand Rapids: Eerdmans, 1972.

Lind, Millard C. *Yahweh Is a Warrior*. Scottdale: Herald, 1981.

McConville, J. G. *Law and Theology in Deuteronomy*. Sheffield, England: JSOT Press, 1984.

Nicholson, E. W. *God and His People*. Oxford: Clarendon, 1986.

Sternberg, Meir. *The Poetics of Biblical Narrative*. Bloomington, Ind.: Indiana University Press, 1985.

von Rad, Gerhard. *Deuteronomy*. OTL. Philadelphia: Westminster, 1966.

———. *Studies in Deuteronomy*. Chicago: Henry Regnery, 1953.

Thompson, J. A. *Deuteronomy*. Downers Grove, Ill.: InterVarsity Press, 1974.

Wesley, John. *Explanatory Notes Upon the Old Testament*. 3 vols. 1765. Reprint. Salem, Oh.: Schmul, 1975.

Welch, Adam C. *The Code of Deuteronomy*. New York: George H. Doran, 1924.

Articles

Fretheim, T. E. "The Ark in Deuteronomy," CBQ 30, (1968): 1–14.

McCarthy, D. J. "Notes on the Love of God in Deuteronomy and the Father-Son Relationship Between Yahweh and Israel." CBQ 27, 1965.

Wenham, G. J. "Deuteronomy and the Central Sanctuary," TB 22, n.d.:103–18.

———. "The Date of Deuteronomy: Linch-Pin of Old Testament Criticism," *Them* 10, no. 3 (1985): 15–20.

JOSHUA

Joseph Coleson

INTRODUCTION

I. TITLE, CONTENT, CANONICAL PLACEMENT

The book of Joshua is named for the man who led Israel into Canaan after the death of Moses. The English title is a rendering of the Hebrew *Yᵉhôshû'a*. The name means "Yahweh is salvation."

The Greek form of the name, used both in the Septuagint translation of the OT and in the NT, is *Iesous*. From this it is readily apparent that Jesus and Joshua bore the same name. Joshua was God's captain to bring the people of Israel into their inheritance within the land of Israel. Jesus is God's Captain to bring all God's people into their eternal inheritance. Thus Joshua was a forerunner and a foreshadowing of God's salvation that was to come in Jesus.

The book spans the years from the death of Moses to the death of Joshua and the times of those elders associated with him who survived him. Joshua may be divided into two major subdivisions. The first is an account of the main features of the Israelites' invasion of the land of Canaan. This phase begins with the destruction of Jericho, then moves on to a major southern and a major northern campaign. These successes meant that the Canaanites would not be able to prevent Israel from beginning to settle in the land.

The second major section of Joshua records the allotment to the twelve tribes of territories within the land. Six cities of refuge and forty-eight Levitical cities were also designated. Then follow Joshua's final charge to the people and a renewal of the covenant. The book ends with notices of the death and burial of Joshua, the burial of Joseph's remains, and the death and burial of Eleazar the high priest. The land that had been promised had become their possession. There could be no better confirmation of this than burying their honored dead within its borders.

The placement of Joshua within the canon of the Hebrew Scripture is significant. The events in Joshua follow the death of Moses recorded at the end of Deuteronomy. The high and low points of the settlement process—the period of the Judges—follow chronologically upon the deaths of Joshua and the elders. The book belongs chronologically where it is.

Joshua is the first book of the section called "Prophets" in the Hebrew

310

arrangement of the Scriptures. This section is divided, in turn, into two subsections, the Former Prophets and the Latter Prophets. The Former Prophets are the books of Joshua, Judges, Samuel, and Kings (both originally undivided). The Latter Prophets are Isaiah, Jeremiah, Ezekiel, and the Book of the Twelve (the so-called "Minor" Prophets).

The fact that the books we often class as books of history are included within the Hebrew arrangement as prophetic books is of great importance. They are history written from a *prophetic* point of view. These books share the view of those men and women called by God to deliver God's oracles to Israel. Israel was God's people. They had been brought into existence by God, they were blessed of God, and they were accountable to God.

Just as the oracles of the Latter Prophets were God's word to God's people, so the recorded history of the Former Prophets was (and is) God's word to God's people. Whatever is important to carry forward the understanding of God's involvement in Israel's history is included. Many details (and even important subjects) about which we would like to know are not included; to have included them would detract from the prophetic message of this history of Israel. In that it teaches, exhorts, encourages, and warns God's people of all ages through its recounting of this period of Israel's history, Joshua is a prophetic book. As these are the primary functions of all prophecy, rightly understood, it is fitting that Joshua stands at the head of the section titled "Prophets" in the Hebrew Bible.

II. AUTHOR, COMPOSITION, AND DATE

The Talmud records the tradition that Joshua wrote the book of Joshua, with the exception of the last few verses. The book itself names no author, and there is no way, at this late date, to know who wrote it or whether the book had more than one author.

Whoever the author(s), the book itself names one of the sources to which he/she had access. The book of Jashar is cited in 10:13. Another book is mentioned in 18:9, though its name is not recorded. It is reasonable to assume that the descriptions of these territories as they were allotted to the remaining seven tribes could have been taken from this unknown book. The same could be true of the list of the cities of refuge and the list of the Levitical cities. These and other records would have been available to the author(s) of Joshua. It is also possible that Joshua and/or some of his officers wrote some accounts of their adventures, which survived long enough to be used in writing the book.

If indeed so many sources were available, we can, in one sense, speak of a compiler(s) of the book. Yet a historical writer, even though utilizing historical sources for the whole of an account, still is an author. It is the author who decides what material to use, what emphasis to give it, how the various events shall be arranged, and what shall be the theme(s) of the work, and from what perspective he/she will write the account. This is the task to which the prompting of God's Holy Spirit set the author(s) of Joshua.

When was Joshua written? Dates as early as Joshua himself and as late as the postexilic period of Judah's history (sixth-fifth centuries B.C.) have been proposed. An extremely late dating of the book may be rejected, though there is not space here to enumerate the reasons. The availability of the kinds of written source material mentioned above and the repetition of the phrase "until this day" (it appears twelve times) seem to indicate that the author was not Joshua. A date some time in the period of the united monarchy would be a reasonable assumption, though the later monarchy cannot be ruled out on the basis of present evidence.

III. LITERARY STRUCTURE AND PURPOSE

The simplest and yet an important analysis of Joshua's literary structure is to note that the book is a bifid, a literary composition structured purposely as two halves. Other OT books with this structure are Isaiah, Ezekiel, Daniel, and Zechariah.

The first half of Joshua relates major events of the Conquest, those battles that denied to surviving Canaanites any possibility of preventing Israel from entering the land and beginning to settle it. Here the emphasis is on God's action on behalf of Israel that enabled them to possess the land.

The second half of the book centers around the allotment of the land among the tribes, with a view to their beginning settlement. Thus it has an aura of expectancy. This is heightened by the way in which the book is concluded, with Joshua's final words of warning and encouragement and his leading the people in renewing the covenant at Shechem.

There are also other more complex structural features of the book that mark it as a deliberate creation with purpose. For example, there are a number of "frames," the most important of which frames the entire book. Ch. 1 records God's and then the people's exhorting of Joshua as he was commissioned to lead them into the land. Chs. 23 and 24 record Joshua's exhortations to the leaders and then to all the people as his death approached. Thus both the beginning and the conclusion of the book highlight God's faithfulness and the necessity of faithfulness on the part of God's people.

The allotment of the land also has a frame. It begins with the apportioning of Caleb's inheritance (14:6–15) and ends with the apportioning of Joshua's (19:49–51).

The major theme of Joshua is the recounting of God's actions in fulfilling the promise to the patriarchs: this land would be the inheritance of their descendants, though they themselves were dwelling in it as sojourners. God's opening charge to Joshua in ch. 1 and the notice in 24:31 that the elders with Joshua had known all the work Yahweh had done for Israel make it clear that the initiative was God's and not Joshua's.

Other themes of the book are the need for holiness on the part of God's people, the reality of judgment upon sin, the land as part of the spiritual inheritance God gives his people, and the importance of passing on the memory of God's actions in the past as a means to faith for the future. This last theme may be described as the author's purpose in writing the book.

IV. OUTLINE

This outline emphasizes that through Joshua God brought the people into the land and allotted it to them as their inheritance, though some of the land was yet to be taken and all of it was yet to be settled.

I. The Entrance Into the Land (1:1–6:27)
  A. God's Charge to Joshua (1:1–18)
  B. The Sending of the Spies Into Jericho (2:1–24)
  C. The Crossing of the Jordan (3:1–4:24)
  D. The First Circumcision and the First Passover in the Land (5:1–15)
  E. The Taking of Jericho (6:1–27)

II. The Campaigns for the Land (7:1–12:24)
  A. Achan's Sin and Judgment (7:1–26)
  B. The Conquest of Ai (8:1–35)
  C. The Gibeonites' Deception (9:1–27)
  D. Joshua's Southern Campaign (10:1–43)
  E. Joshua's Northern Campaign (11:1–23)
  F. The List of Defeated Kings (12:1–24)

III. The Allotment of the Land (13:1–21:45)
  A. The Land That Remained; the Allotment of the Transjordan Tribes (13:1–33)
  B. Caleb's Portion (14:1–15)
  C. The Allotment of Judah (15:1–63)
  D. The Allotment of Joseph (16:1–17:18)
  E. The Allotment of the Remaining Tribes (18:1–19:51)
  F. The Cities of Refuge and the Levitical Cities (20:1–21:45)

IV. Joshua's Farewells and Burial in the Land (22:1–24:33)
  A. The Return of the Transjordan Tribes; Their Memorial Altar (22:1–34)
  B. Joshua's Farewell to the Leaders (23:1–16)
  C. Joshua's Renewal of the Covenant (24:1–28)
  D. Joshua's Death; Three Burials (24:29–33)

COMMENTARY

The emphasis of this commentary is the *theological themes* and *motifs* of the book of Joshua—the message of the book. Only limited discussion of necessary historical, geographical, and cultural background is given. See the standard introductions, dictionaries, encyclopedias, and commentaries for more detail. The Hebrew text of the book will be considered when it is of specific help.

I. THE ENTRANCE INTO THE LAND (1:1–6:27)

A. God's Charge to Joshua (1:1–18)

Ch. 1 introduces most of the themes of the book. God's sovereignty and initiative are highlighted. It was God who commanded Joshua to end thirty-eight years of Israelite inactivity by leading the people across the Jordan to possess the land. The beginning of the charge to Joshua contains three promises: (1) All the land will be theirs, (2) no enemy will withstand them, and (3) God will be with them and will not forsake them.

We should not spiritualize this historical narrative when we consider whether it offers anything of promise for God's people after Joshua. We cannot conclude that because God promised all this to Joshua he promises a Christian today a particular house, spouse, or position. The transfer of a specific promise in a particular ancient context to a particular modern context is risky because the contexts usually are not parallel.

But we can make a legitimate transfer of promise or principle from the specific context of the ancient situation to the general human context in all ages.

God gives Christians all the "land" of their experience for an eternal inheritance. Even though Christians may suffer reverses in this life, ultimately no enemy of the soul can stand before those who trust in God. No Christian ever awoke to find that God had forsaken him/her.

The land of Israel was always more than a physical entity; it was also a central part of the spiritual inheritance of Israel. If we err by spiritualizing the material or the temporal, we err equally by unspiritualizing them. God created the human race with one foot in the world of space, time, and matter and the other foot in the eternal world. The spiritual creature is also the material creature; for this life, at least, our material destiny is an important part of our spiritual destiny. While we are here, the two really cannot be separated. The spiritual importance of the land of Israel for the redemption of the human race is central in its Conquest and allotment.

God commanded Joshua three times (vv.6, 7, 9) to be **strong and very courageous.** Then, for good measure, the people said they would follow Joshua if he would be strong and courageous. Israel had failed to enter the land years before because they lacked the courage to trust in God. Failure to receive the good gifts God would give his people was not only Israel's problem.

The command for care in keeping God's laws (vv.7–8) is not works righteousness. The keeping of the law was the *external evidence* of Israel's *faithfulness* to God. A right relationship with another person will show in actions and attitudes pleasing to that person.

The land as the promised rest for God's people is also presented in this first chapter. What Israel had held in hope for many years was soon to be reality.

B. The Sending of the Spies Into Jericho (2:1–24)

Ch. 2 recounts Joshua's sending of two spies into Jericho. In an approach from the east, Jericho is the key to the hill country. It could not be bypassed. Like any good military commander, Joshua needed information about his objective.

The two men—6:23 refers to them as young men—came into the house of Rahab, who was a harlot. A harlot's house would be a place for strangers to avoid unwanted attention. Josephus relates the tradition that Rahab was also an innkeeper; women sometimes were both harlots and innkeepers in the ancient Near East.

Rahab's statements to the spies indicate how much God's acts on Israel's behalf, even in an earlier generation, had inspired fear in the inhabitants of Canaan. They recognized the parting of the Red Sea and the destruction of the kingdoms of Sihon and Og as the work of a God much greater than their own.

V.11 also contains Rahab's personal confession of faith, **The Lord your God is God in heaven above and on the earth below.** This declaration of faith, shown to be genuine by her aid to the spies, brought Rahab, despite her Canaanite birth and her profession, into the people of God. Though Canaan as a whole was under judgment, individual Canaanites would be saved by faith in Israel's God.

The author notes (6:25) that Rahab was spared: **She lives among the Israelites to this day.** If the book was written after her death, this means she lived through her descendants. Mat-thew tells us (1:5) that Rahab was the mother of Boaz.

More than a third of the chapter details provisions of the promise to spare the lives of Rahab and her family. This again demonstrates Rahab's faith in Israel and Israel's God. It also shows the seriousness of an oath taken in God's name.

C. The Crossing of the Jordan (3:1–4:24)

The recounting of the crossing of the Jordan occupies two chapters. This is in keeping with the prominence of God's actions on behalf of Israel throughout the narrative. It also is further evidence that the author's interest is not the military history of the Conquest, but its theological or faith history.

The crossing of the Jordan is also emphasized because of its pivotal nature. The crossing meant there would be no turning back, as with the previous generation. Under Joshua, and by the power of God, Israel really would occupy the land that had been promised for so long. The crossing became a spiritual and psychological as well as a physical entrance.

The Ark of the Covenant led the people as they entered the Jordan. Then the priests bearing the Ark stood in the middle of the dry river bed as the people crossed over. The Ark, as the visible symbol of God's presence, was a further reminder that this was a divine and not a human enterprise.

Joshua erected two memorials to this event, one in the river bed and one at Gilgal. These memorial stones were to be a visual aid in teaching Israelite children. The stones were to serve also as a witness to **all the peoples of the earth** (4:24).

The author is careful to point out that the crossing of the Jordan was a miracle. **Yet as soon as the priests** who carried the Ark reached the Jordan and their feet touched the water's edge, the water from upstream stopped flowing (3:15–16). The river was not at normal level but at spring flood stage (v.15) so that it overflowed its banks. The location of the stoppage was pinpointed at Adam, modern Damiyeh, about eighteen miles upstream from Jericho (v.16). The priests carrying the Ark **stood firm on dry ground in the middle of the Jordan** (v.17). **No sooner had they set their feet on the dry ground than the waters of the Jordan returned to their place and ran at flood stage as before** (4:18).

The usual explanation for this miracle is that the Jordan was dammed at Adam by a landslide of its banks, probably caused by an earthquake. Such landslides, stopping the river's flow from sixteen hours up to about two days, occurred in A.D. 1160, 1267, 1546, 1834, 1906, and 1927.

Was the stoppage of the waters on Israel's behalf due to the same cause? Since there is no way to verify a natural cause for that stoppage, we cannot be sure. God could have acted without utilizing natural means. That natural means *have* caused such stoppages six times in the last nine hundred years, however, would suggest that perhaps Joshua's stoppage, too, was caused by a landslide.

If so, was it a miracle? If we define a miracle as God's direct intervention in earthly events, then it was. With the Jordan in flood, Israel could not have crossed otherwise. Just as God has the right to choose whether or not to intervene, so God has the right to choose whether his intervention shall be by natural or supernatural means. Either way, it is a miracle. A natural event, timed to bring glory to God and

to be of benefit to God's people, is still a miracle.

D. The First Circumcision and the First Passover in the Land (5:1–15)

First actions in new circumstances are usually of great symbolic value. Ch. 5 records two initial actions in the new land. The first was circumcision of all males born in the forty years of the wilderness wanderings. For males, circumcision was the sign of participation in the covenant. Included in the covenant was the gift of the land. To enter the land, the men had to be circumcised; i.e., personal acceptance of the covenant was necessary.

The second action was the celebration of the first Passover in the land. As the Passover in Egypt marked the exodus from slavery, so this Passover in Canaan marked attainment of the goal toward which God had been leading them ever since. Passover always has commemorated God's ancient act; this one also anticipated God's new act of giving his people the promised rest in the new land.

This Passover is connected also with cessation of the daily provision of manna. Miraculous provision is, by definition, not normal. Now that the produce of the land was available, manna was no longer needed.

These first five chapters lead up to the siege of Jericho, the first engagement with the Canaanites. The chapters are framed by God's encounter with Joshua in a strong and lengthy speech of encouragement and by a short encounter with **the commander of the LORD's army** (v.15). This, too, was for Joshua's encouragement on the eve of military action against the enemy.

E. The Taking of Jericho (6:1–27)

One of the most widely known narratives in the Bible is the taking of

Jericho. The march around the city for seven days, the shouts and blowing of the ram's horn trumpets, the crumbling of Jericho's walls—all are dramatic and unforgettable.

The fall of Jericho is also a prime example of difficulties that sometimes arise when biblical records are compared with archaeological findings. Ancient Jericho is today a tell, or ruin mound, beside the copious spring that waters the oasis of Jericho on the edge of the Jordan Valley, 670 feet below sea level. Jericho was the second site in the Holy Land (after Jerusalem) to be excavated; archaeologists have dug there in four campaigns. The first was under Charles Warren in 1867 and 1868. He concluded that the tell was the remains of an ancient castle, and he did not connect it in any way with the story recorded in Joshua.

The first major excavation was by Sellin and Watzinger in four seasons from 1907 to 1911. They concluded that the tell was unoccupied when the Israelites entered the land. John Garstang excavated from 1930 to 1936. He judged that the city had indeed been destroyed as recorded in Joshua; therefore, it probably had been destroyed by Joshua. Kathleen Kenyon was the last to excavate Jericho, from 1952 to 1958. She concluded that the destruction all the excavators had found was too early to be ascribed to Israel under Joshua. Most recently new studies of the site are again affirming the accuracy of the biblical records.

Before proceeding, we should note that it is not necessary to have archaeological "proof" in order to have confidence in the biblical record of an event. Archaeology seldom can prove events; archaeology and history are different disciplines, with differing methodologies.

In by far the greater number of instances, when archaeology, history, or another discipline *can* be brought to bear on the biblical record, its findings tend rather to confirm than to contradict it. Despite the statements of some, there exists no solid, substantial evidence from history or archaeology that disproves the biblical record. Christians can be glad of that, but it is more to be expected than marveled at. The Bible's reliability and authority have been demonstrated over millennia. Archaeological or historical affirmation, though welcome, is not essential to the Christian's confidence in the revelation of God.

But evaluation of *all* the excavation records from Jericho (most of Kenyon's data was not published until the early 1980s) reveals that many details of the Joshua account of Jericho's destruction have parallels in the archaeological record of the city's destruction about 1400 B.C. That record reveals:

1. Jericho was strongly fortified (cf. 2:5, 7, 15; 6:5, 20);
2. The attack occurred just after the spring harvest (cf. 2:6; 3:15; 5:10);
3. Jericho's citizens could not flee with their newly harvested food supplies (cf. 6:1);
4. The siege was short (cf. 6:15);
5. The city walls were leveled, possibly by an earthquake (cf. 6:20);
6. The city was not plundered (cf. 6:17–18);
7. The city was burned (cf. 6:24). (Wood, 57)

The archaeological record seems to preserve an independent witness to the circumstances of Joshua's capture of Jericho.

A second serious concern arises from the narrative of Jericho's destruction. This is the nature and intention of the ban (Heb. *herem;* cf. Eng.—from Arab.—"harem") under which Joshua placed Jericho, at God's command. The events are clear: All the inhabitants of the city were killed; the city and all it contained were burned; the only exceptions were Rahab and her family who were spared because of her faith and the oath of the spies; all metal objects were put into the treasury of the tabernacle; the metal would not have perished, only melted, in the fire.

But why were *all* the city's inhabitants put to the sword? Why would God command such a thing? In considering these questions, we first must trust the justice, integrity, love, and wisdom of God. We probably never will understand fully.

Two partial answers can be suggested. The first lies in God's sovereignty. This is emphasized by the fact that Jericho was God's battle, not Joshua's. Joshua only directed the disposition of the city after God had given him the victory. The God who created human beings has the sovereign right to destroy them. The theological heirs of John Wesley affirm, along with other Christians, the truth of God's absolute sovereignty.

The second answer lies in God's justice. A God who called for wanton, capricious destruction would be reprehensible to the sense of justice with which humans have been created. We are not told the details of Canaan's sin, but already God had informed Abraham (Ge 15:16) that "the sin of the Amorites has not yet reached its full measure" (here "Amorite" stands for the entire Canaanite population).

After a great space of years in which to repent, Canaan instead had completed its iniquity. God, the righteous Judge, declared the day of grace for Canaan over. Joshua and the Israelites were God's instruments of judgment.

Whatever the extent of Canaan's sin, God's judgment upon them was just. Whenever God declares, "Enough," and brings judgment upon a people, we may be sure that continued grace and mercy would not really have been either gracious, merciful, or just. With that, we must trust God to judge rightly.

II. THE CAMPAIGNS FOR THE LAND (7:1–12:24)

This second major section of the book gives, in broad outline only, the southern and the northern campaigns that followed the taking of Jericho. Joshua's victories in these campaigns assured that the Canaanites would not be able to deny Israel access to the Negev and to the hill country of Judah, Samaria, and Galilee.

A. Achan's Sin and Judgment (7:1–26)

The sin of one man and its consequences for the nation demonstrate how seriously God viewed the ban (*herem*) placed upon Jericho. Of all that had been in Jericho, Achan took only a small amount of gold and silver and one imported garment. But sometimes an action is more than it seems on the surface, more than its perpetrator realizes.

Achan's action caused the deaths of thirty-six Israelite soldiers. God's response to Joshua's lament over this defeat suggests that it might have been avoided had Joshua not been overconfident, had he consulted God before sending the small force to attack Ai. Still, the reason for Israel's defeat was Achan's sin. The fate of Ananias and Sapphira comes to mind (Ac 5:1–11).

This suggests another aspect of the ban. Anything placed under the ban was considered so completely to belong to God that it could not be redeemed. It must be destroyed so there never would be any possibility of its reverting to profane, or common, use. Jericho, dedicated to God in this way, was a sort of firstfruits of the Conquest of the land. This understanding of the ban, of which Achan must have been aware, increased the seriousness of his transgression.

Any sin affects more than the perpetrator. Not only did the thirty-six men die unnecessarily in battle, Achan's family perished with him as punishment for his sin. We are not told the ages of Achan's children. However, it is reasonable to assume they were old enough to share in their father's guilt. Though he, not they, had taken the goods, they became accessories after the fact, if they knew about his theft from God and did not reveal it. Since Achan hid the treasures under the earthen floor of his tent, it would have been difficult for his family not to know about them.

This sin, its consequences for Israel, and the punishment for Achan and his family, underscore in a somber way that God's people *must* be holy. To trifle with things that clearly belong to God is dangerous because it really is rebellion against God. Such sin always brings trouble (*achor*) upon God's people.

B. The Conquest of Ai (8:1–35)

In the second effort to conquer Ai, God gave detailed instructions, and Joshua carefully followed them. As Jericho guarded the entrance into the hill country from the valley, Ai guarded the entrance from the hilltop. If Israel were to gain access to the hill country, Ai could not be bypassed; it must be taken.

Ai has been identified traditionally with et-Tell, east of Bethel (modern Beitin). Whether this identification is correct is perhaps still open to question.

Et-Tell does not appear, from the excavations carried out on the site, to have been occupied as a city at the time of the Israelite entry into Canaan. Whatever the proper identification of Ai, it guarded the upper reaches of one or more of the passes from the Jordan Valley up into the hill country.

The author described in considerable detail the preparations for the battle against Ai, the stratagem of the ambush, the battle itself, and its outcome. Throughout, his emphasis is on God's direction of the Israelite forces; Joshua took his orders in every detail directly from God. Ai also was put under the ban, and all its inhabitants were killed. However, Israel was allowed to keep the cattle and the spoils of Ai for themselves. The site of Ai itself and the burial place of its king were left as memorial heaps for the instruction of future generations.

Ch. 8 ends at the pass of Shechem with the ceremony that Moses had commanded (Dt 31:12). This began with the building of an altar on Mount Ebal, the northern of the two mountains that form the pass. Then Joshua read the stipulations of blessing for obedience and of curse for disobedience. Apparently the whole camp of Israel came up to Shechem for the ceremony. The implication is that Shechem did not have to be conquered; we do know that Jacob had bought land there (Ge 33:18–20).

This occasion marked a sense of taking possession of the land, though the campaigns against the Canaanite coalitions were still to come. As a ritual of sacrifice and reading of the law, it brought to Israel's memory, individually and collectively, the promises and obligations of the covenant that had been mediated to them through Moses. As a ritual of anticipated possession, it demonstrated their faith in God's promise, whose fulfillment was beginning to unfold before them. The solemnity and inclusiveness of the affair are emphasized throughout this short account.

C. The Gibeonites' Deception (9:1–27)

Ch. 9 recounts another sorry episode, this one brought on by Joshua's failure to consult God when an unexpected situation arose. The narration of these less than flattering events shows clearly that the author's intent was not to portray Israel's heroic leadership. Joshua and the elders are shown in their shortcomings as well as in their triumphs. God is the real hero whose exploits the author wishes to recount.

There were two reactions by the citizens of Canaan to the news that Israel was coming into the hill country. The first notice is that most of them began preparing to fight. But the Gibeonites, with three neighboring cities, decided on a different course. Knowing that Israel was charged with destroying the Canaanites, they attempted to gain a covenant with Israel by deceit. This is further evidence of others' fear of Israel, of which the author has already spoken (cf. 2:24; 5:1).

Gibeon is only a few miles from Ai. But the Gibeonite messengers took worn-out equipment and old provisions. When they reached the Israelite camp at Gilgal, a little north of Jericho (the exact location of Gilgal is not known today), the envoys told Joshua and the elders that they had come on a long journey to reach them.

The Israelite leaders did raise the possibility of deception, but they should have been even more cautious. They believed the Gibeonites without pressing for the name of the envoys' city or country. The Israelites examined only some of their provisions, accepted

their story as true, and entered into a treaty with them.

The author seems to chide Israel's leadership gently for this foolish decision. He notes only that they **did not inquire of the LORD**. But in light of all that transpired, one sees that this is not really such a gentle chiding after all. Not asking for the counsel of the Lord had cost lives at Ai. The victories at Jericho and Ai both had been won when Israel followed precisely the counsel of the Lord. How could they so soon forget?

But the covenant was made, and only afterward did Joshua and the elders of Israel discover that they had been tricked. One might suppose them entitled to declare null and void a covenant made under false pretenses. But the covenant had been sworn **by the LORD [Yahweh], the God of Israel** (vv.18–19). To break it would be to treat lightly the name and honor of God. Israel's leaders kept the covenant and the oath they had sworn in God's name and preserved the Gibeonites alive. Joshua reduced them from free men to servants of the tabernacle, **woodcutters and water carriers** (v.27).

D. Joshua's Southern Campaign (10:1–43)

The treaty with the Gibeonites precipitated events that led to the breaking of Canaanite resistance in the South. To understand the Canaanite reaction to the news of Ai's defeat and Gibeon's treaty with Joshua, we must understand the geography of the hill country. Gibeon and its neighboring cities occupied the Plateau of Benjamin (as it is called now), a relatively flat rectangle immediately to the north of Jerusalem, about a hundred square miles in area. Control of this plateau is essential to control of the entire hill country. With Gibeon now allied to Israel, control of the plateau and thus of the hill country belonged to Israel. The Canaanite kings had to conquer Gibeon before Joshua could reach the area with his forces. Otherwise the Canaanite cause was lost.

The Canaanite coalition did reach Gibeon and besieged it. But the Gibeonites were able to get word to Joshua to ask for his assistance. Joshua's response underscores again the seriousness of the oath taken in God's name. Joshua might have delayed his response until Gibeon and its neighbors had been destroyed by their fellow Canaanites. Instead, he responded quickly, in good faith to the obligations he had undertaken.

Joshua's response actually was more vigorous than required by any treaty. He brought the Israelite army up from Gilgal by an all-night forced march. In this way he surprised the Canaanites besieging Gibeon and routed them. Militarily, it was in Joshua's interest, too, not to have to recapture the plateau.

In this battle also, God took the initiative. In the engagement before Gibeon, God confounded the Canaanites, and the battle turned into a rout. As the enemy fled, God sent hailstones, killing more than the Israelites did with the sword.

God's direct intervention in the battle reminds us again of the nature of miracle. It would be possible to construe the hailstorm as a fortunate coincidence for Israel, who then interpreted it as God's intervention. But the one who takes seriously God's control over all his creation and his interest in the affairs of individuals and of nations cannot understand this event in that way. God, who reserves the storehouses of the hail for the day of war and battle (Job 38:22–23), opened them on that day.

God's intervention in this battle is the clearest notice in all of the book of Joshua that the judgment upon Canaan was God's doing and no one else's. God did use Israel as an instrument of judgment. But even more, he judged directly. Israel did not cause the collapse of Jericho's wall. Israel did not propose the successful strategy against Ai. And now God's hail killed more Canaanite soldiers than did Israel's swords. God's right to rule includes the right to use his methods when the day of judgment dawns. (See comments on ch. 6 regarding the ban.)

The record of the sun and the moon standing still raises unanswerable questions (vv.12–14). The omnipotent God could do such a thing. But how could it be done without tremendous disruptions throughout the world? Why would such a cataclysmic event be necessary after God had already used the hail on the fleeing enemy? Not all miracles can be understood, either in purpose, in scope, or in mechanism.

The five kings had led the southern coalition against God's people. As a sign of their utter defeat and submission, Joshua had his captains put their feet on these kings' necks. Then Joshua executed them; the cave where they had taken refuge became their tomb, a memorial to the great victory God had given Israel.

Joshua now began a series of actions throughout southern Canaan. He captured a number of the important cities, though the author seems to be careful to refrain from saying that Joshua burned any of these cities. This would be in keeping with God's promise that Israel would dwell in cities they had not built (Dt 6:10).

In view of the later notices concerning the land that remained, we must remember that this was a military campaign and not yet the settlement of the tribes. Some of these cities apparently had to be retaken later. But this campaign made it impossible for surviving Canaanites to prevent Judah and the other southern tribes from settling when the time came. Joshua's southern campaign, following God's decisive victory at Gibeon, secured the hill country, the Negev, the shephelah (lowland), and the slopes. These were the areas the southern tribes occupied first when the settlement process began. Joshua's southern campaign had cleared the way.

E. Joshua's Northern Campaign (11:1–23)

The northern kings now organized a coalition against Israel. The northern coalition was under the leadership of the king of Hazor, which sat astride the international trade route north of the Sea of Galilee. They brought their forces together at the waters of Merom, north-northwest of the Sea of Galilee.

The account of the northern campaign has many features in common with that of the southern campaign just concluded. However, they are reported in briefer fashion. The point has been well made that God had given this land to his people. Details could be omitted in the account of the northern campaign.

One detail not omitted is that Joshua hamstrung the horses and burned the chariots captured at Merom (v.9). This was at God's command; Israel was not to trust in human weapons of war, but in God, who alone would give victory against their enemies.

The summary statement of the northern territory taken indicates that the campaign lasted a long time. Though initial victories in both campaigns were quick and decisive, the taking of many fortified cities was a longer process. The total campaign for

Canaan may have lasted about seven years (cf. 14:10). Both faith and perseverance were needed.

It is fitting that the descriptions of the warfare for the land should end with the notice that the Anakim were vanquished and destroyed from the territory Israel would settle. The ten spies (Nu 13:28, 33) had discouraged Israel from entering the land in the previous generation with their report of the Anakim and their great size. What must Joshua's victorious soldiers have thought of their fathers' lack of faith, which had cost them entry into the land of promise?

F. The List of Defeated Kings (12:1–24)

Ch. 12 begins with a reminder that Israel's first Conquests had been in Transjordan under the leadership of Moses. It concludes with the roster of the thirty-one kings of Canaan defeated by Israel under Joshua's leadership. The roster is almost poetic in its form. It is interesting that the names of the kings are not preserved.

In this first half of the book, the author has taken care to emphasize that the Conquest of Canaan was for God's purposes. For Israel, God's purpose was to give them their promised inheritance. For Canaan, God's purpose was to bring the long-delayed judgment. In view of this, the roster of defeated kings should be understood as a litany of the accomplishment of God's purposes. It is a solemn yet joyful recital, summarizing and symbolizing God's mighty acts on behalf of his people.

III. THE ALLOTMENT OF THE LAND (13:1–21:45)

With the Canaanites unable to prevent Israelite settlement, it was time to apportion the land to the tribes. The bifid structure of Joshua now becomes significant. We are familiar with the narratives of Conquest that make up the first half of the book. But most of the second half seems to be only uninteresting lists of territorial borders and cities. Yet these lists must be of great importance to be given so much space that their inclusion defines the literary structure of the book as a whole.

The tribal allotments give concrete expression to the fulfillment of the promise to Abraham, Isaac, and Jacob. They represent a title deed to the land. It is one thing to say, "This land is ours." It is much more convincing to have in an authoritative document a description of the land to lend credence to claims of ownership (under God).

The people of God in the Old Testament period were a people of the land. The covenant was given in the context of the land, and the land was a major part of the covenant. The word "land" (*erets*) occurs 6,400 times in the Hebrew Bible (though it does not always refer to the land of Israel). The lists of tribal allotments give geographical reality to the importance of the land for the people of Israel in covenant with God, who owns the land.

Because God does own the land, this apportionment to the tribes is spoken of consistently as a gift. God gave them the land to dwell in; its distribution was at God's direction. For this reason, we may question the appropriateness of the terminology and metaphor of "claim" and "claiming" as used sometimes in the church today. We do not flaunt God's covenant with his people as though it were a contract by which we can drag God into court and force him to live up to his obligations. We do not "claim" God's gifts to us, as though they were ours by some prior right. We accept them with thanks, remembering that they are gifts of grace.

In the discussion of the tribal allot-ments, proper names sometimes refer to the sons of Jacob from whom the tribes reckoned their ancestry. Sometimes they refer to the tribes, the descendants of these men. In considering the land as both part of, and shaper of, the spiritual inheritance of the tribes, the distinction between tribe and ancestor is not always a wide distinction. The character and destiny of the ancestor are reflected in the character and situation—spiritual, geographic, political, economic—of the tribe.

A. The Land That Remained; the Allotment of the Transjordan Tribes (13:1–33)

The section begins with a notice about the land that remained to be conquered (vv.1–6). The book of Joshua does not claim that all the land had been conquered, though we could get that impression if we read only the narratives of the two decisive campaigns. The areas of least Canaanite occupation were the areas opened up by Joshua's campaigns, and these were the first settled by Israel. The areas listed here were the most populous Canaanite regions; Israel did not conquer those in Joshua's day.

The two-and-a-half tribes in Transjordan had received their allotments several years before the Conquest of the land west of the Jordan (Cisjordan). Thus, it was fitting that their portion should be described first.

In the tribal allotments some borders are described closely enough that they can be plotted on a map; others are not. Locations of many of the cities are known today; many are not known.

B. Caleb's Portion (14:1–15)

Caleb's portion within the tribal territory of Judah is a special case. Caleb reminded Joshua that only the two of them had been faithful to God at the first opportunity to enter the land (Nu 14:6–9). God had promised Caleb that he would enter it. Now Caleb requested Hebron as his inheritance, with the opportunity to drive out the Anakim who had so frightened the other spies long ago. Joshua gave him Hebron as a reward for his faithfulness.

That the Anakim still could be present to challenge Caleb at Hebron after the notice of 11:21–22 is puzzling. Though Joshua had conquered Hebron in the southern campaign, Caleb had to take it again. Perhaps some of the surviving Anakim (11:22) had come back to Hebron. Or perhaps the notice of Joshua's complete victory over them is intended to include Caleb's victory recorded in 15:14. In any case, Caleb's victory marked a promising beginning to the process of allotment on this side of the Jordan.

C. The Allotment of Judah (15:1–63)

Judah's allotment is described in much more detail than most of the rest of the others. This is one of many testimonies to Judah's prominence throughout Israel's history. Jacob had promised and prophesied that importance (Ge 49:8–12). Subsequent history, down to the present day, bears it out.

With Judah especially we see the land as part of the spiritual inheritance of Israel. When Jacob blessed his sons (Ge 49), he passed over Reuben, Simeon, and Levi, Judah's older full brothers, to give the blessing of the firstborn to Judah. One way this blessing is brought to reality is in the tribal allotments. The descriptions of Judah's borders are the most detailed, and the list of Judah's cities the most nearly complete, of any tribe. Judah's geographical position among the tribes is central,

guaranteeing Judah's leadership in the affairs of the nation. Reuben, Simeon, and Levi, whose transgressions had caused Jacob to pass them over, each became, as tribes in the land, dependent upon Judah. The geography of the tribal allotments both reflected and helped to shape the fulfillment of each tribe's spiritual inheritance as given by Jacob and confirmed by Moses (Dt 33).

D. The Allotment of Joseph (16:1–17:18)

Joseph was the firstborn of Rachel, Jacob's favorite wife—the only wife he really desired. Joseph had two sons by his Egyptian wife, Asenath. Half of the tribe of Manasseh had received its inheritance across the Jordan. Ephraim and the rest of Manasseh now received allotments, mostly in the northern part of the hill country. Both Ephraim and Manasseh received portions in order to bring the number of tribal allotments to twelve. This was necessary because the priestly tribe of Levi did not receive an inheritance of land. It also brought to reality the bountiful blessing Jacob had pronounced upon Joseph (Ge 49:22–26). As Judah in the South, so Joseph exercised leadership in Israel from its central position in the North.

The provision for the daughters of Zelophehad (17:3ff.) was in fulfillment of God's command to Moses (Nu 27:1–8). Israelite society was not a patriarchal monolith.

The account of Joseph's allotment ends with their request for more land. Even though they considered themselves to be a numerous people, they were afraid to challenge the Canaanites in the valleys of Jezreel and Beth Shan, because the Canaanites had iron-plated chariots. As a result, they were restricted to the hill country.

Rather than rebuke them for their fear, Joshua instructed Ephraim and

Manasseh to clear the hill country forests. Hard work would enlarge their inheritance. He also promised that eventually they would drive out the Canaanites in spite of their iron chariots. This gave them a hope by which they could enlarge their faith and conquer their fear.

E. The Allotment of the Remaining Tribes (18:1–19:51)

Seven tribes still were without territory. Joshua commanded each to appoint three men; these walked through the land, writing down descriptions of seven allotments. When they returned, Joshua cast lots for each tribe's assignment. The descriptions that follow may well have their ultimate source in the book that the survey party compiled.

Benjamin, as second son of Jacob's favorite wife and twelfth of Jacob's sons, received a central but small portion between Judah and Joseph. Simeon, though older than Judah, had forfeited his right to a central role by his violence against Shechem. His inheritance was on the southern periphery of Judah.

The five final tribes were descendants of five of the six sons born in the contest between Rachel and Leah for their husband's affection. Dan and Naphtali were Bilhah's (Rachel's maid). Gad and Asher were Zilpah's (Leah's maid); Gad already had received his allotment in Transjordan. Issachar and Zebulun were Leah's own, conceived when she "hired" her husband for the mandrakes her son Reuben had found (Ge 30:16). All these—with Reuben, who had forfeited his birthright (Ge 35:22; 49:3–4)—received tribal allotments on the periphery of the national territory. They were small tribes and generally had little influence in the affairs of the nation.

As Caleb's allotment opened the

apportioning of land to the tribes, so Joshua's closed it. This is another example of the author's literary framing of his material. Joshua was of the tribe of Ephraim; thus he requested and received Timnath-serah in the hill country of Ephraim. With that, Joshua finished apportioning the land.

F. The Cities of Refuge and the Levitical Cities (20:1–21:45)

Two tasks remained. God commanded Joshua to designate cities of refuge, and the Levites needed places to live. As servants of God ministering at the tabernacle, they received no tribal allotment of land.

The law had made provision for the safety of anyone who killed a person unintentionally. By fleeing to a city of refuge and remaining there until the death of the current high priest, he was safe from the avenger of blood. The duty of a near relative of the victim was to avenge the murder. Murderers were not protected in the cities of refuge but were bound over for execution, even from a city of refuge. Only those who caused deaths accidentally could be sheltered in the cities of refuge.

Six cities of refuge were designated so this provision could be implemented. Three were on the west side of Jordan, three on the east. All six were well-known cities in their regions so they could be easily and quickly found. They were located so that from anywhere in the land one of the six was not far away.

Levi had no tribal inheritance of land. But the priests and Levites who served the tabernacle and later the temple needed places to house their families and pasture their flocks and herds. So forty-eight cities were given to the Levites out of the inheritances of the other tribes; six of these were the cities of refuge previously designated.

From the cities included in this apportionment to Levi, we should not assume that only Levites lived there. The subsequent history of Israel makes it clear that some of these cities at least had non-Levites among their inhabitants. Some were important cities throughout most of Israel's history, active in its economic and political affairs. Exactly how this Levitical apportionment functioned through the generations we do not know. The author's concern here is to emphasize the gracious provision of God for those who were not given a tribal territory because of their service to him.

With all distributions completed, the author notes that the three promises made to Joshua (1:3–5) have now been fulfilled. The promise of land and rest had in fact been made to the fathers, the author notes. God is shown to be faithful to his people and true to his word.

IV. JOSHUA'S FAREWELLS AND BURIAL IN THE LAND (22:1–24:33)

The Conquest and allotment of the land were accomplished, though the hard work of settlement lay ahead. For Joshua, all that remained was to say farewell.

A. The Return of the Transjordan Tribes; Their Memorial Altar (22:1–34)

Joshua's first farewell was to the Transjordanian tribes as he sent them home. His admonition to continued faithfulness is characteristic of Joshua and of the themes of the book.

As they came to the Jordan, the Transjordanian tribes built an altar, which nearly precipitated a civil war. The other tribes initially interpreted this altar as a move away from allegiance to God. They saw it as a threat

of rebellion and reminded its builders of Achan's sin, which had troubled Israel at the beginning of the Conquest. They did not want a similar event at the end of the Conquest.

The Transjordanian tribes protested that this was not an altar of sacrifice but of witness. They were concerned that the other tribes in days to come might deny them participation in the covenant because they lived across the Jordan. Though they were on the fringe, they intended to remain faithful to God. Because they were on the fringe, they needed a strong witness to the other tribes of their faithfulness to God. The representatives of the western tribes accepted this explanation. The eastern tribes had the witness they desired, and war was averted.

B. Joshua's Farewell to the Leaders (23:1–16)

As Joshua's death drew near, he called the leaders of Israel to him for final instruction and encouragement. First, he reminded them that God would continue to drive out the Canaanites who yet remained in the land. It was imperative that Israel not make any accommodation with them in the meantime lest they become a snare and lead Israel astray into the worship of other gods. Israel's continued faithfulness in the land was essential to her continued dwelling in the land. These leaders of the people bore special responsibility for keeping Israel faithful.

Joshua's farewell exhortation exhibits a solemn theme that is both hope and warning. God is holy; therefore, Joshua could speak with optimism and hope of God's good words and of the good land into which God had brought them. God is holy; therefore, God cannot change his character even if his people change. If the people rebel against God, it will not damage God; but rebellion will destroy the rebellious.

C. Joshua's Renewal of the Covenant (24:1–28)

Joshua bade final farewell to all the people as he led them in a renewal of the covenant at Shechem. Several elements common to second-millennium B.C. covenant treaties are present in this record. The first is a recital of the gracious acts that God, the Great King, had performed for his people; its purpose is to inspire gratitude and trust. Remembrance and recital of God's gracious acts on behalf of his people always have been an important part of worship and covenant renewal.

To underscore the seriousness of this commitment, Joshua argued with the people that it would be impossible for them to serve God, since God is a holy and a jealous God. They responded that they could serve him, and they gave legal witness to their commitment. This ceremony of covenant renewal had a lasting effect on its participants, for the author records (v.31) that Israel did serve the Lord as long as that generation lived.

D. Joshua's Death; Three Burials (24:29–33)

The book of Joshua concludes with the record of two deaths and three burials. Joshua died at the age of 110, as had his ancestor Joseph; he was buried on his homestead at Timnath Serah. The book of Joshua is not intended as a biography of Joshua nor as an apology for his leadership. As noted, the author recorded Joshua's shortcomings as well as his strengths and successes. But here we see that the final assessment of Joshua and his leadership is positive. His legacy was so strong that **Israel served the Lord throughout the lifetime of Joshua and of the elders who outlived him and who had experienced everything the Lord had done for Israel** (v.31).

The second burial was the bones of Joseph, brought up with the Israelites from Egypt and carried along all those years. Joseph was buried at Shechem in the plot his father Jacob had purchased. This was within the inheritance of Joseph's descendants. Finally, Eleazar the high priest died and was buried at the home of his son Phinehas in the hill country of Ephraim.

All three men were buried on Mount Ephraim in the central part of the newly conquered and newly settled land. The death and burial in the land of these three important leaders is a final important signal of God's fulfillment of his promise to give Israel the land. Joshua's major themes of God's faithfulness, God's fulfillment of his promises, God's gift of the land, and the spiritual importance of the land are carried down to the very last verse of the book. These are themes of everlasting encouragement to God's people.

BIBLIOGRAPHY

Aharoni, Yohanan. "Book of Joshua," *Encyclopedia Judaica.* Vol. 10. Edited by C. Roth. Pp. 271–77.

———. *The Land of the Bible.* Philadelphia: Westminster, 1979.

Garstang, John. *Joshua, Judges: Foundations of Biblical History.* Grand Rapids: Kregel, 1978.

Gray, J. *Joshua, Judges and Ruth.* The Century Bible. London: 1967.

Harrison, Roland K. *Introduction to the Old Testament*. Grand Rapids: Eerdmans, 1969.

Martens, Elmer A. *God's Design: A Focus on Old Testament Theology*. Grand Rapids: Baker, 1981.

Miller, J. M.; and G. M. Tucker. *The Book of Joshua*. CBC. New York: Cambridge University Press, 1974.

Noth, Martin. *Das Buch Josua*. Tübingen: Mohr, 1953.

Smith, George Adam. *Historical Geography of the Holy Land*. London: Fontana Library, 1966.

Soggin, J. A. *Joshua*. *The Old Testament Library*. Philadelphia: Fortress, 1972.

Vaux, Roland de. *Ancient Israel: Its Life and Institutions*. 2 vols. New York: McGraw-Hill, 1961.

_____. *The Early History of Israel*. Philadelphia: Westminster, 1978.

Wood, Bryant G. "Did the Israelites Conquer Jericho? A New Look at the Archaeological Evidence." *Biblical Archaeology Review* 16, no. 2, 44–58.

Woudstra, Marten H. *The Book of Joshua*. NICOT. Grand Rapids: Eerdmans, 1981.

JUDGES

Lawson G. Stone

INTRODUCTION

I. TITLE, ORIGIN, AND PLACE IN THE CANON

The book's name derives from the title given to the heroes dominating its central section. In Israel "judging" denoted both rendering verdicts and directly effecting justice. Ideally, Israelite judges personified God's government by embodying his salvation and government in military deliverance and administration.

The author remains unknown. The latest event to which Judges alludes (18:31) is a deportation, either of northern Galilee in 734–732 B.C. or of the whole northern kingdom in 721 B.C. The book's confidence in the superiority of the southern kingdom and in the spiritual effectiveness of the monarchy suggests composition under one of Judah's righteous kings, Hezekiah (716–687 B.C.) or Josiah (640–609 B.C.).

While English Bibles, following the Septuagint and Vulgate, place Judges among the historical books, the Hebrew Bible numbers it among the former prophets with Joshua, Samuel, and Kings. These books constitute a unified historical narrative striving not simply to inform, but to confront the reader with a proclamation of the ways, truth, and judgment of God.

II. MATERIALS

Three types of material appear in Judges. Independent hero stories dating from near the events they narrate (1200–1040 B.C.) form the core of the book. In heroic literature a people celebrates the exploits of its individual heroes. Such accounts served entertainment as well as historical needs. George Steiner, writing about Homer, aptly observes that heroic literature

> revels in the gusto of physical action and in the stylish ferocity of personal combat. [It] sees life lit by the fires of some central, ineradicable energy. The air seems to vibrate around the heroic personages, and the force of their being electrifies nature. (p. 180)

This literature relishes physical prowess and bodily defects, craftiness and eccentricity, victories but also failures. It delights in striking details and savors the grotesque. These features make Judges rollicking reading but unsettling for pious meditation. Nevertheless, heroic literature serves biblical theology well. It inseparably fuses real history with the tastes, hopes, and faith of God's people. Vibrantly experiential, it provokes engagement. A preface (2:6–3:6) and standardized introductions and conclusions bind the stories into a series, conforming each to a common pattern linking each story's opening crisis to apostasy and characterizing the heroes as champions of God. Several sections, however, lack this framework and either ignore the judges or depict them negatively (1:1–2:5; 8:33–9:57; 16:1–31; 17:1–21:25). These passages brand the period anarchic, playing a minor-key counterpoint to the rest of the book. Ironically aloof from the heroic ideals, they offer "a critique of the archaic values of the [hero stories] in the light of new energies and perceptions" (Steiner, 184).

III. THEOLOGICAL MESSAGE

Judges concerns itself with the most momentous issue faced by early Israel: the nature of the community. Is Israel to continue as a confederation of tribes led by charismatic leaders, or should the nation take the bold step toward national statehood and kingship? Readers of the eighth century B.C. also debated whether the southern monarchy of a single (Davidic) dynasty was superior to the charismatic approach to kingship taken in the northern kingdom. Was the northern way closer to Israel's ancient ideal and more faithful to the covenant?

The author answers the question by exploring Israel's spiritual fortunes during the period of the tribal confederacy, analyzing Israel's evil, and examining two solutions. The book clearly views the time of the tribal confederacy as spiritually disastrous. In pushing beyond apostasy to national self-will, the analysis of Israel's evil in Judges undergirds that offered in the NT, which probes beneath acts of sin to the underlying self-will. Likewise, the NT depicts sin's consequences objectively as bondage to oppressive principalities and powers beyond the person, and subjectively as living "in the flesh," emphasizing the self-destructive propensity of self-will. Judges portrays a communal embodiment of the spiritual impotence of life in the flesh described in Ro 7, where "I," "me," and "my" appear more than thirty-five times. Wesleyan theology understands sin as imprisonment in self-will, broken only by the sanctifying grace of Christlikeness. In depicting how self-will ravages the community of faith, Judges portrays that carnality that threatens the full realization of the Gospel.

Judges and the NT also concur in the solution to self-will. In 3:7–16:31 Spirit-driven charismatics appear increasingly impotent to save Israel. Occasional onrushes of the Spirit cannot stop the downward spiral and actually accelerate it. Israel's deep madness cannot be dislodged by a tour de force of the Spirit. In contrast to charismatic leadership, chs. 17–21 offer an alternative: kingship. Israel needs a king who will confront Israel's idolatry, self-will, and penchant for self-destruction. The king must save Israel from its most lethal foe: itself. Judges proclaims the primacy of the spiritual dimensions of kingship—messiahship—in Israel. The OT persistently links kingship to national spiritual fidelity. In a similar vein, the NT never discusses the Holy Spirit apart from the kingly rule of Christ and his summons to deny self. John Wesley developed his theology of the sanctified life primarily as a life of Christlike purity, not power in the Spirit. Holiness advocates after Wesley rightly related sanctification to the Spirit but emphasized the Spirit's power specifically as power over the inward tendencies to sin. Following the author of Judges, Wesleyan theology recognizes the primacy of character over charisma, purity over power.

IV. OUTLINE

COMMENTARY

I. PROPOSITION: A DISLOYAL COMMUNITY (1:1–3:6)

Compromise and apostasy set in after Joshua and the Conquest generation die. The introduction delineates Israel's deterioration territorially, in terms of the Conquest (1:1–2:5), and theologically, in terms of the covenant (2:6–3:6).

A. Faltering Conquest: The Failure That Is Sin (1:1–2:5)

Joshua's death (1:1–3) suspends Israel between the past fulfilled promises and their continued realization. Will Israel persevere? Yahweh sanctions Judah's preeminence and promises victory, while Judah promises mutuality and good faith with the other tribes. A victorious Judean campaign marked by tribal cooperation realizes these expectations (vv.4–21). Judean preeminence is confirmed by the confession of a defeated enemy and the burning of Jerusalem (vv.4–8), and is personified by Caleb's nephew, Othniel, who lives in the apostate, post-Conquest period but represents the faithful Conquest generation (vv.9–15). Intertribal cooperation dominates as Judah keeps faith with the Kenites, Simeon, and Caleb. Judah's conquest of Philistine cities foreshadows David's breaking of Philistine power (vv.16–21). Southern failures are excused or laid on Benjamin (1:21; cf. Jos 15:63). Two references (vv.16, 20) associate Judah with Moses, and Judah's victories closely parallel Joshua's. Three elements anticipate David: the Davidic cities, Hebron (vv.9–10, 20) and Jerusalem (vv.7–8, 21); Judah's foreshadowing of David's achievements; and the failure of Benjamin (Saul's tribe). Judah links David and his successors to the two heroes embodying God's past saving work: Moses and Joshua.

Jdg 1:22–36 narrates the deepening failure of the northern tribes. Victory at Bethel (vv.22–26) gives way to victory qualified by a continuing Canaanite presence (vv.27–30). That Asher and Naphtali live surrounded by Canaanites points to deeper failure (vv.31–33). Finally, the Amorites expel the Danites (vv.34–35), whose fate remains unresolved until ch. 18. This failure progresses from south to north, coupling the northern tribes to failure. In contrast with Hebron and Jerusalem in vv.1–21, the names of the two northern royal sanctuaries, Bethel (vv.22–26) and Dan (v.34), bracket this narrative, associating them with the loss of the land. In contrast to southern cooperation, the catalogue of isolated northern tribes discloses no cooperation. The northern failure culminates in an angelic reproof (2:1–5). Although the Hebrews in Jdg 1 evince no intention to break covenant, the angel's speech brands them disobedient. Compromise never announces itself as it unravels the life of God's people. The weeping concluding this section augurs ill for the future. Too little, too late, Israel's sacrifices are vacant gestures. Their only hope lies latent in Judah's continuation of the work of Moses and Joshua, pointing ahead to David.

B. Fractured Covenant: The Failure That Is Judgment (2:6–3:6)

The prologue shifts to a theological assessment, returning to Joshua's death as a spiritual watershed. Since he and the conquest generation inspired faithfulness, they become the standard for the next generation, which proves faithless, knowing neither Yahweh nor his acts. **"Not knowing Yahweh"** denotes refusal of submissive acknowledgment of Yahweh's sovereignty (cf. Ex 5:1–2). This categorical refusal precipitates a spiral of wrath and apostasy. Rejection of the true God leads not to atheism, but to the enthronement of false gods so that Yahweh's **wrath blazes,** a point watered down by the NIV (2:14). Yahweh's wrath, his personal opposition to infidelity, works through external historical forces— turning the Hebrews over to their enemies—and through social and spiritual forces, rendering Israel impotent. Yahweh's wrath does not lead directly to destruction. Jdg 2:16–19 describes the judges as God's overture to unfaithful Israel. The writer from the outset declares the judges failures. Their influence did not extend beyond their deaths, and Israel ignored the judges even while they lived (v.17).

In the face of Israel's obduracy, Yahweh's wrath breaks out a second time (2:20–23). It finds expression not in mute historical forces but in a direct divine condemnation, which, like 2:1–5, accuses Israel of breaking covenant and withdraws divine support from the conquest. This speech makes explicit what 1:1–2:5 implied: the nations remaining after Joshua represent a test. Jdg 2:6–23 merits comparison with Ro 1:18–32, which describes the spiral of accelerating sin, wrath, and social collapse among pagans. Apostate Israel, no better than pagans, surrounded by foes, must add another enemy to its list: Yahweh!

Jdg 3:1–6 summarizes 1:1–3:6, expanding the notion of the unconquered nations as a **test.** The Hebrew term connotes the discernment of the quality or suitability of something. The test also had pedagogical aims. Learning of the **wars in Canaan** meant learning fidelity to Yahweh and confidence in his power. The new generation had the opportunity, like their ancestors, to know God's direct saving action, but Israel squandered the opportunity and **lived among the Canaanites,** intermarried with them, and **served their gods.**

C. Summary

Jdg 1:1–3:6 epitomizes the period after the death of Joshua as one of deepening faithlessness and frustration. Jdg 1:1–2:5 explores the covert apostasy of compromise, while 2:6–23 expounds how overt apostasy sabotaged Israel's mission. No simplistic connection exists between sinfulness and failure, faithfulness and success. In 1:1–2:5 failure is sin; in 2:6–23 failure is judgment. In 3:1–6 failures of one generation provide an opportunity, a test for the next. Living in Canaan, without serving Yahweh, the Hebrews abort their mission. Holding God's gifts without faithfully holding to God trivializes Israel's election. Hope resides in the converse principle: keeping faith with Yahweh even when bereft of his gifts constitutes Israel's true being. Judah's faithfulness, therefore, realizes God's promise and anticipates its ultimate embodiment in the royal house of David.

II. DEMONSTRATION: A DISINTEGRATING COMMUNITY (3:7–16:31)

A. The Exemplary Judge (3:7–11)

The story of Othniel looks like a report form for the judges with the "blanks" of a complete set of framework expressions filled in with the names of the oppressor and judge. The name Cushan-Rishathaim ("Cushan of Double-Wickedness") cannot be a historical name, but a caricature emphasizing the consummate criminality of Othniel's foe. Othniel is the only southern judge, and his genealogy suggests that he alone represents the faithful conquest generation. Therefore he sets the standard by which subsequent leaders are judged. But will the standard set by Othniel be equaled by his successors?

B. Triumph by the Word (3:12–5:31)

The Ehud and Deborah stories depict a victorious Israel and triumphant judges. Close inspection reveals the true source of deliverance: Yahweh's word.

1. The devastating word (3:12–30)

Despite the twice-repeated claim that Israel **did evil in the eyes of the LORD,** 3:12–15b creates positive expectations. The evil is unspecified, and the oppressor is satirized: **Eglon** means "Big Calf." The tide turns when Israel cries to Yahweh. Though explicitly raised up by Yahweh, Ehud experiences no onrush of Yahweh's spirit. He also embodies an irony: he is a **Benjaminite,** meaning "son of the right hand," but is left-handed. A "left-handed right-hander" suggests an unpredictable hero.

Jdg 3:15c–17 sets the scene, an audience with Eglon to present tribute, then focuses on the double-edged dagger concealed on Ehud's right thigh. V.7 captures Eglon's vulnerability: the "big calf" is fatted! The assassination (vv.18–26) is bracketed by references to turning back from the idols and crossing the idols, spatial references with theological overtones (Polzin, 158–61). Ehud seizes his opportunity, returns alone, and cleverly gains privacy with Eglon by announcing a **secret message.** His claim of a **message from God** draws Eglon into striking range. Ehud's secret divine message turns out to be fatally pointed. The dagger executes its mission in one thrust. The king's bulk holds the dagger fast— Ehud's message hits home! The NIV omits the next phrase of the Hebrew in

which the king's feces spill on the floor, though the narrative to follow requires this detail.

Jdg 3:23–26 frames the discovery of Eglon's body with Ehud's escape. He does not escape through the **porch.** Royal halls had two levels: a lower audience room and an elevated, enclosed dais. This **upper room** had a toilet emptying into a chamber below, which would have opened into the lower audience room for maintenance. After stabbing Eglon, Ehud locks the doors of the upper room from inside, passes through the passage from the upper to the lower levels and out into the audience room, then departs through the front door. The attendants return, discover the upper doors locked, and assume, probably from the odor, that the king is relieving himself. They wait until embarrassed, then open the door to discover their assassinated sovereign. (Halpern, 43–60).

Ehud's individual achievement embraces all Israel (vv.27–30). Like their hero, the Israelites employ a clever strategem, capturing the fords of the Jordan against the Moabites, who all, like their dead king, are fat! That all Israel participates in Ehud's victory elevates Ehud above swashbuckling individualism. The summary of his career records an unparalleled eighty years of rest, and notice of Ehud's death does not occur until 4:1.

This story is as double-edged as the dagger it celebrates. Ehud, despite the introduction's religious billing, performs a secular deed. But this political act is bounded by theological innuendos. Though his divine message has a brutally secular point, he proclaims his deed an act of Yahweh! No Spirit-endued charismatic deliverer, Ehud's divine enablement resides in his wits, his left-handedness, and his double-edged **word of God.** The story presents the mystery of God's ways. He works not only through the Spirit-inflamed charismatic, but through the clever ruthlessness of an Ehud. That which seems "religious" may not be; the "secular" may yet conceal the double-edged word of God that still finds its mark and cannot be withdrawn.

2. Minor judge, major achievement (3:31)

Shamgar's ox goad has made him the patron saint of those who do their best with what they have. In three ways this notice adds to the atmosphere of triumph pervading 3:12–5:31. (1) Shamgar comes **after** Ehud, but no apostasy intervenes, implying restraint of Israel's apostasy; (2) he defeats the Philistines, anticipating David's victory; and (3) he **save[s] Israel.**

3. The delivering word (4:1–5:31)

The introduction (4:1–3) still does not accuse Israel of idolatry, though 5:8 hints at it. The death of Ehud is noted in 4:1 parenthetically. The judge's death signaled a reversion to evil, limiting Ehud's death notice to a parenthetical remark. This combined with his eighty-year peace suggests Israel did not revert to evil immediately. The oppression gets detailed treatment, however, and the enemy now comes from within the land, Hazor, a city destroyed by Joshua (Jos 11). Israel's cry does not lead immediately to the divine elevation of a leader but is followed by more details of the oppression before the introduction of Deborah in 4:4.

Before launching into the story of deliverance, 4:4–10 depicts Deborah's judicial and prophetic role. Though a judge, she would not be the deliverer. Deborah prophetically summons Barak, who refuses to engage in battle unless Deborah joins him. Deborah's agreement has a price: the **honor** will belong to a woman. But again, who? Barak musters the armies and assumes the role of deliverer. Jdg 4:11–24 narrates Barak's divinely granted victory. Most suppose that Sisera learns of Barak's advance from Heber, who abandoned his fellow Kenites. One related to Moses' father-in-law now allies with Israel's oppressors. Jdg 4:17–22 switches to the flight of Sisera to the tent of Jael, wife of Heber, from whom Sisera expects refuge because of his treaty with Heber. By double-crossing Sisera, Jael abrogates an unfaithful alliance. Ehudlike, Jael maneuvers Sisera into lowering his defenses, then spikes his head to the ground. The **honor** that bypasses Barak and Deborah goes to a non-Israelite woman whose defiance of her husband's treaty with a Canaanite king wins her a place in Israel's lore.

This story undercuts the ideal of the lone hero. The prophet instigates and sustains the victorious military leader, who plays a secondary role. The real honor goes to an obscure woman who rejected her husband's compromise with Canaan. The story dramatizes the catalytic power of Yahweh's word to elicit daring faithfulness and extols the heroics of an ordinary person choosing the Lord's side.

In 4:23–5:31 we find Deborah's song, which fits into the concluding summary (4:23–24; 5:31b). Its themes reinforce the emphases of ch. 4. In 5:2–5 Deborah lauds the leaders and volunteers of Israel, then proclaims to pagan rulers that Yahweh's coming, not military might, procures Israel's victory. Jdg 5:6–9 accentuates Deborah's role in reawakening the volunteer spirit and stresses the paralysis and powerlessness caused by oppression and, possibly, apostasy, if NIV is correct with **They chose new gods** in the textually difficult 5:8. Jdg 5:10–12 affirms the efficacy of reciting Yahweh's righteous acts. The roll call of the tribes (5:13–18) praises initiative and daring and castigates Reuben's indecisiveness, Gilead's isolation, Asher's unwillingness to risk its security, and Dan's complacency. On the latter, NIV's **"Why did [Dan] linger by the ships?"** is better translated "Why did he abide at ease?" (Craigie, 84–86). Praise for Zebulun and Naphtali's willingness to take mortal risk climaxes the list, since they figure in ch. 4. Jdg 5:19–23 celebrates the saving action of Yahweh, not through charismatic deliverers, but through the stars and the river Kishon. That Yahweh is the principal protagonist heightens the urgency of the battle call. To stay away betrayed not humans but Yahweh. Thus the village of Meroz is cursed, and the wife of a Gentile collaborator with the enemy, by helping Israel, becomes **most blessed of women** (5:24–27). The gutsy faith of Jael contrasts with Sisera's mother, who callously assumes that Sisera is taking extra time despoiling the Hebrews and molesting their maidens to find her some little curio! The reader already knows that Israel will provide no souvenirs for the oppressors' mantles.

Jdg 5:31a declares the point of the story: To oppose Yahweh is to perish; to love him is to know ever-growing strength. That love is embodied in the faithful and risky choices made by Barak, the volunteers of Israel, and Jael. The divine word, embodied by Deborah, is both catalyst and celebration of that love. No death notice appears. A hero's influence fades with death. The action of God, the commitment of his people, and the empowering Word transcends all generations.

C. Transition (6:1–10:5)

In the transitional Gideon-Abimelech section the judge appears riddled with ambiguity and fraught with possibilities for evil. Charismatic enablement and power-grasping populism become indistinguishable.

1. Anointed ambiguity (6:1–8:32)

The introduction in 6:1–10 signals a new stage in the story. The NIV wrongly inserts **"again"** in 6:1, which does not continue the previous period, but opens a new stage in Israel's evildoing. The resultant military crisis is fearsomely detailed. Midianite raids force the Israelites into mountain lairs, leaving crops vulnerable to pillagers aided by a new military commodity, the camel. The resultant destitution—and not repentance—wrenches from Israel a cry to Yahweh. But rather than leap to Israel's defense in raising up a savior, Yahweh first issues a scathing prophetic denunciation (cf. 2:1–5, 20–23). The dangling invective places the career of Gideon under Yahweh's growing displeasure. Gideon does not unambiguously represent "Yahweh to the rescue." Indeed, ambiguity is the undercurrent of the whole story.

The preparation for battle (6:11–7:14) begins with the angelic summons to save Israel. That call (6:11–24) contrasts Gideon and Yahweh's angel. Gideon is resentful and regards the oppression as unmerited and questions God's character, despite the apostasy and rebuke recorded in 6:1–10. He doubts his own capacity to save Israel. By contrast, the angel greets him as **"mighty warrior,"** affirms his strength, and promises Yahweh's presence. Unpersuaded by the divine word (contrast Deborah/Barak), Gideon tests the angel with an offering that is consumed in flames, convincing Gideon of the divine identity of his visitor.

The divine-human contrast continues in Gideon's first task (6:25–32). Called to destroy the local Baal altar, Gideon obeyed by night **because he was afraid.** A secret act hardly mounts a public challenge, and in the ensuing investigation, Gideon's idolatrous father declares the position Gideon should have taken: let the god defend himself. Gideon's new name, **Jerub-Baal, "Let Baal contend,"** captures his ambiguity. The Gideon-God contrast advances into sacred territory in 6:33–7:14. Empowered by the Holy Spirit, Gideon musters an army of 32,000. The NIV's **"the Spirit of the Lord came upon Gideon"** muffles the graphic emphasis on divine power and human passivity in the Hebrew, which reads, "The spirit of Yahweh put on Gideon [like clothes]." Despite the Spirit's enabling and a large turnout, Gideon demands two more signs from Yahweh. In 7:1–18 Yahweh rejects 94 percent of the soldiers responding to the Spirit-inspired draft. The concern that great numbers would deceive Israel into ascribing deliverance to their own capabilities captures the tension between Gideon's perspective and God's. Worse yet, miraculous signs left Gideon still afraid (7:10), grouping him with those whom Yahweh dismissed! By contrast, Yahweh's encouragement involves simple intelligence gathering, which suddenly energizes Gideon for battle.

The two-part battle narrative concentrates on the divine-human contrast in Gideon himself. Jdg 7:4–8:3 describes the stratagem of a night ruse with pitchers, torches, trumpets, and war whoops in which the panicked Midianites attack one another before fleeing. Gideon pursues, mustering the Ephraimites, who seize the fords of Jordan against the enemy exactly as Ehud's troops did. Gideon's self-effacing tact in answering the Ephraimites' irritation over their late summons preserves the victory. Gideon appears as the champion of God who, with a clever stratagem and direct divine inter-

vention, defeats the enemy and sweeps all Israel to victory, even despite tribal divisiveness. All interpreters note an abrupt shift in 8:4–21. Gideon still pursues the kings of Midian, but suddenly not in irresistible triumph. The three hundred are exhausted and hungry, and Midian seems about to escape. Gideon's men cannot even obtain food, much less military assistance, from Succoth and Penuel. Gideon appears not as peacemaker and securer of unity, but as vengeful and threatening. Jdg 8:4–21 nowhere mentions Yahweh as the author of victory, and Gideon fulfills his threats against Succoth and Penuel. Jdg 8:18–21 also reveals Gideon's stake of personal vengeance in the battle: Zebah and Zalmunna murdered his half-brothers. His last act is to slay them in anger for mockery. The divine-human tension centers now in the person of Gideon. Is he a divinely anointed deliverer and reconciler or a determined pursuer of personal revenge? Israel has won deliverance from the Midianites, but the reader's confidence in the judge is shaken.

The issue of leadership culminates in the final contrast in 8:22–27, when the elders offer Gideon permanent, hereditary rule. Contrary to Yahweh's express intention (7:1–3), the Hebrews credit the victory to Gideon: **"You have saved us"** (emphasis mine). Gideon's response sounds like a pious rejection of kingship based on the belief that God alone is King over Israel, but his response is as flawed as the people's offer. Human rule is not at stake here. That Yahweh is "the Judge" (11:27b) did not preclude human judges. Gideon offers an alternative to his own rule: his own religion! The ephod was the means by which worshipers learned Yahweh's will and thus the vehicle of Yahweh's rule. Gideon makes an ephod, which promotes not Yahweh's rule, but spiritual harlotry. The conclusion (8:28–32) notes forty years of peace following Gideon's victory but for the first time limits the period of peace to the judge's lifetime.

2. The self-made king (8:33–9:57)

The Abimelech story and the list of minor judges (8:33–10:5) loosely follow the pattern of the deliverer narratives: Israel sins (8:33–35); a tyrant arises, though from within Israel (9:1–57); and a deliverer, Tola, arises to save Israel (10:1–5). The deeper relationships among these sections differ from the usual pattern. The tyranny of Abimelech embodies Israel's sin as much as it results from it. Likewise, Tola saves Israel, not by charismatic action, but by uneventful administration (Boling, 187). The story identifies an oppression more grievous than any foreign foe. Israel's faithlessness can raise up oppression from native soil.

Jdg 8:33–35 binds Abimelech's rise to Israel's sin, which now appears unequivocally as idolatry under the image of harlotry (cf. 2:17; 8:27). Additionally, a dynastic element materializes. The NIV's **"failed to show kindness"** (8:35) is better translated "did not keep faith with" the family of Jerub-Baal. The verse thus remarkably coordinates spiritual harlotry with the political betrayal of Gideon's descendants. This latter crime occupies center stage in the moral drama of ch. 9.

In describing Abimelech's grasp of power, 9:1–6 foreshadows his demise. His approach is indirect, through the mediation of his mother's family. His overt appeal to order—one ruler rather than seventy—thinly cloaks a covert appeal to ethnic prejudice. The appeal succeeds, and Abimelech, bankrolled by the lords of Shechem from the temple treasury of the Canaanite deity Baal Berith, murders his seventy half-brothers **on one stone** in a savage ritual dynastic execution. Having slain the legitimate heirs of Gideon, Abimelech alone remains to be elected king. This usurpation by dynastic fratricide triggers a sequence of consequences unfolding in 9:7–57.

Jotham, sole survivor of Abimelech's purge and legitimate heir of Jerubbaal, directly challenges Abimelech's pretension to superiority (9:7–21). Taking his stand on the mountain from which the curses of the law were proclaimed (Jos 8:30–35), Jotham utters a fable usually taken as an attack on kingship. The fable, however, curses not kingship, but followers of *unfit* kings. Whoever makes a bramble king should not be surprised when the bramble cannot provide shade. Jotham transforms the fable's foolhardiness into moral guilt. In backing an unfit ruler, the Shechemites perpetrate treachery and violence.

Jdg 9:22–24 apprises the reader of God's ratification of Jotham's curse, beginning with an evil "charisma." **"Evil spirit"** (v.23) here denotes a divisive disposition, not a malevolent spiritual entity. Divine retribution does not hurry, but waits three years, working secretly in the bad spirit brooding between Abimelech and his coconspirators. Vv.25–55 unfold the human drama in which God's retribution carries out its hidden design. Two threats to Abimelech's rule appear in 9:25–30. The lords of Shechem begin sponsoring raiding forays around Shechem, and Gaal ben-Ebed steals the confidence of the Shechemites. The first threat issues explicitly from the divinely prompted disaffection noted in 9:22–24, but the second brings an ironic twist. More than a malcontent, drunken drifter boasting against authority, Gaal poses a threat because the Shechemites **trust** him and his ugly (Abimelech-like) ethnic slurs. These threats issue explicitly from the divinely prompted disaffection noted in 9:22–24. Abimelech, faced with treacherous Shechemites and a popular detractor, responds in force. After squashing Gaal and routing the Shechemite ambush parties Abimelech burns the Shechemite leadership alive in the very temple whose treasury financed Abimelech's murderous rise to power. Jotham's dynastic curse finds literal realization. The vengeful Abimelech moves on to Thebez, besieges its tower, and prepares to burn it as well. This violent excess undoes him. His gratuitous violence is now brought to mind forcibly and finally by the Thebezite woman's millstone.

Jdg 9:56–57 summarizes the whole narrative. All the events of 9:1–55 feature human actors, but the narrator penetrates beneath human causes to the vengeance of God working secretly to redress the evil done to Gideon's family. The account starkly criticizes one kind of relationship between leader and people. Charismatic leadership easily degenerates into craven populism. Condemning Abimelech in a self-effecting curse by the sole surviving legitimate heir of Gideon, the story unmistakably asserts the inherent superiority of inherited rule. Shechem, the scene of this story, served as the early capital of the northern kingdom. In contrast to Judah, which enjoyed an unbroken succession of legitimate Davidic kings, at least seven dynasties ruled the North. The one threat to the Davidic line in Judah came when Athaliah, daughter of Jezebel, slew all the royal heirs but one, Joash, whom the priests hid (2Ki 11–12). The stories of Abimelech/Jotham and Athaliah/Joash parallel each other closely, presenting the conviction that charismatic rule, such as the North seemed to favor in some form, easily becomes corrupted into rule by violent usurpation.

3. Salvation by administration (10:1–5)

Jdg 10:1–5 reinforces the emphases of the Abimelech story by noting the careers of two "minor" judges. Tola follows Abimelech and is credited with **sav[ing] Israel.** After twenty-three years under Tola, Jair governs twenty-two years with no apostasy intervening. The orderly and uninterrupted succession of the nonmilitary "minor" judges suggests the conviction that God's people need order, not heroics; character, not charisma.

The second stage of the history of the judges (6:1–10:5) began with a fresh departure in evil-doing and a divine rejoinder in response to Israel's cry. A two-named judge embodied the growing ambiguity of the charismatic hero, and Abimelech realized the threat fully. When charisma rules, anyone with a power base can tyrannize the community. God's judgment of Abimelech affirms precisely the form of community rejected by Gideon: hereditary rule.

D. Tragedy in the Spirit (10:6–16:31)

The account of Jephthah (10:6–12:7) and Samson (13:1–16:31), with the second list of "minor" judges in between (12:8–15), comprises a third stage in the history of the judges, revealing all the weaknesses of charismatic leadership. In Jephthah, the deliverer becomes a destroyer. Samson never fulfills the potential of his birth. By focusing on the personality of the individual occupying the charismatic office, the writer exposes the rampant egoism that destroyed it.

1. Spirit-driven savagery (10:6–12:7)

Everything about 10:6–18 points to a climactic crisis. The notation of Israel's evil explicitly includes idolatry as Israel worships its enemies' gods! For the second time in 3:7–16:31 Yah-weh's wrath blazes. The introduction to the judges' stories (2:6–3:6) projected two outbreaks of divine wrath. The first initiated Yahweh's chastening oppressions and merciful deliverances (2:14–19). When Israel's faithlessness only deepened, a second outbreak of wrath signaled a withdrawal of Yahweh's saving presence. In the narrative itself, the first reference to divine wrath comes in the Othniel account (3:8), followed by deepening apostasy. This second outbreak signals the beginning of the end. The inclusion of the Philistines (10:7), who figure in Samson's career (13:1–16:31), indicates the gravity of the oppression. Thus 10:6–18 introduces both the Jephthah and the Samson stories. Since the Philistine crisis contributed to the establishment of the monarchy, this reference foreshadows the end of Israel as a tribal confederation led by charismatic heroes.

Israel's outcry contains a confession of sin and meets with an emphatic divine refusal: **"I will no longer save you. Go and cry out to the gods you have chosen."** Israel's rejoinder betrays its double-mindedness: **"Do with us whatever you think best, but please rescue us now."** Jdg 10:16a can therefore describe only a fleeting fit of foxhole fidelity, not true repentance. Israel rearranges the furniture on its sinking spiritual ship. The divine response in 10:16b finds near universal misinterpretation to mean Yahweh **could bear Israel's misery no longer** (NIV). The Hebrew expression used is "his soul became short at Israel's toil," an idiom denoting extreme aggravation, not compassion (cf. 16:16). Finally, Israel's outcry no longer leads to the emergence of a divinely sent hero, but to a purely human canvass for a leader. Jephthah emerges under a cloud of apostasy, alienation, and divine aggravation.

Jephthah is the first hero not to come into his role by direct divine initiative (11:1–11). As a **mighty warrior** he has the "right stuff" to lead Israel. His irregular parentage, however, eclipses his native potential, and rejection by his kindred consigns him to a brigand's life. When the crisis forces the Gileadites to send for Jephthah, he vents his bitterness in a complaint echoing that of Yahweh in 10:11–14. Jephthah shows himself a hard negotiator, alive to his counterparts' vulnerability, mercilessly tightening the screws until he gets what he wants. Not rash, he demands for every promise the appropriate definition and guarantee.

In 11:12–28 Jephthah's proclivity to bargain appears again. In two exchanges he tries to dissuade the Ammonite king from war. Strangely, Jephthah's whole message addresses Moab, not Ammon. He appeals to Israel's original, nonaggressive policy, its right to possession by divinely enabled conquest, and three centuries of actual occupation. His concluding charge (vv.23–27) borders on insult, and the claim **"May Yahweh judge ..."** amounts to a declaration of war. Unintimidated by Jephthah's rhetoric, the Ammonite king refuses to listen.

With Jephthah's bluff called, war is imminent (11:29–40). The onrush of the Spirit of Yahweh certifies Jephthah as a charismatic hero as he successfully musters an army. The most conspicuous concomitant, however, of the Spirit's possession of Jephthah is his vow. Hard-bargaining Jephthah acts as though Yahweh were the same. Far from rash, Jephthah's vow constitutes a calculated gambit with God with a priceless chip on the table. But those who attempt to manipulate God ensnare themselves in their own devices.

Jephthah, the victor in battle, loses his gambit. Three different Hebrew idioms in 11:34 underscore the magnitude of his loss. Worse, Jephthah grieves only for himself and upbraids his daughter. She heroically accepts her fate, death as a human sacrifice. The notion that she became perpetual virgin, based on 11:39, comes late in the history of interpretation and lacks foundation. The daughter, not Jephthah, finds perpetual remembrance in Israel.

Jephthah's final act seals his fate as a disastrous antihero. In 12:1–6 the Ephraimites test Jephthah's exercise of government, a role for which he bargained. He faces a crisis identical to that faced by Gideon (7:24–8:3), both of which contrast with an event in Ehud's career (3:27–29). Ehud eagerly enlisted the Ephraimites in battle, and the latter employed a strategy of entrapment at the Jordan. Gideon's call for Ephraimite assistance receives the identical response but is followed by a bitter complaint that Gideon answers with consummate tact. Jephthah, faced with Ephraimite jealousy, responds with bitter recrimination and employs the Ephraimite strategy to destroy forty-two thousand of his fellow Israelites. The man who negotiated with Israel's enemy preemptorily slaughters his countrymen! More Israelites die here at Jephthah's hand than in the rest of the book of Judges. The charismatic deliverer has become a destroyer.

The conclusion (12:7) notes only that Jephthah **led** Israel, conspicuously omitting the regular reference to Israel having **peace** (cf. 3:30; 5:31; 8:28). How could the land rest during the reign of such a leader? The chronological reference also insinuates failure. Prior to Jephthah, the periods of peace are at least twice as long as the time of oppression. Jephthah's career is shorter by a significant margin than the time of oppression. The balance sheet on Israel's judges now registers a loss. Jephthah embodies fully the threat in charismatic leadership. He becomes an incomprehensible monster, sacrificing his daughter and slaughtering his fellow Israelites. Most troubling of all is that this horror begins with the onrush of the Spirit! The spark of divine power lit a fuse, not a fire. Power alone, even God's power, without the accompanying grace of character, destroys.

2. The measure of mediocrity (12:8–15)

The lists of "minor judges" undergird the emphases of the sections in which they appear. Shamgar (3:31), standing between two triumphant judges, is an effectual deliverer. The second list (10:1–5) features Tola, who "saves Israel," after the anarchic reign of Abimelech. This third list, between Jephthah and Samson, reflects the negative tone of 10:6–16:31. None is said to "rise up" to "save Israel." The low numbers given for their rules total less than half that attributed to Tola and Jair (fifty-five years), just as Jephthah and Samson experienced abbreviated careers.

3. Charisma and corruption (13:1–16:31)

Israel's unremitting apostasy, continued from 10:6–9, brings on the Philistines, who broke down Israel's loose tribal confederacy, ultimately forcing Israel to choose a king. Likewise, Israel continues alienated from Yahweh, who had rejected Israel's plea (10:10–16). Thus no outcry is heard here. Apostate Israel stands mute before its offended Lord. The book's progressive exposé of the weaknesses of charismatic leadership culminates with Samson, whose birth narrative (13:2–25) also climaxes the book's increasingly detailed description of each judge's background. Like Jephthah, Samson lives under a vow, though not one of his own making. Samson's anonymous mother receives God's promise of a child (13:2–5, 7), which decrees the child a Nazirite, requiring abstinence from alcohol, strict avoidance of the dead, and uncut hair (Nu 6). Although Nazirites undertook these obligations voluntarily for a limited period, prenatal divine election foreordains Samson a lifelong Nazirite. Annunciation stories usually herald the arrival of salvation. Samson, however, will barely begin this task. With Jephthah, the deliverance became disaster; with Samson, deliverance itself slips away.

Rather than receive Yahweh's word from his wife, Manoah requires direct confirmation (13:8). The ensuing encounter reveals Manoah's spiritually insensitive assertiveness. The confirmation emphasizes the primacy of the original word to his wife, but Manoah attempts to fit Yahweh's word into a set of religious and traditional expectations: he injects an offering, demands the messenger's name, and fears for his life upon realizing his impertinence (vv.8–23). Samson's birth and blessing (vv.24–25) fulfill God's promise and sound a warning. The NIV's **"The Spirit of the LORD began to stir him"** conceals the awful oppressiveness of Samson's experience of the Spirit. "Harass, plague, afflict" render the Hebrew better.

The first phase of Samson's life recounts his harassment of the Philistines (14:1–15:20) in a tight, cause-effect sequence emphasizing riddles (14:1–20) and revenge (15:1–21). Jdg 14:1–9 sets the stage, characterizing Samson's headstrong insistence on marrying a Philistine woman, despite parental protest, as Yahweh's opportunity to confront the Philistines. Samson's secret, Spirit-energized slaying of a lion inspires the riddle at the heart of the

story. The wedding banquet reveals Samson's rarely noted cleverness as he frustrates his Philistine companions with an impossible riddle (14:10–14). Only threats to burn Samson's fiancèe and her family alive persuade her to nag him into telling his secret (vv.15–17). Confronted with humiliation and betrayal, Samson explodes in Spirit-energized rage, murdering thirty Philistines to pay off his wager and abandoning his new bride (vv.18–20). The Philistines won their bet, but at a frightening cost to their nation.

Samson's anger, by prompting the loss of his bride, triggers the next episode, which circles around Samson's revenge (15:1–19; see esp. vv.3, 7). Samson avenges his loss by burning the crops of the Philistines, who avenge themselves by burning Samson's erstwhile fiancèe and her family alive, per their original threat (vv.1–6). Samson's vengeful slaughter sends him into hiding and exposes Judah, an innocent bystander, to Philistine military wrath. As the Judeans hand Samson over to the exuberant Philistines, the Spirit of Yahweh energizes Samson to break his bonds, seize the nearest weapon, a donkey's jawbone, and kill a thousand Philistines (vv.7–17), leaving him mortally exhausted and thirsty. Dying of thirst or falling captive to the Philistines would negate all his triumphs. His bold prayer for deliverance and vindication is heard (vv.18–19).

Superficially, 14:1–15:20 seems to exult in its roguish hero. The total context, however, suggests several warning signs. (1) Jdg 3:5–6 damns intermarriage with Gentiles as compromise and defeat. (2) The NIV obscures the Hebrew idiom behind **"She's the right one for me"** and **"He liked her"** (14:3b, 7). The same idiom in 17:6 and 21:25 is traditionally translated "Everyone did what was right in his own eyes," denoting wanton self-will. (3) Samson violates two provisions of his vow noted in ch. 13: touching the dead and drinking alcohol. *Feast* in Hebrew actually refers to drinking. Also, by concealing the source of the honey, Samson causes his mother to violate her vow (cf. 13:4, "you"). (4) Samson is one "afflicted" by the Spirit (13:25), and the account's driving force is the Spirit. Strangely, the three occasions of the Spirit's onrush affect the narrative negatively. By enabling the slaying of the lion, the Spirit sets up the first violation of the vow— touching the dead—and suggests the riddle dominating ch. 14, thus initiating the chain of recrimination driving chs. 14–15. Samson's Spirit-stimulated violent rage left his fiancèe abandoned (14:19–20), triggering the revenge motif of ch. 15. The use of the jawbone of a donkey in the climactic battle (15:15–16) involves another Spirit-inspired breach of Samson's vow. (5) Samson himself seems trapped in his own Spirit-instigated violence. In 15:7 the NIV's **"I won't stop until I get my revenge"** is better translated "I will be avenged upon you, and after that I will quit" (RSV). Samson expects one final act to end the cycle of vengeance. Bondage always cries, "Once more, and I'm through!" (6) The periods of peace were longer than the periods of oppression from Othniel to Gideon but ceased with Jephthah's career, which was much shorter than the time of oppression. Stepping further down, the period of Philistine oppression fully encloses Samson's twenty-year career (v.20).

The undercurrent of impending ruin in chs. 14–15 breaks out unambiguously in 16:1–31, whose structure runs roughly parallel to chs. 14–15. Both units begin with Samson's relationship with a Philistine woman. The liaison narrated in 16:1–3 suggests a deterioration, however. The former relationship was marital, but here Samson consorts with a harlot. In 2:17 and 8:27, 33 harlotry is an image for apostasy. Like chs. 14–15, 16:4–22 depicts Samson, now in a second immoral relationship, divulging a secret to a persistent paramour. Delilah plays for keeps, probing not for the answer to a party puzzle, but for the key to Samson's destruction. Ironically, Samson willfully, even enthusiastically, violated the first two provisions of his vow. The last provision, however, was secretly snapped as he slept in Delilah's bosom. Such is the fragility of human spiritual freedom. Shorn of his strength, Samson awakes, expecting to defeat the Philistines in the sudden energy of the Spirit as always. But Samson **did not know that the LORD had left him.** The text provides one small sign of hope: as Samson labors in the Philistine prison, powerless and blind, his hair silently returns. The final scene (16:23–30) parallels 15:18–19. No longer a triumphant charismatic, Samson occasions the praise of a pagan god. While Samson's death provokes awe in readers, he nevertheless appeals to God only for vengeance for his eyes. To the end, Samson champions not God but himself. The best thing the last charismatic judge does for Israel is die (16:30). Samson remains the emblem of a self-will that denies its addiction to lust, revenge, and power and refuses to face its own bondage.

E. Summary of 3:7–16:31

Jdg 1:1–3:6 asserts the progressive failure of the Hebrews to build faithfully on the achievements of Joshua and the Conquest generation. Jdg 3:7–16:31 depicts Israel's deepening apostasy and traces its expanding consequences. Oppressions deepen, political crises grow in gravity, tribal discord increases, and Israel's saviors become destroyers (Jephthah) or disasters (Samson) as the divine protest grows in stridency (6:7–10; 10:11–14). The theme of Spirit-led leadership epitomizes Israel's collapse. As matters worsen, references to the Spirit of Yahweh multiply and the Spirit's onrush actually contributes to the tragedy.

III. SUMMATION: COMMUNITY IN CHAOS (17:1–21:25)

Jdg 17–21 culminates the process of deterioration narrated in 3:7–16:31 and demonstrates the thesis advanced in 1:1–3:6. Chs. 17–18 resume the narrative of failed conquest broken off in 1:34–35 and depict the only "conquest" of which the Danites were capable. Chs. 19–21 depict an outrageous breach in the covenant community, matching the covenant-breaking of 2:6–3:6. Israel's failure finds expression not in claims of continued apostasy, but in the observation that **everyone did as he saw fit** (17:6; 21:25). These stories feature no charismatic judges but make a powerful statement on leadership by constantly reminding the reader that **in those days** of self-annihilating anarchy, in which **everyone did as he saw fit,** Israel had no king (17:6; 18:1; 19:1; 21:25).

A. Perverted Conquest (17:1–18:31)

This account castigates the worship, tribe, and city of Dan. Dan later became one of the two shrines established for the northern kingdom by Jeroboam, thus earning him the epithet "he who caused Israel to sin" (1Ki 12:25–33). This narrative, no doubt, directs its critique at the heretical northern center. Danite worship originated in theft and flagrantly violated Yahweh's prohibition of images (17:1–6). The thief's ordination of his son as priest

for his idolatrous shrine could also censure the northern kingdom's irregular priesthood (1Ki 12:31). The scene closes by observing that such events could happen only in the absence of a king, where everyone becomes his own standard for right. In 17:7–18:1a Micah hires a traveling Levite to serve as his priest. The only claim to legitimacy held by this shrine is a Levite, who comes from Bethlehem—David's home city. The scene concludes, repeating the reminder that **in those days, Israel had no king.**

The stage being set, 18:1b–31 returns to the landless Danites of 1:34–35. Impotent before the Amorites, Dan's defeat epitomized the collapse of the conquest in the North. Their trek northward embarked from precisely the places, Zorah and Eshtaol, that witnessed Samson's early urgings by the spirit. The great charismatic left his tribesmen without an inheritance. This story has close parallels to several Conquest narratives in Numbers and Joshua, identifying 18:1b–31 as a conquest story (Malamat). But what kind of conquest? The mission of the spies suggests that this is a perverted conquest. The cities confronted by the Danites' forebears were strong, fortified, and populated by the daunting Anakim, making the spies feel like grasshoppers (Nu 13:28–33). The Danite spies gleefully characterize Laish as wide open, unsuspecting and defenseless, the perfect victim (18:1–10). Conquest narratives typically begin with inquiry at a divine oracle to receive assurance of victory. This ritual, however, involves idols tainted by theft and an opportunist priest. Removing all the sacred trappings from Micah's shrine with the Levite's consent suggests that neither the priest nor the Danites were overly concerned with the opinion of the idol or its oracle (vv.11–21). Once clear of their Amorite enemies and fortified by their newfound religious resources, the Danites intimidate the pitiable Micah (vv.22–26) and ruthlessly slaughter the defenseless occupants of Laish (vv.27–28a). Conquest stories often culminate in the erection of a monument or holy place to commemorate Yahweh's assistance. The Danites, who needed little help from God in defeating the Laishians, establish a city in their own name and install their own priesthood there. Ironically, the opportunistic, idolatrous priest has Moses as a grandfather! In the context of 1:1–2:5, this story reveals that God's people, when they fail in their mission through compromise, tend to erect a perverted substitute, a caricature of the sacred task given them by God. Such arrogant anarchism testifies to the absence of a king in a time when **everyone did as he saw fit.**

B. Perverted Covenant (19:1–21:25)

As 17:1–18:31 developed the theme of failed conquest begun in 1:1–2:5, so 19:1–21:25 returns to the question of Israel as a covenant community, initiated in 2:6–3:6. The narrative begins with a simple domestic dispute between a Levite living in Ephraim and his estranged concubine, who abandons him and returns to her home in Bethlehem (19:1–11). Signs of the collapse of Israel as an extended family of tribes appear as the Levite fails to find a hospitable reception in Gibeah, a town in Benjamin's territory that later became the capital of Saul, Israel's first king. Finally an old man of Ephraimite extraction takes in his fellow tribesman (vv.12–21). Gibeah's indifference then erupts into outrage in a story manifesting remarkable affinities with the story of Sodom's destruction (Ge 19), except that Jdg 19 ends in a mob's gang rape

of the Levite's concubine, a crime that shatters covenant loyalty and brotherhood (vv.22–26). Moreover, the host participates in the outrage, saying to the mob, **"Here is my virgin daughter, *and his concubine"*** [emphasis mine]. Offering a guest's lover, even a concubine, to a sadistic mob hardly constitutes hospitality. Nor is the Levite a hero, as witnessed by his peremptory command—**"Get up; let's go!"**—while she lies lifeless on the doorstep having saved his skin by serving as his sexual surrogate in the unsavory doings of that grim night (vv.27–28).

The rape of the concubine plunges Israel into war. The Levite's dismemberment of his concubine—another allusion to the Saul story (1Sa 11:6–8)—energizes the nation's tribal judicial machinery to avenge the crime (19:29–20:13a). Benjamin's refusal to turn Gibeah over to tribal justice prompts an all-Israelite civil war. Israel musters in classic holy war fashion but against one of its own tribes. Inspired by Yahweh's repeated encouragement, the Judeans lead Israel against their Benjaminite brothers twice, both times being defeated (20:13b–25). The Israelites resort to frenzied offerings, prayers, and inquiry under the direction of Eleazar, an Aaronic priest, and ambush the Benjaminites much as Joshua defeated Ai (Jos 8). Twenty-five thousand Benjaminites die, and the victorious Israelites subject the territory of Benjamin to burning and annihilation as only six hundred survive (vv.26–48).

On the surface, the mechanisms of covenant justice appear to function flawlessly. The culprits in the original crime are never definitively identified and punished; however, the Levite, whose grievance began the whole episode, falls out of sight after 20:7. Most significantly, the system of tribal justice creates a problem by eliminating a tribe from Israel, a kind of social dismemberment. The same Israelites who asked Yahweh, "Who will go up first to fight against Benjamin?" now wail **"Why should one tribe be missing from Israel?"** (vv.1–3) Frenetic seeking of Yahweh brings no divine answer, despite the Aaronic pedigree of the officiating priest (cf. 20:27–28). On its own, Israel seeks to restore the tribe it has just annihilated by procuring wives for the few remaining Benjaminites. This ad hoc solution entails yet another atrocity, the slaughter of the men of Jabesh Gilead (21:4–12), the town later saved from destruction by Saul at the beginning of his reign (1Sa 11:1–11). When this proves inadequate, the elders of Israel authorize the kidnap and rape of the maidens of Shiloh—a

grim reversal, considering how the episode began (21:13–24). In the end, the tribal judicial apparatus, even when operating correctly, no longer preserves Israelite unity. The traditional structures for redressing injury serve only to multiply it. The narrator's last words recall Israel's true problem: **"Everyone did as he saw fit,"** a situation possible because **in those days Israel had no king.** Unfavorable allusions to the Saul story clearly imply the writer's preference for Davidic kings.

C. Summary of 17:1–21:25
The final section (17:1–21:25) probes beneath apostasy, discovering anarchic self-will, which the writer constantly blames on the absence of a king. The tribal confederation and its charismatics having failed, kingship deserves its chance.

BIBLIOGRAPHY

Boling, R. *Judges: A New Translation With Introduction and Commentary.* Garden City, N.Y.: Doubleday, 1975.

Buber, M. "Books of Judges and Book of Judges." *Kingship of God.* 3d ed. Pp. 66–84. London: Allen and Unwin, 1967.

Burney, C. *Book of Judges With Introduction and Notes.* London: Rivingtons, 1920.

Craigie, P. *Ugarit and the Old Testament.* Grand Rapids: Eerdmans, 1983.

Cundall, A. and L. Morris. *Judges and Ruth: Introduction and Commentary.* Downers Grove: InterVarsity Press, 1968.

Halpern, B. *The First Historians: The Hebrew Bible and History.* San Francisco: Harper & Row, 1988.

Malamat, Abraham. "The Danite Migration and the Pan-Israelite Exodus-Conquest: A Biblical Narrative Pattern." *Biblia* 51 (1970): 1–17.

Moore, G. *Critical and Exegetical Commentary on Judges.* Edinburgh: T. & T. Clark, 1895.

Polzin, R. *Moses and the Deuteronomist.* New York: Seabury, 1980.

Soggin, J. A. *Judges: A Commentary.* Philadelphia: Westminster, 1981.

Steiner, G. "Homer and the Scholars." *Language and Silence,* 171–87. New York: Atheneum, 1962.

Webb, B. *The Book of Judges: An Integrated Reading.* Sheffield: JSOT Press, 1988.

RUTH
Bill T. Arnold

INTRODUCTION

I. AUTHORSHIP AND DATE

Jewish tradition credits Samuel with writing the Book of Ruth (Talmud, *Bab. Bath.* 14b). But if the references to David (4:17, 22) are original (see below), it seems unlikely that Samuel was responsible. The book contains no decisive evidence regarding authorship, so it is best to accept it as anonymous.

Ruth's date of composition is a moot issue. Dates have been suggested ranging from 950 B.C. to late in the postexilic period, even down to 250 B.C. The events themselves are dated to the period of the Judges (1:1), but the author was obviously conscious of David's significance. Myers has convincingly argued that this little idyll was transmitted orally for centuries in poetic form before it was finally written down as a narrative (referring to the book as "a narrative poem," p. 42 and see also pp. 33–43). Although he feels the present edition was not written until the exilic or postexilic period (p. 64), there is just as much evidence for an earlier transition to a narrative format.

Some have argued for a late date because of the presence of Aramaisms and other internal linguistic evidence. But the identification of Aramaic forms in Ruth is far from certain. Moreover, scholars are becoming more convinced that the presence of Aramaisms, even where they can be demonstrated, is a precarious argument for a late date of composition. On the contrary, a careful analysis of Ruth's linguistic peculiarities yields evidence for a date earlier than the exilic period (cf. Campbell, 24–26). For more on these difficult issues, see the commentaries.

II. CONTENT AND STRUCTURE

This story is best categorized as an idyll, a simple description of rustic life. The plot centers around three main characters: Naomi, Ruth, and Boaz. The action may be viewed in four scenes, each scene revolving around an important dialogue. The events of ch. 1 take place in Moab (more technically on the road back from Moab), and the dialogue involves primarily Naomi and Ruth. The rest of the action is set in Bethlehem or its environs.

The material in Ruth is organized according to a "problem-solution" framework. The basic problem and its severity is presented in stark terms in 1:1–5. Driven from home by famine, Elimelech's family is forced to live in Moab for ten years. While there, all three males die, leaving the mother, Naomi, without progeny. Naomi returns to Bethlehem to face the prospects of a life of privation and sorrow. The events of ch. 1 fail to address the problem, but merely explain how Ruth the Moabitess came to live with Naomi in Bethlehem. At the close of the chapter, the problems are abundantly clear. Naomi is without child, Ruth without husband. Together they face the realities of poverty. The rest of the book describes the slow, gradual unfolding of the solution to these problems. The denouement occurs in the climactic fourth chapter where Ruth gets a husband, Naomi gets a (grand)son, and Boaz (a man of "standing") serves as their kinsman-redeemer (4:13–16).

Many have questioned the originality of the concluding paragraphs. The birth of Obed (4:13–17) and David's genealogy (4:18–22) are commonly taken as secondary to the story. But recent studies have demonstrated that these sections serve an important literary function as closures (known as "codas," Berlin, 101–10). We agree that 4:13–22 is an integral part of the author's purpose, and these verses will be treated in the commentary as original.

III. THEOLOGICAL SIGNIFICANCE

The author's purpose for writing is not at first apparent. Some have suggested it was written as an antiexclusivistic tract, demonstrating that even a Moabite woman could become attached to God's people. Others feel the author was simply accounting for the ancestry of King David. But the recurring emphasis is Yahweh's unobtrusive activity in the lives of devout but otherwise ordinary individuals. Through their faithfulness and humble loyalty, he gradually accomplishes his purpose. In this way Ruth illustrates biblical and theological synergism. Far from canceling human-kind's free will, God's sovereignty is demonstrated and accomplished through the willful faithfulness of his servants.

In some ways the title of the book is misleading. Ruth is one of three main characters, and she takes the initiative in the events of ch. 2. But in ch. 3, it is Naomi who takes initiative; in ch. 4, Boaz. One could easily argue that the book centers around Naomi rather than Ruth, since Naomi eloquently states the problem to be addressed (1:20–21) and overshadows her daughter-in-law at the book's climax (4:14–17). But in another sense, neither of them is the central character. "The implication throughout is that God is watching over His people, and that He brings to pass what is good. The book is a book about God" (Cundall and Morris, 242).

Other theological themes in Ruth are derived from this emphasis on God's sovereignty. For those who are committed to his service, there are no mundane or commonplace occurrences. For the Christian, the distinction between sacred and secular is unnecessary, for all of life is sacred. This is beautifully illustrated in the surprise ending of Ruth (4:17), where we learn that these very ordinary folk became the ancestors of Israel's greatest king and, indeed, of the future Messiah.

Finally, some have overemphasized the theological significance of the kinsman-redeemer (*gōʾēl*) in Ruth. It is true that this little book provides valuable insight into the meaning of redemption (see commentaries). But the parallel should not be pressed since Ruth had a legal claim on her kinsman-redeemer, whereas the people of God have no such claim. We rely solely on the mercy of our Redeemer. A more pertinent lesson from the book is the emphasis on family values. Throughout this charming story, the characters are conscious of family ties and their responsibilities. This was, in fact, an integral element in their righteous conduct. This message is needed today.

IV. OUTLINE

COMMENTARY

I. INTRODUCTION (1:1–5)

The author lists the cast of characters and places them in their historical and geographical context. Unlike other historical books in the OT, the main characters here are not important judges, kings, or prophets. Elimelech and his family are pictured as average Israelites, negotiating their way through the everyday affairs of life. They have authentic Northwest Semitic names with appropriate meanings (given the events of the book), though they are not necessarily symbolic names (Campbell, 52–54, 59). Elimelech's name ("My God is King") is perfectly suited to a story about God's sovereign-ty. The significance of Naomi's name is unclear, but it may be an abbreviated name meaning "[God is my] delight," or "Pleasant[ness]." Likewise, precise meanings for the names of the two sons and Orpah are lost to us. There has been much speculation about Ruth's name which is assumed to mean "woman companion/friend," or "satia-tion." (See commentaries for more on the names.)

During the premonarchic period, this family had been forced by famine to leave their home temporarily in order to make a living elsewhere (as others had done from time to time, Ge 12:10, 2Ki 8:1). This relocation con-tinued for a full decade, during which the father died and the two sons mar-ried local Moabite women. Through a series of unexplained tragedies, the two sons also died. Thus this brief introduc-tion graphically explains the problem (see "Content and Structure" above), which will gradually be addressed in the book. In rapid and succinct narra-tion, the author describes how these three women came to be alone and helpless. Bereaved of husband and chil-dren and past her childbearing years (1:11), Naomi found herself in the most extreme and desperate circum-stances possible for an Israelite woman. Having just met Naomi, the reader is already sympathetic to her plight and anxious to see it resolved.

II. NAOMI AND RUTH RETURN TO BETHLEHEM (1:6–22)

The point of this unit is revealed in the repetition of the word *return* (*šûb*, variously translated **"go back," "return home,"** and **"turn back"**), which is used twelve times in seventeen verses. In vv.6 and 22 it serves as an inclusio, a kind of literary envelope for the inter-

vening verses. The unit opens with Naomi returning to her homeland with her daughters-in-law (although the Hebrew verbs of v.5 are all singular and the exact role of the two younger women is unclear). Midway (vv.12–14) Orpah obeyed her mother-in-law's advice and returned (v.12) to her home, not to be mentioned again. Finally, v.22 contains a double refer-ence to returning, which is obscured by the NIV (cf. RSV). The Hebrew applies the expression "who had returned from Moab" to Ruth (Campbell, 77–80). Thus Naomi and Orpah **return** to their respective homes. But in a peculiar and surprising way, Ruth "returns" by ac-companying her mother-in-law to a land she had never seen before.

A. Ruth's Determination (1:6–18)

With nothing to keep her in Moab, Naomi prepared to return to Bethle-hem. News had reached her that Yah-weh had visited (*pāqad*, NIV's **"come to the aid of"**) Judah. This is covenant language, often used to denote divine activity that may be positive or negative depending on the circumstances when God arrives. "When God visits, every-thing depends on the state of affairs He finds" (Cundall and Morris, 252).

Having lost every source of security and comfort, Naomi was returning to a life of loneliness and despair. As much as she must have longed to take her daughters-in-law with her, she realized the sacrifice involved. Marriage was the only career available for a woman in the ancient Near East and the only source of stability and security. Moabite women living in Judah would have few suitors. But if they remained in Moab, their chances for a new life were much better. For this reason, Naomi took it upon herself to remove her last source of comfort—her daughters-in-law (vv.8–9).

At their refusal to say good-bye (v.10), Naomi countered with the impracticality, even impossibility, of their experiencing a life of joy and security with her. Her reference is to the OT practice of levirate marriage, whereby the brother of a deceased (and childless) man marries the widow in order to raise up an heir for the deceased (Dt 25:5–6). But since in this case there were no more brothers, nor prospects for more, Naomi insisted that the two young women seek marriage in their homeland (vv.11–13).

The author of this book expresses his theology through the speeches of his characters. Naomi's **"The Lord's hand has gone out against me!"** (v.13) reflects the main theological motif of the book; viz., with Yahweh, there is no such thing as happenstance.

There is nothing in the text that leads us to condemn Orpah for obeying her mother-in-law. Instead, v.14 contrasts her with Ruth to heighten the surpassing love and commitment of Ruth. One simply chose "to become a wife again, the other to remain a daughter" (Cassel, 19). Ruth's expression of devotion (vv.16–17) has become classic. Her decision to be buried in Naomi's homeland reflects a commitment of life itself. Even in death, Ruth will never abandon Naomi.

B. The Arrival in Bethlehem (1:19–22)

Upon their return, Naomi was hardly recognizable due to the years of hardship. She instructed the women of the city (presumably the men were working the harvest, v.22) to stop calling her "Pleasant." Her new name, "Bitter," graphically illustrates the contrast between her former life and her present circumstances. Again, Naomi does not credit her misfortune to fate or chance (cf. v.13). She is convinced

that Yahweh is over all, and she uses a rare name for him (*šadday*) that emphasizes his irresistible strength.

This section's concluding verse (v.22) summarizes; Naomi has recently returned from Moab and is fully aware of her dire circumstances. By her side stands the faithful but hardly noticeable **Moabitess.** The author has given no suggestion that Ruth may ultimately provide the answer to Naomi's plight. He has, however, prepared us for the next unit by relating the time of year, **as the barley harvest was beginning.**

III. RUTH GLEANS IN THE FIELD OF BOAZ (2:1–23)

This chapter may be divided into three units. The first and last scenes (vv.1–3 and vv.18–23 respectively) are of Naomi and Ruth in conversation. These serve as a frame for the events in the field of Boaz (vv.4–17).

A. Ruth Goes Out to Glean (2:1–3)

Ch. 2 opens with an additional bit of background information necessary for the full impact of the story. Naomi had an in-law named Boaz, a man of considerable means and reputation. (The significance of his name is uncertain. See commentaries.)

V.2 provides insight into the OT's provisions for the very poor. During the harvest period, a farmer was prohibited from reaping his field to the edges and gathering the leftover sheaves (Lev 19:9; 23:22). These were left for the needy. Ruth, as the younger of the two, nobly volunteers to go into the fields to collect what she can. It just so happened (NIV **"As it turned out"**), Ruth worked in the field of Boaz that day. This phrase in v.3 makes it clear that Ruth was unaware of the significance of the "chance" encounter about to be described. At the same time, the author is driving home his point that God was at work behind apparently insignificant events.

B. Ruth and Boaz Meet (2:4–17)

When Boaz comes from the city to inspect his laborers, he notices the industrious young woman gleaning in his field. Upon inquiry he learns that she is **the Moabitess** recently returned with Naomi. The author reminds us of Ruth's nationality six times, and it was obviously integral to his message.

Boaz addresses Ruth directly (v.8) and takes actions to provide for her safety and well-being during the workday. It is possible that his form of address (**"my daughter"**) reflects a disparity in their ages (Cundall and Morris, 274). He encourages her to remain close to the young women reaping in his field (v.9). This would provide her a more favorable position than any other gleaners and would insure her success. Upon her expression of gratitude and bewilderment that he should show such kindness, Boaz explains that he was aware of her personal sorrow and misfortune (vv.10–11). He concludes with a brief prayer that Yahweh would honor her faithfulness and sacrifice (v.12). Little did Boaz know that he would be Yahweh's instrument in answering this prayer.

Ruth responds in deep humility and gratitude, acknowledging how much his kindness has comforted her (v.13). Her words **"spoken kindly to"** (lit. "spoken to the heart of") portray a beautiful picture that is lost in English translation. His actions must have meant a great deal to her. "They represent the first cheerful thing recorded as happening to her since the death of her husband in Moab" (Cundall and Morris, 277). After widowhood, exile, and acute poverty, her encounter with Boaz was a turning point in her life.

But Boaz's kindness did not stop here. At mealtime he gave her special attention and extra food (v.14). After lunch, he made provisions for Ruth to have more than the leftover sheaves; the harvesters were ordered to leave stalks behind intentionally for her to gather (vv.15–16). The result of her day's work was **an ephah** (v.17), an impressive amount for a gleaner.

C. Ruth Relates These Events to Naomi (2:18–23)

Upon seeing Ruth's ephah of barley and her leftovers from lunch, Naomi was anxious to know the human source for such unexpected blessings (vv. 18–19). When she understood that her **close relative,** Boaz, was responsible, she broke out in praise of Yahweh, who is consistently the great moving force behind the events of this story. Boaz is identified as a **kinsman-redeemer** (gōʾēl). This is the designation used for the kinsman who was responsible for, among other things, insuring family property. In Israelite society, all real property belonged ultimately to Yahweh; it was not possible legally to purchase another family's land. But in hard times, one could sell the land temporarily (i.e., as a sort of lease). It was the responsibility of the gōʾēl to redeem the property and restore it to the original family owner or the heir. This responsibility naturally merged with the institution of levirate marriage (see above at 1:11–13), whereby the gōʾēl married his dead brother's widow if she was childless. The events of ch. 4 imply that it had become customary for the kinsman-redeemer also to marry the widow in fulfillment of levirate requirements, in order to insure a family line (see discussion there).

Naomi's comment that Yahweh had **"not stopped showing his kindness to . . . the dead"** (v.20) may indicate that she already had hopes that Boaz would fulfill the duties of the *gō'ēl* and preserve the line of Elimelech and Mahlon.

Although Ruth continued to work in the fields of Boaz during the barley and wheat harvests, the author is careful to state that she continued to live with Naomi (v.23). This serves as a reminder of her absolute and undivided loyalty to her mother-in-law. Although some modern readers would be skeptical about Ruth's sincerity and suspect ulterior motives, the text gives no indication of this. In fact, Hebrew narratives do not generally employ characters with hidden agendas unexposed to the reader. Every indication is that the author is describing ordinary people moving in and out of the complexities of life in an exemplary fashion. Boaz the local farmer, the bereaved Naomi, and her daughter-in-law recently returned from Moab all behave in a manner worthy of emulation. This is especially important for a proper understanding of ch. 3.

IV. RUTH'S REQUEST OF BOAZ THE KINSMAN (3:1–18)

Similar to the structure of ch. 2, an encounter between Ruth and Boaz (vv.6–15) is framed by paragraphs of dialogue between Ruth and Naomi (vv.1–5; 16–18).

A. Naomi's Instructions to Ruth (3:1–5)

After the seven weeks of barley and wheat harvests (2:23), Naomi decides to take the initiative. She has Ruth's best interests in mind. After Naomi's old age and death, Ruth's life as an unprotected, widowed foreigner would be difficult. But marriage could alter her situation. She expresses her desire to provide for Ruth a **home** (*mānôah,* cognate to word for "rest" in 1:9). The

season of harvest was ending, and Boaz would be spending the night on the threshing floor, away from the crowded city. The time seemed appropriate for Ruth to make her request for marriage.

Naomi encouraged Ruth to look her best and secretly to observe Boaz's actions. At the desired moment, when Boaz was comfortably asleep, Ruth was to **uncover his feet and lie down** (v.4). The full significance of these instructions is not known to us. Commentators have offered many explanations; among them the following are plausible: the exposure of his **feet** to the cold was to awaken Boaz; her position at his feet was one of humility in preparation to present a petition; or **feet** is a euphemism for sexual organs. It is best to admit that we do not know the full implications of Ruth's actions. They reflect an ancient custom now lost to us. What is clear is that Boaz understood Ruth to be proposing marriage as a function of his kinsman's role (vv.10–13).

B. Ruth and Boaz at the Threshing Floor (3:6–15)

The author has carefully and artistically created an air of mystery in this unit that centers around a "contrived ambiguity" (Campbell, 130–31). Each element in the narrative contributes to the desired effect. The secrecy of Ruth's mission, the privacy **at the far end of the grain pile,** the darkness of midnight and early dawn in which the encounter takes place, the danger of being discovered, and the ambiguity of Ruth's actions all contribute to the aura of suspense and anticipation. Ruth's request is an honorable one and does not constitute anything of an illicit nature. But she has placed herself in a compromising situation, and the audience is immediately aware that impropriety is possible, perhaps imminent.

This is heightened by the recurrence of the word **"to lie down"** (eight times in vv.4–14), which frequently in Hebrew has clear sexual connotations. The audience is suddenly left with the question: will the characters continue to act in righteousness or not?

Ruth carefully followed the instructions of her mother-in-law. But at the moment of disclosure (v.9), she uses a graphic metaphor when she asks Boaz to **spread the corner** (lit. "wing") of his **garment** over her. Again we are confronted with an ancient custom, the meaning of which is not entirely clear. Garments were frequently used symbolically in the Bible (2Ki 2:13; 9:13) and elsewhere in the ancient Near East (e.g., occasionally in Nuzi customs). This particular metaphor is used in Eze 16:8 for the commitment of marriage. This symbolic language further creates a wordplay with Boaz's statement in 2:12 where he asserts that Ruth has found security under the "wings" of the God of Israel. In essence, her request was to find further security under the wings of Boaz.

The suspense and ambiguity of the narrative are soon resolved. Not only does Boaz behave nobly, but decisively and honestly. He is genuinely honored and surprised by Ruth's request for marriage, for he assumed she would have preferred a younger man. He states that **this kindness** (*ḥeseḏ*, "loyalty") is greater than her earlier expression, presumably referring to her faithfulness to Naomi (v.10). The implication is that Ruth has consistently given higher priority to family obligations than to her own personal well-being. The audience is given assurance of a happy ending by his **"I will do for you all you ask"** (v.11). He assures her that over the last two months it has become obvious to everyone in Bethlehem that she is an attractive prospect for mar-

riage. But in a surprising twist, he informs Ruth that there is another man closer in relationship than he (vv.12–13). This was apparently news to Ruth, though Naomi must surely have known it. Reasons for Naomi's silence about this relative are unknown. She must have favored Boaz as the prospective husband for Ruth. Boaz apparently did not consider marrying Ruth without first giving preference to the closer relative, even though he held the advantage. His integrity is exemplary.

To avoid any appearance of impropriety, he advises Ruth to leave before dawn to remain undetected (v.14). He sends her back to Naomi with a generous portion of the grain (v.15). Again, Ruth and Boaz have acted admirably in admittedly delicate circumstances. "It is not prudery which compels the conclusion that there was no sexual intercourse at the threshing floor; it is the utter irrelevance of such a speculation" (Campbell, 138).

C. Ruth's Report to Naomi (3:16–18)

When Ruth returns, Naomi advises her to wait patiently and expectantly for an answer that day. Naomi apparently has great confidence in Boaz's character.

V. BOAZ MARRIES RUTH (4:1–22)

The narrative now moves quickly to its climax in which all of the problems of ch. 1 are resolved.

A. The Legal Transaction in the City Gate (4:1–12)

Unlike the secluded events of the previous chapter, the scene here is the most public arena in any ancient Israelite city, the city gate. This was the site for important assemblies and the only proper place for legal business. Boaz knew the nearer kinsman would pass that way, so he positioned himself strategically in view. When the unnamed relative was seated, Boaz assembled the necessary elders (v.2) and began the legal proceedings.

In v.3 we learn for the first time of a piece of agricultural land belonging to Naomi. It was apparently a share in the common field that was Elimelech's. OT law was clear that a family's real property was inalienable (cf. 1Ki 21:3 for the strength of this sentiment). In Naomi's poverty, the land would be sold, but must be redeemed by a kinsman-redeemer so that the property was not lost to the family. These are the circumstances Boaz brought to the attention (lit. "I will uncover your ear," v.4) of the closer relative.

After the unnamed kinsman declared his intention to redeem Naomi's property, Boaz added a condition to the transaction: marriage to Ruth. Though scholars are uncertain, it appears that popular custom had associated levirate marriage (Dt 25:5–6) as a further responsibility of the kinsman-redeemer. The practices of the kinsman-redeemer and levirate marriage shared the same legal and societal principles. And since these were the same principles undergirding all Israelite law and custom, "the juxtaposition of redemption and levirate practices in Ruth is a natural one" (Campbell, 132–37, but see Hubbard, 49–51). Indeed, Ruth assumed Boaz's role as kinsman-redeemer included marriage (3:9, "since you are a kinsman-redeemer").

But the closer relative was unwilling to act as kinsman if it required marriage to the Moabitess. On the surface of it, acquiring the field would be a significant expansion of his own property. But an additional wife would fragment the inheritance, and he felt it might jeopardize his own family. We may assume he was not a man of unlimited resources.

An alternative interpretation translates v.5b as "Ruth the Moabitess, wife of the deceased, *I have acquired (as a wife)* to raise up the name of the deceased over his inheritance" (see Hubbard and Sasson, ad loc.). In this case, the unnamed kinsman would acquire the field, and Boaz would acquire Ruth. The first kinsman would have to buy and maintain the field but eventually pass it to Ruth's offspring who would have legal rights to the field. The kinsman would incur much expense, with only temporary gain, jeopardizing his estate and family. While this approach has much to commend it, it misses the thrust of the threshing floor agreement (3:9, 12–13) and violates "the internal consistency of the Ruth story" (Campbell, 146). The NIV is supported by LXX and the consensus of ancient versions. (See Hubbard, 58–61, for summary of the arguments).

At this juncture, the narrator supplies legal background which had become obsolete by his own day (v.7). Presumably a considerable length of time elapsed between the events described and the present edition of the text. Although it is a matter of debate (see commentaries), a legal agreement was ratified by the strange sandal ceremony. The very uniqueness of this act would draw attention to the transaction, which was probably the intention (Morris, 306).

After the two men had agreed upon the appropriate course of action (v.8), Boaz addressed the assembly and summarized the agreement to which they were witnesses (vv.9–10). The assembly responded with a blessing first for Ruth and then for Boaz (vv.11–12). For Ruth, they invoked Yahweh to make her like Rachel and Leah who **built up the house of Israel.** They also prayed that the family of Ruth and Boaz would be like that of Perez. Specifically they recalled that Perez, who was in fact an ancestor of Boaz (vv.18–21), was the son of Judah by Tamar (Gen 38). In other words, they compare Boaz and Ruth to another unusual example of levirate marriage that Yahweh had blessed abundantly.

B. Marriage and the Birth of Obed (4:13–17)

In one laconic verse (v.13), nearly every problem presented in ch. 1 meets a solution: Ruth remarries, Yahweh grants immediate conception, and a son is born (a distinct contrast to Ruth's ten barren years in Moab). But after this verse, Boaz leaves center stage. Nor is Ruth the central figure. Suddenly Naomi comes again to the foreground. **The women** (v.14) who heard her complaint against Yahweh in 1:20–21 now return to acknowledge Yahweh as the source of her blessings. When enumerating those blessings, they mention first her new grandson who will sustain her in her old age. But the newborn baby is not the greatest of Naomi's blessings. It is a beautiful irony that they speak next of her daughter-in-law, Ruth, who stood quietly by when Naomi bitterly complained about her lot in life (1:20–21). Yet by Ruth's faithfulness and excellent character, Naomi's circumstances reversed, and her complaints were answered. It is interesting that in such a tender book (and one in which words are so carefully chosen) "love" is reserved for this climax to describe Ruth's feelings for her mother-in-law. What an astounding assertion it is to say that Ruth **"is better to you than seven sons"** in a book in which the birth of a son has been the all-consuming need! V.16 contains an interesting word

that forms an inclusio with 1:5 to round out the book. Naomi takes into her arms the **child** (*yeled*, "lad"), the same word applied to Mahlon and Kilion in 1:5. The narrator has taken us from the point where Naomi was bereaved of her two sons to this stage where she now holds this new child, the son of Ruth and Boaz (Campbell, 56, 164). Naomi was finally part of a family again, with a loving and fulfilling role to play. "The babe in a sense symbolized it all, and Naomi gave herself over to caring for him" (Cundall and Morris, 314).

All of the problems of ch. 1 have been resolved, and we have arrived at a happy conclusion. But before the genealogy, the story ends with a terse sentence containing an unexpected disclosure. Naomi's friends named the child Obed, who was none other than the father of Jesse, the father of David (v.17). The son born in these bizarre circumstances to a Moabite woman became the grandfather of Israel's greatest king. And, of course, the gospel writer most taken with Jewish concerns did not fail to see the significance of Ruth's presence in the lineage of the Messiah (Mt 1:5). Yahweh's purpose had been accomplished through the lives of ordinary but faithful individuals. A life committed to his service meets no insignificant turns. All of life becomes sacred.

C. Genealogy of David (4:18–22)

The closing genealogy has been commonly called a later addition. Though it bears the marks of an appendix, this does not necessarily mean it is secondary. Indeed, it appears to form a closure (along with the birth of Obed) and thus forms an important literary unit in the book (see introduction and Berlin, 107–10).

BIBLIOGRAPHY

Berlin, Adele. *Poetics and Interpretation of Biblical Narrative*. Sheffield: Almond, 1983.

Campbell, Edward F. *Ruth: A New Translation with Introduction, Notes, and Commentary*. AB 7. Garden City, N.Y.: Doubleday, 1975.

Cassel, Paulus. "The Book of Ruth," *Commentary on the Holy Scriptures*, vol. 2. Edited by J. P. Lange. Grand Rapids: Zondervan, 1960.

Cundall, Arthur E. and Leon Morris. *Judges and Ruth: Introduction and Commentary*. TOTC 7. Downers Grove: InterVarsity, 1968.

Hubbard, Robert L., Jr. *The Book of Ruth*. NICOT. Grand Rapids: Eerdmans, 1988.

Keil, C. F. and F. Delitzsch. *Biblical Commentary on the Old Testament*, vol. 2. Grand Rapids: Eerdmans, 1976.

Myers, Jacob M. *The Linguistic and Literary Form of the Book of Ruth*. Leiden: E. J. Brill, 1955.

Sasson, Jack J. *Ruth: A New Translation with a Philological Commentary and a Formalist-Folklorist Interpretation*. Baltimore: Johns Hopkins University Press, 1979.

Smith, Louise P. "The Book of Ruth." IB. Vol. 2. Nashville: Abingdon, 1953.

1 AND 2 SAMUEL

Frank Anthony Spina

INTRODUCTION

I. TITLE, LITERARY HISTORY, AND HISTORIOGRAPHY

A. Title

First and Second Samuel were originally a single work, as the Qumran Samuel scroll (4QSamᵃ), Talmudic references, and Masoretic notes indicate (McCarter, *1 Samuel*, p. 3). But because of length, Samuel was incorporated into the Jewish community's Greek Bible (Septuagint [LXX]; third–second centuries B.C.E.) as a two-volume work. The Latin Bible (Vulgate) continued this practice. Not until the sixteenth century was Samuel treated as two books in Hebrew traditions. Dividing the corpus in this way led to the curious result that Samuel does not appear in the second volume that bears his name.

According to some ancient Jewish sources, "Samuel" was so titled because the prophet featured in the work wrote it (and Judges). But today scholars suggest rather that the name derives from the fact that Samuel was featured prominently in the book. In the Septuagint, 1–2Sa is called 1–2 Kingdoms, being grouped with 1–2Ki as 1–4 Kingdoms.

B. Literary History

Traditionally, Jews and Christians believed that Samuel was comprised of eyewitness accounts of the prophets Samuel, Nathan, and Gad (1Ch 29:29). But most modern critical scholars contend that Samuel consists of disparate sources. They isolate sources supporting the monarchy (1Sa 9–10) and some discouraging the monarchy (1Sa 8); an ark tradition (1Sa 4–6; 2Sa 6); cryptic hero accounts (2Sa 21:15–22; 23:8–39); originally independent poems (1Sa 2:1–10; 2Sa 1:19–27; 22:2–51 [cf. Ps 18]; 23:1–7); a cycle of stories about Saul; the account of David's rise; the story of succession to the throne of David (2Sa 9–24; 1Ki 1–2); and more).

Using the model of Pentateuchal source criticism, this heterogeneity was observed because of thematic tensions, duplications, or outright contradictions in the materials themselves (McCarter, *1 Samuel*, p. 12). For example, Saul was chosen by lot in 1Sa 10:17–27 but by public acclamation in 1 Sa 11. Yahweh appears to reject him twice (1Sa 13, 15). David is Saul's armor-bearer and personal musician in 1 Sa 16, but unknown to the king in 1Sa 17. There seem to be two versions of David's engagement to Saul's daughters (1Sa 18), two accounts of David's defection to the Philistine king at Gath (1Sa 21, 27), and two incidents of his refusal to kill Saul (1Sa 24, 26).

Nevertheless, Martin Noth suggested that Samuel is part of a "Deuteronomistic History" extending from Dt to 2Ki [excluding Ruth]. The exilic author/editor organized the traditions into a unified work propounding a distinctive viewpoint. Others accepted most of Noth's thesis but disagreed either over its precise theological thrust or over how many editorial revisions it underwent (Cross, 274–89; Halpern, 107–20; Nelson, passim; von Rad, 334–47; Van Seters, 249–91; 322–53).

C. Historiography

Many nineteenth-century scholars asserted that Samuel imparted historical information only about the period when it was written (late seventh, early sixth centuries). Thus Samuel was not a suitable source for reconstructing the eras of Samuel, Saul, or David (Halpern, 16–35). Others subsequently argued that at least some Samuel traditions were reliable. Regardless of theological or historiographical overlays, it was believed that much of Samuel was a relatively trustworthy account of Israel's early monarchic period (Rost).

More recently, scholars interested in newer literary approaches have remarked that posing historiographical questions to material like Samuel is illegitimate. Its meaning inheres in its textual structure and "narrative world," not in ostensive historical references.

Advocates of social scientific historical methods urge the use of various sociological models as a means of evaluating biblical texts (Wilson). No text is to be dismissed out of hand as a potential historical source; it has to be tested by appropriate external models, including archaeological data.

Still others assert that the Deuteronomistic history generally and Samuel specifically manifest historiographic intention (Halpern, 266–80). For our purposes, suffice it to say that history is doubtless encoded in Samuel. But the artful nature of the text and the complicated history it reflects suggest that the historicity issue is more complex than previously thought.

II. CANONICAL, THEOLOGICAL, AND LITERARY FACTORS

A. Canonical

Scholarly discussion about canon once focused predominantly on what, why, and when writings were included in the biblical corpus. More recently interest in canon has taken a more theological turn (Childs, *Crisis; Introduction;* Sanders, *Torah; Community;* Spina). Scholars have studied

(1) the hermeneutical *processes* involved in canonizing written traditions;
(2) the final *product* of those processes (=received canonical text); and
(3) the effects of canonical *shape* on innerbiblical exegesis (=interpreting
any biblical part within the context of the biblical whole).

I shall pay more attention to canonical product and shape than
process. Thus the text's final canonical form is the object of study. I also
emphasize that in its present canonical shape Samuel is no longer part of
the Deuteronomistic history, but part of the former prophets (Jos–2Ki)
(Sanders, *Torah,* 52–53; Childs, *Introduction,* 131–32). This means that
one key for interpreting Samuel is the extent to which Israel conforms to
the Mosaic revelation or Torah (cf. Jos 1:7–8). Further, Samuel must be
viewed in the context of the material that precedes (Jos, Jdg) and follows
(1–2Ki).

B. Theological/Literary

As canon, the Bible's ultimate function is theological. Scripture
explicates the nature and interrelationships of God, humankind, and the
world. Samuel is therefore an indispensable and authoritative source for
the believing community's theological reflection. Unfortunately, this
theological aspect has often been downplayed or ignored. Samuel and
other similar texts have been viewed primarily as "historical background."
However, while the historical dimension is important, theological concerns remain paramount. Though Samuel, like the rest of the Bible, is not
systematic theology, it is broadly theological nonetheless. Indeed, properly
understood, Samuel is as theological as Ro or Mk.

Samuel's theology is derivative of its literary makeup (Morgan and
Barton, 203–68). The "Samuel story" focuses on God's direct and indirect
involvement with Israel from the time of Hannah and Samuel to the time
immediately preceding Solomon's accession to the throne. The particularities and vicissitudes of this story raise a number of theological issues.
Considering these issues enhances the believing community's faith and life.
It is precisely the literary artfulness of Samuel that conduces to a profound
theological reading.

Samuel's theology is not direct, didactic, or rationalistic. It is narrative
specific, suggestive, oblique, highly nuanced, often purposefully ambiguous, and carries several possible meanings. This dynamic theological
dimension is embedded in the myriad details of the unfolding story.

In the exposition I will emphasize the role of the "omniscient"
narrator, the allusive nature of the text, the use of vocabulary repetition,
the means of character development, implicit textual features, the importance of what is included in and excluded from a given episode, and the
story line itself (Alter, *Art;* Alter and Kermode, *Literary Guide;* Steinberg).
I have tried to be more suggestive than definitive so that readers can
employ their own textually informed imaginations to reflect on the text's
theological import. Familiarity with the Samuel story is the path to its
theological treasure.

III. OUTLINE

COMMENTARY

I. THE RISE OF SAMUEL, SAUL, AND DAVID (CHS. 1:1–3:21)

A. The Rise of Samuel (Chs. 1–3)

The book of Judges sets the stage for 1–2Sa generally and the first chapters particularly. Judges is structured on the pattern: Israel sins, God sells them into the hand of an enemy, the people "cry out" (z^cq), the deity raises up a deliverer, the latter defeats the enemy, and the land has rest (Jdg 2:10–19; 3:7–16:31). Thus the book asks whether Israel is doomed to this cycle of disobedience, punishment, and delivery, and also whether its leaders are becoming increasingly immoral, as stories featuring Gideon, Jephthah, and Samson suggest (Jdg 8:22–27 [cf. 8:28–9:57]; 10:6–12:7; 13–16).

Jdg also contains episodes in which Israelites severely mistreat other Israel-ites, underscoring the disunity of God's people (Jdg 17–21). A stock phrase intimates that such wickedness was because Israel had no king (Jdg 17:6; 18:1; 19:1; 21:25). This section asks whether a king might reverse this sad state of affairs.

At first the new episode with which 1Sa begins (1:1; see Jdg 13:2; 17:1; 19:1) seems to bypass such concerns (Eslinger, 65). It simply introduces Elkanah, who had two wives: Hannah and Peninnah. Though it seems innoc-uous, the potential for conflict is insin-uated when the narrator reverses the names to emphasize that only Peninnah had children (1:2; cf. Ge 16:1–16; 29:31–30:22).

Trouble soon surfaces (1:3–8). Dur-ing a yearly sacrifice at Shiloh, Elkanah gave his wives unequal sacrificial por-tions as a present. Peninnah and her children received a portion each, while

Hannah received either a double (NIV) portion or a single one with great ceremony (Walters, 388, 390). Regardless, Hannah clearly was singled out for being childless. Peninnah's cruelty added to Hannah's misery.

Hannah suffered silently for years, not even responding to her husband's ministrations (1:7–8). Eventually she vowed to dedicate any son whom God would grant her to lifelong religious service (vv.9–11; cf. Jdg 13:2–5). Still, the only concession she made to actual speech was moving her lips, something that Eli the priest took as a sign of inebriation. When the priest rebuked her, Hannah finally spoke in self-defense. Though he had initially misunderstood, as perhaps Elkanah had (v.8), Eli finally blessed her (vv.12–17). Having spoken at last, Hannah's mood changed and she ate (v.18). The scene ends with worship, after which the party returned home where the Lord answered her prayer, a fact Hannah acknowledged in the naming of the child (vv.19–20; Walters, 405–6).

Does Samuel's birth address the issues raised by Jdg? Will he become a new, righteous judge or a king who keeps the people from doing as they see fit? The narrative tantalizes at this point. We still do not know what role Samuel will play, though his birth is the result of God's remembering his mother (v.19).

We are further tantalized when Hannah appears to renege on her promise by refusing to accompany Elkanah on the next trip to Shiloh. But it turns out that she wanted only to wait till the child was weaned. Her husband accepted her decision, but intriguingly added, **"Only may the LORD make good his word"** (v.23). But what **word** was that? We are not told. In any event, after weaning, the child is presented to Eli (vv.24–28).

Hannah moved from pained silence to inward prayer to bitter expression. She concluded with a doxology (2:1–10) in which she extolled God as a sovereign deity who reverses the fortunes of the powerless and poor, defeats the arrogant and mighty, and disposes of enemies. Moreover, the Lord's strength will prevail, the Lord's enemies will be shattered, and the Lord's anointed will be empowered.

But what did Hannah have in mind? Who were her enemies: Peninnah, Eli, Elkanah? How is the military imagery to be understood? And what do the references to **"king"** and **"anointed"** (="messiah") portend (v.10)? Has Hannah somehow said more than she knew? Do her remarks intimate that Samuel will be the new king?

Instead of answering such questions, the narrative returns to Hophni and Phineas, who were introduced earlier (1:3). Now we learn that they are wicked and have **no regard for the LORD.** They have been seizing sacrificial portions that belong to God (2:13–16). These sinful priests and God's reaction to them (v.17) are sharply contrasted to Samuel, whose service and that of his parents evoke a priestly blessing for more children, the fulfillment of which in addition brings to mind one of the inversions of Hannah's doxology (2:5, 18–21).

As Samuel's position before God and people improved (2:26), the status of Hophni and Phineas deteriorated, for they were lecherous as well as greedy (v.22). Eli attempted to restrain them, but to no avail, for they were now under a divine death sentence (v.25). Eli's failure put him under judgment, too, according to a **man of God** (=prophet; vv.27–29). His priestly house, therefore, would not last as designed but would be replaced by another. As for Hophni and Phineas, they would die on the same day (vv.30–33). The new priestly line was to serve the Lord's anointed, with those left from the old line reduced to begging (vv.35–36). Another reference to God's **anointed** (v.35, *mšḥ*) by the "man of God" seems to confirm Hannah's "prophecy" (v.10, *mšḥ*), even if she did say more than she realized.

Ironically, the appearance of a **man of God** (2:27–36) did not alter the fact that prophetic vision was **rare** in those days (3:1). But this was about to change.

As Samuel was previously contrasted to Eli's corrupt sons (2:12–26), so now he is contrasted to the old priest himself. Eli's inability to perceive that the voice which Samuel heard was God's indicates that his failing eyesight was a spiritual as well as a physical condition (3:2, 5–6). Had this dual malady also been responsible for his surmise that Hannah was drunk (1:14)? Not until the third summons did the priest realize that Yahweh was speaking (3:8–9). At least then he managed to tell Samuel what to do (v.9).

When God called again and Samuel responded, he received a vision (*ḥzn*; cf. 3:1) that confirmed the previous judgment against Eli (2:27–36; 3:11–14). The priest insisted that the reluctant Samuel hold nothing back (vv.15–18). The condemnation notwithstanding, Eli was resigned to God's will (vv.17–18; cf. 1:17; 2:20, 22–25; 3:8–9).

Ch. 3 began by noting that there was more darkness than light in Israel, symbolized by the infrequency of **vision** (*ḥzn*) and Eli's weak eyes. The only light available was provided by the **lamp of God,** which was not yet extinguished (v.3). By the end of the account, God made Samuel's word efficacious, all Israel recognized the

new prophetic ministry, and God's revelation became regular (vv.19–21). For now at least, prophetic light has overcome priestly darkness.

Finally, a phrase in the vision (3:12) reminds us that Elkanah's cryptic remark (1:23) to Hannah was pregnant with meaning: **"May the Lord make good [*yāqēm*] his word [*dᵉḇārô*]."** This corresponds to God's statement: **"I will carry out ['*āqîm*] against Eli everything I spoke [*dibbartî*]."** The idea of God's "confirming"/"making good"/"carrying out a word" occurs in contexts having to do with divine fulfillment of prophetic speech (Walters, 410–12). In this instance, whether Elkanah knew it or not, the **word** that God would confirm was the judgment against the house of Eli particularly (3:12) and the establishment of a prophetic ministry in Israel through Samuel generally.

B. The Ark of God—the Word of Samuel (chs. 4–7)

Virtually without exception, commentators agree that 4:1a concludes ch. 3, and 4:1b begins ch. 4. This is because 4:1a—**"And Samuel's word came to all Israel"**—seems a fitting conclusion to Samuel's establishment as a prophet (cf. 3:19–21) and makes little sense as the beginning of the ark story in chs. 4–6, where Samuel not only says nothing but does not even appear! **Samuel's word,** announced in 4:1a, is not uttered until 7:3. This has led most critics to view the intervening material as having had an independent source of origin and development, only later being inserted into the present narrative (McCarter, *I Samuel,* 23–26; Miller and Roberts, 18–26).

But even if correct, that assessment ignores the final literary and canonical form of the text. As presently shaped, the text emphasizes that God's newly appointed prophet was disregarded. Since the ark story centers on Israel's attempt to ascertain God's will (4:3) and to ensure God's presence in battle, and since when Samuel eventually spoke he called for repentance, the present literary shaping highlights Israel's neglect of prophetic ministry.

Initially, it is unclear why Israel has been defeated (4:2–3). It is also unknown whether being accompanied by the ark will make a difference (cf. 3:3; 4:3–4). Granted, the Philistines and Israelites obviously believed the ark mattered (4:5–9). But the notation that Eli's sons, Hophni and Phineas, were with the ark makes one wonder whether their predicted fate was imminent (cf. 2:25, 34; 3:11–14; 4:4).

In fact, Hophni and Phineas were killed. Further, instead of being benefited by the ark, Israel suffered more than seven times the casualties of the first battle (4:10–11; cf. v.2). One might conclude at this point that the ark was a meaningless relic of Israel's condemned priesthood. Indeed, did not the ark's capture illustrate that this sacerdotal symbol had no efficacy, while the death of Eli's sons demonstrated the power of God's prophetic word that had been spoken by the **man of God** and Samuel?

Was not the response to the ark's capture therefore all the more pitiful? In language reminiscent of Jdg, the Shilonites cried out (z'q) when they heard the news (4:12–13). Eli maintained his composure when he learned of Israel's devastating defeat and even the death of his two sons, but when he heard about the ark, he collapsed, breaking his neck, and died (v.18). Phineas's pregnant wife went into premature labor when she heard the news of the ark and of Eli's and her husband's deaths. Just before she died, she named her baby Ichabod: "[There is]

No Glory" (kbd, **"glory,"** may be an epithet for God). From her point of view, God/The Glory (kbd) had left Israel with the captured ark (vv.19–22).

But a curious ambiguity remains. We have already seen that Eli was not completely reprobate (cf. 1:17; 2:20, 23–25; 3:8–9, 17–18). Here, too, though one is reminded of his poor eyesight, with its hint of spiritual dimness (4:15), the priest's inordinate concern for the ark seemed laudatory (vv.3, 18). His daughter-in-law's reaction, though possibly based on a false theological premise, also seemed genuine (vv.19–22). More significantly, the very next episode (chs. 5–6) cautions against drawing premature conclusions.

When the ark was captured, the Israelites and Philistines both appeared to have concluded mistakenly that God was "in the box." No deity who had done what Yahweh had done to the Egyptians (4.8) could ever be taken prisoner. But the narrator quickly lets us know that the Philistines immediately and the Israelites later would realize their error.

First, the Ashdodites discovered that, after the ark had been placed in Dagon's temple, he fell down. After being stood up, Dagon fell again, this time losing head and hands in the process. This led to a practice that constantly reminded the Philistines of their god's humiliation (5:1–5).

But Dagon did not suffer alone, for Yahweh's **hand** harassed the Philistines, too (5:6–7, 9, 11). They even contributed to their misery by circulating the ark (vv.6–12), in spite of associating (correctly?) God's **hand** with it. Ironically, as Israel had "cried out" (z'q; 4:13) in response to the ark's absence, the Philistines **cried out** (5:10; z'q; cf. v.12) in response to its presence and concluded that they had to get rid of it (v.11).

It is also ironic that the Philistine "clergy" seemed as (more?) informed about the ark as the Israelites (ch. 6). They understood that proper ritual—returning the ark with golden models of tumors and mice—had to accompany recognition of Yahweh's power (6:3–12). They surmised that just as Pharaoh had to release the Israelite slaves or suffer dire consequences, so they had to respond in kind. The priests and diviners were also aware that the ritual only opened up the *possibility* that Yahweh would relent (vv.5–6; cf. v.3b). Thus they established a test to determine whether the events were coincidental. If two untrained and nursing cows, separated from their calves, pulled the cart straight to Beth Shemesh, then Yahweh had to be responsible (vv.7–12).

Does this episode criticize the priestly house of Eli? for not knowing any more about Yahweh and the ark than pagans? Or does it intimate that God cannot be manipulated though a sacerdotal object? Curiously, though Israel used proper rites and personnel when they recovered the ark (6:13–15), an awesome and unpredictable power was still unleashed when some acted disrespectfully (6:19–20). Whether God had ever been "in the box," the Deity simply would not be controlled (6:21–7:1).

Twenty years passed since Samuel was first poised to speak (4:1; 7:2)! All that time the ark remained at Kiriath-Jearim with Eleazar (7:1). During the same period Israel lamented, though they had **rejoiced** initially (6:13; 7:2). When Samuel finally spoke, he summoned Israel to repent of idolatry as a precondition for future military success. Either Israel's idolatry during the period of the Judges (cf. Jdg 2:10–13,

17–19; 3:7; 6:10, 25–32; 8:23–27, 33–34; 9:4; 10:6, 10, 13–14, 16; 17–18) or some unspecified act of idolatry was in view. In any case, Israel repented (7:3–4).

The efficacy of this became immediately evident, for the Philistines approached again while Samuel interceded (7:5–6). Israel reacted this time (cf. 4:1–3) by imploring Samuel to continue **crying out** (z^eq) (v.8) to God on their behalf. Samuel complied and offered a sacrifice (v.9), whereupon God panicked the encroaching army (v.10; cf. 2:10), allowing the Israelites to finish the operation (vv.7–11). This pattern of **crying out** and God's answering accords with that in Jdg, a point underscored by the remark that Samuel had judged (v.6; NIV **"leader"**) at Mizpah.

The "judges" model, as opposed to the "ark" model, spelled victory. Indeed, Samuel and the "judgeship" he represented are affirmed by the comment that throughout his lifetime the Lord's hand was against the Philistines, that captured territory was regained, and that there was even peace with the Amorites (7:13–14). First as prophet (3:19–21) and later as "judge" (7:15–17), Samuel succeeded where Israel with the ark failed.

But Samuel also built an altar (7:17; cf. vv.9–10), perhaps to show that he was capable of priestly functions as well. Still, the actual "hero" of the story is Yahweh, a fact commemorated by Samuel's naming the site Ebenezer (="stone of help"; 7:12; cf. 4:1).

C. The Rise and Sudden Fall of Saul (chs. 8–15)

Samuel's success was short-lived since he, like Eli (2:22–25), had to be told that Joel and Abijah, his sons whom he had appointed judges, were corrupt. As the Eli episode led to a new era of prophetic leadership in Israel, so this episode led to a new period of royal leadership. Samuel's age and his sons' failures compelled the people to ask for a king to judge them (8:1–5).

In the larger canonical context, in addition to Hannah's reference to a king (2:10), Moses had put forth conditions should Israel ever opt for a monarch (Dt 17:14–20). Gideon rejected a request that he and his sons rule, since that was Yahweh's role (Jdg 8:22–23). Gideon's wisdom was confirmed by the disastrous kingship of his son Abimelech (Jdg 9). Also, as noted, though Jdg 17–21 indicated the need for a king, 1Sa 1–7 emphasized that the prophet Samuel was providing adequate leadership. Thus, up to this point the canon (1) qualifies kingship (Dt 17:14–20); (2) condemns it (Jdg 8:22–23; 9); (3) anticipates (Jdg 17–21) and predicts it (1Sa 2:10); but delivers a prophet (1Sa 1–7). Kingship in Israel was a complicated proposition.

Though the people obviously acknowledged Samuel's authority in their request, he was displeased. So was the Lord, who construed the request as a rejection of divine kingship (8:6–8). Nevertheless, God told Samuel to accede, but also to inform the people that one day they would **cry out** because of their king (z'q; cf. Jdg 3:9, 15; 4:3; 6:6–7; 10:10–14; 1Sa 7:8), but God would not respond (vv.9–18). Undaunted, Israel insisted on a king, and Yahweh told Samuel to relent (vv.19–21).

1Sa 9:1 appears to launch a new story (cf. 1:1). Indeed, it takes a while (9:15–17) to realize that the newly introduced protagonist Saul was slated to be the new king. First, one learns only that he was Kish's son, tall and good looking, and dutifully searching for his father's runaway livestock (vv.1–5). The encounter with Samuel seemed accidental and completely related to the lost animals (vv.6–14).

Yahweh (and Samuel) simultaneously established and attempted to control the kingship. Yahweh told Samuel to appoint a "leader" (ngd not mlk [= "king"]) because Israel's cry under Philistine oppression had been heard (9:15–16). But Yahweh had already saved Israel from Philistia (7:8). God acted at this point as though the kingship were not due to the people's rejection of divine rule. At the same time, the Lord said that this "leader" would "govern" ('ṣr; lit. "restrain" [an ironic pun?]) rather than "judge" (8:5). Was Yahweh refusing to grant the people exactly what they requested? Regardless, there are two counter impulses present: (1) the kingship was based on sinful demands and therefore was problematic, and (2) Yahweh elected an obedient son to be the new leader.

When Samuel anointed Saul (10:1; cf. 2:10; 9:16), he told him that he would find the asses, receive bread from three men bearing uneven burdens, and prophesy with other prophets while being **changed into a different person** (vv.2–6; cf. 9:3, 7). Such signs confirmed Saul's appointment. Then Samuel issued two orders, one open-ended (v.7) and one specific (v.8). How was Saul to know which was operative, or was the first merely a statement that the king was empowered to act (Eslinger, 323)? However this question is answered, Saul began on a positive note. At the same time, Samuel's ability to predict the signs reminds one of his prediction that the kingship would fail (8:10–18).

God changed Saul's heart before the signs were fulfilled (10:9), perhaps to hasten the course of action (Eslinger, 326). Or it may be that the statement is a presummary. Curiously, only the third sign is elaborated on. Is this to emphasize the reaction of the people (vv.10–12)? And do the people simply ask a rhetorical question, or do they in fact connect the prophetic movement and Saul (Eslinger, 331)?

The text invites other questions. Did Saul keep the matter of the kingship secret (10:14–16) because he thought his uncle would not believe him, or because he was himself incredulous or thought himself unfit (cf. 9:21; 10:20–24)? Did Samuel's negative word (10:17–19) counter God's positive one (9:15–16)? Since Saul was already chosen, did God and Samuel manipulate the lots (10:20–21)?

Samuel exercised control by informing the people of divinely sanctioned **regulations** governing **the kingship** (10:25). But the people still got most of what they wanted and were pleased (vv.24, 26; cf. v.27). It remained an open question whether Saul, who had done everything asked of him, could survive the countervailing forces at work.

His first test came when Nahash the Ammonite threatened the Jabeshites with humiliation and enslavement (11:1–2). But Nahash was as stupid or arrogant as he was diabolical, for he gave the elders time to find a deliverer (v.3). When Saul was informed, God's Spirit spurred him into action (vv.4–7; cf. Jdg 14:6, 19; 15:14). The king issued a call to arms by invoking Samuel's name along with his own; the summons was sanctioned by Yahweh (vv.7–8). Then, after making the Ammonites believe that Jabesh would surrender, Saul attacked and defeated the enemy (vv.9–11).

Saul succeeded by being under God's Spirit, demonstrating military acumen (11:11) and mustering ten times more troops from his own territory as from elsewhere (v.8). He also credited God

and refused to punish detractors (vv.12–13). Samuel affirmed Saul by reconfirming the kingship and leading worship. Still the question remains: Was the kingship affirmed because it had operated on the "judges" model rather than a "nations" model (cf. 8:5: **"a king . . . such as all the other nations have"**)?

Samuel's speech suggests an affirmative answer. When the people agreed that he was above reproach (12:1–5) and that the former way of dealing with difficulties worked well (vv.6–11), they had to admit that there was no legitimate rationale for demanding a king. The victory against Philistia (7:2–17) and Ammon (11:1–15) proved that the "judges" model worked (cf. 12:11).

At the same time, Samuel glossed over his sons' corruption (v.2), which the people *and* the narrator said was the reason for requesting a king (8:1–5). Samuel made it sound as though the people first demanded a king in response to Nahash's threat (12:12). In spite of the way he played down his sons' role, by emphasizing the kingship's conditional character he ensured its subordination to other values (vv.13–15). Yahweh confirmed Samuel's argument with a miracle (vv.16–18). The prophet's last words about the kingship reflected his earlier point of view, and in addition provided a hermeneutical key for interpreting the subsequent history of the monarchy (vv.20–25; Eslinger, 408–10).

Samuel's notion of a kingship informed by a "judges" model was immediately compromised. The formula in 13:1 is the same as that used for succeeding Israelite kings, indicating that a new era had been inaugurated (cf. 2Sa 5:4; 1Ki 14:21; 15:1, 9–10, 25, 33, etc.; Childs, *Introduction*, 271). Now, instead of acting under the impetus of God's Spirit (cf. 11:6–7), Saul conscripted troops ahead of time (13:2). But he was still unprepared, for when Jonathan provoked the Philistines, he had to draft more troops (note how Saul took credit for his son's attack; vv.3–4). This worsened the odds. Why had Saul allowed troops to return home (v.2)? Was it because of inexperience or incompetence? Things were made worse when some soldiers hid while others deserted (vv.5–7).

Samuel had promised to come to Gilgal (10:8), the battle site (13:4, 7) where Saul was dutifully waiting. But when Samuel inexplicably did not show, the king offered sacrifices (vv.8–9). Samuel then appeared; demanded an explanation; and, brushing aside Saul's excuse, announced that his dynasty would not endure. Worse, God had already selected a replacement "after his own heart" (vv.10–14).

Had Saul usurped a priestly or prophetic prerogative? That is a typical interpretation, but others made similar offerings without censure (cf. 1Sa 14:33–35; 2Sa 6:12–14, 17–18). Besides, was not Samuel partially to blame for being late? If Saul violated an official regulation (10:25), we are not told what it was. Was Saul set up by vague or contradictory instructions (10:7–8; Gunn, 40–56)? Had Samuel fulfilled his own prophecy (8:10–18)? Or had Saul departed from the old ways (e.g., the Spirit of the Lord had not fallen) so that the sacrifice indicated a lack of faith rather than a liturgical violation? The narrator has temporarily withheld the answer to such questions.

In any case, Samuel withdrew, leaving Saul and Jonathan to face the Philistines alone with only six hundred troops. Worse, the Philistine monopoly on iron technology left Saul's army with only two swords (13:19–22)!

This discouraging situation affords an insight into Saul's behavior.

Whereas Saul felt compelled to seek the Lord's favor in Samuel's absence (13:12), Jonathan was unfazed by Philistine superiority and was blithely dependent on God. Ignoring standard military procedure, Jonathan and his armor-bearer (with only one sword!) crept to a **Philistine outpost** without telling anyone (14:1). Such daring if not brash initiative underscores the timidity of Saul and his forces. Also, perhaps it should not go unnoticed that Saul had in his company Ahijah, a priest who belonged to Eli's deposed line (vv.2–3).

Jonathan believed that odds meant nothing to Yahweh (v.6), so he devised a test whereby enemy reaction would signal attack or retreat. Receiving a positive sign, he attacked and inflicted minimal damage, whereupon a divinely induced panic beset the whole Philistine army (14:8–15).

When the Israelite army noticed the tumult, they checked and discovered that Jonathan was missing. Saul reacted by calling for the ark and presiding priest (14:19), which was reminiscent of Israel's prior futile actions (ch. 4). Jonathan's actions in contrast motivated defectors to return (v.21). While Jonathan's initiative enabled Saul to exploit the confusion, the victory was clearly God's (vv.20–23; cf. vv.6, 10, 12, 15, 23).

Whereas Jonathan prompted a divinely inspired victory, Saul underachieved and fostered sin. The king's rash order that forbade eating till evening endangered Jonathan and drove the troops to cultic violations (14:24–33). Saul corrected the desecration (vv.33–35), but he and his priests received no revelatory word about the next course of action (vv.36–37). Ironically, though the priests failed, Saul prayed directly to God and learned that Jonathan had violated his oath. However, as though God had provided the information to embarrass Saul, the troops protected Jonathan because of the way God had used him (vv.38–45).

Saul's ineptitude and ill-conceived oath prevented a decisive victory and forced him to face the Philistines again. To be sure, he tallied a few victories and his family grew, but unquestionably his record was undistinguished (14:46–52).

After this, Samuel mysteriously reappeared (cf. 13:15) and commanded Saul as though nothing untoward had happened. Noting that Yahweh had sent him to anoint Saul over God's (not Saul's!) people, Samuel ordered the king to destroy the Amalekites (15:1–3; cf. Jos 2:10; 6:18, 21, 26; 10:1, 28, 35, 37, 39, 40; 11:11, 12, 20, 21).

Saul obeyed unhesitatingly and even demonstrated initiative by warning the Kenites in advance (cf. Jdg 4:11, 17–22). But the king's obedience was at best partial, for he spared Agag the Amalekite king and did not destroy the best part of the booty (15:4–9). So the Lord condemned Saul's action, prompting Samuel to cry out (*z'q*; vv.10–11; cf. 13:11–14).

Instead of being poised for rebuke, Saul was so obtuse that he was off erecting a monument to himself (15:12). When Samuel confronted him, he protested his innocence and then blamed the soldiers, saying that their actions were motivated by cultic concerns (vv.13–21; Sternberg, 482–515). Saul at last confessed when Samuel said that God demanded unqualified obedience rather than compliance with perceived cultic regulations. But by then it was too late: Samuel rejected the confession! When Saul tore Samuel's robe, it symbolized that his kingship had been torn from him (15:24–28).

Saul's blaming the soldiers/people (*'m*; 15:15, 21, 24) was somewhat ironic in that it was their demands that had led to a king (8:7–10, 19, 21). It is also ironic that the Lord **was grieved** (*nhm*; cf. RSV: "repented"; 15:11, 35) over having made Saul king but would not **change his mind** (= "repent"/*nhm*; 15:29) regarding the judgment. And it is curious that God is referred to here as the **Glory of Israel**, the very epithet (*kbd*) used when Israel thought that God had disappeared with the ark (cf. 4:21).

Samuel finally allowed Saul to worship, but it was the last time the two men would be together. Having slain Agag as Saul was to have done, Samuel left the king alone (15:30–35).

D. The Rise of David and Further Decline of Saul (chs. 16–31)

1. David Anointed (chs. 16–17)

As the story turns to the selection of Saul's successor, the narrator and Yahweh know what no one else, including Samuel, knows (16:1). Samuel was even afraid to anoint a replacement. So Yahweh instructed him to say that he had to celebrate priestly rites with Jesse and his sons (cf. 15:29). The townspeople's reaction proved that the situation was indeed tense, but Samuel's dissimulation worked (16:2–5).

Samuel thought Jesse's first son was the nominee, presumably because of appearance (cf. 9:2; 10:23). But Yahweh insisted on "internal" criteria (16:7); subsequently Samuel at least knew who was *not* the Lord's choice (vv.6–10). Inexplicably, Jesse had to be prodded to introduce David (Rosenberg, 130–32). Yet this handsome lad was the one chosen (Sternberg, 354–64). He was anointed on God's explicit instruction and empowered by the Spirit (vv.11–13).

Simultaneously, God victimized Saul with an evil spirit! This paved David's way into Saul's court, since someone was needed who could minister to the king. One servant recommended David because of his musical ability, military record, good looks, and the fact that Yahweh was **with** him. (If true, why had Jesse been reluctant to present David?) So Saul summoned David, whose father sent him to the king loaded with bread, wine, and a goat, interestingly all items involved in the signs attesting *Saul's* election (cf. 10:1–11). David became Saul's armor-bearer, ingratiated himself to the king, and with music induced the evil spirit to leave Saul after an attack (16:19–23). The king was now at the mercy of God *and* David!

As he suffered in comparison to Jonathan (ch. 14), Saul (and the Israelite army) was (were) shamed by contrast to David in the Goliath incident (ch. 17). When the absurdly oversized and heavily armed Philistine champion (vv.4–7) challenged the Israelites, they **were terrified** (v.11). And Saul was no better than they.

Though David has already been introduced as a military man (16:18, 21), a stock formula reintroduces him here as though for the first time, perhaps suggesting a new role or stage in his life (17:12). This "new" David, unlike his three brothers, had not even been drafted; he still tended sheep (vv.13–15). But that was about to change.

David delivered supplies to his siblings just in time to witness Goliath menacing Israel (17:17–24), which had been going on **for forty days** (v.16)! As the scene unfolds, David seems at times naïve (vv.29–30), at other times opportunistic (vv.26–28; cf. v.25) or heroic (v.26b). Having finally told Saul of his willingness to **fight** (v.32), the king unwittingly con-

demned himself by dismissing David as a **boy** (v.33).

After David argued that the God who had saved him from dangerous animals could save him from Goliath, Saul made himself look even worse by saying, **"Go, and the LORD be with you"** (17:34–37; cf. 16:14, 18). Obviously, the Lord was not with Saul, and he knew it. It is also noteworthy that David found Saul's armor useless—it had done Saul no good either!—and that he defeated the Philistine with lighter weaponry than Saul and Jonathan had had previously (vv.38–50; cf. 13:19–22).

Under Saul the Israelite army was dispirited. After David killed Goliath and cut off the giant's head with his own sword, the army revived and routed the Philistines (17:51–53). David was already a better leader than Saul. Further, the note that David put Goliath's head and weapons in his tent in Jerusalem, which is anachronistic, foreshadows David's future success (v.54; cf. Jdg 1:8; 2Sa 5:6–10). That he is still holding the head when he identifies himself to Saul emphasizes his and the Lord's stunning victory (v.57).

Saul's inexplicable failure (17:55–58; cf. 16:19) to recognize David probably means that ch. 17 was a later insertion (McCarter, 284–309). However, in the text's present form, his inability either highlights David's new identity or the fact that Saul has been so affected by the evil spirit from Yahweh that he could no longer recognize those close to him (17:55–58). But this presupposes that those of Saul's attendants who knew David were not around during the battle.

2. David and Jonathan (chs. 18–20)

After the Goliath incident, David's career soared. Saul had **liked him very** much (16:21; *’hb*); now Jonathan loved him (18:1, 3; *’hb*). Soon all Israel and Judah, including Saul's daughter Michal, and the king's servants loved David as well (vv.16, 20, 22, 28; *’hb*). David became part of Saul's household (v.2). Jonathan even gave his own robe and (sole?) sword to the newcomer (v.4), an action poignantly symbolic. But David earned such treatment, for he continued to stack up military successes (v.5).

However, Saul worried that David was opportunistic or at least too popular for the king's political good (18:6–9). Already jealous because of unfavorable comparison (vv.7–8), Saul, troubled by an evil spirit sent by God, tried to kill David. His failure to do so only highlighted his ineptitude (vv.10–11)! Still, he realized that his main problem was that God had abandoned him to be with David (vv.12, 14, 28).

Saul's attempts to neutralize David had the opposite effect. Assigning his nemesis to military duty only made him more famous (18:13, 16). The king offered his daughter in marriage in exchange for more military service, hoping that David would be killed (v.17). (By rights David should have won Saul's daughter when he defeated Goliath [cf. 17:25, 27], but he humbly declined [18:18–19]).

When Michal fell in love with David, Saul anticipated that he would again beg off. So the king tried to jeopardize David by leaking word that a marriage present of 100 Philistine foreskins would suffice. David instead acquired 200 Philistine foreskins, thus foiling Saul and winning Michal's hand. Nothing could impede David's rise (18:20–30).

When he finally issued direct orders to kill David (19:1, 11), Saul was thwarted by Jonathan, Michal, and God's Spirit. Jonathan warned David and pointed out to his father that David not only had not harmed him but had actually benefited him. Saul relented, so David returned to the king and fought on his behalf as before (vv.2–8).

But Saul, under the influence of the evil spirit from God, tried to murder David again. When David fled, Michal tipped him off about the king's posse, lied about his whereabouts, rigged a dummy to look like her bedridden husband—the inept servants did not notice this until they arrived home!—and then lied to her father (19:9–17).

Finally, though an evil spirit from God had formerly instigated Saul (19:9–10), God's prophesying Spirit latterly frustrated his efforts against David (vv.18–24). Also, though Samuel was with David at the time, something of which Saul was aware (v.22), the king apparently was not conscious that he had actually prophesied before the great prophet (cf. 15:35) or symbolically had removed his royal attire (vv.24–25).

David had to rely on Jonathan once more (ch. 20), but this time his friend seemed naïve (vv.2, 9, 13; cf. 19:1). David pleaded his innocence and tried to get the incredulous Jonathan to appreciate the danger (vv.1–3; cf. v.8). He finally convinced Jonathan to try something that would indicate which man correctly understood the situation (20:5–23). Though Jonathan appeared imperceptive about the present danger (and therefore unworthy to be king?), he was prescient about the future, "predicting" that David would not be killed and that his enemies would be vanquished (vv.2, 9, 13, 15–16). Poignantly, however, Jonathan hoped that he would be spared and that his family could depend on David's kindness (vv.14–15).

Just as an ostensive liturgical occasion was the pretext for Samuel's anointing of David (cf. 16:2–3), so Jonathan attributed David's absence from court to his attending a **family sacrifice** (20:6, 28–29). Apparently genuinely inquisitive at first about David's being missing, Saul got angry when he heard the alibi, surmising (correctly!) that Jonathan was undercutting his own chances of being king (vv.30–31). Previously Jonathan got Saul to change his mind about David (19:4–6), but this time Jonathan's efforts almost led to his own execution. Underscoring his naïvete, Jonathan perceived Saul's true intentions only after eluding a spear meant for him (vv.32–33). Jonathan had to admit that David had been right, whereupon the two friends renewed their vows (vv.34–42).

3. The Fugitive David (chs. 21–27)

After leaving Jonathan (21:1; NIV 20:42), David was **alone** (except for Yahweh? cf. 20:13). The priest Ahimelech, to whom David had fled, was troubled by that, perhaps sensing that David had become a marked man, as any would be who helped him (McCarter, *I Samuel*, 349). But Ahimelech did not knowingly abet David, for the latter lied that he was on a secret royal mission. When David requested food, the priest could offer only consecrated bread. But David and his men were eligible for such in that they met the ritual standards (21:2–6). David honored priestly regulations in stressful situations, while Saul violated them (cf. chs. 13, 15).

David was also unarmed. So he requested and received a weapon: Goliath's sword (vv.8–9; cf. 17:54, 57). Only later do we discover Ahimelech's family connections, but we cannot miss the ominous notation that one of Saul's servants happened to be nearby (v.7).

David had a close call when he sought refuge with Achish, king of Gath. The Philistines recognized that David was an Israelite famous for military exploits (against them; cf. 18:6–7). Sensing the danger, David feigned madness to effect his release. Ironically, the Philistines seemed to lose their minds in allowing a past and future enemy to escape so easily (21:10–15).

Having been **alone** (21:1), David was soon surrounded by family and a number of disaffected folk, whose Robin-Hood-like leader he became (22:1–2). Unlike Saul, who had tried to kill his own son (20:33), David cared for his family, seeing to it that his parents were protected by the Moabite king. Moreover, he was solicitous of God's will, receiving and heeding a prophetic word (22:3–5).

Learning of David's whereabouts, Saul accused his servants of conspiracy (22:12–16). As usual, he had spear in hand (cf. 19:9; 20:33); somehow he was always ready to spring into action against David, Jonathan, or servants; but Goliath had had nothing to fear! The charge was based on a half-truth, for Jonathan had made a pact with David. But his son had not suggested an ambush (22:6–8). Saul's paranoia increased when Doeg reported that Ahimelech had fed and armed David, and also inquired (*š'l*: pun "Saul") of God for him (vv.9–10). Then we discover that Ahimelech was Ahitub's son (cf. 14:3) and therefore an Elide, but it is impossible to know yet whether he in fact inquired of God as Doeg contended (cf. 21:1–9). In any case, given David's deception, Ahimelech was not truly an accomplice (21:2, 8).

When confronted, Ahimelech admitted what he had done but denied any conspiracy; moreover, he defended David as a loyal servant of the king. Unimpressed, Saul ordered the death of *Yahweh's* priests, something sufficiently outrageous that his own officers balked. (Saul did not know that the Elides were condemned.) But the Edomite Doeg was unfazed—he annihilated the whole family, something Saul had not done even to the Amalekites (ch. 15). Only one—Abiathar, Ahimelech's son—escaped and sought asylum with David. Though condemned, the priestly family which had served Saul, defected to David (22:11–23; cf. 1Ki 2:26–27).

Though David had acquired a priest, he inquired (*š'l*) of Yahweh on his own and received God's sanction to defeat the Philistines (23:1–6). Saul, on the other hand, merely *surmised* that God had trapped his enemy (vv.7–8). But David sought the Lord again, this time with the priest's help. And again God responded (vv.9–12). The Elides had been of little use to Saul but were instrumental in David's escape. Contrary to what Saul had supposed, God was on David's side (vv.13–14).

Jonathan found the fleeing David and encouraged him by saying that he would get away unharmed and eventually be king. According to Jonathan, Saul had even come to believe in this inevitability (23:15–18). But Jonathan was not completely right; he would *not* end up second to David.

At this juncture, the Ziphites tried to do what the Lord had not done: deliver David to Saul (23:19–20). Saul still believed the Lord would cooperate: **"The LORD bless you"** (v.21). Saul gave chase once more but was distracted by a Philistine raid (vv.22–29).

That chore aside, he resumed his obsession. Incredibly, en route Saul stopped to relieve himself in the very cave where David and his party were

hiding. David's compatriots saw the opportunity, but David restrained himself and unobtrusively cut off a corner of the King's robe. (David had "cut" [*krt*] a covenant with Jonathan [cf. 18:3; 20:16; 22:8; 23:18], but "cut" [*krt*] Saul's robe [24:1–4] as he had "cut" [*krt*] off Goliath's head [cf. 17:51]).

Yet, given Saul's status, David was troubled by even this minimal act. Thus, using deferential and familial language, David implored Saul to trust his good intentions in spite of the advice he, David, had received (24:5–15). Surprisingly, Saul responded in kind—he called David "my son" (cf. 20:27, 30–31; 22:7–9, 13)—and confessed his obstinacy. Saul even acknowledged that he knew David would be king and hoped only that he would not take vengeance on his family. David gave his word, and the two separated (24:16–22). Was Saul at last resigned to Providence?

Samuel at last died (25:1). And his death raises a question. Since God usually spoke through Samuel (3:1, 19–21; cf. 14:41–42 [=lots]; 23:2, 4, 11 [=David]), would the divine word become less accessible? Also, would Samuel's efforts to check the kingship come to naught? Answers are not forthcoming. Rather, the narrative focuses on the first incident involving David that was not at least indirectly related to Saul (ch. 25).

The introduction of two opposites, a wealthy curmudgeon Nabal ("Mr. Fool"!) and his lovely, intelligent wife, Abigail, immediately suggests tension (25:2–3). Such emerged when David through his men requested a payment from Nabal for having protected his flocks, only to be rebuffed as a runaway slave (vv.4–11).

Reacting in kind (25:12–13), David and his men set out to avenge the slight. When Abigail was told, she prepared a lavish present (vv.14–19; cf. v.3). Then she intercepted David—whose reference to males as "any that pisseth against the wall" evidences his disdain (v.22, KJV)—and tried to dissuade him. Conceding her husband's foolishness, Abigail argued that David had not yet sinned by seeking personal vengeance and that it would be better to leave his future in God's hands (vv.20–31). David finally agreed, accepted the gift, and saw providence at work in Abigail's actions (vv.32–35). Her reasoning and the wisdom of David's concurrence were confirmed when Yahweh struck Nabal dead after he had collapsed (vv.36–38). Appropriately, David praised God (v.39).

In addition to being kept from sin, David benefited by acquiring Abigail and Ahinoam as wives. But there were also setbacks. David's anointer and supporter had of course already died (25:1); moreover, his connection to Saul's house was severed when Michal was taken from him and given to another (vv.39b–44; cf. 18:27).

Though Saul was previously penitent (24:17–21), a Ziphite intelligence report led him to hunt David again (26:1–2). However, the hunter soon became the hunted (vv.3–5). After Saul had secured a position, David and some volunteers sneaked to the spot where Saul was sleeping. This time Saul's spear was in the ground nearby rather than in his hand (cf. 18:10; 19:9; 20:33). Seeing this rare opportunity, Abishai urged David to assassinate the king. But David refused. Since Saul was divinely anointed, only God could strike him. David merely wanted to grab the spear and water jug to prove he had been there (vv.6–11).

The inclination to praise David's cunning and disparage Saul's and his compatriots' competence subsides

somewhat when one observes the Lord's role (26:12). Though he repudiated Abner for his failure to guard Saul, David too was unaware of God's involvement (vv.13–16).

As before (24:16–21), Saul—who again used the familiar **"my son"**—was touched by David's restraint (26:17). David protested his innocence, lamented his being forced from God's inheritance, and asked who had made Saul act so: God or men (vv.18–20). From our perspective, Saul was victimized by his own jealousy and paranoia as well as by the evil spirit from God. Yet he confessed once more that he had indeed been foolish (v.21; cf. 13:13). David showed his good faith by returning the implements and reminding Saul that he had not harmed the king though God had provided an opportunity. Saul, too, appeared to mellow when he "predicted" a triumphant future for David (vv.22–25).

But actually David was not convinced, thinking that it was only a matter of time before Saul got to him. He figured he had no choice but to seek refuge with the Philistines (27:1–2). David's cynicism about Saul is highlighted not only by his defecting to a longstanding enemy (cf. ch. 17; 18:26–27, 30; 19:8; 23:1–5), but also by his siding with the very Philistine king with whom his first encounter had almost proved disastrous (21:10–15). Perhaps the difference this time was that David was no longer alone but was a captain of mercenaries who had families in tow, which provided the Philistines some leverage. In any case, after David switched allegiance, Saul quit looking for him (27:2–4).

Once with the Philistines, David, saying he did not deserve to live in the royal city, asked Achish for a town: Ziklag. That Ziklag remained in Judah's possession demonstrated

David's ability to increase Israelite territory at an enemy's expense even before he was king (27:5–6). Equally clever, David attacked Israelite enemies from his base in Ziklag, all the while lying that he had engaged Israelites. So Achish concluded that David no longer had any choice but to remain an ally (vv.7–12).

4. The End of Saul (chs. 28–31)

David's future was endangered when the Philistines confronted Israel again. Achish expected David to **accompany** him (28:1–2; cf. 14:21). David had to agree or risk blowing his cover. But going along meant Israelites would view him as a traitor. How would David extricate himself from this impossible situation?

The answer is not immediately given. Instead, the narrative recalls Samuel's death (28:3; cf. 25:1) and its import for Saul since he had expelled mediums and spiritists, which cut off his access to the divine world. Ironically, the hapless Saul was even disadvantaged by observing Torah (cf. Lev 19:31; 20:6, 27)!

As before, Saul panicked when facing the Philistines without Samuel (28:4–5; cf. ch. 13). He sought (*šʾl*) the Lord through **dreams, Urim,** and **prophets,** but received no reply (cf. 14:37). So in desperation he sought (*šʾl*) **a medium** (28:6–7). This required secrecy and setting aside the penalty for necromancy, but eventually Saul succeeded in having an **old** and robed Samuel conjured from the grave (cf. 8:1, 5; 12:2; 15:27–28). Samuel listened to the king's woes (note that Saul mentioned **prophets** first; v.15; cf. v.6), but then offered that his Amalekite prophecy was being fulfilled. There was, however, one final twist. Samuel added that Israel would lose its pending battle and Saul and Jonathan would be with him (i.e., in the nether world) on that day

(vv.18–19; cf. 2:34). Saul finally got an answer from God, but hardly the one he wanted!

Saul's reaction was worse than the medium's had been (28:20; cf. v.12). Indeed, he was reduced to receiving comfort from the very woman whose actions led to a confirmation of prophetic judgment against him. Worse, this king who had disobeyed Samuel and God ended up obeying an outlawed medium (vv.20–25).

David's situation finally was resolved when Achish's colleagues questioned the Israelite's loyalty. Though Achish defended him, the others were dubious (29:1–3; cf. 14:21; ch. 17). Their mentioning David's **"taking the heads of our own men"** and the singing of a victory song after the Goliath triumph were hardly subtle (vv.4–5)! Achish had to dismiss David because of the latter's surely disingenuous protest (vv.6–11). Once again events had worked in David's favor.

An Amalekite raid against Ziklag (cf. 27:6) presented David with another opportunity. The raid had resulted not only in the city's destruction but in the abduction of women and children, including David's wives. David was as distraught as anyone, but emotion was so high his men contemplated assassination (30:1–6a). However, unlike Saul's reaction in stressful moments, David found strength in the Lord and, with Abiathar's help, asked (*šʾl*) God whether he should pursue the offenders. Instead of silence, he received instruction and a promise about the positive outcome (vv.6b–8). With the help of an abandoned slave turned informer, David caught the raiding party and retrieved everything that had been taken (vv.9–20). God's word was good.

David demonstrated his magnanimity (and his suitability to be king?) by insisting on dividing the booty—which after all belonged to God (30:23)—equally with his troops. He made this a regular practice (vv.21–25). He also ingratiated himself with Judah's elders by distributing booty among them, something that would pay dividends later on (vv.26–31).

As David's lot improved, Saul's deteriorated. When the Philistines attacked, Samuel's prophecy (28:16–19) came tragically true, except that Saul was only wounded (30:1–3). There is a bitter irony in Saul's command that his armor-bearer finish him off, for his original armor-bearer (16:21) was indirectly responsible for the king's present plight. When the armor-bearer refused—again unwittingly mirroring David (cf. chs. 24, 26)—the king took his own life, his aide pathetically following suit (30:4–6). In a reversal of the Goliath incident, the Israelites fled while the Philistines occupied the abandoned territory and the next day did to Saul what David had done to their champion: desecrated the corpse and stashed the armor (31:8–10; cf. 17:51–54). The only respect accorded Saul in this final sorry episode was that some of his countrymen recovered his and his son's bodies and buried them in Israelite territory.

II. THE KINGSHIP OF DAVID (2SA 1–24)

A. David Becomes King (2Sa 1:1–5:5)

After Saul and Jonathan died, a messenger with torn clothes and head covered with dirt approached David in Ziklag, where he had been since defeating the Amalekites (1:1–2; cf. 1Sa 30). Bowing before David (as though before a king?), the courier related that Saul, Jonathan, and many others had died; he did not mention Saul's other sons (v.4; cf. 1Sa 31:2). Apparently wanting to ingratiate himself, the messenger lied that he had killed the wounded Saul at the latter's request. He presented the king's belongings as proof (vv.5–10). However, since the narrator described Saul's death as suicide (1Sa 31:4–5), the messenger had to have found Saul already dead (McCarter, *II Samuel*, 62–64). Surely the messenger did not expect David's reaction. Though a fulfillment of prophecy, David and his men lamented what had happened (1:11–12). Instead of earning favor, the messenger—whose situation scarcely improved when he admitted that he was an Amalekite—was rewarded with death (vv.13–16). If the anointed David had not taken Saul's life, how could this foreigner do so? His fabrication only underscored his stupidity.

The episode concludes with David's formal lament (1:17–27). The dirge begins and ends with Israel's glory and weapons abandoned on the battle site, highlighted by the refrain, **"How the mighty have fallen!"** (vv.19, 27; cf. v.25). In between, David pleaded that the terrible news be kept from the Philistines so that their women could not gloat, as Israelite women once did at Philistine defeats (v.20; cf. 1Sa 18:7; 21:11; 29:5). David even cursed the battlefield (v.21). Finally, he extolled Saul and Jonathan for their heroism, then Saul for his largess and Jonathan for his intimate friendship (vv.22–26).

Personal feelings aside, the death of Saul and Jonathan paved the way for David's takeover. But David made no immediate moves; instead, he sought (š'l) the Lord and was told to go to Hebron (2:1). When David and his entourage arrived, the men of Judah anointed him king, apparently confirming what Samuel had done (vv.2–4a; cf. 1Sa 16:1–13). But David continued to show respect for Saul and his family by affirming the people at Jabesh-Gilead who had buried the slain leader (2:4b–7).

David became king of Judah (=southern territory) while Ish-Bosheth, Saul's son, became the king over Israel (=northern territory), a move engineered by Abner, Saul's military leader. In Ish-Bosheth's case there was no divine direction, no seeking God, and no anointing (vv.8–11).

From a human standpoint, conflict between these factions was understandable. From the standpoint of God's will, it was inevitable. After an initial stalemate, illustrated by a bizarre form of ritualized combat, David's forces gained the upper hand (2:12–17). But Saul's forces scored, too. Abner slew a persistent if not impulsive (cf. 2Sa 2:18–32) Ashael, brother of David's officer Joab. Yet this presaged an ominous future (2:18–23). Curiously, Saul and Jonathan died *though* swift (*qll*; cf. 1:23), while Ashael perished *because* he was swift (*qll*; 2:18–23).

In this initial confrontation the House of Saul lost 360 troops, the House of David only 19 (vv.24–31). Hostilities then ceased temporarily.

Though the ensuing war was long, victory for David's house was only a matter of time (3:1). A measure of strength was reflected in David's many wives and sons. By contrast, in the house of Saul a dispute arose over one of Saul's concubines—no wives of Ish-Bosheth are mentioned (vv.2–8). Ish-Bosheth's position was seriously compromised when Abner withdrew his loyalty as a result of the quarrel. But the loyalty may have been questionable anyway, given Abner's awareness of God's promise that David was destined to rule over Judah and Israel. In any case, Ish-Bosheth was so intimidated that he kept silent (vv.9–11).

Ish-Bosheth got weaker, and David even stronger, as illustrated by David's demand for Michal in response to Abner's offer (cf. 1Sa 25:44). Ish-Bosheth actually acquiesced in this, apparently too dim-witted to realize the political implications (3:12–16). When Abner finally encouraged Israel's elders (and later folk in Benjamin, Saul's home) to make David king, something they apparently believed was God's will, Ish-Bosheth's days in office were numbered (vv.17–21).

But the negotiations went awry when Joab found out about Abner's role, for Joab had a personal *and* a political stake in the affair (cf. 2:18–23, 32). Without David's knowledge, Joab lured Abner to camp and assassinated him with the same technique Abner had used on Ashael: a sword in the belly (3:27; cf. 2:23). Unlike David, who foreswore or was prevented from taking personal vengeance against his enemies, Joab plunged (quite literally!) ahead (3:27, 30; cf. 1Sa 24–26).

The effects of Joab's blunder were mitigated when David lamented publicly, asserted his innocence, and exposed the guilty party (3:28–35). Whether David truly grieved or was merely being politic is not clear. But the upshot was that he was exonerated (vv.36–38). Interestingly, though Joab had killed an enemy, David feared these sons of Zeruiah (v.39; cf. 2:18).

Robbed of Abner's skill and power, Ish-Bosheth (now reduced to "Saul's son" in the Hebrew text) and Israel lost heart. They had good reason to fear. Ominously, the narrator mentions two semiforeign leaders of raiding bands and also interjects information about how Jonathan's son Mephibosheth had become crippled: a nurse dropped him when she hastily fled upon hearing the news of Saul's and Jonathan's deaths

(4:1–4). This juxtaposition of external and internal troubles portends further reverses for the house of Saul.

David once escaped being killed in his own bed (cf. 1Sa 19:11–16), but Ish-Bosheth was less fortunate. Baanah and Recab stabbed him (cf. 2:23; 3:27), decapitated him (cf. 1Sa 31:9), and triumphantly presented the head to David. But David treated these assassins as he had the messenger who lied (though David did not know he had lied) about killing Saul. The king dismissed the accusation that Ish-Bosheth had sought his life or that Yahweh had wrought vengeance. So David had the men killed, desecrated their corpses, and then buried Ish-Bosheth's head (4:5–12).

The death of Ish-Bosheth and Abner made it possible for David to rule all Israel. Nevertheless, he remained an object while **all the tribes of Israel** were the subject of the action. Israel cited its symbolic kinship with David (cf. Ge 29:14; Jdg 9:2), acknowledged that he *acted* like a king militarily (cf. 1Sa 17; 18:13–14, 16, 27, 30; 19:8; 23:1–5; 27:8–9; 30:1–20) though Saul *was* king, and finally appealed to a hitherto unknown divine statement (had they paraphrased or invented it?). They anointed David (cf. 1Sa 16:12–13; 2Sa 2:4) and made a covenant with him (cf. 1Sa 10:25). The standard "royal" formula which is used emphasized David's tenure: he would not be prematurely killed (5:1–5; cf. 1Sa 13:1; 1Ki 14:21; 15:1, 9–10, 25).

B. The Consolidation of David's Kingship (2Sa 5:6–10:19)

David's first act as the Israelite king was to capture Jerusalem, which was foreshadowed earlier (cf. 1Sa 17:54). Though Jerusalem was considered impregnable, David effortlessly took the city, illustrating either that the inhabitants' confident words were sheer bluster or that David's strength was extraordinary (5:6–8). Once in the city, he fortified it. And he got even stronger because God was with him (5:9–10; cf. 1Sa 16:18; 17:37; 18:12, 14, 28; 20:13).

Another king immediately recognized David's status and built David a palace as a present. This was not the first time foreign rulers saw him as Israel's potential or actual king (cf. 1Sa 21:10–15). However, though elevated in diplomatic prestige, David regarded his kingship in theological perspective (5:11–12).

Acquiring more wives and children underscored David's increasing strength (vv.13–16; cf. 3:1–5). At the same time, a cautionary note is sounded. David **"took"** (*lqh*) these women. Samuel had used this word in reference to royal extravagance (cf. 1Sa 8:11, 13–14, 16). Also, David's precipitate downfall began when he **"took"** (*lqh*) another woman, the name of whose son was already mentioned (5:14; cf. 11:4).

Unlike Hiram's peaceful overtures, Philistia initiated hostilities. In response, David inquired (*š'l*) of the Lord and received reassurance. Consequently, he defeated the Philistines and carried off their idols, thus repaying them in kind, as it were, for their capture of the ark (cf. 1Sa 4–6). A pun emphasizes that the Philistines abandoned (*'zb*) their idols (*'ṣb*) because their idols had abandoned them (5:20–21)! When the Philistines attacked again, David inquired (*š'l*) a second time and won a divinely aided victory (vv.22–24).

Later David brought the ark (cf. 1Sa 7:2; 14:18) to Jerusalem with great ceremony. But an attendant touched it, whereupon God struck him dead (6:1–7). Both angry and apprehensive,

David sent the ark elsewhere. Not even this great king could control God!

When the Lord blessed the ark's keepers, David retrieved it, apparently to secure a similar blessing. This time he was successful, perhaps because he performed the requisite priestly functions himself (6:8–19).

But the celebration over the ark's return was marred by Michal's reaction. She had loved David but later was taken away from him (1Sa 18:20, 28; 25:44). When David negotiated her return, she came back docilely while her husband pitifully followed (3:14–16). Had she cooled toward the king? Or had she thought that he wanted her back for political reasons alone? In any case, she detested David for what she regarded as his lewd (in her mind) dancing before the ark. David defended his actions "before God" and reminded her that he had been chosen to replace her father. Henceforth, Michal remained childless, presumably because David never slept with her again. She would produce no children to represent Saul's line (McCarter, *II Samuel*, 172).

When David turned to domestic affairs, he expressed misgivings about living in a house (NIV **"palace";** cf. 5:11) while the ark remained in a tent (6:17). Therefore, with the prophet Nathan's encouragement (**"go,"** v.3), he decided to build Yahweh a **house** (=temple; 7:1–3). However, though Nathan was doubtless correct that God was **with** David generally (v.3), the Lord had other plans (**"go and tell,"** v.5).

God had never lived in or asked for a **house** but had instead chosen David, been **with** him, planned to **make [his] name great** (cf. Ge 11:4; 12:2), wanted to make Israel secure, and would construct a **house** (=dynasty) for the king (7:5–16). David's successor could build the temple; God, not David or Nathan, was in charge of such things (v.13). Certainly the most important feature of this revelation was that David's dynasty was to be perpetual (**"forever";** vv.13, 16). Even when future kings in the Davidic line sinned and incurred punishment, God would never withdraw **love** as happened with Saul (v.15). God's posture toward Israel's kingship had clearly changed: Saul's kingship was conditional and potentially ephemeral, David's unconditional and everlasting.

David responded to this word with humility and gratitude, affirmed God's past and future actions, emphasized his role in carrying out the divine will, implored God to make the divine name great, and asked for continued blessing (vv.18–29). Even in his response David accents **"forever"** (vv.24, 25–26, 29).

As promised (7:10–11), God made David victorious (8:1–14; cf. vv.6, 14). In turn, the king kept Torah (Dt 17:16–17) by refusing to stockpile horses (8:4) or gold (vv.11–12). He also consolidated his government with a "cabinet" (vv.15–18).

Still, as good as everything seemed, there was cause for concern. David was already worried about Joab (3:39). Another danger was the possibility of conflict between rival priests: (1) Abiathar, the son of Ahimelech (rather than the other way round [Eli—Phineas—Ahitub—Ahimelech—Abiathar]   cf. 1Sa 14:3; 22:9, 20); (2) Zadok, the son of another, non-Elide Ahitub. Tension between rival priesthoods could be complicated by David's priestly sons (8:18; *kôh⁽ᵃ⁾nîm*; NIV **"advisers";** RSV "priests"; McCarter, *II Samuel*, 253–55; Hertzberg, 294).

When David favored Mephibosheth (4:4) by giving him Saul's lands and arranging for their upkeep and by inviting him to the royal table, he repaid Jonathan's generosity and at the same time strengthened himself (9:1–13). Ironically, David had often referred to himself as **Saul's servant** (cf. 1Sa 17:32, 34; 26:18–19); now Saul's servants and grandson were "David's servants."

But David was not always politically wise. He expressed sympathy to Hanun, the new Ammonite king, after the death of his father Nahash. But Nahash had been Israel's bitter enemy (1Sa 11), contrary to what David believed (10:1–2). Perhaps David's political sensibilities were not sufficiently honed. In any case, after Hanun, who suspected ulterior motives in David's overture, humiliated Israel's emissaries, he realized that he had overstepped his bounds (vv.3–6). Hanun allied himself therefore with Aram, but David defeated the coalition handily and made Aram a vassal state (vv.7–19). Notwithstanding David's carelessness, Joab knew why he landed on his feet: **"The Lord will do what is good in his sight"** (v.12).

C. The Decline of David (chs. 11–20)

Key terms in the story of David's downfall are *send* (*šlḥ*), *lie* (*škb*), and *take* (*lqḥ*). David **sent** Joab to fight the Ammonites (11:1; cf. ch. 10) while he stayed behind. Then he arose from his bed (*mškb* = "place where one *lies*"), espied a beautiful woman, and **sent** someone to inquire about her. Told that she was married (her husband was mentioned last!), David **sent** messengers to get (*lqḥ* = "take"; cf. 1Sa 8:11, 13–17) Bathsheba. He then **slept** (*škb*) with her, presumably on the same bed *mškb*) already mentioned. Though they had intercourse right after Bathsheba's menstrual period, when she was supposedly infertile, she **sent** word that she

was pregnant (11:2–5; Sternberg, 198).

So David **sent** for the husband, whom Joab **sent** to the king. David asked Uriah (*š'l*: he would have done better to inquire of the Lord) about the war, then abruptly urged him to go home. But Uriah was as honorable as David had been dishonorable; he **slept** (*škb*) with David's servants in the palace and later explained that he could not bring himself to **lie** with his wife while his comrades fought. Promising to **send** Uriah back on the morrow, David induced him with drink to go home, but Uriah again went out to **sleep** with the servants (11:6–13). He had more integrity while drunk than David did while sober!

Having failed, David **sent** Uriah with his own death warrant back to Joab. That Uriah's death would endanger other Israelite soldiers compounded this outrage. Joab finally **sent** word back, having instructed the messenger to neutralize any negative reaction by specifically mentioning Uriah's death. Initially angry, David responded that tragedy is inevitable in war and that Joab should not be overly concerned (= "Let not this matter be evil in your eyes"). Now David was free to **send** for Bathsheba permanently. However, what David did not want to be evil in Joab's eyes most emphatically "was evil in Yahweh's eyes" (11:14–27).

Thus Yahweh **sent** Nathan to tell David a story about a rich man who had abundant livestock and a poor man who had purchased (difficult for a poor man) a single ewe. This animal was like a daughter (*bat*) to the man (a pun on *Bat*sheba's name?). But this did not deter the rich man from "taking" the ewe to entertain a guest, leaving his own herds untouched. David became irate and demanded justice on hearing this, which led Nathan to accuse: **"You are the man!"** (12:7).

A devastating judgment oracle followed. In spite of all that Yahweh had done for David, including putting Saul's wives into his arms (= "into his bosom" [*ḥq*], v.8; cf. v.3 [*ḥq*]), the king had done evil in Yahweh's eyes (12:9; cf. 11:25, 27) by **taking** Uriah's wife and using Ammonites, against whom David should have been fighting, to destroy him. Hence, violence would "forever" afflict David's "house" (cf. ch. 7). Worse, Yahweh would **take** David's wives, give them to someone close, and allow him to **lie** with them in full view (12:7–12). The only consolation was that David would retain his kingdom (cf. 7:14–15).

David's immediate confession elicited God's forgiveness, but Bathsheba's child was condemned. David pleaded for the boy's life in the hope of changing God's mind. He fasted, secluded himself, and **lay** (*škb*) on the ground, but gave up when the child died. After comforting Bathsheba, he **lay** with her again. This eventuated in another child, whom David named Solomon (cf. 5:14). But Yahweh loved the child and **sent** Nathan to name him Jedidiah (12:13–25).

This episode concluded when Joab urged David to join him and claim victory over the Ammonites, which David did (12:26–31). Had David tended to business all along (cf. 11:1), judgment might have been averted.

The predicted troubles soon afflicted David's house (12:10–11). His son Amnon, whose love for his half-sister Tamar went unrequited, heeded a cousin's advice and got the woman alone. Despite her protests, he **raped** (*škb*: "laid her"—the phrase is as vulgar and harsh in Hebrew as it is in English) and then cavalierly discarded her (Trible, 37–63). Absalom, Tamar's full brother, counseled her to forget the matter, though he himself despised Amnon. David was angry but did nothing, just as Eli and Samuel failed to discipline their sons (cf. 1Sa 2:22–25, 29; 3:13; 8:1–5). David's passivity allowed Absalom to plot against and murder Amnon two years later (after getting him drunk, as David had done to Uriah!). David's initial fury turned to hysteria (he lay [*škb*] on the ground) when he was misinformed that *all* his sons had been murdered. Though he quickly learned the truth, he still wept bitterly. Indeed, he was so consumed with grief over Amnon, who had behaved so despicably, that he neglected Absalom until it was too late (ch. 13).

David eventually softened toward Absalom (13:39) but still did nothing (14:1). Indeed, Absalom would have remained exiled had not Joab hired a **wise woman** (v.2; cf. 13:3) to fool the monarch. She said that one of her sons had killed his brother because no one separated them, a point that hardly could have been lost on David. She begged the king to prevent the family from seeking vengeance. David was willing, but when the woman got more specific he guessed that Joab had set him up. Nevertheless, he let Joab retrieve Absalom, but he himself would not receive him (vv.3–24).

Several clues suggest that the worst was yet to come. Absalom's extraordinary looks remind us that earlier handsome men came to power (1Sa 9:2; 10:23; 16:12). Also, Absalom's sole daughter, Tamar, was the only one of his children named, which was unusual in itself. But the name would be a constant reminder of the rape. Finally, Absalom's restiveness led him to destroy Joab's property to attract attention after the commander had twice refused to see him. To see his father, Absalom was willing to risk alienating the man responsible for his return (14:25–33).

Absalom's next moves confirm one's suspicions. He acquired a small militia, publicly criticized state policies, and campaigned for (and won) popular support (15:1–6). He was so confident that he lied to David about a trip to Hebron. Saying he wanted to worship there, he went instead to be proclaimed king. Ahithophel's support indicated that he had some backing from palace personnel as well (vv.7–12).

By the time David caught on, it was too late. The king, household staff (excepting concubines), bodyguard, and a few elite forces had to flee (15:13–18). Of course, David was not without resources. Some foreign mercenaries remained loyal; ironically, he could not count on similar loyalty from his own family (vv.19–22). David also retained considerable popular support (v.23). Most importantly, David trusted Providence. Demanding that the ark be returned to Jerusalem, he left it to God to decide whether he would see it again (vv.25–26). And he prayed that the Lord would confuse the traitor Ahithophel's counsel (v.31).

David banked as well on his military and strategic gifts by sending his priests and their sons, as well as Hushai, to Jerusalem as spies (15:27–29, 32–37).

As David fled, he was informed that Mephibosheth (cf. ch. 9) saw the king's plight as opportune (16:1–4). Saul's house still had life, something also indicated by Shimei's accusation that David was being punished for violence against the Saulides. But was this so? In fact, David had killed those who took (or said they took) the lives of Saul or his family (cf. 1:1–16; 4:5–12), and he had refused to kill Saul when he had the chance (cf. 1Sa 24, 26). In any case, David, severely shaken by his son's actions and resigned to God's will,

ignored the slander, though some of his retinue wanted to respond (16:5–14).

Hushai meanwhile positioned himself inside Absalom's inner circle by insisting that his loyalty extended to the one anointed by the Lord, the people, and the men of Israel, not to one man (16:15–19). Absalom failed to see how ironic it was for him to charge Hushai with disloyalty (v.17)!

Ahithophel's (15:12, 31) first advice to Absalom resulted unwittingly in the fulfillment of the oracle of judgment against David (12:11–12). The usurper king slept with his father's concubines on the roof of the palace to publicize his irreparable break (16:20–22).

In spite of his sterling reputation (16:23), Ahithophel's next piece of advice was rejected for Hushai's. Though Ahithophel's plan was clearly superior (17:1–13), the Lord induced Absalom and his men to favor Hushai. This was an answer to David's prayer and the triumph of his strategy (v.14; cf. 15:31, 34). The informant priests' sons then risked their lives to get word to David (17:17–22).

Ironies abound at the end of the episode. Ahithophel killed himself because his advice was rejected—had it been followed, Absalom would not have been killed (17:23; cf. 18:9–15). Amasa, Joab's cousin (presumably there are difficulties in this genealogy; cf. 1Ch 2:13–17), was appointed commander of Absalom's forces so that both David and Joab had to fight kinfolk (17:24–26; McCarter, *II Samuel*, 391–92). Finally, David received better treatment from foreigners than from Israelites or from his own son (vv.27–29).

In contrast to the scene where David shirked military duties (11:1) and got himself in trouble, he took charge again (18:1–2). But he was advised against this, since he was thought to be the principal target of the revolt. Almost pathetically compliant, David agreed to desist, asking only that Absalom be treated leniently (vv.3–5). This too was ironic in that David's paternal indecision brought about the precarious situation in which he now found himself.

Though prospects had at times looked bleak, David's forces prevailed (18:6–8). But in the process Absalom became entangled in a tree and was helplessly exposed. The first to find Absalom heeded David's admonition and let him be, foregoing potential wealth and fame. But David's instructions did not faze Joab, who was perhaps still smarting from the previous altercation (14:28–31). He and his armor-bearers mercilessly slew the royal scion, foregoing an easy capture (18:9–15).

When Joab and his troops piled stones on Absalom's corpse, erecting a victory monument, it was a tragic counterpoint to the monument that Absalom had built to preserve his memory (18:16–18). It is ironic, too, that David's first premonition of what had happened came on a roof (v.24; cf. 11:2). Ahimaaz, who had been so insistent on giving David the news first, hedged when he got there, making it possible for a Cushite to tell the king insensitively that Absalom was dead. Finally, was David conscious of his pun when he asked: "Is **Abšālôm** [= 'The (Divine) Father Is Peace'] **safe** [šālôm]?" (18:19–32)?

David's reaction to Absalom's death threw a pall over the victory, making his men ashamed rather than jubilant (18:33–19:4; Heb. 19:1–5). Joab excoriated the king for not realizing that regaining power necessitated Absalom's death. Further, David would lose support if he remained naïve about Absa-

lom and unappreciative of his troops. David appeared to accede to Joab's argument (19:5–8).

Their fortunes reversed with Absalom's death, the Israelites believed they had to invite David to rule again. But the king told Zadok and Abiathar to urge Judah to act before Israel, apparently because of kinship ties. In another strategic move, David replaced Joab with Amasa. Then, as Absalom had (15:6), David won over Judah and was invited to rule (19:9–15).

On the way back to Jerusalem, Shimei, who had reviled David as he fled (16:5–14), asked forgiveness. Though Abishai protested, David forgave, arguing that his return should be a day of celebration not vengeance (19:18–23; cf. 1Sa 11:13; 26:8). Mephibosheth, whose servant had accused him of seeking political advantage (16:1–4), was also restored to favor when he accused Ziba of lying (19:24–30). Finally, David blessed Barzillai, who had helped the king before (vv.31–39; cf. 17:27; 1Sa 21, 25).

But the path of David's return was not smooth. Israel and Judah fought over who had the superior claim to reinstall the king. Since Judah won the dispute, a certain Sheba incited Israel to rebel again (19:40–20:2). Before David dealt with this new crisis, he attended to his concubines (cf. 15:16; 16:21–22). The king provided for them but no longer slept with them, which perhaps suggests a truncated future (20:3).

David dealt with the revolt by commanding Amasa to solicit help from Judah. Because Amasa tarried, David ordered Abishai to organize a search for Sheba. When Amasa finally caught up with the deployed forces, he was assassinated by Joab, who had accompanied Abishai (cf. 2:16; Jdg 3:12–30). Joab used the murder to rally support for himself and ostensibly David, and resumed the chase. Once David's forces had Sheba holed up in Abel, they besieged it and urged a **wise woman** to convince the townspeople to hand over the fugitive or pay dire consequences. The woman persuaded the Abelites to throw Sheba's head over the wall! The episode ended as it began: with the trumpet blast (20:1, 4–22; cf. 14:1–3).

Though this rebellion too was squashed, since that fateful day when David stayed home (11:1), nothing had been the same. Even in a seemingly mundane note about the cabinet, a reference to the officer in charge of forced labor is another indication that David had not lived up to the ideals set for him (20:23–26; cf. 1Sa 8:10–18; 1Ki 4:6; 5:13–18; 9:15, 22–23; 12:18).

D. The Davidic Kingship: Retrospect and Prospect (chs. 21–24)

Chs. 21–24 have long been regarded as an appendix. However, in their present canonical form, they play a strategic literary and theological role. The section is bracketed by two stories (21:1–14; 24:1–25); a list of heroes and their exploits follows the first and precedes the second (21:15–22; 23:8–39); and these halves are joined at the center by two poems (22:1–51; 23:1–7) (Childs, *Introduction*, 273).

The first story tells of a three-year famine that God inflicted on Israel for Saul's [unrecorded] violence against the Gibeonites (21:1). This violation of an ancient agreement (v.2; cf. Jos 9) underscored Saul's failure by showing that he spared those he was ordered to destroy (1Sa 15) and destroyed those he should have spared. David therefore gave the Gibeonite survivors an opportunity for redress. Diffident at first, the Gibeonites eventually requested the execution of two of Saul's sons and five of his grandsons. Though somewhat out of character, given David's solicitous stance toward Saul and his family (1:1–15; 4:1–12; 9:1–13; 1Sa 24; 26), but because the Lord had been clear about the reason for the famine (21:1), David complied. His only concession to his prior attitude was the respect he accorded the remains. Afterward, God once more answered Israel's prayers (21:3–14).

The story takes pains to show that David was not responsible for Saul's fate, whose sins were to blame (cf. Nu 35:33; Childs, *Introduction*, 274).

When the narrative resumes, a note about another confrontation with the Philistines cites David's exhaustion (21:15), an embarrassing contrast to his prior prowess. Abishai even had to save David from a Philistine warrior, after which his men patronizingly insisted that the king remain home (vv.16–17). Other Philistine champions emerged, all to be killed by soldiers other than David. Indeed, as though to qualify David's famous victory over Goliath (1Sa 17), we are told that David's warrior Elhanan slew him (cf. 1Ch 20:5). The only concession to David's previous reputation is the remark that the Philistines **"fell at the hands of David and his men"** (vv.18–22). David's decline mirrored his rise.

But the poetic sections sound another note. David's praise to God (22:1–51) is juxtaposed to the account of his weakness. The text moves from the king's deglorification (21:15–22) to God's glorification. Since the doxology is sung after **all** (v.1) the **enemies** have been defeated, David's review of his career emphasizes God's promises (cf. 7:10–11). This theocentric perspective, now seen in retrospect, is also underscored by the connections between David's and Hannah's song (e.g., 1Sa 2:2 = 2Sa 23:3; 1Sa 2:6–8 = 2Sa 22:17, 28; 1Sa 2:10 = 2Sa 22:8, 51; Childs, *Introduction*, 274).

David's considerable talent notwithstanding, his true greatness is reflected in the hymn's themes: The Lord is the king's refuge and source of help (22:1–7, 17–20, 31–37); the Lord's appearance is awesome (vv. 8–16); the anointed one's righteousness is central (vv.21–25); a sovereign God "inverts" the ways of humankind (vv.26–30); victory is ultimately God's (vv.38–46); the only future for the Davidic dynasty is the one God envisions and secures (vv.47–51). David's retrospective hymn dovetails with Hannah's prospective hymn.

David's last words—symbolically, not literally (cf. ch. 24; 1Ki 1–2)—function as a blessing and establish the program for the future of the chosen dynasty (23:1–7; cf. Ge 27:27–29, 39–40; 49:1–27; Dt 32:1–43; 33:1–29; Hertzberg, 399). Divinely inspired, David stressed the anointed's righteousness, when he would truly shine (23:1–4). Further, in spite of everything that had transpired, the future was as secure as the God who had made the everlasting covenant, evil detractors notwithstanding (vv.5–7; cf. 7:5–16).

To show that this glorious future transcended the historical David, after David's final oracle a second list of heroes and their accomplishments is presented. David's exploits are ignored here, as though one should no longer rehearse them. Also, he is contrasted unfavorably to his compatriots. During a battle he alone became thirsty (23:15; cf. 21:15) and was supplied with water by men who risked their lives to get it. Shamed by their selfless courage, he poured the water on the ground. More conspicuously, the final hero mentioned was none other than Uriah the

Hittite (v.39). It can hardly be accidental that the last mentioned of David's mighty men compels us to recall how the king treacherously murdered a loyal, principled, and honorable servant (vv.8–39).

The final story in this section (and 1–2Sa) concerns judgment and restoration. It parallels ch. 21, and in addition sets forth how the future messianic blessing will be retained in spite of the anointed one's sinfulness (cf. 1Sa 2:10; Childs, *Introduction*, 275–76).

Becoming angry with Israel again, God incited David to take a general census (24:1), perhaps to isolate a particular segment of the population for punishment (cf. Nu 26). Why was Israel's sin not specified? Was it immaterial? Is it to be inferred from the context, especially in light of formal connections with ch. 21 (McCarter, *II Samuel*, 509; Gordon, 317)? Is the sin unmentioned to highlight Yahweh's exasperation for Israel's unfaithfulness and obstinacy in demanding the kingship in the first place? Does the vocabulary ("Yahweh's nose/forehead [*'p*] burned hot") allude to the encompassing nature of Israel's sin since its formation as God's people (cf. Ex 32:12; Nu 25:4; 32:14; Dt 13:17 [Heb. v.18]; 29:24 [Heb. v.23], 27 [Heb. v.26]; Jos 7:26; 1Sa 28:18 [against the Amalekites])?

Regardless, David exacerbated matters by commanding Joab to count fighting men (*'m* can mean "troops"), which prompted even the officer's objection (vv.2–4; cf. v.1: **"Israel and Judah"**). The count indicated 800,000 in Israel and 500,000 in Judah who could handle a sword, a far cry from the days when Saul had 3000 troops and two swords (1Sa 13:2, 22)! Unfortunately, the monarchy's military might had outpaced its moral might.

When David's conscience pricked

him (cf. 1Sa 24:5), he confessed: **"I have done a very foolish thing"** (24:10). This is the term (*śkl*) that Samuel had used to accuse Saul and that Saul had used of himself when he was chasing David (1Sa 13:13; 26:21), which intimates that David had stooped to Saul's level. When the verdict was announced, Yahweh through the prophet Gad (cf. 1Sa 22:5) gave David three options: (1) three years of famine (cf. 21:1), (2) three months of fleeing enemies (cf. 1Sa 20–31), or (3) three days of plague. Confident that Yahweh would be more merciful than his enemies, David opted for plague. After terrible carnage, a grieving Lord demanded that the destroying angel desist just before inflicting Jerusalem (24:11–16).

But David also played a role in averting the plague. Chagrined that Israel suffered for his sins, he asked God to limit the punishment to him and his family. So God had the prophet tell David to present offerings. After purchasing a site and the material for an offering—David refused to present something that had cost him nothing— he built an altar (cf. 1Sa 14:35) and made sacrifices. The Lord responded by answering prayer and stopping the plague (24:17–25; cf. 21:14).

David's last act in 1–2Sa was a priestly and repentant one. He and his family had been under a curse since the Bathsheba/Uriah incident. Yet, in spite of these human failings, God did not withdraw the ultimate promise to David, the anointed one (cf. ch. 7).

BIBLIOGRAPHY

Alter, Robert. *The Art of Biblical Narrative*. New York: Basic Books, 1981.

———. and Frank Kermode, eds. *The Literary Guide to the Bible*. Cambridge, Mass.: Harvard University Press [Belknap], 1987.

Childs, Brevard S. *Biblical Theology in Crisis*. Philadelphia: Westminster, 1969.

———. *Introduction to the Old Testament as Scripture*. Philadelphia: Fortress, 1979.

Cross, Frank M. *Canaanite Myth and Hebrew Epic*. Cambridge, Mass.: Harvard University Press, 1975.

Eslinger, Lyle M. *Kingship of God in Crisis*. Vol. 10. Bible and Literature Series. Edited by D. M. Gunn. Decatur, Ga.: Almond, 1985.

Gordon, Robert P. *1 and II Samuel*. Grand Rapids: Zondervan, 1986.

Gunn, David M. *The Fate of King Saul*. Vol. 14. JSOT Supplement Series. Edited by David J. A. Clines, Philip R. Davies, and David M. Gunn. Sheffield: JSOT Press, 1980.

Halpern, Baruch. *The First Historians*. San Francisco: Harper & Row, 1988.

Hertzberg, Hans Wilhelm. *I and II Samuel*. Translated by J. S. Bowden from German. Philadelphia: Westminster, 1964.

McCarter, P. Kyle, Jr. *I Samuel*. Vol. 8. AB. Garden City, N.Y.: Doubleday, 1980.

———. *II Samuel*. Vol. 9. AB. Garden City, N.Y.: Doubleday, 1984.

Miller, Patrick D., and J. J. M. Roberts. *The Hand of the Lord: A Reassessment of the "Ark Narrative" of 1 Samuel*. Baltimore: Johns Hopkins University Press, 1977.

Morgan, Robert, and John Barton. *Biblical Interpretation.* Oxford: Oxford University Press, 1988.

Nelson, Richard D. *The Double Redaction of the Deuteronomistic History.* Vol. 18. JSOT Supplement Series. Edited by D. J. A. Clines, P. R. Davies, and D. M. Gunn. Sheffield: JSOT Press, 1981.

Noth, Martin. *The Deuteronomistic History.* Vol. 15. JSOT Supplement Series. Edited by D. J. A. Clines, P. R. Davies, and D. M. Gunn. Translated by Jane Doull from German. Sheffield: JSOT Press, 1981.

von Rad, Gerhard. *Old Testament Theology.* Vol. 1. Translated by D. M. G. Stalker from German. Edinburgh: Oliver & Boyd, 1962.

Rosenberg, Joel. "1 and 2 Samuel." Pp. 122–45 in *The Literary Guide to the Bible.* Edited by Robert Alter and Frank Kermode. Cambridge, Mass.: Harvard University Press [Belknap], 1987.

Rost, L. *The Succession to the Throne of David.* Vol. 1. Historic Texts and Interpreters in Biblical Scholarship. Translated by M. D. Rutter and D. M. Gunn from German. Sheffield: Almond, 1982.

Sanders, James A. *Torah and Canon.* Philadelphia: Fortress, 1972.

————. *Canon and Community.* Philadelphia: Fortress, 1984.

Spina, Frank Anthony. "Canonical Criticism: Childs Versus Sanders." Pp. 165–94 in *Interpreting God's Word for Today.* Edited by W. McCown and J. Massey. Anderson, Ind.: Warner, 1982.

Sternberg, Meir. *The Poetics of Biblical Narrative.* Bloomington, Ind.: Indiana University Press, 1985.

Trible, Phyllis. *Texts of Terror.* Philadelphia: Fortress, 1984.

Walters, Stanley D. "Hannah and Anna: The Greek and Hebrew Texts of 1 Samuel 1." *Journal of Biblical Literature* 107, no. 3 (1988): 385–412.

Wilson, Robert. *Sociological Approaches to the Old Testament.* Philadelphia: Fortress, 1984.

Van Seters, John. *In Search of History.* New Haven: Yale University Press, 1983.

1 AND 2 KINGS

Terry L. Brensinger

INTRODUCTION

I. TITLE AND CONTENT

In the Hebrew canon the title of these books is simply 1 and 2Ki. However, the presence of two seemingly distinct books merely hides the fact that they, like 1 and 2Sa, were originally one. The division first appeared in the LXX, where 1Sa through 2Ki comprised the four books of the "Kingdoms." Not until the mid-fifteenth century did a similar division appear in the Hebrew text. That such a division occurred at all stems, not from any noticeable shift in content, but from a purely logistical consideration. In consonantal Hebrew all of the material contained in 1 and 2Ki could be copied on a single scroll. In Greek, however, with both consonants and vowels, far more space was needed. The resulting two scrolls led to the division that remains in our Bibles today. In actuality, 1 and 2Ki constitute a single unit and will be examined here in that light. When I refer to Kings, I mean 1 and 2Ki in our English Bibles.

The book of Kings covers a considerable period of time and a great variety of experiences and events. Included within its pages are moments of victory and defeat, though the story itself wanders down a path that leads to the destruction of both Israel and Judah. In general, the contents of Kings can be divided into two alternative groupings of three sections each. To begin with, the contents can be viewed from the traditional political point of view: (a) The United Monarchy Under Solomon (1Ki 1–11), (b) The Divided Monarchy (1Ki 12–2Ki 17), and (c) Judah Stands Alone (2Ki 18–25). Second, the major section dealing with the prophets Elijah and Elisha can be highlighted, resulting in the following units: (a) Kings: From Solomon to Ahab (1Ki 1–16); (b) Prophets: The Adventures of Elijah and Elisha (1Ki 17–2Ki 10); and (c) Kings: From Athaliah to Zedekiah (2Ki 11–25).

Building upon the reign of David in 2Sa, a high point during Israel's united monarchy, Kings begins with the ascension of Solomon to the throne c. 971 B.C. The eleven chapters devoted to Solomon's reign attempt to present him as a model king. His wisdom, for example, earned for him an international reputation, and he is commended for both his building endeavors as well as for his commitment to Yahweh. His undoing, however, eventually stemmed, at least on the surface, from his many marriages to foreign women and the pagan religious influences that accompanied them.

Following the reign of Solomon, the united monarchy gave way to the divided monarchy. Where once stood the nation of Israel, dominant and to some extent united under David and Solomon, one now finds two distinct and independent nations—Israel in the north and Judah in the south. As would be expected, such a division results in considerable tension and conflict between these neighboring groups, tension of both religious and political varieties. In the twenty-eight chapters of Kings dealing with this period (1Ki 12–2Ki 17), both northern and southern kings are interchanged until the northern kingdom of Israel is finally destroyed by the Assyrians in 721 B.C.

The concluding section of Kings, 2Ki 18–25, continues to follow the nation of Judah for roughly another 140 years. Interspersed during this period are occasional times of prosperity and religious awakening, but the overall development is not so unlike what took place in the northern kingdom. Indeed, the same fate that fell upon Israel awaited Judah, even though she witnessed Israel's ordeal and, at least from a religious perspective, had considerable time to reflect upon it. In short, 2Ki 18–25 moves from the destruction of Israel to Judah's own demise at the hands of the Babylonians in 587/86 B.C.

II. AUTHORSHIP, COMPOSITION, AND DATE

The book of Kings, as is typical of other materials in the Hebrew canon, is anonymous. According to a Talmudic tradition, authorship is to be attributed to the prophet Jeremiah (*Baba Bathra*, 15a). This view, though generally dismissed by modern scholars who cite the Talmudic tendency to associate all of the biblical writings with prophets, has recently been defended with considerable enthusiasm by Friedman (pp. 146–49).

Rather than speaking in terms of a named individual author, it is customary to associate Kings with a person or group of people known today as "Deuteronomists." This purely descriptive title derives from the belief that Kings, rather than standing independently, actually serves as the concluding volume in a series that begins with Deuteronomy. More specifically, the story running from Joshua through 2Ki constitutes an edited whole intended to demonstrate how the principles recorded in Deuteronomy can be traced in Israel's actual history. Accordingly, Kings is ultimately attributed to an editor or editors, the precise number of whom cannot be finally determined, who compiled these materials in order to depict the general theological orientation of Deuteronomy.

Beyond the question of authorship, however, considerably more can be said concerning the date and composition of Kings. The concluding event, King Jehoiachin's release from a Babylonian prison in 561 B.C., helps establish the earliest point at which the book could have been completed. However, a good portion of the materials included in Kings dates to the periods of the united and divided monarchies, the same periods that they describe. Furthermore, many of these materials, as we will see, were housed in already existing collections. Indeed, some scholars have argued the difficult position that an original edition of Kings, concluding with Josiah (2Ki 22–23), was completed during that king's reign (Gray, 5; Cross, 274–89; Friedman, 107–16). In any case, the final composition as it now stands took place during the Exile or, in the case of possible editorial changes, beyond (Ackroyd, ch. 5; Harrison, *Old Testament*, 730–32).

Throughout Kings, the editor makes it clear that he is drawing upon various sources for his information. In fact, three such sources are specifically mentioned in the text itself:

1. The "Book of the Annals of Solomon" (1Ki 11:41), which probably contained materials from the temple archives itself.

2. The "Book of the Annals of the Kings of Israel" (occurring repeatedly throughout 1Ki 14–2Ki 15, including 1Ki 14:19), which served as the major source of material from the northern kingdom.

3. The "Book of the Annals of the Kings of Judah" (occurring repeatedly throughout 1Ki 14–2Ki 24, including 1Ki 14:29), which served as the major source of material from the southern kingdom following the reign of Solomon.

In addition to these, other sources no doubt provided various materials found in Kings. For example, a cycle of prophetic tradition must have developed, which included stories about Elijah and Elisha, not to mention other prophets. Furthermore, court records from David's reign contributed to the conclusion of the succession narrative in 1Ki 1–2.

Sources such as these would have been maintained in various places, including official court archives. Insofar as the editor, working during or near the time of the Exile, came from the southern kingdom, records from Judah were understandably accessible. With respect to information from Israel, we need only imagine that members of the northern kingdom fled south across the border to escape the oncoming Assyrians. With them came records and stories descriptive of northern affairs. Relying to a degree upon such materials as well as those traditions preserved by prophetic groups themselves, the editor was able to fashion the book of Kings generally into the form that we now see.

III. LITERARY STRUCTURE AND PURPOSE

Even a casual reading of Kings will suggest that the editor had interests other than simply preserving the past. What is found here makes no pretenses about being historical in the modern, scientific sense of the term. Indeed, the fact that additional sources are so willingly referred to indicates a selectivity in choosing materials deemed appropriate for a particular purpose. Beyond this, the amount of attention given to various individuals is also instructive. Omri, as a most notable example, is known from extrabiblical sources to have been one of the northern kingdom's most influential kings. How unusual, then, that Kings devotes only eight verses to his reign (1Ki 16:21–28)! Similar comments could be made concerning Jeroboam II, whose reign for many must have represented a renaissance of sorts (2Ki 14:23–29). By way of contrast, several chapters are devoted to such kings as Hezekiah and Josiah as well as the prophets Elijah and Elisha. The reason, in one word, is "theology."

In understanding the perspective and purpose of Kings, it is important to keep in mind that the southern kingdom of Judah had recently been destroyed by the Babylonians. That Jerusalem, Judah's capital city, could ever fall was in the minds of many a theological impossibility (La 4:12, 20). Jerusalem, after all, was God's chosen city. Yet fall it did, and its destruction raised perplexing questions that begged for answers. Questions of this sort receive attention in Lamentations, where we find an emotional response similar to a mother crying over a dying child. In a similar fashion, Kings presents in a more journalistic style an account that attempts to trace both the major events that ultimately shaped Israel and Judah as well as their causes. For the editor, those causes were not so much poor political decisions, nor were they the unknown and uncontrollable chances of life. Rather, such causes were theological in nature, and the resulting account is "history" from a theologically reflective perspective.

As an illustration, were an atheist and a Christian to write histories of the United States, chances are that the end products would be drastically different. Even more so, were these same two individuals instructed to set aside the contemporary emphasis upon "scientific objectivity" and to write accounts that reflected their own world views, imagine the outcome. What the atheist sees as a mere natural occurrence might very well be seen by the Christian as an act of God. Does this mean that either or both accounts are necessarily unhistorical? No. It simply suggests that those events and experiences that were included in the finished product had been selected for a specific purpose and interpreted from a particular point of view. The ultimate intention, then, is not merely to preserve information, but to use that information to make a point. In describing the book of Kings from this perspective, DeVries suggests that "the facts may speak for themselves, but [the Deuteronomist] is not going to let them speak for themselves, lest someone misunderstand" (p. xlvii). As a result, these same facts are housed within a theological framework.

In pursuing this framework, various significant themes can be identified in Kings. These include:

1. The primacy and continuity of the Davidic dynasty (see, e.g., 1Ki 2:2–4; 3:6; 6:12; 11:12–13; 15:4–5; 2Ki 8:19; 22:2). Yahweh's faithfulness to the Davidic covenant serves to explain his subsequent faithfulness to Judah, ruled by David's successors. Furthermore, David himself becomes a positive standard by which later kings are evaluated (see below).

2. The centralization of worship in Jerusalem, Yahweh's chosen city (1Ki 11:13, 32, 36). Post-Solomonic kings are then frequently denounced

for their failure to comply with this regulation (1Ki 12–13; by way of contrast, note 2Ki 22–23).

3. The ultimate accountability of the royal leaders of both Israel and Judah to Yahweh and the Mosaic covenant. While David serves as the positive standard, such a standard exists at all only insofar as it coincides with the Mosaic tradition reflected in Deuteronomy. As von Rad points out, "The king is now regarded as the responsible person to whom has been entrusted the law of Moses and who has the duty to see that it is recognised in his kingdom" (p. 339). To place confidence, then, in the Davidic line without complying with Mosaic expectations (e.g., Dt 17:14–17) was theological shortsightedness.

4. The importance and reliability of the prophetic word and the consistent failure of many of the kings to listen to the true prophets among them (1Ki 11:29–39; 17:24; 18:16–46; 2Ki 6:8–23; 9:25–26; 17:13–14). According to Dt 18:14–22, prophets had been graciously promised in order to deliver the word of Yahweh to his people in Palestine. Such a promise finds fulfillment in Kings, and the frequent dismissal of the prophetic presence by those in power was to the editor a fundamental rejection of an avenue of guidance, correction, and hope.

5. The overarching conclusion is that, given these standards and expectations, Yahweh blesses those who walk obediently before him but judges those who do not. Rooted deeply in the blessings and curses motif of Deuteronomy, the kings of Israel and Judah are evaluated on the basis of covenantal faithfulness rather than political prowess. Subsequently, the events and experiences of these nations are seen as blessings or curses from Yahweh, whatever the case may be.

These major themes can be clearly seen when the literary structure of Kings is analyzed. On the surface, the editor weaves together materials from both the northern and southern kingdoms. In so doing, he discusses in a rough chronological fashion each of the kings, providing basic information regarding their reign (for a discussion of the chronological difficulties associated with the book of Kings, see Gray, 55–75). While occasional variations are noticeable, this information includes (1) the date when the king came to power and the length of his reign, (2) the place of his reign, (3) a theological evaluation, (4) mention of significant accomplishments, (5) sources from which additional information can be obtained, and (6) a reference to the king's death and burial. Of particular importance is the fact that, in the theological evaluation, the northern kings are consistently condemned whereas the southern kings receive mixed reviews.

But beyond this surface structure it is fascinating to note the manner in which additional theological ideas are incorporated. Once again, it is clear from the start that David was the exemplary king (1Ki 2:2–4; 3:14), a role attributed by Wesley primarily to the fact that David avoided habitual and continual sins (Wesley, 1146; cf. 1Ki 15:5). His son Solomon, then, was commissioned to follow his lead. In spite of his various accomplishments, however, he failed to do that, and the editor concludes that he "did not follow the LORD completely, as David his father had done" (1Ki 11:6). Solomon, however, does not become a negative example to be contrasted with his father. Among other possible reasons, this no doubt is related to the editor's high regard for the Davidic dynasty.

The "privilege" of serving as the negative example is reserved for Jeroboam I, the first ruler of the northern kingdom. Jeroboam disregarded Jerusalem as the center of Israelite worship, establishing competing shrines at Dan and Bethel. This deviation, according to the editor, led to Jeroboam's downfall (1Ki 13:34), and it would also serve as a stumbling block for his successors. From this point on, northern kings are condemned for walking in the ways of Jeroboam (e.g., see 1Ki 15:25–26; 16:19; 2Ki 13:2), and the many difficulties facing Israel are due to these sins (1Ki 14:16). For the northern kingdom, interestingly enough, there is no positive example!

In Judah, however, David continues to serve as the pattern although the majority of his successors fall far short of the standard. For this majority, the northern king, Jeroboam, is not mentioned in any comparative way. Apparently his sins were too severe to associate with the southern kingdom, even in the case of Manasseh, whose wickedness is compared instead to the pagan nations who had earlier been expelled from Palestine (2Ki 21:2)! Typically, evil southern kings are simply described as being either "unlike" David (1Ki 15:3; 2Ki 16:2) or "like his father," as in the case of Amon, who was like his evil father, Manasseh (2Ki 21:20). Even the worst of the southern kings cannot be compared with their northern neighbors who abandoned the Davidic cause.

This structural scheme can be traced through Kings until it reaches two climactic points. First, the northern line continues to follow Jeroboam until Israel is ultimately destroyed by Assyria (2Ki 17). Then the editor provides a summary statement in which he reinforces the motif (2Ki 17:7–23). Israel suffered defeat, not because of a military mismatch, but because her people had sinned. Briefly, her sins involved following the ways of Jeroboam and refusing to listen to the many prophetic warnings (17:22–23).

With respect to the southern kingdom, the line continues somewhat longer. Judah enjoys the reigns of selected good kings, and her direct tie to the Davidic dynasty encourages Yahweh to preserve her from certain defeat during Hezekiah's reign (2Ki 20:6). Nevertheless, these Davidic ties are insufficient to prevent eventual destruction, for Judah has all too often rejected covenantal expectations (2Ki 23:26–27; 24:20). As such, a second climactic point is reached when Judah herself is taken captive by the Babylonians (2Ki 25).

In short, the editor arranges the material in order to demonstrate that destruction has come upon the people of God because they failed to follow his covenant with them. Yahweh had indeed been faithful to his word, and he had provided continual opportunities for reform. Nevertheless, his commandments were broken and his gracious overtures rejected, making judgment a justifiable outcome. That such judgment need not be Yahweh's final word, however, is suggested by the fact that the very same covenant had provisions for repentance, even in a foreign land (1Ki 8:46–51). Similarly, the closing release of Jehoiachin (2Ki 25:27–30) is perhaps but a foretaste of things to come. In this sense then, the purpose of Kings is both confessional and, to a lesser degree, kerygmatic (Nicholson, 75). While acknowledging guilt, Kings subtly invites the community of faith to envision a future of hope.

IV. OUTLINE

COMMENTARY

I. THE UNITED MONARCHY UNDER SOLOMON (1KI 1:1–11:43)

The first eleven chapters of 1Ki describe various aspects of Israel's history from the time of Solomon's ascension to his death some forty years later (c. 971–931 B.C.). Chs. 1–2, which together with 2Sa 9–20 form a previously independent source generally referred to as the "Succession Narrative" (Porter), recount the struggles associated with Solomon's coming to power. Chs. 3–10 then discuss particular positive qualities or characteristics of Solomon that served as the impetus for his international reputation. Finally, ch. 11 explains why it is that a man of Solomon's apparent religious and political stature lost favor with both his people and his God.

A. Solomon Becomes King (1:1–2:46)

With the squelching of Sheba's revolt in 2Sa 20, David's kingship was relatively secure. However, the question as to who would succeed him had not yet been answered. It must be recalled that this was a new problem for Israel's fledgling monarchy; both Saul and David had been divinely selected apart from any formal family ties. Now, given the eternal promises to the Davidic line (2Sa 7:11–15), the heredity principle takes over. As such, the responsibility of naming a new king fell on David. That he delayed in doing so caused significant tension. That he was now old and in failing health, unable even to stay warm, made matters all the worse (1:1–2)

Out of such a context arose two rival factions, one supporting Adonijah (1:5–7) and the other Solomon

(1:11–14). Insofar as both Amnon (2Sa 13:28–29) and Absalom (2Sa 18:15) had been killed earlier, and Kileab is never mentioned outside of a genealogical record (suggesting that he probably died at a young age), Adonijah was David's oldest living son. Furthermore, like Absalom before him, he clearly saw kingship as the right of the eldest. That Adonijah proclaimed himself to be king, however, indicates that he doubted whether David saw things in the same way.

With a certain charisma that again calls Absalom to mind (2Sa 14:25–26), Adonijah attracted a significant group of supporters. Yet, in spite of a following that included both Joab and Abiathar (1:7), influential leaders under David, Adonijah's scheme failed. Reminded by Bathsheba and the prophet Nathan of an earlier promise (vv.13, 17), a promise that goes unmentioned elsewhere in the biblical text, David finally announces that Solomon will reign in his place (v.30). With this pronouncement, Adonijah's supporters disperse (v.49), and Adonijah himself seeks leniency from his younger brother.

Following this relatively rapid sequence of events, ch. 2 suggests how Solomon strengthened his hold on the throne. Up to this point, he had played a quiet and rather inactive role. With the death of his father (2:10), however, all of that changes. Systematically, Solomon removes or banishes his potential rivals.

To begin with, Adonijah, who had earlier sought mercy (1:50–51), approaches Bathsheba with a seemingly innocent request. He asks to marry Abishag (2:17), the Shunammite girl given to David (1:3). The nature of the request, however, is immediately recognized by Solomon (2:22). Because she had belonged to David, Abishag remained royal property. In asking for her, Adonijah actually laid yet another claim to kingship. In that light, Solomon's reaction (v.22) and ultimate response (v.25) can be better understood.

Following Adonijah, Solomon banishes Abiathar the priest to the town of Anathoth (2:26−27). Abiathar's religious role and his specific connection to the ark of the covenant explain why his punishment was more lenient than those to follow. It would have been far more difficult and dangerous for Solomon to kill a priest than to kill mere political rivals.

Finally, Solomon has both Joab (2:34) and Shimei (v.46) killed. In the case of Shimei, an almost humorous plan is invoked (vv.36−37). While remaining in Jerusalem was theoretically possible, the entire scheme indicates Solomon's ultimate intentions. Indeed, the fact that three years later he is immediately aware of Shimei's whereabouts, an apparent triviality for a king, reinforces the notion. Aware of David's final charge (vv.8−9) and seeing an opportunity to remove a Benjamite who could incite trouble among those just north of Jerusalem, Solomon removes this perceived threat. And with that, the editor concludes: **The kingdom was now firmly established in Solomon's hands** (v.46).

B. Solomon the Wise Man (3:1−4:34)

With Solomon's position established, chs. 3 and 4 constitute the first in a series of units that look at various aspects of his life and reign. Of particular importance here is the hypothetical and unwritten question that most readers would be asking: "How did Solomon become so wise and so wealthy?" The answer, at least on the surface, lies in the prayer that soon follows (3:6−9).

Ch. 3 begins abruptly by mentioning Solomon's alliance with Egypt and his subsequent marriage to Pharaoh's daughter (3:1). Such a marriage was extremely unusual, for although pharaohs were known to marry foreign wives, they did not share their daughters in like manner. In fact, a text from before the time of Solomon suggests as much: "From of old, a daughter of the king of Egypt has not been given to anyone" (Amarna Letter IV). While Israel had reached a point of strength by this time, such a marriage indicates that Egypt, like Assyria to the northeast, was in a somewhat weakened condition. In addition, Solomon's ties with Israel's former taskmasters and his proudly bringing his new queen to Jerusalem must have produced a degree of hardship in the hearts of some of his followers.

Prior to the building of the temple, the religious situation in Israel remained somewhat unsettled (3:2). The ark was in Jerusalem (2Sa 6), the tabernacle most likely in Gibeon (1Ch 16:39; 21:29), and public worship had been going on at various places. Of these places or shrines, some were clearly heathen, but others were neutral and could be dedicated to Yahweh (DeVries, XXVI−XXIX). According to 1Ki 3:2, while heathen shrines should have been destroyed, shrines of the latter type would cease to function only when the temple itself was completed.

Of these earlier legitimate shrines, Gibeon was one of the more important because of its connection with the ark and the tabernacle. While there, Solomon offers a monumental sacrifice (3:4) and is invited by God in a dream to make a request (v.5). Rather than asking for wealth or power, as one might expect, Solomon desires a discerning heart (v.9). Such a request pleases God to the extent that he gives Solomon not only wisdom, but a promise of unsolicited wealth and honor as well (v.13). A further benefit—longevity—would be Solomon's too if he lived up to the righteous standard established by his father (v.14). David, once again, serves as the positive example to be emulated.

With Solomon's request having been granted, it remained for his newly found wisdom to be demonstrated. Proof, in other words, can be found in the familiar story recorded in 3:16–28. Here Solomon makes the legendary decision with respect to the two prostitutes arguing over the same child. Importantly, the decision affected not only the conflicting individuals, but also the entire community. Solomon was now held in awe (3:28).

Organizationally, the internal positions of Solomon's kingdom reflected in 4:1–6 closely resemble those of David's (2Sa 8:16–18; 20:23–26), with perhaps a few additions. Of particular significance, however, are the administrative districts listed in 4:7–19. In order to finance his various endeavors, Solomon devised a scheme whereby his kingdom would be divided into twelve districts. Not to be confused with the earlier twelve tribes, each of these districts was responsible to provide supplies for one month every year. On the basis of 4:22–26, this was no small matter! In spite of 4:20, a degree of resentment began to set in as a result of this and other policies, although it goes largely unmentioned until 1Ki 12.

Having depicted Solomon's wise ruling and described his organizational structures, the editor now supplies an almost breathtaking synopsis of Solomon's wisdom (4:29–34). Needing to spend far less time dealing with military matters than did his father, Solomon had the luxury to direct his attention elsewhere. He enjoyed various literary and musical pursuits, composing both proverbs and songs (v.32), and he was accomplished in the natural sciences (v.33). Not only did native Israelites marvel at his insight, but people from all over the world came to hear him speak (v.34). In short, Solomon's wisdom knew no limits (v.29).

But beyond a simple picture of Solomon himself, this description of him as a sort of Renaissance Man also reflects the ever-increasing importance of the wisdom movement during his reign. Even though wisdom in ancient Israelite society was understandably rooted in family life, where parents and grandparents would pass insight on to the children, the demands of the monarchy required good and dependable counsel. As such, groups of particularly wise individuals gathered in a formal sense and, most likely, schools gained importance (Crenshaw, "Wisdom in the OT," and particularly *Old Testament Wisdom,* 27–65). Solomon, then, embodies so much of the wisdom that had become important to people at that time. He was nothing less than wisdom in human form.

C. Solomon the Builder (5:1–7:51)

In addition to his remarkable insight, Solomon is also remembered for his building exploits. Many of the materials used in such projects came from Tyre, the capital of the important Phoenician state that controlled the Mediterranean coastline north of Israel. Already in effect when David built his palace (2Sa 5:11), Solomon renewed the alliance with King Hiram and used it as a way of obtaining needed lumber (vv.1–10) and skilled workmen (v.18). In exchange, he exported wheat and olive oil (5:11). Note that such peaceful international relationships are once again attributed to Solomon's God-given wisdom (v.12).

In order to complete these various projects, however, workers were needed. In response to this, Solomon established something new. Forced labor was of course common throughout the ancient Near East, and both David himself (2Sa 12:31) and Solomon (1Ki 9:20–22) had continued this practice. In such cases, conquered people constituted the laborers. Now, however, Solomon also developed a labor force made up of otherwise free Israelites (5:13). While perhaps not slaves in the technical sense (1Ki 9:22) insofar as they were required to work only one month out of every three (5:14), such a practice must have been burdensome for a group of people who had earlier been delivered from slavery and oppression. No doubt, Samuel's words rang in the ears of many who observed these developments (1Sa 8:16).

With the materials and laborers in hand, chs. 6–8 discuss Solomon's building projects in general and the temple in particular. While the date recorded in 6:1 has been the object of considerable debate (Kitchen, 72–75), its function here is to link the building of the temple with the exodus from Egypt. Both, in other words, are seen as monumental and memorable events.

What follows then is a detailed list preserving specifications for the construction of the temple (6:2–36), a temple apparently patterned to a great extent on a Phoenician model (Wright, ch. 3). Roughly 90 feet long by 30 feet wide by 45 feet high, it was not particularly large (6:2). However, if the details in this list are viewed functionally, the sight of the temple must have created varying impressions in the hearts and minds of those who came to worship there.

Solomon's building interests were not limited to the temple. Included among his many projects were the five structures mentioned in 7:2–8: (1) a gathering hall called the "Palace of the Forest of Lebanon" that was far larger than the temple itself (v.2); (2) a colonnade (v.6); (3) the **Hall of Justice**, where he carried out judicial matters (v.7); (4) his own personal palace (v.8); and (5) a palace for his Egyptian queen (v.8).

This entire complex rested south of the temple compound and in some ways must have overshadowed the religious structure. In light of this, one can only attempt to sort through Solomon's true views and intentions with respect to Yahweh and his own personal position.

Following this general list of projects, 7:13–51 describes the many furnishings located within and around the temple. Included among the many items were selected pieces that earlier belonged to David (7:51). Given all of his various endeavors, Solomon's notoriety continued to expand. He was, in short, the consummate builder.

D. Solomon the Religious Example (8:1–66)

Not only was Solomon remembered for his wisdom and building projects, but he apparently served as a religious model as well. In 8:1–21, for example, he made sure that the ark was placed in the temple. Generally speaking, Saul took little account of Israel's religious traditions, paying virtually no attention to such matters as the ark and the tabernacle. David, by way of contrast, displayed far more sensitivity in this area, and Solomon did likewise. In addition, 8:22–66 recounts Solomon's majestic prayer of dedication and the actual dedication ceremony. From these indications, Solomon rose as a religious figure.

The sum of Solomon's religious accomplishments, then, resulted in the centralization of Israelite worship. At least in theory, the various shrines situated throughout the land were now to disappear, and the temple was to serve as the focal point of all Israelite religious practices. With such a development, however, came the possibility of a major problem—a permanent structure frequently leads to a permanent institution. Similarly, that structure and institution frequently replace the God they were originally intended to serve. When the joy of this remarkable occasion fades, the likes of Jeremiah and others will echo this concern (Jer 7:4). But in the meantime, Solomon is surely a religious example.

E. Solomon the Incomparable One (9:1–10:29)

In this final unit depicting the positive qualities and characteristics of Solomon, the editor recounts all three of those mentioned previously—wisdom, building projects, religion—but in reverse order. Religiously, Yahweh appears to Solomon a second time and voices his general approval (9:1–9). Included are a reiteration of the promise to bless Solomon further if he lives up to David's example (9:4–5), as well as the tragic consequences if he does not (9:6–9).

With respect to building activities, 9:10–26 describes various projects, labor forces, and trade agreements. The extent of Solomon's control is depicted not only in the number of towns that he either built or rebuilt, but also in both the international flavor of his laborers (9:20–21) as well as the geographical parameters of his business

enterprise (9:26–28). Solomon is credited with controlling the entire region from Ezion Geber on the northern shore of the Red Sea to the Euphrates (1Ki 4:21).

Finally, Solomon's wisdom is once again verified with the testimony of the Queen of Sheba (10:1–13). Hearing of Solomon's wisdom in her homeland in southern Arabia, the queen came to find out for herself. Left virtually breathless by all she sees and hears, she affirms Solomon's wisdom and achievements and offers praise to the God of Israel.

At this point the editor nearly runs out of words to describe his subject. In summing up his appraisal of Solomon (10:14–29), he concludes that he was without equal in the entire world. People from every land sought his counsel, and with them came priceless gifts (10:23–25). Solomon, in short, was incomparable.

F. Solomon's Wives and Adversaries (11:1–43)

As has been implied in the previous discussion, Solomon's reign is complicated and difficult to evaluate. It was a prosperous time, at least for some, but in spite of the fact that Solomon controlled such a vast region and therefore the trade routes that went with it, his income could not keep pace with his lavish expenditures. As a result, his people faced burdensome policies that included severe taxation and forced labor.

Religiously, several factors indicate a sense of commitment on Solomon's part to the God of Israel. His initial prayer for wisdom and subsequent prayer to dedicate the temple suggest spiritual sensitivity, and his connection with the ark reveals at least some concern for Israel's religious traditions. Yet his reign clearly ends on a negative note, and his kingdom is far from unified when he dies. What happened?

As mentioned in the introduction, the book of Kings reflects the theological perspective presented in the book of Deuteronomy. With that in mind, Dt 17:14–17 clearly suggests Solomon's shortcomings. According to this passage, three things were to be avoided by Israel's king: (1) marrying many wives, (2) accumulating large amounts of silver, and (3) acquiring great numbers of horses.

Yet in precisely these three areas Solomon is found wanting. First, Solomon married many wives who in turn led him away from Yahweh (11:1–13). To be sure, David also had several wives, but his wives were typically not foreigners who were married for international political reasons as were Solomon's. Beyond that, however, Solomon clearly did not marry all of these women at once, in spite of the fact that the problem goes unmentioned prior to ch. 11. These marriages denote a gradual shift rather than a sudden alteration; Solomon increasingly sought the political security that such alliances offered. In the process, he accommodated the gods that foreigners worshiped. Besides building a temple for Yahweh, therefore, Solomon erected many temples dedicated to various gods from throughout the ancient world (vv.7–8).

Second, Solomon accumulated great amounts of silver (1Ki 10:27). To be sure, the promise of wealth was included in God's earlier address (1Ki 3:13). But the context of 10:27 makes it clear that Solomon's riches were not so much the product of divine generosity as they were of human achievement. Solomon, in other words, accumulated great wealth on his own initiative and often at the expense of those under him. The point is the same as that

expressed by Jesus in Mt 6:33. When one seeks first the kingdom of God, other things will be added. However, the presence of other things, as the psalmist attests to (Ps 73:3), does not necessarily indicate that the kingdom was actually sought first. The presence of wealth, therefore, must not be taken as a sign of God's approval.

Third, Solomon acquired large numbers of chariots and horses, the majority of which were obtained from Egypt (1Ki 10:26, 28–29). Here, the taskmaster has now become the provider! In earlier periods in Israel's history, war was carried out by the infantry, and the outcome clearly rested upon God. Stories such as the conquest of Jericho (Jos 6) and the battles of Gideon (Jdg 7) reinforced the notion in the Israelite mind that victory was dependent on God rather than on military excellence. Yet just as he sought political and financial security, so too did Solomon strive for military security. In the process his commitment to God naturally diminished. With Solomon, what on the surface appears to be a time of remarkable vitality and achievement turns out to be what Mendenhall and others have referred to as the "paganization of Israel" (Brueggemann, 31; Mendenhall, 160). The quest for self-security and a lasting trust in God are, as we see here, mutually exclusive.

As a result, Solomon's reign ends in disarray. 1Ki 11:14–43 briefly records several of those individuals and nations who caused trouble during Solomon's last days. Internationally, Edom and Aram were noteworthy nemeses (vv.14–25). On the local scene, a northerner named Jeroboam received a message from the prophet Ahijah that he would gain a considerable portion of Solomon's kingdom (11:29–39). Apparently unwilling to wait for such an event to occur, Jeroboam rebelled and was exiled for a time in Egypt (11:40). Although Solomon retained somewhat tenuous control of his kingdom, the end was clearly in sight. The facts that the destruction of Solomon's kingdom was delayed until after his death and that such a destruction would affect only a portion of the actual kingdom are attributed by the editor to God's faithfulness to David, the positive example of kingship in Israel (vv.13, 32, 36). Had Solomon followed that example, these difficulties would have been averted (v.33). As Clarke aptly concludes:

> How few proofs does [Solomon's] life give that the gracious purpose of God was fulfilled in Him! He received much, but he would have received much more, had he been faithful to the grace given (p. 395).

However, probably due either to his relationship to David or to his connection with the temple, Solomon is at least spared the embarrassment of serving as the negative example of kingship. That role will soon be delegated to Jeroboam.

II. THE DIVIDED MONARCHY (1Ki 12:1–2Ki 17:41)

This second major unit of the book of Kings deals with the period in Israel's history beginning with the division of the kingdom into the two distinct nations of Judah and Israel and ending with the eventual destruction of Israel at the hands of the Assyrians (c. 931–721 B.C.). The events of the split itself are recounted in 12:1–24. The remaining chapters trace the journeys of each nation, interchanging sections dealing first with the kings of one nation and then with the other.

Interspersed throughout the entire unit are selected prophetic speeches as well as various stories describing the

actions of the prophets. Particularly noteworthy of these are the two major blocks of material dealing with Elijah (1Ki 17:1–2Ki 2:18) and Elisha (2Ki 2:19–8:29). At first glance these sections appear to be out of place or at least unreasonably extended. But the importance of the prophetic word to the Deuteronomistic perspective must always be kept in mind. Apart from these sections we find isolated stories and repeated references to the role of the prophets in the affairs of the kings. Here, however, we receive a particularized or in-depth view of prophetic activity. In effect, the editor pauses to focus on a relatively brief period of the entire story before resuming the more rapid pace.

The overall unit comes to a close with an account describing the fall and subsequent repopulating of the northern kingdom of Israel (2Ki 17:1–6, 24–41). Coupled with this description is a theological statement explaining why such a dreadful event ever took place (17:7–23).

A. The Kingdom Divides (12:1–24)

With Solomon's death the kingdom established by David almost immediately comes to an end. It should be recalled that Jeroboam had already received a prophetic word concerning his gaining control over a major portion of the kingdom (11:29–39) and that he fled to Egypt to escape Solomon's wrath. Now, however, Jeroboam freely returns, and he serves as the northern tribes' representative at a summit of sorts at Shechem (vv.1–3).

During this summit, Jeroboam and other northerners confronted Rehoboam, Solomon's son, whose kingship had already been recognized by those in Judah (11:43). But the Davidic family typically enjoyed less acceptance in the

North. Recall, for example, that a similar division of the house occurred during David's time when he himself ruled over Judah for seven years before extending his authority over all of Israel (2Sa 5:5). As such, the northern delegation now presented Rehoboam with certain demands that had to be met before they would recognize him as king.

At this point the severity of Solomon's policies, only alluded to in chs. 1–11, is completely unmasked (v.4). For Rehoboam to exercise control over a unified Israel, he first had to agree to free the people of such oppressive policies. When he refuses, the northerners remove their allegiance.

What now begins is the period known as the divided monarchy, and what remains are two far less powerful and important states that spend much of their time quarreling with each other. The name Israel comes to refer specifically to the northern kingdom, a nation under the kingship of Jeroboam. In the South the original tribal name Judah comes now to designate the resulting nation under the kingship of Rehoboam. This situation continues for over 200 years until the northern kingdom of Israel is destroyed. Following that event, Judah will continue to exist, generally in a weakened condition, for nearly 150 years longer.

B. Jeroboam Reigns Over Israel (12:25–14:20)

Upon becoming king in the North, Jeroboam took several steps to ensure the completeness and permanence of the division and with it his own political position. The primary problem he faced was that the religious center remained in the southern city of Jerusalem (12:26–27). Insofar as one cannot simply invent a new religion, particularly within a community somewhat

steeped in religious tradition, Jeroboam devised an alternate or revised version in order to compete with the Yahwism of the South. He sought, as Wesley rightly points out, to alter circumstances rather than substance (p. 1133). This revision included various components:

1. Shrines were established in the cities of Dan and Bethel. Both cities had earlier religious importance (Ge 28:16–22; 35:1–4; Jdg 18:27–31), and the fact that they were located at opposite ends of the kingdom made going to one or the other far more convenient. Furthermore, Bethel was situated in close proximity to the border with Judah. For those who might still prefer the long, uphill journey to Jerusalem, such a sight might be a tempting alternative after an exhausting day.

2. Tangible objects were needed to compete with the famous ark in Solomon's temple. From the beginning of time, people have longed for physical expressions verifying the presence of deity, and Israel's inhabitants were no different. Therefore two golden calves were erected at each shrine. Presented not so much as isolated images, these calves symbolized the gods **"who brought [the Israelites] up out of Egypt"** (12:28).

3. Priests were appointed to serve at these religious centers (12:31). While they were not Levites, they could nevertheless satisfy the needs of those who came to offer sacrifices.

4. A religious festival was instituted (12:32). Although the precise nature of such a festival remains uncertain, it was clearly intended to compete with those celebrated annually in Jerusalem.

Jeroboam's policies, therefore, constituted not simply a political break with Judah, although his motives were clearly political in nature. Rather, what in effect occurred was a religious break as well. As subsequent chapters will point out, these developments will become a thorn in the side of both Jeroboam and his successors.

In Jeroboam's case, a pronouncement of judgment follows immediately in ch. 13. In a striking and perplexing story, an unnamed man of God is sent from Judah to condemn Jeroboam at Bethel (13:1–3). Having completed his task, the man begins his journey home only to violate some seemingly trivial instructions that God had given to him. As a result, he is killed by a lion and buried in the city of Bethel by an old, unnamed prophet.

Following as it does the account describing the initial policies of Jeroboam, this story serves at least two primary functions. First of all, it does denounce Jeroboam's activities, making it clear from the start that such religious revisions are no less idolatrous than the worship of totally alien gods. And, second, it underscores the importance of following even the lesser details of God's instructions. Such obedience is especially expected of those who have been commissioned to deliver divine messages, i.e., prophets.

In 14:1–20 Jeroboam receives yet another prophetic word of judgment. No doubt recalling Ahijah's earlier favorable pronouncement (11:29–39), Jeroboam sends his wife with the hope of securing an encouraging word concerning his ill child. That he disguises her, however, betrays his sense of pessimism. Such efforts notwithstanding, Ahijah, as an enabled prophet, identifies the woman even before seeing her. He then forcefully condemns Jeroboam's idolatrous activities and predicts the death of the child (14:7–16).

Before leaving Jeroboam, it is important to emphasize precisely what it was that brought him such prophetic pronouncements. Never is the establishment of the northern kingdom condemned, nor was Jeroboam denounced for his participation in that event. In fact, the northerners' earlier criticism of Solomon reflects a perspective on social justice that was faithfully Israelite; his policies were harsh and oppressive. In that sense, it could be argued that the founding of the northern kingdom was a legitimate attempt to establish a more equitable system. Rather, Jeroboam was condemned for his religious activities (13:34; 14:9). By establishing counterfeit shrines and images, he rejected Jerusalem and its temple, invited religious syncretism, and led his people astray. Insofar as he did not walk in the ways of David (14:8), Jeroboam now becomes the negative example with whom future evil kings will be compared.

C. Rehoboam, Abijah, and Asa Reign Over Judah (14:21–15:24)

After hearing of the events that had taken place in the northern kingdom, one would expect that things were considerably better in the South. However, the account of Rehoboam, Judah's first king, immediately sets such misconceptions aside. In fact, the editor suggests that Judah's wickedness, which included the establishment of religious high places, idols, and cult prostitution, equaled that of the Canaanites who had been driven out during the initial conquest of the land (14:22–24). That the nationality of Rehoboam's mother is specified suggests that such evil can once again be attributed to the Solomonic practice of marrying foreign wives (v.31).

On the international scene, Jerusalem was attacked by Pharaoh Shishak during Rehoboam's reign (14:25), and Judah and Israel were continually at war with each other (v.30). Concerning Shishak, Egyptian records suggest, perhaps in a glorified manner, that he captured some 150 cities in Israel and Judah during his reign (c. 940–915 B.C.). Though he gathered considerable booty (v.26) and apparently collected tribute, his military campaign had no major lasting impact on the area.

Like his father Rehoboam, Abijah is also condemned as a religious failure (15:1–8). In a fashion that characterizes the editor, Abijah was unlike David (v.3). As is typical throughout the book of Kings, the evil kings of the North are compared to Jeroboam, but the evil kings of the South are contrasted to David (see the introduction). Yet, in spite of Abijah's wickedness, God's favor to the Davidic line produced an heir rather than the termination of the dynasty (v.4).

That heir bore the name Asa (vv.9–24). Asa destroyed virtually all of the religious objects created by his predecessors, and that his heart was committed to Yahweh meant that he was like David (v.11). Beyond this, Asa established a treaty with Syria in order to stave off Baasha, Israel's king at the time. As a result, the northern kingdom suffered considerable loss (v.20). Although Scripture repeatedly views such treaties and alliances as a lack of trust, Asa receives no word of correction here. The chronicler, however, supplies it (2Ch 16:7–10).

D. Nadab, Baasha, Elah, Zimri, Omri, and Ahab Reign Over Israel (15:25–22:40)

The editor now rapidly disposes of five northern kings before slowing down to discuss Ahab and Elijah. Nadab (15:25–26) emulated his father Jeroboam and was soon assassinated by Baasha (15:27–16:7). In turn, Baasha replaced Nadab and immediately destroyed Jeroboam's entire family

(15:29). Though he removed the family, he was unable to remove the influences, for Baasha himself **walked in the ways of Jeroboam**. After a reign of some twenty-four years, he was succeeded by his son Elah (16:8–14). After just a few years, Elah's own official, Zimri, murdered him, destroyed Baasha's entire family, and took the throne. But within days, Zimri, seeing that a rival faction favoring Omri had gathered considerable support, died in a building that he himself set on fire (vv.15–20). Such is our picture of kingship in Israel.

The reign of Omri, however, deserves a bit more discussion (16:21–28), for Omri is the classic example of how the editor swiftly dismisses even politically competent kings who fail in the religious realm. Having attracted greater support than yet another rival, Tibni, Omri became king and established a dynasty that would last some forty-four years. During his twelve-year reign, he moved his capital from Tirzah to the strategically located site of Samaria, where it remained throughout the northern kingdom's existence. Furthermore, he undertook significant building projects, formed an alliance with Syria, pursued a general course of conciliation with Judah and Phoenicia, and exercised control over the territory of Moab. While the biblical text has little to say concerning these matters, archaeological evidence in general and the Moabite Stone in particular have shed additional light (Miller and Hayes, 250–75). Indeed, Omri's influence reached such proportions that an Assyrian text dating to the reign of Menahem, over a hundred years after this time, referred to the land of Israel as "Omri-Land" (Pritchard, 284). Yet he is dismissed here in eight verses, unaccused of specific sins, but said to have **walked in all the ways of Jero-**

boam. Omri's political accomplishments, needless to say, were unimpressive to the Deuteronomistic editor.

Omri was succeeded by his son Ahab (16:29–22:40). Included in this account and set during Ahab's reign are many of the Elijah stories. This, along with his politically motivated marriage to the Phoenician Jezebel, explains why Ahab remains the most famous of all the northern kings. Throughout this entire section, which actually covers only some twenty to twenty-five years, the southern kingdom virtually disappears from the discussion as concentration is centered on the North. In addition, the monarchy is greatly overshadowed by the prophetic office as we receive a more complete picture of prophetic/political interaction.

From the start, it is clear that the primary issue in these chapters is the religious struggle between Yahwism and Baalism. Although information in the biblical text concerning Baal is scant, texts found at Ugarit in 1929 have added much to our understanding (Craigie; Harrison, "Ugarit," 460–61). Baal was the Canaanite god who "rode on the clouds." He controlled the lightening and the thunder, and it was he who regulated the rain. Therefore, in a land like Palestine, which lacks major rivers such as those in Egypt and Mesopotamia, Baal was someone that everybody wanted to know.

Baal's importance, furthermore, was accentuated by the fact that Canaan maintained what was predominantly an agricultural economy. Simply recall that Solomon exported wheat and olive oil in exchange for timber (1Ki 5:11). What was at stake, then, was often the very issue of security and survival. For an Israelite community called to trust Yahweh, the threat of drought often proved too great a temptation when one could find security by approaching Baal.

Although this religious tension had existed since Israel first entered the land, it had clearly reached the gravest proportions by the opening half of the ninth century B.C. Ahab, according to 16:30, did more evil than any of his predecessors. Indeed, the sins of Jeroboam were trivial to him (16:31). In part due to the Baal-worshiping Jezebel, it appears that Baalism was nothing less than the national religion in the northern kingdom by this time. An official temple had been erected in Samaria (16:32), prophets of Baal were functioning in a recognized capacity (18:19), and those faithful to Yahweh were systematically executed (18:3–4). In this context, both Elijah and Elisha after him have their setting.

The severity of the situation also helps us to understand why such a great number of miracles are associated with the period in question. While isolated miracles could very well occur at any time, there are three noticeable concentrations of miracles in the biblical record. The first of these is found in connection with the exodus from Egypt. In this case, the community of faith is freed from actual political oppression. The third and final concentration of miracles appears in the Gospels and is of course associated with the ministry of Jesus. In this case, the community of faith is freed from the oppression of sin and death. The second such concentration appears right here with Elijah and Elisha. The implication, of course, is that the people of God are once again in a potentially fatal crisis. In this case, the community of faith is in danger of losing its identity by thoroughly assimilating the cultural religion of the day.

Elijah appears rather abruptly in ch. 17, and the text simply records that he came from Gilead on the eastern side of the Jordan. His opening words were a direct challenge to Baal, the rain-giver: **"There will be neither dew nor rain in the next few years except at my word"** (v.1). Elijah is then divinely cared for by both the ravens (v.6) and a foreigner in her hometown of Zarephath (vv.7–24). Through the subsequent raising of the child, Elijah has the opportunity both to demonstrate his power and publicly to verify his prophetic office (v.24).

Given such a demonstration, the stage is now set for the confrontation between Elijah and the prophets of Baal. With the hesitant assistance of Obadiah, another faithful follower of Yahweh (18:3–4), Elijah approaches Ahab and instructs him (not a mere suggestion!) to gather the prophets of Baal as well as the population in general on Mount Carmel. There a contest of sorts is to take place.

According to Elijah's plan, first the prophets of Baal and then he as Yahweh's representative were to place bulls on wood that had been arranged before them. Each side would then call on their respective gods, and whichever deity responded with fire would be declared the winner (18:22–24). As the prophets of Baal carried out their turn, it became apparent that no response was forthcoming. As such, Elijah taunted them, suggesting that perhaps Baal was either visiting the bathroom, traveling, or sleeping (v.27). Their increased efforts notwithstanding, Baal remained silent.

Elijah's sense of the dramatic is further seen when, given his turn, he has the bull thoroughly drenched with water (18:33–34). Yet, without any further theatrics or arm-twisting, he prays and Yahweh sends fire to consume the bull. At the sight of such a demonstration, the entire community affirms that Yahweh, not Baal, is indeed the true God (v.39). As an apparent coup de grace, Elijah attempts to rid the land completely of Baal worship by slaughtering the defeated prophets (v.40). That he was unsuccessful is made unmistakably clear in later accounts, particularly those dealing with Jehu (2Ki 10:18–29).

Following what was certainly an invigorating experience, ch. 19 presents Elijah in a drastically different situation. While considerable debate has centered on the placement of this story in the overall narrative (DeVries, 234–35; Gray, 374), one can at least imagine such a radical emotional shift. Exhausted from the events on Mount Carmel and drained from the victory, Elijah has nothing left with which to confront Jezebel. Instead he flees southward to the sacred site of Horeb and eventually finds refreshment. In the assurance of God's presence, which came in the form of a gentle whisper (19:12), Elijah returns and anoints Jehu as king over Israel and Elisha as his own personal successor for the prophetic office (vv.15–21).

With the drama of Mount Carmel in the past, 20:1–22:40 preserves various stories concerning both Ahab and Elijah. Much of Ahab's reign was spent in conflict with the Syrians. In fact, 20:1–34 mentions three such battles. In the last of these, Ahab was unreasonably merciful and established a treaty with the defeated Ben-Hadad (20:34). In response, an unnamed prophet predicts that disaster will come upon both Ahab and his people (20:42). Ahab's sullen reaction is instructive, showing once again a prophet dominating a king (20:43).

Ch. 21, contrary to popular opinion, shows Ahab during one of his better moments. With his efforts to purchase Naboth's vineyard thwarted, he returns to the palace angry. Yet he apparently realizes that, according to Israelite law, it is impossible for Naboth to sell land that belongs in his family (Lev 25). Though he is clearly dissatisfied with the results, Ahab nevertheless appears willing to accept the undesirable. Unfortunately for Naboth, Jezebel does not share even Ahab's modest regard for earlier Israelite traditions. Rather, she plots his death and delivers the vineyard to Ahab. With this, a prophetic word is once again uttered. According to Elijah, Ahab's entire family, including Jezebel, will be destroyed (21:20-24). According to the editor, no previous king can compare to the evil Ahab (v.25). Only a thoroughly unexpected last-minute confession delays the predicted judgment until after Ahab's death (vv.27-28).

The series of stories concerning Ahab comes to a close in ch. 22. In spite of the warnings of the prophet Micaiah, who represented Yahweh in the most hostile of surroundings, Ahab and the Judahite king Jehoshaphat, now allies, went to yet another battle with the Syrians. While at Ramoth-Gilead, Ahab, though thoroughly disguised, suffered a mortal wound and was later buried in the capital city of Samaria. To the detail, events occurred as they had been prophesied (22:38).

E. Jehoshaphat Reigns Over Judah (22:41-50)

Jehoshaphat is remembered in 1Ki for two primary reasons. To begin with, he lived at peace with Israel (v.44) and in fact formed an alliance with Ahab (v.4). This, as has become clear, was a monumental accomplishment. Second, he furthered the religious reform begun by his father Asa (vv.43-46). Although more could have been done (v.43), Jehoshaphat

receives high marks, having done **what was right in the eyes of the LORD**.

F. Ahaziah and Joram Reign Over Israel (1Ki 22:51-2Ki 8:15)

In returning once again to the northern kingdom, Ahaziah has now succeeded his father Ahab as king (1Ki 22:51-2Ki 1:18). In spite of Elijah's heroics, Ahaziah not only walked in the ways of Jeroboam, but he also worshiped Baal (1Ki 22:53). For that, he of course receives the editor's condemnation.

Other than dealing with a Moabite rebellion, the worst of which actually fell on Joram (3:1-27), Ahaziah's legacy actually rests upon a personal tragedy. Following a severe fall, he desired a divine word concerning his fate. However, rather than summoning a prophet of Yahweh, he sends messengers to consult Baal-Zebub, a Philistine god (1:2). While this is perhaps not surprising considering the flow of events, its implications are startling nonetheless. For Ahaziah, Baal-Zebub rather than Yahweh directed the course of human affairs. Elijah, however, is commissioned by God to present the messengers with an unsolicited word: **"You will certainly die!"** What follows, then, is a perplexing story that underscores the importance of treating God's prophets and the prophetic office with the utmost respect (1:9-16). Given the reliability and significance of the true prophetic word, Ahaziah, as expected, did in fact die as a result of his fall (1:17).

Insofar as Ahaziah had no son, he was succeeded by his brother Joram (or Jehoram). During this time, the various stories dealing with Elisha have their setting (2:1-8:15). In ch. 2, Elijah is dramatically removed, and Elisha remains to carry on the work. Elisha's request for a double portion of Elijah's spirit (2:9) reflects the fact that the firstborn son of an Israelite received twice the inheritance (Dt 21:17). By implication, Elisha saw himself as Elijah's son, and he wanted to be thoroughly equipped for his task.

Following this transfer of authority, two brief stories illustrate his power and verify his position. The city of Jericho, first of all, had been cursed earlier by Joshua (Jos 6:26), and apparently that curse included the spring located there. Using a **new** bowl, which signified both a special occasion as well as the absence of earlier influences, Elisha restored the water for the benefit of the city's inhabitants (2:19–22).

Second, in a somewhat more disturbing account, Elisha curses some youths who apparently ridiculed him (2:23–25). It must be remembered, however, that travelers in the ancient world covered their heads. The "baldness," then, does not designate Elisha's personal physical condition, but rather some distinguishing mark or patch that symbolized the prophetic office. In this way the youths did not mock Elisha as much as they mocked the office. To do so was nothing less than mocking God (Lev 24:10–16; Dt 18:19). If the story of the man of God from Judah suggests the need for total obedience on the part of God's chosen servants (1Ki 13), then the present story indicates that those same servants are to be treated with the highest respect.

During Joram's reign, the Moabite rebellion mentioned earlier in connection with Ahaziah (1:1) reached its peak (3:1–27). In response, a coalition consisting of Israel, Judah, and Edom, Judah's vassal (1Ki 22:47; 2Ki 8:20), fought the Moabites in battle and was initially successful (3:24). Out of desperation, the Moabite king publicly sacrificed his son to the god Chemosh as a way of winning his favor. At such a

sight, the coalition mysteriously withdrew (v.27). While the underlying dynamics are difficult to discern, perhaps many of the Israelites either feared Chemosh or were sickened by the sight of such an abomination (Lev 18:21; 20:3).

A series of loosely arranged stories pertaining to Elisha's ministry follow. The first six of these find Elisha assisting various individuals or friends (4:1–6:7), while the others more closely show him functioning in international affairs (6:8–8:15).

The first group of stories begins with Elisha assisting a woman of desperate economic standing (4:1–7). Her husband died, leaving her in debt, and her creditors are about to take her two sons as payment. In addition to the emotional loss associated with losing family members, she would also lose her final sources of support. By miraculously supplying her with valuable oil, Elisha demonstrates his concern for the poor and oppressed. Beyond that, the nature of the story implies the close connection between Elisha and Elijah, who had also ministered to a woman and her son (1Ki 17:8–16).

In the second story, we find that Elisha also addressed the needs of those in the upper strata of society (4:8–37). In this case, a wealthy but barren Shunamite woman had shown Elisha gracious hospitality. When his initial attempts to repay her are rejected, Elisha promises her a son. However, that son later dies while working in the field, apparently of sunstroke. In raising the boy to life, Elisha demonstrates that Yahweh, not Baal, is the giver of life. Furthermore, he once again calls to mind his predecessor Elijah, who performed a similar miracle for a grieving widow (1Ki 17:17–24).

Two brief stories next show Yahweh providing for others through the hands of his prophet. In 4:38–41, such provisions take the form of an otherwise poisonous vine. When the benefactors, a collective gathering of prophets, realize the danger, Elisha decontaminates the food. In 4:42–44 provisions for many come through the multiplication of an insufficient amount of bread.

The fifth and longest story in this series recounts Elisha's ministry to a foreign leader (5:1–27). Of particular importance here is the power of the prophet as contrasted to the weakness of the king. Suffering from a serious skin disease, the Syrian army commander, Naaman, receives word that an Israelite prophet could provide the cure. In response, Naaman writes to the king of Israel, hoping to secure an audience. With the king frightened by his own inability to heal diseases, Elisha gives Naaman simple instructions that are at first rejected. When convinced by his assistant that a simple but effective solution is far better than a sophisticated but ineffective one, Naaman complies and is healed (vv.13–14). That same disease, however, soon infects Elisha's servant Gehazi, who in his greed sought financial reward for the prophet's services (v.27).

The final story in this first group shows Elisha's sensitivity to the concerns of a fellow prophet (6:1–7). Insofar as iron was extremely valuable in ancient Israel, losing such a borrowed axhead would have resulted in a sizeable debt. With that in mind, Elisha's retrieving the axhead approximates the provision of oil for the impoverished widow (4:1–7).

The second series of stories, once again, consists of those in which Elisha acts in international affairs. In each, the northern kingdom is under Syrian (or Aramean) attack. 2Ki 6:8–23, to begin with, presents the prophet amusingly revealing Syrian war strategies to the Israelite king. Out of frustration, the Syrians attack anyway, but they are miraculously blinded and captured. When they are fed and released rather than executed, the fighting comes to a close (6:23). The story implies that enemies can be converted into friends through feasts rather than fists.

2Ki 6:24–7:20 records yet another struggle with the Syrians. Encircled by enemy soldiers, Samaria is plagued by an ever-worsening famine. In this context, Elisha prophesies that a drastic change of events will soon take place (7:1). Shortly thereafter, four lepers leave the city gate in hopes of surrendering, but they find that the Syrians had mysteriously fled. Enjoying all of the provisions that the enemy left behind, the lepers decide that notifying those living in the city would be far better than hoarding the goods for themselves (7:9). As a result, the famine passes, the prophetic word is substantiated, and the example of the lepers is preserved.

The entire series comes to a close in 8:1–15. With his servant, Gehazi, in Israel making certain that the Shunamite woman's property is returned to her following a famine (vv.1–6), Elisha finds himself in the Syrian capital of Damascus (vv.7–15). While there, he foresees the trouble that King Ben-Hadad's assassin and successor, Hazael, will bring to Israel. The true prophet, quite clearly, can both minister in the present as well as envision the future.

G. Jehoram and Ahaziah Reign Over Judah (8:16–29)

While Joram was on the throne in Israel, two kings followed Jehoshaphat in the South. Jehoram and Ahaziah are swiftly dismissed by the editor because of their wicked deeds. One thing, though, is particularly noteworthy here. Rather than being "unlike

David," the typical descriptive phrase used for Judah's evil kings, Jehoram and Ahaziah walked in the ways of the kings of Israel (vv.18, 27). Note, however, that both were related to Ahab through marriage! The evil of the North had infiltrated the South through such relationships. Nevertheless, because of David, Judah was once again spared (v.19).

H. Jehu Reigns Over Israel (9:1–10:36)

In addition to the prophets, there were others in the northern kingdom who disliked Omri's dynasty. There must have been considerable public displeasure, for example, over the incident involving Naboth's vineyard (1Ki 21). And indeed, the coup here in ch. 9 was led by Jehu, the commander of Joram's own army. Among his supporters, mention is made here of the Recabites (10:15), a clan that later, in the time of Jeremiah, was still recognized as an example of steadfastness (Jer 35). Clearly, when Jehu rebelled, others went with him.

According to the rationale for Jehu's kingship given here in 9:7, he was to destroy the house of Ahab. This he did with considerable zeal. After being anointed king, Jehu killed Joram (9:24); the Judahite king Ahaziah, who was a relative of Ahab (9:27–28); Jezebel (9:33); Ahab's friends, priests, and associates (10:11); Ahaziah's relatives (10:14); and all the ministers of Baal (10:25). Although surely concerned about advancing his own political cause, Jehu was, in the mind of the editor, simply an instrument in God's hands.

Yet the final evidence with respect to Jehu is mixed at best. While he was certainly anti-Baal, he was perhaps not as pro-Yahweh as he might at first appear. Even here in 10:31–32 we see

that he was somewhat unconcerned about keeping the law and ridding his kingdom of Jeroboam's influences. Likewise, the reduction in territory is seen as a sign of God's displeasure. But the reviews given by the prophet Hosea are even more severe. According to Hos 1:4, God intended to punish the house of Jehu because of the aforementioned massacre. Apparently Jehu not only disregarded the law, but he also went well beyond the parameters of the task assigned to him.

I. Athaliah and Joash Reign Over Judah (11:1–12:21)

With the death of her son Ahaziah at the hands of Jehu, Athaliah attempted to slay the entire royal family in order to gain power for herself. When the scheme became apparent, however, Ahaziah's infant son was concealed by his aunt, Jehosheba, and spared from the carnage (11:2–3). Although Athaliah managed to rule Judah for some six years (c. 841–835 B.C.), years in which she sought to reinstitute Baal worship (11:18), she had wrested the throne and disregarded the principle of Davidic succession. While common in the North, such activity was intolerable in the South. Therefore, the fact that she was given no official recognition is reflected in the editor's refusal to include either the typical introductory or concluding formulas concerning her reign.

At the age of seven, the previously protected Joash ascended to the throne (11:21). Of particular note during his lengthy reign (c. 835–796 B.C.) are the repairing of the temple, which had no doubt been neglected in recent years, and the paying of a treasury-emptying tribute to protect Jerusalem from the approaching Syrians (12:18).

J. Jehoahaz and Jehoash Reign Over Israel (13:1–25)

With the death of Jehu, Jehoahaz and Jehoash in turn rule over Israel. Both followed the sins of Jeroboam (vv.2, 11), although Jehoahaz's brief period of repentance brought Yahweh's favor and a temporary reprieve from the Syrians (vv.4–5). Of greatest significance during Jehoash's reign are the renewed Syrian attacks and the death of Elisha. In this latter instance, Jehoash's words to a dying prophet are instructive: **"My father! My father! The chariots and horsemen of Israel!"** (v.14). Using precisely the same expression that Elisha had used earlier when speaking to Elijah (2:12), at this moment even the destitute king of Israel realized that his country's true strength rested in the prophets.

K. Amaziah Reigns Over Judah (14:1–22)

Brief mention is now made of Amaziah, who succeeded Joash as king of Judah. While he generally walked in the ways of Yahweh, it is interesting to note that, by degree, he disobeyed sufficiently to prevent a direct comparison with David (v.3). In addition to executing those who had murdered his father Joash, Amaziah apparently exercised some control over Edom (v.10) and sought a confrontation with Israel (v.8). That confrontation, however, ended with Judah's defeat. Several years later, in a manner reminiscent of his father's death, Amaziah was himself assassinated by a group of conspirators (v.19).

L. Jeroboam II Reigns Over Israel (14:23–29)

Though dismissed with but a few verses, Jehoash's successor, Jeroboam II, ruled Israel with considerable skill and strength. According to 14:25, he fulfilled the prophet Jonah's predictions by extending his kingdom's borders well beyond their present limits, and he was even able to capture Damascus (v.28). Yet he too draws somewhat conflicting reviews. On the basis of 14:27, Jeroboam II was seen as a bit of a savior, no doubt for freeing Israel from Syrian oppression. The prophet Amos, however, levels a scathing attack against him because of internal wickedness. More specifically, Amos accuses him of social injustice (Am 2:6–8). While Jeroboam II's reign was characterized by remarkable prosperity, a large percentage of the population never reaped the benefit and in fact suffered as a result of it.

M. Uzziah Reigns Over Judah (15:1–7)

Known also as Azariah, Uzziah succeeded his father, Amaziah, as king of Judah. The account here tells us virtually nothing about him other than that he reigned for over fifty years, walked generally in the ways of Yahweh, and suffered from some sort of skin disease. In a more extended treatment, the Chronicler presents Uzziah as an able ruler who experienced considerable military success (2Ch 26:1–23). Such success, however, apparently led to his downfall, for Uzziah came to symbolize the dangerous and destructive journey from fidelity to faithlessness that results from excessive pride (2Ch 26:16).

N. Zechariah, Shallum, Menahem, Pekahiah, and Pekah Reign Over Israel (15:8–31)

Following Jeroboam II, everything fell apart for the northern kingdom. All of the five kings listed here receive disastrous marks, and they once again demonstrate the political instability characteristic of the northern kingdom. In contrast to the Davidic dynasty in

Judah, which, apart from Athaliah's brief and unwelcome interlude, reigned throughout her history, Israel's kingship was continually changing hands.

Assyria, though somewhat weaker during Jeroboam II's reign, had now regained considerable strength. Israel was therefore constantly looking over her shoulder, paying attention to this eastern enemy's every move. During the reign of Menahem (c. 752–742 B.C.), the anticipated invasion actually occurred, but a sizeable Israelite tribute temporarily appeased the attackers (vv.19–20). An even more serious situation arose while Pekah was in power. Under Tiglath-Pileser III, the Assyrians ravaged the entire countryside and deported a good percentage of the population (v.29). All that remained undone was the conquering of Samaria and, with it, the final fall of Israel. That job, however, would be left for Tiglath-Pileser III's successor.

O. Jotham and Ahaz Reign Over Judah (15:32–16:20)

With the long reign of Uzziah over, Jotham and then Ahaz ruled over Judah. Whereas Jotham walked obediently before the Lord, Ahaz was **unlike David** (v.2). Both, however, shared at least one thing in common: trouble from the alliance between Israel and Syria. In the face of an escalating Assyrian threat, these otherwise notorious rivals combined forces. When Judah refused to join with them, Jerusalem was attacked. Although the attack proved unsuccessful, the conflict continued. Finally, Ahaz assured his safety, at least from the alliance, by purchasing Assyrian protection (vv.7–9).

P. Israel Falls During Hoshea's Reign (17:1–41)

The continual fighting with Syria and the damage inflicted by the Assyr-

ians left the northern kingdom a shadow of its former self. While hanging by a thread, the end came when Hoshea refused to pay the expected tribute to the new Assyrian ruler, Shalmaneser V (v.4). With such a rebuke, the Assyrian forces marched into what remained of Israel's former territory. Though Shalmaneser V died in the process, his successor, Sargon II, destroyed Samaria in 721 B.C. and deported its leading citizens (vv.5–6). As the defeated Israelites made their way to a dismal Assyrian captivity, the northern kingdom came to an end.

In the rare event that anyone might still wonder why all of this took place, the editor now inserts an explanatory note or sermon (vv.7–23). Israel's defeat must not be attributed to an inferior military, nor can it simply be associated with incompetent leadership in the political or administrative sense. Rather, disaster came upon Israel because of sin and a refusal to listen to the prophetic voices that Yahweh provided. Had she walked in the ways of the Lord rather than choosing her own evil course, the story would have ended differently. This, as all of the previous accounts have sought to demonstrate, is the lesson to be learned.

One final word remains concerning the repopulation of the land (vv.24–41). As was typical of the Assyrians, foreigners were brought in to replace those who had been deported. Though the lower class of Israelites surely remained, additional labor was perhaps needed to work the territory long decimated by war. But what is of far more importance to the editor, who, you will recall, is from the southern kingdom, is the apparent religious consequence of such a population shift and the subsequent polluting of what was still a portion of the Promised Land. With the transplanted foreigners came foreign gods, and what resulted was an unacceptable ethnic and religious amalgamation. Although the people of Judah had long considered their northern neighbors to be religious orphans separated from the temple in Jerusalem, present developments clearly worsened their perspective (on the doubtful relationship between these imports and the later Samaritans, see Purvis).

III. JUDAH STANDS ALONE (18:1–25:30)

Following the fall of Samaria, the southern kingdom continued to exist, though surely in a weakened condition. Throughout the preceding turmoil, which eventually led to the destruction of Samaria, Judah tried diligently to keep peace with the Assyrians. Such efforts, as we have seen, left her a vassal state of Assyria at least by the time of Ahaz (16:7–9).

With the northern kingdom suffering the consequences of her sin, the editor's attention now shifts totally to Judah. At the same time, various questions in the readers' minds anxiously anticipate answers. Given a combination of seemingly conflicting factors—namely, the theological perspective of the editor, the fact that already in 1Ki 14:22–24 and several times thereafter Judah received negative evaluations, and the primacy of the Davidic kingship—what will now happen to the southern kingdom? Will the experiences of Israel in any way help Judah alter her sinful course and avoid a similar fate? And in light of his preserving the southern kingdom previously because of David, will Yahweh even allow her destruction? With such pressing questions in view, 2Ki 18:1–25:30 will, readers hope, provide some answers.

In this final major section of the book of Kings, Judah does in fact experience certain moments of victory and revival. Yet the efforts of both Hezekiah and Josiah prove inadequate to offset years of disobedience and the influence of several evil kings. As such, although the southern kingdom remains for some 150 years after the destruction of Israel, a similar fate does in fact await her. With the Assyrians leaving the historical scene, however, it will be left for someone else to serve as Yahweh's hand of judgment.

A. Hezekiah Reigns Over Judah (18:1–20:21)

Following the death of Ahaz, his son Hezekiah rules over Judah (c. 716–687 B.C.). From all accounts, he was both an able leader and a true follower of Yahweh. In fact, from the editor's perspective, with the probable exception of Josiah, Hezekiah was the southern kingdom's finest king (18:5–8).

With the fall of Israel fresh in his mind, Hezekiah set out to accomplish two primary goals. To begin with, he sought religious purification. To accomplish such an objective, he not only destroyed the competing shrines and removed the pagan idols (18:4), but he also served as a positive example in terms of trusting the God of Israel (18:5).

Second, Hezekiah sought freedom from Assyrian domination (18:7). During c. 720 to 711 B.C., the Assyrian king Sargon II had a considerable amount of business to tend to at home, so Hezekiah no doubt had been entertaining thoughts of revolt for some time. Yet he postponed any action until 705 B.C., when Sargon died. In hopes of squelching this and similar rebellions by other vassal states, Sargon's successor, Sennacherib, engaged in a military campaign throughout the region (18:13). This event, then, serves as the backdrop for much of what the editor has to say about Hezekiah (on the relationship between this account and the parallel passage in Isa 36–39, see Sawyer, 19–42).

Hezekiah's revolt clearly placed him in a theological predicament. From the outset, he seemingly expected Egyptian assistance in carrying out the revolt, and no doubt his political advisors encouraged the formulation of a treaty. However, to the religiously astute of the day, such an alliance, particularly with Egypt, would suggest a total lack of confidence in Yahweh's delivering power. In this context, for example, the prophet Isaiah issued the strongest of rebukes:

"Woe to the obstinate children,"
   declares the LORD,
"to those who carry out plans that
      are not mine,
   forming an alliance, but not by my
      Spirit,
   heaping sin upon sin;
who go down to Egypt
   without consulting me;
who look for help to Pharaoh's
      protection,
   to Egypt's shade for refuge.
But Pharaoh's protection will be to
      your shame,
   Egypt's shade will bring you
      disgrace."

(Isa 30:1–3)

For Hezekiah, to revolt without Egyptian aid would be military and political suicide. To revolt with aid, however, would be a breach of confidence with God. Hezekiah, surprisingly enough, chose the former.

In preparation for the anticipated attack, Hezekiah took various precautions. Foremost among them was the manner in which he dealt with a potential water problem. The spring of Gihon, Jerusalem's source of water, lay outside the city walls. Not only would such a location allow the Assyrians to replenish their own water supply upon

arrival, but they could also restrict access for the city's inhabitants. As a solution, Hezekiah oversaw a major engineering achievement, having his workmen tunnel some 1,700 feet through solid rock in order to divert the flow of water to within the city (20:20).

As Sennacherib marched westward, he destroyed virtually everything in his path. After attacking and defeating Judah's fortified cities, Jerusalem alone remained (18:13). In an effort to pacify the Assyrian ruler, Hezekiah admits to wrongdoing, empties the temple treasury, and sends a sizeable gift to Sennacherib (v.16). Sennacherib declines the offer, however, and sends a contingent of military personnel to the capital city. While there, they demand Hezekiah's total surrender, assuring the inhabitants of Jerusalem that their God will fare no better in his effort to protect them than did the gods of those whom the Assyrians had conquered earlier (18:19–25, 33). In fact, the enemy even claims to be acting on Yahweh's behalf (18:25)! In Sennacherib's own words, Hezekiah was now confined "like a bird in a cage" (Pritchard, 288).

Given the circumstances, Isaiah prophesies once again. Having rejected the Egyptian option, the prophet assures Hezekiah that Yahweh will indeed deliver the city from the Assyrians (19:5–7). Shortly thereafter, Jerusalem receives a brief reprieve as Sennacherib has additional business to tend to (19:9–13). He guarantees Hezekiah, however, that he will shortly finish the job.

For a final time, Hezekiah prays and Isaiah prophesies (19:14–34). Before his words have a chance to fade, thousands of Assyrian soldiers mysteriously die. Whether the cause was bubonic plague or an attack of field mice (Herodotus, II, 141), as have been occasionally and at times humorously suggested, this occurrence and the subsequent withdrawal of the Assyrian ruler were perceived as nothing less than divine deliverance (19:35).

With his legacy of faith enshrined in the previous account, two additional glimpses of a thoroughly human Hezekiah are presented in ch. 20. Suffering from a severe illness, he first of all receives word from Isaiah that he will not recover. However, after tearfully pleading for mercy and calling attention to his faithful service in the past, fifteen years are added to his life (20:1–11).

Second, Hezekiah soon entertains messengers from Babylon who apparently had come to wish him well (20:12–21). But no doubt their ulterior motive was to solicit Judah's support in an effort to overthrow the Assyrians. In any case, Hezekiah indulges in a bit of personal aggrandizement by showing the visitors his entire financial holdings. Although not specifically condemned for this or any other sin, he receives a disquieting word from Isaiah: **"Everything in your palace, and all that your fathers have stored up until this day, will be carried off to Babylon"** (20:17). While Hezekiah's response in v.19 appears remarkably self-centered, it may indicate not so much a lack of concern for future generations as it does a sense of gratitude for the delay in judgment (1Ki 11:12; 21:29).

B. Manasseh and Amon Reign Over Judah (21:1–26)

Hezekiah was succeeded by his son Manasseh, who, according to the editor, totally redefined evil (21:1–18). Included among his deeds are the sacrificing of his son and the erection of a pagan idol in Solomon's temple. In fact, Manasseh influenced the people under him to such an extent that they were actually worse than the Canaanites who inhabited the land before Joshua's arrival (v.9). As a result, Yahweh's mercy runs out and the ultimate destruction of Judah is predicted (vv.12–15).

The parallel account in 2Ch 33:10–13, however, suggests that extreme Assyrian pressure led Manasseh to repent of his evil ways. If so, the editor of Kings either knows nothing of it, discredits it, or ignores it. All are understandable in light of 2Ki 23:26, where God's anger with Manasseh continues to burn even after Josiah's reforms. Any such repentance left no lasting impression here.

Manasseh's successor, Amon, simply continued the evil that he learned from his father (21:19–26). That he bore the same name as an Egyptian god rather than an Israelite name, such as Joel ("Yahweh is God") or Obadiah ("Servant of Yahweh"), says something about the situation. After a reign of only two years, he was assassinated in the palace by his own officials.

C. Josiah Reigns Over Judah (22:1–23:30)

Josiah, Amon's son, came to power in 639 B.C., and in the eyes of the editor, he surpasses even Hezekiah in greatness. He also turned out, however, to be Judah's last breath of hope. Josiah's leadership somewhat resembles Hezekiah's, particularly in the area of religious reform. Needless to say, it is precisely this reform that dominates the account of his reign.

Some eighteen years into Josiah's kingship, a certain **Book of the Law** was found in the temple (22:8). Since the time of St. Jerome (c. A.D. 340–420), this book has been identified with at least a major portion of the book of Deuteronomy. How such a book could be found is difficult to understand. How it could be lost is harder still! As might be expected, scholarly views on the subject cover a wide variety of possibilities. In general, these range from seeing the find as an actual rediscovery of some previously written law to suggesting that it simply depicts the origin of that law during Josiah's time, not only in written form but, to a degree, in content. (For a more thorough discussion, see LaSor, Hubbard, and Bush, 177–80.) The view supported here is that, regardless of the actual written history of the book of Deuteronomy, the laws contained therein predate the reign of Josiah by a number of years. The discovery was in some fashion a *re*discovery of materials and traditions that should have been familiar at the time.

Given Josiah's renewed interest in the temple even before this significant discovery (22:3–7), an interest that clearly separated him from his predecessors, he was no doubt ready for some sort of reform. Therefore, when he heard the **Book of the Law** being read, he experienced immediate conviction (22:11). Clearly Judah fell short of this newly discovered law on virtually every count.

After receiving confirmation from the prophetess Huldah concerning the legitimacy of the book (22:14–20), Josiah set out on an all-encompassing policy of reform. Included are each of the following steps:

1. He gathered the elders, priests, prophets, and general population at the temple for a public reading of the book (23:1–2).

2. He renewed the covenant, and all of those gathered comply with the agreement (23:3).

3. He removed the false gods and idols (23:4, 6–7).

4. He slaughtered the pagan priests (23:5, 20).

5. He destroyed the competing shrines or high places (23:8).

6. He desecrated Topheth (23:10). Topheth was a hearth located in the Hinnom Valley just outside Jerusalem. The site was used specifically for the offering of human sacrifices (Gray, 735–36).

7. He went into the northern kingdom's former territory and destroyed the altar at Bethel constructed by Jeroboam (23:15).

8. He reinstituted the Passover (23:21).

According to 23:24–25, no one could possibly compare to Josiah in terms of religious fidelity. Systematically, he removed the abominations left behind by all of his predecessors, both from Israel and Judah. At the same time, he served Yahweh **with all his heart and with all his soul and with all his strength,** no doubt the highest imaginable Deuteronomic evaluation (Dt 6:5).

At this point in the narrative, the sympathetic reader can sense the excitement of the editor. Josiah, it would seem, was the king that he had longed for. The northern kingdom's fate would not be repeated. When even hope itself appeared hopeless, a few lessons had been learned from the many mistakes of the past. Finally Yahweh's mercy had paid off.

Then, incredibly enough, the Egyptian army under Pharaoh Neco headed north to provide assistance to the weakened Assyrians, of all people (23:29). While attempting to thwart the plan, Josiah was killed at Megiddo. With him died the dream of reform. Though surely hoping to finish the story on a positive note, the editor now had a new conclusion to write. In retrospect, the sins of Manasseh simply proved too severe for even Josiah's reforms to counteract (23:26–27). The honest repentance of one individual, Wesley suggests, could not easily alter the condition of a generally corrupt people (Wesley, 1261).

D. Jehoahaz, Jehoiakim, and Jehoiachin Reign Over Judah (23:31–24:17)

After Josiah, the end of the southern kingdom is just around the corner. Each of his successors receives negative marks, and a rising power in the ancient world is just waiting to enlarge its territory. Josiah's son and successor, Jehoahaz, immediately reverses the course established by his father (23:32). After ruling for only a few months, he is banished to Egypt by Neco, who now apparently considers Palestine to be part of his territory. To reign in Jehoahaz's place, Neco selects his brother Eliakim, renaming him Jehoiakim (v.34).

Meanwhile, Babylon has become the dominant force in the eastern region. Having conquered Assyria, the Babylonians invade Palestine during Jehoiakim's years in power (24:1), establishing Judah as a vassal state. When the Judahite king chooses to rebel, he is destroyed and replaced by his son Jehoiachin (v.6). Strongly denounced by the prophet Jeremiah (Jer 22:24–30), he, along with the leading men of Judah, is taken captive to Babylon by King Nebuchadnezzar in 597 B.C. (24:15–16). Judah, needless to say, has virtually nothing left. What does remain falls into the hands of one final king.

E. Judah Falls During Zedekiah's Reign (24:18–25:30)

In this final round, Nebuchadnezzar once again names Judah's king, select-

ing Jehoiachin's uncle, Zedekiah (597–586 B.C.). Ignoring Jeremiah's strongest warnings (Jer 27:8), he too rebels, provoking Nebuchadnezzar's forces to attack Jerusalem in 588 B.C. (25:1). No doubt several of its inhabitants were expecting divine intervention, much like that afforded to Hezekiah during his Assyrian conflict. But this time around, Jerusalem would stand or fall on its own. After a lengthy siege, the city fell in 587/86 B.C., and Zedekiah was blinded and exiled to Babylon (v.7).

With respect to the conquest of Jerusalem, the editor of Kings clearly reveals his theological orientation. While the city itself was no doubt important, emphasis here is placed on the temple (25:8–17). Much attention had been given to its construction during Solomon's reign, and much criticism was leveled against those rulers who established competing shrines. Now, however, the temple has itself been destroyed, and with it the very identity of this covenant people has apparently vanished.

What remained after the smoke cleared was pale in comparison to former days. Judah was but a small part of one province in an empire of several provinces. Gone into captivity were the leaders and those of higher standing in the community. Left behind were the lower classes, commissioned to work the fields and vineyards (25:12). In place of a king, Nebuchadnezzar appointed a governor. The first to occupy such a position was, graciously enough, a Judahite named Gedaliah (25:22). Yet many refused to accept his leadership, and he was eventually assassinated (for a more extensive account of Gedaliah's governorship, see Jer 40:7–41:18). With that, Judah's own involvement in administrating the land came to an end, and an exodus **to**

Egypt occurred in order to avoid possible Babylonian wrath (25:26).

If nothing but desperation remained in Judah, the closing verses of ch. 25 would seem to imply that a flicker of hope was still shining in Babylon (vv.27–30). There King Jehoiachin, the son of Josiah and a descendant of David, had been set free. Is there still time for the lessons of the past to be learned and applied to the present and future? Could it be that Jehoiachin's good fortune might in some way suggest or symbolize a similar conclusion for the community of faith in general? While the prophets of the Exile may later answer with a resounding yes, the editor of Kings simply leaves us pondering the possibility.

BIBLIOGRAPHY

Ackroyd, Peter. *Exile and Restoration*. OTL. Philadelphia: Westminster, 1968.

Brueggemann, Walter. *The Prophetic Imagination*. Philadelphia: Fortress, 1978.

Clarke, Adam. *The Holy Bible with a Commentary and Critical Notes*. 6 vols. New York and Nashville: Abingdon, n.d. Vol. 2: *Joshua to Esther*.

Craigie, Peter C. *Ugarit and the Old Testament*. Grand Rapids: Eerdmans, 1983.

Crenshaw, James. *Old Testament Wisdom*. Atlanta: John Knox, 1981.

_____. "Wisdom in the OT." IDBS. Edited by Keith Crim. Nashville: Abingdon, 1976.

Cross, Frank Moore. *Canaanite Myth and Hebrew Epic*. Cambridge: Harvard University, 1973.

DeVries, Simon J. *1Ki*. WdBC. Vol. 12. Waco: Word, 1985.

Friedman, Richard Elliot. *Who Wrote the Bible?* Englewood Cliffs, N.J.: Prentice Hall, 1987.

Gray, John. *I and II Kings*. OTL. 2d ed. Philadelphia: Westminster, 1970.

Harrison, Roland K. *Introduction to the Old Testament*. Grand Rapids: Eerdmans, 1969.

_____. "Ugarit." NIDBA. Edited by E. M. Blaiklock and R. K. Harrison. Grand Rapids: Zondervan, 1983.

Kitchen, K. A. *Ancient Orient and Old Testament*. Downers Grove, Ill.: InterVarsity Press, 1966.

LaSor, William Sanford; David Allan Hubbard; and Frederic William Bush. *Old Testament Survey*. Grand Rapids: Eerdmans, 1982.

Mendenhall, George. "The Monarchy." *Interpretation* 29 (1975): 155–70.

Miller, J. Maxwell, and John H. Hayes. *A History of Ancient Israel and Judah*. Philadelphia: Westminster, 1986.

Nicholson, E. W. *Preaching to the Exiles*. Oxford: Oxford University Press, 1970.

Porter, J. R. "Old Testament Historiography." *Tradition and Interpretation*, 125–62. Edited by G. W. Anderson. Oxford: Oxford University Press, 1979.

Pritchard, James B. *Ancient Near Eastern Texts*. 3d ed. Princeton N.J.: Princeton University Press, 1969.

Purvis, James D. "The Samaritans and Judaism." *Early Judaism and Its Modern Interpreters*, 81–97. Edited by George W. E. Nickelsburg and Robert Kraft. Philadelphia: Fortress, 1986.

Sawyer, John F. A. *Isaiah*. 2 vols. Philadelphia: Westminster, 1986. Vol. 2, chs. 33–66.

von Rad, Gerhard. *Old Testament Theology*. Translated by D. M. G. Stalker. 2 vols. New York: Harper and Row, 1962–65. Vol. 1.

Wesley, John. *Explanatory Notes Upon the Old Testament*. 3 vols. Salem, Ohio: Schmul, 1975 (reprint of 1765 edition). Vol. 2. Judges XV–Psalm LXII.

Wright, G. Ernest. *Biblical Archaeology*. Philadelphia: Westminster, 1957.

1 AND
2 CHRONICLES
Joel H. Hunt

INTRODUCTION

I. STRUCTURE, CONTENT, AND SIGNIFICANCE

The chronicler wrote to Jews living in Canaan in the Persian Period. His major focus is God's eternal covenant with the Davidic monarchy and how this vow should engender hope for renewed existence in the Promised Land. The covenant initiated by God is conditional, requiring human obedience for the nation to enjoy the benefits of that pact.

Chronicles has three divisions: 1Ch 1–9, genealogical lists; 1Ch 10–2Ch 9, the united monarchy; 2Ch 10–36, the Judahite monarchy from the schism after Solomon's death to the return from exile in Babylon. The second and third divisions may in turn be subdivided: 2.1—History of King David (1Ch 10–29); 2.2—Solomon (2Ch 1–9); 3.1—the southern kingdom from the division to the fall of Samaria (2Ch 10–28); 3.2—the kingdom from the reign of Hezekiah to the Exile (2Ch 29–36).

Some scholars have denigrated Chronicles since, to them, it contains material of uncertain historical worth that supplements the more important works of Samuel-Kings. In their view, the chronicler had so modified or falsified his sources as to make it impossible to reconstruct the events behind his story. In light of this assumption and with the rise of the historical-critical method, there was a prevailing negative assessment of Chronicles (Childs, 637–55; cf. Miller and Hays; Aharoni and Avi-Yonah).

In the nineteenth century, Julius Wellhausen's *Prolegomena* presented the epitome of this negative evaluation. He concluded that Chronicles, heavily influenced by the Priestly Source, was essentially worthless as a historical document. He saw Chronicles as a later Jewish commentary on the superior canonical sources of Samuel–Kings (Wellhausen, 227).

A movement toward a more positive evaluation of Chronicles began at the turn of the century. C. C. Torrey appreciated the chronicler's literary creativity (Torrey, 157–73; 188–217). William F. Albright defended the historical accuracy of some of the separate traditions (Albright, 274).

Others, such as Gerhard von Rad, became interested in the theology of the chronicler (von Rad, 347–54). Recent works attempt to understand Chronicles on its own terms and not simply as a supplement to Samuel-Kings (Ackroyd, 501–15; Williamson). The author tells the nation's story from his point of view and, in the process, encourages his community to obey God.

In 1Ch 1–9 the chronicler delineates the ancestry of "all Israel" (9:1). The writer uses this inclusive term with a religious rather than political connotation. The genealogies, due to the presence of some later additions, lead the reader up to, and perhaps slightly beyond, the chronicler's own day. The lists introduce the author's interest in the constitution of God's people, which he develops in the later narrative. Connections with the primeval past demonstrate to the postexilic audience the continuity of God's dealings with his chosen people.

The chronicler is interested in the Israelite monarchy, particularly developing the stories of David and Solomon. He focuses on their obedience to the divine word and holds up these kings as the standard of evaluation for future Judahite rulers. The chronicler makes reference to the North only when the information is significant for his narrative about the South. It is immediately apparent that the chronicler did not intend to provide a complete history of the nations of Israel.

The temple is central for the chronicler. He almost belabors the story of construction and maintenance of the sanctuary. This is the place of God's choosing and dwelling. The Lord provides David with the "blueprints." It is the site where God manifests himself and around which the community, whether pre- or postexilic, is organized. The king's relationship to the temple is one of the criteria used to evaluate each monarch. The chronicler sadly notes that the fall of the nation was accompanied by the razing of the temple, Israel's symbol of divine grace and glory.

In evaluating the nation's history, the chronicler presumes that actions are directly related to results and that each generation must be obedient to the divine word. If the nation is righteous, God will grant blessing. If, on the other hand, the nation is wicked, he will send wrath. However, the chronicler modifies this harshly simplistic doctrine by noting that God provided repeated opportunities for repentance and restoration. A key interpretative verse for the narrative is 2Ch 7:14. God promises, in response to Solomon's dedication prayer, forgiveness and healing to distressed people if they seek him. Indeed, the chronicler records several instances where humble repentance averts judgment.

In some biblical texts there is a tension between the writer's report and the historical event. In the case of Chronicles, the major tension, which concerns the relationship of the text to other canonical texts, sometimes reaches contradiction. The chronicler shaped the material in a different way from the author of Samuel–Kings. These differences, and the reasons for them, help define the exegetical task for the reader. By adapting the historical books, the chronicler helped his generation to appreciate and appropriate God's word in their situation. In part, he tried to answer the question, "How did we get back to the land and how should we live?"

II. AUTHORSHIP, DATE, AND COMPOSITION

The book does not name an author. A rabbinic tradition maintains that Ezra wrote Chronicles. However, it is doubtful that this tradition is trustworthy. Some scholars assume that the author was a minister, perhaps a Levite, due to his intense concern for the temple and worship.

The language of Chronicles is close in form, vocabulary, and Aramaic influence to other later biblical books such as Ezra-Nehemiah, Esther, and Daniel. It is also similar to the language of the Isaiah Scroll of Qumran and the Samaritan Pentateuch. These similarities in style, and the fact that there are no traces of Hellenistic influence, call for a date of composition within the Persian Period. Chronicles was probably written sometime in the fourth century B.C. (Japhet, 533).

What sources did the chronicler use? He does not mention parallel biblical books, but he cites noncanonical materials. Royal annals, designated by the title "The Book of the Kings," are usually qualified by the name of a specific kingdom (2Ch 16:11; 20:34; 24:27; 25:26; 27:7; 33:18; 35:27). The use of the names Judah and Israel in these phrases is not consistent, so they may refer to varations of the same annalistic work. Other sources are associated with the ministry and writing of prophets (1Ch 29:29; 2Ch 9:29; 12:15; 13:22; 20:34; 26:22; 32:32; 33:19). The author points to other documents, such as "the words of David and of Asaph the seer" (2Ch 29:30), "the directions written by David king of Israel and by his son Solomon" (2Ch 35:4), and "the laments" (2Ch 35:25).

What was the chronicler's main source? Though some have doubted that the canonical books of Samuel-Kings were his primary source, it is apparent that the chronicler was making use of authoritative Scripture to tell the nation's story to his contemporaries. His text was probably related to, but not identical with, the Masoretic tradition.

How did the chronicler handle his authoritative source? Sometimes he omitted materials, perhaps assuming that his audience was familiar with the contents of Samuel-Kings. He virtually ignored the history of the North. He deleted narratives regarding Absalom, Amnon, Adonijah, the apostate Solomon, and David's adultery. The chronicler controlled his source material to stress themes such as God's promise to David and the centrality of the temple.

What about the emendations to the stories recounted in Samuel-Kings? Some of these supplements came from the sources noted earlier. Some scholars have considered these stories as figments of the chronicler's imagination or revealing only the historical circumstances of the author's day. These additions may reflect reliable historical data. However, there is no scholarly unity regarding the nature of the sources. Did the chronicler use oral tradition, other written sources, or an enlarged form of Samuel-Kings? We do not know.

III. TITLE AND CANONICAL PLACEMENT

The Hebrew name of this book, *diḇrê hayyāmîm*, means "the events of the days" and is used of annals. The term *diḇrê* is used in the Bible in phrases such as 1Ch 29:29: "As for the events [*diḇrê*] of King David's reign, from beginning to end, they are written in the records [*diḇrê*] of Samuel the seer, the records [*diḇrê*] of Nathan the prophet and the records [*diḇrê*] of Gad the seer." The unqualified phrase *diḇrê hayyāmîm* is used three times in the Hebrew Bible (Ne 12:23; Est 2:23; 6:1) in the general sense "annals." This phrase is generally qualified by the name of a nation or person. For example, in 1Ki 14 we find *diḇrê hayyāmîm*, qualified by Jeroboam and Israel (v.19) and by Rehoboam and Judah (v.29) to differentiate the court documents used. With a proper name we find, for example, 1Ch 27:24, "the annals [*diḇrê hayyāmîm*] of King David." The term refers to a book recording the series of events in the life of a monarch and/or a nation.

Ironically, in the Greek versions of the OT the book is called *paraleipomenōn*, "things omitted." The Vulgate also uses the name *paralipomenon*. Apparently the early translators viewed Chronicles as supplemental to other biblical texts. This obscures the true character of the book and subordinates it to the earlier books. Perhaps the misunderstanding signaled by this title contributed to the negative assessment of the book through the history of interpretation. Since the book covers the period from Adam to Cyrus, Jerome commented that this book was "a chronicle of the whole of sacred history." The title used by most modern translations of the book comes from Jerome's comment.

Chronicles is usually the last book of the Hagiographa section of the OT. In some manuscripts it is at the beginning of the Writings. No one has offered a compelling explanation for this placement. On the basis of content, the Septuagint puts the book among the historical books, after Samuel–Kings. Most modern translations accept the placement and binary division of Chronicles found in the Septuagint.

IV. OUTLINE

I. The Genealogies (1Ch 1–9)
   A. Adam to Israel (1:1–2:2)
   B. Israel's Sons (2:3–9:1)
      1. Judah (2:3–4:23)
      2. Simeon (4:24–43)
      3. Transjordanian tribes (5:1–26)
      4. Levi (6:1–81)
      5. Six tribes (7:1–40)
      6. Benjamin (8:1–40)

3. Asa (14:2–16:14)
   a. Asa's initial reform (14:2–7)
   b. The Lord and Asa defeat Zerah (14:8–15)
   c. Azariah's sermon (15:1–7)
   d. Asa's reform continues (15:8–19)
   e. Asa fights Baasha (16:1–6)
   f. Hanani's sermon (16:7–10)
   g. The conclusion of Asa's reign (16:11–14)
4. Jehoshaphat (17:1–21:1)
   a. Jehoshaphat's reign (17:1–19)
   b. Jehoshaphat and Ahab (18:1–19:3)
   c. Jehoshaphat's judges (19:4–11)
   d. Jehoshaphat's victory (20:1–30)
   e. The conclusion of Jehoshaphat's reign (20:31–21:3)
5. Jehoram (21:4–20)
   a. Jehoram's evil reign (21:4–11)
   b. Elijah's letter (21:12–15)
   c. End of Jehoram's reign (21:16–20)
6. Ahaziah (22:1–9)
7. Joash (22:10–24:27)
   a. Joash comes to power (22:10–23:21)
   b. Joash's righteousness (24:1–16)
   c. Joash's wickedness (24:17–27)
8. Amaziah (25:1–28)
9. Uzziah (26:1–23)
10. Jotham (27:1–9)
11. Ahaz (28:1–27)
B. Hezekiah to the Return From Babylonian Exile
   (2Ch 29–36)
   1. Hezekiah (29:1–32:33)
      a. Hezekiah purifies the temple (29:1–36)
      b. Hezekiah celebrates the Passover (30:1–31:1)
      c. Hezekiah organizes regular worship (31:2–21)
      d. Hezekiah's faithfulness (32:1–33)
   2. Manasseh (33:1–20)
   3. Amon (33:21–25)
   4. Josiah (34:1–35:27)
      a. Josiah's piety and cultic reform (34:1–13)
      b. The discovery of the Book of the Law (34:14–33)
      c. Josiah's Passover (35:1–19)
      d. Josiah's death (35:20–27)
   5. Jehoahaz (36:1–4)
   6. Jehoiakim (36:5–8)
   7. Jehoiachin (36:9–10)
   8. Zedekiah (36:11–21)
   9. Proclamation for the return (36:22–23)

COMMENTARY

I. THE GENEALOGIES (1CH 1–9)

The extent of these genealogies suggests their significance for the chronicler. These nine chapters set the stage for the drama to unfold. The author tells, in capsule form, the story of God's people from creation until the postexilic period. The chronicler begins to expound God's election and care of Israel that he will emphasize in the following survey of the nation's history. With stress upon God's longstanding relationship to his people, the chronicler prepares his readers to understand the narrative and the call to those who are part of this heritage to be obedient to God's Word.

The vertical dimension of the genealogies stresses the unbroken strand of God's chosen people. Ch. 1 tells of God's election beginning with Adam and extending to Jacob/Israel. The middle section, chs. 2–8, enlarges the circle by including representatives of Israel's twelve sons. Finally, ch. 9 encircles the postexilic community. A horizontal dimension is shown by "an effort to include within the family of Israel all who could mount any legitimate claim to participation" (Williamson, 38). The chronicler integrates persons from all of the original tribes despite the fact that his audience was composed of returnees to Judah. This is an inclusive view of God's people. He places people who joined the nation through intermarriage and reprobate Israelites alongside more faithful people. The author seems more concerned with painting a broad picture of **all Israel** than with the issue of strict purity or fitness for inclusion. This interest with the whole people of God continues in the ensuing narrative.

A. Adam to Israel (1:1–2:2)

After ten antediluvian generations, the chronicler lists Noah's sons (1:4). He reverses the standard birth order when discussing their families (vv.5–27). This climactic arrangement leads to the Israelites' forebear, Abram.

The chronicler lists Abraham's sons in reverse birth order, with the favored offspring last (1:28–37). He arranges the material according to the mother of the children: Hagar, the concubine; Keturah, the second wife; and Sarah, the wife of promise. Vv.38–54, like Ge 36, discuss Sarah's spurned grandson, Esau, and his connections with Edomites.

1Ch 2:1–2 is the high point of the patriarchal genealogy and serves as a bridge to the largest section. The chronicler introduces the ancestors of the twelve tribes. Again, for reasons of emphasis, he does not follow the birth order. Here he places the most important tribe, Judah, at the beginning.

The patriarchal genealogy places Israel within the human family. God's choice of the nation involved a progressive narrowing. The incipient election of Israel at Creation in Adam was realized in Jacob (consistently called Israel by the chronicler) and his family. Later this exclusive family becomes more inclusive.

B. Israel's Sons (2:3–9:1)

This middle section of the genealogies discusses the twelve tribes. The relative length and complexity of each list seems to be a function of both the chronicler's desire to highlight some tribes and due to the lack of material regarding others. The author underscores the makeup of the groups that formed the core of the postexilic community: Judah, Levi, and Benjamin.

If the chronicler desired to portray a complete Israel, with all tribes represented in the resurrected nation, the lack of the tribes of Zebulun and Dan is a problem. Due to the brevity of the Naphtali genealogy in 7:13, some scholars have conjectured that a scribal loss reduced the size of the Naphtali entry and deleted these two tribes (Williamson, 47, 78).

1. Judah (2:3–4:23)

The chronicler emphasizes David's ancestral heritage and the continuity of this line through the Exile and into his contemporaneous era. He will discuss God's promise of this Davidic line in greater detail in the following narrative.

At times this theme is interrupted by seemingly irrelevant or highly tangential material. For example, who is Jabez in 4:9–10? His connection to the preceding lists is unclear. Nevertheless, Jabez's use of prayer, his specific requests for protection and increased land, are familiar themes in the OT and significant for Chronicles. A divine grant of protection and land was crucial to the chronicler's readers, who learn that God honored Jabez's request (see discussion of 2Ch 7:14).

2. Simeon (4:24–43)

In comparison to Judah, Simeon was a relatively small clan. The chronicler reveals that he had access to this tribe's own genealogical materials (v.33).

3. Transjordanian tribes (5:1–26)

The Reuben list explains that Judah ranked above the firstborn because the tribe was strong and gave birth to a ruler (vv.1–2). The chronicler cites a tradition, unknown elsewhere in the OT, that the right of firstborn belonged to Joseph (v.2).

The chronicler discusses the military men of Gad, the half-tribe of Manasseh, and their Transjordanian neighbor, Reuben. He goes beyond simple enumeration and reveals the secret of their military success. They gain victory by trusting God's ability and desire to make them successful in battle (v.20). As with Jabez, God answers the prayers of these mighty men. This is the first of many examples in which God blesses military actions based on faith and prayer (see 2Ch 13:13–19; 14:9–15; 18:31; 20:1–27; 26:7; 32:7–8, 20–22).

In contrast to the glowing report of trust in battle, the chronicler relates the unfortunate fate of the disobedient tribes (vv.23–26). Manasseh's unfaithfulness is first reported, but the entire Transjordanian group is punished for apostasy (v.26). God uses Tiglath-Pileser III, king of Assyria, as the instrument of his wrath.

4. Levi (6:1–81)

This genealogy is long and detailed. Levi, possibly the chronicler's clan, had various special tasks. David appointed some as temple musicians (vv. 31–32), and others had duties in the tabernacle (v.48). The Aaronic clan had the most important position: they **presented offerings in the Most Holy Place** (v.49). The chronicler affirms that the appointment of the Aaronic functionaries originated in God's revelation to Moses, not in David's organization of the cult (v.49).

This chapter gives a sense of the chronicler's belief in the centrality of the Levites and their functions for the well-being of the land. The list of Levitical dwellings shows that those called into divine service were spread throughout the land (vv.54–81).

5. Six tribes (7:1–40)

Ch. 7 provides brief genealogies of six tribes: Issachar, Benjamin, Naphtali,

Manasseh, Ephraim, and Asher. This is little more than a census of fighting men. Surprisingly, Benjamin is included here though the chronicler treats this tribe more fully in ch. 8.

6. Benjamin (8:1–40)

The chronicler completes his genealogical survey with the family of the first Israelite monarch, Saul. This is a more extensive list than 7:6–12. The variations in the lists may result from the chronicler depending upon sources from different times for each list. Vv.28–39, which parallel 9:34–44, show that the author was concerned with Saul's family. The chronicler starts his discussion of the monarchy with a brief account of the tragic end of the first king's reign.

7. Conclusion (9:1)

The chronicler summarizes the middle portion of his genealogical table with the statement that **all Israel** was listed in the royal record. He next lists returnees from exile. This verse is a summary of the preceding chapters and should not be split in half as in the NIV. The middle genealogies end with the captivity and the reason for God's judgment. The people were unfaithful. This same term, *m'l*, describes the reason for Saul's downfall (1Ch 10:13) and the eventual destruction of the southern kingdom (2Ch 26:16).

C. The Postexilic Community (9:2–44)

The chronicler emphasizes that the clergy were among **some Israelites** who first resettled in Judah. These religious functionaries were necessary to organize the postexilic community.

This genealogy balances the introductory list of Adam to Israel. Ch. 1 provides the ancestry of the Israelite tribes, ch. 9 the progeny. Just as the persons of ch. 1 were linked to the

tribes, the postexilic community stands in continuity with the tribes as well (Williamson, 87).

The author ends the lengthy genealogical section with a second listing of Saul's family to introduce the story of the monarchy.

II. THE UNITED MONARCHY (1CH 10–2CH 9)

The United Monarchy forms the paradigm for the remainder of Chronicles. The author devotes almost half of his work to Saul, David, and Solomon as he develops his major themes of obedience, true piety, and restoration.

A. Saul (1Ch 10:1–14)

The story of the monarchy abruptly begins with the account of Saul's death on Mount Gilboa. Perhaps the chronicler assumes that the reader is familiar with the history of Saul's kingship, including David's prekingship escapades and Samuel's ministry. Saul is killed, his dynasty ends, and an exilic situation prevails with Israel's defeat and the apparent triumph over the Lord. Several observations must be made regarding this story.

This story of defeat, which begins the historical section of the book, parallels the recent experience of Israel. Foreigners routed Israel and killed the king. The Israelites abandoned their cities to enemy occupation. This vignette presents the exilic motifs of defeat and dispossession.

The detail regarding Saul's head and armor, left out of 1Sa 31:10, emphasizes this exilic situation (vv.8–10). By proclaiming victory to Dagon, the Philistines declare the defeat of Israel's God. The reader confronts, at the end of Saul's dynasty, the themes of human despair and apparent divine humiliation, which were part of the Exile.

The chronicler provides the rationale

for punishment (vv.13–14). Saul was an unfaithful king because he did not keep the Lord's word. He consulted a medium for guidance instead of inquiring of the Lord. There was a simple causal relationship between Saul's sin and God's punishment on him (death) and on his progeny (loss of kingship). This idea of unfaithfulness (*m'l*) as the justification for punishment and exile is used seventeen times in nominal and verbal forms in Chronicles (1Ch 2:7; 5:25; 9:1; 10:13–14 [twice]; 2Ch 12:2; 26:16, 18; 28:19 [twice], 22; 29:6, 9; 30:7; 33:19; 36:14 [twice]).

Finally, in the midst of the utter bleakness of Saul's collapse, the chronicler shows the path to restoration. Human unfaithfulness invites judgment, but there is divine redemption for people willing to seek God's grace. In this instance, David is crowned and a glorious new age begins. God abandons unfaithful Saul; God is with King David (11:9; 12:18; 14:2, 10, 17).

Recovery is found in other *m'l* passages. The Israelites defeat Ai in the second attack (Jos 7–8). Rehoboam avoids total destruction through humility (2Ch 12:6–12). Hezekiah brings restoration and reform after a period of apostasy (2Ch 29–31). Manasseh, the most wicked king, repents and is restored (2Ch 33:12–13). Return follows exile (1Ch 9:2; 2Ch 36:15–23).

But restoration does not always follow unfaithfulness. In 1Ch 5:25 the North experiences utter destruction without return. These people are displaced **to this day** (5:26). In 2Ch 26:19–23 Uzziah remains ill when he angrily disobeys God's command.

B. David (1Ch 11–29)

David is the central character in Chronicles. Over against the tension and hopelessness prevailing from the failure of Saul's dynasty, David's rule

over all Israel represents the zenith of hope. The chronicler, to contrast these monarchs, does not follow a strict chronology.

David, like a proper ancient Near Eastern monarch, is both benefactor of the cult and administrator of the court. Chronicles records the establishment of David's secular power (chs. 11–16) and the religious dimensions of his rule (chs. 17–29). These subsections overlap somewhat, but the focus of the first is the consolidation of David's position, while the second deals primarily with the temple. The second subsection is unified by the content that frames it. Ch. 17 promises Solomon's reign. Chs. 28–29 record David's transferring leadership to the promised heir.

The author emphasizes that the Lord established David. God assisted David in various arenas and acted to place David on the throne (1Ch 10:14; 11:2–3; 14:2), to provide military victories (1Ch 11:9, 10, 14; 14:11, 15–17; 18:6, 13), and to promise a dynasty (1Ch 17:7–14; 22:10; 28:2–10, 19; 29:25).

1. David's power (11:1–16:43)

a. David's rise to power (11:1–12:40)

The author has organized this unit on the basis of the geography and chronology of David's headquarters. The outer paragraphs, 11:1–3 and 12:23–40, describe David's coronation at Hebron. In 12:1–7 and 12:19–22 David lives in Ziklag. The inner sections, 12:8–15 and 12:16–18, place David in his mountain stronghold in the earliest years of his struggle.

David's kingship gains broad support within all Israel, even within Saul's own tribe, at the earliest stage of his rise to power. The people confirm God's will by crowning David. The chronicler's report differs from the story of 1Sa 16–2Sa 5, since he does not present a David gradually winning the loyalty of the tribes.

David is crowned at Hebron (11:1–3). The chronicler ignores material of 2Sa 1–5 to juxtapose Saul's fall and David's accession. **All Israel** makes three appeals to persuade David to become king. The first is kinship. The second is David's importance in military successes under Saul's administration. The last is God's anointing of David for this position. The chronicler apparently assumes that his reader knew of Samuel's ministry.

David conquers Jerusalem (11:4–9). This unit interrupts the report of David's support and is connected to the preceding paragraph by the theme of David's capitals. This pericope describes the acquisition of the neutral site that was to become the political and religious center of the Davidic monarchy. Politically, Jerusalem unifies the North and South around David. Later, with the founding of the temple, the site acquires religious importance.

Three significant points emerge from this account. David takes the city despite the Jebusites' confidence. Second, Joab becomes commander-in-chief for his leadership in the conquest. Finally, David makes the city the center of his power. The chronicler summarizes the major lesson of this paragraph by noting that David's rise occurred because of divine empowerment, not because of mere human military ability (v.9).

David's men are listed next (11:10–47). Despite some textual confusion of the numbers in this passage, the Three and the Thirty formed the core of a royal guard. Since more than thirty men are listed, the term *Thirty* may be a technical term, or the register may include men from different periods of David's reign. These warriors supply the human support for setting up David's kingdom. V.10 describes the complementary roles of human and divine actors in fulfilling God's promise to David.

The defectors who came to David prior to his coronation may be grouped by the place where they joined him (12:1–22). The events of Hebron frame this portion. Deserters from Benjamin (vv.1–7) and from Manasseh (vv.19–22) join David at Ziklag. Renegades from Gad (vv.8–15) and Benjamin (vv.16–18) join at the earlier stronghold.

The fugitive David was joined by some of Saul's kin who had ambidextrous ability for long-range combat. Gadites, to complement the Benjamites, were experts in close combat. They were brave, quick, more mighty than numerous opponents and able to overcome natural and human challenges.

This invincibility motif recalls other texts that speak of divine power that comes to the obedient. Lev 26:8 states, "Five of you will chase a hundred, and a hundred of you will chase ten thousand, and your enemies will fall by the sword before you." Dt 32:30, Moses' farewell address, focuses on the negative outcome for a disobedient people: "How could one man chase a thousand, or two put ten thousand to flight, unless their Rock had sold them, unless the LORD had given them up?" Isa 30:17, a word to an obstinate nation, stresses judgment on the disobedient through an enemy empowered by the Lord: "A thousand will flee at the threat of one; at the threat of five you will all flee away, till you are left like a flagstaff on a mountaintop, like a banner on a hill." In each case, God enables a minute force to mete out judgment against a greater foe. The key to victory is obedience; disobedience brings ruin.

Amasai's prophetic word emphasizes

God's choice of David (12:18). The Spirit comes upon this chieftain and leads him to pledge allegiance to David's cause. David, who was perhaps reticent to receive the support of these defectors, makes these men commanders of his raiders.

All Israel crowns David at Hebron (12:23–40). Members of all the tribes come **to turn Saul's kingdom over to him** (12:23). (The precise size of this supporting cast depends upon the interpretation of the Hebrew word *'eleph*. The term may designate one thousand; or, in a rather loose sense, a large group or unit; or the number of "chiefs" over various-sized contingents.) To make his point, the chronicler passes over the time David ruled only a portion of the nation while Ishbosheth controlled the North.

b. David's concern for the ark (13:1–16:43)

King David begins to pay attention to the religious matters of his realm. The Hebrew word *peres,* "to break forth," connects the first three chapters of this unit.

The ark goes to Obed-Edom's house (13:1–14). David calls the **whole assembly of Israel** to bring the ark from Kiriath Jearim. The king must correct Saul's neglect of the ark before he can avenge the Philistine victory over the nation. The chronicler stresses the role of **all Israel** in this act more than the report of 2Sa 6:2–11. He views worship as necessary for people at all levels of society and not only for a restricted, royal segment.

Despite good intentions, the first attempt to transfer the ark fails because the people do not carry the ark properly. God kills Uzzah when he steadies the shaken ark at the place since called Perez Uzzah. David responds with anger and fear to the divine outburst.

He leaves the ark with Obed-Edom to avoid further problems. David assumes that continued contact with the ark will bring a curse. Obed-Edom, however, enjoys divine blessing. In the same way, David's house will receive blessing when the Lord, symbolized by the ark, takes up residence in Jerusalem.

The report of David's victories over the Philistines, misplaced from a chronological point of view, provides an interlude in the story of the ark (14:1–17). The focus shifts to David's house and Philistine wars while God blesses Obed-Edom's house. While the ark was diverted, David's house was not bereft of blessing on both domestic and foreign fronts. King Hiram sends materials and workers to build a palace. David enjoys the knowledge that he was not enthroned merely by the efforts of human heroes. The Lord elevated him for Israel's benefit. God begins to build David's house, the dynasty, by granting a large family. This situation contrasts with the annihilation of Saul's house.

God grants David victory over the destroyers of Saul's house (14:8–17). David is a savior king who, by the Lord's power, reverses the exilic-type situation and reestablishes Israel's might.

The report of battle uses the term prominent in ch. 13, *peres* (vv.8–12). The king inquires of the Lord, in contrast to Saul and to David's first attempt to transport the ark. God promises victory and breaks out against the Philistines. As they run, the enemies abandon their gods who once received news of glorious victory. The place name, Baal Perazim, commemorates the triumph.

The second victory comes through ambush (14:13–16). David again inquires of the Lord and does not depend upon his own strength. God proves his unmistakable leadership as the Israelites rout the Philistines.

As a result of these victories, David's powerful reputation spreads (14:17). The chronicler includes this statement, not given in 2Sa 5, to emphasize God's appointment of David as the savior-king to unite Israel, reverse the debacle of Saul's era, and prepare for the Lord's house.

What about the ark? The chronicler now returns to the problem of the ark's fate (15:1–16:43). David constructs his residence and a place for the ark's tent. This passage lacks the motivation, recorded in 2Sa 6:12, that David was moving the ark because of Obed-Edom's blessings. According to the chronicler, David never abandoned his original intention to bring the ark to Jerusalem, but used the interruption to prepare the place and the people for successful transfer.

All Israel participates in the celebration, but David, in obedience to Mosaic injunctions, commands the Levites to bear the ark. The first attempt failed because they did not inquire of the Lord regarding this proper method of transport. The king orders the priests and Levites to sanctify themselves in anticipation of the ark's transfer by washing their clothes and abstaining from sexual intercourse (Ex 19:14–15). The Lord would "break out" (*pereṣ*) against them for noncompliance (Ex 19:22).

Michal, David's wife, is presented as the only Israelite not joyfully participating in this transfer (15:28–29). In contrast to the report of 2Sa 6:20–23, the chronicler tells of her disdain and not her punishment. Perhaps David's public display of religious enthusiasm disturbed her. Perhaps it was his devotion to this cult object, which held no interest for her family.

David puts the ark into the prepared tent and appoints Levites to continue worship before the ark with petition, thanksgiving, and praise (16:1–6). He also arranges for regular worship at Gibeon (vv.37–42). The details of worship at the Gibeon shrine remain unknown. It is not surprising that there was no attempt to centralize worship prior to Solomon's temple. The concern is for regular and orderly worship of the Lord regardless of site. The view of competing worship centers changes with completion of the temple.

David praises God for the inauguration of a new era signaled by the arrival of the ark (16:7–36). The chronicler borrows from the canonical Psalter to construct this praise. He chooses themes appropriate to David's setting to remind the later community of God's grace.

Ps 105:1–15 parallels 16:8–22. David calls for thankful testimony of God's acts (vv.8–10). He encourages continued reliance on the Lord (v.11). He calls for a clear memory of God's past gracious acts (vv.12–13). The chronicler alters the original text slightly by substituting Jacob in v.13 for Abraham of Ps 105:6. This shift agrees with the chronicler's emphasis on **Israel** and his descendants and not on Abraham, in the genealogies.

God's everlasting covenant with the patriarchs and his care for them provides the rationale for praise (16:14–22). In v.15 one should read the plural imperative ("Remember!") of the Masoretic text instead of the third person singular ("He remembers") from Ps 105:8 and some Greek versions, which the NIV follows. The imperative fits the chronicler's hortatory concerns. Both David's Israel and the chronicler's community must remember God's covenant with their ancestors to grant Canaan as an inheritance. God kept his word when he originally brought Israel to the land, and he was in the process of reestablishing the regathered nation.

God protected the small patriarchal band as it wandered homeless throughout the ancient Near East (16:19–22). The people of the Exile and Return also discovered that God's good will did not cease when they were expelled from Canaan. In fact, v.19 of the Hebrew text reads "When you were" instead of "when they were" of Ps 105:12 in both the KJV and the NIV. As in the case of v.15, this shift may be intentional to help the author's contemporaries see themselves in David's prayer. They are new patriarchs who wandered and found God's aid in a foreign land. They may expect his continued protection as they inhabit their reacquired homeland.

The chronicler deletes the verses concerning the descent into Egypt, the Exodus, and the Conquest from Ps 105:16–45. These stories did not fit his purpose of constructing a parallel between the patriarchal era and the postexilic community.

David renews his call to praise the Lord in 16:23–33, which parallels Ps 96:1–13. In this section of the prayer, the disparity between the ineffectual deities of the nations and the Lord of Israel is the major reason for worship. Idol worshipers experience discouragement; God-fearers find comfort. All humanity must celebrate the Lord's mighty deeds, which prove his superiority to idols. People must honor the Creator God and not the created god. The idols are unworthy of worship because they do not have the inherent qualities of true divinity.

The nonhuman world joins the human family in exalting the Lord. The earth trembles before its Creator. The unmovable creation rocks with praise for the Judge. The heavens, sea, fields, and forests resound with song for the Lord. This picture of the Deity's awesome power provides Israel with a message of hope and encouragement. Thir God is able to care for them.

1Ch 16:34, which borrows the call of Ps 106:1, provides a transition from praise to petition. David exalts God for his everlasting goodness and love. The Lord demonstrated his care for the patriarchs and the Davidic monarchy. God's past activity and his enduring love assure the chronicler's audience of his assistance in the present and future circumstances of resettlement.

Because God's love endures forever, one has confidence to cry out to him in days of uncertainty, such as at the founding and refounding of the nation. Foreign gods appeared to be in control for a brief period, but now the people are back in the land promised to their forebears. In exile and return the people learn that God's love endures despite outward appearances.

The final petition and praise, 16:35–36, uses Ps 106:47–48. David prays for the regathering of God's people from foreign lands to the land of promise, the reverse of exile. God's rescue of his people will engender thanksgiving. The final benediction, noting God's eternal love, exhorts people of all eras to participate in a panoply of praise.

The chronicler adapts the closing benediction of Book 4 of the Psalter (Ps 106:48). He changes the focus from a call for response to the report of the affirmative response by David's congregation. In closing, David appoints clergy to maintain regular worship before the ark and at Gibeon (vv.37–42). With the ark in its new abode, the people and David return home.

2. David's provision (17:1–29:30)

The chronicler now shows David doing everything to ensure the building of the temple. He addresses the matters of the builder, the plans and materials, the site, the workers, and the condition of peace.

a. God's house—David's house (17:1–27)

King David feels uncomfortable that the ark rests in a tent, and he desires to provide a proper residence for the Lord. Since God has demonstrated his presence with David in all previous undertakings, Nathan gives the king approval to build.

God, however, appears to express his disapproval of David's project. David must delay building the temple and serve in a preparatory role for another king (vv.4–6). Historically, God never commanded the people to construct a permanent sanctuary. A mobile shrine was adequate up to this point, so David need not hurry to build a temple.

In vv.7–14 God promises a house to David. God had lifted David from his flock to become the shepherd of Israel. He had assisted David in defeating the nation's enemies and will now exalt David's name. God promises to plant the people in the land and to give rest from opposition. This is a reversal of an exilic situation, which the returnees have experienced. They will find peace in their inherited homeland.

The king's offspring will come to the throne and build the temple. God will establish an everlasting filial relationship with David's child. At this point in the narrative the author deletes the correction motif of 2Sa 7:14. David's throne will last forever unconditionally. In other passages, especially those concerning Solomon and later kings, a provisional component stresses the interplay of divine promise and human response (1Ch 22:6–10; 28:2–10; 2Ch 6:15–17; 7:17–18; 13:5; 21:7; 23:3). Here, however, God stresses

that he will set Solomon and his dynasty over Israel forever. Though Israel had a human king, the real ruler was God. Note 1Ch 10:14; 28:5; 29:11, 23; 2Ch 9:8; 13:8. See also the original request for a king as recorded in 1Sa 8:7.

David responds with awe to this remarkable oracle (vv.16–27). He recognizes God's grace in crowning him. God is now promising to exceed the past and the present blessings to produce a future dynasty. The king affirms God's lordship over him. The Lord is the incomparable One. He sought Israel to be his unique people. The prayer moves from the miracles of the Exodus to God's work in establishing the Davidic monarchy. God redeemed the nation and made a name for himself by his awesome deeds in setting up this everlasting kingship. David invites the Lord to accomplish his word regarding the dynasty and the temple. God will establish his name and provide a witness to humankind of his faithfulness to his promises.

David's final words recapitulate the main concerns of his prayer (vv. 25–27). God's promise, a revelation of divine grace, has provided the occasion for the king's words. The king affirms the incomparable nature of the Lord. The Lord makes fulfillable promises; whatever he pledges is as good as done.

b. David's battles (18:1–20:8)

These chapters describe David's reputation as a man of blood, which disqualified him as the temple builder (1Ch 22:6–10; 28:2–3).

(1) David's various victories (18:1–13)

David secures the peace necessary for Solomon to construct the temple. (Note 1Ch 22:9 and the play on the proper name Solomon and the word for peace.) The Lord enables the king to defeat the Philistines, Moabites, Arameans, and Edomites. David dedicates all booty to the temple.

(2) David's kingdom organized (18:14–17)

David's organizational abilities complemented his military skills. Besides providing external peace, he set up a political system to ensure the smooth running of internal affairs.

(3) David defeats the Ammonites (19:1–20:3)

When the Ammonites misinterpret David's kindness, they dispatch the Israelite messengers in shame and hire Aramean mercenaries to assist their forces against a retaliatory strike. General Joab, confident that the outcome is in the Lord's hands, splits his forces to deal with the double threat. The Israelites rout the enemy coalition. When the Arameans call for help from relatives beyond the Euphrates, David leads his army to victory in the Transjordan. The Ammonites lose an ally when the Arameans become David's vassals.

In 20:1–3 the chronicler narrates the springtime war against the Ammonites at Rabbah. However, the account lacks the story of David's liaison with Bathsheba (2Sa 11–12). Some interpreters view this lacuna as suppression of negative details about David. This is possible. However, one must ask why the author did not expunge Bathsheba's name from the genealogy of the royal family in 1Ch 3:5 if he wanted to hide this connection. Given that the chronicler ignores other details known from canonical sources to shape his story, the lack may be due to the author's desire to focus on David as a warrior. The story of David's sin plays a role in Samuel-Kings to explain the succession problems at David's death. In light of

the smooth transition to Solomon recorded in Chronicles, this narrative would not serve the same function for the chronicler and could be eliminated.

(4) David is victorious over the Philistines (20:4–8).

This chapter ends with another record of David's subjugation of the Philistines who were mighty at the time of his accession.

c. Temple preparations (21:1–22:19)

(1) Satan's census and the Lord's sword (21:1–22:1)

This section begins with the troubling story of Satan's census and the Lord's sword (21:1–22:1). The chronicler's narrative diverges from the parallel account of 2Sa 24. The first word signals one major difference in the story. Who was responsible for this census? According to 1Ch 21:1, **Satan** inspired David to take a census. In contrast, 2Sa 24:1 attributes the instigation to **the LORD.** The Chronicles' narrative is reminiscent of Satan's appearance before the Lord to accuse Job. The text of Job 2:3, which uses the word *incited* of Satan, may have influenced the chronicler's composition. Due to his theological sensibilities, the chronicler substitutes Satan where his original source accuses God as being the instigator of the census and its consequences. This is the same theological issue with which the book of Job struggles. Who is ultimately responsible for the suffering of innocent people? The chronicler chooses to blame Satan as the initiator and to focus on the mercy of God in providing both an end to the punishment and the site for the temple. Thus, as in the story of Job, Satan's wicked intentions are turned around to the glory of God. (The only other appearance of Satan in the OT is the postexilic book of Zechariah. Satan appears in Zec 3 as an accuser of the high priest Joshua.)

The chronicler places the plague in the middle of David's life, whereas the author of 2Sa 24 sets this story at the end of the king's life. The issue of David's temple preparations controls this arrangement. This story tells how David selects the temple site. He chooses to erect the Lord's house where God demonstrated mercy in the midst of a terrible judgment against Israel.

Despite Joab's opposition, David sends him to number the troops. Joab avoids completely fulfilling the repulsive command by not reporting the total to David. The census angers the Lord, perhaps because David was tempted to trust human military might alone (21:7). This line regarding the anger of the Lord, unparalleled in the 2 Samuel account, is necessary in Chronicles since the author has attributed the idea for the census to Satan. David begs for God's forgiveness, and God outlines three options for punishment. David chooses to let a merciful God judge him (v.13).

The Lord, grieved by the calamity, stops the destruction. He instructs David to build an altar at Araunah's threshing floor where the angel stood. In a manner similar to Abraham's purchase of the cave at Machpelah (Ge 23), David refuses to take Araunah's property for less than full price. The Lord accepts David's offerings with a heavenly fire, just as he would at the same site when Solomon dedicated the completed temple (2Ch 7:1). The plague ceases.

The chronicler's report and placement concerns the acquisition and future use of Araunah's threshing floor. God's mercy, displayed during David's day, is available to any who turn toward this site after the temple is erected. The temple will be a memorial of an experience of God's grace and a sign of God's continued willingness to forgive and heal his people (2Ch 7:14). In 2Ch 3, when Solomon builds the temple, the chronicler reminds the reader of this connection.

(2) David prepares for the temple (22:2–5)

There is no explicit parallel for the materials of 1Ch 22:2–29:30 in the other canonical books. David conscripts resident aliens and provides materials for the temple construction. He makes these extensive preparations because of Solomon's inexperience as a ruler and builder.

(3) David's charge to Solomon (22:6–16)

After he provides material and human support for this project, David gives a charge to Solomon that is reminiscent of Moses' mandate to Joshua (Dt 31–Jos 1).

God ordained David's peaceful son to construct the temple (22:6–10). God will be the Father of this son and establish his throne forever. It seems incorrect to assume that the act of war itself disqualified David from this act of devotion. Military victory is a gift from God to an obedient king. So why should this rule out David as builder? Perhaps the stain of enemy blood made David unclean. Perhaps David, due to the time spent in battles, was unable to devote adequate attention to this project. The wordplay on **"peace"** expresses the necessity for national rest for the monarch to devote energies to building projects (v.9).

David assures Solomon that the Lord will enable him to build and to govern (vv.11–13). Solomon returns to the second theme at his coronation when he prays for divine guidance. David modifies the unconditional nature of the dynastic promise by emphasizing that success comes through obedience to the divine laws revealed to Moses.

David outlines the wealth provided for the project. He has also recruited craftsmen. In light of this Davidic and divine support, the king exhorts the people to get to work (vv.14–16).

(4) David instructs the leaders to assist Solomon (22:17–19)

The Lord has given the nation rest to build this house. The leaders must devote themselves wholeheartedly to helping Solomon provide a proper residence for the Lord.

d. David divides the Levites (23:1–27:34)

David divides the Levites into four companies as part of his physical and spiritual preparations for the temple. These groups will serve the Lord in supervision, judgment, gate-keeping, and praise (23:1–5).

David distinguishes the Levites by families (23:6–32). The chronicler stresses that the Levites' role changed with the building of a permanent sanctuary. The tribe assisted the priests in the cult (vv.25–32). Aaron's descendants are singled out because of their divine calling to the priesthood (vv.13–14).

In describing the twenty-four divisions of the Aaronic priesthood, the chronicler connects the human assignments to the long tradition of Aaronic priestly service ordained by God (24:1–19). God appointed these service groups, just as he was responsible for the nation's election, the rise and success of David, victory in war, and the origin of proper worship. To complete the picture, the author lists the remaining Levites without reference to their specific tasks (vv.20–31).

Consonant with the tradition of David's musicianship, the chronicler records that the monarch assigned persons to provide the music ministry in the temple (25:1–31). He appointed twenty-four groups of musicians to perform on a cyclical basis.

To control access to temple property, David appointed Levites to guard various gates and storehouses (26:1–19). He also commissioned other important officials (vv.20–32).

In ch. 27 the chronicler discusses David's military preparations. Twelve divisions, one for each month, were on duty (vv.1–15). He appointed tribal officers (vv.16–24). Some men cared for the royal property (vv.25–31). The last part (vv.32–34) lists the inner circle of power.

The author mentions in passing the ill-fated census (27:23–24). He alludes to the beginning and abrupt end of the numbering. He portrays David as believing God's promise of an innumerable Israel and not numbering men below the age of twenty. The author does not reiterate that David ordered the census or that Joab obeyed reluctantly. The chronicler says only that judgment came because of the census.

e. David exhorts Solomon (28:1–29:30)

David's final acts of preparation for the temple were the public commissioning of Solomon and the delivery of the temple plans.

David's commissions Solomon in 28:1–10. David summons all officials to assemble at Jerusalem and again instructs them regarding their responsibilities for completing the temple. First, David recalls his desire to build the sanctuary and the Lord's refusal to grant permission to build. Second, despite David's reputation as a warrior, God chose him as a fitting king for Israel. God made a dynastic promise and selected Solomon to succeed his father. This theme contrasts with the story in 2 Samuel and 1 Kings, which expresses some uncertainty regarding David's successor. Perhaps the chronicler assumes that the reader is familiar with the narrative recorded in the canonical books, but he presents God's intention to place Solomon on the throne as the temple builder.

David expresses the promise of everlasting kingship in conditional terms (28:7). The kingdom could be lost should the Davidic heir swerve from serving the Lord. God's promise is not an immutable, impersonal entity which, once spoken, can never be altered. The promise, intending to provide an enduring Davidic kingship, is personal and dynamic in nature and is to be worked out in a divine-human relationship. God is disposed to continue the Davidic line; he asks for obedience so that the line that continues will be "Davidic" not only in genetic code, but, more importantly, in faithfulness to the Lord of David.

The final charge to the leaders has the ring of commands given to earlier Israelite conquerors. The central ingredient to conquering the land and passing it on to future generations was obedience to God. This injunction was appropriate for the chronicler's generation faced with the fresh challenge of faithfully serving God while rebuilding in Canaan.

David encourages Solomon to serve God completely (28:9–10). The external equipment of worship, which Solomon will construct in splendor, is not sufficient for true religion. Worship must be heartfelt and thoughtful because God knows the motives of the worshiper. God is near to people who

seek him, but he rejects those who spurn him. Solomon must respond with holy courage if he is to complete his divinely appointed task.

Divinely inspired blueprints were familiar to ancient Near Eastern monarchs directed by their god or goddess to construct a house. As the climax of this public service, David gives these plans to Solomon (28:11–21). These instructions delineate the physical layout of the temple, the organization of the temple staff and the design of utensils. The written plans ensure complete correspondence between God's will and Solomon's performance (v.19). Again David enjoins Solomon to work courageously. Human preparations are finished. God will not fail to give strength to complete his temple.

David reminds the assembly of Solomon's inexperience for this great task. The king supports this project from his own resources, and the people joyfully follow David's example of sacrificial giving as an act of consecration to the Lord (29:1–9).

When David came to power his first concerns were religious. Now, at the end of his reign, David prays (29:10–20). He links his nation to father Israel. He ascribes overwhelming power and majesty to God, the King over all heaven and earth. God shares a portion of his honor and strength with a human ruler. The Lord deserves his people's praise (vv.10–13).

David stresses utter dependence on God (29:14–19). The peoples' generosity toward the temple is but a reflection of God's liberality. God, however, inspects each giver's motives. David asserts that the community has given with deep sincerity. He prays that God would keep this religious fervor alive in Israel forever. For the immediate future, he asks the Lord to give

Solomon the internal moorings necessary to be a faithful temple builder.

This prayer communicates themes important for the chronicler's community. In discouraging days of rebuilding, the postexilic community could reflect on the preparations for the first temple and draw strength from David's prayer. Their God was the God of the patriarchs, David and Solomon. Surely the Lord would provide the requisite materials, personnel, and desire for this later community to rebuild life in the land. The God who cared for David and his contemporaries would support the renewed Israel.

Solomon takes the throne amidst this atmosphere of worship (29:21–25). All Israel feasts and offers sacrifices and libations to the Lord. David's entourage transfers its loyalty to Solomon. The chronicler mentions none of the struggles for the throne recorded in 2 Samuel. The Lord makes Solomon Israel's splendid monarch, whose reign is the zenith of Israelite royal power and prestige (v.25).

The chronicler finishes David's story by recording his time of service, his wealth, his power, and his successor. The author points to the records of the prophets Samuel, Nathan, and Gad for additional information (29:26–30).

C. Solomon (2Ch 1–9)

The chronicler's main interest in Solomon is that he fulfilled his charge to build the Lord's house. Chs. 1 and 9 deal with the wisdom, splendor, and piety of Solomon and frame the main narrative regarding the completion of the building project.

1. The greatness of Solomon (1:1–17)

The chronicler relates three aspects of the consolidation of Solomon's power to stress that God had chosen this son

of David to inherit Israel's throne. In contrast to David, Solomon does not use any force to solidify his position. He enjoys the rest promised in 1Ch 17.

a. Solomon's worship (1:2–6)

Solomon and the people begin his reign with worship at the tabernacle at Gibeon. They follow David's example by "inquiring" of the Lord and offering a thousand burnt offerings on the altar.

b. Solomon's wisdom (1:7–13)

Solomon's most well-known characteristic, his wisdom, is the focus of the second part of this chapter. Solomon tells God that he needs divinely inspired insight to govern the nation. The Lord vows to grant this unselfish request and also to bestow unsurpassed wealth and honor on Solomon.

c. Solomon's wealth (1:14–17)

God fulfills the second half of his promise to Solomon. Solomon accumulates great wealth: chariots, horses, precious metals, and wood. The prosperous nation even exports horses. The people enjoy Solomon's good fortune as precious metals and cedar become commonplace. It is interesting that the kingdom's wealth almost becomes a curse later.

2. The temple charge fulfilled (2:1–8:16)

Despite Solomon's wisdom and wealth, the main interest of the author is the king's completion of the work entrusted to him by God and David. The section begins with Solomon's order to build (2:1) and closes with the statement, "So the temple of the LORD was finished" (8:16).

a. Conscription of the labor force (2:1–18)

Statements concerning the laborers drafted for the building projects frame the chapter. In contrast to 1Ki 7:1, little attention is given to Solomon's palace. Initially the chronicler tells only the number of carriers, stonecutters, and foremen. He later clarifies that the workers were aliens in Israel (vv.17–18). Solomon enlisted these sojourners to work just as the Egyptians conscripted his ancestors centuries before.

Solomon requests Hiram to send cedar for the Lord's house. He asks for a specialist in precious metals and fabrics and for woodcutters to work alongside Israelite artisans. Solomon recognizes the inadequacy of his building to house God. The temple will simply provide a focal point for the human devotee when worshiping the uncontainable God.

Hiram, a non-Yahwist, is not offended by Solomon's assertion of the Lord's superiority. Perhaps the richness of his partnership with Solomon caused him to praise the Lord. He lauds the Creator of heaven and earth, who formed the Davidic dynasty and gave David a supremely intelligent son. This praise provides the first evidence that the Lord answered Solomon's request for wisdom to rule the nation. Hiram recognizes the divine command to build the temple. He sends a craftsman, one who is part Israelite, and requests his fee.

b. The building and its furnishings (3:1–5:1)

This section begins with the statement that Solomon began to work (3:1) and closes with a note about the completion of the task (5:1). Araunah's threshing floor on Mount Moriah is the proper site for the temple. The chronicler links David's lot to Ge 22 and Abraham's aborted sacrifice of Isaac. The Lord mercifully appeared to both Abraham and David at this site. Thus, on the basis of both an ancient tradition and a recent deliverance, it is the appropriate place for the sanctuary.

The chronicler outlines the building and furnishing of the temple (3:3–4:22). He highlights various aspects from the foundation to the decorative pomegranates dangling from chains on the front pillars. Solomon provides utensils for worship made with undetermined amounts of bronze and gold. His preparations for worship are extensive and expensive. The stage is now set for the spiritual anointing of the house.

c. Solomon dedicates the temple (5:2–7:10)

Solomon summons the leaders to bring the ark to the temple. All Israel joins the celebration. While the assembly offers innumerable sacrifices, the Levites carry the ark, the tabernacle, and the furnishings. The Levites place the ark in the Most Holy Place. The priests withdraw, and the appointed musicians lead the worship with the refrain **"He is good; his love endures forever."** The Lord responds, as at the tabernacle dedication, by filling the place with his overwhelming presence (Ex 40:34). The ministers are unable to perform their tasks because of God's glory.

Ch. 6 records Solomon's dedication prayer. Solomon evaluates the Lord's splendid house and blesses the assembly by reviewing God's role in their history. God chose Jerusalem and David's family. During the monarchy, the Lord breaks with earlier tradition and chooses the temple site and Davidic builder. This moment of dedication constitutes the final realization of God's promise to David (vv.10–11).

Solomon lauds God's incomparable faithfulness to his word (6:14–15). The Lord, who honors obedient servants, has now fulfilled his promise to David regarding the temple. The king asks God to keep his promise of David's house in light of human obedience (vv.16–17). The conditional nature of God's vow provides an appropriate call to obedience for every generation of God's people.

The temple is an inadequate house for God, whom the heavens cannot contain (6:18–21). The king, however, asks that the Lord would focus his attention on this place for the sake of those who will direct prayers toward it. Solomon illustrates this general request by various scenarios that call for God's forgiving response to penitential prayer (6:22–39).

Solomon asks the Supreme Judge to decide between adversaries to clear the innocent and punish the guilty person (6:22–23). When Israel is exiled, Solomon asks God to forgive the people and to return them to the land (vv.24–25). The chronicler's audience was not far removed from this experience.

Disobedience might bring drought (6:26–27). In response to prayer God will give rain and instruction for living. A variety of other disasters may come upon the nation from an offended God (vv.28–31). Solomon asks the Lord to deal with each person on the basis of individual actions and motives. Judgment and forgiveness will motivate the people to future obedience.

Solomon asks the Lord to include non-Israelites who might pray toward the temple in the circle of his concern (6:32–33). The king also recognizes that foreign relations will not always be friendly. He asks God to make Israel victorious in war (vv.34–35).

Finally, Solomon clarifies the problem underlying the other cases (6:36–39). The people will not obey God perfectly. When they sin, God will send them into exile. They will have a change of heart and pray for forgiveness toward the land, city, and temple, which the Lord gave to them. He asks God to listen to this exilic plea.

Solomon's final benediction, 6:40–42, renews the call for the Lord to heed prayers offered at the temple. The writer adapts a canonical Song of Ascents, which relates two themes significant in Chronicles—David's desire for the Lord's house and the Lord's promise of David's house (Ps 132:8–10). The ark has come to its place of rest in fulfillment of the first promise. Solomon ends his prayer by asking God to fulfill the second vow and establish the dynasty.

Human and divine participants are active in the dedication ceremony. The Lord accepts the house by devouring the sacrifices with heavenly fire and filling the temple with his glory (7:1). This event recalls David's acquisition of the temple site and parallels the inauguration of tabernacle and the beginning of the priests' ministry (Lev 9:23–24). Again the priests cannot carry out their appointed functions because of the Lord's overwhelming presence (2Ch 5:14). The people respond with a familiar thanksgiving refrain (7:3).

The king and people consecrate the temple with myriad sacrifices. Professional singers and musicians accompany the worship. The theme of God's eternal love for his people is prominent when God reveals his presence, such as the inauguration of the central place of worship. After a lengthy celebration, Solomon sends the people home rejoicing over God's good deeds. The chronicler, in contrast to 1Ki 8:66, includes Solomon in 7:10 to draw attention to the continuity of events between David and Solomon in building the temple and reestablishing the monarchy.

d. God replies to Solomon's prayer (7:11–22)

After the festivities, God responds in a night vision to Solomon's prayer. He assures the king that he will hear prayers offered toward the temple. Regarding Solomon's concern for the people, God declares that he will restore them and the land after a time of distress if they humbly and actively seek him (vv.13–16). V.14 is a key to interpreting the later history of the nation as it rebels, repents, and is returned. (Note these terms in other parts of the chronicler's work. "Humble themselves"—2Ch 12:6–7, 12; 30:11; 32:26; 33:12, 19, 23; 36:12. "Pray"—2Ch 32:20, 24; 33:13. "Seek my face"—2Ch 11:16; 15:4, 15; 20:4. "Turn"—2Ch 15:4; 30:6, 9; 36:13.) This section about God's people is unique to Chronicles and emphasizes one of its important themes. The parallel passage, 1Ki 9:2–9, deals only with dynastic concerns. The text also calls the chronicler's contemporaries and later generations to respond with humility to receive divine deliverance from judgment. These verses emphasize again the dynamic nature of the divine and human relationship.

God asserts that Solomon is responsible to assure the continuance of David's dynasty (vv.17–18). He will continue to rule as David's son if he continues to be faithful to the Lord.

God promises judgment for unfaithfulness (vv.19–22). The Hebrew text has plural "you," referring to Solomon and the entire nation. Exile will come for serving other deities. The Lord will make the temple, intended as a sign of hope to Israel and all nations, into an **object of ridicule.** People who see the devastation of this glorious edifice will learn about the disastrous results of forsaking the God of the temple. The hope is that this warning will deter disobedience. People in exile may enjoy forgiveness and return if they seek the Lord; those in the land may avoid punishment altogether by obedience.

The postexilic community, newly planted in the land, could affirm that God granted Solomon's request for forgiveness for humble, exiled people.

e. Solomon's other activities after building the temple (8:1–16)

Solomon rebuilt cities acquired from Hiram or captured in war. He conscripted resident aliens as a labor force and drafted Israelites into military service. Solomon made a marriage alliance with Egypt and prepared a house for Pharaoh's daughter separate from buildings connected with the Lord. Solomon was faithful to his religious responsibilities. He offered the required sacrifices and appointed priests and Levites to their tasks. The chronicler closes this section by noting that the temple was now completely finished. The chronicler does not describe Solomon's apostasy in following the deities of his foreign wives (1Ki 11).

3. Solomon's greatness (8:17–9:31)

This section balances the introductory chapter of Solomon's story. The main points are wealth and wisdom; worship was the focus of the middle chapters of the narrative. Solomon's wealth came from sea trade, tribute from the queen of Sheba, and revenue generated by vassals and merchants.

The queen of Sheba tests Solomon's wisdom (9:1–12). She brings a great retinue and gifts for the king. Solomon answers her challenging questions. The queen is overwhelmed by Solomon's wisdom and splendor. Expecting to test this fabled monarch, she finds that the truth far exceeds the tales. Solomon's subordinates are fortunate to stand and hear him daily. The queen, like Hiram, praises the Lord who delighted in Solomon and blessed him so richly.

Solomon sits as regent upon God's throne over Israel. God loves his people and has provided Solomon's kingship to give them an orderly way of life. The queen gives Solomon valuable items, but the king's gifts surpass her tribute. Materially and intellectually the queen is enriched by Solomon.

Further notes regarding Solomon's splendor are recorded in 9:13–28. Precious metals were so abundant that Solomon used gold for decorative purposes and for household items. Silver was devalued because it was so common. Foreign monarchs treasured Solomon as they came to bring tribute and to learn wisdom from this incomparable king.

In Solomon's summary, 9:29–31, the chronicler points the reader to the sources of Nathan, Ahijah, and Iddo. By mentioning Jeroboam son of Nebat, the author hints at the problem of succession and the coming rift of the nation.

III. DIVIDED MONARCHY (2CH 10–36)

A. Until the Northern Kingdom Falls (2Ch 10–28)

1. Rehoboam (10:1–12:16)

Dramatic changes occur with this king's accession. One united realm under a Davidic ruler becomes two competing kingdoms. The kingdom's glory is reduced, as symbolized by the replacement of Solomon's gold shields with bronze replicas in 12:9–11. The peace Solomon needed to complete his building projects is gone and replaced with continual warfare within Israel, invasion from foreigners, and the need for increased fortifications. Finally, in contrast to the picture of David and Solomon's complete submission to God's will, the chronicler demonstrates

that the monarchs and people alternate between obedience and disobedience.

a. Northern tribes rebel (10:1–11:4)

The nation gathers at Shechem to crown Rehoboam. The rival leader, Jeroboam, returns from Egypt and asks for relief from Solomon's burden. Apparently the people had been heavily taxed and forced to work during Solomon's administration (1Sa 8:10–18). The chronicler does not relate material from Kings that places Solomon in a negative light and explains this division as a divine judgment (1Ki 11). This deletion makes Rehoboam appear more responsible for the schism than is the case historically, but he is not without blame.

Rehoboam's older counselors, who served Solomon, advise a policy of kindness. He follows his young advisors who encourage him to add weight to the burden. God, the unseen partner in this exchange, keeps his promise to Jeroboam (10:15). The northern tribes rebel in light of Rehoboam's severity and their lack of partnership in the Davidic monarchy.

Hostilities intensify when the rebels stone Adoniram, the man in charge of forced labor. Despite affirming God's role in this split, the chronicler views the breach as continual rebellion against the Davidic monarchy (10:19). Rehoboam musters an army to retake the North, but Shemaiah reiterates the Lord's part in the split and convinces him not to fight (11:3–4). This initial obedience contrasts with Rehoboam's behavior after consolidating his position over the reduced kingdom.

b. Rehoboam fortifies Judah (11:5–17)

Rehoboam's fortifications along the eastern, southern, and western flanks of his territory are both a sign of the Lord's blessing and of the hostilities of his time (vv.5–12). Another sign of divine favor is the support of the religious establishment for Rehoboam (vv.13–17). Northern Levites, rejected by Jeroboam's alternative cult, travel south. The chronicler asserts that the righteous people of the land side with Judah and reject the false religion of the North. The people seek the Lord, one of the conditions of forgiveness outlined in 2Ch 7:14. This movement parallels the broad-based support that David received from **all Israel** when he rose to power. David's grandson, trying to establish himself over Judah, gains the backing of the righteous people of the land.

c. Rehoboam appoints the crown prince (11:18–23)

To prevent succession problems at his death, Rehoboam appoints Abijah as crown prince. To avoid palace intrigue, he disperses his sons into various districts of the kingdom and provides abundantly for their needs. The chronicler portrays Rehoboam, in the first part of his reign, as a faithful and capable ruler.

d. Rehoboam becomes unfaithful (12:1–12)

After a period of consolidation, Rehoboam and the people abandon the Lord's law. As a result of this sin, Pharaoh Shishak invades the land and captures the weak fortified cities. Shemaiah reveals that the Lord is abandoning Israel to another ruler because the people chose to reject the Lord. In contrast, 1Ki 14:25–28 lacks the explicit linking of the invasion to the nation's faithlessness as the chronicler has supplied.

The leaders humble themselves and affirm God's justice. The Lord promises

deliverance. The nation, however, will remain an Egyptian vassal to learn the difference between serving a divine and human overlord. Shishak's looting of the palace and the temple lessens the tiny kingdom's splendor, just as Jeroboam's rebellion reduced its dimensions. Gold shields, once proudly displayed, are stolen. These are replaced by bronze replicas fearfully kept under lock and key.

God reduces his punishment in response to Rehoboam's humility (v. 12). Throughout Chronicles, the author stresses the cycle of judgment; repentance; and, ultimately, divine forgiveness, which follows unfaithfulness. These themes were part of Solomon's prayer and God's promise at the temple dedication. The nation's history demonstrates this cycle. The chronicler reminds his audience that they are forgiven and that they are responsible to be obedient to the Lord to avoid renewed judgment. "As so often in Chronicles, the historical narrative is thus made into an example, a paradigm, of a situation that is likely to recur, and to which his readers will be expected to make the appropriate response" (Williamson, 246).

e. Rehoboam summary (12:13–16)

The chronicler gives Rehoboam a negative evaluation even though he firmly held the throne. Rehoboam's lack of internal devotion to the Lord led to acts of disobedience. Despite the fact that he sought the Lord when he was in trouble, this king is an unfit example for future monarchs. There was general unrest during Rehoboam's reign but a smooth transition to Abijah's reign.

2. Abijah (13:1–14:1)

In contrast to 1Ki 15:1–8, which views Abijah in a negative light, the chronicler asserts that Abijah was righteous during his brief reign. He is more than simply an heir to carry on the Davidic monarchy, he is one who trusts God in battle. Abijah, outnumbered two to one by Jeroboam, issues a twofold challenge. He maintains that the only true monarchy is Davidic (13:4–7). Abijah, ignoring the Lord's hand in the split, charges the ten tribes with rebellion against a young, indecisive and impotent Rehoboam.

Abijah challenges Jeroboam regarding true worship (13:8–12). Israel's religion is false. Jeroboam fashioned golden calves to worship and anointed anyone to the priesthood. This system clashes with Judah's worship in which a God-ordained priesthood continues to offer proper sacrifices to the Lord in Abijah's time. In light of Judah's faithfulness, Abijah is fully assured of God's help in battle.

Jeroboam ignores Abijah's appeals, and he attempts to ambush Judah. Judah raises the battle cry and, as in the days of holy war, God routs the enemy. The North sustains heavy casualties because Judah relied on the Lord and not on its outnumbered troops. Differing fates await the warring kings. The Lord kills Jeroboam, but he gives Abijah strength and a large family.

3. Asa (14:2–16:14)

The chronicler includes more information on this ruler than the parallel (1Ki 15:9–24). He reports two battles, each followed by a sermon, to illustrate the nature of this monarch's reign. In the first case, Asa relies on God and receives a favorable word. In the second, Asa leans on a human ally and hears rebuke.

a. Asa's initial reform (14:2–7)

Asa's initial evaluation is positive. In a religious reform, the king removes the materials of the false cult and commands the nation to obey the Lord. As a political benefit from this reform, Asa enjoys the peace necessary to work on building projects. Asa affirms, in the sentiments of 7:14, that the nation holds the land due to fidelity to the Lord (v.7).

b. The Lord and Asa defeat Zerah (14:8–15)

Zerah's army greatly outnumbers Asa's forces. Asa prepares for battle just as Abijah did when confronted by Jeroboam's troops (2Ch 13). Zerah opposes the Lord himself, so Asa prays for power to defeat this overwhelming foe. In response to righteous Asa, God strikes Zerah down. A huge number of enemy warriors fall, and Judah takes much spoil.

c. Azariah's sermon (15:1–7)

Azariah encourages the nation to continue in faithfulness to the Lord because of the conditional nature of their relationship. God grants the nation its desire. If they seek God, he will bless them; if they abandon him, he will leave them alone. Azariah illustrates his sermon with a story from the nation's distant past. When they first sought God, apparently in the tumultuous days of the judges, he helped them. This early trust is exemplary for a king in the early divided monarchy, for the postexilic community, or for any generation of God's people.

d. Asa's reform continues (15:8–19)

The king, encouraged by Azariah's sermon, removes more idols and repairs the Lord's altar. Israelites who recognize God's presence with Asa assemble to sacrifice a great portion of the plunder from their victory over Zerah.

They make a pact among themselves **to seek the LORD** wholeheartedly. The worshipers kill persons who do not agree with their resolve. This harsh treatment is reserved for those who might lead the nation astray (Dt 13:6–11; 17:2–7). In response to this worship, the Lord gives them rest.

Asa makes his reform personal by deposing the queen mother and burning her Asherah pole. The chronicler gives Asa an overall favorable report even though he did not destroy the **high places.** In contrast to Rehoboam, Asa's heart was pure in intent to serve God. He did not completely purge the nation of false religion, but he did much to reestablish true worship.

e. Asa fights Baasha (16:1–6)

In this struggle against the North, Asa fails to follow his own earlier example. Instead of trusting God, Asa makes an alliance with Ben-Hadad of Aram. This plan seems successful as the Aramean king attacks his former ally, Baasha, to end the threat to Judah.

f. Hanani's sermon (16:7–10)

In a speech not included in 1Ki 15, the chronicler records the Lord's evaluation of this second military action. Hanani rebukes Asa because he relied not on the Lord but on a human ally, who should have been treated as an adversary. The seer contrasts this battle with the Lord's victory against Zerah. Asa, using an improper method, successfully repelled Baasha's troops. He could have achieved a better result by relying on the Lord. In punishment, God will withdraw his peace.

g. The conclusion of Asa's reign (16:11–14)

Despite early devotion and Hanani's rebuke, Asa's life ends in anger and illness. He oppresses the people and suffers a serious, undetermined disease of the feet. He refuses to seek divine healing and trusts only in human physi-

cians, just as he had relied on human allies. The chronicler implies that Asa could have been healed if he had trusted the Lord. The extensive and elaborate burial that Asa received seems to indicate an overall favorable view of this king.

4. Jehoshaphat (17:1–21:1)

The chronicler gives a fuller account of this monarch than 1Ki 16:29–22:50, which focuses on King Ahab and his struggles with Elijah. Jehoshaphat receives a mixed review in Chronicles. His reign illustrates the blessings of faithfulness and the dangers of associating with the wicked. The author underscores the potential for restoration due to repentance.

a. Jehoshaphat's reign (17:1–19)

The Lord enables this king to strengthen his fortifications against Israel. In his early years, Jehoshaphat is righteous, his intentions are pure, and he removes items and places of false worship. Besides his building projects and personal piety, Jehoshaphat sends officials on missions to instruct the people in the Lord's law. As in the case of holy war, but without conflict, the fear of the Lord falls on Judah's neighbors. The Philistines, once powerful conquerors, bring tribute to Jehoshaphat. The king is powerful because of his obedience, and his future looks bright.

b. Jehoshaphat and Ahab (18:1–19:3)

Jehoshaphat, however, makes an alliance with Ahab. The chronicler strongly condemns this relationship. Ahab urges Jehoshaphat to attack Ramoth Gilead. The word *urge* is the same term used in 1Ch 21:1 when Satan **incited** David to number the fighting men. It is also used in 2Ch 32:11, 15 when Sennacherib's servants accuse Hezekiah of **misleading** the people by telling them to trust the Lord. Later in this story, the Lord allures the Arameans away from Jehoshaphat (18:31).

Jehoshaphat agrees to assist Ahab if he asks the Lord's counsel in the matter. Four hundred Israelite prophets tell the rulers to fight. Jehoshaphat, not happy with the prophets' pedigree, requests a prophet of the Lord. Ahab summons Micaiah. The messenger dispatched encourages Micaiah to tailor his message to the majority opinion. In the spirit of a true prophet, Micaiah vows to say only what God reveals. Micaiah initially agrees with the false prophets, but Ahab himself, in a strange twist, forces Micaiah to give him a message of doom. Micaiah places his reputation as the Lord's prophet on the line with his prediction that Israel would become shepherdless and scattered.

When the two kings enter the battle, Jehoshaphat wears his royal vestments but Ahab disguises himself. The enemy troops pursue the man dressed like a monarch. The Lord delivers Jehoshaphat from this chase when he prays for help. The disguised Ahab, however, dies, struck by a stray bow shot.

Jehoshaphat returns safely to Jerusalem to face the rebuke of Jehu, son of the seer who scolded his father (19:1–3). Divine wrath will come because of the king's misguided alliance. God tempers the punishment because Jehoshaphat sought God and removed places of false worship.

c. Jehoshaphat's judges (19:4–11)

This king, whose name means "The Lord is Judge," inaugurates judicial reform. Jehoshaphat himself travels about teaching the people to follow God. He appoints judges and teachers, some introduced in 17:7–9, to settle disputes and admonish the citizenry to obey the Lord. Jehoshaphat warns of the consequences of further sin.

d. Jehoshaphat's victory (20:1–30)

This triumph results from complete dependence on God. In response to a threatened invasion, the king calls a fast and the whole nation seeks the Lord.

Jehoshaphat's prayer (vv.6–12) is structured like a complaint psalm. He praises God's power, which nothing in heaven and earth can withstand. Jehoshaphat lauds God's past assistance during the Conquest. God also made the temple, a place of hope for distressed peoples, a reality. The king expects that the land should enjoy peace. But Judah is besieged. The invaders repay Israel's kindness at the time of the Exodus with hostility (Nu 20:14–21; Dt 2:1–19; Jdg 11:16–18). Jehoshaphat pleads with God to judge these nations for their betrayal. Judah is helpless to defend itself; God must graciously provide deliverance.

The Lord encourages Jehoshaphat with an oracle of salvation through Jahaziel. Just as in a holy war, the king must be fearless in the face of this challenge. The Lord will provide victory as the nation watches.

The chronicler records the humble response to the oracle and accents the religious nature of the battle (vv.18–28). God overcomes the enemy by means of a worshiping community. Anxious to see salvation, the people rise early on the day of battle. Jehoshaphat admonishes them to trust God for a successful campaign. Praising people lead the army into conflict with a familiar refrain of the Psalter and of Chronicles (1Ch 16:34; 2Ch 5:13). This "fight song" replaces the battle shout recorded in other biblical war texts (Jos 6:5; Jdg 7:20; 1Sa 17:20,

52; 2Ch 13:15). While the people sing, the Lord incites the invaders to destroy each other. The only tasks left for Israel are plunder and praise. They spend three days gleaning the booty. On the fourth day, all the men complete the "battle" by glorifying God. Potential enemies fear God, and Judah enjoys divinely granted rest.

e. The conclusion of Jehoshaphat's reign (20:31–21:3)

The only negative feature of this monarch's generally positive reign is that popular worship is not brought into line with orthodoxy. The high places remain, and the people are not motivated to worship the Lord.

The chronicler frames the story of Jehoshaphat's life with accounts of bad alliances (20:35–37). At an unspecified time, Jehoshaphat enters into a trading alliance with Israel. Eliezer's words against this shipbuilding enterprise form the centerpiece of this vignette. The Lord shipwrecks the trading vessels prior to their maiden voyage in what the author presents as an example of immediate divine retribution.

5. Jehoram (21:4–20)

a. Jehoram's evil reign (21:4–11)

Jehoram illustrates that faithlessness leads to ruin. He comes to power smoothly, but in contrast to the pious activities of good kings such as David and Solomon, his reign is completely evil. Jehoram kills all rivals for the throne, marries Ahab's daughter, and leads the nation in following the wicked ways of the North.

God demonstrates his grace by bringing political problems, but not complete destruction, to David's kingdom. Edom and Libnah rebel. The chronicler connects the nation's distress to Jehoram's refusal to obey the Lord.

Jehoram rebuilds the destroyed high places and leads the people astray.

b. Elijah's letter (21:12–15)

Elijah, the prophet who spoke forcefully against Ahab in the North, sends a letter that promises judgment. Jehoram is evil, and the Lord will punish him by striking down his people, sons, wives, and everything else. Jehoram will suffer a fatal bowel disease.

c. End of Jehoram's reign (21:16–20)

The Lord fulfills his promise. The Philistines and Arabs administer the heavy blow, taking the royal family and many possessions into exile. The royal line is almost cut off. However, a son remains to continue David's dynasty. Jehoram dies from his incurable disease and is buried without honor.

The chronicler sums up this reign as eight regrettable years in Judah's history. Jehoram was not buried with the kings. The author does not tell the reader where to find additional information on this ruler; he is not worthy of research.

6. Ahaziah (22:1–9)

Jehoram's surviving son rules for one evil year. Ahaziah's mother, Athaliah, leads him to increase connections with the North. His downfall comes as a result of his alliance with Joram of Israel. God ordains a coup, led by Jehu, to end Ahab's dynasty. Ahaziah, while on a visit, is killed in the revolt. The dynastic situation in the South becomes hazy as a result of Ahaziah's death (v.9). This dark moment for the nation was similar in many respects to the despair at the fall of Saul's house. What would become of the monarchy? Would someone from David's house sit on the throne? In the interim, the evil Athaliah seizes the throne.

7. Joash (22:10–24:27)

a. Joash comes to power (22:10–23:21)

Athaliah puts the Davidic dynasty on the brink of extinction. However, for the six years that this illegitimate ruler sat on the throne of Judah, Jehosheba and Jehoiada hide baby Joash in the temple.

Finally, Jehoiada initiates a pact with the military commanders, the Levites, and the family heads to place Joash on his promised throne. The priests and Levites lead a popularly supported holy revolution. They crown Joash and slay Athaliah and her followers. The people vow to serve God, and, as a result, they tear down the Baal temple and care for the Lord's neglected temple.

b. Joash's righteousness (24:1–16)

The Lord blesses faithful Joash. The chronicler mentions that his mother came from as far south as possible, Beersheba, perhaps to stress a contrast to Athaliah and the North. Joash follows the Lord while Jehoiada lives. The king takes wives and begins to rebuild David's dynasty, which had been decimated by Jehoram and Athaliah (v.4).

Joash begins to restore the neglected and looted temple (vv.4–14). Although the Levites refuse to collect the tax, the people contribute gladly. Like their ancestors, who provided lavishly for the tabernacle, they give more than necessary for the repairs. True worship continues during the lifetime of Jehoiada, but Joash's spiritual gains were short-lived.

c. Joash's wickedness (24:17–27)

As Rehoboam years before, Joash is led astray by different advisors after righteous Jehoiada dies. The chronicler offers a theological explanation for the assassination recorded in 2Ki 12:17–21. This once pious king abandons God's shrine and worships idols. The nation's guilt will bring retribution, but it is not a foregone conclusion. The Lord offers restoration through his prophets. However, the recalcitrant nation rejects the message of hope (vv. 18–19). This continued rejection of God's grace brings a punishment and will ultimately lead to the Exile (2Ch 36:15–21).

The people kill Zechariah when he comes to deliver God's rebuke. Therefore, the Lord sends the Aramean army to judge Judah's faithless leadership. The chronicler describes a familiar scenario, but with a twist. A small, insignificant army defeats an overwhelming favorite. Judah's apostasy causes God to bring this embarrassing defeat (v.24). The Arameans leave a wounded Joash to be assassinated by his own officials as repayment for Zechariah's murder.

8. Amaziah (25:1–28)

The chronicler gives this king, like many others, a mixed review. He is obedient to God concerning Israelite mercenaries but is disobedient with regard to Edomite deities and a battle with Israel.

Amaziah executes his father's murderers but spares their children. To fortify his army, he hires Israelite mercenaries. A **man of God** declares the Lord's displeasure with this alliance. To avert punishment and gain victory, Amaziah dismisses the mercenaries. As a sign of God's blessing, the obedient Amaziah captures Edom.

Unfortunately, Amaziah was not steadfast in his piety. In a paragraph unique to Chronicles, the author relates that this king worshiped the defeated Edomite gods. This time, however, Amaziah refuses to heed God's message of warning and hears a word of judgment.

Amaziah's counselors encourage him to challenge Jehoash of Israel. The northern king, empowered by God to bring Amaziah's downfall, defeats Judah. Judean conspirators kill Amaziah at Lachish. The chronicler explicitly links this tragedy to the king's worship of Edomite deities (v.27).

9. Uzziah (26:1–23)

The author says little regarding the prosperity of this monarch's lengthy reign. Uzziah's reign was generally positive, but his life ends on a sad note. Like Joash, Uzziah sought the Lord while an influential spiritual advisor lived. God's vow in 7:14 to bless those who seek him is realized in this king's life (v.5).

Vv.6–20 are unique to Chronicles. They narrate the two phases of Uzziah's reign and God's response to each. The first, vv.6–15, may be summarized as **"God helped him"** (v.7). Uzziah builds the seaport at Elath and wins victory in war. He inaugurates building projects in the homeland. Uzziah has a huge army. God gives him an extensive reputation. The words **"until he became powerful"** (v.15) alert the reader to Uzziah's future downfall.

Uzziah's pride causes a decisive change (v.16). The chronicler provides a theological explanation for the disease and downfall recorded in 2Ki 15:5. The king becomes unfaithful to the Lord who made him mighty. The author uses the term *m'l* in a slightly different sense since Uzziah does not forsake the Lord. Rather, he attempts to usurp the priestly office and becomes enraged when confronted by the priests. In response to Uzziah's arrogance, the Lord afflicts him with a skin disease. Uzziah's reign ends in disgrace; he loses both his palace and the privilege of temple worship.

10. Jotham (27:1–9)

Jotham's story breaks the pattern of interchange between faithfulness and unfaithfulness in the lives of the past several kings. By accentuating the positive nature of this reign, the author sets up a strong contrast between Jotham and his wicked son, Ahaz. Jotham does not disrupt temple worship, but, on the other hand, he does not promote true religion. Jotham enjoys blessings of building projects and military victory because of his piety.

11. Ahaz (28:1–27)

This monarch's reign is totally evil. He follows the ways of the North: making idols for Baal worship, sacrificing at rival shrines, offering his sons, and worshiping at high places. As a result, Arameans take citizens into exile and the North punishes the South. The chronicler attributes Judah's distress to God's punishment for unfaithfulness.

The prophet Oded rebukes the Israelites for their zeal in their role as the instrument of God's wrath (vv.9–11). The chronicler still considers the North and South as parts of one fractured state, not as separate entities. He calls the exiles taken to Samaria **fellow countrymen** (vv.11, 15) and **kinsmen** (v.8) to show this close connection. Remarkably, Israel returns the prisoners to Judah. The chronicler's readers would recognize this parallel to their history of captivity and return.

Ahaz sends for Tiglath-Pileser III to help fight his various opponents. The Lord judges Ahaz for this alliance. This ally was an adversary, one paid tribute from the temple and palace. Besides this political miscue, Ahaz closes the temple and promotes false religion. In his distress King Ahaz sacrifices to the Aramean gods instead of seeking God's forgiveness and restoration.

B. Hezekiah to the Return From Babylonian Exile (2Ch 29–36)

The chronicler does not report the fall of Samaria. From the time of Ahaz and Hezekiah, the tiny kingdom of Judah abides alone until its destruction over a century later.

1. Hezekiah (29:1–32:33)

Hezekiah's story is the longest of any king after David and Solomon. The author embellishes the report of the religious reform mentioned in 2Ki 18:4. Hezekiah's reestablishment of temple worship parallels Solomon's original building.

a. Hezekiah purifies the temple (29:1–36)

Most of this material is original to Chronicles. Hezekiah, portrayed like David, does not have a faithless period. He begins his rule by caring for his religious responsibilities. He repairs the temple in his first month and gathers Levites to renew service to the Lord. Hezekiah recognizes their forebears' apostasy and subsequent punishment. To emphasize the seriousness of rebuilding, he speaks in terms of defeat and exile (vv.8–11). The people need restoration after Ahaz's wickedness. The Lord's temple must be the center of renewal. Hezekiah intends to return the nation to a covenantal relationship with God. The chronicler's audience would see the parallel to their situation and, he hoped, respond in faith to the Lord.

The Levites finish the temple purification after the beginning of Passover. The next morning the king and the city officials present offerings for the nation's sins. Hezekiah instructs those dedicating themselves to the Lord to bring additional sacrifices and thank offerings. The people rejoice that God made a quick refurbishing possible.

The kingdom enjoys a radical break with Ahaz's apostasy.

b. Hezekiah celebrates the Passover (30:1–31:1)

Since Israel is destroyed, Hezekiah reigns over a land extending from Beersheba to Dan. He invites persons of South and North to celebrate the Passover. Due to a lack of consecrated priests, they celebrate one month late. Hezekiah sends a letter encouraging the nation to return to worship of the Lord (30:6–9). The letter, reminiscent of 7:14, calls the people to submit to God in trust that he will stay his anger and return the captured Israelites to the land. The chronicler's generation experienced a deliverance from exile, and such a letter would also encourage them to be faithful to the Lord.

A large crowd congregates in Jerusalem to share the Passover feast. The king prays for the ceremonially unclean people from the North. His prayer stresses the importance of internal religious motivation with regard to serving God, especially if all external requirements are not met (30:18–19). The Lord heals these people in fulfillment of his promise of 7:14. The feast, a spectacle of praise and worship, is unlike any celebration since Solomon's dedication of the temple. Significantly, for the first time since Solomon's days, an assembly composed of all tribes gathers to worship the Lord. After the feast, the people smash the remaining items of false worship.

c. Hezekiah organizes regular worship (31:2–21)

Hezekiah, like David and Solomon, arranges for regular cult observances at the temple. He organizes the clergy, gives his wealth for daily offerings, and orders the people to support the temple servants. The people respond quickly and generously. Storerooms and supervisors are needed to care for the donations. The report of this prosperous stage of Hezekiah's reign ends with a lengthy evaluation (31:20–21).

d. Hezekiah's faithfulness (32:1–33)

The chronicler briefly recounts an event covered more fully in 2Ki 18–19. Sennacherib invades Judah despite Hezekiah's faithful activity. The Israelites block off the land's water sources, reinforce Jerusalem's walls, and fashion additional weaponry. Hezekiah addresses the citizens, in terms of holy war, to trust in the Lord and not to be dismayed by Assyria's might.

Sennacherib mocks Judah's resistance and interprets Hezekiah's removal of high places as an affront to the Lord. This charge might seem reasonable to any Israelite who had worshiped the Lord at these shrines. Sennacherib questions Hezekiah's leadership and reminds the inhabitants that all other gods had been impotent against his forces. He suggests that the Lord will be equally powerless.

Much to Sennacherib's surprise, God delivers Jerusalem. Hezekiah and Isaiah place the battle on a spiritual level. Whose god is omnipotent, whose is impotent? In response to prayer, the Lord sends an angel to destroy the Assyrian army. In his own temple, Sennacherib's god is unable to protect the king from his murderous sons. In contrast, Hezekiah and Judah enjoy peace.

Hezekiah's final report includes a story demonstrating repentance and restoration. Hezekiah becomes proud after being healed of a deadly disease. God delays his wrath when the king repents. Because of his faithfulness, this monarch enjoys God's blessings: wealth, military success, and building projects. The chronicler briefly mentions the visit of the Babylonian envoys but does not link this event to God's wrath.

2. Manasseh (33:1–20)

The chronicler's story of Manasseh practically contradicts the parallel report (2Ki 21:1–18). The author of Kings gives a completely negative evaluation of this monarch. Chronicles, however, has a mixed, though generally positive, view of Manasseh. The contrary material has been challenged as counterfeit by some scholars. Nevertheless, the chronicler affirms that no one is beyond God's grace, even the most wicked king bound for Babylon. Since Manasseh returns from Babylonian exile, the chronicler's audience would hear this message and respond appropriately to the Lord.

Manasseh leads the people in Canaanite practices, perverting the religious policies of his righteous father. He rebuilds destroyed high places and idols. He constructs altars for rival deities within the temple precincts. This evil provokes God's anger. Manasseh increases apostasy by setting up an idol in the temple. The Lord delivers Manasseh to Assyria when he repeatedly refuses to repent.

Manasseh's Babylonian exile is unique to Chronicles (vv.11–20). Manasseh humbles himself, and God returns the repentant monarch to Jerusalem. God keeps his promise of 7:14, even in response to the most wicked king of all! Manasseh contrasts with Ahaz who became more wicked when in distress.

After his restoration, Manasseh refortifies the land and leads a religious reform. He destroys false gods and restores the temple. The high places are converted into shrines for the Lord. This is one of the few cases where repentance occurs late in a monarch's life.

3. Amon (33:21–25)

This report agrees essentially with the story in 2Ki 21:19–26. Amon was a wicked ruler. Due to the chronicler's unique perspective on Manasseh, however, he includes a note to distinguish Amon from his pious father (v.23). Amon's renewed apostasy sets the stage for Josiah's reformation. Amon's officials assassinate him. The monarch's wickedness brought personal loss and political intrigue to the land.

4. Josiah (34:1–35:27)

a. Josiah's piety and cultic reform (34:1–13)

Young Josiah receives an unqualified positive evaluation (v.2). At sixteen, Josiah begins to seek David's God (v.3). This personal piety becomes public. Vv.3–7, peculiar to Chronicles, concern action prior to Josiah's temple purification. The twenty-year-old king purges the nation of high places and items for false worship. He executes rival priests. The geographical notations show that Josiah is concerned with the spiritual vitality of all Israel.

Josiah begins to purify the temple in his eighteenth reignal year. Second Kings presents this event as if it started Josiah's reform. Chronicles, however, places the temple cleansing in the middle of the revival. The first phase of renewal is removal of alternative forms of worship. The second is rebuilding the Lord's house. Hilkiah manages the funds collected from the whole country to refurbish the temple. Levites supervise the hired men and accompany the work with songs of praise.

b. The discovery of the Book of the Law (34:14–33)

According to 2 Kings, this discovery forms the basis and motivation for Josiah's reform. In Chronicles the book is found while workers are cleaning the temple as part of a reform well under progress. The reform begins at the direction of a young pious king. The law book discovery is not the starting point of reform, but adds further admonition, direction, and impetus to the movement.

Josiah responds with brokenness to the reading of the book. He instructs the leaders to **inquire of the LORD** regarding the nation's duties. If the book's commands are from the Lord, the nation is in trouble. The weight of potential divine punishment overwhelms Josiah even though he is in the middle of religious reform.

The prophetess Huldah affirms Josiah's interpretation of the book. Judgment comes for disobedience. However, in response to Josiah's humility (cf. 7:14), the Lord promises that the king will die before disaster strikes. Josiah leads the populace in a covenant renewal. They vow to obey the Lord's commands. With renewed enthusiasm, the people remove more idols. The story ends on a familiar discordant note. The people are faithful to the Lord only while righteous Josiah lives (v.33).

c. Josiah's Passover (35:1–19)

King Josiah leads the people in celebrating an incomparable Passover. Chronicle's supplies more details regarding this feast than 2Ki 23:21–23. The report of Josiah's concern for the Levites may indicate something of the chronicler's own background and interests. The leaders provide offerings for the lay people. The celebration is unlike anything since premonarchic days (v.18). This statement could be an evaluation of the magnitude of religious fervor, which exceeds the Passovers of preceding kings. It might also refer to the enhanced role of the Levites in the feast, a shift that would be important for the postexilic community in which this group played a significant role.

d. Josiah's death (35:20–27)

Josiah's death seems to contradict Huldah's favorable prophecy. Pharaoh Neco kills the king at Megiddo; he does not die in peace. Josiah challenges Neco as he travels to assist the Assyrians against the Babylonians at Carchemish. Pharaoh attempts to dissuade Josiah with a prophetic pronouncement, but Josiah disobeys the Lord's word. Josiah disguises himself for battle and, like King Ahab years before, falls to an archer's arrow. The chronicler's explanation for this event centers around the monarch's refusal to hear God's voice. Josiah's disobedience to Neco's prophecy contrasts with his obedience to Huldah's promise.

5. Jehoahaz (36:1–4)

The final movement toward exile begins with Jehoahaz's reign. The chronicler briefly describes the last four monarchs. In each case he shows that an exile took place and the temple was desecrated.

Neco deposes Jehoahaz after three months and deports him to Egypt. Judah pays a levy to Egypt from the temple's wealth.

6. Jehoiakim (36:5–8)

Pharaoh Neco places Eliakim on the throne of Judah as his puppet king and changes his name to Jehoiakim. This king's eleven-year reign is evil. As punishment, Nebuchadnezzar takes Jehoiakim into Babylonian exile and plunders the temple.

7. Jehoiachin (36:9–10)

This king's wicked leadership lasts slightly more than three months. Nebu-chadnezzar banishes him and loots the temple.

8. Zedekiah (36:11–21)

This final ruler's eleven-year reign represents the nadir of faithlessness and exile. Religiously, Zedekiah does not obey the Lord's word from Jeremiah (v.12). The leading priests and all the people become **more and more unfaithful** to God (v.14). The chronicler draws attention to his key text, 2Ch 7:14, and demonstrates that the Exile comes as a result of repeated refusal to obey God's call for repentance. The Exile is not due to the Lord's failure, but is an episode in his consistent dealings with his people. Politically, Zedekiah rebels against Nebuchadnezzar. The Babylonians become God's instrument of judgment to expel Israel.

In his description of the fall of Jerusalem, vv.15–21, the chronicler emphasizes that an obstinate people repeatedly refused God's grace. This rebellion continued until, in the terminology of 7:14, there was no healing for the people (v.16). The exile came not as a punishment for apostasy but for the perpetual refusal to heed divine warnings for repentance. No one is spared, the temple is razed, and the land rests. The chronicler ignores the historical reality that some people remain in the land during the Exile, and he paints a picture of the complete transfer of survivors to Babylon. At the end of his narrative, the chronicler describes a hopeless situation similar to the uncertainty prevailing at the start of his story. There is an exile: no king; no temple; and, apparently, no hope. However, the Lord will heal his people when they humble themselves and seek him.

9. Proclamation for the return (36:22–23)

These verses, declaring restoration after exile, form an appendix to the chronicler's work. They are based on Ezr 1:1–4 and direct the reader to the story of the first generation of returnees. Chronicles thus ends on a more positive note than if it finished with the report of the Exile. God again speaks through a foreign ruler. The exiles return by God's grace, apparently in response to humble repentance. Back in the land, the chronicler exhorts his community, and each generation of God's people, to obey the Lord.

BIBLIOGRAPHY

Ackroyd, P. R. "History and Theology in the Writings of the Chronicler." *Concordia Theological Monthly* 38 (1969): 501–15.

Aharoni, Yohanan and Michael Avi-Yonah. *The Macmillan Bible Atlas*. Rev. ed. New York: Macmillan, 1977.

Albright, William Foxwell. *From the Stone Age to Christianity. Monotheism and the Historical Process*. 2d ed. Garden City, N.Y.: Doubleday Anchor, 1957.

Childs, Brevard S. *Introduction to the Old Testament as Scripture*. Philadelphia: Fortress, 1979.

Japhet, Sara. "Chronicles, Book of." *Encyclopedia Judaica*. Jerusalem: Macmillan, 1971.

Miller, J. Maxwell, and John H. Hayes. *A Short History of Ancient Israel and Judah*. Philadelphia: Westminster, 1986.

Torrey, C. C. "The Chronicler as Editor and as Independent Narrator." *American Journal of Semitic Languages* 25 (1908–9), 157–73; 188–217.

von Rad, Gerhard. *Old Testament Theology*. Vol. 1. *The Theology of Israel's Historical Traditions*. New York: Harper & Row, 1962.

Wellhausen, Julius. *Prolegomena to the History of Ancient Israel*. Gloucester, Mass.: Peter Smith, 1983.

Williamson, H. G. M. *1 and 2 Chronicles*. NCBC. Grand Rapids: Eerdmans, 1982.

EZRA–NEHEMIAH
Owen Dickens

INTRODUCTION

Most Christians find the books of Ezra and Nehemiah unfamiliar territory. The NT never mentions either man, nor does it directly quote either book. Nevertheless, these books are important witnesses to the origin of Judaism, the religion that gave birth to Christianity. We can scarcely understand the religious mindset of Jesus' day apart from the legacy of Ezra the priest and Nehemiah the governor.

These books also address the challenge of being the people of God in the contemporary world. The Jewish postexilic community faced this issue in a different world from that in which their forefathers had lived. Adapting to their new situation was a difficult task. The power of God's Word coupled with the skills of energetic spiritual leaders enabled the Jews to recover their identity as God's covenant people.

I. HISTORICAL BACKGROUND

A brief outline of the history of this period is presented here. Consult standard histories of the OT, such as those of John Bright or Martin Noth, for more detail.

The destruction of Jerusalem and the temple by Babylonian forces under Nebuchadnezzar in 586 B.C. left an indelible psychological and spiritual imprint upon the Jews. It shattered their assumption that election guaranteed divine blessing and protection. The Babylonians exiled the civil and religious leadership of Judah. They left behind the poorer classes who found it politically and economically expedient to accommodate them-selves to the practices of their pagan neighbors. The future of God's chosen people lay not in Palestine, the chosen land, but in distant Babylon.

The exiles found life in Babylon a bittersweet experience. Texts such as Ps 137 suggest that the Exile was unremitting torment for some Jews. Other sources reveal that many Jews prospered in Babylon and were unwilling to return to Palestine when given the chance. Yet, despite their success, others longed to see the land of Israel again. These strove to maintain their distinct religious and cultic identity through a renewed emphasis on their traditions.

The events of Ezra–Nehemiah cover a hundred years of history during the reigns of five Persian kings. The first, Cyrus the Great (539–530 B.C.), issued the decree allowing the Jews to return to Jerusalem and rebuild the temple. They completed the temple during the reign of Darius I (522–486 B.C.). There is brief mention of Xerxes I (486–465 B.C.) in Ezr 4:6. His son, Artaxerxes I (465–425 B.C.), reigned during the missions of both Ezra and Nehemiah. Finally, another Darius is listed in Ne 12:22, doubtless Darius II (424–404 B.C.).

II. SOURCES AND AUTHORSHIP

Jewish tradition has considered the books of Ezra and Nehemiah a single work. Their separation was first attested in the third century A.D. by the church father, Origen. Recognition of the original unity of the books is important for interpretation, requiring us to look for the structure and meaning of the whole work.

It is generally agreed that there are several identifiable sources the author utilized in his composition. The largest are two separate first-person accounts, one by Ezra, the other by Nehemiah, usually considered their respective "memoirs." The Ezra memoir comprises Ezr 7–10 and perhaps Ne 8–10. Nehemiah's memoir is found in Ne 1–7 and most of chs. 12 and 13. The first six chapters of Ezra are composed primarily of official documents, mostly in Aramaic (4:8–6:18), together with traditions reflected in the prophecies of Haggai and Zechariah. The remaining material is thought to have originated with the author.

In view of the extensive sources used in Ezra–Nehemiah, the designation "author" is somewhat misleading. It is probably more accurate to speak of the compiler or redactor who selectively used these sources together with other material to convey a particular message. We must also consider the possibility that there were several stages of redaction before the final work appeared.

The Talmud (*Baba Bathra* 15a) attributes authorship of both books, as well as Chronicles, to Ezra. This tradition has been supported by some modern scholars. The consensus in current scholarship, however, is that an unnamed Jew who lived in the fourth or third century B.C. was responsible for these books. The compiler is usually called the chronicler due to the conventions and themes these works share. Recently several interpreters have challenged this theory.

III. STRUCTURE AND THEOLOGY

Although Ezra–Nehemiah covers more than a century chronologically, the books do not record a continuous history. They present a selective account with many gaps. The author has chosen to include certain events for their intrinsic importance and their theological significance. The author's principle of selectivity and organization helps reveal his purpose and intent.

Four distinct sections focus on the primary themes in the book. They are: (1) Ezr 1–6, the initial return and the rebuilding of the temple;

(2) Ezr 7–10, Ezra's mission to establish the law; (3) Ne 1–6, Nehemiah's rebuilding the walls; and (4) Ne 7–13, the reordering of the covenantal community.

There are close parallels between the first three sections, suggesting a careful arrangement of material. Each begins with the return of a group of Jews from Babylon in order to address a specific situation. Each group returns with royal authorization from the Persian king. The purpose of the first group is to restore the temple. Ezra's task centered upon the vital role of Israel's tradition, the law, in the new community. Finally, Nehemiah's mission was to provide a defense system for the capital city and to insure separation from the pagan world that threatened their religious identity.

Each section also records opposition, externally from the peoples of the lands surrounding Judah and internally from the Jews themselves. There is repeated emphasis on the gracious providence of God working in and through pagan kings to enable them to overcome their opponents. There are no supernatural acts in Ezra–Nehemiah, but God is recognized as sovereign over the events of heaven and earth.

The final section (Ne 7–13) draws together the emphases of the first three and brings the work to a climax. Ezra, supported by Nehemiah, reads the Law (Ne 8), preparing the people to renew their covenantal relationship with God (Ne 9–10). The security afforded by the newly completed walls allows the repopulation of Jerusalem (Ne 11). This sets the stage for the climactic dedication of the city walls at the temple. There the Jewish community celebrates the completion of the walls and their restoration as God's covenant people.

IV. OUTLINE

   I. Return and Rebuilding of the Temple (Ezr 1–6)
      A. Cyrus's Decree (1:1–11)
      B. List of Returnees (2:1–70)
      C. Altar Rebuilt; Temple Begun (3:1–13)
      D. Opposition to Rebuilding (4:1–24)
      E. Completion of the Temple (5:1–6:22)

   II. Ezra's Mission to Jerusalem (Ezr 7–10)
      A. Ezra's Return (7:1–8:36)
      B. Problem of Mixed Marriages (9:1–10:44)

   III. Nehemiah Rebuilds the Walls (Ne 1–6)
      A. Report to Nehemiah (1:1–11)
      B. Nehemiah's Return (2:1–20)
      C. Builders of the Wall (3:1–32)
      D. Opposition Without (4:1–23)
      E. Oppression Within (5:1–19)
      F. Completion of the Walls (6:1–19)

   IV. Restoration of the Covenant Community (Ne 7–13)
      A. Records for Repopulating Jerusalem (7:1–73)

COMMENTARY—EZRA

I. RETURN AND REBUILDING OF THE TEMPLE (EZR 1–6)

The events of the first six chapters took place long before the time of Ezra. These chapters span approximately twenty-two years (538–516 B.C.) and deal with the return of several groups of Jews from exile and their attempts to reestablish their religious roots in their homeland. Rebuilding the temple was their first priority since it was the focus of their religious and national identity.

A. Cyrus's Decree (1:1–11)

Throughout the OT Yahweh is a deity who exercises sovereignty over his own people and also over pagan nations and monarchs. This truth is stressed in the first verse. The author asserts that Cyrus's edict releasing the Jews from Babylonian exile and authorizing them to rebuild the temple is a result of the direct action of God as he **moved the heart of Cyrus.** This action was taken **to fulfill the word of the LORD spoken by Jeremiah,** evoking the prophecy of Jer 25:11–12 and 29:10–14. The effect is clear and unmistakable. The author dispels any thought that the events of 538 B.C. were fortuitous coincidence.

The primary provision of the decree (1:2–4; cf. 2Ch 36:23) is for the rebuilding of the temple in Jerusalem. In order to accomplish this task, those Jews who were willing were free to return to Palestine. Those who elected to remain in Babylon were obligated to assist the returnees.

No ancient cuneiform texts have been discovered that record Cyrus's release of the Jews, but few doubt the authenticity of this decree. It corresponds closely in content with the famous Cyrus Cylinder (Pritchard, 315), the account of Cyrus's conquest of Babylon and his restoration of the gods and cult of his new subjects. Other ancient sources also illustrate his tolerance and support for the religions of his subjects.

The second part of the first chapter is linked to the first by the phrase **"everyone whose heart God had moved"** (1:5). God "stirred up" (RSV) a pagan monarch in 1:1. Here it is the Jews themselves who need divine arousal. This verb (*hē'îr*) is used in a number of significant passages describing God's active involvement in the course of history. Yahweh is the God who stirs up Jew and Gentile alike to bring his plans to fruition. (See 1Ch 5:26; Isa 41:25; 45:13; Jer 50:9; Eze 23:22; and Hag 1:14.)

The leader of the first return was an enigmatic figure, Sheshbazzar (1:8, 11). Called here **the prince of Judah,** perhaps implying royal lineage, he is also referred to as **"governor"** (5:14) and is credited with laying the foundation of the temple (v.16). These few references create numerous difficulties because another, more conspicuous figure, Zerubbabel, is credited with these same accomplishments. Although Jewish tradition has equated these two men, modern scholarship is virtually unanimous in the opinion that they were separate individuals. Their exact relationship may never be resolved.

B. List of returnees (2:1-70)

The inclination of modern Christians is to skip over this chapter and similar ones, because it seems only a meaningless list of ancient Jewish names. This list is repeated almost verbatim in Ne 7, and there are other similar lists in Ezr 8, 10; Ne 3, 11, 12. All together these lists constitute almost one third of Ezra-Nehemiah.

Such lists exist for at least two purposes: First, these lists establish continuity between the Jews who returned from Babylonian exile and their ancestors who, almost a millennium before, escaped from Egyptian bondage and became God's covenant partner at Mount Sinai. The catastrophic physical, economic, and religious dislocation produced by the destruction of 586 B.C. burned into the Jewish psyche the need to maintain solidarity with their heritage.

Second, there is a religious reason for these lists. A primary concern of the postexilic community was the purity of the community. To establish membership in the covenant people, accurate family lists and records of priests, Levites, and other cultic personnel were required. The legitimacy of this concern is illustrated by the existence of several cases among both laity and priesthood of those who could not prove their lineage from Israel (2:59-63). This may seem bigoted to us, but for the Jews their national identity and cultic separation were of vital importance.

C. Altar Rebuilt: Temple Begun (3:1-13)

Abraham's first act upon arriving in Canaan was to build an altar and offer a sacrifice to God (Ge 12:7). In like manner, the returnees, having settled into their towns, rebuilt the ruined altar at the temple site and resumed the sacrificial system as prescribed in the Torah. The altar was constructed under the leadership of Joshua, the high priest, and Zerubbabel, the governor (Hag 1:1), who was of royal lineage (1Ch 3:17-18). They represented the two primary institutions of ancient Israel, the priesthood and the monarchy, at this crucial time.

The altar was rebuilt **despite their fear of the peoples around them** (v.3). This phrase foreshadows the friction that was to erupt between the returnees and the people who had lived in Judah during the Exile. These **peoples around them** included both descendants of the Israelites who were not exiled and other ethnic groups such as the Samaritans, a mixed population whom the exiles considered apostate.

After the altar had been rebuilt and regular sacrifices reinstated the returnees celebrated their first festival, the Feast of Tabernacles (v.4; see Nu 29:12-38). This same festival is observed in Ne 8:13-14, in response to Ezra's reading of the law. It is one of the three great pilgrimage festivals in Judaism, commemorating the period of the desert wanderings. This and other parallels suggest that the author of Ezra-Nehemiah viewed the Exile and return as a second Exodus experience.

The preparations for rebuilding the temple (vv.7-9) are reminiscent of those made for Solomon's temple over four hundred years earlier. They brought materials from Lebanon, made payment in kind, and began the work in the second month (see 1Ki 5-6;

2Ch 2–3). These parallels demonstrate continuity between this temple and the first. Supervision by the priests and Levites (vv.8–9) insured the cultic purity of the work.

The returnees laid the foundation of the temple in the second year of the return (536 B.C.). The community responded with religious celebration, complete with appropriate vestments, musical instruments, and liturgy (vv.10–11). This action, too, is reminiscent of the dedication of Solomon's edifice (2Ch 5:13). The festive atmosphere was tempered, however, by the somber note introduced in 3:12–13. Mixed with the shouts of joy was the sound of weeping. The older returnees who had seen the first temple were bitterly disappointed by this new temple. Hag 2:3 informs us that the postexilic temple paled when compared with the grandeur of Solomon's.

Ch. 3 ends with a seemingly insignificant note, **"And the sound was heard far away."** This phrase, repeated almost verbatim in Ne 12:43, has structural significance for the book of Ezra–Nehemiah. Here in 3:13 it serves to foreshadow opposition to the rebuilding effort and, hence, is a gloomy portent. But in the climax of the book, Ne 12:43, it is a triumphant note. There the walls have been dedicated and the noise of celebration signals the frustration of all efforts by the surrounding nations to thwart God and his people.

D. Opposition to Rebuilding (4:1–24)

The opposition twice foreshadowed in ch. 3 becomes a reality here. A long sequence of harassments begins in this chapter and lasts virtually until the end of the book of Nehemiah. Uncharacteristically the opponents are nameless here, but the reference to Assyrian deportations in 4:2 strongly suggests Samaritan involvement.

In our present age of toleration and ecumenicity, their offer to assist the Jews in rebuilding the temple seems entirely reasonable. As they point out, they too seek God and sacrifice to him. The response of Zerubbabel and Joshua, in contrast, smacks of intolerance and parochialism when they say, **"You have no part with us in building a temple to our God"** (v.3). Yet in light of the description of Samaritan religion in 2Ki 17:24ff. (tendentious though it may be) and the longstanding political and religious differences between the North and South, it becomes more understandable.

Samaritan religion, an admixture of biblical and pagan religion, constituted a severe threat to the returnees because of its implicit assertion that it is acceptable to mix the holy with the unholy, the clean with the unclean. This tendency toward syncretism had plagued the Israelites since their days in the desert, and once again the menace confronted them. The returned Jews faced, not so much the question of tolerance versus intolerance, but the issue of maintaining their identity as the people of God. They could offer but one response.

Faced with Zerubbabel's stunning rebuff, the Samaritans initiated a vigorous, persistent (as indicated by the repeated use of participles), and successful campaign to halt work on the temple. This hiatus lasted some sixteen years (536–520 B.C.). The prophet Haggai placed the blame for the interruption of the rebuilding program squarely upon the Jews themselves. They were more concerned with their own homes than with the house of God (Hag 1:3–4).

Vv.6–23 present a major interpretive problem. The events through 4:5

took place during the reign of Cyrus the Great (539–530 B.C.), but this section records opposition during the times of Xerxes I (486–465 B.C.) and Artaxerxes I (465–425 B.C.). The following material, Ezr 5–6, resumes with the reign of Darius I (522–486 B.C.), culminating with the completion of the temple in 516 B.C.

But why is material inserted here that is clearly out of place chronologically? Some commentators have maintained that this dislocation is simply one of several such accidental digressions in Ezra–Nehemiah, the primary example being the problem of Ne 8–10. On the other hand, several recent commentators have suggested that the present order is intentional. They convincingly argue that the similar language and content of 4:5 and 24 effectively bracket 4:6–23, indicating that this passage is a deliberate aside. The effect is to group 4:1–5 topically with other examples of opposition in order to justify Zerubbabel's rejection of Samaritan help and to further substantiate the call for separation from non-Jews.

This section preserves letters to and from King Artaxerxes, written not in Hebrew, but in Aramaic, the diplomatic language of the day. The letter from Rehum and Shimshai, otherwise unknown officials of the Persian province, refers to attempts to rebuild the walls of Jerusalem, suggesting that Nehemiah was not the first to undertake the project. Artaxerxes' response is not surprising since he had never authorized the work and because he had faced a number of revolts in the western part of his empire. Later this same king sponsored both the reforms of Ezra and the work of Nehemiah.

E. Completion of the Temple (5:1–6:22)

The Jews resumed work on the temple under the impact of the pro-

phetic ministries of Haggai and Zechariah (5:1–2). The authentic prophetic voice overcame foreign opposition and domestic apathy. Reference to these prophets dates the events to the second year of Darius I (522–486 B.C.), that is 520 B.C. (see Hag 1:1; Zec 1:1).

Resumption of work on the temple prompted an official inquiry by Tattenai, the governor of the Persian province of Trans-Euphrates, in which Judah lay. Tattenai's inquiry into the activities in Jerusalem may seem intrusive, but in reality he was acting as a competent civil servant. The first two years of Darius's reign were punctuated by revolts throughout the empire. Therefore loyal officials were alert for anything suspicious. Accordingly, Tattenai investigated and forwarded a report to the king (5:7–17). But due to God's province (v.5), Tattenai allowed the work to continue while he awaited a response to his letter.

Darius's response (6:1–12) contains several elements. First, there is an Aramaic version of Cyrus's decree (vv.3–5) that substantially agrees with the Hebrew version in 1:2–4, focusing upon the reconstruction of the temple. The second part (vv.6–12) gives specific instructions to Tattenai and his associates. They must not impede the work but rather must provide royal subsidy for it. The only request is that the Jews offer sacrifice on behalf of the king and his family. Thus the returnees received both royal authority and funding. What had begun as a potential threat proved to be the means to complete the project.

As commanded, Tattenai fulfilled the king's decree **with diligence** (Aram. *'osparnā'*, cf. 6:12). Bolstered by official Persian support and the preaching of Haggai and Zechariah (6:14), the Jews completed the temple. In a statement consonant with the theological outlook of the book, the author attributes this outcome to the command of God and the decrees of the Persian kings. God works through the decrees of pagan monarchs and the words of Israel's prophets.

In the month of Adar, the last month of the year, in the sixth year of Darius (516 B.C.), the temple was finished, twenty years after the work had first begun. It was nearly seventy years after Solomon's temple was destroyed. The temple was dedicated (Aram. *ḥănukkāh*) with joy and extensive dedicatory sacrifices. Twelve goats were offered for all Israel (6:17), representing all the tribes of Israel, even though the returnees included only Judah, Benjamin, and Levi. Although these tribes constituted the remnant, all the tribes were God's covenant people.

A few weeks later, in the first month, the Passover was celebrated, signaling the resumption of regular cultic observances at the new temple. With this celebration the first part of Ezra–Nehemiah ends.

II. EZRA'S MISSION TO JERUSALEM (EZR 7–10)

In the final four chapters we finally meet the man whose name the work bears. Ezra's journey to Jerusalem is recorded in chs. 7 and 8; in 9 and 10 he deals with the problem of mixed marriages. He reappears in Ne 8–10 to play a significant role in the reorganization of the covenantal community.

A. Ezra's Return (7:1–8:36)

The opening phrase **"After these things"** conceals a chronological gap. The temple was completed in 516 B.C., but Ezra's return dates to the seventh year of Artaxerxes (7:7). Traditional chronology has understood this king to be Artaxerxes I (465–424 B.C.), which would place Ezra's return in 458 B.C.

However, for several reasons many scholars date Ezra's mission to the reign of Artaxerxes II (404–359 B.C.). They argue that Ezra followed rather than preceded Nehemiah. This view would date his return in 397 B.C. In either case, sixty to one hundred years pass between chs. 6 and 7.

An overview of Ezra's journey and mission is presented in 7:1–10, followed by more detail in 8:15–36. Ezra's lengthy genealogy (7:1–5) demonstrates his priestly lineage and importance. In addition to his priestly credentials, Ezra is described as **"a teacher well versed in the Law of Moses"** (v.6). The word translated **teacher** (Heb. *sôpēr*) reflects Ezra's expertise in the Torah. He is the archetype of the NT scribes.

A theologically significant phrase appears in 7:6. The author notes, **"The king had granted him everything he asked, for the hand of the LORD his God was on him."** This phrase, with slight variations, occurs eight times in Ezra–Nehemiah. In each instance the emphasis is the same. God's providential care is extended to Ezra and Nehemiah because they are fulfilling a divine calling. Yahweh is acknowledged as the one who prompts Artaxerxes to grant their requests (7:6, 28; Ne 2:8, 18), who provides Levites to return with Ezra (8:18), and who restrains bandits along the way (7:9; 8:22, 31).

The description of Ezra's character in 7:10 is worthy of emulation. He devoted himself to a threefold goal: To study (Heb. *dāraś*), practice (*'āśāh*), and teach (*limmēḏ*) the Torah. Ezra was intimately involved in the effort to understand and apply the law of God to the contemporary situation and problems that confronted the postexilic community. In Ezra there was none of the common disjunction between orthodoxy and orthopraxy. Similarly, one of the primary concerns of Wesleyan theology is to bridge the gap between belief and practice. In true Christianity the two are one.

The royal letter reproduced in 7:12–26 authorized Ezra's mission to Jerusalem. Like the official documents in Ezr 4–6, it is in Aramaic. The letter reflects an accurate knowledge of Jewish affairs and may have been drafted with input from Ezra himself. It focuses on the cultic activities of the temple. As a polytheist, Artaxerxes believed that the favor of all gods was essential to his continued success.

The great reformer finally speaks in the closing verses of the chapter (7:27–28). The text returns to Hebrew as Ezra pronounces his doxology to God. Here begins a series of first-person passages usually considered part of the Ezra memoir. Speaking theologically, Ezra attributes all the good that has happened to the intervention of Yahweh.

Ezra's memoir includes a list of those who returned with him (8:1–14) before providing further details of the return. The fast Ezra proclaimed to seek God's protection for the return trip affords us an intimate view of the reformer (vv.21–23). Because he knew Yahweh to be a God who safeguards his people, Ezra was ashamed to request an armed guard from the king. The need for protection is apparent in view of the amount of gold and silver the caravan carried.

Ezra accented the biblical concept of holiness in 8:28 when he told the twelve priests responsible for the treasure, **"You as well as these articles are consecrated to the LORD."** Both people and things can be separated for God, transferred from the realm of the everyday, the common, to the sphere of the divine. Though it was primarily the priests in the OT who were considered

holy, the NT boldly proclaims that all believers are holy ones (Gk. *hagioi*), a "royal priesthood, a holy nation" (1Pe 2:9; quoting Ex 19:6). Wesleyan tradition has affirmed this emphasis and has insisted on the objective reality of holiness in the life of the believer.

The thousand-mile journey to Jerusalem is recorded without comment (8:31–32), except that God delivered them from enemies and bandits. Upon arrival, the group offered sacrifices on behalf of all Israel.

B. Problem of Mixed Marriages (9:1–10:44)

A recurring problem among the postexilic Jews was intermarriage with the non-Jewish population of Palestine. Ezra dealt with it upon his return, Nehemiah during his second tenure as governor (Ne 13:23–28), and Malachi prophesied against it (Mal 2:11). Legislation prohibiting intermarriage appears in Ex 34:11–16 and Dt 7:1–4. (The book of Ruth stands as a notable exception.) In the legal passages this prohibition is part of a larger command. God forbade his covenant people from making covenants with the peoples of the land because of the corrupting influence of their idolatrous religions. Intermarriage is a subset of this larger concern.

The metaphor of marriage describes the believer's relationship with God. This is because marriage is a covenant, the most intimate union of two individuals. Therefore, marriage serves as an appropriate symbol for one's relationship to God. The prohibition of intermarriage is not a reflection of Jewish racial bigotry, but rather symbolizes their need to maintain religious identity. This concern is forcefully expressed in the words of the Jewish leaders who confessed that the Jews had **mingled the holy race with the peoples around them** (9:2).

Ezra's activities during the months between his arrival in Jerusalem and the surfacing of this problem are not specified (cf. 7:8 with 10:9). It may be that his teaching the Torah aroused a sensibility in the leaders to their transgression, prompting them to approach Ezra (9:1–2).

When Ezra received news of the problem (9:1–2), his reaction was dramatic and effective. His actions (v.3) are well known symbols of mourning. Ezra verbalized this symbolic message in a prayer. The dominant theme is confession, the acknowledgement of sin, and the justness of God's punishment. As is also true of Nehemiah, Ezra identified himself with his people's sins, using the first-person "we." The covenant is not merely an individual relationship with God; it is a communal one, a fact that the contemporary church has largely forgotten.

A secondary theme in the prayer is that the returnees constitute the **remnant** of which the prophets spoke. God, through his unmerited favor, has left them as a remnant (Heb. *p'lêṭāh*), anchored literally by a "tent peg" in his sanctuary (9:8, NIV **"firm place"**). God has granted them new life to reestablish their lives in Judah. Yet Ezra knew that intermarriage posed a grave threat to the covenant. Even this remnant might be subject to God's wrath, leaving **no remnant or survivor** (9:14).

Ezra's actions and prayer produced a decisive response from the people

(10:1–4). Their spokesman, Shecaniah, acknowledged their sin and proposed a covenant with Yahweh to divorce their foreign wives. The proposal is a call for covenant renewal. The sin of intermarriage had broken the covenant, necessitating renewal. Covenantal renewal involves two steps: (1) a public renewal ceremony and (2) elimination of the offense that vitiated the covenant.

The public assembly was held in the ninth month (10:9), corresponding to December, the rainy season in Palestine. The people were uncomfortable because of the wet weather and the weight of their guilt. In his speech Ezra presented both the problem and the solution (vv.10–11). Because they had transgressed the law, they must first make confession (Heb. *todah*), and then separate themselves from their foreign wives. God hates divorce (Mal 2:16), but in this instance it is the lesser of two evils.

The congregation strongly affirmed Ezra's proposal (10:12). In order to expedite the process (and get the crowd in out of the rain) the people suggested that the officials of the community consider each case separately. This procedure was adopted; in three months all cases were resolved (vv.16–17).

The book of Ezra closes with a list of those guilty of intermarriage (10:18–44). The list begins with the priests, led by the family of the high priest of the first return, Jeshua ben Jozadak. In all there were about 110 cases, indicating the extent of the problem.

COMMENTARY—NEHEMIAH

III. NEHEMIAH REBUILDS THE WALLS (NE 1–6)

This part of Ezra–Nehemiah is delineated from the first by the title, **"The words of Nehemiah son of Hacaliah"** (1:1). It is an appropriate introduction because much of the book reads like a personal account of this great civil leader of postexilic Judah.

The events of most of the book took place in the spring and summer of the twentieth year of Artaxerxes I (465–424 B.C.), i.e., 445 B.C. Artaxerxes had a long reign, but his administration was not tranquil. He faced repeated revolts. An Egyptian rebellion in 460 B.C. took five years to quell, and in 448 B.C. the satrap of Trans-Euphrates, the satrapy that included Judah, mutinied. Such turmoil points to the strategic importance of Judah and the political expediency of a friendly, stable province. Nehemiah's mission to rebuild the walls of Jerusalem and his authority should be seen in this setting.

A. Report to Nehemiah (1:1–11)

The first three verses of the book are the catalyst for what follows. Nehemiah's brother Hanani, recently returned from Jerusalem, reported on the sorry state of affairs in the Jewish capital. Nehemiah's extended period of mourning, fasting, and prayer in response to the news (v.4) prepared him for his encounter with the king and for his mission to Jerusalem.

The prayer itself is formally similar to the communal laments, one of the most frequent psalm types, but the emphasis on repentance makes it unique. Nehemiah begins with an invocation (vv.5–6a), then moves to confession (vv.6b–7). This is a natural progression; when sinful humanity is confronted by the holy God, the only authentic reaction is prostration and confession (see Isa 6:5; Rev 1:17).

The chapter ends with the note that Nehemiah occupied the position of cupbearer in Artaxerxes' court. The cupbearer was a trusted official responsible for tasting the king's wine to make sure it was not poisoned. This position gave Nehemiah access to the monarch and considerable influence. His position indicates the good standing Jews enjoyed in the empire.

B. Nehemiah's Return (2:1–20)

Four months elapsed from the time Nehemiah received Hanani's report (in Kislev, the ninth month) and his opportunity to appeal to the king (in Nisan, the first month of the new year). These months of fasting and mourning had exacted a physical and emotional toll on Nehemiah, as the king noticed immediately. In response to Artaxerxes' question, **"What is it you want?"** Nehemiah offered his famous "lightning" prayer (v.4b) even while formulating his request.

Nehemiah first requested permission to rebuild his native city. He never mentioned Jerusalem by name, perhaps because Artaxerxes had earlier ordered building projects there stopped (Ezr 4:21). Nehemiah then asked for official letters to the governors of Trans-Euphrates for safe conduct and to the keeper of the royal forest for timber. When the king granted his requests, Nehemiah attributed his success to "the gracious hand of God" that was upon him (v.8).

Attempts to contrast Nehemiah's use of a militant escort (v.9) with Ezra's rejection of it (Ezr 8:22) miss the point. As an official of the king on a royal mission, Nehemiah was obliged to travel with full military honors. For Ezra the priest and scribe, such was not the case.

In 2:10 Nehemiah's chief antagonists are introduced, Sanballat the Honorite and Tobiah the Ammonite. Sanballat is mentioned in the Elephantine Papyri where he is called "governor of Samaria" (Pritchard, 492). The Tobiad family, likely descended from this Tobiah, figured prominently in Jewish affairs during the intertestamental period. The arrival of a Jew in Jerusalem with royal authority **to promote the welfare of the Israelites** was perceived as a threat by these men.

Nehemiah's initial act was to gain firsthand knowledge of the situation. He made a clandestine inspection of the walls of Jerusalem (vv.11–16). His secrecy was designed to forestall opposition until he was able to initiate a plan of action. Archaeological work in Jerusalem over the past two decades has illumined Nehemiah's nocturnal walk. He began his tour on the west side of the city and proceeded counterclockwise around the old city of David.

Armed with this information, Nehemiah was able to present his plan for rebuilding the walls to the Jewish leaders (vv.17–18). He emphasized that both God and the king were behind the endeavor. The leaders responded, **"Let us start rebuilding."**

Sanballat and his allies soon heard of the work and launched a verbal attack against the Jews, accusing them of rebellion (v.19). The addition of a third opponent, Geshem the Arab, meant that opponents confronted the Jews on three sides: Samaritans on the north, Ammonites on the east, and Arabs to the south. Later (4:7) the circle would be closed when enemies to the west joined these.

Nehemiah set the tone for future dealings with his opponents in his unequivocal response to their charges (v.20). He appealed to the Jews' divine mandate to rebuild, and then, utilizing legal terminology, informed his opponents that they had no **share** (*ḥēleq*), **claim** (*ṣᵉḏāqāh*), or **historic right** (*zikkārôn*) in Jerusalem.

C. Builders of the Wall (3:1–32)

This passage identifies the group responsible for rebuilding each section of the city wall. It is testimony to the organizational abilities of Nehemiah and the broad consensus of support he was able to enlist among the Jews. The list includes every spectrum of society: priests, led by the high priest himself; temple servants; civil officials; laity; craftsmen; merchant groups; and even one man's daughters (v.12). A spirit of cooperation is evident, but there were some who withheld their support, such as the nobles of Tekoa (v.5).

Not every feature of the wall can be identified, but the overall plan is clear. The list begins at the Sheep Gate where Eliashib, the high priest, sponsored the work. This gate was on the northeastern corner of the wall, near the temple (see John 5:2). The list continues counterclockwise around the wall, section by section, until it returns to the Sheep Gate (v.32).

D. Opposition Without (4:1–23)

Sanballat had not fully anticipated Nehemiah's resourcefulness and determination (2:10, 19). News of the rebuilding **greatly incensed** him. Caught off guard, his only recourse was a barrage of derisive rhetorical questions (v.2). Tobiah added his own contemptuous word picture (v.3).

Nehemiah responded to this crisis as he did at other times, with prayer (vv.4–5). His call for vindication may not coincide with the ethic of the

Sermon on the Mount (Mt 5:38ff.), but it is paralleled in the OT (e.g., Jer 18:23, Ps 109). The prayer is founded upon the conviction that it was God's work. Anyone who opposed it opposed God. Characteristic of Nehemiah, prayer was backed up by action (v.6). The people continued to work **with all their heart** so that the wall reached half its height.

This pattern of threat and counter-measure recurs throughout the rest of the chapter. As the gravity of the threats increases, so does the intensity of Nehemiah's response. In 4:7 the circle of enemies was closed with the inclusion of representatives from Ashdod, formerly a Philistine city, in the conspiracy. But the classic riposte of the Jewish leader, **"We prayed to our God and posted a guard,"** parried the threat. The medieval monastic motto, *ora et labora,* "pray and work," typifies Nehemiah's philosophy.

The specter of outright attack (v.11) was met through exhortation and reorganizing the work force. Nehemiah's exhortations express the now familiar synthesis of inspiration and perspiration in his call, **"Remember the LORD . . . and fight"** (v.14)! Organizationally, Nehemiah instituted a shift system. Half the workers stood guard while the other half continued building (vv.16–17). Even those working had their weapons ready. The workers were also asked to remain in the city overnight to bolster the defense force. These steps frustrated the plots of their enemies and hastened the work to completion.

E. Oppression Within (5:1–19)

The external threats were serious; this chapter reveals the existence of equally severe threats from within. Social and economic problems, exacerbated by the concerted effort to rebuild

the wall, boiled to the surface. Common folk cried out against upper-class Jews (vv.2–5). Three complaints are enumerated: (1) hunger due to their large families, (2) debts incurred to avoid starvation, and (3) Persian taxes. As a result of these problems many resorted to selling their children into slavery to raise money and to have fewer mouths to feed.

Nehemiah's angry reaction (vv.6–13) calls to mind the righteous anger Jesus displayed on several occasions. He immediately instigated a legal case (Heb. *rîb*) against the nobles and officials. The nature of the charge against them is not clear. The NIV translation, **"You are exacting usury"** (vv.7, 10), is possible, but the technical term for usury employed in the laws of the Pentateuch (*nešek*) is not used here. Possibly the wealthy Jews had demanded security for their loans in the form of land, thus depriving the borrower of its income. These Jews may not have violated the letter of the law, but they had transgressed its spirit. As covenantal partners, all Jews were considered equal in the sight of God, yet these practices perpetrated class distinctions. Since the ancient mindset equated material success with spiritual blessing, this was more than an economic problem; it was a religious problem.

The remainder of the chapter (vv.14–19) is a digression in which Nehemiah describes his manner of administration. This aside clearly dates from a later period (v.14) but is included here because it substantiates his method of dealing with the current problems. Nehemiah's guiding motivations shine through; reverence for God (v.15) and concern for the welfare of the people (v.18). He integrated the two great commandments, love for God and neighbor.

F. Completion of the Walls (6:1–19)

With the wall nearly completed Nehemiah was once again confronted by external threats, this time directed against his own life. Unable to stop the work itself, Sanballat and company resolved to assassinate Nehemiah. Five times Sanballat attempted to lure Nehemiah to the plain of Ono, some twenty-seven miles north of Jerusalem, supposedly for a summit meeting.

Sanballat and Tobiah also enlisted confederates among the Jews. One of these, Shemaiah, acted and spoke like a prophet, though he is not called one (vv.10–13). His intent was to entice Nehemiah to seek refuge from potential assassins in the temple, thereby compromising himself. Among the others hired to intimidate Nehemiah was a prophetess, Noadiah (v.14). Nehemiah recognized the architect of these plots and preserved his integrity.

The succinct statement in 6:15 records the completion of the wall of Jerusalem. Despite opponents without and within, economic problems and social upheavals, the Jews finished the walls in the month of Elul (the sixth month), in the short period of fifty-two days. Nehemiah was always convinced that Yahweh was responsible for their success. Now even the enemies of the Jews were forced to acknowledge God's hand at work (v.16). Throughout the book their opponents attempted to frighten and discourage the Jews, but, ironically, in the end it was the non-Jews who were afraid and discouraged.

Note: A key word in this chapter and the book is *yārē'*, "to be afraid." The translators of the NIV have ignored the vocalization of the MT and the reading of the LXX in 6:16 and have translated, "the surrounding nations *saw* it," thereby losing the emphasis. Preferable is the RSV, "all the nations round about us *were afraid*."

IV. RESTORATION OF THE COVENANT COMMUNITY (NE 7–13)

This final section is the climax of Ezra–Nehemiah. All of the main themes of the book are found here: the temple, the law, and the completed walls. These elements are brought together as the Jews renew their covenant with God and dedicate the walls of Jerusalem.

A. Records for Repopulating Jerusalem (7:1–73)

City walls are of little defensive value if not properly manned, and a city serves no function if no one lives in it. Thus Nehemiah's next task was to organize the city and repopulate it. Nehemiah appointed his brother Hanani, who had first alerted him to the disgrace of Jerusalem (1:2–3), over the capital city. Nehemiah also issued strict regulations concerning operation of the gates (v.3).

To repopulate Jerusalem it was necessary to compile an accurate census of the populace. The basis of such a census was the genealogical record of the original returnees, which is reproduced in 7:6–73. With minor variations this is the same list found in Ezr 2.

B. Ezra Reads the Law (8:1–18)

Careful readers of the text have observed that the material in ch. 11 should immediately follow ch. 7. But the natural order is interrupted by chs. 8–10. Although these chapters may be chronologically out of place, it seems certain that the present arrangement is intentional. In this chapter postexilic Israel's two great leaders unite to confirm the central role of the law for the life of the restored community (v.9). Childs has perceptively observed that here the Law is not read to effect repentance, but to evoke joy and celebration from the restored community. His words are worth repeating: "Ezra does not read the law in order to reform Israel into becoming the people of God. Rather, the reverse move obtains. It is the reformed people to whom the law is read" (p. 636).

Here we again meet Ezra the priest and scribe. His royal mandate was to teach and establish the Law (Ezr 7:14; 25–26). In 8:1 an assembly was convened for that very purpose. The Jews gathered not at the temple, as might be expected, but at the Water Gate, a public place where all could hear the Law. Women would have been excluded from the temple court.

The contents of the **Book of the Law** (v.3) from which Ezra read are not specified, but the people regarded this book as authoritative. The Levites' role as the Law was read is also unclear (vv.7–8). Many have assumed that postexilic Jews no longer spoke or understood Hebrew, having adopted Aramaic as their common language. Therefore, it was thought that the Levites were translating from Hebrew to Aramaic for the people. More recently this assumption has been questioned. The prevailing opinion is that the Levites provided a running commentary or homily on the law as it was read.

This fresh encounter with the Word of God produced a profound reaction among the people. They wept (v.9). Confronted with the will and character of God, the people were all too aware of their shortcomings. But mourning is inappropriate on a holy day, so three times Ezra and the leadership exhorted the people to cease weeping and rejoice because, "This is a day sacred to the LORD" (see vv.9, 10, 11). Reading the

law should produce joy and celebration among God's people. As Derek Kidner has remarked, "Holiness and gloom go ill together" (p. 107).

On the following day a select group of Jewish leaders met with Ezra to examine the Law more carefully (v.13). The portion studied evidently included Lev 23:33–43, because the result was a proclamation to observe the Feast of Tabernacles beginning the fifteenth day of that seventh month. The original returnees had also celebrated this feast after they had rebuilt the altar (Ezr 3:4). It is no coincidence that the first and last cultic event in Ezra–Nehemiah is this important festival reminding the Jews of the Exodus. The author has combined the concept of a second exodus with the centrality of the Torah.

C. Covenant Renewal (9:1–10:39)

Two days after the conclusion of the Feast of Tabernacles the Israelites reassembled, this time in a state of mourning (9:1–2). The ceremony included reading the Book of the Law for three hours followed by another three hours confessing their sins and the sins of their ancestors.

The prayer of confession (9:5b–37) has a poetic quality and is set out as verse in some versions. It shares features with several types of OT literature. The initial doxology (vv.5b–6) evokes the hymn form, but the tone of penitence is more characteristic of the laments. The overall thrust is exhortation: instruction through a review of the great themes in Israel's salvation history. The Hebrew verb for confession, *yāḏāh*, has a dual meaning. It can refer to the confession of sins, but it can also be translated, "to praise," that is, to acknowledge God's greatness and power. Both aspects of the verb are incorporated here.

It is impossible to comment fully on

the content of this prayer, but several observations can be made. Its structure is straightforward, following an outline of Israel's history. The prayer draws upon parallels throughout the Pentateuch and historical books, some extending even to the exact choice of words. (For an extensive list of parallels see Myers, 167–69). The recurring theme is the contrast between God's mercy and grace and the stiff-necked obstinacy and disobedience of the Israelites. At every turn God provided for their needs, defeated their enemies, and was faithful to the covenant; yet the Israelites turned their backs and rebelled. Therefore their present state of virtual slavery under the Persian kings is acknowledged as just.

The final verse of ch. 9 serves as a literary link between the prayer of confession and the **binding agreement** into which the Jews enter in ch. 10. The Hebrew expression translated, **"making a binding agreement,"** is unique, but the verb employed (*kārat*) immediately brings to mind the idiom of covenant making. The restoration and reordering of the community can be complete only as the people renew their covenantal relationship with God.

Although a religious document, it also has a legal character, as seen in the fact that it was put in writing and sealed by the leadership. The list of those who sealed the agreement is headed by the governor, Nehemiah, followed by priests, Levites, and lay leaders (10:1–27). But the covenant is not restricted to the hierarchy. All true Israelites, male and female, adult and children, are able to enter into a renewed relationship with God (v.28). Therefore all segments of society **"bind themselves with a curse and an oath to follow the Law of God"** (v.29).

The stipulations of the covenant spelled out in the rest of the chapter (vv.30–39) include mixed marriages (v.30), Sabbath and Year of Jubilee regulations (v.31), temple taxes (vv.32–33), and other offerings (vv.34–39). These stipulations parallel the catalogue of problems with which Nehemiah dealt in ch. 13. This cannot be accidental and suggests that the list may be a synopsis based on problems encountered in real life. The emphasis is on the cult and cultic personnel. Deprived of political autonomy under the Persian Empire, the Jews discovered their identity in the religious institutions which served as symbols of their relationship with and election by God.

D. Repopulating Jerusalem (11:1–12:26)

The task of repopulating the capital city after the completion of the walls (see 7:4) is taken up again. Although the leaders of the people had settled in Jerusalem, there seems to have been a dearth of ordinary citizens necessary to make it a living city. The solution was a lottery in which one out of every ten was chosen to live in Jerusalem, the **holy city** (11:1).

The rest of this section preserves three different lists, once again stressing the importance of continuity between the past, present, and future.

E. Dedication of the Walls (12:27–13:3)

The dedication of the walls of Jerusalem (12:27–43) is the highpoint of Ezra–Nehemiah. This climactic ceremony commemorates the final step in the restoration and reorganization of the people of Israel. The temple had been rebuilt, the walls of Jerusalem finished, the city repopulated, and the authority of the Book of the Law established. Therefore, the community joined together with unmitigated **joy** to celebrate what God had done for his people.

The religious nature of the dedication is immediately evident. The participants as well as the walls and gates themselves were first purified by the priests and Levites. Ritual purification (Heb. *ṭāhēr*) is symbolic of the holiness and purity of God that can be appropriated by his people. As God's restored covenantal community the Jews can be ritually pure.

The procession began on the western wall facing eastward toward the temple. From there it divided into two symmetrical "thanksgiving **choirs**" (Heb. *tôḏōṯ*). The first (12:31–37), led by Ezra, proceeded to the right, counterclockwise, along the wall toward the temple. The other (vv.38–39), which included Nehemiah, advanced to the left, clockwise, toward the sanctuary. Meeting at the house of God, they expressed their **joy** through song and sacrifice. The word **joy** is the central focus of the dedication.

F. Nehemiah's Final Reforms (13:4–31)

Following the events of chs. 7–12, everything else seems anticlimactic. After the joyous dedication of the walls of Jerusalem one might think that the Jews, like storybook characters, lived happily ever after. This chapter serves as a reminder that life with all its temptations and compromises goes on.

The Nehemiah memoir records a series of problems the governor faced in his second term of office. After his initial twelve-year term (13:6; cf. 5:14), he returned to Babylon for an unspecified period. Upon arriving back in Jerusalem he discovered that time had dulled the Jews' memory of the great events that marked God's decisive actions to reestablish his people in the land. The result was the reappearance

of sins they had sworn to renounce (see 10:30–39). The prophet Malachi, ministering at about this time, faced many of these same problems.

In his energetic style, Nehemiah addressed three problems in turn. Each involved a rebuke of the guilty parties, and each was punctuated with prayer (13:14, 22, 29). The verb translated **"rebuked"** in 13:11 (Heb. *rîḇ*, see 5:7; 13:17, 25) is typically used in the context of a lawsuit. It was often employed by the prophets to describe God's dispute with his wayward people who have broken the covenant.

The first problem concerned the temple and cult (13:4–14). His old nemesis, Tobiah, capitalizing upon his intimate connections in Jerusalem (see 6:17–19) and aided by a priest, had acquired a room in the temple complex itself. Nehemiah's reaction, comparable to Jesus' cleansing of the temple, was literally to throw the interloper out, reaffirming the principle of separation from anything or anyone foreign. The other two problems involved blatant compromise of Sabbath observance (vv.15–22; cf. 10:31) and new cases of mixed marriages (vv.23–29; cf. 10:30; Ezr 9–10). Nehemiah acted with righteous indignation to curb these abuses.

The final verses of the book record Nehemiah's own evaluation of his accomplishments. He says nothing of his work on the walls, that for which most remember him. Rather, his epilogue mentions the purification and organization of priests and Levites and provision for regular offerings. These are among the primary themes in the covenant renewal oath of ch. 10.

This correlation suggests an important theological truth for the Christian in this final chapter. Judaism, which properly begins with Ezra, is characterized as a religion of the Book. Ezra's reading of the Law and the covenant-renewal ceremony of Ne 8–10 were formative events in the development of Judaism. Yet this book ends with an admission that the Law and the old covenant are not in themselves sufficient to maintain a people in close relationship with God. Elsewhere the OT speaks of a new covenant, based not in adherence to a written code, but on an intimate knowledge of God (Jer 31:31–34). Thus the book of Ezra–Nehemiah points forward to this new covenant, realized in the person of Jesus Christ, with the promise of divine enabling for God's people truly to live as God's people.

BIBLIOGRAPHY

Bright, J. *A History of Israel*. Philadelphia: Westminster, 1972.
Childs, B. S. *Introduction to the Old Testament as Scripture*. Philadelphia: Fortress, 1979.
Fensham, F. C. *The Books of Ezra and Nehemiah*. Grand Rapids: Eerdmans, 1982.
Kidner, D. *Ezra and Nehemiah*. TOTC. Downers Grove, Ill.: InterVarsity, 1979.
Myers, J. M. "Ezra Nehemiah." AB. Garden City, N.Y.: Doubleday, 1965.
Noth, M. *The History of Israel*. New York: Harper, 1960.
Pritchard, J. B., ed. *Ancient Near Eastern Texts Relating to the Old Testament*. Princeton: Princeton University Press, 1955.
Williamson, H. G. M. "Ezra, Nehemiah." WdBC. Waco: Word, 1985.

ESTHER

G. Herbert Livingston

INTRODUCTION

I. TITLE, CONTENT, CANONICAL PLACEMENT

The book is named for Queen Esther, who dominates the story. Her Hebrew name was Hadassah, which means "myrtle." The name Esther is based on the Persian word *stara,* which means "star."

This narrative is beautifully constructed and is filled with suspense and surprising turns of events.

The story begins with a feast attended by the military leaders of the empire. Queen Vashti was demoted because of disobedience, and Esther was chosen to replace her.

A struggle for power developed with Esther and her uncle Mordecai against Haman, the new grand vizier. Haman hated Jews and persuaded the king to issue a decree that would lead to their destruction. With great courage, Esther succeeded in exposing Haman's plot, and he was executed. Mordecai was made the new grand vizier, and, with the aid of Queen Esther, gained permission from the king to issue a new decree that granted the Jews the right to protect themselves. The Jews successfully overcame their enemies, so Mordecai and Esther proclaimed the Feast of Purim to celebrate the victory.

In the Hebrew arrangement of the OT, the book of Esther has been grouped with Ruth, Song of Songs, Ecclesiastes, and Lamentations. In the oldest Greek translations of the OT, about A.D. 430, Esther is placed before the Minor Prophets. In English versions the book comes after Nehemiah.

II. HISTORICAL SETTING, AUTHORSHIP, AND DATE OF ESTHER

Assuming that Esther was the Queen of Xerxes I (486–465 B.C.), the first banquet would be dated 483–482 B.C. (1:3–4), and Esther made queen in December 479 or January 478 B.C. (2:16–17). The next date (3:7) would be April 17, 474 B.C., and the next date (3:13) would be March 7, 473 B.C. The decree (8:9) was written June 25, 474 B.C.

The book does not name its author. Since it has no indications of

Greek influence on vocabulary or customs, it seems best to keep the date of the book between 465 and 333 B.C.

III. STRUCTURE AND THEOLOGICAL THEMES OF ESTHER

The book of Esther is a unified narrative with three sections: The rise of Esther to the rank of queen; the rise and fall of Haman; and the rise of Mordecai to power.

The book is subdivided by ten references to feasts: 1:1–4; 1:5–8; 1:9–12; 2:18; 5:5b–8; 7:1–9; 8:16–17; 9:17, 19; 9:18; 9:20–32.

A series of decrees was issued: 1:19–22; 2:1–4, 8; 3:2, 9–15; 8:1, 7–14; 9:20–25, 29–32. These decrees made legal the events related to the several feasts.

Ten duplications give a sense of organization to the book: (1) two royal banquets (1:1–8), (2) two banquets for women (1:9–12; 2:18), (3) two listings of royal servants (1:10, 14), (4) two references to Esther concealing her identity (2:10, 20), (5) two references to virgins (2:8, 19), (6) two houses (2:12–14), (7) two royal consultations with leaders (1:13–20; 2:2–4), (8) and two with groups (6:1–5; 7:9), (9) Mordecai consulted twice with Esther (4:5–9, 10–17), and (10) Haman consulted twice with his wife and friends (5:10–14; 6:12–14).

These duplications serve as literary "stitches" that tie the narrative together.

Esther has always caused biblical scholars embarrassment because none of the names of God occur in the book. A recent computer search made by James D. Price and Leroy E. Eimers (see bibliography) has brought forth eight instances of four different divine names. These acrostics occur in 1:20; 4:9; 5:4, 13; 6:1, 14; 7:5, 7, all crucial spots in the story.

The theological themes in Esther seem almost as hidden as God himself. Much as in the story of Joseph (Ge 37, 39–50), the activity of God is providential. God is at work behind the scenes, overruling the decrees of potentates and wicked people, bringing about crucial turns of events, and always watching over his people to preserve them in times of crisis. It is this providential presence of God that has convinced both Jews and Christians that the book belongs in the OT canon.

As the story of Joseph ignores the polytheism of Egypt, so the book of Esther ignores the polytheism of Persia, except for passing reference to wise men who were astrologers. Both stories largely ignore the standard religious practices of the Hebrew people, especially those related to the priesthood. As noted above, the book does have two references to fasting, which would have religious significance. Even the Feast of Purim was set up as a folk observance with little religious significance.

IV. OUTLINE

Major Theme: God Does Not Forsake His People
    I. Esther Becomes Queen of Persia (Chs. 1–2)
    II. Haman's Rise and Fall (Chs. 3–7)
    III. Mordecai's Rise to Power (Chs. 8–10)

COMMENTARY

I. ESTHER BECOMES QUEEN OF PERSIA (CHS. 1–2)

This section covers a period of six months. Possibly the banquet was a planning session for an invasion of Greece.

The next banquet was held for all the people in the citadel. Archaeological research has supported the description of the ornateness of the palace.

The king's permissiveness hints that the celebration was an unrestrained orgy. Queen Vashti's banquet for the women occurred at the same time.

By the end of the week of banqueting, Xerxes was intoxicated and ordered seven male servants to bring the queen so he could present her. She refused to appear, making Xerxes furious.

Xerxes called a conference of his seven closest advisors. They were **wise men who understood the times,** an oblique way of saying that they were skilled in astrology. The seriousness of the crisis that faced the government is highlighted. To ignore the disobedience of the queen would send a signal to all wives that they need not unwillingly obey husbands. That would create **disrespect and discord** and thus destroy male authority. Vashti must be replaced by a **better** (a completely submissive) woman.

Interestingly, the divine name Yahweh appears in a reverse acrostic order at the end of v.20. These are the Hebrew words in English symbols: *hy' wkl hkunshym ykuttnw* (literally, "all the wives will honor"). Working backwards, note that the underlined letters are *yhwh*, or *Yahweh*, which is translated "LORD" in English.

After Xerxes had recovered from his drunkenness and **anger,** he felt remorse about what he had done, which according to Persian law could not be undone (1:19). He needed a queen, but how should he go about choosing a replacement? His trusted **personal attendants** (astrologers) were summoned to a conference. They proposed a search for beautiful girls who would be brought to the palace and prepared for the king's evaluation. Whoever he chose would be Vashti's replacement.

Mordecai was **a Jew of the tribe of Benjamin** and thus a descendant of one of the captives (Kish) transported from Judah to Babylon by Nebuchadnezzar's armies in 597 B.C. He had adopted a young cousin, whose parents had died.

The selection process netted a number of beautiful girls, among whom, providentially, was Hadassah, who would receive a new name, Esther, and special treatment from the servant in charge of the harem. Mordecai took the precaution to instruct his cousin not to reveal her ethnic identity, the first hint that there was prejudice in Susa against people of Jewish origin.

The king had his own method of evaluating the young women brought to the palace. He slept with each girl one night before offering his opinion. Esther's turn came, and though the procedure was extremely humiliating, she managed to keep her composure and won the approval of Xerxes. He thought he alone made the choice, but future events were to show that the Almighty was quietly carrying out his own will in the matter.

The fact that Mordecai customarily sat at the palace gate indicates that he already held an important position in the government, for that was the custom of the time. Gates were the places where many business and legal transactions took place daily. It was also a good place to overhear conversations between people.

Mordecai heard two officials plotting the death of the king. Mordecai quickly got word to Esther, and the officers were executed. The royal court dutifully recorded the details of the plot and the punishment.

II. HAMAN'S RISE AND FALL (CHS. 3–7)

The villain, Haman, appears on the scene. The text does not explain why Mordecai refused to bow down when Haman passed by in a royal parade. Perhaps it was because he deeply distrusted Haman.

Fellow officials who saw Mordecai's act reported his behavior to Haman and identified him as a Jew. Fierce anger gripped his soul.

Anger and prejudice combined to engender in Haman's mind an evil desire. Here was an opportunity to implicate all Jews and justify a procedure to wipe them all out.

With like-minded friends, court officials cast lots to determine a proper time when this deed could be carried out. The lots designated the month of Adar (February/March) almost a year later.

At a chosen time, Haman presented a report of a serious threat to the well-being of the empire. An unnamed people had customs that caused them to disobey the king's laws. Such lawlessness should not be tolerated. Haman offered to pay the costs, an amount equivalent in weight to 375 tons of silver. Haman suggested that a royal decree be issued authorizing the destruction of these lawless people. Evidently Haman expected to obtain the silver from the plunder of the possessions of the people killed. Xerxes gave permission to issue the decree, and it was immediately written and distributed throughout the empire.

Haman celebrated by drinking wine. He had gained control of the procedure to do away with the hated Jews. The emperor had been easily persuaded to issue a decree that could not be altered. His enemies, including Mordecai, could not escape. The people of Susa were **bewildered.** Who were these people with such customs that they would disobey the commands of the king?

When Mordecai heard the royal heralds read the decree publicly, his heart was broken. How could his people could escape destruction? Unable to contain his emotions, he **tore his clothes.** In their place he robed himself in sackcloth (a rough burlap-like material), rubbed himself with ashes, and roamed the streets of Susa **wailing loudly and bitterly.** Jews everywhere did the same. This easily identified the people against whom the decree was directed. The death of all Jews was certain.

When word came to Esther, she was puzzled about Mordecai's behavior; she did not yet know about the decree. Mordecai sent her a copy of the published decree and gave instructions to an attendant to ask Esther to appeal to Xerxes for help.

In 4:9 an acrostic of a name of God occurs in reverse sequence in the first letters of four words. In transliteration, these words are *ḥtk wygd l'str 't,* "**Hathach . . . reported to Esther** [**what**]." Reading the underlined letters in reverse sequence, one finds *'lwh,* or with vowels, *'eloah.*

Ordinarily, people must be summoned to appear before the emperor. The penalty was death unless the king gave mercy by holding out his **gold scepter.**

Esther's problem was that the king seemed to have lost interest in her. For **thirty days** he had not requested her to visit him.

Mordecai saw the extreme danger inherent in his request. If the ruler was angered by Esther's bold approach to him, she could be executed immediately. If nothing was ventured, Esther, Mordecai, and all Jews would lose their lives. There was only one small ray of hope: perhaps Xerxes would be in a good mood and grant mercy. Maybe **relief and deliverance** could come from another source (a hint of faith in divine providence) for other Jews, but that would not protect Mordecai, Esther, and their family.

Mordecai's appeal was directed to Esther's deepest sense of family loyalty, but also to her importance as queen and her unique access to Xerxes.

The text lacks a description of Esther's agony or a reference to prayers she may have offered to God. The author does indicate that Esther was religiously sensitive. He notes that she asked Mordecai to send a notice to all Jews in Susa to fast for three days and

nights. Esther and her maids would do the same.

Her final statement is one of profound commitment: **If I perish, I perish.** She was ready to offer her life as a sacrifice for the possible deliverance of her people.

At the chosen time, Esther prepared herself to approach the throne. By implication her courage is highlighted by the apparent casualness of her act.

Her heart must have leaped with unbelief and joy when she saw Xerxes extend his **gold scepter.** A marvelous thing had happened; Xerxes was in a good mood. The king even offered Esther **half the kingdom** if she wanted it. Esther's request was brief; she invited Xerxes and Haman to a banquet she had prepared.

In 5:4 another acrostic occurs in forward sequence. The following Hebrew words, in English symbols, have the key letters underlined: *ybw' ḥmlk whmn ḥywm* ("**let the king, together with Haman, come today**"). The first letters of each word in forward sequence spell *yhwh* (Yahweh).

Xerxes summoned Haman, and they went to the banquet. Esther promised she would reveal her real petition at a banquet the next day. The king accepted her promise.

Haman left in **high spirits;** he really was an important man. However, he saw Mordecai at **the king's gate** still refusing to show him respect. Joy turned to **rage,** but he did nothing at the moment. Instead he bragged before his wife and his friends about his importance to King Xerxes and Queen Esther. There was only one problem; Mordecai refused to show him respect and honor.

The divine name is present in 5:13. The last letters of the four Hebrew words, in English symbols, are *zḥ 'ynnw shwḥ ly* ("**this gives me no** satisfaction"). These letters in reverse sequence spell *yhwh* (Yahweh).

Haman's audience had a ready solution: build a high gallows and hang Mordecai on it.

That night, unable to sleep, Xerxes ordered that the daily government records be read to him. Xerxes noted that Mordecai had not been rewarded for his report of the plot against the king's life.

The divine name, Eloah, is repeated in 6:1 in reverse sequence. The Hebrew words in English symbols follow: *ḥmlk wy'mr lhby' 't spr* (**"The king ... ordered the book ... to be brought in"**). The letters underlined spell *'lwh* (Eloah).

Haman arrived at the palace to ask permission to execute Mordecai. Before he could speak, Xerxes requested advice on how best to honor a person who had benefited the king. Haman assumed that the king wanted to honor him, so he suggested an opulent parade. Haman was amazed at what he heard but had no choice. He obediently prepared the parade, led the horse on which Mordecai rode, and proclaimed that this man was honored by the king.

Haman dared not express his emotions publicly, but as soon as his painful ordeal was finished, he went home and poured out his **grief** to his wife and friends. They too were shocked and told Haman that he was doomed and that Mordecai would win.

At this crucial point in the story, the basic consonants of the divine name, Eloah, appear. The Hebrew words in 6:14 are shown below in English symbols and the key letters are underlined: *ḥgy'w wybhlw lhby' 't hmn* (**"[eunuchs] arrived and hurried Haman away"**). In reverse sequence, these letters spell *'lwh* (Eloah).

Xerxes seemed intrigued by Esther's delaying tactics; so during the banquet,

he requested Esther to state her petition. Begging the king's mercies, she pleaded that her life be spared. She then identified herself as a member of the Jewish people who had been **sold for destruction and slaughter and annihilation,** and she pleaded for their deliverance too. If slavery had been involved, she would have said nothing; but this was death.

Xerxes demanded the name of the man who proposed to destroy the Jewish people.

A word associated with the divine name Yahweh is in both forward and reverse sequence in 7:5. The key consonants appear on the last letter of each word and with an overlap of three letters, each of which is underlined as follows: *my hr' zh w'y zh hw'* (**"Who is he, and where is the man?"**).

The underlined consonants spell *'hyh* in both directions. This Hebrew word means "I am" and is the same Hebrew word that occurs in Ex 3:14 where God says to Moses, "I am who I am."

The impact of Esther's identification of Haman as the culprit was dramatic. Haman **was terrified,** and Xerxes left the table in a **rage.** While the king was in the nearby garden, Haman threw himself on Esther's couch, pleading for mercy. The man, who was angry because Mordecai would not prostrate himself before him, now fell prostrate before Mordecai's cousin.

In 7:7 the divine name occurs in two forms in sequence, as the last consonants of these Hebrew words shown in English symbols: *ky r'h ky klth 'lyw* (**"realizing that the king had already decided his fate"**). The two divine names are *yh yhwh* or Yah, Yahweh (Lord, Lord). The acrostic is like a great shout of triumph because the enemy is now doomed.

Xerxes saw the act, interpreted it as an assault, and reprimanded Haman.

Guards immediately arrested and blind-folded Haman, and their leader suggested that the man be hanged on the gallows prepared for Mordecai. Xerxes ordered it, and it was done. The execution assuaged the king's anger.

III. MORDECAI'S RISE TO POWER (CHS. 8–10)

This time Xerxes was quick to hand out awards. First, Esther was given Haman's possessions. The estates of criminals automatically reverted to the crown and were at the disposal of the king. Next, Mordecai was rewarded, for Esther had revealed her relationship to him. The presentation of the royal **signet ring** symbolized an important promotion. Note that when Haman received the ring, he was given charge of royal funds (3:10–11). Queen Esther took her turn and granted Mordecai supervision of the newly acquired estate that had belonged to Haman.

The salvation of the Jewish people was not yet assured. Again, Esther dared to approach the throne. The gold scepter was extended to her, and she presented her plea with many tears. The decree issued by Haman could not be annulled, so it remained a threat to the existence of her people. Esther was overburdened with concern for them. She pleaded with great effectiveness.

Xerxes had a solution: to issue another decree **in behalf of the Jews.** Queen Esther and Mordecai could word the decree as they wished. Work on the decree began immediately. The date given in 8:9 is the same as June 25, 474 B.C. The decree granted the Jews the right to defend themselves against any who might attack them on the date mentioned in Haman's decree. Jews could also **plunder** the possessions of their enemies.

The Persians had an excellent communications system, a "pony express"

that could reach all parts of the empire in the span of a few days. The decree was proclaimed and posted by royal heralds for all to hear and read.

Mordecai was no longer a low-level official sitting in the city gates. He now wore **royal garments of blue and white and a purple robe of fine linen** along with a **crown of gold.**

In sharp contrast to the lack of joy in any of the several banquets reported in the story (they always seem to end in tragedy), a burst of joyful celebration erupted among the Jews. Their neighbors were so amazed that they began to identify themselves with the Jews.

At last the **thirteenth day of the twelfth month** (March 7, 473 B.C.) arrived. It was the date designated in the first decree for the slaughter of all Jews in the empire (3:13). But **the tables were turned.** Instead of Jews being slaughtered by the thousands, their enemies fell before the sword. Amazingly, the officials of the empire and their military forces helped the Jews. They were taking no chances. The man who had issued the first decree died as a criminal; the man who issued the second decree ruled with great power. The text repeatedly takes note that the Jews refused to plunder their enemies.

The scene was not a pretty sight, for thousands of bodies lay everywhere. Among the bodies were those of the **ten sons of Haman.** Prejudice in Susa was so strong that Esther requested one more day for the Jews to resist their enemies. Xerxes granted the request, and when the extra day ended, the Jews were free of threat from the old enemies. To emphasize their victory, the Jews displayed the bodies of Haman's sons on gallows. The source of evil had been wiped out. To the Jews these were days of justice, not days of mercy.

The extra day the Jews of Susa spent

defending themselves created a disjunction of celebration of victory in the empire. The results caused confusion; Jews outside Susa celebrated on Adar 14 and Jews in Susa on Adar 15.

Mordecai noted this difference as he considered making the celebration an annual event. He sent out letters establishing both Adar 14 and 15 as days of celebration. These were to be days of joy and generosity to each other and to the poor.

The section 9:23–28 seems to be a later summary of the reason behind the Feast of Purim (casting of lots) and an exhortation that the celebration should be observed **in every generation by every family.** And, indeed, this has been the case to the present time.

Queen Esther joined with Mordecai to send out another letter **with full authority to confirm** the legitimacy of the Feast of Purim. This was dutifully recorded in the royal annals.

Chapter 10 is an appendix to the main story and summarizes the importance of Mordecai during the reign of Xerxes. First, the power of this monarch to tax his subjects is stressed, and then it is noted that a full record of the deeds of both men was preserved in annals of the empire.

Mordecai served the king as second in command, a grand vizier. Throughout his tenure he was noted for his protective support of all Jews.

BIBLIOGRAPHY

Anderson, B. W. "The Book of Esther" (Exegesis). IB. New York: Abingdon, 1954.

Baldwin, Joyce G. "Esther: An Introduction and Commentary." TOTC. Downers Grove, Ill.: InterVarsity Press, 1984.

Brockington, L. H. "Introduction to the Book of Esther." NCBC. London: Thomas Nelson, 1969.

Broomall, W. "Esther." BE. Philadelphia: Holman, 1960.

Clarke, Adam. "The Book of Esther." *A Commentary and Critical Notes.* New York: Abingdon, n.d.

Demaray, C. E. "The Book of Esther." BBC. Kansas City: Beacon Hill, 1965.

McDonald, A. "Esther." NBC. Grand Rapids: Eerdmans, 1953.

Price, James D.; and Leroy E. Eimers. *The Acrostic Names of God in The Book of Esther.* Unpublished paper. Chattanooga, Tenn., 1983.

Whitcomb, John C. "Esther." Wycliffe. Chicago: Moody, 1962.

Wilson, Charles R. "The Book of Esther." WBC. Grand Rapids: Eerdmans, 1967.

JOB
Carl Schultz

INTRODUCTION

I. TITLE AND CANONICAL PLACEMENT

This book bears the name of its hero, Job. The inclusion of Job in the canon is secure. A larger issue is its location in the OT. In the Hebrew Bible, Job is located in the last of the three divisions, the Sacred Writings, or Hagiographa. The Hagiographa is a diverse and complex corpus. Job, Psalms, and Proverbs are juxtaposed, appearing as a tripartite whole. In the various arrangements of the Hagiographa, the book of Psalms always stands first, but the positions of Job and Proverbs are interchangeable. Uncertainty about the date of the hero, Job, kept the book from heading this trio. Its poetic form and the nature of its materials caused it to be a part of this indivisible group (Dhorme, IX).

In the Greek texts, the location of Job ranges from the end of the OT to a position between Psalms and Proverbs. In our English Bible it is the eighteenth book and the first in a corpus of five books known as Books of Poetry. Since Job is primarily poetic in form, its location here is understandable. The literary genre of Job is critical to its interpretation.

II. CONTENTS AND COMPOSITION

As with other biblical books, a distinction needs to be made between the date of the contents and the date of the composition of the book.

From textual evidence the man Job could be dated in patriarchal times. Note the following data: (1) Job offered his own sacrifices (1:5) as did the patriarchs (Ge 24:35). (2) Job's wealth was measured in terms of livestock and servants (1:3) as was Abraham's (Ge 14:14). (3) Job's longevity (42:16) compares to persons in patriarchal times (Ge 25:7–8). (4) The Chaldeans are seen as nomadic pirates (1:17) rather than as the controlling element of the Neo-Babylonian Empire of the eighth and seventh centuries B.C. (5) Job is classified by Ezekiel (14:14, 20) with the ancient hero Noah (also with Dan'el—an early heroic figure and possibly not the Daniel of the OT). While these data seem somewhat conclusive, precise dating of the man Job is not critical to the understanding of the book.

Not knowing the identity of the author/s, it is impossible to date the writing of the book. A wide range of dates has been suggested, from the patriarchal age (due to the dating of the man Job as noted above) to the second or first century B.C. (Rowley, 21). Utilization of such data as orthography, historical events, identifiable institutions, theological ideas, and alleged quotations from other biblical books has not resulted in any consensus (Andersen, 61–63). The complexity of this book may argue for an extended time of composition with more than one writer involved. Our inability to identify the author/s and date in no way detracts from its inspiration and does not seriously affect its interpretation.

III. LITERARY BACKGROUND AND CHARACTER

Job is classified with the Wisdom Literature of the OT. This genre of literature has a variety of forms, ranging from simple sayings to learned discourse (Andersen, 23). Such literature is not restricted to the OT or to the Bible. Wisdom Literature has common concerns, and the geographical location of Israel and some parallels in form and thought with extrabiblical literature indicate that a book such as Job would not have been produced in isolation. These points of contact with other sources will help us to interpret the book and possibly help us to understand something about its origin.

Job is didactic, but it is profoundly more religious than the other Wisdom Literature. Virtually every genre of literature in the OT can be found in it. Efforts have been made to characterize Job as an epic poem, a drama, a dialogue, and a lawsuit. But Job is in a class by itself.

IV. LITERARY STRUCTURE

The arrangement of this book includes a large poetic section (3:1–42:6) flanked by shorter prose sections. The prologue (1:2–2:13) pictures Job in his original happiness and details his calamities; the epilogue (42:7–17) depicts Job's restoration and final satisfaction.

The bulk, of the poetic section is given over to the speeches of Job and his comforters (4:1–27:23), aligned in three cycles:

Participants	*Cycle 1*	*Cycle 2*	*Cycle 3*
Eliphaz	4–5	15	22
Job	6–7	16–17	23–24
Bildad	8	18	25
Job	9–10	19	26
Zophar	11	20	?
Job	12–14	21	27

They are flanked by Job's opening soliloquy (3:1–26) and his closing peroration (29:1–31:40). Ch. 28 disturbs the symmetry of the book with its Hymn on Wisdom and the uncertainty of the speaker. Chs. 32–37 contain the presentations of Elihu, who is neither anticipated in the prologue nor assessed in the epilogue. Possibly Elihu should be seen as an adjudicator, providing a human estimate (32:12; 33:12) of the previous speeches. The book ends with the Lord's critique (42:7).

V. OUTLINE

VI. MESSAGE

It is easy to express the negative message of this book. The idea that Job's sufferings are due to sin, as claimed by the three comforters, is held up to ridicule by the writer who has already indicated in the prologue that Job was "blameless and upright." God also rejects this assessment in the epilogue (42:7). Elihu moves slightly beyond these three and suggests that there is a remedial purpose to Job's sufferings. Such an explanation, valid perhaps in some situations, is not appropriate for Job's sufferings.

What is the positive message of the book? One would expect the answer to be found at the end of the book and in the mouth of the most credible character of the book. If so, the answer is most likely to be found in the speeches of the Lord. But establishing the location of that answer is easier than determining its nature. The speeches of the Lord with their zoological and meteorological questions are difficult and seemingly unrelated to Job's sufferings. This has caused some to insist that the answer is not verbal but personal—the theophany itself. It is enough that God appeared to Job. Others have noted that the concern of these speeches is not with the "why" of Job's suffering, but with the "how" of those sufferings. Suffering, no matter how extreme, does not warrant the attitude displayed by Job, thus it is that Job repents, following the Lord's speeches (42:6).

Given the interrogative nature of the Lord's speeches, they perhaps need to be viewed as educative. Job had hoped to question the Lord, but instead he is questioned. Job sees the complexity of the world and the immensity of God's task and realizes that he has been too preoccupied with himself and has spoken from ignorance. His rebellion is replaced by submission and his despair by faith.

COMMENTARY

I. THE PROLOGUE (1:1–2:13)

A. The Hero Job (1:1–5)

The character of Job is described in universal terms. Four qualities are mentioned. He was **blameless** (perfect in the sense of completeness), **upright** (straight), devout (**feared God**), and moral (**shunned evil**). Job's goodness is critical to a proper understanding of the book. His sufferings cannot be attributed to sin.

B. The First Divine Council Meeting (1:6–12)

The sovereignty of God is seen in this section as he presides over the angels (cf. Pss 82:1; 89:5). Satan is among these angels, as a regular or possibly as an intruder. He responds to God's question about Job's goodness with skepticism. He cannot deny Job's goodness, but he insinuates that Job's piety is part of a bargain. Job is righteous because it is to his advantage. Confident of the outcome, the Lord grants Satan permission to **strike everything** Job has.

C. The First Disasters and Job's Reactions (1:13–22)

Four disasters in rapid succession strip Job of his family and possessions. Disasters one and three are caused by marauding humans, while two and four are due to natural phenomena. The death of his children is the climax of this sequence. Children were viewed as a part of a person's wealth (Pss 127:3–5; 128:3–4). Job responds to these calamities by performing the mourning ritual and by worshiping. He is oblivious to the contest between the Lord and Satan (as he must be) and ignores the secondary causes of the disasters. It is the Lord who initially gave and has now taken away.

D. The Second Divine Council Meeting (2:1–6)

The Lord notes that Satan's initial efforts to discredit Job were without effect. Job still maintains his integrity. Satan counters by suggesting that up to this point he has only begun to harass Job. The person of Job has not yet been touched, only his possessions. If he is permitted to touch his innermost being, the results will be different. Observe again that Satan can do only what he is allowed to do. He cannot kill Job.

E. Job's Illness and Reaction (2:7–10)

Job does not yield to his wife's advice as did Adam. He characterizes her as **foolish**. This is not a reflection on her intelligence but rather on her moral and spiritual deficiency (Rowley, 37). The masculine form of this word (foolish) is used to designate the fool who suggests that God does not figure in the affairs of this life (Ps 14:1). As far as Job's wife is concerned, Job's integrity is of no value in the eyes of God. It has not

protected him against adversity. Job counters by stating that it is appropriate to receive not only good from God but trouble.

F. The Arrival of the Comforters (2:11–13)

The comforters show their sympathy by performing the grief ritual. They clearly had come to comfort him even though their subsequent words seem to deny it. Following established practice, they remain silent until Job speaks.

II. DIALOGUE (3:1–27:23)

A. Job's Opening Statement (3:1–26)

A radical change in Job is observable in this chapter. While he does not curse God, he comes close to it by cursing his own birth. Perhaps he is becoming more aware of the magnitude of his suffering.

Clearly his mind is occupied with death as can be seen in his three wishes. First, he wishes that he had never been born (vv.1–10). Treating his day of birth as if it had autonomous existence, he wants it stricken from the calendar. He would have preferred to remain in his mother's womb.

Second, since he was conceived and did leave his mother's womb, he wishes that he might have been stillborn and taken his place in Sheol with the other dead (vv.11–19). This chapter provides us with one of the best descriptions of Sheol found in the OT. Nowhere in this book is it suggested that the inequities Job suffered would be adjusted in the next world. Both reward and punishment must be experienced in this life. Death does not right the wrongs of earth; it simply ends them (vv.17–18). Death is no respecter of persons. All ages and classes are found in Sheol. While the concepts of heaven and hell are yet to be developed, this chapter recognizes that death does not mean extinction (Andersen, 106).

Third, Job wishes that he could die now (vv.20–26). Life is intolerable. Death is preferable but elusive (v.21). It would be an occasion for celebration (v.22), but Job does not have access to death because God has **hedged** him in. Perhaps Job anticipates the comforters' frenzied response to his outburst since he notes that trouble is coming.

B. First Cycle of Speeches (4:1–14:32)

It is difficult to label these exchanges. The designation "discussion" seems too scholarly, while the designation "debate" seems too structured. To label them "speech" seems too formal. The designation "dialogue" suggests short and interrupted exchanges, but the presentations in this section are rather long. Recognizing the absence of a precise term for these exchanges, for convenience we will use the designation "dialogue."

1. Eliphaz (4:1–5:27)

Eliphaz is the most sympathetic comforter. He initially affirms Job, reminding him of his past involvement with those who suffer (4:3–4) and urging him to practice in his sufferings that which he previously taught others (v.5). In his later presentations he will challenge Job's integrity, but now he recognizes it (v.6) and suggests that Job need not despair. Job can anticipate a speedy intervention by God.

It is at this point that Eliphaz divulges his theology of suffering. Using the analogy of agriculture, he states that those who suffer have cultivated sin (4:8). Calamities do not happen without a cause. Life is lived in a world of cause and effect, of stimulus and re-

sponse. Moving from effect back to cause, Eliphaz in subsequent presentations will find it necessary to establish that Job has sinned.

Eliphaz's source for his theological position was a dream (4:12–13). His reference to and description of the dream produces an expectation of a profound revelation. But it is only a simple truism: A mortal cannot be more righteous than God (v.17).

Eliphaz stresses here a theme common among the comforters—that any success of the fool (in Wisdom Literature the wicked and the fool are equated) is momentary and illusory (5:3–5). This emphasis is followed by an apparent contradiction. In v.6 he argues that suffering is not to be compared to that which grows of its own accord, but rather to that which is deliberately planted. Suffering has a cause! But in v.7 he seems to suggest that suffering is both innate and inescapable. V.6 may be an allusion to Ge 3:17–19, thereby associating human suffering with sin. Vv.7ff. trace human suffering to God. Hence, appeal must be made directly to God (v.8). It is God who is active in nature (5:9–10) and active in human affairs (vv.11–16).

The reference to rain demonstrates both the destructive and beneficial acts of God (Andersen, 120). A sharp contrast is made between God's treatment of the lowly and needy and his treatment of the **crafty** and **wily**. Eliphaz identifies God with the poor as is common in the OT. Given Job's present lowly condition, Eliphaz may be seeking to offer him hope and guidance relative to the handling of his present sufferings.

Eliphaz seems to anticipate Elihu by recognizing suffering as a form of divine discipline (5:17). The person who accepts suffering as a discipline from God is blessed. This is a truism, but in the light of the prologue it is not appropriate in Job's case. The blessings that he projects for Job are prosperity (vv.23–24), posterity (v.25), and longevity (v.26). He seems to have forgotten that all of Job's children are dead, unless he anticipated the new family (42:13). While he does not offer Job hope beyond the grave, he promises a long life with full vigor until death (42:16–17).

2. Job (6:1–7:21)

That Job is irritated by Eliphaz's presentation is evident from his emotional defense. If the hungry donkey and ass can instinctively bray and bellow (6:5), Job argues that he has the right to give verbal expression to his anguish. Even though Eliphaz warned Job about the futile consequences of resentment (5:2), he insists that his anguish (same Hebrew word) is immeasurable and justifies his outburst (6:1ff.). He traces his sufferings to God (v.4), bewildered at such treatment. Before praying Job states that Eliphaz's consolations are insipid and nauseating (vv.6–7).

Job now prays (6:8–13). While the comforters talk about God, Job talks to God. As he requested God to remove the protective hedge from about him (3:23), so here he prays that God will **loose his hand** (6:9) and allow him to die. Being flesh and not stone or bronze, he has reached the limits of his tolerance (vv.11–12).

Following the prayer, Job issues a stinging indictment of the comforters' friendship. What he expected from them was loyalty (a covenant term) even if, as Eliphaz had insinuated, he had turned from God (6:14). But instead of loyalty he experienced betrayal. His friends failed him as wadis that gush with water in the rainy season but become bone dry in the heat of summer (vv.15–17) and fail the thirsty and expectant desert caravans (vv.18–21).

The friends' failure to be loyal and sympathetic was due to Job's frightening physical condition. They could neither cope with the sight of it (6:28) nor reconcile their prepackaged theology with what they knew of Job. Further, if they sided with Job, they might incur the wrath of God (v.21). As the drama unfolds they clearly opt for their theology and allow Job to be expendable. No wonder Job begs them to concentrate on him, not on their theology (v.28), and to give up their unfair assumption that he must be guilty and hence deserving of his suffering (v.29).

The balance of Job's first presentation amounts to soliloquy in which he renews his complaint against God and his appeal to God. Life was such now that he felt that he had been conscripted and employed but without benefits of wages or rest (7:1–2). Instead he receives **"months of futility, and nights of misery."** He suffers from insomnia, perhaps due to mental anguish and physical pain (vv.4–5).

Given the brevity of life (7:6) and the finality of death (vv.7–10), Job urges God to remember him, to restore the previous fellowship between them. The characteristic of Sheol emphasized here is that it is a place from which there is no return (vv.9, 21; 10:21).

After begging God to remember him, Job urges God to leave him alone (7:16–17). These sudden changes are due in part to Job's duress and in part to his perplexity and confusion about God. While the psalmist is pleased with God's attention (Ps 8:4), Job is distressed with it. He insists that he is no threat to God and hence does not need to be treated like the primeval chaos (7:12) that was restrained by God.

Does Job acknowledge sin here? Possibly, but not sins of such a magnitude to warrant his present sufferings (7:20). His attitude appears to be somewhat insolent. So what if he has sinned? He has not hurt God. God should forgive him now before it is too late (v.21) and should desist from attacking him (v.20).

3. Bildad (8:1–22)

While Eliphaz in his opening presentation was ready to concede Job's piety, Bildad challenges it, arguing that if Job were innocent, God would restore him. The tone of Bildad's remarks is set in his opening words when he accuses Job of being a windbag (8:2). Implying that Job has charged God with injustice, Bildad insists that God consistently dispenses justice (v.3). What Job's children received, they deserved (v.4). Job must seek God and implore mercy (v.5). Restoration will result (v.6), and his future condition will greatly exceed his previous condition. While his prediction was correct, his basis for it was clearly wrong.

While Eliphaz's theology was predicated on the mystical and the empirical, Bildad bases his on tradition. The accumulated wisdom of humankind must be consulted (vv.8–10).

Citing an ancient proverb, Bildad claims that the wicked will perish in the midst of their prosperity even as papyrus and reeds wither when deprived of water (vv.11–13). Any prosperity of the wicked is only apparent and at best momentary. It is no more lasting than the flimsy spider's web (vv.14–15) and the luxuriant growth of an uprooted tree (vv.16–19).

In concluding Bildad contrasts the fate of the righteous and the wicked. His words that God does not reject a **blameless** (same Hebrew word as 1:1, 8) person are hurled at Job as the taunt of Jesus' enemies were hurled at him, charging that if he were innocent God would rescue him (Mt 27:43).

4. Job (9:1–10:22)

Job directs his comments to a statement Eliphaz made that one cannot be righteous in God's eyes (4:17) and to the claim of Bildad that God is always just. In a legal dispute with God, humans must lose since God determines all the rules and is the final arbiter. In his profound wisdom, God would pose unanswerable questions (9:3).

But not only is it a matter of God's wisdom; it is also a matter of his power (9:4). A hymn of God's power is presented in vv.5–10. Here Job parallels the comforters' remarks about God's infinite power. God's actions are numberless. Earthquakes (vv.5–6), eclipses (v.7), and the constellations (vv.8–9) are all the work of God. God is neither visible (v.11) nor restrainable (vv.12–13). Any solution to Job's sufferings must reckon with God's vast power though theodicies that argue for a limited God have been advanced.

Job sees the futility of any judicial proceedings. As a defendant he could not establish his innocence and would be forced to plead for mercy (9:15). As a plaintiff he could not force God into court or once there could not force him to testify.

Job now advances his explanation for sufferings. There is a kind of randomness both in nature (9:23) and in human events (v.24). His claim that natural disasters strike bad and good indiscriminately reminds us of Jesus who noted that God sends the sun and rain on both the righteous and the unrighteous (Mt 5:45).

Job has already employed the imagery of a weaver's shuttle to depict the brevity of life. Now he uses three more figures: the runner (9:25), the speedy papyrus boats of Egypt (v.26), and the swift eagle (v.26).

Since God is not human, Job needs someone to represent him in court, to arbitrate, to effect reconciliation (9:32–33). More important to Job than receiving answers that explain his suffering is the restoration of his previous relationship with God.

Ch. 10 is addressed directly to God and is cast in the form of a prayer. As the psalmist frequently does, Job here resorts to frank speech. He calls for acquittal (v.2), charging God with showing favoritism to the wicked (v.3). He questions whether God is able to understand and sympathize with the human condition (vv.4–5)

Job uses three handicrafts to depict humankind's creation: the potter and clay (10:8–9); the conception and prenatal development of a human metaphorically presented as the curdling of cheese (v.10); and pleating cloth to show the development of the prenatal body (v.11). Job reminds God of his providential care in earlier days.

Job seems convinced that his present sufferings were planned by God during his prosperous days but were concealed from him (10:13). God had indeed watched over him (v.12) but now with hostile intent (v.14). In his planning, God was indifferent to Job's moral condition (v.15). Now he suffers from shame and loss of self-respect (vv.15–16) and does not know what to expect next (v.17).

He renews his desire to die, returning to his soliloquy of ch. 3. Sheol is depicted as a gloomy place. Four synonyms for darkness are used to demonstrate this (10:21–22).

5. Zophar (11:1–20)

Zophar begins by charging Job with glibness. Job will later acknowledge

that he has been verbose and that his language has been strong (42:3). But Zophar fails to recognize that while his words are theoretical, Job's are existential. By challenging the theology of the comforters, Job seems to them to claim both purity and superior understanding (Rowley, 88). Zophar is mistakenly convinced that, if God should speak, the comforters will be vindicated (v.5; cf. 42:7), for God knows both the hidden and the manifest sides of every matter (Pope, 84).

Zophar seems to deny to Job what he allows for himself—the ability to fathom the mysteries of God (v.7). He describes Job as witless and having no more chance of becoming wise than a wild ass's colt has the chance of being born a human (v.12).

Assuming the role of the evangelist, Bildad calls on Job to repent. By doing so he would experience the peaceful life, be delivered from shame (v.15) and find rest (v.18) and freedom from fear (v.19). The importance of repentance must never be minimized, but it must not be seen as a panacea for life's problems.

6. Job (12:1–14:22)

Job resents the assumed superiority of the comforters and sarcastically recognizes that they think they are representative of the race and have a monopoly on wisdom (12:2). He insists that he is their equal (v.3).

In 12:7–25 the issue is not God's power. All the participants are in agreement here. The debate is over the part moral purpose has in God's actions.

In 13:1 Job is convinced of the randomness of suffering and warns the comforters that they will gain no favor with God by attempting to defend on moral grounds his treatment of Job (13:7–8). Smearing Job with lies (v.4), they could show greater wisdom by remaining silent (v.5), and it would be safer for them. It is dangerous to patronize God who might well turn on them (vv.9–11). Here Job does not dissociate God's actions from moral purpose.

Job is now ready to state his case forthrightly. He considers himself innocent (13:16). He does not expect anyone to challenge this case (v.19). He knows that he will be vindicated (v.18). Job becomes defiant. Even at the risk of death (much welcomed) he is going to argue his integrity before God. Nothing is more important to him than that. He would prefer to argue his case with God than with the comforters (v.3). He seems desperate rather than triumphant and assured.

Job now turns aside from his friends to address God, requesting that God withdraw his hand from him and that he stop frightening him (vv.20–21) before he summons him (v.22). Job gives God two choices relative to the format of this encounter. He can either question Job or allow Job to question him (v.22). When the encounter occurs, God ignores the latter and uses only the former (38:3). To prepare himself, Job wants a list of the charges against him (13:23). Job feels that he is a victim of God's whim (v.25), although he does seem to allow for the possibility that his sufferings may be due to the sins of his youth (v.26). If so, those sins were not so serious as to merit his present sufferings.

Beginning with 13:28 Job expresses a longing for the Resurrection. He is clearly groping toward the idea of an afterlife (Pope, 108). He wishes for temporary asylum in sheol, from which state God would subsequently call him (14:13–15). While he yearns for this, the balance of the book indicates that he does not expect it.

Job laments the brevity of life, comparing it to a flower and a shadow (14:1–2). He is astonished that God should take note of and scrutinize an insignificant, defenseless, and unclean creature such as he is (vv.3–4). He prays again that God will leave him alone (v.6).

From Job's perspective the human situation is more like a parched riverbed (14:11) than a cut tree (v.7). The cut tree will sprout again with the coming of rain (vv.8–9), but the riverbed, probably due to some erosive situation, will remain dry (v.11).

Even the mountains, noted for their antiquity and longevity, will erode and crumble (14:18–19). So the human creature will yield to death, which will erode the visage (v.20). In death the only awareness is personal pain (v.22), with no awareness of posterity (v.21).

C. Second Cycle of Speeches (15:1–21:34)

The first cycle of speeches has disclosed the theological position of the comforters. All three agree that sin is behind Job's sufferings. The presentation of the comforters reveals self-righteous and patronizing attitudes. The men show considerable anger and impatience with Job but little compassion and understanding.

And Job disclosed his position in the first cycle. He is unable to reconcile his predicament with the traditional answers provided by the comforters. His conclusion that there is a randomness about suffering forces him to view God differently from the comforters.

These respective positions will be maintained and reinforced in the second cycle. The relationship between Job and his friends will deteriorate. Virtually no progress will be made in resolving Job's sufferings.

1. Eliphaz (15:1–35)

While Eliphaz remains the most courteous comforter, there is a marked decline in his politeness. He dismisses Job's words as hot air and nonsense (vv.2–3). But Job's words are not simply useless, they are harmful. Job is undercutting religion! He is discouraging devotion to God (v.4). His words are not only sinful in themselves, they are symptomatic of a deep awareness of guilt (vv.5–6). His protestations are prompted by his guilt.

Through several questions addressed to Job (vv.7–9), Eliphaz seeks to show Job his arrogance (vv.12–13) and his delusion relative to his innocence (vv.14–16). Obviously Eliphaz is more concerned with his traditional theology than with Job.

Eliphaz again presents his favorite theme—the ultimate fate of the wicked (vv.17–35). What is that fate? Suffering and pain. Any prosperity is at best temporary (vv.27–29) and is not fully enjoyed because of the realization that retribution is imminent (vv.22–24). Not only is Eliphaz's tirade here irrelevant and inapplicable, it is clearly incorrect. All too often the wicked prosper while the righteous suffer. The psalmist presents a more realistic and accurate picture than the one given by Eliphaz (Ps 73).

2. Job (16:1–17:16)

Job dismisses the speeches of the comforters as pious platitudes. Were the roles to be reversed, Job insists that he would know how to extend comfort to these friends (16:4–5).

Job not only blames God for his sufferings (16:7) but also for his mistreatment by others (v.11). While the graphic language here (vv.10–11) may suggest physical assault, it is more likely that Job is referring to verbal assault, the kind he is experiencing by way of the comforters. The picture of God presented in this passage (vv.7–14) is frightening. God's treatment of Job is characterized as a vicious attack with the descriptive figures being drawn from the behavior of wild animals and human enemies. Job does not know how to react to God's treatment. Neither speech nor silence has helped (v.6), nor has mourning or the humbling of himself (v.15).

In spite of his suffering, Job still categorically denies his guilt (16:17). He wants his blood to remain exposed as Abel's blood (Ge 4:10) that it may be a cry to the Lord (16:18). He is confident that he has a witness in heaven (v.19) who serves a purpose similar to that of the arbitrator of 9:33 and the vindicator of 19:25.

This witness could possibly be God himself. Job continues to struggle with two conceptions of God (Rowley, 121). He appeals to the God of justice and steadfast love against the God of wrath. But, as Pope observes, since God is already accuser, judge, and executioner, it is more likely that an intermediary is implied (p. 125).

Job now appeals to God to favor him in his dispute with the comforters by giving a pledge (17:3). This seems to refer to some material token used in business transactions (Ge 38:18) to verify agreements (Andersen, 184). The comforters have closed their minds (17:4) and are confident of their claim that Job is guilty of sin. It appears that they will triumph unless God lends Job his support, unless he affirms Job's integrity. Not only do the comforters insist on his guilt, but the oversensitive Job concludes that everyone does, with the exception of some upright people who are appalled and support him (vv.6–9). This support gives Job a momentary surge of defiance as he taunts his comforters to continue their efforts (vv.9–10).

Job now seems to resign himself to imminent death. Some commentators conclude that Job has lost all hope (Pope, 131). But noting that he calls the grave his home (17:13) and alludes to family members (v.14), Andersen (p. 187) argues that Job may yet hold to some hope after all.

3. Bildad (18:1–21)

While Bildad has nothing significantly new to say, he becomes more direct. He addresses Job in the plural ("you" of v.2 is plural), thereby including him with the wicked. Bildad accuses Job of wanting the moral order changed so as to accommodate him (v.4). For one who was such a traditionalist as Bildad, this was tantamount to overturning the order of nature.

The moral order is indeed fixed. The fate of the wicked is clear and certain. Job will experience darkness as his lamp will be snuffed out, a certain indication of disaster (vv.5–6). He will be caught in a trap. Six different terms for traps and snares are used here (vv.8–10). Terrors will pursue him, and he will not be able to avoid them (vv.11–13). His tent will be destroyed (vv.14–15) and he will have no descendants (v.19). Bildad concludes with the claim that his representation of the fate of the wicked is certain (v.21).

4. Job (19:1–29)

After beginning with an expression of impatience with the comforters (vv.2–6), Job charges God with vicious treatment. The imagery employed by Job is graphic. God destroys him as a building is destroyed and as a tree is uprooted (v.10). He moves against Job as an army moves against an enemy (vv.11–12).

God's treatment has brought about ostracism. He has been alienated and estranged from all human relationships (vv.13–17). He has been denied the normal convention of courtesy (v.18) and the anticipated response of love (v.19). His experience has been so harrowing that he has barely survived (v.20). He begs his friends to desist from attacking him; they already have their pound of flesh (vv.21–22).

But in spite of his physical weakness, Job is certain of vindication. So certain is he that he wants his words of protestation preserved for future generations (19:23–24). His vindication will be brought about by his **Redeemer** (v.25). In Israel the redeemer was usually the nearest kinsman who was obligated to exact vengeance in a blood feud (Dt 19:6–12; 2Sa 14:11) and to look after the interests of the family members for whom he was responsible. This term is often applied to the Lord as the deliverer of Israel from bondage in Egypt (Ex 6:6; 15:3) and in Babylon (Jer 50:34). It is also used of the Lord's deliverance of a person from imminent death (Ps 103:4; La 3:58). Given Job's present situation and his rejection by the comforters, it is quite obvious why Job asserts his belief in the **Redeemer.** What he needs is not so much physical help as moral vindication.

V.26 has been translated in several ways, but these translations fall essentially into one of two categories: from (perspective) my flesh I shall see God or from (privative, i.e., out of) my flesh I shall see God. If it is the former, then Job is referring to the theophany he experiences in chs. 38–41. After it is over, he concludes **"Now my eyes have seen you"** (42:5). On the other hand, if the latter translation is followed, then Job seems to anticipate an afterlife which will result in his seeing God.

5. Zophar (20:1–29)

Zophar explodes with his response. He moves immediately into his invective against the wicked. He observes that any prosperity enjoyed by the wicked is only momentary (vv.4–11). Using the metaphor of sweet food that proves to be poisonous, he asserts that evil, while attractive, is deadly, having a built-in retribution (vv.12–22). Finally, in cataloging the woes of the wicked (vv.23–29), he cites several of the calamities Job has experienced. By paralleling Job's experience with the wicked, he clearly groups Job with them. At no point in this speech does Zophar hint that the wicked could repent and make amends.

6. Job (21:1–34)

Job flatly contradicts Zophar's picture of the wicked. The wicked grow old and increase in power (v.7). Their homes are safe (21:9). Their children thrive and enjoy themselves (vv.8, 11–12). Their herds are productive (v.10) and their death is peaceful (v.13). These are the wicked who deliberately reject God (vv.14–15).

By using the phrase **"how often"** (vv.17–18), Job may be acknowledging that Zophar is correct concerning the fate of the wicked. Or he may be sarcastically asking for proof. Job objects to any concept of hereditary guilt even as Jeremiah (31:29), Ezekiel (18:2–3), and Jesus (Jn 9:1–3) did. He also objects to the comforters imposing their pattern of reward and punishment on God (v.22). Death is the common experience of all regardless of morality (vv.23–26).

Job senses that the comforters have really been talking about him when talking about the wicked (v.27). He concludes that the arguments of the comforters are contradicted by universal experience (vv.28–33) and dismisses them as nonsense (v.34).

D. Third Cycle of Speeches (22:1–27:23)

The definite interchange of speeches found in cycles 1 and 2 is missing here. While Eliphaz has his turn (ch. 22), Bildad's presentation (ch. 25) is short and perhaps abbreviated. Zophar has no assigned speech in this cycle. Further complicating the issues is the material assigned to Job (chs. 23, 24, 26, 27). Job now seems to agree with his antagonists. He may be quoting his opponents.

In this final cycle the comforters openly accuse Job of wickedness, ascribing to him deeds that even the author denies. Clearly the comforters' theological assumptions are more important than their friendship with Job. Job is expendable. Position is more important than a person.

1. Eliphaz (22:1–30)

Eliphaz now insists that a person's piety is of no benefit to God. He portrays God as unaffected by human actions and is therefore apathetic (vv.2–3). Such a concept is out of keeping with the biblical portrayal of God (cf. Luke 15:7). Further, it is not helpful to Eliphaz's argument. If God is indifferent to piety, must he not also be indifferent to wickedness? Eliphaz may simply be seeking to counter Job's claim that God seems indifferent to wickedness (21:23–26) by suggesting that God is in reality impartial and fair in his treatment of all.

Following his cataloging of Job's sins (vv.4–11), Eliphaz accuses Job of taking advantage of God's transcendence (vv.12–14) and thereby associates him with the wicked men of old (vv.15–18).

As in his first speech (5:17–27),

Eliphaz appeals to Job to repent (vv.21–23). His call for Job to love God rather than gold (vv.24–25) may indicate a belief that Job's sufferings were due at least in part to his love of wealth. While such an assumption was wrong, Eliphaz's call (vv.26–27) is in keeping with the biblical attitude toward wealth.

2. Job (23:1–24:25)

Job's response does not seem to be directed to the comforters but appears to be a soliloquy directed to God. He longs to find God (23:3), underscoring his belief that God has deserted him (vv.8–9). In spite of his protestations and his refutations of the comforters' positions, he is inclined to associate God's presence with pleasantness and prosperity. The absence of these indicates the absence of God.

While he cannot find God, Job is certain that God can find him (23:10). He is confident of his own integrity and that he will pass the present test he is experiencing. His mettle is being tested, and Job expects vindication rather than pardon and grace. Such an expectation must be kept within the context of Job's struggles with the comforters. Job obviously needs grace (as do all persons), but to refute the fallacious position of the comforters, he seeks vindication, which he will receive at the end of the story.

Job notes here the sovereignty of God, its implications, and his response to it. God does what he pleases (23:13); and what God has decreed for him, Job will experience (v.14). This frightens Job (vv.15–16) but does not silence him (v.17). Significant shifts are discernible in Job's attitude toward God in this chapter, but as Andersen (p. 211) observes, Job's dread here is an essential part of his faith.

Job now returns to an earlier emphasis. The comforters' insistence that God regularly administers justice in the world is not supported by facts (24:1). Job cites several wrongs perpetuated against the defenseless, wrongs that are clearly forbidden by laws given to Israel by the Lord, but that are committed with impunity and without redress (vv.2–4). While the perpetrators escape judgment, believing that no one sees their wrong doing (vv.13–17), the defenseless poor lack food (v.6), clothing (v.7), and shelter (v.8). Their children are removed by force as payment for debts (v.9). Yet in spite of their cries, God remains inactive (v.12). The claim of the comforters that the wicked inevitably come to a bad end (vv.18–24) is simply not verified by empirical data. Job is certain that he is correct (v.25). Indeed, it is difficult to establish a precise relationship between cause and effect. Evil is not always punished, nor are the poor always delivered. Job is aware of randomness here.

3. Bildad (25:1–6)

In his truncated speech, Bildad emphasizes both the power and purity of God. In sharp contrast to Job's assessment in the previous chapter, Bildad argues that God maintains order through his greatness. Seeking again to establish Job's guilt, he deprecates humankind. Both the maggot and the worm are associated with the grave (v.6). Thus Bildad refers here to the certainty and finality of death. The psalmist, comparing people to the moon and stars (Ps 8:3–4), also realized humanity's relative insignificance, but he quickly added an important qualification when he observed that the human creature was made a little lower than God and crowned with glory and honor (Ps 8:5).

4. Job (26:1–27:23)

Following a sarcastic response directed to Bildad (26:2–4), Job also magnifies the power of God. The netherworld (vv.5–6), the heavens (v.7), and the earth (v.10) are all under the scrutiny and jurisdiction of God. If anything, Job's assessment of God's power exceeds that of Bildad. There is no threat to God's dominion. He destroys Rahab and Leviathan, mythological sea monsters used as symbols of chaos, not only by his power, but also by his wisdom (vv.12–13). While chaos was a serious threat to the pagan gods, it was no problem to the Lord. This chapter, which is a preparation for the speeches of the Lord that will also focus on creation (chs. 38–41) concludes that humans are able to comprehend only a small part of God's creative greatness (v.14).

While some scholars assign these comments on God's greatness to Bildad, it is not really necessary to do so. There is no disagreement between Job and his protagonists relative to God's greatness. At issue is God's justice and his involvement in human affairs. The comforters have a programmed and predictable God, one whose actions can be anticipated, while Job's God is free, not subject to any restraints. In a sense, the comforters have reduced God to a reasonable and manageable level. This is idolatry. While Job's concept of God is troubling and less reassuring than that of the comforters, it succeeds in allowing God to be God. He cannot be manipulated or adjusted to suit theological positions.

Ch. 27 has been variously handled. Introduced as it is with a totally new statement—**"And Job continued his discourse"**—it is seen as the beginning of Job's conclusions, thus designating ch. 26 as the close of the third cycle. However, grouping ch. 27 with chs.

29–31 is problematic because of the intervention of ch. 28, which is probably not to be seen as words of Job. Since Zophar does not have a part in the third cycle and this chapter sounds like him, some scholars assign vv.7–23 to him (Rowley, 175).

If these words are given to Job, then 27:7–12 is clearly directed at the comforters and should not be read as descriptive but rather as imprecative. Job, in keeping with Israelite law, calls down upon his enemies the very punishment that would have come to him had their charges been correct. To call upon his enemies the fate of the wicked is to wish for them the worst fate.

In 27:13–23 Job takes words similar to those used by the comforters against him and turns them back upon his friends. They do not perceive themselves as wicked, but they are because of their attacks on Job. The fate described here is not so much personal as it is domestic. The wealth of the wicked will be transferred to the righteous (27:16–17), his family will be destroyed (vv.13–15), and his house will disappear (v.18).

Job's imprecation and bitter attack on the comforters must be kept both within the context of the book and the culture in which he lives. Since the writer has established Job's integrity and must retain it to refute the comforters' position, such outbursts on the part of Job are not surprising. By establishing the wickedness of the comforters who are not suffering for their sins, the writer refutes their position.

III. HYMN ON WISDOM (28:1–28)

Three pertinent questions arise relative to this hymn on wisdom. Who uttered it? Why is it located here? What is its role in the book?

The present arrangement of the book

would argue for Job to be its spokesman since the chapters preceding it and following it are assigned to Job. However, the material of this chapter is incompatible with Job's earlier and subsequent thoughts. If this chapter is given to Job, then the balance of the book is extraneous since Job would already have his answer. It seems equally unacceptable to assign this chapter to one of the comforters. The suggestion that this chapter was presented by a chorus must also be rejected since Job is not a drama. It appears best to assign these words to an editor.

The location of this material is also problematic since it interrupts Job's speeches. Perhaps this chapter is deliberately detached, serving as an interlude marking the end of the dialogue and preparing for the peroration of Job that follows. It certainly is a break from the heated exchange that had occurred. This hymn reflects an aura of calmness and sanity.

More significant for our consideration is the role this chapter plays. Retrospectively it serves as a rebuke to the arrogance of the debaters who by their dogmatism reflected their hubris. It shows that one, unaided by God, can never arrive at an answer to the reason for innocent suffering. Human beings can locate and mine mineral treasures hidden in the earth, but they cannot find wisdom (vv.1–11). Not only can they not find wisdom by their ingenuity, they cannot secure it with their wealth (vv.12–19). While wisdom remains hidden from them, it is seen by God (vv.20–28). This divine wisdom is beyond their grasp, and they must settle for the practical wisdom of piety (Pope, 206).

This chapter not only rebukes the past dogmatic claims of the participants; it also sets the stage for the appearance of the Lord.

IV. JOB'S PERORATION (29:1–31:40)

As Job was given the first word (ch. 3), he is now given the last word (chs. 29–31). Here he summarizes his position, beginning with ch. 29 where he recollects his former happy condition. In ch. 30 he speaks of his present miserable condition. Finally in ch. 31 he uses a series of oaths of clearance to establish his innocence.

A. The Way It Was (29:1–25)

Reflecting on his former happiness when he was in his prime (v.4), Job recalls his family relationships (vv.5b–6), his community relationships (vv.7–16, 21–25), but most of all his relationship with God (vv.2–5). It was God's protective care and friendship that accounted for his former condition. As already noted, his present sufferings were seen as proof that God was not with him now. Not being privy to the divine council meetings in the prologue, Job is unable to account for his sufferings any other way than by the absence of God. This shows the fallacy of measuring God's nearness by observing existing circumstances.

During his prosperous days Job was loved and respected by residents of his town (vv.7–11, 12–25). The reason is apparent. Job was active in the administration of justice (vv.7, 12). He was benevolent, extending his assistance to the exploited (vv.12–13, 16), to the handicapped (v.15), and to the stranger (v.16). His faith found practical expression, qualifying for what James called **pure and faultless** religion (James 1:27).

Job had anticipated that given his compassion and service for others, his favorable circumstances would have continued (vv.18–20). Here Job is guilty of linking prosperity with goodness even as his friends were guilty of associating suffering with wickedness. He found it difficult to break away from the religious convictions of a lifetime.

B. The Way It Is (30:1–31)

In ch. 30 Job's attention turns to his present plight. Instead of the respect he enjoyed during his prosperous times, he is now greeted with disdain by the young and offscouring of the town. He is hurt by such treatment (vv.1–15). He had been acclaimed by notables; now he is ridiculed by a segment of the town whom he had "disdained."

Not only is he ridiculed by the people, he is attacked by God (vv.16–23). Job continues to assign his suffering to God, being ignorant of the divine council meeting in the prologue. Reflecting OT thought, Job ignored secondary causes of his suffering and focused on God, whom he sees as the primary source. All events were attributed ultimately to God.

The suffering Job is not greeted with the same concern and care that he had extended to those in affliction. No one pities him now in his desperate circumstances (vv.24–31). Such treatment only intensifies his sorrow and pain.

C. Job's Ultimate Claim of Innocence (31:1–40)

Having secured no justice from God and having no support of his claim of innocence from his friends, Job now (ch. 31) asserts his innocence in such a way that God is forced to act. He uses the oath of clearance. This oath was taken by the accused of the OT but was invoked only after all rational means of proof had been exhausted. This use of nonrational proof brought the Deity into the process, which is precisely what Job wanted.

The format of the oath is this: If I have done X, let Y happen to me. So forceful are the **if** clauses and so frightening are the **then** clauses that the **then** clause is generally omitted. In this chapter Job omits most of the **then** clauses but does retain a few (vv.8, 10, 22, 40).

The list of sins is not exhaustive nor is their sequence systematic. Job denies lust (vv.1–4), dishonesty (vv.5–8), adultery (vv.9–12), oppression (vv.13–15), miserliness (vv.16–23), avarice (vv.24–25), idolatry (vv.26–28), vindictiveness (vv.29–30), parsimony (vv.31–32), hypocrisy (vv.33–34), and exploitation (vv.38–40).

He is so confident of his innocence that he calls for an indictment in writing—a bill of particulars (v.35). He knows he can respond to any charge and establish his innocence.

The debate is now ended. No significant progress has been made. In the prologue Job's integrity was asserted. Here it is reaffirmed. Claims of the comforters that Job's sufferings were due to wickedness have been dismissed. Job stands innocent. But why does he suffer? The book continues.

V. SPEECHES OF ELIHU (32:1–37:24)

Elihu has been called an angry young man. His youth is indicated by his hesitation to speak until the three comforters had nothing more to say (32:4–5). However, if he was an adjudicator he would not normally have spoken until the end of the debate. That he was angry is underscored by references to his anger (vv.2–3, 5). He was angry with the three because they had not successfully refuted Job (v.3). His anger with Job is due to his perception that Job believed himself to be right in the dispute with God (v.2).

Elihu's defense of youth is admirable. Indeed, advanced years are no guarantee of wisdom (32:7). Elders are not necessarily correct. More important is spirit (vv.8–9).

Elihu addresses Job by name (33:1), something the three friends had not done. His approach initially is courteous. The characteristics Elihu assigns to himself are indeed desirable: integrity, sincerity (v.3), and humanity (v.7).

Elihu's assertion that Job had claimed innocence (33:9) is an overstatement. While Job had insisted on his righteousness (9:21; 10:7; 16:17; 23:10; 27:5–6; 31:1–40), he had never insisted upon sinlessness (7:21; 13:16). His contention was that his sufferings were not commensurate with his sins; he did not deserve such terrible suffering. Since it is inconceivable to Elihu that God would punish an innocent man, he categorically denies Job's claim that God is unjust (33:10–11; cf. 13:23–27; 19:6, 11).

Elihu is clearly not modest in spite of his claims. While the others have searched and reasoned, their answers have been inadequate (32:11). He seems to imply that the three friends gave up the discussion because they believed that Job could not be refuted (v.13). He will be more successful than they! While he insists that his arguments are new (v.14), they are not radically different but are targeted more directly to Job's objections. His conviction that he will be so successful that there will be no need to invoke God is contradicted by what follows. Elihu assures them that he will not be partial nor will he recognize distinctions of age or class (vv.21–22).

Ch. 33 is linked with 32:6–22 and is considered Elihu's first speech. In this speech Elihu challenges Job's claim that he is innocent and has been unjustly treated (33:8–12) and his complaint that God does not answer when addressed (vv.13–28).

Elihu denies Job's charge that God does not answer (33:13) by stating that God responds by dreams (v.15), by illness (v.19), and by an angel (v.23). These visits of God are purposeful warnings to deter or to dissuade from sin (vv.16–18). They are remedial, serving a disciplinary purpose (vv.19–22). Elihu's emphasis on the remedial character of suffering is an improvement over the penal emphasis of the three friends but is still not appropriate to Job. Job's sufferings are not for correction but for demonstration.

In Elihu's second speech (34:1–37) he defends the character of God against the charges of Job that God is unjust (v.5) and that piety is without reward (v.9). He believes that Job's assertion that he is no liar has in effect made God a liar (v.6). Job's insistence on his innocence and undeserved sufferings is tantamount, given Elihu's theology, to making God a liar.

Elihu's insistence that God is just is self-evident (34:10–15). It is unthinkable that God would do wrong (v.10). While Elihu has the luxury of being theoretical and general (which he is) in his comments, Job, by virtue of his sufferings, is personal and existential in his. At issue in the book is, not the justice of God in general, but his justice as it pertains to Job's sufferings.

To defend his teaching that God is impartial and infallible Elihu advances the concept of God's omniscience. God does not need to hold a trial as Job requested to determine guilt (v.23). He knows all, and his actions are predicated on that knowledge (vv.24–26). No inquiry is needed (v.24). God's actions are beyond human comprehension and he does not need to offer any explanations (vv.29–30) as Job demanded.

This chapter concludes by Elihu arguing that Job cannot dictate the terms that govern God's activities (34:33). The fact that Job continues to suffer proves his impenitence and stubbornness. He speaks without knowledge (v.35), and he is guilty of rebellion (v.37). As with the other participants, Elihu is forced to picture Job as a wicked person if his theological assumptions are to stand.

In his third speech (35:1–16) Elihu responds to two questions he has heard Job ask. The first one has to do with the value of virtue (vv.2–8). The second one deals with the unanswered cry of the afflicted (vv.9–16).

His reply to the value of virtue begins by establishing the remoteness of God (35:5). Since God is so distant, he is not harmed by human sin (v.6) nor is he benefited by human righteousness (v.7). Humankind's good or evil affects only humans (v.8). Elihu has both insulated and isolated God. By stressing God's transcendence, he has protected God from the actions of people. But the reasoning here contradicts his earlier claim that God reacts to the sins by punishment and discipline and to righteousness by reward. His point may be that beneficial or destructive forces are inherent in the actions themselves and do not necessitate divine response. Such a position, given Job's suffering, would necessitate establishing his sinfulness, which is what each of the other participants has endeavored to do. By suggesting that God is indifferent, Elihu comes close to Job's position of challenging his justice.

Elihu now turns to Job's earlier claim (24:12) that God ignores the cry of the oppressed for help. His answer is one that is given frequently and one that is often pertinent. They do not deserve an answer (35:9–10). Animals by instinct turn to God (v.11), but the wicked (i.e., the oppressed) are so preoccupied with their misery that they ignore God (v.10). When the oppressed do pray their motives and attitudes are im-

proper. They are characterized as arrogant (v.12) and their prayers as empty, i.e., deceitful (v.13). The onus of unanswered prayers rests squarely on the shoulders of the person praying. How can Job expect God to hear him since his cry is directed against rather than to God (v.14)? While his prayers have been many, they have been without knowledge (v.16).

Elihu's fourth speech has two distinct parts. In the first part he moves beyond the penal concerns of the three comforters and emphasizes the remedial implications of suffering (36:1–25). In the second part Elihu focuses on God's activities in nature, thereby anticipating the speeches of the Lord that follow (36:26–37:24).

Although God is mighty, he does not despise his creatures (36:5). Contrary to what Job claims (21:7), the wicked are not allowed to live (36:6). When the righteous suffer, it is to alert them to their sins (v.9) and to lead them to repentance (v.10). Through such suffering God speaks (v.9). If the righteous learn from their discipline, prosperity and contentment will follow (v.11). If they do not, doom will overtake them (v.12). Elihu now applies this principle to Job (vv.16–21), but this strophe is so problematic that it is not clear whether Elihu is encouraging or warning Job. While there is strong scriptural support for suffering being remedial in nature, the prologue precludes its application to Job. Job's suffering is neither penal nor remedial. It is a demonstration of his integrity.

Elihu now turns to the greatness of God as revealed in nature (36:26–37:13). This portion begins with an emphasis on the power of God as seen in the storm. God has not only created the forces of nature, he controls them. He sends the rain (vv.27–28), the thunder (v.29), and the lightning (v.30). The destructive qualities of the storm suggest God's anger and his judgment (vv.31–32). There is no break in thought here even though the speech extends into the next chapter where there is a shift from an attitude of awe to expectation. The thunder is recognized as the voice of God (vv.29, 33; cf. Ps 29) and the medium of a theophany. It is in the storm that God frequently reveals himself (Ex 19:18ff.; Ps 18:7–15; Jn 12:29). These verses are a preparation for the theophany Job will experience. A seasonal shift is discernible in 37:6 when the precipitation now becomes snow. Agricultural activities are suspended (37:7) and the animals hibernate (v.8). In these forces of nature, Elihu sees God at work, punishing the wicked and showing his love to the righteous (v.13).

In anticipation of God's visit, Elihu directs a series of ironic questions at Job to humble him (37:14–18). The season has now shifted to summer (v.17). Job is warned that his continued challenge of God (vv.19–20) could result in destruction. God is beyond our reach and unsearchable, but he never acts unjustly (v.23).

VI. SPEECHES OF THE LORD (38:1–42:6)

Appropriately the Lord appears to Job at the end of the book. All the participants have had their say, but Job still is not satisfied. He will remain thus until the Lord has spoken (42:5–6). Throughout the exchanges with the comforters, Job had been seeking an audience with God. He had offered either to question God or to allow God to question him (13:22). While he preferred the former, he finally had to settle with the latter format.

A. First Speech and Job's Response (38:1–40:5)

Acting as a wisdom teacher, the Lord employs the didactic method of interro-

gation. His questions are concerned with nature, a common medium in Wisdom Literature (1Ki 4:33). The questions put to Job are ironic in nature since the situation is not simply instructional but also polemical (Bergant, 180).

The Lord does not directly address Job's situation. No reference is made to his suffering or his alleged sinfulness. None of Job's questions is answered directly, yet when the Lord is finished, Job is satisfied. Something about the speeches satisfies and rehabilitates Job. But what? Several suggestions have been offered. Among them are the following.

Since the Lord's speeches are difficult and seemingly unrelated to Job's sufferings, the answer is not to be found in their words but rather in the appearance of the Lord himself. It is not so much what the Lord says as the fact that he showed up. The theophany itself rehabilitates Job.

God's concentration in his speeches on nature is for the purpose of causing Job to realize the complexity and immensity of this world. Throughout the book he has been engrossed with his own affairs. Now he sees himself and his suffering in terms of God's management of the world. Perspective makes the difference.

The issue addressed by the Lord is not the "why" of suffering, for which there is no answer, but rather with the "how" of suffering. Proper conduct is not arrogant or challenging, but humble and silent. Job is rebuked for being confrontational. This is the reason for his repentance.

A final suggestion is that these speeches demonstrate that the Lord is not subject to the patterns of earthly courts when it comes to the administration of justice. He determines what is right and gives to each creature what is appropriate. Since each contains some compelling truths, perhaps elements from each are needed to represent the purpose for the speeches.

In the first speech the initial group of questions addresses the creation of the land (38:4–7) and of the sea (vv.8–11). The next set turns from creation to management—the management of the inanimate world (vv.12–38) and the animals (38:39–39:30).

The Lord concludes his first speech with a challenge to Job to answer him and to correct him (40:2). Job chooses not to do this, opting for silence (vv.4–5). Job does not suggest that he has nothing to say but that he will not verbalize his thoughts. Job may be subdued, but he is not vanquished. Thus the Lord begins again.

B. Second Speech and Job's Response (40:6–42:6)

The second speech begins with a challenge to Job to take his turn at the running of the world (40:8–14). Does he have the power and resources to do so. Can he manage the proud and the wicked? Job must show an ability to cope with evil. Here we arrive at the heart of the book. God's way of handling evil has been challenged. Can Job do better? Then let him do it, and God will acknowledge his power (v.14).

The rest of this speech is devoted to a treatment of the behemoth (40:15–24) and leviathan (41:1–34). These beasts are viewed by some as natural, by others as mythical. They appear in ancient myths and apocalyptic writings. Behemoth is pictured as the land monster of chaos, while leviathan is considered the sea monster of chaos.

After this speech Job concedes that he addressed matters he did not understand (42:3). Since Job had always recognized that God can do all things (v.3), he gained insight into the justice

of God through his sufferings. His hope, expressed in 19:27, is now realized. He had previously only heard, but now he has seen (v.5). Hearing suggests the inherited, the second hand. While such a knowledge may be adequate in prosperous times, it is not sufficient for times of suffering. Having seen God, Job can now confront his sufferings.

Job's acute awareness of God leads him to repentance (42:6). This repentance must pertain to the words of haste and ignorance he spoke after his suffering began. Since sin did not cause his suffering, his repentance cannot be in that area. Job now sits and worships. He is satisfied.

VII. THE EPILOGUE (42:7–17)

The trial is now concluded. Job's sufferings have served their purpose, and there is no reason to continue them. Job's wealth and health are restored, not because of his personal merit, but to acknowledge that the trial is ended and to discredit Satan.

As the divine adjudicator, the Lord now indicates that Job's position is right while that of the comforters is wrong (42:7). This statement should not be read as a blanket endorsement of all that Job said or a blanket condemnation of all that the comforters said. Job acknowledges that he has said things that were wrong (v.3), but his claim to innocence is sustained by the Lord. Ironically Job serves as priest and intercessor for the comforters (vv.8–9).

It was after Job prayed for others that his situation changed (42:10). Throughout the exchanges Job had been understandably preoccupied with himself. Now freed of that self-engrossment, he returns to serving as a priest for others as he had done in the prologue. This undoubtedly contributed to his healing.

BIBLIOGRAPHY

Books

Andersen, Francis I. *Job*. TOTC. Downers Grove, Ill.: InterVarsity, 1975.

Baker, Wesley C. *More Than a Man Can Take*. Philadelphia: Westminster, 1966.

Bergant, Dianne. *Job, Ecclesiastes*. OTMS. Wilmington, Del.: Michael Glazier, 1982.

Davidson, A. B. *The Book of Job*. The Cambridge Bible. Cambridge: Cambridge University Press, 1918.

Delitzsch, Fran. *The Book Of Job*. Biblical Commentary on Old Testament. 2 vols. Translated by F. Bolton. Grand Rapids: Eerdmans, 1956.

Dhorme, Edouard. *The Book of Job*. Translated by H. Knight. Camden, N.J.: Thomas Nelson, 1967.

Eaton, John. *Job*. Old Testament Guides. Sheffield: JSOT Press, 1985.

Glatzer, Nahum. *The Dimensions of Job*. New York: Schocken, 1969.

Gordis, Robert. *The Book Of God And Man*. New York: The Jewish Theological Seminary of America, 1978.

Morgan, G. Campbell. *The Answers Of Jesus To Job*. New York: Revell, 1935.

Neiman, David. *The Book of Job*. Jerusalem: Massada, 1972.

Peake, Arthur S. *Job*. London: Caxton, n.d.

Pope, Martin H. *Job*. AB. Garden City, N.Y.: Doubleday, 1973.

Rowley, H. H. *The Book of Job*. NCBC. Grand Rapids: Eerdmans, 1980.

Articles

Bowes, Paula J. "The Structure of Job." *The Bible Today* 20 (1982): 329–33.

Freedman, D. H. "Elihu's Speeches in the Book of Job." *Harvard Theological Review* 61 (1968): 51–59.

Gordis, Robert. "The Lord Out of the Whirlwind: The Climax and Meaning of Job." *Judaism* 13 (1964): 48–63.

Sarna, Nahum M. "Epic Substratum in the Prose of Job." *Journal Of Biblical Literature* 76 (1957): 13–25.

Thompson, K. T., Jr. "Out of the Whirlwind: The Sense of Alienation in the Book of Job." *Interpretation* 14 (1960): 51–53.

PSALMS
David L. Thompson

INTRODUCTION

I. TITLE AND PLACE IN THE CANON

A. Title

Following ancient precedent, most English versions of Scripture entitle this anthology of sacred songs "(The) Psalms" (e.g., ASV, RSV, NASB, JB, NEB, NIV) or "The Book of Psalms" (KJV, DV, NAB, NKJV). In the NT Luke uses the titles "The Book of Psalms" (Lk 20:42; Ac 1:20) and "The Psalms" (Lk 24:44), calling each individual composition therein a "psalm" and showing awareness of their numbering in the expression "the second psalm" (Ac 13:33). Luke may reflect the custom of the Greek-speaking Jews of the Diaspora here. Their Scriptures, the Septuagint (LXX), contained these titles, if manuscript evidence from the early Christian era (Vaticanus) attests pre-Christian tradition at this point.

The Greek word *psalmos*, meaning "a stringed instrument," "a song sung to stringed accompaniment," or simply "a song," stands behind these titles. The LXX translates the Hebrew designation *mizmôr* (see section II below), found in the superscription of 57 psalms and apparently taken as characteristic of the majority of the collection. LXX tradition (Alexandrinus) also shows the title *psaltērion*, "a stringed instrument." Common Christian reference to "the Psalter" and Luther's translation reflect this.

Hebrew- or Aramaic-speaking Jews came to call these 150 songs *t°hillîm*, "Songs of Praise," using a special plural form of a word that appears only once in a psalm title (145:1). This use to designate a favorite type of song in the collection (see II.E below) reflects a time when the Psalter had become the "hymnal" of the Jewish worshiping community.

B. Place in the Canon

Jewish tradition universally located the Psalms in the third section of the Hebrew Scriptures called "The Writings" (the *K°tûbîm*), following the Former and Latter Prophets (Genesis–2 Kings and Isaiah–Malachi respectively, excluding Daniel) but placed it variously within those books. Lk 24:44 apparently reflects a tradition (also in the LXX) that placed the Psalms at the head of the Writings. Modern English versions follow a tradition seen also in the Vulgate where Job, Psalms, and Proverbs, in that order, lead the Writings and in which this set of books stands between the Former and Latter Prophets.

II. HEBREW POETRY

Even in translation many of the psalms have a beauty and elegance that mark them at the very least as elevated prose. But in fact these songs and prayers are true Hebrew poetry, standing along a spectrum from slightly more than lofty prose to elegant poetry, often as far removed from Hebrew prose as Shakespeare and Longfellow are removed from the morning newspaper. At no other point in Psalms study does the fact appear more clearly than here that the Psalter, like all of Scripture, is the Word of God in the words of humans. Here God breathed his truth through the minds of inspired artists whose own skill in grammar, syntax, and vocabulary and whose own sense of poetic beauty and balance were the vehicle of choice for divine revelation. As at every other point in Scripture, the medium is itself inseparably part of the message (see section E below).

Parallelism and rhythm most distinctively characterize Hebrew poetry. Numerous other rhetorical devices belong to the artistic repertoire of the Hebrew poets and appear more or less frequently in the Psalms. But without parallelism and rhythm, Hebrew poetry does not exist.

A. Major Characteristics of Hebrew Poetry: Parallelism

Parallelism is the foundation of Hebrew poetry and registers most obviously to the English reader as a balanced repetition:

> The earth is the LORD's, and everything in it,
>   the world, and all who live in it;
>   for he founded it upon the seas
>   and established it upon the waters.
>   (24:1–2)

The symmetrical arrangement of parallel lines of about the same length (called "cola" or "stichs") in which meaning, grammar, syntax, form, and stress balance and reinforce one another constitute parallelism. The cadence of the Psalms even in translation rises in the main from these overlapping parallelisms—semantic, syntactic, morphological, prosodic. Usually two parallel lines appear together, forming a "bicolon" or a "dystich:"

> Who may ascend the hill of the LORD?
> Who may stand in his holy place?
>   (24:3)

Less frequently three lines comprise a "tricolon" or a "tristich:"

> He who has clean hands and a pure heart,
>   who does not lift up his soul to an idol

> or swear by what is false.
>   (24:4)

Types of parallelism emerge from the common patterns of meaning sustained between these parallel lines. *Synonymous parallelism* describes bicola or tricola in which the same or similar thoughts are repeated:

> Therefore the wicked will not stand in the judgment,
>   nor sinners in the assembly of the righteous.
>   (1:5)

Antithetic parallelism describes couplets or triplets with contrasting thoughts:

> For the LORD watches over the way of the righteous,
>   but the way of the wicked will perish.
>   (1:6)

In *synthetic parallelism* the second or third lines of the unit are not synonymous or antithetic to the first line but advance the thought in a variety of other ways. For example, one of the lines may give a comparison to illuminate the other. This is *emblematic parallelism:*

> As a father has compassion on his children,
>   so the LORD has compassion on those who fear him.
>   (103:13)

Other lines of synthetic parallelism relate by reason or result, as in 34:9:

> Fear the LORD, you his saints,
>   for those who fear him lack nothing.

Many lines of synthetic parallelism simply advance or complete the thought without recourse to any of the semantic ties noted above, as, for example, in 23:6:

> Surely goodness and love will follow me
>   all the days of my life,
> and I will dwell in the house of the LORD forever.

Climactic parallelism designates a highly repetitive, slowly advancing set of lines such as in 29:1–2:

> Ascribe to the LORD, O mighty ones,
>   ascribe to the LORD glory and strength.
> Ascribe to the LORD the glory due his name;
>   worship the LORD in the splendor of his holiness.

B. Major Characteristics of Hebrew Poetry: Rhythm

Hebraists recognize that classical Hebrew poetry probably had some system of meter. What that system was remains hotly contested for lack of clear evidence, with some scholars actually denying that Hebrew poetry contains such a system. Some conclude that line length, perhaps counted in syllables, was the basis of Hebrew "metrics." Others think Hebrew meter was counted in word or word-group units ("feet"), with some corresponding balance in line length naturally arising as a result. Whether an actual system of accent or stress was involved we do not know.

Our uncertainty in the whole matter means that designations used in the study of Hebrew poetry are primarily descriptive. Customarily, poetic cola are two or three (less than four) word/word-group units in length. One often encounters treatments of the Psalms describing bi- and tricola as $(3 + 3), (3 + 2), (3 + 3 + 3),$ or $(2 + 2 + 2)$. Dividing and rearranging the English words of the NIV to indicate the Hebrew word/word-groups, we would scan parts of Ps 19 as follows:

The law of—the LORD—is perfect,	
reviving—the soul.	$(3 + 2)$
The ordinances of—the LORD—are sure	
and righteous—altogether.	$(3 + 2)$
They are more precious—than gold,	
than pure gold—much;	$(2 + 2)$
they are sweeter—than honey,	
than honey from—the comb.	$(2 + 2)$
Your servant—is warned—by them;	
in keeping them—is reward—great.	$(3 + 3)$
(vv.7, 9–11)	

Whether or not such designations correspond to the ancients' understandings of their art, they serve well to indicate the relative length of lines whose balance in length (and with it one might surmise some sort of rhythm) and use of length for artistic and rhetorical purposes can scarcely have been accidental.

C. Artistic Repertoire of the Hebrew Poets

Beyond the foundational elements of parallelism and rhythm a whole repertoire of artistic and stylistic devices of sound, form, and arrangement lay open to the composers of poems such as the psalms. Some writers used them sparingly, others literally flood their works with them in multiple layers and complex interaction. While they are often important for discerning meaning, they are essentially art, expressions of the beauty of God and his creatures. What follows is a partial list from the writers' portfolio in order to heighten our awareness of this important dimension of God's Word. Some of them are apparent even in translation.

Acrostic. In Hebrew acrostics, succeeding lines (or other units like stanzas) of the poem begin with successive letters in the alphabet, from "A to Z" (aleph to tau), first the aleph line, then the beth line, and so on to the end. Pss 25, 34, 37, 111, 112, 119, and 145 are acrostic poems. Pss 9 and 10 are an acrostic, now divided in the Hebrew text and English translations. The union of Pss 9–10 as a single poem in the LXX and the

Vulgate accounts for the majority of the numbering differences in the Psalms between modern versions heavily dependent upon them (the LXX or the Vulgate) and other English versions that follow the Hebrew textual tradition's numbering. The acrostic "centerpiece" of the Psalter is Ps 119. Its twenty-two stanzas of eight lines each march through the alphabet with all eight lines of succeeding stanzas starting with the same, succeeding letter of the alphabet. So impressive is this that some translations, such as the NIV, which do not mark the lines of lesser acrostics, do head this poem's stanzas with the appropriate letter of the Hebrew alphabet. Interpreters must be aware that the thought flow of the acrostic poem often yielded coherence to the demands of the alphabet's sequence and thus beware of forcing an outline where none exists. Other famous biblical acrostic poems include Pr 31:10–31 and La 1–4.

Alliteration. Beginning a series of words with the same or similar sound is alliteration. Assonance is the use of a series of words with the same or similar *internal* sounds (versus the initial sounds). The "r" (resh) line, v.19, of the acrostic in Ps 34 combines these three devices (acrostic, alliteration, assonance): *rabbôt rāʿôt ṣaddîq,* "A righteous man may have many troubles. . . ."

Chiasm, named from the Greek letter chi (χ), arranges elements in an "x" or inverted pattern: abc//c'b'a'. Chiasm most often appears and is most easily discernible at the clause level in bi- or tricola where grammatical elements are arrayed chiastically, as in Ps 19:1, here divided and rearranged to reflect the Hebrew text.

> The heavens—declare—the glory of God;
>   // and the works of his hands—proclaim—the skies.
> subject—verb—object
>   // object—verb—subject

But poets also arranged topics of their work chiasticly, structuring an entire poem in such an abc//c'b'a', sometimes perhaps thus calling attention to the items at the center of the pattern.

Inclusio or "envelope." Here the poet begins and ends the unit (paragraph, division, or entire psalm) with the identical or nearly identical words, such as Ps 8:1, 9. "O LORD, our Lord, how majestic is your name in all the earth!" begins and ends the psalm.

Fixed Word-Pairs (A-B Words). Hebrew poets employed numerous word-pairs, placing one in the *a* colon and the other in the *b* colon. Not only the vocabulary but also the order of these pairs was usually set, much like the English expressions "law and order" or "ham and eggs," which rarely appear in the reverse order. Examples of such fixed pairs are: "enemies/foes" (Pss 18:40; 21:8), "one thousand/ten thousand" (Pss 91:7; cf. 144:13), "days/years" (Pss 61:6; 77:5; 78:33).

Numerical Progression. The most commonly used numerical progressions are the patterns x//x + 1 and 1,000//10,000. Thus Ps 62:11:

> One thing God has spoken,
>> two things have I heard:
>>> that you, O God, are strong . . .

and Ps 91:7:

> A thousand may fall at your side,
>> ten thousand at your right hand,
>>> but it will not come near you.

Repetition/refrain. Much like the refrain of a contemporary song, a repetition can mark out main units of the poem. Recall the repetition in Pss 42:5, 11 (MT 42:6, 12); and 43:5–6a:

> Why are you downcast, O my soul?
>> Why so disturbed within me?
> Put your hope in God,
>> for I will yet praise him,
>>> my Savior and my God.

Such an obvious refrain has led some to think these two poems are in reality a unit.

Rhyme. Unlike some forms of English poetry in which rhyme is essential, Hebrew poetry does not demand it. But rhyme is often used, and sometimes in important ways to signal unit boundaries or for emphasis. Ps 23:2 is a lovely example:

> *bineʿoṯ dešeʾ yarbîṣēnî*
>> *ʿal-mê menuḥôṯ yenahˤlēnî*
> He makes me lie down in green pastures,
>> he leads me beside quiet waters.

In addition to these obviously identifiable artistic devices, Hebrew poetry abounds with symbolic and lofty expression that, together with all its other marks, issues in a power and vigor not found in prose. Concepts that could be expressed in perhaps more straightforward fashion in prose take on life and power and grip the heart and imagination in Hebrew poetry in a way not possible in prose. Ps 23 could perhaps be summarized in prose as follows: "Yahweh cares for my basic physical and spiritual needs, leads and is present with me even in threat of death, vindicates my trust in him and promises unending relationship with him as well." But this would be no match for

> The Lord's my shepherd, I'll not want.
>> He makes me down to lie
> In pastures green; he leadeth me
>> The quiet waters by.
>>> James Leith Bain
>>> From the *Scottish Psalter*, 1650

D. Poetry and the Interpretation of the Psalms

As a matter of fact, there is much more to be reckoned with here than mere power or beauty of expression, though that surely meets us in these sacred poems. Judging from the poetic form of major oracles in the classical prophets, poetry was considered in some sense the language of God. When prophets spoke for him, they often spoke poetically, not just in direct words from Yahweh but also in sermons and reflections of their own upon Yahweh's word. To find prayer and liturgical celebration couched in poetry, as the language of intercourse with God, does not surprise us. The very literary form calls the reader to reverent attention, to openness to the voice of God.

Paradoxically the interpretation of the Psalms and other poetry calls for both caution and creativity. On the one hand, the interpreter must take care not to overanalyze features of the works rising more from the artistry of the poet than the logic of precise reasoning. One thinks here of the demands of the acrostic progression or of the A-B words here, to say nothing of the susceptibility of symbol to overanalysis. On the other hand, little if any in these poems should simply be attributed to "poetic license." The very ambiguity of symbols, for example, is not only their danger but their power. Symbols intentionally invite reflection. They are purposefully open to imaginative exploration that leads the listener-reader to a whole new world of insight, as the core image is stretched and turned in meditation upon it.

E. Some Implications of Biblical Poetry as a Mode of Revelation

First, consider Biblical poetry and theological reflection. The fact that God has chosen to reveal himself, among other ways, through the vehicle of poetic literature in both the OT and NT bears reflection. Not only *what* God says, but *how* he says it instructs us. For one thing, from God's revelation of himself in poetic form we can affirm his appreciation of beauty, for poetry (including biblical poetry) is art. Although there are numerous passages where the biblical poets use the various devices of poetry in themselves to signal or enhance meaning, e.g., marking the beginning and ends of passages and tying lines together, at many other points no semantic motivation for the poetic turn *appears to be* present. It is simply part of the art and beauty of the form. Why did the poet say it that way? Because of the beauty of the expression. Surely God can understand our attempts to be beautiful and to produce beauty in our work and world. Ugliness and distortion are sin's scars in this world, not the will of God. We reflect his person in this quest.

Second, from God's revelation of himself in poetic form, we can affirm God's desire to hallow both our intellect and our emotions for his use. Poetry expresses both emotion and intellect, inseparably combined in the production of powerful communication. The beauty, imagery, and balance tap the deep psyche of God's people in a way that simple theological essay would rarely do. Yet the psalms are not mere sentimental drivel or emotional effusion. Profound theology, often elaborately structured in intricately crafted poems betrays intellectual breadth and depth as well as strong feeling. False choices between a "warm heart" and a "clear mind" do not find support in these psalms or in God's very mode of revelation in them. God made both the head and the heart and relishes the opportunity to sanctify them for his use. The psalmist affirms God had made his "inmost being" (KJV "kidneys," 139:13), the location of feelings, internal sensitivities in ancient physiology. The Wesleyan Revival in eighteenth-century England illustrates this well, for it was not John Wesley's analytical, orderly sermons alone that spread the flame of renewal and the call to Christian perfection across the British Isles. Without Charles Wesley's hymns, passionately but intelligently touching the hearts of England, one may wonder how far the effort would have gone. The movement joined the head and the heart of the Wesleys. God calls us by this mode of revelation to surrender our whole being to him for his service.

Third, from God's use of Hebrew poetry in revelation we can affirm God's willingness to redeem all cultures and art forms by filling them with his Word. Of course, strictly speaking, we cannot speak of what God wishes to do with *all* cultures and art forms based solely on his use of this one. But we can infer his openness to do so with some art forms we might have considered "out of reach" to him or too depraved for his use. What we have called "Hebrew" poetry should more accurately be called "Northwest Semitic" or "Canaanite" poetry. The canons of Hebrew poetry (see A, B, and C above) are the same as those found in other Canaanite poetry, indeed in poetry pressed into the service of debauched idolatry. Our most extensive exposure to this larger body of Canaanite poetry has come from the city of Ugarit, where copious poetic epics predating David's time and telling of the gods El, Baal, Yamm (Sea), Mot (Death), and goddesses Anat, Shapshu (Lady Sun), and others have been found. Other poetic worship literature devoted to the Canaanite high gods is known from there as well. Considering the virulent rejection of that culture's faith and its depraved manifestations, one marvels at the Lord's appropriation of this very art form with all its disreputable associations to express himself. The move is analogous to the appropriation of "off-limits" music forms by the church from earliest times (again like Wesley's use of "pub music"). But there is more than mere "appropriation" involved. The art forms and the slice of culture they represent are not only appropriated, but redeemed; not simply neutralized, but pressed into the holy service of God. This feature of God's ways of revelation calls for artists among people of God to unleash their creativity in both redeeming and creating art forms to the glory of God.

III. THE SUPERSCRIPTIONS

Only thirty-four psalms lack editorial notation at the beginning. The precise meaning of many of these superscriptions appears already to have been a mystery to the LXX translators. The notations apparently relate to such matters as authorship, archival care, musical notation, and historical setting, though at almost every turn the precise meaning is difficult to ascertain and at some points only an educated guess can be made.

"Editorial" notation does not here mean "peripheral" or "incidental" to the main body of the Psalter, as the total omission of the superscriptions in the NEB implies. Rather these notes, thoughtfully added by the believing community in the course of the gathering and editing of the Psalms, now provide the canonical context in which the poems are to be read, individually and collectively. The role they play in understanding the Psalter as a whole is just beginning to be understood. On their significance see also V and VI below.

A. Authorship and Archive Tag

The notation *ldwyd* (*ləḏāwîḏ*) appears on seventy-three psalms (3–9, 11–32, 34–41, 51–65, 68–70, 86, 101, 103, 108–10, 122, 124, 131, 133, and 138–45)! Linked in some cases with specific situations from the life of David, they obviously intend now to convey authorship. 2Ch 29:30 already understands them this way. The NT reflects this view (Mt 22:44; Mk 12:36; Lk 20:42–43; Ac 2:25–35), as do translations ancient and modern: "a psalm/miktam of David." Other psalms are similarly connected to Asaph (50, 73–83), the "sons" of Korah (42, 44–49; 84–85; 87–88), Solomon (72, 127), Moses (90), Ethan (89), and perhaps Heman (88) and Jeduthun (39, 62, 77).

The preposition (*l-*) used with the proper name in all of these notations has many meanings, including "to," "for," "from," "about," and "by (in the sense of authorship)." The common superscription, "to/for the director of music," apparently uses this preposition (*l-mnṣḥ*) to assign archival responsibility. The closest *literary* parallel to these *l*-noun notations is found in the tablets from Ugarit, the coastal city destroyed about 1250 B.C. whose written remains have shed significant light on Canaanite and Israelite culture. There, tablets recording mythological and epic poems carry similar superscriptions, *lbʿl* and *lkrt*. In these cases the notation seems to designate either the content of the tablets—"about Baal" or "about Keret" or perhaps an archival-literary location, "belonging to the Baal/Keret cycle"—not authorship.

Thus the original meaning of these notations is open to question. David, famous for his artistic gifts, may well be the author of numerous poems in the Psalms that bear his name and that do not. But most of what we know of authorship of temple literature in the ancient Near East would lead us not to expect single authorship. It is possible that no single explanation will cover them all. Some "Davidic" poems, for example, may originally have been composed not "by David" but "for David" or "for the Davidic (King)." Whatever their original sense, they stand now as authorship notes in light of which the poems are to be read. It is possible that at this point the Hebrew hymnic tradition differs from its Ugaritic (and Akkadian as well) counterparts. The use the final editors of the Psalter have made of these tags and other features of the superscriptions, using them to group materials and to define seams [i.e., boundaries] in collections, even influencing the perspective from which the poems are to be read, is of even greater import than their original meaning.

B. Technical-Musical Notation

Our lack of adequate information about these superscriptions is particularly obvious in what appear to be the technical and musical notations. Already obscure to the LXX translators, they are sometimes simply transliterated (as opposed to being translated) in the KJV and ASV. Even so, some contours of meaning seem likely. Some notes appear to designate tunes, some instrumentation, some technical musical or liturgical information. Nearly all of the interpretations given here must be tentative.

Tunes. Although the structure and nature of Canaanite/Israelite music is not know to us, the following appear to name known tunes, songs (cf. 137:3), or cantilation patterns according to which a given poem would be sung: *'ayyelet haššaḥar,* "The Doe of the Dawn" (Ps 22); *'al-tašḥēt,* "Do Not Destroy" (Pss 57, 58, 59, 75), perhaps a reference to the promise in Isa 65:8; *ḥagittît,* "The Gittite [Tune]" or "The Winepress" (Pss 8, 81, 84); *yônat 'ēlim rᵉḥōqîm,* "The Dove of the Distant Terebinth Trees" (Ps 56); *mût labbēn,* "Death for the Son" (Ps 9, perhaps Ps 46); *šōšannîm,* "Lilies" (Pss 45, 69); *šûšan 'ēdût* and *šōšannîm 'ēdût,* "Shushan/Lillies—A Testimony" (?) (Pss 60, 80).

Technical Notation. Some expressions appear to designate instrumentation ("musical instruments," e.g., Am 6:5): *binᵉgînôt,* "with stringed accompaniment" (Pss 4, 6, 54, 55, 61, 67, 76); *'el-hannᵉḥîlôt,* "for flute" (Ps 5); *'al-haššᵉmînît,* "for the eight-stringed (instrument)" (Pss 6, 12); *'al-šōšannîm* and *'al-šûšān* may refer to six-sided or six-stringed instrumentation (Pss 45, 69, and 60, 80, respectively); *'al-māḥᵃlat,* perhaps related to flute or dance (Ps 53, 88). "Selah" clearly gives some technical musical or more likely liturgical direction, perhaps for an interlude, or for repetition, or for a posture like bowing.

C. Use

Eight notations in the superscriptions seem to designate the use for the song or the occasion for its use or composition. These are usually infinitives naming an act, or nouns naming an occasion. Their precise meanings elude us. Ps 38 and 70 carry in their superscriptions an infinitive meaning "to call to remembrance, to cause to remember, to make a memorial offering." Ps 88 has in its superscription an infinitive meaning "to call to remembrance, to cause to remember, to make a memorial offering." Ps 88 has in its superscription an infinitive most likely meaning "for singing," as the word is used in Ex 15:21, but which could also mean "for responding," even "to afflict." Ps 60 is designated "for teaching" or "for instruction," Ps 100 "for giving thanks," or "for the thank offering." Ps 30 is for "the dedication of 'the house'" (NIV "temple" or, perhaps, the palace), Ps 92 for the "sabbath Day." Judging by its content, Ps 45 is not simply a "love song," but a "wedding song." Pss 120–34 are commonly known as "songs of Ascents" from the notation they all carry (with slight variation in Ps 121), *šîr hamma'ᵃlôt,* having somehow to do with "going up." The *ma'ᵃlôt* should most likely be linked either with the steps of the temple gates (Eze 40:6, 22), vestibule (Eze 40:49), or altar (Eze 43:17) or with the act of pilgrimage (cf. e.g., Pss 24:3; 122:4), particularly its final stage of procession into the temple. These then would be "procession songs" or "pilgrimage songs."

D. Setting

Fourteen psalms carry notes giving, for the most part, specific historical information setting the context in which the psalms are to be understood. In some cases the event noted is not known from the OT, as in Ps 7, or is a general situation, as in Ps 102. In most cases the contexts called to mind reflect other OT texts as follows:

Ps	3	2Sa 15:1–18:33—Flight from Absalom
Ps	18	e.g., 1Sa 19:1ff.; 24:1ff.; 26:1ff.; 2Sa 5:17ff.; 8:1ff.; 10:1ff.—Deliverance from enemies like Saul
Ps	34	1Sa 21:10ff. (Psalms have Abimelech; 1 Sa has Achish)—Expulsion by Abimelech
Ps	51	2Sa 11:1ff.—Confrontation by Nathan
Ps	52	1Sa 22:6ff.—Betrayal to Saul by Doeg
Ps	54	1Sa 23:14ff.—Betrayal to Saul by the Ziphites
Ps	56	1Sa 21:10ff.; 22:1ff.; 27:1ff.—Capture by Philistines
Ps	57	1Sa 24:1ff.—Hiding in a cave from Saul
Ps	59	1Sa 19:8ff.—Surveillance by Saul
Ps	60	2Sa 8:3ff.; 10:15ff.—Battle against Aram Naharaim
Ps	63	e.g., 1Sa 22:1ff.; 24:1ff.—In the Judean desert
Ps	142	e.g., 1Sa 22:1ff.; 24:1ff.—Hiding in a cave

Just which of these were actually penned by the composer of the psalms in question and which have been provided as commentary on the psalms we can no longer determine with certainty. Evidence from the LXX and the Targums suggests these and other parts of the superscriptions either (1) continued to be added as the OT text was copied and edited or (2) differed in the different textual traditions behind these translations.

Whatever their origin, these "historical" notes along with other information in the superscriptions now stand every bit as much a part of the canonical text as the poems themselves. In many cases the content of the psalm itself, though compatible with the historical setting given, would not necessarily suggest the event noted more than any other similar situation. The classic penitential prayer, Ps 51, for example, has no marks demanding association with David's sins with Bathsheba and his response to Nathan, though of course it is eminently appropriate to that terrible set of events. Nevertheless, the poem must now be read in that context, a frame of reference that influences, indeed enhances, the reader-prayer's understanding of the poem.

E. Classifications

Several terms in the superscriptions seem to designate either psalm types or collections or both. The *mizmôr*, "psalm," is the most common designation for these works, appearing on sixty-one songs (e.g., 3–6), including five that also carry the designation *šîr*. The LXX translation with *psalmos* reflects the understanding that these songs are to be sung to the accompaniment of stringed instruments. This may well preserve an important distinctive of the *mizmôr*, since the verb to which the name is related deals especially with singing accompanied by musical instruments.

The *šîr*, "song," names the next most common psalm type in the Psalter (e.g., 65–68). Frequently used with *mizmôr*, (e.g., 66 and 75) to describe a psalm, the differentiation between the two escapes us. Combined classifications like the "Song of Zion" (137:2), "Song of Ascents" (120–34), and "Song of the Temple of Yahweh" (1Ch 6:31 [MT v.16]), which focus on acts or places of worship, could indicate the *šîr* specifically as a "cultic (temple) song" (Kraus, 21–22).

The *miktām* (16; 56–60). This word's meaning is obscure. The earliest versions connected the title with inscription, perhaps connecting this song type to related written artifacts in the temple or in the liturgy. All are Davidic songs related to the need for deliverance.

The *maśkîl* has generally been connected with didactic or wisdom categories due to the related verb's meaning of being and acting prudently or skillfully. The contents of the thirteen poems thus designated do not seem to support this view (32, 42, 44, 45, 52–55, 74, 78, 88, 89, 142). 2Ch 30:21–22 adds the concept of art to intellect in this term and perhaps points to the nuance "art song" (Kraus, 25–26).

The *šiggāyôn* (Ps 7) is most likely a lamentation or similar stirring song form, judging from the content of this psalm and the word families to which the name can be related.

The *tᵉpillâh*, "prayer song," is the most common type of psalm found in the Psalter. It dominates Books 1 and 2, which still close with the note, "The 'prayer songs' of David son of Jesse are ended" (72:20). Psalms 17, 86, 90, 102, and 142 carry superscriptions that indicate that they are prayer psalms. In addition Ps 72:20 applies this name to an entire collection of "prayers of David" now incorporated in Book 2 of the Psalter (Pss 42–72). In this more general sense, *tᵉpillâh* better than any other description found in the Psalter describes the majority of psalms that are first and foremost "prayers."

The word *t'hillâh*, "praise song" or "hymn," belongs to the word family known in the nearly universal loan-word *hallelujah*. An unusual plural form of this designation came to be used by the Hebrew- and Aramaic-speaking traditions as the title for the entire Psalter (See I.A).

IV. RECENT STUDY OF THE PSALTER AND PSALM TYPES

A. Recent Study of the Psalter

Two European scholars, Hermann Gunkel and Sigmund Mowinckel, writing mainly in the first three decades of this century, have exercised dominant influence on modern study of the Psalms. Gunkel pioneered the method of "form criticism" in the study of the Psalms, in numerous separate studies and then in a major commentary (*Die Psalmen übersetzt und erklärt*, published in 1926), along with a later introduction to the Psalms (*Einleitung in die Psalmen*, completed and published in 1933 by his student, J. Begrich, after Gunkel's death). His method has now been applied to virtually the entire Scripture. This approach to the Psalms takes its name from Gunkel's contention that it was possible to discern basic literary types in the Psalms, each having its own form (common inner structure, flow, and treasury of ideas), arising out of and shaped by its own setting in the worship/cultic life of the community. He identified five main psalm types (*Gattungen*) or genres: (1) hymns, (2) communal laments, (3) royal psalms, (4) individual laments, and (5) individual songs of thanksgiving, along with several minor types.

Gunkel emphasized the study of the psalms within the context of the other OT songs and particularly within the literary and cultural context of the ancient Near East, notably Egyptian and Babylonian materials. From such inquiry Gunkel concluded that virtually the entire Psalter had its traditional source in the cult, thus radically altering the traditional understanding of the settings for many psalms. The Davidic psalms of Book 1, for example, were in his judgment individual complaints originally reflecting different specific rites or situations in the cult such as incubation rites, prayers for healing, and exorcism of demons. Psalms that are traditionally taken as messianic Gunkel saw as spoken by and to the king in songs analogous to the royal hymns of Babylon and Egypt and reflecting a view of divine kingship common to those cultures. Gunkel's work in many ways was simply the culmination of earlier critical study of the psalms, but his discernment of distinctive psalm types and the anchor of these types firmly in the temple cult was programmatic for following studies, including eventually those by evangelical and Wesleyan scholars.

Sigmund Mowinckel's work, *The Psalms in Israel's Worship* (Nashville: Abingdon, 1967), appeared in English in the sixties but was first published in six volumes from 1921–24 as *Psalmenstudien*. Mowinckel extended Gunkel's early work by seeking to tie individual psalm types and the present psalms much more specifically to their cultic settings. He sought to reconstruct as fully as possible the liturgical contexts that produced the psalms and in which they were used. Mowinkel concluded that an Israelite autumn New York Festival was the major source of the psalms. Relying heavily on the Babylonian *Akitu* festival, he reconstructed a celebration in which Yahweh died and rose in conquest of the forces of Chaos and was enthroned, confirming his kingship and continuation of the cosmic order for another year. In his *Psalms* (Philadelphia: Westminster, 1962), Artur Weiser extended Gunkel's work much as Mowinckel had done but reconstructed an autumn covenant renewal ceremony rather than a divine enthronement festival.

While later scholars have worked under the influence of these pioneers, findings of Gunkel and Mowinckel have attracted substantial critique and refinement. The failure of the OT to mention explicitly any of the major festivals or cultic events thus reconstructed as exercising pervasive influence on the Psalter and in the life of people has been pressed by persons like Roland de Vaux (*Ancient Israel*, 502–6). Thus many who continue to see significant evidence of cultic influence in the Psalter refrain for lack of clear evidence from detailed reconstruction of the events. Placing the inner theological frame of reference of the OT more clearly over against the assumptions of Israel's Canaanite and larger ancient Near East setting leads others to part company with the "myth and ritual" orientation in Gunkel's and Mowinckel's work and pursued avidly by some of their successors in Psalms research. This commentary shares these critiques.

In addition, even though Gunkel's idea of the psalm types and their common forms seems obvious, once pointed out, further research has demonstrated the difficulty, if not actual inability, of establishing clearly the common literary form alleged for each major type, such as the royal psalms or the hymns. While there are many common rhetorical and structural features among the works grouped under a particular type, there is also considerable variation, stretching the forms many times beyond recognition. And the types themselves prove open to question. The "laments of the individual," for example, turn out in many cases neither to be "laments" nor to be really tied to "individuals" standing apart from the community of Israel (e.g., Ps 130).

One reason for these difficulties is that Gunkel's literary categories derived as much from larger European literary studies as from the Bible itself. The superscriptions of the psalms themselves and other references in them together with their own subject matter should provide the most promising source material for discerning such psalm types, if they exist.

No scholar I am aware of has made more headway than Hans-Joachim Kraus at attempting thus to discern and group psalm types/genres on the basis of *the text's own awareness* of these matters. His work is most accessible to the English reader in the introduction and commentary of *Psalms 1–59*. This volume, a translation of the fifth (1978) edition of volume 1 of his German work is particularly noteworthy. In a radical departure from his stance in the first four editions of that work and in several other of his previous studies, Kraus here works from a thorough-going critique of Gunkel at numerous points (see esp. pp. 38–43). The following presentation of psalm types reflects at many points this work by Kraus (*Psalms 1–59*, 43–62), as do the resulting psalm groups expounded theologically in the commentary below. Numerous psalms are of "mixed types" (e.g., Pss 19 or 66), eluding easy categorization but still much illuminated by the attempt. Still others do not fit easily into any category known yet. These will be located in a type without extended defense, with the awareness that we still have much to learn about such matters and with the attempt to let the text speak for itself in each song, our discernment of its "type" notwithstanding.

B. Psalm Types

Hymns of Praise (the *t°hillâh*). Only Ps 145, is actually designated a "song of praise" in its superscription (cf. III.E above). But numerous other references to the *t°hillâh* in the Psalms and the parallels partly noted above lead to the discernment of the general designation (Kraus, 26, 43–47). The term appears frequently as the name of the songs of praise of individuals (e.g., 22:25; 65:1) and the community (e.g., 33:1; 100:4). The label highlights the distinctive yet general praise orientation of these songs. The "song of praise" can be a synonym for the "thanksgiving" (*tôdâh*) as in 100:4, and can stand in parallel to the "new song" (40:3; 149:1). Other designations also appear for the song of praise, some of them included in the treatment of superscriptions above, for example, the cultic song (*šîr*) or the "psalm" (*mizmôr*). But these are not exclusively used for this song type and seem to call attention to other features of the song than its form and content, such as its accompaniment.

Four major themes find expression in the Psalter's hymns of praise: praise of the Creator (Pss 8, 29, 33, 65, 100, 104, 136, 148); Yahweh, the king (Pss 24, 47, 93, 95–99, 145); and Yahweh's sovereign activity in history (Pss 105, 106, 114, 135, perhaps 136), with several themes sometimes woven together in a single song (Pss 68, 146–48). At times the theme is more generally the praise of God, his glory, or his works (Pss 75, 103, 113, 117, 134, 150).

Prayer Songs (the *t°pillâh*). The prayer song is specifically designated the prayer for deliverance (80:4) and the prayer of intercession (109:4), i.e., prayer for another's deliverance (Kraus, 26–27, 47–56). The song arises from deep distress (102:1; cf. 1Ki 8:38) and is at times uttered in a setting of sackcloth and fasting (35:13). Often (with Gunkel) called lament, these are much more than lament. The worshipers here do not simply complain or bemoan their plight. They declare in faith their distress and cry to God for deliverance. The *t°pillôt* (plural) include prayer songs of the individual and of the people (i.e., community prayer songs, cf. 80:3). Because of the arrangement the book of Psalms achieved in its final editing, the prayer songs, which predominate in number, do not in the end set the tone and overall impression gained from the Psalms.

With regard to themes, some prayer songs are general prayers of distress (Pss 16, 28, 36, 82), but most are not. The majority of the prayer songs of the individual carry the theme of deliverance from accusation and persecution (Pss 3–5, 7, 9–13, 17, 22, 25–27, 31, 35, 42, 43, 54–59, 62–64, 69–71, 86, 94, 109, 120, 139–43). Others concern sickness and healing (Pss 6, 38, 39, 41, 88, 102), inextricably related to the prayer song of the sinner (Pss 40, 51, 130). The "prayers of the people" deal mainly with national defeat or distress and the need for restoration (Pss 14, 44, 53, 60, 74, 79, 80, 83, 85, 90, 126, 129, 137), though other more general concerns appear as well (Pss 123, 125). Several of these prayers cry for deliverance and vindication with such passion that they have come to be known as "imprecatory" psalms (5, 10, 17, 35, 58, 59, 69, 70, 79, 83, 109, 129, 137, 140) in which curses are called down upon the enemy. Prominent in many prayer songs are affirmations of deliverance or of God as deliverer.

Thanksgiving Songs (the *tôdâh*). The Thanksgiving Songs echo the themes from the prayer songs in the course of offering thanksgiving for rescue (Pss 18, 23, 30, 32, 52, 66, 92, 107, 116, 118, 124, 138). On the one hand, they differ from the prayer songs in that the deliverance sought has now come. On the other hand, they differ from the various praise songs in their frequent inclusion of narrative of their plight and deliverance in the thanksgiving and in their thanksgiving for specific deliverance experienced by the worshiper as opposed to praise for the various attributes and historic acts of Yahweh.

Royal Songs (the *maʿăśay lᵉmelek*). The Royal Songs (Pss 2, 20, 21, 45, 61, 72, 89, 101, 110, 132, 144) include works of widely differing character but find their unity in their concern for the king—most likely David and his sons (Kraus, 56–57). The king's relationship to Yahweh and the Davidic covenant, his enthronement, victory in battle, wedding, splendor, righteous rule, longevity, and salvation are important themes in these songs. Changing speakers and form indicate liturgical use for several of these (e.g., 2, 61, 72, 110, 132), though the exact nature of the celebration in which they would have been used is a matter of debate. Included here are songs that have come to be regarded as messianic.

Songs of Zion (the *šîr ṣiyyôn*). Even the Babylonians knew of the "songs of Zion" (137:3), of which at least six have survived in the Psalter (Pss 46, 48, 76, 84, 87, 122; Kraus, 58). Extolling Zion—her beauty, election, and sanctuary—the worshiper sang these songs, among other times, when entering the sanctuary after pilgrimage (Pss 84, 122).

Didactic Songs (the *ḥokmâh*). The "Didactic Songs" may be a variety of prayer song and praise song, using the language and thoughts of Israel's instructional heritage, more than an independent psalm type (Kraus, 58–60). Often called wisdom psalms, two traditions in Israel's life find expression here, the teachings of the wise and instruction from and in Yahweh's law. One is familiar to us from Proverbs, Ecclesiastes, and Job. The other expresses instruction associated first with the priesthood (Mal

2:1–9). Ps 1, a classic "wisdom psalm" focused in the blessings of Torah meditation, illustrates the merging of these two in what has come to be known as "Torah piety." ("Torah" here means not simply the Law of Moses, but sacred instruction in general grounded in that law.) Thus these songs address the congregation in an instructional mode, some explicitly (e.g., 34:11, 78:1–2) and others implicitly (e.g., Pss 15 or 37). We take Pss 1, 15, 34, 37, 49, 73, 78, 111, 112, 119, 127, 128, and perhaps 92, as didactic songs.

Festival Songs and Liturgical Pieces (Pss 50, 81, 115, 121, 131, 133). Not surprisingly we are unable with any confidence to categorize several psalms (no doubt including some we have confidently labeled!). *If* they constitute a grouping of their own, the indigenous name for it eludes the modern reader. Pss 121, 131, and 133 are all Songs of Ascent, but not the others. In some cases they relate obviously to a specific festival, such as the New Moon (Ps 81). The connection of the others is vague. Pss 50 and 81 appear to provide settings for delivering divine oracles. Pss 121, 131, and 133 are (perhaps benedictory) affirmations, with no obvious liturgical setting. Ps 115 could perhaps be located in the praise songs but looks more like a liturgy of affirmation and response.

C. Psalm Types and Judeo-Christian Prayer and Song

These psalms are both songs and, in almost every case, prayers. They correct skewed or overly narrow understandings of prayer that equate "prayer" with "petition" or some other specific feature of communication with God. Prayer in the Psalter is obviously much larger than "merely" asking God for help or praising God. It includes, of course, cries for help. But prayer also includes affirmation of faith, confession of sin and need, promise of action and attitude, and thoughtful reflection on inner and outer life in the fear of the Lord. Prayer includes instruction and liturgy, wisdom and celebration, and much more.

And these are also song. Again the Psalter stands over against overly confined understandings of "sacred song." The music of the saints here includes songs focused solely on God, his person and his works, and, just as readily, solely on the biography of the people of God, their walk with him, and their life in the world before him. Others flow effortlessly between these poles, oblivious of modern predilections for "objective" or "subjective" music. The genius of Charles Wesley's hymns in good measure was their ability to reflect this great breadth of prayer and song in the idiom of the people.

V. THE PSALTER AS A COLLECTION: DEVELOPMENT AND DESIGN

A. Development

The amazing work we call "The Book of Psalms" represents the product of a long and complex process of inspiration, worship, composition, collection, and editing, a process of which we are poorly informed. Some clues do surface in the anthology, but many questions remain.

For instance, the present compilation clearly incorporates earlier smaller collections. Four collections of psalms of David, which may originally have been a single "Davidic psalter," presently stand in the Psalter: Pss 3–41 (possibly excluding Ps 33), the major Davidic psalter, along with Pss 51–70 (excluding 66–67), Pss 108–10, and 136–45. Only seven Davidic psalms stand outside these groups (Pss 86, 101, 103, 122, 124, 131, 133). Ps 72:20 reads, "This concludes the prayers of David son of Jesse," and shows awareness of such Davidic collections, calling these psalms "prayers."

Two collections of the psalms of Korah appear, Pss 42–49 (perhaps except Ps 43) and 84–88 (excluding Ps 86). The psalms of Asaph now stand as Pss 73–83. Beyond these collections grouped by authorship or archival attribution, the Songs of Ascent (Pss 120–34) form an obvious set, apparently related to pilgrimage or procession. Finally two Hallel collections, the "Egyptian Hallel" (Pss 113–18), traditionally associated with Passover observance, and Pss 146–50 take their name from the exhortation "Hallelujah," i.e., "Praise Yahweh," which figures prominently in both. This rubric opens or closes Pss 113–18 (excluding Ps 114), and *both* opens and closes the final five songs of the psalter.

These smaller collections along with other psalms are now compiled in five "books": Book 1, 1–41; Book 2, 42–72; Book 3, 73–89; Book 4, 90—106; and Book 5, 107–50. Books 1–4 each conclude with a doxology, 41:13 (MT v.14); 72:19; 89:52 (MT v.53); and 106:48, e.g.,

> Praise be to the LORD, the God of Israel,
>   from everlasting to everlasting.
> Let all the people say, "Amen!"
>
> (106:48)

The final Hallel forms the climactic doxology for Book 5 and the entire collection.

Repeated psalms and psalms composed by combining other works in the Psalter give additional clues to the growth of the Psalter. Ps 14 is nearly identical to Ps 53, except Ps 53 has been edited to increase the use of the divine name Elohim and reduce the occurrence of the name Yahweh. Ps 40:13–17 appears again as Ps 70. Pss 57:7–11 and 60:5–12 are combined to produce Ps 108. In these cases originally independent psalms found their way into collections now joined in the Psalter, and/or material from previous collections has been edited for inclusion in still another.

Perhaps the most striking evidence of editorial activity in the Psalms is the thoroughgoing revision of Pss 42–83 to reduce use of the divine name Yahweh, replacing it with Elohim, as noted regarding Pss 14 and 53 above. In Book 1 the name Yahweh occurs 272 times and Elohim 15 times (standing alone). In Books 4 and 5 again the name Yahweh predominates. But Pss 41–72 and 73–83 show just the reverse preference, with occurrences of Elohim outnumbering Yahweh 200 to 43, or 5 to 1! These data suggest the deliberate formation of an "Elohistic psalter," perhaps edited in a period when public or perhaps even private use of the name Yahweh was unacceptable, or where Elohim was at least preferred (cf. Chronicles). Such a revision, it seems, would have followed the gathering of Davidic psalms (51–65, 68–70) and those of Korah (42–49) and Asaph (50, 73–83) but may have preceded the formation of Books 2 and 3 whose boundary that revision now spans. There is obviously much concerning all this and the rest of the process about which we simply do not have adequate information. At some point the materials were given their final shape, with the whole collection given the design we now have before us.

B. Design

Does the book of Psalms have a "design"? Until recently scholars despaired of discerning the editorial design of the Psalter, if indeed it was arranged according to a plan. The repeated suggestion that the five "books" of the Psalter were intended to correlate with or somehow reflect the five books of Moses simply fails for lack of convincing evidence and the need to force what evidence there is to fit the desired patterns. The designation of the Psalter as "Israel's Hymnbook" conjured the idea of a work from which one picks and chooses, without much thought to overall design.

Recent Psalms research has called attention to two phenomena that hold promise for answering the puzzle. First, the introduction (Ps 1) and centerpiece (Ps 119) of the Psalms transform the entire work into a resource for individual piety, specifically "Torah piety" (Mays, 4, 12). Placed without superscription at the outset, Ps 1 places the following psalms in the category of Torah in which the righteous person delights and meditates day and night (1:2). By this a person is distinguished from the ungodly and opens the door to the blessing of Yahweh 1:1, 3–6). By its sheer size and unusual design, Ps 119 stands as the pillar of the collection, dominating especially the concluding books. It gathers from a wide spectrum of previous biblical teaching forms and sources and presses them all into the service of a prayer for the salvation of the one who loves and lives Torah, not just the Law of Moses, but all the "way of the LORD." So the psalms as we have them are not simply songs to be sung or recited in worship, though they have continued to be that in both the synagogue and in early Christian worship (Mk 14:26; Eph 5:19; Col 3:16). They are profound resources of prayer, meditation, and reflection on the full set of agendas raised by the Psalter regarding the Lord, his will, his world, and his people.

This transformation of the Psalms from a collection of liturgical pieces to a Torah anthology correlates well with the omission of extensive liturgical notes from these poems. Regardless of the source of scattered individual poems, the psalms have obviously come to us through the worshiping community by way of the temple archives (note "For the director of music" on 55 psalms). That we have the few remnants of that liturgical history catalogued in the superscriptions above (See II.A–D) is not remarkable. That we do not have more is the striking thing, as is the fact that what remains has been transmitted in ways totally useless for liturgical direction, already obscure to the translators of the LXX, Jews living centuries before Christ. Such an introduction, centerpiece, and editing policy hint at design.

Second, Gerald Wilson (*The Editing of the Hebrew Psalter,* particularly 139–228) has, in this writer's opinion, demonstrated that the final editors of the Psalter used the superscriptions, especially the author and genre notation (as well as the lack of superscription) together with thematic considerations, to group materials according to an overall editorial plan. In addition to the fact that the whole corpus is put before the reader as a resource of Torah piety with its introductory frame and pillar, the editors have tackled the OT community's most staggering question and provided an answer applicable to all persons of all times, "Our God reigns!"

The theological problem driving the Psalter's design appears to be kingship, the issue raised by Ps 2. In fact, it is possible that Ps 2 should be thought of as linked with Ps 1 as part of the introduction (Pss 1 and 2 both seem to be set apart from Book 1 by lack of superscription and are perhaps intended to be at least loosely tied together by the inclusio of blessing, 1:1; 2:11.) The Psalter's first unit, after Ps 1, opens with the "proclamation of [Yahweh's] special covenant with his king in Ps 2" and closes with "David's assurance of God's continued preservation in the presence of [Yahweh]" (Wilson, 210), a theme extended through Book 2. Book 3 with its startling conclusion (Ps 89) turns to the crushing problem inherent in the history of Israel's kingship—the failure of the eternal covenant with David.

> You have rejected . . .
> You have been very angry with your anointed one.
> You have renounced the covenant with your servant . . .
> You have broken through all his walls . . .
> You have exalted the right hand of his foes . . .
> You have turned back the edge of his sword . . .
> You have put an end to his splendor . . .
> (89:38–40, 42–44)

To this staggering loss and agony of the Exile and Restoration communities, Books 4 and 5 give answer. Pss 90–106, in Wilson's opinion, "function as the editorial 'center'" of the present Psalter, the heart of the answer to the problem posed in Ps 89 (Wilson, 215). Elaborated throughout Books 4 and 5, these psalms present a four-pronged answer to the Exile and Restoration community's plight: (1) Yahweh's kingship, (2) his ancient and enduring faithfulness to Israel, (3) the faith that he will continue as their refuge now, and (4) the blessing of those who trust

Yahweh (Wilson, 215). Now the Psalter develops the splendor and universal scope of Yahweh's eternal kingship, concluding in a symphony of praise (Pss 145–50) to this One who reigns forever (Ps 146:10). The design of the Psalter was produced by arranging groups of material and juxtaposing individual songs and previous collections with various themes and emphases. Such a work cannot proceed with the precise and economic logic of a theological essay like Romans. But the movement and design appear to be there nevertheless, and they yield to those who "meditate in it day and night."

In it all an astounding transformation has taken place under the inspiration of God's Spirit. In spite of the fact that we often read the Psalter as though we were reading the ancient temple or synagogue's full book of liturgy, it is not so. We have no such documents. We do have words that in many, if not most, cases originated in the cult or passed through the cult. They are prayers, praises, and doxologies—the words of worshipers to their God. But these poems no longer stand in a primarily liturgical collection, a simple anthology of psalms. They are "The Psalms," standing in Scripture as God's holy Word. Indeed, "Israel's words of response to her God have now become the Word of God to Israel"—and to God's people of all times and places (Wilson, 206).

VI. INDEX TO TREATMENT OF PSALMS IN THE COMMENTARY

Psalms	Commentary	Psalms	Commentary
1	VII	21	V
2	V	22	IV
3	II.B	23	IV
4	II.B	24	I.C
5	II.B,D	25	II.B
6	II.E	26	II.B
7	II.B	27	II.B
8	I.B	28	II.A
9	II.B	29	I.B
10	II.B,D	30	IV
11	II.B	31	II.B
12	II.B	32	IV
13	II.B	33	I.B
14	II.C	34	VII
15	VII	35	II.B,D
16	II.A	36	II.A
17	II.B,D	37	VII
18	IV	38	II.E
19	I.B; VII	39	II.E
20	V	40	II.E

Psalms	Commentary	Psalms	Commentary
41	II.E	85	II.C
42	II.B	86	II.B
43	II.B	87	VI
44	II.C	88	II.E
45	V	89	V
46	VI	90	II.C
47	I.C	91	VII
48	VI	92	IV
49	VII	93	I.C
50	III	94	II.B
51	II.E	95	I.C
52	IV	96	I.C
53	II.C	97	I.C
54	II.B	98	I.C
55	II.B	99	I.C
56	II.B	100	I.B
57	II.B	101	V
58	II.B,D	102	II.E
59	II.B,D	103	I.A
60	II.C	104	I.B
61	V	105	I.D
62	II.B	106	I.D
63	II.B	107	IV
64	II.B	108	II.C
65	I.B	109	II.B,D
66	IV	110	V
67	I.A	111	VII
68	I.A	112	VII
69	II.B,D	113	I.A
70	II.B,D	114	I.D
71	II.B	115	I.A.; III
72	V	116	IV
73	VII	117	I.A
74	II.C	118	IV
75	I.A	119	VII
76	VI	120	II.B
77	II.A	121	III
78	I.D; VII	122	VI
79	II.C,D	123	II.A
80	II.C	124	IV
81	III	125	II.A
82	II.A	126	II.C
83	II.C,D	127	VII
84	VI	128	VII

Psalms	Commentary	Psalms	Commentary
129	II.C,D	140	II.B,D
130	II.E	141	II.B
131	III	142	II.B
132	V	143	II.B
133	III	144	V
134	I.A	145	I.C
135	I.D	146	I.A
136	I.B,D	147	I.A
137	II.C,D; VI	148	I.B
138	IV	149	I.A
139	II.B	150	I.A

COMMENTARY

I. THE HYMNS OF PRAISE (the t^ehillâh)

The Hymn of Praise is the psalm par excellence—the celebration of God his mighty works and incomparable character. Though not the most numerous of the psalm types, these hymns so color the impact of the Psalter that they gave the collection its name in the Hebrew tradition, sēp̱er t^ehillîm, "Book of Praise Songs."

A. The General Hymns (Pss 67, 68, 75, 103, 113, 115, 117, 134, 146, 147, 149, 150)

1. The language of praise

"Sing [√šr] to God, sing praise [√zmr] to his name," "extol [√sll] him who rides on the clouds . . . and rejoice [√ʿlṣ]" (68:4). "Praise [√hll] the LORD" and his name (113:1). "Extol [√šbḥ] him" (117:1); "Bless the LORD" (134:2 [NIV "praise"]). "Sing [√ʿnh] to the LORD . . . ; make music to our God" (147:7). "Sing [√šr] to the LORD a new song" (149:1). "Let Israel rejoice" (√śmḥ), "be glad" (√gl, 149:2). "Let

the saints exult" (√ʿlz) and "sing for joy" (√rnn, 149:5)!

Already in the imperatives of these few general hymns the tone emerges that in the end pervades the Psalter. The other thematically focused hymns in many cases carry this distinctive also, leavening the whole anthology. In the providence of the inspiring Spirit, these invitations that once called the people of God to celebrate in his courts now call the reader/listener to join that praise. The transformation from liturgy to canonical Word has liberated the call from time and place and set it free for myriad uses, calling the reader not only to join the song, but prayerfully and continuously to reflect upon it.

These biblical poets press an extensive vocabulary of joy and exultation into service to draw the worshiper to praise, clumsily noted above by the indications of the Hebrew roots (√) used. Many of the finer distinctions simply escape us and are usually lost in translation (note the repeated "sing" and "praise" for different roots). But we know enough to catch the mood.

"Shout for joy" (e.g., 100:1, √*r'*) must have carried intense energy in worship, for it is a word at home as much on the battlefield (e.g., at the wall of Jericho, Jos 6:10) as it is in the house of Yahweh. "Sing" (√*rnn*) is more akin to a ringing cry than simple "singing." "Extol" (√*sll*) seems to command "raising a song." "Sing" or "make music" (√*zmr*) calls for instrumental accompaniment. And so on. Charles Wesley echoes the jubilant spirit of these songs when he writes

> O for a thousand tongues to sing
>   My great Redeemer's praise,
> The glories of my God and King,
>   The triumphs of his grace!

2. The Worshipers

Whom do these invitations and those in the other hymns address? Who is called to praise? In some few striking cases the invitation nearly stands on its own. Ps 19's praise reflections on the revelation of God's glory in the heavens (vv.1–6) and transforming nature of Yahweh's Law (vv.7–10) proceed without explicit referent until v.11. There the reader discovers the referent all along has been Yahweh. Ps 19 has been, and now explicitly becomes, a prayer: "By them ['the ordinances of the LORD,' v.11, and the Law as described before that] is *your* [Yahweh's] servant warned." Ps 93 opens acclaiming the majesty of King Yahweh (v.1), turning to address the LORD directly in v.2, turning away again in v.3, and back to Yahweh for the concluding v.5. Such disjuncture may be due to the liturgical origins of the piece, as we shall see clearly in some other psalms, with various speakers speaking with different referents or different parts of the worshiping congregation in view (cf. Pss 67, 115).

Ps 8 stands alone among the praise songs as addressed entirely directly to Yahweh, a *prayer* of praise, if you will. "O LORD, our Lord, how majestic is your name in all the earth! You have set. . . . You have ordained. . . . You made him. . . . O LORD, our Lord. . . ." From beginning to end the worshiper is faced toward Yahweh with no other person asked to attend and no distracting voice heard.

Some hymns lack specific addressees and are presumably directed to the worshiping congregation, the "assembly of the righteous" of Ps 1: "Come, let us sing for joy to the LORD" (95:1); "Give thanks to the LORD" (105:1); "Praise the LORD" (106:1). But this is not typical. Much more often specific parties are called to praise in these hymns, covering the entire spectrum of possible worshipers.

The heavenly court among whom Yahweh sits enthroned (103:19) is summoned en masse (148:1) and by particular name to worship and render praise to Yahweh: the divine council or heavenly court ("sons of God," 29:1), messengers, i.e., angels, heavenly hosts—the army of God and Yahweh's servants (103:20; 148:2), along with the heavenly bodies—sun, moon, stars, heavens (96:11; 148:3–4).

The cosmic reach of Yahweh's praise finds expression in the common call to all creation to praise the LORD. Parallel to the address to the heavenly creation (i.e., "from the heavens"), praise is evoked in general "from the earth" (148:1, 7) and specifically from all sectors of created earth (148:7–10)— earth (as over against the sea) and the sea (96:11; 98:7), distant shores (97:1), fields (96:12), rivers and mountains (98:8). More than idyllic metaphor is at work here. There is apologetic as well. Faith options in Israel's day judged most of these creatures of Yahweh worthy of divine worship or fear themselves. The Mediterranean was not just "sea" but "Lord Sea." The river was "Judge River." "Lady or Lord Sun" shone by day, and the Divine Moon by night. In the Psalter these "gods of the nations" are themselves the creatures of Yahweh, called to bow in praise to him.

This assumed apologetic implies the warning directly issued elsewhere *not* to trust (or praise) rivals to Yahweh's undivided claim to worship. "Do not put your trust in princes, in mortal men, who cannot save," warns 146:3. Similarly Ps 135:15–18 mocks the gods of the nations, warning of the foolishness of trusting them and exposing the end of those who do. One cannot serve two masters.

The "servants of the LORD" on earth, temple personnel who serve Yahweh night and day there, receive summons as well (113:1; 134:1; 135:1–2). Ps 134 is totally devoted to such a "call to worship," ending in a blessing upon these ministers of the Lord. Ps 135 concludes by embracing the entire worshiping community in its call—lay worshipers ("house of Israel"), Aaronite priests and their assistants, the Levitical priests, i.e., all who "fear" Yahweh (135:19–20). These songs call those known by their character to praise: all the devout, "the saints" (149:1–2), and the righteous (33:1; 97:12). Zion, Yahweh's city, and her people (117:1; 146:10; 147:12; 149:2), even her city gates and temple doors (24:7) hear the call to rejoice in their King.

But the horizon of the call to praise does not stop at the people of God. In a movement stamped on the Psalter as it now stands, the collection proclaims the possibility, indeed the necessity of the universal praise of Yahweh. All the earth (96:1; 97:1; 98:4; 100:1); all peoples (117:1) great and small, young and old, male and female (148:11–12); all nations (47:1; 117:1) and

people (96:7) receive the invitation to full participation in the worship of Yahweh. God's judgment of the nations here and now (68:23–30) and the participation of his saints in that warfare (149:6–9) are not abandoned. But the vision here transcends the vision of nations beaten into submission. Joyful, glad service of Yahweh by all the earth, knowledge of his works and character, identification with his people, and appreciation for (and apparent acceptance of) his covenant faithfulness appear in Ps 100!

Twice the direction of address is interior, a self-reflective call to praise.

"Praise the LORD, *O my soul;*
  all my inmost being, praise his holy
    name."
      (103:1; cf. 103:22; 104:1, 35)

The worshiper and now the one meditating on Yahweh's Torah are led to lift praise to Yahweh, who is active in their lives (103:1–4). But even though the call here is interior, self-referential, the hymns themselves focus on Yahweh and his works, not on the worshiper. In fact, couched within the inclusio of Ps 103's "Praise the LORD, O my soul" is perhaps the most expansive invitation in the entire Psalter:

Praise the LORD, all his works
  everywhere in his dominion.
      (103:22)

This anticipates the climactic note with which the entire collection ends— "Let everything that has breath praise the LORD" (150:6)! Out of such a stance the promise to Abraham has chance of fulfillment, "All peoples on earth will be blessed through you" (Ge 12:3). In the framework of this invitation, the command of our Lord to "make disciples of all nations" (Mt 28:19) and John Wesley's "world-parish" spirit are certainly at home.

3. Reasons for praise

Why praise the Lord? A distinctive feature of many of the hymns of praise is the implicit and explicit substantiation of the call to praise by specific reason(s) that prompt the praise. At this point one can often distinguish the various hymn types, because the bases for the praise provide the more specific themes of the various types—Yahweh as Creator and Deliverer, Yahweh as King, harvest and Yahweh's sovereign activity in history. Nor are these reasons incidental to old covenant faith. They account for the vitality of praise generated in the psalms. Amorphous awareness of some vague transcendental force or mysterious being could never produce the resounding songs found here. The psalmists' faith in the living God of Abraham and Jacob, Creator, Redeemer, Covenant Maker, and much more, and their encounter with the God of the Exodus, Conquest, Davidic dynasty, Exile and Restoration, and the present generate dynamic, focused praise grounded in life.

4. Themes of praise

The general hymns of praise extol less specifically the exalted, incomparable greatness of the LORD (113:2–6; 150:2), his mighty deeds (150:2), and his marvelous rescue for the needy (113:7–9). Or Yahweh's covenant love and faithfulness (117:2) find praise without elaboration. In Ps 134 the call to praise stands entirely on its own—with no justification, for the praise of God is its own justification and needs no stated reason in the hearts of the saints. Beside Yahweh, the blind, mute, impotent idols are disdained, as those who trust in them are to be pitied (115:3–8).

In several general hymns the themes particularly emphasized elsewhere are intertwined. Ps 103 extols Yahweh for the psalmist's own rescue from ravages of sin and disease (perhaps linked) to satisfying vigor (103:1–5). But the psalmist's experience is simply a particular example of Yahweh's compassionate and forgiving deliverance known in the community's entire history, the second topic of praise (103:6–18). Historic covenant grace to frail human beings extends still to all who keep Yahweh's commandments (103:15–18). The song climaxes in praise of King Yahweh, urging praise from all his realm (103:19–22). Ps 146 follows its warning against trusting mortal humans who cannot save (vv.3–4) with blessing upon the one "whose help is the God of Jacob" (v.5). The following description of this "God of Jacob" then is the implied basis for his praise, setting him forth as "Maker of heaven and earth, the sea, and everything in them"; as faithful upholder of the oppressed, and as King forever— "Praise the LORD" (146:6–10). In Ps 147 the LORD's building, gathering, healing work in the restoration community (vv. 2–3); his amazing wisdom and sustenance of the lowly (vv.4–5); his provision of food through the creation (vv.7–9); his protection of Zion (vv. 12–14); his manifestation by command in wind and storm (vv.15–18); and, finally and emphatically in climax, the unique disclosure of his word to Israel (vv. 19–20) all expound the exclamation in 147:1:

> How good it is to sing praises
> to our God,
> how pleasant and fitting to
> praise him!

Placed primarily together as they are at the conclusion of the Psalter (Pss 146; 147; 148), these eclectic pieces draw together major motifs from all over the collection, binding them together as with a multicolored cord placed around a treasure and picking up its own hues.

5. Liturgy of Praise

Even though the saints God inspired to edit and arrange the Psalter have left the work without sufficient, specific liturgical direction to serve as the church's book of worship (see introduction, section V), evidence abounds in these songs of their pre-Scriptural cultic use.

Pss 67 and 115, included in this treatment of "general hymns," could well have stood by themselves as "liturgical hymns," for they seem so obviously to have functioned not merely as hymns in a liturgy but as praise liturgies themselves. In each case the frequently changing referent in the addresses and highly mixed form give the surest clues to their liturgical function. Ps 67 begins with invocation with purpose (vv.1–2), moves to indirect call to praise (vv.3–5), and concludes with an affirmation of blessing and call to reverence (6–7). Ps 115 opens with an ascription of praise (v.1) and then moves to affirmation of God's sovereign superiority to idols (vv.2–8), basing an antiphonal call to "trust in the LORD" and affirmation of help on that superiority (vv.9–11). Vv.12–13 affirm the LORD's mindful blessing, poetically balancing the preceding section's call to trust. An invocation of blessing and "increase" follows (vv.14–15), with a concluding instruction and affirmation of praise (vv.16–18).

At the very least, worship at the Jerusalem temple before and after the Exile finds expression at many points, even when the use of the specific psalm in question cannot be discerned. And while the editors apparently did not intend that users of the Psalter should recreate the worship of the Jerusalem temple, they left numerous clues by which we may enter the spirit and atmosphere of that worship.

At no place are these points of entrance clearer than in these hymns of praise and in passages that echo them. As the Psalter stands, the reader concludes this work by entry into a jubilant worship procession of singers and dancers. They do not simply accompany praise to the LORD with their instruments. Rather, the very playing of their instrument and the very movement of their dance *is* their praise to Yahweh (150:3–5). Not sufficient to refer generally to "musical instruments" (Am 6:5), this song (Ps 150) calls the pieces of the "orchestra" by name, enlisting their use in praise: trumpet (the "shophar" or ram's horn, v.3; cf. 81:3; 98:6), harp (v.3; cf. 57:8; 92:3; 81:2; 98:5; sometimes a "ten-stringed" harp is specified, 33:1), lyre or harp (v.3; cf. 33:2; 43:4; 49:5; 71:22; 81:2; 147:7; 149:3), tambourine (v.4; cf. 81:2; 149:3), strings (v.4; cf. 45:8), flute (v.4), and two kinds of cymbals (differing in size or volume? v.5). In spite of the fact that the readers do not know how or where these instruments are to be placed or what specific "notes" are to be played, the sights and sounds of a sanctuary full of instruments and musicians rise in persons' minds, drawing them into the sanctuary. Movement of dance (149:3; 150:4) and lifting of the hands (134:2) in praise appear in the picture. Ps 30 shows the dominant association of these sights and sounds with praise and jubilation by contrasting them with sackcloth and wailing (30:11).

> You turned my wailing into dancing;
> you removed my sackcloth and
> clothed me with joy.

Elsewhere we hear of a grand procession of King Yahweh approaching the temple (68:24–27), with details from the route to the sanctuary to supplement the picture of Ps 150 taken inside its gates. Ps 24 places us right at the walls of the city and/or the temple gates, with the worshipers inquiring in an entrance liturgy (24:3, 7, 9).

B. Hymns in Praise of the Creator (Pss 8, 19, 29, 33, 65, 100, 104, 136, 148)

These powerful songs either logically ground their call to praise God significantly in his role as Creator (8, 33, 136, 148) or are praise reflections on creation itself (19, 29, 65). These latter songs do not explicitly designate God as "Creator" or "Maker," but assume his role as Creator in their celebration of his sovereignty over creation. The Creator/creation theme finds important though more abbreviated expression in other psalms also, such as Pss 24, 50, 95, 135, 146, and 147. Judging from these hymns, no other feature of Israel's faith was more foundational than its trust in Yahweh God as Creator of all that is. Understanding of Yahweh's very deity builds from here:

Know that the LORD is God.
It is he who made us. (100:3)

Thus a startling range of claims about God cluster around faith in Yahweh as Creator, either directly linked as faith correlates or closely associated by context. Strike this plank from Israel's faith, and biblical faith exists no more.

Confidence in Yahweh as King of the universe (29:10; 104:2–4), superior to all other "gods" (136:2-3; cf. 95:3–5) rests in Israel's awareness that he is Creator. Sometimes the Creator's royalty is plainly claimed as in Ps 29's celebration of Yahweh of the Storm:

The LORD sits enthroned over
the flood;

the LORD is enthroned as King
forever (29:10).

This explicit link between God as Creator and God as King finds repeated, explicit praise in several songs where creation thought is subordinate to other themes, as in Ps 95:2–5:

Let us come before him [the LORD]
with thanksgiving
and extol him with music
and song.
For the LORD is *the great God,*
the great King above all gods.
In his hand are the depths of
the earth,
and the mountain peaks belong
to him.
The sea is his, *for he made it,*
and his hands formed the dry land.
(italics mine)

See similar construction in 24:1–2, 7–10; 93:1; 96:5; 146:10.

Other songs draw from the imagery of the heavenly court—the *royal court* in which God sits enthroned—and in this way praise the Creator as King, even when the words "king" or "throne" do not appear. This is the assembly of the "mighty ones" (the "sons of God") who offer homage in King Yahweh's presence (29:1–2). From this court God, the King, regally arrayed, sends his messengers and servants to do his royal bidding (104:1–5; cf. 103:19–22).

God as Creator-King acted and acts in Israel's history—the Exodus, the deliverance at the Sea, the wilderness wandering, and the victorious entry to the land (136:10–24; cf. 135:7–12 in context). It is Yahweh the Creator who did these marvelous wonders (136:4). He is sovereign, able to carry out his will, thwarting the devices of the nations and thwarted by no one. He not only wills but is able to deliver his people and to achieve his purposes for them (33:10–11).

This sovereign Creator knows the inner life of all, the way the potter knows the vessel he has fashioned (33:13–15; cf. 139:13–16). As such he is the sure hope of those who fear him, and he stands over against all vain hopes such as military might or natural vigor to which persons are tempted to turn for salvation (33:16–18, 20–22). This is Israel's helper (29:11; 33:16–20; 148:14; cf. 146:6).

The creation hymns extend Yahweh God's creative power beyond the originating, founding act of creation that brought all that is into existence. The Creator now provides for and sustains the life of all flesh (136:25; 104:10–18; 147:14–18). Ps 104:10–23 particularly expounds the life-giving forces in the psalmist's world as the work of Yahweh the Creator. Springs, grass, plants, wine, harvest, seasons, and more are all God's continuing work. Without his sustaining gifts and Spirit no life survives (104:27–30). Not only so, but a profound sense of the complex, interdependent ecosystem appears there, a wonder that reveals the marvelous wisdom of the Creator (104:24). Ps 65 builds its (perhaps New Year) celebration of anticipated harvest on the Creator's (v.6) care in saturating the parched ground with water and thus bringing plenty (65:9–13). "*You* crown the year with *your* bounty," sings the poet (65:11, italics mine). Grain, showers, crops, overflowing carts, verdant grasslands, and meadows covered with grazing flocks are all Yahweh's continuing provision. But this is not simply a praise for harvest bounty. Praise for "nature's" bounty comes after worship for God's gracious atoning for overwhelming human transgressions (65:1–4) and his saving deeds apparent to persons near and far (65:5–8).

In none of these songs is a stinging attack on the "gods of the nations" far from the surface. Sometimes in the Creation hymns this exaltation of the superiority of Yahweh God to all other "gods" explicitly appears. Yahweh is the "God of gods" and the "Lord of lords," that is, "the highest, supreme God," "the highest, supreme Lord" (136:2–3; cf. 95:3–5). But the apologetic is always present by virtue of the fact that the various parts of the "natural order" subordinated as God's creatures (his creative work) are among Israel's neighbors worshiped and feared as gods. Lord Sea, Judge River, Baal (god of storm, wind, lightning, fertility), Lady Sun, Moon, the Stars, Miss Earth (as underworld/plague), and twins Dawn and Dusk all appear in mythological or liturgical texts from the Canaanite city of Ugarit. Affirming that "the heavens" (i.e., the sun, moon, stars, and all the heavenly order) declare the glory of God," Ps 19 directs worship from these "gods" to the one who made them and then specifically subordinates the divine Sun to Israel's Creator God (19:4b–6). Ps 29 presses all the domains of the storm god Baal into the praise of God: flood waters, thunder, wind, and lightning (29:3–9). These express *Yahweh's* power, *not Baal's*, the informed ancient reader understands. Similar is Ps 104:2–9. At other points the psalmists borrow categories of creation from Canaanite theology (e.g., mighty conquest of the primordial sea, the raging floods) to praise Yahweh as Creator, and to deny any ground to the gods of the nations (65:5–6; 104:7).

The apology continues in the celebration that the Creator's genius and life-giving Spirit sustains the created order and now provides life and food for all flesh (104:10–27). *Wine, vine, oil, grain, bread,* and *offspring* (flock and family) are among the code words in the polemic regarding life and food in the OT and the ancient Near East. Canaanite religion tied continuing fertility and life not to creation and the Creator's continuing care but to the dying and rising, the captivity and rescue and/or the sexual union and procreation of the gods. In mythology expressing this "fertility" faith, Baal figured prominently. The sole option to the contrary in the ancient Near East, so far as we know, was faith in Yahweh of the sort we have come to call "biblical faith."

Israel continually succumbed to confusion at this point, often falling before the temptation to think that the wine and oil, the wheat and grain, the lambs and their wool and meat, the goats and their milk, and their own children were "gifts" of the various baals (manifestations of Baal worshiped at local shrines at the "high places"). Hosea, among others, exposes this delusion by which the provisions of Yahweh are thought to derive from Israel's harlotrous worship (Hos 2:5–13). All such matters come under the works of the one Creator, Yahweh, who "gives food to every creature" (136:25). The worship of the baals received such severe castigation not simply because fertility worship involved promiscuous and degrading sexual behavior in its liturgy. More fundamentally, fertility faith is the worship of oneself, the supreme blasphemy, for its aim is the guarantee of the worshipers' own survival, the perpetuating of life as it is through worship. The Creation hymns call the worshiper away from such preoccupation with one's own survival to the worship of Yahweh who made and sustains the world and all flesh by his power.

As a matter of fact, these songs in praise of the Creator draw precisely the opposite conclusion regarding human beings. The life, fertility, and survival of human beings is not the primary concern here. Praise of God is. In the presence of the Creator and his vast creation, the frailty and finitude of human beings is obvious (8:3–4; cf. 104:27–30). That the Creator pays attention to them is an astounding act of grace (cf. 139:12–17). And yet God has placed humans as the crown of his creation, chief administrator of the Creator's works (8:4–8). This creation paradox has the seeds of a true humanism in which the marvelous grandeur of human beings and their obvious and often painful frailty are held together in the worship not of them but of their Creator. So not only do these songs present cardinal "theology" (doctrines about God) but clear "anthropology" (doctrine about human beings) as well.

Ps 19, a song of "mixed form," raises important issues for creation thought. This song is apparently formed from the joining of a Hymn to the Creator (19:1–6) and a Torah Song (19:7–11) with concluding reflections (19:12–14). The key issue: What can you know about God from creation? It is the question of "natural theology." Clearly the psalmists believed the created order did reveal something about God; the question is what. Ps 19:1 carefully phrases the affirmation that the heavens reveal "the glory of God" and the fact of creation, i.e., God's creative activity (They present themselves as the "work of his hands."). Similarly Pss 8:1, 9; 29:1–9; 104:1; 148:13 sing the majesty, splendor, and power of God based on creation. Ps 104:24 sees God's wisdom in creation. Ps 136, called here a Hymn in Praise of the Creator because of the primary place accorded Yahweh's creative work in his "marvelous works," affirms repeatedly "his love endures forever." But the affirmation stands on its own, grounded if anywhere in the whole range of God's self-disclosure in history, not only or primarily in creation.

But there are limits to what one may know of God from creation. The exaltation of the Torah (19:7–11) stands beside the celebration of the Creator's glory seen in the heavens (19:1–6) as absolutely essential commentary. One may know of God's glory, power, and intelligence from creation, but one does not know clearly God's character or his will from creation. One knows that only from the Law, from God's revelation of himself to his servants and in the history of Israel. True revival of the soul, moral awareness, concepts of righteousness and justice as Yahweh sees them are found only in his law, statutes, precepts, commands, and ordinances.

And still there is more. Neither creation nor the law by itself gives illumination and accomplishes moral transformation on its own. God himself must grant insight and foster moral transformation. The psalm closes with appeal to the Creator-Lawgiver himself to forgive and for moral restraint beyond the psalmist's own sheer will power. The plea is that God will be Rock and Redeemer to his servant in such ways that his words and thoughts prove pleasing to Yahweh (19:12–14; cf. 104:34). Perhaps such surrender is implicit in all of these songs that call worshipers and all creation to sing (e.g., 33:1; 104:33), to praise (e.g., 104:1, 35), and to trust and hope in Yahweh the Creator (33:12–22).

C. Songs of Praise to King Yahweh (Pss 24, 47, 93, 95, 96, 97, 98, 99, 145)

From the day David first brought the ark to Jerusalem proclaiming the kingship of Yahweh (1Sa 6; 1Ch 16:1–37, particularly v.31), one suspects Israel celebrated the rule of Yahweh and remembered the installation in Zion of his "throne" (the ark). Pss 24, 47, and 95 apparently reflect such a celebration, with the procession of worshipers approaching Zion, most likely with the ark and Yahweh enthroned on it (cf. 99:1). If there was a separate festival devoted to this celebration, we have no clear record of it.

The central announcement of songs most closely associated with the celebration of the kingship of Yahweh and probably of the procession itself was "Yahweh reigns!" "Yahweh is king!" (93:1; 96:10; 97:1 99:1; and 1Ch 16:31, where almost the entirety of Ps 96 is housed, 16:23–33). Israel proclaims the "kingdom of God" and celebrates the ongoing rule of God, whose kingship is never threatened or lost. "Enthronement festivals" are known from biblical times, most notably involving the Babylonian god Marduk's assumption of divine kingship by conquest of the primordial chaos and rescue of the threatened rule of the gods. Pagan theologies associated seasonal cycles and their perceived annual threat to life and order in nature. They apparently saw the rule of the gods also at risk with the death of vegetation. These psalms in praise of King Yahweh and the whole OT's understanding of God stand in direct conflict with such views and hence do not proclaim "Yahweh *has become* king!"

Important aspects of the psalmists' faith in the kingship of Yahweh surface already in the names of God in these songs. He is "Glorious King" ("King of glory," 24:7, 8, 9), "Yahweh, Strong and Mighty" (24:8), "Yahweh, Mighty Warrior" ("mighty in battle," 24:8), and "Yahweh of Hosts/Heavenly Army" (24:10, NIV "The LORD Almighty")—all titles that celebrate King

Yahweh's victory over the nations, now and in the conquest of the land long ago (as in 47:3–4).

Yahweh is "the King" (98:6; 145:1), a "great king" (47:2; 95:3). But beyond that he is "King of all the earth" (47:7), "Yahweh Most High" (47:2), "Most High over all the earth" (97:9), and "great King above all gods" (95:3). Tied to Yahweh's kingship is his superiority and universal sovereignty. The Lord is the highest of all gods, superior to all rivals whose existence may at some stages have been granted and at others was simply raised as rhetorical nothing to be smashed (96:4–5). All the earth is his. As noted in connection with the Hymns in Praise of the Creator (I.B above), this superiority and universal sovereignty is inevitably connected to Yahweh's role as Creator of all that is, the world and his people (95:1–7; 96:1–6).

Yahweh the King is also the God of the Fathers, the God of Jacob (24:6) and of Abraham (47:9). Celebration of his kingship was linked to Israel's history with God, the memory of his election and redemption of them, his giving them the land (47:1–4). This is God the Savior (96:2–3; 99:6–7), indeed "God, the Forgiver" ("a forgiving God," NIV, 99:8).

These songs extol not only King Yahweh's exalted superiority and might, but also his majesty (93:1; 96:6; 99:1–3), holiness (93:5; 99:3, 5, 9), righteousness (96:13; 97:10–12; 99:4), and the sureness of his Word, his statutes (93:5). The acrostic Ps 145, which could perhaps be considered a general hymn, extols Yahweh the King's greatness and transgenerational praise (vv.3–7), his grace and compassion (vv.8–13), and his faithfulness (vv.14–16) and love (vv.17–20) related specifically to "all he has made" (vv.9, 13, 17).

Yahweh's rule, particularly his worldwide kingship, ordered the earth itself (24:1–2; 93:1–4; 96:11–13; 98:7–9) and was cause for great celebration there: "the trees of the forest . . . sing for joy" (96:12), "the rivers clap their hands" (98:8). It also guaranteed equity and order in the affairs of persons on the earth (96:11–13; 98:9). And the two though separate are related, much as in Paul's vision of creation groaning in sympathy with the suffering of persons now and in anticipation of the redemption of humanity (Ro 8:18–25). All creation, nature, and those in whose stewardship the earth has been placed celebrate the righteous judgment of King Yahweh, who rules the course of events with justice and will one day make his judgment apparent to all. "He comes to judge" celebrated his present rule and was an affirmation of hope in the face of circumstances that were at odds with the justice of God (96:11–13; 98:9).

All of these features of Israel's faith in King Yahweh buttress the calls to praise and worship, even the singing of a "new song" (New compositions? new insights? 96:1; 98:1). The calls to worship prominent in all these songs (47:1–4, 6; 95:1–2, 6; 96:1–6; 97:1, 8–9, 12; 98:1, 4–9; 99:1–3) use much of the vocabulary of celebration outlined in connection with the "General Hymns" (I.A.1 above). The worship will involve ascending Yahweh's hill, standing in the temple courts (24:3), kneeling before the King as to an earthly monarch (95:6), and bringing offerings (96:8). Before such a King one not only celebrates but trembles in awe before the majesty (97:2–6; 99:1–3).

While the whole earth is called to acknowledge Yahweh's rule, his kingship has particular meaning for the upright in heart (97:11), the faithful who see his rule in their lives (97:10). Indeed only those whose inner and outer lives conform to his will truly qualify to enter his courts and seek his favor (24:3–6). The superiority of Yahweh to other "gods" is not only important theological affirmation, it is also a call to put away all such gods from one's life (24:4), a call not to be entangled with such unworthy loyalties (96:5). Such vain hopes ultimately bring shame (97:7). Thus the worship of King Yahweh included the prophetic(?) word, warning against following the hard-hearted ways of the wilderness generation and calling those **today** truly to hear the King's voice (95:7–11).

In the flow of the Psalter as it now stands, this call to faith and obedience is perhaps closest to the point of the Songs in Praise of King Yahweh (cf. introduction, I.V). The bulk of these songs stand immediately after the conclusion of Book 3 and Ps 89's cry of agony. The shocking destruction of Jerusalem and the temple and the termination of the Davidic dynasty raised to a totally unprecedented level the question of the rule of God. These songs affirm that Yahweh's kingship, celebrated from of old, stands more than ever at the center of Israel's hopes. Yahweh rules whether there is a king or not. In his restoration of his people (98:3?), his rule is still apparent and will continue to be. It is for God's people to worship him and celebrate his providence, his coming judgment, through and beyond their tragedy.

D. Songs in Praise of the Lord of History (Pss 105, 106, 114, 135; cf. 78, 136).

All of these songs base their call to praise Yahweh in his **mighty deeds**, particularly his calling, saving, judging deeds in Israel's history. This logic

separates them from, e.g., Ps 78, which reviews the same history for mainly teaching purposes. Here, whatever else is made of the history, and it is pressed to diverse ends even in these songs, the context of them all is praise. The poets draw personal and corporate applications, but before and around these uses they draw important theological conclusions inspiring praise.

What can one say regarding Yahweh from Israel's history, according to these songs? Three primary conclusions dominate. Regarding his character, Yahweh is **good** and **gracious,** known for **faithful love** (106:1; 135:3; cf. 78:38 and 136 throughout). Regarding his person, Yahweh is **great** and awesome (114:7–8; 135:5), judging from his astounding works (105:5; 106:2). Indeed, he is absolutely sovereign!

> The LORD *does whatever pleases him,*
> in the heavens and on the earth,
> in the seas and all their depths.
> (135:6, italics mine)

Regarding his relation to other **gods,** his history with Israel demolishes all rivals and calls in judgment all who make idols or give themselves to such folly (135:15–18; cf. 115:3–8). For these reasons, based in Israel's knowledge of God's work in their history, the worshipers and now the reader are called to praise.

While the calls to praise provide the occasion for these hymns and set their ambience, the bulk of each hymn recites history more than it delineates praise. What history inspires these conclusions? Israel's history receives primary attention, even though these songs know that Yahweh of Israel's history is the God of all history, indeed the God of creation (136:5–9).

Emphasis in these songs rests definitely on the deliverance from Egypt and the gift of the land. Ps 105 reaches back to the everlasting covenant with Abraham, Isaac, and Jacob (105:8–11) and evokes their history, noting God's providential care of them in their vulnerable condition (105:12–15), even addressing the hearers as **descendants of Abraham** and **sons of Jacob,** highlighting their election by the God of the Fathers and the continuity between them and their God and the God of the ancient covenant (105:6–7). Unique in these songs is Ps 105's interpretive review of the Joseph era and the circumstances of entry into Egypt (105:16–25). The conclusion to Ps 78 extends the history to the chaos of the period of the judges and beyond to the election of David (78:56–72). But in the remainder of these songs and in the others all together, the emphasis is from Moses to the entry into Canaan.

The **miraculous signs** done through Moses and Aaron among the Egyptians are noted in general (105:27; 135:9; cf. 78:12, 43, 49; and Ex 7–15). But in addition, all the plagues known from the book of Exodus, save the murrain on the cattle and the boils (9:1–12), are recounted, with the final smiting of the firstborn receiving particular emphasis (105:36; 135:8; cf. 78:51; 136:10). Due to these events, Yahweh's renown will endure forever (135:13–14). As in the Exodus tradition itself, by these means God **brought out** his people (114:1–2; 78:52–54; 136:11). The deliverance at the sea commands special attention (106:8–12; 114:3–6; cf. 78:13; 136:13–15), Ps 106 even noting the rebellion preceding that rescue (v.7). In the wilderness experience these songs single out God's provision of food in the desert (105:39–40); cf. 78:23–29), the cloud and fire (105:39; cf. 78:14), and the water from the rock (105:41; 114:8; cf. 78:15–16, 20) for particular memory. Finally, Yahweh's

gift of the nations' land as a possession for Israel is stressed (105:43–44; 135:10, 12; cf. 78:55; 136:21–22). Specific events connected to these more generally noted mighty deeds of Yahweh appear as the purposes of each poem dictate.

Of course there is more here than mere recitation of history. The recitation proclaims to the nations the "good news" of the God of Israel, much as the proclamation of the Christian Gospel is at heart a recitation of God's saving deeds in Jesus Christ (105:1–2). This is the main burden of Pss 114 and 135, where the history calls for reverence and celebration. But beyond this proclamation, the call is to **remember** what God has done (105:5). No simple bringing to mind of forgotten facts is intended here, for no Israelite would actually forget these stories. To remember is to bring the awareness of these sacred deeds so forcefully to bear on the present that the community's life is meaningfully impacted and that of individuals as well. This very same significance attaches to the Christian disciple's "remembrance" of the life, death, and resurrection of Jesus in the celebration of the Lord's Supper (1Co 11:24).

Ps 105 brings the review to bear on the question of present obedience:

> He brought out his people with
> rejoicing,
> his chosen ones with shouts of joy;
> he gave them the lands of the
> nations,
> and they fell heir to what others
> had toiled for—
> *that they might keep his precepts*
> and observe his laws.
> Praise the LORD.
> (vv.43–45, italics mine)

Memory of this historic purpose calls the worshiper now to new loyalty to this Deliverer's law. Emphasis throughout this song is on the acts of Yahweh himself. It is *his* history in reality, and that history calls all hearers to obedience and praise. Praise and exhortation are combined, for it is grace that God's purposes should thus have been ("Praise the LORD").

In Ps 106 awareness of deep need for forgiveness and deliverance colors the whole recollection. **"We have sinned, even as our fathers did"** (v.6). The entire history is a story of ingratitude and unfaithfulness in spite of Yahweh's mighty deliverances (vv.7, 13, 16, 19, 21, 24, 38, 32, 34–39). On Israel's side it is a story of **giving no thought** (v.7), forgetting (v.13). "Forget" thus means much more than simply "lose track of facts." "Forget" here means "despise," "ignore," "refuse to act upon." Forgetting is sin with full responsibility, turning from faith. On Yahweh's side it is a story of grace and compassion, acting in great love in view of his covenant (vv.44–46). But now in this song both the terrible consequences of sin and the reality of possible deliverance are brought to bear on the desperate plight of God's people in exile. Responsibility is assumed for the catastrophic fall of Jerusalem, elsewhere evaded (Eze 18:1–4). But the history supports hope as well, hence the plea: **"Save us . . . gather us"** (vv.47–48). This hope concludes in Book 4, endorsed by the congregation's **"Amen!"** (v.48). The individual worshiper found hope as well in this confession of sin and memory of saving history. Yahweh could **remember** the individual's plight and hear his or her prayer to participate in the salvation of the people of God (106:4–5).

II. PRAYER SONGS (the *t^epillâh*)

A. General Prayers of Distress (Pss 16, 28, 36, 77, 82, 123, 125)

Unlike the prayer songs (the *t^epillôt*) considered below in which the plight facing the petitioner is clearly revealed in the course of the prayer, these few prayers present only general distress or hints of specific problems. The other main features of the prayer songs appear, however, so that these poems form a fitting introduction to the consideration of the others.

Here, as in the prayer songs that follow, affirmations of faith fill the songs, assertions of confidence in Yahweh and rationale of various sorts, which form the context in which the prayer can be offered. As a matter of fact, in these prayers this theological foundation accounts for the bulk of the psalm, supporting, undergirding or leading to the petitions, which themselves consume little space. For example, Ps 16's opening petition (v.1a) is supported by the entire remainder of the work.

The major context in which the petitioners lay their request before the Lord is their undivided trust in him, their loyalty to him, and their claim of seeking refuge in him, which claim has leverage on its own (16:1, 2, 8; 28:1, 7; 123:1–2). This involves a rejection of the wicked and their ways (36:1–4) and an acknowledgment that without God's help they are doomed (28:1). These prayers claim confidence in Yahweh's ability and disposition to come to the aid of those who call upon him. His rule (82:1, 8; 123:1), his unfailing love (36:5–7a), his protection of the upright (125:2, 5), and his destruction of the wicked (125:5) are not in question, indeed are the very basis for looking to him at all. They are buoyed by the undeniable blessing experienced by the people of God, the recipients of his continuing love (36:7b–9; 125:1–2). And they themselves fully expect not to be shaken or abandoned to death (16:8–10), to give thanks now and on the other side of deliverance (28:7).

The generally presented plight facing the worshiper in these prayers is the ever-present danger from the proud (36:11), the general threat that the wicked always constitute (28:3–5), an assumed need for refuge (16:1, 10), and contempt endured (the most specific ill confronted in these poems, 123:3–4). None of these is specified or elaborated, allowing a wide range of worshipers with vastly differing problems to enter these prayers sympathetically and use them to lay their distress before God.

The petitions are equally vague, but important, pleading for safety (16:1), a listening ear (28:1–2), salvation (28:2, 8) and blessing (28:9), continuing of love and containment of the wicked (36:10–11), and for mercy (123:3). None of these petitions is elaborated either. But never mind; they have been uttered. Yahweh, who knows the heart, hears; and that is what counts. A most unusual prayer is set in the heavenly court, where God presides over the divine counsel (82:1). The bulk of the poem is a "speech of God," upbraiding the members of his court for their failure to enforce justice among earth's rulers (82:2–7). At the conclusion the petition calls on God himself to rise and judge the nations (82:8).

As with the other prayer songs, indeed the other psalms, these few *t^epillôt* defy overly precise categorization as individual or communal. While Ps 16 reads totally in the first person ("**I**," "**me**," "**my**") and Ps 125 is totally of communal referent, the other prayers here move without fanfare between these viewpoints. These prayers lead the worshiper, even when praying **alone,** to remember his or her tie to **the people,** God's **inheritance.** And even while the congregation stands praying as God's people, each **I** and **me** is able to speak to Yahweh and is confident of being heard by him.

These and the other prayer songs reveal some small part of the temple experience behind them. Even after their collection in the Psalter, they call the believer to the temple's courts and prayer there, literally and in spirit. One petitioner prays, lifting hands toward the temple's Most Holy Place (28:2). Another prayer has the believer bowing toward the sacred place (5:7), a daily pattern of prayer (5:1–3). From that **holy hill** answer would come (3:4). There in his temple, Yahweh sits enthroned (63:2), though his throne is also in the heavens above all. He dwells between the cherubim (80:1). There between the cherubim the worshiper encounters Yahweh himself, hears God speak (60:6–8); 63:2; 108:7–9), and turns to this place with special attachment (26:8).

B. Prayers for Deliverance From Accusation and Persecution (Pss 3–5, 7, 9–13, 17, 25–27, 31, 35, 42–43, 54–59, 62–64, 69–71, 86, 94, 109, 120, 139–143)

These pleas for deliverance are the most numerous single song type, dominating the first two books of the Psalter (forty-two percent of the opening seventy-two psalms). Some of them may have come from the harrowing dangers King David endured, as the editors who provided the superscriptions thought—Absalom's coup attempt (Ps 3), flight from Abimelech (Ps 34), betrayal to Saul (Ps 52; cf. introduction III.D). They have Israel's king in mind

(63:9–11). During the kingdom period they perhaps formed part of the congregation's prayers for the son of David then on the throne. But now, in the time of the formation of the Psalter as a collection, the king of Israel is long gone. All of these prayers, including those set in the life of David, express the cries of the worshipers for deliverance from their own plight. Indeed the very drama of these harrowing experiences of David now heightens the sense of gravity and desperation in the songs.

One could attempt to separate these songs according to whether they are individual or community prayers. In most cases the distinction is obvious by the pronouns "I," "me," "my" as opposed to "we," "us," "our." In several of these prayers the composition flows with apparent disinterest between these two, e.g., Ps 4: **"Answer *me* when *I* call to you, O *my* righteous God. . . . Let the light of your face shine upon *us*, O LORD"** (vv.1, 6). Compare 62:8. In two cases an "individual" song has been strikingly appropriated for the edification of the community, 25:22 and 69:34–36. They remind us that such distinctions are artificial as the Psalter now stands, for all of the pieces are now meant for individual and communal nourishment, quite apart from their origins. The individual's experience often mirrors the life of the whole family of God, and each needy one prays in the context of and with the support of the whole worshiping congregation.

In some songs the telling of the problem consumes almost the entire effort (10:2–11; 70:1–4; perhaps most elaborate in Ps 69), with only brief space devoted to the cry for help or affirmation of faith (70:5). In others relatively little attention is paid to the problem itself, with most of the song devoted to the faith and affirmation

that makes possible the casting of one's soul upon God in the first place (e.g., 9:13–14, 19–20; 139:1–18). Ps 62 has no actual petitions, but only affirmation, self-exhortation, and instruction to others, with the petition implicit (62:12; cf. Ps 63:9–11).

Taken as a whole these prayers for deliverance express a terrible range of human fear, pain, danger, and sadness. They reveal a horrible picture of the predatory ways of sinful human beings. Sometimes the worshiper prays generally of his or her plight (59:4), citing terror (55:4), many foes (3:1; 7:9; 55:3), oppression (12:5; 143:3), pain and distress (69:29), helplessness (142:4), and need for vindication (26:1). But other lines spell out these general situations in frightening detail. The petitioner is under attack or at least *feels* under attack—ambushed (59:3), the center of a lethal plot (35:4; 56:5–6; 59:3; 64:1–6; 70:2; 71:10–13; 109:31), with life itself threatened (31:13; 35:4; 55:4; 69:4). Literally or figuratively the worshiper lives under siege (31:21), stalked like an animal for whom a trap has been set (31:4, 8, 11; 35:7–8), the bow drawn (11:2). In these prayers the worshipers see themselves as desperately needy, **the oppressed** (9:9), **the needy** (9:18), **the afflicted** (9:18), **the helpless** (10:12), and **the weak** (12:5).

In many cases these situations may well have been actual, life-threatening plights. At other times, or related to these, the attack is verbal, the weapons words. The petitioner stands before God slandered (31:13; 35:11, 15–16; 56:2; 57:4; 140:3), falsely accused (7:1–2, 8; 35:19–21; 109:2–5, 25) of wrongdoing and lack of integrity (7:3–5). Here the servant of God needs vindication and a righteous judge (7:6–8). The verbal attack sometimes has a double edge, assaulting the believer by blaspheming his or her God (10:2–11). Taunts assail the psalmist's psyche (11:1–3; 12:3; 35:15; 38:16; 42:3, 10; 55:3). The wags deny that God will help, thus impugning either the psalmist's character and "right" to rescue or his God's ability or desire to save (3:2; 42:3, 10; 69:10–12; 71:11), or taunting him for refusal to join idolatrous worship (4:2–7). Perhaps most poignant are those situations where the psalmist calls to God, betrayed by trusted compatriots and family (55:12–14, 20–21; 109:4–5), or where the psalmist's plight itself has alienated loved ones (31:11–12; 55:12–21; 69:8).

These drastic straits find a face in the various names given to "the enemy": the arrogant (5:5), the bloodthirsty (5:6; 26:9; 59:2; 139:19), the greedy (10:3), the ruthless (35:11; 54:3; 86:14), and the violent (11:5). "The foes" are the deceitful (5:6; 26:4), the fierce (59:3), the wicked (5:4) and cruel (71:4), people without regard for God (54:3; 86:14). Included here are strangers (54:3) and companions alike (55:13), traitors (59:5), slanderers (56:2), liars (5:6; 120:2–3), pursuers (7:1; 31:15; 56:2; 142:6), sinners (26:9), and hypocrites (26:4). These persons are like angry bulls (22:12, 21), ferocious lions (22:13, 21; 57:4; 58:6), poisonous snakes (58:4–5), and hungry dogs (22:16, 20; 59:6, 14). In some few places the psalmist indicates that his own sin may be part of the problem, i.e., he himself may in part be "the enemy" (25:11, 18; 69:5ff.).

Life thus under attack by the enemy and bowed down by cares exacts a heavy toll, even on the people of God. That toll itself is the focus of prayer as worshipers cry out about their tears (42:3), their discouragement and brokenness (69:19–20; 143:4), their despair of ever finding help (4:6), their distress at the ungodly (4:1; 55:9–11), or their desire to run or hide (55:6–8).

But these prayers reject hiding as an adequate response to life in the face of hostility and attack, implicitly by their very existence and explicitly in their content. Instead the worshipers' hearts turn to God, in earnest, even desperate prayer (54:2; 69:13) and supplication (31:22). More than calm "prayers," these songs are cries for help (5:1–2; 57:2) and mercy (31:22). They record sighing (5:1), groanings toward God (12:5), laments as in the face of death (56:8), complaints (64:1; 142:2) and pouring out the heart to God (62:8).

At times the plea is an unspecified call for God to act: **"Arise!"** (3:7; 7:6; 9:19; 35:23; 59:4), **"Answer!"** (4:1; 13:3; 55:2; 69:16; 109:1; 143:1, 7), **"Hear!"** (4:1; 5:1–2; 27:7; 31:2; 54:2; 55:1, 2; 64:1; 86:1, 6; 141:1–2; 143:1; cf. 71:2), **"Awake!"** (7:6; 35:23; 59:5), **"See!"** (9:13; 13:3; 25:18–19), or **"Have mercy!/Be merciful!"** (4:1; 9:13; 25:16; 31:9; 56:1; 57:1; 86:3). The negative counterparts to these general pleas implore God not to ignore (55:1) or hide his face (69:17; 143:7) or hide himself (27:9) or forget (10:12) or turn away (27:9) or forsake (27:9; 71:18).

Frequently these more general petitions open the song, as the references indicate. They form introductions to more specific requests for God to move vigorously in defense of the petitioner or actively against the foe. In the face of danger the psalmist prays for rescue (25:20; 31:4–5; 35:17: 43:1; 69:15, 18; 140:1) and deliverance (3:7; 7:1; 12:1; 54:1; 59:1, 2; 69:1; 71:4; 109:26; 120:2). The petitioner calls for relief (4:1), for redemption (25:22; 69:18)—for God to **lift his hand** in defense of the helpless (10:12), to lift **from the gates of death** (9:13), to **free** the sufferer from a **trap** (31:4). The

need is urgent—**"Hasten!"** (70:1, 5;
141:1). The psalmist needs to be kept
safe (16:1; 25:20), to be placed under
guard (86:2; 140:1), to have God's
protection (5:11; 64:1–2) and preservation (143:11), to have God himself
take up the battle (35:1). Helpless to
find the way in the present darkness,
the worshiper looks to be led out of
that plight and into a continuing walk
with God (5:8; 25:4–5; 31:3; 43:3;
139:22–24; 143:10).

In the present discouragement the
petitioner asks to be made glad again
(5:11; 70:4; 86:4). In the face of
accusation he calls for God to take up
his case (35:1; 43:1), to judge him
fairly (7:8), to vindicate him in the face
of all his accusers (26:1; 35:24). In the
present sense of isolation from God, he
longs for the sense of God's acceptance
and presence. The prayer is for the
light of God's face to **shine upon** him
again (4:6; cf. 13:3; 31:16; 43:3).

The petitions call God not only to
redeem the worshipers themselves but
also to act vigorously against the foe. In
some cases these pleas also are general
requests for God to prevent the antagonists from triumph (9:19), to show
traitors no mercy (59:5), to bring the
wicked's violence to an end (7:9), to
strike terror into the foe (9:20), to
confuse the wicked (55:9), to bring
disgrace to the enemies (35:4, 26;
70:2–3; 71:12–13), to declare the
enemy guilty (5:10), to set them in a
dark and slippery path (35:6; cf.
69:23), to pour wrath on the wicked
(69:24), or not to grant them their
desires (140:8). Obliquely the prayer
asks for **ruin [to] overtake** attackers
(35:8; cf. 69:22–28; 140:9–10), their
dwelling to be deserted (69:25). But
more often these psalms have clearly in
mind the utter destruction of the foe,
lethal action by God to bring to an end
the assault upon the psalmist's life

Plainly put, the prayer is for God to **cut
off** (i.e., kill, 12:3–4), to slay
(139:19), to destroy (54:5; 143:12),
to consume the wicked (59:13), to let
them vanish (58:7–8), let death **surprise** the enemy (55:15). Using imagery of mortal conflict on the battlefield or in the hunt, the worshiper
asks God to strike the enemy's jaw
(3:7), break his teeth (3:7; 58:6) and
arm (10:15), tear out his fangs (58:6).
In the language of the celestial court
the request is for him to be blotted out
of the Book of Life (69:28). In the
language of covenant hope denied, he
is not to **be established in the land**
(140:11).

Prayers like these do not rise in a
vacuum. They require a place to stand.
While not all the petitions carry explicit
rationale, many do. Significant reasons
are given as to why Yahweh should
answer the prayer or why the prayer
should be made in the first place. Some
songs base the petitions in the situation
itself, the gravity of the need (5:8;
12:1–2; 31:9; 109:22–25), and the
despicable deeds confronting the
psalmist (59:12–13; 109:16–20). In
some cases the petitioner stands in
confidence based in the integrity of his
own life and walk with Yahweh (26:1–
8, 11–12). This is not arrogance and
does not deny the foundation of Yahweh's grace upon which the entire
ability to turn to him for rescue stands.
It rather acknowledges the reality of
faithful life with God. No one will
endure an open judgment by Yahweh if
it is simply on the basis of the petitioner's character alone (143:2). In
other places the very security of a
person's past and present relationship
with Yahweh (25:4–5; 143:12) undergirds the petitioner. Again, the very
fact that the psalmist seeks refuge in
Yahweh and trusts in him supports the

prayer (16:1–4; 31:4; 57:1; 143:8–10), as Ps 86:1–4 so eloquently sings.

The deeper foundation upon which these petitions rest is Yahweh himself, his person, character, and saving history with his people. These reasons often explicitly undergird the prayer (25:4–5), with appeal to Yahweh's faithfulness (54:5), might (54:1), mercy, goodness, and love (69:13; 109:21, 26; 143:12).

Beyond these explicit groundings in Yahweh himself and the worshipers' relationship to him, the titles with which the petitioners address Yahweh here reveal a solid faith that implicitly supports the prayers for deliverance. Profound confidence in Yahweh and his longstanding relationship with his people as well as strong ownership of the worshipers' own relationship with the God of Israel emerge, solidly intertwined. The prayers address God as **"My Glorious One"** (3:3), the **"Most High"** (9:2), **"God Most High"** (7:10), **"God of Israel"** (59:5), **"Sovereign LORD"** (109:21), **"Yahweh God of Hosts"** (59:5), **"my King"** (5:2), **"my God and LORD**" (35:24), and simply **"my God"** (e.g., 3:7), all calling attention to the sovereign grandeur of Yahweh and the petitioner's relationship to that kind of God. That relationship itself is sometimes underscored in the very address of God: the One **"whose word I trust"** (56:4) and **"whom I praise"** (109:1). Other titles highlight Yahweh's character and his saving ways: **"Yehweh, God of Truth"** (31:5), **"Righteous God"** who searches minds and hearts (7:9), **"my Rock"** (42:9), **"my Strength"** (59:9, 17), **"our Shield"** (59:11; cf. 140:7), **"God, my Savior"** (25:4; 27:9), **"my Strong Deliverer"** (140:7), and the One who **avenges blood** (9:12). Under it all is confidence

in the God who will fulfill his purposes for the one who calls upon him (57:2).

Substantial amounts of these "Prayers for Deliverance" hold positive affirmation about Yahweh and the worshipers' relationship to him, not merely bare petition. These affirmations elaborate the theological and experiential bases for petition discerned in the "reasons" and "direct addresses" treated above. The "affirmations" do not arise as explicit "reasons" supporting the prayer. They simply state convictions of the worshiper, undergirding the whole approach to God. At times the affirmations stand strikingly at variance with the present situation (e.g., 9:1–12, 15–18 over against 9:13–14, 19–20), recalled expressly for the encouragement of the petitioner (56:3–4).

These prayers affirm the worshipers' own walk with God, past and present. The worshipers have experienced Yahweh's deliverance (54:7; 86:13) and have a history of trust and praise toward him (71:5–8, 17). In the very course of crying for help, they celebrate Yahweh and their utter commitment to him (16:1–4, 8; 31:5) and their distance from the wicked (31:6). In the face of adversity they claim sleep sustained by Yahweh (3:5–6) and gladness of heart (16:8–10; 31:7–8). They ask God to see and hear, and they are confident that he does just that—in spite of the wicked's claim to the contrary (4:3; 10:12–14, 17; 11:4–5; 35:22). They take refuge in Yahweh (7:1; 11:1; 16:1; 31:1; 141:8; 143:9), trust in Yahweh's loving-kindness (13:5; 25:1–2; 31:14–15; 56:4, 11), remember his works (143:5–6), and acknowledge his present blessing (16:5–6). They are confident that Yahweh reigns forever (9:7) and will judge equitably (9:8), no matter what the present may hold. They are sure of Yahweh's particular bond to the godly

(4:3; 16:3; 86:5, 15; 142:3; cf. 25:8–14) and his proven disdain for the wicked (5:4–6; 16:4; 59:8; 64:7–8). They cite their habit of expectant prayer (5:1–3, 7; 25:1; 59:9; 142:1–2; 143:6), their utter longing for Yahweh himself (42:1–2; 63:1; 143:6). They express hope that what they now pray for they will live to see (58:9; 62:2–6; 63:3–5, 7; 86:12; 109:28). When these prayers are answered, they are confident that those who know will fear, ponder, and proclaim Yahweh's works (64:9), declaring his power to the next generation (71:18). In song after song, these affirmations conclude the prayer, sending the worshiper from the temple and leaving the reader with a powerful benediction (e.g., 3:8; 4:8; 5:12; 10:16–18; 11:7; 12:7; 62:11–12; 71:22–24; 140:12–13).

The prayers for deliverance include promised response to Yahweh's rescue: joyful praise (e.g., 7:17; 13:6; 35:18; 57:7, 9), glad proclamation of Yahweh's character and wondrous deeds (9:1; 35:28; 71:14–18), sacrifices fitting the delivered (43:4; 54:6; 56:12–13), buoyed hope (71:14), and a faithful walk in Yahweh's truth (86:11). These promises pledge the grateful response of persons snatched from hopeless straits.

Several Prayers for the Deliverance of the Persecuted carry traces of their liturgical life in asides directed to various persons other than God, to whom the prayers are primarily addressed. Admonitions to the wicked appear, urging them to be aware of Yahweh's peculiar relationship to the godly, to search their hearts, cease from sin, offer correct sacrifice, and trust Yahweh (4:3–5). Accusation (58:1–2; 62:3–4) and warnings of punishment (120:3–4) are found. Exhortation to the saints occurs also, encouraging them to be strong and love Yahweh (31:23–24), to trust and pour out their hearts to him (62:8; cf. 27:14; 64:10), and to praise Yahweh (9:11). They receive instruction regarding the lifelong perversity of the wicked (58:3–5; cf. 62:9). Exhortation is even directed to the psalmist himself, encouraging hope and rest in Yahweh and questioning the despondency the petitioner feels in facing his foes (42:5, 11; 43:5; 62:5).

The strength of these "Prayers for Deliverance From Accusation and Persecution" rises from their pervasive confidence that God rescues the worshiper from the ambushes laid even for the saints in this sinful world. God does hear, he does care, and he does act—literally slaying the foe and delivering those who trust him. This, of course, is the OT's "majority report." It breathes an understanding of life in which God is intimately, observably, and directly involved in human affairs. Here there is encouragement for the oppressed and hope for the needy.

In the scattered "whys" regarding Yahweh's distance or hiding (10:1), his delay (13:1–2), his possible forgetting (42:9), or puzzling rejection of the psalmist (43:2), we catch the hint that life may not be this straightforward nor the ways of Yahweh this simple.

Complicating this issue further is the clear connection drawn between life circumstances and individual and corporate moral character in orthodox wisdom literature (Proverbs) and standard covenant faith (e.g., Deuteronomy). Trust of Yahweh and obedience to him bring immediate, concrete blessing; distrust and disobedience bring immediate, concrete curse and punishment. In this frame of reference, attack by enemies, distressing adversity, and calamity cannot simply be viewed as happenings in a fallen world. They must or at least may very well indicate

Yahweh's displeasure at sin in one's life. While Scripture from beginning to end teaches the dreadful, present results of sin, to construe this linkage in an overly simple manner results in painful consequences. Among these are the shame and embarrassment caused by adversity itself, if it necessarily implies sin (cf. 31:11; 69:6–8).

Other songs in the Psalter will face this problem head-on and will echo the "minority report" found elsewhere in the OT (e.g., Job, Ecclesiastes; cf. section VII below). The Psalter as a whole may even address the issue in its final shape. However that vexing question is finally settled, with all the mystery added to the faith in God's participation in the lives of his people, these songs were left to stand as they were. None of the problems, of which the Psalter's compilers were surely aware, were edited out. For faith in a God who cannot or does not or will not participate meaningfully in the lives of his people is worse than this overly simple faith and the confidence it inspires.

C. Prayers for Restoration From National Distress and Defeat
(Pss 14, 44, 53, 60, 74, 79, 80, 83, 85, 90, 108, 126, 129, 137)

Of these songs for national restoration, Pss 74, 79, 137, and probably 126 spring demonstrably from the disasters associated with the fall of Jerusalem (586 B.C.) and the Babylonian exile. Talk of the destruction of the city and the (Solomonic) temple (74:3–8; 79:1–3) and of forced march and harassment in Babylon (137:1–4) indicates this setting or later, as most likely does note of a specific return of captives to Zion (126:1). At first glance Pss 44, 60, 80, and 85 would seem to register catastrophe of sufficient proportions to indicate the Exile also, but the evidence

is not conclusive. Other deportations, north and south, were known before the Babylonian exile (cf. Am 1:6, 9) so that such notes in themselves do not fix the date of the distress laid before God.

More important, these prayers for national restoration have been preserved in the Psalter for the edification of the saints long after the specific historical setting that prompted them in the first place. They now serve as means by which the defeated, the oppressed, and the displaced of all times and places lay bare their souls before God, their only hope.

These *t*ᵉ*pillôṭ* share the components common to the other "prayer songs" (see the more extensive discussion in section II.B). Affirmations of faith and rationale for the petitions (noted by "for" or "because," e.g., 44:26) provide theological foundation for the prayers. In these times of national distress, the history of God's saving deeds among his people seemed particularly important, usually standing starkly over against the present, urgent need (e.g., 44:1–3, 9–16). The Exodus and God's conquests of his creation are recalled as evidence of his ability to do the impossible (74:13–17; 80:8–12). Yahweh rescued his people through the judges (83:9–13; cf. Jdg 4)—"Do it again!" rings the prayer (83:9). In Ps 80:8–18, a "vine" metaphor expresses both God's historic care for his people and the present calamity (cf. Isa 5:1–7; Eze 19:10–14). The very language of self-description in these prayers calls forcefully to mind Yahweh's historic, loving relationship with the congregation: **"your people"** (60:3; 79:13), **"your dove"** (74:19), **"your afflicted people"** (74:19), **"those you cherish"** (83:3), **"the sheep of your pasture"** (74:1; 79:13).

Faced with national defeat, God's people see more clearly what they have known all along, that human beings for all their strength are frail at best, especially when set beside the terror of God and the magnitude of their own need (90:7–12). These prayers set aside hope in human beings as futile in these darkest hours of life (60:9–11; 108:10–13). Only trust in Yahweh, the King who alone brings victory, avails (44:4–8; 60:6–8, 12; 74:12–17; 108:7–9, 13). Perhaps most eloquently put, from the very beginning God alone has been their very **dwelling place** (90:1–2), their home and rest and security.

In these prayers the entire nation stands at risk or in collapse. Surrounded or under attack (60:10–11; 80:14–18; 83:2–8); suffering destructive murderous invasion (79:1–4), the brunt of animosity against Zion (129:5); the land itself torn and shaken (60:2), the people defeated, disgraced, plundered, scattered, and sold into slavery (44:9–16), the people cry to God. The enemies are not only Judah's or Israel's but God's as well (83:3, 5), even when the catastrophe is construed as judgment (44:9–10; 60:1; 79:5). The entire history of the people of God found them often under attack (129:1–3), able to appropriate these descriptions of disaster to recount their own siege situation under succeeding tyrants to the very present.

Not only national collapse but collective disillusionment finds solace here. Dreams turned sour when the prophets' grand promises failed to materialize upon return from the Exile and when euphoria from first setting foot in the Holy Land again subsided. These also threatened the very life of the people of God as surely as military attack and called for restoration (126:1–6). The memory of unspeakable anguish suffered and the lingering need for redress adequate to the crimes endured finds prayer expression in these songs as well (137).

In these desperate situations the psalmists call God to act, using general pleas similar to those in the other "prayer songs"—**"Awake!"** (44:23; 80:1), **"See!"** (83:2), **"Redeem us!"** (44:26), **"Save us!"** (60:5; 80:2; 108:6), for example. Others uniquely arise from these national disasters, calling for regard for the covenant, which promised not only judgment but also restoration (74:20), for remembrance of the people Yahweh himself had historically **purchased** (74:2). **"Pick your way through these everlasting ruins"** calls God as dramatically as one can imagine to enter inch by inch into the terrible plight of his people (74:3). They call for attention to international implications of God's destruction and/or restoration of his people, the fools' mockery of God himself (74:18, 22), the culpability of other nations (79:6), and potential for Yahweh's unveiling his glory and sovereignty over all the earth in the affairs of his people as a nation (83:18; 108:5).

These prayers share the ambiguity of the other *tĕpillôt* in their attempts to discern whether and how the defeat they now endure is the judgment of God for their sin, as the historic covenant would indicate (Dt 28). This of course was the major theological problem raised by the national destruction, exile, and the prospects of those disasters. First and Second Kings recount the nation's history to the Exile and explain that national disaster as judgment for Israel and Judah's idolatry (2Ki 17; 21:10–15), a conviction preached continually by Jeremiah (e.g., Jer 25, 26). The ambiguity surfaces clearly in a prayer like Ps 44, where the calamities are attributed to God's actions (44:9–16) even though innocence of wrongdoing worthy of such judgment is claimed (44:17–22). *Whose* sins account for the tragedy is the question—ours (79:9) or our **fathers'** (79:8).

The Gospel of Jesus Christ penetrates this ambiguity with the good news that God is "for us" no matter what our circumstances. This confidence stands on God's saving revelation of his love in the life, death, and resurrection of Jesus. Paul dramatically demonstrates this by quoting Ps 44:22 (Ro 8:36) from the very prayer in which the problem seems most obvious and then declaring that "in all these things we are more than conquerors through him who loved us" (as demonstrated unambiguously in Jesus!) (Ro 8:37; cf. 8:31–39).

D. Imprecatory Psalms (Pss 5, 10, 17, 35, 58, 59, 69, 70, 79, 83, 109, 129, 137, 140)

These "imprecatory psalms" are prayer songs so designated because of their particularly vigorous attitude toward the enemy. The verb "imprecate" means "to pray evil against" or "to invoke curse upon" another, hence the name for these prayers. There is no indication that the editors of the Psalter or the ancient petitioners in the first or second temple would have distinguished these particular prayers from the other *t^epillôt*, where frequent petition to God for the death and destruction of the foe rises. Their identification itself is a matter of judgment and moral sensitivity. For that reason this commentary includes them in the treatment of the groups to which they best belong, "Prayers for Deliverance From Accusation and Persecution" and "Prayers for Restoration From National Distress and Defeat." Still, for the Christian reader at least, these poems deserve comment, for they jar the sensitivities of those whose Master

taught them to love their enemies and pray *for* (not *against*) their persecutors (Mt 5:44).

The Christian reader must begin by accepting these prayers as they are, by and large the cries of God's people for vengeance for unspeakable atrocities against them as God's people and those places sacred to them and to him. The best reading will refrain from spiritualizing the enemy or the petitions or the blessings thereby diminishing the depth of the agony felt and the vehemence of the action sought.

The disciple of Jesus must also realize that any disquiet he or she feels in reading these prayers is due to the redeeming influence of the Lord and his apostles, not to any particular moral sensitivity naturally possessed by the "enlightened" reader. Contemporary readers would have no problem, were it not "given" them by the same Scripture that preserves both these poems and the teachings that call them into question. This sensitivity surely does not rise out of pure Enlightenment refinement or "modern maturity." Secular humanism can never on its own support values sufficient to impugn these prayers. Thus one will do well to refrain from patronizing or moralizing approaches to these works.

Contemporary readers, particularly those in more affluent societies, can allow these prayers to help them enter the suffering life of the people of God, to transport them from their relative ease into the ghastly suffering and consternation of persons who have been uprooted, mocked, or abused. These prayers awaken the conscience to the human cry for redress, the cosmic demand for moral order and justice. They can lead one to feel as deeply as one ought the horrendous insult to Yahweh and his creation perpetrated by those who lie and cheat and kill and abuse and blaspheme. Made callous by exposure to continual evil, one may lose the sense of outrage these evils deserve, whether done to us or to others or to God. These prayers awaken that outrage, which is to be offered to God and which motivates to redemptive action.

Beyond these instructive appropriations the imprecatory prayers must point the followers of Jesus beyond themselves to a loftier vision of prayer, as noted above, *for*, not *against*, "the enemy," a form of prayer taught by our Master (Mt 5:11, 43–48) and modeled by the earliest church (1 Pe 2:19–25). This vision does not set aside the call for justice and vindication, but places these matters in God's hands for the eschaton (Ro 2; Rev 2:19ff.; 18).

These prayers can also articulate our own disquiet when we are caught in the agony and emotional upheaval of life's incongruities and injustices. When, for whatever reasons, we find ourselves unable to appropriate the mind of the Master for "the enemy," these prayers can provide a place of prayer from which to start, leading through the desire for vengeance to the prayer for blessing and redemption to which we are called. Further, having begun with their primary point, the forceful response to actual sin and evil against the people of God, one can walk through this door to the larger arena of our own desires for the destruction of evil in our own lives and our disdain for those enemies within.

E. Prayer Song of the Sinner (Pss 6, 38, 39, 40, 41, 51, 88, 102, 130)

The psalmists' awareness of sin as the (or a) cause of their plight marks these prayer songs (*t°pillôt*) as a group. In some the awareness of sin prompts a clear confession or at least acknowledgment of sin (38:18; 39:8; 41:4; 51:1–

5). In others this acknowledgment is less direct (40:12). In still others the sense of sin, though obviously present, is implicit, evidenced by the psalmists' conviction of being under Yahweh's **rebuke** or **discipline** (6:1; 38:1; 39:11), the object of Yahweh's **wrath** (6:1; 38:3; 88:5–9; 102:10), the target of Yahweh's actions (88:6–9), 15–18)—all implying sin in the one praying. The petitioner feels rejected by Yahweh and alienated from him (88:4). In Ps 130 the sense of sin is present in the affirmation (vv.4, 8).

The need for healing is a second distinctive of most of these songs (not present in Ps 130 and not clear in Ps 40). These *t°pillôt* could perhaps have been called "Prayers of the Sick and the Sinner," though the awareness of sin is the more consistent of the two themes. They can be properly understood only within the theological framework outlined under the Prayer Songs for Deliverance From Accusation and Persecution (section II.B.), the OT's standard wisdom and historic covenant faith. Here obedience, wisdom, and covenant trust lead to present, concrete blessing, including health. Disobedience, folly, and unfaithfulness to the covenant bring divine cursing, *including disease* (e.g., Lev 26; Dt 28).

Standard wisdom and the historic covenant connection between sin/sickness and obedience/health says something other than the enduring insight that a relationship exists between moral choices people make and the quality of their health, the truth that sin often wreaks havoc in body and mind, and that godliness often saves persons from physical and mental ills. This last truth is a matter of creation; God in his wisdom and grace has made the world so that it reflects the goodness of his will.

The theology undergirding these

prayers holds not simply a faith in created processes but in present, physical divine blessing and retribution. Pss 38 and 41 most clearly state this:

> *Because of your wrath* there
>   is no health in my body;
> my bones have no soundness
>   *because of my sin.*
>   (38:3, italics mine).

> O LORD, have mercy on me;
>   *heal me, for I have sinned*
>   against you.
>   (41:4, italics mine).

These lines reflect a worldview in which illness itself was a sign of God's displeasure and issued in the assumption that one had sinned, even where there was no clear awareness of specific sin that might have brought God's judgment.

Perhaps this is why some of these songs cry for healing and proceed under the conviction of God's rebuke and wrath and discipline but lack any clear confession of sin or clear acknowledgment of specific sin (Pss 6, 40, 88, 102). Ps 88 unveils the particularly poignant pain of a person suffering chronic illness, plagued from childhood. Such persons would have carried as well the continuing question as to the reason for God's "obvious" anger and rejection (88:13–18). Perhaps this accounts also for the strange conjunction of continuing trust and confidence in Yahweh side by side with terrible consciousness of his wrath and rebuke and rejection, as in Pss 38, 40, and 88. In spite of the fact that these prayers acknowledge sin and seek help, these songs are not the prayers of "wicked" persons, "the foolish," or "idolaters," persons who deny and reject God. These are the saints, suffering under the perceived burden of their sins.

Since illness of necessity called the moral character of the sick one into question, another repercussion of disease registered in these prayers is the response of others to one's plight (after the model of Job's "comforters," e.g., Job 8). Family and friends found the situation awkward at best, alienating at worst (38:11; 41:9; 88:8, 18). Enemies capitalized on the occasion to slander the good name of the sufferer (39:8; 40:14–15; esp. 41:5–8).

No doubt related to this theological frame of reference is the fact that most of these prayers of the sinner do not actually ask for forgiveness. The obvious exception to that pattern is Ps 51, with its classic confession of sin and profound cry for forgiveness. Ps 41 cries for mercy (v.4); Ps 130 anticipates redemption (v.8). In the main these prayers are concerned not with forgiveness of sin but with rescue from the perceived *results* of sin, particularly illness. Thus they cry for deliverance and salvation (6:4; 40:13), for help (38:22; 40:13), for God to hear (39:12; 88:2; 102:1, 2; 130:1). They ask for an end to rebuke and wrath (6:1; 38:1).

Moreover, while the distinctive features of the problems faced in these songs are sickness and the wrath of God prompted by sin, the problems are broader than sickness, including enemies and persecution much like those found in the Prayers for Deliverance From Accusation and Persecution. That is, the sickness with which these persons struggle is only one, even if in these cases the chief, manifestation of God's displeasure and one feature of their plight. At one point the healing is desired so that the psalmist may live to exact vengeance (41:10). So these psalms contain prayers for general salvation and rescue and mercy.

The affirmations and rationale undergirding these prayers parallel those detailed for the Prayers of Deliverance

From Accusation and Persecution (see section II.B). They emphasize the petitioners' trust in Yahweh (38:15; 130:5, 6), their denial of all other gods as help (39:7), and their proclamation of Yahweh's loving deliverance (40:9–10). They assume Yahweh's unchallenged rule (102:12–14) and his unchanging self (102:24–28) as the basis for hope. In other ways as well they reflect the confidence seen in the previous *t°pillôt̠*. Distinctive, however, in this song type is the affirmation of the worshiper's own moral deprivation and need (51:5–6, 10) as a prominent conviction motivating the prayer.

Ps 51 is Scripture's premier model for confession of sin. The setting of David's "classic sin" with Bathsheba, involving not only adultery but also lying, murder, and theft (2Sa 11), only enhances its power. Throwing himself without reserve upon the mercy of God (v.1), David takes full responsibility for his sin, implicating no one else, though others could have been cited, and offering no rationalizations or evasions of accountability (*"my* **transgressions . . .** *my* **iniquity . . .** *my* **sin"** [vv.1–3]; **"I have sinned and [I have] done what is evil"** [v.4]). Using virtually the OT's entire vocabulary for sin, David calls his terrible deeds by their terrible names, eschewing euphemisms to blur the question. He acknowledges that God the Judge alone is the One with whom he must finally deal in this, in spite of the fact that others are involved (v.4). Acknowledging that this set of deeds is no isolated event, he accepts his sinful history from birth (v.5) and points beneath his deeds of sin to his more fundamental need, his sinfulness (vv.5, 10). He accepts legitimate social ramifications to his sin (v.14) and traces disruption of his health and emotions to his own vice (vv.8, 12, 15). He acknowledges one and only

one source of rescue from all his sin and its many implications, the God of mercy and unfailing love, **"the God who saves me"** (v.14). Then in a vocabulary broader than that cataloguing his sin, he implores God to save him. Legal language—"expunging from the record" (**"blot out"**), sacral language borrowed from laundering—**"cleanse,"** ceremonial language—**"make clean,"** atonement language—to **"un-sin with hyssop,"** and traditional epic language of creation—**"create,"** all find use in this cry for full salvation.

But Ps 51 contains more than a paradigm for confession. This Prayer of the Sinner carries potent theology of sin and salvation, some features of which are anticipated in the model of confession. The prayer exposes the central human predicament, the contrast between human sinfulness from birth and the desire of God for inner and outer integrity (vv.5–6). It assumes human action to be symptomatic of inner life, tracing in this case human acts of sin to sinfulness of heart and spirit. The prayer everywhere assumes God's ability and willingness not only to forgive the acts of sin and grant acceptance and continuing life to the offender, but also the ability and willingness to rectify the sinner's inner need, creating and renewing the very core of the needy one's person—heart and spirit (vv.1, 10, 11). The prayer makes the confession and pleas a truly individual and personal matter, emphasizing the priority of inner brokenness and integrity, while not privatizing or divorcing the entire endeavor from the worshiping community or its liturgy (vv.7, 16–17). The role of God in not only reconciling and renewing, but also in sustaining the rescued one in a continuing walk with God, is taught (v.12). Finally, the song sets forth the link between reconciliation with God and authentic worship, evangelism, and service (vv.13–15).

As in Ps 130, this prayer of confession and restoration is appropriated for the community's needs. Distraught over the destruction from the nation's sin, without temple and sacrifice, the exiled community made the confession and confidence expressed in the prayer its own confession and hope (51:18–19; 130:6).

III. FESTIVAL SONGS AND LITURGICAL PIECES (PSS 50, 81, 115, 121, 131, 133)

Although these pieces resist location in one of the established psalm categories, they reveal in fascinating ways the liturgical and temple background of the works now in the Psalter. They also convey the import of support in prayer and loyalty to God.

At points we can only guess the worship setting. Pss 131 and 133 seem scarcely more than benedictory affirmations, indeed benedictory sayings. The one contains an individual's affirmation of contentment in quiet, expectant waiting on Yahweh (131:1–2). The fretting of the nursing child has given way to the tranquillity of the weaned. This personal certitude the piece then appropriates for all Israel, with the exhortation to **"put your hope in the LORD"** (v.3). But together the piece is more comfort and benediction than challenge. Ps 133 celebrates the sheer goodness of unity among brothers in a world so fractured by intrigue and fighting (remember the Prayers for Deliverance). Ps 121 is a little longer. Two verses affirming the psalmist's sole reliance on the **Maker of heaven and earth**—not the hills and the idolatrous, earthbound "helps" they represent—open the song. The remainder holds instructive, encouraging

affirmations addressed to the worshiper of vv.1–2, supporting that faith and reassuring the listener of Yahweh's unending protection.

As to when such affirming, encouraging, comforting words may have been spoken, virtually to stand on their own in the worship, one can only speculate. Perhaps they followed the *t*ʿpillôt* when the worshiper had poured out his or her groaning, calling for protection or deliverance. Such benedictory affirmations would bring comfort. Other situations could be suggested. Perhaps as much as anything, these pieces underscore the value of corporate affirmation, the healing, helping force of affirmative, benedictory sayings in worship. For those who truly listen, the "speaking of the peace" has power, especially when one may find oneself unable to speak such words on one's own. Now in the Psalter, out of the temple courts, these poems bring that comfort to the reader.

Ps 115 opens a window upon the lively interaction probable in the liturgy of the temple. Trace the interplay. A congregational ascription of glory to the Lord opens the psalm (v.1), followed by a corporate affirmation of faith in **"our God,"** denying, indeed ridiculing, the worthless gods of the nations (vv.2–8). Growing out of this affirmation of faith comes a recitative liturgy of exhortation to trust this God (vv.9–11). Sectors of the worshiping community are addressed in turn—the (royal) house of Israel, the (priestly) house of Aaron, and the lay community of Yahweh fearers, with each exhortation to trust followed by the assertion (apparently by another party) that **he is their help and shield.** These exhortations are then balanced by a mirror-image response, affirming that the Lord will indeed bless the house of Israel, the house of Aaron, and those who fear the

Lord (vv.12–13). Finally a concluding affirmation undergirds the import of the entire community's praise of Yahweh (vv.16–18) and closes now with the editors' line that places it in the series of Hallel songs (v.18b). With imagination one can still sense the liveliness of such a liturgy, in spite of the mystery regarding its setting.

Whether there was a festival devoted solely to covenant renewal in ancient Israel we do not know. Some passages of Scripture present themselves as candidates for arguable liturgies for such occasions (e.g., Dt 26:16–30:20; Jos 24). Covenant renewal itself surely was a part of Israel's worship. Ps 50 no doubt addressed such a situation. V.5 refers the gathered ones back to their covenant roots; v.16 implies that recitation of the law and the covenant words was part of the service.

The piece is structured by an opening appearance of God, with emphasis on his "speaking" and "coming," with echoes of the Exodus and Sinai (vv.1–4), followed by three clearly introduced oracles in which God directly speaks. First stands the divine invitation (v.5), then admonition to Yahweh's people (vv.7–15), and finally the contrasting denunciation of the wicked (vv.16b–23). El, the universally recognized High God (NIV **"The Mighty One"**), Yahweh God himself, will utter righteous judgments (vv.4, 6). We must think most likely of a temple prophet or a Levitical preacher speaking Yahweh's word.

The sermons are heavily freighted theologically. The message to Yahweh's people hinges on realizing the implications of who their God actually is (50:7). It demolishes current, popular misunderstandings of the sacrificial system, rejecting the idea that Yahweh in any way literally feeds on the sacrifices offered (vv.8–13). Israel's neighbors

often envisioned the clothing, feeding, moving of their gods as indispensable functions of the priests and worshipers. God separates the whole endeavor from mythological approaches to worship, implying the sacramental (versus literal) quality of the drama. He urges authentic sacrifice and promises deliverance with it (vv.14–15).

The contrasting oracle to the wicked expounds the equally important issue of integrity in worship (50:16–23). Persons who neither do nor intend to keep the law find scorn here. Their basic problem is also their distorted view of God, whom they project as devious like themselves (v.21b). They seal their judgment by such folly. This hypocritical trifling with sacred words and litanies appears worse than simple ignorance, reminding one of Paul's strong words to the Corinthians' disdain for the Lord's Table (1Co 11:17–34).

At the climax of the year, Ps 81 (no doubt with many more songs and readings)) called Yahweh's people to festival joy and the hearing of his word. The blast on the ram's horn at the **new moon** and **full moon** (v.3) locates Ps 81 at the seventh month. Opened with the horn blast at the new moon's first sliver, the month included the high Day of Atonement on the tenth day and the Feast of Tabernacles on the fifteenth day (the full moon), according to Lev 23:33–34.

Following the call to festival joy (81:1–5), Yahweh himself speaks (again, we presume, through a temple prophet or Levitical preacher) a message in four movements (vv.6–7, 8–10, 11–12, and 13–16). Building on the review of his saving history with his people, Yahweh calls his people to **listen** to him, putting away foreign gods (vv.6–10). Rehearsing their tragic habit of not heeding his voice (vv.11–12), he indirectly calls the hearers to obedience by a lament over the truly satisfying blessing forfeited by those who will not hear (vv.13–16).

These pieces presenting the Levitical preacher or temple prophet bring to the fore the power of the spoken Word of God in worship. The form of these sermons is astounding, for they speak directly as the oracles of God, quoting God, as modern English editions of the Psalter indicate by punctuation. Though these pieces now stand as the *written* Word of God to us, they were not first thus delivered. They constituted in worship the spoken word. But unlike the contemporary sermons, where the prophets or preachers give "the word of God" in "their own words," these come with the conviction that the very "words" (plural!) of God are being spoken. Behind them we can perhaps assume the same agony to **hear** God, the same searching and openness to God experienced by persons now who address others in the name of God. At the very least they call attention to the marvel of God's speaking at all through human lips.

The burden of these last liturgies, Pss 50, 81, 115 (and implicitly, 121 as well) is clearly the continuing need to call God's people away from culturally accommodated, character-eroding understandings of him to the foundational commitments of the covenant. **The hills** seemed so near (121:1–2), where Canaanite and confused Yahweh worship claimed to present more tangible and believable help (Jer 3:6–10). To Israel's neighbors her "invisible god" (115:2) lacked credibility. One might like to think of the people of God as able to stay true to the One who saved them—without reminder and repeated reinforcement . Their history does not support that dream. In these psalms God clearly gives his Word and calls his people to continual renewal of their bonds with him. Just as the benedictory affirmations noted earlier may well have undergirded the believers' desperate prayers, these liturgies support God's people in continuing obedience.

IV. THANKSGIVING SONGS (the *tôdâh*) (Pss 18, 22, 23, 30, 32, 52, 66, 92, 107, 116, 118, 124, 138)

The Thanksgiving Songs constitute the joyful reflex of the Prayer Songs (See section II), especially those for Deliverance From Accusation and Persecution, for here those cries have been heard. The terrible plights encountered in those prayers are now history. They surface here only to recount God's faithful deliverance. Certain death and destruction (18:4–5), enemies and illness (30:1–2), a sense of forsakenness by God (22:1), sin and the terror of God's anger (30:5; 32:3–4), and the scorn of it all (22:7–8) appear in testimony of the Lord's saving answer. In every case he has made the day in which gladness appears (118:24).

No single structure guides this process, though the components of praise on the basis of recounted deliverance are common to almost all of these songs. The entire opening two-thirds of Ps 22 recounts the desperate, deadly attack in which the psalmist felt deserted by God (22:1–21), a picture so bleak one despairs ever hearing from him. Reflecting God's rescue later, the latter third of the song is as victorious and confident as the first section is despondent (22:22–31). In Ps 30 the opening and closing lines declare praise to Yahweh for deliverance in general terms, with the intervening lines detailing and supporting these invitations to praise. Ps 52 devotes seven of its nine verses to warning the wicked, with praise and testimony of deliverance briefly concluding the work (52:8–9).

Ps 23, if it belongs here, simply assumes the plight and devotes all its energy to testimony of Yahweh's salvation past, present, and future. Ps 107 is a meticulously crafted liturgy of thanks, with recurring refrains and culminating exhortation. The grand point of it all, as Ps 52:9 puts it, is that these marvelous rescues are **"what you [Yahweh] have done."** And the point of the songs, by and large, is **"Come . . . let me tell you what he [God] has done for me"** (66:16).

Just as the plights recounted before in petition now surface in testimony to problems resolved, so the petitions themselves appear now in testimony to what God has done. He *has* heard (18:6; 66:19); *has* healed (30:2–3); *has* forgiven (32:5); *has* delivered from the enemy and given victory (18:32–45); and *has* protected, provided, vindicated, and given hope (23:1–6). Nowhere is this more clearly portrayed than in the matching refrains of Ps 107, where predicament is mirrored repeatedly in the language of deliverance: for example, **"Some sat in darkness and the deepest gloom. . . . He brought them out of darkness and the deepest gloom"** (vv.10, 14).

In the course of these testimonies and related to them, rich faith in Yahweh finds song. Affirmations regarding Yahweh's saving relationship to the psalmists now rise from life experience, Yahweh as the Rock and Fortress (18:2–3)—the place on which one stands safe from the swirling waters of a wadi's flash flood or the impregnable city behind whose high and strong walls one is secure. Yahweh is the **hiding place** from haunting sin (32:7). Yahweh's holy dominion, the ancient reports of the ancestors, and the psalmist's own history of trust, which in the crisis stood so ironically out of place, now in the light of deliverance

seem surer than ever (22:4–5, 9–11 versus 22:1–2, 6–8, 12–18 in light of vv.22–30). Ps 118's account of rescue (118:5) undergirds the call to affirm Yahweh's enduring mercy (118:2–4), the Lord's nearness, and the psalmist's freedom from fear (118:6). The fitness of praising Yahweh and his exaltation (92:1–3, 8) springs directly from the psalmist's gladness at Yahweh's works, the demise of Yahweh's enemies, and the psalmist's own elevation (92:4–7, 9, 10–11). Deliverance leads to assurance that God treasures the life of his dear ones, relinquishing them only with great reluctance (116:15–16). What else could explain this poor soul's survival?

But according to these songs, it is not simply that the experiences inspired or confirmed faith, but that in the deliverance Yahweh actually made himself known. Ps 18 uses classic language borrowed from historic theophanies (appearances of God) to make this point (18:7–15). None of this finds clearer expression, perhaps, than in Ps 23, where the image of the royal shepherd unites the entire work. (That is, the poem does not begin with a shepherd picture and switch to a host picture.) No lowly peasant shepherd here, this is Yahweh, the King, in the figure of Shepherd (as known since earliest days in the ancient Near East and frequently, e.g., in the prophets' hope for the mighty David to rule after the Exile). This **Shepherd** has the resources, authority, power, and goodness to supply life's deepest needs; to rescue from death and guide through mortality; to judge and vindicate lavishly in the presence of foes; and to offer unending bliss by his very presence. According to Ps 107, only the upright of heart are able to see God even in these experiences; the wicked miss it all (107:42).

From these experiences of God's deliverance, the psalmists find eyes to see the future in faith. They envision Yahweh's "global" dominion and worship (22:27–28), universally rendering service to him (vv.29–31). They see Yahweh's providence continually with them for good and life forever in his presence (23:6). The flourishing lot of the righteous in God's all-embracing goodness now appears to them (92:12–15). This new hope shines through the repeated "will" and "shall" language of these songs. They find themselves inspired to pronounce blessing on the forgiven (32:1–2) and on those who join the liturgy of praise (118:27–28).

Nor is this all a private matter. The drama of the *tôdâh* engaged the worshiping assembly so that the private experiences of these rescued ones was to edify other people of God. The liturgy frequently associated with the *tôdâh* still peeks through Pss 52, 66, 107, and 118. Ps 52:9 registers the simple import of praise in the presence of the saints. The back and forth interaction between the celebrant and other worshipers and leaders present is obvious in Ps 66 (vv.8–9, 10–15, 16). The refrain structure of Ps 107 would almost certainly have involved antiphonal or responsive worship. The celebration could involve a procession of praise (118:26–28), marching with waving boughs to the altar. There the grateful one offered a thank offering (of the same name as these Songs of Thanks, the *tôdâh*) and other sacrifices, paying vows made during the distress now past (66:13–15; 116:17–18). The whole priestly leadership and worshiping congregation are called to join the praise and affirmation with this delivered individual (118:1–4).

Oddly enough, many of these deliverances are actually reversals of distress also traced to Yahweh's anger and displeasure (e.g., Ps 30). Yahweh rescues from the storm he has spawned and now controls to a whisper (107:23–30). On the other hand, for those who trust him, Yahweh's presence is affirmed through all the woes that the righteous endure (32:10). In the end, the afflictions seem momentary in a lifetime of awareness of the Lord's loving favor (30:5).

V. ROYAL SONGS (the *ma'aśay l'melek*) (Pss 2, 20, 21, 45, 61, 72, 89, 101, 110, 132, 144)

These **verses to the king** (45:1) span all five books of the Psalter and originally served diverse purposes. Pss 2 and 110 seem to have come from enthronement ceremonies. From David or his court on, they may well have been part of coronations of succeeding kings. If so, they no doubt served multiple purposes, warning vassals compelled to be present on such occasions (2:1–6, 10–12). Ps 20 honored the king by benedictions and prayerful support. Offering praise to Yahweh, Ps 21:1–7 undergirded the king's relationship to God, and concluded by encouraging and supporting the crown with promised and implied divine support (21:8–12). The king and his rule were placed in the hands of Yahweh (21:13; 72:1, 15–17; 110; 132). One song unabashedly celebrates the king and kingship, cementing his marriage and fostering stability in political affairs of the realm (Ps 45). More soberly, Ps 61 prays for the king's life and health and rule in the presence and protection of Yahweh. Similarly, Ps 132 appeals to David's important oath regarding the ark to reinforce its prayer for Yahweh to fulfill his oath to David's descendants, a song undergirding the dynasty. Pss 72 and 101 pledge just rule as an expression of the rule of Yahweh and must have functioned to instruct as well as encourage and exhort the king indirectly. Ps 89 celebrates Yahweh's historic deeds, his blessing of his people, and especially his singular covenant with David his servant, all in the course of agonizing over that covenant's apparent disarray, perhaps a pivotal point in the Psalter as a whole. Ps 144 recalls the idyllic days of David, the warrior-musician, but seems to have in mind a situation in which the Davidic son is held captive and David's worst fears have come to pass, a poignant prayer for the king's liberty and preservation.

The language of the crown in these few songs points to the several key relationships focused in the king. The ruler here is, of course, **the king** (20:9; 21:1; 45:11, 14; 61:6) and thus the chief man (45:2) in the realm, with power virtually unlimited within the bounds of his ability to command loyalty and faithfulness to the historic faith. The king's prowess and vigor were presented well in David's story, **a young man, a warrior** (89:19), **O mighty one** (45:3). At best he was the people's best hope beside Yahweh himself, reflected in the ownership and confidence seen in such titles as *"Our King"* and *"Our Shield"* (89:18). The profile of ideal kingship celebrated and pledged in these songs places squarely on his shoulders the maintenance of justice in the realm, the care of the disenfranchised, and defense of the crown and therefore those under it with their property (45:4, 6–7; 72:2–14). To the king fell primary accountability for the character of not only his own affairs, but those of his court, his home, and of his selected associates (Ps 101). Truly such a person would be **a horn** and **a lamp** (132:17). Ps 45 addresses the royal groom as **God** (v.6), an understanding maintained in the earliest version we have (the Septu-

agint). Though such language was quite at home in the ancient world, it surprises us in Israel, where Yahweh shares his glory with no one. Yet it stands as an extravagant celebration of the king's honor, and tells us something of the awe in which he was held. Derek Kidner frames it well: "As for divine honours the language . . . was understood, we may suppose, as terminology not to be pressed (until the New Testament insisted that it should be), yet as not entirely inappropriate" (Kidner, 1:19).

But in these **verses for the king** David's relationship to God receives primary accent. The king is *"My* [i.e., **God's] Anointed One,"** and therefore set apart to sacred service, endued by God's Spirit. He is *"my* Son" (2:7; **"the Son,"** v.12), **"my chosen one"** (89:3), **"my servant"** (89:3; 144:10), **"my firstborn"** (89:27). Each of these registers the unusually honored or intimate relationship the king sustained with Yahweh, a relationship declared at enthronement (2:7; 110:1) and sustained by covenant.

Not only is the king uniquely related to Yahweh, but Yahweh also relates himself to the crown. To plot against the king is to rebel against Yahweh (2:1–2). Yahweh "begets" and installs the king (2:6; 89:27; 110:1–2). He is the source of all royal blessings (21:1–7), the breadth of his rule (2:8–9; 110:2–3, 5–7), victory in battle (20:1–5), his salvation and preservation (61:2–3). He endows with a sense of justice (72:1). He establishes the king's priestly duties, whatever they are (110:4). He founds and perpetuates the Davidic kingship by covenant and pledges to chastise David's successors without destroying the dynasty (89:3, 17–29). In him, as much as in the priesthood, God's people see Yahweh at work and find his word confirmed.

One may ask what significance all of this has in view of the fact that by the time God's servants were putting the Psalter in the form we now have before us, the kingship was no more. Though we have been given works from the coronation hall itself, the entire institution lay in the past, an agony acknowledged by this work itself (Ps 89:38–51). The editors of the Psalter have underscored this fact in the ironic contrast in the songs closing the second and the third books (Ps 72 versus Ps 89)!

One fascinating implication of this fact is that these songs must *already have been understood* as messianic by the ancient editors. Not the extravagant language (even the "forevers"), but the by-then-past demise of the kingship shows it. The Targum indicates this already by actually inserting "Messiah" with "King" at points (e.g., 72:1). These songs carry the faith that Yahweh will one day keep his covenant to David and fulfill the promises made through his prophets (e.g., Jer 23:1–6; Eze 37:15–28).

The NT declares unequivocally that this hope has been realized in Jesus of Nazareth (Mt 2:1–6; Lk 1:67–79). The totally nationalistic orientation of these Royal Songs as well as the prophetic hopes obscured the identity of Messiah to many, including the disciples (Mk 8:27–9:2). But the non-nationalistic, universal reach of Messiah Jesus was already apparent in his ministry and certainly in his commission (Mt 28:18–20) and risen presence (Acts). This enabled the appropriation of these songs for the worship of the church (cf. Ps 110 in Heb 1 and 2 and elsewhere).

But the Psalter itself had already broached this point in the second major implication of the fallen kingship's songs here preserved. As noted in the introduction (section V), the Psalter's arrangement proclaims the kingship of Yahweh himself, not simply "over" the king but "without" the king. And Yahweh is King of all the earth, receiving praise from all his creation, calling into question overidentification of his rule with any state and offering his kingdom to all who will love his law and walk in it.

VI. SONGS OF ZION (the *šîr ṣiyyôn*) (Pss 46, 48, 76, 84, 87, 122; cf. 137)

Jerusalem's most beloved name, "Zion," evoked history, tradition, pride, faith, and loyalty in her people. "Zion" designated the Jebusite fortress, straddling the hill crest between the Kidron and Tyropeon Valleys captured by David (2Sa 5:5–9). The name was extended up the hill to what became the temple mount and eventually to the whole city of Jerusalem and its residents. Of course references to Jerusalem and Zion abound in the Psalms. (Some of these will be noted, as they reflect themes found in the songs at hand.) But these Songs of Zion are uniquely devoted to extolling this **city of [God] the Great King** (48:1–2). No other city or place, including the temple, receives this adulation. The poets include language of ancient tradition to enrich the lines, one indication of the distinguished topic. The Creation story's life-giving river (46:4; cf. Ge 2:10; Eze 47:1–12); Canaanite religion's Northern Mount of the Gods, Mount Zaphon (48:2); and antiquity's Salem of patriarchal fame (76:2; cf. Ge 14:17–20) all appear here. The fact is that "Zion Songs" existed and were known as such, were even famous among Israel's neighbors and enemies. Babylonian soldiers may have overheard these songs sung for encouragement by besieged Jerusalemites before the collapse of 586 B.C. In

Babylon these captors demanded, perhaps at spearpoint, the exiles in forced march (?) by the canals to sing . . . one of the songs of Zion! (137:3). What humiliation to face those extravagant lyrics now.

The Songs of Zion exalt her in part because of the city's relation to David, Israel's first "real" king, and the model for all who followed. It was he who presided over the transport of the ancient ark of the covenant from Kiriath-Jearim to "the City of David" (2Sa 6), fulfilling the ancient vision (Dt) and uniting the tribal worship. As a matter of fact, David's transport of the ark, God's covenantally buttressed choice of David, and God's choice of Jerusalem stood closely intertwined in the hearts of the faithful (132).

The Zion Songs, however, celebrate this city primarily because of its special relation to Yahweh, God of Israel. Zion belonged to Yahweh. Zion was *his*— "the city of our God" (48:1–2, 8; 87:3; cf. 2:6, **my holy hill**), the object of his special love (87:2), chosen (78:68–70; 122:3–5; 132:13–18) and established (87:5) by him. Thus selection and preservation of David's capital city, designed to unite the scattered tribes, could not be seen simply in political or sociological terms. This place with its role in the life of Israel (and later Judah) was Yahweh's.

In Zion Yahweh was uniquely present (46:5; cf. 99:2; 135:21). Known specifically as Yahweh's dwelling (76:2), the temple of Solomon stood here (cf. 102:21; 135:21). For that very fact Jerusalem was extolled (48:9; 84:1–4), and it was sufficient reason to pray for Jerusalem's peace (122:9). Specifically, Yahweh **dwelt** between the cherubim (99:1). At the dedication of the temple Solomon acknowledged the utter inability of any human construction to "house" Yahweh, God of heaven and earth (1Ki 8:27); God would still see and hear "from heaven" (1Ki 8:29–30). Even so, Yahweh was felt also to be uniquely present in his house, present in a way unknown elsewhere. There Yahweh was seen; there he revealed himself uniquely (48:3; 84:7; cf. 50:2; 102:16). This speaking, disclosing presence of Yahweh we have already seen expressed in liturgy, where God (we assume through his priests and prophets) directly speaks to worshipers with instruction or rebuke or encouragement (e.g., 32:8–9; 60:6–8 = 108:7–9). *From* Zion Yahweh exercises sovereignty among all the nations of the earth, achieving his victory and accomplishing his will (46:9; 48:10; 76:5–6, 11–12; cf. 9:11). From this place he brings salvation (53:6; 134:3).

Thus, these Songs of Zion celebrate Yahweh's unique presence in Jerusalem, and rightly so, for much depended on that presence. Zion's stability and security are connected directly in these songs to Yahweh's presence in spite of international turmoil (46:6; 48:4). The congregation's safety was at stake (46:7). God himself was the citadel's defense (48:3; 76:3). These themes, among many others, no doubt, brought Zion intense love and deepest loyalties from her residents and those who made frequent pilgrimages there. The poets of these works describe her beauty and majesty with extravagant endearment (48:2, 12–14; 84:1–4; 87:1–3; cf. 50:2). The songs express intense longing for Jerusalem, for Yahweh's house, and for their good (84:1–4, 10; 122:1–2, 6–9). The absolutely sacred and unimaginably precious nature of Zion, her temple, and even her songs stands behind the potent emotions driving Ps 137:

If I forget you, O Jerusalem,

may my right hand forget its skill.
May my tongue cling to the roof of
    my mouth,
  if I do not remember you,
if I do not consider Jerusalem
    my highest joy.

(vv.5–6)

Those who enter her gates are
blessed indeed (84:4–7, 12; cf.
137:7–9).

Christian readers recognize passages
of the Songs of Zion from music of the
church, classical and modern, appropriating this ancient city as something of
the capital of the universal people of
God. Their faith can no longer be
confined to the chief city of any political state. The final Son of David foresaw the day when persons would worship neither in Jerusalem nor in
Samaria (Jn 4:21–24). Worship in the
Spirit and according to the truth would
not be tied to one place. Further, the
people of God themselves, Messiah's
people, would be in reality the temple
of God, individually (1Co 6:19) and
collectively (1Co 3:16; Eph 2:19–22;
1Pe 2:4–5). The vision of history's
climax exalts this truth. There the New
Jerusalem is no place at all, but the
redeemed people of God of all ages and
cultures become in reality the eternal
dwelling of God and the Lamb (Rev
21). These ancient Songs of Zion seem
still capable of expressing much of the
truth of that reality, as they are sung
now to a theologically different key.

VII. DIDACTIC SONGS (the ḥokmâh) (Pss 1, 15, 34, 37, 49, 73, 78, 91, 111, 112, 119, 127, 128; cf. 19)

Teaching purpose, distinctive language, and the "Piety of the Two
Ways" mark the Didactic Songs. Their
faith may be the most influential in the
Psalter.

The teaching purpose is explicit in

Pss 34 and 78 (vv.1–7). After opening
invitations to worship and participation
in the way of the Lord (34:1–10), Ps
34 invites the listeners/readers to come
to instruction, raising the topic question and presenting instruction based
on it (vv.11–22). In Pss 15 and 49 no
explicit invitation appears, but again
the instructional question enters (15:1;
49:5–6), followed by the crafted answer (15:2–5; 49:7–20). The instructional intent may perhaps also account
for the fact that five of the Psalter's
eight acrostic poems appear in this
group of songs (34, 37, 111, 112, 119;
cf. "Acrostic," in the Introduction,
II.C). It is Ps 91's apparently clear
instructional mode that places it in this
group. Its lack of "wisdom-Torah"
language raises a question about its
inclusion here.

Words and expressions normally associated with "wisdom teaching" in the
OT, here joined with the language of
Torah ("law") in the sense of "instruction," punctuate these songs. The lines
in these songs are "instructional sayings" (lit. **"wisdoms,"** 49:3), involving
"insight sayings," "proverbs," and
"riddles" (49:3–4), the standard language of wisdom teachers and writers
(cf. Pr 1:5–6). The Didactic Songs
understand "Torah" as instruction, parallel to wisdom (37:30–31) and linked
with proverb and riddle in the task of
teaching (78:2, where NIV translates
tôrâh as "teaching"). They include hallmark sayings of wisdom instruction,
such as **"The fear of the LORD is the
beginning of wisdom"** (111:10; cf.
the key passage of Proverbs [1:7] and
Job 28:28).

Most distinctive of these poems is
their instruction in "The Piety of the
Two Ways." The Didactic Songs expound the totally separate paths known
from wisdom literature as the ways of
"the wise" and "the foolish," from

covenant literature as those of "the obedient" and "the disobedient." Nothing could be clearer in this teaching than that there are fundamentally two groups of persons in Israel (perhaps on earth). These two groups are distinguished by their totally different characters and their consequently divergent lives and destinies.

General descriptions distinguish these groups. On the one hand stand the righteous (1:6), the blameless (15:2), the upright (37:37), the wise (49:10), the saints (34:9), the pure in heart (73:1). Those who fear the LORD probably names these godly ones most comprehensively (34:7, 9; 112:1). These general designations are elaborated with other descriptions. These are "people of the Law" par excellence. They not only live the Law, they live *in it* (1:1–2). These are often, though not always, the afflicted (34:2; 37:11), the brokenhearted (34:18), the poor (34:6; 37:14), the needy (37:14). They are the meek (same Hebrew word as "the afflicted," 37:11), persons who trust Yahweh, look to him and and seek refuge and hope in him (34:3, 8, 10, 22: 37:9, 11). These character traits and general dispositions of life find expression in specific acts, with particular interest taken in the use of the tongue, of money, and of influence (cf., e.g., 15:2–5; 34:13; 37:21). Most telling, these persons actually reflect Yahweh's own character here and now. They, like him, are gracious and compassionate (cf. 111:4; 112:4). They are not only *considered* righteous by Yahweh, they *are* righteous. Such persons alone may truly worship (the question of Ps 15).

On the other hand stand the wicked (1:4–6; 37:13–14). These are sinners (1:5), mockers (1:1), vile persons (15:4), wrongdoers (37:1), schemers (37:7), deceivers (49:5), and abusers of power and wealth (37:16–17, 32–33). These are the enemies of the Lord (37:20). Pss 34 and 37 delineate as clearly as any psalms the persons of the two ways, as the references above show.

Two contrasting destinies (present and future) parallel these two populations, according to the Didactic Songs. These contrasting destinies express the blessing and the cursing of the Lord (37:22), causally, not accidentally, linked to the moral character of the persons involved (e.g., "therefore" and "for" [1:5–6]). Yahweh loves (37:28), upholds (37:17), protects and delivers (34:4, 6–7), saves (34:18), redeems (34:22), vindicates (37:6; 112:3, 8–9), and delights in the way of (37:23) the godly. He blesses them with prosperity (1:3; 112:3), long life (34:11–12), plenty (37:19), fertility (112:2, 3; 128:3, 6), and an enduring inheritance of the Promised Land (37:9–11, 22, 29, 34). *Not so the wicked!* (1:4). Their cursed life differs directly from this blessed walk. Images tell it best—the contrast between a perennially fruitful tree growing by a canal and worthless chaff blown away by the wind (Ps 1; cf. 37:1–2, 20, 35–36; 73:18).

But life does not always appear to vindicate such a clear picture of blessing and cursing (cf. II.B above). The Didactic Songs address this problem also, and well they might, for the contrast between faith and experience here, i.e., between what these dear people believed and what they actually encountered in life, posed a major problem for the faithful (73:1–16). To begin, say these songs, one must view the promised destinies as life processes. Not every person or circumstance will vindicate this faith (37:5–9, 35–36). More profoundly, the simple appearance of the "blessings" in one's life does not actually constitute the blessing of Yahweh. Equating the two is self-delusion (49:18–20). If one is wealthy, for example, but lacks true understanding (including reverence for Yahweh and his covenant and an appreciation for the source of life's goods) one is not blessed at all but rather no better than **the beasts that perish** (49:20). Furthermore, neither wealth nor poverty but only the Lord can redeem one from the power of death itself (49:7–9, 15). It is obvious that all die, the wealthy wicked as well as the godly poor, and that they take nothing with them from this life (49:10ff.). But the fact of death is not the problem; the problem is the power of death to dominate. From this terrible trap only Yahweh can deliver (49:12–15)—whether by a "taking" like Enoch's before death (cf. Ge 5:24) or resurrection after death (Isa 26:19; Da 12:2) is not clear here.

Elsewhere the OT makes significant advance on the idea. Job and Ecclesiastes mount the most formidable attack on the overly simple, overly direct connection between moral character and life circumstance engendered by the standard wisdom and historic covenant faith. In spite of the fact that in the end Job's fortunes are reversed, the book's broadside at the standard view is never retracted. Job's friends hold the "orthodox" view (as does Job when the book opens, else he would not have his spiritual problem), at times reasoning clearly from it, at other times exaggerating it, drawing half-truths. Job 21 is the *tour de force* that simply demolishes any attempt to say life itself vindicates the claim that the righteous experience immediate, concrete blessing now and the wicked the opposite. Ecclesiastes, the journal of a candid believer, quotes standard wisdom repeatedly to refute or qualify it, precisely at the point of debate here (e.g., Ecc 2:12–14; 8:10–14). Finally, the Preacher asserts that

one cannot know the disposition of God toward one—love or hate—based on circumstances (9:1–6). These words of God contribute to the OT's consideration of the difficulty by forcefully calling the theological frame of reference itself into question without forging through to a full answer. Job's major contribution appears to be the mystery of God, for no one in the book except the heavenly court *ever* knew what really lay behind Job's disasters. God's reasons were completely his own, and he refrained from revealing them to any of the earthly parties.

Beyond these major approaches to the issue, other OT passages make significant contribution. The Joseph narratives place these matters beyond simple connections of blessing-cursing to the larger, sovereign purposes of God. "You intended to harm me, but God intended it for good to accomplish what is now being done," said Joseph to his brothers (Ge 50:20). Jeremiah narrates the truth of unvindicated servants of Yahweh who suffer for no sin of their own, with no apparent redress by God. Habakkuk is led to affirm *joy,* not simply trust, in God his Savior, *even if* the covenant blessings (figs, wine, oil, field crops, fertility) do not materialize (3:16–19). Isa 53 raises the reality that God's servant not only suffers because of the sins of others (not his own), but does so *redemptively*!

Against this backdrop the NT's teaching is astounding. These teachings and especially the death of Jesus the Messiah himself constituted the major source of NT insight here. Jesus vindicated the OT's minority report by severing the clear, direct connection between sin and illness (Jn 9:1–3) and essentially "internalizing" and "eternalizing" the blessings and curses (Mt 5:1–12). Moreover, his call set suffering and death clearly before the prospective disciple as no result of the disciple's own sin but the inevitable consequence of following the Son of Man who himself has a cross (Mk 8:31–9:2). The apostles caught this remarkable reversal and continually appealed to Jesus' life as the pattern for the believer's response to suffering (e.g., 1Pe 2:13–25). Nowhere is this issue put more persuasively and movingly than in the climax to Paul's discussion of life in Christ by the Spirit (Ro 8). There, on the basis of the demonstrated love of God for us in the death of Jesus, believers encounter the old covenant's curses—famine, nakedness, persecution, sword, and more—victorious and unseparated from the love of God in Christ (Ro 8:31–38; cf. esp. Dt 28 curses with Ro 8:35).

Ps 73 may give the most adequate answer to these problems in the end. Though the poet really does not solve the problem of the underlying theological structures (either wisdom or covenant) that link so clearly personal character with life circumstances, in worship he lodges himself solely with God (73:16–17). God alone is enough and—the stark truth that still stands—in the end all one really has (73:23–26). Simply to be near God is good (73:28). This heads one toward the revolutionary breakthrough possible only in light of the cross (Ro 8:31–39).

This radical view of all of human existence under God is apparently the piety shaping the whole Psalter. In spite of the utterly clear lines drawn, "Torah piety" offered no simple "goods-for-services-rendered" religion. Torah piety is a life of delight in Yahweh himself and utter abandon-

ment to his covenant ways and his care (37:1–6)! The Psalter opens by setting before the reader these radical alternatives in which life and destiny hinge upon life in the Torah (Ps 1; cf. introduction, V.B). Book 3 opens and closes with profound examinations of deep problems in the theological structures involved (Pss 73, 89). The concluding Books 4 and 5 elaborate an answer in the universal kingship of Yahweh while undergirding the more chastened view of life in the Torah.

Ps 119 seems to be the pillar around which this latter section of the Psalter informally hangs (Mays, 6–7). By size, elaborate acrostic, extensive vocabulary, and mixture of song types from the entire book of Psalms, it unites the whole corpus in a celebration of Torah faith captured in the opening lines:

> Blessed are they whose ways are
> blameless,
>   who walk according to the law of
>   the LORD.
> Blessed are they who keep his statutes
>   and seek him with all their heart.
>   (119:1–2)

Then follow 174 verses of meditating on his law, in loving prayer rejecting all rival counsel and ways and places, and confirming faith in Yahweh (cf. 1:1–2). While the Gospel of Jesus rejects all distortions of this devotion that set obedience to the law in itself as of any consequence to salvation, the spirit of this piety surely finds echo in the Christian's all-consuming quest "to know Christ and the power of his resurrection and the fellowship of his sufferings, becoming like him in his death, and so, somehow, to attain to the resurrection from the dead" (Php 3:10).

BIBLIOGRAPHY

Allen, Leslie. *Psalms 101–150*. Edited by David A. Hubbard et al. WdBC. Waco: Word, 1983.

Craigie, Peter C. *Psalms 1–50*. Edited by David A. Hubbard et al. WdBC. Waco: Word, 1983.

Kidner, Derek. *Psalms 1–72: An Introduction and Commentary on Books I and II of the Psalms*. Edited by D. J. Wiseman. TOTC. Leicester: InterVarsity, 1973.

————. *Psalms 73–150: A Commentary on Books III–V of the Psalms*. Edited by D. J. Wiseman. TOTC. Leicester: InterVarsity, 1975.

Kraus, Hans-Joachim. *Psalms 1–59: A Commentary*. Translated by Hilton C. Oswald. Minneapolis: Augsburg, 1988.

Mays, James Luther. "The Place of the Torah-Psalms in the Psalter." JBL 106, no. 1 (1987): 3–12.

Vaux, Roland de. *Ancient Israel*. New York: McGraw-Hill, 1965.

Weiser, Artur. *The Psalms: A Commentary*. Edited by Peter Ackroyd et al. *The Old Testament Library*. Translated by Herbert Hartwell. Philadelphia: Westminster, 1962.

Wilson, Gerald Henry. *The Editing of the Hebrew Psalter*. Edited by Charles Talbert and J. J. M. Robert. Society of Biblical Literature Dissertation Series, no. 76. Chico, Calif.: Scholars Press, 1985.

PROVERBS

Robert Branson

INTRODUCTION

Tradition has associated the book of Proverbs with Solomon, the son of David, even though it contains materials that come from a later time. This is due to the reputation Solomon gained as Israel's "wise" king, a reputation that had spread beyond the nation's borders even while he lived (1Ki 10:1–10). Solomon's reputation was based on the program he had initiated to place the young nation of Israel in the mainstream of cultural achievement. The temple was built with the help of the king of Tyre. His court was organized along Egyptian lines. He developed his own talents in the international art of wisdom literature and thus became its patron (1Ki 4:29–34).

Proverbs cannot be definitely dated either as to the age of its material or the time of its final composition. In all probability some of the material goes back to Solomon himself (10:1). Yet it is the nature of a proverb to be passed down orally for many generations, and Solomon may have been a collector as well as an originator of them. The book states that the wisdom teachers of Hezekiah (715–687 B.C.) made additions to it (25:1), and the words of both Agur and Lemuel have been added (chs. 30, 31). Thus the book took its final form sometime between the beginning of the seventh century to possibly as late as a century and a half after the return from the Exile (538 B.C.).

Proverbs are found in practically every culture. Often one can find similar sayings in diverse areas of the world. This is because wisdom deals with life as it is lived. One observes what happens in the affairs of people and draws short, memorable word pictures about the situations. Collections of proverbs sometimes were passed from one people to another. Pr 22:17–24:22 is an adaptation of the work of an Egyptian named Amen-em-Opet, who several centuries before Solomon had made a collection of sayings. This borrowing and adapting of material made wisdom literature truly an international art form.

The source of information for wisdom is life itself. Life is observed and a saying is developed to describe what is learned. Knowledge is not gained primarily through visions or supernatural revelations. This secular approach to knowledge has several ramifications for understanding the

Proverbs. While each saying is true, not all can be made universally applicable. A bribe may seem like a charm that brings success and gives one access to great persons (17:8; 18:16), yet it also is the condemned device of the wicked to pervert justice (17:23). Each saying is correct but not universally applicable. One must ask under what circumstances a given saying would be appropriate.

Those who developed proverbs believed that they were observing the principles of wisdom that had been implanted in the order of the world at the time of creation. God created the world in wisdom (Pr 8). By the principles of wisdom the universe was brought into existence, and thus those principles were woven into the very framework of all creation. Through observing creation and finding out what is profitable and what is not, one discovers those same principles. In adjusting one's life in accordance with wisdom, one is getting in tune with God himself. Thus the wisdom teacher urged students to gain wisdom and insight by placing their lives in harmony with the principles God placed in the universe.

Because of this basic theological orientation, the book of Proverbs contains many sayings that a modern person would consider secular. What is religious about 13:11, "Dishonest money dwindles away, but he who gathers money little by little makes it grow"? It contains no "religious" language. To the wise man, however, the saying reflects a principle of life. How did this principle come into being? God put it there when he created the world. Thus to observe it is to place one's life in harmony with God. To learn wisdom is to learn how to succeed in life.

The three perennial questions with which wisdom worked were: How may one succeed in life (Proverbs)? What is the meaning of life (Ecclesiastes)? and Why does humanity suffer (Job)? Each of these books finds its literary counterpart in other cultures of the ancient Middle East; the questions with which they work have perplexed people of many nations through many centuries. The book of Proverbs deals with the problem of success as it relates to the various aspects of life. While it is theologically oriented in the broadest sense, it also addresses religion specifically, noting that "the fear of [or respect for] the LORD is the beginning of knowledge" (1:7). Other categories of interest include business, family life, personal morals, politics, and personal discipline, among others.

Where did the proverb originate? Were there schools that trained young men (a patriarchal society rarely provided formal education for women), or was their education the exclusive obligation of the home? Undoubtedly many of the proverbs are ancient and arose in the home or village. They were probably framed by one gifted with the ability to catch in memorable oral form some insight into life. Since natural talent knows no gender boundaries even in a patriarchal society, the sources could have been both women and men. In early Israel the extended family and clan contributed to the education of the child. As the monarchy arose, a class of trained advisers was needed. Jeremiah refers to this class as an established part of his seventh-century culture (18:18).

The book of Proverbs probably owes its origin to this class of professionally trained wise men. Whereas Solomon may have started the process of collecting and editing wise sayings, they eventually were used to train young men in schools. The term *father,* found often in the first nine chapters, may reflect an original home setting of instruction, but the term came to refer to the headmaster of the school.

OUTLINE

The book of Proverbs is easy to outline because it is made up of collections of sayings. However, inside the larger blocks of materials there often seems to be no principle of organization. Proverbs may have been grouped together due to the use of similar words or even verb tenses while their contents might be diverse. The linking of sayings by verbal similarity does indicate that they were often memorized, the similarities providing mnemonic keys.

COMMENTARY

I. INTRODUCTION (1:1–7)

The introduction (1:1–7) to the book not only identifies Solomon as the patron of proverbial wisdom, but through a series of infinitive clauses (vv. 2–4) supplies the reader with the function of the book. The young and simple (open-minded) are to learn how to live wisely. The book will even help the wise to increase their knowledge (vv.5–6). Climaxing this brief prologue is the theological expression of the ultimate source of knowledge, **the fear of the LORD.**

II. A FATHER'S ADVICE (1:8–9:18)

This section of the book originally was composed of ten poems of instructions styled in the format of advice from a father to a son. As it stands now, both smaller additions have been made to the poems themselves, and whole blocks of materials (e.g., ch. 8) have been incorporated.

The First Instruction begins with 1:8, where a son is encouraged to adopt the values given in the home, for they will prove to be adequate guides for life. Specifically, he is warned against companions who seek to entice him into violent acts (1:10–19). Here home instruction is pitted against peer pressure. The immediate prize is wealth divided equally (vv.13–14). The youth is encouraged to look beyond the immediate rewards to see the end results of their actions. What they plan for others will become their own destiny. Wisdom sees beyond the immediate to the final ends.

Wisdom's first soliloquy (1:20–33) begins with an invitation to learn from her (the Hebrew term for wisdom is feminine). The poem quickly turns to an indictment of the simple ones and fools who have rejected her invitation. When life turns against them and they desire to know wisdom, it will be too late. They will be left to their own fate, which was chosen through their rejection of wisdom. **"They hated knowledge"** (v.29) indicates an action of rejection, not an emotion. Refusing to accept wisdom's offer is the same as not choosing to fear the Lord. The two paths that lie before a person are folly, leading to destruction, or wisdom, leading to **safety** and **ease** (vv.32–33). Other paths are not available because the Lord did not create others.

Chapter 2

In the Second Instruction the instructor encourages the student (**"my son"**) to pursue after wisdom as diligently as those who seek silver or hidden treasure (v.4). The first result of such an endeavor is understanding the fear (reverence) of the Lord. By pursuing the principles by which God or-

dered creation, one gains his help in life and is assured of victory (vv. 7–8). Wisdom will also protects from two destructive influences, wicked men (vv.12–15) and the adulteress (vv.16–19).

The way of the wicked is marked by darkness and perversity. Their end will be their removal from the land (v.22). The land represents the area of the blessings of God. To be removed from it is to be removed from God's presence. The phrase can also signify death.

The young man is repeatedly warned in Proverbs to avoid the adulteress. Accepting her invitation is the height of folly, which leads to death. It must be remembered that this book originated in a patriarchal society and that the instructions are directed to young men. While similar advice is not found explicitly directed to young women, it may be assumed that the culture through home instruction warned them against seductive men. The wise person found sexual fulfillment always within the bonds of marriage.

Chapter 3

Ch. 3 divides into three parts: vv.1–12, commitment to the Lord; vv.13–20, two poems on wisdom; vv.21–35, warnings on proper behavior.

The chapter begins with an exhortation to the student, marking the beginning of the Third Instruction. This section is, however, much more theologically oriented than the previous two. The student is to keep the "teachings," or *torah,* of the instructor in order to have a long, peaceable life (cf. Ex 20:12). **"Love"** in v.3 is better translated "loyalty." The highest expression of wisdom is trusting in Yahweh rather than in one's own knowledge. Religious knowledge concerning ethical behavior takes precedent over one's own insight. By following God's torah, one's moral life or **paths** will be straight, and physical **health** will be enjoyed (vv.6–8).

The blessings of God extend even to one's material possessions (vv.9–10). The **firstfruits** of a crop were given to God in recognition of his blessings (Lev 23:9–14). In a money economy one might bring cash, check, or credit card. Proper management of resources enables God to increase them. However, there is not an inflexible law of cause and effect in operation here. Vv.11–12 speak of God's discipline, which is to be embraced rather than shunned. While blessings will come, so will times of discipline. A good father knows that both are needed in a child's life. In his sovereignty, God will bring into his children's lives that which he considers best. His children should respond by recognizing that both blessing and discipline are signs of his care.

The next section is composed of two short poems. The first (vv.13–18) celebrates the riches of wisdom. The one who seeks after her gains a long and pleasant life. The term **"tree of life"** occurs three other times in Proverbs (11:30; 13:12; 15:4). Each time the phrase functions as a poetic metaphor for life itself.

The second poem (vv.19–20) describes how God created the world according to the principles of wisdom. These verses state the basic presupposition of wisdom study; to understand the order of the world is to understand God's creative actions. This theme is amplified in ch. 8.

The last section of the chapter, the fourth discourse, begins with the words of assurance addressed to the pupil (vv.21–26). Sound judgment and discernment will provide protection along life's journey, because in deciding to follow them he will be choosing the protection of the Lord himself. A series of ethical admonitions follow (vv.27–32). If one can help a neighbor, he must do it immediately amd not delay. He must avoid any act of willful harm against a neighbor and not envy the success of the perverse or violent, for they are an abomination to the Lord. God will eventually give the deserved judgment, shame, and destruction to the wicked but give honor and grace to the wise (vv.33–35).

Chapter 4

This chapter breaks into three roughly equal divisions, each of them one of the original Ten Instructions. The first section (vv.1–9), the Fourth Instruction, admonishes the student to seek wisdom. The instructor recalls how his father or instructor had taught him to grasp his words with his heart (mind) and not to swerve from them. The student benefited from the learning of several generations. In vv.6–9 wisdom is personified as a bride whom the student is to love and for whom he must be willing to pay any price. The prize to be gained is a life lived with honor clinging to him like a beautiful wedding garland or crown.

The Fifth Instruction (vv.10–19) emphasizes the doctrine of the two paths. The student is to choose the path of wisdom, which is straight and in which he will not stumble (fall into trouble) and which leads to life. He is to avoid the path of the wicked, which is beautifully described as an insatiable obsession. Evil becomes so absorbing that sleep does not come unless the wicked do harm to someone. Wickedness and violence become as important as food and drink. It is the way of deep darkness. In contrast, the path of the righteous begins like the first ray of dawn and grows into the full sunlight of a day.

The Sixth Instruction (vv.20–27)

builds upon the metaphor of the parts of the body. The instructor's words, if followed diligently, will preserve the life of the student. They will bring health to his whole body. The heart is the seat of emotions, and the function of the mind and will is attributed to the heart (v.23). The mouth is to avoid corrupt talk, while the eyes (the attention of the student) are to remain riveted on the straight path.

Chapter 5

The Eighth Instruction is devoted to warning the student about the dangers of the adulteress. While the theme is the same as found in 2:16–19, the material is greatly expanded. The first section (vv.1–6) begins by exhorting the student to pay attention to wisdom so that his lips might preserve knowledge, a metaphor for being able to speak well. V.3 makes a play on the word *lips* to introduce the theme, only the metaphor is changed. The lips and **speech** (better, "mouth") of the adulteress are sweet and smooth, not in speaking, but in kissing. What is so pleasurable at first becomes in the end **bitter as gall.** Her path leads, not to **life,** but to **death.** Wisdom considers the end of an action, not just its beginning.

The second movement (vv.7–14) focuses on the ruin one incurs by pursuing adultery. It begins by again exhorting the student to avoid the adulteress. While he thinks he will exploit her sexuality, in reality he becomes the exploited (vv.9–11). His **strength** and **years** (better, "dignity" and "honor," as in NEB) is poured out on one who by profession must keep her compassion under control and treat her lovers with cool cruelty. The expenses of keeping a mistress will eventually bring demands from the creditors. Too late the student will recognize

the wisdom of his instructor's words and at the point of **ruin** and disgrace will wish he had heeded the warnings.

The third section (vv.15–20) offers the positive advice that the student should seek sexual satisfaction exclusively with his wife. If v.16 is taken as a rhetorical question, the images of public springs and streams refer to a man whose semen and thus offspring is given to prostitutes. If it is taken as a statement, then the images refer to numerous children borne by his wife. The wife of one's youth is one's fountain (source of children), the one with whom he should seek sexual satisfaction, the one whose love should captivate (intoxicate) him.

The chapter ends with a theological word (vv.21–23). Ultimately Yahweh will judge each person's path (manner of living). As the guarantor of justice, he allows the wicked one's sins to run their full destructive course. Death is the result of refusing discipline.

Chapter 6

This chapter is made up of four exhortations on ethical concerns and a larger section warning the student to beware of the temptations of the adulteress. It has no particular unifying theme but seems to be a random compilation of instructions.

The chapter begins with a warning against being a cosigner of a loan (6:1–5). One is not to enter into an agreement for a **neighbor** with a stranger (NIV **"another"**). The stranger may be a non-Israelite to whom the student has obligated himself if his neighbor, probably another Israelite, fails to perform on the note. The student is instructed to humble himself before his neighbor and earnestly plead until his neighbor releases him from the obligation, presumably by finding another cosigner. The wise do not place themselves in jeopardy by being dependent on the financial integrity of another.

In the second section (6:6–11), the **sluggard** is castigated for his laziness. The **ant** is held up as a model of industry as it stores up in time of plenty to have in time of need. By continuing to slumber through opportunities, the sluggard will surely experience poverty. The images of the **bandit** and **armed man** indicate that the need will come upon him suddenly and without compassion for his situation.

The **scoundrel** or **villain** (6:12–15) is one who for his own ends provokes antagonism among others. V.13 lists ways in which he might surreptitiously convey signals to confederates in his evil plots. Eventually justice will be done, and the villain will reap the fruits of his deception. This is the basic theme of each of these sections. The world is created in justice, and **evil** and folly will eventually be destroyed.

The fourth section (6:16–19) is a numerical saying listing seven items Yahweh detests. The numerical formula (x, x + 1, where x equals any number) was current in Israel (cf. 30:15–31; Am 1:3–2:6) as well as in other cultures such as Ugarit. The items are ethical in nature, with the last one, one who stirs up dissension, being identical to the previous section. The God of Israel, Yahweh, unlike many of the gods of the nations, incorporated ethical concerns as part of serving him. The worshiper was required to incorporate a high standard of moral living as part of his/her covenant obligation (Ps 15).

The final section (6:20–35) continues the theme of moral concern with the third set of warnings (2:1–22; 5:1–23) about the adulteress. This Ninth Instruction begins with an exhortation to keep the instructions that have been committed to the student, for they will preserve him from harm,

especially from the immoral woman. That which is done in secret can no more be kept secret than one can carry hot coals in his clothes and not be burned. Stolen pleasures will cost one public disgrace when exposed and will earn him a constant enemy in the wronged husband. No gifts will ever erase the enmity that is created between the two. The prudent path is to avoid the adulteress and never subject oneself to the destructive results of folly.

Chapter 7

The Tenth Instruction, consisting of the fourth warning against the adulteress, begins with an exhortation to the student to pursue wisdom. The instructor's teachings are to be closely adhered to, bound on the fingers and written on the heart. Wisdom is the faithful sister who guards the young man from the adulteress.

A descriptive poem on the seduction of a young man makes up the main section of the chapter (vv.6–23). The instructor has observed a young man who lacks **judgment** (empty of mind) being seduced by a woman of **crafty intent** (cunning of mind). It was an unequal contest. With physical attraction, flattering words, promises of sexual delight, and assurances of safety (**"My husband is not at home"**), she persuaded him to follow her home. Even religion formed part of the seduction (v.14). She who carefully observed religious requirements provided fertility as an avenue to God. Accepting the invitation, the youth was led like an animal to slaughter. The house of the adulteress is not the place of pleasure but the entrance to the **chambers of death** (vv.24–27). Wisdom sees beyond the immediate gains that temptation offers to its ultimate end, which is death. Thus it is able to choose the path of life. The fool sees only the immediate and is surprised by destruction.

Chapter 8

In contrast to the adulteress who tempts fools to the path of death, Wisdom invites them to life. She lifts her voice to the simple and foolish, calling them to learn of her, a lesson more valuable than gold and precious gems. In this poem wisdom is personified as a woman who, like the adulteress, walks abroad seeking men. Her invitation though is to life, not death. Her words are not deceptive but can be trusted as just and true. To grasp her is to grasp life.

The reason Wisdom is to be preferred is that prudence, knowledge, and discretion dwell with her, those qualities necessary for successfully mastering life. Properly understanding the universe as created by Yahweh means that one aligns oneself with the good that he has created, as opposed to evil, which is seen as a disruptive force in an otherwise well-ordered creation. **To hate** (v.13) is to oppose and to refuse to associate with, not to feel antipathy. It is an action, not an emotion.

Wisdom provides the principles by which rulers govern justly (vv.14–16). Those who love her, i.e., practice her precepts, find a wealth that surpasses gold and silver, a treasury of righteousness and justice. These principles enhance any kingdom and form the basis for building a sound economic system.

The reason why wisdom is so important is related in vv.22–31. When Yahweh began to creat, he started with Wisdom herself as the first of creation. The metaphor must not be pushed so far as to suggest that here is given a sequential ordering of a process of creation. Wisdom is given preeminence in creation to signify that she is the principle by which all that now exists

was brought into being. All that God does is wise, not because of some eternal principle of wisdom by which his deeds can be measured, but because it is his nature to act in wisdom. Those who follow wisdom thus order their lives in accordance with God himself.

The ordering of creation (vv.27–31) follows the typical pattern of ancient Semitic thought concerning the world. All things are called forth out of the watery deep with the heavens lifted above it and the land marking its boundaries. The earth itself is set on pillars or foundations sunk into the waters. Modern humanity does not derive its cosmology from the Bible, for its understanding of the structure of the universe is different from that of ancient times. We do affirm with the writer that what exists, regardless of the theories of its order and structure, came from God and is not self-generated.

The epilogue of the chapter (vv.32–36) contains an invitation from wisdom to seek her. There are only two options. The one who finds wisdom finds also Yahweh and life. The one who fails to find her is destroyed.

Chapter 9

The final chapter in this section has been artfully constructed with three movements: the invitation of wisdom (vv.1–6), the response to instruction (vv.7–12), and the invitation of folly (vv.13–18). The imagery of the first and last sections has been deliberately developed to draw upon religious symbolism of the fertility cults as well as to stand in direct contrast to each other. The invitations of both are directed to the simple who are invited to a meal. To participate in the banquet of wisdom is to study and learn and thus gain life. To accept the invitation of the woman Folly is to enter into the realm of the dead. This invitation, issued in blatantly sexual language, emphasizes ease and pleasure in contrast to the discipline of wisdom.

The dedication of the house of wisdom calls for a banquet. Servants of Lady Wisdom seek out the simple and those who lack wisdom to learn from her the paths of life. The banquet is rich, consisting of meat and wine mixed with honey and herbs, a pointed contrast to the simple bouquet of water and food of Lady **Folly** (v.17).

Vv.7-9 contain practical wisdom about instruction. One willing to learn will do so, but the one who has rejected learning will react adversely toward anyone who provides correction.

Vv.10-12 add another theological dimension to the chapter by identifying wisdom with Yahweh or the Holy One. The parallelism demands that the last phrase refer to God and not angels. In vv.11-12 Lady **Wisdom** again speaks about the reward she offers, a long life.

In the final section (vv.13-18), Lady Folly is depicted as a cult prostitute seducing the simple to worship at her shrine, which is located at the acropolis or highest point in the city. In earlier passages the adulteress is a real person, but here she is a metaphor for the life lived without knowledge. To accept her invitation is to enter into the realm of the dead, sheol, or the grave.

III. THE PROVERBS OF SOLOMON (10:1-22:16)

With this section begins a different style of proverb, the two-line, often antithetical, saying commonly thought to be the normal form for the proverb. The commentary will often treat the sayings separately. However, where in a chapter several may be grouped together by common subject matter, they will be discussed as a group.

Chapter 10

V.1. There are no isolated lives, for we all live in a web of relationships and our actions affect those close to us.

Vv.2-4. These verses center around **wealth.** The Lord has so structured the universe as to benefit the righteous. Even ill-gotten treasure is not a lasting benefit. Wealth is not showered upon the righteous; it must be earned through **diligent** work. The lazy will go hungry.

Vv.6-7. These verses contrast the fate of the righteous and the wicked. In wisdom literature little is known about an afterlife. The highest hope was for a long life blessed by peace, wealth, and many descendants. When life ended, one's children and friends would bless the memory of the righteous and curse that of the wicked.

V.8. A contrast is made between one ready to receive instruction and one who speaks without knowledge.

V.9. Life is often seen as a pathway characterized by the inner disposition of a person. The wise, righteous, and knowledgeable walk a straight path, while the wicked have a perverted or twisted life.

Vv.10, 11, 13, 14, 18, 19, 20, 21, 31, 32. These verses each deal with speaking wisdom or its opposite, evil or foolishness. The words of the wise are valuable, for their effect is to help a community and to give life. They may be few in number, but they are fitted for the occasion and are based on knowledge of things as they truly are. The fool's words may be many, but wisdom is not measured by volume. The words of the **wicked** bring **ruin, judgment, violence,** and **sin.** In the end wisdom will be established, and wicked words will lead to destruction.

V.12. The end results of the actions of **love** and **hatred** are contrasted.

V.15. **Wealth** insulates the rich from many of the blows that the poor suffer.

Vv.16, 24, 25, 27, 28, 29, 30. These verses contrast the end result or **wages of the righteous** and the **wicked.** Wisdom follows the path of life as established by the Lord and thus finds **life, joy, refuge** in time of trouble, stability, and one's deepest desires. The wicked will be suddenly swept away by destruction as their life lacks permanence. What they dread will come upon them, for they have no refuge.

V.17. Wisdom and folly both affect the lives of others.

V.23. One's values are revealed in one's **pleasures.**

V.26. Trusting an important matter to someone who is lazy is the same as inflicting oneself with an irritant.

Chapter 11

V.1. Yahweh demands honesty in business practices.

V.2. The egotist does not learn except in **disgrace,** but the humble gains **wisdom.**

Vv.3, 5–8, 18, 19, 21, 23, 31. These verses contrast the rewards of the righteous and the wicked. Wisdom concentrates on this world and has little to say about a future life. Therefore, each must receive the fruit of his or her ways in this life. The wicked will be trapped by their evil desires and destroyed. When they die, all is lost. The **integrity** of the righteous **guides** them in life, rescuing them from trouble and granting what is good.

Vv.4, 28. **Wealth** has limitations that are exceeded by righteousness.

Vv.9, 12, 13. The mouth has the power to bless and curse. It can destroy, denigrate, and disclose confidential material. The wise know what to say, when to say it, and when to be silent.

Vv.10, 11. The life-styles of the righteous and the wicked directly affect the well-being of their communities. They can be blessed or destroyed. Thus they rejoice in the success of the **righteous** and in the death of the **wicked.**

V.14. The security of a people lies in the wisdom of their leaders.

V.15. See 6:1.

Vv.16, 17, 24–27. Kindness and generosity not only help others, but they rebound to expand the quality of one's own life. The **cruel** and **ruthless** who hoard their resources earn the curses of the people and store up destruction for themselves.

V.20. Behind the moral order of the universe stands a God who takes pleasure in those who are **blameless** and is displeased with those whose values are perverted. This is the basic theology of the wisdom teacher.

V.22. Physical beauty unmatched by moral purity is as incongruous as **a gold ring in a pig's snout.**

V.29. A fool destroys his own inheritance, and instead of becoming the head of his own family ends up serving one who is wiser.

V.30. RSV follows the Greek, while the NIV attempts to make sense of the Hebrew. **"Wins souls"** means preserving lives.

Chapter 12

Vv.1, 15. Wisdom is not gained easily. One must be willing to take correction to learn. This quality separates the **wise** from the **fool.**

V.2. Behind the moral order stands a moral God guaranteeing it.

Vv.3, 7, 12, 13, 21, 26. These verses contrast the **wicked** who are transitory and destined to be **overthrown** with the **righteous** who are established and unmoved. The **wicked** are betrayed by their pursuit of **evil** (v.12) and their own words (v.13). The first part of v.26 is difficult but suggests that the righteous are careful in making friends and thus are not led astray.

V.4. One's spouse may be a source of honor or disgrace.

Vv.5, 6, 8, 20. The advice of the righteous is just, wise, and salvatory, and it promotes joy. The plans of the wicked are deceitful, violent, and evil, for they arise out of a warped or perverted mind.

Vv.9, 10, 11, 24, 27. These verses deal with diligence in labor, mostly farm labor. The wise perform without boasting. They are industrious and reap the rewards of hard work. The lazy and those who chase dreams end up with nothing, or worse, serving others.

Vv.14, 16, 17, 18, 19, 22, 23. These verses deal with good speech, which is as rewarding as rigorous toil. Wisdom is characterized by listening to advice but being slow to give it, by overlooking an insult, and by being truthful. Yahweh delights in such persons. The fool is right in his own sight, easy to offend, reckless, and a liar who offends Yahweh.

V.25. Encouraging words lift the one bowed down with stress.

V.28. The path of righteousness leads to life, not death. It may be too strong to suggest that this verse speaks of immortality.

Chapter 13

Vv.1, 13, 14, 18. Learning wisdom brings its own rewards, including honor and life itself. The mocker or arrogant person who refuses instruction solicits poverty and death.

Vv.2, 3. Words have power. The wise use them judiciously and gain by them. Misuse brings violence and ruin.

Vv.4, 11. Diligence in work and saving brings wealth. Indolence gains nothing and squanders what it has.

Vv.5, 6, 9, 21, 25. The rewards of the righteous are contrasted with the afflictions of the wicked. The righteous who hate false words enjoy prosperity while being protected from harm by their own integrity. The wicked suffer disgrace, hunger, misfortune, and violence. While the lamp (life) of one increases, the light (life) of the other is extinguished.

V.7. Appearances may be deceiving.

V.8. While wealth enables the rich to buy freedom, the poor do not fear captivity, for no one would kidnap them for ransom.

V.10. The closed mind of the proud begets strife, but the wise seek advice.

Vv.12, 19. The satisfaction of hope or its frustration affects one's mental and physical well-being. A fool, however, refuses to give up a desire, which in the end means disaster.

V.15. The insight of wisdom and the way of treachery are contrasted in their results.

V.16. Knowledge guides the prudent; folly betrays the fool.

V.17. The integrity of a messenger should be considered before entrusting that one with an important matter.

V.20. One's character is affected by one's associates.

Vv.22, 23. These two proverbs deal with justice but in opposing views. In a just world ordered by God, the children of the righteous gain not only their inheritance but eventually even that of the wicked. When injustice rules, even the produce of the fertile fields of the poor is swept away.

V.24. Discipline is a normal part of growing up. Without it a child would not develop into a productive citizen. The proverb does not justify abuse.

Chapter 14

V.1. Wisdom and folly are personified, both words being feminine. It is the nature of wisdom to build and of folly to destroy.

Vv.2, 16, 26, 27, 31. To fear or reverence Yahweh is the beginning of wisdom. Those who do reverence him conduct their lives in an ethically **upright** manner, shunning **evil** and providing for the **poor**. He in turn gives life and protection from deadly snares.

Vv.3, 7. Proper speech is a continual theme. The words of the **wise protect,** but the fool's words return like a punishing **rod. Stay away from** the fool, because he has no **knowledge** to give you.

Vv.4, 23. These verses refer to productivity. An **ox** is needed to pull a plow on a productive farm. **Work** produces results. **Talk** produces nothing.

Vv.5, 25. The setting is the courtroom where honest witnesses are necessary for justice.

Vv.6, 33. It is not difficult to find **wisdom,** but the **mocker** cannot find it because of his attitude.

Vv.8, 11, 14, 15, 18, 22, 24. These seemingly diverse sayings deal with giving **thought** to the outcome of actions. The wise consider their **ways** and the end results. They exercise knowledge in their planning, choosing what is good in life. The foolish and **simple** reap the **folly** of their ways.

V.9. The righteous work at keeping the favor or goodwill of the community, but the fool does not make amends for his guilt.

Vv.10, 13. The **heart** is the seat of thinking, willing, knowing, and feeling in OT anthropology. One's heart can experience both **joy** and **grief** that no one else may know, and discern the reality of a situation.

V.12. Only the **end** of a matter may reveal its true nature.

Vv.17, 29. The wise do not make hasty decisions, but the **quick-tempered** make **foolish** ones.

V.19. In God's justice the **wicked** will eventually honor the **righteous.**

Vv.20, 21. The normal course of events is for the **poor** to be **shunned** and the **rich** to be sought after. Yet those who are blessed by God are those who care for their neighbors, especially those who are poor.

V.30. One's mental state affects one's physical well-being.

V.32. While the RSV and NEB follow the Greek, substituting "integrity" or "honesty" for **"death"** (NIV), there is no good reason to reject the Hebrew unless one has prejudged that Proverbs cannot refer to life after death. The verse clearly indicates that in death the righteous have more to look forward to than simply the grave.

V.34. The moral qualities of a **nation** either add to or detract from its stature among the peoples of the world.

V.35. This verse is a saying on kingship that exults wisdom.

Chapter 15

Vv.1, 4, 18, 23. The power of speech may be used for beneficial or destructive purposes. It can incite **anger** or calm one down, heal or inflict damage to another's **spirit.** How much better it is when appropriate words are spoken at the proper time that they might benefit the hearer.

Vv.2, 7, 28. This set of sayings is similar to the first set, but it contrasts the effects of the words of the **wise** or **righteous** with those of the **fool** or **wicked.** The one brings forth **knowledge** while the latter bubbles out foolishness or **evil.**

Vv.3, 8, 9, 11, 25, 26, 29. Yahweh keeps constant watch over his creation, judging both the **good** and the evil. He opposes the **wicked** and the **proud,** rejecting their prayers and sacrifices. As a moral God, he despises their way of life and their evil designs, defending the helpless (widows) against them. He shows his love to the **righteous** by hearing their prayers.

Vv.5, 10, 12, 14, 19, 21, 31, 32, 33. The person who is **wise** and **understanding** seeks knowledge and is humble enough to listen to **correction.** This one receives honor from Yahweh while walking the **straight,** or righteous, **path,** which leads to life. The fool spurns **correction** and instruction and receives the harsh disciplines with which the path of **folly** rewards its victims. In rejecting instruction the **fool** rejects life itself and treads a **path** that is blocked (hedged) by briers and leads to death.

V.6. Those who order their lives according to the plan of God are the righteous who will receive the benefits of this life, including its wealth. The wicked's prosperity will be swept away by calamity.

Vv.13, 15, 30. The word *heart* for the Hebrew meant more the mind and will than the emotions. These verses speak of the disposition of the mind that looks for and rejoices in the good in life and in turn promotes good **health. Heartache** and oppression, however, can crush one's **spirit.**

Vv.16, 17. This couplet extols quality of life over wealth. Reverence for Yahweh and **love** are to be preferred over **wealth** and feasting, which are accompanied by **turmoil** and **hatred.**

V.20. See commentary on 10:1.

V.22. See commentary on 11:14.

V.27. The values a person has affects the quality of life even in the home. Greed brings trouble while honesty promotes life.

Chapter 16

This chapter begins with two collections of proverbs. Vv.1–9 deal with the sovereignty of Yahweh, and vv.10–15 with kingship. A third collection on

types of evil persons is found in vv.27–30. It is impossible to tell when the verses were compiled or who was responsible for their arrangement. It does indicate that at some point attempts were made to order some proverbs by topic.

Vv.1–9. The theme of the sovereignty of God holds these verses together. It is he who created all things and has determined their purposes and ends, even the destruction of the **wicked.** The results of one's plans are governed by Yahweh's will. This does not mean that the freedom of a person is abrogated. One is still invited to commit one's way to Yahweh, to live a life of **love, faithfulness,** and **righteousness.** He will judge both **motives** and deeds to reward or punish as appropriate. To humanity belongs the choice of aligning with or against Yahweh, to choose a path. But it is Yahweh's to create paths and their results.

Vv.10–15. Parallel to the sovereignty of God is the sovereignty of the king. While the king's sovereignty is relative to that of God, he still holds the power of life and **death** over his subjects. His anger can mean **death,** and one would do well to **appease it** quickly. As God's representative he desires **justice, righteousness,** and honesty in his administration. To those who please him his favor is as rewarding as **rain** in the **spring.**

V.16. See commentary on 8:10.

V.17. Life is depicted as a road with dangerous turns. The upright guard their way and thus their lives.

Vv.18, 19. These verses contrast the way of **pride** and humility. Humility is to be preferred over the ill-gotten wealth of the **proud** who are headed for a **fall** (disaster of some sort).

V.20. Instead of **instruction** read "the word." The one who meditates on the word of Yahweh and **trusts** him is indeed blessed.

Vv.21, 23, 24. Proper speech is a trait of wisdom. The one who knows how to speak well provides **instruction** to others and benefits for himself.

V.22. This verse contrasts the benefits of **understanding** (prudence) and **folly.**

V.25. See commentary on 14:12.

V.26. Necessity **drives** one to work. Find the right motivation, and the job will get done.

Vv.27–30. These verses describe the wickedness performed by four types of evil persons. **Perverse** speech is used to stir up strife to entice others to join in their **evil** schemes.

V.31. Long **life** is a reward of righteousness.

V.32. Inner strength is more beneficial than bold exploits.

V.33. The last verse concludes the chapter by returning to the theme of the first section; the sovereignty of Yahweh ultimately rules.

Chapter 17

V.1. See commentary on 15:17.

V.2. Wisdom is deed as well as knowledge. The servant will inherit, for ability is more important than position.

V.3. There is an appropriate refining process for everything.

Vv.4, 10. The character of a listener determines what will be heard.

V.5. See commentary on 14:31.

Vv.6, 21, 25. The actions of one generation bring honor or shame to the other. See commentary on 10:1.

V.7. Speech reveals the nature of and should be suited to the speaker. Read "eloquent" in place of **"arrogant."**

Vv.8, 23. Bribes are effective means of achieving one's goals, but efficiency is not the ultimate value. Perversion of **justice** is wrong.

V.9. See commentary on 10:12.

Vv.11, 19, 20. **Evil** persons bring about their own **destruction,** reaping the **evil** they have done to others.

V.12. This is a humorous verse ridiculing the **fool.**

V.13. What **evil** one does to a friend will be visited upon that person's family, e.g., David's crime against Uriah (2Sa 12:9–10).

V.14. It is better never to start a **quarrel** than to try to end one.

Vv.15, 26. Yahweh demands justice in the courtroom.

V.16. This is a humorous verse about students who have resources but no ability.

V.17. Friendship and betrayal prove themselves in adversity.

V.18. See commentary on 6:1–5.

V.22. See commentary on 12:25; 15:13.

V.24. **Wisdom** concentrates on the problem at hand; folly daydreams about the future.

Vv.27, 28. Restrained speech is a mark of wisdom.

Chapter 18

V.1. This is a difficult verse in the Hebrew that has the general sense of condemning antisocial behavior.

Vv.2, 6, 7. The speech of the fool brings trouble to the speaker.

V.3. The companions of **wickedness** are a social **disgrace.**

V.4. This is a cryptic verse conveying the general idea that one's words reveal the depth of one's character.

V.5. This is a verse about **justice.** See commentary on 17:26.

V.8. this is a comment on human nature, which likes to listen to whispered information about others.

V.9. Not to finish a task is no different from destroying what has been completed.

Vv.10, 11. Yahweh provides ultimate protection, but **wealth** also offers

its level of security. There is no contradiction between the two proverbs.
Both are true, the first ultimately and
the second pragmatically.

V.12. See commentary on 16:18–
19.

V.13. The fool has the answers
before hearing the question.

V.14. See commentary on 12:25;
15:13.

V.15. The **wise seek knowledge** (cf.
8:10).

V.16. See commentary on 17:8.

V.17. A position may appear sound
until it is closely examined.

V.18. Disputes were sometimes settled by asking Yahweh to decide the
issue by influencing the **casting** of lots.
The disputants were bound by oath to
accept the outcome as the will of
Yahweh.

V.19. This is a cryptic verse that
notes that hurt feelings are more
difficult to overcome than the defenses
of a city.

Vv.20, 21. Words have power and
may be used to bring satisfaction.

V.22. Domestic tranquility is greatly
valued. A good spouse is a gift of God.

V.23. This verse describes a harsh
reality of life. Wealth brings power. See
commentary on v.11; 10:15.

V.24. To make a friend means to
take on an obligation. Too many **companions** who need assistance may bring
one to **ruin.** A true **friend** stands by
one even in adversity.

Chapter 19

V.1. See commentary on 15:16, 17.

V.2. **Knowledge,** not quick action,
brings success.

V.3. It is easier for a fool to blame
God than to take responsibility for
failure.

Vv.4, 6, 7. **Wealth brings friends**
while poverty suffers alone.

Vv.5, 9, 28. Those who violate the

commandment about bearing false witness (Ex 20:16) will be punished. False
witnesses destroy the foundation of
justice.

Vv.8, 20. Valuing **wisdom** brings
richness to life.

Vv.10, 11. In this couplet about
social order the first verse notes an
absurdity that is disruptive; the second
describes how it is maintained.

V.12. See commentary on 16:14, 15.

Vv.13, 14. This is a couplet about
the home. The first describes destructive forces, the second describes
beneficial forces. See commentary on
18:22.

Vv.15, 24. Sloth ends in hunger.

V.16. See commentary on 13:13.

V.17. See commentary on 14:31.

Vv.18, 19. This couplet concerns
discipline. The child may yet be saved
by discipline for bad behavior, but
uncontrolled anger of an adult will
bring repeated punishment.

V.21. See commentary on 16:1–9.

V.22. Honesty and loyalty have
higher value than wealth.

V.23. See commentary on 18:10.

Vv.25, 29. Adjust teaching methods
to fit the student. Corporeal punishment was often used in the schools of
the scribes.

V.26. Dishonor is earned by one
who violates the commandment about
honoring parents (Ex 20:12).

V.27. A word of caution to the
student. Wrong actions produce wrong
results.

Chapter 20

V.1. Especially the young need the
warning against the dissipation that
drunkenness brings. Lack of discipline
is the opposite of wisdom.

V.2. See commentary on 16:10–15.

V.3. See commentary on 18:6, 11.

V.4. Those who are too lazy to
prepare will reap no rewards.

V.5. The wise who study human nature will understand the depths of motivation often superficially concealed.

Vv.6, 11. One's character is proved by deeds, not words.

Vv.7, 9. The greatest inheritance is the example of the **blameless life**. Yet it comes not by one's own efforts. The grace of God sustains.

Vv.8, 26. The ruler is responsible for justice. In wisdom he is to discern between the righteous and the wicked.

Vv.10, 23. See commentary on 11:1.

Vv.12, 13. Instruction to the student to use diligently what God has created. **"Stay awake"** means "open your eyes."

V.14. This is a humorous observation on business.

V.15. See commentary on 3:14, 15 and 8:10, 11.

V.16. This is advice to the lender. See commentary on 6:1–5 for the borrower. **"Woman"** is incorrect here as the Hebrew word "strangers" is masculine.

V.17. Evil in the long run does not pay. See commentary on 9:17.

V.18. See commentary on 11:14; 15:22.

V.19. See commentary on 11:13.

V.20. See commentary on 19:26.

V.21. Instruction on business: Knowledge is needed to manage money, or even an **inheritance** will be gone.

V.22. Vengeance is not wise. Leave it in Yahweh's hands.

V.24. See commentary on 16:1–9.

V.25. To pronounce a thing holy or sacred is to **dedicate** it to God. One should not be hasty even in making religious **vows.**

V.27. **"Lamp"** symbolizes one searching a room. See commentary on 15:11.

V.28. These qualities, not force, must ultimately **secure** a government.

V.29. Each age has its own benefits to be enjoyed. See commentary on 16:31.

V.30. **"Evil"** refers to bad actions, not wickedness. See commentary on 19:25.

Chapter 21

Vv.1, 2. See commentary on 16:1–15. The sovereignty of God directs even the king.

Vv.3, 4, 21. These verses show contrast in values. Justice and **righteousness** are more important than **sacrifice.** See commentary on 15:8. They with **love** (loyalty) lead to **life** and **honor.** **"Lamp"** symbolizes a **wicked** life-style.

Vv.5, 6, 7, 8. These verses contrast wisdom and wickedness in securing wealth. Wise persons make plans and do justly. The **wicked** act in **haste** with lies and **violence.** What they gain is eventually lost.

Vv.9, 19. These verses are observations on domestic tranquility. Peace is preferred over comfort.

Vv.10, 12, 13, 15. These verses are observations on **justice**. The **wicked** who are **evil** and ruled by **evil** do not want **justice** done. But **the Righteous One**, God, ultimately guarantees **justice,** and the righteous rejoice in it.

V.11. See commentary on 19:25.

V.14. See commentary on 17:8.

V.16. The wanderer finds only death.

Vv.17, 20. Lack of discipline spells financial ruin.

V.18. **"Ransom"** means to suffer the evil fate the **wicked** planned for the **righteous.** See commentary on 11:8.

V.22. See commentary on 16:32.

V.23. See commentary on 13:3.

V.24. This is a description of the mocker, an insolent person.

Vv.25, 26. See commentary on 19:15.

V.27. See commentary on 15:8.

V.28. See commentary on 19:5, 28.

The last line is difficult. Either the one who accepts the false testimony also will die, or the one who hears the truth will speak it.

V.29. This verse is difficult in Hebrew. The wicked speak boldly, but the righteous have substance in their manner of living.

Vv.30, 31. See commentary on 16:1–9. Even wisdom's highest values are secondary to obedience to Yahweh.

Chapter 22

V.1. Reputation is more valuable than wealth.

V.2. See commentary on 16:1–9.

V.3. See commentary on 14:15, 16.

V.4. See commentary on 21:21.

V.5. The wise avoid the hardships of the **wicked.**

V.6. One should be trained for a vocation according to his/her talents and inclinations.

V.7. To money belongs power over others. See commentary on 10:15.

V.8. The wicked will finally destroy themselves.

V.9. See commentary on 19:17.

V.10. See commentary on 18:6–8.

V.11. Advice to students to seek high moral standards. See commentary on 14:35.

V.12. See commentary on 15:3.

V.13. This verse contains humorous sayings on the excuses of the lazy.

V.14. See commentary on 2:16–22; ch. 5.

V.15. See commentary on 13:24.

V.16. See commentary on 14:31.

IV. SAYINGS OF THE WISE (22:17–24:23)

Chapter 22

Vv.17–21. These verses form an introduction to this section and are similar to 1:1–6. They encourage the student to memorize the sayings so that they might be a guide for responding to questions. The students were to know their homework and trust in Yahweh to succeed. The following sayings are molded on the thirty sayings of the Egyptian Amen-em-Opet.

Vv.22, 23. One must not use one's power to oppress the poor, for Yahweh will avenge them.

Vv.24, 25. See commentary on 13:20.

Vv.26, 27. See commentary on 6:1–5.

V.28. Land was marked by **boundary** stones established by earlier generations. To change them was to steal from one's neighbor and defy one's ancestors' decisions.

V.29. Excellence in performance brings a rich reward.

Chapter 23

Vv.1–3. Observe table manners and discipline oneself in the presence of one in higher authority. To act as if one were accustomed to such **food** could be interpreted as grasping at the host's position.

Vv.4, 5. Wealth is elusive. One must not make it one's ultimate goal.

Vv.6–8. One should not work for a **stingy man,** for he will get little; and what little he gets, the man will take back.

V.9. Do not waste **words** on one incapable of understanding them.

Vv.10, 11. See commentary on 22:28.

V.12. This verse contains advice to a student to pursue **instruction** and **knowledge.**

Vv.13, 14. See commentary on 13:24.

Vv.15, 16. The instructor takes pride in the achievements of the pupil.

Vv.17, 18. The success of the wicked was a problem. The student was to trust in Yahweh, who brings justice and gives a **hope** that in the **future** he will succeed.

Vv.19–21. The student should guard against drunkenness and gluttony, which lead to poverty. See commentary on 20:1.

Vv.22–25. In ancient Israel the parents' hope for immortality was bound up with their children. Thus they took great pride in their achievements, especially in their **wise** and **righteous** deeds.

Vv.26–28. See commentary on chs. 5 and 7.

Vv.29–35. This is a vivid and humorous description of the alcoholic who seeks only after drink and does not learn from his physical and psychological deterioration. This one is the ultimate fool.

Chapter 24

Vv.1, 2. See commentary on 23:17, 18.

Vv.3, 4. In contrast to 23:29–24:2 the person who follows **wisdom** gains life's **treasures,** both literally in wealth and figuratively in character.

Vv.5, 6. See commentary on 16:32; 21:22.

V.7. The fool has no standing in the community and thus will not be listened to.

Vv.8, 9. Those who scheme **evil** are despised by the community.

Vv.10–12. The responsibility of the wise extends to helping those in need of legal defense. Ignorance can be no excuse for the wise, who will be judged by Yahweh.

Vv.13, 14. Enjoined to indulge in pleasure, the student should find the highest pleasure in **wisdom,** which provides hope for a better life.

Vv.15, 16. The Sustainer of the **righteous** is Yahweh, who will make them ultimately to triumph.

Vv.17, 18. One should not **gloat** over the misfortunes of even one's enemies. Yahweh gives justice to all.

Vv.19, 20. See commentary on 23:17, 18.

Vv.21, 22. The wise are conservative and are taught to support their rulers. Not only does one remain loyal to Yahweh, but also to the ruler lest one suffer **destruction.**

V. FURTHER SAYINGS OF THE WISE (AN APPENDIX) (24:23–34)

Vv.23–26. The administration of justice is one of the factors that holds a society together. This saying is addressed to judges to encourage them to speak honestly in judgment.

V.27. This proverb is taken from agriculture. One should provide for economic security before considering marriage, i.e., building a **house.**

Vv.28, 29. Vengeance is no excuse for perjury. See commentary on 14:5.

Vv.30–34. These verses give a graphic description of the **poverty** that laziness brings. See commentary on 6:6–11.

VI. THE WORDS OF THE MEN OF HEZEKIAH (25:1–29:27)

Chapter 25

Vv.2–7a. See commentary on 16:10–15. These sayings were placed together due to verbal similarities in the Hebrew. It is the task of rulers to inquire into the mysteries of governing in order to rule well. However, they need honest advisers and must purge the wicked from their courts. Note how Jesus in Lk 14:7–10 used vv.6 and 7.

Vv.7b–10. One should not hasten to court but settle disputes privately (Mt 5:25). A quick decision to enter court without all the facts could prove disastrous when the opponent wins. One will suffer both financial loss and a loss of **reputation.**

Vv.11, 12. See commentary on 15:23.

V.13. See commentary on 13:37.

V.14. This verse is a saying on empty promises.

V.15. See commentary on 15:1.

Vv.16, 17, 27. One can have too much of a good thing. The wise discipline themselves even in pleasure.

V.18. See commentary on 14:5.

V.19. A saying on the danger of misplaced confidence.

V.20. There are improper times for even good things.

Vv.21, 22. Hostility is overcome by kindness. Yahweh will reward forgiveness that is followed by deeds of kindness.

V.23. **"Sly"** means "secret." The proper response to gossip is anger.

V.24. See commentary on 21:9.

V.25. The venture in a distant land could be financial or military.

V.26. The divine order of the **righteous** triumphing over the **wicked** is disturbed by a compromise that allows the wicked to succeed.

V.28. One lacking in self-control is vulnerable to personal loss.

Chapter 26

This chapter has three sections: vv.1–12 the **fool,** vv.13–16 the **sluggard,** and vv.17–28 the meddler.

Vv.1, 8. **Honor** should not come to a **fool.**

V.2. An addition to this group. The Israelite considered a curse more than words; it was a force capable of evil.

V.3. See commentary on 19:25.

Vv.4, 5. These contradictory sayings are correct depending on circumstances.

Vv.6, 10. One acts foolishly in trusting an important task to a **fool.**

Vv.7, 9. The **fool** does not know what to do with wisdom.

V.11. A fool does not learn; that is why one is a **fool.**

V.12. The proud are worse than fools.

V.13. See commentary on 22:13.

V.14. This is a humorous description of the sluggard.

V.15. See commentary on 19:24.

V.16. The lazy, due to self-satisfaction, are not motivated to do better.

V.17. Stay out of others' quarrels.

Vv.18, 19. Poor excuses will not avert the anger of the offended.

Vv.20, 21. Gossip fans the fires of quarrels.

V.22. See commentary on 18:8.

Vv.23–28. The meddler stirs up strife due to **evil** intent, even though one may pose as a friend or act innocent. Eventually the **evil** will be discovered and publicly **exposed** so that the disaster planned for others will recoil onto the meddler.

Chapter 27

V.1. **Tomorrow** lies in Yahweh's hand, not ours. See Jas 4:13–16.

Vv.2, 21. It is better to receive **praise** from others and to enjoy a rich reputation than to be known as a braggart.

Vv.3, 4. The **anger** of a **fool** is difficult to bear, but **jealousy** is worse than **anger.**

Vv.5, 6, 9, 10, 14. **Love** means friendship. The wise one will stay on good terms with a **neighbor** or **friend** who is more valuable than distant relatives. An old trusted **friend** brings **joy** to a life, even through rebukes.

V.7. It is the appetite, not the food, that makes the difference.

V.8. Be satisfied with what you have.

V.11. The parent takes pleasure in the **wise** child.

V.12. See commentary on 22:3.

V.13. See commentary on 20:16.

Vv.15, 16. See commentary on 19:13.

V.17. People can provoke each other for the better.

V.18. Faithful service will be rewarded.

V.19. What one is internally is shown outwardly.

V.20. Greed is never **satisfied.**

V.22. See commentary on 26:3, 11.

Vv.23–27. Drawn from a pastoral scene this poem teaches diligence in labor. Study what one has and manage it well, for wealth does not last forever. In times of adversity, that which has been taken care of will in turn provide one's necessities.

Chapter 28

V.1. This verse shows a contrast in confidence, for the **righteous** are secure in their integrity while the **wicked** are apprehensive of retribution.

Vv.2, 3, 5, 15, 16. The **wicked** ruin a country morally, economically, and politically. The experience of the northern kingdom may lie behind v.2. Wisdom and **knowledge** of the way of Yahweh bring prosperity and peace.

V.4. **"The law"** is the covenant law revealed by Yahweh. A continuous tension exists between **those who keep the law** and **the wicked.**

V.6. See commentary on 15:16, 17.

V.7. See commentary on 23:19–25.

V.8. **Interest** on loans was allowed in business, but justice demanded that it be canceled for **the poor.**

V.9. See commentary on 15:8, 9.

V.10. Those who corrupt others will be punished.

V.11. Wisdom, not wealth, is the higher value.

Vv.12, 28. See commentary on 11:10.

V.13. The mercy of God in forgiveness comes only after sin is confessed and forsaken.

V.14. **"The LORD"** is missing in the Hebrew. "Fear" is to respect, obey.

V.17. A murderer, though conscience-stricken, is not to receive mercy.

V.18. See commentary on 10:9.

V.19. See commentary on 12:11.

Vv.20–22, 25. These verses speak to the sin of greed, recognizing the length to which the **greedy** will go for wealth. Justice will be done when they experience the punishment of **poverty** for their sin, and the faithful **prosper.**

V.24. Dishonesty toward one's parents was a heinous sin (Ex 20:12).

V.26. See commentary on 3:5–8.

V.27. See commentary on 11:24–27.

Chapter 29

V.1. See commentary on 1:24–33.

Vv.2, 14, 16. See commentary on 11:10.

V.3. See commentary on 10:1; 23:19–25.

V.4. **Justice** provides the foundation for any government to govern.

V.5. The motives of the flatterer are self-seeking and harmful to a **neighbor.**

V.6. The **righteous** do not fear repercussions of their actions, but the wicked set in motion deeds that come back to punish them.

V.7. Concern for the **poor** is one of the factors that distinguish **the wicked** and **the righteous.**

V.8. The **wise** benefit a community, but **mockers** are troublemakers.

V.9. One cannot reason **with a fool,** even in **court.**

Vv.10, 27. Hostility between **the wicked** and **the righteous** may flair into open persecution. **The righteous** must be wary of **the wicked.**

V.11. See commentary on 14:17.

V.12. Advisers will reflect the moral level of the ruler.

V.13. See commentary on 22:2.

Vv.15, 17. See commentary on 13:24.

V.18. **"Revelation"** correctly translates the Hebrew, not a dream for the future, but a prophet's **revelation** from God. When a people reject God's revelation, they throw off the restraints that guard life from evil.

Vv.19, 21. Physical discipline was often used to force a slave to work. On the opposite sentiment See commentary on 17:2.

Vv.20, 22. The wise bridle their speech and act after thinking. The hasty blurt out their thoughts, and the **hot-tempered** act without thought. Both repent later of their actions.

V.23. See commentary on 11:2; 16:18.

V.24. **The accomplice of a thief** places his own life in danger. He cannot **testify** against a partner without implicating himself.

V.25. See commentary on 16:7; 28:1.

V.26. Ultimately justice and security come from Yahweh, not from a ruler.

VII. THE SAYINGS OF AGUR (30:1–33)

Chapter 30
Vv.2–6. The Hebrew of v.2 is unintelligible. By dividing the letters differently (see NIV footnote), the verse begins the complaint of a skeptic who declares that humanity can know nothing about God. An answer is given in vv.5–6; God has revealed himself through his word. God's word is both that written in Scripture and in nature.

Vv.7–9. This is a prayer to avoid the temptations of both wealth and **poverty**. Wealth breeds pride, and **poverty** provokes dishonesty.

V.10. A **curse** was thought to create a negative force in another's life.

Vv.11–14. This series describes four types of sinners. The compiling of lists was common among wisdom writers who observed life and catalogued their findings.

Vv.15–17. These verses perhaps speak by way of metaphor to human desire that cannot be satisfied but must be disciplined.

Vv.18–19. This numerical saying compares the mysteries of nature with the mystery of love.

V.20. Sin so corrupts the conscience that the sinner denies any guilt.

Vv.21–23. This series describes events that upset society's norm. The **"unloved woman"** is better translated "the divorced woman" or "woman who cannot keep her marriage vows." The Hebrew word indicates one who does not remain faithful to a relationship.

Vv.24–28. This series recommends a study of small **creatures** in order to learn disciplined habits.

Vv.29–31. Each display of majesty has its own glory.

Vv.32–33. The fool is warned that retribution is certain. That which is planned for others will recoil onto the perpetrator.

VIII. THE SAYINGS OF KING LEMUEL (31:1–9)
This advice of a mother to her royal son centers around the theme of justice. He is to beware of the corrupting influence of women, a common theme in the ancient Middle East. Also, he is to avoid indulgence in drink that might cloud his judgment. Finally, he is urged to take up the cause of society's underprivileged. The rich and powerful receive justice, for they can afford it; but the poor need the help of their ruler.

IX. A WIFE OF INDUSTRIOUS CHARACTER (31:10–31)
This passage is an acrostic poem, each verse beginning with a subsequent

letter of the alphabet. The poem describes in typical wisdom style the ideal wife, praising her economic value while depreciating her physical charms. A young man must be practical even in the affairs of the heart if he is to succeed in life.

Vv.10–12 introduce the poem. **"Noble character"** is better understood as "efficient" or "worthy." A **husband** trusts that this type of woman will benefit him.

Vv.13–27 illustrate in concrete terms the desirable characteristics of this type of wife. She is industrious, shrewd in business practices, and capable in managing the home. She plans ahead so that her family is amply provided for and well-clothed.

Vv.28–31 conclude with praise for the woman. The reference to fearing the Lord provides a Yahwistic cast to the poem. The proper wife would guard the home against all illegitimate religious influences.

BIBLIOGRAPHY

Kidner, Derek. *Proverbs*. TOTC. Downers Grove, Ill.: InterVarsity, 1964.

McKane, William. *Proverbs: A New Approach*. OTLS. Philadelphia: Westminster, 1970.

Whybray, R. N. *The Book of Proverbs*. NEBC. Cambridge: The University Press, 1972.

ECCLESIASTES
Carl Schultz

INTRODUCTION

Ecclesiastes is a difficult and therefore frequently ignored book. Reading it without an awareness of its nature and purpose can result in confusion and dismay. Due to space limitations, the introduction here will be brief. It is imperative that the reader consult other sources that address these issues.

I. TITLE

The English designation Ecclesiastes is derived from the Septuagint, the Greek translation of the OT. The Hebrew word behind the Greek is *Qoheleth*. This word appears seven times in this book (1:1, 2, 12; 7:27; 12:8, 9, 10) but nowhere else in the OT and is the title and/or name of the writer. *Qoheleth* is a feminine participle and comes from the Hebrew root *QHL* meaning to gather or to assemble. The object of this action is people, never things. *Qoheleth* is a title meaning "one who gathers people," probably for the purpose of instruction. It is possible that *Qoheleth* should also be regarded as the writer's name. In Hebrew, as in other languages, function may determine a person's name. Consider such English surnames as Cook, Smith, and Fowler. In time the name and function may be separated.

If *Qoheleth* is a proper name, then it should be transliterated (JB). Generally efforts are made to translate it in the English versions: "Preacher" (KJV, RSV), "Speaker" (NEB), "Philosopher" (TEV), and "Teacher" (NIV). While "preacher" is the most common rendition, it is not the best. Since the intent of the book is sapiential rather than sermonic, "Teacher" is a better translation.

II. AUTHOR

Both in Jewish and Christian traditions, this book has been attributed to Solomon, but his name never appears in the book. Further, the style of Hebrew suggests a date after Solomon's time. If he is not the author, what is his relationship to this book? The writer does not claim to be the wise king but uses his experiences as the backdrop for this book. He assumes that role, wanting us to think of Solomon, since Solomon is the example par excellence of the futility of life.

III. NATURE

Ecclesiastes is a difficult book—difficult because of its alleged contradictions and alarming negative conclusions.

A casual reading of the book will reveal apparent contradictions (cf. 2:2 and 7:3 with 8:15 relative to joy; cf. 8:12 with 8:13 relative to the life span of the wicked). The writer not only seems to contradict himself, he also seems to contradict the traditional views of Israel.

The negative tone of the book is also readily detected. "Meaningless! Meaningless! Utterly meaningless! Everything is meaningless." Adjectives such as fatalistic, pessimistic, skeptical, even nihilistic have been used to characterize this book.

Various efforts have been made either to deny the existence of these problems or to account for them:

A. The hermeneutical approach used by both Christians and Jews avoids a straightforward interpretation of the difficult passages and spiritualizes them, thus muting any problem.

B. In the past more than now, scholars were inclined to tear apart the various books of the Bible by seeing them as the composite of many sources. Ecclesiastes so viewed was said to be the product of two or three or as many as nine sources. Today scholars are inclined to see the book as a single literary unit.

C. Another suggested possibility is that the original book was prepared by a sage who was heterodox. To secure a place for Ecclesiastes in the canon a pious believer added a number of glosses that made the book orthodox.

D. The writer is role playing, putting himself in the shoes of the secularist. He will present the claims of the secularist and then proceed to discuss them and refute them. Ecclesiastes is a kind of notebook in which Qoheleth enters the thoughts of others and reflects on them. This could explain in part the apparent lack of overall organization in the book and the fluctuation of thought.

E. Ecclesiastes is essentially a kind of diary in which the writer records his oscillating thoughts, his struggles, doubts, and groping. This accounts for variations in the book both in tone and position and necessitates the reading of this book with the heart as well as the head.

IV. PURPOSE

Qoheleth is an iconoclast, destroying the gods of wealth, wisdom, power, fame, and even religion. Veneration of these will result in emptiness. God alone is to be worshiped. Qoheleth refuses to shackle God and make him conform to human wishes and plans. He allows God to be free and mysterious. As for human beings, they are to discover the simple joys of life and enjoy their work and not be tyrannized by it. Even though his efforts may seem absurd and appear to count for nothing, they are important because "God will bring every deed into judgment" (12:14).

V. STRUCTURE

Clearly Qoheleth was no systematic theologian. Given this fact and the nature of the material considered in the book, it is difficult to analyze Ecclesiastes and determine its structure. But pericopes must be carefully established, identified, and related to the total book.

VI. OUTLINE

I. The Repetitious Nature of Life (1:1–11)

II. A Solomonic Experiment—A Search for Satisfaction (1:12–2:26)

III. A Catalog of Times (3:1–15)

IV. Problems of Injustice and Oppression (3:16–4:3)

V. Competition, Cooperation, and Fame (4:4–16)

VI. Temple Protocol (5:1–7)

VII. The Vanity of Wealth (5:8–6:12)

VIII. Provocative and Perplexing Proverbs (7:1–8:1)

IX. Court Protocol (8:2–9)

X. The Reality of Injustice (8:10–17)

XI. A Common Destiny (9:1–10)

XII. Inadequacy of Wisdom (9:11–18)

XIII. Assorted Practical Sayings (10:1–20)

XIV. A Call to Action (11:1–6)

XV. Youth and Old Age (11:7–12:8)

XVI. The Conclusion (12:9–14)

COMMENTARY

I. THE REPETITIOUS NATURE OF LIFE (1:1–11)

Following the superscription (v.1) the theme of the book is given (v.2), **"Everything is meaningless."** Not only some aspects of life are meaningless, but the sum total is. The Hebrew word *hebel*, translated "meaningless" by the NIV, designates that which is not substantial—breath, vapor, cipher, ab-surdity, irony, futility. By the doubling of this word the writer achieves the superlative.

The monotonous routine of nature and human effort is stressed (vv.3–11). Nature is characterized by sameness—sunrise and sunset (v.5), shifting winds (v.6), and ever-emptying streams (v.7). Not only are the motions of nature repetitious, so is human effort. Though the world remains, its occupants change (v.4). There is the constant search for emotional and psychological satisfaction (v.8) and the redoing of that which already has been done (v.9). Nothing under the sun is new (v.9). This does not refer to scientific achievement but to the human condition.

The phrase **"under the sun"** occurs only in this book in the OT, appearing some thirty-four times. It refers to the observable world and is used to show the absurdity and futility of life if confined to these horizons. There would simply be no gain or satisfaction (v.3), only hopelessness with such existence.

II. A SOLOMONIC EXPERIMENT—A SEARCH FOR SATISFACTION (1:12–2:26)

The writer does not claim to be Solomon but assumes his role to give credibility to his experiment and to show the sagacious approach to this effort. The nature of the experiment is revealed by the verbs **to study** and **to explore** (1:13). The former means to penetrate to the heart of a matter while the latter means to search thoroughly. It is the same word that was used of the Hebrew spies who were sent to gather information about the people, terrain, and resources of Canaan (Nu 13:2, 16–17).

Qoheleth's preliminary conclusions are that the restless quest for meaning is ordained of God, that all human effort amounts to no more than chasing after the wind, and that, given the fixed nature of things, there is little that people can do to effect change (1:13–15). These conclusions will continue to be pressed in the balance of the book.

Areas tested by Qoheleth are: wisdom (1:16–18), pleasure (2:1–3), great projects (vv.4–6), and wealth (vv.7–8). For the test to be valid Qoheleth denied himself nothing (v.10). At the end of the test, looking back, he concludes that he has found no ultimate meaning under the sun in any of his efforts (v.11). There is no advantage to being wise since the same fate of extinction befalls the wise as befalls the fool (vv.13–16). Not only did Qoheleth hate life because of his common fate but also because all that he had toiled for would be left to his successor, whether wise or foolish (vv.17–23).

Given these realities of human existence, emphasis is to be placed not upon the outcome of the work, but upon its performance. That is where satisfaction is to be found (2:24–25). It is the sinner who is occupied with gathering and storing up wealth (v.26). The word *sinner* here is not used so much in a moral sense as in a pragmatic sense, indicating one whose focus in on the outcome of work rather than on its performance. Such an emphasis is tantamount to chasing the wind (v.26).

III. A CATALOG OF TIMES (3:1–15)

Contrary to some popular ideas and lyrics, these verses are not suggesting that there are proper or appropriate times for the specified activities, i.e., that there is a right time for war and a right time for peace. They indicate rather that these tenets and all that occurs have been fixed and determined by God.

Open to question is Qoheleth's attitude toward this fact. Generally it is said to be negative. He has already lamented the futility of life and human effort because of their transience. Lack of permanence makes human toil meaningless. Now he compounds the sense of frustration by noting that all human efforts have been predetermined. Humankind simply executes an already determined schedule of events. Life is both fleeting and fixed.

However, it is possible to read these verses, not as adding to Qoheleth's sense of futility, but as answering objections already raised. Since all has been determined by God, life has purpose and meaning. Since God has set a time for everything, a sense of security results. The continual movements of life do not need to be viewed as meaningless. "Instead of changelessness, there is something better: a dynamic, divine purpose, with its beginning and end. Instead of frozen perfection, there is the kaleidoscopic movements of innumerable processes, each with its own character and its period of blossoming and ripening; beautiful in its time and contributing to the over-all masterpiece which is the work of our Creator" (Kidner, 39). From this perspective, then, God's actions are not simply arbitrary, but appropriate, and not simply confining, but releasing.

IV. PROBLEMS OF INJUSTICE AND OPPRESSION (3:16–4:3)

Qoheleth now addresses the matter of injustice. Continuing his emphasis on sets of opposites and a proper place and time for each event of life, he now suggests that there is a time established for injustice and justice. Presently he is sensitive to oppression (4:1–3) and injustice in juridical procedures under the sun (3:16). But God has established a time when he will administer justice (v.17). Injustice, like all earthly evils, will not continue indefinitely.

God's toleration of injustice has a purpose. It is to show people that they are like the animals (3:18). The presence of injustice in the world (v.16) along with the fact of human mortality (v.19) places humans at the level of beasts. Qoheleth notes that as we have come from dust, so we return to dust

(v.20). Observations made under the sun do not reveal to him whether the human spirit will survive death. Strong affirmations about life after death are reserved for the NT.

V. COMPETITION, COOPERATION, AND FAME (4:4–16)

In this section Qoheleth condemns the competitive spirit (v.4) while calling for a cooperative one (vv.9–12). Either prompted by envy (v.4) or habit (v.8) the solitary worker may secure wealth, but he has neither friends nor family. His drive for wealth has virtually dehumanized him, robbing him of companionship.

Cooperation, on the other hand, provides for great productivity (v.9). Further, companionship provides support for the person who physically falls or has a lapse in judgment (v.10), warmth for a cold winter's night (v.11), and protection against a thief (v.12).

The danger of isolation is seen in the old king who enjoys position but is characterized as foolish because he has lost contact with his constituency. The youth, lacking position but possessing ability and energy, will supplant the old king (vv.13–14). The emphasis here is one of "rags to riches." But even this youth will go the way of the old king (vv.15–16). He will lose favor with his constituency as his attractiveness fades. Qoheleth has given another example of chasing after the wind.

VI. TEMPLE PROTOCOL (5:1–7)

Qoheleth here focuses on the creature as a worshiper and addresses himself to conduct that is appropriate in the presence of God. The language is more restrained than that of the prophet since the observed worshiper is well-meaning but forgetful rather than hypocritical (Kidner, 52). There are three separate sayings in this passage.

First, Qoheleth urges caution relative to the frequency and quality of approach to God (v.1). While not rejecting sacrifice (his objection to the fool's sacrifice is probably due to misuse), Qoheleth stresses the importance of listening, i.e., of understanding and obeying.

Second, he warns against impetuosity and multiplication of words during prayer (vv.2–3). Words should be carefully weighed before they are uttered. In prayer an adequate distance of awe and respect must be maintained.

Third, he speaks against hastily made vows (vv.4–7). Better not to make a vow than to make one and not fulfill it. Evasion of a vow by alleging that it was a mistake does not exonerate the worshiper. Throughout this section Qoheleth calls for few and careful words when in God's presence.

VII. THE VANITY OF WEALTH (5:8–6:12)

The material in this section is centered around poverty and wealth.

Qoheleth seems resigned to an oppressive bureaucratic hierarchy where public office holders are preyed upon by higher ones, resulting in corruption at all levels of government. In turn, the poor seeking justice are victimized by this corrupt system (5:8–9). Bureaucracy, while decried, seems to be accepted as necessary and inevitable.

Three sayings about money follow. First, the desire for money is insatiable (5:10). Second, the advantages of wealth are only temporary since it will soon be consumed by others (v.11). Third, wealth can result in insomnia for the rich, a condition unknown to the untroubled laborer (v.12).

Qoheleth now presents a scenario that he characterizes as a deadly evil

(5:13). In some undefined business venture a rich man loses all his acquired wealth, leaving his family destitute (v.14). He himself dies in poverty (v.15). The trouble and tension associated with acquiring wealth (vv.12, 17) and the trauma associated with losing it do irreparable damage to him. He loses on both scores, causing Qoheleth to be dissatisfied with such a prospect.

But not only does Qoheleth express his dissatisfaction, he also offers an alternative approach to life (5:18–20). In the above scenario no reference is made to God, but in this alternative approach, God is mentioned four times. It is God who gives life, wealth, and the ability to enjoy possessions. Recognizing God and appropriating wealth as his gift make a significant difference. Wealth is to be celebrated and shared with others (v.18) rather than hoarded. While this will not increase the length of life, it will increase the quality of life (5:20).

Qoheleth considers it imperative that wealth be enjoyed, and he recognizes that the power to enjoy it comes from God (5:19) who can choose to withhold it. He now gives instances in which this power to enjoy was withheld by God.

The first one (6:1–2) is similar to the scenario of the previous chapter (5:13–17) except that the person considered here not only had wealth but also honor (6:2). This added dimension is significant and should have changed the situation but did not. He too lacked the ability to enjoy life and God's gifts.

Inability to enjoy life is illustrated further in the next section (6:3–6). Here a man, in addition to being prosperous, has a large family (a hundred children, v.3) and lives a long life (a thousand years twice over, v.6). The figures employed here are exaggerated for emphasis. This man also fails to enjoy God's gifts. The stillborn child without any experience, accomplishments, and fame is better off than the man just described (vv.3–5). At least the stillborn has rest.

A series of unanswered questions further demonstrates the human plight (6:7–12). Efforts are essential to maintain life. People work to eat so that they may have strength to work again, but their appetites are never sated and become even more demanding as times go on (v.7). The wise and the pious poor (v.8) are not exempt from such a treadmill. They too experience insatiable appetites. It is better to use that which is available and realize joy in what they have than to yearn for that which is beyond them. "A bird in the hand is worth two in the bush."

Qoheleth now seems to pause to summarize what he has said to this point. People must accept themselves and their world the way they are. The statements that **"whatever exists has already been named and what man is has been known"** indicate that the essence and character of human life and of the world have already been determined (6:10). People are limited and mortal. They may choose to challenge God but to no avail (v.10). They may multiply words, but words are not effective in producing change (v.11).

This chapter concludes by noting that humans lack knowledge and advisers (6:12). They neither understand this life nor the nature of the future. Two obvious conclusions are found here. People by their own efforts cannot discover God's plans for themselves and their work; neither can they alter or change those plans no matter what they do. Apart from divine help, they are both ignorant and helpless.

VIII. PROVOCATIVE AND PERPLEXING PROVERBS (7:1–8:1)

Qoheleth now cites a number of gloomy proverbs that surprise, anger, and disappoint. This series of **better than** proverbs (7:1–12) is possibly Qoheleth's answer to his own question, **"What is good for a man?"** (6:12).

The advantage of sorrow over pleasure is presented first (7:1–6). Since death is the destiny of all, it must not be ignored (v.2). The consideration of one's death is critical to proper living. Frivolity characterizes the fool whose occupation is with partying, while pensiveness characterizes the wise whose preoccupation is with death (v.4). The funeral, not the party, causes one to number one's days and to gain a heart of wisdom (Ps 90:12).

After a proverb urging the acceptance of the harsh words of the sage rather than the flattering words of the fool (7:5–6), Qoheleth turns his attention to four ever-present dangers: extortion (v.7), impatience (v.8), anger (v.9), and discontentment (v.10). Qoheleth is consistent in this chapter in recommending that the reader take the harder, less humanly attractive road.

As he did in the opening chapters (chs. 1–2), Qoheleth recognizes the value of wisdom but observes that it must be linked with means (7:11–12). Even as fools can lose their money, so the wise can be poor. But wisdom has its advantage over wealth.

Echoing his earlier comments, Qoheleth does not attribute prosperity and adversity to fate but to God (7:13–14). He now speaks of an anomaly that he has observed (v.15). The righteous perish while the wicked live long. Hence he urges moderation in righteousness, wisdom, and wickedness (vv.16–18). The warning against being overrighteous is troubling. Various explanations have been offered. Some see Qoheleth extending his golden mean here to religion, while others see this as a caution against overscrupulosity, legalism, and self-righteousness.

The recognition that no man is completely righteous (7:20) supports the call for moderation (v.16) and also for forbearance (vv.21–22). Qoheleth also concedes the unattainability of wisdom (vv.23–24), thus supporting his call for moderation in that area (v.16).

Turning his mind to the more mundane, Qoheleth demonstrates that folly and wickedness are the same (7:25). His attitude toward women must be kept in the context of his personal observations. He can be positive about women (9:9). The one upright man whom he found among a thousand (7:28) is the wise man of 8:1 who is able to handle the difficult issues raised in ch. 7.

IX. COURT PROTOCOL (8:2–9)

Sages were essentially favorable to the monarchy, and their pupils were probably from the upper classes and had contact with the king. They needed practical advice. Having taken an oath of loyalty, the subject should not be quick to desert his post (8:2–3). Since kings can be capricious and unpredictable, subjects must exercise discretion, even expediency. "With the dangerous caprices of a king to reckon with, wisdom has to fold its wings and take the form of discretion, content to keep its possessor out of trouble" (Kidner, 74). Such a call may be seen as unworthy of the Bible unless it is balanced by the rest of Scripture where principles and examples of courage and integrity in government are given. Not only are a people limited by royal power, but they are also helpless in the presence of the wind, death, war, and evil (vv.7–8). Unable to control these phenomena, they turn to lording it over other humans, and the result often is injustice (v.9).

X. THE REALITY OF INJUSTICE (8:10–17)

Qoheleth now expresses his dismay at the injustice he observes in the world. The wicked are praised and receive an honorable funeral in the very city where they perpetrated their crimes (8:10). Such a delay in retribution incites further wrongdoing (v.11). In vv.12 and 13 Qoheleth either affirms his faith in ultimate justice or is citing a popular position which he then rejects in the next verse on the basis of empirical data he has collected. Retribution and reward are interchanged and not appropriately distributed as some claim (v.14). This does not make sense to the writer, and he labels it meaningless.

If Qoheleth is anticipating ultimate justice, he is then allowing for momentary success of the wicked. But he insists that God's patience should not be misunderstood. There is a limit to the success of the wicked. Justice will ultimately be administered. Meanwhile, he urges enjoyment and contentment (v.15). God is in charge of the events of life. While we will struggle to understand the events of life, we will remain in ignorance even though the wise may claim otherwise (v.17). We must learn to live with mystery and ignorance.

XI. A COMMON DESTINY (9:1–10)

The concerns of the previous chapter are continued here. Having already denied consistent and predictable patterns of reward and retribution, Qoheleth again emphasizes the uncertainty of outcome. The righteous/wise themselves and their actions are in God's hands (9:1), suggesting resignation more than trust. God is not controlled by human concepts of retribution. He is free to act, either to accept (love) or reject (hate). If the terms *love* and *hate* are to be applied to human action, then people do not know either their own future attitudes toward others or the future attitudes of others toward them. Applying these terms to the events and circumstances of life, people cannot know whether they will experience love or blessing. Qoheleth protests such a reality, being outraged that moral distinctions are not made.

Qoheleth now focuses on death. Life with all its frustrations is better than death (v.4). Life at its very worst is preferable to death; in life there is awareness, but in death there is no awareness, no further reward, no opportunity to alter one's image or perpetuate one's memory (v.3), and no emotions or feelings (v.6). The absence of these passions indicates the destructiveness of death.

Given these stark truths about death, Qoheleth urges three responses. First, life is to be enjoyed. While food, wine, garments, and oil can be viewed as necessities of life (Hos 2:5), they are also suggestive of celebration. The certainty of death is not to prevent the enjoyment of life (9:7–8). Second, companionship and fidelity in marriage are urged (v.9). Last, he calls for thoroughness in our efforts (v.10). Whatever we do must be done with all our might. The certainty of death must not lead to inertia.

XII. INADEQUACY OF WISDOM (9:11–18)

Humans must not only cope with death, they must also cope with chance and fickleness.

Wisdom (in the sense of ability or skill) is no guarantee of success. Time and chance cloud the outcome. While these factors could be positive, they appear to be negative here, suggesting bad times and accidents (9:12).

Qoheleth now presents an anecdote of a poor man who saved a city through his wisdom (9:13, 16). Confronted by a powerful king, this man through an act of diplomacy managed to save the city. The story demonstrates the superior of wisdom over might, but this wisdom was not rewarded. The poor man was forgotten, not immortalized. Even wisdom is vulnerable to uncertainty and does not assure success.

XIII. ASSORTED PRACTICAL SAYINGS (10:1–20)

The role of this chapter in the book is difficult to determine. It is a collection of assorted maxims. These proverbs dealing with practical virtues have little organic connection but are the type of sayings expected from a traditional wisdom teacher.

V.1, frequently attached to the previous chapter, indicates that it is easier to ruin something than it is to develop it. The thoughts of the wise will lead to the beneficial, while the thoughts of the fool will lead to the detrimental (v.2). Though the fool does not speak, he betrays himself by his general demeanor (v.3).

A hurried resignation by the bureaucrat only intensifies the king's anger (v.4). The inequities in the structure of society are traced to a ruler who makes decisions by whim.

Risks are associated with any human effort. People do not have total control over the events of life, but they frequently cause their own accidents (vv.8–9). The importance of both preparation and timing is seen in vv.10–11.

The next group of verses (vv.12–14)

addresses a favorite subject of the sage—words. The words of the wise result in grace, while those of the fool result in destruction. Fools exercise no restraint in speech but multiply words concerning matters about which they are ignorant.

The final group of verses (vv.10–20) deals mostly with rulers. A land whose king acts childishly is in trouble (v.16), while a land whose king is disciplined is greatly benefited (v.17). The influence of the ruler has a way of filtering down into the citizenry (vv.18–19), but even if the leader is profligate, the critic must be careful in his disapproval (v.20).

XIV. A CALL TO ACTION (11:1–6)

The futility and uncertainty of life as depicted in the previous chapters could result in paralysis and inertia. Qoheleth will not tolerate this. He now calls for diligence and bold action.

It is difficult to know whether philanthropy or business is in mind in v.1 (bread suggests either agricultural pursuits or a contribution to the hungry). Either way the emphasis is the same. People must be bold and invest their resources since the return they receive will depend on that investment (cf. Lk 16:1–9; Jn 12:23–26). V.2 calls for diversification of charitable or business efforts. It is simply unwise to put all our eggs into one basket.

Reference to the generous clouds pouring rain upon the earth may serve here as an analogy of appropriate charitable giving. On the other hand, it may suggest a storm that topples the tree, an unexpected and inconvenient happening (v.3). In spite of such aggravations, people must not procrastinate. They must not cower before the unknown or inconvenient. The tasks of life must be done now and not be delayed for ideal conditions (vv.4–6).

Since the same Hebrew word can mean wind or spirit, it is not clear in v.5 whether the reference is to the path of the wind or the path of the spirit. The former would attach it to the preceding verse, while the latter would connect it with the formation of the fetus. Human ignorance concerning the wind (Jn 3:8) and the human fetus (Ps 139:13–16) serves to remind us of our inability to understand the work of God (v.5).

XV. YOUTH AND OLD AGE (11:7–12:8)

In this passage the writer contrasts youth with its joy and advantages and old age with its trouble and disadvantages. Youth must be lived with a conscious recognition of the approach of death (11:8) and of judgment, whether eschatological or the continual vicissitudes of life (v.9). Qoheleth does not see such a mindset as destructive of joy. To the contrary, youth can be enjoyed only as reminders are given both of its beauty and transience.

Further, it is critical for the Creator to be remembered during youth. This is not simply a mental exercise; it is a deliberate act of committing the self to the source of its origin—to God. Such a commitment must be made while life is still enjoyed and the faculties and capacity to know and serve God are at their fullest. The days of trouble—the decline and restraining years—will come (12:1).

Beginning with 12:2 the frailty of old age is presented in a series of pictures. The diversity includes the aging of various parts of the body, the destructiveness of an approaching storm, and the ruin of a wealthy estate due to the failure of its guardians. All emphasize the same—the debilitation of the body because of old age.

V.7 is a reversal of Ge 2:7. Humankind returns to dust, and the dust returns to the ground. Since God gave the spirit, he also has the power to reclaim it. Minimally the spirit refers to the breath of life, the animation of the body God provided (Ps 104:29). From a NT perspective, more will be read into this return of the spirit to God.

XVI. THE CONCLUSION (12:9–14)

Since Qoheleth begins this book with an emphasis on the meaninglessness of life (1:2), it is argued that v.8, where this same emphasis is found, is his conclusion. The book is thus framed by this negative assessment of life. Such a position treats vv.9–14 as a postscript from the hand of a different writer who seeks to add an orthodox dimension to the book. While that is possible, it is also feasible that, in keeping with his use of polarities throughout the book, Qoheleth in these verses is again presenting a contrasting view.

He states that he has carefully pon-dered, searched out, and arranged his material (v.9). His arrangement may suggest the juxtapositioning of ideas. He admits that his material is pointed, having a twofold effect: prodding the mind and the will and remaining in the memory. Indeed, he succeeds in making us both uncomfortable and mindful.

While life from some vantage points may seem meaningless, the fact that it is ultimately subject to divine scrutiny gives it meaning (v.14). Humankind's wholeness (the word "duty" is not in the Hebrew text, leaving the wholeness undefined) is to be found in worship (**fear God**) and conduct (**keep his commandments**). In all stages and events of life the human creature is to reverence God and obey him. The **all** of human life stands in sharp contrast to the **all** of vanity. Here we find meaning and purpose. If the deeds of life are deemed consequential enough by God to be judged, then life can never be without significance (v.14).

BIBLIOGRAPHY

Barton, George A. *The Book of Ecclesiastes*. ICC. New York: Scribner, 1908.

Bullock, C. Hassell. *An Introduction to the Old Testament Poetic Books*. Chicago: Moody, 1979.

Delitzsch, Franz. *The Song of Songs and Ecclesiastes*. Grand Rapids: Eerdmans, 1950.

Gordis, Robert. *Koheleth—The Man and His World*. New York: Schocken, 1968.

Kidner, Derek. *A Time to Mourn, and a Time to Dance*. Downers Grove: InterVarsity Press, 1976.

Murphy, Roland E. *Wisdom Literature: Job, Proverbs, Ruth, Canticles, Ecclesiastes, Esther (The Forms of Old Testament Literature)*. Grand Rapids: Eerdmans, 1981.

Rylaarsdam, J. C. *Proverbs, Ecclesiastes, Song of Solomon*. LBC. Richmond: John Knox, 1964.

Scott, R. B. Y. *Proverbs, Ecclesiastes*. AB. Garden City, N.Y.: Doubleday, 1965.

Short, Robert. *A Time to Be Born—A Time to Die*. New York: Harper & Row, 1973.

Selected Articles

Armstrong, James F. "Ecclesiastes in Old Testament Theology." *Princeton Seminary Bulletin* 94 (1983): 16–25.

Bergant, Diane. "What's the Point of It All?" *The Bible Today* 22 (1984): 75–78.

Glasson, T. Francis. " 'You Never Know': The Message of Ecclesiastes 11:1–16." *Evangelical Quarterly* 60 (1983): 43–48.

Rainey, A. F. "A Study of Ecclesiastes." *Concordia Theological Monthly* 35 (1964): 148–57.

Sheppard, H. "The Epilogue to Qoheleth as Theological Commentary." *Catholic Biblical Quarterly* 39 (1977): 182–89.

SONG OF SONGS
Wayne E. Caldwell

INTRODUCTION

I. TITLE, AUTHORSHIP

The Hebrew title *Shîr Hashîrîm* in 1:1 means "Ode of Odes" or "Song of Songs." This superlative form implies it is a song of utmost excellence or of the most exquisite composition. Because Solomon is named in v.1, it is also known as the Song of Solomon. "Canticles" is the Latin Vulgate form of "Songs."

Solomon's name appears seven times in the book (1:1, 5; 3:7, 9, 11; 8:11, 12). The ascription in 1:1, like those of the Pss, is probably not part of the inspired text. 1Ki 4:29–34 states that Solomon wrote 1,005 songs and that he had great wisdom and intimate knowledge of plants and animals. There are more than twenty varieties of plants and fifteen species of animals named in the book. Numerous references to precious metals and stones are also made. Tradition of long-standing, based on such internal evidence, assigns the book to Solomon.

Some critics say, "It would be difficult to find a man in all history who more conspicuously illustrated the exact opposite [of the poem's] praise of the love and fidelity of a country maiden and her lover [with] the simplicity of their rustic life" (Gray and Adams, 3:31).

Other scholars object to assigning authorship to Solomon primarily because in a book of only 117 verses nearly 50 words are found nowhere else in the OT. Also, some linguistic forms seem to suggest Greek or Persian influence of a later era (Kinlaw, 643). There is inadequate evidence, however, to deny Solomonic authorship. But perhaps it is best left open to debate. Additional material to be considered when assigning authorship follows.

II. DATE, HISTORICAL CONTEXT,
PLACE IN THE CANON

It has been assumed that Solomon wrote SS in his younger years, probably about 965 B.C., when he had only 60 wives and 80 concubines (6:8), rather than in his old age when he had 700 wives and 300 concubines (1Ki 11:3). The author is familiar with cities and mountains all over Palestine. He mentions no fewer than fifteen geographical sites from Lebanon in the north to Egypt in the south.

The reference to Tirzah along with Jerusalem (6:4), as though they were of equal importance as northern and southern capital cities, may suggest a tenth-century date after Solomon. But Tirzah was an ancient city known even in Joshua's day (Kinlaw, 654). Tirzah became the residence of some of the early kings of Israel after the division of the kingdoms.

Questions often are raised whether this poem comes from the northern or southern kingdom and whether it is preexilic or postexilic. The author knows the Hebrew language well, and his vocabulary is extensive. Some authorities think the poem is a protest against the luxury and massive harem of Solomon and that love could not exist in such an environment (ISBE, 5:2831).

Song of Songs was highly respected by the Hebrews. Portions were sung or recited on the eighth day of Passover (*Decision*, Dec. 1968, p. 5). Devout Jews regarded SS as an allegory portraying the relationship of Jehovah and Israel (cf. Isa 55:5; Jer 2:2; Eze 16:8–14; Hos 2:16–20). Because of the sensuous imagery in describing the joys of passionate lovers, the Jews forbade the reading of the SS until a man was thirty years of age. It is noteworthy that the Bible covers the whole range of human experience. Parts of Proverbs such as 5:15–20 are also explicit in descriptions of passion. Ps 45 has a similar tone.

There is no clear allusion to SS in the NT, either by Christ or the writers. Philo makes no mention of the book. The earliest distinct references are in Jewish writers of the second century A.D. Its canonicity was debated as late as the Synod of Jamnia in A.D. 90, when it was decided the book was inspired. Rabbi Akiba held the book as a gift of great value to Israel and the holiest of sacred writings (*Decision*, Dec. 1968, p. 5).

III. KEY THOUGHT, WORDS, VERSES, THEME

Song of Songs is the only biblical book that has human love as its sole thought and theme. Song has been a problem to both Jewish and Christian scholars due to the intimate type of love described in such frank and candid terms. It is embellished by rich Oriental scenes that contain charming descriptions of natural beauty. They are handled with skill and insight.

The theme may be expressed in a number of ways by key words or verses. The word "love" or its cognates are used over fifty times. "My darling" or "my beloved," "my dove," "beauty," or their cognates appear frequently. The theme may also be stated as "faithful love" or "courtship and married bliss."

"Kisses Sweeter Than Wine" (1:2), "Sweet Rose of Sharon" (2:1), "The Lily of the Valley" (2:1), "His Banner Over Me Is Love" (2:4), "I Am His and He Is Mine" (2:16; 6:3), "Until the Day Breaks" (2:17; 4:6), "When the Shadows Flee Away" (2:17; 4:6), "Fairest Among Ten Thousand" (5:10), and "Altogether Lovely" (5:16) are a few of the titles or phrases of songs or choruses taken almost verbatim from SS.

Key verses may be chosen in profusion, e.g., "He has taken me to the banquet hall, and his banner over me is love" (2:4), "I belong to my lover, and his desire is for me" (7:10) and "Many waters cannot quench love; rivers cannot wash it away. If one were to give all the wealth of his house for love, it would be utterly scorned" (8:7).

IV. STRUCTURE AND INTERPRETATION

Perhaps nothing but a direct revelation from God will unite scholars in an understanding and interpretation of this love poem. Is this dramatic poetry like the book of Job, with dialogue carried on between Solomon and a Shulammite lover? Is it a lyric poem designed to celebrate the romance and wedding of Solomon and a bride of humble birth? Is it a collection of short erotic verses intended for wedding feasts of Oriental couples? Such questions are raised by anyone making a serious study of its structure.

There have been numerous attempts by scholars to explain the structure of the SS. Some of the explanations follow:

1. A nuptial song of Solomon's marriage to the daughter of Pharaoh, king of Egypt.

2. An allegory of God's conduct toward the Jews in bringing them out of Egypt, through the wilderness, and into their Promised Land.

3. The incarnation of Christ and his "marriage" with human nature in order to redeem it.

4. Christ's love to believers in the church who make up his bride.

5. An allegory of the glories of Christ and his mother.

6. A collection of sacred idylls whose spiritual meaning is unknown (Clarke, 3:842).

These views can be summarized in three primary interpretations.

A. Allegorical—By the first century A.D. Jewish rabbis had established the interpretation in the Targums that the SS was an allegory of the marital love of Jehovah, the bridegroom, and Israel as the bride from the Exodus to the messianic time. Origen wrote the first extant Christian explanation of the book in the second century. He thought it was a wedding song in honor of Solomon's marriage to an Egyptian princess. It was in the Bible as an allegory of Christ's love for the church (Kinlaw, 642). The Mishnah kept Jewish scholars from interpreting SS as a secular song.

Christian scholars from Augustine to the present have found it easy to follow the Jewish method of interpretation because the figure of wedlock is employed in the NT by Paul and John to represent the vital union of Christ and his church (cf. 2Co 11:2; Eph 5:22–33; Rev 19:7–9; 21:2, 9). Wesley regarded it as a picture of Christ and his marriage with the church. He wrote that it breathes "forth the hottest flames of love between Christ and his people, most sweet and comfortable, and useful to all who read it with serious and Christian eyes" (*Commentary*, 1:1, 318). So all through SS, Wesley spiritualizes every term and description of human love, making them parallel with NT Scriptures or a relationship between Christ and his church.

The difficulty with the allegorical method is that there is not a shred of evidence in SS to suggest that it should be understood as an allegory. Most allegorical interpretations have no historical basis. They are construed and superficial. Many who allegorize it take nearly every phrase of every verse and give it a spiritual meaning. They leave the impression that God has inspired them with what they think they see. The various people named or unnamed in SS are introduced casually and incidentally for the sole purpose of bearing some spiritual message, according to this method.

God's name is not once mentioned here, nor is there any reference to any of his attributes. It is true that God has a special relationship with his chosen people. Christ does have a close affinity with believers. But the writers of sacred literature are careful to state the use of a figure of speech when it is so intended. If SS is intended to represent Christ and his bride, it is difficult to understand why he and all the NT writers pass over it completely. The allegorical method of interpreting Scripture is weak unless metaphors, similes, types, or other figures of speech are clearly indicated by the writer (cf. Eze 23:1–4; Hos 3; Ro 5:14; Gal 4:24; Heb 9:9, 24; 11:19).

B. Literal—This view takes Song its rhythm, symmetry, and beauty in all its force as expressive of natural love between two normal human beings. Theodore of Mopsuestia of the Fourth Century of the Christian Era said that SS was the literal response of Solomon to his subjects who criticized him for his marriage to an Egyptian princess. The church condemned his interpretation, but in more recent years some authorities have taken the same position (Kinlaw, 642). Song of Songs may be both moral and didactic in purpose in describing the dignity and purity of physical love. Human love does not have to be merely erotic, sensual, lustful, animalistic, physical, and biological in nature. It can and also should be pure and noble in accord with God's design for married couples.

The literal view sometimes is called the naturalistic theory by those who think that SS is a collection or anthology of erotic songs that have literary merit but no allegorical or typical meaning whatever (*Decision*, Dec. 1968, p. 5). Some authorities think it is a survival of an ancient pagan liturgy, such as that sung to a fertility god (Kinlaw, 643). Such views, however, are farfetched and depend on the Jews preserving a document or collection simply for their literary excellence. Or the unacceptable conclusion would need to be held that the Jews modified a pagan song for use in the worship of Jehovah. This is contrary to the carefulness with which they included only inspired writings in their Scriptures.

One of the more interesting views of SS, taken literally, is dramatic in nature. The chief character is Solomon, the hero, and a Shulammite maiden, the heroine. Both of these names are from the same root, one masculine and the other feminine in form. They mean "king of peace" and "daughter of peace."

The simple story told in poetic, dramatic form is that a village girl, daughter of a widowed mother of Shulam, is betrothed to a young shepherd whom she met while tending the flock. (Some think the name Shulam may be derived from Shunem, a village southwest of the Sea of Galilee in the tribal area of Issachar.) The girl's brothers hired her to work in the vineyard on their farm. While on the way to the vineyard one day she met a cortege of sixty warriors with King Solomon, who was on a spring visit to the country.

Enthralled with her beauty, the king took the girl to his royal palace in Jerusalem in great pomp and ceremony. In the hopes of adding the girl to his harem by overwhelming her with his splendor and wealth, Solomon praised her with the most lavish words of enticement. But all was in vain. True to her virtue, love, and grace the Shulammite resisted all of Solomon's allurements; spurned his promise to elevate her to the highest rank; and assured her humble shepherd that her affections were secure, sacred, and inviolably pledged to him. Solomon allowed her to leave the royal palace, and the two lovers returned to their native land hand in hand.

C. Typical—Whereas the allegorical method of interpretation ignores the historical setting altogether, this method sees SS as a recital of an actual incident in the life of Solomon. It recognizes the distinctives in each of the other views without going to either extreme. The truth of the book is that it took the charms of a humble country girl to teach the king the true meaning of monogamous love. It is the ideal of human love. It is representative of the love between the Lord and his people as he leads every believer into close fellowship with God.

V. OUTLINE

There are many ways to outline SS. Some divide the book into seven parts corresponding to the seven days of nuptials or seven nights of celebration in Jewish marriage (Clarke, 3:845–46). Others think there are twelve sacred idylls, and divide the book accordingly (Gray and Adams, 3:5). For the purposes of this discussion, I have chosen to use several broad strokes to indicate the progression toward maturity that is seen in the lives of two earthly lovers. It is not even certain who speaks as the poem unfolds, whether it is the bride, the groom, or daughters of Jerusalem or other friends who try to advise the bride.

    I. The Communion of Youthful Lovers (1:1–3:5)
        A. The Lovers' Mutual Love Declared (1:1–2:17)
        B. The Bride's Dream (3:1–5)

    II. The Dream of the Union of Lovers (3:6–4:15)
        A. Solomon's Procession (3:6–11)
        B. Solomon's Song (4:1–15)

    III. The Struggles of Lovers (4:16–7:9a)
        A. The Bride's Second Dream (4:16–5:9)
        B. The Bride Sings of Her Lover (5:10–6:3)

C. The Groom Sings of the Bride's Beauty (6:4–7:9a)
IV. The Growth and Progress of Young Lovers (7:9b–8:14)
  A. The Bride Responds to Her Lover (7:9b–8:4)
  B. The Covenant of Lovers in Marriage (8:5–14)

COMMENTARY

I. THE COMMUNION OF YOUTHFUL LOVERS (1:1–3:5)

If Israel and Judah had been satisfied with the delights of human love among themselves as portrayed in the communication that these young lovers enjoyed, they might not have fallen into ruin as they did. Intermarriage with heathen nations around them brought the influence of the corruptions of a morally declining civilization.

A. The Lovers' Mutual Love Declared (1:1–2:17)

The writer begins the love story abruptly without details of what is about to happen or who is involved. The bride as the beloved country girl and the groom as the shepherd lover are engaged in conversation in the opening verses of the book. The bride asks her spouse where he takes the flock at noon to protect them from the heat. She does not want to look for her lover in some strange pasture. Her lover tells her to follow the tracks of the sheep. A day and a night or two may pass as they exchange platitudes of praise for each other, especially as the bride describes a visit of the groom, apparently in the spring of the year (2:8–13).

B. The Bride's Dream (3:1–5)

The dream described may be one that occurred on more than one night while the bride was separated from her lover. When she becomes uneasy, she rises from her bed and asks city watchmen whether they have seen her lover. Just then the lover appears, and she conducts him to her room. A repeated reference to the daughters of Jerusalem throughout the book (cf. 2:7; 3:5, 10–11; 5:8, 16; 8:4) not only suggests the unity of the book, but also indicates that they gave the bride tidbits of friendly advice from time to time (cf. 1:4b; 5:1c, 9; 6:1, 13a; 8:5a, 8–9).

II. THE DREAM OF THE UNION OF LOVERS (3:6–4:15)

A. Solomon's Procession (3:6–11)

For the first time Solomon is identified as the groom or suitor. The king is mentioned in 1:4 and 1:12, but only now does the poet indicate whose person and carriage the delegation of sixty swordsmen protect. The retinue is impressive in its sheer elegance as perfumes, powders, precious metals, and the crown of the king are described.

B. Solomon's Song (4:1–15)

As Solomon had come to take his bride, he breaks out into praise and adoration, noting her eyes, hair, teeth, lips, temples, neck, and breasts. Doves, goats, sheep, lambs, a red ribbon, a pomegranate, the tower of David, and fawns are similes that describe her physical beauty.

III. THE STRUGGLES OF LOVERS (4:16–7:9A)

A. The Bride's Second Dream (4:16–5:9)

The invitation of the bride for her groom to enter her garden is followed by her dream, which she relates to her friends. The dream shows how the bride can hardly believe that her lover is really asking for her. When she responds to his request, she finds that he is gone. She is abused by two guards when she asks where he went. This is followed by an appeal to the daughters of Jerusalem who ask her why her lover is so special.

B. The Bride Sings of Her Lover (5:10–6:3)

The bride breaks into song, describing her lover's physical appearance. She notes his head, hair, eyes, cheeks, lips, arms, body, legs and mouth, concluding that "he is altogether lovely." She doesn't spare the similes in telling the daughters of Jerusalem why he is "outstanding among ten thousand." They offer to help find her lover, but she declines their help, stating that she knows where he is.

C. The Groom Sings of the Bride's Beauty (6:4–7:9a)

The king does not allow the bride's praise of his charm to go unrequited. He sings of her beauty, which surpasses even that of all the king's women. She is the choicest of all the virgins, "my perfect one" (6:8–9). There are others who enter the conversation at this point. They call for the maiden to return so that they can gaze on her beauty. The significant name of the maiden as the Shulammite, probably from the village of Shunem, gives the setting for the groom's song as he continues (7:1–9a). The most intimate chambers of married love are here described as the groom extols his bride's feet, legs, navel, waist, breasts, neck, eyes, nose, head, hair, breath, and mouth. This section should be seen of married bliss in all its candor and grace. The Jews would not condone any description of fornication.

IV. THE GROWTH AND PROGRESS OF YOUNG LOVERS (7:9B–8:14)

A. The Bride Responds to Her Lover (7:9b–8:4)

The maiden replies to her lover with an invitation to run free in the fields and vineyards, to enjoy the fruit of nature, and to accept her love unashamedly. With modesty and purity she invokes the daughters of Jerusalem not to interfere with the love that the pair now has come to enjoy. They are well able to carry on their own lovemaking.

B. The Covenant of Lovers in Marriage (8:5–14)

This final section shows the lovers in conversation with the brides's brothers or friends assuring her that they know of her integrity and purity. The bride's words show the growth and maturity that has come during the courtship. The words of 8:10 are a declaration of her virtuous character and maturity. She and her lover want only the closest bond to keep them committed to each other forever.

The key verse of SS, 8:10, may express something of the same quality and endurance of love as that found in 1Co 13. In my view the original literal intent of SS was to show the splendor of physical love in marriage as Solomon and the Shulammite maiden experienced it. To find applications and analogies of the truth of this interpretation does not do SS an injustice. It should be used more frequently by young

Christian lovers in the enhancement of their romance in courtship, all the while preserving themselves in purity for each other until after their marriage. And best of all it is analogous to a believer's relationship to Christ and of Christ's to the believer.

Seen in this light the words of Dennis Kinlaw have a great deal of meaning:

> It is important to see that the biblical account does not see procreation as the originally primary purpose of sex. Before the forming of the first woman, according to Genesis 2:20, Adam found no "suitable helper." Thus the primary purpose of women is not procreation. . . . She is the one in whom her husband finds his completeness. That completeness may involve progeny, but it is far more than this. The ability of the woman to bear children is an intermittent and passing phase of her earthly existence. Her femaleness and her role as marriage partner are far more extensive than this. The complete giving of one partner in a divinely ordered relationship of love to the other results normally in children. This, however, is a bonus. Married love has its own justification in that it is God's own way of making that higher person, that "one flesh," which is God's normal order for His children (p. 644).

BIBLIOGRAPHY

Clarke, Adam. *A Commentary and Critical Notes. The Old Testament*. Vol. 3. New York: Abingdon-Cokesbury, n.d.

"Introducing the Old Testament, The Song of Songs Which Is Solomon's." *Decision* (December 1968), 5.

"Introducing the Old Testament, The Song of Songs Which Is Solomon's." *Decision* (January 1969), 5.

Gray, James Comper and George M. Adams. *The Biblical Encyclopedia*. Vol. 3. New York: George H. Doran, 1903.

Henry, Matthew. *Commentary on the Whole Bible*. Vol. 3. Old Tappan, N.J.: Revell, n.d.

John Richard Sampey. "Song of Songs." ISBE. Vol. 5. Grand Rapids: Eerdmans, 1947.

Keil, C. F. and F. Delitzsch. *Commentary on the Old Testament in Ten Volumes*. Vol. 6. "Song of Solomon." Grand Rapids: Eerdmans, 1978.

Kinlaw, Dennis. *The Song of Solomon*. WBC. Vol. 2. Grand Rapids: Eerdmans, 1968.

Purkiser, W. T. *Know Your Old Testament*. Kansas City: Beacon Hill, 1954.

Robinson, Theodore H. *The Poetry of the Old Testament*. London: Duckworth, 1947.

Wesley, John. *John Wesley's Commentary on the Bible*. Edited by G. Roger Schoenhals. Grand Rapids: Zondervan, 1987. (Wesley's *Notes* in one volume, previously published by Zondervan under the title *Wesley's Notes on the Bible*.)

ISAIAH
Dan Johnson

INTRODUCTION

The book of Isaiah contains some of the grandest poetry, loftiest theology, and keenest political insight ever recorded. It is an epoch-making work that emerged from the lifework of a prophet-statesman and has influenced the NT and the Christian church in a manner unparalleled by the rest of the OT.

I. ISAIAH THE MAN

Isaiah was born during the reign of King Uzziah, around the year 760 B.C., and pursued his ministry in and around Jerusalem. The dominant political situation was the Syro-Ephraimite crisis, with Assyria the menacing world power. Israel (Ephraim) and Damascus (Syria) plotted to resist them, applying pressure on King Ahaz and Judah to join them. Ahaz refused, but rather than simply trust God as Isaiah directed Ahaz (ch. 7), he called upon Assyria for aid. Assyria responded by destroying Damascus and eventually Samaria, Israel's primary city, in 721 B.C. Then, instead of rewarding its ally, Judah, Assyria reduced it to a vassal state. Chs. 1–12 are from this period. The pronouncements of judgment against a corrupt society see Assyria as God's instrument of that judgment. Imbedded in the material are expressions of hope (2:1–5; 4:2–6; 9:2–7; 11:1–12:6) that come to fruition in chs. 40–55 and most fully in the idea of a messianic age.

During Hezekiah's reign (720–686 B.C.) there were several attempts to rebel against Assyria. Frequent contact was made with Egypt for help despite Isaiah's warnings that it was useless (31:1–3) and that they should trust God instead. As he did with King Ahaz, Isaiah had easy access to King Hezekiah and interceded for him during his illness (ch. 38) and chastised him when he revealed his treasury to Babylonian envoys (ch. 39).

II. THE TEACHINGS OF THE BOOK OF ISAIAH

As a young man, Isaiah received his call to the prophetic ministry through an encounter with God in the temple (ch. 6). This experience was pivotal to his life's work and formative to his theology. Most of his major theological concepts originated here.

A. The Sovereignty of God

The temple experience revealed a holy God whose glory filled the whole earth (6:3). God's rule extended beyond Israel to include all the nations. Thus all nations come under his scrutiny (cf. chs. 13–27, oracles against the nations). Particular nations were used as his instruments, e.g., Assyria (8:6–10), as were individual rulers (44:28). Other gods were as nothing (cf. the denunciation of idols 44:9–20), and the inexhaustible power of God is praised (40:12–31) as the basis on which the restoration of the exiles is proclaimed.

B. The Holiness of God

Isaiah's vision of God in the temple was accompanied by the cry of the seraphs, "Holy, holy, holy is the Lord Almighty." Consequently the title, "The Holy One of Israel/Jacob" occurs twenty-six times in Isaiah (while occurring only six times elsewhere). God's holiness carries three dimensions: (1) Otherness. God is wholly other; the Creator is separate from the creature. (2) Moral and ethical purity. Because of God's holy character, he expected the same from his people. Most of the indictments against Judah in chs. 1–12 and 28–33 were because of moral and ethical concerns. (3) Redemption, a dimension that is often overlooked. Instructive is the number of times in chs. 40–55 that the idea of the Holy One of Israel is accompanied by a promise of salvation. When God acts in his holiness, Israel is restored (cf. 40:25; 41:14, 16, 20; 43:3, 14, 15; 47:4; 48:17; 49:7).

C. Sin

Isaiah's awareness of the holiness of God made him aware of his own sinfulness and the sinfulness of his people (6:5). Isaiah viewed the inner, religious dimension and the outer, social dimension of sin as integrally related, and he made it his life's work to turn his people away from their sinfulness. A paradigmatic portrayal of sin is found in the person of King Ahaz (ch. 7) and his refusal to trust God. Rather, he called on Assyria, which reduced Judah to a vassal state.

D. The Remnant

The account of Isaiah's vision closes with a reference to the holy seed (6:13). Isaiah's son was named Shear-jashub, "A remnant shall return" (7:3). The idea had a twofold meaning. On the one hand it was a message of judgment, for only a remnant would return. On the other hand, it was a statement of hope, for indeed a remnant would be kept to ensure the future. It was an idea that took on increasing significance in the subsequent OT history and in Christianity (cf. Ro 11).

E. Messiah

It is instructive that Isaiah saw the Lord "seated on a throne." He saw God as the King of kings. It soon became apparent to Isaiah that no human king would be able or worthy to govern his people properly. God would have to fulfill that role by providing a divine/human king; an anointed one, a Messiah.

Isaiah's predictions of such a king are found in 9:2–7 and 11:1–16, which became increasingly influential not only throughout the book of Isaiah (32:1–20; 61:1–11), but through subsequent OT history. They came to fruition in the person of Jesus of Nazareth.

F. Suffering Servant

Four servant poems are found in the book (42:1–4; 49:1–6; 50:4–9; 52:13–53:12). While the identity of the servant is unclear, it is certain that his role is that of redemptive sufferer on behalf of his people. This model became central in the life and ministry of Jesus.

III. STRUCTURE, AUTHORSHIP, AND DATE OF ISAIAH

Traditionally the entire book of Isaiah has been viewed as the work of one man who lived from about 760 to 700 B.C. However, for the past two hundred years many interpreters have suggested that this view should be more finely nuanced. The book seems to fall into three major divisions: (1) chs. 1–39, (2) chs. 40–55, (3) chs. 56–66. Chs. 1–39 portray Isaiah as bringing the word of God to bear on Judah (chs. 1–12) and then on the nations around Judah (chs. 13–27), returning to address Judah once again (chs. 28–35), with chs. 36–39 being a historical section repeated from 2 Kings 18:17ff. It is clear, however, that chs. 40–55 mark a major change. The location is no longer Jerusalem but Babylon. The time period is following the destruction of Jerusalem in 587 B.C., some 150 years after the death of Isaiah. The prophet calls the people to take heart; God is about to deliver them and take them home. Chs. 56–66 appear to be later still, during the time of restoration when the exiles have returned home and are trying to rebuild their city.

Readers who believe in the limitless power of God will affirm that God could project Isaiah 150 years into the future to produce the material of chs. 40–66. That is not to be doubted. But did God do that? We do not know. When one reads the material carefully, one has the feeling that the author was there among his people, that he sensed their fears and their doubts about God and about Cyrus, and that he was enraged at their propensity toward idolatry. Is it not possible that a subsequent author could have built on the theology of Isaiah, particularly the ideas of God's sovereignty and holiness, the idea of the remnant and the Messiah, and brought them to bear on a later situation. We must remember that the prophetic word was expansive, that is, spoken to a particular situation but having a life of its own, making it applicable to situations in the future.

IV. OUTLINE

I. God's Plan for Judah and Jerusalem (1:1–12:6)

COMMENTARY

I. GOD'S PLAN FOR JUDAH AND JERUSALEM (1:1–12:6)

These chapters come from the early part of Isaiah's life and contain an account of his call and a record of his teaching. Statements of judgments are joined by promises of blessing.

A. Judah's Sin Is the Cause of the Punishment (1:1–5:30)

This collection of oracles introduces the book and portrays a society that has become infected with a sickness unto death.

1. The problem is defined (1:1–31)

The opening chapter serves as an introduction to the entire book of Isaiah, presenting a picture of a sinful, rebellious nation.

a. The heading (1:1)

The Hebrew word for **vision** (*ḥazôn*) suggests that one has received a direct word from God and carries both a sense of authenticity and authority. The focus of the vision is stated: Judah and Jerusalem. It should be noted that the kingdom under David and Solomon has long since been divided into the North (Israel) and the South (Judah). It is the southern kingdom that is now the object of God's attention.

Isaiah is the recipient of the vision and the one charged with announcing it. His name means "Yahweh will save" ("Yahweh" is the Hebrew name for God). Isaiah's name is an important clue for understanding the entire book. Rather than this being one uninterrupted pronouncement of judgment, as some interpreters have suggested, the primary purpose of God is to save his people. Redemption, wholeness, and restoration are the goal of God's activity. The listing of the kings of Judah provides historical benchmarks for Isaiah's prophetic activity.

b. The case against Judah (1:2–31)

The form that Isaiah employs is that of a court case (a *rîb*). Yahweh, speaking in the first person, pleads his case against Judah and asks the entire creation to serve as a witness (v.2). Even though Yahweh has acted as a loving parent to his children, they have acted with far less intelligence than dumb animals and have turned their backs on God and forsaken him (vv.2–4).

Here we first encounter the appellation for God that occurs frequently in Isaiah: **"the Holy One of Israel."** Note that it comes in the context of moral wrongdoing (see v.4). This suggests that inherent in the word *holy* (*qodesh*), is the idea of moral character. To turn one's back on and to spurn the Holy One of Israel is, according to the context of this verse, to be **sinful, loaded with guilt, evildoers . . . given to corruption.**

The Daughter of Zion (v.8) is another name for Jerusalem. These verses may reflect the situation when Sennacherib laid waste all of Judah except Jerusalem. It was a time of severe hardship. The ultimate indictment of his people is given in the comparison with Sodom and Gomorrah, the infamous cities of Ge 19. Only the grace of God prevented Judah from receiving the same fate.

Isaiah reveals the hypocrisy of their worship (vv.10–15). The religious leaders have increased their religious activities in direct proportion to their disobedience to God. God would have none of this. He hates their duplicity.

In vv.16–20 the prophet gives a prescription for wholeness. Straightforward and powerful, it focuses on both inner motivation (**"wash and make yourselves clean"**) and outer action (**"stop doing wrong, learn to do right"**). He then delineates what the right is in v.17. V.18 is a powerful appeal to their reason. The prescription makes sense. If they follow it, they will be made whole. If they do not, if they rebel, they will be destroyed.

In vv.21–28 history is presented as a prelude to the future. The prophet, in keeping with biblical tradition, recalls the past in order to shape the future. The city has become a harlot, full of impurities and corruption. But it once was faithful, full of justice and fine silver. Therefore God will restore the city. He will purge the dross and impurities so that it will once again be the faithful city.

Vv.29–31 are an addendum. The sacred oaks were objects of worship and therefore of idolatry. Here they have parabolic significance. Judah will become like the object it worships, like an oak now dried up, like tinder that is set on fire and utterly destroyed.

2. Isaiah's twofold vision of the future (2:1–22)

This new title suggests that chs. 2–4 may once have stood separate from ch. 1, with the latter being a more general introduction to the entire book.

a. The glorious distant future (2:1–5)

The phrase **"in the last days"** is an expression used by the prophets to refer to an unspecified future time. While some commentators suggest that it is an apocalyptic phrase referring to the new age at the end of history, it seems for Isaiah to refer to a time within history. As we shall see, throughout this book the prophet is consistent in seeing God's activity as occurring within history. His vision of the future is eschatological rather than apocalyptic in tone.

The Hebrew people were a people of irrepressible hope. In the midst of devastation the prophet is able to see a day when God's design for his people will indeed come to pass. These verses find their parallel in Mic 4:1–3. The mountain of God, that is, Mount Zion, the place of Jerusalem and the temple, will be exalted, and the peoples of the earth will be drawn to it. God's law will reign supreme, and there will be an era of peace. He ends the vision with a call to his people to walk in the light of the Lord.

b. Imminent judgment (2:6–22)

Alas, while the call was to walk in the light, the people of Judah have abandoned the light of God. Instead of relying on Yahweh, they have looked to foreign powers for their aid. With the aid has come the corresponding superstitions and religious practices of those countries.

In this chapter we see a dramatic and powerful display of the literary prowess of the prophet. Note how he plays on the theme of elevation and being brought low to the ground and even below the ground (v.10). This alternating relationship is summarized in v.11: **"The pride of men [will be] brought low; [and] the LORD alone will be exalted."**

The Lord's Day of Judgment will be the great reversal. All that is currently exalted through pride will be humbled, and God alone will be lifted up. The artist conveys his image with particular force by references to the lofty cedars of Lebanon, the oaks of Bashan, towering mountains, lofty towers, and trading ships (vv.13–16). Then again, the re-

frain is repeated: Man in his arrogant pride will be brought low, and the Lord alone will be exalted.

When God comes forth in judgment, arrogant men will simply be disposed of (vv.19–22). Therefore, the prophet concludes, why trust these foreign powers who are ever so transitory when you can trust in Almighty God? (This is the heart of Isaiah's contention with Ahaz in ch. 7.)

3. The future Day of Judgment is now (3:1–4:1)

Starvation and social anarchy rule. This section seems to reflect the actual state of affairs that existed in 701 B.C. during Sennacherib's siege of Jerusalem. Indeed there was little food and water left in Jerusalem during the siege (v.1). It was a time of panic, terror, and related social chaos. Society has dissolved to the point where only children are willing to govern (v.4). In reality, the situation was so horrendous that no one wanted to govern (vv.5–7).

Like the composer of a great symphony, the prophet/poet returns to earlier themes to present them in a slightly different light. He reminds the people of Judah that the current judgment is a result of their sins against Yahweh (vv.8–15). Again the parallel with Sodom is drawn. As in 1:18–19, the contrasting features of the righteous and the wicked are indicated (vv.10–11).

V.12 is difficult. It may be, as some have suggested, that it refers to a child king and queen mother. One suspects, rather, because of the context, that the references are intended to be derogatory terms suggesting that the current leaders were in fact weaklings.

Indeed, subsequent verses demonstrate that the reason the Lord rises to judge his people is because the leaders and rulers have not acted in good faith.

Rather, they have ruined God's people (*vineyard* is a term often employed to refer to Judah/Israel; see below on 5:1–7). They have exploited the poor. In short, they have failed to seek justice. (1:17).

The haughtiness of the women of Jerusalem is excoriated (3:16–4:1). In stark contrast to the crushed and helpless poor are the overbearing, wealthy women of Jerusalem. God's judgment will surely come to them. Note the striking contrast of v.24:

> Instead of fragrance, there will be stench;
> Instead of a sash, a rope;
> Instead of well-dressed hair, baldness;
> Instead of fine clothing, sackcloth;
> Instead of beauty, branding.

These are the terms of exile, an exile that would one day come.

Then the prophet combines, as it were, the tragic sorrow of these devastated individual women into one symbolic whole with the reference to a feminized Zion, who, destitute, sits on the ground and mourns (v.26).

In that day of devastation, so many of the men of Judah will be killed that there will be only one man for every seven women. And they, who once exhibited such arrogant pride will beg of that man simply to let them be called by his name and take away their disgrace.

4. The purging leads to blessing (4:2–6)

We saw in ch. 2 that the prophet established a contrapuntal relationship between the themes of elevation and demotion on a grand scale throughout the book. The same is true of the themes of judgment and blessing. The book begins on a note of judgment, but ch. 2 opens with a vision of blessing (vv.1–5). This is followed by a graphic depiction of judgment (2:6–4:1). But once again the prophet reiterates the theme of blessing. Similar themes of blessing appear in 9:1–7 and 11:1–12:6.

Most critical scholars consider these portions that refer to future blessing to be later postexilic additions. Little evidence is available to support this, and it destroys Isaiah's intention. He has carefully woven the two themes together to show that even though Yahweh's judgment must surely come because of their disobedience, just as surely Yahweh will never forsake them but will restore and rescue them. Always in the midst of devastation there remained a vision of hope. This legacy Isaiah gave to his people and to all of us who are his spiritual descendants.

In this specific text Isaiah looks beyond the imminent devastation to a beautiful and glorious future. He mentions a remnant, that is, **those who are left** (*shear*, v.3). This is the first reference in Isaiah to the holy remnant or righteous remnant.

Note in vv.5 and 6 the allusions to the Exodus/Sinai experience when the children of Israel were led by a pillar of cloud by day and fire by night and when God's presence was symbolized by the presence of the cloud that covered the Tent of Meeting.

5. Judgment is inevitable (5:1–30)

This section conveys Isaiah's indictment of Judah, first with a parable of the vineyard and then with a series of staccato woe sayings.

a. The song of the vineyard (5:1–7)

This is one of the classic passages in Isaiah and shows the prophet's literary skills at their highest. He carefully weaves the story of the vineyard, slowly drawing in the listener/reader ever more fully until at the end he is trapped with no escape.

Isaiah the prophet of God now plays the role of a singer for God. The one he loves is Yahweh, and the song he sings is about Yahweh's vineyard. Yahweh had prepared the ground and planted the best vines. He had every reason to expect a good crop of grapes, but the vineyard yielded only bad ones.

Next, he speaks for God and asks the audience, the people of Jerusalem and Judah, to act as judge. Considering all that he had done, didn't he have the right to expect good grapes? The implicit answer is yes. And because the vineyard failed to yield good fruit, he, the owner, will let it be destroyed. It will become a wasteland.

The trap had been set; now it is sprung. The vineyard is none other than the house of Israel, the people of Judah. They have distorted God's intention for them. Two wordplays bring the message home with particular force, especially in the Hebrew:

> He looked for justice [*mišpāt*],
> but saw bloodshed [*mišpāh*];
> for righteousness [*ṣedāqāh*],
> but heard cries of distress [*seʿqāh*].

The similarity in the vowels and consonants (assonance and alliteration) of the Hebrew words would emphasize the dissonance of their lives.

b. A series of woes (5:8–25)

Each of the woe sayings begins with the Hebrew word *hôy,* commonly translated "woe." It is a term that probably comes from the context of a funeral lament: *Hôy* is a cry of mourners as they lament the passing of the deceased. The term is, no doubt, intentionally chosen by Isaiah, for in his eyes the impending judgment of God is so certain that wrongdoers, when he addresses them,

are as good as dead. The mood of lament conveyed by this term is appropriate as well. Isaiah does not communicate God's message of punishment with sinister joy but with deep sorrow.

The first woe is an attack on those wealthy landowners who accrue as much land as possible at whatever cost. It was a practice that was oppressive to the poor and therefore stood under the judgment of God.

But there was another dynamic at work here. Basic to OT thought was the idea that the land was Yahweh's (Lev 25:23, "The land is mine and you are but aliens and my tenants"). Indeed, the previous parable of the vineyard clearly made this very point. So both the theological and social dimensions of life had been violated. God could not let this go unpunished.

The punishment is stated in vv.9 and 10: The vast accumulations will be destroyed, and the new houses will all be empty. The land that they have seized will yield next to nothing.

The second woe is against indulgent and godless living (vv.11–17). The people have become so hedonistic that their first thought in the morning is the pursuit of pleasure. They have no regard for God (v.12). And because they have chosen to live without God, then indeed they will. Exile and death, life without God will be their lot (v.13).

Note Isaiah's graphic picture of the mouth of death extended without limit, into which the people descend (v.14). Their descent brings to the prophet's mind his earlier depiction of Yahweh's Day of Judgment from ch. 2 (2:11, 17; 5:15–16).

The holy and righteous character of God will not permit unrighteousness and godlessness to go unchecked. V.16 suggests that when God acts in accordance with his character, all that is contrary to that character of holiness and righteousness will be destroyed.

The third woe is against those who have become so accustomed to sinning that it becomes a part of them and they drag it along with them wherever they go. Some interpreters would change the phrase **"cords of deceit"** to "like a sheep on a tether," but this requires a change in the Hebrew text and misses the more subtle nuance. The phrase refers to deceptively thin cords like a spider's web. The first sin seems harmless enough and perhaps the second, but soon the sinner is trapped in the webbing, unable to get out (cf. Sawyer, 59).

V.19 is directed against those who mock God and his prophet. Isaiah has prophesied that God's judgment was imminent, but these foolish ones do not believe him! "If what you say is true, show us. See, it won't happen."

The forth woe is against deliberate falsification of reality (v.20), while the fifth woe is against distorted perspective (v.21). The sixth woe is against those who misappropriate justice (vv.22–23). Those in the law court are portrayed as experts regarding things of no consequence, such as mixing drinks. But more seriously they have imbibed freely of the corrupt spirit of the times and are no longer able or willing to deal justly.

The judgment is now stated: Because they have rejected the word and law of God, the Holy One of Israel, God will destroy them with fire.

c. The distant invader is God's instrument (5:26–30)

God has called a great nation from the ends of the earth, and it is coming swiftly. The powerful description of its approach is a classic one. The nation is Assyria. But the nature of the prophetic word is such that seldom is it exhausted by one historical situation. The vitality of Isaiah's word would enable a passage such as this one to be seen later in 588/87 B.C. in the context of the Babylonian invasion as well. While the specific historical event was of penultimate importance, of ultimate importance was the reality that Yahweh was the one in whose hands the nations are but instruments to do his bidding.

B. King Ahaz Is Unfaithful; Need for God's Future King (6:1–12:6)

1. Isaiah's call (6:1–13)

The location of Isaiah's call at this point in the book rather than in the beginning has sparked a great deal of discussion and debate. Little warrant exists to question its position here. Isaiah's mission was an extremely difficult one: to announce that the devastating judgment of God would soon come upon his people because of their sin and wrongdoing. The first five chapters set the stage for the call. The society had become so immoral and corrupt that Yahweh had to call someone to bring the Word of God to bear on the situation. Isaiah was that person.

There is a second reason why the present position of the call narrative makes sense. Isaiah identifies with his people, even in their sinfulness: **"I am a man of unclean lips, and I live among a people of unclean lips"** (v.5). Their uncleanness has been well established in the preceding chapters. Only through personal cleansing can he or they return to a righteous relationship with God, the Holy One of Israel. Isaiah's cleansing now becomes paradigmatic for the entire community.

a. The encounter (6:1–7)

King Uzziah's death in 736 B.C. brought to an end an era of prosperity and well being and ushered in a time of uncertainty and anxiety. The Assyrian threat was beginning to loom on the horizon. No doubt feeling the weight of these tremulous times, Isaiah made his way to the temple. It was there that he was confronted by God.

It is difficult to catch the full impact of Isaiah's vision simply from reading the English text. The Hebrew word often translated **"train"** of his robe is really "hem," the bottom portion of a robe or dress. The "hem" of his robe filled the temple!

A comparison with the mythology of Israel's neighboring countries brings out the grandeur of v.2. It was common to see images of seraphs with wings outstretched surrounding the deities of other countries to protect them. But here, note that the God whom Isaiah sees is so powerful and awe-inspiring that the seraphs, rather than stretching out their wings to protect him, protect themselves.

We noted that Isaiah's vision was of a high, exalted, and powerful God. V.3 adds another dimension, a dimension that was to play a dominant role in Isaiah's understanding of God's character and God's action: **"Holy, holy, holy is the LORD Almighty."** It is his holy character that will not allow the offenses of the people of Judah, which were chronicled in the previous chapters, to stand. And not only the offenses of Judah, but of all peoples, past and present, for **the whole earth is full of his glory.**

b. The commission (6:8–13)

In the wake of his personal cleansing, Isaiah overhears a dialogue between God and his heavenly court (see 40:1–8 and 1Ki 22:19–22 for a similar situation). God needs someone to fulfill a task: Who will it be? Seemingly without hesitation, Isaiah volunteers: **"Here am I. Send me!"**

Then God gives Isaiah the message that he is to deliver to this people. It is an enigmatic message that has proved to be problematic for interpreters for centuries. Even today there is no consensus as to its meaning. On a first reading, it appears to suggest that God has acted capriciously toward his people. Through Isaiah, God's word will have the effect of blinding the people and making them unable to understand lest they perceive the error of their ways and repent. But this runs contrary to what we otherwise know of the character of God.

Some commentators have reasoned that this text was written down at the end of Isaiah's life and is thus a reflection on his call and subsequent ministry. As such, it appears to the prophet that his words had the effect of dulling his people's sensitivities. As appealing as this idea is, there is nothing in the text to suggest that it is a later reflection. Rather, it all is of one piece, as it were, immediately following upon the call.

The key is found in the context. Unfortunately, many commentators fragment the text of Isaiah, thus lifting the call of Isaiah out of its context. We have seen from the previous five chapters, and we shall see in ch. 7, that the people of Judah and Jerusalem have indeed heard Isaiah's words of woe and warning, but they have been unwilling to understand or come to reason. It appears that the more Isaiah preaches, the more resistant the people become, even to the point of mockery (cf. 5:19). They simply would not believe! It has become all too obvious from the context that this people was not going to turn and be healed. Thus, in this context, v.10 carries a biting note of irony, for God surely wanted them to turn and be healed (1:5–6, 18–20), but by now it has become clear that that will not happen.

The commission is followed by a question of lament: **"How long?"** The answer: **"Until the cities lie ruined and without inhabitant, until the houses are left deserted and the fields ruined and ravaged . . ."** Once again it is consistent with the context. See especially the woes of ch. 5. Yet characteristic of Isaiah's message and of the God who gave it, there is a note of hope. A holy seed, a remnant, will be left.

2. Three prophetic signs (7:1–8:22)

As noted, in the first five chapters the people of Judah and Jerusalem were unwilling to trust God and obey him. This destructive posture of a people is now brought into sharp focus through an episode in the life of Ahaz, their king (736–725 B.C.). The historical setting is that of the Syro-Ephraimite War. The massive and devastating army of Assyria under Tiglath-Pileser III (744–727 B.C.) was a menacing presence, a dark cloud just east of Palestine. Some of the smaller states, such as Ephraim (the northern kingdom of Israel) and Syria (Aram) tried to spark an anti-Assyrian revolt. Wanting Judah to join forces with them, they threatened it with violence unless it agreed.

Ahaz is terror-stricken (his heart shook **as the trees of the forest are shaken by the wind**). Into this situation, Isaiah comes, calling upon Ahaz to trust in Yahweh rather than in the power of men. To communicate his message, Isaiah gives a sequence of three signs based on the names of three children: Shear-Jashub, "a remnant will return" (7:1–9), Immanuel, "God with us" (7:10–17), and Maher-Shalal-Hash-Baz, "Quick to the plunder, swift to the spoil" (8:1–4).

a. The sign of Shear-Jashub (7:1–9)

Jerusalem was under siege by the allied forces of Syria and Ephraim. Because Jerusalem had been uncooperative in their attempts to throw off the yoke of Assyria, these two countries turned on Judah and threatened to replace Ahaz with a pawn of their own, Tabeel.

Frightened, Ahaz has decided to inspect the water supply to his city rather than look to the real Supply of his strength. It is there that Isaiah and his son Shear-Jashub are sent to meet Ahaz. His word to Ahaz is clear: "These two little countries to the north are no more of a threat than are two smoldering sticks of firewood. Their plans to invade you will not come to pass." Isaiah's son was there as a sign that the forces to the north would be reduced to only a bare remnant. Their demise is spelled out with clarity in vv.8–9a.

Isaiah concludes his word to Ahaz with a warning. It is a well-crafted play on the word *'amen,* which means "believe, be established, stand firm" from which we get the word "amen"—let it be established. **"If you do not stand firm in your faith, you will not stand at all."** In that event, Shear-Jashub becomes a name of warning, meaning that Judah itself will be destroyed, with only a remnant left to return.

Clearly Isaiah wants Ahaz to act from a position of faith and trust in God. He must not be threatened by Ephraim and Syria. God would see that they were taken care of. Thus there was no need for Ahaz to run to Assyria (as he unfortunately chooses to do) for help. If he could simply trust in God and not in the power of men, then he would stand firm. But, alas, Ahaz knew no such firmness of faith.

b. The sign of Immanuel (7:10–25)

Perhaps Isaiah saw Ahaz wavering, uncertain. He challenges him to ask God for a sign. With hauntingly hollow piety, Ahaz responds, **"I will not ask; I will not put the LORD to the test."** He failed to recognize that he alone was the one who was being tested. Isaiah could tolerate this religious posturing no longer: **"Will you try the patience of my God also? Therefore the Lord himself will give you a sign: The virgin will be with child and will give birth to a son, and will call him Immanuel."**

The debate over the interpretation of the Hebrew word, 'almâ is extensive and inconclusive. Whether Isaiah meant a virgin, a young maiden, his own wife, or something else cannot be stated with certainty (cf. this debate in Oswalt, 207–9). Whatever one concludes about the nature of the mother, the primary importance has to do with the son and his name: Immanuel, God with us.

The question arises, Does the name Immanuel mean weal or woe, blessing or destruction? One of the literary techniques that Isaiah employs is that of double entendre or twofold meaning. This is but one example. The meaning to be realized depends entirely on the choice that is made. If you stand firm in faith, then "God is with us" in blessing. If you do not stand firm in faith, then "God is with us" in judgment.

Both elements are present in the subsequent prophecy (vv.15–25). Before the boy is of the age of choosing right and wrong, that is, very shortly, **the land of the two kings [Ahaz dreads] will be laid waste.** Therefore, God would be with us in blessing (vv.15–16). Indeed, within three years, Damascus had been destroyed and Samaria reduced to nearly nothing, and Samaria was completely destroyed twelve years later.

However, now it becomes clear that Isaiah has realized that Ahaz would not stand firm in his God but would disobey and turn to Assyria for help. Therefore, "God is with us" in judgment. He will bring upon Judah a time of unprecedented devastation brought about by the very one to whom Ahaz had turned for help, the king of Assyria (v.17).

Vv.18–25 speak in figurative language of the coming Assyrian invasion. To be sure, over the next twenty-five years Assyria brought tremendous devastation to Judah.

c. The sign of Maher-Shalal-Hash-Baz (8:1–4)

To reinforce the prophecy and to make certain that it is known publicly, God orders Isaiah to write it down in the presence of witnesses. The form the prophecy takes is the name-phrase Maher-Shalal-Hash-Baz, which means "quick to the plunder, swift to the spoil." This is reinforced by the giving of this name to yet another son, a sign that soon, within the period of two years (time for conception, birth, and the baby's first words), Isaiah's prophecy of the destruction of Damascus (Syria) and Samaria (Ephraim/Israel) will have come to pass. Their plunder and spoils will have been carried off by the king of Assyria.

d. God's response to Ahaz's lack of faith (8:5–10)

It is a rule of life that choices have consequences. Because Ahaz chose to reject the will of God, symbolized here by **the gently flowing waters of Shiloah**, God will bring against him and his people the overwhelming devastation of the king of Assyria, symbolized by the river that overflows its banks, which the Euphrates River was known to do. The **floodwaters** of the Assyrian army would sweep over into Judah all the way to Jerusalem (**up to the neck**) as it in fact did.

Isaiah concludes v.8 with a cry, **"O Immanuel."** It carries the twofold meaning mentioned earlier. On the one hand, it concludes the previous section on a foreboding note: **God is with us** in judgment and devastation. But implicit in the phrase is the ever-present note of hope, for the fact remains that **God is with us.** And that leads the prophet to perceive that precisely because **God is with us** he will not allow his people to be completely overrun by the enemy. The nations may design their strategies and make plans for battle, but they will ultimately come to naught because **God is with us** (vv.9–10).

e. When proper perspective is lost (8:11–22)

Any hope Isaiah may have had of redirecting Ahaz is now long since vanished. Ahaz and his people have resolutely set out on a path that will lead to their destruction. In their disobedience they have lost perspective. It is likely that they even accused Isaiah of conspiracy (v.12). They fear the wrong king. Isaiah is reminded not to get caught up in the misdirection of the people but to fear Yahweh alone.

In vv.16–18 Isaiah brings his thoughts to a close. He bids his followers to secure these written statements. He has made his vision known; now he will wait for the Lord. He and his children stand as signs of what the Lord will do.

The words of vv.19–22 appear to be an afterthought. In stark contrast to the prophet who has heard the word of the Lord are those who trust in necro-

mancy, a practice condemned in biblical laws (Lev 19:31; Dt 18:10–11; cf. also the story of Saul and the witch of Endor [1Sa 28]). Isaiah cannot resist a sarcastic blast at the destructive futility of their ways, which he portrays in the graphic terms of darkness, distress, and gloom.

3. The vision of a royal savior (9:1–7)

This is one of the best known passages in the OT. As in 2:1–5 and 4:2–6, this bright vision of hope stands in stark contrast to the gloomy portrayal of judgment that precedes it. While human arrogance, pride, and disobedience bring devastation, a gracious act of God brings hope for an otherwise impossible future.

The power of this passage is heightened when one realizes that it serves to conclude the section that began with King Ahaz (ch. 7). Because of his defiant disobedience to the will of God, his reign experienced the devastation and destruction of the Assyrian army. It was a time of great darkness. In contrast, there is one, another royal figure, who will be of divine character and whose reign will bring peace and light and justice.

Let us look at this passage in more detail. The lands of Zebulun and Naphtali are in the northern-most region of Israel and no doubt suffered the brunt of the Assyrian invasion. Even they will experience the beneficence of the coming royal Savior. Isaiah draws upon history to support his prophecy. Just as God worked with Gideon to defeat the Midianites (Jdg 7), so he will once again work to overthrow the present enemy.

What is the meaning of this remarkable prophecy, **"For to us a child is born"**? Is this a reference to Immanuel mentioned in ch. 7? Is this a hymn used on the occasion of the coronation of King Hezekiah, as many scholars would have us believe, with the divine titles being borrowed from the Egyptian royal tradition? One doubts it. There is simply no other occasion in the whole of the OT where such ascriptions of deity are assigned to a human king. Isaiah saw a messianic figure, somewhere in the future, who had divine qualities and yet who would enter human history, thus ushering in an age of peace and righteousness.

Isaiah continues his contrast with Ahaz in particular and human kings in general in v.7. This future ideal king will establish the kingdom the way it was meant to be, in justice and righteousness, a task that will not be realized through human means but will require an act of God ("**The zeal of the LORD Almighty will accomplish this**").

4. The present reality of God's judgment (9:8–10:4)

While Isaiah's vision of God's royal Savior breaking into the present darkness is certain, the present darkness must first be dealt with. God must purge the sinful rebellion of his people.

This section is punctuated by the fourfold occurrence of the sentence, "**Yet for all this, his anger is not turned away, his hand is still upraised.**" It is an ominous refrain that leaves little doubt as to the Agent of the impending destruction.

Because the northern kingdom rejected the earlier prophetic message, God would now bring judgment on them. From east and west the enemy has come, yet Israel has foolishly persisted in its pride. Thus God's hand of judgment continues to be lifted up.

The events of the preceding verses seem to reflect the historical situation of 732–725 B.C., i.e., the initial invasion of the northern kingdom. It is

severely attacked but not completely destroyed. Samaria, the capital, is still standing. It is an appropriate time for repentance, but the people are unwilling to do so. Therefore God will **cut off** the leading (and now only) city of the country. Indeed, in 722, Samaria is completely destroyed. Because the wickedness has spread like fire over parched ground, so will the judgment.

Isaiah returns to the woe sayings he began in ch. 5. This is not a misplaced woe saying, as is often suggested. Rather, the prophet brackets the Syro-Ephraimite crisis with woe sayings as if to say to his people Judah and Jerusalem, "If you will not listen to me, then at least learn from the devastation that has come to your fellow countrymen of the northern kingdom who were themselves destroyed because of their refusal to obey God." The message that God sent against Jacob (9:8) was a message to Judah. And the ominous phrase "**His hand is still upraised**" (10:4) suggests that God did not let Israel escape; neither will he let Judah.

Isaiah returns (10:1–4) to the theme of injustice and oppression that concerned him in ch. 5. The day of reckoning is drawing near, and there will be no place to hide.

5. God's judgment on Assyria (10:5–19)

In a marvelous turn of the phrase, Isaiah now redirects the woe sayings toward Assyria. Even though Assyria was God's instrument against his own people (vv.5–6), this was not how Assyria perceived it. In a great act of pride, Assyria viewed itself as the invincible conqueror, with Jerusalem and Samaria as two more cities to be added to its list of conquests (vv.7–11, 13). With vivid imagery, Isaiah proclaims that Assyria has failed to recognize the One who directs all nations: "**Does the** ax raise itself above him who swings it. . . ?" (v.15). Therefore, God will destroy Assyria (vv.16–19).

6. The remnant of Israel (10:20–34)

Unlike Ahaz, who led the people to trust in Assyria rather than in God, the remnant that will be left after the devastation will rely solely on **the Holy One of Israel**. Because of their sin, devastation is certain. Because of God's faithfulness, a remnant is assured (vv.20–33).

Vv.24–34 summarize what Isaiah has been saying. Assyria's oppression of God's people is transitory. To be sure, they will work havoc in the land, coming to the very edge of the city of Jerusalem (v.32), as Sennacherib did in 701 B.C., but then God will turn his wrath upon them.

7. An ideal ruler is envisaged (11:1–16)

The previous section, concluding as it does with a reference to a razed forest, gives rise to Isaiah's image of hope: a branch growing out of a stump. The remnant is as a stump, all that is left of the great "forest" of Israel. And from that stump will grow a branch that will bear fruit.

The reference **"stump of Jesse"** is an avoidance of the phrase "house of David" and is therefore to be seen as a slap at the current ruler of the royal house of David. His fall from God's intention has become so great that the prophet refrains from mentioning him. As David was taken from the house of Jesse to usher in a period of greatness in Israel's history, so a second David will spring forth. Just as God's Spirit was upon David, so will his Spirit rest upon this second David (1Sa 16:13; 2Sa 23:2–3).

In dramatic contrast to the injustices and corruption that characterized the administration of so many of David's successors, the future ruler, empowered by the Spirit of the Lord, will rule with righteousness and justice (vv.4–5), thus ushering in an age of Shalom (vv.6–9) and a return of God's people from exile (vv.10–16).

8. A hymn of praise (12:1–6)

Such a vision of the future will cause the people to break forth in praise of God. Finally they have gained the perspective that Isaiah has wanted Ahaz and his people to have from the start: **"Surely God is my salvation; I will trust and not be afraid"** (v.2). Because of God's mighty acts to restore his people, they will extol his name throughout the earth.

Significantly, Isaiah concludes this section with reference to **the Holy One of Israel**, the One who made himself known to Isaiah in the temple. It is not accidental that it was a personal encounter with God that led to (1) Isaiah's conviction about righteousness and justice and to (2) his vision of a new and glorious age when the holy God will inaugurate a reign of universal peace.

II. GOD'S JUDGMENT AGAINST THE NATIONS (13:1–27:13)

This passage is a collection of oracles that demonstrate the judgment of God against human arrogance and rebellion. It includes the nations around Israel (13:1–23:18) and concludes with an oblique prophecy against Judah. Isaiah foresees the total collapse of the world in a return to chaos from which God ultimately brings restoration (24:1–27:13).

A. Oracles Against Foreign Nations (13:1–23:18)

Now begins a series of prophecies directed primarily against foreign nations. Such a collection is common in the major prophets (Jer 45–51 and Eze 25–32), but the Isaianic one is the longest. It deals with Babylon, Philistia, Moab, Damascus, Ethiopia, Egypt, Arabia, and Tyre.

Why are these prophecies included in the Isaianic corpus? It appears from Isaiah's vision of the Holy One of Israel in ch. 6 that he saw God as the Creator and therefore Judge of the whole earth. The inclusion of foreign nations demonstrates the extension of God's rule and judgment over all the earth. Second, through the prophecies, Isaiah was able to demonstrate to his people and to succeeding generations that even though any one of the nations mentioned herein might prove a threat, ultimately Israel/Judah's God is sovereign over nations. Therefore, rather than put its trust in one of the nations, Judah was to put its trust in Yahweh alone.

1. The prophecy against Babylon (13:1–14:23)

The primary sin of the nations was that of self-exaltation and pride, and none was more guilty than Babylon. It was Babylon that demonstrated its arrogance and its power most manifestly against Israel, culminating in the destruction of Jerusalem in 587 B.C. So intense was the hatred that Israel had for Babylon that the name itself became emblematic for all that was evil. (Its reputation long outlived the city as witnessed by the caricature in Rev 18.)

a. The gathering of Yahweh's host for battle (13:1–5)

The call has gone out for the Lord's hosts to gather to do battle against Babylon. This introduction employs what is known as "Day of the Lord" language. As such, it is a mixture of historical and suprahistorical refer-

ences. The Lord's army is made up of earthly warriors from faraway lands as well as some of the heavenly host, God's holy ones from the ends of the heavens (vv.3–5).

b. The Day of the Lord is near (13:6–22)

In an ever-increasing crescendo of staccato phrases, the poet/prophet paints a picture of unimaginable destruction. This is the **day of the LORD.** It strikes terror in the hearts of all (vv.7–9) as it comes upon the land.

The author then turns his attention to the heavens. This is especially appropriate in an oracle against Babylon, as this city was well known for its astrology and worship of the heavenly bodies. The stars will not be able to show their light (v.10).

As yet the particular enemy (Babylon) has not been specifically identified. God's punishment will be for all evil, arrogance, and ruthlessness. God is so outraged that he extends his wrath into the cosmic realm (v.13). Vv.14–16 describe the chaos and the savagery that accompany an invading army.

The Medes (v.17) were a people of what is now central Iran. In 539 B.C. they and the Persians captured Babylon. Babylon, with its hanging gardens, one of the seven wonders of the world, was considered to be the most magnificent city of its time.

c. How the mighty one has fallen! (14:1–23)

The taunt song (vv.4b–21) forms the major part of the next section. It is preceded by a reference to God's compassion on Israel (vv.1–4a). In brief form, these verses convey the message of chs. 40–55. As such, they certainly presuppose Israel's exile, anticipate the imminent destruction of Babylon, and look eagerly to the return.

When the day of devastation comes, the exiles are encouraged to take up this taunt against the king of Babylon, at whose hand they suffered so intensely.

What a taunt song it is! It celebrates Babylon's end with unrestrained joy. Such is this wonderful deed of the Lord that all the lands and created things cannot refrain from singing.

The second stanza (vv.9–11) moves to the underworld where the **spirits of the departed** prepare to meet the Babylonian king who has become just like them, with this exception: While they sit on thrones (v.9), he is to be on a bed of maggots and worms (v.11).

The third stanza (vv.12–15) is reminiscent of 2:6–22, where we are told that "the LORD has a day in store for all the proud and lofty . . . they will be humbled." The arrogant pride of the king of Babylon knew no limit. He would ascend to the highest heights and dare to make himself like God. Alas, now he has been brought down, down to the grave.

In the fourth stanza (vv.16–20) we read the words of onlookers as they pass by a great battlefield. Apparently they see the Babylonian king slain there. Unlike the other royalty of the world who have their tombs, this one is covered only with the corpses of others killed in battle (cf. Jer 22:19 for the stigma of a king not having proper burial). Vv.20b–21 declare the end of the monarch's descendants.

As if to add credibility to his song, the prophet now concludes with direct address from the Lord himself. It provides a fitting summary to the entire poem as well.

2. The prophecy against Assyria (14:24–27)

This oracle is a testimony to the certainty of Yahweh's plan. He swears it; it will be done. Assyria will be destroyed. Numerous themes from ch. 10 are restated here: V.25a—**"I will crush the Assyrian in my land; on my mountains I will trample him down"**—is reminiscent of the invasion up to the very gate of Jerusalem in 10:29–32. The references to the removal of the yoke and burden in v.25b alludes to 10:27. And of course the outstretched hand that cannot be turned back finds its antecedent in the refrain: "Yet for all this, his anger is not turned away, his hand is still upraised" (10:4; also 9:12, 17, 21). While the historical situation of this oracle is uncertain, it may well refer to the miraculous defeat of the Assyrian Sennacherib in 701 B.C.

3. The prophecy against Philistia (14:28–32)

This oracle is dated at the time of Ahaz's death. Although there is uncertainty regarding the exact year of his death, it was probably in the mid-720s B.C. At about the same time, Shalmaneser V, the king of Assyria, died. It was this death that occasioned the oracle. Isaiah warns the Philistines not to rejoice, because Shalmaneser V is dead (**"the rod that struck you is broken"**), for his successor would be even more oppressive. Indeed, Sargon II crushed the Philistine rebellion with great severity. It was during this period that Philistia sent messengers to Judah urging the nation to join the rebellion (v.32a). What was Isaiah's word to his countrymen? Trust in the Lord who has established Zion (v.32b), and do not trust any human alliance.

4. The oracle concerning Moab (15:1–16:14)

The reader is struck immediately by the different tone of this oracle as compared to that of the two preceding oracles. Here the prophet is in anguish over Moab's destruction; there he was exuberant over Babylon's demise. In general, the oracles against the nations show no sympathy for the nations. Thus this outpouring of concern over Moab is striking.

What are we to make of this highly unusual approach toward a rival foreign nation? Is the lament a hollow one, being the epitome of sarcasm, when in reality Isaiah is delighted at Moab's unenviable fate? No, the lament seems to be genuine. Isaiah and his people are so overwhelmed by the extent of Moab's devastation that they are in shock. They have no thought of rejoicing, only amazement and pity.

The first stanza (15:1–4) mentions several cities located throughout Moab, thus showing the wide path of destruction. In vv.5–9 the prophet identifies with the feelings of the Moabite warriors. He realizes that even though they flee, there appears to be no end to their suffering. The flow of blood will be unceasing.

In 16:1–5 the Moabites make a plea to Jerusalem to grant them aid and protection. The section concludes with a cryptic reference to the future Messiah, using the words of ch. 11. It is as though a foreign nation, in the midst of its oppression, is enabled to see the Israelite Messiah and is thus given hope for its own future.

What could have brought on such disaster? Moab's pride caused their downfall (16:6). This has resulted in the withering of their fields and the trampling of their vines. Once again the prophet himself takes up the lament.

5. The oracle concerning Damascus and Israel (17:1–11)

This prophecy goes back to the Syro-Ephraimite crisis (see on chs. 7 and 8) in which Syria (Damascus) and Israel (Ephraim) were allied against Judah. In

ch. 7 Isaiah predicted their downfall. Here he presents a more detailed prophecy. V.3 is cryptic: "**The remnant of Aram will be like the glory of the Israelites.**" Clements thinks it makes no sense and alters the text. But the prophet is teasing his readers and goes on to describe the glory of Israel as a tragically faded glory (vv.4–6).

The prophet believes that this judgment will have a corrective influence on Israel so that it will once again turn to the **Holy One** (vv.7–8). In the meantime, devastation will surely come (vv.9–11).

6. The futility of the nations (17:12–14)

In a moment of reflective exasperation, the prophet proclaims the absurd futility of the nations. They actually believe that their roaring threats mean something when in reality, before God, they are like chaff blown away by the wind (cf. 40:15)!

7. A prophecy against Ethiopia (18:1–7)

This is a beautifully crafted oracle against Ethiopia (Cush). The tall, bronzed Ethiopian was legendary: Herodotus, writing in the fifth century B.C., described the Ethiopians as "the tallest and most beautiful of men." Undoubtedly, the envoys were sent to Jerusalem to persuade Judah to join with them in a revolt against Assyria. Isaiah may have been on hand to see them arrive. He is not impressed. He has come to be impressed only by the Holy One of Israel who waits quietly until he is ready to act. When he does, devastation will occur and the envoys will return, not to threaten but to pledge their allegiance to the LORD **Almighty.**

8. A prophecy concerning Egypt (19:1–25)

Whenever Israel was threatened from the north, it was tempted to turn to

Egypt for aid (cf. chs. 30–31). Isaiah was vehemently opposed to this: "Trust God alone and do not rely on human forces" was his persistent message.

Isaiah sees Yahweh coming against Egypt in judgment. The action will result in complete chaos within Egyptian society, which was world renowned for its social stability. The effect will be (1) civil war (v.2), (2) a sense of desperation (v.3), and (3) a tyrannical government (v.4). The death of Egyptian society is symbolized in the death of the heart of Egypt, the Nile (vv.5–10). Without the Nile, there would be no Egypt. Farmers, fishermen, weavers, and merchants were all dependent on the mighty river. There is a total breakdown of society (vv.11–15). The **cornerstones** (v.13), or leaders, have led the people astray. In the end, Egypt will be completely impotent (v.15).

A marked change occurs in both style (from poetry to prose) and tone (from judgment to redemption) in the latter half of ch. 19. Isaiah reinforces his point that Judah should not turn to Egypt. Reason number 1: Egypt will be nearly devastated by God's judgment. Reason number 2: Eventually Egypt itself will turn to God.

"**Five cities**" (v.18) probably refers to a few or a small number, enough for **a sign and witness** to God (v.20). The NIV notes that the Dead Sea Scroll reads "city of the Sun" rather than *City of Destruction*. In Hebrew, the two terms would be easily confused, and the former is correct.

Vv.20b–22 are allusions to the Exodus, with a significant twist, "**When they [the Egyptians] cry out to the Lord because of their oppressors [as the Hebrew slaves had done], he will send them a savior and defender [as he sent Moses], and he will rescue them.**" The Egyptians will acknowl-edge Yahweh as God. The plagues with which God struck them will now be used to heal them. Eventually the great empires of the earth, Egypt and Assyria, along with Israel, will one day worship the Lord.

9. A prophecy against Egypt and Cush (20:1–6)

This chapter summarizes Isaiah's beliefs about trusting Egypt and Cush. They both were doomed. How much more anyone who trusted them! Imagine the visual effect that Isaiah's physical appearance must have had.

The historical referent is probably 713–711 B.C. when Ashdod attempted a revolt against Assyria. Egypt promised unlimited assistance. Sargon, the Assyrian ruler, responded with force, crushed Ashdod, and the Egyptians did absolutely nothing to help Ashdod.

10. A prophecy against Babylon (21:1–10)

Few oracles have proved to be so difficult as this for the interpreter. If it is against Babylon as v.9 suggests, why didn't the prophecy make it clear from the beginning? Also, after chs. 13 and 14, is another oracle against Babylon really necessary? Third, what is the provenance of the oracle? Is it the eighth century, referring to defeats of Babylon in 710, 702, or 689 B.C., and thus a word to Israel not to rely on Babylon for help against Assyria (cf. Oswalt, 389.)? Or does it refer to the defeat of Babylon in 539 B.C. and thus the end of Israel's exile? If so, then why isn't there more of a celebrative tone, similar to that of chs. 13 and 14?

It seems better to recognize that we do not have enough data to make a definitive determination. But clearly the prophet has received a vision of awesome destruction, like a fierce sirocco destroying everything in its path.

Elam and Media (v.2b) are the two nations that defeated Babylon in 539 B.C. This is evidence in support of a later date for the oracle.

The vision is so potent that the prophet feels the pain of it himself. A watchman is posted. He comes with the message that Babylon has fallen.

11. A prophecy concerning Dumah (21:11–12)

Some interpreters have taken Dumah to be a wordplay on Edom, as the words are similar in Hebrew. Or it may be the oasis in northern Arabia, Dumet ej Jendel (Oswalt, 398). Again, it is not possible to know for certain. What is certain is that we are talking about the area southeast of Jerusalem. Given the possibility of an attack from that direction, the fate of this area would be very important. But, alas, the response of the watchman is not clear. Morning is coming (good news), but also the night (bad news).

12. A prophecy concerning Arabia (21:13–17)

With this the prophet brings the prophecies against Babylon and its neighbors in Arabia to an end. All of these nations experience only a transitory glory. Soon it passes, and they are destroyed.

13. A prophecy concerning Jerusalem (22:1–25)

The opening line refers to a **Valley of Vision.** While a specific valley near Jerusalem may have been intended, the reference is probably symbolic, for the focus of the oracle is on the people's amazing inability to see or perceive the true understanding of the events around them.

While it is difficult to determine the historical background of the first stanza (vv.1–4), it is likely the hollow victory over Sennacherib in 701 B.C., when during a siege of Jerusalem he mysteriously abandoned the attack and left. Isaiah saw it as the clear hand of God. The people see this as cause for celebration and thus take to the rooftop (v.1). But Isaiah realizes (1) that the cost has been great (vv.2–3) and (2) that because they persisted in their disobedience, eventual defeat and destruction were not far off (v.4).

In the second stanza (vv.5–8a) Isaiah describes that day of destruction in more detail. The references to Elam and Kir suggest the Babylonian conquest in 587 B.C., an apt description indeed. And when the crisis came, the people frantically considered everything—except the One who created them (vv.8b–11).

The Lord had intended his day of judgment to lead to a day of repentance; instead, his people mocked him, joining in revelry instead of mourning (vv.12–14). Isaiah then particularizes the judgment on Judah by referring to an individual named Shebna. Judah's attitude and fate parallel his (vv.15–19). Because of his arrogance and pride, he has become a disgrace to his master and will therefore be cast out.

Someone else will take his place. Eliakim, as God's servant, is a foreshadowing of the messianic figure as the phrase **"key to the house of David"** suggests (vv.20–24). The meaning of v.25 is unclear, as it appears to reverse the claims of the previous verses. It may be a reference (later?) to the fact that some of the leaders who seemed particularly trustworthy and capable actually failed (such as Hezekiah).

14. A prophecy against Tyre (23:1–18)

With this oracle against Tyre, Isaiah concludes his section on the judgment of the nations, which began with Babylon in the east (vv.13–14) and now concludes with the Phoenician seaports in the west.

As the prophecy indicates, Tyre's influence was extensive, reaching all around the lip of the Mediterranean Sea and beyond. But this **marketplace of the nations** is about to fall. Its chief trading partner, Egypt, will be the first to learn of her demise (vv.1–5). The word will go as far west as Tarshish, which is near the coast of Spain (vv.6–7). Lest there be any doubt, Isaiah makes it known that it is God who planned this (vv.8–9). He concludes the first portion of the oracle as he began it (v.14). The phrase **"ships of Tarshish"** had come to stand for the large Phoenician fleet of mercantile ships. They now have no place to call home. The prose section (vv.15–18) speaks of the restoration of the fortunes of Tyre and of her new-found allegiance to the Lord.

B. From Chaos to Restoration (24:1–27:13)

The next four chapters comprise a unit, one which has been analyzed and debated extensively by commentators (see my book *From Chaos to Restoration, An Integrative Reading of Isaiah 24–27*). It begins with a picture of utter destruction (24:1–20). There are two unnamed cities (24:10; 25:2; 26:1; 27:10). Their fate affects the rest of the world. When the one is destroyed in 24:10, there is unending lament, and the rest of the world is devastated. When the other is destroyed in 25:2, God is praised and the world rejoices. In 26:1 the city is strong, the place of God's salvation. But in 27:10 the city is desolate. The identity of these cities and the meaning of these chapters have proved elusive. But, in my view, Isaiah speaks of Jerusalem and Babylon, two cities whose destinies affected the world.

There are three compelling reasons for seeing 24:10 as a reference to Jerusalem: (1) The everlasting covenant in v.5 was extended to Israel alone, no one else. (2) In v.11 the phrase in Hebrew is "the joy of the earth," which is a well-known epithet for Jerusalem. (3) V.13 focuses the destruction "in the midst of the earth," an expression for Jerusalem, which was believed to be located at the center of the earth. Its eventual destruction in 587 B.C. would be tantamount to the total collapse of the world, chaos.

In 24:21–23 a day in the future (**"in that day"**), God will intervene against the forces of chaos. He will destroy the wicked city (25:2), which must be Babylon, to Jerusalem, the most horrible enemy. It will be a day of great rejoicing with a heavenly banquet (25:6–9). But that day of rejoicing is still in the future, so the prophet admonishes the people to trust in the interim. Isa 26:1–6 is a song of trust.

But until that day of victory comes, Judah's lot is extremely difficult. Isa 26:7–18 is a lament bemoaning the situation of God's righteous ones who currently are in distress because of God's disciplinary action (v.16 refers to the Exile). The nation's pain is like a woman in childbirth, but it has no birth to show for the pain (26:17–18). Isa 26:19 is an oracle of salvation, a shout of joy that the **dead will live**! There will be a national restoration (this is similar to Ezekiel's prophecy concerning the dry bones and is not a reference to individual resurrection).

Indeed, God is about to act. He will move out across the face of the earth in terrible judgment, so they must hide for a little while until he is finished (26:20–21). In that day, God will slay the chaos monster (27:1), a reference to the devastation of Babylon. When he does, Judah will be restored (the vineyard song in 27:2–6 is the reversal of the song of the vineyard in 5:1–7). Isa 27:7–11 is a reflection on the current state of Judah, struck down by God, punished with exile, her precious city in ruins. But the ultimate plan of God will be enacted, resulting in complete restoration and the return of the exiles (27:12–13).

These four chapters are placed here as a summary of the previous chapters, albeit in a heightened, almost apocalyptic key. Jerusalem will be punished for breaking God's laws. She will be utterly devastated (chs. 1–12). But because Jerusalem is the religious center of the world, her demise will mean the destruction of the entire earth. All the earth will be judged (chs. 13–23, the oracles against the nations of the earth). But here, as in the earlier chapters, is a hint of divine action to save and restore Israel (2:1–5; 4:2–6; 9:2–7; 11:1–12:6).

III. JUDGMENT AGAINST JUDAH IS RENEWED (28:1–39:8)

This section is a collection of Isaiah's prophecies, perhaps to recapitulate and reinforce those found earlier in the book. As in the first eleven chapters, here is both a note of warning of imminent destruction and a promise of future hope. The prophecies end at 35:10 and are followed by a historical section (36:1–39:8) from the period of Hezekiah, which serves as a bridge between the two major portions of the book, chs. 1–35 and 40–66.

A. Imminent Danger, Future Hope (28:1–35:10)

Chs. 28–32 indicate that the destruction will be soon and justified due to the breach of covenant. But ch. 32 brings a decided shift and the perspective is futuristic, a time when Zion's

fortunes will be reversed and her glory restored.

1. Prophecy against the northern kingdom (28:1–13)

Isaiah, in a scathing attack on Israel's (Ephraim's) callous infidelity, makes a play on the concept of the wreath or garland of flowers. Party-going revelers often wore such wreaths but, in their enthusiastic intoxication, failed to see that with the passing of time their flowers had faded and died. Such would be the fortunes of the northern kingdom and its chief city, its crowning wreath, Samaria. It would soon be destroyed by invading Assyrians who would sweep in like a devastating hailstorm (v.2). The events of 721 B.C. were surely in view, when Assyria invaded the northern kingdom and took Samaria **like a fig ripe before harvest** (v.4).

Note the striking contrast of vv.5 and 6. The Lord will always preserve a remnant, and he will be its glorious crown.

Vv.7–13 resume the attack with particular focus on the priests and prophets. In vv.9 and 10 they object in mocking fashion, insisting on their ability to perceive reality. True to Isaiah's initial vision (6:9–10), the people in their pride hear but do not understand, see but do not perceive.

Isaiah responds with renewed vigor. If they will not learn the words of love and justice from God, then they must learn the words of oppression from the Assyrians (vv.11–13).

2. Prophecy against Judah (28:14–29)

The arrangement of the text and the transitional term *laken*, **therefore**, suggests that vv.1–13, while originally directed toward the northern kingdom, are placed here as an entree into an indictment of Judah in the south. Isaiah's point is this: the fate that came upon Samaria will just as surely come upon Jerusalem, for its people and, more importantly, its rulers, are just as corrupt.

Mention of a **refuge** in v.15 causes the prophet to develop the imagery of a true refuge, a building that has a true cornerstone, built according to the principles of justice and righteousness rather than lies and falsehoods. Only this refuge will stand in the day of the overwhelming scourge, which will sweep away all of their falsehoods along with the people themselves.

What is the historical referent? It is difficult to know. It may refer to the events of 721 B.C. when Assyria swept into the north and spilled over into the southern kingdom. Or more likely it may refer to the days of Hezekiah and his ill-advised revolt against Assyria in 705 B.C. and the resulting Assyrian invasion in 701 B.C. It may indeed look to the future invasion of Babylon in 597 and 587 B.C. It is important to remember that the prophetic message, while given in a particular historical situation for that historical moment, is always expansive. The vitality of the word lives on beyond the moment and is ever applicable to future events. One thinks of Jesus' parable about building a house on a rock rather than on sand (Mt 7:24–27; Lk 6:47–49).

V.20 is probably a popular proverb, employed here to highlight increasing torment, as in spending a sleepless night because the bed is too short and the blanket too small.

With v.21 the prophet recalls two of the great stories of ancient sacred history although with yet another terrifying twist of irony. Just as God had struck out at the Philistines at Mount Perazim (2Sa 5:20) and routed the Canaanites at Gibeon (Jos 10:10), so will God again attack his enemies. But his enemies now are not foreigners; they are his own disobedient people.

Isaiah concludes this prophecy with a parable of the farmer (vv.23–29). Characteristic of Isaiah, he follows a word of judgment with a word of promise. The judgment will be severe, but it will not be forever. The farmer breaks up the soil, but he does so in order to sow the seed. It is a word of hope.

3. Jerusalem's future foretold (29:1–24)

In vv.1–4 the prophet tells of an imminent siege of Jerusalem. The meaning of the term *Ariel* is still in dispute. It may mean lion, although the context does not support this. Emerging consensus regards it as **"altar hearth."** Jerusalem, the chosen city where David settled, has become corrupt even to its central core with empty and irreverent religion expressed on a profaned altar. Therefore God will reduce Jerusalem to an altar with the inhabitants as the sacrifice.

V.3 portrays what in reality took place as the Assyrians set up their towers and siegeworks. V.4 in Hebrew suggests not so much captives lying on the ground but death and deathlike voices rising out of the grave.

Vv.5–12 show a remarkable reversal. In an instant, God will act to reverse the fortunes of Jerusalem, as indeed he did during the siege of Jerusalem in 701 B.C. when the entire Assyrian army suddenly and inexplicably abandoned its siege and fled (37:36–37; 2Ki 19:35–36; 2Ch 32:20–21).

Playing on the term *dust* in v.4, Isaiah indicates the similar fate of Judah's enemies when the Lord acts to save his city, Jerusalem. The descriptive phrases in v.6, while they do not appear in the historical contexts mentioned above, frequently occur in poetry as an indication of theophany, or the presence of God.

Vv.7 and 8 seem to extend the notion that Assyria is not Jerusalem's only enemy to be reduced to **dust** but that all foreign enemies of any time will experience God's wrath. Such a view was a building block in the view of the inviolability of Zion (Jerusalem), i.e., that it will never be destroyed (cf. Ps 2).

With v.9 Isaiah returns in the harshest of terms to his indictment of the leaders of Jerusalem. He chides them for their blindness and senselessness. The blindness of the people leads to hypocrisy (vv.13–14), a verbal faith that is unrelated to genuine heart religion.

To break through, God finds it necessary to do something astonishing (**"wonder upon wonder"**). It will take cataclysmic devastation and a similar restoration to shock the people to their senses.

The next oracle (vv.15–17), a woe oracle, continues the theme of misguided wisdom. Isaiah mocks those who go to great lengths (and depths) to assure that their plans are somehow hidden from the Lord. Perhaps a secret political plan has been made between Israel and Egypt without consultation with Isaiah.

Vv.22–24 bring this section to a conclusion. The **therefore** of v.22 suggests that after God's astonishing work (v.14) of cleansing and purifying Israel (both the northern and southern kingdoms are intended here), God's people will rediscover their true identity. This may explain the reference to Abraham, for redemption is a rediscovery of one's own past. Central to their self-understanding is a rediscovery of the One who created and redeemed them, **the Holy One.**

4. Woe to those who rely on Egypt (30:1–31:9)

a. Woe to the obstinate children (30:1–18)

The general stance of rebellion and disobedience on the part of God's people in chs. 28 and 29 now takes a specific direction: instead of trusting God, they trust Egypt.

Hezekiah sought the counsel of other prophets who advised him to form an alliance with Egypt and to rebel against Assyria. It would prove to be a foolish and destructive move. Note the reference to **Egypt's shade for refuge** in v.2. This was a direct affront to Yahweh who alone had been Israel's shade (cf. 4:6; 25:4).

V.4 is not immediately clear, but the history behind the text suggests that the Ethiopian Shubako had only recently devastated Egypt and continued to have envoys in strategic locations, thus heightening the foolishness of relying on weakened Egypt.

Vv.6 and 7 comprise a separate oracle. With great artistic skill, Isaiah paints a picture of extraordinary measures to transport extravagant payment to buy the help of a wasted and worn-out mythical figure now rendered impotent (Rahab is the sea monster but is here portrayed as an old woman sitting on the ground.)

In vv.8–11, Isaiah insists that a written record be made of their rebellion as an everlasting witness against them. They somehow thought they could choose not to be confronted with **the Holy One of Israel** (v.11). Such a confrontation by God is not a matter of our choosing. We will be confronted by either his word or his judgment. In rejecting the former, this people chose the latter. God's judgment, says Isaiah, will break in upon them like the collapsing of **a high wall** (vv.12–14).

V.15 is striking in its contrast. **Repentance and rest, quietness and trust**—these are what God wants; these are what they need, but they refuse God's ways. One is reminded of the words of Jesus "Take my yoke upon you . . . for my yoke is easy and my burden is light" (Mt 11:29–30).

In response to God's offer of himself, they chose horses instead! With a masterful play on words, Isaiah spins their fate (vv.16–17). Their horses will have to be fast, but the enemies will be faster still, and the devastation will be swift and total. What remains will resemble a lonely pole on a barren hill.

Isaiah concludes this section with an open invitation to trust in God who desires to show compassion and grace. As such it makes a transition to the following section.

b. God will destroy Assyria and deliver Judah (30:19–33)

This unit falls into two sections, the first written in prose (vv.19–26) and the second in poetry (vv.27–33). The implication of the prose section is that eventually God's people will cry to God for help. Yahweh stands ready and eager to respond. When he does, their aimlessness will end and they will cast away their idols. Vv.23–26 are highly figurative and limn God's blessings in agricultural terms reminiscent of the Garden of Eden.

The poetic section draws on the imagery of worship. The hymnic language anticipates a theophany (visitation) of God, who will come to judge his enemies. He has tolerated Assyria as an instrument of chastisement long enough. Now that nation will receive God's judgment.

c. Woe to those who look to Egypt (31:1–9)

Ch. 31 restates the message of ch. 30 and conveys the similar elements of

(1) a warning against misplaced trust (vv.1–3), (2) the promise of God's deliverance (vv.4–5), (3) an appeal to the people to return to God and cast away their idols (vv.6–7), and (4) a portrayal of the impending destruction of Assyria (vv.8–9).

5. A king who will reign in righteousness (32:1–20)

Isa 32:1–8 is a messianic passage. The prophet has given up on human kings and looks to the future, to a time when a great king, an idealized king, will rule in righteousness. Such a king will be divinelike, providing for each person shelter and refuge in the storm (v.2; cf. 4:6; 25:4, which demonstrate that this is the provenance of God). Life-giving water will transform the desert, the blind will see, and the deaf will hear (vv.2–3). Understanding will be given to the people (v.4) and there will be a great reversal correcting the distortions mentioned in ch. 28. The foolish will be seen as fools and the noble as noble.

Before the messianic vision can be fulfilled there must first come judgment (vv.9–14). For some reason, Isaiah singles out **complacent women** as recipients of God's judgment, as he did in 3:16–4:1. Surely, they, in their unrecognized vulnerability, are fulfilling a representative role. The impending disaster and devastation will destroy the land, terminate the merriment, and cause great mourning.

But this portrayal of destruction is interrupted by a return to the messianic vision of the opening verses of this chapter. Peace and security will come at last to the people.

6. God will deliver his people (33:1–24)

The historical situation appears to be just before Sennacherib leads his Assyrian army in final assault against Jerusalem. He has already devastated the cities of Judah and has broken the treaty with Hezekiah despite taking the tribute money (2Ki 18:14ff.). As a final act of desperation, the king and people of Judah turn to Isaiah and ask him to pray for them. Isaiah does and assures them that God will route the Assyrian enemy and preserve the city of Jerusalem (2Ki 19:1–37).

V.1 is a pronouncement of doom on Assyria. It is followed by a petition for salvation (cf. Hezekiah's prayer in 2Ki 19:15–19). The section closes on a note of praise to God. The reference to a sure foundation (v.6) calls to mind the prior passage in 28:16.

Isaiah returns to the historical situation (vv.7–16). Sennacherib has reduced Judah to a point of desperation. In v.10 the Lord speaks in the first person. He will arise and destroy the destroyer. Sennacherib's plans against Jerusalem are as fruitless as chaff; his own fiery threats will turn to destroy him (v.11). All the nations are invited to take note of God's actions. The appeal to universal understanding of the identity of the true God is a prevalent theme throughout the book of Isaiah. God's appearance strikes fear in the hearts of all who are hostile to him (v.14); only the righteous can stand in that day (vv.15–16).

As we have seen frequently in Isaiah, the prophetic word, while rooted in history and spoken in a particular historical situation, inexorably pushes its vision onward to the very limit of history, toward a messianic age of blessing and shalom where righteousness and justice reign. With vv.17–24, the prophet's gaze is directed into the future once again, where he sees a divine king ruling in beauty (cf. 4:2; 6:5). At that time Sennacherib and his chief officers, the Assyrian rulers with their difficult language, will be a distant memory (vv.18–19). Jerusalem will be transformed into a place of peace and wholeness (vv.20–24). Compare similar Isaianic visions: 2:2–5; 4:2–6; 9:2–7; 11:1–9; 32:1–4, 15–20.

7. Judgment against the nations (34:1–17)

The futuristic vision of ch. 33 now shifts its focus to the correlative idea of judgment. Many modern scholars insist that the eschatological, neoapocalyptic language of chs. 34 and 35 requires that they be given an exilic date. It is further reasoned that these chapters originally provided the introduction to chs. 40–55. As with much of the ancient biblical material, it is extremely difficult to date particular verses with accuracy. In my judgment, however, chs. 34 and 35 provide a continuation of the futuristic vision we saw in ch. 33. So there is no compelling reason to posit a different location and date. Further, the judgment of God against the nations is a theme that occurs repeatedly throughout the book and is part and parcel of the theology of Zion (cf. Ps 2, also Isa 2:12–22; 13:1–27:13; 29:5–8; 30:27–28; 33:10–13; see also the judgment pronounced against the nations in Am 1 and 2).

Reminiscent of the opening lines of the book, the scene is a law court, and the entire world is called to hear God's verdict. Now the judgment is not against Israel; it is against the nations. Consistent with the royal theology that undergirds Isaiah's thoughts is the notion that Jerusalem stands over against the nations (again, see Ps 2). Jerusalem has been properly punished; now the prophet looks to the judgment against the nations.

In v.2 the prophet employs "day of the Lord" language to portray the widespread destruction, which extends even to the heavens (v.4, probably a reference to the destruction of the astral deities of the nations).

Edom, which had a long history of hostility against Israel, is singled out in v.5 but is a symbolic particularization of all the nations. The language is that of sacrifice in vv.6–7, as if the people are in some measure sacrificed before God. The punishment is due in part because of the nations' crimes against Zion as suggested by the reference in v.8 to **Zion's cause.**

The slaughter of vv.1–7 will lead to total desolation (vv.9–15). Like a forerunner of Dante's *Inferno*, the prophet's depictions of destruction employ hauntingly graphic imagery. Vv.12–15 use language typically employed to portray complete desolation. Edom will become a total wasteland.

While it is uncertain what the reference to the **scroll of the LORD** (v.16) means, the point of the concluding verses is that this final destruction will surely come to pass because God stands behind it.

8. The joy of the redeemed (35:1–10)

Just as ch. 34 conveyed unmitigated destruction of the nations, ch. 35 presents a picture of unrestrained joy and unending blessing for the people of Zion. Isaiah held to a belief that was deeply imbedded in the hearts and literature of the Hebrews, i.e., the end time will be like the beginning of time, the new age (messianic) will reflect the earliest age. Just as the eerie chaos of Ge 1:2 gave way to the creative blessing of God in Ge 1:3ff., so the devastation of the final day will give way to the extraordinary blessings of the new age. Few passages convey these blessings more graphically than does ch. 35.

The desert of ch. 34 will be transformed into a place of beauty (vv.1–2).

Those who are weak will be saved/strengthened (vv.3–4). Miraculous healings will occur (vv.5–6), the blind will see, the deaf hear, the lame walk, and the mute speak. It will be a sign that the new age has dawned, the Messiah has come, and the kingdom of God is at hand (see Mt 11:1–6 where Jesus' response to John the Baptist's question as to whether Jesus is the Messiah includes these signs).

The contrast with ch. 34 continues in vv.6–7 with the transformation of the desert into an oasis. The picture of redemption culminates in the restoration of the people of God. The exiles will return upon **a highway, the Way of Holiness.**

B. Sennacherib, Hezekiah, and Isaiah (36:1–39:8)

This concluding historical section of four chapters is found almost word for word in 2 Kings 18:13–20:19. The reader should consult the commentary on 2 Kings for matters of historical importance. Its role here in Isaiah appears to be threefold: (1) It summarizes much of the prophetic material found earlier in Isaiah. Most of chs. 1–12 and 28–33 had to do with Assyria and Judah. (2) Hezekiah's response to the Assyrians is presented as a sharp contrast to that of Ahaz (cf. ch. 7). Hezekiah looked to Yahweh and trusted him, while Ahaz rejected Yahweh and trusted in political alliances. (3) This material makes the transition to ch. 40, the exile in Babylon. Hezekiah unwisely had shown his treasures to the Babylonian envoys (39:1–8). It was an open invitation to this rising power one day to return and plunder the same treasure, which they did in 587 B.C.

1. Sennacherib's siege but Yahweh's victory (36:1–37:38)

In 701 B.C. Sennacherib began his attack on Judah by destroying a number of cities. Suffering extreme devastation was the city of Lachish.

Undoubtedly the news of the destruction of Lachish traveled to Jerusalem faster than did the field commander. So the stage was set for him to call for surrender.

When the message is brought to Hezekiah, he is overwhelmed with fear and enacts the rites of repentance, always a prerequisite to salvation. Then he sends for Isaiah, who assures Hezekiah that God will deliver Jerusalem. The language here is theological. The Assyrians have called into question the power of Yahweh to act (37:12). Likewise, Hezekiah appeals to the honor of God in his prayer (37:14–20), that in delivering his people God may be known throughout the earth. In response to Hezekiah's prayer, Isaiah condemns the arrogance of Assyria and brings assurance of God's protection. The earlier references to a remnant (7:3; 10:20–23) are reiterated here (37:31–32).

This concludes with a narrative account of the destruction of the Assyrian army and the murder of Sennacherib.

2. Hezekiah's recovery and subsequent shortsightedness (38:1–39:8)

This chapter contains an initial prose section relating Hezekiah's illness unto death (v.1), his prayer for healing, and his testament of devotion (vv.2–3). God's response through Isaiah is a promise of deliverance for both Hezekiah and the city of Jerusalem (vv.4–6). The promise is confirmed by a sign, the meaning of which is not entirely clear (vv.7–8). The increasing shadow may have been viewed by the king as paralleling his own demise. To move the shadow backwards was in effect to lengthen the light of day for both himself and Jerusalem.

The prose section is followed by a psalm of thanksgiving, which is not included in the 2 Kings account. It conveys Hezekiah's trust that God will heal him. Vv.10–15 reflect on the illness as a past event, while vv.16–20 look to his restoration of health.

The emphasis on the king's faithfulness (v.3) and the call for a sign (v.22) heighten the contrast with Ahaz. It was the unfaithfulness and disobedience of Ahaz that led to his and Judah's demise initially; now it is Hezekiah's faithfulness and devotion that lead to his and Judah's deliverance.

Ch. 39 provides the transition to the Babylonian chapters that follow. Hezekiah's unthinking disclosure of his country's treasures to the Babylonian visitors leads Isaiah to predict the eventual Babylonian invasion and the removal of Jerusalem's inhabitants to exile in Babylon, all of which is regarded as a reality in the opening verses of ch. 40.

IV. A MESSAGE TO THE EXILES (40:1–55:13)

In these chapters the scene shifts to Babylon where the foreboding prediction of the preceding chapter has become a reality. The history has been both so recent and painful that it is assumed rather than stated. As Isaiah warned, the Babylonians under Nebuchadnezzar destroyed Jerusalem in 587 B.C., leveled the temple, and took its treasure and most of its people back to Babylon as exiles. This section is addressed to them.

Here is some of the world's loftiest poetry, made even more famous by George Frideric Handel's *Messiah*. As indicated in the opening phrase, these are words of comfort: Judah's sins have been forgiven; words of hope: they will soon return to their homeland; words of courage: despite appearances, God will act in their behalf; words of chastisement: they must not be deceived by their captors and place their faith in the false gods of Babylon.

Some of the grandest theology in the Bible appears here. The sovereignty of God is portrayed in an exquisite and powerful way in 40:12–31; the notion of redemptive suffering has never been conveyed more movingly than in ch. 53 and the other servant songs.

A. The Departure From Babylon (40:1–48:22)

This material was written to correct significant misconceptions that the Jewish exiles had about God. First, some believed that God's punishment, expressed in the destruction in 587 B.C., was unending. Thus the opening words, **"Comfort, comfort my people."**

The second widely held belief was that their God, Yahweh, had been defeated by the gods of Babylon. The hymn on the sovereign power of Yahweh in 40:12–31 speaks to this concern, as do other key passages, especially those sections ridiculing the impotence of idols (44:6–20 and 46:1–7) and the prediction of Babylon's fall in ch. 47.

The third misconception was that perhaps Yahweh no longer cared and had given up on his people. This is addressed directly in the question of 40:27, **"Why do you say, O Jacob, and complain, O Israel, 'My way is hidden from the LORD; my cause is disregarded by my God'?"**

1. A message of comfort (40:1–11)

The prologue opens with a word from God. This word is followed by a number of voices, which leads us to believe that we are listening in on the heavenly council of God. It is strikingly reminiscent of the initial call of Isaiah in ch. 6.

Note the personal pronoun *my* in v.1. God has not forsaken his people. The covenant is still operative. Vv.3–5 allude to the return of the exiles. The highway through the desert runs from Babylon to Judah. Such elevated roads were not uncommon in the ancient Near East as processionals for kings. In this case, the king will be God as he leads his people home, an event that all humankind will note and therein give glory to Yahweh. It will be like a second Exodus and thus a reaffirmation of that covenant-forming event.

While these words were meant for sixth-century Jewish exiles, like all prophetic words, their meaning is expansive. This scene was reenacted with paradigmatic force in the preparation by John the Baptist for the coming of the Christ, who continues to lead his people into freedom.

The seemingly despondent tone of vv.6–8 has puzzled interpreters. Some have suggested that they are misplaced. But they fit here perfectly well. They refer to the transitory nature of human contrivances, particularly human kingdoms like that of Babylon. As with all things human, such kingdoms will fade away like the grass, while this word of comfort and hope will stand forever. Vv.9–11 continue the theme of good news. Zion/Jerusalem is to prepare for the imminent return of the exiled children. The phrase "Fear not" (NIV **"Do not be afraid"**) occurs frequently in these chapters. It obviously addressed a need in the exiled community (cf. 41:10, 14; 43:1, 5; 44:2, 8, et al.) Vv.10 and 11, with their emphasis on Yahweh's power, mark the transition to the next section (40:12–31), which has as its main theme the power of God to save, and they bring the prologue to a completion: Judah's time of judgment has come to an end (vv.1–2), the exiles will return home via the desert highway (vv.3–5), the hated kingdom (Babylon) will wither (vv.6–8), Jerusalem will prepare for the return (vv.9–10), and God will accomplish it (v.11).

The symbol of the shepherd is significant, especially suited to convey the tenderness of God. But there is more. The shepherds were the leaders and rulers of Israel. They had let the people down. Now God himself will shepherd his people (cf. Ps 23, Eze 34, Jn 10).

2. The power of God (40:12–31)

The key to understanding this section is found in the rhetorical questions in vv.18, 21, 25, 27, and 28. The concerns are threefold: (1) The confidence of the exiles in Yahweh had been shaken. Now they were questioning whether Yahweh was indeed greater than the gods of Babylon. Comparisons were being made (vv.18, 25). (2) They evidently had forgotten their story, which was the history of Yahweh's relationship with the world in general and this people in particular. Because they had a history, they would have a future (vv.21, 28). (3) Some of the exiles believed that God had disregarded them and did not care about their fate. This magnificent poem is written to address these concerns.

The poem begins with two questions (v.12) that have only one answer: "God! God created all that is." These are followed by more questions (vv.13–14) that have only one answer: "No one! Yahweh alone is God." Though the nation of Babylon looms large now, it is time to gain a clearer perception of reality. As with all nations, Babylon is like **a drop in a bucket**, like fine dust compared to the majesty of God (vv.15–17). Lebanon is mentioned because of the heights of

its mountains, yet does not compare with the loftiness of God.

In vv.18–20 the comparison is brought into sharper focus with the specific reference to the idols of Babylon. Dare we really compare the creator God to a created object?

Vv.21–24 are a recapitulation of history within the context of creation. The creator God is the God who is involved in history. He is responsible for his creation and will not abandon it, as history shows. Vv.25 and 26 refer to the popular astral deities of Babylonian mythology. Rather than worship the starry hosts as the Babylonian captors do, one ought simply to remember who created them. Surely he alone is the one worthy of worship.

The chapter concludes with an appeal to trust God. The exiles may have grown tired and weary in exile, but the prophet reminds them in this moving passage that God will give them the needed strength in abundant supply.

3. Fear not, O Israel (41:1–29)

The frequent occurrence of the phrase **"Fear not"** or **"Do not fear"** throughout these chapters indicates that fear, rather than faith, was the predominant posture of the exiles. This needed to be overcome, and the prophet addresses the problem with a threefold argument: (1) A deliverer sent by Yahweh will come very soon (vv.1–7), (2) Israel is still God's chosen people (vv.8–20), and (3) the nations (particularly Babylon) and their gods are as empty wind (vv.21–29).

The deliverer whom Yahweh is bringing from the East (v.2) is Cyrus, the Persian, who will eventually conquer Babylon and liberate the exiles. The path of his destruction is extensive (vv.2a, 3), and his reputation has reached far and wide (vv.5–6). The prophet concludes with a mocking reference to the Babylonians' futile appeals to idols for protection in the face of impending danger. Not only must this "source of strength and protection" be made by a **craftsman,** he must nail it down **so it will not topple!**

As God's chosen servant, Israel will be strengthened and protected (vv.8–10). Vv.11–16 explore God's protection further, as he intervenes on Israel's behalf against the nations. Again we meet the Isaianic phrase **"Holy One of Israel."** When God acts in holiness and righteousness, he delivers his people. Even the desert will be transformed when God acts.

The prophet concludes by destroying the credibility of the nations and their gods. Were they able to predict the future? Of course not. The gods of Babylon were impotent.

4. The servant (42:1–25)

In these chapters (40–55) are four servant songs, so-called because of their particular reference to God's servant (42:1–4; 49:1–6; 50:4–9; 52:13–53:12). The exact identity of the servant has been intensely debated. Mentioned are historical figures such as Moses, Jeremiah, and Cyrus; an ideal figure of the past, present, and/or future; the nation of Israel itself; and the remnant of Israel in Babylon. The best explanation centers around the Hebrew concept of corporate personality, which subsumes the individual and a group under one reality with little distinction between the two (cf. Rowley). This idea best explains the interrelationship of the singular and plural references to the servant.

Evangelical interpreters will disagree as to the role of the servant vis-a-vis Jesus Christ. It seems clear, however, that Jesus himself and the early church understood his mission to be the fulfillment of the servant role. Note that Matthew quotes this passage in its entirety (12:18–21). That Isaiah looked specifically to the person of Jesus several hundred years in the future may be doubted. Rather, he saw an idealized representative as the servant.

The servant is chosen by God who delights in him. Note that the language is reminiscent of the royal theology (see esp. Ps 2). Confirmed by the Spirit, the servant is to bring justice to the nations. The context suggests that the word *justice* carries not so much the sense of judicial activity as the idea of law or torah, which is to say, the revelation of God.

There is (v.5) a renewed appeal to God's creative activity. It is God as creator who is able to act in history. Because God has invested himself in his creation, he will act to save it. And the instrument he chooses is his servant (v.6). This servant will be the embodiment of divine grace (a covenant), a light to the Gentiles to bring about their release from darkness.

In response to the servant's mission of redemption, the ends of the earth are called upon to rejoice (vv.10–13). It will be a new song, commensurate with the new thing God is doing.

Vv.14–17 suggest that the time of exile is almost over. God has been quiet long enough while Babylon oppressed his people (v.14). Now he will act to take them home. Vv.15–16 recall 40:3–5.

The prophet chides exiles who persist in their dullness (vv.18–22). They seem to have learned nothing from the judgment they have experienced (v.20). Evidence from Jeremiah (44:15–19) suggests that the exiles, rather than regarding their tragic state as a judgment from Yahweh, viewed it as a result of the superiority of the gods of Babylon. They sought any explanation that would spare them from accepting any personal blame (vv.23–25).

5. I am your Savior (43:1–28)

The personal pronouns I and you are used here effectively to highlight the personal, covenantal relationship between God and Israel. Again, the Lord says, **"Fear not,"** which is a frequent introductory formula to an oracle of salvation, as it is in this instance.

V.2 may be an allusion to the exodus through the Red Sea, or it may refer to the sweeping flood of Assyria (8:7–8). The addition of the fiery language at the end of v.2 suggests the latter reference (cf. 9:18–19). Assyria's attack will be like a devastating fire.

The notion of countries given as ransom (v.3) is not to be taken literally but as symbolically, indicating the preciousness of Israel to Yahweh (see v.4). The scope of Yahweh's redemptive act is now extended to all the ends of the earth (vv.5–7). Not only the exiles in Babylon, but those who have been scattered to other countries will return. Vv.9–13 return to the theme found earlier in 41:21–29, namely a comparison of Yahweh and the other gods, which are found to be nothing. The Lord assures Israel that he will act on their behalf against their captor, Babylon. The assurance is based on the fact that God has a history of acting on their behalf, most notably the deliverance at the Red Sea (vv.16–17).

Then suddenly, after this powerful historical recollection, God tells them to forget the former things. Is this a reference to the Exodus or to recent events of history, namely the destruction of their homeland and subsequent exile? It seems to refer to the Exodus. This new work that God is about to do will be so extraordinary as to transcend even the earlier work of the Exodus. Therefore, Israel must let go of the old

imagery in order to understand the new. Note the reversal: Instead of a way through the sea, it will be through the desert. Instead of the sea made into dry land, the desert will bring forth life-giving water.

Vv.22–28 serve as an explanation of Israel's current status. They are in exile now because of their past sins. Prior to the destruction in 587 B.C., their prayers had been insincere (v.22), their worship empty (v.23), their devotion lacking (v.24), and their sins weighty (v.24). For these reasons, Yahweh brought destruction (v.28).

6. Yahweh is faithful; idols are foolish (44:1–28)

Against the backdrop of Israel's unfaithfulness (43:22–28), Yahweh's fidelity is now portrayed. The beginning verses are reminiscent of the first servant song (42:1–4) with the emphasis on being chosen. The name **Jeshurun** (v.2) is obscure. Derived from a word meaning "upright" it is a term of affection (it appears elsewhere only in Dt 32:15; 33:5, 26).

When God acts, nature will be transformed (v.3). The Spirit, which is normally limited to individuals, will be poured out on Israel. Israel will be so blessed that non-Israelites will desire to become a part of them. This section concludes with a statement on God as incomparable and with reassurance of his faithfulness (vv.6–8).

In several translations vv.9–20 are in prose, an essay against idolatry. Vv.9–11 criticize the idea in principle. Vv.12–17 describe the craft of making idols. The mocking tone is obvious and effective. It is incredible to the prophet that anyone would consider a crafted object to be a god. But the practitioners are so blind that they cannot perceive their own foolishness (vv.18–20).

After the excursus against idolatry,

the poet returns to the theme with which he began in 44:1–8, namely, the implications for Israel of their role as Yahweh's servant; forgiveness and redemption (vv.21–22). These saving acts in history will be celebrated in creation (v.23). The theme of creation leads to a reference to Yahweh's lordship in creation (v.24), which establishes his lordship over historical events. V.25 may refer to false prophets within the Israelite community or the ubiquitous diviners in the Babylonian culture, or both. None of them believed Israel had a future. But God had a different idea: Jerusalem would be inhabited and restored (v.26)! And just as amazing, he will use the pagan king Cyrus to accomplish his ends (v.28).

7. God will act as he chooses (45:1–25)

Cyrus has been **anointed** (the Hebrew word is the word for messiah) by God to redeem Israel. However, v.4 makes it clear that God is raising up Cyrus, not for Cyrus's sake but **for the sake of Jacob my servant** (v.4). The passage closes with a response of praise by the created order.

Israel's reaction to this remarkable move by God is anticipated. They are not in a position to question their Maker. Through a series of images from pottery and family life the prophet drives his point home (vv.9–10). Because God is the sovereign Creator, he will do as he chooses, and he need answer to no one.

In vv.14–25 the prophet returns to the theme that Israel's salvation will attract the other nations (cf. 42:6; 44:5). This section (chs. 40–55) contains the most expansive understanding of the revelation and grace of God in the OT, reaching out to all nations. Some have suggested that had Israel heard, believed, and acted upon this

message, it would have become a missionary religion rather than a closed ethnic one. V.14 concludes on a remarkable note: The nations will acknowledge that Yahweh is God and there is no other.

V.18 returns to the theme of creation. Note particularly the reference to chaos (NIV **"empty"**). The Exile was frequently portrayed theologically as a return to chaos (Ge 1:2). Now the prophet builds on that notion, reminding the people that God is a God of creation, not of chaos. His creative activity will become a redemptive activity.

8. The Gods of Babylon will fall (46:1–13)

This is a marvelous passage illustrating the artistic and rhetorical skills of the poet/prophet. In a masterful way in vv.1–7 he plays on the words "to carry" and "to bear," demonstrating that Babylon's gods must be **carried** and **borne** by those who are already weary, while the God of Israel carries and bears his people and gives strength to the weary (cf. 40:28–31).

This statement on God as incomparable is reinforced by an appeal to history: **"Remember the former things,"** a reference to God's mighty acts in the Exodus event. V.11 is another allusion to Cyrus (a bird of prey). He is a part of God's plan.

9. Babylon will fall (47:1–15)

This prediction of the fall of Babylon follows logically that of the fall of Babylon's gods. It is one of the most vitriolic passages in Scripture, understandably so, as Babylon came to be viewed as the symbol of evil (as in Rev 18). From lofty, queenly heights, the woman Babylon is brought low to the status of a slave girl, the most to be pitied of captives for the sexual abuse they endured as well as the hard labor.

In v.4 we again encounter the recurring title **Holy One of Israel.** When God expresses himself as the Holy One, he acts in redemption or in judgment, as he does here.

God used Babylon as his instrument to chastise his people (v.6), but, as with Assyria, Babylon was extreme in its destruction and ascribed to itself the status of deity (vv.8, 10). Vv.9, 12, and 13 are negative allusions to Babylon's well-known practice of astrology.

10. Prepare to leave Babylon (48:1-22)

This section (40:1-48:22) concludes with a rousing call to leave Babylon, but before this final note of exultation the prophet pulls together the various themes he has developed throughout the preceding chapters: Israel's stubbornness and rebelliousness, Yahweh's ability to foretell the future, the victories of Cyrus as God's instruments, and the fall of Babylon.

The prophet attacks Israel's relationship to Yahweh. It is artificial. Their relationship was characterized by stubbornness (v.4), a propensity for idolatry (v.5), obstinacy (v.6), hubris (v.7), deafness, and long-standing rebellion (v.8). In spite of this, Yahweh, for his own sake, will not allow Israel to be cut off.

After this verbal chastisement God appeals to Israel to listen once again. Establishing first his credibility as the Creator (v.13), he reminds them of his ability to foretell the future and particularly of the coming of Cyrus (v.14).

With v.16 the prophet is again the speaker. He offers what amounts to a final warning before he calls them to leave. V.20 makes a radical shift from chastisement and warning to exultation and joy. He proclaims the release from

Babylon as though it had already happened. Note that he returns to the theme of the new exodus and passage through the desert with which he began (40:1-11).

Many scholars view v.22 as out of place. It would so appear. However, it may well be intended as a final warning to those who scoff at the idea that God could and would deliver captive Israel.

B. The Songs of Zion and the Suffering Servant (49:1-55:13)

We enter a new section with ch. 49. The previous chapter ended with a call to leave Babylon. In chs. 49-55 no further mention is made of Babylon or Cyrus. Now the poems become focused on alternating themes: the songs of Zion and the suffering of the servant. Implicit in the interwoven nature of the material is that Israel's salvation is dependent on the servant's suffering.

1. The servant, bringer of salvation (49:1-13)

In the second servant song the servant speaks. Like one of the prophets, he relates his call by God (v.2), expresses his own inadequacy (v.4), and is reminded that God is his strength (v.5). God reminds him of his mission: it is not only to restore Israel, but to bring the light of God to the Gentiles.

Vv.8-13 are a beautiful prophecy of salvation that begins with a reiteration of God's promised help to his servant (vv.8-9a). Then follows a graphic depiction of the journey home, the second exodus: pastoral scenes with cool water, moderate climate, and a highway fit for a king, over which exiles from the farthest points of the earth will travel (vv.9b-12). All of nature is called on to celebrate the restoration event (v.13).

2. The restoration of Zion (49:14–50:3)

The focus shifts from the exiles to Zion. The poem is a mixture of questions that Zion asks (vv.14, 21, 24) and the answers given, which are oracles of salvation. These are followed by a question from God to Zion. Zion's response to the preceding oracle of salvation is disbelief (cf. the response in 40:27 to the initial announcement of salvation): Zion believes it has been both forsaken and forgotten by God. As inconceivable as it may be that a mother might abandon her child, God would never abandon his child, Zion! V.16 may be a reference to the rebuilding of the city of Jerusalem in preparation for the return of her sons, the exiles. The return will be so extensive that there will not be enough room in Jerusalem. Far from forgetting Zion, God will restore her beyond measure.

Zion responds in continuing disbelief: "But I am barren; where are all these children coming from?" The answer is that the Gentiles will escort her children home (vv.22–23).

But doubt remains with Zion, and she questions whether anyone is strong enough to subdue those whom she remembers as the fierce destroyer of her people and her city. She is unable to see that the stage of world history is changing. Babylon, which once was invincible, is so no longer.

Now it is God's turn to ask a question. **"Where is your mother's certificate of divorce?"** It does not exist. Zion's plight was only temporary. In v.2, the prophet chides them for their disbelief. When God came to deliver them, they were not around. The prophet concludes his portion with a barrage of images relating God's power and strength, which are drawn primarily from the Exodus tradition.

3. The servant, one who perseveres (50:4–11)

The third servant song conveys the prophet's frustration in trying to convince his people of Yahweh's faithfulness and ability to deliver them. The servant has been persecuted because of his faithfulness to the task God has given (vv.5–6). He is not deterred but trusts the Lord (v.7), sure of his vindication (v.8). He concludes with an appeal to follow the true light of the word of God, and with a note of biting irony compares the true eternal light of God with small hand-held torches that light one's way only a few feet and will surely lead to no good end.

4. Zion is comforted (51:1–52:12)

This unit is comprised of several short poems, woven together to announce and celebrate proleptically the restoration of Zion with Yahweh reigning again in Jerusalem with his gathered children, the exiles.

The prophet states that because God is righteous, he will be faithful to his covenant and deliver his people. The mention of Abraham and Sarah has the twofold effect of (1) reaffirming the covenant and (2) reminding the exiles that God intervened when the future seemed to be without hope for Sarah and Abraham. So now they who seem to be without hope must trust God once again to intervene.

Again comes the call to listen (vv.4–7). Soon God will act, and transformation will be swift. Even the heavens, which were a symbol of constancy, will appear transitory compared to the everlasting nature of Yahweh's righteousness.

In vv.9–16 the prophet turns from the exiles to Yahweh, though certainly his fellow countrymen were intended to "overhear" his call to Yahweh. He appeals to history, particularly the exodus story. Rahab is Egypt (cf. 30:7), although it is a term drawn from the chaos myth and therefore has great symbolic power to represent any ominous evil force. The deliverance at the first exodus is the basis for a new exodus and a return to Zion. The remainder of the poem finds Yahweh speaking in the first person. There is no need to awaken him. He is already acting in their behalf. Note the reiteration of earlier themes: comfort (40:1), mortals as grass (40:6–7), and God's creative power (40:12ff.).

Finally, the prophet turns to Zion (51:17–23). It is the one that needs to awaken from its stupor. V.18 is a critical reference to the monarchy. No king was able to guide Israel faithfully. Indeed, all reliance on human ability has ended in calamity (vv.19–20). It is time now to turn to God for his help.

The call to Zion is repeated (52:1). The time of stupor and calamity is over. Restoration has begun. Jerusalem is to put on garments of splendor (an allusion to the loss of these in 3:18ff.). Jerusalem will rise up as from the dead (cf. the mention of dust in v.2 and 29:4–5) and sit enthroned.

Vv.4–7 are a rehearsal of history: first Jacob's children as slaves in Egypt, then the oppressive rule of Assyria, and most recently the deportation of God's people to Babylon. Enough! Yahweh will act!

The prophet now sees a magnificent sight, a messenger running to Jerusalem to bring the good news of God's restoration of the exiles to Zion. The crescendo of phrases in v.7 is powerful. The watchmen in Jerusalem see the messenger and, anticipating his message, shout for joy. When Yahweh brings his people home, all the ends of the earth will recognize this as God's salvation. The prophet concludes with

a call to leave (which is similar to the concluding remarks of ch. 48).

5. The suffering and glory of the servant (52:13–53:12)

This is the fourth and final servant song. Note that as chs. 40–55 have developed, the intensity of the servant's ministry of redemptive suffering has increased.

It should be obvious that in this passage the identity of the servant is unclear. On the one hand, much of the description would apply to the exilic community, which has been disfigured and disgraced and reckoned as dead (vv.8–9) but which is now exalted and restored. This exiled community had in some measure the role of redemptive suffering. Yet the opening verses of this section (40:1ff.), and indeed the majority of the book of Isaiah, suggest that the people's suffering was deserved. It was due to their own iniquities, not someone else's.

On the other hand, the singular pronouns must be reckoned with. They allude to a particular individual whose identity is shrouded in ambiguity. Was it the prophet himself, another contemporary, or an idealized individual in the future whose reality was to be fulfilled by Jesus of Nazareth?

The **"arm of the LORD"** (53:1) is a phrase from 51:9 and 52:10. In both instances they implied an act of salvation. The allusion here is intentional. The servant's suffering is an act of salvation.

The **message** (v.1) centers first on the servant's appearance. He was so disfigured that people would turn away from him. His physical suffering led to the social suffering of being an outcast. Like Job's "friends," the chorus of speakers reasoned that the suffering was the deserved punishment inflicted by God. But in v.5 they realize that the servant was taking their iniquities on himself. Their peace and healing was because of his suffering.

The mention of straying sheep in v.6 leads to the notion of a sacrificial lamb in v.7. The servant dies (vv.8–9). Vv.10–12 shift the tone and tell of the servant's exaltation.

Regardless of the numerous ambiguities, the point of the poem is eloquently clear: The community of God experiences healing and forgiveness because God has transferred their deserved punishment onto a sinless servant.

6. Zion, beloved by Yahweh (54:1–17)

The prophet returns to the idea of the barren woman who has more children than her house can possibly hold (cf. 49:21). There will be no more need to fear, for Yahweh who is her maker is also her husband. With language similar to that of Hosea, the prophet mentions Yahweh's temporary fit of anger. But now it serves to highlight his enduring and eternal compassion.

The prophet draws a comparison with the days of Noah where chaos temporarily reigned (the exile was referred to as a time of chaos), only to be followed by an everlasting covenant.

Now, in direct address to Zion, Yahweh details his future plans for his beloved city. It is language that can be described only as eschatological, for it transcends the realm of historical reality. There will be no need of priests, for the Lord himself will teach Zion's children. And the city will be safe from any and every oppressor.

7. God's salvation (55:1–13)

This portion of the Isaianic corpus concludes with a divine invitation. It is an invitation of grace, to receive life-giving water free of charge. It recalls Yahweh's earlier provision of manna and water in the desert and foreshadows the One who said, "If anyone is thirsty, let him come to me and drink" (Jn 7:37).

Vv.6–7 are a final appeal to the exiles to seek Yahweh and return to him. Vv.8–9 remind the people that their deliverance is beyond human comprehension. God's word has promised it. It will not return void. We recall the opening verses of this portion of the book of Isaiah, "The word of our God stands forever" (40:8).

The prophet concludes this section by announcing and celebrating the departure from exile. Again, this act of deliverance will cause all creation to join in the celebration, and restored Israel will stand as an everlasting sign to all the nations that Yahweh is faithful to his covenant.

V. RETURN AND RESETTLEMENT (56:1–66:24)

A. Difficulties in the Restoration (56:1–59:21)

The locale has shifted in this section from Babylon to Jerusalem. It is understood that many of the exiles have returned. It should be noted, too, that there is a decided shift in mood. Ch. 55 was clearly the climax of the previous section with its picturesque announcement of departure. Now with ch. 56 comes the difficult decisions of day-to-day matters, the transformation of the vision into the reality.

1. Blessed is the one who does what is right (56:1–8)

The Isaianic theme of righteousness is boldly set forth once again, but here it carries a new component: keeping the Sabbath. Indeed, the legalistic tone is surprising in that it was never so stated in the rest of Isaiah.

The inclusion in the Jewish community of foreigners and eunuchs suggests that there must have been some difference of opinion on this matter. The old law of Dt 23:1–6 excluded eunuchs, and the writings of Ezra and Nehemiah were attempts to preserve the community from religious and cultural assimilation. But the focus here is on inclusion, based on faithful obedience and keeping of the Sabbath law.

2. The humble and wicked contrasted (56:9–57:21)

The reader is struck by the sudden and bold note of contrast in this section. The ideal faithfulness of 56:1–8 stands over against the wickedness related in these ensuing verses. The leaders (watchmen, shepherds) of the Jewish community are self-seeking and lazy, ripe for judgment. Vv.1–2 suggest that there is so much moral and social chaos that the only positive thing going for the righteous is that in their dying they will be spared the pervasive evil and find their peace.

Isa 57:3–13 is an attack on idolatry that involved participation in the Canaanite fertility cult. The point is well taken. Note v.10 with its ironic play on the words of 40:31. True strength for the weary is found solely by waiting on Yahweh.

In 57:14–21 the prophet shifts his focus. Note the play on the words *high* and *low[ly]*. The high and lofty one who lives in a high place is concerned about those who are lowly in spirit. They are the object of God's affection, and he will act to bring them healing, comfort, and peace. But the wicked will be denied all of these.

3. The spiritual and ethical dimensions of faith (58:1–14)

In 58:1 the prophet refers to a particular type of rebellion that is then explicated in the succeeding verses:

empty religious observance (fasting) designed to achieve selfish ends (vv.2–3a) that have no correlation with righteous, ethical behavior (vv.3, 6, 7). It is the height of hypocrisy for one to fast while at the same time one exploits his workers and engages in strife. A genuine fast will result in correcting injustice, freeing the oppressed and those in bondage, feeding the hungry, and providing shelter and clothing for those in need. When these things are done, then God hears and responds (vv.8–9).

The prophet concludes by insisting that the people rebuild the walls of Jerusalem (v.12) and that they keep their priorities straight by keeping the Sabbath (vv.13–14). If they do, God will bless them.

4. Sin, confession, and deliverance (59:1–21)

The prophet, sensing consternation and dismay among his people due to their unfortunate situation, is quick to state that the fault does not lie with Yahweh but with them. Surely Yahweh is able to save (v.1), but the people's sins have hindered his saving activity. A litany of sins follows: lies (v.3), indifference to justice and a desire for evil (v.4), and threatening to subvert society's structure (v.5, snakes and spiders' webs were frequently used to symbolize this; cf. Sawyer, 177). This inner disposition expresses itself in evil deeds (v.6), the shedding of innocent blood (v.7), and distortion of trust (v.8), with the result that there is no peace.

Vv.9–15a constitute a confession of sin and an admission of guilt. They are like the blind who cannot find their way. The cause of the blindness is stated in vv.12–13: their rebellion against God, which results in the lack of justice and righteousness and trust and honesty (v.14).

The situation had deteriorated to the

point where there was no one to intervene, so God himself would act. His own arm would bring salvation (see 59:1). When God comes in warriorlike fashion, evildoers will be judged, and those who repent (v.20) will be redeemed. The prophet closes by setting the seal of God's authority on his words (v.21).

B. The Future Glory of Zion (60:1–66:24)

1. Arise, shine! (60:1–22)

With this chapter the prophet appears to shift into a higher key with a greater sense of expectancy, highlighted by a lofty vision for Zion's future and punctuated with expressions of abundant blessing.

The darkness of the preceding chapter set the stage for this jubilant announcement: **"Arise shine, for your light has come."** The announcement draws on the idea of 9:1–2 and is preparatory to the arrival of God in Christ in the Gospels (Mt 2:2, Lk 1:28–29, and Jn 1:4–5). Zion/Jerusalem is the one place that will be light in the midst of darkness, and all the nations will be drawn to its light (v.3; cf. 2:2–4). Zion will be flooded with the wealth of nations. It will be as in the days of Solomon (note the reference to Sheba in v.6). The purpose of the nations' coming will be to worship Yahweh, thus the reference to animals for sacrifice and appointments for the temple (vv.6–7).

These that fly along like clouds (v.8) is a reference to the sailing ships of Tarshish from the west, which bring rich gifts and more sons of exile.

There seems to be no end to this glorious picture. Foreigners will rebuild Jerusalem. The arrival of foreign kings and their wealth will be constant and uninterrupted (vv.10–16).

Vv.17–22 employ a number of theological terms to convey a state of peace and rest where righteousness rules and salvation reigns. In a brilliant display of poetic vision, the prophet looks to the day when the glorious light of God alone will brighten Jerusalem and when the sun will no longer be needed (vv.19–20). This vision captured the imagination of John (Rev 21:23–26) and it continues to be a source of hope for all who follow Christ and look for the final triumph of God.

2. The servant's message of hope (61:1–11)

The opening verse is a reference to the first servant song in 42:1, "I will put my Spirit on him." The prophet sees his role as the fulfillment of the servant's task. It seemed to the exiles that the promised vision of 40:1–11; 49:25; 52:2, 7–12; 55:12–13 had been delayed. The prophet is called to announce that the vision is still valid. Comfort, peace, freedom, and security will once again prevail.

Vv.4–7 return to themes of the infusion and subordination of foreign people along with their riches. Finally, the prophet sings a song of gladness on behalf of all Zion. Salvation and righteousness will indeed become the primary rule of society. It is important for the prophet to insist that the earlier glorious vision is still viable and sure. The recurring and persistent insistence upon this fact reinforces our suspicion that in the early days of the restoration, the vision seemed to have waned.

3. Zion is reassured (62:1–12)

The note of reassurance struck in ch. 61 continues here. The prophet continues to speak with heightened urgency. He will not be silent until the glorious vision comes to pass.

An interesting play on names occurs

in v.4. **Deserted** and **Desolate** will be changed to Delight (**Hephzibah**) and Married (**Beulah**). In v.5 **"sons"** should be changed to "builder" as suggested by the context and requires only a slight emendation (cf. Ps 147:2).

The prophet calls the people to persist with God until he establishes Jerusalem in her glory (v.7). Never again will enemies conquer them (vv.8–9). Drawing on earlier images (40:3) of the call to return from exile, the prophet now tells the people to enter the city. The vision of 52:7–10 is now about to be fulfilled. One of the things the prophet likes to do to illustrate the New Day is to give new names (cf. v.12; also 60:14, 18 and vv.2 and 4 of this chapter).

4. Zion's enemies will be destroyed (63:1–6)

Ch. 62 contained a promise that God would not allow Zion's enemies to overwhelm her. Isa 63:1–6 portrays the fate of those enemies. The imagery of Yahweh marching in bloodstained garments and trampling "out the vintage where the grapes of wrath are stored" is somewhat disturbing. But in this original setting as well as in the nineteenth-century song, the imagery is intended more for effect than for an accurate depiction of reality.

5. A prayer for help (63:7–64:12)

This section has the form of a communal lament, which generally contains the elements of (1) citation of past blessings (vv.7–9), (2) mention of present need (vv.10–19), (3) request for aid (64:1–12), and (4) assurance that God hears and will answer (in this case 65:1–25). A recognition of sin underlies the entire lament.

Most scholars believe that the glorious vision of restored Zion has been proclaimed but not attained. This community lament grows out of that situation. Jerusalem still lies wasted. Some of the exiles have returned, but the restoration has scarcely begun, and its completion remains in doubt. Therefore they offer this prayer.

6. Yahweh's response: A mixed blessing (65:1–25)

Yahweh responds to the preceding lament by reciting his overtures to his people and their blatant rebellion (vv.1–7). Yahweh will act to deliver Israel but with discrimination, bringing salvation to those who respond in faithfulness, and judgment to those who continue in evil doing (vv.8–16). The prophet concludes this section with an eschatological vision (vv.17–25).

In vv.1–7 the prophet thinks it ironic that Israel pleads with God (the previous lament) to come, when God had faithfully and persistently made himself available to Israel and had been met only with rejection and the provocation of idolatrous worship. V.4 refers to the forbidden rituals of communicating with the dead. The eating of unclean meat was an act of open rebellion. Note in these verses the emphasis on cultic impurity and disobedience.

In vv.8–16 we see the early stages of the sheep and goats motif, i.e., the distinction between the faithful and unfaithful within Israel. Previously the people of Judah had been viewed largely as a whole, but here and increasingly in subsequent postexilic literature is a delineation of those who are true and those who are not. V.8 was probably a well-known parable, which sets the tone for the passage. God will act to save his people for the sake of his faithful servants (vv.8–10), but those who forsake Yahweh will be destroyed (vv.11–16). The faithful servants will enter the new era as symbolized by the receiving of new names (v.15; cf. the comment on 62:12).

Contemplation of the fate of the faithful servants lifts the prophet to yet another visionary height as he seems to gather many of the previous joyous images in the Isaianic corpus (2:2–4; 4:2–6; 9:2–7; 25:6–9; 32:15–20; 35:1–10; 41:17–20) to limn his view of the future eschatological age. God's new activity will be on a scale similar to that of the first acts of creation. The former things, i.e., the disaster, despair, and dismay, will not be remembered. The messianic vision of ch. 11 will come to pass (v.25).

7. A final word (66:1–24)

This concluding chapter appears to be a collection of material designed to emphasize the future well-being of Jerusalem (vv.7–16) and to issue a final warning (vv.17–24). However, it begins with a surprisingly negative attitude toward worship in the temple (vv.1–6).

The emphasis in the opening verses is on proper worship. The temple is not yet completed, only anticipated. While the temple is important, Yahweh points out that it is not necessary, for heaven is his throne. And the true worshiper is one who is humble, contrite, and obedient to God's word.

Vv.3 and 4 are troubling. Acceptable rites (Lev 1–3) of worship are here denounced in the sharpest of terms. Perhaps something within the postexilic community of which we are not aware lies behind these stern words. Or perhaps there is an understood condemnation of superficial worship. V.5 suggests that a division existed within postexilic Judaism. It would follow that those offering sacrifices were somehow excluding the faithful (the poor) and therefore came under God's strong condemnation.

The prophet now shifts to a vision of the future well-being of Zion (vv.7–16). He believes its glorious future is imminent, as suggested in the imagery of a birth that is not delayed by a period of labor (vv.7–9). The themes of peace and abundance are reiterated (vv.10–13). Once again the inverse themes of salvation and judgment are juxtaposed (vv.14–16). It is clear that there was deep concern about rites that were based on superstition; the prophet returns to this motif yet once again to denounce it (v.17).

The theme of vv.18–24 is the glory of God in the midst of the nations. The enduring sign of that glory will be restored Israel, some of whose people will be sent as missionaries among the nations, which will in turn bow before the God of the universe (v.23). The book of Isaiah ends with a gruesome warning against unfaithfulness (v.24).

BIBLIOGRAPHY

Clements, R. E. *Isaiah 1–39.* NCBC. Grand Rapids: Eerdmans, 1980.

Gray, G. B. *A Critical and Exegetical Commentary on the Book of Isaiah, I–XXVII.* Vol. 1. ICC. Edinburgh: T. & T. Clark, 1912.

Johnson, D. *From Chaos to Restoration, An Integrative Reading of Isaiah 24–27.* JSOT Supp. Ser. 61. Sheffield, England: Sheffield Academic Press, 1988.

McKenzie, J. L. *Second Isaiah.* Vol. 20. AB. New York: Doubleday, 1968.

Oswalt, John N. *The Book of Isaiah, Chapters 1–39*. NICOT. Grand Rapids: Eerdmans, 1986.

Payne, D. F. "Isaiah." IBC. Edited by F. F. Bruce. Grand Rapids: Zondervan, 1986.

Rowley, H. H. *The Servant of the Lord and Other Essays on the Old Testament*. London: Lutterworth, 1952.

Sawyer, J. F. A. *Isaiah, I. II*. DSBS. Philadelphia: Westminster, 1986.

JEREMIAH

Alexander Varughese

INTRODUCTION

I. TITLE AND CANONICAL PLACEMENT

The introductory statement (1:1–3) constitutes the title of the book of Jeremiah. The phrase "the words of Jeremiah" (v.1) refers to the entire book. The words of Jeremiah are "the word of the LORD" (*dᵉbar yahweh*) that "came" (lit. "happened") within a particular historical setting (vv.2–3). In the prophetic literature, the phrase *dᵉbar yahweh* is a common expression for the prophetic word of revelation. The title thus makes clear the divine origin of the content of this book. Jeremiah ben Hilkiah was Yahweh's spokesman and a witness of His sovereign actions in history.

The book of Jeremiah is located between the books of Isaiah and Ezekiel in the Hebrew canon. The English versions follow the Septuagint order in which the book of Lamentations is found between the books of Jeremiah and Ezekiel. An ancient rabbinic tradition mentions Jeremiah before Ezekiel and Isaiah. This order is maintained by many European manuscripts. In the Syriac version (Peshitta) the book is placed immediately after the Minor Prophets.

II. HISTORICAL SETTING

Jeremiah's ministry took place during the reigns of Josiah, Jehoiakim, and Zedekiah (640–587 B.C.; 1:1–3). He began his prophetic career in the thirteenth year of King Josiah (627 B.C.; v.2). Most likely Jeremiah, himself a young man, was inspired by Josiah's religious reformation, which aimed to free Judah from the corrupt influences of paganism. The discovery of the "book of the law" in 622 B.C. (2Ki 22–23) gave this reformation a firm theological orientation. Though there are no direct references that connect Jeremiah with Josiah's reform activities, it is likely that the prophet was a strong supporter of this program (11:1–13).

Josiah's reformation was also an attempt to free Judah from over a hundred years of political bondage to Assyria. The rise of Babylon as a world power and the near collapse of Assyria gave Josiah the hope of freedom. His involvement in the power struggle between Assyria and Babylon, however, led him to his untimely death in 609 B.C. in the battle of Megiddo with the Egyptians, who were on their way to assist the

Assyrians in recapturing Haran from the Babylonians (2Ki 23:29–30). For the next five years Judah remained a vassal of Egypt. The Babylonian victory over the Philistines in 604 B.C. prompted the Judean king Jehoiakim to transfer his allegiance to Nebuchadnezzer (2Ki 24:1). Judah returned to Egypt in 601 B.C. when Babylon could not break up the resistance of the Egyptian army near the Egyptian border. The Babylonians retaliated against Judah in December 598 B.C. Meanwhile Jehoiakim died, and a few months later, King Jehoiachin, the queen mother, and 10,000 leading citizens were deported to Babylon (2Ki 24:10–17). Zedekiah was placed on the throne as a vassal by the Babylonians. His rebellion in 589 B.C. prompted the Babylonians to march again to Palestine. Jerusalem was placed under siege in 588 B.C. (2Ki 25:1). Though the Babylonians raised the siege in order to meet an Egyptian threat, they returned again and destroyed Jerusalem in July 587 B.C. (chs. 39, 52; 2Ki 25:3ff.). Gedaliah was appointed as governor, who in turn was assassinated by a rebellious group under the leadership of Ishmael (ch. 41). Fearing reprisal from the Babylonians, Gedaliah's friends escaped to Egypt, taking Jeremiah with them against his will (ch. 42). The last known oracle of Jeremiah was made from Tahpanhes in Egypt (43:8–13), where presumably his life came to an end.

III. STRUCTURE, AUTHORSHIP, AND DATE

"The words of Jeremiah" are not arranged in any chronological order. Moreover, there is no logical progression of thought running from the beginning to the end of this book. This lack of a proper order and arrangement is a real difficulty in our attempt to study the theology of Jeremiah. However, the book preserves a "form" with at least three clearly identifiable sections. The first section (1:1–25:13a) for the most part contains the oracles of Jeremiah, which he preached during the first twenty-three years of his ministry (25:1–3, 13; see also ch. 36, which gives the account of the writing of a scroll in the fourth year of King Jehoiakim). Obviously 21:1–10; 22:24–23:8; and 24 come from a later period. This section contains the prophet's condemnation of Judah's apostasy, warnings of Yahweh's judgment, and his call for repentance. A distinct group of oracles within chs. 11–20 is labeled "confessions" (11:18–12:4; 15:10–21; 17:14–18; 18:18–23; 20:7–13, 14–18), because these sayings contain expressions of Jeremiah's emotional outbursts in the form of complaints, laments, and prayers.

The second section (chs. 30–33) contains the message of hope to both Judah and Israel; it is sometimes called "The Book of Consolation." Chs. 30–31 are mostly in poetry with emphasis on the restoration of Israel to their own home land. Chs. 32–33 continue the same theme, mostly in prose, based on Jeremiah's purchase of a piece of land, which expressed his conviction of the future restoration of Israel's fortunes.

The third section (chs. 46–51) contains Jeremiah's oracles of judgment pronounced against foreign nations. These oracles are found in the Septuagint after 25:13a; hence the arrangement of the Septuagint after 25:13a is significantly different from that of the Hebrew Bible (Masoretic text).

These three sections (1:1–25:13a; 30–33; 46–51) provide us with a basic form of the book. The remainder of the book (chs. 26–29 and 34–45) contains mostly biographical accounts; these are placed between the first and second and the second and third sections. The biographical accounts do not follow any chronological order (for a chronological arrangement of these chapters, see Bright's *Jeremiah* in the Anchor Bible). The biographical accounts are also strongly theological in character. Judah's political decisions are a proof of their unfaithfulness to God. Therefore, the nation is under judgment. Jeremiah's own actions, on the other hand, are a testimony to his faithfulness to Yahweh. Yahweh preserves his life in the midst of national disaster. This is Yahweh's faithfulness to him.

The words of Jeremiah conclude with a historical appendix (ch. 52), which for the most part is also found in 2 Ki 24:18–25:30.

Scholars have observed three major literary types of materials in the book of Jeremiah, labeled as A, B, and C. "A" materials are for the most part the poetic oracles, which contain the first-person speeches of Yahweh. The biographical accounts make up the "B" materials. These accounts usually provide us with some chronological data. Jeremiah is addressed in these accounts in the third person, which leads us to believe that a biographer is responsible for compiling these materials. The third type ("C") is Jeremiah's prose discourses which are scattered throughout the book and mingled with poetic oracles and biographical materials (e.g., 7:1–8:3; 11:1–17; 16:1–18; 18:1–12; 19:1–12; et al.). The style, language, and theology of these discourses closely resemble that of the book of Deuteronomy.

The existence of these three distinct literary types of materials has prompted scholars to raise questions about the authorship of the book. See discussions of this matter in other commentaries. The present writer follows the view that the book as a whole is a record of the ministry and teachings of Jeremiah. The poetic oracles and the prose sermons preserve Jeremiah's words. The biographical accounts come from a biographer (most likely Baruch). It is highly unlikely that those among whom the words of Jeremiah were circulated would have attempted to create a "Jeremianic theology" different from the basic theological convictions of the prophet. Though political conditions changed after Jeremiah uttered his words, one cannot be certain that Jeremiah's own words, or words about him, were revised, edited, or even reshaped to make them relevant to a late exilic or postexilic situation. The basic spiritual needs of God's people have remained the same throughout Judah's history. This view, however, does not dismiss the activities of later "editors" who were responsible for giving the book its present canonical form.

The process through which the book received its present canonical form is not known. It is likely that the various sections of Jeremiah were put together in the form of a "book" soon after the catastrophe of 587 B.C. Differences between the Hebrew and the Greek texts of Jeremiah (the latter is about one-eighth shorter than the former) point to the existence of two divergent lines of textual traditions. It is plausible, as recent studies have proposed, that the textual basis for the Greek translation was a shorter edition of the book. The expanded edition of the book is preserved in the Hebrew Bible (Masoretic text). Though it is within the realm of conjecture, we may conclude that this later edition was also the work of the prophet, which he sent to the exiles in Babylon from his Egyptian home. Most likely these two text traditions existed side by side in the mid-sixth century B.C.

IV. THEOLOGICAL SIGNIFICANCE

According to Jeremiah, there is a clear connection between the spiritual condition of God's people and the events that happen in their political history. Yahweh is the sovereign Lord of history. His plan is *"to uproot and tear down, to destroy and overthrow"* those who do not acknowledge his lordship and *"to build and to plant"* those who are faithful to him" (1:10, et al.). Jeremiah reminds Judah that Yahweh is their creator (5:22), husband (2:2), father (3:19), and the source of life (2:13). In spite of repeated prophetic warnings, God's people, called to live in the experience of a circumcised heart (4:4; cf. Dt 30:6), remain desperately ill with a corrupt and sinful heart (5:23; 17:1, 9). Their sickness is terminal because of the stubbornness of their evil heart (9:14; 11:8; 16:12; 18:12), which refuses to be healed (8:22). Therefore they are under the curse of the law (see Dt 28:15ff.). This theological interpretation of history is the major goal of Jeremiah.

Judgment is not Yahweh's last word to his people. God's grace is at work even in the midst of sin and judgment to give the people of God a hope and a future. Judah's restoration is pivotal to Jeremiah's eschatology (chs. 29–33), not only so that there will be a new beginning, but also that there will be a new covenant (31:31–34). God's people will live under the faithful leadership of a Davidic king (33:14–16). Jerusalem will once again be called the throne of the Lord to which all nations will make their pilgrimage (3:17).

Jeremiah's theology is rooted in the past saving events of Israel's history. True worship is an expression of gratitude to God for his salvation. Judah has religion but no remembrance of their deliverance from Egypt, the Sinai covenant, the wilderness, and the gift of the land. This forgetfulness of the past is caused by their failure to internalize (*circumcise your hearts*, 4:4) the laws of the Sinai covenant. Yahweh's plan, therefore, is to establish a new covenant relationship, the laws of which will be placed in the inner being of the redeemed people of God (31:31–34).

Jeremiah's book is a vital link between the people of God in the OT and the church in the NT. Its place in the canon is a clear evidence of the hope expressed by exilic and postexilic Judaism in the restoration of their nation as a new covenant people of God. This promise of God through his prophet Jeremiah was fulfilled through his Son, the mediator of the new covenant (Mk 14:22–24). The book challenges the new covenant community (the church) to learn a valuable lesson from the history of the old covenant community and truly to become the kingdom of God in the world.

V. OUTLINE

COMMENTARY

I. JEREMIAH—A PROPHET TO THE NATIONS (CH. 1)

The introductory statement (1:1–3) establishes Jeremiah as a historical person and his book as a theological document. See other commentaries for detailed descriptions of the historical, geographical, and cultural setting of the book.

The ministry of a true prophet in Israel was guided by the strong conviction that he was under constraint by a divine call to speak on behalf of Yahweh. The account of Jeremiah's call (vv.4–19) is much like the call accounts of Moses (Ex 3:1–4:17), Isaiah (ch. 6), and Ezekiel (1:1–3:15). **"Before I formed you"** and **"Before you were born"** (v.5) imply that Yahweh bestowed his grace upon Jeremiah from the time of the prophet's conception in his mother's womb. Yahweh's words, **"I knew you,"** etc. (v.5), are covenantal terms. God has established a special covenantal relationship with his spokesman before his birth. Therefore, the one being called is under obligation to obey the one who calls (see Isa 49:1; Gal 1:15).

Vv.6–7 demonstrate the theological principle that Yahweh's decision to call one to be his spokesperson is not guided by the human tradition that words of wisdom are with the experienced (see Mt 21:16; cf. Ps 8:2). Furthermore, he equips the one being called with the promise of his presence (v.8), with his personal touch (v.9), and by placing his words in one's mouth (15:16; Eze 3:2; cf. Dt 18:18). Jeremiah's task is to announce to the nations the promptness with which Yahweh is about to fulfill his threats and promises (vv.10–16; see Clarke, 256). Contemporary political powers are the instruments of Yahweh's judgment against the wicked and the disobedient (vv.13–16).

Yahweh expects faithfulness and courage from his spokesman—faithfulness in proclaiming judgment and courage to encounter opposition (vv.17–19). **"I am with you"** (v.19; also v.8) is an assurance of protection and safety. God is determined "to defend and support" his prophet (Clarke, 257). Implied here is a call to abandon self-sufficiency and to trust in the presence and power of God (see Ex 3:12; Mt 28:20b).

II. SERMONS ON SIN, JUDGMENT, LOVE, AND FORGIVENESS (2:1–6:30)

This section contains a collection of Jeremiah's oracles, all connected with the theme of Israel's apostasy and Yahweh's judgment. Most commentators place these oracles in the early part of the prophet's ministry.

A. Yahweh's Case Against His People (2:1–37)

Yahweh's remembrance (**"I remember,"** v.2) and Israel's forgetfulness (**"My people have forgotten,"** v.32) are the basis for his case against his people. Yahweh remembers the time when Israel was a devoted, loving, and holy nation (vv.1–3). The words **"devotion"** (*ḥesed*), **"loved"** (*aḥăbâ[h]*), and **"holy"** (*qōdeš*) are all covenantal terms. The reference here is to the making of the covenant at Sinai (Ex 19–24). The prophet's accusation is that Israel does not maintain a living memory of the experience of Yahweh's grace in the wilderness days. The leaders who are entrusted with the duty to initiate faith and to promote true religion in the land (vv.5, 8; see Dt 6:20–25; 17:14–20; 18:15–22; 33:10) do not remember their responsibility. They practice a religion of falsehood (**idols**). There is no recognition of Yahweh who alone is the **spring of living water** (v.13; 17:13; see Jn 7:37–39).

Israel's involvement in the political events of Jeremiah's time is the evidence of their rejection of the freedom brought to them by Yahweh (vv.14–19; 36–37). Jeremiah rejects the popular notion that Israel is a **slave by birth** (v.14). Though freed by the grace of God and adopted as a "son" (Clarke, 259), the people of God behave like a servant bound to a former master (see the law concerning slaves in Ex 21:1–6). Israel shows no trust in Yahweh, whose actions are not immediately visible in the historical scene (see also Isa 8:5–8). The consequence of this **evil** (*rā'*) of God's people is **evil** (*rā'*) from Yahweh (v.19).

God's people (**choice vine**) have become useless and corrupt like a **wild vine** by their refusal to submit themselves to the spiritual principles established by God (vv.20–21). "Instead of becoming true worshippers, and of a holy life and conversation," they have "become idolaters of the most corrupt and profligate kind" (Clarke, 260). The cause of Israel's rebellion against God is the corruption of their moral character. The cultic laws provide no ritual for the total cleansing of this degeneration, which is deeply rooted in their inner being (v.22).

Self-righteousness is the claim of a morally degenerate nation ("**I am not defiled,**" v.23; see also "**I am innocent . . . I have not sinned**" v.35). When they are confronted with the reality of judgment, their response is "**It's no use**" (v.25) because they have gone so far in their **love** for other gods. This is the claim of those who deny the boundlessness of God's grace, the depth of his mercy and love, and his strong will to save the repentant sinner.

Disgrace is in store for all who practice foxhole religion (vv.26–28). Yahweh cannot be manipulated. On the Day of Judgment, neither Yahweh, whom they denied, nor the gods, whom they trusted, will come to the rescue of those who practice superficial religion. The former will not hear their cry; the latter cannot hear at all.

B. Yahweh's Passionate Appeal for Israel's Repentance (3:1–4:4)

This section includes a mixture of prose and poetry and continues the earlier theme of Israel's apostasy. The portrait of Yahweh here is that of a loving and merciful husband and father. However, repentance is the necessary condition for the restoration of sinners.

Yahweh does not behave like a man who, by the mandate of the Deuteronomic law, cuts himself loose of any emotional ties to his unfaithful wife (3:1; see Dt 24:1–4). Though he established the law because of his own demand for righteousness, Yahweh does not restrict himself by the law. His grace (v.12) supersedes his laws, which makes it possible for Israel to return to Yahweh. Return (*šûb*) is not a casual matter, rather an action to be taken with genuine contriteness and sincere desire to restore the broken relationship.

Sincere worship involves the practice of what one says about God (3:2–5) and genuine repentance (vv.6–11). Repentance is the central theme of 3:12–4:4. The call to repentance ("**Return**") is found in 3:12, 14, 22; and 4:1. The essential conditions of repentance are confession of guilt and acknowledgment of Yahweh as the Lord (v.13; see also vv.21–25). **"I am merciful"** is the word of grace Yahweh the Healer offers to the repentant sinner (vv.12, 22).

Repentance is also the condition for the future salvation of Israel (3:14–18). An important aspect of Jeremiah's eschatology here is the promise that **no longer will they follow the stubbornness of their evil hearts**, a promise given to both Israel and the nations (v.17). The gift of the will to obey God is the gift promised to the repentant sinner.

Israel's election is treated in 3:19 as God's favor and an unmerited gift (the daughter was given the inheritance that according to social custom belonged to the sons). Such a display of love (grace) must evoke gratitude, love, and faithfulness. Israel's response was to the contrary; her actions were like that of a woman unfaithful to her husband (v.20).

Yahweh gives an opportunity to Israel once again to become a source of blessing (salvation) to the nations (4:1–2). The requirements are a radical turn around from all evil to God (*šûb*), a life of God's holiness (**"Put your detestable idols out of my sight"**), and acknowledgment of God's sovereignty (**"As the LORD lives"**) in all spheres of life. Yahweh requires from his covenant people truthfulness (*'emet*), justice (*mišpāṭ*), and righteousness (*ṣedāqâ[h]*).

An essential prerequisite to the experience of the full blessings of the covenant relationship is a radical change from the way of life set in evil (4:3–4). Jeremiah calls those who have been "uncultivated in righteousness" to "break up" their "fruitless and hardened hearts" in repentance and to allow the "seed of the word of life" to be sown in them (Clarke, 266). The true sign of a covenant relationship with Yahweh is

obedience that comes from within. Clarke comments that the call to "circumcise" is a call to "put away every thing that has a tendency to grieve the Spirit of God" (p. 266). The metaphors (**break up** and **circumcise**) imply that a decision to obey God and to acknowledge his sovereignty is a critical and painful decision.

C. Yahweh's Judgment Is Coming (4:5–6:30)

Here we have a collection of the oracles of Jeremiah with primary emphasis on Yahweh's judgment imminent upon Judah. It is not certain that these oracles chronologically follow the preceding oracles in which Judah is called to repent; however, there is a theological continuity with chs. 2 and 3. It is equally difficult to ascertain the exact dates of these oracles. See other commentaries for further discussion on this matter.

As Yahweh's spokesman, Jeremiah warns his nation of Yahweh's action of judgment through an enemy, a political nation coming from the **north** (4:5–18). The enemy is described in unusual and colorful metaphors (**clouds, whirlwind, eagles**).

Jer 4:19–22 expresses the physical and emotional crisis of the prophet who announces the coming disaster. The consequence of the sin of God's people is destruction, not only of their own existence, but of the whole universe (vv.23–28). Yahweh's determination is to punish sin, even if it results in a cosmic catastrophe. On the day of judgment, sinners will not find escape from God's wrath in **the thickets** or among **the rocks** (v.29).

Judgment marks the end of Yahweh's patience (5:1–9), which is exhausted because his people do not **know the way of the Lord** (vv.4–5). Instead of justice and faithfulness, Jerusalem has become the center of falsehood (v.2), stubbornness (v.3), ignorance (v.4), rebellion (v.5), unfaithfulness (v.7), and covetousness (v.8).

Yahweh has already given his order to the destroyer nation to remove the **branches** that do not belong to him (5:10–11; see Mt 3:10; Jn 15:1–2). This is God's action against those who trust in the deceptive words of lying prophets who teach a shallow theology of God's grace (vv.12–13). Yahweh is determined to deal with the complacency of his people, who are "atheists at heart" (Clarke, 269). His words of judgment through Jeremiah have power to consume, like fire burns wood. Everything Israel trusted in (**harvests, sons and daughters, flocks and herds, vines and fig trees**, and **fortified cities**) would be devastated by this formidable enemy who is being sent by Yahweh (vv.15–17).

God's people under his judgment can still hope in his grace and mercy (5:18–19). The coming exile of Judah, though the consequence of sin, is also an act of grace in the midst of judgment.

God's people, like the nations around them, have become a **foolish and senseless people**, and they do not show any respect for the authority of Yahweh who is the creator, sustainer, and provider of this world (5:20–26). The root cause of this perversion is their **stubborn and rebellious hearts** (v.23). Moreover, they **love** the way they are being led by their wicked and corrupt leaders who do not **plead the case of the fatherless** and **defend the rights** (*mišpāṭ*) **of the poor** (vv.26–31). *Mišpāṭ* is one's covenant obligation to other members of the covenant society, including God who is the Covenant Maker. Where there is no *mišpāṭ*, there is no proper relationship with God or with one's neighbor.

The impending attack on Jerusalem is the theme of 6:1–5. The reason for the siege and destruction of Jerusalem is stated in vv.6–8. Though the city looks delicate and beautiful, what one finds within it is a fresh supply of wickedness, violence, and destruction. V.8 contains the offer of grace as well as warning. Even at this last minute, the inhabitants of the city are given an opportunity to appropriate divine grace through their obedient response before the judgment is carried out.

God's people have closed their ears (lit. their ears are uncircumcised) to Yahweh's words, and his words have become repulsive to them (6:10). Circumcision is the sign of obedience and covenant relationship. Judah is a nation with uncircumcised heart (cf. 4:4) and ears.

The attitude of deceit and falsehood has become a national characteristic, from top to bottom (6:13–15; see also 5:30–31). This is clearly evident in the preaching and teaching (false prophets and priests) popular in the land. Like vagabond physicians, these leaders proclaim *šālôm* to those who have no *šālôm*. They are not concerned with the spiritual and physical health (*šālôm*) of the nation. The leaders are therefore under Yahweh's judgment.

Sacrifice without obedience has no merit (6:16–21). Israel has rejected Yahweh's *tôrâ(h)* (v.19), which contains both quiet counsel and loud warning. The law given as instructions is an expression of grace (Deuteronomic law), which offers rest to the weary souls by pointing them to the right way (**the ancient paths, the good way**). The law also warns the lost about the impending disaster that is now about to come upon Israel.

Yahweh and the prophet speak in 6:22–26. Yahweh warns the Judeans about the cruel and merciless nation that is stirring up from the northern country (Babylon) as the agent of his judgment against Judah (vv.22–23). The prophet speaks to Yahweh's people (vv.24–26). In the former speech, his passion as Yahweh's spokesman is explicit. In the latter speech, the prophet speaks as a Judean who experiences anguish and pain with the rest of the nation because of **terror on every side** (see also 20:3,10; 46:5; 49:29).

Ch. 6 ends with an oracle of Yahweh to the prophet, appointing him to the task of a **tester** of the redeemability of Judah (vv.27–30). Yahweh is willing to extend his grace to any measure even at this moment before their destruction. However, this nation is far beyond the point of redemption. They are rejected by Yahweh because "they would not yield to either the *ordinary* or *extraordinary* means of salvation" (Clarke, 274).

III. FALSE WORSHIP AND ITS CONSEQUENCE (7:1–10:25)

Judah follows a theology based on false religious claims and presumptions. The nation promotes falsehood about God. Ironically, they claim to have wisdom. Yahweh's judgment is coming upon this arrogant and stubborn people who have perverted the truth about God and his requirements.

A. Jeremiah's Temple Sermon (7:1–8:3)

Consult other commentaries for a review of the historical context and the authorship debate. This section contains a number of originally independent sayings on false worship.

God requires from those who worship him the following: (1) strong determination thoroughly to reform their conduct (7:3, 5a); (2) dismissal of all false theological claims (v.4); (3) preservation of justice (*mišpāṭ*) in the society (v.5); (4) concern for the rights of resident aliens, orphans, and widows (v.6a); (5) an end to violence (v.6a); (6) absolute faithfulness to God (v.6b); and (7) absolute faithfulness to other members of the covenant society (v.9a). True piety is zeal for God rather than false confidence in the house of God. God is zealous of his house, which he will not allow to become a "den of robbers" (Mt 21:13).

God's repeated warnings, when unheeded would prompt him to a total withdrawal of his grace, the consequence of which would be disaster (7:12–20). Judah cannot expect anything but Shiloh's fate (v.14). When God is provoked with abominable actions, no one, not even the prophet, can dissuade him from executing his anger and wrath (v.16).

Obedience is the key to God-man relationship, without which rituals have no effect (7:21–24). An **evil heart** is the cause of disobedience; the disobedient walks backward (v.24). Judah has a long history of disobedience and rejection of God's word (vv.25–28). This is the reason for Yahweh's rejection of Judah (v.29).

Sin, when it is committed in the most detestable and merciless way, would be punished with the same or greater degree of passion by God (7:30–8:3). The passion of the people of Judah for idols led them to a total disregard for the value of human life. God's judgment will come to them with the same terribleness and indignity. No one will be able to withstand God's judgment.

B. Judah's Stubbornness (8:4–9:1)

Stubbornness is a defiant refusal to learn the established pattern for life. Even birds have enough wisdom to follow signs set for them. God's people refuse to acknowledge his way for them

(8:4–7). Stubbornness leads to the claim of wisdom; this wisdom does not promote the fear of Yahweh; therefore, it is false (vv.8–12; 10b–12 is also found in 6:13–15).

Stubbornness brings judgment because it is a sin against the Lord (8:13–17; see v.14). Jeremiah's knowledge of the catastrophic effects of the coming judgment brings pain and agony within his soul (vv.18–21). Judah has brought upon herself the terrible pain of divine judgment because of her refusal to acknowledge Yahweh as her King (v.19). The proverbial statement in v.20 indicates the hopelessness of the people who have rejected all opportunities presented to them for their salvation.

The prophet's anguish over the terribleness of the divine judgment on account of Judah's sin reaches its climax in 8:22–9:1. Even though judgment is at hand, Jeremiah declares that God is the ever-present Healer in whom is an abundance of mercy for the healing of sin-sick souls. Yet he is also aware of the bondage of his people to the power of sin, which prevents them from coming to God for their healing. The outcome is their tragic destruction and death. "It is not because there is a deficiency of grace, nor of the means of grace, that men are not saved . . . but few are saved, because *they* WILL NOT *come unto him* [Jesus Christ] *that they may have life*" (Clarke, 280). Jeremiah can do only one thing: weep bitterly for the lost. His heart is not hardened though his people have rejected his call for repentance (see Mt 23:37).

C. Judah's Depravity (9:2–21)

This section together with the previous oracle reveals a paradox. Judah's depravity is so widespread that he wishes no longer to remain as a part of this treacherous people (9:2). Everyone

in Judah is a "Jacob" (v.4), filled with deceit and falsehood. This depravity remains with them because they do not allow God's grace to transform them (see Hos 12:2–6; Ge 32:22–32). God's people, no matter how chosen and privileged, are no different from heathen nations when they refuse to acknowledge Yahweh as the Lord (vv.6, 9). Yahweh's decision is to refine this depraved nation through the painful process of desolation and destruction (v.7). The one who understands the cause of this divine action has wisdom (v.12; cf. 8:8–9).

Life in the land is secure only when the people are obedient and faithful to the One who is the Giver of the gift (the Sinai covenant requirement). The consequences of disobedience (stubbornness of heart) and unfaithfulness (idolatry) are expulsion, life among strangers, destruction, and death without regard for age (vv.13–16; 17–22).

The wisdom of God admonishes his people that they cannot boast about any of their own resources (wisdom, strength, or wealth) as the means of their salvation (9:23–24). They must reject their self-sufficiency and enter into a personal experience with Yahweh who demands kindness (*ḥeseḏ,* covenant loyalty), justice (*mišpāṭ,* covenant obligation), righteousness (*ṣᵉḏāqâ[h],* covenant conduct) from everyone on this earth. A Christian cannot boast about anything but "the surpassing greatness of knowing Christ Jesus" and "the righteousness that comes from God . . . by faith" (see Php 3:7–11).

Vv.25 and 26 fit with the theme of the preceding oracle. The scope of Yahweh's judgment is universal and upon everyone who is **uncircumcised in heart** (see 4:4). National or religious identity cannot save one from the judgment of God.

D. The Wisdom and Judgment of Yahweh (10:1–25)

God's people cannot formulate a theological system based on the **ways** and **customs** of surrounding cultures. The God of Israel and the gods of the world have nothing in common. The former is the source of wisdom; he is the true, living, and eternal King and God. The proper starting point of theology is the affirmation that Yahweh is the **maker of all things**. Refusal to acknowledge this truth about Yahweh would only lead to fraudulent beliefs and worship of idols (10:1–16; see also 51:15–19).

When leaders fail to respond and remain insensitive to the requirements of Yahweh, the outcome is destruction and scattering of the flock. Jeremiah, though he is the messenger of Yahweh's judgment, is sensitive to the distress of his people and regards it as his **sickness**, which he must endure (10:17–22).

Man is totally dependent on God's grace for his existence. Though man does not acknowledge this, Jeremiah pleads with God to extend his grace to those who are under judgment and to turn judgment into a corrective measure (10:23–25).

IV. THE COVENANT WITH YAHWEH IS BROKEN (11:1–15:21)

A covenant is a formal agreement between two parties that provides a proper basis for an ongoing relationship. Covenant-breaking is an act of unfaithfulness and is punishable. Israel has broken the Sinai covenant conditions; therefore, Yahweh's decision is to punish them. This theme is expressed here through prose sermons, poetic oracles, first-person speeches known as "confessions," symbolic actions, and biographical accounts.

God's covenant relationship with Israel has a historical basis: he is the one who saved them from their bondage in Egypt. His curse is upon those who do not acknowledge his grace at work in their lives (11:1–5). Yahweh's salvation is not a license for God's people to live in the **stubbornness of their evil hearts** (vv.6–8). Neither the intercession of Yahweh's spokesman nor rituals will save those who have abandoned their identity as people **called** by the grace of God to produce fruit worthy of their salvation (vv.9–17; see 2:3)

Yahweh's faithfulness to Jeremiah in the midst of a treacherous plot against his life is the theme of 11:18–23. God watches over his word as well as his spokesman (see 1:12). This crisis was perhaps the context for Jeremiah's complaint expressed in 12:1–4. The prosperity of the wicked leads him to think that God is partial to those who pay lip service to him. However, Yahweh challenges Jeremiah to use this and future crises in life to build up his character and strength (vv.5–6).

Yahweh's judgment is upon his **house,** which does not regard him as Lord (12:7–13). The nations are also under his judgment (v.14). However, God's wrath does not remain forever. He is determined to reach out to his people with love and compassion and to restore them. The day of Israel's restoration (from their foreign captivity) is the setting for the salvation of the Gentiles. Implied here is the charge to the restored Israel to become "a light for the Gentiles" (Isa 49:6). God's desire is to save all those who acknowledge his lordship. Obedience of the nations is the primary condition for the fulfillment of this eschatological promise (vv.15–17).

The message of Jeremiah's symbolic act (13:1–7) is stated in vv.8–11. The primary responsibility of God's people who are **bound** to him through a covenant relationship (**my people**) is to be Yahweh's **renown and praise and honor** (v.11) through their obedience and loyalty to him. The reasons for Yahweh's decision to remove the people of Judah from the place of their honor in the world are their pride (v.9), wickedness, refusal to obey God, propensity to follow the plans of their own hearts, and alliances with other gods (v.10).

Jeremiah reiterates the theme of judgment through the use of a popular proverb (13:12–14). The people of Judah are like empty **wineskins**, useless to God. They do not allow themselves to be filled with the Spirit that motivates them to be useful. Therefore, Yahweh intends to fill them with his wrathful spirit, a spirit of confusion and disillusionment, which would lead them to their destruction.

Pride is another cause of Judah's judgment (13:15–17). Pride prevents them from listening to Yahweh's voice and acknowledging him as the object of their praise and glory. Jeremiah warns that sinners cannot hope for salvation (light) when Yahweh brings his judgment (darkness) upon them. Jeremiah's agony over the disastrous consequence of Judah's pride is the same as in 9:1.

The lament over the royal family in 13:18–19 (most likely pronounced before they were taken to exile in 597 B.C.) is a challenge to show humility as the way of life for God's people. Humility of the leaders is an example for those who look up to them for guidance.

Jerusalem is addressed in 13:20–27. It is the leader among the cities of Judah. The coming judgment is the consequence of their sin, which is very much an inherent characteristic of their moral nature, like the spots on a leopard. They can do nothing whatsoever

to free themselves from the power of their sinful nature. But as Clarke notes, "What is impossible to man is possible to God" (p. 293). What makes it difficult or impossible to be changed is their "obstinate refusal of the grace of God" (p. 293). V.27 strongly conveys the willingness of Yahweh to cleanse his people and to set them free from their predicament (see RSV for a preferable reading of the awkward Hebrew idiom in v.27b).

Judah's dependence on other gods (**cisterns that cannot hold water**, 2:13) for their existence, and their outright rejection of Yahweh (**the spring of living water**, 2:13) leaves Yahweh with no other option but to punish them with drought (14:1–6; see Dt 28:23–24). When calamity strikes them, they will turn to their gods (**cisterns**) for help, but they will be disappointed. Yahweh alone is the hope of Judah (see vv.8, 22). Everyone and everything in the land will suffer the consequence of the sin of God's people.

Jeremiah's prayer of confession (14:7–9) is an example for the people to follow. Yahweh alone is the hope and Savior of Judah. He extends his help only when his people, who are called by his name, confess their sin and plead with him for mercy and forgiveness (see 2Ch 7:13–15). Yahweh indicts against his people (v.10), who are undisciplined in their commitment to him. He has no other choice but to reject those who have rejected him.

Yahweh's decision to bring judgment upon Judah is final. The injunction to Jeremiah (14:11; see also 7:16; 11:14; 15:1) implies that unrepentant sinners cannot escape from Yahweh's final judgment through the prayer of the righteous. This is not an injunction against intercessory prayer aimed to elicit penitence and salvation. At this last moment, whatever actions the people may take also have no use (v.12). Such actions are prompted by a sudden fear of judgment and not by a sincere desire to be restored to God.

Jeremiah objects to this injunction with the claim that the people are the victims of theological seduction by those who preach a shallow theology of God's grace (14:13). Yahweh's response (vv.14–16) is an indictment against such preachers who are not divinely appointed communicators of the truth. They promote a theology that has its origin in their own mind and is falsehood therefore. The God of peace is also the God of judgment. Yahweh's judgment is upon both the seducers and the seduced.

The prophet again expresses agony over the severe calamities that are about to come upon the land (14:17–18; see 9:1; 13:17). The nation is called a **virgin**—one who has the potential to become a wife and a mother. She faces the threat of destruction by famine and enemy attack. The religious leaders (false prophets and priests) do not recognize the seriousness of divine judgment, and they remain unconcerned (see RSV for a preferable reading of v.18b).

The prophet offers to his audience a model prayer that contains a confession of the sins of the present as well as of the past generations (14:19–22). Peace (*šālôm*) shall come to Zion only when genuine repentance characterizes Yahweh's people. Their hope rests on Yahweh's faithfulness to his covenant and on their acknowledgment of him as their God.

God's judgment against sinners, when it is ready to be carried out, cannot be averted by the intercessory prayer of the righteous (15:1–4). At this late moment, even Moses and Samuel (Israel's intercessors par excel-

lence) would find it impossible to persuade Yahweh to be merciful to those who are destined to death and destruction. No one will have compassion for those who are rejected by Yahweh because of their persistent backsliding (vv.5–9).

Jer 15:10–21 is another "confession" of Jeremiah. Consult Thompson's *Jeremiah* (pp. 392–93) for a treatment of the textual difficulty in vv.11–12. Vv.13–14 perhaps belong to ch. 17 (see 17:3–4).

Yahweh's faithful spokesman is under the curse of the entire population. This rejection is painful and unbearable. Moreover, rejection leads to self-pity (15:10), hatred (v.15), and self-righteousness (vv.16–17). Jeremiah cannot help but question the genuineness of his whole religious experience, which began with his birth. What was once a source of his joy is now the cause of his pain. His despondency drives him to regard himself as a victim of deception by his God who seems to be aloof from him.

Yahweh's response to his spokesman (15:19–21) is a reminder of the harsh reality that a true prophet is without honor among his people (see Mt 13:57). Yet he must remain true to his calling and continue to speak Yahweh's word. This is what makes him truly an honorable person. Jeremiah is called here to repent of self-centeredness, which prompted him briefly to lose sight of his task. **"I am with you"** is the divine assurance to the one who experiences spiritual crisis. This promise alone is the real source of the inner strength that keeps persons of God faithful to their calling.

V. SIN, JUDGMENT, AND GRACE (16:1–17:27)

Death, disaster, and an end to every joyous occasion are to be expected when Yahweh withdraws his grace from his people (16:1–13). Even Jeremiah cannot enjoy a normal family life. He cannot extend to his people any feelings that Yahweh does not have for them. Yahweh no longer looks at his people with favor, for they possess an evil heart, which was also found in their fathers. Sin, which corrupted the previous generation, is found in the present generation with a greater degree of perversity.

Judgment is not Yahweh's last word. His people hear the word of hope even in the midst of judgment (16:14–15). Yahweh's love compels him to restore the nation from the land of their exile. This promise of a new exodus experience (see 23:7–8; 31:8–9) clearly attests to the infinite grace of God available even to the most defiant sinner.

God's judgment upon sinners is a present reality (16:16–18). No sin or sinner is hidden from the scrutiny of God. Neither height nor depth can provide a sinner an escape from the wrath of God (see 4:27–29).

A universal eschatology of salvation is expressed in 16:19–21. Gentiles will abandon their idolatry and acknowledge Yahweh as the true God. V.19 may be viewed as a "prediction of the *calling of the Gentiles* by the Gospel of Christ" (Clarke, 300). What prompts Jeremiah to express this confidence is his own experience of Yahweh as the source of his strength and hope (v.19 reflects a faith found in several psalms). Yahweh himself, through his power and might, will teach the Gentiles to acknowledge his lordship over them.

Judah's present existence as God's people is not governed by Yahweh's will revealed to them (on the tablets of stone), rather by the will of their own heart, which is deeply corrupted by the power of sin (17:1–4). Their pagan religious practices, known even to their children, attest to this moral depravity. Judah must pay the price for their sin. The wages of sin is destruction and deportation.

Jeremiah reiterates the wiseman's emphasis on the two ways of life (17:5–8; see Ps 1). The way of the wicked is cursed and hopeless because he relies on his own resources. The way of the righteous is blessed and prosperous because he trusts in Yahweh's resources for his life.

Jeremiah's understanding of the individual (17:9–11) is important to Wesleyan theology. The primary emphasis of this text is on the total corruption of humankind. The **heart** and kidneys (**mind**, NIV) represent the center of human thoughts, emotions, will, and actions. Deceitfulness ('*aqōb* or "Jacob"; see also 9:4) is the characteristic of human beings. Wesley comments: "There is nothing so false and deceitful as the heart of man; deceitful in its apprehensions of things, in the hopes and promises which it nourishes, in the assurances that it gives us . . . (p. 2173). The constant yearning of the heart is to "gratify its propensities to pride, ambition, evil desire, and corruption of all kinds" (Clarke, 302). NIV **beyond cure** also refers to the feebleness of the heart. It is so corrupt that even its owner does not comprehend it (Wesley, Clarke). This "worst enemy of the fallen creature" (Clarke), though concealed from others, cannot escape the scrutiny of Yahweh. Though the wicked may seem to prosper for the moment, ultimately the righteous judgment of Yahweh would bring them to their destruction.

Yahweh is the eternal hope for all those who seek his presence (17:12–13). The destiny of those who reject him, who is the true and everlasting source of human existence (**the spring**

of living water, see also 2:13) is already determined.

Jeremiah's lament (17:14–18) is similar to the individual laments of the oppressed in the Psalms. Yahweh is the Healer, the Savior, and the object of Jeremiah's praise. Jeremiah's opponents demand an immediate fulfillment of Yahweh's word. He is convinced of his own faithfulness as shepherd over the flock of Yahweh. The rest is with Yahweh who will vindicate his faithful servant and bring judgment against his enemies.

The primary emphasis of 17:19–27 is on the conditional nature of divine judgment. Judah is offered an opportunity to repent and to make a concerted effort to obey the covenant requirements. Continuation of their existence is promised as a reward for obedience. The consequence of disobedience is also repeated. The life or death choice is thus given to the nation. The fourth commandment is singled out here because this commandment, above all others, calls for a collective and visible expression of obedience by the nation as a whole.

VI. YAHWEH'S SOVEREIGNTY (18:1–20:18)

It is possible that these chapters belong together. Yahweh's sovereignty over Judah and over the life of the prophet is the major theme that connects the various oracles together.

The message that Jeremiah receives (18:5–12) at the potter's house contains the theology of 18:1–12. Vv.2–4 provide us with the illustration of "the free agency of man" and "the goodness and supremacy of God" over Israel and the nations (Clarke, 304). Corruption is the inherent characteristic of all humankind. It is the corruption of the clay (i.e., the moral corruption of Israel) that caused the pot to be marred

(v.4a). The reshaping of the clay to another pot (v.4b), rather than discarding it as worthless to the potter, shows Yahweh's willingness to extend grace to those who are under his judgment (v.6). The offer of grace is made to all who repent of their sins and demonstrate their willingness to conform to his will (vv.7–8). The universality of God's saving grace is clearly evident here. Those who enjoy his salvation, if they become corrupt again, face the judgment of God (vv.9–10). Obedience is the necessary condition, not only for the initial experience of salvation, but also for its continued enjoyment.

Judgment is upon the covenant people who failed to show constancy and dependability in their relationship with Yahweh (18:13–17). These are qualities found in nature, even in the most unlikely places (v.14). Judah's forgetfulness of their God is a horrible sin (see 2:9–13). On the day of judgment, those who reject God cannot expect to experience anything but rejection by Yahweh.

In 18:18 the people plot to slander Jeremiah as a false prophet. Those who trust the words of corrupt, complacent, and irresponsible religious leaders regard Yahweh's true spokesman as an obstacle that should be removed. Jeremiah makes another "confession" in 18:19–23. His prayer for the destruction of his enemies should be evaluated in the light of other admonitions that call for a more honorable way to treat one's enemy (Pr 25:21–22; see Mt 5:38–48; Ro 12:19ff.).

Yahweh's determination to destroy Jerusalem is the direct consequence of the blatant sins of its inhabitants (19:1–13). The city and its people are like a clay jar, designed and fashioned by a potter. The potter (Yahweh) finds his vessel unusable for any purpose.

Therefore he has no other choice but to destroy it irreparably. An apostate people is a useless people for God. The divine decision is to bring them to their end. The place of worship (Jerusalem) that they have abandoned will be destroyed; the place of worship that they have chosen for themselves (the valley of Ben Hinnom) will become their burial ground.

Yahweh's spokesman is not shaken by disciplinary action taken by leaders of the established religion (19:14–20:6). His call is to preach judgment and that he must preach regardless of what others may think or what actions may be taken against him. He is convinced that in the end the false leaders will suffer shame for corrupting and lying to the people.

The man of God, however, is also a human being who cannot escape his own emotions and feelings (20:7–12). His unpopularity compels him to think that his call was a deception used by God to exercise his sovereign will over his feeble nature (v.7). At the same time, he is also aware of the terrible consequences of his refusal to speak Yahweh's word. Even in this darkest hour he is certain that Yahweh is his defender, who will not abandon those who commit their cause to him. The man of God in conflict can do only one thing—offer his praises to Yahweh who defends and sustains his servants with his grace (v.13).

The lament of Jeremiah in 20:14–18 is much like Job's lament (Job 3). He feels nothing but anger toward God and his fellow human beings. It is a terrible task to be a messenger of doom. He must experience the painfulness of the divine wrath twice—when the word comes to him initially and when the word is realized in the history of his nation. The divine call came to Jeremiah at his birth. That moment is no longer a joyous occasion; his life is filled with trouble, sorrow, and shame. Though no divine response to this lament is forthcoming, the preceding hymn of praise suggests to us that in this loneliest hour, Yahweh did not abandon his faithful servant to despair and defeat.

VII. UNGODLY KINGS AND LEADERS (21:1–23:40)

This section contains two parts. The first part consists of oracles directed against the kings who have ruled Judah in the final days of her history (21:1–23:8). The second part consists of Jeremiah's indictment against those who have illegitimately assumed the prophetic role for their own profit (23:9–40).

The events of 588 B.C. constitute the historical context of 21:1–10. (See other commentaries for details.) Zedekiah is a prime example of those who practice foxhole religion. His message to Jeremiah (v.2) reflects his thinking that God can be manipulated with a cry for help in the time of trouble. His perception of Jeremiah is also the same. Yahweh's response to those under his judgment reveals a fundamental theological principle (vv.8–10; see also Dt 30:15–20). Submission to God, even in the midst of strange and unfavorable circumstances, will lead to life. The Babylonians are executing the divine judgment; therefore submission to the Babylonians is submission to the will of God. This is the way of life. Resistance to the Babylonians, on the other hand, is resistance to the will of God. Death is the destiny of those who choose the path of resistance.

Yahweh's judgment is upon the royal house that he has chosen as an everlasting dynasty (21:11–14; 22:1–5; 22:6–30). The Davidic kings have failed to promote justice and righteousness and to guarantee the rights of the alien, the orphan, the widow, and the innocent. The contrast between Jehoiakim and Josiah, his father (22:15–17), includes a discussion of true religion (**"what it means to know me,"** v.16). The essential quality of a leader is his hunger and thirst for justice and righteousness for all and his particular care for the poor and the needy.

Yahweh's own personal involvement in the restoration of the remnant is the theme of 23:1–4. The shepherds are under judgment because they failed to tend and care for the flock of Yahweh. Yahweh's plan is to restore and to care for the lost and the scattered of his flock. This is the duty of good and faithful shepherds. Moreover, he would place this **remnant** under the leadership of faithful and caring shepherds. This eschatological era of salvation (**The days are coming**) will be ruled by a **righteous branch**, a wise and just king from the house of David who will truly demonstrate the righteousness of Yahweh (vv.5–6; see Jn 10:1–18). The precise meaning of the name **"The Lord Our Righteousness"** is uncertain. (Consult Clarke's commentary for a detailed discussion of this phrase.) In contrast to Zedekiah who failed to live by the symbolic meaning of his name ("My righteousness is Yahweh"), the eschatological community will put their trust in Yahweh as the source of their righteousness and salvation. The restoration of Yahweh's flock from their worldwide dispersion will be far greater in magnitude than the exodus experience from Egypt (vv.7–8; see Isa 43:15–21). The restored community will live in the reality of this new exodus experience and personal salvation.

Jeremiah's courage as Yahweh's true spokesman is clearly evident in his outspokenness against those who have made false claims about their prophetic task and the priests who have abused their office. In 23:9–40 are five separate oracles connected by a common theme, namely, the illegitimacy of false prophets and their impending doom (vv.9–12, 13–15, 16–22, 23–32, 33–40).

Jeremiah is outraged at the dishonor he suffers because of his faithfulness to Yahweh's word while the false prophets who are adulterers, wicked, and godless enjoy popularity throughout the land, even in the Jerusalem temple (23:9–11). These prophets have no true loyalty to Yahweh (v.13) and no sense of right or wrong (v.14). Their primary concern is to please their audience with words of hope, prosperity, and peace, the source of which is their own dreams and visions (vv.16–17, 25–28). They have no divinely given authority (vv.18, 21). They are under the severe judgment of Yahweh (vv.12, 15, 19–21, 30–32, 39–40).

Prophets who are commissioned by Yahweh speak his words truthfully and forcefully because they listen to him when he speaks to them (23:22). The visions of the false prophets are like straw, useless and without any value. Yahweh's word has content; like grain, it has worth; like fire, it burns; like a hammer, it has power to break. In the end, only the genuinely spoken words of Yahweh have power to produce any life-transforming changes in the heart of stubborn sinners (vv.28–29).

The emphasis of 23:23 in Hebrew seems to be on the transcendence of God, though the NIV implies both immanence and transcendence. False prophets treat him as if he is limited in power and presence. There is no escape for them in heaven or on earth from the wrath of God (v.24).

VIII. TO BUILD AND TO PLANT (24:1–10)

The historical background of this vision is clear (597 B.C.). The vision is described in a typical question-answer style (see 1:11–16; Am 7:1–9; 8:1–3).

Jeremiah's description of those who were deported to Babylon in 597 B.C. as **good** does not necessarily mean that they were of superior moral quality. Most likely **good** and **bad** are terms used here comparatively to describe the spiritual response of those who are under Yahweh's judgment. This vision introduces a new theological perspective about the Promised Land. Yahweh's future relationship with those who are under his judgment is not determined by the land of their existence. Life in the land does not mean acceptance by Yahweh. Likewise, exile does not mean rejection by Yahweh. Those who **return to me** [Yahweh] **with all their heart** (*šûḇ*, v.7) are given hope for the continued relationship with God. They will receive the gift of an obedient heart, which in turn will enable them to enter into a covenantal relationship (*yāḏaʿ*, **"know"**) with Yahweh. Those who are righteous in their own thinking, because they still live in the land, are given no hope for their future (vv.8–10).

IX. GOD'S WRATH IS ON THE WICKED (25:1–38)

Consult other commentaries for a discussion of the difference in the order of arrangement between the Hebrew text (MT) and the Greek version (LXX), which commences with 25:14. It is possible that 25:1–14 is a summary statement of the first twenty-three years of Jeremiah's messages (627–605 B.C.). **"This book"** (v.13) might very well be a reference to the scroll that Baruch copied after the original scroll

was destroyed by King Jehoiakim (see 36:1–26). It is commonly held that the contents of chs. 1–25 constitute the above-mentioned scroll.

The true measure of a preacher's success lies in his commitment to preach the word regardless of its outcome. For twenty-three years Judah has refused to accept Jeremiah or his message from Yahweh (25:1–3). Judah's apostasy through idolatry has become for them a way of life (vv.4–7). Yahweh's patience is exhausted (v.8–11). The reference to Nebuchadnezzer as **"my servant"** (v.9) shows Yahweh's sovereignty over the kingdoms and sovereign powers of this world. Yahweh decides to punish those who were called to be his servants in the world. Historical events will teach Judah the painful lesson that destruction is the fate of those who reject Yahweh's sovereignty.

Yahweh's wrath is also upon the ungodly nations, though they are now instruments of his judgment against Judah (vv.12–29). **Seventy years** in v.12 most likely is a reference to the totality and the completeness of Judah's judgment. The kingdoms of this world cannot escape from drinking the cup of Yahweh's wrath. His decision to bring judgment upon his own people and his city (v.29) is cited here as concrete proof of the fact that he is an impartial Judge who does not tolerate wickedness in any form found anywhere in his creation.

The language of 25:30–38 contains an apocalyptic tone. The intensity of Yahweh's wrath against the wickedness of human beings is vividly expressed through the language of theophany (**roar, shout, storm**) and law suit (**bring charges**). **From one end of the earth to the other** he will execute his judgment and bring the wicked to their ultimate ruin. The leaders are the primary objects of Yahweh's wrath, from which they cannot escape. Their distress will be greater because they will witness the destruction of their flock to whom they have promised prosperity and peace.

X. JEREMIAH UNDER TRIAL (26:1–24)

Ch. 26 is a biographical account of Jeremiah. Most scholars think that 26:2–6 is a summary of Jeremiah's temple sermon (see ch. 7), which serves as an introduction to the narrative that follows (vv.7–24). Others regard 26:2–6 as the original sermon. Consult other commentaries for a discussion of Jeremiah's temple sermon.

Jeremiah's sermon (26:1–6) stresses the need to preach relentlessly to those who practice religion without acknowledging that they must repent of their evil. Yahweh is always hopeful that his word might bring about the repentance of sinners. He desires to cancel his judgment against them. It is this wish that compels him to send his messengers again and again with urgency to proclaim his law to his people. The house of God, which does not respond to the display of Yahweh's grace, is on the path to destruction.

Jeremiah encountered opposition because of his faithful preaching and his boldness to attack a shallow theology promoted by the popular leaders (26:7–11). Jeremiah's strong conviction that he was Yahweh's spokesman (**"The LORD sent me to prophesy"**) enabled him to face his judges without fear (vv.12–15). Though he was at the mercy and goodwill of these men, his goal was to lead them to conviction and conversion (**reform your ways**).

Boldness was a characteristic of Israel's prophets (26:16–19). The prophetic tradition, though it was strongly influenced by the Zion theology, re-

fused to accept a blind belief in the inviolability of the temple and the city. The emphasis here is also on the conditional character of Yahweh's threat of punishment; he is not a static and capricious deity but a gracious God who extends mercy to sinners who **fear the LORD and seek his favor** (v.19). The parenthetical story of Uriah shows that the threat against Jeremiah's life was real and that his escape was providential (vv.20–24).

XI. THE CONTROVERSY OVER THE BABYLONIAN YOKE (27:1–28:17)

Consult other commentaries for a discussion of the textual problem of 27:1 and the probable date of this account. This narrative has two sections: (1) Jeremiah's wearing a wooden yoke to symbolize the coming Babylonian captivity and the subsequent message to King Zedekiah (vv.1–22), and (2) his confrontation with Hananiah, the false prophet who has attempted to discredit Jeremiah's message (28:1–17).

Yahweh the Creator is also the sovereign Lord of history (27:1–17). Therefore, submission to Babylon is in a real sense submission to Yahweh's will; rebellion against Babylon, on the other hand, is rebellion against Yahweh. Those who proclaim a contrary message are not authentic prophets. Anyone who proclaims peace to a sinful generation cannot be accepted as a true prophet (28:5–9). Authentic prophets speak judgment and not peace to sinners. The clear basis for the recognition of a true prophet is the fulfillment of his words, which he claims to have come from Yahweh. The fulfillment of the word of judgment against Hananiah (vv.15–17) shows that Jeremiah was indeed a true prophet (Dt 18:20–22).

XII. JEREMIAH'S MESSAGE TO THE EXILED JUDEANS (29:1–32)

The precise date of this letter is not known. The historical reference in 29:2 places the letter after 597 B.C. The message of Jeremiah's letter is clear. The exiled community, though under judgment, must not give up hope. The time of judgment is also a time for them to build and to plant themselves among the heathen and to live as witnesses of God's grace. Even in the midst of judgment, God does not relieve his people of their responsibility to become a "light for the Gentiles" (Isa 49:6). God's people must pray for their enemies, because he is concerned with their *šālôm* (v.7), the wholeness that would come when they acknowledge God as the sovereign ruler of the world.

God has set a time for the punishment of the exiles; when that set time is completed, he will return to them with his **gracious promise**. Judgment is not the last word God proclaims to the sinners. With his grace he reaches out to them to give them a **hope and a future**. This promise is, however, conditional. In order to enjoy the benefits of God's grace, sinners must **call upon** him, and **seek** him with all their heart (29:10–14).

XIII. THE BOOK OF CONSOLATION (CHS. 30–33)

Most scholars regard chs. 30–33 as a distinct section within the book of Jeremiah. The future restoration of Israel is the primary theme of this section. (For an understanding of the debate over the authenticity and date of these oracles, see Thompson, 551–53.)

The opening statements (30:1–3) make clear the eschatological character of this section. The promise of restoration is addressed to all Israel.

Before Israel can experience the grace of salvation, she must endure distress and pain **like a woman in labor** on **that day** of her discipline through God's righteous judgment (30:4–11). This day of judgment will be followed by yet another day (**"in that day,"** v.8) in which the nation will again be **saved** from those who rule over them.

Though no one will care for Israel, Yahweh will care for her and heal her wounds (30:12–17). The One who strikes her with incurable wounds because of her many sins is also her Healer (see also 33:6). **"Because you are called an outcast"** (v.17) is the reason the Healer will act in grace. Yahweh is the champion of the poor, the afflicted, and the despised in the world.

Restored Israel will experience the full blessings of restoration (30:18–20; see also 31:1–14; 33:10–13). The mood of the restored community will be the same as that of Israel when they found Yahweh's **favor** (*ḥēn*), **love** (*'aḥᵃbâ[h]*), and **loving-kindness** (*ḥeseḏ*) during their exodus from Egypt and in the days of wilderness wanderings (31:2–6). Their ruler, by risking death, will approach Yahweh's presence to establish a covenant relationship between Yahweh and his people (30:21–22). This priestly Mediator and King will accomplish the goal of the old covenant (see v.22). The Davidic ruler (**a righteous branch**) and the Levitical priests play a significant role in Jeremiah's eschatology (see 33:14–26).

The description of the New Exodus (31:7–14; see also Isa 40:3–5, 11; 41:18–20; et al.) contains several references to Yahweh's direct involvement to **ransom** and **redeem** (v.11) his people. **"Because I am Israel's father ... so there is hope for your future"** is Yahweh's word of grace to those who weep and lament over their destruction (vv.9, 17). The Redeemer is a father who loves his prodigal son (v.20). The way of their return will be a **highway** (see Isa 40:3). New conditions will be brought into existence by the Creator God who has the power to create (*bārā'*) things that do not exist (vv.21–22). Yahweh's ultimate goal is to dwell among his people as the Righteous and Holy One, and to **refresh the weary and satisfy the faint** (vv.23–25).

The re-creation and reestablishment of Israel as an eschatological community under the watchful eyes of Yahweh is the theme of 31:27–28. Members of the restored community will live with a greater sense of their individual responsibility to make choices that will lead to their own life or death (vv.29–30; see Eze 18).

Once in their history of salvation, Yahweh revealed to Israel his will through his covenant with them at Sinai (Ex 19–24). Jer 31:31–34 contains Yahweh's promise of a new covenant relationship with those who would be restored after their judgment for breaking the old covenant. Wesley comments, "It is not called the new covenant, because it was as the substance new . . . but because it was revealed after a new manner. . . . It was likewise new in regard of the efficacy of the spirit attending it. . ." (p. 2209). Yahweh's commitment is to be a gracious and faithful God to a people who by their own very nature and will are incapable of obeying him. The goal of this covenant is the same as that of the old covenant (**"I will be their God, and they will be my people,"** v.33). The newness of this covenant is in that the inner being (**"in their minds . . . on their hearts"**) will become the depository of Yahweh's instruction (*tôrâ[h]*). Whereas the law of the old covenant directs the people of God to

their duty, the Gospel "brings the grace of regeneration by which the heart is changed, and enabled for duty" (Wesley, 2209). Yahweh's promise includes a thorough cleansing of the heart (33:8; **circumcise**, Dt 30:6) that is corrupted by sin (17:1), and the gift of **singleness of heart and action** (32:39–40). The heart cleansed of sin will instinctively and without pressure from any external source yearn to acknowledge Yahweh's sovereign lordship (**"know the LORD,"** 31:34; see Dt 6:4–5). The new covenant also offers to those who enter into a personal relationship with God the assurance of his total forgiveness of their sins.

The recipients of the new covenant are guaranteed their national existence by the Creator who established the laws of nature (31:35–37). There is no suggestion of the merits of the nation here. Emphasis is on the dependability and eternality of God's word to an undeserving nation. His goal is not only to establish a new covenant, but also to rebuild his city with new measurements as a New Jerusalem (vv.38–40; see Eze 40–48).

"Faith is being sure of what we hope for" (Heb 11:1) finds a practical application in Jer 32. His purchase of the land was not just a courageous act; it was a demonstration of his faith that **nothing is too hard** for Yahweh and that he is able to establish order and life in the midst of chaos and lifelessness (32:15, 17). **"Is anything too hard for me?"** (v.27) is Yahweh's response to Jeremiah.

XIV. EVENTS BEFORE THE FALL OF JERUSALEM (CHS. 34–38)

Faithfulness to the covenant with Yahweh is the theme here. A covenant promise cannot be broken because it is an oath taken before Yahweh (34:15).

A violation of the covenant, therefore, is an outright disregard for the sacredness of the divine name. Zedekiah and the citizens of Jerusalem renewed the Sinai covenant and demonstrated their repentance during the siege of the city by Babylon only to break it when the crisis was over. This was typical of the unfaithfulness that was a characteristic of Israel for many generations. Therefore they are under the curse of the covenant. In ch. 35 Jeremiah contrasts the unfaithfulness of the nation with the faithfulness of the Rechabites to the command of their ancestor Jonadab (v.14). The Rechabites' refusal to yield to any pressure from others and to compromise their ideals is a lesson from which Judah must learn the meaning of fidelity to their covenant obligation to Yahweh. **Because they obey their forefather's command** (v.14) is the reason for the blessing pronounced upon the Rechabites (v.19).

Consult other commentaries on the significance of ch. 36 to our understanding of the composition of the book of Jeremiah. The primary goal of God's spoken and written word is to lead each listener to repentance, which is a necessary condition for the experience of forgiveness by him (36:3; see also 35:15). On a publicly declared day of fast, a day set aside for prayer and penitence, King Jehoiakim was not only unmoved but also acted in defiance of Yahweh's written word, which was read to him on such a solemn occasion (vv.9, 22–25). Rejection of Yahweh's word is rejection of his sovereign authority. Judgment is the final word upon the house of Jehoiakim who refused to listen to the spoken and the written word of Yahweh (vv.30–31).

Chs. 37 and 38 contrast Jeremiah with King Zedekiah. Jeremiah is Yahweh's spokesman, but Zedekiah has not **paid any attention to the words the LORD has spoken** (37:2). Zedekiah is indirect in his approach to Jeremiah with the request to pray on behalf of the nation, but Jeremiah is direct and straightforward in declaring the coming catastrophe (vv.3–10). Zedekiah is weak, indecisive, and fearful of his court officials, but Jeremiah, though he is falsely accused, mistreated, and imprisoned, is firm and unafraid to speak to the king about his fate (vv.11–17; 38:1–6; 14–28). Jeremiah understands clearly what is morally right and wrong, but Zedekiah lacks a clear perception of right and wrong (37:18; 38:5). Ironically, Zedekiah ("Yahweh is my righteousness") learns a lesson on righteousness by Ebed-Melech, a gentile servant of the court (38:1–13). Jeremiah exemplifies a tenacious faith in God. Zedekiah, though he seeks to learn God's plan for Judah, ends up rejecting not only the prophetic counsel, but also the promise of life given to him (a special grace) in the final hour of Judah's history (vv.17–23). Zedekiah demands that Jeremiah disclose everything that he received through revelation (37:14), yet to protect his own personal interest he charges the prophet not to reveal the whole content of his conversation to the court officials (vv.24–27). Jeremiah yields to the wishes of the king despite his protest that the king will not listen (v.15), and he remains true to his prophetic task as well as to his duty to the king. Clarke notes that the king was asking Jeremiah to tell "the truth, and nothing but the truth, but not the whole truth" and that Jeremiah was "most certainly not obliged to relate any thing" other than "what was necessary" to these officials (pp. 358–59).

XV. THE FALL OF JERUSALEM AND OTHER RELATED EVENTS (CHS. 39–44)

The account of the fall of Jerusalem to the army of Nebuchadnezzer (ch. 39) includes a graphic description of the tragic fate of Zedekiah who refused to listen to the prophetic word. At the same time, the Babylonian king, the enemy of all Judeans, extended cordial treatment to Jeremiah (v.12). This theme of the reward for the faithful is further illustrated in 39:15–18. Ebed-Melech, the Gentile, received the promise of salvation in the midst of Yahweh's judgment of his chosen nation. The basis of his salvation is clear: **"I will save you . . . because you trust in me"** (v.18). Peter's words remind us that "God does not show favoritism but accepts men from every nation who fear him and do what is right" as the message of the Gospel of "Jesus Christ, who is Lord of all" (Acts 10:34–36).

Even the pagans knew that the destruction of Jerusalem was **decreed** and carried out by Yahweh **just as he said he would** (40:2–3). Judgment disclosed not only Yahweh's sovereignty but also the sinfulness and disobedience of the people of God (v.3). What the people of God have refused to acknowledge is made public through historical events. Again, the Babylonians recognized Jeremiah as an authentic spokesman of Yahweh and treated him with respect and honor, which was denied to him by his own countrymen (see Mt 13:57).

Jer 40:7–43:7 describes the disobedience of **the poorest in the land** who were left in Judah by Babylon. Babylon left them in the land because they were not a threat to Babylon. Theologically speaking, Yahweh allowed them to remain in the land because they played no part in the disobedience of the ruling and the wealthy citizens of Jerusalem that led to the destruction of the city and the captivity of Judah. But this **remnant** too cannot have a future without demonstrating their obedience and dependence on Yahweh.

Gedaliah's plan was to bring stability through servitude to the Babylonians (40:9–10). The fact that he was killed by one of his trusted men shows the element of greed and treachery that continued to exist even in the midst of the calamity that came upon the whole nation. Out of fear and anxiety, the loyalists approached Jeremiah for his counsel (42:2–3) and promised to obey Yahweh's word **whether it is favorable or unfavorable** (vv.5–6). It is apparent from their later response that they were simply seeking Yahweh's approval of what they had already decided to do, namely, to escape to Egypt. Jeremiah spoke to them of Yahweh's plan to **build** and to **plant** them in their own land (v.10). They do not need to live in fear of the king of Babylon because Yahweh is with them to **save** and **deliver** them. They are the objects of Yahweh's compassion; therefore their enemy also will have compassion on them and restore them in their land (vv.11–12). The consequence of their disobedience and decision to abandon the Promised Land will be disastrous. Yahweh's judgment will follow them into the land of Egypt where they hope to find peace and security (vv.13–22). Even though the people promise to obey Yahweh's word, they regard Yahweh's messenger as a liar and a traitor (43:1–7). Self-centeredness and lack of trust in God continue to exist even among those who have been spared of destruction. They seek God's will, but their intention is to follow their own will.

Jer 43:8–44:30 contains a series of oracles addressed to the Jews who have settled down in Egypt. Those who have escaped the power of Babylon will soon find themselves surrounded by their enemy in the land of their refuge (43:8–13). Death is the destiny of those (1) who lack humility before Yahweh, (2) who are disrespectful and disobedient to his law, and (3) who think that their idolatry will lead them to peace and prosperity (44:10, 15–18). Yahweh is **watching over** the Jews in Egypt, not to protect them, but to carry out his judgment upon them (v.27).

XVI. A MESSAGE TO BARUCH (CH. 45)

Baruch, Jeremiah's trusted friend and scribe, is in agony because he is aware of the reality of the coming judgment, the distress of which will affect even the faithful like himself (45:3). Yahweh's word to him through Jeremiah implies that Yahweh also is in pain because what he plans to **uproot** is what he has **planted** (v.4). When Yahweh executes his judgment, it is not a time for the faithful to **seek great things** for themselves or to worry about their own lives. Yahweh's command, **"Seek them not,"** conversely is a call to "seek first his kingdom and his righteousness" (v.5; cf. Mt 6:33). The only reward Yahweh promises to Baruch is the preservation of his **life** in the midst of death and destruction of the wicked (v.5), which indeed is the greatest gift of God to those who are faithful to him.

XVII. ORACLES AGAINST THE NATIONS (CHS. 46–51)

Jeremiah's oracles addressed to the nations are similar to those found in Isaiah, Ezekiel, Amos, Obadiah, and Nahum. See other commentaries for a discussion of the authenticity of the material in this section and the different order of the arrangement of these chapters in the Septuagint.

Yahweh's sovereignty over his own chosen people and over all the nations of the world is an important theological claim of the prophets of Israel. He is the Creator and the Lord of all nations (51:15–19). He is incomparable; no one can successfully challenge his authority (50:44). The primary sin of the nations is their refusal to acknowledge this truth about the God of Israel and their worship of objects that have no life in them (51:17–18). Yahweh is a holy God, and judgment is upon those who defy his authority over them (48:26, 42; 51:29).

Though nations are instruments of his judgment against his chosen people, they themselves are under the righteous judgment of Yahweh, the God of Israel (51:6–8, 20–24). In addition to their idolatry, the nations are proud and arrogant (46:8; 48:29; 49:4; 49:16; 50:31–32); they trust in their idols, kings, and in their own resources (46:25–26; 48:7; 49:4); they have ridiculed and destroyed Israel (48:27; 51:49). The day of their judgment is the day of Yahweh's vengeance on his enemies (46:7–10). The nations and their idols will be punished (46:25; 48:7; 50:2; 51:44, 47, 52). They are also given the promise of their future restoration (46:26; 48:47; 49:6, 39). It is possible that Jeremiah anticipated the eschatological restoration of the nations in conjunction with Yahweh's plan to forgive the sins of Israel and to bring them back to Zion to establish with them **an everlasting covenant** (50:4–7, 20). The day of Israel's restoration will also be a day of restoration of her enemies.

XVIII. HISTORICAL APPENDIX (CH. 52)

The historical appendix formally concludes the book, though the words and deeds of Jeremiah end with 51:64. This historical section, for the most part, is a reiteration of the events narrated in 2Ki 24:18–25:30. This chapter accomplishes three goals: first, it testifies to the authenticity of Jeremiah as a true prophet and to the truthfulness and the power of the prophetic word. Second, the fall of Jerusalem, the destruction of the temple, and the deportation of the Jews are presented here as the consequence of Yahweh's anger (52:3). Third, the concluding report about the release of King Jehoiachin from prison (52:31–34) gives a clear hint that the promise of the restoration of the exiled Jews in Babylon is about to be fulfilled. It is only fitting that this book, which begins with a word of judgment (1:14–16), end with a note of hope to those who experience God's judgment. After all, the ultimate goal of the prophetic word is to announce to those who live in despair the reality of God's grace, which offers to them a future and a hope. This is the good news we find in the book of Jeremiah.

BIBLIOGRAPHY

Consult Robert P. Carroll's commentary on Jeremiah for an extensive bibliography. The bibliography that follows contains only those works cited in this work.

Bright, J. *Jeremiah*. AB. Garden City, N.Y.: Doubleday, 1965.

Carroll, R. P. *Jeremiah*. Philadelphia: Westminster, 1986.

Clarke, A. *A Commentary and Critical Notes: The Old Testament*. Vol. 4. New York: Carlton and Porter, n.d.

Thompson, J. A. *The Book of Jeremiah*. Grand Rapids: Eerdmans, 1980.

Wesley, J. *Explanatory Notes Upon the Old Testament*. Bristol: William Pine. Reprinted by Schmul Publishers, Salem, Ohio, 1975.

LAMENTATIONS
Alexander Varughese

INTRODUCTION

I. TITLE AND CANONICAL PLACEMENT

The book of Lamentations begins with the word 'êḵāh ("Ah, how!"), a typical expression of lament, in the Hebrew text. Since the book originally had no title, the opening word 'êḵāh became its title in the Hebrew Bible. The title conveys the nature of its contents. It reminds the reader that this book contains sorrowful words about the sudden, tragic, and untimely destruction of someone who was renowned and held in high esteem by others. Such funeral songs were a part of the religious and literary tradition of ancient Israel (see 2Sa 1:17–27; Am 5:1–2; Eze 19:1–14; 26:17–18; 27:1–36; 28:11–19). The Jewish tradition sometimes referred to this book as qînôṯ ("lamentations"). The book has the title Threnoi ("wailings") in the Septuagint translation. The English title comes from the word *lamentationes*, part of the title in the Latin translation (Vulgate).

Lamentations is placed in the *Ketûbîm*, the third division of the Hebrew canon, among the five megilloth or rolls that were used for public reading at the five major festivals of Judaism (Song of Songs, Ruth, Lamentations, Ecclesiastes, and Esther). Lamentations was read on Ab (mid-July) when the destruction of the Jerusalem temple was commemorated. In the Septuagint this book is placed after the book of Jeremiah and the apocryphal book of Baruch. This order is maintained by other ancient versions.

II. HISTORICAL SETTING

The content of this book and the consensus of Jewish tradition point in the direction of the destruction of Jerusalem in 587 B.C. as the immediate historical setting of this poetic work. The introductory statements of both the Septuagint and the Vulgate cite the fall of Jerusalem and the captivity of Judah as the occasion of the writing of Lamentations. The statement of 2 Ch 35:25 has led some to think that this book as a whole, or a portion of it, contains Jeremiah's lament over the death of Josiah, which took place in 609 B.C. However, these poems do not speak about a deceased king, rather about a city and its people who suffer because of their sin.

III. STRUCTURE, AUTHORSHIP, AND DATE

The book is made up of five poems that exemplify a careful style and structure and a rich and elegant variety of metaphors. These poems, all except the last one, are constructed as acrostics, using the twenty-two letters of the Hebrew alphabet. Although the order of the consonants is maintained in the first poem, in the second, third, and fourth poems, the consonant *ayin* follows *pe* (a reversal of the usual order), which has resulted in a slight deviation from the strict pattern of acrostics. The first, second, and third poems are arranged in three-line stanzas, except for 1:7 and 2:19. In the third poem, each of the three lines of the stanza begins with the same consonant; thus the alphabet is repeated three times in this chapter. The fourth poem is made up of two-line stanzas. The fifth poem has twenty-two lines, equivalent to the number of the consonants in the Hebrew alphabet, but it is not an acrostic composition.

The first poem describes Jerusalem as a desolate city because of God's rejection of them brought on by the sins of the people. The theme of God's rejection of Jerusalem is continued in the second poem with emphasis given to his anger. The third poem stresses the greatness of God's love and the need for repentance and contrition for the restoration of the nation. The prophets and priests are blamed for the horrible experiences of the people in the fourth poem. The last poem is a prayer for the restoration of the suffering nation.

The Jewish tradition and the ancient versions ascribed the authorship of this book to Jeremiah. Many recent commentators have regarded Lamentations as the work of an anonymous writer of the late exilic period. Though it does not bear the name of Jeremiah, the content clearly suggests that it is the work of an eyewitness of the tragedy of 587 B.C. One of the reasons cited here for the execution of God's wrath upon his people is the sins of the prophets and priests, a theme also found in Jeremiah. The language of the coming devastation of Judah and Jerusalem in Jeremiah is closely similar to the descriptions of the desolation in Lamentations. In addition to this, there are several other internal similarities between these two books that compel us to agree with those who favor the traditional view (see a detailed discussion of the authorship question in Kaiser, 24–30).

IV. THEOLOGICAL SIGNIFICANCE

This dirge poetry, unlike secular compositions of the same literary type, proclaims significant truths about God, his people, their sin, his righteous judgment, and the source of their hope in the midst of tragedy and suffering. Though the various poems have a calculated structure, as typical of dirge poetry, the thoughts of the author are often mixed and move from one theme to another, largely due to the sudden changes in his emotions. Therefore various themes are not developed or arranged in any systematic manner. However, the acrostic structure of these poems helps us to understand one important theological perspective of the writer.

Destruction has come upon God's people in a tragic and horrifying manner. This has to be dealt with in all of its details without attempting to treat it lightly or to avoid it because it brings to memory the horror of destruction. Kaiser notes that the acrostic form "systematically organizes each detail so as to identify, objectify, and pacify each and every pain . . . The final letter will come and so will the end of this sorrow" (Kaiser, 17). At the same time, the writer of these poems also affirms that the suffering community is under God's judgment because they have rebelled against his commandments. Therefore, the end he foresees is not what is destined to be the natural end of suffering. The finality of grief and suffering is conditional upon his people's confession of their sin and guilt before God (see 2Ch 7:13–14). The sovereign God is also a gracious, loving, compassionate, and faithful God. The One who brings grief is also the One who comforts. The call of the author to his people is to seek God and to wait patiently for their salvation.

This little book reminds the Christian community of the tragic consequences of covenant breaking with God. Though suffering of God's people is a major issue here, it must be understood in its proper context. God's wrath is poured out upon those who have been unfaithful to him. In this sense, Lamentations offers no clear solution to the problem of suffering in the world. However, it provides us with some practical guidelines to encounter both personal and communal suffering. The writer expresses in detail everything he feels and experiences as a member of the suffering community. This is a courageous way to encounter suffering. He takes time to examine, reflect on, and come to grips with his pain. He takes time to pray, confess, and seek God's forgiveness. He is certain that his suffering will come to its end. Most importantly, he is convinced that he is not alone in his suffering but that he is surrounded by the "unfailing love" of God (3:32; Ro 8:28, 38–39).

OUTLINE

I. There Is None to Comfort Jerusalem (1:1–22)

II. God's Anger (2:1–22)

III. A Personal Lament (3:1–66)

IV. The Wages of Sin (4:1–22)

V. A Prayer for Mercy (5:1–22)

COMMENTARY

I. THERE IS NONE TO COMFORT JERUSALEM (1:1–22)

The author laments the desolation of the city in vv.1–10. Beginning with v.11, the city speaks for itself about its misfortune. In both sections, the primary concern is on the cause of the fall of God's people. In the first section, a contrast is drawn between the present and the past. Though the city was once filled with people and enjoyed the status of a **queen** with great splendor and treasures, she has become a **widow,** and a **slave.** The city where there was laughter and joy is now weeping. She had many friends; now she is lonely and without comfort. Once she was the object of praise; now she is a despised city. This city is not an ordinary city; it is the city of God, and the people who live in it were the people of God with whom he had made a covenant. The covenant community, however, did not consider their future while they were enjoying the blessings of God. Instead they **sinned greatly** and became **unclean** (see vv.5, 8, 9, 14, 17, 18, 20). There is no doubt in the mind of the author that the pagan desecration of the Holy City and the temple was the direct consequence of the sins of God's people (vv.5, 12–14, 17, 22). The conditional nature of God's covenantal blessings upon his people is clearly implied here. The most tragic consequence of the sins of God's people is the withdrawal of God's presence from them, which leaves them with no **resting place** (v.3) or **comfort** in the world (vv.2, 9, 16, 17, 21). Rest or comfort (in Hebrew these two are related words) is a state of being that a believer enters into by faith in God (see Heb 3:17–4:2). **There is no one to comfort** Zion because God does not comfort her. Yet the writer calls the suffering community to admit that God is **righteous** in all that he does (see Dt 32:4), and to confess that they have **rebelled against his command** (v.18).

II. GOD'S ANGER (2:1–22)

This poem elaborates on the theme of God's rejection of his people, his city, and the place of his dwelling because he is angry with them. God is angry with his chosen people because they have trusted in the falsehood promoted by the false prophets who did nothing to expose the sins of the people (v.14). The most obvious sign of his anger is the destruction of the temple (**the splendor of Israel**), the ark of the covenant (**his footstool**), and the altar (vv.1, 6–7). These symbols of holiness have been removed from among a people who are no longer holy to the Lord. He has become an enemy to those who have become unfaithful to their covenant with him (vv.4–5). Perhaps the worst tragedy is the cessation of God's communication through the law and the prophetic visions (v.9). The media of revelation are temporarily withdrawn from the apostate who are under judgment, which brings upon them "a famine of hearing the words of the LORD" (Am 8:11). This judgment is the fulfillment of the word of the Lord who **planned** and **decreed** it through his spokesman **long ago** (v.17). He does not allow sinners to escape or survive his judgment (v.22). However, God may have pity for them if they come to his presence with a broken heart and tears of sorrow (vv.18–21).

III. A PERSONAL LAMENT (3:1–66)

The first twenty verses of this poem express the complaint of the writer who also is a member of the suffering nation. The language of this section is much like that of the complaints of Job against God. However, the mood of the writer changes quickly, and he expresses hope and confidence in God (vv.21–42). The complaint is picked up again in vv.43–54.

Unlike Job, the writer is clearly convinced that he and his nation are being punished because they have offended God with their sins (vv.39, 42). Nonetheless, he maintains hope and remembers that his nation has not been totally destroyed because of God's **great love** (*ḥesed*), and **compassion** (*rāḥamîm*) (vv.22–23, 31–32). **"Great is your faithfulness"** (v.23) is the joyous acclamation that comes out of the lips of the one whose heart has been pierced with arrows from God's quiver (see v.13). In the midst of suffering, he proclaims that God is good and calls his people to **wait quietly for the salvation of the LORD** (vv.25–26; see Ro 8:22–25). At the present moment, the suffering community must **bear the yoke** and **sit alone in silence,** because **both calamities and good things come** from God (vv.27–30, 37–38; see Job 2:10). The true character of God's people is best revealed through their patient waiting upon the Lord (see Ro 5:3–5). When suffering is the consequence of sin, the most appropriate thing to do then is to confess sin and to acknowledge guilt before God (vv.39–42). God's ultimate will is not to cast his people off forever or to bring affliction upon them, but to restore them so that they may experience his **unfailing love** (vv.31–33).

Vv.34–36 introduce the theme of justice and human rights, which God will not allow to be perverted or to be denied to any individual. God's will is to liberate the captives and to protect the basic rights of individuals, of which the most significant is their right to live before him as his image. Those who have fallen from the grace of God and are living under bondage to sin are given hope of being restored into his image (see Isa 42:1–4; 61:1–3; Lk 4:18–19).

The lament of the community is continued in vv.43–54. Those under judgment are deprived of any spiritual relationship with God. They are also treated by God as **scum and refuse** in the world, though they were once his prideful possession, a holy nation and a kingdom of priests (vv.43–45; see Ex 19:5–6). Moreover, the nations in the world also treat them with contempt, hatred, and violence (vv.46–54). Those who have been rejected by God are rejected also by the world.

The poem ends with a prayer for the punishment of the enemies of the suffering community (vv.55–66). This prayer and other similar prayers in which God is asked to take action against the enemies have been a problem to the Christians on account of the love commandment in the NT (Mt 5:44). Most likely, the prayer here is not against the writer's own personal enemies, rather against those who defy God and who are stubbornly opposed to God's people. The only recourse for God's people in such cases is to leave that matter with God for him to act in judgment (2Ti 4:14–15).

IV. THE WAGES OF SIN (4:1–22)

This fourth lament is a reminder to God's people that they cannot escape from paying the price when they commit sin against God. As a covenant nation, Israel was once beautiful, sacred, and precious to God; now they have become dull, common, worthless, heartless, destitute, ugly, and unclean in the world. The description of the fate of the young children is a vivid reminder of the intense famine within Jerusalem during the Babylonian siege. Even mothers have lost all compassion for their children. This tragic reversal of their status is the consequence of the sins of their prophets and priests who have failed to give them proper direction and leadership. Like the people they have misled, these leaders also have become the object of ridicule and dishonor in the world. The hopes and aspirations of the elect nation are shattered because the Lord **no longer watches over them** (v.16).

V. A PRAYER FOR MERCY (5:1–22)

This last lament again acknowledges sin as the cause of the present misfortune of God's people. V.7 reflects a common belief held by the exiled community (see Eze 18). The community is under judgment not only because of the sins of the fathers, but also because of their own sins. Hence the confession **"We have sinned"** (v.16) is appropriate. The judgment is the clear evidence of the sovereignty of God and his kingship from **generation to generation** (v.19). The lament ends with an earnest appeal for the restoration of God's people. The apostate nation's future depends entirely on God's will to restore them unto himself. The writer is certain that the Eternal King and the Sovereign Lord will not reject or be angry forever with a repentant sinner (vv.19–22).

BIBLIOGRAPHY

Consult Delbert Hillers' commentary on Lamentations for a detailed bibliography.

Hillers, D. *Lamentations*. Garden City, N.Y.: Doubleday, 1972.
Kaiser, W., Jr., *A Biblical Approach to Personal Suffering*. Chicago: Moody Press, 1982.

EZEKIEL

George Kufeldt

INTRODUCTION

I. EZEKIEL THE MAN

Early in his writing (1:3) Ezekiel tells us that he was a member of a priestly family and that he was one of the early exiles to the land of Babylon, taken there during the deportation of King Jehoiachin in the year 598 B.C.E. His name may be taken to mean "God is strong" or "God strengthens." The name *Ezekiel* is found only once more in the book (24:24), the only instance in which Yahweh refers to him by his name. Otherwise, Yahweh refers to him as "son of man" (93 times), a stereotyped formula which in Hebrew (*ben 'adam*) is used to refer to a male representative of the human race rather than to a specific male.

All we know of Ezekiel is from his book. We know that he was married and that his wife was suddenly taken from him. Her death became a strange symbol of the demise of the nation and the deep mourning this would bring upon the people (24:15–27). He apparently lived in his own house (3:24; 8:1) and seems to have had freedom to go in and out among the other exiles. In contrast to many of the other prophets, especially Jeremiah, Ezekiel never referred to any personal confrontation or contact with the leaders of his people. The closest he came to this was when, after his awesome vision in ch. 1, he went to the exiles at Tel Abib and sat among them overwhelmed for seven days (3:15). He also met with the elders twice in his own house (8:1; 14:1). However, he gave no indication of any conversation with the exiles during those times. Otherwise, Ezekiel's primary contact was with Yahweh through the divine instruction he was given, either through the spoken word or visions. Unlike Isaiah and Jeremiah, he never recorded any specific conversations with any leaders or even ordinary exiles.

It is no wonder that Ezekiel has been so frequently psychoanalyzed by commentators and others. No other writing prophet displayed his personality idiosyncrasies, such as trances, muteness, and bizarre visions and actions. For example, in at least seven passages it is said that "the hand of the LORD [Yahweh] was upon [him]" (1:3; 3:14, 22; 8:1; 33:22; 37:1; 40:1). While this term may be a traditional formula that described the divine empowering of a prophet to give an oracle, "it is quite clear that for

682

Ezekiel being seized by the hand of Yahweh meant more than simply his reception of the divine message. It was a submission in which among other things the receiving of the divine word took place" (Zimmerli, *Ezekiel 1*, 118). While one may assume that it involved some kind of trance state or experience, the text gives us no details to confirm this. Certainly one must admit that it appears that his fellow exiles saw him as something of a strange but interesting person (see 33:30–32).

II. HISTORICAL SETTING

It was Ezekiel's lot to live in a period that straddled both the preexilic period and the Exile. The powerful Assyrian Empire which had destroyed and conquered the northern kingdom in 722 B.C.E., had fallen victim to the combined power of Babylon and Media, which destroyed the Assyrian capital, Nineveh (612 B.C.E.). Three years later Egypt joined Assyria in battle against the Neo-Babylonian Empire in the Plain of Megiddo as Egypt tried to regain control over Palestine and Syria. King Josiah of Judah seems to have been an ally of Babylon and joined the battle against Egypt but unfortunately lost his life (see 2Ki 23:29–30; 2Ch 35:20–24).

Josiah's son, Jehoahaz (Shallum), ruled Judah for three months, after which the Egyptians installed another son of Josiah, Jehoiakim, as vassal-king in Jerusalem (609 B.C.E.). The Babylonians defeated the Egyptians in the famous battle at Carchemish (see Jer 46:2) in 605 B.C.E. Later that year Jehoiakim revolted against Egypt and gave his political loyalty to Babylon and its new king. Some time later when Jehoiakim again shifted his loyalty, this time to the Egyptians, Nebuchadnezzar sent his armies to Jerusalem at which time Jehoiakim was killed (597 B.C.E.). With the capture of Jerusalem, the Babylonians took Jehoiachin, who had succeeded his father Jehoiakim, into Babylonian exile. Nebuchadnezzar then put the youngest son of Josiah, Zedekiah, in power as puppet-king over Judah.

It was not long, however, before pro-Egyptians within the government convinced Zedekiah to revolt against the Babylonians. This revolt was put down by the armies of Nebuchadnezzar after a two-year siege of Jerusalem. This resulted in its destruction and fall in 587 B.C.E. As part of the conquest of Jerusalem, the great temple built by Solomon was burned to the ground, destroying Judaism's primary focus of nationalism and religion. A second deportation took place (see Jer 52) at that time, with a final deportation in 582 B.C.E. ending a sad chapter in the history of Judaism.

Ezekiel's call came in 593 B.C.E., five years after his deportation to Babylon and six years before the destruction of Jerusalem in 587 B.C.E. The latest date in the book is 571 B.C.E. (29:17). Thus his ministry spanned at least twenty-two years. There is no information given us concerning the rest of his life, but there is a tradition that places his grave just south of the city of Babylon (Zimmerli, *Ezekiel 1*, 16).

III. EZEKIEL'S DATES

More than any other OT prophet, Ezekiel frequently dated events, his particular visions, and prophecies. Now that archaeology has made available to modern scholars various Babylonian annals written in cuneiform on clay tablets and other materials, it is possible to calculate precise equivalents in terms of our calendar. The thirteen separate events or times Ezekiel cites have been calculated as follows:

1. His vision call (1:1, 5; 3:16)—July 31, 593 B.C.E.
2. His vision visit to Jerusalem (8:1)—Sept. 17, 592 B.C.E.
3. God's heartbreak over Judah's sin (20:1–2)—Aug. 14, 591 B.C.E.
4. Start of siege of Jerusalem (24:1)—Jan. 15, 588 B.C.E.
5. Judgment against Tyre (26:1)—Apr. 23, 587, to Apr. 13, 586 B.C.E.
6. Judgment against Egypt (29:1)—Jan. 7, 587 B.C.E.
7. Egypt given to Babylon for Tyre (29:17)—Apr. 26, 571 B.C.E.
8. Judgment against Pharaoh (30:20)—Apr. 29, 587 B.C.E.
9. Judgment against Pharaoh (31:1)—June 21, 587 B.C.E.
10. Dirge concerning Pharaoh (32:1)—Mar. 3, 585 B.C.E.
11. Demise of Egypt (32:17)—Apr. 13, 586, to Apr. 1, 585 B.C.E.
12. Arrival of Jerusalem escapee (33:21)—Jan. 8, 585 B.C.E.
13. Vision of the New Jerusalem (40:1)—Apr. 28, 573 B.C.E.

Additional information concerning dating of events in Ezekiel may be found in the following resources: Greenberg, *Ezekiel, 1–20*, 8–11); Zimmerli, *Ezekiel 1*, 9–16.

IV. SUMMARY OF EZEKIEL'S TEACHINGS

1. Yahweh is a God of transcendent glory—ch. 1 et al.
2. Israel's greatest sin is idolatry—chs. 8, 14, 16, 23, et al.
3. The doctrine of individual responsibility for sin and the nontransference of merit—ch. 18; 33:10–20.
4. The true prophet is the watchman of his people—33:1–9
5. Judah's worst enemies are within her, her leaders—34:1–19
6. Israel's hope lies in the promise of the new heart and new spirit—36:22–32; 37:24ff.
7. The new temple will have an influence that will flow out to the whole world—47:1–12.
8. God's sovereignty and judgment are not limited to Israel but extend to all nations of the world—chs. 25–32, 38–39.
9. Judah ultimately will be restored—ch. 37.
10. Ezekiel used spoken parables to convey his message: eagles and the vine (17:1–10); Oholah and Oholibah (ch. 23); the cooking pot (24:1–14); Gog and Magog (chs. 38–39).
11. Ezekiel used many acted parables to demonstrate his message: map on brick (4:1–3); lying on left and right sides (4:4–8); rationing of food (4:9–17); shaving of hair of his head (5:1–12);

no mourning at the death of his wife (24:15–24); inability to speak (3:24–27; 24:27; 33:22).

V. OUTLINE

COMMENTARY

I. EZEKIEL'S VISION CALL (1:1–3:27)

The reader of Ezekiel is impressed immediately with the intensely personal nature of the writing. Indeed, as Joel Rosenberg notes, "The pervasive dominance of the 'I' voice, the persistence of precise dates and of an almost purely sequential chronology and the private, literate and bookish manner of the language and idioms give the text much of the quality of a journal" (pp. 194–95). This journal or record of Ezekiel's pilgrimage as an exile called to be a prophet is unique among the OT prophets. These first three chapters of his journal leave no doubt in the reader's mind that the prophet is above all under the direction of the God who

called him. Indeed, the whole book "stops distinctly short of revealing the prophet's feelings, despite its lush generosity in rendering the divine pathos, and even despite its willingness otherwise to render the prophet's astonishment and dismay over things coming to pass" (Rosenberg, 196).

A. When and Where it Happened (1:1–3)

It is impossible for us to know what Ezekiel meant when he referred to **the thirtieth year.** Many take it to mean his own age, finding support in Nu 4:3, which sets the minimum age of a priest at thirty. The Jewish Targum or Aramaic paraphrase of Eze 1:1 counts the thirtieth year "from the time that Hilkiah the High Priest found the Book of the Torah in the Temple" (Levey, 20). Counting back thirty years from the fifth year of the Exile (v.2), one does arrive at the eighteenth year of Josiah's reign, the point at which the book of the law was found (2Ki 22:3). Still, one must ask why he would count from that event. All we really know is that Ezekiel's vision came during the fifth year of the exile of Jehoiachin, 593 B.C.E.

The location of the vision was at the Kebar River, which was really a canal near Nippur, just south of the city of Babylon. It must be assumed that a community of exiles was living at that place. So overwhelming was the experience that came to Ezekiel while among the exiles that he could explain it only as the result of the hand or power of the Lord being upon him (see introduction).

B. Vision of God (1:4–28)

It is difficult to resist the temptation to analyze each tiny detail, every jot and tittle, of this bizarre vision. A quick perusal of commentaries on Ezekiel demonstrates this all too clearly. (See bibliography for a listing of representative commentaries.) Even after each detail has been identified or, more likely, conjectured about, what is the result? It is not unlike studying Michelangelos' portrait of Mona Lisa by peeling off each of the brush strokes made by the artist and laying them in a row. The result is a collection of brush strokes that have lost all beauty and meaning.

What did Ezekiel really see? Greenberg is exactly right when he says, "Reduced to its essentials, this is the narrative of *the vision of the divine Majesty* (*Ezekiel, 1–20*, 51, italics mine). The problem was that Ezekiel had seen and experienced something that he could describe only in this-worldly terms, terms familiar to himself and to his readers. Trying to describe the indescribable, he was limited by his human experience and vocabulary. Thus the language he used could only be symbolic of what he saw and experienced, not the literal experience. His difficulty in describing his experience was similar to that of the seven-year-old boy who, living during the Great Depression, had never had a taste of soda pop. After he finally had a sample, he was asked what it tasted like. He responded after a period of deep thought, "It tastes like your foot's asleep!" He may have mixed his categories, but every reader knows what he meant!

So too Ezekiel used human, everyday terms to describe his own apprehension and sense of the overwhelming glory, power, and majesty of the Great God of Heaven. The **four living creatures** must represent God's presence in all four quarters of the world of humankind. The four faces represent aspects of the world of creatures God has created. The wheels beside each creature and their unhindered movement surely stand for the universality of God who is everywhere, moving unhindered in his world and among his creation. His repeated references to brightly colored stones, flashing lightning, sparkling ice, etc., all speak of the glory of the transcendent God.

The impossibility of Ezekiel's actually describing the vision is emphasized by terms he used to refer to what he saw: **"looked like," "the appearance . . . was like," "sparkled like," "like the roar of," "what appeared to be."** The climax to his description came in v.28 when he exclaimed, **"Such was the appearance of the likeness of the glory of the LORD!"** So overwhelming, so awe-full, so indescribable was what he saw that Ezekiel could speak of God only by using terms at least three times removed from the Ultimate Reality ("the appearance of," "the likeness of," "the glory of")!

When Isaiah had his vision of God at the temple in Jerusalem, he saw his own lostness and uncleanness before God (Isa 6:5). When Ezekiel had his vision of God in Babylon, far from the temple in Jerusalem, he fell on his face, overwhelmed by the realization that God was not limited to Jerusalem and to the temple. God was also in Babylon, an unclean land (Ezr 9:11).

C. Ezekiel's Call and Commissioning (2:1–3:27)

It was immediately clear that God was in charge of the situation. By referring to Ezekiel here and throughout the book as **"son of man"** (Heb. *ben 'adam*; see introduction), God clearly indicated his sovereignty, not only over Ezekiel but over all humanity. Here was no room for a buddy-type relationship with God as is so common in Christian circles today. When God said, **"Stand up,"** Ezekiel could not debate or refuse. All he could do was obey.

Continuing with the same commanding voice, God carefully laid out the task before Ezekiel. There was no glossing over of the difficulty of the commission laid on Ezekiel. The difficult, indeed, the virtually impossible task was bluntly described in detail. The people may have been rebellious and stubborn, but still God said, **"You must speak my words to them, whether they listen or fail to listen"** (2:7). God calls and sends not because it is easy or because he promises success, but because there is a message to share, a job to be done. Even the scroll that was handed to Ezekiel reflected the difficulty of his mission. While scrolls

normally were written on one side only, this scroll was written on both sides, so many and terrible were the words of God's judgment that Ezekiel was to proclaim.

The command to eat the scroll means that Ezekiel was to make God's message of judgment his own. The honey taste was not a literal sensation to his mouth but was "only a typically emblematic and allegorical affirmation of the objective 'sweetness' of that most precious commodity, *obedience to the divine imperative*" (Rosenberg, 197, italics mine). He had come to know, in the words of the song, "the sweet will of God."

In 3:4–11 God not only restated Ezekiel's commission but also specified that the message of divine judgment was only for the house of Israel and not for Babylon (v.5). While he was to go to his **countrymen in exile and speak to them** (v.11), one may assume that any word of warning and judgment he would give would apply to the people still back in Judah. Again, Ezekiel was reminded that he had no option whether the people listened or not. They may be hard-hearted, but he was to be even more stubborn and hard-headed (v.9).

In five places in his writing Ezekiel says, **"The Spirit lifted me up"** (3:12, 14; 8:3; 11:1, 24; 43:5), but only here in vv.12, 14 was there a mixture of physical movement to a place and vision. The other four are movement within a vision. He was taken from the site of the great vision of ch. 1 and came to the exiles who lived at Tel Aviv. The name is a Babylonian term meaning "Mound of the Flood." He sat among them overwhelmed ("dumb-founded," NEB) for a period of seven days. What a model for us who cannot sit quietly for an hour in ordinary times, to say nothing of times of crisis.

No wonder God cannot get through to us.

At the end of the seven days of silence, God laid on Ezekiel the awesome responsibility of being a **watchman for the house of Israel** (3:17). Every ancient city had its sentries who were responsible for the safety and protection of its people. Ezekiel was to be responsible for both the wicked and the righteous, to persuade the wicked to turn to righteousness and to warn the righteous of the dangers of wickedness. Each Christian also stands in that unenviable and often difficult circle of influence within which friends and family may be turned from sin or patiently warned of falling into sin.

By means of another vision (33:23) similar to that in ch. 1, God concluded his commissioning of Ezekiel. He was to shut himself in his house as one bound and silenced by the rejection and repulsion of the people who stubbornly resisted his message. In God's good timing, however, he would release Ezekiel to speak the divine word of judgment. What a difference between God's timing and ours and the success of any enterprise.

II. FOUR ACTED PARABLES (4:1–5:17)

Two things are to be noted here. First, the traditional chapter divisions unfortunately make for unnatural breaks in the sequence of Ezekiel's journal, which continues from ch. 3. Second, Ezekiel's silence (3:26) was demonstrated throughout the four acted parables in which he never spoke to the exiles who gathered to watch his pantomimes. He spoke only to God when in the third acted parable he protested that he was expected to do something that was not kosher (4:14).

A. Siege of Jerusalem Depicted (4:1–3)

Since Babylonia had little stone, from the beginnings of history in that region clay bricks were used for building purposes (see Ge 11). These bricks were often somewhat larger than the bricks we use today, and it was typical to put inscriptions on bricks used for government and religious buildings while the clay was still wet. Apparently Ezekiel was to use either a wet or air-dried brick on which to scratch a map of the city of Jerusalem. This he was well able to do since he probably was very familiar with that city. After building model siege-works around the city, he was to act as the besieging enemy, representing God who ordained the siege as part of his judgment. The siege literally took place in 588–586 B.C.E. (see Jer 39:1–2).

B. Length of the Exile Demonstrated (4:4–8)

One must assume that the instruction for Ezekiel to lie first on his left side and then his right was carried out in some symbolic way not specifically described for us. Ezekiel's description gives us no clues as to when the numbering was to begin. The main point was that the exile for both the north and the south would last a long time.

C. Rationing During the Exile Dramatized (4:9–17)

The parable of eating rationed food which had been cooked on fire fueled by human dung symbolized both the privation and hunger brought on by lengthy siege and the humiliation of being exiled to an unclean land. There the exiles would have to eat nonkosher food in order to stay alive (Da 1:8–18). As terrible as that would be and was, they would suffer the even greater famine, as Amos had predicted for Israel, "not a famine of food or a thirst for water, but a famine of hearing the words of the LORD" (Am 8:11).

D. The People's Destruction and Dispersion (5:1–4)

The props used in this dramatic skit vividly illustrate the meaning of this parable. Ezekiel was told to use a sword, the universal symbol of war and conquest, to shave his head and beard. In addition, priests were not to shave their heads (Lev 21:5; Eze 44:20), and since Ezekiel was a priest, this must have had a startling effect on his viewers. While most of his shaved hair was to symbolize either the burning, the killing by the sword, or the taking into exile of the people after the walls of Jerusalem were broken down, a small portion of the hair was to be tucked into his robe. In this way Ezekiel portrayed the doctrine of the remnant which most preexilic prophets taught (see Isa 6:13; Jer 23:3; Mic 2:12; Zep 2:3; etc.). In every generation a remnant, a faithful few, would give hope for the future.

E. Consequences of God's Judgment Discussed (5:5–17)

Having finished his silent acted parables, Ezekiel spoke to the people, describing God's judgment. Judgment is coming to Israel, said God, because **"she has rejected my laws and has not followed my decrees"** (v.6). The judgment bites even deeper because Israel had **not even conformed to the standards of the nations around [her]** (v.7). Because she did not live up to her chosenness and privileges, Israel would suffer all the more severely. Israel finally discovered, but too late, that being chosen by God would not protect her from his judgment, a lesson for any nation in any generation.

III. ORACLES AGAINST JUDAH'S WICKED HIGH PLACES (6:1–14)

Ezekiel may have used the term **"mountains of Israel"** as a deliberate contrast to the plains that characterize the land of Babylon. More likely, however, he is using the term to refer to the whole of the land of Israel which had **"altars on every high hill and on all the mountaintops"** (v.13). This was in deliberate violation of the commandment to destroy all such Canaanite sanctuaries with their grossly immoral religion and to worship Yahweh alone (Dt 12:1–7). All such shrines, whether on mountains or in the valleys, would be destroyed. Those who worshiped at these pagan shrines would discover that the gods at these shrines could not protect them against the wrath of Yahweh (6:4).

It is a mistake, however, to see God's judgment and the Exile only as an expression of God's wrath. Indeed, in his heartbreak, God said, **"I have been grieved by their adulterous hearts"** (v.9), and yet he would **spare some** (v.8). These would be taken into exile where its discipline would bring them to repentance. The purpose of the Exile was that the remnant would again **"know ... the LORD"** (vv.10, 14). "To know" often means to have an intimate or experiential relationship with someone. So the Exile too was an expression of the covenant loyalty and steadfast love (*ḥesed*) of God. His love never lets us go.

IV. DOOM IS AT HAND (7:1–27)

There is no mistaking the urgency in Ezekiel's proclamation **"The end! The end has come upon the four corners of the land"** (v.2). This whole chapter shouts the full meaning of the term "the day of the LORD," first uttered by the prophet Amos almost 170 years before (Am 5:18). It will indeed be a day of darkness and not light (Am 5:20). This chapter presents the death warrant for Israel. Their own standards would condemn them. What does this say about the level of morality and ethics they actually lived? When the Day of the Lord's wrath does come, God said, then **"they will know that I am the LORD"** (v.27).

V. EZEKIEL'S RETURN IN VISION TO JERUSALEM (8:1–11:25)

Up to this point Ezekiel's message of judgment has been directed only at the people of Israel, their pagan shrines, and their evil way of life. He has made no mention at all that God's judgment included the temple in Jerusalem, the place where God's glory resided. It is in these chapters that Ezekiel confronts the despoiling of the temple by the elders of Israel and faces the fact that God's glory will not stay there much longer.

A. Four Foul Abominations in the Temple (8:1–18)

There is no need to conjecture as some do that Ezekiel was actually in Jerusalem and literally saw the happenings described in ch. 8–11. Using language and imagery very similar to that which he used in ch. 1, he again spoke of being under the hand/power of the Lord (v.1). In that state of being he was lifted up and transported to Jerusalem where he envisioned the sorry state of affairs existing there. Having been there as a priest before he was exiled, he would have no difficulty in seeing and identifying the various parts and aspects of the temple area. The main point in this chapter is to show how the temple was being desecrated by the elders of Israel who were still

resident in Jerusalem. At the very entrance to the temple he saw **the idol that provokes to jealousy** (v.3). This probably was a Canaanite fertility cult image, something that was not allowed by the commandments (Ex 20:4) and certainly was not permitted within the temple. The disgusting scene of **crawling things and detestable animals** (8:10) pictured on the very walls of the temple was made even worse as the elders of Israel were standing there worshiping these images (vv.11–12).

At the north gate of the temple, Ezekiel was shown women who were mourning the death of Tammuz, a Babylonian fertility god equivalent to the Canaanite god Baal. According to their religion, Tammuz/Baal died each late spring, resulting in drought and the wilting of all vegetation. The late autumn rains were believed to be the result of the resurrection of this god whose rains restored fertility to the land.

The final abomination was the scene showing Israelite men bowing toward the east in worship of the Babylonian sun god. In order to do this they had to turn their backs to the temple, a sign of their rejection of the true God.

All these sins reflected the fact that Israel had rejected God and had turned to the gods of their neighbors. Their alibi was not unlike that used by people even to this day: **"The LORD does not see us; the LORD has forsaken the land"** (v.12). Even the worst of sins can be and are rationalized away by those who reject God.

B. Death Pronounced Upon Jerusalem (9:1–11)

As God continued the vision of Jerusalem and the temple, Ezekiel must have been startled to hear God shout, "Bring on the executioners of the city . . . !" (v.1, Greenberg, 174). The seven men who responded stood at the bronze altar in the temple courtyard. One of them marked the foreheads of those few in Jerusalem who still protested the sins taking place in Jerusalem and the temple. By marking them this remnant would be sealed or protected against the judgment of Yahweh upon the city and temple (9:6). Ezekiel discovered the sad truth that God's judgment and wrath can and will come against God's own house (see Jer 7:1–15). How true that judgment must begin at the house of God (1Pe 4:17), but how true also that those who remain true and faithful will be saved. It is not enough to have a good start; one must continually be faithful.

C. The Glory of Yahweh Leaves the Temple and Jerusalem (10:1–22)

As the vision continued, it repeated many of the same features of the vision Ezekiel saw at the Kebar River (1:1–28). Now, however, "the living creatures" were called **"cherubim,"** a term derived from the Babylonian word for guardian figures at city and temple gates. Among these cherubim was **the man clothed in linen,** who in ch. 9 was the divine messenger who marked the faithful remnant. Now in ch. 10 he was the divine destroyer who was to scatter burning coals over Jerusalem in order to destroy it by fire (vv.2, 7). Then, with the imagery of the wheels within wheels, etc., as in ch. 1, the same imagery depicted the departure of the glory of God from the burning city and temple (vv.9–19). There are no more tragic words than these: **"The glory of the LORD departed from over the threshold of the temple"** (v.18). This vision came true when Nebuchadnezzar destroyed the city and the temple in 596 B.C.E. How often have these words described the spiritual condition of

churches and religious organizations throughout history.

D. Judgment Upon the Wicked Leaders (11:1–15)

The vision of twenty-five of Israel's leaders who had sold out to evil rather than righteousness portrays what happens when leaders reject God as their source of wisdom and direction. Leadership is a terrible responsibility. Leaders dare not forget that they are responsible not only to their followers but to God himself. When leaders fail, they destroy their followers as well as themselves.

E. Divine Promise of Judah's Restoration (11:16–25)

God did not allow Ezekiel to forget that although judgment was brought upon the nation and its leaders because of their sin, he had a word of hope for the future (note again ch. 6). Yes, the Exile was God's judgment on Israel's sin, but it was to be a purifying experience for the faithful remnant. The Exile would teach them a lesson. In fact, it would completely change them, for then they would be willing to receive the **undivided heart** and **new spirit** that God would give them (v.19). When their spirit is completely committed to God they finally will be able to act as God's people. Jeremiah called this same experience "the new covenant" (Jer 31:31–34), in which God's Torah, or instruction, would be written on his people's minds and hearts rather than on tablets of stone.

VI. MORE ACTED PARABLES (12:1–28)

One might wonder why these acted parables were not given along with those in chs. 4–5. The reason may be that some time has passed and that the end is very near at hand.

A. Exile Journey Dramatized (12:1–16)

In this skit Ezekiel acted out the general manner in which each of the Israelites would prepare for the long journey to the land of exile. Unfortunately, the many people who watched him saw only an act and not the fact that Ezekiel was God's sign to them (v.11). The skit made special reference to King Zedekiah as **the prince** (vv.12–13). He would cover his face as a disguise and try to escape. Then he would be captured, brought back, and blinded by the Babylonians before he was taken to Babylon where he would die (see 2Ki 25:4–7; Jer 39:4–7).

B. Fear and Trembling Before the Approaching Enemy (12:17–20)

Again the people watching Ezekiel saw more entertainment than warning as he shook and trembled before them even while he told them that this was the way they would react when the enemy would conquer and devastate their land. Somehow it was still so impossible, so far away from them, that they did not get the point.

C. The Vision of Destruction Will Not Be Delayed (12:21–28)

The continuing tension between the message of the true prophet and that of the false prophet is illustrated by the two proverbs quoted in this section. First, the false prophet played down the warnings of the true prophet by saying, **"The days go by and every vision comes to nothing"** (v.22). The second proverb was similar: **"The vision he sees is for many years from now, and he prophesies about the distant future"** (v.27). In other words, the false prophet said what the people wanted to hear: "Don't worry about it—nothing is going to happen soon!" God's words have a disgusted ring to them when he

says, **"None of my words will be delayed any longer; whatever I say will be fulfilled"** (v.28).

VII. ORACLES OF DIVINE JUDGMENT ON JERUSALEM AND JUDAH (13:1–24:27)

A. Judgment on False Prophets and Idolatry (13:1–14:23)

In ch. 13, Ezekiel came down hard on the false prophets who paraded as true prophets and so misled the people. Like Jeremiah (Jer 23), Ezekiel boldly accused them of listening to their own minds, and using false visions and divinations by which they deceived the people. He also denounced the false prophetesses who practiced witchcraft and fortune-telling. Just what the various charms and devices were that they used is not clear. What is clear is the fact that they **profaned [God] among [his] people for a few handfuls of barley and scraps of bread** (v.19). Also, by lying, they **killed those who should not have died and . . . spared those who should not live** (v.19).

It is not always easy to distinguish between the true and the false prophet. They may all appear to be equally sincere, look the same, and even use the same theological language. Often, too, those who listen to false prophets encourage them by their acceptance of their words and by giving them praise and financial support. Sometimes even false prophets are self-deceived and self-deluded, having convinced themselves that what seems right or what wins public acceptance must be true. There are two basic tests that can and must be made of any prophet: Does the prophet's life measure up to the highest standards of morality? And does the prophet's message measure up to known truth?

Idolatry and false prophecy go hand

in hand. In ch. 14 God's judgment on idolatry is seen as stemming from the same corruption of heart and mind that breeds false prophecy. Indeed, false prophets would have no audience, no support, if they and the people had not given their minds and hearts over to the spirit of idolatry. They refused God's sovereignty, choosing to follow gods of their own making, gods who were a reflection of themselves and their sinfulness. So great was the sin in their hearts and in the land that God's judgment was inevitable. Only the faithful remnant of God would survive (14:22), and they would survive only because of God's sovereign grace.

B. Jerusalem Depicted as a Useless Vine (15:1–8)

Israel is frequently referred to in the OT as a vine, a comparison that was readily accepted by the Israelites who knew the blessings of the beauty, shade, fruit, and wine the grapevine provided. Unfortunately, the comparison was often negative because Israel did not always demonstrate the good qualities of the vine (Isa 5:1–7; Jer 2:21; Hos 10:1). For Ezekiel, too, the image of the vine was seen as an illustration of Israel's uselessness because of her sin: the wood of the vine is useless for building, and it makes poor firewood. Israel is hardly worth throwing into the fire.

C. Jerusalem as the Unfaithful Bride (16:1–63)

In vivid, sometimes coarse terms, Israel's response to God's election is portrayed in an unflattering allegory. First, God chose her in spite of her pagan origins, with no qualities to deserve such a choice. Second, he chose her even though as a people she was rejected, an outcast. As she grew and developed, God provided everything good for her, choosing her as his bride. As his bride, she was given everything she needed, and much more—food, clothing, beautiful adornment. But what did she do? She became a prostitute and gave herself to the gods of all the surrounding nations. Preferring these gods, she went so far as to pay or bribe these lovers contrary to what prostitutes usually do (vv.32–34). The best thing that could be said of her was the familiar proverb, **"Like mother, like daughter"** (v.44)! She had become even worse than her pagan origins.

Fortunately for Israel, God's great covenant loyalty, steadfast love (Heb. *ḥesed*) came through again (vv.59–63). Because she had broken her covenant with God, her true spouse, God said, **"I will deal with you as you deserve"** (v.59), presumably referring to the discipline of the Exile. He still would keep his end of the covenant made with Israel in the wilderness (Ex 19–24) and **"establish an everlasting covenant"** with her, and make atonement for her (vv.60–63). Then she would remember and know he is the Lord.

D. Allegory of the Two Eagles and the Vine (17:1–24)

The allegory given in vv.1–10 is interpreted in vv.11–21 as a picture of how King Zedekiah's policies brought about his downfall and ultimately that of Judah. The eagle designates Nebuchadnezzar of Babylon who took Jehoiachin, king of Judah who is the top of the cedar (the Davidic line) into exile in 597 B.C.E. The **seed of [the] land** is King Zedekiah, another descendant of David, who was placed on the throne in Jerusalem by Nebuchadnezzar. **Another great eagle** represents the pharaoh of Egypt to whom Zedekiah appealed for help against Nebuchadnezzar (17:15). This rebellion against Nebuchadnezzar failed, and Zedekiah was captured, blinded, and then taken to Babylon, where he died in 587 B.C.E. (vv.16; 2Ki 25:7). The allegory concludes with God's promise that he himself would one day take a branch from the very top of the cedar (the line of David) and plant him in Jerusalem. Through this messianic figure God's reign of peace would become a universal reality.

E. Alibis Do Not Work (18:1–32)

From the very beginning, human beings have tried to blame others for their sins (Ge 3:12–13). Both Jeremiah (Jer 31:29) and Ezekiel quote the proverb, **"The fathers eat sour grapes and the children's teeth are set on edge"** (v.2). Both prophets deny that this or any other alibi ever works. No matter what a person may think or want to believe, each person is responsible for his or her own sin. On the other hand, just as responsibility cannot be transferred to anyone else, neither can the merit or righteousness of one person be transferred to or be assumed by another person.

F. An Allegorical Lament Over Jerusalem's Leaders (19:1–14)

In this chapter Ezekiel gives us two different allegories that lament the sorry state of affairs the royal house of Judah had brought upon itself. The lioness portrays the nation or tribe of Judah (see Ge 49:9), or perhaps even Jerusalem, out of which its kings had come. **"One of her cubs"** (v.3) refers to Jehoahaz who, although he ruled only three months, had a reputation for ruthlessness (see 2Ki 23:31–34; Jer 22:11, NIV mg.). When Jehoahaz was taken as a prisoner to Egypt, another "cub," probably Jehoiachin (2Ki 24:15) was taken prisoner to Babylon.

The point in both cases is that these kings trusted in themselves rather than in God and so suffered the consequences. The second allegory uses the figure of a vine to symbolize the Davidic dynasty as a strong, flourishing, and fruitful plant that was uprooted and dried up by the strong east wind, Nebuchadnezzar. The current branch, Zedekiah, has been transplanted in Babylon where he is weak, and the vine is of no consequence

G. God's Heartbreak Over Judah's Rebellion (20:1–49)

Ezekiel dated the events and message in this chapter to the year 591 B.C.E. The elders of Israel came to Ezekiel **to inquire of the LORD,** to get a message from God through Ezekiel. On reading the words of that message, it is clear that the elders received much more than they had bargained for.

Probably no other passage in the Bible better illustrates the meaning of God's repenting, or changing his mind (Ge 6:6–7; Ex 32:14; 1Sa 15:1–35; 2Sa 24:16; et al.). Beginning with his initial choice of Israel (20:5), God recited the whole history of Israel's disobedience and how they ignored his plans and purposes for them. How often Israel's sin had broken his heart so that he decided to **"pour out [his] wrath on them and spend [his] anger against them"** (v.8; cf. vv.13, 21). **"But,"** he said, **"for the sake of my name I did what would keep it from being profaned in the eyes of the nations"** (v.9; cf. vv.14, 22, 44), and so he spared them. He changed his mind and spared them not because they deserved it, but for the sake of all that his name stands for and is. He spared them because he loved them (see Dt 7), and his love would not let them go.

H. Babylon as God's Instrument of Judgment (21:1–32)

This chapter is one long, loud cry of judgment and destruction by the sword. This is not just any sword, but one readied by God himself, the sword of Babylon. Even a cursory look at the rhythm and repetition expressed in the several parts of the Song of the Sword recited by Ezekiel (note the printed form of the text) shows that Ezekiel must have acted out this song by dancing and clapping.

More moving and more important than drama, however, was Ezekiel's own personal involvement in the meaning of the poem. What pain he must have suffered when God said, **"Cry out and wail, son of man, for it is against my people; it is against all the princes of Israel. . . . Therefore beat your breast"** (v.12). It must have been most difficult for Ezekiel to give this terrible song of judgment, especially since it did not include any word of comfort or hope as God's messages through Ezekiel usually did. Unfortunately, such messages sometimes must be given.

I. More Judgment Against Jerusalem (22:1–31)

It is only a short step from the content of this chapter to the content of our evening television newscast or newspaper, so modern and up-to-date is this list of Israel's sins. Indeed, many of these sins take place daily on our own streets. Some of them may have slightly different names, but most of them are all too obvious and recognizable. Well, so what? Just this: How can we as communities and nations think we can avoid the same judgment and fate as that which God announced in this chapter and then brought to pass through the destruction by Nebuchadnezzar? Who among us is willing to **"stand before [God] in the gap on behalf of the land so [God] would not have to destroy it"** (v.30)?

J. Israel and Judah, the Harlot Sisters (23:1–49)

This chapter clearly is a continuation of ch. 22. However, the focus of this descriptive allegory is not so much the sexual immorality of society generally, although this is part of it, but more specifically the gross immorality of the Canaanite religion, which had overwhelmed Israelite religion. By using the terms *Oholah* (Heb. for "her tent") and *Oholibah* (Heb. for "my tent is in her"), Ezekiel specifically referred to the religious shrines in both Israel and Judah. The Canaanite fertility cult with its male and female prostitutes long had characterized both the North (see 1Ki 12) and the South (1Ki 14:22–24). Religious corruption, worship of the gods of other nations, also had dire political implications, for it implied alliances with these pagan nations. Ironically, but so typically true, these lovers of Judah would soon turn against her and wreak horrible torture and suffering upon her once they had used her for their own purposes (vv.22–27). As this chapter so vividly demonstrates, the sin of adultery may be personal, spiritual, or national. It is nothing less than the betrayal of the person, cause, or God to whom we profess complete commitment.

K. Allegory of the Cooking Pot (24:1–14)

Ezekiel was instructed to note the date, which is equal to January 15, 588 B.C.E., **"because the king of Babylon has laid siege to Jerusalem"** (v.2). This sad date is still commemorated in Judaism as a fast day. Two years later Jerusalem and Judah fell to the Babylonians. The parable of the cooking pot dramatically predicted this sorry end, an end brought about and made necessary by the gross sins of the people. God's judgment could be delayed no longer. God said, "**The time has come for me to act. I will not hold back; I will not have pity, nor will I relent. You will be judged according to your conduct and your actions**" (v.14).

L. Death of Ezekiel's Wife and Mourning of the Exile (24:15–27)

This acted parable is an extreme example of the prophet's personal involvement in God's word of judgment and at the same time an ultimate illustration of the prophet's commitment to God's will. The main point is that Ezekiel was not to follow the traditional mourning custom of loud wailing and emotional display. This would provoke the people to ask what his actions meant for them. Then he could tell them that just as he had lost "**the delight of [his] eyes**" (v.16), so they would lose the delight of their eyes, the beautiful temple in Jerusalem (v.21). The result of that would be a grief so deep that they would not be able to weep, to show their sorrows. It would be too late, but then they really would know that God was the Lord, the Master of his world.

V.27 must be seen in connection with 33:22, where his voice is restored to him when the news of the fall of Jerusalem comes to him. Just what his dumbness or loss of speech really signifies is not clear. Perhaps it had to do with the horrible prospect of the judgment and wrath of God. On the other hand, perhaps the restoration of his voice may be related to the fact that in the last half of his book Ezekiel was able to speak great hope of restoration after the discipline of the Exile.

VIII. JUDGMENT PRONOUNCED AGAINST THE NATIONS (25:1–32:32)

The prophecies Ezekiel gives against the surrounding nations in chs. 25–32 seem to be inserted deliberately between the notice that the siege of Jerusalem has begun (24:1) and the news that Jerusalem has fallen to Babylon (33:21–22).

A. Judgment Against Surrounding Nations (25:1–17)

The first three nations cited for judgment had one common trait, and that was their distant relationship to Israel. The Ammonites and the Moabites were descendants of Lot, the nephew of Abraham (Ge 19:30–38), while the Edomites were descendants of Esau, brother of Jacob and grandson of Abraham. Judgment against them would be harsh because they, although relatives, had often been antagonistic against Israel. The Ammonites had rejoiced sadistically when the temple was desecrated and the people of Judah were taken into exile (v.3). According to Ob 11–13 the Edomites had acted the same way. Certainly a blood tie includes a greater responsibility than that felt for other human beings.

The traditional antagonism between the Philistines and Israel that led to establishment of the monarchy under Saul had continued until late in the history of Israel. Even though they had been subdued by David, they continued to act in vengeance and with hostility. Now their time had come and they would be destroyed by the Babylonians.

B. Judgment Against Tyre and Sidon (26:1–28:26)

There is one basic ingredient that must lie behind the fact that Ezekiel prophesied more about Tyre than any

of the prophets: as the capital of Phoenicia (modern Lebanon), Tyre was also
the capital of Canaanite culture and
religion. Canaanite culture and religion
had completely saturated Israel, thus
bringing upon Israel Ezekiel's repeated
pronouncements of God's wrath. God
promised the city a swift end under the
armies of Nebuchadnezzar.

Vv.3–24 of ch. 27 sound on the
surface as though God were agreeing
with Tyre's announced opinion of itself: **"I am perfect in beauty"** (v.3).
Indeed, as one of the world's great
trade centers, it had much to be proud
of, as this chapter shows. The problem
was that she had come to believe and
trust in her own opinion of herself. The
chapter ends, however (vv.25–36),
with the verdict, "Pride goes before a
fall." Those who applauded her will
become appalled at her when the end
comes, so terrible will it be.

Ch. 28 emphasizes the judgment
against Tyre as its king is denounced
for his inordinate pride and self-
deification. Contrary to some interpretations, this chapter is not a description
of Satan and his ultimate fate. The
language Ezekiel used is highly symbolic and poetic and makes use of
language and imagery that echo Ge 2
and 3. The text and its larger context
(chs. 25–28) can refer only to the king
of Tyre and his pride. It is unfortunate
that later traditions about Satan from
the intertestamental period are often
read into this chapter and other OT
passages such as Isa 14:12, while at the
same time the context is ignored. The
student of the Bible must begin with
the context of any passage to understand it.

It is clear from 28:12–15 that the
king of Tyre was an unusual person,
with unusual potential and possibilities.
Although he was a pagan, God said of
him, **"You were the model of perfection, full of wisdom and perfect in
beauty. . . . You were anointed as a
guardian cherub, for so I ordained
you"** (28:12c, 14a). Is this statement to
be taken as sarcasm or irony? More
likely, it probably reflects God's sovereign control of all history and nations,
as the apostle Paul was to write later,
"The authorities that exist have been
established by God" (Ro 13:1). Perhaps within God's grand design God
had special plans for the king of Tyre
(cf. Isa 45:1 and its reference to the
Persian king Cyrus). The tragedy is that
although this king had been created
blameless (v.15), he allowed pride and
wickedness (v.15) to rule his life and to
destroy himself, his potential, and his
nation. The lesson seems all too obvious: "In the pride and fall of the
Prince of Tyre, there is repeated the
story of 'primeval man.' This is 'Every-
man's story' " (Zimmerli, *Ezekiel 2*, 95).
It is always true that "whoever exalts
himself will be humbled" (Mt 23:12).

Sidon (vv.20–26), a city near Tyre,
would be destroyed also. As a Canaanite city it had been a partner with Tyre
in its corruption.

C. Judgment Against Egypt (29:1–32:32)

In a series of seven prophecies in
these four chapters (29:1ff.; 29:17ff.;
30:1ff.; 30:20ff.; 31:1ff.; 32:1ff.;
32:17ff.), Ezekiel points out the sins of
both Pharaoh and Egypt and how the
Egyptians will experience God's judgment for their sins. Like the prince of
Tyre (ch. 28), the pharaoh boasted in
his position and power (29:3–5). Also,
Egypt had offered help to Israel when
the Babylonians began their siege of
Jerusalem, but Egypt turned out to be
unreliable (vv.6–7). Because of this,
God would make sure Egypt would
survive at least partially so that it would
be a reminder to Israel of her sin of

turning to Egypt instead of God for help (vv.13–16).

Repeatedly throughout these chapters, Ezekiel mentioned Babylon as his instrument of wrath against Egypt. He vividly described just what would happen when he decided that the time for judgment had come. Like all the great powers of the world that had forgotten God, who had been guilty of crimes against other nations, especially against Israel, Egypt would end up in Sheol, the place of the dead. Already destroyed and in Sheol were Assyria (32:22), Elam (v.24), Meshech and Tubal (v.26), Edom (v.29), and Sidon (v.30). Again, Ezekiel's words have emphasized his conviction that Yahweh is the Lord of history, that all nations are responsible before him and subject to his power and control.

IX. THE PROMISE OF ISRAEL'S RESTORATION (33:1–39:29)

These chapters comprise a new section of the book, reflecting a look to the future and thus to the restoration of Israel. With the fall of Jerusalem (33:21), Ezekiel turned from warnings of impending doom to a look at the time when the Exile and its discipline would be over and God would restore his people to their homeland.

A. Ezekiel as God's Watchman (33:1–33)

In a review of God's messages to Ezekiel in 3:16–21 and in 18:1–32, Ezekiel was reminded of his terrible responsibility to be a watchman to warn the people. At the same time the people had a personal responsibility to heed his warnings. Against their despair under their burden of sin and guilt, Ezekiel held out God's word of grace: **"'I take no pleasure in the death of the wicked, but rather that they turn from their ways and live. Turn! Turn from your evil ways! Why will you die, O house of Israel?'"** (v.11). Life was possible only as they took action, as they repented of their evil ways. No one else could do it for them.

The news of the fall of Jerusalem to the Babylonians freed Ezekiel from the limitations placed upon him in 3:24–27. He must have chafed under the complacency and lack of response to his message by his own people both in Babylon and back in Judah. Since he had not pronounced any specific judgment against Babylon as he had all the other nations, perhaps now he was free even to do that. As God's watchman he had the task of reproving those Jews who had escaped the conquest of Babylon but lived as fugitives in Judah. They were still unrepentant and claimed wrongly that now the land belonged to them (vv.23–29). Also, he needed to reprove the exiles among whom he lived for their greed and their stubbornness in regarding his words of warning as little more than entertainment (vv.30–33).

B. Judgment on the Bad Shepherds of Judah (34:1–31)

The term *shepherd* is used in this chapter to refer to the leaders of Judah, and it may include both political and religious leaders. It was a common metaphor for such leaders throughout the ancient Near East.

As in ch. 22, Ezekiel again denounced the leaders of the people for their sin in taking advantage of their position and power to satisfy their greed rather than for the good of the people. Instead of feeding the sheep, they had fed on the sheep. Ezekiel also rehearsed the theme of responsibility he had emphasized in ch. 18, this time telling the leaders that God held them accountable for what had happened to the flock (v.10) and that he will remove them from office. Instead, God himself will be the Shepherd, searching out the people in all the places to which they have been scattered (vv.11–16). As the Good Shepherd, he will bring them back home and feed and care for them with justice, probably alluding to the restoration after the Exile.

The Good Shepherd also will correct the social and economic inequalities that resulted when people of wealth and power took advantage of the poor Israelites (vv.17–22). This theme so common among the prophets became Jesus' own emphasis, taking Isa 61:1–2 as the text of his inaugural sermon in Nazareth (Lk 4:16–21).

The main point of this chapter is God's promise to raise up a ruler of the Davidic line, through whom God would rule his people (vv.23–24). At that time God would establish a **covenant of peace** (Heb. *šalom*, which includes all that makes for peace: wholeness, security, welfare, absence of hostility [v.25]). Peace is a reality when God rules, but only then.

C. Another Judgment Against Edom (35:1–15)

Here Ezekiel referred to Edom primarily as Mount Seir, the range that ran the entire length of that country. As seen in 25:12–14, the Edomites were both relatives and traditional enemies of Israel. In this short chapter Ezekiel harshly condemned Edom for its continual desire and effort to overthrow Israel, God's chosen nation. God had not overlooked or forgotten their enmity and cruelty.

D. Divine Consolation and Hope to Judah (36:1–38)

In ch. 6 Ezekiel had spoken judgment against "**the mountains of Isra-**el" because the people were following the Canaanite gods for whom they had erected shrines on every high hill. In ch. 36, however, Ezekiel used "**the mountains of Israel**" as a term to refer to the entire land of Israel (v.8). He spoke of them in a tone that reflected something of the uniqueness of the land, the land God had given to his own special people.

The purpose of this chapter was to encourage Israel to remember that although the surrounding nations had plotted against her to take her land away from her (vv.3–7), these nations would be punished and Israel soon would be brought home from exile and brought back to her hills again. Ezekiel was quick to point out, however, that God would do this not because Israel deserved it but for the **sake of** his **holy name** (v.22), and to show the holiness of his name among the nations.

Perhaps no other passage in the OT expresses so forcefully the idea of God's gracious acts in behalf of Israel as vv.24–28. Notice the verbs: "**I will take you out of the nations; I will gather you . . . bring you back. . . . I will sprinkle . . . I will cleanse. . . . I will give you a new heart and . . . put a new spirit in you. . . . I will remove from you your heart of stone and give you a heart of flesh. And I will put my Spirit in you and move you to follow by decrees. . . . I will be your God.**" When God restores his people, he forgives, regenerates, sanctifies, and empowers.

E. The Vision of the Valley of Dry Bones (37:1–28)

By using the terms "**the hand of the LORD was upon me**" and "**he brought me out by the Spirit of the LORD**" (37:1), Ezekiel clearly indicated a visionary experience similar to that which he wrote about in chs. 1 and 8. Thus there is no need to speculate about the location of the valley or why the bones were there. The vision confronted Ezekiel with several important issues: Is there any hope for Israel that is now dead and scattered to the four winds? Can it ever be brought back to life and restored to its homeland? If so, how will this be done? As Ezekiel carried out God's instructions, he saw and heard the bones come together to form bodies and come to life. So, too, God said, God would raise up the dead nation that was now in exile and restore her to her own land (v.13). This was not a physical resurrection of individual Israelites but a restoration of the nation, or remnant, which had learned through the Exile that God may judge sin but that he never stops loving the sinner.

The curious acted parable of the two sticks, one representing Israel and the other Judah (vv.15–28), promised the reunion of the nation of Israel again under a Davidic king. B. H. Hall notes, "This is not an allusion to a resurrected David, but to a second David, the originator of a new dynasty. . . . The fulfillment of this great promise is accomplished in Jesus Christ, the 'root of David'" (p. 469). God's **dwelling place** (v.27, Heb. *miškan*, "tent"), must be reflected in the Greek word *skēnē* ("tent"), which underlies John's statement that "the Word became flesh and lived for a while among us" (Jn 1:14). In the new kingdom over which the New David will rule, everyone will live up to the **covenant of peace** in holiness and righteousness (vv.24–28). Through the coming Holy Spirit, God's **sanctuary/dwelling** (vv.26–27) will be among them forever (Jn 14:16).

F. Gog and Magog (38:1–39:29)

Few other passages in the Bible have been subjected to such a variety of interpretations as have these two chapters. One cause for such disparate meanings is the frequent failure to recognize the nature of the writing. First of all, these chapters reflect again Ezekiel's characteristic use of highly symbolic language. Thus the reader must try to understand the meanings Ezekiel pictures. Also, since it is so symbolic, the message is not to be equated with any specific historical situation or personages, whether past, present, or future. To say that the message is symbolic is not to say that it is untrue. Rather, because of its nature it has a timeless message, one that may apply to any generation.

What then is this timeless message? Simply this: God has committed himself in covenant to his people, and he will not allow any enemy, no matter how great and powerful, to overcome them. This is a message Israel needed while in exile (vv.25–29), and it is a promise appropriate to any time or place when God's people face an overwhelming enemy. Whether or not these two chapters should be categorized as apocalyptic might be debated. But in the manner of apocalyptic writing, Ezekiel clearly sees God in control of history and sees that God will bring his people to ultimate victory.

At the very outset Ezekiel set the pattern for interpreting these two chapters. By naming the enemy of God's people as **Gog, of the land of Magog** (v.2), he obviously invented or made up the name of the king and his land. There simply is no historical record of a King Gog or a land of Magog. In fact, the place name *Magog* is clearly built on the name *Gog*, using the prefix *ma-* which is commonly used in Hebrew to mean "place of." Interestingly, in Rev 20:8 both Gog and Magog symbolize the nations of the world that have joined in a great battle against God and have been annihilated.

Thus it is futile to try to identify Gog and the land of Magog. Since Ezekiel nowhere else gives a specific judgment against Babylon, it would be easy to speculate that these chapters are really a veiled word of God's judgment against it. Still, these judgments could apply to any and all enemies of God's people in any generation. Early rabbis pointed out that the numerical value in the Hebrew for the name *Gog and Magog* is seventy. They then defined the number seventy to mean the seventy nations of the world. Thus Gog and Magog may mean any or all nations of the world.

In the three oracles against Gog (38:3, 14; 39:1), Ezekiel clearly shows God's sovereignty and superiority over all the forces of evil. Typically, they came from the north, the direction from which most of Israel's enemies came. Even when the Assyrians or Babylonians came against Israel, they had to come from the north since they could not cross the great desert that lay between Israel and the Mesopotamian Valley. The destruction of Gog's hordes is within God's great plan as he brings them from the far north and even sends them against the mountains of Israel (39:2). The extent of the slaughter of the enemy is beyond comprehension, for it will take seven months (*seven* used as symbolic number of completion) to bury the dead (v.12). The last oracle (v.17) is given to the birds and animals that are called to take part in a final victory banquet to celebrate God's victory over Gog and his forces.

This section ends with God's renewed promise to restore the people to their land and to covenant relationship with him (39:25–29). Then God will be able to reveal himself to the nations through the people upon whom he will pour out his Spirit.

X. VISION OF THE NEW JERUSALEM (40:1–48:35)

In his final vision, dated April 28, 573 B.C.E., Ezekiel received the divine plan for the restoration of the temple, the priesthood, and the Holy City, Jerusalem. While the modern reader may have difficulty with the tedious details Ezekiel gives for the restored temple and priesthood, all of this was of utmost importance for him and the returning exiles. For them, the restored temple and cultus was a sign, a means to something much greater, and that was the return of the presence and glory of Yahweh to Jerusalem and to his people. In the vision of chs. 8–11, Ezekiel had to face the fact that the gross sin of Israel would result in God's departure from the temple and the destruction of the temple and Jerusalem. We noted the tragic words in 10:18, "The glory of the LORD departed from over the threshold of the temple." This resulted in its destruction. However, the temple would be rebuilt, and God would again dwell in the midst of his people (37:27–28)!

A. The Restored Temple (40:1–42:20)

All building processes involve measurement, dimensions, and plans. In his vision, Ezekiel was introduced to a divine angel-guide (40:3–4) who showed him how the temple was to be built. Actual building of the new temple was authorized in 539 B.C.E. by the decree of Cyrus of Persia (Ezr 6:3). In that document only a few dimensions were given. When the temple was built under the leadership of Zerubbabel and the prodding of the prophets Haggai and Zechariah, the dimensions were not recorded in the texts of those prophets. Ezekiel's main concern was to point out God's direct involvement in the restoration process, from beginning to end. When Zechariah had his vision (Zec 2:1–13) of "a man with a measuring line" (Zec 2:1), the measuring at that time was to make certain that Jerusalem would be large enough to include all who wanted to enter it. Plans for the new temple were to ensure a residence adequate for God's presence in the midst of his people.

B. The Return of God's Glory (43:1–27)

The vision of the restored temple is climaxed with Ezekiel's triumphal statement, **"I saw the glory of the God of Israel coming from the east!"** (v.2). Some nineteen years earlier God's glory had departed from the polluted temple and then from the city of Jerusalem itself (10:18–19). Now God's glory again filled the temple (v.5) as it had the wilderness tabernacle (Ex 40:34–35) and later Solomon's temple (1Ki 8:11). The vision was fulfilled some fifty-five years later when God commanded Zerubbabel and the returning exiles, "Build the house, so that I may take pleasure in it and be honored" (Hag 1:8).

The new temple was to be a holy place, God's throne and footstool. Never again was it to be defiled by the harlotry and pollution of the worship of other gods. Neither was it to be secularized by connection to the royal palaces as the former temple had been. All of God's instructions concerning the temple were to be written down for the people as a lesson in holiness and so that the people might **be faithful to its design and follow all its regulations** (v.11). Holiness was to be the law of the temple (v.12) as the NT later would teach: "God's temple is holy and that temple you are" (1Co 3:17 RSV).

While the next section (vv.13–27) may be misplaced here, it still emphasizes the need for preserving the holiness of the temple and its worship. The leaders of worship, the priests, must always be spiritually qualified and ready to guide the people in this experience with God.

C. The New Priesthood (44:1–31)

Further instructions regarding the temple include the command that the eastern gate would not be opened again since God's glory had entered through it and would never leave it again. As Ezekiel followed the man, the divine angel-guide, around to the north gate of the temple, he saw God's glory filling the temple. At this, he fell on his face before the holiness of God (v.4). This reemphasis of the awesome holiness of God led to further divine instructions for the preservation of the holiness of the temple. No longer would it be possible for non-Levites to enter the temple even to do required maintenance work. This work was to be done by Levites who were descendants of those Levites who had sinned against God in earlier times (v.10). Only those Levites who were the descendants of Zadok, who had been faithful to God (vv.15–16), would be allowed to officiate at the temple. All that such priests were and did was to validate their holiness and thus the holiness of God. The term *holiness* (Heb. *qodeš*) means "to be set apart for a special function." Since priests were set apart by and for God, they were to be *morally pure* as God is.

D. New Rules for the New Temple (45:1–46:24)

Nothing was to be left to chance in the restored or new community. It seemed necessary, then, to lay down new rules so that everything having to do with worship was done correctly so that a sense of God's holiness was preserved.

When the Israelites settled the land under Joshua, it was divided among the tribes according to divine instructions given in Jos 13–21. No land or territory was given to the tribe of Levi (Jos 13:14). Nor was there any setting apart of crown lands, lands for the king, since there was no king except God. In 45:1–8 and especially in 48:1–7, 23–29, Ezekiel was given specific instructions concerning the redivision of the land. The Levites who were descendants of Zadok were not assigned any lands of their own, for God said, "I am to be the only inheritance the priests have" (44:28). However, certain lands were to be set aside for the Levites who were not Zadokite priests, as well as for the temple complex, the palace area, and the tribes in general. This was to prevent land grabbing, especially by the prince, which had happened in earlier days. In fact, the prince was to be the custodian and example of justice, demonstrating in his own life the principles of divine holiness. It was his responsibility to safeguard the just balance and to guarantee honest weights and measurements.

The three main annual festivals, New Year, Passover, and Tabernacles, were emphasized. But the Day of Atonement is not mentioned. In these festivals as well as the Sabbath and the New Moon festival, the prince was to be a participant and an example for all the people.

E. New Life From the New Temple (47:1–12)

For the last time the divine guide led Ezekiel to the temple where he saw water flowing out from under the temple itself. Following the flow of the water, Ezekiel saw it increase from a trickle to a river more than a mile wide.

This symbolic stream not only watered the desert, but it flowed into the sea and sweetened it, producing great schools of fish. On its banks grew all kinds of fruit trees and trees with healing leaves. Thus Ezekiel envisioned how the return of Yahweh to the new temple would bless the whole world and its peoples. The obvious NT parallel passage is Rev 22:1–5. There the river of the water of life flows out from the throne of God and of the Lamb. No longer, however, is there a need for a temple, for "the Lord God Almighty and the Lamb are its temple" (Rev 21:22). In the new day all are invited to "take the free gift of the water of life" (Rev 22:17).

F. New Boundaries for the New Land (47:13–48:29)

In this section Ezekiel described the ideal boundaries of the new land. This idealization obviously ignored the division of the land into the northern kingdom and the southern kingdom in 922 B.C.E. under Rehoboam (1Ki 12). This division had ended in the destruction of both kingdoms and the virtual dissolution of tribal lines and distinctions. Thus references to "the tribes [of Israel]" are found in the text of the postexilic prophets only three times (Isa 49:6; 63:17; Zec 9:1). Here, however, Ezekiel looks toward an equal redivision of the land along traditional tribal lines, including the double tribe of Joseph. In fact, all the tribes are mentioned along with their territorial boundaries in 48:1–7, 23–28. It is not clear how or why both the northern and southern boundaries of the new land far exceed the widest extent of the kingdom under David. A new note of universalism is struck by the provision that even resident aliens would be granted property rights and citizenship in the new era (47:21–23).

The central place which the temple and Jerusalem held in the theology of Ezekiel is emphasized again in 48:8–22 (which is an expansion of the provisions in 45:1–8). A special block of territory in the center was to be reserved for the temple and the king. The central focus for the life of the new Israel would be the temple and the worship of God who lived in the midst of his people.

G. The New Name for the New Jerusalem (48:30–35)

This last section of the book of Ezekiel is a fitting climax to all that the prophet-priest had seen and written. He described the New Jerusalem as having twelve gates, each named for one of the twelve tribes of Israel. This list of tribes is different from the usual list. Included now were the tribe of Joseph, not the half-tribes Ephraim and Manasseh, and the tribe of Levi, which traditionally was given no land of its own. The naming of the twelve gates after the twelve tribes implied unity of the tribes and equal participation in the new city. Symbolically, the tribes thus surrounded the new city, and so the city, and especially the new temple in the new city, were to be central to the life of all the tribes.

Most important of all is the concluding sentence of the book: **"The name of the city from that time on will be:** THE LORD [YAHWEH] IS THERE" (Heb. *Yahweh-šammah*). Yahweh, who had departed from the temple and the city because of the terrible sins of the people (10:18), would again reside in the temple and Jerusalem in the restored kingdom. And he would never leave again.

A rabbinic tradition adds an interesting variation on the interpretation of the new name of the new city (Zimmerli, *Ezekiel 2*, 547). By only a slight change of the vowel pointing, the Hebrew can be read *Yahweh-šemah*, "Yahweh Is Its Name!" Either reading, or both, may well have expressed Ezekiel's ecstasy as he concluded his book. No further visions were necessary.

BIBLIOGRAPHY

Beasley-Murray, G. R. "Ezekiel." NBC. Edited by F. Davidson et al. Grand Rapids: Eerdmans, 1954.

Bruce, F. F. "Ezekiel." IBC. Edited by F. F. Bruce. Grand Rapids: Zondervan, 1986.

Cooke, G. A. *A Critical and Exegetical Commentary on the Book of Ezekiel*. ICC. 2 vols. Edinburgh: T. & T. Clark, 1936. New York: Scribner, 1937.

Ellison, H. L. *Ezekiel: The Man and His Message*. Grand Rapids: Eerdmans, 1956.

Greenberg, Moshe. *Ezekiel, 1–20*. AB. Vol. 22. New York: Doubleday, 1983.

Hall, Bert H. "The Book of Ezekiel." WBC. Vol. 3. Grand Rapids: Eerdmans, 1969.

Levey, S. H. *The Targum of Ezekiel: Translated with a Critical Introduction, Apparatus, and Notes*. The Aramaic Bible. Vol. 13. Wilmington, Del.: Glazier, 1987.

May, H. G. "The Book of Ezekiel: Introduction and Exegesis." IB. Vol. 6. Nashville: Abingdon, 1956.

Rosenberg, Joel. "Jeremiah and Ezekiel." *The Literary Guide to the Bible*. Edited by R. Alter and F. Kermode. Cambridge: Belknap Press of Harvard University Press, 1987.

Zimmerli, Walther. *Ezekiel 1*. Hermeneia Series. Translated by R. E. Clemens. Philadelphia: Fortress, 1979.

_____, *Ezekiel 2*. Hermeneia Series. Translated by J. D. Martin. Philadelphia: Fortress, 1983.

DANIEL

G. Herbert Livingston

INTRODUCTION

I. TITLE, CONTENT, CANONICAL PLACEMENT

The title is the same as the name of the main character of the book, Daniel.

Six stories make up the first six chapters. See the outline for titles of each story. The other chapters preserve Daniel's visions of wild animals that represented present and future kingdoms, as well as visions of future events and the time of the end. These visions are explained by angels. Ch. 9 has an agonizing prayer offered by Daniel to God.

Regularly in the Hebrew Bible, Daniel appears between Esther and Ezra-Nehemiah. The Septuagint places Daniel after Ezekiel and before I Maccabees, with additions attached. Protestant English translations place Daniel after Ezekiel and before Hosea.

II. HISTORICAL SETTING, AUTHORSHIP, AND DATE

The book of Daniel spans the time period of 605 to 536 B.C., which involves both the Babylonian Empire and the beginning of the Persian Empire. Daniel, with others, was taken into exile when Babylon conquered Judah. The first four chapters are placed in the reign of Nebuchadnezzar (605–561 B.C.); 5, 7, and 8 in the reign of Belshazzar. Ch. 6 relates the fall of Babylon to the Persians in 539. The remaining chapters belong to the next three years.

Through the centuries, most Jewish and Christian scholars have accepted Daniel as valid prophetic prediction and, most have regarded Daniel as a historical person of the sixth century B.C. Most critical scholars and a few conservative scholars differ with this assessment of the book. Both the Hebrew and Aramaic of Daniel can fit into the sixth and fifth centuries B.C.

III. STRUCTURE AND THEOLOGICAL THEMES

The book of Daniel is divided into two sections. Chs. 1–6 are in story form with some poetry. Chs. 7–12 are essentially apocalyptic literature, mostly in prose form and concerned with the relationship of a series of kingdoms to God's people. This literature is futuristic, extending to the end times.

The book is written in two languages, with 1:1–2:4a and chs. 8–12 in Hebrew, whereas 2:4b through 7:28 are in Aramaic.

Each story opens with the chief character troubled by a difficult problem and forced to make a decision related to a life-threatening crisis. In a miraculous way, God provided aid, which resolved the crisis and brought glory to his name.

Each story is written in the third person, except for 4:1–27, 34–37, which are in the first person. Within these stories are five poems in the NIV text: 2:20–23; 4:3, 34–35; 5:25–28; 6:26b–27.

In chs. 7–12, the visions experienced by Daniel and interpreted by angels are in narrative prose. In the NIV text, 7:9–10 is in poetic form. Both the visions and the interpretations are marked by symbolic images, metaphors, similes, and other figures of speech.

The cardinal doctrine in the book is the sovereignty of God over all nations and their potentates. Daniel and his friends were hostages. Repeatedly their lives were in danger because of their total commitment to their God and his laws. God powerfully delivered them, and mighty rulers acclaimed the supremacy of the one true God.

Three vicious beasts and a horrible monster, representing four empires, threatened the existence of the people of God, but a Messiah was promised who would save them. Finally God would resurrect the righteous to everlasting life and the unrighteous to face contempt. To the holy ones the book has a theology of hope; to the wicked it has a theology of divine justice that punishes wicked rulers and brings empires to ruin.

The book amply illustrates the reliability of divine revelation about the future. Not only were the symbols of dreams and visions in accord with present reality, they were in accord with future events that God brought to pass. God has a plan of judgment for the wicked and a plan of redemption for those who trust in him, and he faithfully carries those plans out.

The book also highlights the effectiveness of prayer as a means: (1) to discover the will of God; (2) to obtain courage to make a total commitment regardless of circumstances; (3) to obtain assurance that God will be with those in danger even unto death; (4) to confess one's own sins and the sins of one's people; and (5) to petition God for fulfillment of the prophecy of a previous prophet, in this case Jeremiah (9:2–3). The book testifies that these prayers were heard and answered by a gracious God in his own remarkable way.

IV. OUTLINE

Major Theme: God Reigns Over All Nations Effectively

    I. A Serious Choice (Ch. 1)

    II. The Dream Image (Ch. 2)

COMMENTARY

I. A SERIOUS CHOICE (CH. 1)

Daniel, along with others, was carried into captivity as a hostage in 605 B.C. by Nebuchadnezzar's armies. The Jerusalem temple was also plundered.

Meats and drinks in Babylon were offered to idols before they were consumed. Mosaic law prohibited the Hebrews from eating such foods. Daniel arranged with a guard to test himself and his four friends by allowing them to eat their own diet for ten days.

God granted them better health, wisdom, and understanding than any of the other hostages; therefore the guard allowed the five Hebrew men to continue eating the foods allowed by their divine laws.

When Nebuchadnezzar examined those who had been in training, he declared that they were superior to the **magicians and enchanters** who belonged to the royal court. This was the first of a series of events in which the captives who committed themselves fully to their God triumphed over all the pagan leaders of two empires.

II. THE DREAM IMAGE (CH. 2)

As in the story of Joseph (Ge 40–41), dreams of idol worshipers and dream interpretation play a significant role in several stories in this book.

The emperor determined to put his court **wise men** to a severe test; he demanded that they tell him the content of his dream before they gave its interpretation. Their failure to do so would be death. The wise men were astounded, claiming that only the gods could do such a thing.

Daniel requested an extension of time. The royal guards were unable to distinguish between his spiritual gifts and the tricks of the diviners.

Daniel and his friends prayed, and the God of heaven revealed to Daniel the secret of the dream and its meaning in a vision. Daniel rejoiced in a psalm of praise and thanked him for granting a revelation that would clear up the mystery and save his life.

When Daniel reported to Nebuchadnezzar, he began by disclaiming any personal skill or special power to reveal the ruler's dream. What he had to say was a revelation from the God of heaven. No wise man in Babylon would make such a denial of personal powers or affirm help from any other source than one or more of their nature deities. This marks the difference, noted throughout the OT, between the true prophet and all false prophets. Joseph gave a similar testimony to the pharaoh of Egypt (Ge 41:16).

The dream was of a giant statue with a head of gold, chest and arms of silver, belly and thighs of bronze, legs of iron, and feet of a mixture of iron and clay.

The head was Nebuchadnezzar, but the other parts represented kingdoms yet to come, hence, cast in the future tense as predictions. In effect, this interpretation laid bare the fraud in the wise men's "skills" and demonstrated the wisdom and power of the one true God. Nebuchadnezzar recognized this and honored Daniel and exalted his God as **revealer of mysteries.**

III. THE SUPERHOT FURNACE (CH. 3)

The next event recorded was a confrontation between the emperor with his idols and three Hebrew men who worshiped the God who could not be represented by an idol or identified with an earthly ruler no matter how powerful.

Since all officials and subjects of the emperor were required to worship the image of gold, it clearly was an idol representing some high god, probably Marduk, a favorite of the emperor. A royal decree demanded the worship of this image. Any who refused would die.

Nebuchadnezzar was told that Shadrach, Meshach, and Abednego would not bow to the image. In a rage, Nebuchadnezzar demanded to know whether the report was true. The three admitted as much and declared boldly that their God was able to save them. If God chose not to, they would die rather than worship idols.

Ordinarily the temperature of Babylonian furnaces was controlled by bellows. Instead of one bellows, seven

were attached to this one. The men were tossed into the flames.

Nebuchadnezzar, who was watching the execution, was startled. The three men did not die, and he saw beside them another who looked **like a son of the gods.** The men were ordered to step out of the furnace, and three did, having suffered no harm. The emperor announced that an angel from God had protected the men, and he began to praise God. Then he promptly issued a decree prohibiting anyone from speaking against the God of the Jews. In effect, this decree provided protection for all Jews in the empire, for the penalty was a horrible death. The one true God had dramatically shown his reality and his power to save his followers from death.

IV. THE HUGE TREE (CH. 4)

This royal report is unusual, for it is in the first person and was published as a personal letter. The king first confessed his belief in the God of wonders, the God the Israelites served. In contrast to pagan deities, this God rules over **an eternal kingdom.** Then the king called in Daniel.

The remark in parentheses in 4:8 indicates that Nebuchadnezzar had not given up his polytheistic beliefs, though he was able to voice correct doctrines about the God of the Hebrews. He still regarded Daniel as the best of the magicians with a special divine spirit in him. This was a polytheistic concept.

Nebuchadnezzar said he dreamed of a large tree that a messenger from heaven had ordered chopped down. The stump was depicted as a man who had lost his mind and become like an animal in the field.

When the emperor asked for an interpretation, Daniel became very disturbed. Reluctantly Daniel explained that Nebuchadnezzar was the tree, for he was a mighty ruler, but the sovereign Lord had decreed his downfall. He would become an animal in the fields unless he sincerely **acknowledge[d] that heaven rules.** Clearly though the king had several times admitted that the God of the Hebrews was mighty, he had remained unwilling to let the one true God rule over his own life.

Nothing happened for a year. Perhaps Nebuchadnezzar was too frightened to challenge the sovereignty of the God of heaven during that time. Eventually he began to boast of his **power and the glory of** his **majesty.**

Nebuchadnezzar's probation period was over. The voice of the Judge uttered the verdict. The tree would now be cut and the king would live like an animal. Nebuchadnezzar's mighty power could not prevent it; he was soon in the fields eating like the animals.

Nebuchadnezzar testified that he recovered his sanity and praised the eternal **Most High.** God granted the emperor full restoration to his throne and empire. Nebuchadnezzar now fully confessed his devotion to the one true God whose ways he called **right** and **just.** The act of humbling the proud is included as one of those ways.

V. BELSHAZZAR'S LAST FEAST (CH. 5)

The last event in the reign of the last king of Babylon is brought into focus because God acted decisively to issue a verdict of judgment.

During a drunken orgy, the intoxicated king was startled as he watched a mysterious hand inscribe words on the palace wall. Faint with fear, he summoned his **wise men** to read and interpret the words. They were helpless, and the king was gripped with panic.

The queen recommended Daniel,

and he was summoned. She praised him as the best of the magicians and diviners, not understanding that he was very different from them. The king assumed that Daniel's previous interpretations were due to Daniel's having a special power. A large reward was offered. Daniel refused the gifts, a striking difference between himself and the **wise men.**

Daniel read and interpreted the words. *Mene* can be a unit of money (about one and one-half pounds of precious metal), or it can mean "numbered." Thus the word is tied to both the metal of the sacred vessels and to the countdown of Belshazzar's reign. It had come to zero point.

Tekel could mean "shekel" (1/50 of a "mina") or "measurement by weight." The Lord of heaven had put Belshazzar on the scales of judgment, and he was spiritually empty. *Peres* could mean either "Persia" (a merger of the Medes and Persians), or it could mean "divided" (one-half of a unit of money). The Babylonian Empire would be cut up and given to an invading army.

In contrast to Nebuchadnezzar, this king did not exalt the name of God. His doom was sealed: that night he died in the maelstrom of Babylon's destruction.

VI. THE LION'S DEN (CH. 6)

Who was Darius? He probably was not one of the later emperors of the Persian Empire, but his name may have been an alternate name for Gabaru, the governor of Babylon after its fall.

Daniel was retained as one of the three top administrators and did so well that he was considered for the position of grand vizier. Daniel's enemies decided to embarrass him at the point of **the law of his God.** These laws were basically different from those of Persia's polytheism.

A legal trap was set. By the use of flattery, the wise men convinced Darius to issue a decree outlawing any worship that was not directed to idols or to the king.

When Daniel heard of the decree, he knew that he was the target with all other God-fearing Jews. Deliberately, Daniel went home and prayed to God as usual; he was caught in the act of worship.

The disobedience was reported to Darius who immediately saw the hidden agenda behind the request for the decree. The king tried desperately to find a loophole in the law but could not. Daniel's enemies forced the king to condemn Daniel to death in the **lion's den.**

Darius was not an intolerant man, and as Daniel was thrown into the den, the king expressed a wish that Daniel's God would somehow come to the rescue.

Darius spent a sleepless night, deeply distressed about Daniel's plight. At dawn he unsealed the den and cried out in anguish, seeking whether **the living God** had saved Daniel's life. His request was a mixture of dread and wavering faith. Daniel's voice came booming back. He was alive because God's **angel** had muzzled the lions. Daniel's faithfulness and innocence had been honored by his God. Daniel was taken unharmed from the den. His trust in the one true and just God had not been misplaced, just as in the case of the three Hebrews in the furnace.

Darius gave evidence of his new faith by condemning Daniel's accusers to death in the same **lion's den.** Neither the deities of these men nor their vaunted and mysterious skills could save them.

On the other hand, Darius issued a new decree throughout the kingdom. The decree was stronger in tone than the one sent by Nebuchadnezzar (3:29); it required that everyone **fear and reverence the God of Daniel.** The king then affirmed the eternal sovereignty of the true God and his power to save those who worship God, even as he had **rescued Daniel.**

VII. THE FOUR BEASTS (CH. 7)

Daniel was overwhelmed by a dream about four beasts. This happened before the event described in chs. 5 and 6; it occurred at the beginning of Belshazzar's reign in Babylon. The exact date is unknown.

Daniel wrote an account of the dream in the first person. Much like Ezekiel's vision (Eze 1:1–5), a storm was involved but the four beasts were different. The first was a lion with eagle wings, which were quickly torn off. The lion took on some human features. The second **looked like a bear** whose mouth gripped **three ribs.** The third was like a leopard with four wings and four heads. The last beast was a monster with **large iron teeth** and **ten horns.** Soon a smaller, eleventh horn with a human mouth and eyes **came up among** the other **horns.**

The most remarkable sequel of the dream was the arrival of **the Ancient of Days.** Daniel was so uplifted by this vision he wrote this section as a hymn of praise. The description is much like Ezekiel's portrayal of One on a throne (1:25–28) and that of the apostle John (Rev 1:12–17). In Daniel's dream, the throne is in a court of justice.

A **son of man** appeared from the clouds and was installed by the **Ancient of Days** as the authentic and eternal world ruler. He was worshiped by all people of the world.

Daniel was still puzzled about the

four beasts and sought an explanation. A heavenly being told him that they represented four kingdoms that were different from the one belonging to the **saints** (true worshipers of God). Their kingdoms would be the everlasting kingdom of the **Ancient of Days** and the Son of Man.

The significance of the monster was still a mystery to Daniel, for its eleven horns fought against the saints. Then he saw the **Ancient of Days** punish the horns and give victory to the saints. This horrible beast was a future kingdom with a succession of ten rulers. The final ruler was the boastful little horn who would violently fight against the **Most High** and oppress the saints. His period of power, **time, times and half a time,** add up to three and a half years.

The vicious tyrant would be brought before the heavenly court, convicted and destroyed. In his place God would provide an eternal kingdom for his saints. The rulers of that kingdom would always worship God. In the final showdown between evil and righteousness, God and his people would win. Thus Daniel received a theology of hope that sustained his troubled soul.

VIII. THE RAM AND THE GOAT (CH. 8)

Two years later Daniel had another dream/vision dominated by wild animals, a ram and a goat. Daniel saw them not in Babylon where he was, but near Susa by the **Ulai Canal,** which connected the now-named Kerkha and Abdizful rivers.

There he saw first a ram with two long horns charging in every direction, defeating all foes he met. Then a goat with one horn between his eyes charged out of the west and defeated the ram. Later the one horn was broken off and replaced by four horns and then

a fifth one that grew very large. It gained power even over the **Beautiful Land** (the land of Israel). The temple was desecrated and also worshipers of God, the **saints,** were **given over to it.**

Gabriel explained the vision to Daniel. Daniel was terrified, but addressing him as **son of man,** Gabriel stated that the animals and their activities represented events in **the time of the end.**

Though Daniel was having difficulty coping with the content of the vision, he heard Gabriel explain that the two-horned ram was a symbol of the kings of the Medes and Persians, and the goat a symbol of the king of Greece. The single horn was the first king and the four horns that replaced it were kings of four subdivisions of the Grecian Empire. The little horn that grew great in power would be vicious and destructive, even challenging the **Prince of princes,** the almighty God.

Gabriel confirmed the truth of these predictions and commanded Daniel to **seal up the vision.** Centuries have gone by since then, and history preserves the records of the rise and fall of the ram, the Persian Empire (539–333 B.C.), which was dominated by two peoples (two horns), the Medes and the Persians.

History also records the remarkable conquest of that empire by the Greeks led by Alexander the Great (the single horn on the goat) beginning in 333 B.C. He died suddenly at the age of thirty-three in 323. His vast empire was divided among four generals: Seleucus, ruler of Babylon; Ptolemy, ruler of Egypt; Lysimachus, ruler of Thrace and Asia Minor; and Cassander, ruler of Greece and Macedonia.

The little horn was Antiochus IV Epiphanes (215–163 B.C.) whose center of power was in Syria. He invaded Egypt in 170–169 B.C. and Parthia as well. He took control of the land of

Israel from Egypt and terrorized the Jews who lived there. In December 168 B.C. he ordered his armies to seize Jerusalem, set up an idol of Zeus in the temple, and sacrificed pigs on the altar.

Two years later the Jews revolted under the leadership of the priest Mattathias, and the next year one of his sons, Judas Maccabeus, rededicated the temple in Jerusalem. The date was December 25, 165 B.C. Jews still celebrate this occasion in their Feast of Hanukkah.

Antiochus IV died insane in Persia in 163 or 164 B.C. God and his saints had won again.

IX. THE PROPHET'S PRAYER AND PREDICTION (CH. 9)

In the first years of the same Darius the Mede mentioned in 6:1 (538 B.C.), Daniel was reading the scroll of Jeremiah, regarding it as trustworthy Scripture. Daniel noted that Jeremiah, who had died about two decades before, had predicted a period of seventy years for **the desolation of Jerusalem** (Jer 25:11–13; 29:10).

Jerusalem had fallen in 586 B.C., and more than twenty years remained before the prediction would be fulfilled. It actually occurred in 516 B.C. when the temple was rebuilt in Jerusalem. Daniel began to pray about the matter.

Like Isaiah (Isa 6:5), Daniel was keenly aware of the holiness and righteousness of God and the unfaithfulness and shame of all Israel. But Daniel was filled with faith and hope. He believed God was **merciful and forgiving** in spite of the rebellion of Israel against God.

Daniel did not accuse God of irresponsibility in letting many of his people go into exile. Daniel's God was the Judge who justly punished his wicked people. For centuries the law of Moses had warned Israel against rebel-

lion. Now, in exile, God's people were still rebelling. They had learned nothing from their punishment.

Daniel's hope was based on the act of God at the Exodus from Egypt, and he pleaded that God in mercy would forgive and deliver his people again. The exile of God's people and the ruins of Jerusalem had generated scorn in the hearts of many pagans.

Daniel pressed his petition with emotional intensity, and casting all other reasons aside, even his own merit, rested his plea solely on the mercies of God as related to a long relationship to Jerusalem and Israel. All effective supplication rests upon the same foundation.

Daniel's prayer achieved results. Gabriel arrived and assured Daniel that God had begun to answer as Daniel started to pray. Gabriel's message was based on the numbers seventy and seven. The possible literal or symbolic values of these numbers in the visions of Daniel have generated as many varieties of opinion among Wesleyan scholars as among those of other persuasions. Daniel's prayer could be understood as fulfilled historically. The time span from Daniel's exile in 605 B.C. to the decree of Cyrus (which allowed Jews to return to Jerusalem in 537 B.C.), plus a period of time for Jews to arrive there, amounts to about seventy years.

Gabriel gave an extended future value to seventy and seven, amounting to 490 years. During this time, **transgression** and **sin** were to be brought to an end and atonement made for **wickedness.** Other themes appear in 9:24: (1) the inception of **everlasting righteousness,** (2) the sealing of **vision and prophecy,** and (3) the anointing of the **most holy.**

Another numerical phrase, **seven "sevens" and sixty-two "sevens,"** refers to the time before **the Anointed One,** would arrive.

Jesus seemed to pick up on the remaining verses of this chapter in his Olivet Discourse (Mt 24:7–28) and apply them to an indefinite end time.

Theological themes evident in this section may be summarized thus: (1) In spite of sin, tyranny, and destruction, God's people in any age have a firm foundation of hope; (2) atonement for sin has been provided, and through confession, repentance, and faith it will transform the sinner into a believer; (3) God's everlasting kingdom has an almighty Messiah who will rule in mercy, truth, and justice; and (4) eventually, in spite of evil-minded opposition, God and his people will always be winners.

X. THE HEAVENLY MESSAGE TO DANIEL (CHS. 10–12)

The date, according to our calendar, would be 535 or 534 B.C. The **revelation** was about war, and its interpretation came in a **vision** seen by the Tigris River.

In many respects, the **man** seen in the vision looked like the Ancient of Days (7:9–10; see also Eze 1:15–21, 26–27; Rev 1:13–16). Daniel's companions saw nothing but fled in fear; Daniel fell to the ground in a **deep sleep.** A divine touch brought him to his feet.

The message was a response to Daniel's prayers as he sought understanding of the end times. The angel mentioned a struggle with Persia, and another angel, Michael, came to **help** Daniel.

Daniel could not cope with the overwhelming presence of his visitor; his body became weak, and anguish gripped him. Another touch revived him to hear more of the message. The angel would return to confront Persia, and afterward the Greeks would come.

However, Darius the Mede had been found worthy of support. Clearly the great empires of that era were regarded as enemies of the Most High God and must be subdued.

The next section (11:2–45) is cast in the future tense in keeping with the statement **"The vision concerns a time yet to come"** (10:14). After Cyrus there would be four more kings. Historically, these kings were Cambyses (530–522 B.C.); Pseudo-Smerdis (522 B.C.); Darius I (522–486 B.C.); and Xerxes I (486–465 B.C.), who tried and failed to conquer Greece.

A century is skipped to pick up a **mighty king,** Alexander the Great of Greece (336–323 B.C.) and the four generals who followed him (**the four winds**).

Wars would take place between kings of the North and kings of the South. Historically, the identification of the following seems fairly certain: **The king of the South** (v.5) was Ptolemy I (323–285 B.C.), ruler of Egypt, and his rebel commander was Seleucus I (311–280 B.C.), who took control of Babylonia. The **daughter** (v.6) was Bernice, whose father was Ptolemy II (285–246 B.C.). Her husband was Antiochus II (261–246 B.C.).

The former wife of Antiochus was Laodice, who led a conspiracy that ended in the death of both Antiochus and Bernice in 246 B.C. Ptolemy II died the same year. The next Egyptian king (v.7), Ptolemy III (246–221 B.C.), killed Laodice and defeated the new king of the North, Seleucus II (246–226 B.C.), whose fortress was at Antioch, Syria. The latter's sons, Seleucus II (226–223 B.C.) and Antiochus III (223–187 B.C.) kept pressure on the Egyptian fortress at Raphia in southern Palestine until it fell in 217, during the reign of Ptolemy IV (221–203 B.C.).

The crucial struggle took place in

198 B.C. when Antiochus III took all of Palestine (vv.14–16) from Ptolemy V (203–181 B.C.). In a treaty between the two rulers, Antiochus III gave his daughter (v.17) to Ptolemy V in marriage.

Antiochus III conquered Asia Minor. But he was blocked by the Roman consul Lucius Cornelius Scipio Asiaticus who defeated him at the Battle of Magnesia, Asia Minor, in 190 B.C. (v.18). Antiochus III died in 187 B.C. (v.19). **His successor** was Seleucus IV (187–175 B.C.) who had a **tax collector** named Heliodorus. This man was killed by Seleucus IV (v.20). **The contemptible person** was Antiochus IV Epiphanes who usurped the throne from the crown prince (v.21) and did his best to destroy the Jewish religion. He was the little horn of 8:9–12: In his title "Epiphanes" he touted himself as "God Manifest" and thus claimed divinity.

The **prince of the covenant** (v.22) was Ptolemy VII who ascended Egypt's throne at the age of six (181–145 B.C.). Vv.22–28 seem to deal with the tides of peace and war between the North and the South when treaties were often broken. Making a strong effort to annex Egypt, Antiochus IV was confronted by a Roman navy and told by Poplius Laenas to go home, a command that was quickly obeyed.

The real interest of Antiochus IV was the abolition of the Jewish religion (the holy covenant, v.28) in Jerusalem. The issue was the occupant of the high priestly office, and Antiochus IV entered Jerusalem to enforce his will. The climax of the struggle was the placement of an image of Zeus in the temple and the sacrifice of pigs on the high altar. The event took place in December, 168 B.C. In his Olivet Discourse, Jesus picked up the phrase (v.31) "the abomination that causes desolation"

(Mt 24:15; Mk 13:14) and applied it to a siege of Jerusalem in the last days.

Antiochus IV was able to divide the leaders of Jerusalem by offering awards to those who would support Greek concepts. Some went to his side and **violated the covenant,** whereas others took a stand for their God (v.32), suffering great personal loss, even their lives. Led by the priest Mattathias and his five sons, the Maccabees, the faithful among the Jews were able to throw off the yoke of the Greeks. Another group set up a community at Qumran on the northwest corner of the Dead Sea. Vv.33–34 describe these daring followers of God. The process of refinement, purification and being **made spotless** was not limited to them; it remains in operation to the **time of the end.**

The perspective of the message shifts from Antiochus IV to a tyrant in a far distant future who will be much like him but more vicious and blasphemous in behavior. During his domination of the world, promoting a world religion, the believers in the one true God will suffer greatly. Wars will rage between super powers (symbolized by North and South), and little nations, especially Israel, will be crushed. When all who are good seem doomed to destruction, the Beast (Rev 19:19–21) will be defeated, **and no one will help him** (Da 11:45). God in his power will win the final victory.

The focus moves from the political and military activities of the mighty tyrant to the results of God's final victory for his faithful worshipers.

The names of these saints will be found in **the book** (see Ex 32:33; Ps 69:28; Mal 3:16; Rev 20:12). They will be delivered by means of a momentous event; the dead will **awake.** The wicked will be forever punished, but the wise and the soul-winners will shine like stars. All believers will have everlasting life. This is the only clear statement in the OT on the resurrection of the just and the unjust. Compare with Job 19:26; Ps 16:10–11; 17:15; 73:23–24; Isa 25:8.

Daniel was told to place a seal on the scroll containing this message, but he was greatly confused and asked several angels about the length of time involved. The answer was that for three and a half years (see 7:25) the **holy people** will be powerless.

Daniel wanted to know the outcome, for he was concerned about these **holy people.** The answer was partially evaded; Daniel was to seal the record of these predictions and be satisfied that the saints will be purified and the wicked will continue their wickedness throughout that 1,290-day (three-and-one-half-year-plus-twelve-day) period. The saints who wait another forty-five days will be blessed. This was the angelic hint that the faithful will be rewarded. Daniel will rest (die) but will rise again.

BIBLIOGRAPHY

Archer, Gleason L., Jr. "Daniel." EBC. Grand Rapids: Zondervan, 1985.

Baldwin, Joyce G. "Daniel: An Introduction and Commentary." TOTC. Downers Grove, Ill.: InterVarsity Press, 1978.

Clarke, Adam. "The Book of the Prophet Daniel." *A Commentary and Critical Notes.* Vol. 4. New York: Abingdon, n.d.

Gaebelein, Arno C. *The Prophet Daniel.* Grand Rapids: Kregel, 1907.

Hall, Bert H. "The Book of Daniel." WBC. Grand Rapids: Eerdmans, 1969.

Howie, Carl G. "The Book of Daniel." LBC. Richmond: John Knox, 1961.

Jeffery, A. and G. Kennedy. "The Book of Daniel." IB. New York: Abingdon, 1956.

Jerome. *Commentary on Daniel.* Translated by Gleason Archer. Grand Rapids: Baker, 1958.

Leupold, H. C. *Exposition of Daniel.* Columbus, Ohio: Wartburg, 1949.

Maclaren, Alexander. *Expositions of Holy Scripture.* Grand Rapids: Eerdmans, 1938.

Montgomery, James A. "A Critical and Exegetical Commentary on the Book of Daniel." ICC. New York: Scribner, 1963.

Porteous, Norman W. *Daniel: A Commentary.* Philadelphia: Westminster, 1965.

Rowley, H. H. *Darius the Mede and the Four World Empires in the Book of Daniel.* Cardiff: University of Wales, 1935.

Swim, Roy E. "The Book of Daniel." BBC. Kansas City: Beacon Hill, 1966.

Whitcomb, John C. *Darius the Mede: A Study in Historical Identification.* Grand Rapids: Eerdmans, 1959.

Wilson, Robert D. *Studies in the Book of Daniel.* New York: Knickerbocker, 1917.

Young, Edward J. *The Prophecy of Daniel, A Commentary.* Grand Rapids: Eerdmans, 1949.

HOSEA

John N. Oswalt

INTRODUCTION

The book of Hosea is one of the best-loved of the twelve shorter (unfortunately called "minor") prophetic books. It holds this place, in part, because of its passionate and highly emotional tone. But another reason is because of the picture of God it presents. Like Hosea, God is depicted as the offended spouse whose mate has forsaken him. Every reader can feel the sense of betrayal and outrage that God feels. But God's final word to Israel, like Hosea's to Gomer, is not one of well-deserved revenge. Rather, it is a word of deep appeal, an appeal to return and let all be forgiven. No one can read this book and believe that the God of the OT is but a God of legalistic wrath.

I. AUTHOR, DATE, AND COMPOSITION

Most OT scholars are agreed that Hosea son of Beeri (1:1) is the author of the book and that it was written in the northern kingdom of Israel sometime during the latter half of the eighth century (799–700 B.C.). It is difficult to be more precise than this because of the limited information given in the book. The Judean kings mentioned in 1:1 (Uzziah–Hezekiah) ruled from about 795–700 B.C. Strangely, the only Israelite king mentioned is Jeroboam II, who reigned over Israel from about 790–750 B.C. Perhaps the Israelite kings who succeeded Jeroboam until the fall of Israel in 722 B.C. are not mentioned because Hosea did not consider them to be legitimate rulers (see 8:4). Jeroboam's son Zechariah reigned only six months before being assassinated (2Ki 15:8–10) in the first of a series of palace coups that continued right down to the destruction of Samaria some thirty years later. At any rate, it seems likely that the materials in the book were first spoken from just before the end of Jeroboam's reign until just after the beginning of Hezekiah's reign. Thus the dates would be about 755 to 725 B.C.

Although it is possible that the materials in the book were first produced in written form, it is highly unlikely. Probably they were first delivered orally, then transcribed, either by the prophet himself or by a disciple. It is also possible that the materials are now in the chronological order of their first delivery, but that is not necessarily so. Just as books of collected sermons often follow topical or other arrangements, so it appears, do the prophetic books. In any case, most recent scholarship agrees that the bulk of the book was in writing before Hosea's death and that any editing that may have taken place after his death was of a relatively minor nature.

II. BACKGROUND

The kingdom of Israel, with its capital in Samaria, was entering its final period when Hosea began preaching. But this may not have been obvious to very many. Jeroboam's reign had been long, prosperous, and peaceful. The Jehu dynasty, of which Jeroboam was a member, had been Israel's most stable. The distant enemy Assyria had been dormant for a number of years, and the nearer enemies Syria and Judah had been at peace with Israel for some time. But beneath the surface, a person looking with the eyes of God would be able to see that all was not well. Israelite religion had become so thoroughly mixed with the Canaanite Baal religion that it clearly was not the religion of the Bible. The reasons for this mixing were fairly evident: the transcendent God of the Bible could not be manipulated through magical rituals: he called for a surrender of one's needs to his supply as he knew best. How much more comfortable is a religion where the natural, social, and psychological forces are deified and manipulated according to one's own wishes.

But this idolatrous kind of religion has a number of destructive side effects. One of these is the promiscuous exercise of sexuality. This is done because pagan religion believes sexuality to be the life force. The result is the destruction of marriage and the home. Another effect is the deification of power and the dehumanization of the powerless. Finally there is the loss of any purpose other than self-gratification and with it the loss of the ability to discipline oneself. Given these conditions, it was clear that, should Assyria reassert itself, Israel's end was near.

Of course, that is exactly what happened; within a decade of Jeroboam's death a new, energetic Assyrian monarch, Tiglath-Pileser III, had come to the throne and was vigorously pursuing Assyria's long-held foreign policy goal: to conquer Egypt. Unfortunately for Israel, she stood directly in the way of that design. So between 745 and 722 B.C. Israel suffered a series of hammer blows in which thousands of Israelites died and which eventually destroyed Israel as a nation. During this time, as desperate measures were tried to stave off disaster, palace coups, and frantic alliances, Hosea was crying out to the people to turn back to their one hope, their spurned lover, the Lord. But it was too late. Hosea's words survived; Israel did not.

III. PURPOSE

The purpose of the book is to show a complacent Israel the true nature of their relationship with God and to call them back to the only One who truly loves them. He is the only One who can supply the very things for which they are petitioning their idols. The book is set up as a court case in which God, the aggrieved husband, brings charges against his faithless wife, Israel (see 4:1–3). The charges include idolatry, sorcery, empty ritualism, corruption, faithlessness, brutality, and injustice. Nor are these merely the aberrations of a few; these conditions extend from the highest political and religious leaders right down to the dregs of society.

It would seem plain that nothing but divorce proceedings could issue from such horrendous failures. However, to the reader's surprise, that is not the case. Although the situation is dire, with all-but-inevitable consequences just ahead, still God does not want to dissolve his relationship with his beloved. Moreover, with prompt action, even those awful consequences could be averted. But if they are not, the coming disasters are not to be interpreted as expressions of God's abandonment of his people. Rather, they should be taken as spurs to return to the only One who ever really loved them.

IV. STRUCTURE AND OUTLINE

There is little agreement as to the overall structure of the book. Many would divide it into two segments: chs. 1–3 and chs. 4–14, but few agree on how to differentiate the content of the two sections. It is tempting to call chs. 1–3 the parable and chs. 4–14 the interpretation. However, ch. 2 is as much interpretation as is anything after ch. 3. From this uncertainty, the points of agreement become even fewer, for the materials in chs. 4–14 show no clear organizing principle. Therefore, the following suggestions should be taken as suggestions only.

Chs. 1–3 may be seen as an introduction, setting the stage for the rest of the book, both by means of Hosea's experience and by means of an explanation of the parallels between Hosea and God. Then chs. 4–14 expand upon the basic points already made. This expansion does not seem to follow any particular order, as noted above. However, there are three points at which offers of restoration seem to coincide with the end of a previous discussion. These occur at 6:1–3; 11:8–11; and 14:1–9. On this basis, it may be possible to subdivide chs. 4–14 into three segments: 4:1–6:3; 6:4–11:11; 11:12–14:9. The first segment dwells on the causes of Israel's sin: the corruption of the leaders; the second details the rebelliousness of Israel; and the third emphasizes their failure to learn the lessons of the past.

V. OUTLINE

    I. Introduction (1:1–3:5)
        A. Gomer's Adultery (1:1–2:1)
        B. Israel's Adultery (2:2–23)
        C. Hosea Buys Gomer Back (3:1–5)

    II. Israel's Sins and God's Love (4:1–14:9)
        A. Charges Against the Leaders (4:1–6:3)

COMMENTARY

I. INTRODUCTION (1:1–3:5)

In several cases OT prophets acted out their messages, often at the express command of God (see Isa 20:2–4; Jer 27:2–11; Eze 12:1–6). Many times (as in Isa 20 and Eze 4:9–15) the actions were disgraceful and unpleasant. Thus there is every reason to believe that the situations described in chs. 1 and 3 actually took place. They formed an unforgettable illustration of the real situation between God and Israel.

A. Gomer's Adultery (1:1–2:1)

See the introduction under background for a possible explanation of the absence of any reference to Jeroboam's successors (1:1). The reference to Gomer as **an adulterous wife** (v.2) does not necessarily refer to her behavior prior to her marriage to Hosea. It may simply describe her attitudes and tendencies. **"Vilest adultery"** (v.2) describes Israel's worship of other gods since the nation is "married" to God through the Sinai covenant.

The Jezreel Valley (1:4–5) in northern Israel is where Jeroboam's ancestor Jehu destroyed the previous ruling family, the house of Omri. Although he was acting in response to God's command, the slaughter went far beyond any such command (2Ki 10:11–14). We do not know whether Zechariah died in Jezreel, but it is virtually certain that the devastating defeats at Assyria's hand that signaled Israel's end occurred in that valley (see on 10:14).

Judah was the militarily weaker of the two survivors of Solomon's kingdom. If Israel could not fend off Assyria, what hope did Judah have? Nevertheless, Assyria never succeeded in conquering Judah. Why not? It was **by the LORD their God** (1:7).

Hos 1:9–2:1 deal with the great paradox of individuals suffering for their sins while the unconditional election of the nation still holds sway. Most of the people of that generation were not God's people. Nevertheless, God would not break his promise to Abraham (1:10). The nation *was* his people and would continue to be until the day when one leader would unite the two parts in Jezreel. That Jesus Christ is intended here is indicated by the fact that Nazareth sits directly on the brow of the great escarpment on the northern side of the Jezreel Valley.

B. Israel's Adultery (2:2–23)

Here the parallel between Gomer's and Israel's adultery alluded to in ch. 1

is developed fully. God's people have forsaken the Lord, their covenant "husband," in a misguided attempt to obtain the agricultural blessings that they thought the Canaanite fertility gods could provide (vv.5, 13). Actually, it was God who gave those blessings (v.8). So now he will take them away in order to show the impotence of the idols (v.7) and the shameful folly of Israel's behavior (vv.10, 13). But the ultimate purpose of this deprivation is not punishment. It is an attempt to bring the people to their senses and turn them back to God (vv.7, 14). This is an important point about the redemptive purpose of divine judgment.

This theme is fully developed in vv.14–23. As v.15 shows, God hopes that when Israel once again experiences a desert, she will be reminded of that first desert experience where God demonstrated his love to her. **"In that day"** (vv.16, 21) is one of the first occurrences of what will become a common prophetic formula to express those moments in time when God intervenes, whether in judgment or deliverance. Here God promises that once his people have finally recognized where the real source of blessing lies, he will pour out upon them the blessings of peace (v.18) and abundance (vv.21–23). Although Israel has experienced this promise to a degree, its ultimate fulfillment awaits the millennial kingdom.

Vv.19 and 20 are of special significance because of the key theological terms contained in them. The words *righteousness, justice, love, compassion, faithfulness,* and *knowledge,* are at the heart of OT religion.

C. Hosea Buys Gomer Back (3:1–5)

As a symbol of God's love, Hosea is commanded to do something that the law forbade: live again with an adulterous former wife (see Dt 24:1–4). It might be argued that there is no indication that Hosea had ever divorced Gomer, which is central to the Deuteronomic prohibition. Nevertheless, it is plain that, at the least, what Hosea is commanded to do is irregular and distasteful, not to mention humiliating. If this was true for Hosea, how much more so for God. But his love impels him to "remarry" Israel.

The total price paid for Gomer was about thirty shekels, the value of a slave according to Ex 21:32. V.3 suggests that she was to be deprived even of marital relations for a time, corresponding to the coming exile when Israel, deprived of the temple, could not worship her true Husband even if she wanted to. But this deprivation is temporary, and Hosea looks forward to the day when Israel will have renewed intimacy with God under a Davidic monarch (v.5). This last comment is a telling one because it confirms that there were people from the northern kingdom who realized that there was only one true ruling family for Israel. The only complete fulfillment of this prophecy is through Jesus, since no Davidic monarch ruled Israel or Judah after their exiles.

II. ISRAEL'S SINS AND GOD'S LOVE (4:1–14:9)

For a suggestion concerning the structure of this division, see the introduction.

A. Charges Against the Leaders (4:1–6:3)

1. Lack of the knowledge of God (4:1–5:15)

Chs. 4 and 5 both begin with the same sort of refrain, a call to answer formal charges. God, the Husband, will now detail how his wife, Israel, has committed adultery against him. Like all the other preexilic prophets, Hosea lays the blame for the corruption of the nation squarely at the feet of its leaders, both civil and religious. If Israel does not know (4:1, 6; 5:4) the Lord, it is because the priests have ignored the law (4:6) and the princes (5:10, NIV **"leaders"**), instead of punishing injustice, are *doing* injustice. To "know God" in the Bible is never simply to possess information about him. Rather, it is to have an intimate and ongoing personal experience of him. Thus those who live lives unlike his cannot be said to know him whatever their intellectual grasp may be. Since "know" is also the word used to express sexual intercourse, its connotations are doubly powerful in this book.

One of the promises to the Levites was that they would be priests forever (Nu 25:12–13), but their sin has nullified that promise so that God has no obligation to continue the Levitical line (4:6, see also Mal 2:3). The clear implication of vv.7 and 8 is that instead of teaching the truths of the law in such a way that people would behave in a more godly fashion, the priests simply focused on getting more sacrifices, which were the source of priestly income.

On the **"spirit of prostitution"** (v.12; also 5:4) see above on 1:2. The fathers should not be surprised if their daughters become prostitutes, since the fathers have prostituted themselves to idols (5:13–14). Hosea is deeply concerned that faithful Judeans may be seduced by Israel's sinful worship, which took place near the Judean borders at such ancient worship centers as Gilgal and Bethel (here mockingly called Beth-aven, "house of iniquity," v.15). Bethel was where one of Jeroboam I's golden calves was located (1Ki 12:28–29).

Unless the Israelites make a clean break with their idols, they have no hope of finding God (5:4–7). So long as they think they can have God and the gods at the same time, any real experience of God will elude them. Their attempts to worship God in this way will be burdensome and eventually destructive. Despite Hosea's concern for Judah, he recognizes that Judah's leaders are infected with the same illness as their Israelite counterparts. Thus the destruction of cities in Benjamin, which lay partly in both nations, is made representative of the total destruction ahead (vv.8–12). This destruction is not an arbitrary punishment on God's part. By taking themselves out from under the shelter of God's care, they have opened themselves to the destructive lusts of their stronger neighbors. V.13 is satirical: Assyria is the one destroying Israel, but Israel asks for a treaty and turns to idols like Assyria's for help.

2. A call to know the Lord (6:1–3)

Instead of turning to what are no-gods, Israel should turn to the Lord (6:1–3). It is not Israel's relation to Assyria that is responsible for her difficulties, it is her relation to God. Hosea daringly says that if Israel will return to her true husband, she may yet be delivered and restored (**"two days . . . third day"** is a Semitic idiom for the future). Here, as elsewhere, he calls on the people to look behind the immediate events of history to the One who controls history.

B. Israel's Rebellions (6:4–11:11)

Unfortunately, the possibility of Israel's making the kind of radical turn called for in 6:1–3 is remote at best.

The desires for comfort and security that led them into idolatry have sapped their abilities to discipline themselves in radical self-sacrifice. So instead of turning to God they rebel more and more against the compassionate love that found them helpless in Egypt and reared them (7:13–16; 11:1–4). They practice murder and oppression (6:7–7:7), they enter into foolish alliances with surrounding nations (7:8–12; 8:7–10), and their religion is thoroughly contaminated (8:1–6, 11–13). In short, the purposes of the Exodus are frustrated, and Israel will enter into a new "Egyptian" sojourn, but this time in the East (9:3–9; 10:5–8; 11:5–7). Nevertheless, God loves his bride too much to allow her to be utterly destroyed. Ultimately he will redeem her (11:8–11).

1. They do not turn to God (6:4–7:16)

God assigned his prophets to "kill" the people's sin (6:5), but the people can only regard the prophetic passion as madness (9:7–8). Why not, if the priesthood is engaged in murder (6:9)? Perhaps this reference is to some battle between rival priestly groups. The people want God to help them but do not recognize that until their sins are repented of and cleansed, he can do nothing for them (7:1–2). Symptomatic of their condition is the series of coups that saw one pretender after another slaughtered in Samaria between 748 and 722 (7:3–7; 8:4).

When putting a new king on the throne does not give them the security they crave, the Israelites turn to foreign alliances, **now** with the attacker (Assyria), **now** with the attacker's ultimate intended victim (Egypt) (7:8–11). Many times the tribute for such "protection" was ruinous, so that the nation was in effect mortgaging itself (8:7–

10). The people are blinded to their only true source of hope, a radical turning to the One who truly has their best interests at heart (7:13–16).

2. They have rejected the good (8:1–9:9)

The fundamental perversion of Israelite religion is depicted in 8:1–6. They claim to know God, but they do not live in accord with his character: they choose rulers without considering God's will, and they serve an idol in the name of God. Furthermore, their careful sacrifices are worthless because they are merely pleasing themselves (8:13).

All of Israel's lush religiosity and self-serving celebration (9:1) will soon be gone, says Hosea. The fertility rituals carried out in the places of harvest (9:1–2) are not only corrupt, but they will be useless because what harvest there is will be carried off by their "protectors" (9:6; see also 8:7). The offerings they now make so much of will soon be impossible because they will soon be exiles in an unclean foreign land where there will be no way to sanctify offerings to the Lord (9:3–5).

3. They have planted wickedness (9:10–11:7)

Israel's rejection of the good is not something of recent vintage. For all their promise at Sinai and on the plains of Moab, promise like that of new grapes or new figs (9:10), the possibility of succumbing to orgiastic idol worship was always near the surface as at Baal-Peor (v.10; see Nu 25:1–18). But, just as then, all such attempts to guarantee fertility and productivity will turn back upon them, and the result will not be fecundity, but barrenness; death, not life (9:11–14).

The Bible does not record an outbreak similar to that at Baal-Peor as having occurred at Gilgal (on the contrary, see Jos 6:1–10), but the setting here suggests that that was indeed the case (9:15). If so, it was evidently remembered in the popular history. Gibeah is cited as another example of Israel's persistent habit of rebellion (10:9). Evidently the events of Jdg 19 and 20 are being referred to. Because of their grievous sin, the Benjamites were all but destroyed.

In such circumstances, how can kings who are illegitimate and a cult that is corrupted with idolatry do anything to help (10:3–8)? Instead, the people are burdened with anxiety as to how they can help to save the monarchy and the cult! A sad reversal of affairs (for a similar statement, see Isa 46:1–2, but contrast 46:3–4). One of the great virtues of Jerusalem's having no idol was that no enemy could ever boast of having captured Judah's God. The same could not be said for Bethel (Beth-aven, vv.5–6). Both king and god would be destroyed.

Ephraim's love of fertility worship on the threshing floors (10:11; see on 9:1–2) will condemn it to hard and tedious labor in the Exile. If they would **seek the LORD** (10:12), then whatever the immediate future might hold for them, personal and national righteousness would result. But their persistent dependence on manipulative ritual, military strength, and political intrigue could bear no other fruit than destruction. Beth-arbel (10:14) is located at an important pass leading up from the shore of Galilee toward the Jezreel Valley (see on 1:4–5). If Arbel is lost, then Jezreel, Israel's most important food supply, is lost as well. Shalman is almost certainly Shalmanezer, the Assyrian emperor who succeeded Tiglath-Pileser (see the introduction). Thus Hosea is pointing out the folly of depending on an army that has already lost its most critical battle.

It is apparent that Israel has not learned the lessons of God's compassion that their history should have taught them. Thus there is no other recourse than to allow their sin to have its effect in the hope that this will somehow teach them the lesson mercy did not (11:1–7).

4. God cannot let them go (11:8–11)

Like Hosea, who cannot abandon his wife even when she has left him for other lovers and has ended up on the slave block, so God cannot abandon Israel to her well-deserved fate. Admah and Zeboiim (v.8) were two of the five cities of the plain (Ge 14:8) that were utterly destroyed with Sodom and Gomorrah (Dt 29:23). Here God says (contra Dt 29:23) that Israel's destruction will not be like that. Where a human being might carry out total destruction simply for the sake of revenge, God will not do so (v.9). He is **holy** and never acts from vindictiveness (see Lk 23:34). So God promises that on the other side of the Exile there will be a blessed return to the land of promise (vv.10–11).

C. Forgotten Lessons From the Past (11:12–14:9)

Hosea indicts Israel with references to both Jacob (12:2–4, 12) and the Exodus (12:9–10, 13; 13:4–6). They are indeed the children of their deceitful father and have learned nothing from all God's care. They will now experience the other side of their covenant with God—all the curses that they invoked upon themselves when they promised to obey him at all costs. Nevertheless, it will take but honest repentance on their parts (14:2–3, 8) for all that disaster to be swept away and the covenant blessings to be restored fourfold (14:4–7).

1. Return to the desert (11:12–13:16)

Hosea reminds his people that the key to success of Jacob their forefather was not his ability to wrestle with men but with God (12:3–6). Like Jacob, they must give up their foolish reliance on intrigue, wealth, violence, and alliances (11:12–12:1, 7–8) and choose a life of obedient dependence. If not, they will find themselves, like Jacob, in exile in a far country, condemned to work at hard labor (12:12).

Interspersed with the Jacob imagery are references to the covenant relationship established in the Exodus (12:9; 13:4). "[He is] **the LORD your God**" is covenant language (see Ex 20:2). Because of what God did for them and because they formally accepted the relationship, they are doubly obligated to him. Through Moses (12:13), and by means of other prophets since that time (v.10), God has attempted to get them to live in obedience to his character and recognize the destructive character of wickedness and idolatry (v.11), but all to no avail.

Therefore, just as the Exodus generation was doomed to wander in the desert because it refused Moses' prophetic word (12:14; 13:6), so this generation will return to the wilderness, figuratively speaking (12:9; see above on 2:14–23). They have refused the truth of God and have chosen instead gods that are not God (13:1– 2) and kings who are not the King (vv.9–11). As a result, there is nothing permanent about them (v.3); all of their efforts will be stillborn (v.13). The fecundity and fertility for which they have labored so strenuously will be devoured and destroyed (vv.15–16).

Commentators differ over the correct understanding of 13:14. Is it a word of hope or a word of destruction? Every-

thing hangs on the way the first sentence is construed. If it is to be taken as a question (as per RSV), then the sense is surely negative, as the negative context on either side would indicate. But while a question is possible, there is nothing in the Hebrew to require that reading. If the sentence is to be taken as an affirmation (as per NIV), then the sense of the verse is surely positive. This reading is somewhat favored by Paul's positive use of the address to death and hell in 1Co 15:55. However, since Paul is using the verse only in an allusive way, his usage by no means dictates the reading here. On balance, while the word of hope is certainly possible, the negative context on both sides of the verse seems to favor the word of destruction.

2. The fruits of repentance (14:1–9)

As Hosea is willing not only to take Gomer back, but to *buy* her back, so the Lord is eager to restore adulterous Israel. All that is necessary for that restoration is for Israel to turn back to God. This involves a specific request for forgiveness (v.2) and a conscious turning away from the false dependencies (v.3). The emphasis on **"words"** in v.2 shows that repentance is always conscious and intentional. It begins to become a reality only when it is objectified through verbalization.

When Israel is living in genuine dependence upon God, the very abundance that they vainly sought from idols will be showered upon them (vv.4–7). God does want to bless his people. He does want them to be a fruitful vine (10:1). But when we seek this for ourselves or seek to ensure it through manipulative ways, he cannot give what we seek. However, when we seek *him*, the blessings follow, not as ends, but as by-products (v.8).

BIBLIOGRAPHY

Andersen, Francis I. and David N. Freedman. *Hosea*. AB. Garden City, N.Y.: Doubleday, 1980.

Kidner, Derek. *Love to the Loveless*. Downers Grove: InterVarsity Press, 1981.

Mays, James L. "Hosea." OTL. Philadelphia: Westminster, 1969.

Reed, Oscar F. "The Book of Hosea." BBC. Edited by A. F. Harper. Kansas City: Beacon Hill, 1969. 6:17–82.

Ries, Claude A. "The Book of Hosea." WBC. Vol. 4. Grand Rapids: Eerdmans, 1967.

JOEL
Milo Chapman

INTRODUCTION

I. AUTHOR, DATE, PURPOSE

Nothing is known of the prophet Joel except that which is told or may be inferred from the book that bears his name. He is identified as the son of Pethuel (1:1). Perhaps because of its similarity to Bethuel (Ge 22:22–23), the Septuagint has Bethuel as the father's name. The name *Joel*, meaning "Yahweh is God," is borne by sixteen other men in the OT. However, some of these may be duplications (Brettler, 494–95). Since Joel's prophecy is concerned only with Judah and speaks familiarly about Jerusalem, it is assumed that he was a resident of Judah.

To date this book we are completely dependent on internal evidence. Little is offered. In ch. 3 Joel mentions such places or people as Tyre, Sidon, Philistia, the Greeks, the Sabeans, Egypt, and Edom. About such nations as Syria, Assyria, and Babylonia, which are of such importance in other prophetic books, he is silent. Neither does he allude to the northern kingdom. Joel is concerned about the proper maintenance of temple services, but he does not cry out against specific sins of the people. There is silence with regard to the king, but the priests are prominent (Driver, 12).

From this and similar data a date near 400 B.C. is generally accepted, although dates ranging from the middle of the ninth century B.C. to 350 B.C. are sometimes proposed.

The occasion of this book was an awesome invasion of locusts followed by severe drought which threatened the very existence of life. Joel sees in these natural calamities evidence of God's judgment on his people and a symbol of the impending final Day of the Lord. Joel claims that the source of his message is the Lord himself (1:1).

II. UNITY—LITERARY STYLE

Questions about the unity of Joel result from the difference between 1:2–2:27, which deals with the locust invasion and drought as present events, and 2:28–3:21, which is concerned with a "day of the LORD" that lies in the future. The unity of Joel was attacked in the late nineteenth century and early years of the twentieth century. The assumption was that it was not likely, perhaps even impossible, for one man to describe both a present and a future judgment of God upon his people. In more recent years it has been recognized that there is no overriding reason for dividing the book into segments and attributing them to separate authors. The comment of R. H. Pfeiffer is typical: "Since both parts of the book seem to have been written about the same time, there is no compelling reason for attributing them to different authors" (p. 575).

Joel's style has been described as "fluent and clear" (G. A. Smith, 397). It is further observed that "the lyrical quality of some of his lines places them among the best of their kind in the OT, while his graphic, terse descriptions are exceedingly effective" (Bewer, 68). J. A. Thompson affirms that Joel's style is characterized by the use of rhythm, concrete details, similes and metaphors, repetition, drawing of parallels, contrast, and alliteration (pp. 730–31). Joel clearly takes a favored place among the poet-prophets of Judah.

III. THE MESSAGE OF JOEL

To understand the message of Joel one must decide to what degree the book is a description of actual events, represents allegorical teaching, or is apocalyptic in nature. These elements need not be viewed as mutually exclusive of each other. The position taken here is that the description of the locust invasion and drought (1:1–20) is of actual events. These natural calamities are an expression of God's wrath in the present but are also portents of the coming day of judgment. From this position the prophet moves easily into the ultimate judgment of God upon the nations of the world. In the process of expounding these themes, other of the prophet's convictions are exposed.

For Joel, as for other Hebrew prophets, it was natural to assume that God's judgment upon wrongdoing could take the form of natural calamity. The appropriate response to such disaster is repentance. Repentance in turn would result in forgiveness granted by a gracious God. Like other postexilic prophets (Haggai, Zechariah, Malachi) he regarded temple worship as of the greatest importance. Joel was provincial. His interests centered in his own people and their particular relationship to God. This seems to be true even in his prediction of the outpouring of the Spirit of God upon "all people" (2:28), since in its context this promise seems to be given to those who are in Jerusalem (v.32). Peter, however, on the Day of Pentecost cast this statement appropriately in an inclusive promise to all nations (Ac 2:17). The day of the Lord, when in God's providence it comes, will be a day of destruction for the nations of the earth but a day of blessing and salvation for his people Israel (3:16). (For further elaboration of these themes see the commentary below and Thompson, 734–35).

IV. STATE OF THE TEXT—PLACE IN CANON

The text of Joel is well preserved. Except for a few minor variations, the Masoretic text and ancient versions such as the Septuagint, the Peshitta, and the Vulgate are in agreement with each other.

The Masoretic text places Joel in the second place in the Book of the Twelve. The Twelve were considered as one book, probably because together they can be contained on a scroll of approximately the same length as the books of Isaiah, Jeremiah, and Ezekiel. The Twelve achieved canonicity as a unit.

V. OUTLINE

I. Superscription (1:1)

II. Plague of Locusts and Drought (1:2–20)

III. The Locusts and the Day of the Lord (2:1–11)

IV. Repentance Brings Forgiveness and Restoration (2:12–27)
   A. A Call to Repentance (2:12–17)
   B. Result of Forgiveness (2:18–27)

V. The Lord Controls the Future (2:28–3:21)
   A. Through His Spirit (2:28–32)
   B. Through Judgment of the Nations (3:1–13)
   C. Through the Coming of the Golden Age (3:14–21)

COMMENTARY

I. SUPERSCRIPTION (1:1)

At the very beginning of his oracle Joel identifies the sources of his prophetic compulsion as **the word of the LORD**. This conception precedes Joel by several centuries. It appears in Isa 6:5–9; Jer 1:7, 9; Am 7:15–16. The claim of being pressed by **the word of the LORD** was more than merely claiming that their utterances were inspired. They were saying that all of the power of God himself was resident within that which they spoke and that it was certain to come to pass, guaranteed by the ability of God to control history (cf. Isa 55:11). The prophet in such a situation became an extension of God's power to accomplish the divine will (see further on the power of the Word, such works as Pedersen, 167ff.; Scott, 90ff.). The coming of **the word of the LORD** did not result in the prophet losing awareness of himself or his surroundings. Rather all of his senses were heightened and his understanding of spiritual matters and meanings was immensely expanded. In the words of Micah he became

> filled with power,
> with the Spirit of the LORD,
> and with justice and might,
> to declare to Jacob his transgression,
> to Israel his sin. (3:8)

II. PLAGUE OF LOCUSTS AND DROUGHT (1:2–20)

Under the kind of influence indicated above, Joel describes and interprets the calamities of his day. This is no ordinary catastrophe. It is so great that nothing like it has **happened** in the lifetime of those now living in the land nor in the memory of their **forefathers** (v.2). The consequences are monumental. They should be told and retold in succeeding generations so that these events will never be forgotten (v.3).

Joel 1:4 describes a total destruction of vegetation by **locust** invasions repeated over a period of more than one year (2:25). Under four different names, which likely describe the life cycle of **locusts,** successive waves of devastation are identified. To those who have experienced such a phenomenon Joel's description will not appear as hyperbole, although similes are used to describe the ferocious strength of the insects (v.6). **Locusts** are capable of accomplishing in a literal fashion that which Joel describes (for examples of this type of invasion see Driver, 84ff.).

The nation is called upon to lament as a prospective bride would **mourn** over a bridegroom snatched away from her. **Priests** and **farmers** despair and **wail** over the total destruction of crops and vegetation. All of the people are hopeless (vv.8–12).

A calamity of this magnitude calls for repentance. Even though there is no mention of idolatry in Joel, the connection between deity and the fertility and productivity of the land is assumed. Here it is recognized that Yahweh is in control of the physical well being of people and land. Therefore, catastrophic kinds of natural phenomena indicate that God is displeased with his people. They obviously have been unfaithful to him (cf. Hos 2:8–13). The cure is repentance. The priests are to lead the way in a national fast. People and elders are to be assembled in the temple in order that together they may **cry out to the LORD** (vv.13–14).

The situation is so bleak and dismal that it brings to mind the old and familiar concept of the **day of the LORD** (cf. Am 5:18–20). As with Amos, the Day for Joel is dreadful. For

him the times are so severe that he sees them as ushering in that time of judgment that had been predicted for so long. **The day . . . is near** (v.15). As he views the destruction around him, Joel sees famine on every hand. Even **seeds** are destroyed. **Storehouses** and **granaries** are emptied and despoiled. There is no food for man or beast or wild animals. The **water** supply has **dried up** in drought. It is as though **fire** had destroyed everything (vv.16–20).

III. THE LOCUSTS AND THE DAY OF THE LORD (2:1–11)

It is often said that the **day of the LORD** is the major theme of Joel (e.g., Allen, 36). Having already alluded to the connection between the locust invasion and the Day (1:15), Joel returns to that theme in this section. It is not yet fully in evidence, but the Day is close. Therefore the **alarm** should be sounded throughout Zion. Strong similes are used to describe the relentless march of the insects across the land. They literally create a black **darkness** as they swarm. They are like an **army** as they attack (v.2). The destruction is complete and sudden. The land, which was **like the garden of Eden** before their attack, is a desolate wasteland after they are gone (v.3). The locusts come in ranks and files. No obstacle deters them. They even resemble miniature **horses**—war horses on the attack. The sound they make is reminiscent of **battle** conditions. They invade every wall and house, every corner (vv.7–9). To Joel the invasion becomes a powerful metaphor of God's judgment to be expected on his terrible Day. Like the locusts God's judgment cannot be evaded (vv.10–11).

IV. REPENTANCE BRINGS FORGIVENESS AND RESTORATION (2:12–27)

A. A Call to Repentance (2:12–17)

As is often the case among the prophets, Joel uses a contemporary disaster to warn the people of impending judgment and to call them to repentance. Although **fasting and weeping and mourning** are elements of "returning" (the word translated "**return**" is *shub,* the primary word for repentance [v.12]), Joel adds a profound element to the meaning of repentance. He urges them to **rend [their] hearts and not [their] garments.** Hope is expressed that the Lord will relent in his wrath (vv.13–14). If repentance is thus a genuine expression of inner remorse, then external acts are in order: the whole of the people from the priest to the infant are to assemble and fast and pray that the Lord might spare them (vv.15–17; cf. 1:14).

B. Result of Repentance (2:18–27)

The promise is given that **the LORD will be jealous for his land** (v.18). However, it is appropriate to translate the verbs in vv.18 and 19 in the past tense. In which case the indication is that the prophet's counsel was heeded, the people repented, and God answered with forgiveness and blessings. The land was restored and **grain, wine,** and **oil,** the basic agricultural products of the land, were restored.

The conclusion of the locust infestation is described as **the northern army** being driven into the **sea**—both the Dead Sea and Mediterranean Sea— with a resultant **stench** created by dead insects washed up on the shores (v.20). Eyewitnesses to this phenomenon affirm that this indeed does occur as a result of strong winds blowing seaward. With the termination of the locust invasion there is no longer any need for fear. **Wild animals, pastures, fruit trees,** and **vines** are now in their normal cycle of fertility. The drought has ended with abundant **rains.** All of the normal activities of harvest are restored. The fear of starvation is over (vv.21–25). Because of the blessings of restored prosperity, Israel will realize that **the LORD their God** is with them and besides him **there is no other** deity (vv.26–27; cf. Isa 45:5–6, 18).

V. THE LORD CONTROLS THE FUTURE (2:28–3:21)

A. Through His Spirit (2:28–32)

In this pericope Joel reaches the pinnacle of his prophetic message. As important as material blessings are to him and the people, the spiritual and moral blessings are of even more significance. To Joel the process of achieving God's intended destiny for his people is in place. They have been punished severely for their sins. Repentance has turned away the wrath of God, and the land is experiencing rejuvenation. As has already been shown, all of this has caused the prophet to see these events as harbingers of the Day of the Lord. Now that the immediate consequences have been dealt with, he looks at the long-range and ultimate consequences. He is forced to conclude that God is, indeed, in control of history. In fact, all historical events from the past through the future are an expression of the activity of God in the affairs of men.

To show the truth of this conviction Joel affirms first that God **will pour out [his] Spirit on all people** (lit. "all flesh"). The list of those who are to be the recipients of this outpouring shows that Joel envisions that all categories of persons will receive the **Spirit.**

The Spirit of God in the OT performs a number of functions. He is the vital power of God in creation and is the Sustainer of life (Ge 1:2; Job 33:4; Ps 104:30). It is because of the presence of the Spirit of God that certain persons exhibit unusual abilities and perform unusual tasks (see, e.g., Ge 41:38; Ex 31:3; Nu 11:17; 1Sa 11:6; 16:13; Ps 51:10, 11; Isa 11:2; 63:11; Mic 3:8; Hag 2:3–5). The Spirit of God is the source of inspiration for the prophets. Although Jeremiah does not use the term, we may conclude that a similar kind of experience is referred to by Jeremiah when he says the word of the Lord comes to him. In Joel the hope expressed by Moses as recorded in Nu 11:29, "I wish that all the LORD's people were prophets and that the LORD would put his Spirit on them!" is promised (for more on this, cf. Driver, 66).

Accompanying or following the outpouring of the **Spirit** will be remarkably portents giving warning to the faithful that the **day of the LORD** is at hand. These signs will include marvelous and terrifying **wonders in the heavens. Blood and fire** and **darkness** will obscure the **sun** and **moon.** When these things occur it is a sign of the onslaught of judgment. However, those who understand and know the significance of these events may call upon the Lord. Safety and deliverance for them will be found in Zion (vv.30–32). Although the context of the promise to **everyone who calls on the name of the LORD** indicates that Joel is speaking to his own countrymen, this is the point at which he is most universal (see also 2:28). Indeed Paul reads him so, just as did Peter on the Day of Pentecost (see Ro 10:13). In any event, the promise is to those who call upon the Lord. Provision is made for the sovereign acts of God in this process when Joel includes among the survivors (lit. "the remnants") **those whom the LORD calls** (v.32). It is obvious that Joel is thinking eschatologically at this point, seeing the pattern unfolding of God's ultimate control of history and the created order.

B. Through Judgment of the Nations (3:1–13)

God is in control, not only of those who recognize him and call upon him, but also of all the nations who have been the enemies of his people. These are to be brought together in the **Valley of Jehoshaphat** (lit. "the valley of decision"), there to receive the **judgment** due them as a result of their evil treatment of **Israel.**

A prose section (vv.4–8) specifies the evil perpetuated by the nations surrounding **Judah** and for which vengeance is sought. The next section (vv.9–13) is a call to battle that will bring about the anticipated destruction of the enemies of God and his people. Joel calls for a reversal of that order to be found in Isa 2:4 and Mic 4:3. There the call is to beat swords into plowshares; here in Joel the message is to beat plowshares into swords, to make weapons of war from their agricultural implements (v.10).

C. Through the Coming of the Golden Age (3:14–21)

As Joel contemplates the two sides of **the Day of the LORD** he sees that the issue facing God's people is the matter of choice. They are to decide to which side they belong. They are in the **valley of decision** (v.14). The Day is at hand. Which will it be, God's wrath or his **refuge?** If they choose **refuge,** it will become perfectly clear to them that Yahweh is Lord and that he is capable of doing that which the prophet claims on God's behalf (v.17). Not only so, but for those who heed the warning and respond to his gracious offer, there will be a Golden Age not unlike Eden (v.18), but for **Egypt** and **Edom,** symbols of rejection and disobedience, there is annihilation (v.19). For **Judah,** now made up of those who do call upon the Lord, there is forgiveness and a secure future (v.20).

The book of Joel, short as it is, is a beautifully stated affirmation that God is gracious in his willingness to forgive the repentant and supply them with his Spirit, by whom he is constantly present with his people. It is clear that the Lord will prevail in upholding righteousness and in destroying that which is evil.

BIBLIOGRAPHY

Allen, Leslie C. "Joel." NICOT. Grand Rapids: Eerdmans, 1976.

Bewer, Julius. "Joel." ICC. Edinburgh: T. & T. Clark, 1965.

Brettler, M. Z. "Joel." *Harper's Bible Dictionary.* Edited by P. J. Achtemeier. San Francisco: Harper & Row, 1985.

Calvin, John. *The Theology of the Old Testament.* New York: Abingdon-Cokesbury, 1949.

Childs, Brevard S. *Introduction to the Old Testament Scriptures.* Philadelphia: Fortress, 1982.

Driver, S. R. *Cambridge Bible for Schools and Colleges.* "Joel." Cambridge: Cambridge University Press, 1915.

Jacob, Edmond. *Theology of the Old Testament.* New York: Harper and Row, 1958.

La Sor, William Sanford, et al. *Old Testament Survey.* Grand Rapids: Eerdmans, 1982.

Luther, Martin. *Luther's Works.* Vol. 18. Edited by Hilton C. Oswald. St. Louis: Concordia, 1975.

Pfeiffer, Robert H. *Introduction to the OT.* Rev. ed. New York: Harper and Brothers, 1948.

Rad, Gerhard von. *Old Testament Theology.* 2 vols. Translated by D. M. G. Stalker. New York: Harper and Row, 1962.

Smith, G. A. *The Book of the Twelve Prophets.* New York: A. C. Armstrong and Son, 1906.

Thompson, J. A. "Joel." IB. Vol. 6. New York: Abingdon, 1956.

Vriezen, Th. C. *An Outline of Old Testament Theology.* Rev. ed. Newton, Mass.: Charles T. Bransford, 1970.

AMOS
Roy F. Melugin

INTRODUCTION

I. THE PROPHET AND HIS TIME

The book of Amos is one of the books in the collection of the twelve Minor Prophets. The book contains words attributed to the prophet Amos, whose ministry probably occurred somewhere around the middle of the eighth century B.C. during the royal reigns of Uzziah of Judah and Jeroboam II of Israel. What little we know about Amos comes exclusively from the sparse detail about the prophet and his activity described in the book of Amos. Am 1:1 tells us that he was from Tekoa (probably Tekoa in Judah), that he was a shepherd, that he prophesied in the days of Uzziah and Jeroboam "two years before the earthquake." The narrative in Am 7:10–17 augments our knowledge a tiny bit by calling him a shepherd and dresser of sycamore trees and by informing us that he had not abandoned his vocation as shepherd-farmer until he was summoned away by God and commanded to prophesy (vv.14–15).

The precise date of Amos's prophetic ministry is by no means certain. That he preached during the reigns of Uzziah and Jeroboam is abundantly clear, but they both ruled over a rather lengthy span of time. The phrase "two years before the earthquake" suggests a specific date and even a short period of time not exceeding two years. But when was the earthquake? We simply do not know. Zec 14:5 mentions an earthquake in Uzziah's time but does not specify a date within that king's lengthy reign.

Since Amos was apparently from the Tekoa in the kingdom of Judah, he was a southerner whose divine calling was to prophesy in the northern kingdom of Israel. Why this is so is not explained, nor does the text tell us how this affected the way he was looked upon as he prophesied in an alien kingdom. To be sure, the priest of the Israelite sanctuary at Bethel ordered him to flee to Judah (7:12–13), but we are not told whether he would have been treated more hospitably if he had been a native of Israel rather than Judah.

We know nothing of Amos's life before he became a prophet other than that he was a shepherd and dresser of sycamore trees. Nor are we told whether, after his call, he remained a prophet until his death. We know only that he prophesied in Israel for an unspecified period of time. We know almost nothing, moreover, about what he did when he prophesied in Israel. One brief narrative (7:10–17) tells us that he once was in conflict with Amaziah, priest of Bethel. No additional narratives in the book describe his activities. Speeches condemning the sanctuary cities of Bethel and Gilgal as well as the capital city of Samaria suggest that he may have spoken in each place, but we are not explicitly told that. Thus we are left largely in the dark about Amos's life and activity. We know much more about the book that bears his name and the message that the book contains.

II. THE OVERALL MESSAGE OF THE BOOK

The dominant message of the book of Amos is the *proclamation of judgment* upon Israel by Yahweh their God because of their oppression of the poor. The book of Amos accuses them of "sell[ing] the righteous for silver, and the needy for a pair of sandals" (2:6); of crushing the needy (4:1); of abusing the legal processes held in the town gate for the improper acquisition of large estates (5:10–11); and of indulging in merrymaking, all the while taking no responsibility while the community was breaking apart (6:1–7). Because Israel promoted so much injustice, Yahweh's judgment was near at hand. His wrath would send burning, destroying fire (1:4, 7, 10, 12, 14; 2:2, 5). Israel would suffer military defeat and be led into exile (2:13–16; 3:9–11; 4:1–3; 5:27; 6:7). Indeed, Israel itself would cease to be: the end of Israel is proclaimed in the text (8:2), and the metaphor of death is applied to Israel (5:2, 16–17; 6:9–10; 8:1–3).

Amos criticizes his hearers' confidence that the sanctuaries and their sacrificial cult would gain them Yahweh's approval. Amos uses the very language of the cult itself, but with satirical tone, to poke fun at his hearers' reliance upon the sanctuaries, to show that Yahweh desires justice and righteousness more than sacrifice, and to proclaim the end of the cultic centers (see 4:4–5; 5:4–7, 21–24). He even announces the eclipse of the remembrance of Yahweh's name (6:9–10) and the hearing of Yahweh's word (8:11–12)—undoubtedly a consequence of Yahweh's bringing Israel to an end.

The message is dominantly one of judgment and destruction. Only at the book's end (9:7–15) do we find a clear note of hope, and that seems to be directed primarily to Judah.

III. THE STRUCTURE OF THE BOOK

The material in Amos, for the most part, was originally delivered orally and later written down and preserved by an ongoing group of disciples. Narratives about prophets, such as Elijah, present prophets as speakers rather than as writers. Thus there is every reason to assume the same for Amos. The written text of Amos, however, is far more than a random collection of originally oral sayings. It exhibits a definite structure.

Section I of the book (see outline below) begins with a superscription (1:1) that provides information about Amos's origin, his vocation, and the date of his prophetic activity. Prophetic books often begin with superscriptions (Isa 1:1; Jer 1:1–3; Hos 1:1; Joel 1:1; Am 1:1; Mic 1:1; Na 1:1; Hab 1:1; Zep 1:1; Mal 1:1). Then comes a report of Yahweh's roaring from Zion (1:2).

The main body of the book (section II) consists of A (1:3–4:13), in which Israel is often called "people of Israel" (2:11; 3:1, 12; 4:5); and B (5:1–9:6), which uses "house of Israel" more consistently than any other name (5:1, 4, 25; 6:14). Parts A and B are characterized by "repetitional compositions" (1:3–2:16 for A; 7:1–9:4 for B). Each of these compositions exhibits considerable repetition in form and language: 1:3–2:16 (A) contains a series of similarly worded oracles against various nations, e.g., "for three crimes of X and for four I will not cause it to return" (see 1:3, 6, 9, 11, 13; 2:1, 4, 6) and "I will send a fire" (1:4, 7, 10, 12; 2:2, 5; cf. 1:14). The vision reports in part B (7:1–9:4) also exhibit a series of similarly worded units, e.g., "This is what the Sovereign LORD showed me" (see 7:1, 4, 7; 8:1); "I said, 'forgive/cease, how can Jacob stand'" (see 7:2, 5); and "What do you see?" (7:8; 8:2).

Not only are repetitional compositions shared by both A and B, but also both contain compositions introduced by "Hear this word" (3:1; 5:1). Neither of these compositions (3:1–4:12 for A; 5:1–6:14 for B) exhibits the structural and linguistic homogeneity of the repetitional compositions. Finally, A and B close with hymnlike doxologies that praise Yahweh for his power as Creator (4:13; 9:5–6).

The repetitional compositions are placed in reversed sequence in A and B. In A the repetitional composition comes first (II.A.1.a), while in B it appears in second place II.B.1.b). A similar reversal may be observed for the compositions beginning with "Hear this word." In B it comes first (II.B.1.a), but in A it comes second (II.A.1.b).

The postscript (section III [9:7–15]) moves from announcement of judgment (v.8a) to qualification of the scope of the judgment (vv.8b–10) to outright announcement of salvation (vv.11–15). And the spotlight has shifted from Israel to Judah. Exactly what this signifies remains to be seen, but for now we observe the book closing as it began, with focus on Jerusalem and Judah in sections I and III and on Israel in section II.

IV. OUTLINE

    I. Introduction (1:1–2)

    II. Main Body of the Book (1:3–9:6)
       A. Laying the Foundation for a Theophany: Judgment of the Nations and of Israel (1:3–4:13)
          1. Body of the text (1:3–4:12)
             a. Judgment of the nations (1:3–2:16)
             b. Judgment of Israel and exhortations to enter into Yahweh's presence (3:1–4:12)
          2. Response: doxological hymn (4:13)

COMMENTARY

I. INTRODUCTION (1:1–2)

The introduction provides the reader with certain information and with a particular perspective, both of which color the interpretation of the rest of the book. The superscription (v.1) tells us that Amos was from Tekoa (probably Tekoa of Judah), that he was a shepherd, and that he prophesied during the reigns of Uzziah of Judah and his contemporary, Jeroboam of Israel, **two years before the earthquake.** The knowledge that Amos was from Judah is compatible with the book's claim that Yahweh dwells in Jerusalem (v.2). Why should Yahweh choose a prophet from Israel if his dwelling place is in Judah? Moreover, the knowledge that Amos was from Judah informs the reader that the order by the priest of Bethel for Amos to "go back to the land of Judah" (7:12) meant a return to the prophet's homeland. The statement that Amos was "among the shepherds" indicates that Amos was not a lifelong prophet, thus giving support to Amos's claim in 7:15 that he had been taken from his life with the sheep in order to obey Yahweh's special call to prophesy to Israel. The phrase **"two years before the earthquake"** clarifies language about the shaking of the earth elsewhere in the book (8:8; 9:1, 5). Thus the intention of the superscription is to demonstrate that Amos's words about the shaking of the earth were actually fulfilled in the earthquake that subsequently occurred.

The report of Yahweh's roaring and thundering from Zion/Jerusalem (v.2) portrays Yahweh in the circumstances of a *theophany* (a technical term for a personal epiphany or appearing of a deity). Such language is characteristically used concerning Yahweh's thundering voice in a theophany (Pss 18:13; 46:6; 104:7; Isa 30:30). Moreover, 1:2 portrays Yahweh's dwelling place as Jerusalem. Nowhere else in the book is that said. Thus this verse supplies an important theological claim that colors our interpretation of the rest of the book: *it is the God who dwells in Jerusalem who sends judgment upon Israel.*

II. MAIN BODY OF THE BOOK (1:3–9:6)

The main body of the book is organized around the theme of Yahweh's presence. The judgment speeches in II.A lay the groundwork for an exhortation to prepare to enter Yahweh's presence. II.B, building upon that exhortation, describes Yahweh's presence in the midst of his people as a presence that brings death and destruction rather than salvation and life.

A. Laying the Foundation for a Theophany: Judgment of the Nations and of Israel (1:3–4:13)

As we saw, this compositional unit falls into two parts: (1) the body of the text (1:3–4:12) and (2) a concluding doxology (4:13). The body in turn may be subdivided into (a) judgment of the nations (1:3–2:16) and (b) judgment of Israel and exhortations to enter into Yahweh's presence (3:1–4:12).

1. Body of the text (1:3–4:12)

a. Judgment of the nations (1:3–2:16)

These oracles against various nations consist of a repeated series of short judgment speeches against several nations (1:3–2:5), culminating in a longer oracle against Israel (2:6–16). Each of them begins with the following: "Thus says Yahweh, 'For three crimes of X and for four I will not cause it to return.'" This X + 1 pattern (one-two, three-four, etc.) is widely known in Israel and the ancient Near East (Wolff, *Amos the Prophet*, 34–44). Just why three-four is used here is uncertain.

It appears that Amos 1:3–2:16 employs a metaphor of a journey of Yahweh's anger. The **it** that Yahweh has not caused to return is apparently his anger (Knierim, 170–72). Yahweh has sent out his hot anger to burn with fire the **fortresses** of the nations, which the text enumerates. Indeed, fire is typically associated with Yahweh's anger (Dt 32:22; Isa 5:24, 25; 9:17–18; 66:15; Jer 15:14; 17:4). So Yahweh sends his anger out on a journey—to burn and destroy. But why does he not "cause it to return"? The obvious answer is that the judgment is not completed; the anger must remain where it has been sent to continue burning. But more can be said. When, in Israel's experience, repentance took place, it was sometimes said that Yahweh's anger returned, i.e., that the return journey of his wrath had been made. But what if repentance had not taken place? Then Yahweh might not call his anger back! Am 4:6–11 indicates just this circumstance; Israel had consistently failed to return to Yahweh. Undoubtedly, this is why Yahweh did not cause the return of his anger.

Although Yahweh's anger is directed at several nations, it is especially aimed at Israel. The fact that the oracle against Israel (2:6–16) is placed at the end of the sequence of judgment speeches in 1:3–2:16, together with its greater length, must surely indicate that the center of interest is the divine judgment upon *Israel*. Moreover, Israel is judged by different standards: The foreign nations named in the text are condemned for acts of cruelty against other nations, but Israel stands accused for crimes against fellow Israelites. They **sell the righteous for silver, and the needy for a pair of sandals** (2:6). They trample the poor into the dust (v.7).

Israel's crimes against persons are at the same time crimes against Yahweh's holiness: the people profane his holy name (2:7); they desecrate his sacred altar by their unjust social behavior (v.8); they profane his hallowed house by their reprehensible deeds. Furthermore, they have responded inappropriately to Yahweh's gracious gift of the Promised Land (v.9) and to his care in delivering them from Egypt and choosing some of their sons as prophets and Nazirites (vv.10–11). Rather than accepting God's gifts with gratitude, they made the intoxicant-abstaining Nazirites drink wine, and they commanded the prophets not to prophesy (v.12).

Yahweh will therefore punish Israel. They will be defeated in battle so badly that their mighty warriors will not escape (2:13–16). The text emphasizes the totality of defeat by narrating at some length the persons who will not escape: the swift, the strong, the mighty, the handler of the bow, the swift of foot, the rider of the horse. No one, absolutely no one, can escape with the dignity befitting his bravery; only in shame—naked and humiliated—can the brave (stout of heart) survive.

b. Judgment of Israel and exhortations to enter into Yahweh's presence (3:1–4:12)

The judgment of Israel, first articulated in 1:3–2:16, continues. And the interest in Israel's relationship to other nations, begun in 1:3–2:16, is sharpened. In 3:1–2, Israel is summoned to hear why Yahweh's judgment is especially directed at them: **"You only have I chosen of all the families of the earth; therefore I will punish you for all your sins"** (v.2). How unexpected! Would not Yahweh be expected to bless both Israel and **all the families of the earth** (see Ge 12:1–3)? But the text of Amos is firm and unambiguous: being Yahweh's chosen means special accountability for sin; Israel is measured by a special standard.

Surely the prophet is wrong! Undoubtedly he is not a prophet! Surely his word does not come from God! Amos knows that his detractors say such things. So a disputation—an argument—emerges to overcome his claims (3:3–8). The argument is based on an analogy between cause and effect in ordinary daily experience and the cause of prophetic speech. A series of rhetorical questions appear: **Do two walk together unless they have agreed to do so?** "Of course not," the reader is supposed to answer, **"does a lion roar in the thicket when he has no prey?"** "Certainly not," the text expects the reader to say. Again and again, in vv.3–6, questions are posed, and in each case the text presupposes that the answer is obvious.

Then the poet moves to resolve the matter under dispute (3:7–8). It begins with an assertion: **Surely the Sovereign LORD does nothing without revealing his plan to his servants the prophets** (v.7). An impressive claim about how fully aware prophets are of Yahweh's deeds! Yet this assertion speaks only of prophets in general. Thus there is still need to show that what Amos says, especially in vv.1–2, truly comes from Yahweh. That is the reason for the questions in v.8. Indeed, their significance may be appropriately paraphrased as follows: "Just as when a lion roars anyone would be afraid, so also, when Yahweh speaks, no one could fail to prophesy." The causal relationship that can be observed in daily life can just as readily be applied to the speeches that prophets utter, according to 3:3–8. If the reader is persuaded, then that reader might also be ready to agree that Amos's words have come from God and can no longer be questioned.

Thus far we have examined the logic of 3:3–8. Now let us turn to its imagery and its potential impact on the total imagination. My contention is that the reader is potentially moved from emotional neutrality to intense apprehension. The first question in the disputation leads to no anxiety; the fact that walking together is the result of prior agreement to meet is an insight that poses no threat. But a question that presumes a lion's roaring comes from having taken prey alludes to a threatening circumstance in the animal world. And so do the questions about snares and traps (v.5). Thus the imagery has moved from the innocuous to the threatening. But there is as yet no potential danger for humans. In v.6, however, danger touches humans: **When a trumpet sounds in a city, do not the people tremble?** If such an alarm is sounded, inhabitants of a city are terrified, for they know an enemy is approaching. So also if calamity (sometimes translated "evil") befalls a city, should they not think it comes from Yahweh? *The imagery has escalated to encompass threat to human life.* But the emotional impact may well create a sense of dread that the hearers' own city might actually be the one in which the sound of alarm might soon be blown.

In 3:9–15 such fears are confirmed, for the total defeat of Samaria, Israel's capital, is prophesied. Messengers are commissioned to journey to Ashdod and Egypt to summon those foreign powers to come to the mountains of Samaria to observe the city's misdeeds (v.9). One must not overlook the irony of having gentile nations whom Yahweh has *not* known (cf. v.2) serving as witnesses against Yahweh's chosen! Ashdod and Egypt will most certainly see **unrest** and **oppression** in the chosen people's capital. Those who have been **chosen** by Yahweh (v.2) do not even **know how to do right** (v.10). Indeed, as the metaphor states it, they fill their **fortresses** with **violence and destruction** (v.10). They have hoarded those two terrible commodities as if they were afraid that there might not be enough violence and destruction to go around. All this among Yahweh's chosen, from whom he expected justice and righteousness!

Yes, it is true that Yahweh will punish for their iniquities those whom he has **chosen.** As punishment for **unrest and oppression**, violence and destruction, an enemy will surround Samaria's land (v.11). Their strength

will be brought down and, ironically, the mighty **fortresses** or **strongholds** upon which they relied for defense will be plundered. The defeat will be so massive that virtually nothing will be left. Just as when a shepherd tries to rescue a sheep from the mouth of a lion, he saves nothing more than two legs or a piece of an ear, so shall those who dwell (or **sit**) in Samaria be rescued with nothing more than a fragment or edge of the furniture upon which they sit (v.12).

In 3:13–15 witnesses are once again called to testify against Israel concerning ways Yahweh plans to punish his people. The imagery of the destruction of buildings and furniture that we saw in vv.9–12, continues: the winter houses, the summer houses, the houses of ivory, indeed the great houses. Thus the defeat by an enemy destroys the fortresses, the houses of the wealthy, and leaves nothing but the smallest remnants of the furniture from those imposing structures. But there is more: on the day that Yahweh punishes Israel for their crimes, he will cut off the horns of the altar at the great sanctuary at Bethel. Such language is of great symbolic significance, for it was well known in Israel that clinging to the horns of the altar was a refuge from the manslayer (1Ki 1:50; 2:28). With the horns of the altar cut off, there would be no place of refuge. Thus Israel's last hope of escape vanishes.

To summarize our interpretation of ch. 3: Israel, alone among all the earthly families **chosen** by Yahweh, cannot rest secure in that special relationship. They are instead to be held especially accountable for all their iniquities (v.2). Moreover, they cannot wriggle free from that awesome responsibility by contending that Amos's words do not come from God. Indeed, just as ordinary events in daily life have their cause, so also does prophetic speech (vv.3–8). Therefore, the text implies, the words of Amos are valid.

The growing dread that Yahweh might blow an alarm in Israel's cities, that his speaking (3:8) might signify an imminent catastrophe, turns out to be a reliable hunch. The summons of witnesses to testify to Samaria's misdeeds (vv.9–10) leads to a verdict of guilt and a sentence in which the dreaded defeat occurs, complete with enemy to surround the land and destroy the fortresses (v.11) and most of the fine furnishings as well (v.12). Any last hope for refuge is dashed forthwith, for the horns of the altar of asylum will be hewn off (v.14). And Yahweh himself will bring the great houses to an end (v.15). Truly the land of Israel, whose people were chosen of Yahweh, will be completely defeated and destroyed with no hope for rescue.

4:1–12 continues the theme of punishment for oppression of the poor. A diatribe against the women of Samaria for oppressing the poor and crushing the needy leads into a prophecy of these so-called **cows of Bashan** being led mercilessly into exile by means of **hooks** and **fishhooks,** straight through the breaches of the city wall made by the battering assault of the enemy. Not only will the land be defeated, but its inhabitants will also be led away into captivity.

While it is true that 4:1–12 continues the theme of judgment of oppressors (ch. 3), it is also the case that a fresh pattern of imagery emerges, namely, a mosaic of metaphors of journeys undertaken. We saw above that 1:3–2:16, in introducing 1:3–4:13, employs the metaphor of the journey of God's anger. Now we see that 1:3–4:13 comes to a close with certain journey metaphors. In 4:1–3 the metaphor of the journey into exile

dominates the announcement of judgment (vv.2–3). Am 4:4–5 exhorts worshipers to make pilgrimage into Yahweh's presence by journeying with sacrifices into his sanctuary. The metaphor of journey also characterizes 4:6–12: a series of chastisements are sent by Yahweh to provoke Israel to repent. But they did not. Each time they refused to return; they failed to make the journey back to God.

Multiple ironies are found in 4:1–12. The wealthy women, addressed metaphorically as **cows,** ironically lose the independence produced by wealth and are led away like animals from their dwelling place into an alien land (vv.1–3). Furthermore, the second journey—the invitation to make pilgrimage to the important shrines of Bethel and Gilgal—is also not without irony. A cultic official might ordinarily have been expected to say something like, "Come to Bethel and make sacrifice," but only an ironic manipulation of conventional ways of speaking would have anyone say, **"Go to Bethel and sin."** Indeed, a tongue-in-cheek exhortation to make a sacred journey into God's presence in order to sin becomes still more satirical when the directives about the kind of sacrifices to bring and when to bring them ends with: **"Call out your freewill offerings, make them public, for so you love to do, sons of Israel."** The summons to come to the central shrines and make sacrifice turns out ironically to be an invitation to parade their religiosity in public so that their piety may be seen by others (see Mt 6:1–6).

God is not impressed with Israel's piety any more than he is willing to tolerate their deeds of injustice. But he had made efforts to lead them to repentance. He chastised them with famine (**empty stomachs** and **lack of bread**). But they refused to return to

Yahweh (4:6). Once again he sent drought, but they would not return (vv.7–8). Again and again Yahweh chastised them, but never would they make the journey back to him. Then comes Yahweh's response: **Therefore, thus I do to you, O Israel; because this I do to you, prepare to meet your God, O Israel"** (v.12). What is meant here? Does v.12 signify that God, having failed to elicit Israel's repentance, *will* heap on additional punishment in the future, for which reason Israel must prepare to meet God? Or does it mean that because God does this (namely, the *past* chastisements mentioned in vv.6–11), they must get ready to meet God? The peculiarities of Hebrew tense structure prevent us from knowing whether **"Therefore"** and **"this"** in v.12 refer to future deeds that Yahweh *will* do or whether they signify chastisements that Yahweh *periodically* does. In any event, Israel must prepare to meet God.

Israel's refusal to make the return journey of repentance back to God is ironically the antithesis of their eagerness to journey into his presence with sacrifices so that their piety might be displayed for all to see. Moreover, the journey readily made in pious pretense (4:4–5), together with the journey of repentance, which they refused to make (vv.6–11), are related to the journey away from Samaria that Israel must make (vv.1–3). Their journey into exile is the result of not having made the appropriate kinds of journeys into Yahweh's presence. Finally, their refusal to make the "return" journey of repentance (vv.6–11) cannot be separated from Yahweh's decision not to cause his anger to "return" (chs. 1–2).

The exhortation **"Prepare to meet your God"** (4:12) is a critical turning point in Amos. It is a summons to prepare for a theophany—a summons to make ready to enter into Yahweh's personal presence (cf. Ex 19:15, 17 to see how the words **prepare** and **meet** are associated with language about theophany). What should Israel expect after they have "prepared" and "met" God? Should they expect to experience a reaffirmation of their role as Yahweh's chosen, despite their having been punished for their iniquities (3:2; 4:6–11)? Surely theophany was often associated with God's presence to affirm and protect his chosen (Ex 19; Pss 18:7–19; 46:6–7; Isa 30:29–33). Or should Amos's audience expect Yahweh's theophany to precipitate still more frightful acts of judgment against Israel? The text does not say. Instead it leaves the reader to ponder just what might happen when Israel meets God face to face. Just what Yahweh's presence will actually signify is indeed not disclosed until part B of the book (5:1–9:6). Thus part A (1:3–4:13) closes on a note of suspense and leads us on to read part B.

2. Response: doxological hymn (4:13)

The doxology renders praise to Yahweh the Creator, who **forms the mountains** and **creates the wind.** Certainly he is praised as absolute Sovereign, who changes the morning to darkness and walks majestically on the **high places of the earth.** It is *Yahweh* (that is his name) and no other God who does this.

B. Death and the End for Israel (5:1–9:6)

1. Body of the text (5:1–9:4)

As our structural outline indicates, 5:1–9:6 falls into two major parts: (1) the body of the text (5:1–9:4) and (2) a concluding doxology (9:5–6). The body in turn may be subdivided as follows: (a) utterances concerning the death of Israel (5:1–6:14) and (b) vision reports concerning the end of Israel (7:1–9:4).

a. Utterances concerning the death of Israel (5:1–6:14)

The depiction of Israel as a virgin adds gravity to the portrayal of death. For an Israelite woman to die as a virgin meant dying childless, without having fulfilled her purpose in life (see Jdg 11:29–40).

Substantiating the funeral lament is a word from Yahweh:

> **"The city that marches out a**
> **thousand strong for Israel**
> **will have only a hundred left;**
> **the town that marches out a**
> **hundred strong**
> **will have only ten left."** (5:3)

The picture is that of an army that goes forth to battle and returns with virtually no soldiers left. Thus v.3 portrays in military language what the lament over the dead virgin expresses: the once-vital Israel now subject to impotence or death.

Suddenly, however, the text begins to speak of life. Yahweh exhorts the house of Israel, **"Seek me and live!"** (5:4). But then unexpectedly the text says,

> **"Do not seek Bethel,**
> **do not go to Gilgal,**
> **do not journey to Beersheba."**
> **(v.5a)**

How ironic! An exhortation to seek Yahweh in order to live well might be what one would expect to hear. But surely it was unconventional to admonish worshipers against visiting prominent sanctuaries of Yahweh! To suppose that Yahweh could not be found in such shrines nor life be obtained there in his name manifestly strained all conventional religious credulity. It is much like hearing God say, "Seek me

and live, but don't seek me in the churches!" The text is nonetheless explicit about it, explaining why indeed they should not visit these sanctuaries: **"For Gilgal will surely go into exile, / and Bethel will be reduced to nothing"** (v.5b). The death of Israel and its military defeat (vv.1–3) extends to the sanctuaries; these shrines can by no means preserve life in the face of the slaughter.

There is a second exhortation to seek Yahweh and preserve life (5:6). One should seek Yahweh **or he will sweep through the house of Joseph like a fire . . . and Bethel will have no one to quench it.** Once again the imagery points toward a destruction much like death. Fire is portrayed as having a mouth that consumes, making nonexistent what once existed. In like manner the once-alive virgin ceases to exist (v.2), the armies of the city return virtually nonexistent (v.3), and Bethel becomes nothing (v.5b). Moreover, no one can prevent the catastrophe. **No one** can quench the consuming fire, just as **no one** can raise up the deceased virgin (v.2).

Am 5:6–7 closes with a defamatory description of the persons exhorted to seek Yahweh. They are called those **who turn justice into bitterness and cast righteousness to the ground** (v.7). The doxology that follows (vv.8–9) contrasts unjust Israel with the praiseworthy Yahweh. Israel, who improperly turns justice to bitterness, compares unfavorably with Yahweh the Creator, who appropriately turns deep darkness into morning and darkens day into night. And Yahweh continues his activity as Judge, sending destruction upon the strong and their fortresses (v.9; see 3:11).

Am 5:10–17 continues the themes of injustice, attainment of life, and death. The repetition of **"therefore"** (vv.11, 13, 16), **"hate"** (vv.10, 15), and **"in the gates"** (vv.10, 12, 15) also shows the unity of these verses. The passage begins with an accusation against those who **hate** the reprover **in the gate** (v.10). Since the town gate was the place where Israelites resolved legal disputes, the accusation charges the prophet's audience with despising those who speak justly in the courts of law. Indeed, they **trample** upon the poor and take wheat from them (v.11). But their abuse of the poor, so vividly pictured by the metaphor of trampling, gains them nothing. When Yahweh judges, he declares they will never occupy the houses they acquired through manipulation of the legal system. They will never get to drink the wine of the vineyards they had so unjustifiably possessed. Their ill-gotten gains they ironically do not get to enjoy! Furthermore, the time of judgment is so great that the only prudent response is silence (v.13). Surely silence on such a day would be wiser than speaking up and being noticed by the Judge.

Suddenly, as in 5:4, the text shifts from description of catastrophe to exhortation concerning life (vv.14–15). Indeed, it sounds downright positive:

> Seek good, not evil,
>   that you may live.
> Then the Lord God Almighty will
>   be with you,
>   just as you say he is.

Nothing sounds amiss until one reads **"just as you say he is."** Are the pious who have *said*, "Yahweh is with us," somehow being mocked? Possibly, but at this point in our reading of the text we cannot be certain. What follows, however, begins to confirm our suspicions. An exhortation to **hate evil** and **love good** and **maintain justice in the gates** (v.15a) concludes with a mere

expression of possibility: **Perhaps the Lord God Almighty will have mercy on the remnant of Joseph** (v.15b). Nothing more than a *perhaps* is articulated, and even then the most that might be saved is a bare remnant.

As suddenly as it started, the exhortation ceases and announcement of judgment begins. It describes a scene of death in which mourning is ubiquitous: in the squares, in the streets, in the vineyards (vv.16–17). The opening dirge (vv.1–2) is complemented by a closing portrayal of death (vv.16–17). But the substantiation for the closing proclamation of death is the most important item in the announcement of judgment (v.17b). There Yahweh explains why death will prevail; it is because **"I will pass through your midst."** Yahweh's presence is the very reason why death reigns. Those pious Israelites who thought Yahweh's being with them would bring life (v.14) were hopelessly deluded. Thus the exhortation in v.14 expresses a hope for life whose underpinning—God's presence—ironically leads to death. Now we know that Yahweh's theophany (v.12) results in death.

Am 5:18–6:14 is composed of two parts (5:18–27; 6:1–14), each of which begins with a woe saying (5:18–20; 6:1–7) and closes with a Yahweh speech in which God says **"I hate," "I abhor"** (5:21–27; 6:8–14). The first part (5:18–27) represents throughout an ironic reversal of expectation. The Day of Yahweh, apparently expected as a day of light, is ironically a day of darkness over which **woe** may be pronounced (vv.18–20). It is a day comparable to a time when someone, fleeing frantically from a lion, has the misfortune to run straight into a bear, or if escaping both lion and bear, to arrive safely home and lean thankfully on a wall, only to be bitten by a serpent.

An **"I hate"** speech follows (5:21–27). Contrary to expectation, Yahweh hates the sacrifices brought by his people: **"I hate, I despise your religious feasts"** (v.21). Indeed, he desires justice instead:

> **"Away with the noise of your songs!**
> **I will not listen to the music of your harps.**
> **But let justice roll on like a river, righteousness like a never-failing stream!"** (vv.23–24)

What Yahweh hates and loves are manifestly contrary to what Israel hates and loves. Israel hates the one who speaks for justice in the gate (v.10); justice is what Yahweh wants (vv.15, 24). Israel loves to sacrifice and to publish its own cultic sanctimony (4:4–5); Yahweh hates Israel's sacrifices (5:21–24). His lack of interest in sacrifices is evident in his not requiring them in the wilderness (v.25). The gap between what Israel values and Yahweh cherishes is indeed a mighty chasm. Judgment and exile must be the consequences (v.27).

Am 6:1–7 pronounces woe on Israelite leaders for pushing far away the bad day of judgment while bringing near the seat of violence, for celebrating their magnificence with abandon while not becoming sick over the breaking down of society. Consequently these heads of society suffer punishment. Ironically, however, they maintain their status in the day of judgment; they will be the **head** of those who go into exile.

Am 6:8–14 also judges the magnificence or pride of Israel: **"I abhor the pride of Jacob / and hate his fortresses,"** says Yahweh (v.8). Therefore the city will be delivered over. Even if ten men are left, they too will

die and every house will be destroyed (vv.9–11). Against those who are prideful concerning their military power Yahweh will send a nation who will oppress them from Lebo Hamath in the north to the wadi of the Arabah in the south (vv.13–14).

To sum up: The virgin Israel will die. The city that sends out a thousand soldiers will have but a hundred left; if a hundred are sent only ten will remain (5:1–3). But even if ten survive, they too will die (6:9–10). Nothing can save them. They will go into exile (5:27; 6:7). They will be overrun completely, from north to south (6:13–14). Their sacrifices will not save them, for Yahweh hates their sacrifices (5:21ff.) and their pretentious magnificence as well (6:8). Death will prevail because Yahweh will pass over into their midst (5:17b).

b. Vision reports concerning the end of Israel (7:1–9:4)

Five vision reports constitute the main elements of the text (7:1–3, 4–6, 7–9; 8:1–3; 9:1–4). Between the third and fourth visions is a narrative of a conflict between Amos and Amaziah, priest of Bethel (7:10–17); a series of oracles about death and famine (8:4–14) separate the fourth and fifth visions. The entire sequence contributes to the theme of death and the end of Israel.

The vision sequence manifests an internal development that escalates progressively from Yahweh's forgiveness of Israel at the beginning (7:1–3) to a horrifying portrayal of Yahweh as the relentless death-dealing pursuer from which not even a remnant of Israel can escape at the end (9:1–4). In the first vision (7:1–3) intercession by the prophet leads Yahweh to forgive and to cancel the catastrophe announced in the vision. In the second vision (vv.4–6), the prophet's intercession results once more in the repeal of the punishment, but this time he cannot, as previously, dare to beg God to **forgive** (v.2) but only to **stop** (v.5). By the third vision (vv.7–9), the prophet no longer asks God to relent. There is only the report of Yahweh placing a plumbline in the midst of his people Israel to decide "whether Israel is stable or ready to be torn down" (Wolff, *Joel and Amos,* 301), much as a builder uses such an instrument to test a wall. One can only assume that Israel fails to pass the test. The fourth vision involves a play on words: the basket of **ripe fruit** (Heb. *qayiṣ*) sounds like the Hebrew word *qeṣ* ("end"). For a second time there is no cancellation of punishment; the end comes upon Israel (8:2), accompanied by death and mourning (v.3). The final vision (9:1–4) describes Yahweh as personally present at the altar, ordering that it be struck so that the capitols will collapse on the heads of the people. Persons who should happen to survive will be pursued relentlessly by God himself, with the aim that no survivors be left. The vision sequence, beginning with Yahweh's forgiveness and repeal of punishment and ending with the merciless pursuit and total slaughter of Israel, portrays a change in God's relationship with Israel. Just as Yahweh's chastisements, originally designed to provoke repentance (4:11), lead to a new divine act (v.12), so also Yahweh's attitude toward Israel changes from willingness to forgive (7:2) to a time of irreversible judgment (7:7–9; 8:1–3; 9:1–4).

The narrative appended to the third vision (7:10–17) reports an attempt on the part of Amaziah, priest of Bethel, to compel Amos to return to Judah because of his condemnation of Jeroboam, king of Israel: **"Get out, you seer! Go back to the land of Judah. Earn your bread there and do your prophesying there. Don't prophesy anymore at Bethel"** (vv.12–13). Amos responds that he is not a professional prophet but rather a shepherd who was called by Yahweh to prophesy not to Judah, but to Israel (vv.14–15). Because Amos has been sent by his God, the true conflict is not between Amaziah and Amos but between Amaziah and Yahweh. Amaziah is indeed one who, in the words of 2:12, commanded the prophets, "You must not prophesy."

The oracles appended to the fourth vision (8:4–14) build upon the language of death in 8:1–3. Because of Israel's oppression of the poor, Yahweh swears that he will never forget these misdeeds (vv.4–7). Indeed, there will be an earthquake, and all the land's inhabitants will mourn (v.8). There will be an eclipse in which God will turn festivals into mourning and songs into lamentation (vv.9–10). The theme of death continues in vv.11–14 with the proclamation, **"They will fall never to rise again"** (v.14; cf. 5:2). But the theme of death is combined with the imagery of drought and famine. Yahweh will send a famine, not of bread or of thirst, but of **hearing the words of the LORD** (vv.11–12). Thus Israel's death is not only a calamity of military defeat and exile but also a spiritual loss of the life-sustaining words of Yahweh.

2. Response: doxological hymn (9:5–6)

Am 5:1–9:6 closes with the doxology in 9:5–6. The language of death and mourning is reaffirmed as Yahweh is praised for shaking the earth, like the rising and falling of the Nile (9:5; cf. 8:8; 9:1). But it becomes clear that this Yahweh who sends death is the Creator who establishes his dwelling in the heavens, creates the earth, and controls the life-giving and destructive waters (9:6).

III. POSTSCRIPT: FROM JUDGMENT TO SALVATION (9:7–15)

The postscript to the book of Amos consists of two major parts (vv.7–10 and 11–15). The first of these begins by questioning whether Israel truly is different in Yahweh's estimation from other peoples:

"Are not you Israelites
   the same to me as the Cushites?"
                  declares the LORD.
"Did I not bring Israel up from
   Egypt,
the Philistines from Caphtor
and the Arameans from Kir?"
   (v.7)

The answer is that they have no special standing: Yahweh's eyes are on **the sinful kingdom,** whether it be Israel or another nation, and he will destroy that kingdom from the earth (v.8a). Thus far the message of death of 5:1–9:6 remains without qualification. But v.8b softens what has previously been asserted; Yahweh will destroy **the sinful kingdom,** whether it be Israel or another, except that he will not completely destroy the house of Jacob. Indeed he will shake them among the nations as one shakes with a sieve so that a pebble shall not fall to the ground (v.9). There will manifestly be death by the sword, as in 9:4, but now it is said that only *sinners* will die.

The claim that only sinners will die appears to be a deliberate softening of the message of the death of all Israel. This difference, together with the expectation that the falling dynasty of David will be raised up, has led many scholars to argue that 9:8b–15 was added over a century later to the prophecies of Amos in order to speak to the fall of Judah during the collapse of the Davidic dynasty in the south (586 B.C.) through conquest by Babylon. Only here and in 1:2 is Jerusalem or the southern dynasty and its demise the primary object of attention. Elsewhere the focus is almost exclusively on the northern kingdom and its fate during the time of Jeroboam, well over a century prior to the fall of the Davidic royal house to the Babylonians. Whether or not the ending of the book is of later origin, it is clear that compilers of the book in its present form saw hope for the chosen people of God beyond the collapse of the northern kingdom in 721 B.C. through its continuation in Judah. And the prophecies in this regard convey a divine promise that Judah and its royal house will survive the deportation to Babylon, will be raised up, and will once again be a fertile and prosperous land (9:11–15). Yahweh's devastating destruction of Israel, completed by the defeat of the northern kingdom in 721 B.C., was indeed an expression of his righteous judgment against injustice, but the house of Israel is expected to take on new life through Jerusalem and its Davidic king who, unlike Israel, will survive the exile to Babylon and will prosper in their promised land.

BIBLIOGRAPHY

Coote, R. B. *Amos Among the Prophets*. Philadelphia: Fortress, 1981.

Knierim, R. " 'I Will Not Cause It to Return' in Amos 1 and 2," in *Canon and Authority*. Edited by G. W. Coats and B. O. Long. Philadelphia: Fortress, 1977, 163–75.

Koch, K. *Amos: untersucht mit den Methoden einer strukturalen Formgeschichte*. 3 vols. Neukirchen-Vluyn: Neukirchener Verlag, 1976.

Mays, J. L. *Amos: A Commentary*. Philadelphia: Westminster, 1969.

Reventlow, H. G. *Das Amt des Propheten bei Amos*. Gottingen: Vandenhoeck & Ruprecht, 1962.

Wolff, H. W. *Amos the Prophet: The Man and His Background*. Translated by F. R. McCurley. Philadelphia: Fortress, 1973.

_____. *Joel and Amos*. Translated by W. Janzen, S. D. McBride, Jr., and C. A. Muenchow. Philadelphia: Fortress, 1977.

OBADIAH

Wayne E. Caldwell

INTRODUCTION

I. AUTHORSHIP, DATE, HISTORICAL SETTING

A. Authorship

Obadiah was a popular name in Israel. There are a dozen men named Obadiah in the Bible in addition to this prophet who wrote the shortest book of the OT.

Obadiah means "servant of Jehovah" or "worshiper of Jehovah." Although there is some difference of opinion on authorship, reasons for rejecting the book as genuine are inadequate. The book bears the name Obadiah and begins like Isaiah, stating "the vision" of the prophet.

From the style of writing it may be deduced that the author lived during the golden age of Hebrew language and literature. Few Aramaic words or constructions are mixed with the text. The style is "animated, terse and full of striking figures," especially in the first part of the little scroll (ISBE, 4:2173).

B. Date

From the earliest to the latest date that has been assigned to Obadiah, there is a span of nearly six hundred years. Some authorities date this prophet early in the ninth century B.C. or a few years later when the Philistines and Arabs partially destroyed Jerusalem in the days of Jehoram, 848–844 B.C. (2Ch 21:5, 8–11, 16–17). Others date Obadiah as late as 312 B.C. when the Arabs were firmly settled in the territories of Edom (cf. Ries, 642; EB, 4:600–601).

A more conservative consensus is that Obadiah may have been an actual witness to the Babylonian destruction of Jerusalem in 587–586 B.C. Added to this is the probability that Jeremiah quoted from Obadiah (Jer 49:7–13) as well as Ezekiel (cf. Jer 25:12–14; 35:1–15) and a psalmist (cf. Ps 137) may have in referencing the razing of Jerusalem (Hailey, 28).

C. Historical Setting

Even before the twins were born, Rebekah was told that there were two nations, two entirely different people in her womb (Ge 25:22–26).

The case of Jacob (Israel) and Esau (Edom, Idumea) was one of intense feuding, of brotherly hate, of fierce competition, and of long-standing animosity.

The boys grew up together. Their personalities and habits were different. Jacob was a man with love of family and livestock. He was tricky and conniving in his youth. Esau was a hunter, a man of the mountains. The NT record of Esau is that he was a "godless" or "profane" person (Heb 12:16). He sold his birthright to Jacob for a bowl of red stew when he was hungry (Ge 25:27–34). He lost his inheritance and the blessing that belonged to him (Ge 27). Jealousies and rivalries were inevitable when Jacob deceived his blind father, Isaac, and left home running from his brother who had murder in his heart.

After centuries had gone by, the children of Israel on their way from the wilderness to Canaan politely asked for safe passage through Edom's territory. The request was met with a nasty threat: "You may not pass through here; if you try, we will march out and attack you with the sword" (Nu 20:18).

David subdued the Edomites temporarily during the time of Saul (2Sa 8:13–14). Cruel and bitter conflicts continued until the Edomites joined with Nebuchadnezzar to bring Jerusalem to utter ruin. When it happened, their vengeance was underscored with delight and laughter.

The last and probably the latest OT record of the disposition of Esau is the statement, "Esau I have hated, and I have turned his mountains into a wasteland and left his inheritance to the desert jackels" (Mal 1:3). The descendants of Esau, in nearly every reference in the prophets, are a symbol of the earthly, worldly, nonspiritual type of people with whom God is displeased.

During their later history the Edomites were overrun by the Arabs, known as Nabateans, a people who pushed in from the desert and drove the Edomites from their land. Crowded out of their own country south of the Dead Sea, the remaining Edomites were forced to settle just south of Judah. In the second century (166 B.C.), Judas Maccabeus began the subjugation of the Edomites, and John Hyrcanus completed their defeat (135 B.C.) by forcing them to be circumcised and to accept the Law of Moses. They became nominal Jewish proselytes and gave rise in the time of Christ to the Herods, Idumean puppets of the Roman government who ruled over Palestine. The one quality ascribed to the Edomites, exhibited to a high degree in the Herods, was their clever, crafty, scheming, ruthless manner of life. By the end of the first century of the Christian era the Edomites were lost in the shades of history.

II. THEME AND GENERAL CONTENT

The twenty-one verses of Obadiah carry one of the strongest predictions of judgment to be found anywhere in the Scriptures. There are no words of hope or consolation. No conditions for possible deliverance are prescribed. The doom of Edom is sealed. God will bring total destruction to Edom. There will be no remnant, no progeny. The case is heard, judged, and ended.

For Israel, however, which tried to make peace and had a passion for the ideal, a vision for the future, and a hope for descendants, there would be a future day of triumph.

III. OUTLINE

It is helpful to note that vv.1–9 are descriptive of the disrespect exhibited toward Edom by nations with which they had been in league. Vv.10–14 show the conduct of Edom toward Israel when the nation was under siege. Their consent to watch with delight was changed to enthusiastic cooperation with Israel's enemies.

COMMENTARY

I. THE UTTER DESTRUCTION OF EDOM IS PREDICTED (VV.1–14)

A. The Announcement of Edom's Doom (vv.1–4)

The invasion of Judah by Nebuchadnezzar, or some earlier attack on Jerusalem, provoked this intense outburst against Edom. The prophet is careful to state that his denunciation came from the Lord himself—"This is what the Sovereign LORD says" and "a message from the LORD" (v.1).

The indignation of the Lord was aroused: he summoned the nations to overthrow Edom in battle. Edom's hate and love of revenge made them **utterly despised** by the nations (v.2). They were a small nation (v.2). They lived in the rocky cliffs and caves (v.3). Like

eagles with their **nest among the stars** (v.4) they felt safe and secure. But the pride of their ugly, selfish hearts would bring them down (vv.3–4).

Two factors were involved in Edom's pride. The first was the capital city, Petra, and its situation at the end of a long narrow valley. The Edomites thought their city was impregnable because of this strategic location. Only a few could easily defend their stronghold against a whole army. They had looked down for centuries with condescension and contempt on the rest of the world. But Jehovah God had determined to bring them down.

B. The Account of Edom's Destruction (vv.5–7)

The prophet declares that even a thief steals only to meet his needs, then slinks away leaving many things behind. But those who plunder the Edomites will not even have the honor of a common thief. Their own allies, former fair-weather friends, confederates, will turn on Edom and pillage even hidden treasures. They would not, with all their wisdom, be able to detect or prevent the total destruction to come (vv.6–7). Obadiah writes as though this had already happened.

C. The Aftermath of Edom's Deeds (vv.8–14)

The second cause for Edom's sin of pride was a reputation for wisdom (v.8). Teman was a village or a district south or east of Mount Seir, variously located in Edom by authorities, from five to fifteen miles from Petra. It was noted as one of the centers of wisdom of the ancient world. Eliphaz the Temanite was the first named of Job's three "wise" comforters (Job 2:11) and the first to offer his free advice (Job 4:1). The prophet states that the mighty warriors of Teman would be terrified, afford no protection at all for Esau on the mountain top, and everyone would be cut down in the slaughter (v.9). Because Edom's pride had led to atrocities against its brother nation, Israel, the Edomites would be cut off forever (v.10).

The crimes of this wicked nation fired Obadiah's soul with scorching invective as he lashed out against such wickedness. It also appears that the prophet wrote from the advantage of having seen the terrible actions of Edom and the fall of Jerusalem. What was Edom's sin? They watched from a distance at first, then cast lots and went for the loot as strangers carried off the wealth of the city (v.11).

Seven times Obadiah repeats the words "in the day" following the phrase "On the day" (v.11). In the day of misfortune, destruction, trouble (v.12), disaster, disaster, disaster (v.13), trouble (v.14), the Edomites scorned their brother, rejoiced, boasted, marched through the gates of Jerusalem, looked down on them in their calamity, seized their wealth, waited at the crossroads to cut down the fugitives, and handed over the survivors to the strangers (vv.12–14). When the besieged people of Judah tried to escape across the Jordan, the Edomites cut them off and turned them over to the invaders, probably Babylonians.

II. THE ULTIMATE EXALTATION OF ISRAEL IS PROCLAIMED (VV.15–21)

A. Israel Will Prevail (vv.15–18)

The day of the Lord (v.15), which Obadiah and all the prophets said was near for all nations, including, and especially Edom, is a favorite expression of most of the prophets. It is described as a day when the proud, lofty, and exalted will be humbled (Isa 2:12). The day of the Lord is bitter, a day of wrath, distress, anguish, trouble, ruin, darkness, gloom, clouds, blackness (Zep 1:14–15).

Although the prophets in all of these passages may not have referred to the same "day of the Lord," there is ample evidence that any day sinners persist in wanton disobedience to God is a fateful, dreadful day. Such was the case of Edom, which would reap what had been sown, with increase.

The figure of drinking on God's holy hill has a striking parallel in the prophet Jeremiah who writes of drinking the cup of God's wrath. All kings and officials and people of many (all) nations must drink from the fury of God's cup of wrath (cf. Ob 16 and Jer 25:15–28).

In marked contrast to the dark,

gloomy forecast for the house of Edom, the house of Jacob and the house of Joseph would be **a fire** and **flame** to consume the **stubble** of Esau until there were **no survivors** (vv.17–18). Wesley wrote that the remnant that would be delivered by Cyrus was "a type of Israel's redemption by Christ and that the people who "returned from captivity shall be holy to the Lord" (*Notes*, v.17).

B. Israel Will Possess the Land (vv.19–21)

Four times in vv.19 and 20 Obadiah uses the words **"will possess,"** a key phrase from v.17 that refers to the restoration of Israel and the triumph of Jehovah in righteous judgment.

When the Jewish captives returned from Babylon they found the Edomites had taken over much of the area of southern Judah. Under pressure from Nabatean Arabs from the desert, the Edomites had moved up the Negev, as far north as Hebron, just twenty miles south of Jerusalem (Earle, 38). In the time of Christ the area was known as Idumea.

No enemy of Israel was more persistent in avarice than Edom. Edom always vented hatred and anger (Smith, 178).

But all the land would be possessed by those who returned from Babylon. The places named in vv.19 and 20 suggest the length and breadth of the land so that the Edomites would have no territory at all. Being completely consumed they would have no need of land or possessions.

Finally the prophet declares that **the kingdom will be the LORD's.** This appears to be either a reference to Israel's rule from Mount Zion or to some future day after the Edomites were gone and forgotten.

The lessons of Obadiah are several and varied, including the following:

1. "'It is mine to avenge; I will repay,' says the Lord" (Ro 12:19). This may not be one of the highest principles of hope, but there is a cosmic truth—a cause and effect relationship between sin and its end—that must be noted.

2. Sin brings its inevitable result. As one sows so shall he reap. "Do not be deceived: God cannot be mocked. A man reaps what he sows" (Gal 6:7).

3. Obadiah's prophecy is a declaration of God's everlasting opposition to brotherly hate (Ro 12:10; Heb 13:1).

4. Pride is deceitful, and a haughty spirit goes before a fall. Pride leads to vanity and a sense of independence from God (Pr 16:18).

5. Even if one stands aside and watches injustice without raising a voice, one shares with the instigator in the wrongdoing (Pr 29:27).

6. In the time of judgment, God provides a means of escape for those who will turn to him. God always has the last word (Lk 21:36).

BIBLIOGRAPHY

Clarke, Adam. *A Commentary and Critical Notes.* Vol. 4. New York: Abingdon-Cokesbury, n.d.

Earle, Ralph. *Meet The Minor Prophets.* Kansas City: Beacon Hill, 1955.

Hailey, Homer. *A Commentary on the Minor Prophets.* Grand Rapids: Baker, 1972.

The International Standard Bible Encyclopedia. James Orr, general editor. Vol. 4.
   "Obadiah" and "Obadiah, Book of," John Richard Sampey. Grand Rapids:
   Eerdmans, 1947.

Keil, C. F. and F. Delitzsch. *Commentary on the Old Testament.* Vol. 10. Grand
   Rapids: Eerdmans, 1978.

Knopf, Carl Sumner. *Ask The Prophets.* Nashville: Parthenon, 1938.

Purkiser, W. T. *Know Your Old Testament.* Kansas City: Beacon Hill, 1954.

Ries, Claude A. "The Book of Obadiah." WBC. Vol. 3. Grand Rapids:
   Eerdmans, 1969.

Robinson, George L. *The Twelve Minor Prophets.* Grand Rapids: Baker, 1979.

Smith, George Adam. *The Book of the Twelve Prophets.* Vol. 1 of two volumes.
   New York: Harper & Brothers, 1928.

Wesley, John. *Explanatory Notes Upon the Old Testament.* Vol. 3. Bristol: William
   Pine, 1765. Reprinted by Schmul Publishers, Salem, Ohio, 1975.

JONAH

G. Herbert Livingston

INTRODUCTION

I. TITLE, CONTENT, AND CANONICAL PLACEMENT

The title is derived from the name of the prophet Jonah.

The story is about a Hebrew prophet, who on hearing the Lord's command to prophesy to Nineveh, rebelled and boarded a ship to the farthest port. God sent a storm, and the sailors tossed Jonah into the sea where he was swallowed by a great fish. Jonah prayed, and the Lord caused the fish to vomit Jonah onto the seashore.

This time Jonah made his way to Nineveh where he declared the city's destruction. The king and his subjects repented and pleaded for God's mercy, and the Lord annulled their punishment. Jonah was unhappy; he wanted Nineveh destroyed. His prayer was marred with anger toward the Lord. Jonah begged for death. The Lord confronted Jonah by showing the vast difference between Jonah's selfish attachment to an unreliable vine and the Lord's unlimited and unbiased love for the ignorant people of a pagan city.

All manuscripts of the Minor Prophets place Jonah between Obadiah and Micah.

II. HISTORICAL SETTING, AUTHORSHIP, AND DATE OF JONAH

A prophet named Jonah, son of Amittai, is mentioned in 2Ki 14:25. This prophet was from Gath Hepher in Galilee and presumably was the same prophet named in Jnh 1:1. The prophet would have prophesied in the reign of King Jeroboam II (793–753 B.C.).

Assyria had been forced out of Damascus, and Jeroboam, free of northern enemies, rebuilt Israel. At that time Nineveh was part of an extensive complex of cities that comprised the center of Assyria's power but was not yet the capital of the empire.

Many scholars have rejected the journey of Jonah to Nineveh as a historical account and prefer to understand the story as an allegory or a parable. Jesus referred to Jonah and Nineveh in relation to his own death, resurrection, and the future judgment (Mt 12:39–41; Lk 11:29–32), which, for many, strongly supports the historicity of the book of Jonah.

The text of the book of Jonah does not specify whether Jonah or someone else wrote the book. There is no compelling reason to deny that Jonah was the author of the book, though some scholars have proposed two or more unknown authors.

The scholars who regard the book as historical suggest that it was written some time after the events recorded but no later than about 760 B.C. Scholars who regard the book to be an allegory or a parable tend to date the book in the fourth or third century B.C.

III. STRUCTURE AND THEOLOGICAL THEMES
Basically, the book of Jonah is a unified narrative. A short prayer psalm is inserted between 1:17 and 2:10. The book has two parts: (1) Jonah's disobedience to the Lord (1:1–2:10) and (2) an obedient prophet who learned a vital lesson from the Lord (3:1–4:11). Each section begins with the same command given by the Lord to Jonah and each ends with a statement about the Lord's compassion (2:10 has Jonah's deliverance from the great fish, and 4:11 has the Lord's statement about Nineveh). Polytheists offer desperate pleas for mercy in 1:14 and 3:5–6, and Jonah offers agonizing prayers in 2:2–9 and 4:2–3. In each instance the Lord provides help.

The Lord dominates every aspect of the activities that take place. This fact is the essence of the theological themes of the book. The Lord, who is the Creator of all things and Lord of all nations, desires to offer salvation to even the worst of them.

Jonah's two prayers show that he knew that the Lord was present on the sea, in the fish, and in Nineveh. Jonah admits in his second prayer that he knew all along that the Lord's love could quickly annul his judicial decision to punish wicked people if repentance was genuine.

In the OT Jonah is the only one who heard God's command to go as a missionary to a specific foreign city.

In summary, Jonah teaches (1) God's concern for all peoples, (2) God's desire to send individuals to preach his Word, (3) God's use of nature in miraculous ways to fulfill his purposes, (4) God's role as Judge but his preference to act as Savior, (5) the fact that mission fields are often more responsive than God's own people, and (6) God's yearning to show mercy and love to any and all people.

IV. OUTLINE
Major Theme: God in Love Offers Salvation to All People
   I. Going Down (1:1–17)
   II. A Fervent Prayer (2:1–9)
   III. Message and Response (2:10–3:10)
   IV. Jonah and the Lord (4:1–11)

COMMENTARY

I. GOING DOWN (1:1–17)

Jonah was suddenly confronted by the Lord and told to go to Nineveh to deliver an important message. That city was wicked and needed to be told that the Lord was against it.

Jonah fled from the presence of the Lord. At the seaport of Joppa he boarded a ship sailing for Tarshish, usually identified with Tartessus, a port on the southwest shore of Spain. Jonah did not escape the Lord. It was not the stormy season, but the Lord produced a wild storm that threatened to sink the ship.

The sailors, probably Canaanites, were polytheists and prayed to their many gods for help.

The captain found Jonah hidden below deck sound asleep. The captain wanted Jonah to pray also. If one man's god could not help, maybe some other deity could. The sailors cast lots because they believed that such a storm was caused by someone's sin. This was an opportunity for the one true God to act, so he caused the lots to identify Jonah as the sinner.

The sailors wanted to know who Jonah was and what kind of sin he had committed. Jonah confessed his faith as a Hebrew in the **God of heaven, who made the sea and the land.** Evidently the sailors knew about the God of the Hebrews and the miracles he had done for them. They seemed to know that running from God's presence was impossible, so they asked Jonah what kind of punishment would stop the storm.

Jonah admitted that his sin had caused the storm, and he advised the sailors to throw him into the sea. The sailors rejected the idea and, filled with fear, rowed against the raging waves with all their might.

The sailors prayed again. But this time they directed their prayers to the one true God. With great reluctance, they tossed Jonah overboard.

Whereas Jonah was disobedient and did not beseech God for mercy, the pagan sailors turned from their false deities to the true God and obeyed him. The Lord saved their lives by calming the sea. Thoroughly frightened, they worshiped God.

God saved Jonah's life by having a **great fish** near the boat to swallow him. Jonah remained alive and able to think seriously about his situation.

II. A FERVENT PRAYER (2:1–9)

Finally Jonah began to pray to the Lord. Perhaps Jonah was remembering the psalmist, who asked, "Where can I go from your Spirit?" The psalmist explored several possibilities and testified, "You are there" (see Ps 139:7–12). By whatever means, Jonah gained faith to state his need and plead for mercy.

Clearly Jonah did not write the prayer while he was in the stomach of the great fish. Later he remembered the experience and set down the essence of his petition in stirring verse. The poem is much like Pss 86 and 88, a mixture of desperation, agony, hope, and faith.

In distress Jonah did not turn against the Lord or away from him as he had when the divine command came. This time Jonah directed his thoughts and emotions toward the Lord and received an answer to his prayer. The psalmists and Jonah were aware that the Lord knows all things, yet they made it a practice to recount the nature of the danger facing them.

Jonah regarded the insides of the fish

as **the depths of the grave.** But that did not create a barrier; the Lord heard him very well. Jonah described the storm but did not accuse the Lord of treating him cruelly. The prophet did feel **banished,** but at the same time he decided to look toward the Lord's temple, though he would have no sense of direction while in the fish. The desire to seek would be adequate.

Jonah summarized the impossibility of his predicament; he seemed **barred** in a prison **forever.** But the impossibility was the Lord's opportunity. The wonder of it all overwhelmed the prophet as he thought back, **"You brought my life up from the pit."**

Jonah had been at the very edge of life and had felt his strength slipping away; but he wrote, **"I remembered you, LORD."** The prayer was an effectual prayer.

In a flash Jonah realized that such a deliverance was a reality of experience that idol worshipers totally miss. No way could their idols provide such an amazing salvation. Perhaps Jonah thought of the sailors on the ship who, in the storm, turned from their idols to pray to the living God. They had thus found grace and were saved. But idol worshipers who fail to convert to the Lord **forfeit the grace that could be theirs.** Jonah completed his poem by stating his joyful intention to worship the Lord by singing thankful praise, by offering sacrifices, and by making vows to the Lord. Compare with Pss 42:4; 50:14, 15, 23; 116:14.

III. MESSAGE AND RESPONSE (2:10–3:10)

The Lord of all creation responded to the prayer by ordering the fish to deposit Jonah somewhere on the eastern coast of the Mediterranean. When God decides to act, he can do so in any part of his creation, and it is always an act of wonder.

Jonah had surrendered to God and was ready to serve him. The command was basically the same as the first one (1:2), except that the wickedness of the city is not mentioned.

Even in obedience, Jonah seemed to have mixed emotions about making the trip to Nineveh (see comments on 4:1–11), but he went anyway. He had learned through experience the truth of the doctrine that the living God is everywhere.

Nineveh was located on the east bank of the Tigris River about five hundred miles from the nearest beach on the Mediterranean. Nineveh was a great city in the sense that it was part of a four-city complex, but it was not yet the capital of the Assyrian Empire.

The **three days** seems to be an idiom with a meaning that is no longer clear, especially to those of a Western culture.

The prophet did not delay his mission; on the **first day** of his arrival he began to preach.

The message was brief and clear cut: **"Forty more days and Nineveh will be overturned."** The sentence bears no conditional clauses, no loopholes. The punishment was unequivocal. Overthrowing a city means an enemy captures and reduces it to ruins.

The response of the people of Nineveh was remarkable. They heard the message and perceived within the time span of forty days an opportunity to repent. They went even further; they **believed God,** the living God of this strange prophet and had hope that this God was really the God of mercy. They expressed their repentance the only way they knew, by fasting and covering themselves with **sackcloth,** a rough burlap-like material.

The king heard of Jonah's message and the response of his people. Instead of taking a stand in favor of the deities of Assyria, many of whom were mean and warlike, he too decided to repent. Whatever the economic and political problems of Assyria may have been, it is known that the empire was in serious trouble. Such a situation in an idol-worshiping society would create serious doubt about the power of the idols and the deities they represented. The city seemed ripe for conversion to the living God.

Through the centuries, Christian missionaries have often found idol-worshiping people totally disillusioned with their idols and ready to respond to the Gospel. In many cases, whole tribes or ethnic groups have turned to God in repentance.

Including animals in the act of repentance seems strange to Western cultures but indicate that the king wanted to spare no means to catch the attention of the Almighty. His decree urged the people to **give up their evil ways and their violence.** Deeds of repentance must be matched with deeds of conversion. Jeremiah later urged that his own people do this, but they refused (7:3; 25:5).

The king's statement of hope reveals a concept of possibility. Though the message was one of judgment, perhaps the God who threatened them was compassionate too and would deliver them. Far better to hope than to live in despair.

The king of Nineveh was right; the God who had threatened destruction was a God of compassion. The intent of his threat was first of all to incite repentance and then to forgive; only as a last resort would he carry out his threat. The Lord explained this truth clearly to another prophet; it applied to all nations equally (Jer 18:7–10). The key element in all such cases is a genuine and earnest joining of repent-ance with a total change of practice. On the other hand, the Lord's switch from judgment to salvation is not a contradiction within his being, but the joyful expression of who he is, the God of love.

IV. JONAH AND THE LORD (4:1–11)

The contrast between the Jonah who humbly and effectively prayed while inside the fish and the Jonah who sulked while the Ninevites prayed effectively, is striking. Jonah had sinned in his disobedience and deserved punishment as much as the idol worshipers of Nineveh. When he was delivered from the fish, he rejoiced and did God's bidding. He knew from his heritage and from experience that the God who is offended by sin is quick to forgive a truly repentant sinner.

Jonah confessed now that this knowledge lay behind his unsuccessful flight from the presence of the Lord. From the time of Moses, the core teaching of the covenant of Mount Sinai had been "The LORD, the LORD, the compassionate and gracious God, slow to anger, abounding in love and faithfulness, maintaining love to thousands, and forgiving wickedness, rebellion and sin" (Ex 34:6–7a). The next sentences balance God's love with his insistence that sin must be punished. Jonah's deep dislike for the people of Nineveh led him to insist that punishment take precedence over the compassion of the Lord. Jonah had allowed anger to push love out of his soul. Anger produced a despair so profound that the will to live was obliterated.

The Lord was not harsh, but he did pierce deeply into Jonah's soul. The question tore aside a veil that hid a boiling anger that contrasts with God's anger. Though his anger is due to the falseness of idolatry and the viciousness of sin, God looks for evidence of repentance and repudiation of evil ways. The true goal of his anger is the salvation of the sinner.

Jonah was angry because his prejudice toward the Ninevites as a people was deep seated. He did not want them to repent and change their evil ways. He wanted them dead, period. That was not right, and the Lord wanted Jonah to see his sin.

In contrast to the Ninevites, who regarded the forty days as a door of hope and repented, Jonah regarded the forty days as an unnecessary waste of time. If Nineveh was to be overturned, why not now? Besides, the spectacle of the city ablaze would be quite a show. Gathering some saplings and branches, he constructed a crude shelter and waited.

Meanwhile the Lord arranged the course of events so that he could teach a lesson on true compassion. He caused a broad-leafed vine to sprout and spread over Jonah's shelter. Wonderful shade from the blazing sun protected Jonah, and his anger turned to joy. Surely the Lord was good to him. He was unaware of the Lord's next move.

Before dawn a worm chewed on the roots of the vine, causing it to wither. Next the Lord directed the east wind to blow on Jonah, causing great discomfort. Jonah's self-centered love for personal comfort was vividly revealed. Like the leaves of the vine, he wilted and begged for death. Again the question about the rightness of his anger was thrown at Jonah.

When the Lord first asked the question, Jonah was angry because the hated Ninevites were repenting and the Lord was forgiving them. Jonah's reputation as a prophet seemed threatened, for he had predicted destruction, but the Lord was granting salvation. That made him look like a false prophet; it was not fair. This time Jonah was angry because God seemed to be making a fool of him, appearing to bless him with a vine and then exposing him to extreme suffering. That was not fair either. Jonah loved himself and the vine that shaded him, but nothing else.

The Lord contrasted this selfish **concern** with the Lord's concern for people, even wicked people. Here was a great city filled with people deprived by their leaders of essential skills of learning. They had never received instruction in moral principles and holy practices of dealing with each other. They had a multitude of children who had no hope of hearing the truth about the living God unless a Hebrew taught them. They had wealth enough to possess many cattle, but they did not have true riches, the true knowledge of God.

The moral and spiritual poverty of Nineveh deeply concerned the Lord, and here he had a prophet on his hands who was excited about preaching judgment but was blind to opportunities the revival in Nineveh provided to instruct and nurture the people on how to live a holy life before him. What irony!

BIBLIOGRAPHY

Allen, Leslie C. "The Book of Jonah." *The Books of Joel, Obadiah, Jonah and Micah.* Grand Rapids: Eerdmans, 1976.

Clarke, Adam. "The Book of Jonah." *A Commentary and Critical Notes.* New York: Abingdon, n.d.

Laetsch, Theo. "Jonah." *Bible Commentary: The Minor Prophets.* St. Louis: Concordia, 1956.

Morgan, G. Campbell. "Jonah." BI. New York: Revell, n.d.

Patterson, John. "Jonah, a Plea for Universalism." *The Goodly Fellowship of the Prophets.* New York: Scribner, 1949.

Peisker, Armor D. "The Book of Jonah." BBC. Kansas City: Beacon Hill, 1966.

Thompson, W. Ralph. "Jonah." WBC. Grand Rapids: Eerdmans, 1969.

Wolff, Hans W. "The Prophet Jonah." *Obadiah and Jonah: A Commentary.* Minneapolis: Augsburg, 1986.

MICAH
Wayne E. Caldwell

INTRODUCTION

I. AUTHORSHIP AND DATE, HISTORICAL SETTING

A. Authorship and Date

Micah has been called "the defender of the poor," "the prophet of the coming Deliverer," and "the common man's prophet." We know nothing of Micah's parents or of his family. We can only conclude that he lived close to his people in a small country village. His "fearless and courageous spirit is of one who is indignant over the corruption and heartlessness of inhuman rulers and time-serving religionists" (Hailey, 186).

The name Micah means "Who is like Jehovah" (also spelled Micaiah, with the same meaning). His home was at Moresheth (1:1, 14), a town on the border between Judah and Philistia, twenty to twenty-five miles southwest of Jerusalem. Beit-Jebrin now occupies the site of the ancient village. Ashdod and Gaza were more than twenty miles away; Bethlehem was nineteen; Hebron thirteen; and Tekoa, the home of Amos in the wilderness of Judea, was seventeen miles east. Both Tekoa and Moresheth produced men of deep conviction, compassion, courage, and independence.

Micah may have been a tiller of the soil, for Moresheth Gath (1:14) is in the Shephelah, which lies between the hill country of Judah and the Philistine plain. This is a fertile low range of hills adorned with streams of water, cornfields, olive groves, and grassland for cattle. Shepherds and farmers still call to each other across the valleys or call to their livestock. The men in Jerusalem could not possibly know the mind of men who were in love with the soil. Micah was so detached from city life that he could objectively predict for Jehovah the ruin and doom of his nation (Smith, 1:403).

Micah is the sixth of twelve minor prophets in the Hebrew canon but third in the Septuagint (LXX), following Amos and Hosea. "This LXX arrangement may have been by size, but in Micah's case it is also chronologically in third place as a younger contemporary of Hosea and Amos" (Smith, 1:383).

Micah dates his ministry during the days of Jotham, Ahaz, and

Hezekiah, or roughly the forty-year period from 740–700 B.C. Jotham succeeded his father, Uzziah, who had reigned for fifty-two years in Jerusalem (2Ch 26:3). Jotham's reign was from 739 to 731 B.C., then Ahaz his son was king from 731 to 715 B.C. Ahaz was followed by his son Hezekiah.

Amos had been silent for about thirty years, Hosea for about fifteen, and Isaiah was halfway through his career. Micah had a passion for justice like Amos plus a heart of love like Hosea. His concern was not for politics but for spiritual and moral problems. In contrast Isaiah was in close contact with the city and world affairs, an associate of kings and princes. Both Micah and Isaiah saw the absolute holiness and majesty of God. They saw him as the infinite ruler of nations and men. To violate God's sovereignty and holiness would surely bring down his wrath and inevitable doom.

When Jeremiah was in danger of being put to death for his faithful words of prophecy, he wrote that some of the elders of the land stepped forward and cited Micah's prophecy made during the days of Hezekiah. Then the elders asked whether Hezekiah or anyone else in Judah put Micah to death because of his prediction of Zion's fall (26:18–19). The answer was obvious, so Jeremiah's life was spared (v.24). This reference substantiates the date of Micah, for the reign of Hezekiah extended from 715 to 687 B.C., during which at least part of his prophecy would have been written (Hailey, 187).

Although critics insist that interpolations have been made in the text, there is no conclusive reason why Micah cannot be the total work of the man whose name it bears. Gray and Adams state that "Micah's style is forceful, pointed and concise, frequently animated and sublime. The abrupt transitions with which the book abounds suggest that Micah, like most of the prophets, was founded mainly on discourse or notes of discourse composed on various occasions (3:797).

B. Historical Setting

Some time just after Samaria's doom had occurred (722 B.C.), while it was still going on, or while its destruction was imminent, Micah cried out that Judah, too, was doomed. The feeling seems to be too intense, the emotion too vividly portrayed for the opening words of Micah to have been made late in Hezekiah's reign. The Assyrian attacks under Shalmaneser or Sargon on Samaria and on the fortified cities of Judah were occasions when Micah could well have mourned the eventful fall of Jerusalem. When Judah was still intact in the reign of Hezekiah but shaking in the aftershock of Samaria's defeat, this fearless prophet stood in sight of the Assyrian armies and attacked the sins of his people. He said they would suffer the same fate as Samaria as a judgment of God.

Micah gave no hope for Jerusalem. He was overwhelmed with a sense of danger and mourned over what the leaders had done to bring on the doom of the capital. Social problems had been felt by people in rural areas even before those in the cities, because wealthy, land-hungry men had descended on country districts. They made the poor their debtors and robbed or bought their land for a small price. These reckless plutocrats inflicted injustice and economic plunder in the country with no one to cry out in their defense until God gave voice to Micah. The rich were quick to tell the prophet that his sentence on the nation and on themselves was absurd and impossible (Smith, 407, 415, 418).

II. THEME AND GENERAL CONTENT

The forceful and simple teaching of Micah is that Jehovah is holy and righteous. As long as His people do what is right, they will enjoy his favor. When they turn away from him in stubborn rebellion, they will suffer his judgment. Nearly one-third of Micah is an indictment of Israel and Judah for specific sins, including oppression; bribery among judges, prophets, and priests; exploitation of the powerless; covetousness; cheating; violence and pride. Another third of Micah predicts the judgment that was to come because of these sins, and the final third is a message of hope and consolation.

The "kindness and sternness" of God (Ro 11:22) are shown in Micah's explanation of divine judgment and pardon. God's justice will always triumph because he has promised a Deliverer. True justice and peace will prevail when Messiah reigns. The relationship between social ethics and spiritual integrity is underscored by Micah. He summarizes what God wants to find in his people. It is justice and equity tempered with mercy and compassion as the result of a humble and obedient relationship with him (Mic 6:8).

Thus Mic 6:8 along with 7:18 are key verses set in the context of these last two key chapters. God calls the mountains and the hills together as the jury in the case he brings against his people who have replaced heartfelt worship with empty ritual. They have divorced God's standard of justice from their daily dealings, and they have failed to live up to what they have known to be right. The only possible verdict is guilty. But God also delights to extend mercy to anyone who will repent and obey his directives.

III. OUTLINE

C. Consolation in the Prophet's Plea From God for Repentance and Restoration (6:1–7:20)

COMMENTARY

I. DENUNCIATION— JUDGMENT (1:1–3:12)

It was twilight for Judah. Night was about to descend over the whole land as God's mills of judgment began to grind fine grist. Micah listened, wondered, and waited until he knew what his message would be for Judah and Jerusalem as well as for Israel and Samaria.

A. Denunciation of Idolatry, Materialism, and Covetousness— Judgment on the People of Samaria and Judah (1:1–2:13)

Although Micah's message was directed to Jerusalem and Samaria (1:1), it was in the villages of Judah where the prophet called the nations to witness the judgment of God. Wesley states that the earth (v.2) "seems to be an appeal to the senseless creatures, or a summons to bring in evidences for God against those kingdoms" (Wesley, *Notes*, 3:383).

If the Sovereign of the universe meted out his wrath from his holy place in heaven against his chosen people, the heathen nations should need no further warning. The figures of the earthquake and volcano (1:4), are vivid descriptions of God's anger vented against all his covenant people. Jacob's transgression (1:5), is all-inclusive of Israel and the ten northern tribes, as well as of Judah and the southern tribes. The capital cities of Samaria and Jerusalem with their rulers are held responsible for leading the people into idolatry and apostasy.

So complete would be the destruction of Samaria, so proud and so seemingly secure, so smug in a mountain fortress, that even the stones of the city's buildings down to the foundations would be rolled into the valley below. The idols, the images, and the city's wealth would be broken and carried away, and the site would be so barren that even vineyards could be planted there (1:6–7).

The prophet himself was so griefstricken over the judgment that Samaria was to receive that he stated he would weep and wail like the jackal and the owl in mournful howl and screech. In the garb of a slave, Micah would walk barefoot in his grief, for he saw that God's wrath would reach even to Judah and the gates of Jerusalem (1:8–9).

In a panoramic tabloid, Micah names or refers to twelve towns. All his hearers and readers would recognize these places as examples of the destruction, punishment, and bondage that was about to come upon them because of sin: (1) **Gath**, tell-town, **"tell it not"**; (2) Acco, weep-town, **"weep not"**; (3) **Beth Ophrah**, dust-town, **"roll in the dust"**; (4) **Shaphir**, fairtown, **"in nakedness and shame"**; (5) **Zaanan**, march-town, **"will not come [march] out"**; (6) **Beth Ezel**, neighbor-town, **"protection is taken from you"**; (7) **Maroth**, bitter-town, **"writhe in pain"**; (8) **Lachish**, teamtown, **"harness the team to the chariot"**; (9) **Moresheth Gath**, possessiontown, **"give parting gifts"**; (10) Ac-

zib, false spring-town, **"will prove deceptive"**; (11) **Mareshah,** heir-town, **"you who live in"**; (12) **Adullam,** wild beast cave-town, **"the glory of Israel will come"** (1:10–15; cf. Knopf, 58; Farrar, 130–31).

As a mother who is led away with her children into bondage, Zion will be taken into exile. The people who disobey God will find their neck and head bereft of covering, with the baldness of a vulture (1:16).

Instead of the wealthy tycoons going to bed at night to sleep, Micah pictures them as scheming and plotting seizures of houses and farms. Such arrogance and wickedness is so deliberate and cruel that the Lord will cause even the conquerors to taunt and tease them with their own mournful wail of loss. Because of their pride and deceit there will be no one to divide the fields to them ever again (2:1–5; Hailey, 197ff.). Rather, as Wesley states, God has divided the fields among others because he has turned away in displeasure (3:383).

The rich men, through their false prophets, warn Micah to stick to religion and not to meddle in their affairs. Since these men were Abraham's offspring and were prosperous, they must have God's favor. As a chosen race no harm could befall them, they thought. Micah responded by telling them that they were no better than night prowlers and thieves of the dark. They were greedy parasites who preyed on helpless women and children. They tried to cover their trail of sin by subtlety and deceit in order to gloss over the real issues. The only kind of prophet they would listen to would be one who would tell them the things they wanted to hear, such as of their own goodness (2:6–11; Knopf, 59).

Amid the description of gloom and doom upon the rich, Micah was faithful in declaring for the Lord that a remnant of faithful, obedient believers would be brought back. Like sheep from the flock in a pasture they would be gathered because their king, with the Lord in the lead (Messiah?), would bring them out of bondage (2:12–13). "This was fulfilled in part when the Jews returned out of Babylon," Wesley thought, "but more fully when Christ by his gospel gathered together in one all the children of God that were scattered abroad" (3:383). Always there is mercy and hope for those who will hear (Rev 2:7, 11, 17, 29, et al.).

B. Denunciation of Injustice and Greed—Judgment on the Leadership of Israel and Jerusalem (3:1–12)

Brought up in humble surroundings and isolated from the awful deeds of the rich, Micah was stirred with anger when he saw what was happening. He lashed out against the leaders of the nation, including the rulers (vv.1–4), the false prophets (vv.5–8), and the priests and prophets (vv.9–12).

Reports from the capital city fanned the flame in Micah's heart. The rulers in Jerusalem were greedy, selfish cannibals. They plucked off the skin and tore the flesh from the bones of the people, then broke the bones and chopped them up like meat for the kettle. Micah's words burned with fire as his soul became an echo of God's holy justice (Earle, 57).

Even the prophets had become greedy and grasping. They preached only for hire, then turned with savage fury against those who failed to put food in their mouths. It was all reminiscent of the way of Balaam son of Beor, later to be recalled by Peter (2Pe 2:15–16) as loving the way of wickedness. The nation was really in trouble when those speaking for God became corrupt and were concerned only for themselves.

God's decision was inevitable. There would be no light, no vision, no answer from him, so the prophets would be ashamed and hide their faces in confusion just as God would hide his face from the rulers (vv.4, 7). Here Micah lays down a principle that separates the false from the true prophet of God: It is not enough to teach and preach nice-sounding platitudes, even if they are true. Unless a prophet declares truths the people need to know, condemning the sins of which they are guilty, "he is as much a false prophet as one who declares untruths or that which contradicts truth" (Hailey, 203).

The source of Micah's ministry was the power of God's Spirit (v.8), by which he was able to address the priests as well as the princes and prophets. The priests assumed that because they were among God's chosen people no harm could come to them. Their primary crime against God was the sin of presumption (v.11). God was going to punish Zion. Jerusalem would not escape. Samaria did not. Since Judah was going in the same stubborn path as Israel had gone, the people, too, would come under judgment. The prophet made the announcement over 100 years before it came to pass in 586 B.C. (v.12).

II. Consolation–Restoration (4:1–7:20)

A. Consolation in Zion's Restoration (4:1–13)

After the gloom and doom of Micah's diatribe against the wicked practices of cruel leaders appear beautiful promises of Jerusalem's restoration. The picture is one of the brightest of Israel's future glory to be found in the OT (Earle, 59).

Most authorities see Micah's proclamation as a messianic prophecy, to which Christ himself may have been referring in Lk 24:47 when he declared that repentance and remission of sins would be preached to all nations, beginning from Jerusalem (vv.1–2; Hailey, 205). Wesley wrote concerning the last days, "The expiring of the seventy years' captivity, nearly two hundred years from Micah's time, a type of the days of the Messiah's kingdom" (3:383).

The prophecy concerning many nations "was in part fulfilled when so many proselyted servants of several nations, out of love for their Jewish masters and more for the God of the Jews, came up with them from Jerusalem. So the Jews, released from captivity, encouraged each other; which was a fulfilling of this prophecy in part. The conversion of the multitude of the Gentiles to Christ was a more eminent fulfilling of it" (Wesley, 3:384).

Not only will many nations make their way to the Holy City in those last days, but the Lord will settle disputes among them (v.3) and they will possess their own possessions without fear (v.4). "The redeemed of the Lord, redeemed from Babylonian captivity, [are] the type of a greater redemption by Jesus Christ" (Wesley, 3:384). There will be no need of arms for war. Spears and swords will become tools for cultivation. The exiles and the remnant of those driven away into captivity in Babylon (4:6–10) will be redeemed and restored to Zion. "That is, they shall enjoy peace, security, and plenty. This was more fully made good in the gospel days" (Wesley, 3:384).

The cry of many nations around Judah and Zion was **"Let her be defiled"** (4:11). But God had not allowed the total destruction of Jerusalem. He meant only to afflict and discipline his people, not to reject them utterly. The enemies of his people would be gathered like sheaves for the threshing floor. There the Lord would give his people the ability to break many nations into pieces. What had been taken from them would be restored for his use (4:12-13).

B. Consolation in Messiah's Birth and Restoration of a Remnant (5:1-15)

Micah foretold the destruction of the armies of the Assyrians, which would have dealt a severe blow to Israel's king (v.1). Then he immediately used the long-range telescope of God to state that Messiah was to come from the family and ancestral village of David.

Although it was small in comparison to the clans of Judah, Bethlehem, "house of bread," and Ephrathah "fruitfulness," was located five miles south of Jerusalem and would be an ideal place for Messiah to be born in God's providential care (v.2). To this place wise men from the East would travel some seven hundred years later to find and see God's Gift to humankind (Mt 2:1-7).

Without a king in the suffering that was to occur, Judah was told that the Messiah King as a shepherd over his flock would rule with strength and majesty in peace **to the ends of the earth** (v.4). The standing position of the Shepherd speaks of "the readiness, cheerfulness, and stability of the Christ, his government, and kingdom. His church, made up of converted Jews and Gentiles, shall continue; the gates of hell shall not prevail against them. For the church is so redeemed and established that Christ the Messiah might be glorified throughout the world" (Wesley, 384). The figure of seven shepherds and eight leaders of men carry the significance of an all-sufficient and more than adequate provision for every need (vv.5-6).

The king will be more than a match for Israel's dreaded enemies, with a focus on the Assyrians. The Lord's redeemed remnant of Jacob will be **like dew from the LORD, like showers on the grass** (v.7). The remnant of Jacob will be **like a lion among the beasts . . . like a young lion among flocks of sheep** (v.8).

Micah speaks for Jehovah four times in rapid succession with the words **"I will destroy your horses," . . . "the cities," . . . "your witchcraft," . . . "your carved images,"** and then adds that God will uproot the symbols of Asherah and take vengeance on the nations that have disobeyed him (vv.10-15).

C. Consolation in the Prophet's Plea From God for Repentance and Restoration (6:1-7:20)

In a tender entreaty the Lord speaks through Micah to the people and poses a controversy. He calls on the mountains and hills to listen to his case and the charge he makes against his people. In deep pathos God asks **"What have I done to you? How have I burdened you?"** (6:1-3). He rehearses his faithfulness to Israel in all their history from Egypt to Gilgal and from Moses to Balaam (vv.4-5).

Jehovah does not call attention to their gross sins but asks wherein he has failed them. He does not command, but pleads with them to remember his faithfulness to them. Israel responds to the Lord's controversy by asking three questions: (1) How about our regular sacrifices? (2) How about our special and lavish offerings? (3) How about our spirit of sacrifice, even to our firstborn? (Ries, 6:6-7).

In one of the greatest passages of the OT, the Lord summarizes the nature and requirements of true religion (6:8). No one can **act justly, love mercy,** and **walk humbly** and fail to please God. Before these conditions can be met, every person must seek peace with, and forgiveness from, God. The Talmud states that David reduced the requirements of the Mosaic Law from 613 to 11 in Ps 15. Micah reduced the 11 to 3, and Christ reduced the 3 to 1, or to 2 if one needs the second one (Earle, 60).

Wesley makes these observations on Micah's key verse: "God has already told you in his word with what you ought to come before him. To render to every one their due; superiors, equals, inferiors, to be equal to all and oppress none in body, goods, or name. To be kind, merciful, and compassionate to all, not using severity towards any. Keep up a constant fellowship with God by humble, holy faith" (Wesley, 385).

A second controversy follows as the Lord leads Micah to name the vices of the rich merchants of the city. They had cheated with a **short ephah,** they had **dishonest scales** and **false weights,** and they were deceitful **liars** (6:9–12). Since these sins were so obvious, the ruin of the fields and produce would be a curse upon them. Walking in the ways of Omri and Ahab, they would reap what they had sown (vv.13–16a), and they would be held in derision and contempt by the nations around them (v.16b).

Micah saw these conditions as a great menace to religion and national integrity. The men of the city were crooks. They were mad, sick, lonely, uprooted, shallow, abnormal. They had a form of godliness in their tradition, background, and character; but they were wholly corrupt. They followed their senses, appetites, and passions like animals. They had lost contact with their past. The deep roots of their piety had rotted away (Knopf, 59).

Whether in the OT or NT, true religion before the Lord means a right relationship with the Lord and one's fellows. Justice is the basis of all moral law and life. Mercy is God's goodness to the redeemed, which must be shown to all his creatures. Humility is the "low, sweet root from which all heavenly virtues shoot," and it must be the characteristic of every true believer in walking before God.

In his final message and before ending his oracle with a doxology of praise to such a faithful, loving, forgiving God (7:18–20), Micah confesses the sins of Jerusalem or Zion (vv.1–6), as well as the sins of the spiritual remnant (vv.7–17).

With heavy heart Micah exclaims, **"What misery is mine!"** There are few if any who are righteous. Hopelessness and despair mark the prophet's lament. Instead of being models of upright living, the ruler, the judge, and the powerful lie in wait to take the life and possessions of the helpless (7:1–3). No wonder Micah was pessimistic. Not even a close friend or those of one's own household could be trusted. Only the Master himself could fully comprehend the prophet's attitude of despair (vv.4–6). Jesus cited the inspired words of Micah in his discourse and instructions to his disciples as he sent them out (Mt 10:34–36).

Only as Micah looked to God did he find comfort and hope for his people. As light at the end of a dark tunnel, the prophet saw that God was utterly faithful (7:7, 9). In the day when Zion's glory will be restored, when captivity is ended, when people from all parts of the earth will turn to God in fear, then and only then will Micah's paean of praise be understood (vv.12, 15, 17).

How glorious are these promises of blessing and goodness from Jehovah! All of these are given in spite of the ingratitude and wickedness on Israel's part. The prophet stands in awe at the presence of such infinite love and greatness. In this awe he closes his message with an ode of praise to the Lord. . . . There is none to compare, for Jehovah passes over iniquity, the grossest and basest of sin, and pardons transgressions, . . . He does all this because He is God who retains not his anger forever, and because He delights in demonstrating lovingkindness. . . . Thus the prophecy of judgment and promise, of travail and birth, of gloom and hope, ends with the glow of faith and happy hope (Hailey, 220–21).

BIBLIOGRAPHY

Clarke, Adam. *A Commentary and Critical Notes.* "Micah." Vol. 4. New York: Abingdon-Cokesbury, n.d.

Earle, Ralph. *Meet the Minor Prophets.* Kansas City: Beacon Hill, 1955.

Farrar, F. W. *The Minor Prophets.* New York: Revell, n.d.

Gray, James Comper and George M. D. Adams. *The Biblical Encyclopedia.* Vol. 3. New York: George H. Doran, 1903.

Hailey, Homer. *A Commentary on the Minor Prophets.* Grand Rapids: Baker, 1972.

Henry, Matthew. *Commentary on the Whole Bible.* Vol. 4. Old Tappan, N.J.: Revell, n.d.

Keil, C. F. and F. Delitzsch. *Commentary on the Old Testament in Ten Volumes.* "Micah." Vol. 10. Grand Rapids: Eerdmans, 1978.

Knopf, Carl Sumner. *Ask the Prophets.* Nashville: Parthenon, 1938.

Purkiser, W. T. *Know Your Old Testament.* Kansas City: Beacon Hill, 1954.

Ries, Claude A. "Micah." WBC. Vol. 3. Grand Rapids, Eerdmans, 1969.

Robinson, George L. *The Twelve Minor Prophets.* "Micah, The Prophet of the Poor." Grand Rapids: Baker, 1979.

Smith, George Adam. *The Book of the Twelve Prophets.* Vol. 1 of two vols. New York: Harper, 1928.

Wesley, John. *Explanatory Notes Upon the Old Testament.* Vol. 3. Bristol: William Pine, 1765. Reprinted by Schmul Publishers, Salem, Ohio, 1975.

NAHUM

G. Herbert Livingston

INTRODUCTION

I. TITLE, CONTENT, AND CANONICAL PLACEMENT

The title is the same as the name of the prophet, and the vision is of a court scene in which the Lord calls Assyria to the bar of justice. The book has always had a secure place among the Minor Prophets of the canon.

II. HISTORICAL SETTING, AUTHORSHIP, AND DATE

The armies of Assyria swept into Palestine in 734 B.C., bringing both the northern kingdom of Israel and the kingdom of Judah under their control. Israel was wiped out in 722 or 721 B.C. Judah retained its identity but not its independence. The book claims to contain **the vision of Nahum,** and there has been little reason to deny him its authorship.

The date of Nahum's prophecy and its authorship would be just before the fall of Nineveh in 612 B.C.

III. STRUCTURE AND THEOLOGICAL THEMES

Apart from the prosaic superscription (1:1), the text of Nahum is in a poetic form equal to any produced by other poets in the OT.

The overall structure is a judicial trial, and the overall components of the book correspond to the various legal aspects of the trial.

The central theme of the book, God's sovereign power and his righteous wrath tempered by goodness to his own people, dominates the prophet's vision from beginning to end.

The prophet was overwhelmed by the awesomeness of the divine presence, and mighty Nineveh reeled like a drunk man toward oblivion.

The holy, almighty God had decided to bring justice upon an utterly brutal empire, and the accused could not escape the death sentence that the Judge pronounced against it. God's wrath toward sin was balanced by his goodness to his own people.

In concert with the other Hebrew prophets, Nahum proclaimed without apology that God exercises power as Judge and Savior in the context of human affairs. The evidence of God's activity is not limited to his spoken word. His acted word was involved in the rise and fall of the

Assyrian Empire. The destruction of its opulent capital was predicted, and it happened.

Theologically, the heinous nature of national and international sins was taken seriously. A nation cannot endure if it lacks a spiritual and eternal foundation, and neither Nineveh nor the empire had such a foundation. The empire was an immoral monster that trampled and devoured whomever it could.

IV. OUTLINE

Major Themes: At the Proper Time God Executes Justice
I. God Convenes the Court of Justice (1:1–15)
II. Prepare for Punishment (2:1–13)
III. Woe to the City of Blood (3:1–19)

COMMENTARY

I. GOD CONVENES THE COURT OF JUSTICE (1:1–15)

The terms **"oracle"** and **"vision"** designate a revelation from God in the form of a divine lawsuit against Nineveh.

The Judge's holiness and righteousness had had enough of Nineveh's brutality; he had made a decision to prosecute the city. The vigor of the Lord's action is emphasized by a cluster of words: **jealous, vengeance, wrath, anger, power, indignation,** and **fierce anger.** The Lord's majestic presence is highlighted by severe natural events.

Nahum is careful to point out that God does not base his act of judgment on whim or vindictiveness but on the fact that sin is evil and vicious, fully deserving punishment.

Nineveh is accused of having a ruler who plans to attack the Lord and his people. In the trial of the criminal, the Lord first comforts Judah, whom he had already brought to justice and had punished, and he promises that their oppression will end. Then the Lord declares that Nineveh will be left without descendants and that her man-made deities will be destroyed.

When God convenes his court, he matches judgment of the sinner with redemption for his faithful followers. The wounds of the afflicted will be healed, and sorrow will be turned into joy, provided they fulfill their vows made before the Lord.

II. PREPARE FOR PUNISHMENT (2:1–13)

The court scene has an international scope. The action portrayed alternates between the beginnings of Nineveh's downfall and the repeated pronouncements of God's sentence of destruction.

There is a tinge of mockery, of taunting, in God's commands to Nineveh. The city, surrounded by a mighty fortress and protected by a horde of skilled soldiers, must prepare a defense against an invading army. Nineveh was in mortal danger. However, weak and brutalized Jacob receives God's promise of complete restoration to the former splendor of a united Israel under David and Solomon.

The appearance of the attacking army was awe inspiring. Nahum compares the rushing chariots with **torches** and **lightning.**

Within the city, the **picked troops** move about in disarray. The **river gates** seem to refer to dams on the Khoser River, either already built or quickly constructed by the invaders.

A divine decree is strongly implied in 2:3. The punishment of Nineveh was the destruction of its palaces and temples. The **slave girls,** who were forced to serve as sacred prostitutes in the temples, are depicted as overcome by fear and grief. Many survivors of the horrible slaughter of people were taken into captivity.

Efforts of leaders to organize the city for defense were hopeless. Nineveh had been the gathering place for hoards of precious metals and stones. These were removed by the victorious armies to their homeland. For every Ninevite, the fall of their city was a nightmare of panic and horror.

After the fall of Nineveh, travelers passing by would be struck with astonishment and wonder. Comparing the city in its power to a **lions' den,** Nahum depicts its inhabitants as hungry, ferocious animals tearing apart their **prey.** The Lord, too, expresses wonder that this den had been destroyed.

In 2:12 Nahum presents the Judge as pronouncing the sentence of annihilation upon the city, which was to happen at a future date. The words **lions** and **prey** tie this declaration to the previous passage.

III. WOE TO THE CITY OF BLOOD (3:1–19)

The **woe** focuses on the sordid character of Nineveh. The words **blood,** **lies, plunder,** and **victims** summarize the wickedness of the inhabitants of Nineveh. Nineveh fully deserved her punishment.

Skillfully Nahum used poetic structure to enhance the violence of the assault. The siege took about two and a half months, but it is condensed here as a moment of time.

The city had become so depraved that it is named a **harlot** filled with **wanton lust** and skilled in the tactics of seduction, **sorceries, prostitution,** and **witchcraft.**

God cries out, **"I am against you,"** and promises that he will expose her nakedness and display her as **a spectacle** to the world. Horrified travelers will marvel at the city's extensive ruins.

In 663 B.C. Assyrian armies leveled Thebes, the capital of Egypt. Other nations would do the same to Nineveh.

The Ninevites may have regarded their plight as a tragedy, and their conquerors may have regarded it as evidence of superior military power. By divine revelation, Nahum understood the fall of Nineveh as an act of God, the Judge of nations.

The ultimate reason for Nineveh's demise was the verdict of the divine Judge. However frantically the defenders labored to save the city, all was to no avail, for the Judge had declared that **fire** and **sword** would wipe them out and that the city's enemies would be **like grasshoppers** and **locusts** in number.

The simile of swarms of locusts is extended to Nineveh's **guards** and **officials** who had exploited their own people without mercy.

The ravaging of the city comes to an end, and the Lord unveils the underlying anguish that always accompanies his acts of judgment.

Nahum mourns with the vanquished who have become wandering refugees, for the blow of punishment had left an incurable **wound.** Nineveh was never to rise again.

Wherever the **news** of the fall of Nineveh is heard, those who listen will rejoice. To them, justice has at last been executed. The multitude of Nineveh's victims had suffered untold agonies, but now the international monster is laid low.

BIBLIOGRAPHY

Achtemeier, Elizabeth. "The Book of Nahum." *Interpretation: A Bible Commentary for Teaching and Preaching*. Atlanta: John Knox, 1986.

Clarke, Adam. "The Book of Nahum." *A Commentary and Critical Notes*. New York: Abingdon, n.d.

Dunning, H. Ray. "The Book of Nahum." BBC. Kansas City: Beacon Hill, 1966.

Laetsch, Theo. "Nahum." *Bible Commentary: The Minor Prophets*. St. Louis: Concordia, 1956.

Reis, Claude. "The Book of Nahum." WBC. Grand Rapids: Eerdmans, 1969.

Smith, Ralph L. "Nahum." WdBC. Waco: Word, 1984.

HABAKKUK

Bill T. Arnold

INTRODUCTION

I. AUTHORSHIP, DATE, AND HISTORICAL BACKGROUND

Nothing is known of Habakkuk the man beyond that which can be gleaned from this little book. Even his name is enigmatic. It may be a Hebrew word meaning "embrace," but it has been traced also to an Akkadian root meaning a garden plant (see standard critical commentaries). It is evident from his book that he was a passionate, caring individual who used his considerable theological acumen to reason his way, under divine direction, to conclusions that continue to influence the church. This book traces his theological journey through social concern and personal plan to redemptive faith.

The controversy over the date of Habakkuk centers on the interpretation of one word in 1:6: "Chaldeans" ("Babylonians" in NIV). Who were these "ruthless and impetuous people" whom God raised up to punish Judah? Early in this century, Duhm, Torrey, and others (see standard critical OT introductions) used complex textual emendations in suggesting this was a reference to Alexander's conquests in Asia between 334 and 331 B.C. They dated the prophecy in the late fourth century B.C. But the lack of textual support for this interpretation, enhanced by the discovery of a text of Habakkuk in 1947 among the Dead Sea Scrolls (1QpHab), supports the traditional view that "Chaldeans" referred to the Neo-Babylonian Empire that dominated Mesopotamia between the fall of Nineveh (612 B.C.) and the rise of the Persians (539 B.C.). Thus the NIV's interpretative "Babylonians" in 1:6 is justified, and the book may be dated to the late seventh and early sixth centuries B.C. Habakkuk's ministry should most likely be dated between Josiah's death (609 B.C.) and the deportation of Jerusalem's nobility to Babylon in 597 B.C.

This period of Judah's history began with great hope and confidence in the future. Josiah's revival of Deuteronomic theology and covenant faithfulness had begun in earnest in 621 B.C. (2Ki 22–23). These domestic events were fueled in part by the decline of Assyria, for centuries the single most dominant world empire.

But this age of hope ended as suddenly as it began. After the fall of

Nineveh, Josiah became entangled in the international machinations and was killed by Pharaoh Neco in 609 B.C. Neco's hand-picked replacement, Jehoiakim, was a weak leader who allowed Josiah's reforms to lapse. Judah soon fell back into pagan practices and immorality that resulted in the injustice and lawlessness so objectionable to Habakkuk (1:2–4). Egypt and Media were significant world powers, but it was the Chaldean hegemony at Babylon that would soon dominate the scene and play a fatal role in Judah's history.

II. STRUCTURE AND CONTENT

Habakkuk is an intensely personal prophet who reverses the traditional role of prophecy. Rather than speaking God's word to the people, he dialogues with God on their behalf. The first two chapters are comprised of Habakkuk's complaints of human and divine injustice, followed by God's response (a literary relationship known as "interrogation").

In his first complaint (1:2–4), Habakkuk describes the lawless and corrupt Judahite society. Initially Habakkuk's concerns were internal. There is no mention of foreign invaders, only of social injustice and violence among God's people. Yahweh's reaction was anything but reassuring for Habakkuk (vv.5–11). He assures his prophet that he is at work to arouse a swift and bitter nation to come and bring "justice" on Judah. Babylonia's armies (v.9) will be used by God to chastize and discipline his children.

Habakkuk objects that justice achieved in this manner is no justice at all (1:12–2:1). How can God use a corrupt and self-serving nation (especially the Babylonians!) to reprove his nation Judah? The prophet complains that God is "too pure to look on evil" and that he must not allow the wicked to "swallow up those more righteous than themselves" (1:13). Yahweh's response assures Habakkuk that the Babylonians will certainly receive appropriate punishment for their crimes (2:2–20).

Meanwhile, the righteous individual is encouraged to live by his faith (or "faithfulness"; see below). The taunting woe oracles of 2:6–20 graphically describe the destruction of the Babylonians and confirm that divine justice will ultimately reach all nations, though God's people must learn to await its consummation faithfully.

Even Habakkuk's psalm in ch. 3 may be seen as a dialogue between prophet and God. In light of all that Habakkuk has learned about God and justice and faith, he becomes impatient and longs more than anything else to see God's work in history. He appeals to Yahweh to "renew" his saving acts of history in Habakkuk's own day (v.2). The theophany in vv.3–15 describes Yahweh's awe-inspiring appearance at Sinai and the Exodus, and it results in the prophet's contentment to endure any hardship as long as he can rejoice in the Lord (vv.16–19).

Although an earlier generation of scholars questioned Habakkuk's authorship of ch. 3, a consensus has developed among more recent commentators that the book is a unity and that the same individual composed all three chapters (*contra* Hiebert, 81–82, 129–36).

III. THEOLOGICAL SIGNIFICANCE

Habakkuk was incensed at the inhumanity of the people of Judah and was intensely concerned over the injustice in the kingdom. The acute discrepancies between God's promises and the undeniable realities of injustice forced the prophet into a theological impasse. How could God allow these circumstances to stand? Ultimately Habakkuk realized that God would not allow injustice to persist. Regardless of their oppressive circumstances, the true people of God will live in faithfulness to his covenant, awaiting his redemptive work in history. This was Habakkuk's message, and the writers of the NT saw in it the central truth of the Gospel in germinal form. Habakkuk's principle of the faithful life became the foundational premise of Paul's doctrine of salvation by faith, proclaimed to the Asian church (Gal 3:11) and the European church (Ro 1:17). The author of Hebrews also made this doctrine clear for the Jewish church (10:36–37).

Classical Wesleyanism was deeply disturbed by the injustice and poverty so prevalent in eighteenth-century England and was committed to social action. Indeed, some scholars have argued that the Wesleyan Revival's social ethic and its ministry to the victims of England's rapid industrialization saved the nation from political revolution. Unfortunately, our tradition has not always retained this emphasis.

Some liberation theologians have used Habakkuk to support violent revolution as the divinely ordained answer to social injustice. But God did not command Habakkuk to gather faithful Judahites for the purpose of raising up arms against the wicked and corrupt society. Instead, in his divine prerogative, God employed a more wicked and corrupt nation as an instrument of his wrath. After the Babylonians served his purpose, they too were punished. The more appropriate biblical paradigm for a Christian response to injustice is Jesus' ministry in Palestine during the oppressive Roman rule (Jn 8:32).

IV. OUTLINE

    I. The Dialogue
    (1:1–2:20)
    A. Habakkuk's Complaint: Human Injustice and Divine Inactivity (1:1–4)
    B. Yahweh's Response: Divine Justice Through the Babylonians (1:5–11)
    C. Habakkuk's Second Complaint: The Inequity of Divine Justice (1:12–2:1)
    D. Yahweh's Response: The Certainty of Babylon's Destruction (2:2–20)

II. The Prayer (3:1–19)
    A. An Appeal for Yahweh to Act (3:1–2)
    B. Activity of the Divine Warrior in History (3:3–15)
    C. Habakkuk's Final Response of Faith (3:16–19)

COMMENTARY

I. THE DIALOGUE (HAB 1:1–2:20)

A. Habakkuk's Complaint: Human Injustice and Divine Inactivity (1:1–4)

The prophet is living in a society filled with violence and injustice, and he feels the impact of that injustice as if he were its victim. It is characteristic of godly people to grieve over that which pains God. The prophet feels personally the pain of the violence and injustice because he knows it is unacceptable to God (v.3a). Moreover, he is confused by Yahweh's silence. How long must he wait to receive an answer? Yet God is quiet.

This opening paragraph deals with many of the great themes of OT theology. One of the results of social corruption is the paralyzing of **the law** (*tôrâ*), the teaching of which was the special responsibility of the priests. It had been recently reinforced by Josiah and served as an indicator of the nation's covenant faithfulness (2Ki 23:24). The prophets task was to apply *tôrâ* to the contemporary situation. But if corrupt priests turned the law into a means of increasing personal wealth (Mic 3:11), the prophetic task was thwarted. And once divine instruction was ignored, "justice" was sure to cease. "Righteousness" (*ṣeḏeq*) is the principle of right action, whereas **justice** (*mišpāṭ*) is the embodiment of that principle.

B. Yahweh's Response: Divine Justice Through the Babylonians (1:5–11)

God lifts Habakkuk's attention beyond the domestic, internal problems to the international scene. On the horizon, Habakkuk sees the Babylonian army—swift, merciless, and unstoppable. God implies that this new destructive force is his answer to Judah's sin. The undeniable message was that God had raised this machine of destruction **to seize dwelling places not their own** (v.6).

C. Habakkuk's Second Complaint: The Inequity of Divine Justice (1:12–2:1)

Yahweh's response was unsatisfying and unacceptable to Habakkuk. He objects by appealing first to Yahweh's character. He is the Lord God, the Holy One, the Rock who is eternal and who ordains his instruments for justice (v.12). Yet Habakkuk objects that punishing Judah along with the Babylonians is a greater evil than the first, a worse injustice than before. After confidently stating his case, the prophet positions himself to receive the Lord's answer (2:1).

D. Yahweh's Response: The Certainty of Babylon's Destruction (2:2–20)

God's answer begins with a "vision" (*ḥāzôn*, NIV's **revelation** [v.3]), which stresses the importance, imminence, and certainty of the events about to be described. Then Yahweh agrees with Habakkuk that the Babylonians are a most wicked nation, consumed with pride and avarice (vv.4–5). By contrast, God mentions the righteous individual (*ṣaddîq*) who will live faithfully (lit. "by his faithfulness"). Hebrew has no abstract word for **faith,** and the meaning here is "the temper which faith produces of endurance, steadfastness, integrity" (G. A. Smith, 142). The righteous person will remain loyal in his commitments to God regardless of the circumstances of his experience. This concept of steadfast loyalty influenced NT authors (see introduction).

The next unit (2:6–20) is a series of oracles each introduced by the word **woe** (vv.6, 9, 12, 15, 19). This cry of grief and sorrow introduces a standard prophetic speech pattern that accuses the nation of sin and announces judgment. In most cases this speech pattern is used against Israel (Isa 5:8, 11, 18, et al.), but here it is spoken against the foreign conqueror (Westermann, 189–94). Habakkuk's speeches of doom are intended as encouragement and comfort for Judah, because they emphasize the judgment of God's enemies. In this context the woe oracles take on a more profound significance. They state unequivocally the judgment of Babylon that was only alluded to in vv.4–5. Thus they establish the hope that justice will ultimately be accomplished, though the people of God must faithfully endure the present injustice.

V. 6 ties the five woe oracles to the preceding paragraph by explaining that the very nations who fell victim to Babylon (v.5c) will sing of her destruction. They will **taunt** (lit. "raise a proverb") and **ridicule** Babylon, words associated with mockery. The word translated **scorn** in NIV is really "enigmatic saying" and may betray a didactic

purpose for v.6a; the Babylonians became an object lesson ("proverb") by means of perplexing and allusive speech (Armerding, 516).

Each oracle that follows is marked by a juxtaposing of the sin with its appropriate and inevitable judgment. Each punishment is made to fit the crime. In vv.6b–8, the exploited victims rise up and turn the tables on the Babylonians, making them the victims. The irony is sharpened by the use of **"plunder"** in v.8; the plunderers become the plundered. Greed is also the crime described in vv.9–11, where the rapacious Babylonians use their ill-gotten gains to build a **house** (i.e., royal dynasty) and to make it secure as a high nest. But, as before, the punishment is fitted to the crime: shame for self-motivated pride.

The third woe oracle (vv.12–14) mocks Babylon for strengthening her position by violence because her futile attempt actually weakens her position before God. The **LORD Almighty** (lit. "Lord of Armies") is more impressed with knowledge of his glory than with the military domination of one's neighbors. The next judgment speech (vv.15–17) moves to a new crime. The Babylonians have humiliated their victims by inducing drunkenness and exploiting their vulnerability, all in the interest of self-**glory** (*kābôd*, v.16). But **"Now,"** the prophet warns, **"it is your turn!"** (v.16). That which the Babylonians have sown is what they shall reap. The **cup** of the Lord (figure of judgment) is coming, and the Babylonians shall drink and be exposed. **Lebanon** (v.17) may be a symbol of the Holy Land but is probably a reference to the violent destruction of Syria-Palestine at the hands of Nebuchadnezzar when he claimed the land of Lebanon (Keil, 88–90).

The final oracle (vv.18–19) changes the pattern of the previous four. It begins, not with a woe expression, but with a statement of the futility of idol worship. Human effort and resources are wasted on such impotent and worthless images. The futility of this idolatry is exposed ironically in the phrase **idols that cannot speak,** which is babbling nonsense phonetically (*'elîlîm 'illemîm,* Armerding, 519). The irony climaxes in the picture of the Babylonian idolater commanding his breathless idol to become lively and active. But abruptly our attention is directed to Yahweh's incomparable presence (v.20). While the idolater vainly appeals to his deity to come to life, all the earth is silent before God.

II. THE PRAYER (3:1–19)

The structure of this chapter is arranged chiastically (i.e., according to a concentric movement): introduction, v.1 (A); prayer, v.2. (B); theophany, vv.3–15 (C); response, vv.16–19 (B¹); epilogue, v.19 (A¹). This structure is denoted by the repetition of certain key words or phrases in v.2 (B) and vv.16–19 (B¹). Examples are *šāma'tî* (**"I have heard"** in vv.2, 16), and *rōgez* (**wrath** in v.2 and **pounded** and **trembled** in v.16). The whole prayer is framed by musical notations in v.1 and v.19c (Armerding, 521).

Many scholars have challenged the ascription of the prayer to Habakkuk (v.1, cf. Hiebert, 136–43). But as stated in the introduction, today a general consensus exists among scholars of multifarious traditions that the same individual composed all three chapters. This case has been made eloquently on the basis of philology (Albright, 9). But even structurally, ch. 3 is not unlike chs. 1 and 2 (see introduction). And theologically, this prayer is an ideal closure for Habakkuk's quest to understand the problem of evil. His prayer reflects his acceptance of God's answers

to his personal complaints. His vow to exult in Yahweh in the midst of catastrophe (vv.17–19) is a fitting example of the principle of faith introduced in 2:4.

A. An Appeal for Yahweh to Act (3:1–2)

That ch. 3 constitutes a new unit is denoted by the introductory comment that designates Habakkuk as a prophet (*nābî*), as in 1:1. Habakkuk then acknowledges that God's mighty acts of deliverance in the past are awe inspiring. He longs for God to reveal himself afresh in his contemporary setting.

B. Activity of the Divine Warrior in History (3:3–15)

The archaic elements of this psalm have long been recognized. Recently this psalm has been dated to the premonarchic Israelite league of the tenth or eleventh centuries B.C. (Hiebert, 120–24). It may also be compared to a mythic scheme paralleled in Canaanite and Mesopotamian literature in which a divine warrior emanates from a holy mountain to defeat the chaotic powers of the universe. In this tradition, the psalm becomes a song of victory in which the Israelite "Divine Warrior" fights on behalf of his people against her enemies. But unlike the parallels among Israel's neighbors, this account has deep historical moorings. The theophany here described appears in two scenes: the events of Sinai (vv.3–7) and those of the Exodus and conquests (vv.8–15).

The geographical references in vv.3–7 are located to the south and southeast of Israel (see critical commentaries). They are the same features used in the Songs of Deborah (Jdg 5) and Moses (Dt 32–33) to emphasize Yahweh's movement from the Sinai Peninsula northward through the land of Edom to arrive at Israel (Szeles, 46–47). These are his eternal **ways** (v.6), the route used by Yahweh to redeem his people from Egypt and set them free. Before his **glory** (*hôḍ*, v.3) every feature of the universe was powerless, and the region was left desolate in his wake (vv.6–7).

The geographical notations in vv.3, 7 (known as "inclusios") serve to frame the verses between them as a distinct unit. Certain other stylistic features designate vv.8–15 as a separate unit. As in vv.3–7, the emphasis here is on Yahweh's mighty saving acts in the past. The repetition of vocabulary denoting water and military conquest reflect God's deliverance at the Red Sea and during the conquest. The references to **horses** and **chariots** (v.8) confirm that the picture described in Ex 14:2–15:22 (and Dt 11:4) is in view.

C. Habakkuk's Final Response of Faith (3:16–19)

The language and style of the conclusion return to that of vv.1–2. Certain key words and phrases are also repeated from v.2 so that these verses serve as a frame enclosing the ancient theophany of vv.3–15.

The recitation of God's mighty acts has filled Habakkuk's heart with awe (v.16). After reviewing Yahweh's majestic works of the past, the prophet realizes that even God's judgments are merciful. So he calmly prepares himself for the coming disaster. The graphic tragedy described in v.17 is equivalent to massive and total economic ruin in Judah, the loss of all agricultural produce. But in the midst of desperate circumstances, Habakkuk finds joy and strength in God (vv.18–19). He is mature enough to allow adversity to strengthen his trust and dependence on Yahweh. "Not in spite of misfortune, but because of it, should we exult in 'the god of our salvation'" (G. A. Smith, 159). When Habakkuk's worst fears become a reality, he himself becomes an illustration of the principle of faith mentioned in 2:4b. Thus the prophecy that began with questions and complaints ends in commitment and praise.

BIBLIOGRAPHY

Albright, William F. "The Psalm of Habakkuk," *Studies in Old Testament Prophecy*. Edited by H. H. Rowley. Edinburgh: T. & T. Clark, 1957.

Armerding, Carl E. "Habakkuk," EBC. Vol. 7. Edited by F. E. Gaebelein. Grand Rapids: Zondervan, 1985.

Hiebert, Theodore. *God of My Victory: The Ancient Hymn in Habakkuk 3*. Harvard Semitic Monographs 38. Atlanta: Scholars Press, 1986.

Keil, C. F.; and F. Delitzsch. *Biblical Commentary on the Old Testament*. Vol. 10. Grand Rapids: Eerdmans, 1978.

Smith, George Adam. *The Book of the Twelve Prophets, Commonly Called the Minor*. Vol. 2. New York: Doubleday, 1929.

Smith, J. M. P.; W. J. Ward; and J. A. Bewer. *A Critical and Exegetical Commentary on Micah, Zephaniah, Nahum, Habakkuk, Obadiah and Joel*. ICC. New York: Scribner, 1911.

Szeles, Maria Eszenyei. *Habakkuk and Zephaniah: Wrath and Mercy*. ITC. Grand Rapids: Eerdmans, 1987.

Westermann, Claus. *Basic Forms of Prophetic Speech*. Translated by H. C. White. Philadelphia: Westminster, 1967.

ZEPHANIAH
Robert Branson

INTRODUCTION

The book of Zephaniah appears ninth among the minor prophets, indicating that the synagogue dated the book to the period before the destruction of Jerusalem (586 B.C.). The superscription states that Zephaniah spoke during the reign of Josiah (1:1). There is no serious objection to dating Zephaniah's ministry to that time; the problem comes in determining exactly when during his reign the prophet worked.

I. TIME OF ZEPHANIAH'S MINISTRY

Since Assyria and Nineveh are mentioned in 2:13, Zephaniah's ministry must have begun before 612 B.C. The condemnation of idolatrous religious customs practiced by the royal household (1:4–9) indicates that either Josiah was not on the throne or that he was still too young to exert any influence. Thus Zephaniah's ministry probably began during Josiah's early reign and before he began the reforms. If the reference in 3:6 alludes to the destruction of Nineveh (612 B.C.), this would indicate that 3:1–17 comes from the end of Josiah's reign and that Zephaniah's career would have spanned the entire reign of Josiah.

II. DATE OF THE BOOK

The composition of the book itself was completed some time after the ministry of Zephaniah. Who first reduced Zephaniah's preaching to writing is only a guess. Isaiah had his disciples and Jeremiah his secretary, Baruch. Was there a similar companion for Zephaniah, or did the prophet himself record his sermons? Whichever the case, the book shows little evidence of later editing. Older theories that saw multiple additions being made have been generally discredited. This is particularly true with regard to the idea that any prophecy of hope must be postexilic. The book is a well-structured unit that was shaped by its original author soon after the messages were delivered. Probably only the Deuteronomic superscription (1:1) and 3:18–20, which reflects a postexilic setting, represent the work of later hands.

III. THE PROPHET ZEPHANIAH

Nothing is known about the prophet except what the book tells us. The superscription and the material of the book places him in the early years of the reign of Josiah. His genealogy is traced back to a certain Hezekiah (1:1). Four generations earlier would be about the time of the reign of King Hezekiah (715–686 B.C.). Also, the sermons reflect both a knowledge of the palace and a lack of interest in the poor. For these reasons it may be suggested that Zephaniah was the descendant of King Hezekiah.

IV. STYLE OF WRITING

The book, with the exception of the superscription (1:1), is written entirely in poetry. The lines of the poems are not uniform in length, but do not exhibit a wide range of variation. While the poems do cover a range of topics, there are few definitive breaks in the development of its thought. Rather, the book presents a unified structure with overlapping themes. An idea may be introduced in one section and expanded or returned to in another. This makes outlining the content of the book somewhat arbitrary.

V. OUTLINE

I. Superscription (1:1)
II. Judgment Against Judah and Jerusalem (1:2–18)
III. Judgment Against the Nations (2:1–3:8)
IV. The Blessing of Yahweh's Presence (3:9–20)

VI. MAJOR THEMES

The leading concept of the book of Zephaniah is the coming of the Day of Yahweh. This image, which may have risen out of the theology of the tribal league, emphasized the ominous nature of the manifestation of Yahweh. He comes to fight for and deliver his people Israel. Popular thought viewed the day as one when God would defeat Israel's enemies and establish her as the supreme military power (Am 5:18). The prophets widened this expectation to include the visitation of Yahweh's wrath on all the sinful, including the chosen people themselves. The nation by which God would bring judgment is not mentioned. The older theory, based on a statement of the Greek historian Herodotus, that Zephaniah saw the invasion of the Scythians as the judgment of God, has now been generally rejected. Like Amos and Hosea, Zephaniah leaves undefined the exact instrument of Yahweh's wrath.

Zephaniah's catalogue of the sins of humanity is not extensive. Judah is indicted for idolatry (1:4–9), sinful pride (1:12; 3:2), and oppression through perversion of the law (3:3–5). The nations are guilty of hubris or pride (2:8, 15), scornful of the rest of humanity. Yahweh desires humility in righteousness and sets himself as the defender of those who humble themselves before him (2:3; 3:12).

The major theological theme that unites the book is that of the presence of Yahweh. That presence may be manifested either in judgment or salvation, depending on the spiritual condition of the people and the purpose of God. The judgment visited upon Judah and Jerusalem conforms to the conditions of the Mosaic covenant, which Yahweh had committed himself to observe (Dt 28:30, 39). The curses of the covenant, however, are remedial (Dt 30:1–6). God's purpose is to restore the people to righteousness in order to dwell in their midst (3:15, 17). In Zephaniah the covenant has not yet been democratized so that those nations that lie outside the covenant experience only the judgment of Yahweh with no hope of restoration (2:5, 9, 12, 13).

COMMENTARY

I. SUPERSCRIPTION (1:1)

II. JUDGMENT AGAINST JUDAH AND JERUSALEM (1:2–18)

The book of Zephaniah begins with a judgment oracle threatening universal destruction of all the earth's inhabitants (vv.2–3). The oracle draws upon the imagery of the flood story, particularly when it employs the phrase **"from the face of the earth"** (see Ge 6:7; 7:4; 8:21). The destruction is, however, more inclusive than the Flood, involving even the fish.

Judgment begins with the people of God, Judah and Jerusalem. The covenant had become not a shield to protect them from the wrath of God, but the basis for indicting them. The curses of the covenant would come upon them.

Three sins are specified in vv.4–6, the first of which is idolatry. During the rule of Manasseh (687–642 B.C.) the indigenous Canaanite cults of Baal worship received royal patronage, the worship of Asherah was represented in the temple, and foreign cults were encouraged. The king became so spiritually bankrupt that he practiced child

sacrifice, participated in sorcery and divination, and inquired of mediums and spiritualists (2Ki 21:6). The Assyrian cult, with its worship of the stars as representatives of deities, was also officially incorporated into the temple worship. It evidently found popular support as the people would go out at night on the flat roofs of their houses to enjoy the cooling evening breezes and participate in a family-altar style of worshiping the stars.

The second sin of the Judeans was religious syncretism. The polytheistic world saw no problem with worship of other gods, Yahweh being accepted as just one of the many. The Judeans, while taking oaths in the name of Yahweh, also took oaths in the name of Molech, a god of the Ammonites (1Ki 11:5). But Yahwistic faith had always been an uncompromising religion, unwilling to share a worshiper's loyalty with any other deity. Worship of Yahweh might be all right with Molech, but Yahweh would not tolerate worship of Molech or any other god.

Finally, some of the Judeans rejected the religion of Yahweh altogether. The words *seek* and *inquire* are technical terms that refer to the practice of securing directions from Yahweh. Zephaniah indicts the people for rejecting altogether the worship of Yahweh. The progression of the sins of Judah seems to be first the toleration or acceptance or the worship of other gods, followed by the incorporation of their practices within the worship of Yahweh, and finally the rejection of the worship of Yahweh. The claim to be the people of Yahweh brings with it the obligation of complete commitment to the exclusive worship of and faithful obedience to this one God.

V.7 opens with a command to be silent, for the Day of Yahweh has drawn near. The concept of the Day of Yahweh arose out of the tribal league theology when "holy wars" were conducted under the leadership of the Divine Warrior who fought for Israel against her foes. Israel came to regard the Day of Yahweh as a time of victory over her enemies. Zephaniah, however, like Amos before him (Am 5:18), broadened the concept into a time of judgment upon all of Yahweh's enemies, even his chosen but disobedient people.

The Day of Yahweh begins with the sacrifice of those whom he has called and consecrated. This idea has cultural parallels. The Canaanite goddess Anath slaughtered the guests she had invited to a feast. Jehu also invited worshipers of Baal to a sacrifice that became a massacre (2Ki 10:18–25).

The first group to experience Yahweh's punishment or visitation was to be the princes or king's sons. The latter designation includes all the royal household, not just the direct descendants of the king. In v.9 judgment falls on those who leap upon the threshold in an act of violence and then give part of their booty to their gods (lit. "their lords"). The worship of other gods had

brought a different moral code for the leaders. Polytheism, with its many gods, does not offer a consistent moral basis of action since it does not have a single source of authority. Thus, when the people of God embraced other deities, they also incorporated other standards of conduct. Yahweh indicts them for two breeches of the covenant, idolatry and immorality.

Judgment begins with the city of God, Jerusalem (vv.10–13). The various locations named by Zephaniah— the Fish Gate, New Quarter, the hills, and the market district—were to the north side of the city, the section most vulnerable to attack. **"Merchants"** translates the phrase "all the people of Canaan." "Canaanite" refers to those who were engaged in trading. Thus the last part of v.11 is directed against the merchant class of the city.

God commanded Jeremiah, Zephaniah's contemporary, to search the city for a single honest person (Jer 5:1). In v.12 Yahweh himself will search the city for the religiously complacent. They are compared to juice, which if not separated at the appropriate time from the pulp of the grape, becomes too thick to be made into good wine. These rich and powerful leaders of society ought to have been leaders in righteousness, trusting in Yahweh to guide the nation. Instead, they were skeptical that the God who had given them the land would not even notice whether they survived or perished. Their trust lay in weapons and political negotiations. God was irrelevant. Yahweh's sentence was that the Conquest would be reversed. The houses and vineyards Yahweh had given them (Jos 24:13) would now be taken away.

No biblical description of judgment surpasses that of vv.14–18 for intensity of feeling of horror. The Divine Warrior shouts as the Day of Yahweh hastens to come. He will fight against them as he had fought for them in the Conquest. Then the former inhabitants of the land were totally destroyed. Now the present inhabitants will experience that same sentence of judgment. No hope for deliverance is expressed. This Warrior cannot be bribed with silver and gold. His people have sinned, and they will be annihilated.

The poet binds up this entire chapter, making it a unit when in the last half of v.18 he returns to the theme of 1:2–3, the whole world will experience this divine fury. The world will return to the primeval chaos when Yahweh brings judgment, but the first to experience his wrath will be his own chosen people who have rejected him.

III. JUDGMENT AGAINST THE NATIONS (2:1–3:8)

With judgment about to fall upon the world, the prophet issues an invitation to Judah to repent (2:1–3). The time for calling upon God is **before the appointed time arrives,** not afterwards. The **humble,** identified as those **who do what he commands,** are urged to seek Yahweh, righteousness, and humility. Here is the essence of OT faith. Seeking Yahweh begins with the turning away from boasting of one's own accomplishments. The humble trust quietly in God's work of salvation. The seeking, however, is not only an inward journey, but must be demonstrated in righteous living among the people of God. Love of God is bound up with love of others.

Oracles of judgment (2:4–15) are hurled against four other nations: Philistia to the west, Moab and Ammon to the east, Cush or Ethiopia to the south, and Assyria to the north. The cursing of enemies in the religious ceremonies of the cult usually stood in contrast to the pronouncement of blessing on God's people. Zephaniah used the form to indicate the sweeping nature of the coming storm. All will experience it, not only Judah, but also her ancient foes.

The Philistines entered Canaan from the west around 1200 B.C., shortly after the Israelites had entered from the east. The two peoples struggled for control of the land, Philistia gaining the upper hand until the time of David. According to this oracle (2:4–7), the inhabitants will be totally destroyed, a fulfillment of the Conquest, in which all inhabitants of the land were to be put to death. **The remnant of the house of Judah** will possess the four remaining cities of the Philistines and use them for places to shelter their flocks.

The peoples of Moab and Ammon are lumped together in the second oracle (2:8–11), which indicts them for insulting and taunting the people of God. Israel and these two peoples who were the descendants of Lot through his daughters (Ge 19:30–38) had fought often through the centuries over the territory of Gilead. God would cause the judgment of Sodom and Gomorrah, from which their forefather escaped (Ge 19:23–29), to fall upon them. Moab and Ammon are indicted for the sin of pride (v.10), and their judgment is seen as the just retribution of their arrogance. However, v.11 limits the destruction to their gods.

Assyria also is indicated for the sin of pride (vv.13–15) as she declares that she alone exists with none (god? city?) like her (v.15b). Her safety or security is falsely placed in her own military prowess. This is a challenge to the sovereignty of Yahweh, and he sentences her populous cities to be reduced to habitations of wild animals.

The final sentence of doom for this book is a woe oracle that falls upon Jerusalem (3:1–8). In vv.1–4 the sins of the city are described. Specifically indicted are the royal officials (cf. 1:8), the prophets, and the priests. These three groups, which should provide moral and spiritual guidance for the community, have instead betrayed their trust. They are arrogant, not fearing God or respecting others. Their arrogance is expressed in oppression, treachery, and the distortion of their religion. Counterbalanced against them in v.5 is Yahweh's righteousness. He has continued to be faithful to them by daily demonstrating his care through the regular administration of the universe.

In 3:6–8 Yahweh himself addresses the city. He argues that his justice can be seen in his destruction of others. Their horrible fate was to serve as an object lesson for the people of God so that they might repent of their sins. Yet the lesson had been wasted on an unattentive pupil. She with the rest of the world will be reserved for final destruction.

IV. THE BLESSINGS OF YAHWEH'S PRESENCE (3:9–20)

Zephaniah closes with a joyful note of redemption. Jerusalem, the city of God, will be cleansed from the arrogant so that Yahweh himself might dwell among his people. They also will be cleansed so that their language and their deeds might reflect the moral nature of the God they serve. With Yahweh, the Mighty Warrior, dwelling among them, the people will not fear their enemies but will rejoice in the care he will provide.

There is no distinctive break between vv.8 and 9. They are linked by the concept of fire, which on the one hand consumes the world but on the other purifies God's people. The prophet, in vv.9 and 10, draws upon the imagery

of the Tower of Babel incident (Ge 11:1–9) to portray a once-scattered but soon to be united people whose lips (speech) have been purified. This reestablished community will be characterized by worship, the natural activity of a redeemed people.

The theme of purification continues in v.11 in that the proud will be removed from their midst. The holy habitation of God (**"holy hill"**) is in the midst of the meek and humble (v.12). He will not dwell with the arrogant but must first humble and purify the people of all that is contrary to his nature. Because he will purify them of their sin and dwell among his people Israel, they will be free from wrong, lies, and deceit (v.13) The ethical character of the people of God will reflect the nature of Yahweh himself. Thus these verses teach the normative paradigm of redemption: Yahweh removes sin and arrogance from the midst of his people and then comes to occupy that vacated throne of values, filling it with his holy presence and shaping their lives to conform to his own righteous nature.

In a brief hymn of salvation (vv.14–17), the people of God are summoned to rejoice in the presence of Yahweh. The recurring word *qirbek*, "your midst" (NIV "within you," v.12; "with you," vv.15, 17), contains the central theological idea of the passage, Yahweh dwells among his people. They may rejoice and not be afraid, for they will be protected from any harm. Yahweh will be their God, a warrior of salvation. His people will rest securely in his covenantal love (v.17).

The final verses of the book (vv.18–20) are spoken by Yahweh himself as he promises to reverse the fortunes of his people who must go through the destruction measured out to the nations in the Day of Yahweh. For them judgment becomes remedial, not final. Strong emphasis lies in the repeated **"I will."** All that they will gain—relief from burdens, salvation from oppression, return from exile, honor and praise—will be due to the direct action of Yahweh. Salvation belongs to him alone.

BIBLIOGRAPHY

Achtemeier, Elizabeth. *Nahum–Malachi*. Interpretation. Atlanta: John Knox, 1986.

Dunning, H. Ray. "Zephaniah." BBC. 10 vols. Kansas City: Beacon Hill, 1966. Vol. 5.

Fensham, F. C. "Zephaniah, Book of." IDB Supp. Vol. Edited by Keith Crim et al. Pp. 983–94. Nashville: Abingdon, 1976.

Smith, Ralph. *Micah–Malachi*. WdBC. Waco: Word, 1984.

HAGGAI
Robert Branson

INTRODUCTION

The book of Haggai, composed of five oracles given on specified days, records the work of one of the Bible's most successful prophets. The task given to him by God to motivate the people of postexilic Judah to rebuild the temple was accomplished. He alone of the prophets received the necessary political and popular support so that the object of his message was achieved in a short time.

I. THE MAN AND HIS TIME

The name Haggai is derived from a word that means "a festival." No genealogy accompanies his name. Twice in Ezra (5:1; 6:14) he is called "the prophet" and is associated with Zechariah in motivating the people to rebuild the temple.

Haggai began his ministry in Jerusalem on the first day of the sixth month of the second year of the reign of Darius, king of Persia. The first Persian ruler, Cyrus, had allowed an expedition of detainees to return to Judah to resettle the land and rebuild the temple (538 B.C.). Economic conditions were so deplorable that the task of rebuilding was halted and not resumed for a number of years. When Darius ascended the throne (522 B.C.), war broke out in many sections of the empire. After two years of strenuous campaigning, peace was restored. It was at this time that Haggai encouraged the people under the dual leadership of the governor, Zerubbabel, and the high priest, Joshua, to begin rebuilding.

II. THE BOOK AND ITS WRITING

The oracles of the book are dated with such precision that there is no debate as to the time of the ministry of Haggai. Each is dated to the second year of Darius, 520 B.C.

The book was prepared either by the prophet himself or one close to him no later than 500 B.C. and maybe as early as 515 B.C. as part of the liturgy for the dedication of the temple.

III. THE THEOLOGY OF THE BOOK

Haggai spoke at a time when the identity of the postexilic community was in jeopardy. The people were a part of a vast empire and could have followed the path of others who lost their own distinctiveness and drifted into the forgotten pages of history. God had something better for them. The way out of the crushing poverty that sapped their communal life was, not the neglect of their religious duties, but the performance of them. The people who had placed their own economic security and well-being ahead of their obligations to Yahweh had to reassess and change their values.

The diagnosis of and the cure for the community's economic problems as given by Haggai arise out of the Deuteronomic concept of covenantal obligations. If the community sought God in obedience and trust, then peace and prosperity would be given to it. The austere conditions faced by the community was a sign that the people had not obeyed God. His curse and not his blessings rested upon them.

The temple was the symbol of the presence of God dwelling among the people. Even though Israel knew that the whole of creation was not vast enough to hold him (2Ch 6:18), the temple remained the abode of Yahweh. Thus, as the people gave themselves to the work of rebuilding the temple, Haggai's message to them was "'I am with you,' declares the LORD" (1:13).

Previously the people existed as an unholy nation (2:10–19), suffering the economic curses of the covenant. Obedience, the concrete expression of faith and trust in God, brought a reversal of their situation. God came among them and made them a holy people again, a right candidate for the blessings of the covenant. Those blessings included not only the acceptance of the worship of the people and the promise of renewed economic prosperity, but also the reestablishment of legitimate political leadership in the person of Zerubbabel (2:20–23).

IV. OUTLINE

    I. God's Challenge to Rebuild the Temple (1:1–11)

    II. The Response to the Challenge (1:12–15)

    III. The Future Glory of the Temple (2:1–9)

    IV. Holiness and Proper Worship (2:10–19)

    V. God's Proper Leader (2:20–23)

COMMENTARY

I. GOD'S CHALLENGE TO REBUILD THE TEMPLE (1:1–11)

The superscription (1:1) locates the date of Haggai's ministry in the second year of the reign of Darius, whose civil authority is recognized throughout the book. Haggai gives no indication of theologically legitimatizing a new earthly kingdom. The shaking of the nations would produce a theocracy with God ruling through his representative, Zerubbabel.

Haggai's sermon begins (v.2) with the standard messenger formula, **"This is what the** LORD **Almighty says."** This identification of the words as God's is repeated three times in the passage (vv.3, 5, 7).

The opening statement of the sermon quotes the people concerning the task of building the temple. After the first return in 538 B.C. an abortive attempt had been made to rebuild. Due to the lack of economic resources, it was left unfinished. The people saw the continued economic plight as reason enough for the continued delay. Haggai had a contrasting point of view. The people thought that economics prohibited religious activity, whereas Haggai proclaimed that their economic plight was caused by their lack of religious commitment.

The theological basis of Haggai's message lies in the Deuteronomic expression of the Mosaic covenant. How the nation responded to the demands of God as expressed in the covenant determined God's response to them; obedience brought national peace and prosperity, but disobedience meant economic and political disaster along with disease and pestilence (Dt 28). Haggai applies this theology in vv.6, 9–10. The people survived, but they never had enough to satisfy their desires. Harvests were inadequate, and their money's value eroded through inflation (v.6). This was not due to the normal course of affairs, but because of God's direct intervention. He was responsible for the droughts and poor harvests (vv.9–11).

II. THE RESPONSE TO THE CHALLENGE (1:12–15)

This section is a narrative on the response that the people made to the

message of Haggai. On the twenty-fourth day of that same month **the whole remnant of the people** (the entire Judean community) began the actual work of restoring the temple. The only oracle of Haggai recorded is the short pronouncement, **"I am with you."**

A community may decide to build a house of worship, but if it is not acceptable to the deity, they labor in vain. The place of worship is a point of contact between the community and its God. Haggai's message assured the people that God accepted their work, removed their iniquities, and dwelt among them to sanctify their efforts. The task became a joint venture as God himself encouraged (**stirred up the spirit**) the leaders and the people.

III. THE FUTURE GLORY OF THE TEMPLE (2:1–9)

On the fifteenth day of the seventh month, Tishri, the Feast of Tabernacles, or Succoth began (Lev 23:39–43). This feast recalled the wilderness wanderings of Israel when God graciously provided for his people. It also celebrated the gourd and vineyard harvest, the fruits of the land for which the Conquest under Joshua's leadership was carried out. The occasion formed the background for Haggai's next address as the twenty-first of this month (2:1) was the last day of the feast.

Haggai began the message (2:3) with three rhetorical questions that collectively were designed to identify the complaints of the people. Some were grumbling that the community was not economically able to finish the temple in the same grandiose style as Solomon, who had used fine woods and gold to decorate its interior (2Ch 3:5–9).

In v.4 Haggai exhorted three times that the leaders and people were to **be**

strong. This exhortation is similar to the Lord's command to Joshua on the eve of the Conquest (Jos 1:6–9). Haggai intentionally drew lessons from the Feast of Tabernacles and the beginning of the Conquest to encourage the community in the work it was facing. Israel would have perished in the wilderness or failed in the invasion if God has not been with her. What guaranteed success was not the people's ability but God's presence. Similarly he was now present with them to complete their task. They possessed adequate resources, for God was among them. The temple would be rebuilt if only they did not lose the inner drive to complete the task. The question was not one of resources but one of faith.

Haggai concluded his message with an appeal to the future (vv.6–9), when the LORD **Almighty** will **shake** the whole creation. The metaphor of an earthquake is extended to describe another political upheaval similar to when Darius took the throne. In a future shaking of the nations, God will cause the wealth of the nations to flow into the temple so that it might be decorated in a manner more splendid than Solomon's. The **"desire of all nations"** means the precious things, or silver and gold, of the nations.

The emphasis of the passage falls on the presence of **the LORD Almighty** or *Yahweh Seba'ot,* Haggai's favorite name for God, which he uses five times in these three verses.

IV. HOLINESS AND PROPER WORSHIP (2:10–19)

Haggai's fourth message to the community began when he asked the priests for a ruling concerning ritual holiness. The source of holiness is God himself, for he alone in the universe is holy. That which is dedicated to him shares in his nature and becomes holy. This holiness was viewed as a force or charge so that the more holy an object was, the more charged with this power it became. The immediate ruling given to Haggai was that objects that come into contact with holy objects do not themselves thereby become holy, but that objects that are ritually unclean (Lev 11) may defile holy objects so that they are no longer acceptable to place before a holy God. Haggai then proclaimed (v.14) that the people were considered by God to be unclean and their efforts were unacceptable.

What, then, were the people to do? They were obeying God's word that came through Haggai to build the temple, yet that effort was not acceptable. The answer lay with God and is given in vv.15–19. Haggai called on the people to remember how poor the previous harvests had been. God had cursed their efforts. How in the ninth month the seed for the new crop lay in the ground. As an unclean people they could not expect the blessings of God; thus the forecast for the next harvest was dismal. The word from God, however, promised a reversal of this situation. He would bless them. God had sanctified his people through his presence and made them clean. They now were proper candidates for his blessings, and work on the temple would be acceptable. Sanctification was the work of God whereby he shared his holiness with his people.

V. GOD'S PROPER LEADER (2:20–23)

The word of the Lord came to Haggai a second time on the same day with a message for Zerubbabel. Again Haggai picked up the idea of God shaking the nations (2:6–9), only this time not only would the economic situation be changed, but political power would be restructured. The shaking of the nations would be an eschatological intervention by God into world history, causing the nations to destroy themselves through war, massive fratricide (cf. Ge 4:8; Jdg 7:22).

The new order to be established would be ruled by God from his new temple. Zerubbabel would be God's viceroy. The terms **servant** and **signet ring** in the political terminology of the day indicated that Zerubbabel would function as the royal representative with broad powers but always exercised in the name of the true Sovereign. As he had been the governor under the king, Darius, so would he continue to function under the true Sovereign, Yahweh—the Lord Almighty. Haggai's final word affirmed the presence of the Lord in the midst of the community. He was there to sanctify the work of building the temple, to bless the economic conditions of the community, and to rule through his chosen leader.

BIBLIOGRAPHY

Achtemeier, Elizabeth. *Nahum—Malachi*. Interpretation. Atlanta: John Knox, 1986.

Baldwin, Joyce G. *Haggai, Zechariah, Malachi*. TOTC. Downers Grove: InterVarsity Press, 1975.

Dunning, H. Ray. "Haggai." BBC. 10 vols. Kansas City: Beacon Hill, 1966. Vol. 5.

Meyers, Carol L. and Eric M. Meyers. *Haggai, Zechariah 1–8*. AB. Garden City, N.Y.: Doubleday, 1987.

Petersen, David L. *Haggai and Zechariah 1–8: A Commentary*. OTL. Philadelphia: Fortress, 1984.

ZECHARIAH
Bill T. Arnold

INTRODUCTION

I. HISTORICAL BACKGROUND

Cyrus, the prince of Anshan and ruler of the recently united Medo-Persian Empire, captured the city of Babylon in October of 539 B.C. The ancient world, and the Jewish expatriates living in Babylon in particular, would never be the same again. Cyrus immediately released the exiles and charged them to return to Jerusalem to rebuild the temple (Ezr 1:1–4). Approximately fifty thousand Jews returned under the civil leadership of Zerubbabel (governor of the satrapy known as Yehud) and the religious leadership of Joshua (the high priest). At this point, progress on the temple was modest. The foundation was repaired and the altar rebuilt in 537 B.C. (Ezr 3). But the early restoration community labored under unfavorable conditions, racial opposition being primary among them. They were also small in number. Many of the Jews had acclimated well to their exile and had become successful in their new surroundings. Jerusalem was in a shambles, was sparsely populated, and seemed uninviting to many Jews comfortably settled in Babylonia. Lacking resources and energy for the task, work on reconstruction soon came to a complete stop (Ezr 4:1–5; 24).

Cyrus died in battle in 530 B.C. and was succeeded by his son Cambyses II. The new Persian ruler successfully added Egypt to the growing empire in 525. But Cambyses' reign was not so secure as his father's, and he feared any threat to his authority. Bardiya, his brother, was so popular with the people that Cambyses had him assassinated. While in Palestine in 522 B.C., Cambyses received news of revolt at home. His death near Mount Carmel is locked in mystery, but we may assume that he was the victim of murder or suicide.

An officer of the army, Darius Hystaspes, claimed the throne in the midst of political revolution. Unrest was widespread early in his reign, but Darius apparently established firm control of the empire by 520 B.C. His policy of tolerance and the stability of his reign created favorable conditions that made it possible for the Jews to resume work on the temple. Darius, in fact, confirmed the original decree of Cyrus and provided royal resources for the temple project (Ezr 6:1–10). Under the local leadership of Zerubbabel and Joshua, the work was resumed in September of 520 B.C. (Hag 1:14–15). This is the context in which Haggai and Zechariah ministered to the Jews of Jerusalem. Their date formulae (Hag 1:1, 15; 2:1, 10, 20; Zec 1:1, 7; 7:1) place much of their ministry specifically between August of 520 and December of 518 B.C.

II. COMPOSITION AND THE PROBLEM OF UNITY

Zechariah's name ("Yahweh has remembered") is appropriate for a prophet whose message was one of encouragement and action. His genealogy (1:1, 7) and certain internal allusions suggest that, like Jeremiah and Ezekiel, Zechariah was from a priestly family. Scholars are generally agreed that the visionary and sermonic materials compiled in chs. 1–8 originated with this "Zechariah son of Berekiah, the son of Iddo" who was contemporary with Haggai.

No such consensus exists concerning chs. 9–14. Scholars have dated these chapters from the eighth century B.C. down to the Maccabean period (mid-second century). Nor is there agreement that these six chapters constitute a unity, many assuming they are a composite work of numerous subdivisions and diverse historical contexts. Arguments universally stress differences in style, atmosphere, vocabulary, and contents between chs. 1–8 and chs. 9–14. Those who assume a position of unity for the book point out that Zechariah was a young man in 520 B.C. (based on his family's return from Babylon and the reference to "young man" in 2:4; Barker, 597) and that his ministry may have continued for several decades. Thus it is possible that twenty or thirty years elapsed between the time when the prophet received his visions and the time when he expressed his "burdens" (9:1; 12:1). But this is as much conjecture as are the various disunity theories. Regardless of one's views on the authorship of chs. 9–14, it is best to analyze the book as it has come down to us; viz., as a single composition.

III. CONTENT AND STRUCTURE

The first six chapters of Zechariah may be called a "book of visions." Through these eight visions (whether actual visions or literary technique is a moot issue) the prophet reveals God's intention to deliver the beleaguered restoration community. The first and last visions emphasize God's sovereignty over all the earth, hence enveloping the other six visions with a tenor of certainty. Chs. 7 and 8 contain the prophet's sermons or sermonic notes on a variety of issues. They have been arranged, however, around the theme of fasting. Chs. 9–14 fall naturally into halves, each introduced by the expression "An Oracle—The Word of the LORD" (9:1; 12:1). In highly symbolic language, the prophet speaks of Yahweh's ultimate victory over evil and the deliverance of his people. The Messiah plays a central role in this ultimate salvation, and Zechariah's description of God's Anointed One is as clear as any other in the OT.

Zechariah contains a strong apocalyptic tone. Technically, only Daniel and Revelation may be said to be "apocalyptic." Those books provide the definition and characteristics of "biblical apocalyptic" (as distinct from the literature of the intertestamental period). Those characteristics include a cosmic scope, God's miraculous intervention on behalf of his people, a sense of finality since the divine purposes were already achieved in heaven, and a liberal use of visions and symbolic numbers or animals. Daniel and Revelation also employ a discernible arrangement of material beginning at a specific point in history (Nebuchadnessar's Babylon for Daniel and the seven local churches of Asia Minor for John). Both books then proceed from the local scene in Babylon or Asia Minor to the universal scene, from a point in time to the end of time.

Zechariah may be said to be a "rudimentary stage" of this type of literature (Baldwin, 71). Chs. 1–8 are set in the prophet's own day in the city of Jerusalem (though two of the visions are broader). Chs. 9–14 involve Israel's history, but the scope gradually broadens to include all the nations. In highly poetic language, the author jumps to "the day of the LORD" when the whole world will acknowledge Yahweh's lordship (ch. 14). The presence of the other characteristics of apocalyptic in Zechariah (visions, symbolism, cosmic scope, etc.) have led scholars to refer to Zechariah as "early apocalyptic" or "proto-apocalyptic" (e.g., Hanson, 472–73).

Zechariah's use of this apocalyptic arrangement from a point of time to the end of time is another reason for assuming the essential unity of the book (see "Composition and the Problem of Unity" above). Moreover, each section of the prophecy is systematically structured on a chiastic pattern. That is to say, there is a concentric movement among each section's subunits. This is best illustrated by the outline of chs. 7–8 (see below). The unit opens and closes with paragraphs dealing with the question about fasting, designated as A and A¹. The sermons of 7:4–14 and 8:9–17 correspond in a general way (B and B¹). In the center stands Zechariah's "sayings of encouragement" (C). So chiasm is arranged according to an ABCBA pattern. The section in the center (C in our example) is usually central to the author's message. The visions of chs. 1–6 are thus organized according to an ABBCCBBA pattern. The arrangement of the materials in chs. 9–14 is a bit more complicated (see outline below). I am indebted to Joyce Baldwin for this analysis and invite the reader to consult her excellent commentary for more detail on this structure (Baldwin, 74–81).

IV. THEOLOGICAL SIGNIFICANCE

The contributions of Zechariah (and Haggai) to Israel's understanding of the Messiah are obvious. The "Anointed One" is the servant of Yahweh (3:8); "the Branch" (3:8; 6:12) connotes renewed life from the stump of David's family tree. His advent means fertility and abundance (8:4–5, 10–13), and he is the Mediator of Yahweh's blessings and power (6:1–14). His service is related to the temple (4:7–10; 6:12–13). Zechariah's combination of two strands of Israelite leadership (priest and king, 6:13) paved the way for the two eventually to merge into one figure. Yet these prophecies in the first eight chapters (and those of Haggai) clearly have Zerubbabel in view. They stop just short of laying "on Zerubbabel's shoulders the mantle prepared for the Messiah" (Mowinckel, 119–22). Subsequently, after it became clear that Zerubbabel was not the ideal king, these prophecies took on greater messianic significance.

The more eschatological oracles of chs. 9–14 contain vivid pictures of the future king. He enters the city humbly (9:9–10), is rejected (11:8), and eventually is murdered (12:10). His followers are then scattered and confused (13:7–9). Yet on that day, a way of forgiveness will be opened for his people (13:1). Ultimately Yahweh will be identified as the King and will rule the whole earth (14:9). If Zechariah wrote these chapters later in his ministry (see above), he would have seen more clearly that a distant future Messiah was intended instead of Zerubbabel.

The impact of Zechariah was clearly felt by NT authors. His prophecy is quoted seventy-one times, most often in the Gospels and Revelation. Interestingly, the Passion narratives contain a high concentration of quotations from chs. 9–14, reflecting again the book's messianic nature.

God's absolute sovereignty and his election of his people are also dominant motifs here. The affairs of the nations are under God's direction, and his messengers traverse the earth (1:10; 6:4–5, 7). By a mere gesture of his hand, Yahweh overthrows the established world empires (2:9). His quintessential adversary ("Satan," 3:2) is powerless before him. In the conflict with wickedness, there is no resisting his authority (5:8). The strongest of Israel's bordering neighbors are helpless before him (9:1–8). Yahweh who "stretches out the heavens" and "lays the foundation of the earth" (12:1) will ultimately return to rule the whole earth (14:9).

The idea that God was absolutely sovereign was a powerful instrument in Zechariah's hands as he attempted to comfort and encourage the returned exiles. But so was the doctrine of election. Yahweh had chosen (*bahar*) Jerusalem as a place where his name would dwell (1:17; 2:12; 3:2; and Dt 12:5). The accusation that Wesleyanism minimizes these doctrines (sovereignty and election) is to misunderstand classical Wesleyanism. Asserting that man is a free moral agent takes nothing away from God's sovereignty and avoids unscriptural views of determinism.

V. OUTLINE

I. Introduction: Call to Repentance (1:1–6)

II. Visionary Revelation of God's Purposes (1:7–6:15)
   A. Vision One: Yahweh's Patrol Reports False Security (1:7–17)
   B. Vision Two: Retribution Against Israel's Enemies (1:18–21 [Heb 2:1–4])

COMMENTARY

I. INTRODUCTION: CALL TO REPENTANCE (1:1–6)

The eighth month of 520 B.C. began on October 27. Unlike the other dates given in Haggai and Zechariah, this one does not give the specific day of the month. While in Ezr 5:1 and 6:14, Zechariah is identified simply as a "descendant of Iddo," here and in v.7 he is identified both by his father's and grandfather's names. Other OT authors followed the common custom of mentioning only the grandfather. (For other explanations, cf. Meyers and Meyers, 92.)

Zechariah begins by reminding the Judahites that Yahweh had become very angry (*qāṣap*) with their forefathers (v.2). This anger is most often associated with God's covenant name (Yahweh) and reflects his revulsion at rebellion among his creatures to whom he had bound himself in covenant. But Zechariah's point is that Yahweh's wrath, illustrated so unforgettably in the destruction of Jerusalem and the Babylonian exile, was directed toward their **forefathers.** For his generation, there was still time to avert further disaster by returning to God (v.3). The repetition of the word **return** (*śûb*) in this introduction reveals the burden of the opening message. It was used often by the prophets to call the nation to repentance (Jer 3:12; Joel 2:12). Zechariah renews that message and assures his hearers that if they would only return to God, the covenant would once again be in effect (**"I will return to you,"** v.3).

The expression **"then they repented and said"** (v.6b) probably introduces a liturgical confession used in the post-exilic cultic worship (Albert Petitjean, quoted and discussed in Baldwin, 92).

II. VISIONARY REVELATION OF GOD'S PURPOSES (1:7–6:15)

This unit contains a "book of visions." The verb "see" (*rā'āh,* variously translated "I had a vision," 1:8; "I looked up," 1:18; "I see," 4:2; et al.) may be taken as a technical term in this type of literature for receiving a revelation (cf. Isa 30:10). These visions remove the scales from the prophet's eyes so that he may observe the normal-

ly unseen spiritual world in which God is gradually accomplishing his purposes.

Each of the eight visions follows a set pattern: introductory words, description of the vision itself, Zechariah's inquiry about its significance, and an explanation by an interpretive angel. For the chiastic structure of the visions, see introduction above. The date in v.7 (February 15, 519 B.C.) was probably the occasion for all eight visions that occurred during that night. This was three months after the oracle in 1:1–6.

A. Vision One: Yahweh's Patrol Reports False Security (1:7–17)

This opening vision involves a series of exchanges between the prophet, an angelic horseman, the interpreting angel (**"the angel who was talking with me,"** v.9), and Yahweh. The **ravine** was probably the Kidron Valley on the outskirts of Jerusalem. The vision contains seven instances of direct speech in characteristically Hebraic fashion (Meyers and Meyers, 129–30), climaxing in the last (vv.14–17), in which Yahweh's intentions are announced. The rider of the red horse (v.8) is to be identified with **the angel of the LORD** standing among the myrtle trees (v.11). He and his patrol of horses have been commissioned to patrol the earth on Yahweh's behalf. This reflects the practice of Persian monarchs who used equestrian reconnaissance teams to keep them informed about matters of the empire. In Zechariah's vision, Yahweh's emissaries appear to have completed their task, and they wait to be dismissed. They report that the world is at rest and in peace, a condition that Yahweh condemns as false security (v.15).

The message of this first vision was a powerful word of encouragement to the Jewish expatriates who had returned to Jerusalem to find it in ruins.

After twenty years (539–519 B.C.), the temple was still not rebuilt and the city was in shambles. At the same time, the rest of the world was enjoying relative peace and security, even though enforced by the strength of Persia. This injustice prompts the question in v.12. Yahweh's comforting answer (v. 13) is related to the prophet in the final address (vv.14–17). The central theme is that God's wrath (*qeṣep̄*, cf. v.2) has now been lifted from Judah and directed toward her enemies (v.15). Buttressing this theme is the emphasis on Yahweh's omniscience. Like the Persian equestrian teams that kept the monarchs apprised of all significant happenings, Yahweh is fully aware of the world's empires, and he is about to act on behalf of his people. The interpreting angel concludes the message of this first vision with the threefold promise of prosperity, consolidation, and election (v.17).

B. Vision Two: Retribution Against Israel's Enemies (1:18–21 [Heb 2:1–4])

This brief section supplies what is missing in the first vision where Yahweh, after declaring his anger against the nations, announces his intentions to restore Jerusalem and Judah. But his anger is not resolved until this second vision where the just destruction of Israel's oppressors is declared (Smith, 279–80). Horns (*qeren*) were symbolic of invincible strength. The number **four** represents the sum total of Israel's enemies, not unlike the four chariots in the eighth vision representing the points of the compass (6:1–15). The method used by the **craftsmen** is unclear, but the smith's hammer would suit the imagery. Zechariah's message of encouragement begins to build now as he assures Jerusalem's inhabitants that they are safe from the world's strong empires, even without city walls.

B¹. Vision Three: Measuring Jerusalem's Dimensions (2:1–13 [Heb 2:5–17])

This section falls naturally into two parts. The first is the vision proper (2:1–5 [Heb 2:5–9]) which underscores the message of the former vision. The man with the measuring line probably represents those who advocated rebuilding the city walls before working on the temple. Jerusalem at this time was sparsely populated and susceptible to enemy attack because her walls had been destroyed sixty-seven years before, in 586 B.C. (2Ki 25:1, 4, 8–12). But the man in the vision was informed that the inhabitants of Jerusalem would be protected by superhuman walls of fire and the city would become so densely populated that physical walls would become impractical. God's plans for the renovated city far exceeded the narrow and limited expectations of her inhabitants. Today God's work in the church must never be limited by our own concerns to guard his sacred institutions of the past.

The second section (2:6–13 [Heb 2:10–17]) is marked by a change of speaker and audience. Instead of the angel speaking to Zechariah, the prophet addresses first the exiled Jews in Babylonia and then those in Jerusalem. As in most prophetic speech, he mingles God's words with his own. In vv.6–9 he exhorts the Jews of Babylonia to flee from their land of exile because God is about to overturn the established order of the nations. The prophet then inserts his own conviction that after these things take place, they will know that he was sent by God. In the closing verses (vv.10–13) he assures those already living in Jerusalem of divine presence and election. But this newly established covenant will not be exclusive because **many nations will be joined with the LORD in that day.** The prophet concludes on a solemn note of expectation (v.13). When God moves into action, people must wait in reverence and silence (Hab 2:20).

C. Vision Four: The High Priesthood Reestablished (3:1–10)

In the previous three visions the prophet moved from a valley outside the city of Jerusalem (1:8) to a vantage point from which the city's dimensions could be measured. The next two visions deal with Israel's moral condition and her standing before God. It is therefore appropriate that they bring Zechariah into the temple courts, the domain of the high priest (Baldwin, 112–13). In this capacity Joshua (Hag 1:1) represents the Jews in a courtroom setting. He stands before **the angel of the LORD** who represents God himself and seems to be called simply **the LORD** in v.2. Joshua's "prosecuting attorney" is also present and is called **Satan** (*śātān*, "adversary"). As elsewhere in the OT (Job 1:6–12; 2:1–7, but with the possible exception of 1Ch 21:1), this word is used as a common noun, serving as an accuser in the celestial court. The doctrine of a personal devil was a distinctive development of NT theology, which is not without bearing on the present passage. As in the NT, here "the satan" is resolutely opposed to God's purposes (Mt 4:1–11) and seeks to harm God's people (2Co 11:14; 12:7). The Jews of Jerusalem in 519 B.C. had endured poverty through intemperate weather and poor agricultural seasons. Their profound discouragement led to the failure to continue work on the temple (Hag 1:2–11; 2:3). But in v.2 the Lord rebukes their enemy who seeks to destroy them. The satan disappears from the scene without a word, not to be heard from again. When God rebukes, there is no retort!

But this vision goes deeper. Israel is rescued but is still impure; is saved, but still unclean. Joshua, the representative of the people, stands helpless in filthy rags before the judge, symbolic of the corporate guilt of the people (v.4b). **Sin** in v.4 is the word often translated "iniquity" (*'āwôn*), and it signifies the twisted disposition that always leads to offense and guilt. When the prophet witnesses the removal of this iniquity and realizes that Joshua's filthy clothes are being replaced with "rich garments," he cannot contain himself. For the first time, Zechariah becomes an active participant in the vision. He suggested a **clean turban** be added to Joshua's attire to complete the picture of an acceptable high priest, one with special access to God (Ex 29:6).

The vision closes with the angel's recommissioning address to Joshua (vv. 6–10). If the high priest meets the moral and ritual requirements, he will be given privileges that exceed those of the preexilic priests. He will have indisputable authority in the temple and its courts, and he will have direct approach to God's presence **among these standing here,** viz., access to God's heavenly court instead of merely his earthly Holy of Holies (vv.6–7). In this, Joshua foreshadowed his greater namesake, Jesus (Heb 4:14–16).

The passing reference to **the Branch** (*ṣemaḥ*) makes no attempt to identify him (v.8). He is simply **"my servant,"** which recalls the themes of Isa 40–55 (see at 6:12–13). The meaning of the stone with seven eyes is uncertain. But the significance is made clear by the last phrase of v.9, **"I will remove the sin of this land."** The prosperity described in v.10 was always the ideal in Israel (1Ki 4:25; Mic 4:4). The commissioning of a new high priest was futile as long as there was no temple, which leads us to the fifth vision.

C¹. Vision Five: The Lampstand and Two Olive Trees (4:1–14)

In conjunction with the fourth vision's imagery of priest and temple, Zechariah now sees a cultic lampstand, reminiscent of the one in the tabernacle (Ex 25:31, although Solomon's temple had ten [1Ki 7:49]). The exact nature of Zechariah's lampstand is impossible to determine. It was probably a single column with a large bowl on top, branching out into **seven lights** each with seven **channels,** or pipes, for oil (Meyers and Meyers, 229–38).

Zechariah's question (v.4) concerning the significance of the lampstand and the **two olive trees** is not addressed until later in the chapter. In the intervening verses, a pertinent message is given for Zerubbabel, the second leader involved in rebuilding the temple (Hag 1:1). Joshua's role and significance had been made clear in ch. 3. Now Zerubbabel comes center stage. He would be instrumental in completing the work on the temple but not through **might** (*ḥayil,* human resources in general) nor **power** (*kōaḥ,* human strength in general). When viewed from a human perspective, rebuilding the temple was impossible at this time, given Zerubbabel's limited resources. But more than this was available. The temple would be completed by God's **Spirit** (*rûaḥ*), who was instrumental in the creation of earth and the parting of the Red Sea. The completion of the impossible task will stand as a witness to God's activity.

The succeeding verses (vv.7–10a) emphasize the invincibility of Zerubbabel as leader and the certainty of his success. Every mountainous obstacle will **become level ground,** and he will provide the final stone of the temple amidst a ceremony of praise. Even the skeptic who considers Zerubbabel's attempts to be insignificant (v.10; cf. Hag 2:3) will have reason to rejoice.

Now the interpreting angel returns to Zechariah's initial question (v.4) concerning the meaning of the vision (vv.10b–14). The two olive trees supply the oil for the lampstand through two pipes, as is made clear by Zechariah's question in v.12, repeated for emphasis. The two trees seem to represent Joshua and Zerubbabel; and the lampstand, the people of God (as the seven lampstands in Rev 1:20 represent churches; cf. Baldwin, 123–24). The success of Joshua and Zerubbabel will depend on their receptivity to God's Spirit. Through Joshua, the people are forgiven of sin and given access to God's presence (3:1–10). Through Zerubbabel, the temple project will meet with glorious success. The two **anointed** ones seemed to enjoy equal status. But after Zerubbabel's death, the office of high priest assumed greater power, and Zerubbabel was without a successor. Both offices contributed significantly to the NT understanding of the person and work of Jesus.

B². Vision Six: The Curse of the Flying Scroll (5:1–4)

The two visions of ch. 5 deal with persistent lawlessness in Judah and correspond to the second and third visions (cf. introduction). The **scroll** (*meḡillâ*) Zechariah saw is related to ancient documentation procedures in which sheets of parchment were stitched together, rolled up, and stored in jars or on shelves (Meyers and Meyers, 278). But in the prophet's vision, the scroll was "flying" like an unfurled flag, as large as a billboard for all to see. The dimensions of the scroll have led some commentators to make comparisons with those given for the tabernacle in Ex 26:15–28, or the porch of Solomon's temple in 1Ki 6:3 (Mitchell, 169; Petersen, 247). The best explanation of the scroll is that it represents the law and is a **curse** (*'ālâ*) because it has been broken. Stealing and invoking God's name in false witness are the seventh and third commandments respectively. As such, they are symbolic of the two "tablets" of law (Ex 32:15), and they summarize duty to one's neighbor and to God. In the form of this flying scroll, the law will bring justice where the corrupt judicial system has been ineffectual, in the privacy of the guilty party's home.

B³. Vision Seven: The Woman in the Measuring Basket (5:5–11)

The previous vision dealt with the punishment of the criminal, but the principle of evil persisted. Jeremiah spoke in terms of a new heart (Jer 32:39–40), and Ezekiel thought of washing away uncleanness (Eze 36:25). Zechariah had already represented sin as filthy clothes to be removed and replaced by rich garments (3:4). In this vision, wickedness (*riš'â*, the counterpart to righteousness) was personified as a woman and entrapped in a measuring basket. Two other women (angel-like creatures) then appeared and bore the basket containing Wickedness to far-off Babylonia where she would be housed permanently. Babylonia is the counterpart to the Holy Land and represents antagonism to God's purposes (Ge 11:1–9; Rev 18).

But the problem of sin is insufficiently solved by the punishment of crime and the expulsion of the criminal (5:1–4). The deeper problem of the human disposition to civil, ethical, and religious evil must be banished from the people of God (5:5–11). The sixth vision deals with the consequences of sin, and this vision with its prevention.

A¹. Vision Eight: The Four Chariots and Joshua's Coronation (6:1–15)

Just as this "book of visions" opened with a picture of God's universal sovereignty (1:7–17), so it concludes. The four chariots with their variously colored horses act upon God's command to patrol the whole earth. Many attempts have been made to explain the significance of the steeds' colors, but none is satisfactory. They are dispersed in all directions except east. Appropriately, the black horses are sent to the north, which represents the center of the world's power. Neither the red horses nor the east are specifically mentioned, which has led some to take v.7 as referring to them (Smith, 297–98). In this way, the red ones are charged with patrolling the earth in general, while the others are dispatched in specific directions. The interpreting angel reveals his identity in v.8 with **"Those going toward the north country have given my Spirit rest."**

The troubled **north** is now at rest and, by implication, God's forces are universally victorious. Thus the deliverance promised in the first two visions is accomplished, and the way is now clear for the children of Israel to assume their proper role in God's salvation history. This note leads naturally to the oracle about the Branch (6:9–14), which was not originally part of the vision.

The prophetic oracle (6:9–14) is fraught with difficulties. When three of the exiles arrive from Babylon, Zechariah is commanded to meet them and fashion a crown from their supplies. He is then to place the crown, not on Zerubbabel's head, but upon Joshua, the high priest. Commentators have for many years assumed that the text originally contained Zerubbabel's name instead of Joshua's. It is assumed that the

Persians objected to the messianic claims made on Zerubbabel's behalf and prevented his coronation. Subsequently, a scribe would have exchanged Joshua's name for Zerubbabel's to avoid the appearance of mistaken prophecy (Mitchell, 185–86; Thomas, 1080). But this reconstruction has no textual support to commend it. Moreover, if a later scribe had wanted to excise any reference to a Davidic prince, it is unlikely that he would have left the reference to the "Branch" with all of its messianic significance (and which may also be a wordplay on Zerubbabel's name, "Shoot of Babylon"). Elsewhere (4:9) Zechariah has given Zerubbabel credit for building the temple, which is emphatically stated in vv.12–13. Finally, the references in v.13 to majestic clothing and a throne are only appropriate for a Davidic prince.

For these reasons (among others) I conclude that it is unlikely that a later scribe altered the text to exclude a reference to Zerubbabel. A more recent theory argues that Zechariah made two crowns, one silver and one gold (Meyers and Meyers, 350). The Hebrew word for "crown" ('ăṭārôt, v.11) is in fact plural. In this case, the priestly crown was placed on Joshua (v.11), and the royal crown was stored in the temple in anticipation of the arrival of the Messiah (v.14, the [other] crown). Regardless of the number of crowns involved, the point seems to be that Joshua was officially inaugurated as high priest. But his contribution could never fulfill the promise of the coming Branch, so the prophet speaks in general terms of the Davidic Messiah ruling in harmony with the priesthood. In this way the priestly and royal offices were joined in the work of the Branch. In later views they would be completely united in the Messiah.

III. SERMONS RELATED TO THE QUESTION OF FASTING (7:1–8:23)

The question raised in 7:3 is not actually answered until 8:18–19. As may be seen in our outline, we take the question and its answer as inclusios (a sort of envelope construction) for this unit. The intervening materials are various sermons and prophetic sayings that relate directly or indirectly to the question of fasting.

A. The Question Posed (7:1–3)

The date in v.1 may be tabulated as December 7, 518 B.C. The source of the question on fasting is much disputed. The NIV of v.2 pictures the inhabitants of Bethel (twelve miles north of Jerusalem) sending **Sharezer** and **Regem-Melech** to Jerusalem to inquire about fasting. But many modern commentators read "Bethel-Sharezer sent Regem-Melech and his men," which is another possible rendering of the Hebrew text (Baldwin, 142; Thomas, 1082). The Babylonian form of the name Bethel-Sharezer has been attested for this period. If this is true, then the problem concerning fasting originated among prominent Jews in Babylonia who sent to Jerusalem to receive an answer. This accords well with the four-month gap between Zechariah's answer in the ninth month (v.1) and the mourning ritual itself in the fifth month (v.3), since the journey from Babylon to Jerusalem took precisely four months (Ezr 7:8–9). This would also remove the need for the NIV's addition of **"the people of"** (v.2) which is not in the original text. This view is not, however, without recent critics (Meyers and Meyers, 379–83).

The temple had been destroyed on the seventh day of the fifth month (2Ki 25:8–9). For nearly seventy years this day had been commemorated as a solemn fast day. But now that the temple was almost rebuilt, the question arises whether it was appropriate for devout Jews to continue this mourning ritual. Although the priests made pronouncements on matters of ritual, it was the prophets who provided the divine mandate for religious innovations. Thus the rest of this unit preserves Zechariah's teachings on the topic of fasting.

B. The Sermon Concerning the Purpose of Fasting (7:4–14)

Zechariah begins by reminding the people that fasting was an external expression of an internal, spiritual reality. They did not fast to satisfy God's requirements. On the contrary, just as feast days were to satisfy themselves, so fasts were often prompted by self-interests. The prophetic quotes in vv.9–10 sum up the four precepts that were meant to shape Israel's social principles. The positive commands reflect the concern for justice (*mišpāṭ*) so prevalent in the prophets and a commitment to covenantal love and loyalty (*ḥeseḏ*) that should pervade all our relationships. The negative prohibitions denounce the exploitation of weakness and forbid thinking of wronging others. The point of Zechariah's sermon seems to be that the preexilic fathers had rejected these principles and had refused to hear God's Word. Thus he goes beyond the question of fasting and dwells on the stubborn disobedience that brought on the tragedy commemorated by the fast days. Those who would consider fasting should dwell on these moral standards because the fall of Judah could have been avoided if these had been maintained.

C. Related Sayings of Encouragement (8:1–8)

But Zechariah's ministry was one of comfort. He moves almost suddenly to a series of memorable sayings (perhaps these were texts of various sermons) intended to reassure God's people of his love. The divine **jealousy** (cf. 1:14) may be thought of as passionate zeal or ardor moving God into action on behalf of his people. The expected arrival of the Lord will herald a new age for Jerusalem. The sounds of prosperous and happy families will once again fill her streets. As is always the tragic truth, the young and elderly would have suffered much at the fall of Jerusalem in 587 B.C. Few of the elderly would have endured the arduous trip back to Jerusalem. But the new age will witness God's people returning to Jerusalem from **the east and the west,** and the repopulated city will once again enjoy the blessing of long life. For some, these tremendous promises were difficult to believe (v.6).

B¹. The Sermon Promising to Restore Judah's Fortunes (8:9–17)

This sermon uses a recurrence of contrast between the unhappy past and the hopeful present. The past for Judah was filled with poverty, violence, and divine condemnation (vv.10, 14). But now Yahweh is committed to dealing differently with his people (v.11). Abundant agricultural produce will mark this generation (v.12), and Yahweh will work on their behalf (v.15). The emphasis of this sermon may be summarized by the statement **"As you have been an object of cursing . . . you will be a blessing"** (v.13).

As in the first sermon (7:4–14), there is here a strong ethical emphasis. The moral precepts of vv.16–17 are very similar to those of 7:9–10. Yahweh punctuates his feelings about injustice and cruelty with **"I hate all this."** God's people keep his commandments because they wish to please him and because they reflect his character (Jn

14:15). This is the "theological basis of ethics" (Baldwin, 154).

A¹. The Answer Given (8:18–23)

The question of 7:3 is now answered in light of all that Zechariah has said about the past. Each of these occasions for mourning rituals is associated with the events of the fall of Jerusalem in 587/6 B.C. The city wall was breached in the fourth month (Jer 39:2), the temple destroyed during the fifth (2Ki 25:8). Gedaliah was murdered and the Babylonian siege began in the seventh and tenth months respectively (2Ki 25:25; 25:1–2). But because of what God was doing in Zechariah's day, the time for mourning was over. These fast days, having been observed for nearly seventy years, were to be turned into occasions for joy and feasting.

The joy of the renewed covenant would not be restricted to the Jews (vv.20–23). The inhabitants of far-off cities would evangelize each other because of the news of Yahweh's goodness to Jerusalem. Thus the covenant between Yahweh and the courageous citizens of the postexilic community had the potential to fulfill the promises to Abraham (Ge 12:3).

IV. THE LORD'S SHEPHERD REJECTED (9:1–11:17)

The many differences between the two sections of the book have already been discussed (see the introduction). One of the important distinctions to keep in mind is that the promises and predictions of chs. 1–8 have a sense of immediacy about them. The prophet was anchored in the events of his day, namely the reconstruction of the temple. But chs. 9–14 have a pronounced eschatological tone and contain stronger messianic themes.

A. Yahweh's Triumphant March Through Palestine (9:1–8)

Oracle (*Maśśā'*, v.1) is repeated in this same grammatical expression in 12:1 and Mal 1:1 only. It signifies a "burden" imposed on the prophet compelling him to speak a message he might otherwise avoid (Baldwin, 162–63). Although there are many inspiring passages in chs. 9–11, their conclusion in 11:4–17 must have been an onerous word to speak.

See the commentaries for details on the geographical references in these verses. In general, Yahweh is pictured coming from the north, moving west and south along the Mediterranean coast, and finally arriving at the temple in Jerusalem (**"my house,"** v.8). Along the way, he defeats all of Israel's traditional enemies, demonstrating his sovereign power and his love for Judah. The reassuring message of the paragraph climaxes in v.8: **"Never again will an oppressor overrun my people, for now I am keeping watch."**

B. The Arrival of Zion's King (9:9–10)

Having brought us into Jerusalem with peace and security (v.8), the prophet moves to a description of the coming messianic King. V.9 exhorts the city to celebrate his arrival and describes his character. V.10 details his accomplishments. The preexilic prophets had anticipated the arrival of an ideal son of David (Isa 9:6). But this is the most explicit postexilic reference to the coming messianic king. The prophet has apparently drawn on the familiar imagery of Ge 49:11; Ps 72; and Isa 40–55.

The ideal Ruler will be **righteous**, providing a dramatic contrast with Israel's long line of wicked monarchs. He will be in possession of **salvation**, which denotes victory accomplished, even if unrealized. His humility is graphically illustrated by his mode of transportation, suitable for a man of peace. The King's donkey may be contrasted with the **chariots** and **war horses** of v.10.

Among the king's achievements will be the complete disarmament of his kingdom (v.10a). He will also extend the boundaries of his territory beyond the ideal limits promised to Israel but rarely held by her (Ex 23:31). The NT authors recognized the fulfillment of v.9 in Jesus' triumphal entry into Jerusalem (Mt 21:5, Jn 12:15). Interestingly, they did not cite his achievements of v.10, indicating this passage was only partially fulfilled.

C. The Deliverance of Zion's People (9:11–10:1)

Prior to the arrival of this King, his people were like victims at the bottom of a **waterless pit** (v.11). After his advent, he will deliver and restore them because of the blood of his **covenant** with them (v.11). Elsewhere in the OT this expression (**"blood of my covenant"**) is used only in the covenant at Sinai (Ex 24:8). Its full significance was made clear by Jesus (Mt 26:28).

In 9:14–10:1 the prophet uses apocalyptic language to describe Yahweh's magnificent warfare against Israel's enemies. His appearance in **the storms of the south** (v.14) probably recalls his awe-inspiring theophany at Sinai (Ex 19:16–19; 24:9–10). The certainty of his victory ensures the celebration of his people (vv.15–16). The cessation of poverty (9:17–10:1) will also accompany this new age of victory and peace.

D. Warning to Leaders and Encouragement for People (10:2–4)

There is a dramatic contrast between v.1 and v.2a. The prophet moves from Yahweh's deliverance and provision in the future to his present situation in which the worship of idols was producing disappointment and despair. The prophet rebukes the present leaders who are largely responsible (vv.2–3a) but comforts the people (vv.3b–4).

The **shepherd** theme introduced in v.2b was a common symbol for rulers in the ancient Near East before it was used in Scripture. It becomes an important element in the prophet's messianic passages later in the book. **Leaders** in v.3 is literally "he-goats" (*'attûd*) and is a pejorative term expanding the metaphor. It contrasts the character of earthly leadership with that which it could and should be. A powerful wordplay in v.3 is missed by the English translations: the Lord will **punish** (*pāqad 'al*) the leaders but **care for** (*pāqad*) his flock.

C¹. Israel's Victory and Deliverance (10:5–11:3)

The prophet continues for the moment to address his present circumstances. In the preceding paragraph he denounced the unscrupulous and unprincipled leaders of Judah. Now he strengthens the people and prepares them for victory. **Judah** and **Joseph** represent the southern and northern kingdoms respectively. Having addressed the problem of leadership in Judah, the prophet concerns himself with the return of Ephraim's exiles (vv.8–9). In the remainder of the unit he deals with nations affected by the Lord's restoration of Israel. Egypt and Assyria stand for those nations who are forced to release the exiles, the latter especially symbolizing also Babylonia and Persia. Gilead and Lebanon are regions that will have to relinquish territory to God's people who will have outgrown their borders.

The poetic section ends (to be resumed briefly in 11:17 and 13:7–9) with a taunting song against Israel's enemies (Dentan, 1101; Mitchell, 295). The pride of Lebanon and Bashan is graphically symbolized in the **cedar** and **oak**, which will be reduced to nothing by ax and fire.

B¹. The Fate of the Shepherd-King (11:4–17)

This allegorical passage presents some of the most difficult interpretive problems in the OT. But this much is clear. The flock represents Israel, and the shepherds are their leaders. The Lord charges his prophet to become their new shepherd, who illustrates the symbolism with two staffs named **Favor** (or "Graciousness") and **Union.** But to their detriment the people reject his gracious and unifying leadership. The message of this enigmatic unit is clearly the need for (and responsibility of) godly leaders among the believing community. This imagery was the backdrop for Jesus' self claims in Jn 10:11–18 and may also have been operative in Jn 21:15–19. This message is as pertinent today as it ever has been.

In vv.4–6 Yahweh shows pity on a flock that has been raised specifically for meat, fattened, and soon to be sold at the slaughterhouse. The merchants, and even their own shepherds, care little for the sheep, but only for making a profit. The exclamation **"Praise the LORD, I am rich!"**(v.5) seems to have more adherents in the modern church than ever before. Few in the Wesleyan heritage today follow John Wesley's injunction to give to the poor *everything* beyond the necessities of life (Wesley, *Sermons,* 50, 87, 116). Whether or not Wesley's austere economic practices can be applied to our technical and complex culture, his love and commitment to the flock is exemplary of Christian leadership.

Yahweh's remedy was to send his prophet to care for the flock **marked for slaughter** (vv.4, 7). But vv.7–14 trace the deterioration and disruption of the relationship between the new shepherd and his flock. Lest we overemphasize the importance of godly leadership in the church, it should be remembered that rejection of God's true representatives will result in irreparable loss.

The identity of **the three shepherds** (v.8) is one of the most complicated problems of Zechariah, yielding up to forty variations of interpretation (for an excellent survey of the data and conclusions, see Baldwin, 181–83). Under the present circumstances it is impossible to determine the historical background of this reference.

The oracle closes with the prophet impersonating **a foolish shepherd** chosen by the flock in their rejection of Yahweh's Shepherd. He will neglect every responsibility of a good shepherd and will in fact feed on the sheep, tossing aside their carcasses when he has had enough (v.16). In the closing poetic stanza, this worthless shepherd is left debilitated, unable to protect the sheep from attack or to watch over their daily activities.

V. FINAL SUFFERING AND DELIVERANCE (12:1–14:21)

The phrase **on that day** is repeated sixteen times in this unit, indicating its setting in the eschaton. The themes of chs. 9–11 are repeated here but with greater intensity (cf. Baldwin, 187, and introduction above). The second section of the book builds to a climax in ch. 14 where the events of **that day** are described.

C². Deliverance for Besieged Jerusalem (12:1–9)

V.1 prepares us for the apocalyptic material to follow by bringing into focus the sovereign Mover in these events, **the LORD, who stretches out the heavens** (v.1). The nations of the earth have surrounded and besieged Jerusalem so that her inhabitants are hopelessly outnumbered. But just as Jerusalem had been made to drink from the cup of God's wrath (Isa 51:17), so now the nations will have their turn. The **cup** (v.2) is a biblical symbol for an experience that God has purposed for someone (Ps 116:13; Mk 14:36). Yahweh will make Jerusalem an **immovable rock** that causes injury to whoever tries to displace it (v.3). The Lord also intervenes directly during a cavalry attack against the city (v.4).

Oddly enough, Judah had been compelled to join the siege against Jerusalem (v.2). But Yahweh's sudden appearance will ignite their resistance (v.5), and their position in the midst of the nations will become Jerusalem's advantage (v.6). Any residual animosity between Judah and Jerusalem will be alleviated by God's undeniable protection (v.7). However, the ideals and dreams for the future continue to rest on **the house of David**, which will become **like God** (v.8). Yahweh's ultimate and irrevocable protection for Jerusalem (v.9) is the central message of the unit.

B². Mourning for the Pierced One (12:10–14)

Though God is quick to act on behalf of his people and bless them physically, he is never content to leave them unchallenged spiritually. The physical blessings of the previous unit lead inevitably to the need for renewal and cleansing (13:1). After God gives them a new gracious spirit, the people will realize the gravity of their actions in rejecting God's representative. Because they have pierced the Shepherd-King, the people—royalty, priests, and common citizens—will all mourn bitterly. The apostle John saw Jesus' death as the fulfillment of this prophecy (Jn 19:37; Rev 1:7).

Hadad Rimmon (v.11) may be a city near the plain of Megiddo, an allusion to a fertility god whose death was mourned seasonally (2Ki 5:18) or a subtle reference to the tragic death of Josiah.

D¹. Rejection of Fraudulent Prophets (13:1–6)

As the result of Israel's repentance in the previous paragraph, **a fountain** (v.1) will appear to deal with sin and impurity (cf. Eze 36:25; 47:1–6). Even the murderers of Yahweh's Shepherd-King may be cleansed by this fountain, and some have suggested a connection between that crime and the fountain's cleansing power (Barker, 685).

The prophet then turns his attention to his professional colleagues. **Prophet** is used in this unit in a derogatory sense. In addition to the purging of all Yahweh's competing powers (**the idols,** v.2), the false prophets will also be banished. Anyone daring to prophesy will be executed by his own parents in fulfillment of scriptural mandate (cf. Dt 13:6–9). Under such conditions, prophets will be hesitant to be identified as such (vv. 4–6).

B³. The Shepherd Is Slain (13:7–9)

This final poetic section resumes the shepherd motif of ch. 11. **"My shepherd"** indicates the special relationship between Yahweh and his servant, further modified by **"the man who is close to me"** (v.7). The word for **close to me** ('ⁿmîtî) denotes an intimacy in relationship and has sometimes been taken as **"my equal"** (cf. Jn 10:30). The identity of this Shepherd is not in doubt, at least not in Jesus' mind (cf. Mk 14:27, where he applies 13:7 to himself).

Subsequent to the death of the Shepherd-King, the people of God will be diminished in size by two-thirds (v.8). The remaining third will be refined by fire like silver and gold, a metaphor popular among biblical authors for removing impurities (Pr 17:3; Jer 6:29–30; et al.). Having been purified, they will become uniquely God's and will find their identity in relationship to him (v.9b).

C³. The Struggle for Jerusalem (14:1–15)

The oracle that began in 12:1 reaches its climax in this description of the Day of Yahweh and the eschatological battle for Jerusalem. The city will be besieged by insurmountable odds (**all the nations,** v.2) and will in fact be captured. Half of her inhabitants will be deported, and half will watch as the nations divide their possessions.

In this dehumanizing and truly hopeless situation, Yahweh will intervene as the Mighty Warrior of Old (v.3). In vivid apocalyptic imagery, the Lord's appearance is accompanied by cataclysmic geographical alterations in Jerusalem's landscape (v.4). The **Mount of Olives** is east of the city across the Kidron Valley and is higher than the temple mound. Because it is actually a ridge extending over two miles north and south, it was impractical as an escape route from the city (2Sa 15:14, 23, 30). But on that day **a great valley** running east and west will be created and will provide a quick means of escape for Jerusalem.

That occasion will be unique, admitting no darkness even when evening

arrives (cf. Isa 60:19–20). Time will no longer be measured by twenty-four-hour periods, and this **day** is understood only by Yahweh. This announcement of "the Day of Yahweh" (vv.6–7) marks the turning point in the narrative and in the fortunes of Jerusalem. Her defeat is dramatically turned into glorious and eternal victory. From this day forward, Jerusalem becomes the source of living water and security. Her perennial problem with water supply (2Ch 32:30) will be over. Unlike Ezekiel's river, which flowed only eastward (Eze 47:1), Zechariah's will flow east and west, to the Dead Sea and the Mediterranean respectively (v.8).

The Israelite monarchy had ideally been perceived as a theocracy; the monarch was merely a representative for Yahweh (Dt 17:18–20; 1Sa 8:7). Israelite worshipers sang "Yahweh Reigns" (Pss 93:1; 97:1; 99:1). This had been more theory than reality. But on that day Yahweh will make himself known as King of all the world (v.9). Suitable for the King's royal city, Jerusalem will be elevated above her geographical surroundings (**"raised up,"** v.10). The mountains around her will no longer be necessary for defense and will be leveled accordingly. For the geographical designations of v.10, see the commentaries.

At the beginning of the chapter, God's people suffer military defeat. But ultimately Israel's enemies will experience unspeakable agony and death. The plague described in vv.12–13 may recall the devastation of Sennacherib's army in Hezekiah's day (2Ki 19:35). At the beginning, Jerusalem was stripped of all her possessions. But on that day she will be filled with the gold, silver, and clothing of other nations. Even the animals, which could have provided a means of escape for the enemy, will suffer this ghastly fate (v.15).

A¹. The Universal Worship of Yahweh as King (14:16–21)

The oldest pilgrimage festival was probably **the Feast of Tabernacles** (or "Booths"), which commemorated the season of harvest and was connected to the deliverance from Egypt. During the postexilic period it became the occasion for reading the Torah and reestablishing the covenant (Ne 8:14–18). Thus it was the perfect festival to unite the survivors of the nations in their worship of Yahweh. Any possibility of apostasy will be avoided by drought, making the reticent worshiper recognize his need to depend on Yahweh for life. Egypt is specially mentioned because she was not dependent on rainfall. The Nile was her source of life and pride. But even Egypt will be no exception in Yahweh's universal kingdom.

In that day of final victory in Yahweh's new kingdom, even horses will be uniquely consecrated to him and will wear on their harnesses the legend "HOLY TO THE LORD, which was engraved on the turban of the high priest (Ex 28:36). There will no longer be a distinction between sacred and secular, and common cooking utensils will be used in the temple (Baldwin, 207). The **Canaanite in the house of the LORD** denotes any moral or spiritual impurity that might mar this perfect scene. When God is made King, every aspect of life becomes sacred, down to the pots and pans.

BIBLIOGRAPHY

Baldwin, Joyce G. *Haggai, Zechariah, Malachi: An Introduction and Commentary*. TOTC 24. Downers Grove: InterVarsity, 1972.

Barker, Kenneth L. "Zechariah." EBC. Vol. 7. Edited by F. E. Gaebelein. Grand Rapids: Zondervan, 1985.

Dentan, Robert C. "Zechariah 9–14." IB. Vol. 6. Nashville: Abingdon, 1956.

Hanson, Paul D. "Old Testament Apocalyptic Reexamined." *Interpretation* 25, no. 4 (1971): 454–79.

Keil, C. F.; and F. Delitzsch. *Biblical Commentary on the Old Testament*. Vol. 10. Grand Rapids: Eerdmans, 1978.

Meyers, Carol L.; and Eric M. Myers. *Haggai, Zechariah 1–8: A New Translation with Introduction and Commentary*. AB 25b. Garden City, N.Y.: Doubleday, 1987.

Mitchell, H. G.; J. M. P. Smith; and J. A. Bewer. *A Critical and Exegetical Commentary on Haggai, Zechariah, Malachi and Jonah*. ICC. New York: Scribner, 1912.

Mowinckel, S. *He That Cometh*. Nashville: Abingdon, 1956.

Petersen, David L. *Haggai and Zechariah 1–8*. OTL. Philadelphia: Westminster, 1984.

Smith, George A. *The Book of the Twelve Prophets, Commonly Called the Minor*. Vol. 2. New York: Doubleday, 1929.

Thomas, D. Winton. "Zechariah 1–8." IB. Vol. 6. Nashville: Abingdon, 1956.

Wesley, John. *The Works of John Wesley*. Vols. 1 and 2 (*Sermons*, vols. 1 and 2). Edited by Albert C. Outler. Nashville: Abingdon, 1984–85.

MALACHI
Milo Chapman

INTRODUCTION

I. AUTHORSHIP

One question that arises when considering the authorship of Malachi is the identity of the prophet. Does the name of the book derive from the name of the prophet, or does *malachi* only suggest the role of the prophet as messenger? (The literal meaning of the word is "my messenger.") Opinions differ and range from those who insist that there was a prophet named Malachi to those who are certain that "malachi" is not a proper name—that the book is anonymous. The latter view is generally accepted.

II. HISTORICAL SETTING—TIME OF WRITING

Even though it is difficult to say who wrote the book, the historical situation is readily discernible, notwithstanding the fact that "there is no archaeological evidence to throw light on the two hundred years of Persian rule in Palestine" (Eban, 66).

The political history of the Jews in the fifth century B.C. is bound to the Persian Empire. Beginning with the conquest by Cyrus and lasting to the victories of Alexander the Great, Persia was the dominant power from the Indus Valley to the Aegean and down to Africa (Bright, 356–57). Cyrus initiated an enlightened policy of generosity toward displaced peoples, allowing them to return to their homeland and to enjoy a high degree of self-determination in the areas of social patterns and religious practices. He demanded complete loyalty in political matters.

As a result of this generous practice Jewish subjects were permitted to return to Palestine and to rebuild the temple (Ezr 1:1–11; 2Ch 36:23). Utopian hopes were fanned and kept alive by prophets of the exilic period (cf. Eze 40–48; Isa 40:3–5; 41:18–20; 42:16; 49:7–13; 54:1–17; 55:1–13), but the reality of return did not match the expectation. In spite of help given by Persian officials, the returnees faced economic hardship and failure. Haggai interpreted their misfortune as evidence of God's displeasure at their selfish concern for personal welfare at the cost of neglect of the temple (1:1–11). At the urging of Haggai and Zechariah the temple was rebuilt and dedicated in 516/15 B.C., and presumably a full scale revival of temple services was enjoyed. If so, the conditions described by Nehemiah upon his return (444 B.C.) to secure the defenses of Jerusalem would indicate that the revival was short-lived. These conditions bracket the time when Malachi was probably written. On the one hand, the temple had been reconstructed and was in service; on the other, the quality of that service had degenerated to a low level (1:6–7), much like the situation found by Nehemiah upon his second visit to Jerusalem (c. 432 B.C.). Further, Malachi and Nehemiah agree on the problem of mixed marriages and their lack of temple support with regard to tithes and offerings. The writing of Malachi fits well in the period between Nehemiah's visits, i.e., some time around 433 B.C. (Verhoef, 160). The best alternative would be a date just prior to the time of Ezra—about 460 B.C.

III. THE ARGUMENT

The prophet shows concern over the spiritual condition of the nation. Even though the temple and its services were restored, there is a marked cynicism on the part of the people. Consequently they begin to doubt seriously whether or not they are really the recipients of God's love. Such disillusionment resulted in a failure to give God honor and respect. Their lessened devotion caused a withholding of tithes. They cheated on the quality of offerings that were given. This attitude was reflected in the services of the priests. Furthermore, the people violated the covenant by divorcing their wives and marrying aliens. Under such conditions judgment from God is inevitable. Repentance is mandatory. There is hope for the triumph of righteousness.

IV. STYLE

In trying to win back the people to loyalty and devotion to God, the author uses a lively form of disputation with them. This style is illustrated at the outset when the prophet says:

> "I have loved you," says the LORD.
> "But you ask, 'How have you loved us?'
> "Was not Esau Jacob's brother?" the LORD says. "Yet I have loved Jacob, but Esau I have hated, and I have turned his mountains into a wasteland and left his inheritance to the desert jackals" (1:2–3).

This pattern of question and answer is repeated several times within this short book.

Scholars disagree in their evaluation of the literary quality of the book, ranging from those who give it slight praise (Smith, *ICC*, 4) to those who appreciate its lively dialogue and freshness of expression (cf. Bewer, *Literature of the Old Testament*, 258; Verhoef, 166–67).

V. AUTHENTICITY—PLACE IN THE CANON

The text of Malachi is in good Hebrew and is well preserved. The book is a unit and was written by one author (Verhoef, 168). Some see evidences of editorial arrangement and additions, such as the superscription. It is sometimes affirmed that 4:4–6 is a later addition of an editor who wished to include a parting admonition, since this is the last of the writings in the Book of the Twelve as well as the final book in that section of the Hebrew canon known as the Prophets. Of course, it is also the final book in the English OT. The right of this book to a place in the canon is not disputed. The conviction rose that with the death of the last prophets, Haggai, Zechariah, and Malachi, the Holy Spirit was withdrawn from Israel (Margolius, 23).

VI. OUTLINE
Malachi deals with a subject of immediate importance to the author. His concerns rise out of issues that he sees in the religious life of the community. It may be outlined in the following manner.

    I. Superscription (1:1)
    II. God's Love for Israel (1:2–5)
    III. Honor Belongs to the Lord (1:6–2:9)
    IV. The Sin of Divorce (2:10–16)
    V. The Day of Judgment (2:17–3:5)
    VI. On Robbing God (3:6–12)
    VII. Triumph of Righteousness (3:13–4:6)

COMMENTARY

I. SUPERSCRIPTION (1:1)
Generally believed to be an editorial addition, the superscription nevertheless identifies the true source of the prophecy. It comes from Yahweh, the Lord, and is addressed to the Jewish community. The Lord's messenger is the instrument through whom the message comes. **Malachi** probably is borrowed from 3:1 where the meaning is simply "my messenger" or "my angel."

II. GOD'S LOVE FOR ISRAEL (1:2–5)
The prophet starts his message to his people by reminding them of God's love for them. This is the message against which the rest of the book must

be seen. The dialectical style begins here. God's claim that he loves Israel is disputed by the people in their retort, **How have you loved us?** They imply that the promises made to their ancestors and reinforced by such prophets as Hosea (11:1) and in Dt 7:8 are not operating on their behalf in the present. After the chastisement of the Babylonian captivity and the hope generated by the return of the exiles, poverty and hardship led to discouragement. However, the prophet uses a verb tense that emphasizes God's continuous love that was actively demonstrated in their past and continues into the present.

The choice of Jacob over Esau is the historical proof that Malachi brings to their attention. This "election" is not to be understood as evidence of predestination as found in Calvin's interpretation. The prophet has no such thought in mind. Rather, the choice is a free expression of God's gracious love. The history of the two brothers and their posterity is clear proof of God's continued love for the descendants of Jacob.

The exact historical reference to the destruction of Edom is difficult to ascertain. It may reflect animosity that went back for centuries. It may refer to the time of the Babylonian conquest of the territory as a whole. However, the feelings expressed by Malachi may reflect a more immediate situation, perhaps as a result of the Persian conquest. At any rate, God attests to the desolation of Edom through the centuries by one group after another. Even though Judah was similarly attacked by enemy armies, their fate was not, in the long view, so serious as that of Edom. No matter how much Edomites try to rebuild their ruins, the Lord Almighty will always be against them and will thwart their efforts.

The love-hate designation used here in Malachi is a difficult concept for modern Christians as they contemplate the nature of God and his relationship to the peoples of the earth. Can God really show favoritism? (Cf. Acts 10:34.) Many commentators contend that "hate" should be read as meaning "loves less." To support such an interpretation they point to Jacob's loving Rachel more than Leah (Ge 29:30), asserting that the meaning of the statement amounts to hatred of Leah (lit. meaning). However, this issue is not Malachi's concern. That which he emphasizes is that God's free choice is Jacob over Esau (cf. Snaith, 133–34). The subsequent welfare of the descendants of these two brothers demonstrates God's continued love for Israel. Recog-

nizing the divine judgment upon Edom should cause Israel to recognize the ways in which the Lord has blessed them.

III. HONOR BELONGS TO THE LORD (1:6–2:9)

The message continues in the guise of the Lord's accusation against the people. He charges that they dishonor Him. They, as children, would honor their father or as servants they would honor their master, but they show no respect for God. The priests are identified as the most guilty in this respect. They engage in practices that reflect a callous indifference to the religious observances that are their charge. Their actions actually result in offerings being made to the Lord that defile rather than show reverence. In spite of the ancient instruction that sacrifices should represent the first and the best of that which the people have (Dt. 15:21; Lev 1:3; et al.), the priests have been offering animals that are **crippled or diseased,** ritually unfit for sacrifice. How can they expect to be the recipients of God's gracious beneficence when they treat him as they do?

A comparison between the KJV and NIV at v.10 will show that difficulty exists in interpreting the Hebrew text. The KJV implies that the priests had sunk to such a low level that they refused to do simple duties without receiving compensation for their services. The context, however, favors the NIV translation. God is so displeased with the quality of their sacrifices that it would be better for the doors of the temple to be closed and no sacrificial fires lighted than for them to go through a mockery of sacrificial service that God will not accept (cf. Am 5:21–22; Hos 6:6; 8:11ff.; Isa 1:11ff.).

Thus by both attitude and action Yahweh was being demeaned. He who should be lauded as Lord and King over all the earth was belittled by those who had been chosen by him to receive the blessings of his great love.

It is not likely that the prophet whom we know as Malachi believed in a universal monotheism (1:11, 14) in spite of the fact that he achieves an insight that points in that direction. Some particularistic ideas are incorporated in this small book. For example, the God who loves Jacob hates Esau. He is the God who disapproved of entangling intermarriages with foreigners. The statement about his fatherhood (2:10), which could be applied to all humankind, is applied immediately to the Jews (Bewer, *Prophets*, 592). With such a mixture of the general and the particular, it is difficult to know exactly what the prophet understood. He may have been reaching for the lofty concept of one God and the unity of the human family as expressed in the book of Jonah. He may have been claiming that the nations recognized the sovereignty of Yahweh. Or perhaps the prophet was only contrasting the honor accorded Yahweh in other places with the insulting neglect in evidence in Jerusalem (Smith, *ICC*, 30ff.).

The attitude priests display toward Yahweh and the temple services will not go unpunished. Beginning with 2:1 God's judgment is pronounced. Blessings will be turned into cursings. In fact this has already been done. The adverse conditions now being experienced by the people come as a result of God's judgment (cf. Dt. 28:1ff.). Blessings and curses are direct and immediate and are physical consequences of God's pleasure or displeasure with his people. As Dentan expresses it, the curse is a "missile which can be sent out and will damage the thing which it strikes" (p. 1130). For a more detailed treatment of the meaning of blessings and curses see Pedersen, 182ff.; 437ff.

Yahweh's rebuke of the priests is of such great consequence that they are in danger of suffering public shame (2:3). Furthermore, their posterity may be cut off from the priesthood. The purpose of the **admonition** is to preserve the **covenant** made with Levi (2:4; cf. Nu 3:45; 18:21–24; Dt 33:8–11). Malachi seems to have the Deuteronomic description of the Levitical duties in mind rather than those found in Numbers (see above reference), since stress is laid upon the instructional obligations of the priesthood (v.7). The priests' failure to fulfill these duties has already brought shame and humiliation upon themselves.

IV. THE SIN OF DIVORCE (2:10–16)

The Hebrew text of this portion of Malachi is difficult. NIV has made a plausible and understandable translation. Even though the text is problematic, this section remains the most outspoken condemnation of divorce to be found in the OT. It comes at the point in the prophet's argument where he turns from his castigation of the priests to condemn the people for their wickedness. He does so in the context of dealing with the question raised by the people as to why Yahweh pays no attention to their acts of worship (vv.13–14).

Some would see in the question **Have we not all one Father? Did not one God create us?** (v.10) an explicit affirmation of the oneness of humankind. But the context clearly limits the statement to the Jewish people. They are inextricably bound together by the covenant God established with their ancestors, a covenant they habitually violate. Not only have they been derelict in the way they have slighted the services of the temple, but now the prophet points out that which is even more vile. They have **desecrated** the sanctuary where God has placed His name by **marrying the daughter of a foreign god** (v.11). Thereby they have profaned that which was holy.

In 2:13ff. the prophet likens the Jews' unfaithfulness to their spouses and the breakup of their marriages to the nation's forsaking God, their husband (see Hosea).

V. THE DAY OF JUDGMENT (2:17–3:5)

The problem of vindicating divine justice is addressed. How can God be just and loving in the presence of so much evil? The people think that the Lord favors those who do evil. How, therefore, can he be considered to be just (2:17)?

The prophet answers with an affirmation that God is not unmindful of the circumstances facing his people. He has a messenger who will come. (Is this the origin of the name for the prophet?) The Lord will appear in his temple. The people will get their desire. But will they be able to **endure the day of his coming** (3:2)? The purpose of the Day of Judgment is to purge and refine in order that the worship of Yahweh in Jerusalem will be restored to its former purity (vv.2–3). Social and moral evils perpetrated against the innocent will be rectified. This moral judgment coming within the events of their history is a part of the revelation God has graciously given to his people (Eichrodt, 382). God is shown as more than protector of the rights and privileges of his people. In the context of judgment and revelation, the prophet confronts Israel with the fact of the moral character of Yahweh (Eichrodt, 382).

VI. ON ROBBING GOD (3:6–12)

This pericope begins with the affirmation that God is unchanging in his loving care of Israel. God's steadfast love (cf. Hos 2:19–20 RSV) is the expression of his fidelity to the covenant made with his people. He expects the same kind of devoted loyalty from Israel. Instead they have been consistent in their stubborn turning away from Yahweh's decrees. Nothing can rectify such waywardness except returning to God. There is in this contrast of consistencies the graphic picture of the primary meaning of sin and repentance. Sin is departure from God. Repentance is returning to him.

The people's inquiry as to how they are to return—a question indicating that they are insensitive to the fact of their departure—gives the prophet an opportunity to be specific. They have actually robbed, or cheated, God of that which is due him. **Tithes and offerings** have been withheld on a nationwide scale (cf. Ne 13:10–13). This is the cause of their poverty (v.9). The antidote for the "curse" upon them is to be faithful in the gifts required by the law (Lev 27:30; Nu 18:21–24; Dt 12:6, 7, 11–14). Their prosperity, if they are faithful in their obligations to God, will become known throughout the world, giving them a reputation of living in a **delightful land** (v.12).

The emphasis on material blessings should not be construed to mean that the prophet was concerned only with external matters either in worship or in the blessings of God, although the time of the prophet may well mark the point in history where such an emphasis began to be made. The Deuteronomic theory linking righteousness with blessings and sin with curses was deeply embedded in the theology of this day. Malachi may well have realized that material prosperity does not always accompany right conduct, but he was sure that the total well-being of Israel was dependent on their faithfulness to God in all of their relationships. The law of the Sabbath is expanded into the need to keep every day holy. In the NT the priesthood is expanded from one tribe, the Levites, to include all of God's people (cf. 1Pe 2:5, 9). The concept of the tithe is enlarged to include faithful stewardship of all resources. Everything belongs to God (Verhoef, 311).

VII. TRIUMPH OF RIGHTEOUSNESS (3:13–4:6)

Malachi is not finished with identifying specific sins of the people. He returns to the theme of their inattention to the proper worship of and reverence for God (cf. 2:1ff.) and to charges that they have actually gone so far as to say **harsh things against** the Lord (v.13). The word translated as **harsh** is in the intensive mood indicating the severity of the charge.

Again the people question the truth of the prophet's word by asking what they have said to bring about such condemnation (v.13). Four things are enumerated in reply. They have said that it does not pay to serve God; repentance gets us nowhere; it is the evildoer not the righteous who prosper; even those who insolently challenge God's demands escape punishment (vv.14–15).

The prophet, however, recognizes that a faithful remnant remains. The remnant will be God's **treasured possession** to be spared in the coming judgment. No matter how it may appear at times there is a **distinction between the righteous and the wicked** (vv.16–18).

Judgment will be fierce and all-consuming. None of the evildoers will

escape (4:1; cf. 3:5). The Day of Judgment is a consistent tradition among the Prophets, covering a period from about 740 B.C. and now reiterated by Malachi near 450 B.C. Judgment is not to be construed as raw, vindictive retaliation for wickedness, but as an inevitable consequence of a just God upholding moral law. But judgment includes also a promise of hope and protection for the faithful in that glory. The Day of the Lord will be a day of purification. The evildoer will be consumed like a fire burning stubble. The faithful will be preserved and will survive that day. Their righteousness will show forth as a blazing sun (Verhoef, 328). The early Christians saw the **sun of righteousness . . . with healing in its wings** (v.2; cf. KJV) as a clear reference to the Messiah. The reference to **Elijah** as the forerunner of that day (vv.5–6) was further proof of the messianic intent. This view was intensified by Jesus' reference to John the Baptist in this connection (Mt 11:14; 17:10ff.; Lk 1:17; 9:18–19).

In the Hebrew Bible 4:1–6 is a part of ch. 3. These verses become 3:19–24. Many scholars consider vv.4–6 as an editorial addition to Malachi that serves as a conclusion to the Minor Prophets. It is true that these twelve books were considered as one in the Hebrew tradition—it was the Book of the Twelve. Furthermore, the scroll of the Twelve was the concluding scroll of the Latter Prophets, i.e., Isaiah, Jeremiah, Ezekiel, and the Book of the Twelve. A final remonstrance is given to obey the law of Moses, along with a promise to send back Elijah from the heavens to which he was miraculously transported (2Ki 2:11). This event will mark the coming of the Day of the Lord. Elijah's mission will be to restore concord between children and their parents, thus averting the sending of a curse upon the earth. The word for curse, *cherem*, means to give irrevocably things or persons to the Lord (cf. Jos 7:1, 11–13, 15 where the word is translated "devoted").

Malachi is the bridge between the religion of the prophetic movement and later Judaism. Strong emphasis is laid upon the active involvement of Yahweh in the history of his people and upon the necessity of building a cohesive community that is responsive to the will of God (see further in Napier, 265).

BIBLIOGRAPHY

Baab, Otto J. *The Theology of the Old Testament*. New York: Abingdon, 1949.

Bentzen, Aage. *Introduction to the Old Testament*. Copenhagen: G.E.C. Gad, 1958.

Bewer, Julius, *The Literature of the Old Testament*. 3d ed. New York: Columbia University Press, 1962.

————. *The Prophets*. New York: Harper, 1955.

Childs, Brevard S. *Introduction to the Old Testament Scripture*. Philadelphia: Fortress, 1982.

Crenshaw, James L. *Story and Faith, A Guide to the Old Testament*. New York: Macmillan, 1986.

Dentan, Robert C. "Malachi." IB. Vol. 6. New York: Abingdon, 1956.

Eban, Abba. *My People, the Story of the Jews*. New York: Behrman, 1968.

Eichrodt, Walther. *Theology of the Old Testament*. Vol. 1. Translated by J. R. Baker. Philadelphia: Westminster, 1961.

Eissfeldt, Otto. *The Old Testament, an Introduction*. Translated by Peter R. Ackroyd. New York: Harper, 1965.

Gottwald, Norman K. *The Hebrew Bible: A Socio-Literary Introduction*. Philadelphia: Fortress, 1985.

Jacob, Edmond. *Theology of the Old Testament*. New York: Harper, 1958.

Kohler, Ludwig. *Old Testament Theology*. Translated by A. S. Todd. Philadelphia: Westminster, 1957.

La Sor, William Sanford, et. al. *Old Testament Survey*. Grand Rapids: Eerdmans, 1982.

Margolis, Max L. *The Hebrew Scriptures in the Making*. Philadelphia: Jewish Publishing Society, 1943.

Napier, B. Davie. *Song of the Vineyard*. Rev. ed. Philadelphia: Fortress, 1981.

Otwell, John H. *And Sarah Laughed*. Philadelphia: Westminster, 1977.

Pedersen, Johs. *Israel, Its Life and Culture*. Vols. 1–2. London: Oxford University Press, 1926.

Pfeiffer, Robert H. *Introduction to the Old Testament*. New York: Harper, 1948.

Smith, J. M. P. "Malachi." ICC. Edinburgh: T. & T. Clark, 1962.

————. *The Prophets and Their Times*. Chicago: University of Chicago Press, 1941.

Snaith, Norman H. *The Distinctive Ideas of the Old Testament*. New York: Schocken, 1964.

Verhoef, Pieter A. *The Books of Haggai and Malachi*. NIC. Grand Rapids: Eerdmans, 1987.

von Rad, Gerhard. *Old Testament Theology*. 2 vols. Translated by D. M. G. Stalker. New York: Harper, 1962.

Vriezen, Th. C. *An Outline of Old Testament Theology*. Newton, Mass.: Bransford, 1970.

PART III

The New Testament

MATTHEW
David R. Bauer

INTRODUCTION

Ernest Renan described the gospel of Matthew as "the most important book in the world." And as far as the church is concerned, Renan's description is accurate. No other book in the NT has exerted more influence upon the life and thought of the church throughout its history than has this gospel.

We turn our attention now to an examination of the origins, structure, and theology of this important book.

I. THE ORIGINS OF THE GOSPEL

Although this gospel is anonymous, it traditionally has been ascribed to the apostle Matthew. This ascription stems almost entirely from a statement made by Papias, a Syrian Christian who wrote around A.D. 125: "Matthew composed the Logia in the Hebrew tongue, and everyone translated (or interpreted) them as he was able." Although later church fathers took this declaration to refer to the gospel of Matthew, the meaning of the statement from Papias is not clear. Many modern scholars believe that either Papias was in error or was not speaking of this gospel at all.

Those who object to Matthean authorship cite the following considerations. First, the most natural meaning of Logia in the statement from Papias is "sayings," not "book" or "narrative." Second, in contrast to Papias's statement, the language and style of the gospel indicate it was written in Greek and not a translation from a Hebrew (Aramaic) original. Third, many contemporary scholars, including some conservative ones (e.g., Martin, 139–60; Bruce, 3–4), believe that the author of this gospel used the gospel of Mark as his primary source. Yet it seems strange that an apostle would depend on a document written by a nonapostle. Fourth, the gospel of Matthew contains little in the way of personal remembrances and narrative detail that one would expect from an eyewitness. Indeed, this gospel contains less narrative detail than does the gospel of Mark.

Although these considerations do not rule out the possibility of Matthean authorship, they do raise questions concerning it. Discussions regarding the identity of the writer can be found in Guthrie (pp. 33–44), Kümmel (pp. 120–21), and Martin (pp. 238–40).

Who, then, wrote the gospel of Matthew? Conservative scholars are divided on this issue. It seems best to conclude that Matthean authorship is possible but improbable. Evidence for Matthean authorship is thin, and there are indications within the gospel that point in the opposite direction. Thus the exact identity of the writer remains a mystery. (For the sake of convenience, however, we will refer to the evangelist as "Matthew.") Fortunately, our inability to identify with certainty the person of the writer in no way diminishes the authority of this book or our capacity to understand its message.

The author of this gospel appears to have been a Jewish Christian. His Christology bears a distinctive Jewish coloration far beyond that found in the other gospels: Jesus is "the son of Abraham" (1:1, 17), "Son of David" (1:1, 6; 15:22), "king of the Jews" (2:1–12; 27:11, 29), "Immanuel" (1:23), and the culmination and fulfillment of the whole history of Israel beginning with Abraham (1:1–17). The writer repeatedly interrupts the narrative to indicate how specific events in the life of Jesus fulfill OT Scripture (1:22–23; 4:14–16; 12:17–21). Moreover, the evangelist underscores expressions that were especially at home in Judaism, such as "righteousness," "the kingdom of heaven" instead of "the kingdom of God" (see commentary on 4:17), and "your heavenly Father."

This gospel apparently was addressed to a church composed of both Jews and Gentiles. The many Jewish terms and motifs point to a large Jewish element in the congregation. On the other hand, constant allusions to the inclusion of the Gentiles into the community of God (8:5–13; 21:43) and interest in the Gentile mission (4:14–16; 22:9; 28:18–20) suggest that many in the church had come to Christ through that mission.

The church to which this gospel is addressed was experiencing persecution from both Jews (10:16–29; 23:34–36) and Gentiles (10:18, 22; 24:9). In addition, it was forced to deal with internal strife and divisions caused by false prophets (7:15–23; 24:11) and others who argued that ethical conduct was of no concern to Christians ("antinomianism," 5:17–20; 28:20). Nonetheless, this church seems to have been a "missionary" church, engaged in evangelistic efforts toward its Jewish and Gentile neighbors (ch. 10; 24:14; 28:18–20). Unfortunately, these evangelistic efforts were resulting in general rejection and persecution (10:16–39; 23:34–36). Most scholars believe that all these factors point to a church located in Syrian Antioch between A.D. 75 and 85.

What was the purpose behind the writing of this gospel? Some scholars argue that Matthew presents Jesus as a new Moses who presents a new law to combat the lawlessness that was rampant in Matthew's church. Others suggest that the gospel was written as a catechism to provide instruction in Christian beliefs and lifestyle to new converts. Some argue that this book was designed as a manual to help church leaders carry on instruction and administration within the church. Still others contend that

Matthew wished to provide a theological foundation for the mission to the Gentiles.

Certainly the gospel addresses all these issues. Yet the gospel of Matthew is primarily the story about Jesus. The primary purpose of the gospel was to present the story of Jesus in such a way as to address the problems and challenges that faced Matthew's church. And since these same problems and challenges have remained with the Christian church throughout its history, the church has returned to this gospel repeatedly for guidance and inspiration.

Discussions regarding the background of the gospel are found in Kingsbury, *Matthew*, 1–32, 96–107; and Martin, 224–43.

II. THE STRUCTURE OF THE GOSPEL

The gospel of Matthew contains three major divisions set off by the parallel statements at 4:17 and 16:21: "From that time on Jesus began. . . ." Mt 1:1–4:16 introduces the person of Jesus Messiah, Son of God; 4:17–16:20 is the proclamation of Jesus Messiah, Son of God, to Israel; and 16:21–28:20 is the passion and resurrection of Jesus Messiah, Son of God. The specific structure of each of the three major divisions is discussed in the course of the commentary.

This structure implies that Matthew is interested chiefly in Christology and that he presents Jesus primarily as Son of God: (1) the divine sonship of Jesus pervades the first major division, which introduces the person of Jesus (1:18–25; 3:17; 4:1–11); (2) each of the three major divisions climaxes in the declaration that Jesus is the Son of God (3:17; 16:16; 27:54); and (3) the book reaches its climax with Jesus addressing the post-Easter disciples in his capacity as Son of God (28:18–20). The meaning of the divine sonship of Jesus is discussed below under III. The Theology of the Gospel.

In addition to this threefold division, there are other structural features that pervade the gospel. The first of these involves the relationship between Jesus and his disciples: Matthew repeatedly *compares* the person of Jesus with Jesus' expectations for the disciples. In other words, Matthew emphasizes the similarity between Jesus, as he is presented in this gospel, and what the disciples are expected to be and do. In terms of mission, the disciples (the church) are to engage in a ministry that is modeled on the ministry of Jesus (9:35–11:1; 28:18–20). In terms of behavior, they are to lead lives that are in complete accord with the kind of life Jesus lived (e.g., 20:16–28).

By means of this comparison, Matthew communicates two important ideas. First, the ministry of the disciples (and later the church) is, in a real sense, a continuation of the ministry of the earthly Jesus, deriving its power and guidance from the ministry of Jesus as presented in this gospel. Second, the Christian life is defined by the model of Jesus so that the good life, the life that is acceptable to God, consists of Christlikeness.

A second structural feature involves the relationship between Jesus and the religious authorities. Matthew repeatedly *contrasts* Jesus and these authorities. In other words, Matthew emphasizes the differences between Jesus and his opponents.

The theological function of this contrast is twofold. For one thing, by presenting Jesus over against the religious authorities, Matthew is able to show with clarity the majesty and righteousness of Jesus. Furthermore, the religious leaders serve as a negative model for discipleship, i.e., the disciples are to be like Jesus by being *unlike* the religious authorities. Thus the religious authorities, and indeed Israel as a whole, become representatives of disobedience and judgment. Believers must do everything they can to avoid the behavior and consequent tragic end of unrepentant Israel.

Another structural feature in the gospel is climax. The narrative moves towards its climax in the Cross and Resurrection and finally in the missionary commissioning of 28:16–20.

III. THE THEOLOGY OF THE GOSPEL

As indicated above, the structure of the gospel suggests that the principal concern in this book is Christology. It is therefore appropriate to begin this examination of Matthean theology with Matthew's understanding of Jesus.

We have seen that Matthew presents Jesus primarily as Son of God. Jesus is Son of God in that he has his origin in God, having been conceived by the Holy Spirit (1:18–25). Moreover, Jesus is Son of God as the one who perfectly obeys the will of his Father (in ancient times, sonship implied obedience). Jesus submits to baptism "to fulfill all righteousness" (3:15; cf. v.17), and as he faces the cross, Jesus prays to his Father, "Not as I will, but as you will" (26:39).

Matthew presents Jesus also as Son of Abraham and Son of David. As Son of Abraham, Jesus fulfills the promise made to Abraham regarding a son in Ge 22:18 ("through your offspring all nations on earth will be blessed") and thus serves as the means whereby God's salvation is extended to all peoples throughout the earth, not just to Israelites. As Son of David, Jesus is the messianic King in the line of David who gently shepherds his people (2:6; 11:29–30), pouring out his blood for them (26:28) in order to save them from their sins (1:21).

For Matthew, therefore, Christian faith and life are rooted in the person of Jesus. Christians throughout the ages, including Wesley and his followers, have recognized the centrality of Jesus Christ. Nevertheless, there has been a tendency at certain points in the history of the Wesleyan movement to emphasize the work of the Spirit that the centrality of Christ has been set aside. The gospel of Matthew, then, draws us back to the heart of our faith, reminding us that the Spirit always points to and bears witness to the person and work of Christ (10:20; 12:28; cf. Jn 14:25–26; 16:12–15).

In addition to Christology, the author voices three other major theological concerns. Each of these concerns involves discipleship, and each of them relates to primary emphases in Wesleyan thought.

First, there is here a distinct concern for Christian ethics, i.e., a concern for questions of right and wrong in the Christian life. Matthew emphasizes, as later Wesley would also emphasize, that discipleship involves a profound commitment to obey God's will in every dimension of life. The will of God is summed up in the command to love God with all our being and to love our neighbor as ourselves (5:43–48; 7:12; 22:34–40).

Second, related to the concern for Christian ethics is the issue of divine and human cooperation in salvation. Although Matthew makes it clear that salvation stems entirely from God's gracious acts, especially the death and resurrection of Christ (1:21; 20:28; 26:28), he makes it equally clear that Christians have a part to play in maintaining their salvation. Thus Matthew warns his Christian readers that disobedience will lead to their condemnation on the Day of Judgment (7:21–23; 24:45–25:46), while they can be assured of final salvation only as they continue to do "the will of my Father in heaven" (12:50; cf. 24:13). Theologians refer to this divine and human cooperation as "synergism" (lit. "working together"), and no one has drawn out the implications of this synergism for Christian salvation more fully than Wesley.

A third theological emphasis involves the Christian mission. The concern for evangelism is evidenced by the fact that the book reaches its climax with the resurrected Christ commanding his followers to "make disciples of all nations" (28:19). Moreover, the whole of ch. 10 is given over to instructions regarding missionary activity. Matthew locates the basis for the Christian mission in the person of Jesus. Jesus is the Son of Abraham who draws all nations to his worship (1:1; cf. 2:1–12). Moreover, as one who has been given "all authority in heaven and on earth," Jesus commands his disciples to bring all persons everywhere under his sovereign rule (28:18–20). It was Matthew's desire that all Christians could say, with Wesley, "The world is my parish."

IV. OUTLINE

I. The Person of Jesus Messiah, Son of God (1:1–4:16)
    A. Origins of Jesus (1:1–2:23)
        1. Genealogy (1:1–17)
        2. Birth and infancy (1:18–2:23)
    B. Preparation of Jesus for Ministry: Baptism and Temptation (3:1–4:16)

II. The Proclamation of Jesus Messiah to Israel (4:17–16:20)
    A. General Heading (4:17)
    B. Calling of First Disciples (4:18–22)
    C. Announcement of the Kingdom Through Teaching, Preaching, and Healing (4:23–9:35)

COMMENTARY

I. THE PERSON OF JESUS MESSIAH, SON OF GOD (1:1–4:16)

This first major division provides background or setting for the book as a whole. It prepares the reader in various ways for the account of Jesus' ministry, which Matthew presents in the remainder of the gospel, principally by introducing the person of Jesus.

A. Origins of Jesus (1:1–2:23)

1:1–2:23 describes the origins of Jesus: his genealogy (1:1–17), and his birth and infancy (1:18–2:23).

1. Genealogy (1:1–17)

Matthew begins by making a three-fold claim about Jesus (v.1): Jesus is the Christ, the Son of David, and the Son of Abraham. But Matthew does not base this assertion on his own authority; he supports this threefold claim by tracing the genealogy of Jesus. This genealogy, drawn largely from the OT (see Ru 4:18–22; 1Ch 2:1–15; 3:1–24), establishes the truth of these assertions regarding Jesus.

The term **Christ** (*Christos*) is the Greek translation of the Hebrew "Messiah," meaning "anointed one." In the OT, persons whom God chose for special service were frequently anointed for their tasks. At the very outset of the gospel, then, Matthew indicates that Jesus has been uniquely anointed by God for the work that he will begin in 4:17.

In this particular context, however, the role of Jesus as Christ takes on a specific meaning, which is indicated by the very structure of the genealogy. Matthew brings the genealogy to its climax with the birth of Jesus, **who is called Christ** (vv.1–16). By means of this climactic development, Matthew shows that Jesus is Christ in the sense that God has chosen him to be the climax, or culmination, of the history of God's dealings with his people, beginning with Abraham (v.16). The whole of OT history thus finds its purpose, meaning, and significance in Jesus as Christ. This affirmation stands behind Matthew's repeated insistence that individual happenings in the life of Jesus fulfill OT prophecy (e.g., 2:5–6). In his role as Christ, Jesus gives meaning to the OT as a whole and to every event and passage found within the OT.

This passage also declares that Jesus is the **son of David** and **son of Abraham** (1:1, 6, 17). The meaning of these titles is discussed in the introduction.

2. Birth and infancy (1:18–2:23)

Immediately after the genealogy, Matthew records the birth story (1:18–25). Yet he says little about the actual birth of Jesus. The focus is rather upon the significance of Jesus' conception and birth as that significance is communicated through the testimony of the angel.

The testimony of the angel contains two major elements. First, the mission of this child is reflected in the very name Joseph is commanded to give the child: Jesus (a Greek form of the Heb. Joshua, meaning "Yahweh saves"). This Jesus will **save his people from their sins** (1:21). Second, Jesus can function as Savior of his people for two reasons: (1) he has been conceived by the Holy Spirit and is therefore infinitely superior to all other humans and unique in his relationship with God (vv.18, 20) and (2) God himself is present with his people in the person of Jesus to grant them victory in their struggle with evil (vv.22–23).

Matthew moves from the conception and birth of Jesus in 1:18–25 to events surrounding his infancy in 2:1–23. Ch. 2 contains the witness of the wise men and is bound together by two major contrasts: the contrast between Herod and Jesus and the contrast between Herod and the wise men.

The contrast between Herod and Jesus centers upon the question of kingship. Matthew introduces the theme of kingship at the outset of the chapter: The wise men ask Herod where the **king of the Jews** has been born (2:2), Jesus is indirectly identified as **a ruler** (v.6), and Matthew repeatedly refers to Herod as **the king** (vv.1, 3, 9). Matthew thus directs our attention to two types of king and two types of kingdom: the kingship of Herod versus the kingship of Jesus.

The kingship of Herod is presented

in harsh terms. His tyrannical rule is characterized by an all-consuming desire to preserve his own status and power. Herod will stop at nothing, including the murder of innocent children, to realize his self-serving goals.

The nature of Jesus' kingship, on the other hand, is defined by the word from Micah quoted in 2:6: He will be **"the shepherd of my people Israel."** He is the gentle and loving Ruler of his people, who, like a shepherd, saves his people from destruction. Specifically, Jesus reigns as King over his people by dying for them (27:11, 29, 37), thereby saving them from their sins (1:21; cf. 20:28). The contrast with Herod could not be more pronounced: Jesus gives his life for the sake of others; Herod takes the lives of others for his own sake.

This tension between the kingdom of Herod and the kingdom of Jesus points to the conflict between the kingdom of this world (i.e., the desire for power and self-rule on the part of evil persons everywhere) and the kingdom of God. The passage challenges readers to reflect upon the character of their own lives in order to determine whether the spirit and attitude of Herod (an attitude of militant self-rule) is present to any degree in their hearts. Those readers who see a bit of Herod in themselves will soon encounter a word of challenge and hope: "Repent, for the kingdom of heaven is near" (3:2; 4:17).

The second contrast in ch. 2 centers upon response to the person of Jesus. Matthew distinguishes between Herod and the wise men in terms of their responses to Jesus. The response of the wise men to Jesus is entirely appropriate, and their actions serve as a model of true discipleship. They seek Christ (v.2), and when they have found him they rejoice (v.10), worship (vv.2,

11a), and offer him gifts that befit a king (v.11b; cf. Pss 45:7–9; 72:15). The response of Herod is completely different. He is disturbed at the news of the wise men (v.3), then engages in deception (v.7), lying (v.8), and murder (v.16) in order to destroy Jesus. The wise men worship Jesus while Herod seeks to kill him. Here as elsewhere in Matthew there is no middle ground: those who will not worship Jesus as the royal Messiah necessarily reject him and seek his destruction.

B. Preparation of Jesus for Ministry: Baptism and Temptation (3:1–4:16)

A gap of several years exists between the end of ch. 2 and the ministry of John in ch. 3. Apparently it did not contribute to Matthew's purpose in writing to include accounts describing the boyhood and adolescence of Jesus. But Matthew is very much interested in the baptism of Jesus, which contains the witness of John (3:1–12) and the witness of God (vv.13–17; 4:1–11).

John declares that Jesus is **the coming one** (*ho erchomenos*, a term that is essentially equivalent to "Christ"; cf. 11:2–3), whose power goes far beyond anything John could boast and who is infinitely majestic and glorious. John is unworthy even to be his slave (3:11). In this way John points to the incomparable greatness of Jesus and suggests that Jesus is much more than a prophet. In fact, to think of Jesus as a prophet in the line of the OT prophets is to miss entirely the true meaning and significance of Jesus (cf. 16:13–17). This is not business as usual; in Jesus God is doing something utterly new and extraordinary.

John proclaims that this coming one brings with him blessing and judgment. All persons will experience his baptism. For some it will be "baptism of the

Spirit," a pouring out of the Spirit that will enable the recipients to participate fully in the community of God that Jesus, as the Messiah, establishes. For others it will be "baptism of fire," the eternal punishment that Jesus, as Judge, will dispense to those who reject God and the Christ whom he has sent (3:11b–12).

In light of this reality, what ought persons to do? John answers, **"Repent"** (3:2). It is only through repentance that one may escape the judgment of this mighty Christ and experience the blessings that he is able to give.

God gives his own testimony to Jesus in 3:17. Here the heavenly voice declares, **"This is my Son, whom I love; with him I am well pleased."** Jesus is the Son of God in the sense that he has his origin in God, having been conceived by the Holy Spirit (1:18–25). By virtue of this divine conception, Jesus experiences an intimacy and unity with God that is absolutely unique (cf. 11:25–30).

Moreover, the immediate context indicates that Jesus is the Son of God as one who perfectly obeys the will of his Father. In 3:15 Jesus submits to baptism, not because he has sin to confess, but **to fulfill all righteousness.** The obedience of Jesus as Son of God is especially prominent in the temptation story, which follows immediately. There Jesus is tempted precisely in his role as Son of God (4:3, 6), and as Son of God he refuses to yield to the temptations of the Devil (4:1–11).

One additional comment should be made regarding 3:1–4:11. Jesus' baptism and temptation serve to equip him for his ministry. The descent of the Spirit upon Jesus in 3:16 indicates that the entire ministry of Jesus is an expression of the power of the Spirit. Indeed, the work of the Spirit in the life and ministry of Jesus is manifested already in the temptation. It is through the might of the Spirit that Jesus rejects Satan's urgings that he fulfill his messianic calling by the performance of great, spectacular signs rather than through God's ordained path of suffering and death (see 16:21–23; 27:32–54). Hence, after his baptism and temptation Jesus is ready to position himself for messianic ministry in Galilee (4:12–16).

II. THE PROCLAMATION OF JESUS MESSIAH TO ISRAEL (4:17–16:20)

4:17 is a general heading to the second major division of the gospel. Matthew expands 4:17 by describing Jesus' preaching of the kingdom to Israel (4:18–11:1) and the dual responses to this proclamation within Israel (11:1–16:20): rejection on the part of Israel as a whole (11:1–12:50; also 13:10–17; 16:13–14) but acceptance on the part of the twelve disciples (11:25–30; 13:10–17; 16:15–20).

A. General Heading (4:17)

The proclamation of Jesus contains two major and interrelated elements. The first is the announcement that the kingdom of heaven is near. The kingdom of heaven is a central theme in this gospel; therefore this phrase deserves special comment.

In Matthew's gospel, **"the kingdom of heaven"** and "the kingdom of God" are used interchangeably. They mean the same thing. The kingdom of God is a dynamic concept referring to the active reign of God. In fact, it is better translated "the rule of God."

This concept stems primarily from the Jewish understanding of the two ages. The Jews divided all of history into two periods: (1) the present evil age, under the immediate control of Satan; and (2) the age to come, when

God will break the power of evil and usher in his kingdom through his Messiah. Mt 4:17 therefore declares that the long-awaited rule of God has now drawn near (to the point of having already arrived; cf. 12:28) in the person of Jesus.

The second major element in 4:17 is the call to repentance. It is not enough to hear that the kingdom of God has arrived; persons also must respond to this message. And the only appropriate response is repentance. The term literally means "changing of the mind" (*metanoeo*), and in this context it involves orienting all of life, both thinking and behavior, around one ultimate reality: God now rules in the person of his Son, Jesus.

B. Calling of First Disciples (4:18–22)

The first specific act of ministry that Jesus performs is the calling of two sets of brothers to discipleship. This passage provides the background for 4:23–11:1 and indicates that the issue of discipleship lies behind all that is reported in these chapters.

C. Announcement of the Kingdom Through Teaching, Preaching, and Healing (4:23–9:35)

Mt 4:23 and 9:35 are practically identical, and together they bracket the Sermon on the Mount (5:1–7:29) and the account of ten miracles that Jesus performs around the Sea of Galilee (8:1–9:35). Both of these units focus on the power of Jesus' word. The Sermon on the Mount demonstrates the authority of the teaching word of Jesus (see 7:28–29). The ten miracles point to the supremacy of Jesus' word over natural and supernatural powers, especially sickness and death; Jesus performs most of these miracles by simply speaking a word.

1. The Sermon on the Mount (5:1–7:28)

The reference to the teaching of Jesus in 4:23 and 9:35 is spelled out in the Sermon on the Mount. This body of teaching, standing at the beginning of the ministry of Jesus, sets forth the nature of the kingdom of God and the character of life within the kingdom.

a. Realities of the kingdom (5:3–12)

The eight statements at the beginning of the sermon are called "beatitudes." This is an apt designation, for the word comes from the Latin, meaning "blessedness." The kingdom is primarily characterized by blessedness (i.e., profound joy and self-fulfillment).

Each beatitude contains a statement of blessedness, followed by the reason for this blessedness in terms of the action of God. In other words, Christians experience joy and self-fulfillment as they contemplate what God is now doing and what he will do when he fully establishes his kingdom at the second coming of Christ.

The **poor in spirit** (5:3) are those who recognize their moral and spiritual poverty before the holy God and hence cast themselves entirely upon his mercy and grace. Such persons are blessed because they experience the rule of God in their own lives now (cf. 4:17; 12:28) and are assured of participating in the future kingdom God will establish at the end of history (cf. 25:31–46).

Those who mourn (5:4) realize the awfulness of their past sins and are deeply sorry for them. They know there is no relief from their grief outside of God. Consequently, they place their hope in God. He forgives their sins, erases their guilt, and assures them of vindication at the Final Judgment (cf. 3:11–12; 26:28).

Jesus continues the theme of dependence on God in the next beatitude, which has to do with **the meek** (5:5; cf. Ps 37:11). Meekness involves the rejection of all forms of worldly power, such as violence, manipulation, or cunning, to achieve one's ends. It may seem that those who employ such devices have their way on the earth. But the person who views life from God's perspective knows that in the end the heavenly Father will give the earth to those who submit humbly to his methods and rule.

The fourth beatitude describes **those who hunger and thirst for righteousness,** i.e., those who experience a craving for the total elimination of evil and oppression from the earth. These persons promote justice and the liberation of all the exploited. Wesley reflected the spirit of this beatitude when he declared, "There is no holiness without social holiness." Such persons are blessed because they know that God has committed himself to the ultimate reign of righteousness on the earth.

Jesus declares that **the merciful** are also blessed (5:7). The gospel of Matthew indicates elsewhere that only those who forgive wrongdoers freely will experience forgiveness and mercy from God at the Last Judgment (6:14; 18:21–35).

The pure in heart are those who are completely undivided in their loyalty toward God and his will (5:8; cf. Ps 24:4). No alloy will prevent them from seeing God, i.e., enjoying intimate fellowship with him, when they come into his presence on the Last Day (cf. 6:22–23).

The reference to **the peacemakers** involves more than simply avoiding conflict or even attempting to reconcile warring parties (5:9). It stems from the OT understanding of peace (*shalom*) as comprehensive wholeness and well-being. Those who pursue this kind of peace do all they can to promote the welfare of others (cf. 5:38–48). Since God actively desires wholeness for all persons, he gladly will claim as his own sons those who share in this enterprise.

Jesus recognizes that one who lives according to the principles set forth in 5:3–9 will encounter opposition from those outside the kingdom. He therefore closes the beatitudes with an assurance of blessing for **those who are persecuted because of righteousness** (vv.10–12). Such persons should consider themselves fortunate, since (1) hostility from the enemies of God demonstrates to disciples that they are on God's side and will receive reward from God on the Last Day; and (2) disciples who are persecuted share in the grand fellowship of the prophets, who experienced God's peace through persecution and finally were vindicated by God.

b. Responsibilities of the kingdom (5:13–16)

With blessings go responsibilities. Those in the kingdom have a responsibility to function as salt and light to the world. The purpose of discipleship is to bring stability, wholeness, and the knowledge of God to all the earth through the performance of good works. Those who reject this responsibility and cease to fulfill this purpose in their lives are by definition no longer true disciples and therefore will be cast out by God.

c. Requirements of the kingdom: Righteousness (5:17–48)

Jesus gives specific content to the meaning of **"good deeds"** (5:16) throughout 5:17–7:12. He begins at the most fundamental point: good works as the fulfilling of the will of God as God's will is reflected in the law.

This passage contains two sections: general declarations (5:17–20) followed by examples from specific OT commandments (vv.21–48). Jesus makes two points in 5:17–20. First, far from "abolishing" the law, Jesus has come to **fulfill** the law. He has come to fill the commandments up with meaning by revealing the will of God that stands behind the letter of the OT commandments. Second, disciples must assume a righteousness that **surpasses that of the Pharisees and the teachers of the law.** Such a surpassing righteousness is necessary for participation in the kingdom.

Jesus spells out the character of this surpassing righteousness in the six examples he gives in 5:21–48. In each case Jesus contrasts the righteousness of the scribes and Pharisees (who understood the letter of the OT commandment as a mechanical legal requirement) with the exceeding righteousness that he demands. Jesus shows that God requires obedience from the heart and especially an obedience that stems from (1) recognition of the holiness of God (vv.33–37) and (2) love toward all persons.

The principle of love stands behind all of Jesus' statements in 5:21–48. Hence the love command forms the climax to this segment (vv.43–48). The entire law is summed up in the command to love (cf. 22:37–40).

It is within this context that Jesus speaks of perfection (5:48). Disciples must be perfect (complete, entire) in their love. This means that they are to love not only those who love them, but also those who hate them and persecute them. When disciples do this, they share the perfection of God's love; for God is perfect in that he actively shows love toward all persons, doing good to both the righteous and the wicked (v.45).

This is the Christian perfection of which Wesley spoke, a perfection of love. Wesley was right when he declared that, humanly speaking, such perfection is impossible. But Wesley was also in line with the thinking of this gospel when he argued that nothing is impossible with God and that God graciously gives to his people the power to fulfill this command (cf. 1:21–23; 5:17–20).

d. Requirements of the kingdom: Piety (6:1–18)

Jesus now turns his attention to the implications of the kingdom of God for piety. The passage begins with a general warning regarding practicing piety with an eye toward human recognition and approval (v.1). Jesus then expands upon this warning by discussing three forms of piety that were especially prominent in Judaism: almsgiving (vv.2–4), prayer (vv.5–15), and fasting (vv.16–18).

The structure of these three passages is strikingly uniform. Each begins with the negative admonition, **"Do not look somber as the hypocrites do,"** who perform acts of piety in order to receive praise from humans. Jesus gives the reason for this admonition: Those who practice piety for the praise of humans can expect no reward from the heavenly Father. Jesus then contrasts the negative admonition with a positive command: Disciples should be careful to perform their pious acts in private, for only in so doing can they be sure that God will see and reward.

By repeating the same elements in all three examples, Jesus emphasizes the following points. First, although disciples are to perform acts of piety, they should realize that such acts are not automatically pleasing to God. The value of such acts is linked to motive. Second, the only appropriate motivation is the desire to win the approval of God and to glorify him. These acts must be done with God, rather than humans, in mind. To practice acts of piety with the intention of receiving human praise necessarily involves hypocrisy or contradiction between outward appearance and inner motive. Third, the desire to receive praise from humans will result in loss of reward from God. Fourth, because the temptation to perform pious acts for human applause is so great, disciples must do all they can to avoid giving occasion to such temptation.

Jesus' discussion about prayer in 6:7–15 is different in both form and content from the surrounding material. Here Jesus warns against the practice of the Gentiles (v.7) rather than the practice of hypocrites. This passage has not so much to do with the motive of prayer as with the attitude of prayer.

Effective prayer requires faith in God (6:7–8) as well as forgiveness of others (vv.14–15). Persons who refuse to forgive others cannot expect God to heed their pleas for forgiveness. The Lord's Prayer (vv.9–13) models the two characteristics of effective prayer just mentioned. It also indicates that prayer should be characterized by recognition of the holiness of God, profound desire to see the will of God accomplished, dependence on God for all things, and simplicity.

e. Requirements of the kingdom: Possessions (6:19–34)

Participation in the kingdom is dependent not only on true righteousness and a piety that seeks God's glory, but also on a proper attitude toward material things. Jesus addresses two problems in this passage: wealth (vv.19–24) and worry over basic needs (vv.25–34).

In 6:19–24 Jesus demands that his disciples give their full allegiance and devotion to God (**"Store up for yourselves treasures in heaven"**) rather than to the accumulation of wealth (**treasures on earth**). He gives three reasons for this admonition: (1) material things offer no security, since they are themselves susceptible to destruction (v.20); (2) the quality of personal character (**the heart**) is determined by the object of commitment and devotion (v.21); (3) the attempt to divide allegiance between God and money is doomed to failure; it can lead only to self-deception (vv.22–23) and the despising of God (v.24).

Jesus goes on to indicate that worry is just as destructive to the spiritual life as is greed. Disciples must not worry about the basic needs of life (vv.25, 31–32), for such worry stems from **little faith** (v.30). Rather, disciples should recognize that the heavenly Father is able and willing to provide for all of their needs (vv.25b–30). Indeed, as disciples invest themselves in the work of God in the world, they will be freed from all anxiety regarding the future (vv.33–34).

f. Requirements of the kingdom: Judging of persons (7:1–12)

The life of Christian discipleship, characterized as it is by a surpassing righteousness (5:20), could easily lead to an attitude of moral and spiritual superiority, to a judgmental attitude toward others. Jesus therefore ends his discussion of requirements of the kingdom by warning against such a tendency (7:1–5; cf. 6:14–15). Mt 7:5 qualifies the prohibition regarding judging: Although disciples must not assume a condemnatory spirit toward others, they should employ discrimination in their ministries (cf. 10:11–15). In the final analysis, however, the principle of active love, which God himself models, must be determinative in all interpersonal relationships (7:7–12).

g. Warnings regarding the kingdom (7:13–27)

Jesus concludes the Sermon on the Mount with graphic warnings to his hearers. Failure to take seriously what he has said in the sermon will result in disastrous consequences. Jesus warns of three specific dangers: (1) the tendency not to take the rigorous demands of discipleship seriously (vv.13–14); (2) the possibility of being led astray by **false prophets** who teach, both by word and example, that one can be a disciple while persisting in sin (vv.15–23); and (3) the notion that it is enough simply to hear the teaching of Jesus, without putting his teaching into practice (vv.24–27). Mt 7:28–29 indicates the authority of the teaching word of Jesus and prepares for the next section of the gospel, which describes the authority of the healing word of Jesus (chs. 8–9).

2. Ten mighty acts (8:1–9:35)

Jesus not only teaches with authority, he also acts with authority. These ten miracles are divided into three groups separated by two passages that deal with discipleship (8:18–22; 9:9–17).

The first block of miracles consists of three healings: the leper, the centurion's servant, and Peter's mother-in-law. These miracles emphasize the *mission* of Jesus: to relieve suffering and to bring wholeness (cf. 8:17; note also that all the miracles in this block are healings). These miracles also indicate that Jesus directs his ministry toward those who were held in low esteem by Jewish culture: the leper (vv.1–4), the Gentile (vv.5–13), and a woman (vv.14–15). Jesus associates with the rejected and downtrodden in order to bring healing to them.

Mt 8:18–22 emphasizes the cost of discipleship. Because Jesus acts with complete authority, he can expect total commitment from those who would be his disciples.

The miracles in 8:23–9:8 point to the *comprehensive nature of Jesus' authority*: He has power over nature (vv.23–27), demons (vv.28–34), and disease (9:1–8). The power manifested in these miracles should cause persons to realize that Jesus also has authority to forgive sins, and to trust him for forgiveness (vv.6–8).

Mt 9:9–17 speaks of the newness of the kingdom. The miracles in this chapter indicate that Jesus acts with power and authority never seen before (v.33); they demonstrate that God is doing something new in Jesus. Therefore, persons must adjust their understanding of reality and of God's work in the world to the new age of the kingdom that God is bringing in through Jesus.

The last block of miracles focuses on the power of Jesus to *deliver* (9:18–34). In the face of human weakness and hopelessness, Jesus shows that he is able to save, even from the bondage of death.

D. Announcement of the Kingdom Through the Ministry of the Disciples (9:35–11:1)

In this segment Jesus sends his disciples out on a mission of preaching and healing that is modeled on his own. In this way the disciples continue the work that Jesus began. Although ch. 10 is addressed to the twelve disciples, this passage points ahead to the mission of the church in every age. It thus has relevance for contemporary believers as they minister in the name of Christ.

The motivation for Jesus' sending

out of the Twelve is found in 9:35–38: his compassion for the needy crowds. Jesus has compassion for them because of their miserable condition. Like sheep without the protection of a shepherd, they are **harassed** (i.e., tormented) and **helpless** (i.e., cast down, as wounded or dead, and thus unable to help themselves) in the face of evil and destructive forces (10:7–8; 11:2–6). This is a graphic description of all those who are outside of Christ. This perspective on the crowds causes a deep sense of pity to arise within Jesus, a pity so strong that it leads to the decisive action of sending out his disciples on a mission to free these persons from the bondage of evil (10:1–8).

The first part of the discourse describes the *acts* of ministry, the manner in which the disciples are to minister (10:5–15). They are to minister boldly, as persons who have been sent out under the authority of Jesus (v.5; cf. v.1). They are to minister aggressively, not content to remain where they are, but to engage in evangelistic travels (vv.5–6). They must depend entirely on God for all their needs, knowing that God is able and willing to give them all they need as they labor for him (vv.8b–10). Because time is short and many will be unreceptive to the Gospel, disciples must concentrate their ministries where the likelihood of acceptance is greatest (vv.11–15; cf. v.23).

Having discussed acts of ministry, Jesus proceeds to describe *contrasting responses* to the ministry of the disciples. The response will be largely negative (10:16–39), but some will respond positively (vv.40–42).

Negative reaction to the disciples' message will involve persecution of the disciples themselves. In the face of violent persecution, disciples must do all they can to remain faithful to their calling as emissaries of Christ. They must **stand firm to the end**, knowing that only those who thus remain faithful will escape judgment on the Last Day (10:22).

Jesus concludes this discourse with a statement about those who accept the message of the disciples. Not everyone rejects and persecutes. Some respond positively, and those who do so will receive great reward from the Father (10:40–42). This consideration encourages the disciples as they minister in the face of opposition and makes all their efforts and sufferings worthwhile.

E. Dual Responses to Jesus' Proclamation of the Kingdom (11:2–12:50)

Mt 11–12 provides an overview of the various responses to the proclamation of Jesus. In these chapters we see for the first time that Israel as a whole is rejecting Jesus.

This rejection characterizes the people (11:7–24), but especially the religious authorities (12:1–45). These authorities are on the attack in ch. 12. Their sin has blinded them to the true significance of Jesus (12:6, 41–42; cf. vv.33–38): therefore they believe wrongly that Jesus' miracles are due to collaboration with the Devil (12:24–32). Only one group within Israel, the disciples, accepts Jesus' announcement of the kingdom (11:25–30; 12:46–50).

These chapters explore the meaning of this general rejection and describe the origins, character, and results of unbelief. Here readers are warned not to fall into the trap of rejection and unbelief. Rather, they are encouraged to hear and understand accurately (11:15), and to **come** to Jesus, who alone is able to grant them the rest that they desperately seek (vv.28–30).

The key passage within this section is 11:25–30. Here Jesus gives one reason for the rejection of Jesus by Israel: It is due to the will of God, who has **hidden** his revelation from the greatest part of Israel (**the wise and learned**), but has granted it to the disciples (**little children**). Jesus is not suggesting that God has chosen certain individuals for salvation and others for condemnation. Rather, God has decided that those who choose to place their trust in the wisdom of this world will be blinded to the reality of his kingdom, while those who reject such reliance on worldly wisdom (and depend on God) will receive understanding (vv.25–27).

Jesus ends this paragraph with an invitation to all persons to **come** to him (11:28–30). Negatively, this coming involves casting aside all vain and wearisome attempts to find **rest** (wholeness) on the basis of human striving. Positively, it means assuming the **yoke** (teaching of the cross) of Jesus, which alone provides the wholeness all seek.

F. Consequent Reactions of Jesus (13:1–16:20)

In these chapters Jesus reacts to the dual responses set forth in 11:1–12:50. In judgment for their unbelief, Jesus turns away from the crowds. But Jesus graciously reveals himself to his disciples, finally drawing from them the confession that he is the Christ (16:16).

1. Parables of the kingdom (13:1–52)

The parables in this chapter can be divided into two groups. The first group contains parables addressed to the Jewish crowds as well as to the disciples (vv.1–35). The second group contains parables addressed only to the disciples (vv.36–52). In vv.1–2 Matthew makes much of the fact that Jesus teaches the crowds; but in v.36 Jesus

leaves the crowds and goes into the house, where he teaches only his disciples. Because the crowds have not received Jesus' proclamation with faith and understanding (vv.10–17; cf. chs. 11–12), Jesus removes revelation from them. This is the judgment for failure to accept Jesus' proclamation. Herein lies a warning to all who hear the Gospel but close their ears to its truth.

The parable of the soils (vv.3b–9; cf. vv.18–23) explains the several reactions to the proclamation of the kingdom. The seed represents the **message about the kingdom** (v.19), i.e., the preaching of the gospel (cf. 4:17). Although all persons hear the same Word, they respond to the Word in various ways. Some, like the Jewish crowds, have hearts that are so hard the seed is unable even to germinate. Others begin the life of discipleship but fall away either because of suffering or concern over material things. Only a minority remain faithful to the Word, obedient to the will of the Father until the end (v.8; cf. 12:33–37).

To those on the outside this parable declares that the rejection of the Word by the greatest part of Israel (and, indeed, the greatest part of all hearers) does not mean there is anything wrong with the Word. On the contrary, the problem lies with the poor quality of the human heart-soil on which the Word falls. To the disciples this parable teaches vigilance: They must guard against the possibility of falling away because of persecution or possessions.

The parable of the weeds (vv.24–30; cf. vv.36–43) emphasizes the contrast between present coexistence of the wheat and the weeds and future separation. The wheat represents the followers of Jesus, while the weeds refer to evil persons in the world. The servants of Jesus (i.e., the church) must not attempt to exterminate wicked persons from the earth, since in so doing they may destroy those who would find their way into the kingdom. Jesus, through his angels, will separate the evil from the righteous at the end.

The parables of the mustard seed and the leaven (vv.31–33) are twin parables; they teach essentially the same thing. Although the kingdom has small and apparently insignificant beginnings, eventually it will cover the whole earth. Only those who participate in the kingdom now (in its "smallness") will experience the blessings of the end-time kingdom that Christ will establish upon the whole earth at his second coming.

The parables of the hidden treasure and the pearl (vv.44–46) are also twin parables. The kingdom of God is so supremely precious that a person should be happy to make any sacrifice necessary to obtain and maintain a place in the kingdom.

The parable of the net (vv.47–50), like the parable of the weeds, involves a contrast between present coexistence of the righteous and wicked and future separation. Here, however, the focus is not on cohabitation of the righteous and wicked in the world but in the church. Jesus declares that there are false disciples in the church, persons who will not pass muster at the Last Judgment. Therefore, all in the church should examine themselves to be sure they are true disciples, bearing the fruit of righteousness (cf. vv.9, 23, 43).

This segment comes to a climax with vv.51–52. The disciples who have accepted Jesus' proclamation and are thus able to understand the parables (cf. vv.10–17) will find that the parables are rich in meaning. As they reflect on the parables, they will constantly discover new insights regarding the kingdom.

2. Movement toward Peter's confession (13:53–16:20)

Throughout these chapters Jesus continues to meet with rejection and opposition from Israel. The stage is set at the beginning of this section when the people of Nazareth, Jesus' hometown, conclude that he is no more than the son of Joseph and thus refuse to believe in him (13:53–58).

Matthew indicates the reasons for this rejection in three passages. The opposition of Herod to John the Baptist in 14:1–12 points toward Israel's rejection of Jesus (cf. 17:12–13); in the case of both John and Jesus, the God-appointed herald of the kingdom is persecuted unto death because he boldly reveals the lawlessness of his hearers (14:4; cf. 15:12; 21:45–46). In 15:1–20 the religious authorities reject Jesus because they want nothing to do with the will of God that Jesus proclaims; they have long ago **nullified the word of God** by insisting on human tradition instead. In 16:1–4 the religious leaders ask for a sign, thus requiring that Jesus submit to their sinful expectations and demands.

In response to Israel's sinful rejection, Jesus repeatedly withdraws from them (14:13; 15:21; 16:4). Nevertheless, he graciously continues to bring wholeness to the people, healing and feeding them (14:13–21, 34–36; 15:29–39).

In contrast to Israel, the disciples follow and believe in Jesus. Jesus therefore continues to instruct his disciples (14:28–33; 15:10–20; 16:5–12), finally drawing from them the confession that he is the Christ (16:13–20).

The whole of 4:17–16:20 comes to a climax with Peter's confession in 16:13–20. The ultimate issue throughout all these chapters is the identity of Jesus. In vv.13, 15 Jesus raises explicitly the question of his identity, and two answers are given. The answer of **people** in general is that he is a prophet. Although this answer might seem positive, it is entirely inadequate. It is not enough to see Jesus as a "good teacher," or even as "a proclaimer of the way of God."

The only appropriate answer is that which Peter, speaking on behalf of all the disciples, offers: **"The Christ, the Son of the living God."** Jesus declares that he will build his church upon this confession and that all the forces of evil will be unable to stand before the mighty power of the church that is built upon such a foundation (16:17–19). Nevertheless, the disciples were not yet to declare openly that Jesus is the Christ (v.20). Although the disciples recognize that Jesus is the Messiah, they do not yet know what it means for him to be the Messiah. Therefore it is only after they have been instructed regarding the necessity of his suffering and death that Jesus commands them to make disciples (28:19).

III. THE PASSION AND RESURRECTION OF JESUS MESSIAH (16:21–28:20)

Mt 16:21 represents a general heading that is expanded throughout the third major division of the gospel. The theme of this division is the passion and resurrection of Jesus; everything within these chapters reflects that concern.

A. General Heading (16:21)

Mt 16:21 contains two major elements: (1) the journey of Jesus to Jerusalem, where he will suffer, die, and be raised; and (2) Jesus' explaining to his disciples the necessity for such a journey. The third major division thus has a two-pronged emphasis. Here Matthew describes the nature of Jesus' calling as Messiah: It is the will of God that the Messiah suffer, die, and be raised. But Matthew also draws out the implications of Jesus' passion for the disciples.

B. Movement of Jesus Toward Suffering, Death, and Resurrection (16:22–25:46)

Matthew employs two devices to tie this material to the events of the passion and resurrection of Jesus in Jerusalem (chs. 26–28). First, all the episodes within these chapters are set within the framework of the journey from Caesarea Philippi to Jerusalem (cf. 16:13, 17:22, 24; 19:1; 20:29; 21:1). Second, this material is tied to the events of chs. 26–28 by means of the repeated Passion predictions. Three times Jesus foretells the suffering, death, and resurrection that he will experience at Jerusalem (16:21; 17:22–23; 20:17–19). All the events and teachings within 16:21–25:46 must be understood in light of Jesus' willingness to undertake the journey to Jerusalem, with the cross and resurrection that awaited him there.

1. Cross and glory (16:22–17:23)

The prediction of Jesus regarding his passion causes strong and immediate objections from Peter (16:22–23). Peter has just confessed Jesus to be the Christ (v.16), but he has done so primarily on the basis of Jesus' transcendent power (cf. 14:33). He was unprepared to accept the notion that messianic glory could be achieved only through suffering.

Yet Jesus insists on this point. Indeed, not only must Jesus assume the path of suffering and death, but disciples must follow him on this road to Jerusalem (16:24). Everyone who wishes to be a disciple must **deny himself and take up his cross and follow [Jesus].**

The Transfiguration points ahead to

the resurrection glory of Jesus (17:1–8). The fact that the Transfiguration is set between two statements concerning Jesus' passion (16:21–28; 17:9–13) indicates that Jesus can reach resurrection glory only through suffering and death.

Mt 17:9–13 continues the theme of imminent suffering. Jesus compares his own death to the suffering of John the Baptist at the hands of those who **did not recognize him.** Jesus soon will be removed from his disciples (as far as his earthly ministry is concerned) by the murderous acts of an "unbelieving and perverse generation." Therefore the disciples must have faith that is strong enough to continue the ministry that Jesus initiated (vv.14–21). This section ends with the second Passion prediction (vv.22–23; cf. 16:21).

2. Cross and community (17:24–18:35)

The cross involves not only suffering, but also humility and submission to others (cf. 20:28; 21:5; 23:12). The cross of discipleship thus has implications for relationships disciples have with other persons, including those within the Christian community. Disciples must cast aside all selfish concern for personal rights and prerogatives in favor of doing that which will benefit others in the church.

Jesus presents in 17:24–27 the principle that disciples must forego personal rights so as not to cause offense to others. This passage thus sets the stage for Jesus' instructions in ch. 18.

Ch. 18 consists of a question from the disciples regarding greatness (v.1), followed by Jesus' answer to this question (vv.2–35). Jesus begins with a general answer (vv.2–4), then details specific implications of this answer for life within the community (vv.5–35).

The question in 18:1 indicates a concern for rank, status, and position. There are indications elsewhere in the gospel that such concerns played a significant role in the thinking of the disciples during this period (20:20–28; 23:1–12).

In reply, Jesus indicates that greatness in the kingdom involves childlike humility. A child was the perfect model for the kind of humility Jesus advocated, since children had virtually no rights. Even as children (because of their status) were forced to submit to others and were unable to claim any rights or prerogatives, so disciples must choose to submit to others and willingly waive any claim to personal rights. In 18:5–14 Jesus declares that this humility involves submitting to the spiritual good of others within the Christian community. Jesus continues to speak of children (**little ones**), but the meaning of this language is different in vv.5–14 than in vv.2–4. Here Jesus uses the image of a child to indicate the vulnerability of all believers. Since all believers are capable of falling away, disciples must do everything they can to avoid causing any of their fellow believers to fall away from Christ. God will judge severely those who are instrumental in the spiritual downfall of a fellow believer (18:5–9), since God desires that not one of these persons be lost (vv.10–14).

The image shifts in 18:15–35 from **child** to **brother**. Here Jesus declares that humility in the Christian community involves redemptive actions and attitudes toward the erring brother.

The first of these redemptive actions is reconciliation (18:15–20). Rather than selfishly seeking vengeance for wrongs done, disciples should pursue reconciliation with Christians who have done wrong to them. If attempts at reconciliation fail, the church has the responsibility to discipline the wrongdoers, even if such discipline involves removing an erring brother from the privileges of Christian fellowship.

The second of these actions is forgiveness (18:21–35). Rather than selfishly holding grudges and nursing ill feelings, disciples should forgive repeatedly and without measure. The parable of the unforgiving servant teaches that they are required to do so, since (1) they themselves have received infinite forgiveness from God, and (2) refusal to forgive will result in the judgment of God (vv.23–35).

3. Cross and commitments (19:1–20:16)

The Cross relates not only to community, but also to the commitments and responsibilities that disciples have toward other persons and toward Christ. The episodes in this section show how radical obedience to the will of God (part of what is meant by taking up one's cross, cf. 16:24) has implications for one's commitment to marriage (19:3–12), to children (vv.13–15), and ultimately to Christ (19:16–20:16).

Jesus broached the question of divorce in the Sermon on the Mount (5:31–32). But now when the Pharisees attempt to draw Jesus into controversy regarding marriage and divorce, he discusses the issue in more detail (19:3–9). In his response, Jesus appeals to the Creation account to show that God wills monogamous marriage for his human creation and that such marriages are to be permanent. Jesus does state an exception: divorce is allowable in the case of **marital unfaithfulness**, since adultery would contradict the very essence of the marriage union as God originally envisioned it (see v.6).

The disciples recognize the profound level of commitment such a view of marriage entails, and they consequently wonder out loud whether some might not find it preferable to refrain from marriage (19:10). Jesus explains that marriage is, in fact, not for everyone. Indeed, some may choose to avoid marriage in order to give all their attention to the work of the kingdom (vv.11–12; cf. 1Co 7:25–35).

Mt 19:13–15 moves from the issue of marriage to children. Jesus has already indicated that childlike humility is necessary to enter the kingdom (18:1–4). Now he declares that disciples must have a commitment to children as such. Everything should be done to bring children to him and to remove any obstacles that stand in the way of their coming to him.

Jesus' encounter with the rich young man, and the discussion Jesus has with his disciples in consequence of this encounter, indicate the profound commitment to Christ required for a person to become a disciple (19:16–20:16).

The young man is searching for **eternal life**, i.e., the quality of life that is characterized by fulfillment and wholeness now and by eternal reward in the hereafter. Jesus declares that the good life can be found only by submitting to God, who is the source of all goodness. This submission to God involves obeying the commandments, yet it is not enough merely to obey the commandments. One must submit to God by becoming a disciple of Jesus, giving oneself entirely to Jesus, and following him along the path of self-denial and the Cross.

To be a disciple, then, one must cast aside everything that stands in the way of complete surrender to Jesus. Jesus recognizes that the one thing that was standing between this man and discipleship was love for his possessions. The man's refusal to **sell [his] possessions and give to the poor** made discipleship to Jesus, and eternal life, impossible for him.

Jesus uses the incident with the rich young man to instruct his disciples regarding the danger of wealth. It will be difficult (though not impossible) for a rich person to enter the kingdom, since those who have wealth tend to find their hearts knit to their possessions (19:23–24). In fact, no one can be freed from this desire for possessions that blocks the way to discipleship, except by the grace of God (vv.25–26).

In 19:27–30 Jesus assures his disciples that those who have forsaken all things to come after him will be well rewarded, in blessings both of the present life and of the life to come. Thus, **many who are first will be last, and many who are last will be first** (19:30; 20:16). In other words, those who put themselves first by grasping for earthly things will be last in terms of spiritual and eternal rewards; whereas those who put themselves last by forsaking earthly things to follow Jesus will be richly rewarded by Christ. The parable of the laborers in the vineyard (20:1–15) illustrates the truth of 19:30 and 20:16. In the parable, those who were hired first are paid last while those who were hired last are paid first.

But the parable of the laborers has another application as well. Peter's question in 19:27 may suggest that those who have given up the most for the kingdom and have rendered the most significant service can expect (indeed, demand) greater rewards than other disciples. The parable answers that God is under no obligation to pay such persons "higher wages." Yet no one can charge God with unfairness, for he is just, giving to his disciples the eternal life he promised them (20:2, 13). Moreover, he is free to dispense his rewards in whatever way he pleases (v.15).

4. Cross and servanthood (20:17–21:22)

This section begins with the third and most complete Passion prediction (20:17–19). Here Jesus once again teaches his disciples that it is necessary for the Messiah to reach his glory through suffering and death.

It is remarkable that immediately after this prediction, James and John (through their mother) request the places of greatest honor in the kingdom (20:20–28). The subsequent context suggests that the rest of the disciples also crave places of honor (vv.24–28).

Jesus responds that greatness in the kingdom has nothing to do with status or power over others. Rather, it involves (1) submission to the will of God, even if this submission includes suffering (drinking the **cup** of Christ; cf. 26:39); and (2) humble service toward others in the Christian community. Jesus himself models this kind of self-sacrificial service. Indeed, the very salvation Christians enjoy is the result of Jesus' willingness to pursue the path of servanthood, even unto death.

Jesus exemplifies the spirit of servanthood in the healing of the blind men (20:29–34), in his triumphal entry (21:1–11), and in the cleansing of the temple (vv.12–22). In 20:29–34 Jesus, the royal **Son of David**, humbly stops to serve needy blind men along the way by healing them. In ch. 21 Jesus enters Jerusalem as its King, and yet his kingship is entirely different from "the rulers of the Gentiles" who exercise self-serving, brutal oppression over their subjects (cf. 20:25). Jesus enters not on a horse, the symbol of brute force and authoritarian rule, but on a common donkey, pointing to his humility (21:5). As the servant of God, Jesus "cleanses" the temple, driving out those who have turned the true worship of God into a means of selfish advancement (vv.12–13; cf. Mal 3:3–4). In this connection, Jesus declares that the essence of true worship and religion is not empty ritual that has lost its meaning, but vital faith in God (21:18–22; cf. 9:13; 12:7).

5. Growing conflict (21:23–23:39)

Jesus has experienced opposition from the religious leaders almost from the very beginning (cf. 9:1–8). But now, in consequence of his cleansing of the temple and his great popularity with the crowds (21:1–17), the opposition becomes more direct.

This section begins with the challenge from the chief priests and elders. They ask the question regarding Jesus' authority (21:23–27). The unwillingness of the religious leaders to answer the question Jesus throws back to them indicates that they were not finally interested in the issue of Jesus' authority, but only in maintaining their status among the people.

The encounter with the chief priests and elders in 21:23–27 leads Jesus to pronounce three parables against Israel (21:28–22:14). In the *parable of the two sons* (21:28–32), Israel is like a child who promises to obey but fails to make good on the promise. The religious outcasts, on the other hand, have repented and do the will of the Father. This parable teaches that God demands actual obedience.

The *parable of the vineyard* (21:33–46) teaches that Israel's rejection of Jesus is consistent with the behavior of Israel throughout its history. Nevertheless, the rejection of Jesus will have far more tragic consequences than the earlier rejection of the prophets. God will no longer establish his rule on the earth through Israel, but through his church, made up of both Jews and Gentiles who do the will of God (21:43). God

will establish his rule through the community of those who obey him.

The *parable of the wedding feast* (22:1–14) indicates that Israel's repudiation of the call of God to enter the kingdom through Jesus will cause God to invite Gentiles into the kingdom. The last part of this parable contains a warning to the church: Those who have accepted the invitation must continue to do the will of God. Otherwise, they (like the man without a wedding garment) will be cast out and judged.

These three parables are followed by three challenges from the religious leaders (22:15–40). By their questions they attempt to trap Jesus. He responds to the question about paying taxes to Caesar by indicating that participation in God's kingdom is not necessarily incompatible with the fulfilling of civic responsibilities (such as paying taxes). Moreover, just as coins bearing the image of Caesar should be given to Caesar, so also persons created in the image of God should give themselves to God (Ge 1:26–28).

The Sadducees' question causes Jesus to affirm the centrality of belief in the resurrection (22:23–33). And the question from the lawyer prompts Jesus to declare the centrality of love in the law (or will) of God (vv.34–40). Here Jesus makes three points. First, the entire law of God is summed up in the command to love so that every demand is an expression of love to God and/or love to the neighbor. Second, God demands a love that is deep and comprehensive. Persons are to love God with their whole being and are to love their neighbors with the same quality of love they naturally have for themselves. Such deep, comprehensive love toward God and others is the essence of what Wesley called "entire sanctification." Third, love to God and the neighbor are inseparably bound together.

In each case, the religious authorities were unable to respond to Jesus' answers. Being ignorant of the true nature of Jesus, they are unable to answer the question Jesus puts to them in 22:41–46. After that point they ask him no more questions (v.46).

The confrontation between Jesus and the religious leaders in this section comes to a climax in the seven woes Jesus pronounces against the scribes and Pharisees (ch. 23). The number seven often indicates completeness, and it points here to the complete sinfulness of the religious leaders and their complete condemnation by God. The chief sin of these leaders is *hypocrisy*. Their acts of piety, ostensibly directed toward God, are actually directed toward people. They do not seek the approval of God; they seek honor from humans (23:1–7). There is no correlation between their inner attitude and outward appearance (vv.25–28).

The hypocrisy of these leaders has devastating consequences. The persons they attempt to win to God are actually made worse than they were at first because of the corrupting influence of these hypocrites (23:13–15). Moreover, their hypocrisy has distorted their understanding of God's will. They focus on legalistic hair-splitting and major on minor concerns, while ignoring those things that are important to God (vv.16–24).

In spite of all their efforts, however, these hypocrites ultimately cannot hide their sinfulness (23:29–36). As long as they persist in their hypocrisy, they can look forward only to the destruction of their nation and temple (vv.37–39; cf. ch. 24), and hell (v.33).

Although Jesus here speaks *about* the religious authorities, he is not speaking *to* them. Rather, Jesus addresses these remarks to the crowds and especially to his disciples. Ch. 23 thus serves to warn disciples against the dangers of hypocrisy.

6. Faithfulness in light of the end (24:1–25:46)

Ch. 23 ended with a reference to the destruction of the temple (23:38) and to the second coming of Christ (v.39). These two themes are taken up and expanded in chs. 24–25.

Jesus' prediction regarding the destruction of the temple (24:1–2) leads to two questions from the disciples in 24:3. The disciples wish to know (1) When will the temple be destroyed? and (2) What will be the sign that the Son of Man is about to return? In his response Jesus does not dwell on these questions but rather focuses on a related and more practical concern: In light of the second coming of Christ, how ought persons to live?

Mt 24:4–44 provides four answers to this question. First, disciples must take every precaution that they not be **deceived** by false Christs who will appear (vv.4, 5, 11, 24). Jesus predicts that persecutions and catastrophes will occur throughout the remainder of history (vv.5–14) and will be especially oppressive at the time of the destruction of Jerusalem (vv.15–28; Jerusalem and the temple were destroyed in A.D. 70). Such events will spawn **false prophets** (v.11) who will declare themselves to be the returning Christ. Jesus warns his disciples beforehand that such persons are mere pretenders, for when Jesus returns it will be with unmistakable glory and majesty (vv.27–31).

Second, followers of Jesus must not be alarmed at tribulations, wars, and disasters (24:4–14). These are simply part of ongoing history and in themselves do not indicate that the end is near.

Third, disciples are to remain faithful to Christ in the midst of tribulations and persecutions, knowing that only those who endure will receive eternal salvation when Christ returns (24:9–14).

Fourth, disciples must be sure they are ready at all times for Christ's return. They should realize that Christ may return at any moment, and therefore they should live constantly as though they expect him to return immediately. This is what Jesus means by **watch** (24:42). Such watching is essential, because no one knows when Jesus will come again for judgment (24:36–44).

Jesus expands upon this theme of constant readiness in 24:45–25:46. The *parable of the wicked servant* (24:45–51) indicates that leaders in the church should perform their service always with an eye toward the fact that Jesus may return at any moment. The *parable of the ten virgins* (25:1–13) poignantly expresses the tragedy of experiencing the second coming of Christ unprepared. Both of these parables refer to the delay of Christ's coming: Persons must beware that the long wait for the return of Jesus does not lead to apathy and carelessness.

The *parable of the talents* (25:14–30) suggests that readiness involves active service. Christians who (because of laziness and lack of affection for God) refuse to use the gifts God has given them for his work will encounter an angry and judging Christ when he returns.

This section reaches its climax with a scene of the Last Judgment (25:31–46). This passage dramatically reveals that disciples prepare themselves for the second coming of Christ by doing good to those who are in need. All will be judged according to the way in which they have treated Christ. The surprise of the Last Day is that they have unknowingly encountered Christ in the persons of the poor and needy. As persons have treated those in need, so they have treated Christ.

C. Events of the Passion and Resurrection (26:1–28:20)

In the preceding chapters Jesus has commanded his disciples to remain faithful to the will of God, even in the midst of tribulations and persecutions. He has assured them that such faithfulness will be rewarded with eternal blessing and life. Now as Jesus faces the cross, he models that faithfulness to God's will in the midst of trials. In these chapters Jesus remains perfectly obedient to the will of the Father. In consequence of his obedience even unto death, Jesus is raised from the dead.

1. Crucifixion of Jesus (26:1–27:66)

Events in this section move rapidly toward the cross. In 26:1–5 Jesus once again predicts his imminent suffering and death.

Mt 26:6–16 presents the stories of two persons who relate to Jesus' death in entirely differently ways. The woman with the alabaster jar recognizes the ultimate significance of the death of Jesus, and in response she spends a large sum of money to anoint him for burial (vv.6–13). The death of Jesus calls for sacrificial response.

In contrast to the woman, Judas advances the plot to kill Jesus by betraying him for thirty pieces of silver (26:14–16). Love of money is thus linked to the awful falling away of Judas and to betrayal of Christ. Judas becomes a living example of the seed that fell among thorns in the parable of the soils (13:22).

The account of the Last Supper points to the meaning of Jesus' death (26:17–30). Jesus is the Passover lamb whose blood establishes a (new) covenant between God and persons; this covenant is characterized above all by forgiveness of sins. When Christians partake of the Lord's Supper they affirm their participation in this covenant and anticipate the great banquet all believers will share with Christ when he returns (v.29; cf. 22:1–10; Lk 22:29–30).

Jesus has prepared his disciples for his death during the Last Supper; he now prepares himself in the Garden of Gethsemane (26:30–46). Jesus has taught his disciples that they must **watch** in the midst of their tribulations if they hope to remain faithful and obedient to the will of God (24:42; 25:13; cf. 24:3–28). Now Jesus acts on his own advice (26:38, 40–41). Jesus is able to remain obedient by being aware of the danger of yielding to temptation in the face of tribulation and by depending on God (in prayer) for strength. The fact that the disciples do not **keep watch** with him (vv.38–45), but depend on their own resources (vv.33–35), accounts for their failure later in the story (vv.56, 58, 69–75).

The arrest of Jesus (26:47–56) leads to his trial before the Sanhedrin, the Jewish council of supreme authority (vv.57–75). Here Jesus is condemned on the charge of blasphemy for claiming to be **the Son of God** (vv.63, 65). These religious leaders cry out that **"he is worthy of death"** (v.66). Yet the reader knows that Jesus is entirely righteous, whereas it is the religious authorities who are guilty and deserving of death (cf. 23:29–36). Their sin has blinded them to the truth regarding Jesus and to any sense of justice and righteousness.

During this trial (and the trial before Pilate; cf. 27:12) Jesus remains silent; he neither says nor does anything to defend himself. There are two reasons for Jesus' silence. First, Jesus shows utter disdain for the false charges that are being leveled against him. The Lord of truth will not dignify false testimony with an answer. Second, Jesus assumes the role of the poor, powerless one. Like the Suffering Servant of Isaiah, Jesus has cast aside all forms of power and violence (cf. 26:47–56) and every attempt to vindicate himself (cf. Isa 53:7). He places his trust entirely in God (27:43).

Because the Sanhedrin did not have authority to carry out the death sentence (Jn 18:31), it was necessary to deliver Jesus over to Pilate (27:1–26). The focus of the trial before Pilate is whether Jesus is the **king of the Jews.** Jesus affirms that he is (v.11) and is subsequently condemned to death (vv.15–26). Yet it is clear that Jesus is not the kind of King who usurps thrones and grabs power for himself. As King, Jesus submits to suffering and death in order to give his life for his people (20:28), thus saving them from their sins (1:21). The crown of Jesus is composed of thorns (27:29), and his throne is a cross (vv.36–37).

Jesus dies not only as King of the Jews, but also as Son of God (27:32–54; cf. 26:57–75). The mockeries of the passersby echo the temptations of Satan in 4:1–11: **"Come down from the cross, *if you are the Son of God"*** (27:40, italics mine; cf. v.43). Here again Jesus is tempted to demonstrate his divine sonship by means of a sign. And once again Jesus refuses to yield to the temptation, choosing rather to fulfill his divine sonship by perfect obedience to the will of his Father. And so, trusting in God (27:43), Jesus dies.

The signs come not from Jesus but from God (27:51–53). And on the basis of these signs, the centurion and the others who were responsible for carrying out the execution confess that Jesus **was the Son of God** (27:54).

2. Resurrection of Jesus (28:1–20)

Mt 27:55–66 has made it clear that Jesus was in fact dead and that his tomb was secured in such a way that no one could steal his body. This is important background for ch. 28, for it indicates that there is no plausible explanation for the empty tomb other than the one offered by the angel: Jesus has been raised by the power of God (vv.5–6).

The events surrounding the Resurrection do not turn the Jews away from their opposition to Jesus. In an attempt to contradict the proclamation of Jesus' resurrection, the religious authorities bribe the soldiers to spread a lie (vv.11–15). Thus opposition to Jesus and his proclamation did not end with his death, but continued on into the life of the church.

The whole of ch. 28 points ahead to the missionary commissioning of vv.16–20. The resurrected Jesus appears to his disciples in Galilee, fulfilling the word of the angel in v.7 and the word of Christ himself in v.10 (also 26:32). Thus Matthew shows that Jesus can be trusted to fulfill the promises he has made to his disciples throughout the gospel.

The declarations of Jesus in 28:18–20 contain two major elements. First, Jesus announces that **all authority** has been given to him (by God) (v.18). The notion of authority involves both the power to act and the right to act. Although Jesus exercised authority throughout his ministry (e.g., 7:29), in consequence of his resurrection he now possesses all authority everywhere.

Second, because Jesus possesses all-inclusive authority, all persons everywhere should be brought under his sovereign rule (vv.19–20a). Previously the disciples were to go only to Israel (10:5–6), but now they are to **make disciples of all nations**. Jesus indicates that making disciples involves (1) baptizing in the name of the Father, Son, and Holy Spirit (this is initial and relates to conversion), and (2) teaching them to obey the commandments Jesus has given his disciples throughout the gospel (this is ongoing and relates to the nurture of Christians). As the disciples perform this missionary work, they can be assured of the continuous presence of the resurrected Christ (v.20b). Jesus will be with the disciples to help them overcome all obstacles that stand in the way of fulfilling this mission. Even now Jesus remains in the midst of his people, speaking words of comfort and guidance as the church performs its missionary work in the world.

BIBLIOGRAPHY

Bauer, David R. *The Structure of Matthew's Gospel: A Study in Literary Design.* Sheffield: Almond, 1988.

Beare, Francis Wright. *The Gospel According to Matthew.* San Francisco: Harper & Row, 1981.

Bruce, Frederick Fyvie. *St. Matthew.* Scripture Union Bible Study Books. Grand Rapids: Eerdmans, 1970.

France, R. T. *Matthew: Evangelist and Teacher.* Grand Rapids: Zondervan, 1989.

Gundry, Robert H. *Matthew: A Commentary on His Literary and Theological Art.* Grand Rapids: Eerdmans, 1982.

Guthrie, Donald. *New Testament Introduction.* 3d ed. Downers Grove: InterVarsity Press, 1970.

Hill, David. "The Gospel of Matthew." NCBC. Grand Rapids: Eerdmans, 1972.

Kingsbury, Jack Dean. *Matthew.* 2d ed. Proclamation Commentaries. Philadelphia: Fortress, 1986.

————. *Matthew as Story.* 2d ed. Philadelphia: Fortress, 1988.

————. *Matthew: Structure, Christology, Kingdom.* Minneapolis: Fortress, 1989.

Kümmel, Werner Georg. *Introduction to the New Testament.* Translated by H. C. Kee. Nashville: Abingdon, 1973.

Martin, Ralph P. *New Testament Foundations: A Guide for Christian Students.* 2 vols. Grand Rapids: Eerdmans, 1975–78.

Tasker, R. V. G. *The Gospel According to St. Matthew.* TNTC. Grand Rapids: Eerdmans, 1961.

MARK

Joel B. Green

INTRODUCTION

I. THE OCCASION OF THE GOSPEL OF MARK

Of the four gospels contained in our NT, the gospel of Mark was probably the first to be written. With these other gospels, its primary purpose was to interpret and proclaim the significance of Jesus in story form. A tradition dating to the second century A.D. has it that John Mark wrote this gospel in Rome. The gospel itself provides little reason to support or challenge this tradition, and modern scholarship has continued to refer to its author as Mark for the sake of convenience.

It is obvious that this gospel was written for a gentile audience outside of Palestine. Mark feels compelled to translate words from Aramaic, the language of Palestine—such as "Talitha koum!" ("Little girl, I say to you, get up!" 5:41) and "Golgotha" ("The Place of the Skull," 15:22). Moreover, he explains Jewish customs and beliefs (e.g., 7:3–4; 12:18), presumably for his non-Jewish audience. However, it is difficult to be more specific about the location of Mark's audience.

Attempts to date the gospel of Mark, like those of Matthew and Luke, revolve largely around its chronological relation to the Jewish War (A.D. 66–70) and the destruction of the temple (A.D. 70) (see Hengel, 1–30). In fact, the gospel could have been written at any point within the two decades preceding the fall of Jerusalem, though many scholars opt for a date in the early A.D. 60s (see Anderson, 24–26).

Greater precision on these issues might help to satisfy our curiosity, but, for interpreting the message of the gospel, this is enough.

II. ON READING THE GOSPEL OF MARK

A previous generation of Christians learned to read the gospel of Mark as though it were a simple collection of episodes in the life of Jesus. Mark, it was supposed, wrote his story merely by placing these episodes end-to-end, in the same way that children string beads together to make a necklace. More and more, however, we understand that the gospel of Mark itself is a unified narrative, and that it must be read as such. Mark tells the story of Jesus from a distinct perspective, preaching the Good News of God by narrating certain aspects of Jesus' ministry (see Green, *Gospels*).

This truth is important for lay reader and preacher alike, for it determines how the gospel of Mark should be read. The meaning of an event is not complete in the few verses within which Mark narrates it. Rather, the whole story Mark tells sets the context for understanding its parts. Readers are encouraged to study the whole gospel, paying attention to the themes Mark traces throughout. With this larger mural in view, they will be much better equipped to understand, as Mark intended, the significance of the various scenes of the gospel.

III. MAJOR THEMES OF THE GOSPEL OF MARK

Mark is a mosaic picturing the ministry of Jesus as a relentless progression of events destined to reach their climax in the Cross of Christ. While a stumblingblock to those who believed that the Christ would be a victorious King, Jesus' crucifixion is, in fact, the fulfillment of God's plan. In the Cross, Jesus is revealed as the Son of God. Furthermore, in his death, Jesus obtains salvation for the new community of faith that is called to follow him in sacrificial discipleship.

Weaving its way through this gospel is the question of Jesus' identity, and it is clear that Mark wants his readers to understand properly who Jesus is. This is not simply a matter of getting the Christological titles right; rather, disciples must understand the connection between Jesus' identity and destiny, his person and work, his messiahship and the Cross. This is crucial since the faith of Mark's readers apparently has led them into struggle and persecution (Best). Against the backdrop of Jesus' steadfastness and submission to God in the face of death, his disciples are encouraged to faithfulness as they await Jesus' triumphant return.

IV. OUTLINE

    I. Jesus: God's Good News (1:1–15)
      A. Jesus: God's Good News (1:1–3)
      B. John Prepares the Way (1:4–9a)
      C. The Advent of Jesus (1:9b–15)
        1. Jesus' baptism and temptation (1:9b–13)
        2. Jesus' proclamation of the kingdom (1:14–15)

    II. Jesus on the Side of the People (1:16–3:12)
      A. The Galilean Preaching Tour (1:16–45)
        1. The summons to discipleship (1:16–20)
        2. The authority of Jesus (1:21–34)
        3. Prayer and mission (1:35–45)
      B. Jesus and the Opposition (2:1–3:6)
        1. Authority to forgive sins (2:1–12)
        2. Jesus with tax collectors and "sinners" (2:13–17)
        3. The question of fasting (2:18–22)
        4. Authority over the Sabbath (2:23–28)
        5. Healing on the Sabbath (3:1–6)

COMMENTARY

I. JESUS: GOD'S GOOD NEWS (1:1–15)

The opening section of Mark's story clearly communicates Jesus' significance and prepares for Jesus' first public act of ministry: calling disciples (1:16–18). The prologue begins and ends with matching references to the "good news": **the gospel [*euangelion*] about** Jesus in v.1 and **the good news [*euangelion*] of God** in vv.14–15.

A. Jesus: God's Good News (1:1–3)

V.1 links the **gospel about Jesus** with OT anticipation (vv.2–3), especially Isaiah's "good news": "Here is your God!" (Isa 40:9; see 40:1–11; 52:7). In a way consistent with Jewish ideas of the kingdom as "the coming of God" (see Beasley-Murray, 1–62), Mark heralds Jesus' coming as the advent of God. "The gospel about Jesus Christ" (NIV) is better read as **the good news of Jesus Christ**, with Jesus as both author and content of the *euangelion*.

V.1 attributes two important titles to Jesus. **Christ** appears eight times in Mark. The story constantly reinterprets this title, suggesting the need for a more adequate understanding of the Christ among Mark's audience. **Son of God** is the ruling title for Jesus in this story (Kazmierski). As Mark's story defines these titles, Jesus' followers will better appreciate his significance and better understand the nature of discipleship.

B. John Prepares the Way (1:4–9a)

In three ways, John's ministry announces and brings closer the coming of God in Jesus. First, John is intentionally portrayed as Elijah, the one who would come before the Messiah (Mal 4:5; see 2Ki 1:8). Second, drawing on the popular notion that the final intervention of God was tied to the repentance of Israel, Mark emphasizes the universality of the Jewish response to John's message of repentance in 1:5 (see **all** and **whole**). Finally, the allusion to the coming of the Spirit reflects John's anticipation of the age of salvation (see Eze 36:24–38; Joel 2:28–32). Moreover, the structural parallelism of vv.7 and 9a (**one will come . . . Jesus came**) clearly communicates the significance of Jesus as the bringer of the kingdom—*before* he opens his mouth or acts!

C. The Advent of Jesus (1:9b–15)

1. Jesus' baptism and temptation (1:9b–13)

Mark's economy of language should not mask the importance of these events. Jesus' baptism is viewed as his solidarity with the people (1:4–5) and as his commissioning to public ministry. To those familiar with Jewish thought in Jesus' day, the opening of the heavens and the descent of the Spirit mark Jesus' identification as the Messiah, for it was said of the Promised One, " . . . the heavens will be opened upon him to pour out the spirit as a blessing of the Holy Father" (*Test. Jud.* 24:1–3). Jesus' identification as the Servant of the Lord is suggested by his anointing by the Spirit (Isa 42:1–4; 61:1) and by God's declaration, "You are my son" (Ps. 2:7). This is Jesus' royal coronation, the significance of which cannot be overstated: From God's perspective, Jesus is the **Son of God.** As the Isaianic Servant, Jesus will exercise his Davidic kingship in humble service.

Jesus' temptation is narrated with astonishing brevity, but the main contours of the event are clear. **Desert** is a recurring theme in Mark's story, representing struggle with Satan and the test of faith. The presence of wild beasts (an OT symbol for evil) and angels underscores this battle's cosmic dimensions. Interestingly, Mark records no victory for Jesus or for Satan; this struggle will continue throughout Jesus' ministry.

2. Jesus' proclamation of the kingdom (1:14–15)

The phrase **after John** points to the continuity between John and Jesus, placing Jesus' ministry at the center of the divine plan of salvation. **The good news of God** is summarized in 1:15. **"The time has come"** announces the long-awaited time (*kairos*) of God's visitation and declares an end to the time of anticipation. **"The kingdom of God is near"** suggests that the new era has been introduced but is not fully present. These are parallel statements

(Ambrozic, 3–31); together they proclaim the initiation of the sovereign action of God that brings salvation.

The presence of God's kingdom is not dependent on human action as such but does lay a claim on humanity. Would-be disciples are called to a radical reorientation of their lives appropriate to the newness of this time (see 8:34–38). The focus of this commitment is the **good news,** Jesus as the bringer of the kingdom and his message of salvation.

To the Jews, **"kingdom of God"** denoted the lordship of God and his intervention in history to establish his rule in a visible, powerful way. At his coming, God would rescue his faithful and condemn their oppressors. Righteousness and mercy would be the order of the day, for then God's peace would be experienced eternally (see Green, *Gospels,* 149–58). Jesus proclaimed the presence of this kingdom. Good news indeed!

After 1:1–15 Jesus' identity is clear, but only to Mark's readers. The characters of the story struggle to understand Jesus' significance; they are able to do so only partially throughout the story.

II. JESUS ON THE SIDE OF THE PEOPLE (1:16–3:12)

A. The Galilean Preaching Tour (1:16–45)

1. The summons to discipleship (1:16–20)

Jesus initiates his public ministry by calling disciples, demonstrating that to repent and believe entails nothing less than following him. This story's simplicity underscores the immediacy of the response of these four men and illustrates how following Jesus entails a reorientation of life. Here they leave their source of livelihood and the family business, with its tradition and security, then enter a new community in which they will be involved in, and not simply observe, Jesus' mission.

2. The authority of Jesus (1:21–34)

These verses, too, are programmatic for Mark's gospel, for they show that the Good News involves authority over demonic forces and physical ailments. The kingdom Jesus preaches is God's redemptive power at work in the present. Moreover, as elsewhere in the gospel, here the question of Jesus' identity is raised—by the people, who do not know who he is; and by evil spirits, who do. Jesus silences the demons; he is not after mere acclamation, but repentance and faith. Notice that no human recognizes Jesus' true significance here nor elsewhere until his crucifixion.

3. Prayer and mission (1:35–45)

Public ministry and solitary prayer both testify to Jesus' relationship with his Father. That Jesus arises from prayer with a straightforward declaration of his mission suggests that he had been seeking God's direction for his work.

Lepers were outcasts of society, ritually unclean, supposedly cursed of God (Lev 13–14). Jesus touches the leper, welcoming this outcast into his circle and healing him. In instructing the cleansed leper, Jesus attempts to avoid publicity. He insists that the man present himself to the priest, perhaps as a sign that God was doing something new. "For, whereas the Law of Moses and its institutions could only certify disease or health, Jesus displays the power to *heal,* effecting a release from the verdict of the Law that a person with [leprosy] was 'unclean'" (Hurtado, 17).

B. Jesus and the Opposition (2:1–3:6)

The events narrated previously led to Jesus' acclaim and popularity. These incidents, however, lead to increasing opposition and the plot to kill Jesus in 3:6. Again we see Jesus siding with the common people and outcasts against the religious establishment.

1. Authority to forgive sins (2:1–12)

The relation between disease and sin is unclear in this passage, but Jesus shows how the Good News (1) opposes evil and its evidences in any form and (2) embraces salvation for the whole person. In doing so, he assumes for himself divine prerogatives, thus raising again the question of his identity. **Son of Man,** an important title for Jesus in Mark, is ambiguous; it could be understood merely as a substitute for "I" or as a title of divinity (Marshall, 63–82). In choosing this self-designation, Jesus refused to reveal his identity clearly.

2. Jesus with tax collectors and "sinners" (2:13–17)

Wesleyan Christians might see here a specific illustration of Wesley's insistence on the universality of God's gift of grace. Jews and Gentiles alike scorned tax collectors as a group for their nosy and criminal behavior. For the Jew in particular, they were suspect for their collaboration with Rome in an oppressive system of taxation. **Sinners** were probably defined as people who had adopted publicly immoral lifestyles. By calling Levi to discipleship, then eating with people deemed socially and religiously unacceptable by the religious leaders of his day, Jesus reinterprets God's grace. It is extended not to a select few who believe they deserve it, but to all in need.

3. The question of fasting (2:18–22)

Since fasting was a symbol for true piety and proper regard for the coming kingdom, some were concerned that Jesus' disciples did not observe fasts. For Jesus, the kingdom was already breaking in; hence, it was not time to mourn over its delay but to celebrate its arrival. The following brief parables highlight how inappropriate old beliefs and practices were in the context of this new reality.

Jesus' words about the wedding feast contain a surprising twist. In noting the departure of the bridegroom, he predicts his own death. This is the first clear anticipation of the Cross, which broods over the whole gospel.

4. Authority over the Sabbath (2:23–28)

Jesus has previously shown his concern for outcasts; this story demonstrates fully his solidarity with them, for it casts him as a man religiously and socially unacceptable. He and his disciples are poor and must therefore take advantage of that portion of the harvest reserved for them (Dt 24:19–22). But in doing so, they break the Sabbath, the litmus test for taking holiness seriously according to many first-century Jews. Interestingly, however, Jesus places his reading of the OT over against that of the learned and "holy." They are concerned with a literalistic interpretation of the Sabbath law (Ex 20:8); he is concerned with the character of the God of which the law is an expression. This is the God who heard Israel crying out in need and responded with deliverance. Jesus reminds them that human need is basic to God's concerns.

5. Healing on the Sabbath (3:1–6)

Having asserted his authority over the Sabbath legislation as interpreted by his contemporaries, Jesus goes on to push for a decision regarding himself. Are his work and words a manifestation of the kingdom and thus appropriate for the Sabbath, or not? As these five conflict stories have shown (2:1–3:6), one cannot remain neutral toward Jesus, and the onlookers respond with unbelief. The religious and political interests join forces against Jesus; the remainder of his ministry must be carried out under the dark cloud of his impending death.

C. The Crowds Follow Jesus (3:7–12)

The closing passage of this larger section, begun in 1:16, summarizes Jesus' ministry in Galilee. In spite of the opposition narrated in 2:1–3:6, Jesus continues to enjoy notoriety, and people come to him from the east, north, and south—i.e., from the areas of Jewish settlement. This marks the beginning of a theme that will weave its way through the gospel: the opposition to Jesus among Jewish leaders versus his popularity with the people. Here Jesus' healing and exorcisms are at the root of his appeal, and Mark notes that the evil spirits, like God, refer to Jesus as the Son of God. Not until the Crucifixion will any human recognize this truth.

III. JESUS' TEACHING AND MIRACLES (3:13–5:43)

A. The Appointing of the Twelve (3:13–19)

As with the previous section (1:16–3:12), so with this one, the theme of the opening passage is discipleship. The topographical setting, **on a mountainside** is symbolically important, for a mountain is often a place of revelation in biblical thought; additionally, a mountain is associated with the making

of God's people in Ex 20. Jesus appointed the Twelve to two tasks. His first purpose is **that they might be with him.** That is, they are called to share life with him as his companions; the emphasis falls first not on their importance or achievements, but on their relatedness to him. Focused on this relationship in this way, the Twelve then participate with Jesus in his ministry to others (Schweizer, 39–43). This, combined with the fact that Jesus chose *twelve* apostles, signifies that he had in mind the beginning of a new, restored Israel. This new people of God would be established through his work and the ministry of these appointed ones. That Judas Iscariot is denoted as the betrayer points ahead to Jesus' suffering and calls all followers to self-examination lest they also fail in the time of testing.

For Wesley, self-examination of this sort is vital (see also below, 14:19), for discipleship is a continuous journey in which the grace of God must be appropriated continuously. This understanding of the Christian life, combined with an intense appreciation of the communal nature of Christianity, lies at the root of Wesley's well-known emphasis on mutual accountability in small-group discipleship.

B. A Redefinition of Family (3:20–35)

Mark sets the Beelzebub controversy within the two-part story of Jesus' family. These episodes interpret one another, raising the inseparable questions of Jesus' identity and the nature of his followers.

Jesus was popular with the crowd, but his behavior broke acceptable conventions so that his family regarded him as mentally deranged.

For their part, the teachers of the law accuse him of having an evil spirit and of being in collusion with Beelzebub. In response, Jesus plays on the incredulity of the phrase **His end has come**: He cannot be in league with Satan, for this would be self-defeating for Satan; Satan would be rendered impotent. Moreover, one who is possessed (the lesser) cannot conquer his or her possessor (the greater). In fact, Jesus claims that his ministry is one of tying up the strong man and robbing his house. The teachers of the law, in rejecting the work of Jesus as demonic activity (3:30), deny the power and work of the Holy Spirit (see 1:10).

After Jesus' family arrives, one notes the unmistakable contrast between those who are outside (vv.31–32) and those who are inside, or sitting around him (vv.32, 34). Clearly, Jesus' **family** embraces his disciples, but the **whoever** of v.35 extends the family circle to include obedient persons in every generation.

C. He Taught Them in Parables (4:1–34)

1. The parable of the sower (4:1–20)
This subsection has three parts: the parable, an interlude on the secret of the kingdom, and the interpretation of the parable. These speak with one voice, proclaiming the necessity of hearing the Word and producing fruit. The **secret of the kingdom of God** must be understood against the backdrop of Jesus' person and ministry: in him, the kingdom of God has begun to penetrate the world.

2. Recognizing God's presence in Jesus' ministry (4:21–25)
Given the ambiguity of Jesus' identity thus far, one could easily understand how the question might be raised, If he is the Son of God, why does he not say so plainly? These

enigmatic sayings provide the answer. At present, Jesus and his message are not easily understood. But they will be. In the meantime, attend to what you see and hear, for a positive response now will bring even greater understanding, but lack of attention will lead to loss.

3. The parables of growth (4:26–32)
These parables underscore a similar point with respect to the kingdom of God—the first by emphasizing the process of growth, the second the contrast between the tiny seed and the mature plant. How the kingdom grows from its small beginnings to a glorious end is God's secret. In the present, then, one should not be deceived by the apparently insignificant inroads of the kingdom in the world.

4. The parables (4:33–34)
In this summary passage, Mark notes that the meaning of Jesus' parables is not out of reach but requires careful listening. These were veiled forms of communication appropriate to this period of Jesus' ministry, prior to his death and resurrection, when the full significance of Jesus was not yet clear.

D. The Disciples' Lack of Faith (4:35–41)
The initial time designation, **that day,** serves to tie this episode closely to the preceding section on parables. Following his teaching, will the disciples understand Jesus clearly? Mark's narration of Jesus is as one who acts with divine authority. Just as elsewhere Jesus rebukes and silences evil spirits (e.g., 1:25), so now he rebukes and silences the wind and the waves. Like God, he has power over the sea and the chaotic evil it represents (Pss 65:5–7; 104:24–26; 106:9; Rev 21:1). Never-

theless, the disciples fail to perceive Jesus' true identity.

E. Jesus and Legion (5:1–20)

The surprising length and detail of this story suggest its importance for Mark. Three themes are present. First, Mark leaves no doubt as to the enormity of evil at work here and the even greater extent of Jesus' power over evil. Second, the question of identity, raised again in 4:41, is answered by the spirits in 5:7: He is the **Son of the Most High God.** On the other hand, the people (v.17) fail to perceive the work of the Lord in their midst, being more concerned about their loss of property. Finally, it is significant that, in crossing the lake, Jesus enters gentile territory. As if to anticipate the church's mission among the Gentiles, Jesus unexpectedly instructs the man to tell others what the Lord has done for him (v.19).

F. The Healing of a Woman and Raising of a Dead Girl (5:21–43)

Mark weaves these stories together because of their chronological proximity and their thematic relationship. The girl, terminally ill, is pronounced dead; the woman has exhausted all human possibilities for healing. The disciples fail to understand what Jesus has done for the woman; the girl's friends and family could not anticipate Jesus' authority over death. However, the woman had faith and exercised it, just as Jairus had faith in coming to Jesus and later is encouraged to believe. Finally, in spite of the critical states of both the woman and girl, Jesus is able to restore them to health. That he devoted himself in this way to two females is startling and points to his giving new value to women—and to others considered less unimportant by his contemporaries.

IV. JESUS ENCOUNTERS BLINDNESS (6:1–8:26)

A. Discipleship With Jesus (6:1–56)

From the triumph of faith in ch. 5, Mark returns to the twin themes of unbelief and hardness of heart in ch. 6. The various sections of this chapter are closely interrelated: Jesus' ministry in Nazareth defines that of his disciples; the fate of the prophet Jesus is anticipated by the killing of another prophet, John the Baptist; John's death, set in the midst of the report of the disciples' mission, also interprets the nature of discipleship as suffering; and, in spite of success in mission, the disciples continue in their lack of perception.

1. Jesus and the Twelve in ministry (6:1–13)

Remarkable parallels tie these two episodes together, demonstrating again the closest relationship between Christology and discipleship. This is suggested already in 6:1, with the mention of the disciples accompanying Jesus. At the heart of the Nazareth scene is the question of Jesus' identity and source of authority, which leads to his rejection by the townspeople and the limited character of his ministry among them. The giving of this same authority to the Twelve heads the following passage, together with instructions to risk themselves in faith by taking no provisions. While they enjoy success on their mission, the disciples have Jesus' warning that they, too, will be rejected.

2. The passion of John the Baptist (6:14–29)

The subsequent recounting of John's execution is clearly an anticipation of Jesus' own. In both cases, (1) the Roman authority is sympathetic to his prisoner, whom he regards as innocent (6:20; 15:14); (2) the death sentence is pronounced under outside pressure (6:26–27; 15:14–15); and (3) after death, the body is taken and laid in a tomb (6:29; 15:42–47). Like the Old Testament prophets (Ne 9:26), John and Jesus are killed.

3. The feeding of the five thousand (6:30–44)

The provision of bread in this "desert" (**Remote place**, NIV) recalls God's provision of manna in the Exodus. In the Prophets, the "shepherd" could be God's agent of salvation. Jesus is thus portrayed as the Shepherd who compassionately provides for the needs of his people (see Ps 23:1; Eze 34:23). The objections of the disciples illustrate their failure to see Jesus in this role.

4. Jesus walks on the water (6:45–52)

This episode is tied to the feeding miracle chronologically and by the note in 6:52 that the disciples' bafflement resulted from their inability to grasp the significance of Jesus as revealed in that miracle. As with the previous sea miracle (4:35–41), so here Jesus is portrayed as possessing divine power.

5. The crowds come to Jesus (6:53–56)

This summary passage serves as a foil to the rejection of Jesus by the people of Nazareth (6:5–6) and the disciples' hardness of heart (v.52). In spite of those setbacks, Jesus is widely hailed as a wonderworker. As we will see, however, this understanding of Jesus is one-sided and is in need of correction.

B. The Gentile Mission (7:1–8:26)

1. The question of cleanliness (7:1–23)

Although in this passage Jesus is engaged with Pharisees and teachers of the law, their debate prepares the way for ministry with Gentiles in 7:24–37. The topic of controversy is not proper hygiene but the Pharisaic lifestyle that made strict standards of ceremonial purity the embodiment of true religion. Unfortunately, by making such behavior as ritual washings the measure of orthodoxy, these Pharisees not only overlooked, but indeed violated, other areas of God's Word. (Contrast their concerns for ritual cleanliness at meals with Jesus' habit of eating with religious outcasts! Clearly the arrival of the kingdom was an expression of what Wesley referred to as God's prevenient grace.) Jesus sets the issue of cleanliness on a new plane, insisting that sin, not certain foods or other objects, separates a person from fellowship and worship.

2. The faith of a gentile woman (7:24–30)

The weight of this story falls on the description of the mother as a Gentile and on her recognition that the benefits of the kingdom go to **the children** (i.e., Israel) *first,* but that there is enough for **the dogs** (a well-known term for Gentiles) as well. The universality of the Gospel is proclaimed and the later mission of the church anticipated, while a woman is presented again as a model of faith.

3. A deaf and mute man healed (7:31–37)

Jesus' journey into the region of the Decapolis is roundabout, keeping him in primarily gentile territory. Mark's recounting of the story highlights the relation of Jesus' ministry to OT prophecy, as both the description of the man's malady and the people's response to the healing allude to Isa 35:5–6. The time of salvation has indeed come!

4. The feeding of the four thousand and problems of perception (8:1–21)

Mark records no change of scene, and we can only assume this feeding is carried out in gentile territory. This is supported by the general flow of the narrative to this point and by the description of some as having **"come a long distance"** (using OT language for gentile regions and the inclusion of Gentiles in salvation, 8:3). Hence, the two feeding stories are parallel: salvation is extended to both Jews (6:30–44) and Gentiles. Moreover, in spite of their previous experience, the disciples continue in their blindness (cf. 6:37–38; 8:4–5).

Against the backdrop of the revelation of Jesus in the feeding story, the immediate appearance of the Pharisees requesting a divine authentication for his mission highlights their blindness. Jesus' reference to **"this generation"** (8:12) places them in the same group as the rebellious Israelites in the wilderness (e.g., Dt 1:35). His response **No sign will be given** is ironic, for Mark's narrative has repeatedly reported signs of the inbreaking kingdom of God. His subsequent warning to the disciples falls on undiscerning ears, for the disciples have yet to understand that Jesus has divine power to provide for their needs and more.

5. A blind man healed (8:22–26)

Jesus' ability to heal is clearly attested, and one is reminded that the healing of the blind signifies the presence of the era of salvation (Isa 35:5–6). In addition, the story functions for Mark as a parable, communicating the need for Jesus to heal the disciples of their spiritual blindness.

V. JESUS AND HIS DISCIPLES: THE WAY OF THE CROSS (8:27–10:52)

This section is controlled by the three Passion predictions (8:31; 9:31; 10:33–34). These begin to make explicit what has been only implicit thus far—namely, the full significance of Jesus' identity and destiny as the Christ.

A. Peter's Confession and Rebuke (8:27–33)

At last, Jesus himself raises the identity question, and the disciples reply with "popular" answers (see 6:14–15), all of which are incorrect. Peter acclaims Jesus as Christ, and he is surely right, as 1:1 indicates. When Jesus begins to teach them plainly about his suffering, however, it is clear that Peter still misunderstands who Jesus is. Apparently, for him, Jesus is the Christ of popular expectation, the glorious King (see Green, *Prophecy*, 83–96). For Jesus, this view of messiahship had to be modified by the portrait of the Son of Man who, of divine necessity, suffers.

B. Disciples of the Cross (8:34–9:1)

If the way of the Christ is the way of suffering, so is the way of discipleship. Both disciples and crowds receive the same call to reorient themselves around the Gospel, even at the cost of their lives. Mk 9:1, a needed reassurance, is fulfilled in the Transfiguration (9:2–13), which itself anticipates the resurrection of Jesus.

C. The Transfiguration of Jesus (9:2–13)

Mark's recounting of this episode contrasts God's open revelation of Jesus' significance with the disciples' continuing incomprehension. Jesus' appearance and God's acclamation of him as Son and the prophet like Moses (**Listen to him!** [see Dt 18:15]) confirm the truth of Jesus' earlier talk of suffering and vindication. They also give the disciples a foretaste of the coming glory. The reaction of the disciples (9:5–6) betrays their lack of understanding.

D. The Healing of a Young Demoniac (9:14–29)

From the mountaintop Jesus descends, like Moses, to find faithlessness (see 9:19; Ex 32). The turning point of the story comes when the boy's father declares his faith and requests help in overcoming his unbelief. In whatever situation, then, disciples are called to respond with faith in Jesus. The passage also points forward to the time when Jesus' ministry will be passed on to his disciples. He reminds them of the centrality of prayer for equipping them for mission.

E. Jesus' Death and the Life of the Twelve Disciples (9:30–50)

1. The second Passion prediction (9:30–32)

For the second time, Jesus plainly predicts his death, and for the second time, his disciples fail to understand. A new clause is introduced here: the Son of Man **"is going to be handed over into the hands of men."** This "divine passive" signifies God's instrumentality in Jesus' death; the Cross is at the center of God's plan for redemption.

2. Giving honor to disciples (9:33–37)

The discussion turns from Jesus' suffering to sacrificing self-interest as the demands of discipleship are spelled out in the context of an argument over relative greatness. Jesus uses a pun on the Greek word *pais*, which can mean either "servant" or "little child." When it is recognized that children in antiquity were treated with gross disrespect, Jesus' insistence on this role reversal is striking: Even the most insignificant among you is to be treated with the greatest honor!

3. Who are Jesus' followers? (9:38–41)

How does one draw the circle around those to be treated with such respect? Who are Jesus' followers? Jesus gives no formal definition, but it is obvious that one's behavior is key and that the benefit of the doubt goes to the unknown person. This is a message all heirs of Wesley do well to take seriously, for, even though Wesley was fond of speaking of doctrinal "essentials," he emphatically taught the necessity of a *faith working itself out in deeds of love.*

4. A disciple's responsibility (9:42–50)

These seemingly unrelated sayings are held together by catchwords: first, causes . . . to sin (vv.42–48), then **fire** (vv.48–50). Together they communicate that entering the kingdom is worth any cost and that it is crucial to avoid behavior that would drive away **"these little ones who believe in me"** (i.e., Jesus' disciples; see on 9:36–37).

F. The Character of Discipleship (10:1–52)

1. The kingdom has come: Divorce as a test case (10:1–12)

Ch. 10 is specifically devoted to discipleship, and this passage appears first since it outlines the context in which discipleship is lived out. Three "times" are recorded: the time of the beginning, when the marriage bond was unseverable; the time of hardness of heart, when divorce was permitted but regulated; and this new time, when hardness of heart is overcome and the original ideal of marriage is again upheld. How can Jesus set aside the Mosaic regulation? The answer is clear: Jesus has come and with him the long-expected time of God's kingdom (1:15). New possibilities for discipleship are available.

On the other hand, inasmuch as Jesus goes on to talk of divorce, he recognizes the continuance of **hardness** of heart. In light of Jesus' coming, divorce is "out of date" (as are other acts working against God's new creation). Nevertheless, we live "in the middle," in tension, in the time between hardness of heart and the new creation. Thus we are called to live according to the ideals of the kingdom of God, and we are enabled to do so by its presence. But the battle with evil continues.

2. Children, possessions, and entry into the kingdom (10:13–31)

Children in Jesus' day were highly insignificant, lacking security, dependent on the will of others. To enter the kingdom one must die to self-autonomy and self-security, and this is precisely what the rich young ruler refused to do. He had impressive credentials, but seemed to know that they were inadequate to qualify him for eternal life. In fact, according to Jesus, he lacked only one thing, the only thing: total self-abandonment. His great wealth, then, is developed as a symbol of the problem of faith. The root problem in Mark is **hardness of heart,** of which wealth is here an expression. Salvation, therefore, is impossible for everyone, but more so for the rich. Yet with God the self-abandonment necessary for entry into the kingdom (for salvation) is possible. So the rich young ruler is contrasted with the children of 10:13–16 and also with Jesus' disciples—who have renounced everything. In the reversal of the kingdom, what is renounced is again received with the establishment of a new family having God as Father. Persecutions, too, are gained, underscoring again how the shape of discipleship is determined by the Cross.

3. Jesus' passion and the way of service (10:32–45)

With this third prediction, the sense of drama is acute: Jesus and his disciples are traveling to Jerusalem, the place of betrayal. The blindness of the disciples is manifest both by their astonishment (v.32) and by the ensuing discussion of places in honor. Still believing that "Christ" signified "glorious King," James and John hope to reserve seats of honor. Jesus redirects their attention to suffering and calamity, his and theirs, for the kingdom has not yet been fully realized. Within the community of faith, discipleship entails service for one another, best exemplified by Jesus himself, who came **to serve, and to give his life as a ransom for many.** This is the secret by which salvation is made available: Jesus' sacrificial death. For Mark, to understand *this* is to understand Jesus' true significance.

4. On receiving sight and following Jesus (10:46–52)

Blind Bartimaeus's faith, persistence, and recognition of Jesus' significance provide the foci for this important story of discipleship. At the outset he is **sitting by the roadside** (Gk. *hodon*), but in the end **he received his sight and followed Jesus along the road** (*hodo*). This is a clear portrait of the healing power of the merciful King, but this story also functions as a parable of discipleship: To be healed from spiritual blindness is to grasp the true identity of Jesus and join him on the way to the Cross. (On 10:1–52, see Via in bibliography.)

VI. JESUS IN JERUSALEM (11:1–13:37)

A. The Entry Into Jerusalem (11:1–11)

Bartimaeus anticipated the messianic, royal image of Jesus' entry into Jerusalem when he referred to Jesus as the "Son of David" (10:47–48). The colt (Ge 49:11; Zec 9:9), the spreading of garments and branches (2Ki 9:13), the petition for salvation (Ps 118:25–26)—these details and more portray Jesus as the Bearer of the kingdom. What sort of ruler is this? The Bartimaeus episode depicts Jesus as the one who rules with compassion.

B. Jesus, the Fig Tree, and the Temple (11:12–26)

Mark interprets the episode in the temple by setting it between the two parts of the story of the fig tree. The fig tree had the appearance of fruitfulness but lacked fruit **because it was not the season for figs.** Hence Jesus cursed it. Upon entering the temple, Jesus discovered temple merchandising actually hindering gentile access to the temple. So, in a prophetic act, he disrupted these business affairs and reminded the people that access to the God of the temple was intended **for all nations.** Mark understands this event as Jesus' cursing of the temple, just as he cursed the fig tree, for the time of the temple was past. He thus prepares us for a new understanding of **temple.** The withered fig tree provides the basis for sayings on prayer and faith, in which Jesus is portrayed as the exemplar of strong faith, to be emulated by his disciples in mission.

C. Jesus and the Jewish Authorities (11:27–12:44)

1. The question of authority (11:27–12:12)

Jesus' action in the temple gives rise to a question about his authority. While refusing to answer the Jewish leaders directly, the parable of the tenants gives his indirect answer: He is the Son of God. At the same time, he alludes to his impending death (like the

prophets and John the Baptist before him), and to God's giving salvation to the Gentiles. That the Jewish leaders grasp the intent of the parable is clear from their response in 12:12.

2. The question of taxation (12:13–17)

Taxation was an economic burden, but also, at least potentially, it was an opportunity for venerating the Roman emperor who designated himself as semi-divine. The dilemma facing Jesus, then, is to support taxation and thus compromise his talk of the kingdom, or challenge it and face charges of sedition. Circumventing the trap, Jesus allows for the paying of taxes but at the same time calls into question the divine claims of the state and reaffirms the claims of God to ultimate loyalty.

3. The question of the Resurrection (12:18–27)

The Sadducees' question seems designed more to ridicule the idea of resurrection than to trap Jesus, and Jesus' reply strikes at the root of their belief system. Their denial of resurrection on the grounds that it is not mentioned in the first five books of the OT (their "Bible") betrays their ignorance of the Scriptures and God's power, according to Jesus. First, he instructs them on the power of God to create a new order of life and relationships in the hereafter. Then, citing a text even they would consider authoritative (Ex 3:6), Jesus argues that God's covenant is without meaning if it is canceled by death.

4. The greatest commandment (12:28–34)

What is the one commandment on which the others hang? Jesus' answer holds together love for God and love for neighbor as inseparable and thus affirms the central message of the OT.

This, along with the positive portrayal of this teacher of the law, indicates that Jesus' purpose in his ministry was not to reject the OT but rather to challenge its misinterpretation and present himself as its fulfillment.

5. The teachers of the law challenged (12:35-44)

As a group, the teachers of the law not only marketed an inadequate view of the Christ but also maintained a false piety. Their showy religion won them public esteem and support from the poor but would lead them to judgment. By contrast, this poor, widowed woman, at the bottom rung of society's ladder, whose commitment was complete, becomes an exemplar of discipleship.

D. Discipleship Amidst Destruction and Persecution (13:1-37)

1. The beginning of the end (13:1-4)

The questions posed by the disciples relate the destruction of the temple to the coming of the end of the present age (**fulfilled** signifies the end).

2. Tribulation and perseverance (13:5-23)

In apocalyptic thought (see Green, *Prophecy*, 61-67), the present age is a battleground with no neutral territory. The disasters enumerated are manifestations of this battle, birth pangs that give rise to the fullness of God's kingdom. Threading its way through this discourse is the theme of readiness. Disciples are to stay on guard; stand firm; and, with the empowerment of the Holy Spirit, serve as witnesses.

3. The coming of the Son of Man (13:24-37)

Evil and suffering are not the last word. God himself will intervene, dem-onstrating his sovereignty over history. Jesus uses a collage of OT texts to communicate the sure hope of the coming of the Son of Man, the day of salvation. In this light, even though the time of the end is unknown by all except the Father, disciples must maintain alertness.

VII. JESUS' SUFFERING, DEATH, AND RESURRECTION (14:1-16:8)

A. Conspiracy and Devotion (14:1-11)

The plot against Jesus, first noted in 3:6, now takes shape as Judas agrees to deliver Jesus to the Jewish leaders apart from the crowds they feared. Mark observes that Judas is **one of the Twelve**: even past, close companionship with Jesus does not guarantee faithfulness in trial. Judas's malicious deed contrasts with the work of the anonymous woman, whose profound generosity and devotion is remembered. Jesus interprets her service as an anticipation of his death, a burial anointing, so significant an act that it took precedence over almsgiving.

B. The Last Supper (14:12-31)

Mark shows that this last meal is the celebration of the Passover feast, a factor that helps interpret Jesus' words and actions in 14:22-25. First, however, the thrust of the passage centers on the treachery of one of the disciples, now unnamed; this is a betrayal of intimacy. As the disciples respond to Jesus' prediction by asking, one by one, **"Surely not I?"** we are drawn into the story to repeat this same question. His passion, Jesus maintains, is the work of God and of human agents; here we see the conjunction of divine and human causation.

During the meal, Jesus departs from

the normal Passover rite, declaring himself to be the fulfillment of Passover. In Jesus' death, God's redemptive plan for all humanity is effected, the new covenant enacted, and the kingdom established. In receiving the bread and wine, his disciples participate in the benefits of his death. Looking beyond his death even here, Jesus anticipates life in the kingdom.

The consequence of his death, depicted as fulfillment of Scripture, is the scattering of his disciples, including Peter. Death (and with it, the disciples' failure), however, is not the last word, for Jesus is able to promise the regathering of the disciples after his resurrection.

C. Prayer in Gethsemane (14:32–42)

Gethsemane marks the critical point in the Passion story, as Jesus recognizes the approach of the fateful hour and prays that he might be delivered from suffering and death. His prayer bespeaks his extraordinary intimacy with God (**Abba**) as well as his focus on following God's will. In so doing, he shows his disciples how to stand in the time of testing—not by sleeping, but by submissive prayer.

D. Betrayal and Arrest (14:43–52)

The full force of Judas's treachery is seen in Mark's description: He is **one of the Twelve,** he greeted Jesus as **Rabbi,** and he **kissed him.** Jesus already has resolved to submit to death as integral to God's plan, so he offers no resistance to the posse. With the flight of the disciples, Jesus' predictions and the Scriptures are fulfilled.

E. Peter and Jesus on Trial (14:53–72)

Mark weaves these two stories together, showing how disciples are to face trial (see 13:9–11; 1Ti 6:13). Jesus' trial is a travesty of justice: first, no evidence is found; then false and inconsistent testimony is given. The temple charge paints Jesus as a messianic pretender, so the high priest asks him if he is the Christ. Jesus accepts the title but qualifies it with reference to the exalted Son of Man judging those who now judge Jesus. On this basis he is condemned, but some go on to mock him as a false prophet, thus fulfilling Isa 50:6.

Peter's story represents the culmination of the theme of discipleship failure developed in the gospel. Even now Peter does not **know** or **understand** (vv.68, 71), so he refuses to acknowledge Jesus before his questioner. Yet, remembering Jesus' words, he later repents, showing the possibility of a new beginning and anticipating the regathering of the disciples after the Resurrection.

F. The Kingship of Jesus (15:1–20a)

1. Pilate's interrogation (15:1–5)

As Jesus had prophesied (10:33–34), the Sanhedrin now hands him over to the Roman court. The charges against Jesus have a decidedly political ring, and he is questioned as a pretender to the throne. His silence identifies him with the Suffering Servant of Isa 53:7 and suggests his readiness to undergo suffering as a part of God's plan. The parallel between these verses and 13:9 is remarkable: Jesus is the first in a long line of those who would suffer unjust accusations and be brought to trial for the sake of the Gospel.

2. The release of Barabbas (15:6–15)

The obvious criminal character of Barabbas serves as a foil to Jesus' obvious innocence. But now the crowds, stirred up by the chief priests, turn against Jesus, so Pilate's plan to release Jesus fails. The result is an implicit portrait of Jesus' vicarious death.

3. Jesus' mockery (15:16–20a)

Already in vv.2, 9, and 12, Jesus is referred to as the King of the Jews (see Matera), and this acclamation comes to a head as the soldiers dress him up as a king and exclaim, **"Hail, King of the Jews!"** Unwittingly, they address him correctly, but the authority Jesus exercises is not the sort one might expect (see 10:44–45).

G. The Crucifixion and Death of Jesus (15:20b–41)

This section contains numerous citations from and allusions to Ps 22, demonstrating that the crucifixion of God's Christ was no surprise to God; rather, Jesus' death is central to God's plan, as prophesied in the OT.

1. The Crucifixion (15:20b–32)

The brevity of Mark's report is striking. Jesus chose to endure death fully conscious rather than drink the sedative offered him (see Pr 31:6). The division of his garments (see Ps 22:18) underscores the humiliation of the Crucified One. The notice affixed to the cross, the taunts of the passersby, and the mockery of the chief priests and teachers of the law are all ironic. They communicate a fundamental truth that would not have been lost to the Christians of Mark's day: In the suffering and weakness of the Cross, God's power is manifest.

2. The death of Jesus (15:33–39)

Darkness covered the land, symbolizing the separation from God that Jesus felt at his death. His cry, a citation of Ps 22:1, with its emphasis on *my* God, speaks of Jesus' horror and trust at the end. Thinking that Jesus has appealed to Elijah, the onlookers look for Elijah to rescue Jesus; this would be a sign that Jesus had divine authentication in his death. It marks the end of the old aeon, the end of the time of the temple, when Jesus himself replaces the temple. Moreover, at his death, Jesus is acclaimed as **"Son of God"** by a centurion, a Gentile(!)—the first human in Mark's gospel to identify Jesus correctly. That he does so after seeing only **how he died** is highly suggestive.

3. Witnesses at the cross (15:40–41)

The absence of the disciples highlights the fidelity of these women. Interestingly, the very women who first witness Jesus' death also witness the empty tomb.

H. The Empty Tomb (15:42–16:8)

The story of Jesus' burial certifies the reality of the Crucifixion account: Jesus is dead. Joseph appears here for the first time and is notable for his willingness to associate himself with the crucified Jesus. Did he recognize the centrality of the Cross to the realization of God's kingdom? Originally the gospel of Mark probably ended with v.8 (see Lane, 601–5). The NIV (like many other English translations) includes 16:9–20, though it notes that "most reliable early manuscripts and other ancient witnesses" do not include these verses. They are only loosely related to the Gospel as a whole and, more interestingly, do not even show how the women of v.8 overcame their fear in order to deliver their message. Instead, these verses seem to borrow material from the appearance and commissioning stories of Matthew, Luke, and John—an attempt by a later scribe to give the Gospel of Mark an ending more in keeping with its companion Gospels.

Nevertheless, even given the more probable conclusion of Mark's Gospel with 16:8, all of the necessary details are present. According to the story, the women expected no resurrection; they came to anoint a corpse and even wondered among themselves how they might obtain access to the tomb. The young man they encounter (1) announces the Resurrection (**"He has risen!"**), (2) provides proof of Jesus' absence from the tomb (**"See the place where they laid him"**), and (3) commissions the women (**"Go, tell. . . !"**). The fear of the women appears to jeopardize their mission, but the story is written in such a way as to recall Jesus' promise in 14:28 and to anticipate the restoration of the disciples in Galilee. In concluding his story of Jesus so abruptly, Mark calls upon his readers, too, to believe the Gospel and take upon themselves this commission to proclaim God's good news.

BIBLIOGRAPHY

Ambrozic, Aloysius. *The Hidden Kingdom*. Washington, D.C.: Catholic Biblical Association of America, 1972.

Anderson, Hugh. *The Gospel of Mark*. NCBC. Grand Rapids: Eerdmans, 1976.

Beasley-Murray, George R. *Jesus and the Kingdom of God*. Grand Rapids: Eerdmans, 1986.

Best, Ernest. *Mark: The Gospel as Story*. Edinburgh: T. & T. Clark, 1983.

Green, Joel B. *How to Read Prophecy*. Downers Grove, Ill.: InterVarsity Press, 1984.

––––––. *How to Read the Gospels and Acts*. Downers Grove, Ill.: InterVarsity Press, 1987.

Hengel, Martin. *Studies in the Gospel of Mark*. London: SCM, 1983.

Hurtado, Larry W. *Mark: A Good News Commentary*. San Francisco: Harper, 1983.

Kazmierski, Carl R. *Jesus, the Son of God*. Würzburg: Echter, 1979.

Lane, William L. *The Gospel of Mark*. NICNT. Grand Rapids: Eerdmans, 1974.

Marshall, I. Howard. *The Origins of New Testament Christology*. Downers Grove, Ill.: InterVarsity Press, 1976.

Matera, Frank J. *The Kingship of Jesus*. SBLDS 66. Chico, Calif.: Scholars, 1982.

Schweizer, Eduard. *Jesus*. London: SCM, 1971.

Via, Dan O., Jr. *The Ethics of Mark's Gospel—In the Middle of Time*. Philadelphia: Fortress, 1985.

LUKE
Arthur W. Wainwright

INTRODUCTION

I. AUTHORSHIP, DATE, PLACE OF ORIGIN, AND DESTINATION

This gospel is the first part of a two-volume work; the second half is the Acts of the Apostles. The author of these two writings is traditionally supposed to have been Luke the physician, a companion of Paul (Col 4:14; Phm 24). Some scholars reject this tradition. But since Luke was not an apostle, these writings are unlikely to have been ascribed to him, unless he actually was the author.

The date of the two books is a matter for dispute. Since Acts does not record the death of Paul or of James the brother of Jesus, some scholars date them in A.D. 62 or earlier, before these events took place. But most date the books in the seventies, eighties, or nineties, on the assumption that Luke made use of Mark's gospel.

It has been suggested that either Rome or Greece was the place of origin of Luke's gospel and that Antioch or Rome was its destination. There is, however, little evidence in support of these conjectures.

II. SOURCES

It is widely supposed that Luke used Mark's gospel and other material as sources. According to this theory some of this other material, often designated "Q" (from *Quelle*, German for "source"), was also used by Matthew. Some of it, sometimes designated "L" (for "Luke"), was used only by Luke. Another source may have provided the birth, infancy, and boyhood stories. It is even suggested that there may have been an earlier edition of Luke's gospel combining the material designated as "Q" and "L."

There are other views of the relationship between the first three gospels. The traditional theory is that Matthew was written first, then Mark, and that Luke had access to both of them. Some scholars have suggested that Luke made use of Matthew but was written before Mark. Yet others have claimed that the first three gospels were written independently of each other. But the theory that regards Mark as the earliest of the gospels continues to have the greatest acceptance.

III. LUKE AS A HISTORIAN

Luke explicitly states that he wished to give "an account" of Jesus' life and teaching (1:1–4). He wanted Theophilus, to whom the work was dedicated, to "know the certainty" of the things he had been taught. And presumably he wanted that certainty to be known by others who read or listened to his gospel. Luke was a historian in the sense that he desired to record events accurately and to place them in their historical setting. He did not attempt to write a detailed biography of Jesus; rather, he endeavored to give a faithful account of the most important aspects of Jesus' life and teaching. Scholars have differed about the reliability of his account (see Fitzmyer, 1:14–18; Marshall, *Luke: Historian*, 53–76). This commentary, however, is based on the events and teaching as recorded and interpreted by Luke.

IV. THE PURPOSE OF THE GOSPEL

Luke's stated purpose has been discussed in the previous section. It was "to draw up an account" of "the things that have been fulfilled among us" and to enable Theophilus to "know the certainty" of what he had been taught (1:1–4).

Additional reasons have been suggested. Luke's emphasis on Pilate's recognition of Jesus' innocence may have been made to prove to the Romans the law-abiding nature of Christianity. The gospel also may have been intended to assert Jesus' superiority over John the Baptist at a time when the followers of the Baptist constituted a rival movement to the church. Again, it may have been directed against Gnostics, who belittled the humanity of Christ and discouraged martyrdom.

Moreover, Luke certainly would have been glad for his gospel to be instrumental in converting either Jews or Gentiles to faith in Christ. On the other hand, assuming that Theophilus, to whom the gospel was dedicated, was already a Christian, Luke's primary concern would have been to strengthen the faith and increase the knowledge of existing converts, not only Theophilus, but others as well.

V. THEOLOGY

Although Luke's gospel is not a theological treatise, it gives emphasis to some important theological themes.

A. God's Work in History. Prophecy and Fulfillment

Both Luke's gospel and the Acts make it clear that God is working out a plan of salvation in history. Some scholars claim that Luke divided history into three periods: Israel, Jesus, and the church. According to other interpreters, he divided history into two periods: prophecy and fulfillment. But whether there were two periods or three, the themes of prophecy and fulfillment and of God's activity in history have great prominence in the writings of Luke.

B. Christ

A central feature of Luke's theology is his doctrine of Christ. He depicts Jesus as the Messiah, Son of David, Son of God, Son of Man, and the Servant of God. He puts repeated emphasis on Jesus' status as Lord and suggests that various events recorded in the Hebrew Scriptures prefigure his ministry. He shows Jesus to be a real human being with human feelings but also declares his divine origin and power. Luke's gospel as a whole gives the impression that in the great events of Jesus' ministry he accomplished the work he was sent to do. That included healing of the body and forgiveness of sins, both of which are saving activities. This work culminated in his death, resurrection, and ascension; and it led to the gift of the Holy Spirit at Pentecost, an event recorded in Luke's second volume, the Acts of the Apostles.

Jesus had a universal mission. He ministered to Samaritans as well as Jews. He preached the Gospel to the poor, and he also directed his message to the rich and powerful. He befriended the outcasts of society, including lepers, demoniacs, tax collectors, and sinners. He admitted women to the circle of his followers and ministered to them as readily as to men. His ministry was intended to enable the whole of humanity to "see God's salvation" (3:6).

C. God

Luke gives prominence to Jesus' teaching about God's mercy to repentant sinners and God's initiative in seeking them out (15:1–32). God's mercy is exercised through the actual ministry of Jesus, as well as through his death and resurrection. But Jesus repeatedly warns men and women that they are accountable to God and liable to judgment.

Luke's gospel depicts God as transcendent, "the Most High," whom nobody knows except through revelation by the Son. But it also depicts God as the Father, with whom men and women can enter into close and familiar relationship (1:32, 35; 2:49; 11:2; 23:34, 46).

D. The Holy Spirit

The activity of the Spirit is affirmed in the opening chapters of the gospel. The Holy Spirit came upon Mary (1:35). John the Baptist, Elizabeth, and Zechariah were filled with the Spirit (1:15, 41, 67). Simeon received revelation from the Spirit and was moved by the Spirit (2:25–27).

In a unique sense Jesus was the bearer of the Spirit because he was the Messiah. He was conceived by the Spirit. The Spirit anointed him at his baptism and led him during his temptation and his ministry (3:21–22; 4:1–2, 18). He rejoiced in the Spirit and promised the gift of the Spirit to all who asked for it, and in particular to the victims of persecution (10:21; 11:13; 12:11–12). That gift had been prophesied by John the Baptist (Luke 3:16) and began to be imparted at Pentecost (Acts 2:4).

E. The Kingdom, Present and Future

Central to the teaching of Jesus are his affirmations about the kingdom (or reign) of God. In one sense he indicates that the kingdom is already present in the ministry he carries out (11:20). It is among or "within" people (17:20–21).

In another sense the kingdom lies in the future and will come with the return of Christ. That event, Jesus affirms, will surely take place. His coming may not occur so soon as some people expect. Nevertheless, he will return (17:22–37; 18:1–8; 19:11–27; 21:25–36).

Most of Jesus' teaching about the future deals with his final advent, the Last Judgment, and the final resurrection. But two passages in this gospel speak of a continuing existence between the moment of an individual's death and the resurrection of the dead. The dying thief is promised a place in paradise (23:43). And in the parable of the rich man and Lazarus, the rich man goes to hell and the poor man to Abraham's side (16:22–23).

F. Discipleship

At the heart of Jesus' teaching about daily life are the commandments to love God and love one's neighbor. But love of neighbor is extended to enemies, as is demonstrated in the parable of the good Samaritan (10:25–37). Jesus exhorts men and women to show mercy, to humble themselves, and to be of service to others. And he himself sets an example for this kind of conduct. To follow Jesus is to take up the cross, deny self, and be ready to give up all things (9:23–25).

This gospel lays stronger emphasis than the others on the danger of worldly wealth. The words of Mary in her song of thanksgiving (1:51–53); the woes Jesus utters against the rich and prosperous (6:24–25); and the parables of the rich fool (12:13–21); the shrewd manager (16:1–15); and the rich man and Lazarus (16:19–31) all address the issue of the use of worldly wealth.

Luke's gospel also gives special attention to prayer. As well as other teaching on the subject, the parables of the friend at midnight (11:5–13); the persistent widow (18:1–8); and the Pharisee and the tax collector (18:9–14) are concerned with prayer. Jesus is portrayed as a man of prayer, especially at key moments in his life such as his baptism (3:21); his appointment of the Twelve (6:12–16); Peter's confession of him as the Christ (9:18–20); his transfiguration (9:29); his agony (22:39–46); and his crucifixion (23:34, 46).

In fact, Jesus is an example to be followed (22:26–27). When Acts is compared with Luke's gospel, it becomes evident that the behavior of some of the early Christians follows the pattern of Jesus himself. The words of Stephen at his death are like the words of Jesus on the cross (Ac 7:59–60; cf. Lk 23:34, 46). The resoluteness of Paul on the way to Jerusalem is like the resoluteness of Jesus on his journey there (Ac 20:22; 21:13; cf. Lk 9:51). Just as Jesus appeared before the Jewish council, the rulers, and the people, so the early Christians appeared before the council, the rulers, and the people. Just as Jesus healed the sick and raised the dead, so did the apostles.

During the ministry of Jesus his disciples were not examples of noble conduct. Often they failed to understand him. Sometimes they were divided among themselves and preoccupied with selfish ambition. At Jesus' trial Peter denied him. Even after the discovery of the empty tomb they continued to be overwhelmed with doubt.

The picture is not entirely negative. Apart from Judas Iscariot, not one of them turned against him. They shared in his ministry of preaching and healing. Except during his trial and crucifixion, they showed no hesitation in remaining with him. And when they finally recognized that he had risen from the dead, they accepted the work to which he commissioned them.

G. The Church

The appointment by Jesus of twelve disciples symbolized the formation of the nucleus of a true and spiritual Israel. Although the gospel does not use the word *church,* it presents Jesus as establishing a community with a mission to all classes of society and to all nations (14:23; 24:47). The early life of the church is the theme of Acts, and Luke's gospel describes the work of Jesus that made that life possible.

VI. LUKE AS A WRITER

Luke's gospel is not organized according to a tightly structured pattern, but there are signs of a studied and often concealed artistry in his work. There is a symmetry about the opening and closing events of the gospel, both of which take place in the temple. Many of the themes stated in the opening chapters are repeated later in the work. And special emphasis is placed on Jesus' last journey to Jerusalem, which frames nearly half the contents of the gospel. Some of the allusions to the OT are made in such a way that the gospel can be read at two levels, either as a simple story or as a statement of the ways in which the events of Israelite history were reenacted in the life of Jesus. It is not surprising that Luke is one of the most widely read of biblical writers.

VII. LUKE'S GOSPEL IN CHRISTIAN TRADITION

Luke's gospel has played an important part in Christian tradition from the days of the early church to the present. The stories and teaching found only in this gospel have been specially treasured. Among them are the accounts of the angel's announcement to Mary, the shepherds' visit to the manger, the anointing of Jesus by a sinful woman, the encounter with Zacchaeus, the prayer of the crucified Jesus for the forgiveness of his killers, his promise to the dying thief, and his appearance to the disciples on the road to Emmaus. Jesus' parables found only in this gospel include the two debtors, the good Samaritan, the friend at midnight, the unfruitful fig tree, the rich fool, the lost coin, the lost (prodigal) son, the shrewd manager, the rich man and Lazarus, the persistent widow, and the Pharisee and the tax collector. Moreover, some of the hymns in this gospel, the songs of Mary and Zechariah, the song of the angels heard by the shepherds, and the prayer of Simeon, have been used for centuries in Christian worship.

The main themes of Luke's gospel are at the heart of traditional Christianity, and some of them have been given special emphasis in Wesleyan thought and practice. Luke's gospel stresses the ministry of Jesus to all classes of society and all peoples of the world. It proclaims the mercy of God to all sinners who repent, it shows a deep concern for the plight of the poor and the outcasts, it attaches great importance to the life of discipleship, it speaks of the need for a proper stewardship of material wealth, and it gives prominence to prayer. And in the story of the journey to Emmaus it tells of the encounter with the risen Christ and the experience of the burning heart. These themes are central in the Wesleyan tradition and are vividly presented in Luke's gospel.

VIII. OUTLINE

G. Peter's Denial (22:54–62)
H. The Trial (22:63–23:25)
I. The Crucifixion (23:26–56)
J. The Resurrection (24:1–53)

COMMENTARY

I. INTRODUCTION (1:1–4)

Luke explains that he wrote his gospel to give an orderly account of the events and teaching of Jesus' ministry and to enable Theophilus to know the truth about them. Theophilus may have been a high-ranking Roman, as the words **"most excellent"** suggest. His name literally means "friend of God." He already had been instructed in Christianity and was probably a Christian.

II. BIRTH, INFANCY, AND BOYHOOD (1:5–2:52)

A. The Annunciation of the Births of John the Baptist and Jesus (1:5–56)

The gospel story begins where it ends (24:52–53), in the temple. But while it ends with belief, it begins with doubt. The priest Zechariah could not believe that he and his wife, Elizabeth, were to be the parents of a child who was to fulfill the expectation of a returning Elijah (Mal. 4:5–6). Because of his unbelief Zechariah was deprived of speech (1:20).

Mary, the cousin of Elizabeth, was told that she was to be the mother of the Son of God, the promised Messiah of the house of David. His conception would not take place through the agency of a man but through the Holy Spirit. She reacted to the news at first with uncertainty (v.34) but then with acceptance, belief, and joy (vv.38, 45,

47). Her song of thanksgiving is known as the "Magnificat" (vv.46–55). This hymn celebrates God's exaltation of the lowly and God's care for the hungry. It is reminiscent of Hannah's song after the birth of Samuel (1Sa 2:1–10), and Luke may be implying that Samuel and Hannah prefigured Jesus and Mary.

B. The Birth of John the Baptist (1:57–80)

After the birth of John, at the time of his circumcision, Zechariah recovered his speech. His hymn of blessing and prophecy, traditionally called the "Benedictus" (vv.68–79), affirms that John will be the herald of the promised Messiah. Luke's account of John's growth (v.80) resembles the description of the growth of Samuel (1Sa 2:21, 26), to whom John as well as Jesus appears to be likened.

C. The Birth of Jesus (2:1–20)

Luke sets the events of the gospel against the background of world history. The pagan emperor's decree about a census created the situation in which the Messiah was born in David's city of Bethlehem. Matthew records the recognition of Jesus by Magi, men of high reputation and standing. But Luke describes the visit of shepherds, people of low esteem, to the manger where Jesus lay. The angel's song (v.14), according to many manuscripts, was "peace on earth, goodwill to men"; but the NIV translation, **"on earth peace to men on whom his favor rests,"** follows the earliest and most reliable manuscripts. Jesus did not bring political peace to the world, but he made it possible for men and women to have peace with God. Charles Wesley (1:183) interprets the message as "Peace on earth and mercy mild, / God and sinners reconciled."

D. The Infancy of Jesus (2:21-40)

Though Jesus was to liberate men and women from their obligation to the Jewish ritual law, he himself fulfilled its requirements. As Paul says, he was "born of a woman, born under law" (Gal 4:4). He was circumcised, his mother went through a ceremony of purification, and he was consecrated to God (vv.21-24).

Two people gave testimony to Jesus at this time. Simeon, a man full of the Spirit, was waiting to see the Messiah. In his hymn, the "Nunc Dimittis" (vv.29-32), he recognized Jesus as the Savior who would give light to all nations. Simeon's words imply that Jesus is the Servant spoken of in Isa 42:6; 49:6; 52:10. Simeon also prophesied the conflict and opposition that Jesus would arouse and the sorrow that Mary would experience (vv.34-35). The other person to give testimony to Jesus was the prophetess Anna (vv.36-38), but Luke gives no account of what she said.

E. The Boyhood of Jesus (2:41-52)

In words similar to those used to describe both Samuel and John the Baptist, Luke describes the growth of Jesus (vv.40, 52; see note on 1:80). He also records the only story in the Bible about Jesus' boyhood. The occasion may have been the preparation for his bar mitzvah a year later, when he would be initiated as a "son of the commandment" and assume the responsibilities of an adult. The story tells of Jesus' spiritual insight and the tension in his relationship with Mary and Joseph. In his first recorded words Jesus speaks of God as Father (v.49). While Mary, like Joseph, failed to understand Jesus (v.50), she pondered and treasured the memory of these events in her heart (vv.19, 51).

III. PRELUDE TO THE MINISTRY (3:1-4:13)

A. The Mission of John the Baptist (3:1-20)

Once again Luke sets his story in the context of world history (vv.1-2). He then declares John to be the person expected to prepare the way for the Lord. With his concern for the church's universal mission, Luke extends the quotation from Isaiah 40:3-5 as far as the statement that all humanity **will see God's salvation** (vv.4-6).

At the heart of John's message was the call to **a baptism of repentance for the forgiveness of sins** (v.3). This baptism symbolized both initiation and cleansing. It was used as a rite of initiation for gentile converts to Judaism, and the Jews practiced frequent ritual washings to cleanse themselves from defilement. The Baptist's claim that God could raise up from stones children to Abraham (v.8) suggests that he regarded baptism as an initiation into a spiritual Israel. He also saw it as a symbol of cleansing from moral defilement. He put great emphasis on judgment and the need to bear fruit in conduct (vv.7-9). He addressed social questions, including the sharing of clothes and food, honesty among tax collectors, and avoidance of injustice by soldiers (vv.10-14). His denunciation of Herod Antipas for marrying his brother's wife and for other unnamed **evil things** was his most provocative ethical teaching. It was this denunciation that led to the Baptist's imprisonment and death (vv.19–20; see Mt 14:1–12; Mk 6:14–29).

The Baptist prophesied the coming of **one more powerful** than himself who would baptize with the Holy Spirit and fire (vv.16–17). This baptism took place at Pentecost and, of course, on subsequent occasions.

Spirit baptism may be accompanied by outward manifestations, but, being spiritual, it is essentially an inward change. It is described as a baptism with fire, says Clarke (1:53, on Mt 3:11), because the Spirit is "to *illuminate* and *invigorate* the soul, *penetrate* every part, and *assimilate* the whole to the image of the God of glory." The Spirit, says John Wesley (*Notes*, 24, on Mt 3:11), inflames people's hearts with the "fire of love." The image of fire is often used for divine judgment. But insofar as judgment effects purification, it is not separate from baptism with the Spirit; it is part of the Spirit's work of inward change.

> O that it now from heaven might fall,
>   And all my sins consume!
> Come, Holy Ghost, for Thee I call,
>   Spirit of burning, come!
>
> Refining fire, go through my heart,
>   Illuminate my soul,
> Scatter Thy life through every part,
>   And sanctify the whole.
>   Charles Wesley (1:329)

B. The Baptism of Jesus (3:21–22)

Luke emphasizes that Jesus was praying when the Holy Spirit descended on him at his baptism. The Spirit, having been active in Jesus' birth, now empowered him for his ministry. As a rite of initiation, his baptism declared that Jesus was a member of the true, spiritual Israel. As a rite of cleansing, it indicated that, though sinless, he identified himself with sinners. The voice from heaven proclaimed that he was the Son of God. The descent of the Spirit on him showed him to be the Messiah or Christ (*Messiah* is based on the Aramaic and *Christ* on the Greek for "Anointed One").

C. The Genealogy of Jesus (3:23–38)

Both Matthew and Luke give the genealogy or family tree of Jesus. Attempts have been made to explain the differences between the two accounts, but there is no clear solution to the problem. Luke's genealogy was traced through Joseph rather than Mary because Jesus was legally the son of Joseph. There are three important features about his genealogy. First, it traces Jesus' descent from David, showing him to be the Messiah of the house of David. Second, it traces his descent from Adam, showing his relationship to the whole human race (the genealogy in Mt 1:1–17 goes back only to Abraham). Third, it describes Adam as the son of God, implying a contrast between Adam, the son who yielded to temptation, and Jesus, the Son who resisted temptation.

D. The Temptation of Jesus (4:1–13)

In the power of the Holy Spirit, Jesus retreated to the desert. The forty days of fasting recall the experiences of Moses and Elijah (Ex 34:28; 1Ki 19:8). Temptation came to Jesus as the Son of God, but he refused to use his position to perform spectacular signs, and he refused to win political authority by worshiping the Devil. In rejecting these temptations he remembered the words of Scripture. Deuteronomy especially came to mind (for vv.4, 8, 12, see Dt 8:3; 6:13, 16).

IV. JESUS IN GALILEE (4:14–9:50)

A. Preaching and Healing in Nazareth and Capernaum (4:14–44)

In the power of the Spirit Jesus began his ministry in Galilee. It is not certain that he was an ordained rabbi, but he did expound the Scriptures in the synagogues. At Nazareth (vv.14–30) he claimed to be the Anointed One of Isa 61:1–2 and therefore by implication the Messiah. His mission, he declared, was to the poor and oppressed. At first his preaching met with admiration. But when he spoke of the ministry of Elijah and Elisha to the Gentiles, there was an attempt on his life.

At Capernaum (vv.31–44) he displayed authority as both Teacher and Healer (vv.32, 36). His message was the **good news,** or evangel (Gk. *euangelion*), of the kingdom of God (v.43). People reacted to his activities with amazement (vv.32, 36). But when the demons he expelled recognized him as the **Holy One of God** and the **Son of God,** he told them to be silent (vv.33–35, 41).

B. The Call of the First Disciples (5:1–11)

The story of the catch of fish (5:1–11; cf. Jn 21:1–14) contrasts Jesus' power with the helplessness of his disciples. It depicts Simon Peter's recognition of his own sinfulness and the astonishment of Peter and his companions at Jesus' miraculous activity. And it tells how Jesus called Peter, James, and John to the work of evangelism.

Their task was to **catch** men and women.

C. A Leper and a Paralyzed Man (5:12–26)

The healing of the leper (vv.12–16) came in response to the leper's faith, and the healing of the paralyzed man (vv.17–26) acknowledged the faith of those who helped him. The story of the leper is reminiscent of that of Elisha and Naaman (2Ki 5:1–14) and shows Jesus' willingness to touch a man who was contaminated. The story of the paralyzed man shows how Jesus linked physical healing with the forgiveness of sins. It also shows how Jesus claimed authority to forgive sins, a claim the scribes and Pharisees condemned as blasphemous.

Jesus described himself as the **Son of Man.** Those words affirmed not only that he was a human being but that he was a person specially chosen by God. It was the form of address God used for Ezekiel (2:1), and in Daniel's vision "one like a son of man" is given dominion by God (7:13–14; cf. v.27).

D. The Call of Levi (5:27–39)

Having already called Peter, James, and John to be his disciples, Jesus called Levi, a tax collector, also known as Matthew. The scribes and Pharisees criticized Jesus because of his readiness to eat with tax collectors and sinners. Tax collectors had a reputation for embezzlement, and **sinners** were probably people with notorious reputations. With a touch of sarcasm, Jesus affirmed that his mission was not to the righteous (as the Pharisees judged themselves) but to sinners.

When he was challenged about fasting, he did not advocate it with the same rigor as John the Baptist (vv.33–39). Although he recognized it as a religious discipline (Mt 6:16–18), he defended the less ascetic behavior of his own disciples. As new wine needed new wineskins, so his teaching needed a new life-style. He was not obliged to keep all the ways of his predecessors.

He recognized, however, that the moment of his death would be a time for fasting. And so he made the first of his prophecies about the fate that awaited him. He also referred to himself as a bridegroom, an image which recalls the idea of God as the husband of Israel (e.g., Isa 54:5).

E. Conflict About the Sabbath (6:1-11)

Jesus ran into conflict with scribes and Pharisees about Sabbath observance. Although the law allowed people to pluck the heads of grain (Dt 23:25), the Pharisees objected to the disciples indulging in that activity on the Sabbath. Their objection was based on the assumption that the disciples' activity was work. Jesus replied that the law was disobeyed by David and his friends when they were hungry (Lev 24:5-9; 1Sa 21:1-6). The obligation to preserve life took precedence over other laws. He also affirmed that he was **Lord of the Sabbath**. And when he healed a man with a shriveled hand on the Sabbath, he defended the lawfulness of his act because he was saving life.

F. The Appointment of the Twelve (6:12-16)

Once again Luke depicts Jesus as a man of prayer. He shows him in communion with God on the mountain top. It was there, when day broke, that he chose the twelve apostles, giving Simon the name Peter, which means "rock" or "stone." Luke's list of disciples includes another Simon, described as the Zealot. The Zealots were members of a revolutionary movement that sought to expel the Romans by force. Whether or not Simon the Zealot remained in the movement is not known. But Jesus himself refused to support their violent methods.

G. The Sermon on a Level Place (6:17-49)

After various acts of healing, Jesus preached a sermon on **a level place,** or plain. This sermon contains much material that is also in the Sermon on the Mount (Mt 5-7). It begins with four blessings, all of which have parallels in the Sermon on the Mount. In Mt 5:3, 6 the blessings deal with spiritual poverty and hunger. In Lk 6:20-21 it is an open question whether Jesus' words about the poor and hungry refer to spiritual or material need. They may refer to both. The word translated **"blessed"** can also mean "happy." The blessings are followed by four woes, a stern warning to all who pride themselves on worldly success and affluence.

The sermon contains important teaching about discipleship. It includes the Golden Rule (v.31). It stresses the need to love enemies, refrain from violence, and give to the poor. Those who love in this way will become children of God. Indeed God is to be regarded as the pattern of merciful conduct. People should exercise forgiveness rather than judgment, and self-criticism should precede criticism of others. There is a strong emphasis on good works. It is not sufficient to pay lip service to Jesus as Lord. Obedience to his teaching is required. The parable of the two men, one who built his house on rock and the other on sand, dramatizes this message (vv.46-49).

H. The Centurion's Servant and the Widow's Son (7:1-17)

The centurion's servant, like the paralyzed man, was healed in response to someone else's faith (vv.1–10), in this case the faith of the gentile centurion. Not only did Jesus heal the sick; he also raised the dead (vv.11–17). Just as Elijah had restored the life of a widow's son (1Ki 17:17–24), so Jesus gave life to the son of the widow at Nain. Luke emphasizes Jesus' compassion: His **heart went out to** the woman who had lost her son.

I. Jesus and John the Baptist (7:18–35)

The Baptist, now in prison, sent his disciples to ask Jesus if he really was **the one who was to come**. In reply, Jesus first spoke about himself. He pointed out that he healed the sick, raised the dead, and preached good news to the poor. And he spoke of these activities in terms that recalled prophecies from Isa 29:18–19; 35:5–6; and 61:1.

Jesus then turned his attention to John the Baptist. He described him as a prophet and **more than a prophet**, the herald of the Lord's coming promised in Mal 3:1. Yet because John belonged to the old covenant of the law, the least person in God's kingdom was greater than he.

The incident closes with Jesus' observations about the reactions of people to the Baptist and to himself. His critics were never satisfied. They were like children who would play neither wedding nor funeral. They refused either to dance or to cry. They said that John the Baptist, an ascetic, had a demon. They called Jesus, on the other hand, a glutton and a drunkard. But, as Jesus observed, the wisdom of God is **proved right by all her children**, including Jesus and John.

J. The Sinful Woman (7:36–50)

Luke makes a strong contrast between a Pharisee and a woman who anointed Jesus' feet. The Pharisee was not utterly hostile to Jesus, since he had invited him to a meal. But he had failed to perform the courtesy of providing water to wash Jesus' feet. The woman, on the other hand, was overflowing with gratitude to him.

There is a contrast, too, between the Pharisee and Jesus. The Pharisee did not want to associate with the woman. But Jesus befriended her and accepted her gestures of gratitude. When he pronounced her forgiven, he was probably confirming the forgiveness that he had already granted her and which had evoked her adoration.

K. The Women (8:1–3)

This is the only gospel to mention that certain women supported Jesus' movement **out of their own means**. In particular, Joanna, being the wife of Herod Antipas's manager, was probably affluent. Luke includes both Mary Magdalene and Joanna among the women who discovered the empty tomb (24:10). He does not identify Mary Magdalene with the sinful woman of 7:36–50.

L. The Parable of the Sower (8:4–15)

According to some interpreters, the parable of the sower affirms that the kingdom of God has arrived in Jesus' ministry. According to others, it speaks of the coming of the kingdom in the future. In the opinion of yet others, it assures the disciples that their preaching will bear fruit in spite of setbacks. Charles Wesley (12:260) relates it to preaching:

> Lord, if at Thy command
> The word of life we sow,
> Water'd by Thy almighty hand,
> The seed shall surely grow.

The interpretation of the parable recorded in the gospel (vv.11–15) concentrates on the different reactions to preaching. Some people hear the message but do not receive it. Others receive the message at first but fall away in times of testing, such as persecution. Others fail in their allegiance because of their obsession with worldly wealth and pleasures. But others react positively to the preaching. They **retain** the word, show perseverance, and bear fruit.

Jesus' statement (vv.9–10) that parables are told so that people may not see or understand is influenced by Isa 6:9. This saying of Jesus has caused much perplexity. It could be interpreted to mean that he told the parables to conceal his message. But it could also mean that the people's lack of understanding was the result rather than the purpose of his teaching. According to John Wesley, they failed to understand because God had confirmed their previous decision to reject the message. "They would not see before; now they could not, God having given them up to the blindness which they had chosen" (*Notes*, 151, on Mk 4:12).

M. Sayings About Discipleship and Jesus' Family (8:16–21)

Jesus stressed the need to bear witness and to set an example for others. His followers should not be like people who hide a lamp in a jar. He also affirmed that his family was not confined to his blood relatives. It included everyone who obeyed God's Word.

N. The Storm (8:22–25)

The miracle of the calming of the storm demonstrates Jesus' power over nature. It contrasts the disciples' powerlessness with Jesus' ability to cope with the storm. There are theological implications in the story. The disciples' reaction to the miracle implied that Jesus was divine, since they spoke about him (v.25) in terms the psalmist used for God (107:28–29). Moreover, it is possible that Jesus' rebuke to the storm implied that there was a demon at work in it. Christian interpreters have also used this story to illustrate the power of Christ to bring salvation to people who are overwhelmed by the storms of daily life.

O. The Gerasene Demoniac (8:26–39)

On the eastern shores of the Sea of Galilee in gentile territory Jesus encountered a formidable demoniac. The numerous demonic forces that possessed him seemed like a whole Roman legion. When Jesus cured him, the demons entered a herd of pigs, who rushed to their destruction. Being unclean animals, the pigs symbolize the world apart from God.

P. Jairus' Daughter and the Woman With a Flow of Blood (8:40–56)

Jesus responded to Jairus' faith in behalf of his daughter by bringing his daughter back to life. In healing the woman with a flow of blood, Jesus responded to the sick person's own faith. His words to her, **"Your faith has healed you"** (v.48), can also be translated "Your faith has saved you." In Greek they are the same words he spoke to the sinful woman (7:50). Healing as well as forgiveness was part of his saving work.

Q. The Mission of the Twelve (9:1–9)

The mission of the twelve disciples, like that of Jesus himself, included both preaching and healing. They traveled with a minimum of possessions, relying on the hospitality of friends. They did not stay where they were unwelcome but left to the judgment of God those who rejected them.

About this time the activities of Jesus caused concern to Herod Antipas, ruler, or **tetrarch,** of Galilee, who had put John the Baptist to death. Herod finally met Jesus at his trial (23:6–12).

R. The Five Thousand (9:10–17)

The feeding of the five thousand illustrates Jesus' power over the forces of nature. There are other implications. The manner in which Jesus broke the bread suggests that this was a sacred meal that foreshadowed the Last Supper. Moreover, Jews expected a messianic feast in the kingdom of God: Jesus apparently understood both this occasion and the Last Supper itself as such a feast. This feeding miracle is also evidence of Jesus' compassion for men and women (Mk 6:34).

S. Peter's Confession of Jesus as the Christ (9:18–27)

This incident is located by Matthew and Mark near Caesarea Philippi, north of Galilee (Mt 16:13; Mk 8:27). It marked an important development in the relationship between Jesus and his disciples. Speaking for his colleagues, Peter confessed that Jesus was the Messiah. In accordance with his policy, Jesus told them to keep the matter a secret. He did not even speak of himself as Messiah, but chose instead to predict his death and resurrection. Characteristically, Luke shows Jesus at prayer on this occasion.

Sayings follow about discipleship (vv.23–27). The denial of the self Jesus commended is the removal of self from the center of ambition and the setting of him in that place. It involves taking up the cross and following him on the road of sacrifice and suffering. Only through the refusal to rely on earthly security is salvation attainable. Anyone who is ashamed of him will be accountable at the Last Day.

Jesus' promise that some of the onlookers will see the kingdom before their death is ambiguous. If it refers to his final coming, then in fact the onlookers died before that event. But the prophecy may have been fulfilled by Jesus' transfiguration, his resurrection, or the outpouring of the Spirit at Pentecost.

T. The Transfiguration and the Epileptic Boy (9:28–45)

In his account of the Transfiguration (vv.28–36) Luke mentions that Jesus was praying. This story depicts the divine glory of Christ. It implies that he is the fulfillment of the law, as symbolized by Moses, and of the prophets, as symbolized by Elijah. Moses and Elijah were speaking of Jesus' **departure** (Gk. *exodos*). The death of Christ was the beginning of a new exodus. For him it was an exodus from this earthly life and an entry into heavenly glory. For his followers it was an exodus from captivity to sin and an entry into new life.

The response of the disciples was not commendable. At first they fell asleep. When they awoke, Peter's immediate reaction was to be up and doing, not listening. But the divine voice told them that it was a time to listen to Jesus. Peter's suggestion about three **shelters** supports the theory that the Transfiguration occurred during the Feast of Tabernacles.

From the mountain, the place of vision, they came down to the valley, the place of suffering and need. But God's **greatness** (v.43) was seen in the valley as well as on the mountain. It was in the valley that Jesus healed an epileptic boy (vv.37–45). Jesus' power to heal the boy is contrasted with the disciples' failure to effect a cure because of their lack of faith. There is also a contrast between the wonder and amazement of the people and Jesus' awareness of the suffering that awaited him. And, as in the story of the Transfiguration, the disciples failed to understand.

U. The Dispute About Greatness (9:46–50)

Luke has shown the powerlessness of the disciples, their lack of faith, and their misunderstanding. Now he depicts their ambition and intolerance. When they disputed about precedence in God's kingdom, Jesus told them that true greatness consisted in childlike humility. And when they tried to prevent an outsider from healing in Jesus' name, he told them to desist.

V. THE JOURNEY TO JERUSALEM (9:51–19:27)

This gospel devotes nearly half its pages to the last journey of Jesus to Jerusalem. Luke says the time was approaching **for him to be taken up to heaven** (9:51). Aware of the destiny that awaited him, Jesus embarked on that period of his life that was to lead to a cross and an empty tomb and was to culminate in his ascension. In making this journey he set a pattern for obedience for his followers, a pattern that was followed by Paul as he made his own last journey to Jerusalem (Ac 20:22–23; 21:10–14).

A. Samaria (9:51–56)

After the Assyrians destroyed the northern kingdom of Israel in 722 B.C., they deported a large number of Israelites. Others were left behind, and some of them may have intermarried with Gentiles who settled in the area. In Jesus' day the Jews regarded the inhabitants, now called Samaritans, as Gentiles, though the Samaritans themselves claimed to be of Israelite descent. The religious practices and beliefs of the Samaritans, though similar to those of the Jews, were different in some important respects. They recognized only the Law as Scripture and not the rest of the Hebrew Scriptures. They said that sacrifice should be performed on Mount Gerizim in Samaria, not in the temple at Jerusalem. Great hostility existed between Jews and Samaritans, which led to eruptions of violence between them.

Luke shows a special interest in Samaritans. His gospel includes the parable of the good Samaritan and the account of the healing of a Samaritan leper (10:25–37; 17:11–19). And in Acts he reports that the mission of the church to the gentile world would begin in Samaria (Ac 1:8; 8:4–25).

Jesus himself wanted to proclaim his message to the people of a Samaritan village. When they were unwilling to welcome him (9:53), James and John remembered how Elijah called fire down on two unfortunate companies of the Israelite army in Samaritan territory (2Ki 1:1–18). They suggested that Jesus should do the same to the inhabitants of the inhospitable village. But he rejected their suggestion. His way was different from that of Elijah.

B. Following Jesus (9:57–62)

Not all prospective followers of Jesus were aware of the nature of discipleship. He used harsh words to make the issue plain. They would be following a leader who spent nights without a place to sleep. Loyalty to him must take priority over the burial of family. Indeed burying the dead was a task fit for the spiritually dead. And while Elijah allowed Elisha to visit his parents at home (1Ki 19:19–21), Jesus even excluded that possibility. It has been questioned whether Jesus intended his words to be taken literally. But he was certainly affirming the precedence of his right to obedience over all other claims.

C. The Mission of the Seventy (10:1–24)

Ch. 9 began with the mission of the Twelve; ch. 10 begins with the mission of the Seventy, a group not mentioned elsewhere in the Scriptures. A tradition says that Luke himself was a member of this group, but no biblical evidence supports it. The number seventy, like the number twelve, may have a symbolic meaning. It could represent the seventy nations of the Gentiles, although this mission does not appear to have been to gentile territory. Or it could stand for Israel, since there were seventy elders with Moses on the mountain. Jesus sent out the Seventy two by two, not just for companionship, but because in Jewish law at least two witnesses were needed to establish the truth of evidence.

Like the Twelve (cf. 9:1–6), the Seventy were told to travel light, without money or extra sandals. They were instructed to shake the dust off their feet if they were rejected. They were also informed of the fate that awaited the cities that rejected them. The mission of the Seventy was successful. They were able to cast out demons. Jesus recognized it as a defeat of Satan and invested the Seventy with authority over the powers of evil, symbolized by serpents and scorpions, perhaps in fulfillment of Ge 3:15. In memorable words Jesus affirmed the closeness of his relation to God the Father (v.22). No other saying in this gospel more clearly asserts his uniqueness as the revealer of God.

D. The Commandments of Love and the Parable of the Good Samaritan (10:25–37)

Jesus elicited from an expert in the law the assertion that the two great commandments were to love God and to love one's neighbor. These com-mandments were at the heart of Jesus' own teaching (Mt 22:34–40; Mk 12:28–34) and were based on Dt 6:5 and Lev 19:18. Obedience to these commandments, said Jesus, leads to eternal life.

To illustrate neighborly love, Jesus told the parable of the Good Samaritan. The road from Jerusalem to Jericho passed through rugged country. But although robbery was a typical incident on that road, it was by no means typical that a Samaritan would rush to the help of a Jew (see comments on 9:51–56).

For a Jewish audience, there was an element of shock in the story. It depicts a reversal of values, a world in which a Samaritan is the hero. But it did much more than unsettle people's values. It provided a positive ideal by which to live. It portrayed a vivid example of neighborly love. It demonstrated the meaning of love more vividly than any dictionary definition.

Love of neighbor crosses the boundaries of nation, race, and social class. Anyone in need is our neighbor. By depicting the Samaritan as the example to be followed and the representatives of conventional religion as the examples to be avoided, the parable issues a challenge not only to Jews but to Christians as well. "Let us go and do likewise, regarding every man as our neighbor who needs our assistance. Let us renounce that bigotry and party-zeal which would contract our hearts into an insensibility for all the human race, but a small number whose sentiments and practice are so much our own, that our love to them is but self-love reflected" (Wesley, *Notes*, 241–42).

E. Martha and Mary (10:38–42)

These two sisters and their brother Lazarus lived at Bethany (Jn 11:1–2). It was this Mary, not Mary Magdalene, who anointed Jesus a few days before his crucifixion (Jn 12:1–11). On that occasion, as on this, Martha performed the household duties, and Mary expressed her devotion to Jesus by listening. But in this earlier incident, recorded by Luke, Martha criticized Mary and provoked a rebuke from Jesus. Martha's fault was not her preoccupation with household chores. It was her hostile attitude toward her sister's readiness to listen to Jesus. This story, like that of the Transfiguration, indicates the importance of listening to Jesus and meditating on his words. Discipleship is not merely action. It involves contemplation.

> O that I could for ever sit,
> With Mary at the Master's feet!
> Charles Wesley (4:342)

F. Prayer (11:1–13)

The Lord's Prayer (vv.2–4) is normally said in a form similar to that of Mt 6:9–13. In Luke's gospel it is shorter and more informal than in Matthew. It addresses God as **"Father"** rather than as "Our Father." **Father** is the equivalent of the Aramaic *abba*, uttered by Jesus in Gethsemane (Mk 14:36). *Abba* was a mode of address to one's human father and was considered too informal to use in speaking to God, for whom "Our Father" was thought more appropriate. But Jesus addressed God as *Abba* and in this version of the Lord's Prayer encouraged his disciples to do so.

The prayer gives glory to God, whose name is holy. It looks for the coming of God's kingdom, inwardly in the heart and outwardly on earth. It asks for God's forgiveness but expects those who pray to show mercy to others. It seeks deliverance from temptation; and the most serious temptation is to abandon loyalty to Christ. John Wesley described the Lord's Prayer

"uttered from the heart" as "the badge of a real Christian" (*Notes*, 242).

The parable of the friend at midnight (vv.5–8) affirms that God will answer persistent prayer. Here is the scene. A Palestinian family is living in a one-room house. Husband, wife, and children sleep together on the same mattress. A neighbor knocks on the door, asking for a loaf to feed a friend who has just arrived. The husband is reluctant to be disturbed, since the rest of the family would also be awakened. But when the neighbor persists, he gives him the loaf. So, says Jesus, if we ask, we shall receive; and if we seek, we shall find (v.9).

Jesus did not mean that people will receive everything they ask for in prayer. But his teaching in 11:9–13 reaches its climax in the promise that prayer for the Holy Spirit will be answered in the affirmative. God is more than willing to give us this most important of gifts, if only we ask him.

G. Controversy About Demons (11:14–28)

In response to criticism Jesus affirmed that his success in casting out demons was not the work of the prince of demons. It was done by the **finger** (i.e., power) of God and was evidence that the kingdom of God had already come (v.20). But, he added, it is not sufficient for the soul to be rid of demons. An empty soul is an invitation for more demons to enter.

H. The Sign of Jonah and the Lamp of the Body (11:29–36)

Although Jesus performed miracles out of compassion for people's needs, he refused to perform them merely for the sake of publicity. The sign that he gave the people was the preaching of repentance, the sign of Jonah. Indeed, he was greater than either Solomon or Jonah.

His words about the lamp of the body describe some characteristics of the life of discipleship. In that life men and women do not hide the light of revelation which they have received from Christ; they make it available to others (v.33). And in that life the whole person is illuminated by the spiritual vision that is obtained by looking to Christ (vv.34–35). "Let your eye be singly fixed on him, aim only at pleasing God; and while you do this, your whole soul will be full of wisdom, holiness, and happiness" (Wesley, *Notes*, 245–46).

I. Woes to Pharisees and Legal Experts (11:37–54)

Controversy continued when a Pharisee invited Jesus to a meal. Jesus seized the occasion to denounce people who were obsessed with outward show but were inwardly impure. They sought a reputation through their good works but neglected love and justice. He also chided the legal experts for their oppressiveness in imposing unnecessary obligations on people, their hypocrisy in giving honor to martyrs, and their reactionary habit of hindering people from understanding the Scriptures.

J. Warnings and Assurances (12:1–12)

Jesus gave his disciples warnings and assurances to help them as they confronted opposition. He warned them about the Pharisees, whose harmful influence could expand as rapidly as yeast (v.1). But he assured them that his message, which they were proclaiming in comparative obscurity, would in the future be given widespread publicity (vv.2–3). He exhorted them to fear God rather than human beings and assured them of God's genuine care for

them (vv.4–7). The blasphemy against the Holy Spirit, which he denounced (vv.8–10), was the accusation made by his critics that the healing activity of the Spirit was in fact the work of demons. He promised his disciples that the Spirit would teach them what to say in time of persecution (vv.11–12), and in that way he prepared them for the experiences described in Acts.

K. Worldly Wealth, Watchfulness, Judgment, and Repentance (12:13–13:9)

In the parable of the rich fool (12:13–21) Jesus gave a warning against preoccupation with the accumulation of material wealth. Further, he exhorted his disciples to overcome anxiety by trusting in God's ability to provide for the necessities of life. They must give priority to the search for God's kingdom (vv.22–34). Like good servants, they should always be ready for the final advent of Christ (vv.35–48).

Jesus declared that he had not come to bring peace, but division (12:49–53). He had **come to bring fire on the earth** and wished **it were already kindled** (v.49). Many scholars (e.g., Coke, 1:575) think the imagery of fire refers to the division and persecution provoked by Jesus' ministry. Clarke (1:443) relates it both to the destruction of Jerusalem by the Romans and to the influence of the Spirit "in the destruction of sin." Others explain it as the purifying activity of the Spirit. John Wesley (*Notes*, 252) regards it as the fire of "heavenly love." The same idea influenced Charles Wesley (9:58–59):

> O Thou who camest from above,
>   The pure, celestial fire t'impart,
> Kindle a flame of sacred love
>   On the mean altar of my heart.

The baptism of which Jesus spoke (12:50) was his suffering and death. Thus Paul could write of "having been buried with him in baptism" (Col 2:12).

Jesus warned the people that the signs of the Day of Judgment were present. In readiness for that day they must be reconciled to God (12:54–59).

Finally he called on them to repent (13:1–5). In the parable of the unfruitful fig tree (vv.6–9), he offered them a new beginning in life but warned them of the consequences of rejecting his offer.

L. The Crippled Woman (13:10–17)

Jesus received criticism for healing a crippled woman on the Sabbath. In answer he pointed out the inconsistency of his critics. They themselves worked on the Sabbath when they cared for their animals. If it was legitimate on that day to look after animals, it certainly should be legitimate to heal the sick.

M. Teaching About the Kingdom of God and Judgment (13:18–35)

In the parables of the mustard seed and the yeast (vv.18–21) Jesus contrasted the small beginning of God's kingdom in his ministry with its great climax in the future. The birds of the air in v.19 may symbolize the Gentiles who enter the kingdom (see Da 4:20–22).

Jesus stressed the urgent need for a response to his message (vv.22–30). **"Make every effort"** (v.24) translates the Greek *agonizesthe*. "Agonize, therefore, now by faith, prayer, holiness, patience" is the interpretation given by John Wesley (*Notes*, 255). Jesus warns the Jews that Gentiles might enter the kingdom of God while they might be left outside. The feast he mentions is the messianic feast expected by Jews in the coming kingdom (v.29).

Fear of Herod Antipas did not deter Jesus from his mission. He predicted his own death in Jerusalem and the destruction of the city itself. At the same time he predicted that ultimately the people of Jerusalem would give recognition to him, though he did not specify when that would happen (vv.31–35).

N. Jesus at a Pharisee's House (14:1–24)

On another Sabbath, when Jesus was a Pharisee's guest, he healed a man suffering from dropsy (swollen limbs). Once again he defended his action. He added some advice about behavior at meals, counseling humility and advising people to invite the outcasts of society to their meals. In the parable of the banquet (vv.15–24) he warned his critics that if they excused themselves from accepting the invitation to God's kingdom, others would be invited. **The poor, the crippled, the blind and the lame** (v.21) may stand for the sick and the outcasts to whom Jesus ministered in Palestine, and the people on **the roads and country lanes** may represent the Gentiles. And in fact the sick, the outcasts, and the Gentiles did receive the good news of the kingdom. Charles Wesley (4:275) interpreted the parable as an invitation to all men and women to accept the Gospel message:

> Come, sinners, to the gospel feast,
> Let every soul be Jesu's guest;
> Ye need not one be left behind,
> For God hath bidden all mankind.

The command **"Make them come in"** (v.23) does not sanction religious persecution. It means that people should be made to come in "with all the violence of love, and the force of God's Word" (Wesley, *Notes*, 258).

O. Counting the Cost (14:25–35)

In further teaching about discipleship, Jesus asserted the priority of loyalty to himself over the closest family ties. The word **hate** (v.26) is an exaggeration. Jesus meant that love for family should take second place to devotion for him. People should count the cost of discipleship: giving up everything for Christ. Otherwise disciples become like salt that has lost its strength.

P. Parables of God's Mercy (15:1–32)

These three parables were told by Jesus to explain his friendship with tax collectors and sinners. They speak of God's mercy to sinners and imply that it was active in Jesus' ministry.

The parable of the lost sheep (vv.3–7) reflects the imagery of Eze 34:11–16. It proclaims God's joy over the recovery of the repentant sinner. It also demonstrates God's initiative in seeking the sinner. There is sarcasm in Jesus' reference to **righteous persons who do not need to repent**. He was repelled by the self-righteousness of his critics.

The parable of the lost coin has the same message as that of the lost sheep (vv.8–10). The woman's coin was precious to her for more than its monetary value: it may have been part of the dowry of coins that she wore on her headdress. It is noteworthy that this parable uses the action of a woman to represent the activity of God.

The parable of the lost or prodigal son (vv.11–32) is really about two sons. The first is a spectacular sinner, whose sins are newsworthy. The parable tells of God's readiness to welcome such people as children, even when

they have no merits to plead. The robe given by the father is a mark of honor and the shoes symbolize liberty. John Wesley (*Notes*, 263), elaborates even further: "He arrays him with the robe of a Redeemer's righteousness, with inward and outward holiness, adorns him with all sanctifying graces, and honours him with the tokens of adopting love."

The second son is a self-righteous, law-abiding person, like Jesus' critics. And Jesus may well have told the parable primarily as a challenge to such people. The parable is a story without an ending. Although the younger son has been received into the house, the elder son stands outside complaining. It is not clear whether he accepts or rejects his father's invitation to step inside. But it is clear that the father extends the same love and mercy to both his sons.

The central theme of this chapter is God's mercy to sinners, whoever they may be. It is reflected in Charles Wesley's words (1:92):

Outcasts of men, to you I call,
  Harlots, and publicans, and thieves!
He spreads His arms to embrace you all;
  Sinners alone His grace receives;
No need of Him the righteous have,
He came the lost to seek and save.

Q. The Use and Danger of Riches (16:1–31)

The parable of the shrewd manager (vv.1–15) commends shrewdness of action in times of crisis. It is uncertain whether the **master** who commended the manager (v.8) is the character in the parable or Jesus himself. In either case the parable commends, not the dishonesty, but the shrewdness of the manager. The **people of the light** (v.8), says Jesus, should heed his example and should use their wealth, not as he did, to cheat, but in such a way that God will receive them into the eternal kingdom. Those who abuse their riches are not fit managers of spiritual things. People cannot be servants of **both God and Money** (v.13). In a sermon on 16:9 entitled "The Use of Money" (*Works*, 2:266–80), John Wesley says that faithful stewardship of money involves adherence to the precepts "Gain all you can," "Save all you can," and "Give all you can."

According to Jesus, a new age had begun, the age of the kingdom of God (vv.16–18). The law remains, but the kingdom is its fulfillment. In fact, the standards of the kingdom are more demanding than the law, as Jesus' teaching about divorce shows.

This section on riches ends with the parable of the rich man and Lazarus (vv.19–31). The contrast is staggering. The rich man, expensively tailored, feasts sumptuously. The poor man, Lazarus, lies at the rich man's gate, covered with sores. The rich man's fault, though not explicitly stated, is his neglect of the poor man and his idolization of wealth. After this life, in death, the two men's fortunes are reversed: the rich man is in hell, and the poor man is at Abraham's side in a state of blessedness. The parable is both a warning to the rich and a promise to the oppressed. It also indicates that spectacular miracles, like the return of a man from the dead, will not change a person's heart. And it provides evidence of belief in a life after death that begins before the final resurrection.

R. Forgiveness and Faith (17:1–10)

Jesus uttered stern warnings to people who caused others to sin. At the same time he encouraged the practice of faith and spoke of the importance of service.

S. The Ten Lepers (17:11–19)

Jesus' ministry extended to Samaritans as well as Jews. Once, when Jesus had healed ten lepers, it was the Samaritan among them who returned to give thanks. The words translated **"Your faith has made you well"** may also be translated "Your faith has saved you." The man received spiritual as well as physical healing.

T. The Kingdom, the Present, and the Future (17:20–37)

To the Pharisees Jesus affirmed that the kingdom was already present (vv.20–21). Some translations say the kingdom is **"within you,"** others that it is "among you." In any case, it is unlikely Jesus regarded the kingdom as present in his critics. As John Wesley (*Notes*, 269) comments, "It is present in the soul of every true believer." The kingdom of God is not a particular domain or territory. It is, says Coke (1:622), "the new dispensation of religion, productive of the dominion of righteousness" in the minds of men and women.

Having spoken of the presence of the kingdom, Jesus turns his attention to the future (vv.22–37) and warns of the coming judgment. Some people think he is referring to a separate rapture when the faithful will be snatched to heaven several years before his final coming. But the most likely interpretation is that he speaks of that final advent itself.

U. The Parables of the Persistent Widow and the Pharisee and the Tax Collector (18:1–14)

The parable of the persistent widow (vv.1–8) speaks of prayer and the return of Christ. A widow who has been exploited takes her complaint to court. The judge has little regard for her, but when she presses him, he consents to give her justice. The parable draws attention to God's response to prayer. God is different from the judge, for God is just. But, like the judge, God listens to persistent prayer. And Jesus encourages his followers not to grow weary in prayer. In Jesus' day, in the early church, and in later ages, men and women have been perplexed by God's delay in bringing the justice for which they pray. Jesus affirms that God will answer their prayer, and that Christ, the Son of Man, will come.

The second of these parables deals with the Pharisee and the tax collector (vv.9–14). In one sense it is a parable of prayer, since it gives examples of how to pray and how not to pray. The Pharisee is the bad example, with his self-righteousness and contempt for others. The tax collector is the good example with his contrition and admission of dependence on God. In another sense the parable tells of the condition on which God accepts people. It is the repentant tax collector, not the self-righteous Pharisee, who is accepted by God. Humility, not self-exaltation, is the way to God's mercy.

V. More Teaching About the Kingdom (18:15–34)

The disciples, still devoid of understanding, tried to stop the children from being brought to Jesus. But Jesus welcomed them. It is the childlike attitude of dependence that is needed for entry into God's kingdom (vv.15–17).

The rich ruler (vv.18–30) approached Jesus with the words **"good teacher,"** but Jesus refused to be called **good**. He ascribed goodness only to God. The ruler's concern was to attain eternal life, which is the same as entering the kingdom. The obstacle that stood in his way was not his conformity to the law. He had kept all the com-

mandments from his boyhood. The obstacle was his refusal to abandon his material security. It is difficult, Jesus indicated, for rich people to enter God's kingdom. But they are not without hope, for God is able to do what seems impossible.

Those who leave home and family for the sake of God's kingdom, said Jesus, will receive homes and family in this life, and eternal life in the world to come (vv.29–30). He did not mean that in this life they would live in great material prosperity. That certainly was not the lot of his disciples. But Clarke (1:323, on Mk 10:30) points out that in fact the disciples found "spiritual relatives" among the members of the church and were able to enjoy the shelter of their homes and the produce of their lands.

Once again Jesus prophesies his death and resurrection, and once again his disciples fail to understand (vv.31–34).

W. Jesus in Jericho (18:35–19:27)

As he approached Jericho, Jesus healed a blind man who had greeted him as the Son of David (i.e., the Messiah). It was a healing in response to the man's faith (18:35–43). When Jesus entered Jericho, he gave recognition to Zacchaeus, the chief tax collector, calling him by name and asking to be his guest. Jesus' ministry to Zacchaeus was part of his work as Savior of the lost (19:1–10).

Jesus told the parable of the ten minas (19:11–27), a mina being the equivalent of three months' wages for a laborer. The parable presented a challenge to both the opponents and the disciples of Jesus. And it has presented an equal challenge to Christians of later generations. It is a warning to them of the dangers in neglecting the spiritual heritage with which they have been entrusted.

The parable may also have an allegorical significance. The nobleman's departure may signify Jesus' ascension. The enemies may be the opponents of Jesus. And the nobleman's return may refer to the coming of Christ in the future.

Jesus told the parable because **the people thought that the kingdom of God was going to appear at once** (19:11). Even during his ministry some of his disciples expected a dramatic divine intervention into the course of history. And in Luke's day, as well as in subsequent ages, members of the church have awaited the return of Jesus in the near future. With the passage of time such people begin to be restless. This parable gives them reassurance. The future kingdom may be delayed longer than they expect, but it will ultimately come.

VI. JESUS IN JERUSALEM (19:28–24:53)

A. The Entry (19:28–48)
The journey to Jerusalem, which began in 9:51, now reaches its climax. Jesus' entry into the city on a donkey was a fulfillment of the prophecy of Zec 9:9 and an act that declared him to be the Messiah. The people greeted him with words taken from Ps 118:26, a psalm composed for the welcome of a victorious king. His protest against the use of the temple for commercial purposes arose from his concern to preserve the building as a place of prayer (Isa 56:7). His implicit claim to be Messiah and his challenge to the temple authorities led the Jewish leaders to conspire against him.

B. The Opposition (20:1–21:4)
Jesus found himself in controversy with the Jewish leaders who tried to trap him into making statements that could be used against him in court (20:1–8). When they questioned him about the source of his authority, he did not give a direct answer but asked them to name the source of John the Baptist's authority, a question they were reluctant to answer.

He told the parable of the vineyard (20:9–19) as a warning to the Jews. Its form is allegorical. The vineyard stands for Israel, or the privilege of being God's people. Its owner is God. The servants beaten by the tenants are the prophets. The beloved son, who is killed, is Jesus. The destruction of the tenants is the overthrow of the Jews, which in fact occurred in the war of 66–73 A.D. And the **others** who receive the vineyard are the followers of Christ, whether Jews or Gentiles. But this parable is not just a warning to Jews. It challenges everyone who, by hostility or disloyalty to Jesus, crucifies him "all over again" (Heb 6:6).

Luke records two questions put to Jesus and one raised by Jesus himself. When the Jewish leaders asked Jesus about taxes (20:20–26), he indicated that taxes should be paid to Caesar. His reaction was consistent with his refusal to rebel against Rome. In answer to another question, put by the Sadducees (vv.27–40), he affirmed his belief in resurrection and took the position that marriage was a relationship for this present life rather than for the future. He then took the initiative and asked a question himself (20:41–44). He did not receive an answer, but the question implied that he was no mere son of David; he was David's Lord.

In the incidents that follow (20:45–21:4) there is a contrast between the exploitation of widows by the teachers of the law and a particular widow's own unstinted generosity.

C. Teaching About the End (21:5–38)

Jesus predicted the destruction of the temple and the persecution of his followers. Jerusalem, he said, would be trampled on **until the times of the Gentiles are fulfilled** (v.24). This prediction implied an end to gentile occupation of the city. But Jesus' prophecies extended beyond the fate of Jerusalem. He foretold his coming in a cloud and the signs that would precede him. **"This generation"** (v.32) probably refers to a period in the plan of salvation rather than a literal human generation.

D. The Last Supper (22:1–38)

The account of the Last Supper reveals the different attitudes of Jesus and his disciples during the final events of his earthly life. Jesus was resolved in his purpose. He had already planned for the supper. He knew that he was going to suffer, and he was determined to follow that destiny. The behavior of his disciples was varied. Judas, acting under the guidance of Satan (v.3), betrayed him. The other disciples remained faithful, but their behavior fell short of the ideal. Some of them were consumed with ambition, disputing who was the greatest (v.24). Peter would deny Jesus (vv.31–34).

The disciples misunderstood the purpose of Jesus' instruction to obtain swords (vv.35–38). He may have wanted them to be equipped for protection against wild animals on their future missionary journeys. Or he may have used **"sword"** as a metaphor for courage in time of conflict. His disciples thought he was talking about armed resistance.

Central to the story of the Last Supper is the account of the institution of a ritual meal (vv.14–23). Jesus gave thanks at the meal; and the Communion service has been called the "eucharist" (from Gk. *eucharistia*, "thanksgiving"). On the basis of his command to **"do this in remembrance of me"** (v.19), the service has also been regarded as a memorial rite. But the words of Jesus show that its significance extends far beyond mere remembrance.

The account of the Last Supper links Jesus' death with the sacrifices for the Passover, the sin offering, and the covenant. The description of the supper as a Passover meal (v.15) suggests that he effected a new Passover deliverance, not from Egypt but from sin. His statement that his body was **"given for you"** and his blood was **"poured out for you"** (vv.19–20) implies that he was a sacrificial offering for sin, like the Servant in Isa 53:12. His reference to **the new covenant in [his] blood** (v.20) indicates that his death ratified the new covenant of Jer 31:31–34, just as a sacrifice had ratified the covenant at Sinai (Ex 24:1–8).

Jesus asserted that the next time he drank wine would be when **the kingdom of God comes** (v.18). These words may have been fulfilled in a meal he shared with his disciples after his resurrection. Or they may refer to a messianic feast at his second advent. They may also look forward to a communion into which people may enter at death. Charles Wesley (5:24) had this last alternative in mind:

> Yet onward I haste
> To the heavenly feast;
> That, that is the fullness; but this is
>   the taste.

John Wesley rejected the idea that the bread and wine at Communion actually became the body and blood of Christ. In his comment on 22:19 he describes Jesus' words as "figurative language" (*Notes*, 286). At the same time he regarded participation in the service as a "means of grace" (*Works*,

1:389−90). The Wesleys believed in the "real presence" of Christ for those who received the bread and wine in faith.

> Come, Holy Ghost, Thine
>   influence shed,
>   And realize the sign;
> Thy life infuse into the bread,
> Thy power into the wine.
>
> Effectual let the tokens prove
>   And made, by heavenly art,
> Fit channels to convey thy love
>   To every faithful heart.
>   Charles Wesley (3:266).

After the institution of the supper Jesus exhorted his disciples to be servants, even as he was a servant (vv.24−27). His promise to them of authority in his kingdom may refer both to their leadership in the church and to their position at the Last Day (vv.28−30).

E. The Agony (22:39−46)

Christ's agony, says Luke, occurred at the Mount of Olives. Matthew and Mark indicate that Jesus was in Gethsemane, a garden at the foot of the mount (Mt 26:36; Mk 14:32). The story depicts the inner struggle of Jesus. His closeness to God is shown by his use of the intimate form of address **"Father"** (see on 11:1−13). His reluctance to take the cup of suffering reveals that he shared normal human fears. His submission to God's will shows him to be truly the Son of God. The reference to Jesus' **anguish** (v.44) (Gk. *agonia*) has led to the description of the incident as his agony. Some important early manuscripts omit vv.43−44; but in any case v.42, which is in all the manuscripts, reveals that he was experiencing an inner conflict.

Jesus' anguish has been attributed to his fear for himself and also to his sorrow for the sins of humanity. John Wesley claims that Jesus was "grappling

with the powers of darkness" (*Notes,* 288).

F. The Arrest (22:47−53)

In the darkness of night Judas approached Jesus in order to identify him with a kiss. But Jesus' followers were ready for a fight. One of them (Peter, according to Jn 18:10) struck the high priest's servant, but Jesus was the Healer even in the moment of his arrest (vv.50−51). Yet it was an hour when **darkness** (i.e., Satan) reigned (v.53).

G. Peter's Denial (22:54−62)

The explanation of this unfortunate event is found in Jesus' prediction in vv.31−32. When Peter denied his connection with Jesus, he was being sifted by Satan. This was a moment of temptation for Peter, and he yielded. But when he remembered Jesus' words, he wept. His weeping was a sign of repentance.

H. The Trial (22:63−23:25)

Luke mentions four stages in the trial of Jesus: the appearance before the Sanhedrin, the Jewish supreme council, presided over by the high priest; the appearance before Pilate, the Roman governor; the appearance before Herod Antipas, ruler, or tetrarch, of Galilee; and the appearance before the crowd. In Ac 4:25−28 these events are said to be a fulfillment of Ps 2:1−2. Jesus' reluctance to speak (23:9) is reminiscent of the Suffering Servant of Isa 53:7. But the words Jesus did speak aroused the anger of the Sanhedrin. He did not explicitly admit that he was the Christ, yet he spoke of himself as the Son of Man, seated at the right hand of God (22:66−69). When he was asked whether he was the Son of God, his reply, literally translated, was, "You say that I am." The NIV interprets it **"You are right in saying I am"** (v.70). According to another interpretation, however, his reply was deliberately ambiguous. Whatever may be its precise meaning, he said enough to reinforce his opponents in their desire to do away with him (v.71).

While the Jewish leaders treated Jesus as guilty (22:71), Pilate and Herod regarded him as innocent (23:4, 13–15, 22). Nevertheless, Pilate sent him to his death (vv.24–25).

I. The Crucifixion (23:26–56)

Simon of Cyrene, a Jewish visitor to Jerusalem, was forced to carry the beam of the cross, the stake itself being already in position (v.26). Simon thus represents everyone who takes up the cross and follows Jesus.

Jesus warned the weeping women of the fate that awaited the Jewish nation. The meaning of 23:31 is not clear. It may mean, "If crucifixion is the fate of the innocent Jesus (the green tree), what will be the fate of people who are guilty (the dry tree)?"

Jesus was crucified at the place called **the Skull** ("Golgotha" is based on the Aramaic and "Calvary" on the Latin for "skull"). Luke records three sayings of Jesus from the cross. The first is his prayer for the forgiveness of his enemies (v.34). The second is his promise that the dying thief will be with him that day in paradise (v.43). And in the third he commits his spirit to God (v.46; see Ps 31:5). The first and the last of these sayings were echoed by Stephen when he was stoned to death (Ac 7:59–60). The other saying promises life immediately after death.

The reactions of the onlookers to the crucifixion were varied. The rulers sneered at Jesus. The soldiers mocked him. One of the criminals crucified with him hurled insults at him. But the women mourned and wailed for him. The other thief asked Jesus to remember him. The centurion at the foot of the cross recognized him as a righteous man and praised God for him. And his friends **stood at a distance**.

The darkness over the land from the sixth to the ninth hours (12:00–3:00 P.M.) symbolized the activity of the power of evil (vv.44–45). But the tearing of the temple curtain symbolized the possibility of a new and direct relationship to God. The curtain was the barrier that separated people from the Holy of Holies, the most sacred part of the temple. The high priest entered there only once a year, on the Day of Atonement. But now the barrier was removed.

This story is told in such a way as to show that Jesus' death was in accordance with the Jewish Scriptures. The casting of lots, the offering of vinegar, and the centurion's words of praise all suggest that this was a time of fulfillment (vv.34, 36, 47; see Ps 22:18; 69:21; Isa 53:11).

The account of Jesus' death ends with the description of his burial (vv.50–56) by Joseph of Arimathea, a sympathetic member of the Sanhedrin. As a child Jesus was taken into the arms of Simeon, who was "waiting for the consolation of Israel" (2:25). After Jesus' death his body was laid in the tomb by Joseph of Arimathea, who was **waiting for the kingdom of God** (v.51).

J. The Resurrection (24:1–53)

The final chapter of Luke's gospel records the discovery of the empty tomb and the appearance of the risen Jesus. Certain important themes emerge from these stories.

It was the women who discovered the empty tomb and the women who brought the news to the apostles. And the immediate reaction of the apostles, as well as that of the disciples who walked to Emmaus, was to disbelieve the women (vv.1–11).

Two men, probably angels, stood beside the tomb. And two disciples met Jesus on the road to Emmaus (vv.4, 13–16). The emphasis on the presence of two people suggests the fulfillment of the law's requirement of two or three witnesses in support of evidence.

Luke records four appearances of Jesus: to Peter, to the two disciples on the road to Emmaus, to the apostles as a group, and again to the apostles at his ascension. All of them took place in Jerusalem or its neighborhood.

The appearance to Peter is not described, but it is mentioned in 24:34. Peter's first reaction when he saw the empty tomb was one of uncertainty rather than belief (v.12). But before the end of the day he had seen Jesus.

The appearance described most fully by Luke was to two disciples on the road to Emmaus (vv.13–35). One of the disciples was Cleopas. The name of the other is unknown. Jesus showed them how the Scriptures foreshadowed and prophesied his coming. As he interpreted the sacred writings, the hearts of his two disciples burned within them. His breaking of bread with them was probably a reenactment of the Last Supper, although he did not actually eat with them. But as he gave them the bread, they knew who he was.

On the burning hearts of the disciples John Wesley observes, "Did we not feel an unusual warmth of love?" (*Notes*, 297), language reminiscent of his description of his own heart "strangely warmed" in Aldersgate Street. The Emmaus story was seen by Charles Wesley (1:304) as a pattern of Christian experience.

Talk with me, Lord; Thyself reveal,
  While here o'er earth I rove;
Speak to my heart, and let it feel
  The kindling of Thy love.

It is noteworthy that Cleopas and his companion did not keep their experience to themselves but told it to the others.

The story of Jesus' appearance to the disciples later that day (vv.36–49) shows that even in the midst of their joy there was an element of doubt. But Jesus asserted the reality of his resurrection. He was not a ghost: he ate fish with his disciples. He explained how he had already fulfilled the Scriptures in his suffering, death, and resurrection. Moreover, the Scriptures would continue to be fulfilled in the preaching of the Good News to all nations. He commissioned his disciples as witnesses to the events that had occurred. He promised them the power of the Spirit and instructed them to remain in Jerusalem until they had received that power.

Jesus' final appearance to the disciples culminated in his ascension (vv.50–53). Although in his gospel Luke does not clearly separate it from the previous appearance, in Ac 1:6–11 he dates it to the fortieth day after the Resurrection. The Ascension was the climax of Jesus' ministry and prepared the way for the outpouring of the Spirit at Pentecost.

The gospel ends where it began, in the temple. It began with Zechariah, who doubted the angel's promise. It ends with the disciples, who praise God for the resurrection of Christ.

BIBLIOGRAPHY

Commentaries

Barclay, William. *The Gospel of Luke*. Philadelphia: Westminster, 1975.

Caird, G. B. *The Gospel of St. Luke*. Baltimore: Penguin, 1963.

Ellis, E. Earle. *The Gospel of Luke*. 2d ed. NCBC. Grand Rapids: Eerdmans, 1974.

Fitzmyer, Joseph A., S.J. *The Gospel According to Luke*. AB. 2 vols. Garden City, N.Y.: Doubleday, 1981, 1985.

Geldenhuys, Norval. *Commentary on the Gospel of Luke*. NICNT. Grand Rapids: Eerdmans, 1951.

Marshall, I. Howard. *The Gospel of Luke*. NIGTC. Grand Rapids: Eerdmans, 1978.

Morris, Leon. *The Gospel According to St. Luke*. TNTC. Grand Rapids: Eerdmans, 1974.

Schweizer, Eduard. *The Good News According to Luke*. Translated by David E. Green. Atlanta: John Knox, 1984.

Other Works

Barrett, C. K. *Luke the Historian in Recent Study*. London: Epworth, 1961.

Conzelmann, Hans. *The Theology of St. Luke*. Translated by Geoffrey Buswell. New York: Harper, 1960.

Danker, Frederick W. *Luke*. PC. Philadelphia: Fortress, 1976.

Marshall, I. Howard. *Luke: Historian and Theologian*. Grand Rapids: Zondervan, 1971.

Wesleyan Writings

Clarke, Adam. *The New Testament of Our Lord and Saviour Jesus Christ . . . With a Commentary and Critical Notes*. Vol. 1. New York: T. Mason & G. Lane, 1837.

Coke, Thomas. *A Commentary on the New Testament*. Vol. 1. New York: Daniel Hitt, 1812.

Wesley, John. *Explanatory Notes Upon the New Testament*. London: Epworth, 1966.

————. *The Works of John Wesley*. Vols. 1 and 2 (*Sermons*, vols. 1, 2). Edited by Albert C. Outler. Nashville: Abingdon, 1984–85.

Wesley, John and Charles. *The Poetical Works of John and Charles Wesley*. Collected and arranged by G. Osborn. 13 vols. London: Wesleyan-Methodist Conference Office, 1868–72. Cited as "Charles Wesley."

JOHN

Anthony Casurella

INTRODUCTION

I. THE SPIRITUAL GOSPEL

In a phrase now famous, Clement of Alexandria (ca. A.D. 150–215) referred to the Fourth Gospel as "the spiritual gospel." This he set in distinction to the other gospels, which had recorded, he felt, the "bodily facts" of Jesus' life and ministry. Since his day, we have come to understand that the Synoptic writers were also theologians with spiritual agendas, even where they seem most factual. Nevertheless, the Fourth Gospel has a distinctive style that shows it to be without question the result of profound theological reflection.

To see this, one need look no further than its use of language. It is not written in excellent Greek, at least not by classical standards; neither is its Greek poor, to judge from the remains of nonliterary writing of the first century. Even in English translation, the style is straightforward and the vocabulary fairly simple. But this in itself presents the reader with a challenge. For, although the text may seem plain and easy to comprehend, it repeatedly rises to heights of thought and spiritual insight that test even the most adept. Perhaps the prime example is the prologue (1:1–18), which introduces many of the themes to be developed later in the book. The modern reader does need some explanation of the name *Word*, it is true. But, apart from that, everything else seems at first sight readily accessible. Yet these verses address some very weighty topics: for example, Christ's preexistence and incarnation and the believer's life and salvation. The author did not come to comprehend such things in an instant; neither will his audience.

In addition, everything in John's gospel, even when Jesus speaks, is presented more or less uniformly in the idiom of the author. For this reason, it is not always possible to tell where a character leaves off speaking and the author begins. It is debated, for instance, whether Jesus' words to Nicodemus end with 3:21 or some verses earlier or whether the testimony of John the Baptist ends with 3:36 or with the climactic words of 3:30. In both cases, ending the speech earlier requires one to understand that the author has added a paragraph of interpretation to the account. But there is insufficient distinction between the speeches of the characters and John's regular manner of expression to be certain. His own language has colored everything; everything has passed through his thinking and received his impress.

The author's theological interests are readily apparent. Even quite ordinary, everyday things become symbols of spiritual realities beyond physical sight. Bread becomes a symbol of the spiritual food given by God in Jesus, who is the "bread of life" (6:35–58), and water the symbol of the Spirit (7:37–39), who was to be given to believers when Jesus had been glorified. This spiritual dimension, always present when Jesus speaks, is made prominent by a feature found frequently in his conversations. He will make an assertion that can be taken in more than one way. Although it rapidly becomes clear that for him the words carry a spiritual meaning, what he has said is misunderstood because it is viewed in a purely earthly way. This leads to a further statement, which clarifies the issue. Thus, for example, the conversation with Nicodemus turns on a Greek word that may mean either spiritually "from above" (Jesus' meaning) or simply "again" (Nicodemus's understanding) (3:3–8). Jesus is similarly misunderstood when he speaks to the woman of Sychar about "living water" (4:7–15) and when he tells the Jews about his impending return to the Father (7:33–36).

II. THEOLOGY

Through the years, the Fourth Gospel has led countless ordinary Christians to extraordinary heights of personal devotion and has inspired masterpieces of theology, music, art, and literature. Not least influential have been its powerful themes, among which are light, love, truth, and glory. All four of these converge on Jesus, who is the expression of God's love (3:16), who is the Light of the World (8:12), who is the Truth (14:6), and who both brings glory to God (14:13) and receives glory from God (12:28).

This gospel also has a good deal to say about the Spirit. It teaches that Jesus himself bore the Spirit (1:32–33; 3:34), that he both promised the Spirit (as the Counselor) and portrayed his functions (14:15–17, 26; 15:26; 16:5–15), and that he bestowed the Spirit (20:22). The Spirit's presence also marks the church. Without the Spirit there is no new birth and no entry into the kingdom of God (3:3–5). It is the Spirit who mediates life (6:63; cf. 7:38) and is effective in Christian worship (4:23–24). The Spirit is the power behind the church and the source of its authority; by receiving the Spirit, the church is equipped for its mission (20:21–23). The detailed teaching is in the passages on the Counselor (14:15–17, 26; 15:26; 16:5–15). The Fourth Gospel makes it plain that the Spirit is no option for the church.

Four major themes of John's gospel come together in 20:30–31, where the author states his purpose in writing. The first is a reference to the miraculous signs recorded in the gospel. In John the word *signs* regularly designates Jesus' miraculous works, which, as evidences (signs) of who he is, become pointers to faith in him (e.g., 2:11; 4:53–54; 6:14; 7:31). A second theme is that of belief in Jesus. Belief is the source of salvation, unbelief of condemnation (3:14–18). Life, the sure issue of belief, is yet a third theme. John 3:16 exalts this idea; so do many other texts in John.

This brings us to the fourth theme mentioned in 20:30–31, the identity of Jesus himself. As Christology is central to John, central to Johannine Christology are two dominant paradoxes: the paradox of Jesus' unity with and distinction from God and the paradox of his simultaneous deity and humanity. These particular verses underscore his relationship to God, whose Son he is.

The unity of Jesus with God is addressed at the very beginning of the Gospel. Jesus is the incarnation of the Word (1:14 and context; cf. 1:18) who both was God (vv.1–2) and was responsible for creation (vv.3, 10). But *Word* theology, as an expression of the link between Jesus and God, occurs only in the opening section. The fundamental Johannine designation of their relationship and of their unity is *Father* and *Son*. As Son, Jesus is very close to the Father. He does what the Father does and only what the Father does (5:17; 19). He judges rightly because in his judging he is in agreement with the Father (8:16; cf. 5:30). And his working in accordance with God's will is absolute: the purpose of his mission is to do the will of the one who sent him (6:38); the denouement of his life would make it plain that he acted precisely as taught by the Father (8:28); even the laying down and taking up again of his life are dependent on the Father's command (10:18). So close are Jesus and his Father that he can reassure Philip and the perplexed disciples that to see him is to have seen the Father (14:9; cf. 12:45); he can inform the Pharisees that, if they would, they could know the Father through him, because to know him is to know the Father (8:19); and he can berate the Jews for their unbelief in the Father, because it is belief in Jesus that equals belief in God (12:44). And eternal life, which consists in knowing the only true God, has as a second element knowing Jesus Christ (17:3).

It is part of the method of John's gospel that we are allowed to watch individuals and groups struggling with the question of Jesus' identity. The matter of Jesus' physical origin and its implications for various individuals is a good case in point. In the beginning, when Philip identifies Jesus *of Nazareth* as the one of whom Moses and the prophets spoke, Nathaniel responds with incredulity; yet he acts on Philip's simple invitation to come and see for himself and is convinced (1:45–51). He, like the man born blind (9:1–38), comes to see and so comes to believe. Others, however, use knowledge of Jesus' Galilean home as a way of not acknowledging his claims (7:40–43, 50–52). As the text makes clear, some are self-blinded (e.g., 9:39–41).

These passages raise the question of Jesus' messiahship. Deity is at issue in 5:18 and 10:33. In both places he is charged with claiming to be, or making himself equal to, God. Neither charge is rebutted; for, though

Jesus was not exactly making himself equal to God, the author does not want to say that he is not God. In fact, his own understanding is reflected in two passages that bracket the gospel. The first is the opening assertion of deity for the Word and thus for Jesus (1:1–2). The second is Thomas's spontaneous worship of the resurrected Jesus with language no faithful Jew would ever ascribe to any but God Almighty (20:28).

III. AUTHORSHIP

It is uncertain who wrote the Fourth Gospel. We know that behind it stands the authority of "the disciple whom Jesus loved" (21:24), about whom we are given some details (13:23–26; 19:25–27; 20:1–9; 21:1–14, 20–24; cf. 1:35–40 and 19:34–37). But in spite of exhaustive debate by experts, we cannot with certainty name him. Answers to questions of date and place of writing are also indefinite, partly because they depend on some of the same vagaries of evidence that beleaguer the issue of authorship. As these matters are really too technical to pursue here, the reader is referred to the commentary by Beasley-Murray (pp. xxxii, lxvi–lxxxi), which discusses them at greater length.

IV. OUTLINE

I. Prologue (1:1–18)

II. Public Ministry (1:19–12:50)
  A. John's First Testimony (1:19–34)
  B. Jesus' First Disciples (1:35–51)
  C. Water Changed Into Wine (2:1–12)
  D. Clearing of the Temple (2:13–25)
  E. Interview With Nicodemus (3:1–21)
  F. John's Second Testimony (3:22–36)
  G. Stopover in Samaria (4:1–42)
    1. Visit with the woman at the well (4:1–26)
    2. Reaction of the disciples (4:27–38)
    3. Response of the villagers (4:39–42
  H. Healing of an Official's Son (4:43–54)
  I. Events in Jerusalem at a Jewish Feast (5:1–47)
    1. Sabbath healing at the Pool of Bethesda (5:1–15)
    2. Controversy with the Jews (5:16–30)
    3. Various testimonies about Jesus (5:31–47)
  J. Feeding of the Multitude and What Followed (6:1–71)
    1. Feeding (6:1–15)
    2. Jesus' walk on the lake (6:16–24)
    3. Teaching about the Bread of Life (6:25–59)
    4. Desertion by many disciples (6:60–71)
  K. Feast of Tabernacles (7:1–8:59)
    1. Jesus' journey to the feast (7:1–13)

1. Empty tomb (20:1–9)
2. Appearance to Mary Magdalene (20:10–18)
3. Appearances to the disciples (20:19–29)

V. Purpose Statement (20:30–31)

VI. Epilogue (21:1–25)
    A. Catch of Fish (21:1–14)
    B. Jesus' Conversation With Peter (21:15–23)
    C. Authorship and Omissions (21:24–25)

COMMENTARY

I. PROLOGUE (1:1–18)

The prologue sets the earthly ministry of Jesus against a cosmic background and so gives us the theological key for understanding it. John begins, not at the baptism of Jesus as does Mark, nor even with his conception and birth as do Matthew and Luke, but "in the beginning" (v.1), a phrase reminiscent of Ge 1:1. In this passage Jesus is identified as the incarnation of the eternal *Word*. On the rich background and significance of this term, see the commentaries (Barrett, 152–55; Beasley-Murray, 6–10).

This Word is brought into relationship with God in the closest possible way. He both was God and was present with God in the beginning (vv.1–2). He was God's agent in creation (v.3; cf. v.10) and was the uncomprehended source of the life that was light for humankind (vv.4–5). He brought salvation into his world (vv.9–13), but, despite John's testimony (vv.6–8), he was not universally received. It is this Word who became incarnate in Jesus (v.14). John the Baptist gave testimony to his greatness (v.15; cf. vv.27, 30), and the author adds to John's testimony that Jesus superseded even Moses. Moses gave only the Law, but the Incarnate One gave grace and truth

and revealed God the Father, whom no human has ever seen (vv.16–18).

With this beginning, the author makes it clear that the story of Jesus is no mere earthly story about a merely human figure. Jesus is the incarnation of a divine person present with God before creation and identified with him. This must be kept firmly in mind as one reads the account that follows. In addition, the author sounds several themes that will recur throughout the gospel: life, the opposition of light and darkness, the world, belief and spiritual birth, truth, glory, and Father and (by implication) Son. For a brief but helpful summary of some of the characteristic ideas in John, see Turner (26–43).

II. PUBLIC MINISTRY (1:19–12:50)

The first half of the Gospel is an account of the more or less public portion of Jesus' life and ministry.

A. John's First Testimony (1:19–34)

John the Baptist's testimony to Jesus has already been mentioned in a general way in the prologue (1:6–8, 15). Now the narrative turns to his witness on two specific occasions. First he speaks negatively, about himself, and then positively, about Jesus.

John's ministry must have attracted considerable attention (cf. Mt 3:5–6; Mk 1:5). At any rate, he was visible enough that the Jews sent official emissaries to his workplace at the fords of the Jordan east of Jericho to question him about his identity (vv.19–28). Judging from their question (v.25) and John's denial (v.20), there seems to have been at least some speculation that John was the Christ (i.e., Messiah). He refused to be mistaken as the Christ or as either of the figures specifically mentioned, Elijah (cf. Mal 4:5–6; Mt 11:14; 17:12) or "the Prophet" (cf. Dt 18:15, 18). He was instead, he insisted, the forerunner spoken of by Isaiah (Isa 40:3), and he announced one among them far greater than himself.

Indeed, the reason for John's ministry of baptism was to make this greater one known. This he did the very next day (vv.29–34). In imagery strongly influenced by his Jewish heritage, John called Jesus **the Lamb of God, who takes away the sin of the world!** He identified him as the one he had spoken of before (see 1:15, 27). He testified that he had seen the Spirit descend and remain on him and prophesied that he would baptize with the Holy Spirit.

The image of the Lamb of God has held great power for Christians through the years since John. Charles Wesley used it as the climax of his great hymn "Jesus, the Name High Over All."

> His only righteousness I show,
> His saving truth proclaim;
> 'Tis all my business here below
> To cry, "Behold the Lamb!"

> Happy, if with my latest breath
> I might but gasp His name;
> Preach Him to all, and cry in death,
> "Behold, behold the Lamb!"

B. Jesus' First Disciples (1:35–51)

John's repeated reference to Jesus as the Lamb of God led two of his disciples to attach themselves to Jesus (vv.35–42). One of them was Andrew, the brother of Simon, whom Jesus renamed Cephas (Aramaic for *rock*). The other might have been John the son of Zebedee, but this cannot be proved. Two other disciples were added **the next day** (vv.43–51). When Jesus was ready to leave for Galilee, he called Philip of Bethsaida to follow him. Philip in turn informed Nathaniel of Jesus, naming him as the one foretold in the Law—that is, the Messiah. Nathaniel's initial skepticism gave way to a confession of faith when he saw a display of Jesus' supernatural knowledge. This in turn led to a solemn assertion that Nathaniel would see even greater things than this, for Jesus is the Son of Man, the Mediator between heaven and earth.

C. Water Changed Into Wine (2:1–12)

Jesus' miraculous works began in a town named Cana very soon (**On the third day**) after the prediction to Nathaniel of greater things to come (1:50). Of the location of this place, mentioned in John alone (vv.1, 11; 4:46; 21:2), it is known only that it lay in Galilee. The occasion was a wedding feast at which Jesus and his mother were guests. His disciples were also present, though in what numbers is not specified.

The narrative is straightforward and is simply recounted. Jesus' mother drew to his attention that the wine at the feast had run out, an affront to the standards of hospitality of that day. He supplied the lack by miraculously changing into wine a large quantity of water, somewhere between 120 and 180 gallons. The master of ceremonies recognized the superior quality of the new supply and commented on it to the bridegroom.

Jesus' response to his mother (v.4) needs some explanation. The address, **Woman,** which sounds disrespectful to modern ears, was in reality neither harsh nor discourteous (cf. 19:26). It is rendered felicitously in the NIV with **Dear woman.** But the words that follow are not so well translated with **Why do you involve me?** As the sequel shows, Jesus was not rejecting involvement, but only the initiative of his mother. He is now independent of family (cf. 7:1–9) and, indeed, any earthly claims, and he acts only when it is time. The time (literally *hour*) of Jesus in John refers to his death and exaltation (cf. 7:30; 8:20; 12:23, 27; 13:1; 17:1) and to anticipatory manifestations of his glory (vv.4, 11).

As usual in John, this miracle signifies something beyond itself. It is, in fact, a miniature of the Gospel. Jewish legalism (symbolized by the water of purification) is replaced by the wine of the new order. It is a sign that reveals the glory of Jesus and moves the disciples to put their faith in him (v.11). *Sign* is the word for a miracle of Jesus in John; it is a precursor to belief (20:30–31; cf. 2:23; 3:2; 4:53–54; 6:14; 7:31; 9:16; 11:47–48; 12:18, 37).

After the wedding at Cana, Jesus, his mother, his brothers, and his disciples went down to Capernaum on the shore of the lake (thus at a lower elevation), and for a few days Jesus remained in Galilee and relative obscurity (v.12). His mother and brothers appear only once more each in this gospel (brothers, 7:1–10; mother, 19:25–27; cf. 6:42).

D. Clearing of the Temple (2:13–25)

Jesus made the customary Jewish pilgrimage to Jerusalem for a Passover Feast, the first of three mentioned in John (v.13; 6:4; 11:55). He opened his ministry there by driving the money changers and animal traders from the outer court of the temple. Their activity there was doubtless intended as a convenience for pilgrims, who needed animals for sacrifice and currency conversion. Jewish law required the annual temple poll tax to be paid in Tyrian coinage, noted for its silver content. Perhaps there were abuses of the system, but Jesus' primary concern (v.16) was that the trading activity was inimical to worship, the true purpose of the temple. The quotation from Ps 69:9, based on reflection by the disciples but cited approvingly by the author (v.17), underscores the messianic significance of this deed.

The Jewish leaders, understandably troubled by what Jesus had done, asked him for a miraculous sign confirming his authority to do it (v.18). His reply is worked out in 2:19–22 in a pattern typical of this gospel. It is stated (v.19), misunderstood (v.20), and then explained more fully (vv.21–22). Jesus used the temple, at that moment present to all minds, as a prophetic symbol of his coming death and resurrection. The Jews overlooked the symbolic aspect and heard only a reference to the temple itself, begun by Herod in 20/19 B.C. but not completed until ca. A.D. 63 and not yet finished at the time of Jesus' ministry.

The disciples recalled this event and came to understanding and fuller belief after the Resurrection (v.22). Many others believed in Jesus as a result of the miraculous signs (see the comment on v.11) that Jesus did at the Passover Feast (v.23). What they were, apart from his action in the temple, is not specified.

E. Interview With Nicodemus (3:1–21)

All we know about Nicodemus is what the Gospel of John tells us (3:1ff.; 7:50; 19:39). This prominent Jew held a conversation with Jesus at night. He was apparently one of those influenced by Jesus' signs at the feast (2:23). At any rate, his opening words (v.2) were favorable toward Jesus. That the interview was **at night** may be simply circumstantial; we know that the rabbis sometimes conducted their discussions until late in the evening. Perhaps Nicodemus either could not meet Jesus during the day or because of timidity did not want to. Or the words may possess a wider Johannine significance and indicate the darkness in which all dwell who are apart from the true Light (cf. 8:12; 9:4–5; 11:9–10; 13:30).

Nicodemus opened by acknowledging that Jesus' miraculous works revealed his origin in God and endorsement by God. In response Jesus maintained that the object of Jewish desire, the kingdom of God, was unattainable without rebirth. The Greek behind this has two possible meanings, either "born again" or "born from above." From what follows, it is clear that, while Jesus was thinking of spiritual birth, Nicodemus understood him to be speaking of a simple physical rebirth and was understandably incredulous. Jesus explained and expanded. Here again we see the common Johannine pattern of statement, misunderstanding, and an explanation that brings understanding.

First, Jesus stated again that rebirth from the Spirit is the prerequisite for entry into the kingdom of God (v.5). This means conversion, which marks Christians off from non-Christians. The meaning of **water** is debated; it refers either to natural birth or baptism. Jesus was speaking of something that can be received and understood only spiritually (vv.7–8). (These verses were expounded by John Wesley in his sermons on new birth [sermon no. 18: vol. 5, pp. 212–23; sermon no. 45: vol. 6, pp. 65–77], and again in his disquisition on the doctrine of original sin [vol. 9, pp. 404–9, 438].)

Second, (vv.10–13), the true interpreter of heavenly matters is the Son of Man, who came from there. But how can he speak directly of heavenly matters when he has not been believed even when using earthly terms to explain spiritual realities?

Third, he is also the source of life and light (vv.14–21), which all who believe in him receive. Those who do not believe love darkness and are self-condemned.

Lifted up (v.14) refers to the events at the end of Jesus' life, which are at once crucifixion and exaltation (cf. 8:28 and 12:32). Jn 3:16, perhaps the best-known biblical text in the history of the church, is an excellent summation of both John and the Gospel of Christ. Adam Clarke devoted considerable space to expounding the verse in exactly these terms in his commentary (p. 533). Thus the brief narrative portion of this text prepares the way for profound teaching.

F. John's Second Testimony (3:22–36)

Jesus and John were engaged simultaneously in ministries involving baptism (but cf. 4:2). Jesus was at work somewhere in the Judean countryside (v.22), and John at Aenon near Salim (v.23), whose precise location is not now known. A dispute between John's disciples and **a certain Jew** about ceremonial washing (v.25), stimulated no doubt by John's ministry, led to a pointed reference to Jesus' baptism and popularity (v.26).

But John felt neither threat nor jealousy. The honor that both were receiving was decreed in heaven, that is, by God (v.27), and God's arrangements were not to be disputed. In any case, John was not the Christ but only the forerunner (v.28; cf. 1:20, 23). Jesus was the Christ (implied). Now that he was present, John must diminish (v.30).

John 3:31–36 is probably a commentary on the Baptist's words rather than part of the quotation itself. They reiterate Jesus' heavenly origin over against John's earthly origin (vv.31–32). Indeed, the unlimited bestowal of the Spirit on Jesus guarantees that what he has to say is straight from God (v.34). Refusal to accept his testimony (v.32) leads to disaster, but whoever believes in him receives eternal life (v.36). In this passage Jesus is spoken of as **the one whom God has sent** and as the Son of the Father; both are modes of expression characteristic of this gospel.

G. Stopover in Samaria (4:1–42)

The Fourth Gospel has shown Jesus to be the culmination of orthodox Judaism (2:1–11; 3:1–21). In the account of his visit with the Samaritan woman, he is seen to supersede heretical Judaism as well. The pattern familiar in John of statement-misunderstanding-clarification occurs several times in this section.

1. Visit with the woman at the well (4:1–26)

The first several verses set the stage for the conversation at the well in Sychar. Jesus was moving from Judea to Galilee (v.3) because the Pharisees had learned of his success in winning and baptizing (cf. 3:22, 26) disciples (4:1, but cf. v.2). For the journey, he chose the route usually followed by travelers between Judea and Galilee, which went west of the Jordan through the region of Samaria (v.4). Perhaps by the words **had to** the author intended the reader to understand that divine compulsion was involved. Jesus' path led him through the village of Sychar (probably modern Askar), close to land purchased by Jacob and apparently given by him to Joseph (v.5; seemingly the reference is to Ge 48:21–22; cf. 33:18–19 and Jos 24:32). Jacob's well, where he rested at about noon (v.6), is identified by ancient tradition but is mentioned nowhere else in Scripture.

The Samaritan woman was not a controversialist determined to argue with anything Jesus might have said. Rather, she was a person who, despite initial misapprehension of who he was, followed his explanations all the way to acceptance of him as Christ. In that regard, she is in John a paradigm of faith.

A dialogue ensued, with the woman expressing surprise (v.9) that Jesus had asked her for a drink (v.7). Jews in the first century thought it unseemly for a rabbi to talk to a woman (cf. v.27). Furthermore, there was a history of tension between Jews and Samaritans. Because Jews could never be certain that Samaritans had properly observed the purity laws, they would not use vessels in common with them. (The final clause in v.9 should be translated "Jews do not share [utensils] with Samaritans"; with the translation **Jews do not associate with Samaritans,** contrast v.8.) The situation demanded clarification, and that was given in the ensuing conversation (vv.10–15), which develops the theme of water (cf. 3:5; 7:37–39; 19:34).

In response to her surprise that he should ask her for a drink, Jesus offered the woman living water (v.10). He was speaking of water that gives eternal life, but she understood him to be offering running water, which would have made him greater even than Jacob, who provided a well, not a spring, and she was incredulous (vv.11–12). Of course, the author knows that Jesus was greater than Jacob, but not in the way she thought. Jesus then stated the issue plainly (vv.13–14), but the woman still misunderstood (v.15). One is reminded of the familiar words of Charles Wesley:

> Thou of life the fountain art,
> Freely let me take of Thee;
> Spring Thou up within my heart,
> Rise to all eternity.
> ("Jesus, Lover of My Soul")

Jesus' change of subject (v.16) led to the revelations that the woman was at present unmarried and that Jesus knew about her marital history (vv.17–18). Impressed at his prophetic knowledge, she raised the main question that divided Jews and Samaritans, whether Jerusalem or Mount Gerazim was the right place to worship God (vv.19–20). Once again Jesus deepened the discussion (vv.21–24). If it were simply a matter of deciding between Jewish and Samaritan worship, the Jewish way is right. But even that is being superseded by a spiritual manner of worship in which God and humanity find their true union in Jesus, who is the Truth (cf. 14:6). After this, there was only one thing left to say: Jesus is the Christ. The woman guessed it (v.25), and Jesus acknowledged it (v.26).

2. Reaction of the disciples (4:27–38)

The disciples returned and were surprised to find Jesus talking with a woman (v.27; cf. the comment on v.9). The woman reported her conclusion about Jesus and his identity to the villagers and invited them to come see him (vv.28–29). When the disciples encouraged Jesus to partake of some physical nourishment (v.31), his response in terms of spiritual food (v.32) mystified them. They wondered if someone else might have fed him (v.33). But he was referring to doing the will of God (v.34) and was speaking of the work of evangelism that God had outlined for both him and them (vv.35–38).

3. Response of the villagers (4:39–42)

The story of the conversations at Jacob's well is brought to a close by an account of wider Samaritan response to Jesus. The villagers, first attracted by the woman's testimony about Jesus, came to believe for themselves that he was the Savior of the world (not the Savior of the Jews alone). During his subsequent two-day stay with them, even more became believers.

H. Healing of an Official's Son (4:43–54)

From Samaria Jesus went into Galilee, where he was well received because of the signs he had performed at the Passover in Jerusalem (cf. 2:23). At Cana he performed yet a second (v.54; cf. 2:11) miracle, this time by healing from a distance of some miles the son of a person who may have been a non-Jew (cf. Mt 8:5–13; Lk 7:1–10). As a result of this miraculous sign, an entire household became believers (v.53).

I. Events in Jerusalem at a Jewish Feast (5:1–47)

Ch. 5 falls into two parts: a Sabbath healing and the ensuing controversy and discourse.

1. Sabbath healing at the Pool of Bethesda (5:1–15)

Back in Jerusalem for an unnamed festival of the Jews, Jesus approached, among the sick at the Pool of Bethesda, a man who had been an invalid for thirty-eight years (vv.1–5). He took the initiative by seeking from the paralytic a desire for healing (v.6) and then granting it (vv.8–9), though the man misunderstood what Jesus could do for him and made excuses for his continuing illness (v.7). Note: 5:4 and the end of 5:3 are not present in the best ancient manuscripts; they were added subsequently by scribes in an attempt to explain 5:7.

That the cured man carried his mat (v.9; cf. v.8) is no incidental detail. It was, of course, solid evidence that he had been cured. But it is also important to what follows; for, as the text stresses, it was a visible violation of Jewish law. When accosted, the former invalid absolved himself by casting the blame onto the one who had healed him, but he was at that time still ignorant of Jesus' identity (vv.10–13). When he did discover it, through another initiative by Jesus (v.14), he made it known to the Jews (v.15). The command to stop sinning (cf. Mk 2:5) speaks of the man's spiritual condition but does not imply that his past illness was caused by his sin.

2. Controversy with the Jews (5:16–30)

As far as the Jews were concerned, Jesus was a Sabbath breaker (v.16). His justification of his deeds on the basis of the activity of God (v.17) served only to anger them further (v.18). They rightly saw that he referred to God as his Father and that he was making himself equal with God, and they thought this blasphemous because they conceived of him as a mere human. But Jesus was not a mere man, he was the incarnation of the divine Word (cf. 1:1–2, 14). In the profoundly Christological discourse that follows, Jesus reaffirmed his special relationship to God.

To begin with, Jesus (as Son) was entirely dependent on the Father for everything he did (v.19) and had (vv.22, 26, 27). But at the same time, the Father was showing the Son all his deeds and would show him even greater things than the healing of the paralytic (v.20). Indeed, the Son shared the divine prerogatives of giving life to the dead and passing judgment (vv.21–22). All this was because the Father purposed that everyone should honor the Son just as they honored the Father (v.23).

The themes of life (cf. 1:4; 3:16; 20:31) and judgment (cf. 3:17–18; 16:11) are more fully worked out in 5:24–29. Jesus was speaking primarily of ultimate judgment (vv.27, 30), but the life he gives is both spiritual life here and now (v.24) and resurrection life for the blessed dead at some future time (vv.28–29). The key to life is hearing Jesus' words and believing the Father (vv.24–25). The key to right judgment by Jesus is his desire to please the Father (v.30).

3. Various testimonies about Jesus (5:31–47)

Jn 5:31 does not contradict 8:14, which, in a separate context, makes a different point. In the present passage, Jesus claimed that not only his actions (vv.17–30) but his endorsement came from beyond himself (vv.31–32). John the Baptist gave testimony to Jesus (vv.33–35), but weightier authorization came from the work given him, from his Father who gave it, and from Scripture. The attitude of the hearers toward Jesus showed that they had not accepted this testimony (vv.36–40). They were intransigent in their unbelief (vv.41–44). But that is hardly to be wondered at. Their culpable rejection of the testimony of Moses to Christ was a precursor to their present unbelief (vv.45–47).

J. Feeding of the Multitude and What Followed (6:1–71)

The feeding of the multitude is symbolic of the fact that Jesus gives spiritual food, and serves as an introduction to the discourse on the **bread of life.**

1. Feeding (6:1–15)

This **sign** (v.14) is recorded in all four gospels (Mt 14:13–21; cf. 15:32–38; Mk 6:32–44; cf. 8:1–9; Lk 9:10–17). The account does not require much explanation. In view of Jesus' interpretation (6:25–59), which is reminiscent of the Last Supper, reference to the Passover (v.4) has theological as well as chronological significance. This is the second Passover mentioned in the gospel (cf. 2:13, 23). As usual, Jesus took the initiative (v.5). **Eight months' wages** (v.7) nicely translates the Greek for "200 denarii," where a denarius was roughly equivalent to one day's wages for a laborer. The loaves and fishes (v.9) serve to underscore the inadequacy of merely human supply as compared to the more than sufficient provision of Jesus (vv.12–13). The miraculous feeding moved the crowd to see Jesus as Messiah (vv.14–15). This is clear from their desire to make him king and their designation of him as **the Prophet who is to come into the world** (cf. Dt 18:15, 18 but contrast Jn 1:21, where, in light of the denial of 1:20, "the Prophet" in mind is not the Messiah).

2. Jesus' walk on the lake (6:16–24)

As in the Synoptic accounts (Mt 14:22–33; Mk 6:47–51), the miraculous feeding is followed by a miraculous walk by Jesus on a stormy Galilee. That the boat reached the safety of its destination as soon as Jesus was in it (v.21) recalls the cessation of the storm in the story as told by Matthew and Mark. The crowd, uncertain of Jesus' movements, still sought him (vv.22–24; cf. v.2).

3. Teaching about the bread of life (6:25–59)

The people successfully sought Jesus (v.25), but from a wrong motive. According to him, they had eaten their fill the day before and longed to repeat the experience. But if they had properly perceived the significance of the miracle of the loaves, they would instead be seeking food of eternal value, not mere physical food (vv.26–27).

The true bread from heaven and source of life was not the manna given by Moses, which perished, but Jesus himself (vv.30–33). The people did not yet understand that Jesus actually was this bread rather than just the giver of it (v.34; cf. the similar request in 4:15). He continued with the first of the well-known **I am** sayings of John: **I am the bread of life** (v.35; cf. 6:48; 8:12, 24, 28, 58; 10:7, 9, 11, 14; 11:25; 14:6; 15:1, 5). As such, he came down from heaven in accordance with the Father's will to bring life to all who believe in him (vv.36–40).

This saying provoked the Jews. Because they knew Jesus as Joseph's son, they could not accept his seemingly absurd claim to have come from heaven (vv.41–42). It was true, Jesus responded, that no one could believe in him who had not been attracted and tutored (he quotes Isa 54:13) by the Father (vv.43–45; cf. Mk 10:27). But he knew himself: he was the living bread from heaven from whose self-giving would come eternal life (vv.46–51).

Once again the Jews missed the spiritual import of Jesus' words (cf.

2:20) and debated whether he might be speaking of cannibalism (v.52). He used eucharistic language in his explanation to reassert that life lies in believing in him (vv.53–58). The entire discourse is summarized in 6:57.

4. Desertion by many disciples (6:60–71)

The reaction of many of Jesus' disciples to his teaching (v.60) prompted further explanation. It is not certain how 6:62 is to be interpreted, but 6:63, which sharply distinguishes flesh and spirit, gives the key to understanding the discourse on the bread of life: the words must be understood spiritually. The desertion of many of Jesus' disciples (vv.64–66) provoked Peter's confession of belief (vv.67–68; cf. Mk 8:29 and its Synoptic parallels).

K. Feast of Tabernacles (7:1–8:59)

The Feast of Tabernacles occasioned a permanent move for Jesus from Galilee to Jerusalem and Judea.

1. Jesus' journey to the feast (7:1–13)

For a time Jesus avoided Judea because of the animosity of the Jews there (v.1). His unbelieving brothers could not understand such behavior in someone supposedly wanting publicity, and they urged him to go to Judea for the feast, where he would be more visible (vv.2–5). But Jesus would act only at the **right time** (cf. 2:4; 7:30; 8:20; 12:23, 27; 13:1; 16:32; 17:1), and he knew that his ministry would provoke hatred rather than acclaim (vv.6–9). Accordingly, though he did go eventually, he went secretly and only after the feast was already underway (vv.10–11).

2. Jesus' teaching and the reaction of the crowd (7:14–44)

When Jesus did begin to teach openly at the feast, the Jews were startled at a display of learning unexpected in someone who had studied at none of the schools of sacred instruction (vv.14–15; cf. Ac 4:13). Jesus confronted their question directly (vv.16–18). He was not self-educated, an obvious conclusion for an unbeliever, but his teaching came from God. This would be apparent to anyone serious about doing God's will (cf. 6:29). The authentication of Jesus' claim lay in the fact that he was not self-seeking but worked to promote the honor of God.

Jesus then carried the war into the enemy camp (v.19). The Jews sought to do God's will (cf. v.17) by obeying the Jewish law, but in seeking to kill Jesus (cf. vv.1, 13, 25, 30, 32, 44; 8:37, 40, 59), they were violating the Law. Perhaps **the crowd** (v.20) is to be distinguished from **the Jews,** the religious leaders opposed to Jesus (cf. 7:12–13, 26). Jesus is also accused of being demon-possessed elsewhere in John (8:48; 10:20; cf. Mt 12:24; Mk 3:22). He explains himself in 7:21–24. Their indignation had been aroused by what they saw as a flagrant breach of the law when he healed a man on the Sabbath (ch. 5). But their judgment was superficial. The rules allowed them to circumcise a child on the Sabbath when that was the eighth day after birth. If it was right to attend to one member of the body on the Sabbath, it was surely right to minister to an entire person.

That Jesus was allowed to continue to teach publicly suggested to some that the authorities might have against reason recognized him to be the Messiah (vv.25–26). But this could not be, because the Messiah was expected to be of obscure origin, while Jesus' background was well known (v.27). To this Jesus responded that, though his earthly derivation was known, his true origin was in God, whom he represented (vv.28–29). This was provocative language, but no attempt to seize him could succeed until the time God had designated (v.30; cf. the note on 7:6–9).

A significant response of faith (v.31) prompted the religious leaders to send a detachment of temple guards to arrest Jesus (v.32). The wardens apparently listened as Jesus predicted his imminent departure (vv.33–34; cf. vv.45–46). He referred to his death and return to the Father, but the Jews thought he was speaking of a mere earthly journey (vv.35–36).

Jesus gave his next teaching at the Feast of Tabernacles (vv.37–38) while standing, an unusual posture for a teacher and one that drew attention. The imagery may have related to the ritual of the feast, which featured libations of water. John identifies **living water** (cf. 4:13–14) with the Holy Spirit, who would not be present until Jesus had left this world (v.39; cf. 16:7). John Wesley interpreted this passage in harmony with the synoptic account of the apostolic mission to the towns and villages of "Israel" (sermon no. 40, par. 11; vol. 6, p. 10). On the reference to **Scripture** (v.38), see the commentaries. With 7:41–42 cf. 1:45–46; 7:52.

3. Unbelief of the Jewish leaders (7:45–52)

The chapter ends with the opposition of the Jewish leaders to Jesus. Neither the awe he had inspired in the guards nor the appeal by Nicodemus (cf. 3:1; 19:39) to the fair play required by the law moved them. On the basis of what they thought was his place of origin (v.52; cf. 1:45–46), they dismissed him contemptuously from consideration.

4. Woman accused of adultery (7:53–8:11)

This account was not originally part of this gospel but was added later. The situation was designed to trap Jesus into opinions contrary to the Law of Moses (8:6; cf. Lev 20:10; Dt 22:22ff.), but he avoided the snare. We have no way of knowing what he wrote on the ground (8:6). He did not condemn the woman, though her guilt was hardly in question, but he did bid her to cease sinning (v.11; cf. 3:17; 5:14). And in his presence her accusers were silenced (vv.7–9; cf. 3:18).

5. Validity of Jesus' testimony about himself (8:12–30)

Jn 8:12 continues where 7:52 left off. Jesus' declaration, one of the great **I am** sayings of John (see the note on 6:35), expresses again the theme of light (v.12). The imagery may have been an allusion to the prominence of light at the Feast of Tabernacles (cf. the note on 7:37–38).

It was contrary to Jewish regulations to accept the testimony of individuals about themselves, and the Pharisees challenged Jesus' pronouncement on this basis (v.13). But his testimony concerning himself was not to be measured by the human standards applied by his opponents; it was based on his unity with the Father, from whom both it and he were derived (vv.14–16). There were thus two who spoke for Jesus: Jesus himself and the Father, who sent him (v.17). This fulfilled the Law, which required two witnesses (cf. Dt 17:6; 19:15). The apparent contradiction between v.14 and 5:31 is not real; the two passages are about different kinds of self-witness.

Jesus' adversaries judged by appearances (v.15; cf. 7:24), and their human ponderings repeatedly become the occasion for further teaching by Jesus in the present context. Their perverse request for Jesus to produce his father exposed their ignorance and lack of faith (v.19). A desire to arrest Jesus is implied (v.20; cf. 7:6–8, 28–30, and notes).

The Jews also misunderstood Jesus' words about his departure and coming inaccessibility (vv.21–24; cf. 7:35–36). They wondered whether he might have been speaking of suicide, but, while his words did refer to his coming death, the laying down of his life (cf. 10:18) was not suicide. His main point was that he and his opponents were from different settings. His was heavenly; theirs was earthly and sinful, and their only hope of escape was through believing Jesus when he said, **I am** (see the note on 6:35). With these words Jesus identified himself unequivocally with God (cf. Ex 3:14; Isa 43:10).

As to who he is, they have already heard from him reliably (vv.25–26; cf. 3:32–34), and they would know him and his unity with the Father when he, the true Mediator between heaven and earth (cf. 1:51; 3:13; 6:27, 62), was **lifted up** (vv.27–29). Lifting up refers to Jesus' crucifixion and glorification (cf. 3:14 and note; 12:34). It becomes evident in what follows that those who believed in him as a result of this interchange (v.30) had only a superficial faith.

6. Parentage of the Jews (8:31–47)

Jesus told the new believers that application to his teaching (literally: "remaining in his word") would set them free (vv.31–32; cf. 15:4–7, which also speaks of remaining). But this was an affront to them, who, as descendants of Abraham, thought of themselves as already free (v.33). Jesus acknowledged their physical descent from Abraham, but their murderous designs on him implied a quite different spiritual lineage (vv.34–41). They then tried to claim God as their spiritual Father (v.41; cf. Ex 4:22; Jer 31:9), but he rejected their claim (vv.42–47). Children of God would love and listen to Jesus; their demeanor toward him revealed their derivation from the devil.

7. Jesus' response to the charge of being a Samaritan (8:48–59)

Stung by what he had said, the Jews leveled at Jesus the linked and perhaps equivalent accusations of being a Samaritan (cf. 4:9) and being demon possessed (cf. 7:20; 10:20). His reply (vv.49–51) did nothing to reassure them.

The promise that disciples (cf. 8:31–32) would never see death referred to spiritual death (cf. 11:26) and was a restatement of the theme of life (cf., e.g., 3:16). But with crass literalness they misunderstood him to be speaking of physical death and responded scornfully, reiterating the charge of demon possession (vv.52–53).

The claim that Abraham had foreseen the day of Christ would not have offended current Jewish teaching. But Jesus claimed that Abraham had foreseen **my day** (v.56), and this left the literal-minded Jews incredulous (v.57). His further claim, which implies preexistence, is not outrageous for the one who is the incarnate Word (cf. 1:14). But in a mere human such as Jesus' adversaries took him to be, the assertion was blasphemous and punishable by stoning (Lev 24:16). Once again he escaped their animosity (v.59; cf. 7:30; 8:20).

L. Healing of a Man Born Blind (9:1–41)

Ch. 9 develops the themes of light and judgment, and it illustrates Jesus' claim to be the Light of the World (8:12; 9:5). Physical healing and spiritual healing are intertwined. The one leads to the other as the blind man moves from darkness to light, first physically and then spiritually. The narrative is uninterrupted by interpretation, which occurs only at the beginning (vv.3–5) and the end (vv.39–41).

1. Healing (9:1–12)

It is stressed that the man in question was congenitally blind. This heightened appreciation for the significance of the miracle (cf. 9:32). To first-century Jews, including the disciples (v.2), it also implied some antenatal sin either on the part of the parents or of the unborn child. Jesus saw things differently: this blindness was not the specific result of some sin, but its healing would bring glory to God (v.3; cf. 11:4). Healing was part of the work of God, and by doing it Jesus brought light to the world (vv.4–5).

Saliva was thought by the ancients to have curative properties (v.6; cf. Mk 7:33; 8:23). Siloam (9:7; cf. Ne 3:15; Isa 8:6; 22:9, 11) was built during the reign of Hezekiah (2Ch 32:30) and provided Jerusalem with a supply of water within the walls. The translation of its name recalls the theme of sentness prominent in John (cf. 20:21 and elsewhere). With 9:12 cf. 5:12–13.

2. Investigation by the Pharisees (9:13–34)

A remarkable feature of this narrative is the positions taken by the actors in the drama. The parents of the man cured by Jesus abandoned their son to his own devices rather than risk excommunication (vv.20–23). The Pharisees, divided at first about the significance of Jesus' action, quickly and increasingly became entrenched in their hostility to Jesus and to the man they were interro-

gating. The man himself is one of the best examples of response to Jesus in this gospel. Holding firm to what he knew to be true (v.25), he refused to be browbeaten and moved from blindness to an enlightened and costly defense of his Healer (vv.30–34).

3. Spiritual sight (9:35–41)

The man's faith was not yet complete, but completion was only a short step away and followed the fuller self-revelation of Jesus to him (vv.35–38). Jesus' presence divided people (v.39; cf. 3:18; 5:22; 8:15–16). Those who acknowledged their own darkness turned to him, as the Light of the world, for illumination. Such was the case of the man born blind. But those who, like the Pharisees of 9:40, insisted on their own ability to see turned away from him and were blinded. As the proverb says, there are none so blind as those who will not see. See the exposition of this passage in Turner (208–11).

The Fourth Gospel and Jesus' claim to be the light of the world was the inspiration for Philip Bliss's famous hymn, "The Light of the World." The chorus is an application of ch. 9 and specifically quotes 9:25:

> Come to the Light, 'tis shining for
>   thee;
> Sweetly the Light has dawned upon
>   me;
> Once I was blind, but now I can see;
> The Light of the world is Jesus.

M. Discourse on the Good Shepherd (10:1–21)

Jesus' teaching on the Good Shepherd is, strictly speaking, neither parable nor allegory, though it has some of the elements of both. It is, rather, figurative discourse (v.6; cf. 16:25, 29) in which spiritual truths are expressed in terms of everyday things, a common feature in John (cf., e.g., 3:8; 4:10; 6:35; 8:12). The symbolism of the sheep and the shepherd is present in the chapter as far as v.30. (For background to the thought of Jn 10 cf. Eze 34.)

The first section (vv.1–5) is a commentary on the events of ch. 9. False shepherds are perfidious both in their manner of access to the fold and in their intentions toward the sheep. But the authentic shepherd is known to both the watchman, who admits him to the fold, and the sheep, who listen to his voice and respond to it. After being expelled by the Pharisees, the man healed of congenital blindness came to Jesus and found him to be the true shepherd. It is hard not to think that the false shepherds Jesus had in mind were the religious leaders of the Jews. Evidently they were not part of his flock, because they did not understand his figurative language (v.6). (On listening to Jesus cf. 5:24; 18:37.)

Jesus continued his discourse with a series of **I am** sayings (cf. the note on 6:35) with comments. The first, **I am the gate,** reiterates and makes explicit the uniqueness of Jesus in bringing life (vv.7–10). The second, **I am the good shepherd,** stresses his self-sacrificing care for his sheep (vv.11–18; cf. v.28). The bond that unites him and his sheep is like that between him and the Father (vv.14–15). V.16 is a reference to the Gentile mission (cf. 11:51–52) and the union of Jews and non-Jews in one community. Vv.17–18 stress anew Jesus' freedom from human control and his complete obedience to the Father (cf. 5:19–30).

Jesus' words once again left his hearers divided (vv.19–21; cf. 7:43; 9:16). This is the third time the charge of demon possession has been leveled against him in this gospel (cf. 7:20; 8:48).

N. Unbelief at the Feast of Dedication (10:22–39)

The unbelieving Jews renewed their question about Jesus' identity in the winter at the Feast of Dedication, still celebrated today as Hanukkah or the Feast of Lights (vv.22–24). His answer included a reference to the evidential value of his miracles (v.25; cf. 5:36; 14:11), which did not produce faith in them because they did not belong to his flock (v.26; cf. 8:47). To those who do belong and listen he gives eternal life (cf. 3:15, 16, 36; 6:40, 47), and they may rest secure in this (vv.27–28). But it is a security that depends on the power of God, with whom Jesus was united in preserving "his own" (vv.29–30).

When the Jews heard all this, culminating in **I and the Father are one,** they set out to stone Jesus (cf. 8:59) for the blasphemy of claiming to be God (vv.31–33; cf. 5:18; Lev 24:16). His defense was twofold (vv.34–38). First he appealed to Scripture and to a mode of interpretation with which they would have been familiar. If God himself referred to unjust judges as sons of God in Ps 82:6, why were they out to stone the one God endorsed for referring to himself as the Son of God? Then he pointed to his deeds and asked the Jews to judge his origin in God on their basis (cf. v.25; 14:10–11). The Jews were still hostile, but once again he eluded them (v.39; cf. 7:30; 8:59).

O. Ministry on the Other Side of the Jordan (10:40–42)

After this display of hostility against him, Jesus retired across the Jordan to John's former place of ministry (cf. 1:28). To the wonder of the people who gathered to him there, his life had lived up to the pronouncements John had made about him (cf. 1:26–27, 29–34; 3:27–36), and many came to faith (cf. 7:31; 8:30; 11:45). This summary, coming at the end of the Jerusalem debates, serves to emphasize the gospel's message about Jesus.

P. Resurrection of Lazarus (11:1–57)

Ch. 11 develops the theme of life as ch. 9 did that of light. The distinction between physical and spiritual life is in some ways irrelevant; Jesus had complete mastery over both.

1. Death of Lazarus (11:1–16)

While still across the Jordan, Jesus received a message from Mary and Martha of Bethany in Judea that their brother Lazarus, his beloved friend, was ill (vv.1–3). He had supernatural insight into what would happen (v.4) and remained where he was for a while despite their appeal (vv.5–6). John's mention of his affection for this family has the effect of intensifying the apparent incongruity of his inaction.

After two days Jesus determined to return to Judea, which alarmed the disciples (vv.7–8). His rejoinder spoke of the need to be performing God's work while the opportunity lasted (vv.9–10; cf. 9:4). In this instance, doing so meant raising Lazarus from death, which he spoke of as sleep (v.11; cf. Mk 5:39 and parallels). The disciples thought he meant natural, healing sleep, but he made it plain that he was referring to the sleep of death and that what was about to take place would result not only in glory for God and his Son (v.4) but in belief on their part (vv.12–15). But that was yet to come. For the moment, the disciples' mood was one of resigned loyalty (v.16). On Thomas called Didymus ("the twin") cf. 14:5; 20:24–28; 21:2.

2. Jesus' meeting with Martha and Mary (11:17–37)

When Jesus arrived in Bethany, the one near Jerusalem (contrast 1:28),

Lazarus had already been buried for four days, and the mourners were together in the house (vv.17–18).

Martha's first words to Jesus conveyed regret that he had not been present to prevent her brother's death (v.21; cf. vv.32, 37). But even yet she was not entirely hopeless (v.22), and her expression of confidence in him prepared the way for the conversation that ensued. To Jesus' ambiguous declaration that her brother would live again, Martha responded with a confession of belief in the general resurrection at the end of time (vv.23–24). But even in the last day, the dead do not rise by themselves; they are raised by Christ, and from him come both physical resurrection and the spiritual life that makes the death of the body inconsequential (vv.25–26; cf. 5:25, 28–29; 6:39). (For the **I am** saying, cf. the note on 6:35.) Martha's response to Jesus was a full confession of faith in him (v.27).

Mary also voiced the regret over Jesus' delayed arrival that seems to have been present to the minds of many (v.32; cf. vv.21, 37). The thought that Jesus might have healed Lazarus revealed in the sisters a genuine though imperfect faith; their insight was shared by **some** Jews who did not doubt his power to heal but were more hesitant (v.37; cf. 9:7). V.37 does not necessarily imply criticism. It is uncertain why **Jesus wept,** but the sympathetic among the Jews interpreted it as a sign of love for Lazarus (vv.35–36).

3. Resurrection (11:38–44)

After all that had passed between them (vv.21–27), Martha still did not expect Jesus to perform a miracle, and she offered resistance to his command to unseal the tomb (vv.38–39). But a miracle was about to be performed that would reveal the glory of God (v.40; cf.

vv.4, 23, 25) and the dependence of Jesus on the Father (vv.41–42). At Jesus' call Lazarus appeared, alive and needing only to be set free of the grave clothes (vv.43–44).

4. Reactions to the miracle (11:45–54)

As in the case of other works of Jesus, Jewish reactions to this miracle were mixed. Some believed, but others carried the story to the Pharisees, who called an emergency meeting of the governing council (vv.45–47). Out of this undoubtedly turbulent meeting came the final plot against Jesus (vv.47–53).

There was only one item on the agenda: what to do about Jesus. To leave him unchecked raised the twin dangers of mass conversion to Jesus and destruction by the Romans of all that the Jews held dear. The irony is that by crucifying him they precipitated both things. Though most of that tale is beyond the scope of John, Caiaphas touched on part of it in his unwitting prophecy—namely, the worldwide mission of the church (cf. vv.51–52). In the face of this threat, Jesus withdrew (v.54).

Q. Final Week (11:55–12:50)

Jesus' final week began in an atmosphere of intense excitement (11:55–57). In addition to the normal turmoil associated with the days preceding Passover, there was speculation about his intentions and an order out for his arrest.

1. Anointing at Bethany (11:55–12:11)

The uncertainty did not last long; almost a week before his final Passover (cf. 2:13; 6:4), Jesus returned to Bethany, where he attended a dinner in his honor at the home of Lazarus (12:1–

2). For the Synoptic parallels to the account that follows, see Mt 26:6–13; Mk 14:3–9; Lk 7:36–39.

The behavior of the sisters was characteristic (cf. Lk 10:38–40). Martha served; Mary performed an act of devotion at once lavish and extravagant (v.3). It was lavish because of the cost of the perfume: the equivalent of a year's wages (300 denarii). It was extravagant in its humility.

To Judas's reaction (vv.4–5) there were two responses. The Evangelist specifically impugns his motive (v.6). And Jesus defended Mary by balancing care for the poor, an ongoing concern, with care for the dead, by nature an immediate concern (vv.7–8). Both categories of good deeds were valued in Judaism.

The effects of the resurrection of Lazarus still lingered (vv.9–11).

2. Triumphal entry (12:12–19)

Jesus was welcomed to Jerusalem in a display of messianic fervor by a tumultuous crowd (vv.12–13). Palm branches had become a national symbol, and the quotation from Ps 118:25–26 had messianic significance. **Hosanna** transliterates the Hebrew for the exclamation "Save!" or "Give victory!" with which Israel used to thank God for success in war; it had become an expression of praise. The next sentence was used as a welcome home for a successful warlord. In this case the acclaimed hero was acknowledged to be the **King of Israel,** a messianic interpretation of the psalm. Jesus' peaceful intentions were demonstrated by his choice of a donkey rather than a horse for a mount and underscored in John by the quotation from Zec 9:9 (vv.14–15). The use of this passage was the result of reflection by the post-Easter church (v.16; cf. 2:22; Mt 21:5). The influences of the miracle of resurrection in Bethany and of the hostility of the Pharisees were potent even yet (vv.17–19).

3. Prediction of approaching death (12:20–36)

The request of some Gentiles to meet Jesus (vv.20–22) was the occasion for a solemn announcement of his impending death. He spoke of it as his **hour** of glorification (v.23; cf. 13:32; 17:1). But glorification for Jesus meant suffering and death, as well as exaltation, and Jesus knew this. Human nature would seek to avoid such trauma, but Jesus' obedience to the Father was complete even in the face of death (vv.27–28; cf. 4:34; 5:30). As a result of his death, there would be judgment for this world and its leader (cf. 16:11) and salvation for humankind. With 12:24 cf. 1Co 15:36; with 12:25–26 cf. Mk 8:34–38 and parallels; and with 12:27–28 cf. Mk 14:36 and parallels.

John maintains that by "lifting up" Jesus meant crucifixion (v.33). Whether or not the crowd understood that, they did at least understand that lifting up referred to removal from the scene, and they rightly understood that **Son of Man** meant **the Christ** (v.34). But they had expected the Christ to stay permanently, and they claimed that Jesus' words confused them. The confusion was feigned; they were unbelievers and were trying to confound him. Jesus addressed their dilemma by a renewed call for them to put their trust in him while there was still time (vv.35–36; cf. 9:4; 11:9–10).

4. Unbelief and belief (12:37–50)

On the whole, the Jews persisted in their unbelief in spite of the miracles Jesus had performed among them, as it had been prophesied that they would (vv.37–41; see Isa 53:1; 6:10). Although it is asserted that their lack of faith was because God had blinded their eyes, this is not simple determinism, since many did believe (vv.42–43). But their faith was clandestine and limited. Jesus' final public speech reiterates what he has already said about his link with the Father and the consequences of belief and unbelief (vv.44–50).

III. MINISTRY TO THE DISCIPLES (13:1–17:26)

His public ministry complete, Jesus spent the hours until his arrest privately with his disciples. Questions of chronology and of the relationship of this evening to the Last Supper described by the Synoptics are too complex to raise here: for them, see the commentaries (Barrett, 48–51; Beasley-Murray 224–26; Brown, 555–58; Lindars, 441–46).

A. Foot Washing (13:1–17)

The first verse of the account contains three pieces of information: (1) It was the day before the Passover (cf. 18:28; 19:14, 31, 42); (2) the **time** had come toward which Jesus' entire ministry had moved (cf. 2:4; 7:6; 12:23 and the commentary); and (3) the foot washing that followed was an expression of Jesus' love for his disciples. The action itself was straightforward. At a supper shared by Jesus and his disciples, he set about washing their feet (v.5). Now, foot washing was not unusual in Palestine, where the roads were unpaved and where the feet of reclining guests could not be hidden under a table. But it was a service performed for guests by household servants, not the host, or by disciples for their master, not the other way around. That there should have been embarrassment when Jesus began to attend to the feet of his neglectful disciples is understandable. In addition, the Evangelist gives two other pieces of information. He lets us know that not all was harmonious that evening, because Judas, motivated by the devil, already harbored treacherous intentions (v.2). And John tells us that Jesus acted not only under the impulse of love but with full awareness of his commission from God (vv.3–4).

With this buildup, the reader is alive to the symbolic significance of Jesus' simple act. But Peter, an actor in the drama, was not aware of it. It was embarrassment and, perhaps pride, that prompted his first reaction to Jesus' approach (vv.6–8). Then partial understanding and enthusiasm led him to ask for more to be washed than just his feet (v.9). But that, Jesus explained, would be unnecessary; it was not a matter of a bath but of inward cleansing (v.10). But not everyone was clean! The treachery of Judas cast its shadow over even the foot washing (v.11).

This event on the eve of Jesus' death may have seemed simple, but it carried profound significance. It was an act of Jesus' love that would stoop to even the most menial service. It was a spiritual cleansing. And it was an example of how Christians should treat each other (vv.12–17). In these ways, the washing of the disciples' feet prefigured the Crucifixion.

B. Jesus' Prediction of Betrayal (13:18–30)

Jesus was in control of his fate and even knew and predicted his betrayal by one close to him. Of several things of interest in this passage, we may notice these. (1) Jesus himself stressed the applicability of Ps 41:9 to the case of Judas (v.18; cf. 26–27). (2) Jesus' prophecy of treachery was to lead to belief just as his miracles had done (vv.19–20; cf. 2:11). (3) This is the first time **the disciple whom Jesus**

loved is mentioned in those terms in John (v.23; cf. 19:26; 20:2; 21:7, 20), and he is characteristically connected with Peter (v.24). (4) When, moved by Satan, Judas went out from the presence of Jesus, he went symbolically from light into darkness, as 13:30 underscores with the words, **And it was night.**

C. Jesus' Prediction of Denial (13:31–38)

With Judas's departure, the die was cast; everything was moving to the conclusion God had designed. Jesus' glorification and removal from the scene were at hand, and he would no longer be accessible to the disciples (vv.31–33; cf. 7:33–34). For Jesus, his ministry, especially the foot washing and the Crucifixion, spoke of love, and it is no mistake that the love command makes its first appearance in this context (vv.34–35; cf. 15:12). Mutual love among Christians is essentially Christlike. But Peter was more concerned with the pronouncement about coming separation, and he challenged Jesus on it (vv.36–37; cf. 7:35–36; 16:17). Peter sincerely believed that he was prepared to die for Jesus and that not even death could separate them. But Jesus with supernatural knowledge knew that denial, not death, was ahead for Peter (v.38; cf. 18:17, 25–27).

D. Farewell Discourses (14:1–17:26)

On their last evening together, Jesus summed up the meaning of his life and ministry for the disciples and spoke to them of the future. The things he had to say have become known as the Farewell Discourses.

1. Jesus, the Way to the Father (14:1–14)

Dismay was the natural reaction of the disciples upon hearing Jesus predict his departure (cf. 13:36–37) and Peter's denial. But that is because their perspective was limited (cf. 16:6–7), unnecessarily so in light of Jesus' consistent teaching. And so Jesus comforted them by putting their perspective right. Trust, not dismay, was the order of the day (v.1). There is ample space in the Father's house, and the purpose of Jesus' journey was to establish a place there for them and to return to take them to be with him (vv.2–3). Even death and its aftermath had a place in the plan. In the words of Nicolaus von Zinzendorf, as translated by John Wesley:

> When from the dust of death I rise
>   To claim my mansion in the skies,
> Even then, this shall be all my plea,
>   "Jesus hath lived, hath
>   died for me."
>
>   ("Jesus, Thy Blood
>   and Righteousness")

That much they endured in silence, but when Jesus insisted that they knew the way to the place where he was going, Thomas protested that they knew neither destination nor route (vv.4–5). Jesus' rejoinder put his teaching about himself in a nutshell (v.6): the way to the Father was through him, just as he was also the avenue into the world for the truth and life of the Father. To know him was to know the Father (cf. 1:18).

Philip's request to be shown the Father (v.8) revealed persistent misunderstanding and led Jesus to declare himself once again (vv.9–11). Not even his works and words were his own; they came from the Father, who was living and working in him. If his saying so had been insufficient to engender belief, then observation of his miraculous works ought to have done it.

Jesus' next words were astounding

(vv.12–14). First, on the basis of Jesus' return to the Father, the believer would do not only the kind of works Jesus did but also greater ones. This did not mean more sensational miracles but works more revealing of the purposes of God; on this see the commentaries. Second, and this was new, Jesus would grant the requests of the believer.

2. Loving Jesus and its result (14:15–31)

Three times in what followed Jesus spoke of the reciprocal relationship between the believer and himself. Just as he loved the Father and was in turn loved by him, so there would be mutual love between him and the believer. Such love is not a matter of mere emotions, though emotion is not ruled out. Rather, true love is expressed in obedience. As Jesus loved the Father and obeyed him, so those who loved Jesus would in turn obey him. And, for the disciples, that separation from his physical presence that they so dreaded would be replaced by a deeper spiritual presence.

The first of the three statements of this theme was a declaration to the disciples that, if they loved him, they would obey his commandments (v.15). He in turn would request the Father to send **another** Counselor, whose function would be to abide with them always (vv.16–17; cf. vv.25–26; 15:26–27; 16:5–15). Jesus was the first Counselor, but he would not stay forever, at least not bodily. Of that the disciples were poignantly aware on that fateful evening. Furthermore, the new Counselor would relate only to the disciples, because nonbelievers could have no cognizance of him. In addition, Jesus promised that their bereavement would not be permanent but would be replaced by a mutual indwelling of Father, Son, and disciple (vv.18–20).

(On the exegetical questions surrounding the teaching on the Counselor, see the commentaries, e.g., Barrett, 461–63). All this is stated positively twice more (vv.21–23) and negatively once more (v.24).

In the second promise concerning the Counselor (vv.25–26; cf. vv.16–17), Jesus alluded to all he had taught while on earth, much of which the disciples had failed to understand (cf. 2:22; 12:16). But the Counselor, here expressly identified as the Holy Spirit, would make clear to them everything Jesus had taught them (cf. 16:13–14). Charles Wesley may have had this verse among others in mind when he wrote:

> Spirit of faith, come down,
> Reveal the things of God;
> And make to us the Godhead known,
> And witness with the blood.

The chapter ends as it began with Jesus comforting the disciples. He bequeathed to them a peace for their bereavement that was quite beyond anything earthly (v.27). And he reminded them again that his departure was really a matter of rejoicing, because he was going to the Father (vv.28–31). The interpretation of the closing command is disputed.

3. Allegory of the vine (15:1–17)

One of the famous **I am** metaphors of John opens this discourse. In it Jesus likened himself to a grapevine and his Father to the farmer who tended it (v.1; cf. Ps 80:8–11; Isa 5:1–7; see on 6:35). Grape husbandry was widespread in Palestine, so much imagery would have been vivid to the disciples. But what Jesus had to say was not just a disquisition on one form of agriculture. It was a spiritual message with three distinct but related parts.

The first section (vv.1–4) builds on a knowledge of basic methods of grape culture. Branches that do not produce fruit are useless and are removed by the farmer from the vine. Branches that do bear grapes are pruned so that they might be even more fruitful. Jesus did not specify the identity of any of the spiritually unfruitful who may have been in his mind, but he implied that the disciples were among the fruitful, for he pronounced them already clean (or pruned; the Greek word is the same) through his ministry (cf. 13:10). As Jesus was the source of Christian fruitfulness, it was essential to remain vitally in touch with him.

Jesus emphasized this idea in the second part of the discourse (vv.5–8). He began by restating the first element of the metaphor of 15:1, but in the second he spoke of the disciples rather than of his Father. No branch, he said, can be fruitful that is severed from its vine. It is the same in the spiritual realm: the secret of fruitfulness is living in connection with Jesus, who is the source of fruitfulness. Remaining in Jesus and being fruitful is the essence of discipleship, brings glory to the Father, and guarantees answered prayer (cf. 14:13).

In the third section (vv.9–17), Jesus reaffirmed the importance and nature of love (cf. 14:15–24) and fruitbearing. The Father's love for Jesus was the model for Jesus' love of the disciples; his obedient love for the Father was to be the model for their love for him; his self-sacrificing love for them was to be the model of their love for each other. The initiative in all this was his. He chose them and not they him. His design was that they should bear fruit, and his command was that they should love each other (cf. 13:34–35).

4. World's hatred of Jesus' disciples (15:18–16:4)

From the mutual love characteristic of Christian society at every level, Jesus turned to a warning about the hate the disciples could expect from the world. The hatred and persecution would be gratuitous and undeserved, but it could at least be explained. And Jesus did explain it, after reminding them that the world had hated him first of all (15:18). Basically, the world would hate the disciples because it was the world and was therefore at enmity with God.

Jesus then explained the issue. The world would hate the disciples because the disciples were no longer part of the world (v.19; 17:14). And it would hate them on account of Jesus, who was already the target of their ill will (vv.20–21; cf. 13:16). But as the hatred of the disciples was really hatred of Jesus, so the reaction to Jesus was really a reaction to God, of whom the world was ignorant (vv.21–25). Its ignorance, which might have been innocent except for the teaching and miracles of Jesus, was inexcusably culpable (cf. 9:39–41) and its hatred groundless (Ps 35:19; 69:4).

This state of affairs would not go unaddressed. The world's hatred depended on a misapprehension of the person and work of Jesus, but correctives would be forthcoming both from the disciples and from the Counselor sent by God. The disciples could testify to the truth about Jesus because of their long association with him during his ministry (v.27). The Counselor's qualifications to testify about him (v.26; cf. 14:16–17, 25–26; 16:5–15) are of sterling quality. He is the Spirit of truth sent by Jesus from the Father, who is the ultimate source of all truth; he was acknowledged by John the Baptist as the guarantor of the trustworthiness of Jesus' own teaching (cf. 3:33–36).

The world's hostility would be intense. Its murderous deeds would even be done in the name of God. But Jesus endeavored to strengthen the disciples and prevent potential apostasy by forewarning them and by explaining the reason for the treatment they would receive (16:1–4). On 16:2 cf. 9:22, 34.

5. Work of the Counselor (16:5–15)

Commentators have been perplexed by the apparent contradiction between the reproach of v.5, **None of you asks me, 'Where are you going?'** and that very question on the lips of Peter in 13:36 (cf. 14:5). Perhaps the issue cannot be resolved to the satisfaction of everyone (see the commentaries), but the immediate sense of the passage is plain. The disciples were so preoccupied with their grief that they had not grasped the joyful news that Jesus was going to the Father and not just vanishing into oblivion (vv.5–7; cf. 16:10, 17, 28). Indeed, his going was to their advantage, for only so could he send the Counselor to them. This person, already mentioned three times in the Farewell Discourses (cf. 14:16–17, 25–26; 15:26–27), was to have a twofold work.

First of all, the Counselor would have a function vis-à-vis the world, that of convincing it of the truth concerning sin, righteousness, and judgment (vv.8–11). Unbelief is the sin that gives rise to all others, and it is this sin that he would lay to the world's account. In this case "convince" is rightly translated **convict** and speaks of guilt. But it cannot be said that the world was guilty of righteousness. Although it had made Jesus out to be a sinner, it was wrong and therefore not righteous. On the contrary, Jesus was the Righteous One, as was evident in the fact that he was returning to the Father from whom he came. As to judgment, the Counselor would show that this world's prince had been put decidedly in the wrong (cf. 12:31). On all three counts the world's cause was lost.

Second, as regards the disciples, the Counselor would be a teacher (vv.12–15). During his earthly ministry Jesus was limited, not least by restricted capacity in those he tried to teach. But as Spirit of truth the Counselor would continue Jesus' work. He would communicate divine truth (cf. 14:26), but not independently. He would glorify Jesus and bring home Jesus' complete unity with the Father; for, revealing Jesus' **things** is tantamount to revealing the Father's **things**.

6. Joy that cancels grief (16:16–33)

After teaching about the Counselor, Jesus returned to the theme of his imminent departure and unattainability (v.16; cf. 7:33–34; 13:33). This time he also referred to a return. As before, his words caused bewilderment (vv.17–18; cf. 7:35–36; 13:36–37), but his explanation did not do much to clear up the uncertainty (vv.19–22). As the suffering of a woman in childbirth gives way to joy when her child is born, he said, so the disciples' mourning when Jesus was taken from them would later turn to permanent joy. When that happened, the nature of prayer would be changed, and Jesus urged them to take advantage of the change (vv.23–24; cf. 14:13–14). One cannot be sure whether the return Jesus spoke of was his resurrection on Easter Sunday or his reappearance at the Last Day. Both would be appropriate in the context, and we may have here a case of deliberate ambiguity. Either way, the response of the disciple would be the reverse of that of the world: when the disciple sorrowed, the world would rejoice, and vice versa.

Jesus then restated two of the themes from 16:16–24. First, there would come a time when Jesus would no longer use figurative language but would speak plainly (v.25; cf. v.29; 10:6). Second, in that day those who had believed on Jesus would have direct access to the Father in his name (vv.26–27). The Father was both Jesus' point of origin and his destination (v.28).

At this the disciples felt that they finally understood Jesus because they felt he was at last speaking directly (v.29). On this basis they expressed confident faith in both his person and his origin (v.30). But Jesus knew that their confidence was misplaced and that they would soon desert him to face his fate without them (vv.31–32). He would not be alone, but it would be his Father, not the disciples, who would be with him. His words, **You believe at last!** were pregnant with irony.

Jesus' final words in these Discourses (v.33) contained a message of comfort. He had already warned the disciples of the animosity of the world (15:18–16:4), and it was inevitable that they would experience it. But peace was possible because of his triumph. He had overcome the world; in that thought lay the essence of the Gospel.

7. Jesus' prayer (17:1–26)

Jesus followed his Farewell Discourses by addressing the Father directly, apparently aloud and in the presence of the disciples. His prayer demonstrated the deep communion between Son and Father, summarized his teaching about himself, and recapitulated several Johannine themes. It was in four parts: a prayer for himself (vv.1–5), a prayer for the disciples (vv.6–19), a prayer for subsequent believers (vv.20–24), and a review of his mission to the world (vv.25–26).

First, Jesus prayed that his approaching death (**the time,** literally "the hour," v.1; cf. on 2:4; 7:6-9; 12:23; 13:1) might result in glory for himself and for his Father (vv.1-5). He had glorified the Father on earth by completing the work assigned to him (v.4), including bestowing eternal life where it was appropriate to do so (v.2). Eternal life, he said, consists in a vital acquaintance with God and his emissary Jesus Christ (v.3). Now that he had nearly completed his work, he petitioned the Father to restore to him the glory he had had in his preexistence (v.5; cf. 1:1-2, 14).

Second, Jesus prayed that the Father would protect the disciples (vv.6-19). (In his essay on perseverance, John Wesley rightly insisted that **those whom you gave me** signifies the Twelve alone [vol. 10, p. 292].) To them he had revealed the Father (v.6), and they knew that the mission of Jesus originated in the Father (vv.7-8). It was for these who had believed on him that he prayed and not, at that moment, for the world (v.9), though he was not unconcerned about the world (cf. 3:16; 17:25-26). Since they belonged to him, they also belonged to the Father (v.10; cf. 16:15), and now that Jesus was no longer going to be around to protect them, he asked the Father to look after them and preserve their unity (vv.11-12). Jesus had lost only Judas, and that had been in fulfillment of Scripture (cf. 13:18).

Jesus was returning to the Father, but the disciples were remaining behind in the world. This was the background to Jesus' further prayer for the Father's watchful care over them. It had two clauses. (1) As recipients of God's Word, they could no longer be described as **of the world,** and they were targets of the world's hatred (vv.13-14; cf. 15:18-16:4). But the world was their sphere of ministry, as it had been his, and he asks that they be protected from **the evil one** (v.15; cf. Mt 6:13). (2) Like Jesus they were not of the world (v.16), but he was sending them into it for ministry, just as he had been sent (v.18; cf. 20:21). And he petitioned the Father to sanctify them completely by the truth—that is, by his word (v.17; cf. 13:10; 15:3). In this regard, one recalls the operations of the Spirit of truth (cf. 14:26; 15:26; 16:12-15).

Jesus prayed, thirdly, for the unity of the future generations of Christians who would come to faith through the testimony of the disciples (vv.20-23; cf. 20:29). In nature this was identical to the oneness that united Son and Father, and it was characterized by the same glory. Its purpose was that by observing it the world might come to know that God had indeed been behind the mission of Jesus and that his blessing was on the church. And Jesus' ultimate desire was that believers should join him in heaven and behold his eternal glory (v.24).

In the final section, Jesus summed up both his prayer and his ministry (vv.25-26; cf. 1:18). By definition the world did not know the Father, but Jesus knew him and came into the world to make him known. Or, in other terms, he came to bring light instead of darkness and life instead of death. He had done this; he would continue to do it. His goal was the salvation of the world.

IV. PASSION AND RESURRECTION (18:1-20:29)

With both his public and private ministries behind him, Jesus set his feet on the path to the final events of his earthly career: crucifixion and resurrection. His hour had come, the time toward which everything had pointed.

A. Arrest and Trial (18:1–19:16)

The final confrontation with the authorities began shortly after Jesus and his disciples had left the Upper Room.

1. Arrest (18:1–11)

Jesus' arrest took place in an olive grove on the other side of the Kidron Valley (v.1), known from the other gospels as the Garden of Gethsemane. Judas knew the place and guided a posse of Roman soldiers and officials from the Jews to the exact location (vv.2–3). John stresses the authority of Jesus through this entire scene. With supernatural knowledge of what was to happen, it was he who confronted the officers, and not the other way around (v.4). To their declaration that they were after Jesus of Nazareth, he frankly admitted his identity, and with that word they fell to the ground (vv.5–6). When, at his prompting, they repeated their object, he showed concern for his followers, rather than himself, and asked that they be allowed to go free (vv.7–8). In this way he kept his promise to preserve his own (v.9; cf. 6:39; 10:28; 17:12). Finally he repudiated Peter's vigorous defense of him, though it was the action itself and not the ineptitude of the swordsmanship that drew his reaction (vv.10–11). Because submission, not resistance, was the Father's will, it was his will, too (cf. 12:27–28).

2. Rejection and denial (18:12–27)

In this section two accounts are interspersed. Both begin with the arrest of Jesus and his delivery to Annas, father-in-law of Caiaphas, the current high priest (vv.12–14; cf. 11:49–51). Caiaphas had been high priest since A.D. 18, and he was to fill that office until A.D. 36. Annas himself had been high priest from A.D. 6 to 15 and still retained great prominence and authority.

The first account is about Simon Peter. Through the kindness of an unnamed disciple with connections, Peter was allowed into the palace courtyard (vv.15–16). The other disciple drops out of the narrative, but Peter's story is pursued in some detail. Three times he was charged with being a disciple of Jesus, and three times he denied it, presumably out of fear (v.17, 25–27). It must be noted that he did not deny the truth about Jesus but only repudiated any connection with him. The reference to the crowing of a rooster is a reminder that Jesus had predicted Peter's desertion (v.27; cf. 13:38).

The second account is a report of Jesus' hearing before Annas, here given the title of the position he had once held (vv.19–24). He asked Jesus directly about his teaching and his followers. But it was not proper judicial procedure to question an accused person directly; nor was it necessary in Jesus' case, and he said so. Everything Annas wanted to know was a matter of public knowledge and might be ascertained from others. This mode of answering was not viewed favorably, and subsequently, but not necessarily because of it, Jesus was bound over to Caiaphas.

3. Trial before Pilate (18:28–40)

Nothing is said about Caiaphas's own course of action. We are told only that Jesus was conveyed from Caiaphas to the palace of the Roman governor Pilate and that he, in deference to Jewish religious scruples, came out to the Jews to ascertain the charge against Jesus (vv.28–29). Insolence, not substance, was their response (v.30). They wanted a judicial execution, which was apparently outside their jurisdiction (v.31). With 18:32 cf. 3:14; 8:28; 12:32–33. Jesus was not being disrespectful when Pilate asked whether or not he was **king of the Jews** (vv.33–34). Before he could answer the question, he had to know what was behind it. Once that was cleared up, he accepted the title but rejected the meaning given it (vv.35–36). His kingship was bound up with truth, God's truth, and that was beyond Pilate, as his cynical question showed (vv.37–38). Nevertheless, Pilate judged Jesus innocent of any violation of the law, and attempted to free him through a custom not attested outside the New Testament (vv.38–39; cf. Mk 15:6 and parallels). But the Jews would have none of it (v.40).

4. Flogging and sentence (19:1–16)

Pilate, caught between his sense that Jesus was innocent of any crime and the clamor for his blood, had Jesus flogged (v.1). He may have hoped that a punishment less severe than execution might both restrain Jesus and satisfy his accusers. Even so, the penalty was vicious, and the soldiers added their own refinements of torture and humiliation (vv.2–3).

If this was Pilate's motive, then his further action was an attempt to placate the crowd with the spectacle of a man marred by harsh treatment but not worthy of death (vv.4–5). His presentation of Jesus was heavy with unconscious irony (v.5). Jesus was God's own Son and was indeed King of Israel, but he was believed by both Pilate and the Jews to be a mere man and a pretender to the kingly office.

The Jews, far from being pacified, cried out even more vehemently for Jesus' death (v.6). By naming crucifixion, they acknowledged that the

affair had passed irrevocably into Roman hands. Pilate responded with a taunt. He knew well that capital punishment was beyond their jurisdiction (cf. 18:31). In any case, stoning, not crucifixion, was the Jewish punishment for blasphemy.

The further accusation that Jesus had claimed to be the Son of God persuaded the superstitious Pilate to delve into the matter more deeply, but he had no success (vv.7–10). To his plea for some response, Jesus told him that ultimate authority in his case came from beyond Pilate (v.11). Jesus was amenable to God's will and God's timing, and God was the real mover in the events of that day. Even Pilate, acting for Rome, had no real autonomy in the case.

After further questioning, Pilate was of a mind to release Jesus, but the Jews wanted a conviction on the capital charge of sedition (v.12). With their veiled threat to convey the tale of an unsatisfactory result to Caesar, the outcome was assured. Pilate's standing at the imperial court was already shaky, and he had no wish to face further scrutiny. So he capitulated, and about noon on the Friday of Passover week he condemned Jesus to death by crucifixion (vv.12–16). The Jews revealed their spiritual condition by rejecting their true King and pledging allegiance to Caesar.

B. Execution and Burial (19:17–42)

Crucifixion was designed to inflict as much lingering agony as possible. This one was carried out at Skull-place, Golgotha, whose location is not certainly known but whose name probably derived from its topography (vv.17–28).

There was an interesting altercation between Pilate and the Jews (vv.19–22). He ordered a placard attached to the cross, written in the three chief languages of the region. The caption affirmed Jesus' true status better than Pilate could have known. The Jews, who undoubtedly thought it false, were nevertheless stung. They asked for an alteration in the wording that would make the caption less an apparent affirmation and more an accusation of blasphemy. But Pilate, who had already been forced to concede the main point, would not be goaded further, and he refused.

Two events of interest took place at the foot of the cross. One involved the soldiers performing the execution (vv.23–24). It was up to them to decide what to do with the clothing of the crucified. In their decision to cast lots for Jesus' undergarment rather than cut it apart, the Evangelist recognized a connection with Ps 22:18. The other involved a compassionate transferal of care for his bereaved mother into the hands of the disciple whom Jesus loved (vv.25–27; cf. 13:23–26; 20:1–10; 21:1–14, 20–24). His request was complied with forthwith.

Two matters of importance also took place on the cross (vv.28–37). The first was Jesus' recognition that he had accomplished his work in full. This is stated in so many words by the Evangelist and was illustrated by the Lord's cry of triumph (v.30). Adam Clarke stressed the significance of this cry as the consummation of the work of salvation (p. 653). The other is the fact that everything that happened was a fulfillment of Scripture and therefore according to God's will: Jesus' thirst (v.28; cf. Ps 69:21), the unbroken bones of the perfect paschal sacrifice (v.36; cf. Ex 12:46; Nu 9:12; Ps 34:20), and the sword thrust (v.37; cf. Zec 12:10). The events on Golgotha were reported by an eyewitness (v.35). The lavish burial by a secret disciple,

Joseph of Arimathea, assisted by Nicodemus (vv.38–42; cf. 3:1; 7:50) was according to Jewish custom.

C. Resurrection Sunday (20:1–29)

The most remarkable day ever was not a Sabbath, as Jews might have expected, but a Sunday. After the conflicts of Jesus' life and ministry came peace, and after death, resurrection.

1. Empty tomb (20:1–9)

When Mary Magdalene visited the tomb early on that Sunday morning, she and her companions (cf. her words, **we don't know**) found the seal disturbed and hurried to carry the report to Peter and the disciple whom Jesus loved (vv.1–2; cf. 13:23–26; 19:25–27; 21:1–14, 20–24). They started for the tomb immediately (v.3).

Note the renewed connection between Peter and the beloved disciple. In this case, though their actions were parallel, their responses to what they found at the tomb were different. Both saw the unoccupied grave windings and head cloth (vv.4–8; cf. 11:44). But, in contrast to Peter, it is said of the beloved disciple expressly that he believed and that he did so without yet understanding from Scripture that Jesus had to rise from the dead (v.9). He was the first Christian believer.

2. Appearance to Mary Magdalene (20:10–18)

Mary's experience at the tomb was different, but it also led to belief. After the two disciples had gone home, she remained behind weeping. She, too, looked into the tomb, but instead of grave cloths she saw two angels sitting where the Lord's body had lain. When they asked why she wept, she told them about her loss (vv.10–13).

The question was repeated by a man standing behind her who wanted to know why she wept and whom she was seeking. Perhaps her tears kept her from recognizing Jesus; perhaps it was something else (cf. Lk 24:16), but she assumed he was the gardener and asked him to show her where he had put Jesus' body (vv.13–15). If he would tell her, she intended to recover it, and in her grief she probably meant to do so single-handedly.

Jesus merely spoke her name and, in a flash of recognition, her grief turned to joy (v.16; cf. 10:3, 27; 16:20, 22). It would have been natural for her exuberant exclamation to have been accompanied by an embrace of some sort, and we may guess from Jesus' next words that it was. For in effect he said, "Don't cling to me, Mary; I haven't left yet" (v.17). But he soon would leave, and he commissioned her to carry that word to his brothers. By **brothers** he meant his disciples, now friends and no longer "servants" (cf. 15:14–15).

3. Appearances to the disciples (20:19–29)

John reports two appearances to the disciples in Jerusalem. The first was on resurrection Sunday itself (vv.19–20). They were frightened and had locked themselves in. But locked doors were no bar to the risen Lord, and into their fear he spoke peace (cf. 14:27). Like Mary, their mood changed instantly to joy. Then followed a solemn tripartite commissioning. Jesus first passed on to them a task like his (v.21). He had been sent into the world by the Father; now in the same way he was sending them. They were to be apostles of the one Apostle. To this commission there is only one appropriate response:

> Forth in Thy name, O Lord, I go,
> My daily labor to pursue;
> Thee, only Thee, resolved to know
> In all I think or speak or do.
>
> (Charles Wesley)

He then formally bestowed on them the promised Holy Spirit (cf. 1:33; 4:14; 7:37–39; 14:15–17, 25–26; 15:26–27; 16:5–15). Finally, he linked their ministry to that of the Spirit-Counselor. When the Counselor convicted of sin, for instance (cf. 16:8–9), it would be through believers who were open to him (cf. 15:26–27) rather than directly to the world, which was not (cf. 14:17).

Thomas was not present the first time Jesus appeared to the disciples, and he doubted their account (vv.24–25). But he was convinced when the Lord appeared in the same way a week later (vv.26–27), and he made a profound confession of faith in Jesus (v.28). Adam Clarke emphasized the significance of Thomas's declaration (p. 659). The entire Gospel is bracketed between 1:1–2 and 20:28–31, and these verses define for John what belief really means. With v.29 cf. 17:20–23.

V. PURPOSE STATEMENT (20:30–31)

These verses are the original ending to John's gospel, and they make explicit his purpose in writing. It was so that the reader might know who Jesus is, might believe in him, and as a result might have life through him.

VI. EPILOGUE (21:1–25)

As John came to an effective close with 20:30–31, ch. 21 must be seen as additional. However, since there is no evidence that the gospel ever circulated without it, we must think of it as an epilogue (cf. the prologue, 1:1–18) rather than as an addendum. On the discussion concerning who wrote it, the author of the first twenty chapters or someone else, see the major commentaries.

A. Catch of Fish (21:1–14)

John recounts a third resurrection appearance to a group of disciples (vv.1–14; cf. 20:19–29), this time in Galilee. For a similar miracle, compare the account in Lk 5:4–7. Peter and a group of six other disciples, perhaps tired of inaction, went night fishing on the Sea of Tiberias (cf. 6:1), but they were unsuccessful (vv.1–3). However, when directed from the shore by the risen Lord, whom they did not yet recognize, they netted a remarkably large haul of fish (vv.4–6). And that was enough to prompt recognition and response (v.7). Once on shore, they were invited to partake of a breakfast already prepared and to add to it from their own recent catch (vv.8–13).

The beloved disciple was one of the seven, but which one? He is not to be identified with Thomas, the slow to believe (cf. 20:8, 24–29). He cannot have been Peter, with whom he was frequently in company (13:23–24; 20:1–9). Since the Evangelist seems reluctant to name him elsewhere in the Gospel, it is unlikely that he does so here; so Nathaniel is probably ruled out. He must have been one of the remaining four (see introduction above). As at the empty tomb, the beloved disciple was quick to perceive while Peter was quick to act (v.7; cf. 20:1–9).

This account may be partly symbolic; see the commentaries.

B. Jesus' Conversation With Peter (21:15–23)

After breakfast, Jesus had a stroll (cf. v.20) and private conversation with Peter.

Corresponding to Peter's threefold denial (cf. 18:15–18, 25–27), Jesus three times questioned him about his love for him (vv.15–17). Although this caused Peter some consternation, his response was consistently affirmative, and he was installed as a shepherd of Jesus' flock (cf. 10:1–18). **More than these** (v.15) probably refers to the other disciples. If so, Jesus was probing Peter for signs that his former boastfulness had vanished (cf. 13:37; Mt 26:33). Two Greek words for *love* are used in this conversation. In view of their interchangeability elsewhere in John, it would be precarious to stress a supposed difference in their meaning here.

The third invitation to Peter to care for Jesus' flock was immediately followed by a reference to his personal future (v.18). The meaning of this would remain obscure, except that the author specified that it referred to Peter's death (v.19). But the editorial comment was not part of the original conversation, and Jesus added without interruption the command to follow (cf. 1:43). Obedience for Peter would mean both pastoring and martyrdom, possibly by crucifixion. It is probable that by the time ch. 21 was written he had already been executed.

Jesus commanded him to **follow,** and at that moment Peter observed the beloved disciple **following** (v.20). The juxtaposition of the words was probably intentional. There are many ways of following Jesus, and martyrdom is not the only one. But Peter was given no information about the future of his friend; he was told only to tend to his own mission (vv.21–22). However, it seems evident that the beloved disciple lived for many years and that this, coupled with an incorrect interpretation of Jesus' reply to Peter, gave rise to a rumor that this one would not die. But the emphasis of the account (v.23) makes it likely that he had died and that his death had caused distress among the faithful, which the author was trying to alleviate.

C. Authorship and Omissions (21:24–25)

Whether or not that is so, this disciple is emphatically identified as the authority behind the gospel (v.24; cf. 15:27; 19:35). We cannot now identify the **we** who endorsed his testimony as **true.**

Indirectly 21:25 underscores the Gospel's message about the greatness of Jesus. The verse is an obvious hyperbole, as Adam Clarke was at pains to point out (664–65, cf. Turner, 415).

BIBLIOGRAPHY

Students of John who desire a deeper exposition of some topic than has been possible to give in these pages should refer to one or more of the following books. Commentaries in this list differ widely in the demands they make upon the reader. At one extreme are the commentaries by Barclay and Young, which can be used by anyone. At the other are those by Barrett, Brown, and Beasley-Murray, which have become scholarly standards and require greater skill in the reader. The work by Barrett is without doubt the most comprehensive commentary on John ever written by a Wesleyan.

Barclay, W. *The Gospel of John.* Daily Study Bible. 2d ed. 2 vols. Edinburgh: St. Andrew Press, 1956.

Barrett, C. K. *The Gospel According to St. John: An Introduction With Commentary and Notes on the Greek Text.* 2d ed. London: SPCK, 1978.

Beasley-Murray, G. R. "John." WdBC. Vol. 36. Waco: Word, 1987.

Brown, R. E. *The Gospel According to John.* AB 29, 29A. 2 vols. New York: Doubleday, 1966 and 1970.

Bruce, F. F. *The Gospel of John.* Basingstoke: Pickering & Inglis, 1983.

Clarke, Adam. *The New Testament.* Vol. 1. Matthew to the Acts. New York: Abingdon-Cokesbury, n.d.

Lindars, B. *The Gospel of John.* NCB. London: Oliphants, 1972.

Morris, L. *The Gospel According to John.* NICNT. Grand Rapids: Eerdmans, 1971.

Tasker, R. V. G. *The Gospel According to St. John.* TNTC. London: Tyndale, 1960.

Turner, George Allen and Julius R. Mantey. *The Gospel According to John.* The Evangelical Commentary. Vol. 4. Grand Rapids: Eerdmans, 1964.

Wesley, John. *The Works of John Wesley.* 14 vols. Grand Rapids: Zondervan, n.d. (photographically reproduced from the London edition of 1872).

Young, Samuel. *John.* Beacon Bible Expositions. Vol. 4. Kansas City: Beacon Hill, 1979.

ACTS

M. Robert Mulholland, Jr.

INTRODUCTION

I. RELIABILITY

For seventeen centuries the Acts of the Apostles was presumed to be a historically reliable account of early Christianity. The rise of modern biblical criticism in the late eighteenth and early nineteenth centuries overturned this presumption. One of the most radical critical approaches to Acts was that of F.C. Baur and the Tübingen School (Kümmel, 112). According to Baur, Acts was a composition of the second-century church created to resolve the tension between Jewish (Petrine) and gentile (Pauline) Christianity.

Baur's view was quickly rejected by critical scholars, and a variety of competing viewpoints emerged. Source critical scholars argued against Lucan authorship, presuming a variety of sources behind Acts (Conzelmann, xxxvi-xl). Historical critics doubted that Acts accurately reflected the first-century Mediterranean world (Guthrie, 354–63). Literary critics viewed the work as typical of Hellenistic historiography, whose authenticity and veracity were as suspect as the secular histories of the period (Kümmel, 112–23).

By the first decades of the twentieth century, Acts came to be viewed as a theological treatise of the late first or early second century written in the literary form of historiography (Harnack, Haenchen). There is still wide diversity among scholars regarding the theological focus of Acts. Nevertheless, most critical scholars of less conservative persuasion presume Acts is a theological treatise by an unknown author of the early church.

Conservative biblical scholarship in the nineteenth century either ignored or reacted against these developments in the understanding of Acts. The work of Sir William Ramsey toward the end of the nineteenth century began to provide conservative scholarship with data to support the historical reliability and Lucan authorship of Acts. Ramsey, a classicist and archaeologist, initially presumed the findings of higher critical German scholarship regarding Acts. Ramsey discovered, however, that his archaeologist findings repeatedly substantiated the reliability of Acts.

Ramsey, carried away with his findings, emerged as a crusader for the reliability of Acts. Unfortunately, his zeal was not always matched with a sound handling of the evidence; so his findings were largely discounted. Others took up the challenge, however, and began the process of substantiating the book's reliability. Sherwin-White, another classicist, found the administrative and legal dynamics of Acts perfectly consistent with what is known of Roman administration in the middle of the first century (*Roman Society and Roman Law in the New Testament*). More recently, Martin Hengel, a critical biblical scholar of high repute, has argued powerfully and persuasively for the historical reliability of Acts (*Acts and the History of Earliest Christianity*).

II. AUTHORSHIP

The earliest references of Acts by the early church unanimously indicate that Luke, the companion of Paul, was the author. Internal evidence, while not conclusive, does nothing to contradict this belief. Scholars are united in their view that the same person wrote both Luke and Acts (Bruce, 2). The vocabulary and style of both writings is the same (Hawkins, 16–29, 174–89). The concerns of both writings are parallel: e.g., concern for those outside of Judaism, the prominence of women, and the role of the Holy Spirit.

The "we" sections of Acts (16:10–17; 20:5–21:18; 27:1–28:16) suggest that the writer was a companion of Paul. There is no means, however, to prove or disprove conclusively that this companion was Luke.

Several scholars have commented on the medical language in Luke-Acts, suggesting that there is a higher incidence of precise medical terminology used in the description of ailments and conditions than in the rest of the NT (Hobart: Harnack, *Luke the Physician*). This might point to Luke, the beloved physician (Col 4:14). More careful scholarship, however, has called into question the strength of this observation (Cadbury).

The author of Acts probably was Luke, the companion of Paul, as the early church attested. However, this cannot be proved conclusively on the basis of the available evidence.

III. DATE

Eusebius, the early fourth-century Father, intimated that Acts was written in the seventh decade (60s) of the Christian era (H.E. 2,22,6). While there are arguments for various dates (Guthrie, 340–48), internal evidence points to a date in the middle of the first century. The historical data in Acts that can be confirmed accurately portrays the conditions of the Roman world at that time (Bruce, 17). The chronological sequence of persons and events in Acts is in precise order. When these "tracers" are followed through to the end of Acts, the book closes about A.D. 62, with Paul imprisoned in Rome.

One of the intriguing features of Acts is the nature of its ending. Harnack suggested that if the Gospels had been written like Acts, they would have concluded with Jesus appearing before Pilate. The author gives a great proportion of his work to describing the events surrounding Paul's imprisonment, trials and hearings, appeal to Caesar, and voyage to Rome. Yet he fails to give the conclusion to this sequence of events. There are numerous theories regarding this situation. Perhaps Luke intended to write another book (Knox) or wished to avoid the outcome of the trial (Guthrie, 342). One theory suggests that Acts is a "defense brief" prepared for Paul's attorney (Theophilus?) in preparation for Paul's appearance before Nero (Guthrie, 352).

The most logical reason for the unusual ending of the book is that the author brought history up to the present (at the time of writing) and closed there, which would date Acts about A.D. 62.

This early dating is further substantiated by the primitive terms that appear in Acts: Christ (Messiah) is used predominately as a title rather than a name; Christians are known as disciples rather than saints; Jesus is called Son of Man, the only use of the term other than on the lips of Jesus in the Gospels; Christianity is called The Way and the sect of the Nazoreans (Bruce, 12–13; Guthrie, 344).

IV. SOURCES

A great number of theories have been developed regarding the sources used by the author (Conzlemann, xxxvi–xl). Many of these theories are colored by presuppositions regarding the historicity, authorship, and purpose of Acts (Guthrie, 363–77). Even for those who presume that the author was a companion of Paul, the question of sources is important. Obviously the author would have firsthand knowledge of the "we sections," and secondhand knowledge through Paul for those narratives where Paul was present (6:7–8:3; 9:1–30; 11:19–30; 12:1–24[?]; 12:25–28:31 as well as much of 2:1–6:6, if Paul was dwelling in Jerusalem for some time prior to his emergence as leader of the persecution). But the question remains: Where did Luke get his information for those portions where Paul was not present?

Luke tells us in his gospel that "many have undertaken to compile a narrative of the things which have been accomplished among us, just as they were delivered to us by those who from the beginning were eyewitnesses" (1:1–2 RSV). This description suggests the existence of both written and oral accounts. Elsewhere the writer implies that he was present with Paul in Palestine for two years during Paul's imprisonment in Jerusalem and Caesarea (Acts 21:17 ["we"]; 27:1 ["we"]). This provided time to meet and talk with those who were present in the early days of the Christian movement prior to Paul's involvement.

Thus, presumably, the writer had available both written and oral accounts of the events, speeches, sermons, and trials in the first part of Acts. The style of the speeches in the first part is inferior to the narrative material in the rest of the book. Moreover, these briefer speeches are perfectly consistent with their setting, suggesting that the author was faithful to his sources (Bruce, 18–21).

V. HISTORICITY

Acts is written in the general style of historiography prevalent in the first century (Conzlemann, xl; Bruce, 15; Aune, 77–111). Secular histories of the time varied in their historical reliability. Acts is highly reliable. The historical events, sociopolitical dynamics, cultural settings, legal structures, and religious practices that can be attested by external evidence consistently confirm the historical reliability of Acts (Bruce, 17).

VI. PURPOSE

The basic purpose of Acts is to portray the development of the Christian movement in its first three decades. There are four interlocking phases in this development.

1. The movement from Jews to Gentiles. This phase contains initial outreach to the Jews (1:1–8:3); outreach to "second-class" Jews, such as Samaritans and proselytes (8:4–40); outreach to God-fearing Gentiles (9:32–11:18); finally, outreach to Gentiles with no connection to Judaism (13:2–21:15).

2. The movement from Jerusalem to Rome. This movement also has four stages: (1) from Jerusalem throughout Judea, Samaria, and Galilee (1:1–9:31); (2) extension to Antioch (11:19–13:1); (3) the Antioch-based mission (13:2–21:16); (4) Paul to Rome (21:17–28:31).

3. The problems within the Christian movement. There are four dimensions to these problems that thread through the book: (1) Jews versus Jewish Christians, (2) Hebrew Christians versus Hellenistic Christians, (3) Jewish Christians versus gentile Christians, (4) Christians versus Roman authorities.

4. The establishment of Paul's primacy in the emergence of Christianity out of Judaism into the Roman world. One way in which the author establishes Paul's authority is to select events from Paul's ministry to the Gentiles that parallel Peter's ministry to the Jews. Each heals a lame person (3:2–10; 14:8–10), each is the source of miraculous healings (5:15; 19:12), each performs exorcisms (5:16; 16:18), each contends with sorcerers (8:18–24; 13:6–11), each raises the dead (9:36–42; 20:9–10?), and each has miraculous deliverances from prison (5:19: 12:7–11; 16:25–26).

The author skillfully interweaves these four phases to record how, through the empowerment and guidance of the Holy Spirit, a small Jewish, messianic sect became a major movement in the Roman world.

VII. OUTLINE

COMMENTARY

I. INTRODUCTION (1:1–2:47)

Luke here describes the formation of the Christian community as a new covenant community experiencing a radical new life of relationship with God through the gift of the Holy Spirit. The rest of Acts portrays the witness and impact of this community upon the world; first, upon the world of the Jews, and second, upon the larger Roman-Hellenistic world.

A. Context of the New Community (1:1–11)

Luke's link to the **former book** suggests Acts is the continuation of **all that Jesus began to do and to teach** (v.1). The focus on the role of the Holy Spirit (vv.2, 5, 8) provides the means by which Jesus' ministry is continued in the life of the Christian community.

Even the presence and teaching of the risen Lord fail to move the disciples out of their old ideas about the kingdom of God (vv.3, 6). They still think in terms of the restoration of Israel. Jesus' response (vv.7–8) points them to the promise of the Spirit who will inaugurate a new order of being, a new kingdom, which will include not only Israel (**Jerusalem, Judea**) but also apostate "half Jews" (**Samaria**) and even Gentiles (**the end of the earth**). The disciples will experience the reality (**power**) of this new order of being when the Holy Spirit comes upon them and will manifest (**witness to**) this new life in the world.

The Ascension (1:9–11) is the next to last event in Jesus' incarnation. The final event is the gift of the Holy Spirit, which extends the Incarnation throughout ongoing history until the final consummation. Paul stresses this reality with the image of the church as the body of Christ.

B. The Waiting Community (1:12–26)

The inclusive nature of the community that is to receive the Holy Spirit (vv.12–14) is seen in Luke's inclusion of women and the previously antagonistic family of Jesus (Mk 3:21; Jn 7:3). Luke also reveals the very human nature of this community. While they wait in prayer for the fulfillment of the promise, they also take matters into their own hands to create a replacement for Judas (vv.15–26). Apparently, this arises from their earlier concern about Israel and the kingdom since Jesus had promised that they would sit on twelve thrones judging the tribes of Israel (Mt 19:28).

Paul is often suggested as the one whom God chose to fill the number of apostles. But in Luke's presentation "the apostles" are restricted solely to Palestine and the outreach to those associated with Judaism (14:4, 14 is the exception that proves the rule), while Paul undertakes the outreach to the gentile world.

C. Content of the New Community (2:1–42)

The promised gift of the Holy Spirit comes at Pentecost (vv.1–4); the culmination of the Passover cycle; the celebration of the giving of the Torah, which shaped the old covenant community as the people of God; and the Festival of the Firstfruits. For the Christian community, it came as the culmination of the Crucifixion/ Resurrection at Passover; it shaped a new covenant community as the people of God; and it was the "firstfruit" of the consummation of God's purposes in Christ (Eph 1:13–14).

As the history of Acts unfolds, we see that the disciples were filled with the presence, the power, and the purpose of God. They entered into a new experience of relationship with God in which their lives came under God's control. Yet they retained their individual freedom and human foibles—as seen in the freedom of Ananias and Sapphira to lie to the Spirit (5:1–11), the prejudiced view of the Hebrews toward the Hellenists (6:1–6), and the perspective of some Jewish Christians toward God-fearers (11:1–18) and gentile Christians (15:1–29). While filled with the Holy Spirit, they still evidence the need to bring various areas of their lives into obedience to the guidance of the Spirit, a reality that confirms Wesley's emphasis on sanc-

tification that continues beyond the experience of entire sanctification. Experiencing one's life under the presence, power, and purpose of the Holy Spirit does not immediately confer "perfection" upon all the characteristics and dynamics of one's being.

The initial experience of the Holy Spirit by the Christian community was attended by visual and aural phenomena that attracted the attention of the larger Jewish community in Jerusalem (vv.2–6). The disciples immediately began to **prophesy**, that is, they began to communicate their experience of God's presence, power, and purpose (**God's mighty works**) to those around them. There is much debate whether the disciples were empowered to speak in various languages or whether the listeners were empowered to hear. Since the Spirit was given to the disciples, it seems reasonable that they were gifted with languages so as to communicate their experience of God to the gathered Jewish community.

The old covenant community of Jews and proselytes, gathered in Jerusalem from across the world, is perplexed by what they see and hear (vv.7–13). They have no frame of reference for understanding such an experience. Not knowing the reality of this new life graced by God, they can explain it only by reference to the only kind of human existence they know.

Peter, however, provides the old covenant community with a frame of reference that enables them to understand what they are seeing and hearing (vv.14–36). Not only does Peter claim that this experience is the fulfillment of old covenant promises (vv.16–21), but, by changing the text of Joel, Peter indicates that it inaugurates the **last days,** a phrase that intimates to Jewish hearers that the new realm of God's kingdom has begun. While this sets the experience into a context the Jewish community can understand, it is a radical proclamation. Peter further highlights the radical nature of what God has done by his exegesis of the text, **Everyone who calls on the** *name* **of the** *Lord* **will be** *saved* (v.21). First, Peter indicates that Jesus, the *name* of the one **attested by God through signs, wonders,** and resurrection, is responsible for this experience of the Holy Spirit (vv.22–33). Second, Peter indicates that Jesus is the *Lord,* an identification that applies a title for God to Jesus (vv.34–36). Third, he indicates that *salvation* is in the name of Jesus (vv.37–40). All of this is confirmed by the Holy Spirit who has been given by Jesus, the risen Lord, and who is now available to **everyone who calls on the name of the Lord.**

In answer to the people's response, Peter calls the old covenant community to a new covenant (vv.37–38). In the old covenant, to repent and be baptized for forgiveness was to leave an old order of being behind and to become part of a new order, God's covenant people. Now Peter calls the old covenant people to enter into a new order of being, which is characterized by the gift of the Holy Spirit.

Peter's invitation reveals the diversity of those invited into the new covenant (vv.39–40). Not only are his Jewish hearers and their descendants included, but also **those far off,** a term that includes the diaspora Jews, apostate Jews, proselytes, and even Gentiles. All humanity is invited.

D. Structure of the New Community (2:43–47)

The people of this new order of being structure themselves along the lines of the old covenant holiness communities (2:42). The holiness movement of the day, the Pharisees, gath-

ered as a "house" around the scribes who were their teachers. They formed fellowships (*chaburim*) that supported and reinforced their commitment to live lives of priestly holiness in the world. One of the essentials of these fellowships was their common meals, which assured meticulous observance of the purity laws. Finally, they were characterized by their communal prayers. In **the apostles' teaching**, the **fellowship**, the **breaking of bread**, and the **prayers**, we see the Christian community using the old structures of their lives for the shaping of their life together as a new people of God. The Christian community, like their Pharisaic counterparts, initially had two foci: the **temple** and the **house** (v.46).

II. JEWISH OUTREACH AND OPPOSITION (3:1–9:31)

Luke shows the impact of the Christian community and its new experience of God upon the Jewish community of Jerusalem and its environs together with the response and reaction of the Jews and their leaders. At first there is great positive response by the Jewish people, contrasted with the animosity of the Sadducees who repeatedly take action against the Christians for their proclamation of the Resurrection. Then the synagogues, under the leadership of the Pharisees, enter into the picture, and Christians are opposed on the more serious issues of the role of the Law of Moses and the sacrificial cultus of the temple.

Luke also portrays the outreach of the Christians to the more marginalized members of the Jewish community. After the initial outreach to "pure" Jews (3:11–8:4), those who, by any definition, would be included in the old covenant community of God's people, the witness extends to questionable "half-Jews," such as Samaritans and proselytes (e.g., the Ethiopian eunuch), who would not have been welcomed into the communities of more conservative Jews (8:5–40).

A. Outreach to Jews in Jerusalem (3:1–8:4)

1. First opposition (3:1–4:31)

While the disciples continued to participate in the liturgy of the temple (3:1), they manifested a power of wholeness, which the temple and its cultus could not (vv.2–10). They not only proclaimed the Resurrection; they were empowered by God to raise up to new life and wholeness those prevented by their brokenness from full participation in the life of God's people. The lame man was prohibited by the religious laws from entering the temple proper where the men of Israel offered sacrifices in God's presence. At the same time, the temple's community and worship never reached out to this man with healing. His healing through Peter and John not only manifested the power of wholeness in this new experience of God, but also illuminated in bold relief the impotence of the old covenant community and its cultus.

Peter's address, following the healing, clearly links the healing with the resurrection of Jesus (3:11–16). The healing is a witness to the Resurrection, an attestation by God to the validity of what the Christian community claims. At the same time, Peter emphasizes that it is the God of Abraham, Isaac, and Jacob who has acted in this way. He links the event with the God of the old covenant and then calls the old covenant community to realize that God has acted to fulfill the promises given through the prophets (vv.17–26). The proclamation of God's fulfillment of the old covenant, clearly manifested in the healed man standing before them, pro-

vides the basis upon which Peter calls the old covenant community to participate in the new covenant, even implying that failure to respond removes one from the old covenant community (v.23). For Peter, it is clear that the new covenant community is the fulfillment of the old.

The keepers of the religious status quo, overly sensitive to their responsibility for the religious welfare of the community, convinced of the impossibility of God acting in a way incompatible with their perspective and intolerant of anything that threatens their authority and power, move to exert their control and remove the threat (4:1–3). Even in the face of such overt opposition by the religious authorities, however, there is a great response to the witness of this new experience with God (v.4). People whose hearts are hungry for God are wiser than those whose lives are devoted to religion!

The trial of Peter and John (4:5–22) is a classic example of the adage "Don't confuse us with facts, our minds are made up." Peter again takes the opportunity to set forth the healing as a witness to the Resurrection, this time in the presence of those who were responsible for the crucifixion of Jesus. Empowered by the Holy Spirit, Peter not only implicates the religious leaders in the death of Jesus, but affirms that their actions have been overturned by God; the healed man before them is the unimpeachable evidence. God has used their rejection of Jesus as the foundation for a salvation that supersedes the salvation of their structures and systems of religion. God always has a disconcerting way of breaking out of the structures in which we think we have regularized and codified our relationship with God.

How vigorously we try to avoid the breakout. The religious authorities first attempt to rationalize away God's absence from their system by considering the credentials of the ones who claim God's presence and power. They cannot be taken seriously; after all, they are not trained in the subtleties of religious knowledge. In addition, they are associates of that heretical, so-called rabbi from Nazareth who was crucified. Surely this discredits their claims.

Though such rationalization may soothe troubled consciences, the evidence of God's breakout is the healed man, who cannot be denied. The only recourse is to attempt to prevent any further publicizing of the fact.

Peter and John, while recognizing the authority of the religious leaders to take whatever action they think appropriate, make it clear that they must live out the reality of their new relationship with God. The religious leaders are trying to deal with the problem as though it were a theological issue alone and not the matter of a whole new order of being. The mind disconnected from the heart often can be coerced to change its position, but when knowledge conjoins with vital piety it cannot be stifled easily.

In the face of coercion and threat, it is significant to note the solidarity of the Christian community (4:23–31). Often a community leaves its leaders "hanging out to dry" when they become the focus of opposition. The unity of the Christian community in their experience of new life in Christ, however, bonds them together in a powerful, mutually supportive consecration of themselves to God. Their response to the threat is to cleave to God in absolute trust and unwavering obedience.

Such submission and consecration never fails to result in the outpouring of God's presence, power, and purpose into and through the lives of the consecrated. Not only are they filled with God's presence, but they show it in the face of threat.

2. Community life (4:32–5:11)

Because of their consecration to God, the members of the community experienced a deep bonding of their lives together (4:32). They were **one in heart and mind;** their commitment manifested itself in a stewardship that enabled them to be God's help to others (vv.34–37). There was a radical new perspective toward possessions. No longer were they possessed by their possessions. They had experienced a liberation that enabled them to offer their possessions for the welfare of others. Such radical behavior presented to the world another confirmation for the reality of the apostles' proclamation of the Resurrection (v.33). The power of the Resurrection was seen in the transformed living of the Christian community. What great need there is in every age for the community of Christ to incarnate the proclamation of its message.

Such incarnation, however, is not achieved easily, as the case of Ananias and Sapphira reveals (5:1–11). Even in a community that had experienced such fullness of God's presence and power, there were persons who, in their compulsive care for themselves, sought refuge in the semblance of participation without the sacrifice. Ananias and Sapphira wanted to appear as fully participating members of the community, but they also wanted to maintain some vestige of control over their own welfare rather than entrust themselves completely to God.

The community, through Peter, discerns their lack of integrity, and the discipline is immediate and radical. How different from the church today, which so often compromises with attitudes and actions that are contrary to the Spirit-filled life. No wonder, then, that the world is little moved by the church's pronouncements.

There must have been such an awareness of the presence and power of God in the life of the community that Ananias and Sapphira were already guilt-ridden and highly stressed as they attempted their deceit. The shock of discovery and the realization of having manipulated God overstressed them and they died.

If they had not realized it before, the Christian community now knew it was participating in a reality of ultimate significance. No playing of religious games here! Those outside the community who may have dismissed it simply as a new sect or passing fad now realized that something serious was going on.

3. Second opposition (5:12–42)

The apostles, manifesting the presence and power of God, attract even more attention by the old covenant community (5:12–16). Increasing numbers of people respond and enter into the new experience of relationship with God. Even those who do not respond, either out of concern for the depth of consecration required or out of fear of the religious authorities, have high regard for the Christians.

For the religious authorities, it is bad enough to have people flocking to this new movement; but when even those who do not join hold it in awe and high regard, it is time to do something (5:17–18). Not only are the religious leaders blind to the presence and power of God in the life and activities of the Christian community, they also seem incapable of seeing God's action in the miraculous release of the apostles from prison and their unintimidated boldness in going right back to teaching in

the temple (vv.19–26). The only concern of the authorities seems to be the security of their own roles and their maintaining control of the people. This concern is revealed not only in the charge that the apostles have disobeyed the injunction to be silent, but also in their fear that the apostles' witness to the Resurrection will put the Jewish authorities in a bad light with the people (vv.27–28).

The apostles refuse to be intimidated by those in authority, repeating their earlier response (4:19) of obedience to God and directly charging the authorities with the death of Jesus (5:29). As if that were not enough, the apostles also reiterate their witness that God has acted not only to undo this work of the religious leaders through the resurrection of Jesus, but that God has instituted a new structure of covenant relationship through repentance and forgiveness, a relationship that is attested by the experience of the presence of God in the lives of those who obey God (vv.31–32).

It is no wonder that the authorities are enraged and ready to kill the apostles (5:33). They now realize that the apostles are the "authorities" of a movement that threatens their whole structure of existence. To accept the truth of the apostles' claims requires them to acknowledge that they rejected and killed God's Messiah, accept God's overturning of their action, and recognize that God is doing something new that does away with the whole structure of religion upon which their roles rely. Providentially, Gamaliel, Paul's teacher (22:3), brings wisdom to the deliberations (5:34–39). He is at least open to the possibility that God just might be active in all this. Of course Gamaliel, as a Pharisee, accepts the possibility of resurrection while the aristocratic Sadducees do not.

Gamaliel at least succeeds in reducing murderous rage to vindictive wrath (5:40). Even the first experience of punishment, however, does not dissuade the apostles from bearing witness to the Resurrection and to Jesus as Messiah (vv.41–42)—both in the temple, center of the old covenant community, and in the gathering of the new covenant community, the house (see above on 2:42, 46).

4. Community life (6:1–6)

Old perspectives die hard, even in new covenant community. People tend to bring their old prejudices and attitudes right along with them. Even in an order characterized by the presence and power of God, the purpose of God is not always quickly discerned nor readily followed. In first-century Judaism the more conservative Jews sought strict adherence to every jot and tittle of the law and resisted any hint of accommodation to the Hellenistic culture. More liberal Jews, however, saw no problem with adopting the Greek language, Hellenistic clothing, and some of the nonprohibited aspects of Hellenistic culture. The **Hebrews** looked askance at these accommodations of the **Hellenistic Jews,** considering them second-class Jews at best and outright apostates at worst.

It appears that these prejudices were carried over into the new covenant community: the Hebrews were discriminating against the Hellenists in the distribution of resources (6:1–7; see 2:44–45; 4:32–37). The apostles discern that such dissension within the Christian community would distract them from their witness and undermine their proclamation (6:2). (This must be the thrust of the apostle's remark, since at least one of the seven chosen to supervise distribution becomes a powerful witness and proclaimer, appar-

ently doing both tasks.) To avoid any countercharges of favoritism, they wisely assign the distribution to the Hellenists who, presumably, would be meticulously equitable in that distribution.

Luke's first major summary sketches the life of the new covenant community (2:43–47). His second portrays the extension of that community throughout Jerusalem and among the priesthood (6:7). The first summary leads into opposition to the Christian community by the high priestly aristocracy. The second leads into the broader opposition by the Pharisees.

5. Third opposition (6:8–8:4)

Sooner or later, it was bound to happen. The Sadducean aristocracy had opposed the Christian community because its witness to the Resurrection implied that God had overthrown their actions, and the popular response threatened their control of the status quo. Now the synagogue, the focus of the Pharisees' power and authority, becomes the source of opposition (6:8–15). Also, rather than individual incidents of opposition, the opposition becomes a programmatic attempt, under Saul, to eradicate the Christian community.

Aside from Stephen's irrefutable witness in ministry and his unassailable integrity in debate (6:8–10), which parallels that of the apostles, a new element emerges here. The issue now is the relationship of the Christian experience to the law and OT cultus: **Moses and God/the holy place and the law** (vv.10–14). If the Christian proclamation is true, if God is acting in a new way to create a new covenant community, what are the implications for the faithful observance of the Law of Moses and the sacrificial system of the temple? Some Jews began to realize that the Christian claim to be the fulfillment of the promises of the old covenant might undermine the whole structure of the old covenant community as they knew it.

Stephen's defense (7:1–53) takes three lines. First, with respect to the significance of the temple, Stephen illustrates from the Jewish scriptures that the God of the old covenant is not confined to any one special place but is a God who dwells in the midst of the covenant people. Second, the old covenant people have a long history of refusing to heed God's agents and of slaying them. Third, the old covenant people also have a long history of rebellion against the Law of Moses. His conclusions are that God does not dwell in the temple of Jerusalem (vv.47–50) and that the Jews are resistant to God, both refusing to listen to God and to consecrate themselves to obedience (v.51). Moreover, the Jews are closed to the indwelling presence of God in the Holy Spirit, all of which can be seen clearly in their rejection and murder of God's Righteous One (v.52).

If Stephen's "defense" does nothing to endear him to his opponents, the witness of his presence does even less. His radiant appearance (6:15) and this claim to a vision of God and Jesus (7:55–56) leave them no choice. A witness whose testimony can be either refuted or rejected can be treated with contempt and thus discredited. But a witness whose very being and life manifest the incarnation of his testimony must be eradicated (vv.57–58). Even in death, however, the power and reality of Stephen's relationship with God is proclaimed as he prays for his executioners (vv.59–60). What an insurmountable dilemma for religious authorities who attempt to deal with God's breakout from their systems and structures. Threats do not work; punishment fails; trials boomerang, and the accusers become the accused; and even execution provides another manifestation of the unavoidable reality of God's escape.

Such an agonizing dilemma must have tortured Saul, the prosecutor at whose feet the executioners laid their garments as required by the law. Obsessed with his zeal for the law (22:3; 26:9–11; Gal 1:13–14; Php 3:6), Saul becomes the leader of a general program to eradicate the Christian community (8:1–3), seeking out the community as it gathers as a house of teaching, fellowship, breaking bread, and prayer.

The very persecution that sought to eradicate the Christian movement, however, becomes the impetus for its expanded witness and outreach far beyond Jerusalem and even Judaism (8:4). It was as if Saul tried to extinguish a fire by stomping on it, only to scatter the flaming embers far and wide. Up to this point, the Christian movement had been confined within Judaism, particularly the racially "pure" Jews of Jerusalem and its environs. Even the Christian Jews had difficulties when Hellenistic Jews whose cultic purity was questionable joined the community. As a result of Saul's persecution, however, the Christian outreach now begins to move toward the outer fringes of Judaism.

B. Outreach to Samaritans and Proselytes (8:5–9:31)

1. The Samaritans (8:5–25)

Now for the first time, Luke indicates the Christian outreach to other than "pure" Jews. The Samaritans were, in some sense, half-Jews, able to claim Abraham as part of their heritage and having essentially the same sacred Scriptures as the Jews. Their racial impurity made them outcasts to racially pure Jews, although, in more liberal circles of Judaism, Samaritans were equated with proselytes (Gentiles who had been incorporated into the Jewish community of faith). More conservative Jews had extreme difficulty accepting even proselytes as part of the old covenant community. For them, there would be no possibility of the Samaritans' inclusion: "For Jews do not associate with Samaritans" (Jn 4:9). With the outreach to the Samaritans, the Christian community takes a decisive step.

It may be significant that Philip, one of the Hellenists, evangelizes the Samaritans and the Ethiopian eunuch. As noted (see 6:1–6), the Hellenists were more open to the larger culture of the Hellenistic world. Philip's witness and ministry replicates that of the apostles in Jerusalem, and the response of the Samaritans is similar (8:5–8). The added note about Simon (vv.9–11) emphasizes the non-Jewish influences prevalent among the Samaritans, which caused the Jews to scorn them.

Although the Samaritans **paid close attention to** the Word, **believed,** and **were baptized** (8:6, 12), there is no mention of their receiving the Holy Spirit. This is not an oversight as the following section reveals (vv.14–17). The Holy Spirit does not come upon them until Peter and John are sent from Jerusalem and **lay hands on them.** This is not due to something inferior about the Samaritans. Rather, it serves as a sign to the Jewish Christians in Jerusalem that even the Samaritans are included in the new covenant community of God's people. It seems likely, since Jerusalem had done nothing to evangelize Samaritans prior to this, that Peter and John were sent by Jerusalem to "investigate" what was going on. Since they **evangelize many Samaritan villages** on their return to Jerusalem (v.25), obviously the pair is convinced by God's outpouring of the Holy Spirit upon the Samaritans.

Simon's desire to control the gift of the Holy Spirit for his own enhancement (8:18–24) should be a warning to those in any age who attempt to contain the Holy Spirit within their own definitions, structures, and behaviors of Christian experience. Such activities are, as Peter noted, a sign that those who do such things are not participating in the reality of Christian experience, for their hearts are not right before God. Instead of being consecrated to God for God's purposes, they seek to manipulate the gifts of God for their own purposes.

2. The proselyte (8:26–40)

It takes divine intervention to extend the witness of Christian experience to a proselyte (8:26, 29). We can infer that the Ethiopian was a proselyte from the fact that he had been to the temple in Jerusalem to worship and possessed a copy of the Jewish Scriptures. But what a proselyte! Not only was he a high official of a pagan foreign government, but a eunuch. For any pious, observant Jew, this man would be excluded from the cultus and would be unclean in the community because he was physically impaired. With the Ethiopian eunuch, Luke portrays the Christian community extending itself to the utmost limit of what could possibly be considered Judaism.

Philip's obedience to God indicates why God was able to use him so powerfully. Instead of raising questions about the sense of going out on a desert road, he went. Instead of discussing the wisdom of a strange, lone person approaching an undoubtedly well-protected caravan, he ran up to it. If we wonder why there seems an absence of direction by God in our day, perhaps we need to look at the quality of our obedience.

Seemingly strange events follow the baptism of the Ethiopian (8:39–40). Translation seems to be part of the problem. The idea of Philip being transported by the Spirit disappears when it is seen that the Greek text says, **The Spirit of the Lord seized Philip, and the eunuch did not see him again, but went on his way rejoicing, and Philip was found in Azotus**. It seems likely that just as the Spirit sent Philip into the desert to meet the Ethiopian, the Spirit sent Philip off on another assignment as soon as the task was completed.

3. Saul's conversion (9:1–31)

Since the persecution of Christians in Jerusalem spread the "disease" to other Jewish communities, Saul undertakes to stop the spread (vv.1–2). **The Way** as a title for the Christian movement is probably another reflection of the manner in which Jewish Christians structured their community on the model of the Jewish holiness movement. At the heart of the Pharisaic quest for a life of priestly holiness was the "traditions of the elders," the whole structure of oral tradition which shaped daily life. The operative portion of the tradition for a life of holiness was the *Halakah,* "the walkings" or *"the Way"!* Is it any wonder that Saul, the zealous Pharisee who could honestly claim, "as to righteousness under the Law, blameless" (Php 3:6), was incensed to murderous rage against those who claimed to be **the Way?**

Damascus was the largest Jewish population center next to Jerusalem. It was also a center of trade and movement of people; these would facilitate further spread of the Christian witness. Saul must have realized the threat; for

later, as Paul, he focused his witness on the two major centers of movement in the eastern Mediterranean—Corinth and Ephesus.

Saul's encounter with the risen Christ must have been a profound trauma (9:3–9; 22:6–11; 26:12–18). The blindness, healed through a Christian, would have been an enacted parable of Saul's blindness to the reality of the Christian claims and experience. During the three days of fasting and blindness Saul certainly must have wrestled with his blindness and emptiness toward the presence and power of God, which had been at work before his eyes.

The unsung hero and the real miracle in Saul's conversion is Ananias (vv.10–19). Ananias is obviously open and obedient to the Lord, but sometimes the Lord seems to demand the impossible. It is doubtful whether anyone could fault Ananias for questioning the Lord, and most would probably absolve him had he failed to obey. Just the idea of going to Saul, the murderous persecutor, would give one pause. But to be told that this man is God's chosen one to carry the Gospel to Gentiles must have given Ananias real cause to question. Nevertheless, he obeyed, and from the simple but difficult act of obedience came the apostle to the Gentiles. The obedience of an otherwise unknown disciple transformed the nature of the Christian outreach.

Somewhere between 9:19b and 9:26, Saul, by his own account (Gal 1:15–18), spent time in Arabia and did not return to Jerusalem until three years after his encounter with the risen Christ. It seems likely that the time in Arabia comes between 9:19 and 20. After **several days with the disciples in Damascus,** Saul goes into Arabia, most likely to process his experience and to work through his understanding of what God had done in Christ. Upon returning to Damascus, **at once he began to preach Jesus in the synagogues**. Who could better prove to Jews that Jesus was the Messiah than a zealous Pharisee rigorously trained in the Scriptures? The best witnesses are always those who return to those from whom they came, to tell them about new life in Christ. They best know the ethos, the subtle nuances of the subculture, the idioms of communication. An outsider who tries to bring an unwanted paradigm shift of perception can simply be dismissed; an insider cannot be so easily discounted. The Jews seek to kill Saul (vv.23–25).

But now Saul, who is outcast by the Jews and anathema to the Christians in Jerusalem, is a person without a community (v.26). Like Ananias, Barnabas takes his life in his own hands to introduce Saul to the leadership of the Jerusalem Christians (v.27). After all, the whole thing could have been a cleverly developed plot by Saul to infiltrate the Christian community.

Saul quickly finds himself in trouble with his own group, the Hellenists (vv.28–29). These were the Jews who came from the Roman-Hellenistic diaspora, bringing with them their adaptations to the Hellenistic culture (see on 6:1–7). This is the group from which the opposition to Stephen (a Christian Hellenist, 6:5) arose (see 6:9, "the synagogue" of those from Asia, Cyrene, Alexandria, and Cilicia—of which Tarsus, Saul's home, was a major city). It seems that Saul returned to his own group of Jews and sought to convince them of the truth of the Christian claim. Again Saul has to flee for his life, this time back home to Tarsus.

Luke uses the conversion of Saul to bring to a close the Christian mission to the Jews. The Jewish Saul's rejection

of Christianity and Judaism's rejection of Saul the Christian Jew brings to a close the purely Jewish mission of Jerusalem Christians. Luke concludes this major section (3:1–9:31) with a summary statement (v.31) indicating the fullness of the church throughout the Jewish homeland—**Judea, Galilee, and Samaria.** In the next section, the Christian movement takes its first step across the outer boundary of Judaism.

III. OUTREACH TO GOD-FEARERS AND OPPOSITION (9:32–11:18)

The central focus of this section is the Christian outreach to God-fearers (10:1–11:18). God-fearers were Gentiles who participated in varying degrees in the Jewish way of life and undertook at least the minimum requirements of abstaining from pagan worship and nonkosher food, which enabled them to worship with the Jewish community. But they did not go through the process of baptism, circumcision, and sacrifice, which would have made them proselytes. In a limited sense, God-fearers could be considered part of the gentile world. No orthodox Jew would have considered a God-fearer a member of the old covenant community of God's people. In their outreach to God-fearers, and especially in baptizing them and allowing them to partake of the table fellowship of the Christian community, the Christian Jews crossed a dividing line that opened the way for outreach to the larger gentile world.

A. Peter's Travels (9:32–43)

Luke provides the accounts of **Lydda** (vv.32–34) and **Joppa** (vv.36–43) for a particular purpose. Lydda was a primarily Jewish town in an area of mixed Jewish and gentile population. Joppa, the principal port city of southern Palestine, was largely Greek in its composition. Luke is paving the way for the reader to realize that the Christian outreach is moving toward the gentile world. This is highlighted in Luke's reference to the Jewish and Greek names for **Tabitha/Dorcas** (v.36).

Both of Peter's miracles witness to the Resurrection: Aeneas is raised from a bed of paralysis and Tabitha/Dorcas from a bed of death. Luke takes no time to detail Peter's preaching and teaching. The accounts are given in brief capsule form, simply to indicate that the witness of the Resurrection in the practical ministry of the apostles is the source of belief.

B. Peter and Cornelius (10:1-48)

It is significant that Peter lodges in the house of a tanner (9:43). Tanning was an "unclean" occupation for Jews, and contact with a tanner would have made one ritually impure. This fact may have been troubling Peter as he prayed on the roof while a meal was being prepared (10:9-10). In a larger sense, however, it serves to represent the fact that Peter is standing on a threshold between his Jewish holiness and the unholiness of the gentile world.

Caesarea (10:1) was the Roman capital of Palestine, the seat of the procurators sent to rule the province of Judea; it was mostly Gentile in its population. A thoroughly Hellenistic city, it had a temple to Caesar, a theater, a hippodrome, and the other features of a pagan city in the Roman world. Since Philip was in Caesarea (8:40), one wonders why he was not sent to Cornelius. It may be because Philip was already open to those on the fringes of Judaism, as evidenced in his preaching to the Samaritans and the Ethiopian. Peter, however, represents the Jerusalem church of solidly Jewish Christians who, as we shall see, have difficulty with God's including those outside Judaism in the new covenant community.

Cornelius was a **centurion,** a position representing the heart and power of the Roman military and one of importance in the Roman world. It would have been impossible for Cornelius to have become a Jewish proselyte without losing his rank. Yet Cornelius was a **God-fearer**, as was **his entire household** (10:2). He was a devout God-fearer, even observing the Jewish hours of prayer in his home in such a manner as to be acceptable to God (vv.3-4).

God initiates the Christian outreach across the borders of Judaism by calling to the church from the other side. God has Cornelius send for Peter (10:4-8). At the same time, God is preparing Peter for the border crossing (vv.9-23). Peter, undoubtedly troubled about the possibility of eating food prepared in the unclean home of a tanner, receives a vision. The thrust of the vision (since, presumably, both clean and unclean animals are seen) is illustrated by the fact that Peter simply could have taken of the clean and left the unclean. The issue is the *mixing* of clean with unclean! For the observant Jew, like Peter (**I have never eaten anything impure or unclean**), the unclean pollutes the clean. But God is showing Peter that the clean transforms the unclean. As he ponders the vision, the Spirit tells Peter to go with the Gentiles who are asking for him at the gate.

It is clear from God's initiative with Cornelius and with Peter, that crossing the border from Jew to Gentile was not something that would have happened "normally" from within the Christian movement. Nowhere else does Luke indicate God's intervention to such an extent as here. This is a major step for the Christian movement.

In his encounter with Cornelius, his family and friends (10:24–33), Peter highlights the crucial issue for himself and the Jewish Christians in general: **You are well aware that it is against our law for a Jew to associate with a Gentile or visit him.** But Peter has begun to understand the lesson of the vision. God is expanding his perception, at least to the point of associating with Gentiles; for Peter acknowledges that Gentiles who **fear [God] and do what is right are acceptable**. In a sense, Peter is expanding his perspective of Judaism to include God-fearers. Rather than cross the border, however, Peter attempts to shift the border to include God-fearers in a broader definition of what constitutes God's people.

That this is the case is seen clearly in Peter's sermon (10:34–43). The entire orientation is related to the Jewish people. **The message of God is sent to the people of Israel** (v.36), proclaimed throughout all **Judea** (v.37), **in the country of the Jews and in Jerusalem** (v.39); and the apostle's proclamation of the Resurrection was to **the people** (a technical term for the old covenant community), as a fulfillment of the promises of the Jewish prophets (vv.42–43).

Before Peter himself can make any connection of his message with the God-fearers, before he can "give an altar call," God pours out the Holy Spirit upon the God-fearers (10:44–48). As with the Samaritans, the gift of the Holy Spirit does not follow the expect form: Repent, be baptized in the name of Jesus, and receive the Holy Spirit (2:38). And as with the Samaritans, the reason for departure from form is to expand the perception of the

Jewish Christians. The focus of attention is on the Jewish Christians (**the believers from among the circumcised**) who are absolutely amazed at this event. They cannot argue with the reality of what God has done, and they offer no resistance to Peter's suggestions that the God-fearers be baptized in the name of Jesus. The crucial issue is circumcision. Baptism was the first step for Gentiles to become Jewish proselytes but was to be followed by circumcision. Peter does something radically new. He baptizes God-fearers into the Christian community, which has heretofore been totally Jewish, without requiring them to be circumcised. A major step has been taken, a major barrier crossed.

C. Jewish-Christian Opposition in Jerusalem (11:1–18)

The radical nature of Peter's action becomes immediately clear when word reaches the community in Jerusalem that gentile God-fearers **had received the word of God** (vv.1–3). Once again it is clear that entering into the experience of relationship with God in Christ and receiving the fullness of the Holy Spirit does not guarantee the elimination of deeply ingrained prejudices and narrow perspectives. While receiving the Word of God might be interpreted in a positive manner, this was not the case for the Jewish Christians in Jerusalem. For them it was not proper that the Gentiles receive the Word of God. This is revealed in their charges against Peter: **You went to uncircumcised men and ate with them.** How often we assume the correctness of our deeply ingrained and long-held perspectives. It often takes a radical intervention by God to break us out of our limitations.

This is the first appearance of the circumcision party, undoubtedly a group of conservative Jewish Christians who held that it was necessary for persons to become Jews before they could become Christians. They appear again in 15:1, 5. Their perspective is reasonable. If the Christian experience is the fulfillment of the promise of the old covenant, obviously people have to be members of the old covenant if they are to experience its fulfillment. Their only problem is in limiting God to their understanding of fulfillment.

Peter's defense, after reiterating the events with Cornelius (vv.4–16), is that God poured out the Holy Spirit into the God-fearers' lives just as at Pentecost. If God dealt with the God-fearers just as with the Jews, who was he to go against God (v.17)? Peter keeps his focus clear; the issue is the reality of the experience of new relationship with God in Christ. If that is genuine, no other structures and procedures, no matter how well established, long held, or cherished, are to become a restriction to what God has done.

There is a possibility of two responses in Jerusalem (v.18). One group (the circumcision party) is silenced; the other rejoices that God has included the God-fearers in the new covenant.

IV. ANTIOCH AND JERUSALEM (11:19–12:25)

Up to this point Jerusalem has been the focus of the Christian community and its outreach. Luke now shifts attention from Jerusalem to Syrian Antioch. Antioch was one of the major centers of Jewish diaspora in the Roman world. The large Jewish community there generally had very good relations with the gentile population of this wealthy and sophisticated city, which trailed only Rome and Alexandria in size. It was through the Christian community in Antioch that the outreach to Gentiles completely outside the Jewish commu-

nity came about. The conflict between Jerusalem and Antioch over this event was the first major watershed of the Christian movement.

A. From Jerusalem to Antioch (11:19–26)

Luke signals a shift by repeating in 11:19–20, the words of 8:4, which inaugurated the wider outreach of the Jerusalem church following Stephen's death: "Now those who were scattered went about preaching the Word" (8:4); **Now those who were scattered ... went about ... (speaking) the Word ... preaching the Lord Jesus** (11:19–20). By this means, Luke indicates that the scattering had two results, which took place at the same time. On the one hand, the Jerusalem church began a wider outreach that extended through Samaritans (8:9–25) and proselytes (8:26–40) even to God-fearers (9:32–11:18). In a much briefer summary, the Christians in Antioch do the same thing. Like the Jerusalem community, they first preach only to Jews (11:19); but in Antioch some reach out to **Greeks** (v.20). (The term *Hellenists,* which appears in some manuscripts, is a contradictory textual variant, since elsewhere [6:1; 9:29] they are clearly Jews.)

Luke's use of the term **Greeks** is revealing. He uses it in the expected way to describe persons of the Roman culture (19:10, 17; 20:21; 21:27ff.). He also uses it to describe Gentiles who participate in the worship of the Jewish synagogue (14:1; 17:4–5; 18:4), who, on two occasions, are further described as being devout (i.e., God-fearers, 17:4; worshipers of God, 18:7). The same use seems to apply to Timothy's parents. His mother was "a woman of the Jewish faith" (i.e., a proselyte; cf. 24:24 for Luke's term for a Jewish woman); his father was a "Greek," presumably a God-fearer, a situation that often existed in diaspora synagogues. It seems likely, in the parallelism of Antioch with Jerusalem, together with the contrast of a predominately Jewish outreach in 11:19, that the "Greeks" in Antioch were God-fearers. In Antioch, however, there is not simply one person with family and friends who believed, as with Cornelius, but a "great number" (11:21).

The Jerusalem church is still seen exercising oversight of the Christian movement (v.22), and they send Barnabas to check up on this situation. Being a man **full of the Holy Spirit,** Barnabas is open to this greater outreach of the Gospel to God-fearers and joins the work with such effectiveness that he has to bring Saul from Tarsus to assist in the work (vv.23–26).

The final proof that the Christian outreach is still within the context of Judaism is their title in Antioch: **Christians.** The term literally means "messianists" (those who hold that Jesus is the Messiah), a term that would have had significance only within a Jewish context.

B. From Antioch to Jerusalem (11:27–12:25)

Luke signals the growing importance of the Christians of Antioch by the account of their caring ministry to the Christians in Judea (11:27–30). The stewardship of the new covenant community, seen first within the Christian community in Jerusalem, is now expanded by the Antioch community to include Christians outside the local community.

Before completing his shift of focus from Jerusalem to Antioch and its outreach through Paul, Luke gives one final glimpse of the situation in Jerusalem (12:1–24). Persecution of Christians has now extended from the Jewish

religious leadership to the Roman political leadership of King Agrippa I (A.D. 37–44). Also, with the broadened persecution following Stephen's death, the apostles seem to have been unaffected (8:1); now they become the martyrs.

Peter's miraculous prison escape reveals the continued presence and power of God in the new covenant community. The community's unbelieving surprise at answered prayer indicates that even a faithful, Spirit-filled community of believers may lack absolute trust in God. In the face of persecution and martyrdom, it is possible to become fatalistic rather than faithful and to presume the worst rather than expect the best.

Luke's use of **multiplied** is the third and final use in the same manner. It appears in 6:7, at the end of the purely Jewish outreach; in 9:31, at the end of the larger Jewish outreach, which included Samaritans and proselytes; and here in 12:24, at the close of the largest Jewish outreach, which includes gentile God-fearers. The new covenant community has now extended its outreach to the ultimate limit of that world encompassed by the old covenant community. It stands on the threshold of a radical step.

V. ANTIOCH'S OUTREACH TO GENTILES (13:1–14:28)

Luke brings us now to the great step of the Christian movement: the inclusion of Gentiles outside the Jewish community into the Christian community. Syrian Antioch now replaces Jerusalem as the center of Christian outreach, and Paul replaces Peter as the primary agent of God's grace in Christ.

A. Cyprus Mission to Jews (13:1–12)

Again the Holy Spirit is the initiator of the new step (13:1–3). The Spirit had led Philip to the Ethiopian and Peter to Cornelius; now Paul is led to the Gentiles. The Holy Spirit also has available for use a church open to God through its worship and discipline (v.2), which is diligently seeking God's guidance through prayer and fasting (v.3).

The mission to Cyprus appears to have been solely among Jews (13:5), and the outcome was Jewish opposition, which brought the Christians before the Roman authorities (vv.6–12). A Jew named Elymas appears to have been responsible for the summons Saul and Barnabas receive to appear at a hearing before Paulus. (The use of technical language clearly indicates that Saul was summoned officially to a formal hearing). There is no substantial evidence that Paulus became a Christian. His "belief," therefore, merely represents a favorable outcome of the hearing for Paul and Barnabas. Surely, had Paulus become a Christian, much would have been made of this.

Paulus's response, however, seems to have convinced Paul of the possibility of outreach to Gentiles outside the Jewish community. This conviction, shared with his companions, may have been the cause of John Mark's abrupt departure (v.13). The term for **left** appears again only at 15:39, the breach between Paul and Barnabas over John Mark. His departure here appears to be a breach and perhaps explains how Jerusalem came to know that Gentiles were being evangelized through the Antioch mission of Paul (15:1).

B. Galatian Mission to Gentiles (13:13–14:28)

A number of significant features cluster around Paul's ministry in Pisidian Antioch. First, Pisidian Antioch was a Roman colony, the highest political status in the Roman world. Second,

this is the longest account of Paul's work in any place he visited. Third, up to now, Luke's order of names has been **Barnabas and Saul** (see 9:27; 11:25, 30; 12:25; 13:1, 2, 7); now it becomes **Paul and Barnabas** (see 13:13, 43, 46, 50; 14:19–20; 15:2, 22, 35–36), except when Jerusalem is the focus (14:12, 14, where "apostle" is applied to Paul for the only time, a term elsewhere associated only with Jerusalem; 15:12, 25, in Jerusalem). Fourth, the term *God-fearers* (10:2, 22, 35; 13:16, 26, a Jewish reference) is replaced by the secular term **devout** (13:43, 50; 16:14; 17:4, 17; 18:7) to describe the Gentiles who worship with the Jewish community. This signals a shift from a Jewish to a gentile perspective. Fifth, "the word of God" (4:31; 6:2, 7; 8:14; 11:1; 12:24; 13:5, 7, 44, 46) becomes **the word of the Lord** (13:44 [variant], 48, 49; 15:35, 36; 19:10). By all these activities, Luke is indicating the profound nature of what takes place in Pisidian Antioch. This is the radical shift of the Christian outreach from a Jewish to a gentile frame of reference.

The shift becomes reality because the Jews rejected the proclamation of God's fulfillment of the old covenant in the new (13:16–45). Jewish Christians in Jerusalem had experienced the same rejection, but Paul has an option not available to them: outreach to the gentile world (13:46–49). God often has to leave behind a community of "faithful" who have become closed to the possibility that God might do something new. The response is great because God had already prepared the way. **All who were appointed for eternal life believed** (v.48), rather than some kind of deterministic predestination that would leave some doomed, more likely represents the awareness that God had already been at work preparing the way for this response by Gentiles; in Wesleyan terms, they were the recipients of prevenient grace.

A typical pattern now emerges. The old covenant community allies itself with the political power structure to act against the new work of God (13:50). A community of faith that takes refuge in the secular power structure to maintain its status quo reflects the institutionalization of belief.

Iconium (14:1–7) was an instant replay of Pisidian Antioch. First Jews and Greeks (i.e., God-fearers) in the synagogue believe; then unbelieving Jews drive the Christians out and enlist the support of secular authorities to persecute them.

Lystra (14:8–20), however, is different. For the first time, Luke portrays the Christian outreach to a purely gentile community. The synagogue, with its God-fearers who form the usual bridge to the gentile world, is absent. Paul clothes the Gospel in the worldview of his audience who clearly perceive Paul (Hermes) and Barnabas (Zeus) from their own pagan outlook. This is always a difficult enterprise. The Gospel must be presented in a frame of reference capable of being received by the hearers, yet it must not be confined to that frame of reference. When God's work begins to become indiginized in such a way, institutionalized belief tends to become most violent in its reactions.

The one who had stoned Stephen at the point where Christian outreach was pressing against the limits of purely Jewish involvement, now himself is stoned for crossing the boundary to the gentile world. Paul's restoration and return to Lystra, however, was a witness to the Resurrection and to the reality of the new order being proclaimed. This kind of witness should be a characteristic of Christian life. When-

ever we are left for dead by those who attack us, we should, in God's grace, rise up and return to them as a witness to the reality of God's presence and power.

Luke notes the ministry in Derbe (14:20–21), which prepares the way for Paul's second mission (16:1).

It is significant to note that an essential part of Paul's mission was the establishment of structure for the communities of faith (14:22–23), a structure that would enable the believers to continue in the faith and to endure the tribulation that accompanied faith.

The return to Syrian Antioch highlights the radical nature of what had happened: God **had opened the door of faith to the Gentiles** (14:27)!

VI. ANTIOCH VERSUS JERUSALEM (15:1–35)

The outreach to Gentiles by the Antioch church did not set well with certain elements in Jerusalem. The first great conflict in the Christian community emerges over how Gentiles are to be included in God's new order of being. This results in the first Christian council in Jerusalem in A.D. 48.

A. The Nature of the Issue (15:1–5)

The crucial question was whether Christianity was understood as the heart and center of Judaism or whether Judaism was the center out of which Christianity emerged. In the first perspective it was obvious, since Christianity was a central circle within the larger circle of Judaism, that those outside the circle of Judaism must first become Jews before they could become Christians. In brief, Christianity was subsumed under the larger context of Judaism. It was the representatives of the strength of Judaism, the Pharisees, who held this view. In the second perspective, however, it was just as obvious, since Christianity was the larger circle within which Judaism was encompassed, that Gentiles came into the new covenant community the same way as Jews, through faith in Jesus as Messiah. As Luke notes, **This brought Paul and Barnabas into sharp dispute and debate with them.** It is to be noted that Paul and Barnabas prepare for their encounter in Jerusalem by telling **how the Gentiles had been converted.**

B. The Jerusalem Council (15:6–29)

Luke provides us only the focus of the council, which centers on a brief summary of Peter's presentation (vv.7–11) and James's decision (vv.13–21). Peter recalls the conversion of Cornelius, the God-fearer, focusing on the fact that God cleansed the heart by faith and gave the Holy Spirit. While Peter lifts up the crucial issue, he implies that Gentile equals God-fearer. James sees this as a point of compromise, since the Jerusalem church has already acknowledged the work of God with Cornelius (11:18). James's decision is that Gentiles who come to faith are to observe the minimum requirements that were placed upon God-fearers to enable them to worship with the Jewish community (v.20). In other words, Gentiles did not have to become proselytes (and be circumcised), but they did have to become God-fearers and thus be brought within the widest possible boundary of Judaism.

The Jerusalem church and the representatives from Antioch sense this is of the Holy Spirit (v.28), although the issue is not resolved, as history shows. The circumcision party obviously saw this as a bare minimum requirement and continued to press Gentiles toward the stricter requirements of the Law of Moses. Paul and his followers obviously saw this as an unrealistic maximum requirement that was itself questionable at some points (1Co 8). From this point, the Christian movement moved down two different roads: Paul leading the majority movement into gentile Christianity, Jewish Christians leading a minority into gradual extinction.

C. Return to Antioch (15:30–35)

With the return to Antioch, the Jerusalem church has appeared for the last time in Acts. Even when Paul returns to Jerusalem for a final visit, there is only a passing reference to the Christians in Jerusalem (21:20). Antioch, and especially Paul's missions from Antioch, now take center stage as Luke portrays Christianity's outreach to the Hellenistic Roman world. Not only has God had to move beyond the old covenant community to fulfill the new covenant, but God also has had to move beyond the limitations of the Jewish Christian community to extend the new covenant to the Gentiles. There should be lessons here for any denomination or group that begins to believe it has the last word on how the presence, power, and purpose of God are fulfilled in the world.

VII. THE PAULINE MISSION (15:36–21:16)

A. Paul's Second Mission (15:36–18:22)

The chief aspect of Paul's second mission is Christianity's move from Asia to Europe, together with the first negative encounters with the Roman power structure. One-third of the account of the second mission is given to the encounter with Roman officials in Philippi. Luke also portrays one of Paul's strategies for the outreach of the

Gospel. Paul now focuses his work in the major centers of cultural influence in the eastern Roman world. On the second mission it is Corinth, where Paul spends at least eighteen months and probably closer to two years. Corinth was one of the major centers of trade, economy, culture, and movement of peoples. By focusing his work there, Paul insured a center from which the reality of God's new order of being could spread far and wide throughout the Roman world. This was undoubtedly why Paul agonized so over the church in Corinth (see 1–2 Corinthians).

1. Antioch to Troas (15:36–16:8)

Was Paul unforgiving or Mark unrepentant (15:36–41)? Since Barnabas and Mark returned to Cyprus for a second mission, and since, after the expulsion of the Jews from Cyprus in A.D. 117, there seems to be no evidence of Christianity there until Constantine (A.D. 325), it would appear that Barnabas and Mark worked only among the Jewish synagogues—just as on the first mission. Apparently Barnabas and Mark were uncomfortable with the mission to the Gentiles.

Why did Paul circumcise Timothy (16:1–3)? Since Timothy was the son of a proselyte mother (**a woman of Jewish faith**) and a God-fearer father (cf. above on 11:19), he was in limbo religiously. Obviously he was born before his mother became a proselyte, else he would have been circumcised. Thus he was neither fully Jew nor clearly Gentile. Such ambiguity would hinder the Gospel in Jewish synagogues as well as give ammunition to Jewish opponents that Paul was advocating the overthrow of Judaism (21:21). Paul solves the problem incisively.

Again Luke stresses the role of the Holy Spirit in the outreach of Chris-

tianity (16:6–8), together with the dream vision that calls Paul to Europe from Troas (vv.9–10). How often, in our intention to "do God's will," does God have to restrict us and guide us into that will? Even Paul seems to have difficulty in discerning the mind of the Spirit, although his pliability in God's hands enables him to relinquish his own agenda for God's.

2. Greece (16:9–18:17)

In Philippi, the Christian movement has its first direct encounter with Roman authorities not instigated by a hostile Jewish synagogue (16:11–40). In fact, the Jews appear to have been expelled from Philippi as this Roman colony had followed Rome's example of the expulsion of Jews by Claudius earlier in the year (18:2). This is seen in the charges against Paul and Silas (16:20–21). The Romans were very sensitive to disturbances of the status quo and to any proselytizing that induced Romans to leave their traditional religious practices. Paul was guilty of both when he exorcised the slave girl.

Why didn't Paul claim his Roman citizenship before he was beaten and imprisoned (16:19–24)? The outcome (vv.35–40) suggests that Paul sacrificed himself to place the authorities in a position where they could take no action against the Christian community for fear that Paul would bring charges against them for their treatment of a Roman citizen.

That Paul and Silas could rejoice in such extreme adversity reflects the profound reality of Christian experience. Life in Christ provides a frame of reference that sets all experiences in a new light, enabling them to become means of God's grace, not only for believers but also for those associated with the experience (16:25–34).

Paul's experience in Thessalonica

(17:1–9) replays the pattern of initial outreach to the Jewish community, response and rejection, outreach to Gentiles, and Jewish instigation of action by local authorities against the Christians. A more serious issue emerges here, however. Paul and his companions are described as **these men who turn the world upside down** by **defying Caesar's decrees, saying that there is another king, one called Jesus** (17:6–7). The escalation of charges from social/religious disruption in Philippi to political revolution in Thessalonica reflects the world's awareness that the reality of Christian experience threatens the structures of the world's order. There is a sense in which the Gospel is always seditious to fallen social, economic, cultural, and political structures. Christians are citizens of a new order whose reality signals the demise of all lesser orders. This is the key to social holiness, not simply "tinkering with the machinery" of the world order, but living out the reality of God's order in ways that bring cleansing, healing, liberation, and wholeness to the world's uncleanness, disease, bondage, and brokenness.

Even when there is positive response to the Gospel as in Beroea (17:10–12), the threatened old order cannot tolerate any "cancer" of liberation, which might spread and destroy its status quo (vv.13–14).

Athens (17:16–34) is the only major city evangelized by Paul without any evidence of the establishment of a Christian community. In spite of his work in both synagogue and marketplace, there is no note of positive response. The only response noted is the skeptical and critical response of the philosophers who drag Paul before the Council of the Areopagus (the censorship board) to question the legitimacy of his public teaching.

Paul's response (17:22–31) is a masterful attempt to clothe the Gospel in the perceptual framework of his Stoic and Epicurean hearers. Remarkably, Paul makes no mention of the Crucifixion, the one thing that would be incomprehensible to his hearers. His attempt is largely a failure. Only a few believed (vv.32–34). While the Gospel must be clothed in the perceptual framework of the hearers, care must be taken not to remove the challenging, confrontive heart of the Gospel. Paul later acknowledges that the Cross is folly to the Gentiles (1Co 1:18). Paul must have realized his mistake, for when he came to Corinth (18:1–17), he decided "to know nothing . . . except Jesus Christ and him crucified," which brought him "in weakness and fear, and with much trembling" to this city (1Co 2:2–3) that vied with Athens for cultural and philosophic superiority.

When we consider that Paul came to Corinth from the "defeat" of Athens, that Paul's companions are refugees for their faith (18:2–3), and that there is much opposition, the results of faithfulness are manifest. Many Corinthians believe and are baptized, the Lord strengthens Paul's ministry in the face of opposition, and Paul ministers in Corinth for a year and a half.

In contrast to heightened concern of Roman authorities in Philippi and Thessalonica, Gallio reflects another side of Roman response (18:12–17). The Jews, having expelled Paul eighteen months earlier, seem intent to clarify for the new proconsul the distinction between Jews and Christians, undoubtedly to preclude Gallio's viewing Christian growth as Jewish proselytizing and hold the Jews accountable. Their worst fears are actualized. Gallio presumes Christians are Jews, in spite of an implied charge of sedition. He affirms the Jews' rights to govern their own affairs and confirms that right by allowing them to discipline Sosthenes without interference.

3. Return to Antioch (18:18–22)

In quick order, Paul moves from Corinth to its southern port, Cenchreae, where Luke notes Paul's continued observance of a Jewish holiness vow—the Nazirite vow (Nu 6:1–21; Ac 21:23–24); then to Ephesus, where Paul lays the groundwork for his return visit; on to Caesarea; up to Jerusalem (**went up** to greet the church—in Palestine one went "up" only to Jerusalem and "down" to everywhere else); and back to Antioch (18:18–22).

B. Paul's Third Mission (18:23–21:16)

Luke notes the strengthening of the Christian communities of the first and second mission in Galatia and Phrygia (18:23), together with those of the second mission in Macedonia and Greece (20:1–4), but he focuses on the third mission in Ephesus. The fruit of Paul's strategy of evangelizing major centers of mobility in the Roman world is seen in the brief comment, **All the Jews and Greeks who lived in the province of Asia heard the word of the Lord** (19:10). When evangelism is seen merely as drawing people into the church, it misses its purpose. While the gathering and nurturing of the church is one result of evangelism, the major focus should be spreading the Word. The communities of faith formed through evangelism become the sources of continued outreach.

1. Through Galatia and Phrygia to Ephesus (18:23–20:1)

Luke's introduction of Apollos (18:24–28), a Jew from Alexandria in Egypt, suggests the spread of the Christian movement into Egypt during the period when Paul was active in Asia Minor and Greece. Apollos, apparently, was not acquainted with the reality of the Pentecost experience, the gift of the Holy Spirit. He **was powerful in the Scriptures** (OT), and was **able to teach accurately about Jesus**; but cognitive understanding is not enough. The Gospel conjoins head *and* heart, thought *and* experience. Priscilla and Aquila explain to him **the way of God,** presumably introducing him to the gift of the Spirit, which was the essential dynamic of the Christian ordering of life known as "the Way" (9:2; 19:9, 23; 22:4; 24:14).

The proof of Apollos' lack of acquaintance with the gift of the Spirit is seen in the disciples Paul finds in Ephesus (19:1–7). Paul goes to the crux of the problem: **Did you receive the Holy Spirit when you believed?** This is the essence of Christian experience (Ro 8:9), which often is replaced by proper theology, correct doctrine, or right belief. Apollos reminds us that knowing accurately the things about Jesus is not sufficient. There must also be the reality of the indwelling presence of the Spirit, which incarnates that knowledge in our lives.

Paul's ministry in the synagogue of Ephesus (19:8–10) is the longest recorded in Acts. For three months they wrestled with the Gospel before expelling Paul and his disciples. Paul moves to the hall of Tyrannus where, according to some manuscripts, he taught from the fifth to the tenth hours. This was the time of rest during the heat of the day (11:00 A.M.–4:00 P.M.) when people were free to gather, Paul was free from his trade to teach, and the hall was available from its regular use.

Paul's ministry over two years had great effect (19:10–20). His work obviously consisted of more than gathering people into a "church." It had a powerful outward thrust so that the entire province of Asia was impacted—an important lesson for evangelism in our day. The ultimate goal is not church growth but spreading scriptural holiness throughout the land. Such ministry, like Paul's, makes a powerful impact on the culture. There are those who attempt to cash in on the movement by mimicking the methods but who lack the reality of experience that empowers the methods (vv.11–16). The old values and structures of the culture are overthrown (vv.18–19), and the transformed lives of disciples are a vital witness to the wider culture (v.20).

Any such dynamic witness to the transforming power of new life in Christ will inevitably become a threat to the power structures of the status quo. This was true in Ephesus (19:23–20:1). A major industry, the metalsmiths who made votive offerings for people to bring to the great temple of Artemis, one of the seven wonders of the ancient world, experienced depression because large numbers of believers no longer worshiped Artemis. Christianity was unraveling the fabric of the culture, and, if allowed to spread unchecked, could result in the demise of a whole way of life.

Consequently, the metalsmiths stir up the city and foment a meeting (*ecclesia*) of the citizenship (*demos*) of Ephesus in the theater. As a free city, Ephesus was allowed to govern her own affairs through such meetings of her citizens, which, archaeological and inscriptional evidence reveals, were held in the theater. Such meetings, however, had to be cleared in advance with the Roman authorities to avoid any possibility of sedition or revolt. Since this was an unscheduled meeting, the town clerk (who regularly chaired such meetings) warned the people of

the danger of Roman displeasure (19:40–41).

Note that the Jews feel compelled to **make a defense before the people** (*demos*) (19:33–34). Again it is likely that the Jews are concerned lest Christian proselytizing be viewed by the officials and Gentiles as Jewish activity and the Jews become objects of attack. The response of the Ephesians tends to confirm these fears.

When the disturbance was over, why did Paul **send for the disciples** to exhort them prior to his departure? Why, on his return through this area on his way to Jerusalem, did he call the Ephesian leaders to meet him at Miletus (20:17)? A growing number of scholars suggest that Paul was imprisoned in Ephesus (cf. 2Co 1:8–10). From this imprisonment the letters to the Philippians, Colossians, Philemon, and "Ephesians" were written. (There is no addressee in earliest manuscripts of Ephesians, and internal evidence clearly indicates that the letter is not to a church founded by Paul [cf. Eph 1:15; 3:2; 4:21]). This might help explain why the Asiarchs (19:31) are involved in preventing Paul from appearing in the theater, and it suggests that one result of the event was Paul's expulsion from Ephesus.

2. Macedonia, Greece, and back to Jerusalem (20:2–21:16)

Luke summarizes, briefly (20:2–6), a trip of several months: from Ephesus through Troas (2Co 2), to Macedonia, and on to a three-month stay in Greece (Corinth?—cf. 2Co 12:14: 13:1), with a return to Troas by way of Philippi. Since we know that Paul celebrated Passover at Philippi, he obviously spent the winter on this itinerary. Luke, who had been left in Philippi (cf. 16:16, "we," and 17:1, "they") now rejoins

Paul and continues with him on the journey to Jerusalem (20:5, **us**).

Perhaps too much is made of Eutychus (20:7–12). It appears that the people thought he was dead, but Paul corrects their fears. Since Luke is not at all hesitant to affirm miracles, one would expect more explicit attestation if this were a miracle. It appears that the miracle is that Eutychus survived a three-story fall, having been overcome by both the hour and the fumes of the lamps, which were wafting through the window where he sat.

Luke continues to emphasize the role of the Holy Spirit in Paul's ministry, noting the Spirit's witness to Paul that troubles await in Jerusalem (20:22–23). This only heightens the previous note (vv.19–20) of the trials and difficulties that attended Paul's ministry in Ephesus. When we look at the tremendous ministry of Paul, the impact he made upon the Roman world, and the apparent success of his work, it is easy to forget the extreme difficulties, hardships, and dangers that formed the context of Paul's ministry (cf. 2Co 11:23–28). We tend to view church growth and evangelism as a progress from victory to victory when, for Paul and for the church through the ages, it has always been victory in the midst of toil, danger, hardship, persecution, and defeat.

Paul also warns the Ephesians that the life of faith will not be without its tribulations (20:29–31), and he urges upon them the structures and disciplines that will enable them to be built up and participate in the experience of sanctification (vv.28:, 31–32). In an unstructured and undisciplined age, the church easily loses sight of the need for structures and disciplines that enhance discipleship and growth toward wholeness (holiness) in Christ, especially to the extent that such structures and disciplines run counter to the prevailing values of the surrounding culture.

Paul's trip from Miletus to Caesarea (21:1–8) gives a glimpse of the nature of travel in those days: Taking one ship as far as it advances one's progress, changing ships, waiting for ships to unload and reload, and finding lodging while waiting. The crux of the trip, however, is the repeated warnings to Paul of what will happen in Jerusalem. Admittedly, there seems to be some tension among the following statements: **Through the Spirit they urged Paul not to go on to Jerusalem** (v.4); **The Holy Spirit says, 'In this way the Jews of Jerusalem will bind the owner of this belt and will hand him over to the Gentiles'** (v.11); and **The Lord's will be done** (v.14). It seems likely that the Holy Spirit was revealing what lay ahead for Paul, as Paul himself had told the Ephesians (20:23). The disciples wanted Paul to take this as a warning not to go to Jerusalem; but Paul, disciplined through suffering and tribulation, sees it simply as the way forward in his discipleship. Some assume that suffering and difficulty, presumably not God's intentional will for us, are to be avoided; others seek to create such situations as proof of their faithfulness.

It is in this context that Paul returns to Jerusalem for the last time.

VIII. PAUL'S ARREST AND IMPRISONMENT (21:17–26:32)

A. Imprisonment and Hearing in Jerusalem (21:17–23:22)

This section reveals how the animosity of Christian Jews toward Paul leads to the attempt by the Jewish leadership to eliminate Paul. Jewish Christians obviously had developed means for living harmoniously within their larger Jewish culture. Paul represents a threat to what must have been a tenuous arrangement at best.

1. Problems with Jewish Christians (21:17–26)

While the leadership of the Jewish-Christian community rejoices over Paul's ministry to Gentiles (vv.19–20), they are more concerned that Christian Jews, who are **zealous for the law** (their means of peaceful coexistence with Judaism), believe Paul teaches Jews who become Christians to renounce their Judaism (vv.20–21). The solution is for Paul to join four Christian Jews who have undertaken the Nazirite vow (Nu 6; cf. Ac 18:18). As one of the strictest Jewish vows of holiness under the law, this would prove to everyone the depth of Paul's Judaism.

By his reiteration of the action of the Jerusalem council (v.25), James emphasizes that while Gentiles do not have to become Jews to be Christians, Jews do remain Jews, and, by implication, he seems to indicate that they still live under the Law of Moses. The hardening of this position led Jewish Christians to subordinate faith in Christ to observance of the law, a position attacked by the writer of Hebrews. Often when God does something new, his people attempt to domesticate it under the old, familiar structures, retaining the form of godliness but avoiding its radical transformation.

2. Riot and Arrest (21:27–22:29)

Paul's Jewish opponents from the mission field (Asia) initiate the action against Paul (21:27), claiming, as James had noted (v.21), that Paul's teaching undermines the old covenant community ("people") and its law, adding the charge of defiling its temple cultus (vv.28–29). Paul was dragged out of the Court of Israel, the inner

part of the temple that surrounded the sanctuary and Holy of Holies, and into the Court of the Gentiles, which surrounded the sacred precincts (v.30). This larger portion of the temple area (900 ft. x 1,500 ft.) was capable of holding a tremendous crowd. Apparently, a large number of people were mobilized for the attack upon Paul, for at least two hundred Roman soldiers are brought to put down the disturbance ("centurions" [KJV] implies at least two, each at the head of one hundred men). The Roman soldiers were housed in the citadel located at the northwest corner of the temple area and had direct access to the temple area via stairs from the citadel down to the Court of the Gentiles. It was up these stairs that the soldiers carried Paul as the crowd sought to kill him (vv.31–36).

The profound balance of the Spirit-filled life, which Paul attests in Php 4:11–13, is evident in his response to this deadly situation. He has the courage to ask his Roman captor for permission to address those who seek to kill him (21:37–40). The commander (tribune) believed that he had captured the Egyptian false prophet who had led an uprising of fanatic religious revolutionaries ("assassins," or Sicarii) about A.D. 54 (Josephus, *Wars* 2.13.4; *Antiquities* 20.8.6). At the time, tensions were increasing between these radical religious Jewish nationalists and the Roman authorities, and the tribune was sensitized to this.

Paul recounts for his attackers his own transformation from a zealous Jewish persecutor of Christianity to its most ardent promulgator (22:1–21). He stresses his profoundly orthodox position within Judaism, emphasizing that he once had acted toward Christians exactly as they were acting toward him (vv.3–5). (On **the Way,** see note under 9:1–31). He accents the reality of his encounter with the Lord, emphasizing God's intrusion into his zealous pursuit of Christians (vv.6–11). He stresses the piety and Jewish affirmation of Ananias, emphasizing his role as God's agent in revealing to Paul the nature of God's purpose (vv.12–16). He points to his continued Jewish piety through his worship in the temple, emphasizing that God appeared to him there, and, even though he had been a persecutor of the Christians, commissioned him to go to the Gentiles (vv.17–21). In brief, Paul tells them he was exactly like they were—but his God and theirs had redirected his life.

The idea of including Gentiles in God's purposes is too much for the Jews. They react violently to a truth they cannot accept, and the tribune resorts to violence to extract a truth he cannot apprehend (22:22–24). Contrary to Philippi (see on 16:9ff.), Paul claims his Roman citizenship (vv.25–29), realizing that this time no purpose will be served by being scourged. The original source of Paul's citizenship is unknown. Obviously his father and/or his mother had citizenship, but how they came by it is unknown.

3. Hearing before the Sanhedrin (22:30–23:10)

The tribune calls upon the Jewish court (Sanhedrin) to determine the facts in the case (22:30). Ananias was a notoriously unscrupulous and rapacious politician who had been deposed by Rome in A.D. 52, then acquitted and restored as high priest. His unlawful action (23:2) is in keeping with his character. Paul had begun his hearing with an attestation of his Jewish orthodoxy (23:1), but when he realized he had unknowingly alienated the president of the Sanhedrin and could never receive a fair hearing, he plays to the

Pharisees of the Sanhedrin (v.6), hoping to split the house since the Pharisees and Sadducees had radically different views. He succeeds admirably, bringing the Sanhedrin to such violent contention that the tribune had to whisk Paul back to the citadel for safety (vv.7–10).

4. The plot against Paul (23:11–22)

As in 18:9; 22:18; 27:23–24, Paul's life of deep obedience makes him available for direct revelation from God (23:11). Such revelations, however, then require absolute trust in God during subsequent situations that appear to nullify the promises. Yet God provides in the midst of such situations. How else did Paul's nephew get wind of the plot?

Such a plot would not have been unusual among the radical religious fanatics such as the Zealots and Sicarii. Like the early Paul (Saul), they would go to any lengths to remove supposed causes of apostasy from among God's people.

B. Imprisonment and Hearings in Caesarea Philippi (23:23–26:32)

The scene now shifts from the Jewish center at Jerusalem to the Roman center at Caesarea Philippi, the seat of Roman power in Palestine. With this shift, Paul the Jew, rejected and endangered by his fellow Jews, becomes Paul the Roman citizen under the protection of Roman jurisprudence.

1. Paul to Caesarea (23:23–35)

The tribune takes no chances with a threatened Roman citizen (vv.23–24). He sends a formidable armed escort with Paul at midnight, and not without cause. During this period there are instances where bands of Jewish rebels fell upon small contingents of Roman troops and destroyed them.

Lysias's letter to Felix (vv.26–30) is an epitome of a Hellenistic letter: writer, recipient, greeting (v.26), and body (vv.27–30). Lysias provides Felix with the gist of the situation, hedging somewhat at the point of when he discovered that Paul was a Roman citizen. If he had conveyed the truth, Felix might have rebuked him for interfering in Jewish affairs and creating a situation that would not have existed if the Jews had simply been allowed to kill Paul in the temple.

Antipatris (v.31) was about halfway between Jerusalem and Caesarea. Having brought Paul beyond the dangerous area around Jerusalem, the soldiers and spearmen return, letting the cavalry continue with Paul to Caesarea (v.32). Upon receiving Paul and the letter, Felix (procurator of Judea, c. A.D. 52–59) places Paul under guard awaiting the prosecutors from Jerusalem after first ascertaining Paul's home, most likely for the purpose of checking on Paul's citizenship (vv.33–35).

2. Hearing before Felix (24:1–27)

The hearing follows the legal form of the day. First, the prosecutor (Tertullus), after opening praise to the judge, brings the charges (vv.1–8), which are substantiated by witnesses (v.9). Next, the accused (Paul), after opening praise to the judge, brings the defense (vv.10–21). Finally, the judge (Felix) gives the ruling (vv.22–23).

Tertullus sets the charges against Paul in the worst possible light, leaving the original charge of defiling the temple as the least. The first charge, being a **troublemaker, stirring up sedition among the Jews all over the empire,** is clearly designed to get the attention of a Roman official. The second charge, being the **ringleader of the Nazarene sect,** would place Paul in the same company with the Egyptians and other messianic pretenders who were stirring up trouble for the Romans throughout Palestine. The third charge, profaning the temple, could be seen by Felix as an action that substantiates the first two charges, that Paul was attempting to overthrow the established order in Jerusalem.

Paul's defense takes several tracks. First, he notes that he had been in Jerusalem only a few days: The **twelve days** include five days in Caesarea (v.1), one day in custody in Jerusalem (22:30), leaving only the seven days of purification, which had not quite been completed (21:27), hardly time to undertake all of which he is charged. Second, Paul notes that he was not causing any trouble in Jerusalem; their charge is false. Third, he affirms that what the accusers call a sect is a Jewish *halakah,* a walk or **Way,** a worship of the Jewish God that holds to the Law and the Prophets. Fourth, Paul states that he was engaged in purification in the temple, not pollution. Finally, Paul says that the Jews from Asia are the cause of the problem, and they are not present.

Felix's decision is to await Lysias, the tribune, before making judgment in the case (vv.22–23). Since Felix somehow had fairly good awareness of the Christian *halakah,* or **the Way,** it appears that he sensed the trumped-up nature of the Jewish charges and subsequently relaxed the nature of Paul's confinement.

It may have been through Drusilla, his Jewish wife, that Felix had some knowledge of the Christian way, and was interested in learning more about the movement (v.24). Felix's true motive for interest, however, is revealed in the expectation of a bribe from Paul (v.26), which probably explains why Lysias never seems to come from Jerusalem; Felix never delivers judgment but keeps Paul under custody for two years. At the end of his procuratorship, Felix was deposed because of Jewish pressures and sent to Rome for trial. He obviously wanted to **grant a favor to the Jews** (v.27) so that they might relent toward him in his trial.

3. Hearing before Festus (25:1–12)

The Jewish leaders attempt to sway Festus before he has had time to become acquainted with the case, still plotting to kill Paul before he could reach Jerusalem (25:1–3). Festus, however, wisely acts within proper legal procedures (vv.4–5). The Jewish charges at the hearing (vv.6–7) must have repeated the earlier charges of heresy, defilement, and sedition since Paul's defense (v.8) claims he has **done nothing wrong against the law of the Jews** (heresy), **the temple** (defilement), **or Caesar** (sedition).

Festus is also sensitive to the Jewish influence, which removed his predecessor, and signals his willingness to accede to the Jews' demand for trial in Jerusalem (v.9). Paul's appeal to Caesar is *not* a petition to be tried in Rome. Festus, as the emperor's appointee to the procuratorship of Judea, represented the emperor in such legal matters. He was himself Caesar's tribunal, and Paul is demanding that Festus handle the matter as he has jurisdiction to do so (vv.10–11).

Festus is impaled upon the horns of dilemma. If he gives in to the Jews, he transgresses the rights of a Roman citizen; if he gives in to Paul, he alienates the people he has to govern. Paul's appeal gives him an escape. Festus, or someone on his council, takes Paul literally (v.12). By sending Paul to Rome, Festus can tell the Jews he has no other choice since Paul is a Roman citizen; and he has not mishandled Paul's case, since every Roman citizen has the right to appear before the emperor.

4. Hearing before Festus and Agrippa (25:13–26:32)

Agrippa II, king of numerous small territories north and east of Galilee, was the son of Agrippa I (12:1–23) and a great-grandson of Herod the Great. Drusilla, the wife of Felix (24:24), was his sister; he lived in an incestuous relationship with Bernice, another sister, who later became the mistress of Titus before he became emperor in A.D. 79. Festus acquaints Agrippa with the gist of the case against Paul (25:14–22), admitting that there is no legal case (v.7), only the question of resurrection. Obviously Luke has not given the entire account of the first hearing before Festus (vv.7–12). It must have followed the pattern of the hearing before Felix, however, since there the issue of the Resurrection was raised (24:21).

In solving his dilemma between Paul and the Jews, Festus has created another problem for himself. He has no valid charges on which to send Paul to the emperor. Now he seeks the help of Agrippa and the leading officials to develop charges (25:23–27).

Paul notes that Agrippa, who, as a Roman king, tried valiantly to appease the Jewish nation, was well acquainted with the dynamics of Judaism and was well suited to understand Paul's case (26:2–3). Paul takes his stand as a staunch Pharisee who has been attacked for his belief in resurrection (vv.4–8). He shares with Agrippa the zeal of his Pharisaism, which persecuted followers of Jesus to death (vv.9–11), and gives the witness of his encounter with the risen Jesus (vv.12–18).

As Paul explains his understanding of the suffering and resurrection of the

Messiah and his obedience to the risen Lord among the Jews and Gentiles, which resulted in his persecution by the Jews (26:19–23), Festus sees an opportunity to acquit Paul by reason of insanity (v.24). After all, who but a madman would risk his life and face such opposition for the sake of a strange hallucination? Paul refuses such acquittal, affirming that he speaks of reality that is not merely a personal aberration but the life-shaping experience of a new community of God's people (vv.25–26). He infers that Agrippa is aware of the Christian movement and calls upon him to affirm that the movement is the fulfillment of the prophets (v.27).

Paul puts Agrippa on the spot. If he denies the prophets, he loses face with the Jews; if he agrees with Paul, he becomes a "madman" and loses face with Festus. Agrippa evades the issue (v.28), but Paul presses the point by calling all his hearers to this "madness" of life in obedience to the risen Lord (v.29).

The hearers agree that Paul should be released, leaving Festus with his problem of having to send Paul to Rome without any charges (26:30–32).

IX. VOYAGE TO ROME (27:1–28:16)

A. Caesarea to Crete (27:1–13)

The return to **we** indicates Luke's presence with Paul throughout his imprisonment and hearings (21:17–18; 27:1). Paul and his companions, under the guard of Julius and, presumably, the hundred soldiers under a centurion, set off on a coastal ship. Such ships sailed close to the coast from port to port and were unsuitable for a straight voyage to Rome on the open sea. They obviously hoped to find at one of the ports a seagoing ship that would carry them to Rome. After port-hopping from Caesarea to Myra, they find a large grain ship that plied the route from Alexandria to Rome with the Egyptian wheat that kept Rome alive (vv.1–6).

The difficulty in sailing from Myra in Asia to Fair Havens in Crete (vv.7–8) was due to the onset of winter. From mid-September to mid-November the Mediterranean becomes dangerous as the Sahara high pressure mass moves from its usual summer position over the Mediterranean to its winter position over Africa, allowing the storms from the North Atlantic and the Russian steppes to ravage the Mediterranean. Luke notes that the fast of the Day of Atonement (October 5, in A.D. 59, cf. Bruce, 455) was already past; therefore they were into the danger season. After mid-November, there was no sailing throughout the winter.

Paul apparently receives discernment about the voyage, but who will listen to a prisoner (vv.10–11)? Instead, lulled by a fair day, they try to sail from Fair Havens, which provided no shelter from the winter storms, to Phoenix, which had a good winter harbor (vv.12–13).

B. Shipwreck (27:14–44)

Caught between Fair Havens and Phoenix by a northeaster, in the shelter of Cauda, the ship finds brief respite to rig for the storm (vv.14–16). Fearing that the storm would drive them onto the deadly quicksands (Syrtis) of the north coast of Africa, they lowered the sails, threw out the cargo (other than the wheat that was so vital to Rome) and the ship's equipment, and gave themselves to the mercy of the storm (vv.17–20).

Since Paul's prediction had come to pass, the centurion begins to listen when Paul claims that God has promised the lives of all on the ship and follows Paul's orders, which enables all to arrive safely on Malta (vv.21–44). Undoubtedly the steadfastness of Paul's reliance upon God and the witness of his trust in God in the face of death must have moved Julius.

C. Winter on Malta (28:1–10)

In Lystra, Paul was first thought to be a god and then stoned (14:8–20). Here he is first thought to deserve death and then proclaimed a god (vv.1–6). It is most interesting that in spite of their veneration for Paul and his healing ministry, Luke gives no indication that any on Malta became Christians (vv.7–10).

D. Malta to Rome (28:11–16)

After winter Paul and his party sail on another Alexandrian grain ship that had wintered in Malta (v.11). They make their way from Malta to Syracuse on Sicily, to Rhegium on the toe of Italy, and finally to Puteoli on the bay of Naples across from Pompeii and Mount Vesuvius. A sizable Jewish community lived in Puteoli, which, presumably, was home for the Christian **brothers** whom Paul meets (vv.11–14). Apparently word was sent from Puteoli to Rome about Paul's arrival, and Christians from Rome come to meet Paul and escort him to the city where he is kept under some form of house arrest (v.15).

X. PAUL IN ROME (28:17–31)

Paul immediately contacts the leaders of the Jewish community to acquaint them with his situation and apparently to determine where they stand on his case (vv.17–20). The Roman Jews know nothing about the charges against Paul, only the accusations against Christianity about which they desire to know more (vv.21–22). It is most interesting, presuming a Christian community in Rome (Romans was written prior to Paul's arrest in Jerusalem), that the Jews of Rome seem to be ignorant of Christianity. Had the Christian community already become so distanced from Judaism? Did Christianity in Rome begin with Gentiles and not Jews, thus not causing disturbances among the Jews? We simply do not know.

The closing scene with the Jews is a reprise of Paul's ministry and Luke's account of Christian history. As throughout his ministry, Paul seeks to convince the Jews from Moses and the Prophets regarding the kingdom and the Messiah. As throughout his ministry, some believe; others reject. And, as throughout his ministry, Paul announces his outreach to the Gentiles (vv.23–29). The success of the gentile mission is epitomized in Paul's open and unhindered preaching and teaching in Rome for two years (v.30). Thus Luke closes his account with a vignette that summarizes the whole work, revealing how the new covenant community emerges out of Judaism to impact the gentile world of Rome.

BIBLIOGRAPHY

Aune, David E. *The New Testament in Its Literary Environment*. Philadelphia: Westminster, 1987.

Bruce, F. F. *The Acts of the Apostles*. Grand Rapids: Eerdmans, 1952.

Cadbury, H. J. *The Style and Literary Method of Luke*. Cambridge: Harvard University Press, 1920.

————. *The Book of Acts in History*. New York: Harper, 1955.

Conzelmann, H. *Acts of the Apostles*. Philadelphia: Fortress, 1987.

Eusebius. *Ecclesiastical History*. Loeb Classical Library. Cambridge: Harvard University Press, 1965.

Guthrie, D. *New Testament Introduction*. Downers Grove: InterVarsity, 1970.

Haenchen, E. *Acts of the Apostles*. Philadelphia: Westminster, 1971.

Hawkins, J. C. *Horae Synopticae*. Reprint. Grand Rapids: Baker, 1968.

Harnack, A. *The Acts of the Apostles*. New York: Putnam, 1909.

————. *Luke the Physician*. New York: Putnam, 1907.

Hengle, M. *Acts and the History of Earliest Christianity*. Philadelphia: Fortress, 1979.

Hobart, W. K. *The Medical Language of St. Luke*. Dublin: Hodges, Figgis, 1882.

Knox, W. K. *The Acts of the Apostles*. Cambridge: Cambridge University Press, 1948.

Kümmel: Feine, Behm, Kümmel. *Introduction to the New Testament*. Nashville: Abingdon, 1966.

Ramsay, W. *Pauline and Other Studies*. London: Hodder and Stoughton, 1908.

————. *The First Christian Century*. London: Hodder and Stoughton, 1911.

Sherwin-White, A. N. *Roman Society and Roman Law in the New Testament*. Grand Rapids: Baker, 1978.

Smith, J. *The Voyage and Shipwreck of St. Paul*. Baker, 1978r.

ROMANS
Joseph S. Wang

INTRODUCTION

I. THE AUTHOR AND THE ROMAN CHURCH

Seldom has anyone questioned the Pauline authorship of this epistle. Even though Paul had not visited the Roman church before, he knew many Christians in the capital city (16:3–16). Probably Paul had met them and even had ministered with them in the East during his missionary journeys. They had since moved to Rome.

II. TIME AND PLACE OF ORIGIN OF THE EPISTLE

When Paul wrote Romans he was ready to go to Jerusalem with the fund he had collected for the poor in Jerusalem (15:25–26). Thus Romans must have been written at the end of his third missionary journey, early in A.D. 57 (Guthrie, 307).

Romans probably was written from Corinth and was delivered by Phoebe of nearby Cenchrea (16:1–2). Paul's host at the time (16:23) was Gaius, who had been converted during Paul's ministry in Corinth (1Co 1:14).

III. OCCASION AND PURPOSE

Paul aimed to preach the Gospel where Christ was not known. He had covered the eastern territories well. So he looked toward the west as his next mission field. He was planning a missionary journey to Spain (15:19–24) and was hoping that Rome would become his home base for this mission as Antioch had been for his missionary endeavors in the East. He wrote this epistle, systematically presenting the Gospel in order to win the support of the Romans.

Paul was about to go to Jerusalem to deliver the fund he had collected for the poor in Jerusalem. Before his departure, he was apprehensive about his own safety in Jerusalem (15:30–31). Probably he thought it good to have a systematic presentation of the Gospel he proclaimed, so that if he should die, the Gospel would be preserved.

IV. DEVELOPMENT OF THE THEME

The theme of this epistle is that the righteousness of God is revealed in the Gospel. This is witnessed by and promised in the OT. In the OT the righteousness of God punishes sinners and provides salvation for those trusting in him.

Even though Gentiles know God from his revelation in nature, they refuse to acknowledge him. The Jews have God's law, but they do not keep it because they do not honor him. Therefore, the righteousness of God is revealed as his wrath in judgment (1:18–3:20).

On the other hand, the righteousness of God provides salvation for those trusting in him. God's actions are consistent with his character. He puts forth Christ Jesus as the propitiation for sin. Through faith believers become united with Christ. Their sins are forgiven, and they have the good standing of right relationship with God. This way of salvation does not contradict the law. Rather, it is in harmony with the law, correctly understood in the context of covenant (3:21–31). This is demonstrated in the life of Abraham. He was justified by faith and received circumcision as a seal of the justification he received while uncircumcised (4:1–25).

Being justified, we now have a good relationship with God and a firm standing in his grace. We can rejoice in our hope of sharing in God's glory in the future. Such hope is grounded in God's love for us and will not disappoint us. Therefore, we can rejoice even in our present sufferings (5:1–11).

This salvation is universally applicable. Just as Adam's sin affected all of his descendants, so salvation benefits all who are united with Christ by faith. Indeed, grace is much more powerful than sin (5:12–21).

If grace is much more powerful than sin, shall we continue to sin so that grace may abound? No, not at all! In order to experience grace, we have to be united with Christ in his death and resurrection. Christ died to sin and lives to God. So we need to live out this union by being dead to sin and alive to God (6:1–14). Furthermore, we are enslaved either to sin or to God. If we commit sin, we become enslaved to sin, which leads to death. But if we offer ourselves to God and become slaves of righteousness, we will reap holiness now and, in the end, eternal life (6:15–23).

When we died with Christ, we died to the law and were married to Christ in order to bear fruit to God. When we were living in the flesh, that is, on our own resources, we ended up in death. For in such a condition, sin takes control over us. Sin uses the law to arouse our passions and leads us to sin. The result is that we cannot do the good we want to do, but instead we do the evil that we do not want to do (7:1–25).

Because of our flesh (human nature under the control of sin), the law is not strong enough to deliver us from this misery. God sent his own Son to take on human nature and condemned sin in the human nature so that the righteous requirements of the law can be fulfilled in us who do not walk by the flesh but by the Spirit. Since we are led by the Holy Spirit, we are children of God and coheirs with Christ. If we share in his suffering now, we will share in his glory in the future. Our future glory is such that our present suffering is not worth comparing with it (8:1–27).

This scheme of salvation is not an afterthought. God planned it before the foundation of the world, based on his love for us. Therefore we can be confident that we will experience full salvation, including our future glory (8:31–39).

Faithfulness promotes right relationship. The righteousness of God includes his faithfulness. At present, the Jews are not saved. Is God, then, faithful to his promise to Abraham? Yes, indeed. We need to recognize that not all the descendants of Abraham are his heirs. God is sovereign, and he is free to determine the condition of heirship. That condition is faith. At present the unsaved Jews are unsaved because of their unbelief, not because of God's unfaithfulness to his promise. They insist on their own way to earn righteousness before God and reject the way of righteousness established by God (9:1–10:21).

God, however, has not completely rejected Israel. At present, some Jews are saved. In addition, God can use the Jews' present rebellion to bring about good for all. This occasions the proclamation of the Gospel to the Gentiles, which, in turn, makes the Jews envious. After the Gentiles are saved, the Jews as a whole also will be saved (11:1–36).

God is morally pure. Therefore, those who are in good relationship with God should be morally pure too. The power of the Gospel makes believers morally holy, and this is manifested in discerning and doing the will of God in daily life (12:1–15:13).

V. THE EPISTLE TO THE ROMANS AND WESLEYAN THEOLOGY

Romans provides the biblical bases for two distinctive emphases of Wesleyan theology.

A. Christian Holiness

In the opening section, the main point of the Gospel is stated. Paul introduces Christ Jesus by mentioning the two stages he went through to become the subject of the Gospel (1:3–4). First, he became human by being born as a descendant of David. Then, after his resurrection (cf. 1Co 15:45; 2Co 3:17), he became "the Spirit of holiness"—the Spirit who brings about holiness. At the very beginning of Romans, when Christ Jesus is introduced, his mission to bring about holiness is emphasized. Toward the end, Paul summarizes the objective of his mission: "That the Gentiles might become an offering acceptable to God, sanctified by the Holy Spirit" (15:16). Sanctification, or holiness, is the central emphasis of the Gospel treated in Romans.

In salvation, God not only forgives our sins, he also delivers us from the power of sin. The latter is called sanctification and the result, holiness. The miserable condition of persons under the control of sin is described in 7:7–25. They want to do good, to obey the law of God, but they cannot do it. Instead, they do the evil they do not want to do. All Christians believe that salvation includes deliverance from the wretched condition of 7:7–25. However, some theological traditions believe that this is a long, continuous process and that complete deliverance will take place only after or at the time of death. Wesleyans believe that entire sanctification can take place in this life. So does Paul.

Romans presents the state of this full salvation without indicating how many steps it takes to get there. In Romans "Paul holds up to view the normal Christian life—full-orbed and free. . . . It is the offer of Christian fullness" (Dayton, "Entire Sanctification," 8). The issue of sanctification is treated in 6:1–8:17.

Paul describes the condition of 7:7–25 as being *en tē sarki* (NIV "controlled by the sinful nature"; RSV, NASB "in the flesh") in 7:5, 25; 8:8, 9; and as walking "according to *sarka* (NIV "the sinful nature"; RSV, NASB "the flesh") in 8:4–13. In 7:5 Paul writes, "When we were *en tē sarki* (NIV "controlled by the sinful nature"; RSV "living in the flesh"; NASB "in the flesh"). . . ." In the past we were, but now we are no longer, in this condition. The condition of 7:7–25 is described as being under "the law of sin" (7:23, 25). In 8:2 Paul declares (using the past tense), "Through Christ Jesus the law of the Spirit of life set me free from the law of sin and death." The deliverance took place in the past. In 8:1–17 Paul presents the opposite of the condition of 7:7–25 as the present normative experience of those who are in Christ.

Holiness (*hagiasmos*) is a fruit of enslavement to God (6:22). It is not a process, but a state attainable in this life by the grace of God (see comment on 6:22).

In 1Co 3:1–3 Paul indicates explicitly that some Christians are subnormative. They are Christians, but they have not yet grown up. They are still infants in Christ. He describes them as *sarkinos, sarkikos* (NIV "worldly"; RSV "of the flesh"; NASB "fleshly"). They are still fleshly, living in the miserable condition of 7:7–25. These subnormative Christians need to be set free from the law of sin and death (8:2). Here is a biblical basis for "the second work of grace" in Wesleyan theology.

B. Sovereignty of God and Human Freedom

Some theological traditions emphasize the sovereignty of God at the expense of human freedom and responsibility. Wesleyan theology properly emphasizes both.

Romans uses the word "predestined" in 8:29–30 and emphasizes God's sovereignty in 9:6–29. Some people interpret these passages to mean that God arbitrarily determines beforehand who will and who will not be saved. Human beings cannot do anything and consequently are not responsible for their own salvation. This is a misinterpretation of the passages. The sovereignty of God consists in his absolute freedom to set the conditions of salvation, blessing, and judgment (see comment on 9:6–29). After he has done that, it is the responsibility of human beings to respond to God and to comply with the conditions. If some are not saved, it is not because God arbitrarily determines to exclude them. It is because they do not respond to God's offer and comply with the condition. So there are both divine sovereignty and human freedom/responsibility. Romans teaches this, as does Wesleyan theology.

VI. OUTLINE OF THE EPISTLE

COMMENTARY

I. INTRODUCTION (1:1–17)

A. Opening Section (1:1–7)

As in the opening section of ancient letters, Paul names himself as author and the Christians in Rome as the recipients. The usual Pauline greeting, **Grace and peace,** follows. In addition, Paul indicates the main point of the Gospel that he preaches and will expound in this epistle.

The Gospel is about the Son of God, Jesus Christ our Lord. In vv.3–4 Paul uses two Greek parallel participles to describe him. These two phrases indicate the two stages Jesus went through to become the subject of the Gospel (Murray, 1:7). First, he became human by being born **a descendant of David.** Then he became the **Spirit** cf. 1Co 15:45; 2Co 3:17), who brings about **holiness** when, through his **resurrection,** he was **declared to be the Son of God with power.** (In Greek, **with power** can go with **the Son of God.**) During his incarnation, he was the Son of God in humiliation. After the resurrection, he is the Son of God with Power.

This Gospel is predicted in the OT. Paul has been appointed to proclaim this Gospel worldwide to bring about **the obedience that comes from faith.**

B. Paul and the Romans (1:8–15)

Paul thanks God for the faith of the Roman Christians and constantly prays for them. He longs to go to Rome to visit them and to preach the Gospel because he considers himself **obligated** to all people regarding the Gospel.

C. Theme of the Epistle (1:16–17)

Here Paul gives the reason for his last statement. In Greek, the three major clauses in this section start with the conjunction **for.** So each explains the preceding statement. In the process, this section also spells out the theme of the entire epistle. The Gospel **is the power of God for the salvation** of all believers. **Salvation** removes destructive powers and negative conditions (God's wrath, 5:9; condemnation, 8:1; power of sin, 6:6; et al.) and bestows positive blessings (righteousness, 3:22; reconciliation, 5:10; sanctification, 6:22; justification and glorification, 8:30). Since the **gospel** is powerful and effective, Paul is **not ashamed of** it and, consequently, he is obligated to share it with all.

In the Gospel a righteousness from God is revealed (v.17). This Gospel had been promised in the OT (v.2). The Law and the Prophets testify to this **righteousness from God** (3:21).

Therefore the **righteousness** treated in Romans is the same as that in the OT.

The basic concept of **righteousness** in the OT is right relationship and the acts promoting it. Those who fear the Lord, trust in him, and thus have a good relationship with him are **righteous** (Ps 112:1–6). God's **righteousness** brings **salvation** and blessing to those who trust in him (Isa 46:13; Ps 103:17–18), but judgment and punishment to those who rebel against him (2Ch 12:5–6; Da 9:14). Faithfulness promotes a good relationship, and God's **righteousness** includes his faithfulness (Ps 143:1). God hates sin and is morally pure. Therefore, those who are in good relationship with him should be morally pure (Eze 18:21–22).

In Romans the **righteousness** of God primarily refers to his act to promote right relationship between himself and human beings, that is, God's provision for their salvation (e.g., 3:21). Surely God's act is in harmony with his character. So the **righteousness** of God also refers to God's character (e.g., 3:5, 25, 26). It can also refer to the right relationship that is granted by God (e.g., 3:22; 10:3). **Righteousness** is having a good relationship with God (5:1). It also refers to the behavior appropriate to this relationship. Therefore, **righteousness** is the opposite of sin (4:6–8; 8:10), impurity, and wickedness (6:13, 19).

Romans expounds this theme. God's character reacts negatively to sin, so he judges sin (1:18–3:20). God provides the way to establish the right relationship with believers, which is consistent with his own character (3:21–5:21). His power enables believers to live the life of holiness, which is consistent with their relationship with God (6:1–8:39). Faithfulness promotes this right relationship, and God is faithful to his

promise to Israel (9:1–11:36). The life of holiness, which is consistent with their relationship with God, is manifested in the daily lives of believers (12:1–15:13).

This **righteousness from God** is to be appropriated by **faith. Faith** is to accept God's revelation, his provision, and to act accordingly. Therefore, Paul mentions **the obedience that comes from faith** in 1:5.

A **righteousness** ... *ek pisteōs eis pistin* (RSV "through faith for faith"; NASB "from faith to faith"; NIV **by faith from first to last)**" in v.17 finds its parallel thought in 3:21–22. There Paul restates the theme of Romans. He mentions the **righteousness of God** as manifested (answering to **revealed** in v.17), then repeats the word *righteousness* and characterizes it as the **righteousness that is by faith** and is for **all who believe.** So the first **faith** in v.17 corresponds to the first "faith" in 3:22 as the means of receiving God's salvation. The second **faith** in v.17 corresponds to "all who believe" in 3:22. V.17 mentions **faith** twice to emphasize its importance.

II. GOD'S RIGHTEOUSNESS JUDGES SIN (1:18–3:20)

A. God's Wrath Against the World (1:18–32)

In Greek this section begins with **For.** This is interpreted in two ways. The first is to understand this section as giving the reason why the **righteousness of God** is needed. This provides the background for the declaration in 3:21 that the righteousness of God, as the salvation provided by God, has been revealed in Christ Jesus.

The other interpretation is to understand vv.18–32 as the substantiation for the statement in 1:17. The righteousness of God **is being revealed** as **the wrath of God** toward sin. In the

OT the righteousness of God does punish sins (e.g., Ne 9:33; 2Ch 12:5–6; Da 9:14). In 2:16 Paul indicates that his Gospel declares God's judgment. Therefore, the second interpretation is better. The righteousness of God is revealed in the Gospel. To those who believe, it is the power of God unto salvation (cf. 1Co 1:18). To those who do not believe but are disobedient and rebellious, it means the **wrath of God** (cf. 2Co 2:16).

Most people are ashamed of their anger. Some scholars think that wrath is unworthy of God, and interpret the wrath of God as some kind of impersonal law of retribution (Dodd, 21–24). Yet Paul's use of **from heaven** (v.18) seems to contradict this. **The wrath of God** is not an irrational emotional outburst. It is his personal reaction to sin based on his holy character. Its judicial character is intimated in 13:4–5. **The wrath of God** is radically different from human wrath. Human anger wants its objects to receive its full blow. But God provides the way for the objects of his wrath to avoid its effects. This kind of wrath is not unworthy of God.

The wrath of God is being revealed (v.18). It is manifested in the terrible corruption and perversion of human life. This, however, is only the beginning. There still is the Day of Judgment awaiting the sinner in the future (2:5).

The wrath of God is manifested against the **godlessness** and **wickedness** of the world. The first is expounded in vv.19–25, and the second in vv.26–32.

Since the creation of the world, God's **eternal power** and his **divine nature have been seen** and **understood from what has been made.** But many people refuse to acknowledge him, and they even rebel against him. Therefore, God gives them up. **There-**

fore (v.24), **because of this** (v.26), and **since** (v.28) all indicate that human sin is the cause, and God's giving them up is the effect. God gives them up by withdrawing his restraining grace (Wesley, *Notes,* 364). As a result, all sorts of corruption take over. The thinking of men and women become so corrupt that they exchange the truth of God for a lie and worship creatures instead of the Creator. In their idolatry they defile **their bodies** through cultic prostitution (vv.24–25). Indeed, their sexual relationships become corrupt, and they practice homosexuality (vv.26–27). Finally, their personal relationships with others become corrupt (vv.28–31). They not only sin; they also encourage others to sin (v.32).

In this section, Paul maintains that God's revelation in nature is adequate to condemn human beings if they refuse to follow its lead to God. However, Paul does not say that the revelation in nature is adequate to lead them to salvation.

B. God's Righteous Judgment (2:1–16)

Encouraging others to sin is condemned in the last section. Judging others, however, does not put one in a favorite position either. **God's judgment is based on truth.** Sinners will be judged whether they condemn the sins of others or not. Because, however, God is waiting for them to repent, he postpones the judgment (vv.1–4).

On the Day of Judgment God will render to each according to what each has actually done. **To those who by persistence in doing good seek glory, honor and immortality, he will give eternal life** (v.7). These are Christians, not non-Christians (Greathouse, 74). In 3:12 Paul explicitly says that apart from God's grace "there is no one who does good, not even one." Only Christians will seek **glory, honor and immortality** because these are connected with the Christian Gospel (8:18, 21; 1Co 15:43, 53). Those who **reject the truth and follow evil** will be punished (vv.5–11).

God's judgment is fair. **All who sin apart from the law** (the Gentiles) **will also perish apart from the law, and all who sin under the law** (the Jews) will perish under **the law**. "The law" refers to the Mosaic Law, which the Gentiles do not have (v.14). People are responsible and will be judged in direct proportion to the light they have. Jews do not have any advantage over Gentiles. On the Day of Judgment, it is not the hearer but the doer of the law who will be declared righteous before God.

This does not disfavor Gentiles either. By nature **Gentiles do not have the law.** (In v.14, *physis* ["by nature"] modifies **who do not have the law,** not **do things required by the law.** The parallel thought occurs in 2:27. There *physis,* translated as "physically," modifies "who is not circumcised," not "obeys the law.") Yet it is possible for Gentiles to do **the things required by the law** (2:12–16). In 8:3–4 Paul explicitly says that the righteous requirements of the law are fulfilled in Christians, Jews or Gentiles, who walk not according to the flesh but according to the Spirit. These Gentiles who do the things of the law are Christians (8:3–4). Apart from God's enabling, no one can fulfill the requirements of the law and be declared righteous before God (3:20; 7:14–25).

C. The Jews and the Law (2:17–29)

The Jews boast in their possession of the law. Yet they do not observe the law and thus **dishonor God** (vv.17–24). They are proud of their **circumcision.** But **circumcision** is meaningful only if they **observe the law.** The uncircumcised gentile Christians who obey the law (8:3–4) will condemn the circumcised Jews who do not obey **the law** (vv.25–27). In God's sight true **Jew** and true **circumcision** are inward realities, not outward signs (vv.28–29).

D. Objections Answered (3:1–8)

Paul answers possible objections to his preceding statements. In v.1 he raises an objection based on 2:29. If true Jew and circumcision are inward realities, not outward signs, then what is the **advantage** of being a Jew physically? The answer is in v.2. Among many blessings, they are **entrusted with the very words** (promises) **of God** (Wesley, *Notes,* 368). In v.3 Paul raises a question based on v.2. If the Jews are not faithful, will it affect **God's faithfulness?** The answer is found in v.4. God is always faithful; therefore he can judge people. Again, v.5 raises an objection based on v.4. If my unfaithfulness magnifies **God's righteousness,** then why does God judge me? And v.6 answers that. If this logic is valid, then God should not judge the gentile world. Yet the Jews maintain that God should judge them. In vv.7–8 we see a repetition of an objection similar to that in v.5. Such unreasonable arguments come from a twisted moral nature, which deserves condemnation.

E. All Under Sin (3:9–20)

If a privilege of the Jews is to have the words of God (3:2), are Jews better off than Gentiles? Not at all. Paul has previously charged that both Jews and Gentiles are under the power of sin.

He now quotes from the Scriptures to press his point upon the Jews. In vv.10–12 Paul quotes Ps 14:1–3 to make evident the presence of sin in human character. And vv.13–14 appeal to Pss 5:9; 140:3; and 10:7 to point to sin in human speech. Isa 59:7–8 is cited in vv.15–17 to show sin in human conduct. And v.18 quotes Ps 36:1 to summarize and point to the source of human sin. The basic problem with the human race is that **there is no fear of God before their eyes.** "Fear of God" is an OT expression for piety. In v.19 Paul emphasizes that these OT quotations speak particularly to the Jews **who are under the law.** If these scriptural quotations accuse the Jews as sinners, how much more the Gentiles. In v.20 Paul cites and slightly modifies Ps 143:2 to conclude that **no one will be declared righteous in God's sight by observing the law.** Rather, **the law** brings the knowledge of **sin.**

III. GOD'S RIGHTEOUSNESS PROVIDES SALVATION (3:21–8:39)

A. Righteousness Through Faith (3:21–26)

Against the background of sin and judgment, another aspect of God's righteousness is revealed. As in the OT, the righteousness of God provides salvation for human beings.

But now (v.21) marks both temporal and logical contrasts with the preceding section. Before this time, God's righteousness in providing salvation was not yet manifested. It was revealed only as the wrath of God. Yet the wrath of God is not entirely in the past. There still will be a future **wrath** of God (5:9). Therefore, the contrast is not merely temporal. It is logical as well.

Through his provision of salvation, God grants to men and women the good standing of right relationship with him. This relationship is not earned by them through the works of **the law** of the OT. Yet the OT testifies to it. It is a free gift of God. All who believe can receive it through faith in Jesus Christ.

This provision of salvation is necessary because **all have sinned and fall short of the glory of God** (v.23). In v.23 Paul summarizes 1:18–3:20. In 1:18–3:20 Paul indicates that men and women refuse to acknowledge and glorify God. The Jews' lack of obedience to the law is a manifestation of this negative attitude toward God.

Fundamentally, sin is not relating to God properly. The relationship between God and human beings is estranged. As a result, they **fall short of the glory** God intended for them to have—the glory Adam had before his fall (Barrett, 74). This includes the good standing of right relationship with God, which issues in intimate fellowship with him. When that relationship was destroyed, God made a provision through Jesus Christ so that he could graciously grant to them the good standing of right relationship with him. The granting of this relationship is called justification. In this section Paul uses two concepts to explain the provision God made in Jesus Christ.

The first concept is **redemption** (v.24), which is release of a captive by payment of a price or ransom (Clarke, on v.24). The **redemption** came by Christ Jesus. He came to give his life as a ransom for many (Mt 20:28). The recipient of the ransom price is not a part of this concept. God redeemed Israel from Egypt (Ex 15:13). However, God never paid any ransom to the Egyptians. The expression merely indicates that it cost God something to bring Israel out of Egypt. Probably this is the meaning of God's redeeming Israel with an outstretched arm (Ex 6:6). Likewise, Paul merely indicates that it cost God a great deal, the life of his own Son, to provide this salvation.

What we are freed from is treated later in Romans.

The second concept is **sacrifice of atonement** (v.25). This is a translation of the Greek word *hilastērion*. The NIV footnote indicates two possible interpretations: "as the one who would turn aside his wrath" or "taking away sin." NASB translates it as "propitiation," and RSV as "expiation." A person who is angry or offended is propitiated, i.e., appeased. Propitiation may refer to the gift given to appease or to the act of appeasing the angry or offended person. Sin and guilt that weigh upon the conscience of an offender are expiated, i.e., removed or wiped away. Expiation refers to the means or the act of removing the sin and guilt.

In many biblical passages where words related to *hilastērion* occur, the idea of God's wrath is present. The meaning of *hilastērion* is the removal of wrath (Morris, *Apostolic Preaching*, 125–85). But some scholars think wrath unworthy of God; appeasing God is even more unworthy. Therefore, they prefer to translate *hilastērion* as expiation (Dodd, 54–55). However, as pointed out earlier, God's wrath is fundamentally different from human anger. Paul explicitly talks about the wrath of God in the preceding section, 1:18–3:20 and again in 5:9; 12:19; and 13:4. If the wrath of God is not taken care of by *hilastērion*, it is left uncared for. This propitiation in Christ does not originate, as in heathen sacrifices, with the sinner who brings the sacrifice. Neither is it Christ Jesus who originated the propitiation. Therefore propitiation cannot be ridiculed, as some do, as the loving Son placating the angry Father. It is God himself, motivated by love, who provided the propitiation as a free gift. Thus both the severity of God's personal reaction

against sin and his love for the sinner are preserved (Cranfield, 1:213–17).

These two concepts, **redemption** and propitiation (NIV **atonement**), are mutually supplementary and corrective. Propitiation prevents us from seeing the ransom as paid to the Devil or to someone else. **Redemption** makes it impossible to think that the mind of the Father needs to be changed toward us.

The NIV of v.25 says that God presented Jesus as a sacrifice of atonement **through faith in his blood.** In the NIV **in his blood** is treated as the object of faith. However, for Paul the object of faith is always a person: Jesus Christ or God, but never a thing. So there should be a comma after **faith,** and **his blood** should be connected with *hilastērion*/propitiation (Cranfield, 1:210). The NASB reads "a propitiation in His blood through faith." This is in harmony with the general teaching of the NT that the blood of Jesus has sacrificial significance (cf. 1Co 10:16; 11:25; Mt 26:28; Mk 14:24; Lk 22:20; Heb 9:11–14; 10:19, 22; 13:12, 20; 1Pe 1:2, 19; 1Jn 1:7; 5:6). Ro 5:9 indicates that we are **justified** by (in) the **blood** of Jesus. As 5:9–10 indicates, the **blood** of Jesus refers to the death of Jesus. The **blood** of Jesus Christ, i.e., the death of Jesus, is the means of propitiation. Propitiation, however, is also effected **through faith.** It is effective only for those who have faith.

God made this provision for two reasons. The first is **to demonstrate his justice** (*dikaiosunē*, the same Greek word as righteousness). **In his forbearance,** God **left the sins committed beforehand unpunished.** God did this in order to give people a chance to repent (2:4). This, however, could easily lead to the misunderstanding that God does not care about sin. Now, by presenting Jesus as the propitiation,

God's attitude—his righteous wrath toward sin—is clearly demonstrated.

The second reason is that God can be **just** (*dikaios,* the same Greek word as righteous) in justifying the person who has **faith in Jesus Christ.** God's holy character cannot tolerate sin. Sin has to be punished. God made Jesus Christ who had no sin to be sin for us (2Co 5:21) and directed the full weight of that righteous wrath, which we deserve, upon himself in the person of his Son, Jesus Christ. Thus he can forgive sinners righteously (Wesley, *Notes,* 370), that is, without in any way condoning their sins. If the first reason is to demonstrate God's righteousness publicly, the second is to satisfy his own character.

In order to avoid some misunderstanding, two points need to be clarified. When God the Father poured out the full weight of his righteous wrath upon Jesus Christ, he was pouring it out upon himself, since the Father and the Son are one. Propitiation is effective only for those who have faith. Through faith we unite with Christ and become one with him. Therefore, when Jesus paid the penalty of sin for believers, it was like a husband paying the debt for his wife.

B. Justification (3:27–5:21)

1. Justification by faith (3:27–31)

Once the problem of sin is taken care of, God can righteously justify sinners—grant them the good standing of right relationship. All they have to do is believe. Men and women are **justified by faith apart from observing the** Mosaic **Law.** If justification were by observing the law, God would be **the God of** the **Jews only.** In that case, only the Jews could possibly be justified, since only they have the Mosaic Law. But **there is only one God. The God of** the **Jews** and **the God of** the

Gentiles is the same person. Therefore, God justifies Jews and Gentiles on the same basis—**by faith,** not by **observing the law.** Thus no one can boast.

This principle of justification by **faith** does not nullify but upholds (is consonant with) **the law.** Correctly understood, the principle of **faith** and that of **the law** are the same. God took the initiative to establish the covenant with the Jews and extended grace to them. The Mosaic Law is a part of this covenant, instructing them how to live. If Israel observes the law, the covenant of grace continues and the promised blessings follow. Otherwise, God can cancel the covenant and terminate the blessings. Without the promise in the covenant, merely obeying the law would not bring the blessing (Noth, 131). Obedience to **the law** is a manifestation of faithfulness to and trust in God. Thus **faith** is consonant with **the law. Faith** achieves what **the law** intends. So **faith** establishes **the law.** As 7:7–25 indicates, human beings, on their own, cannot observe **the law.** The righteous requirements of the law can be fulfilled only in those who live according to the Spirit (8:4), which is done by **faith.**

2. Illustration from Abraham (4:1–25)

In 3:21 Paul states that justification by faith is not contrary to but upholds the law. This is demonstrated from the life of **Abraham,** the respected father of the Jews. His example carries great weight with them. God regarded Abraham as righteous on the basis of his faith (Ge 15:6), before he was circumcised (Ge 17:10). Abraham was justified by faith first and later received circumcision as a seal of his righteousness. He did not do any work to earn the good standing of right relationship with God. Therefore he did not have any reason to boast. Since Abraham was justified while he was uncircumcised, this blessing of justification is available to **uncircumcised** Gentiles. Then Abraham was circumcised. So the blessing of justification is also available to **circumcised** Jews. Since this blessing is available to both **uncircumcised** Gentiles and **circumcised** Jews, it has to be through **faith,** not **the law** (vv.1–12).

If the blessing were through **the law, the promise** would be worthless, since no one can perfectly observe the law. **The law** can only convert sin into **transgression** and bring **wrath.** Thus **the promise** would be nullified. **The promise comes by faith,** not by **the law.** Therefore it is based on grace, not on human achievement, and thus can be guaranteed. God promised to make Abraham the **father of many nations.** Those who follow the faith of Abraham become his descendants, and thus God's promise is fulfilled (vv.13–17).

The faith of Abraham consists in **being fully persuaded that God had power to do what he had promised** (v.21). In spite of their physical conditions, he still took God's promise at face value and acted accordingly. He circumcised himself and his household before Isaac was conceived (Ge 17:23–27). Thus he **gave glory to God** (v.20). Abraham believed in God **who gives life to the dead and calls things that are not as though they were** (v.17). Today, **we believe in him who raised Jesus our Lord from the dead** (v.24). Both Abraham and we believe in the same God **who gives life to the dead.** Since Abraham was justified by **faith,** we, too, can be justified on this basis (vv.18–25). Since v.24 mentions that we **believe in him who raised Jesus our Lord from the dead,** a statement about him is added in v.25: **He was delivered over to death for**

our sins and was raised to life for our justification. No doubt this statement was formulated according to Isa 52:13–53:12. The two clauses in v.25 are not to be understood in such a way as to separate the function of Christ's death from that of his resurrection. While in v.25 our justification is connected with Christ's resurrection, in 5:9 it is connected with his **death** (blood).

3. Benefits of justification by faith (5:1–11)

Christ brings us to the place of divine grace where we stand firm. We are so confident of God's grace that we can **rejoice in the hope of** sharing in God's **glory** in the future. God's grace is so powerful that, for those who stand firm in it, **suffering produces perseverance.** Such **perseverance** shows that we can meet the test of adversity. The Greek word behind NIV's **character** is *dokimē,* which refers to the quality of approval by test. Meeting the test reinforces the **hope** (vv.3–4). Such **hope does not disappoint us** because it is grounded in the **love** God has for us. We experience that **love** when we receive the **Holy Spirit** (v.5).

Vv.6–8 give objective evidences for the love of God. **Rarely** would anyone **die for a righteous** person, though some may **possibly dare to die** for their benefactor. But surely no one would die for the enemy. Yet **Christ died** for us, **ungodly** sinners and God's enemies! **God demonstrates his own love for us in this** (v.8). The tenses of the verbs are noteworthy. The event of crucifixion was a past one, but the fact that it took place remains as a present proof of God's love for us.

It is hard to die for one's enemy. It is much easier to save one's friend. When **we were still sinners** and God's enemies, **Christ died for us** in order to reconcile us to God and make us his friends. Since God has done this much harder thing, surely we can count on him to do the much easier thing, to save us, his friends, from his **wrath** in the future. Meanwhile we can now **rejoice in God** and in his present grace (vv.9–11). V.10 states, **We are reconciled to him through the death of his Son**; and **How much more, having been reconciled, shall we be saved through his life!** This should not be interpreted so as to make a rigid distinction between what Christ's death and what his life accomplished (see comment on 4:25).

Three important theological issues need further attention. V.9 mentions the **blood** of Jesus Christ. Some scholars, starting from Lev 17:11, "The life of a creature is in the blood," maintain that Jesus' blood was shed in order to release his life to be shared with others. However, the parallelism of vv.9–10 indicates clearly that the **blood** of Jesus stands for his **death**, not his life.

Reconciliation (v.10) removes enmity. The enmity removed is both human hostility toward God (cf. 8:7) and God's hostility toward sinners (cf. 11:28; 1:18). God takes the initiative in reconciliation. Paul uses the active voice of the verb only of God and the passive only of human beings. Yet in 2Co 5:20 Paul represents God as calling men and women to be **reconciled** to him. So the human role in reconciliation is not totally passive.

In vv.9–10, the word *saved* is in the future tense. The **wrath** of God from which we shall be saved is in the future. Even though the wrath of God is being revealed from heaven now (1:18), there will still be God's **wrath** in the future, at the end of the present age. V.10 also mentions that we shall be saved in the future. Yet Paul uses "saved" in the past tense in 8:24, "we were saved"; in v.9

Paul says, **We have now been justified**. Evidently salvation took place in the past, has its effect at present, and will be completed in the future. For other aspects of salvation see comment on 1:16.

4. Universal applicability of justification (5:12–21)

Just as Adam's sin affected the entire human race, so the work of Jesus Christ also affects all who believe in him. In this way, Adam **was a pattern of the one to come** (v.14). In this section, Paul uses **one** twelve times to emphasize this point. **One** affects **many** or **all**. **Sin entered the world** (the human race) **through one man,** Adam, when he sinned. The wages of sin is death, so **death came to all men.**

Paul says that **sin entered the world through one man, and death through sin, and in this way death came to all men, because all sinned** (v.12). Several theories have been proposed to elucidate the clause **because all sinned** to explain how the sin of Adam brought about death to all. Only the two most popular views will be considered here.

The first view maintains that when Adam sinned all people sinned (Murray, 1:187). All descendants of Adam participated in the sinful act of Adam. This is demonstrated by the following fact. The law was given through Moses. Between Adam and Moses there was no law. When there is no law, sin is not taken into account, that is, not charged or punished. Yet between Adam and Moses, men and women died. Since they were not punished for the sin they committed individually, their death had to be the punishment for Adam's sin in which they participated (vv.13–14; see Clarke on v.13). This view seems to be supported by v.19, **Through the dis-**

obedience of the one man the many were made sinners.

This view, however, has its weaknesses: (1) The statement Sin is not taken into account when there is no law in v.13 cannot mean that without law sin is not punished. In 1:18–32 and 2:12 Paul explicitly states that the wrath of God is against the sin of Gentiles who do not have the law, and they will be punished for their sin. Even before the time of Moses the people in the age of Noah were punished for the sins they committed. The people of Sodom and Gomorrah, too, were destroyed for the sins they committed (Ge 19). (2) Paul declares in 1:32 that "those who do such things deserve death." They deserve death, not because of the sin of Adam, but because of their own sinful acts. (3) The identical expression, "all [have] sinned," occurs in 3:23. There the preceding context clearly indicates the meaning. All sinned individually, not merely as participants in the sin of Adam.

The second view interprets all sinned in v.12 as all sinned individually. When Adam sinned, sin entered the human race and corrupted the human nature. Wesley understood this sin to be "actual sin, and its consequence, a sinful nature" (Notes, 375). This corrupted human nature inherited from Adam caused all men and women to sin individually (Cranfield, 1:274–82). If this second view is adopted, the weaknesses of the first view disappear. The meaning of vv.13–14 becomes as follows. Between Adam and Moses all men and women sinned individually. When there is no law, however, sin is not easily recognized. (In v.13 ellogeō, translated as taken into account, can mean "recognize.") Yet the death of all men demonstrates that all sinned individually. Through the disobedience of the one man the many were made

[kathistēmi] sinners (v.19). Kathistēmi can mean "to cause to become" as in Ac 7:27 (NIV Who made you). So v.19 means that through the disobedience of Adam, human nature was corrupted. This causes all men and women to sin and thus become sinners.

No matter how all sinned is interpreted, the main point is clear and valid. The sin of Adam affected the entire human race by bringing sin and death upon all men and women.

Just as Adam's sin affected all, so also Jesus' act affects many. The parallelism, however, is not entirely balanced, because trespass and grace are not the same. It takes greater power to undo the effect of sin than it took originally for sin to enter. Grace is much more powerful than transgression. So if death came upon the entire race through Adam's sin, how much more will life come to those who accept God's provision in Jesus Christ (vv.15–17)!

Earlier Paul touched on the law (v.13). So in this closing part he makes a provisional statement about the law in relation to sin and grace. Before the law was given, sin was in the world (v.13). However, where there is no law, there is no transgression (4:15). When the law came, it converted some sins into transgressions. In this sense, the law increased the transgression (v.20).

The law also increases transgression in the sense of 7:7–8. A prohibition tends to provoke one's desire to do it. Thus through the law we become conscious of sin (3:20; cf. 5:13). Since all transgressions are sins, where transgression increases, sin increases as well. However, grace is more powerful than sin. Therefore, where sin increased, grace increased all the more. Grace brings about righteousness and eternal life through Jesus Christ (vv.20–21).

C. Sanctification (6:1–8:17)

1. Union with Christ (6:1–14)

The last section concludes with Paul's statement that "where sin increased, grace increased all the more" (5:20). Naturally this raises the question, **Shall we go on sinning so that grace may increase?** (v.1). **By no means!** says Paul, and he goes on to explain the reason.

There are two races: one headed by Adam, the other by Christ. One is dominated by **sin,** the other characterized by **righteousness.** By birth, all men and women belong to the race of Adam. Through baptism, believers unite with Christ and become members of the race of Christ. The members of each race share in the experience and the destiny of the head.

Christ **died to sin** [tē hamartia] **once for all** (v.10). In Greek this means that the death of Christ has something to do with **sin.** In his death, Christ paid the penalty of sin for us (3:24–26; 4:25; 5:6–8; 1Co 15:3; 2Co 5:21; Gal 3:13) and condemned sin in his flesh (8:3). Therefore, those who are united with Christ have died to, and have been **freed from,** sin (v.7). When we became the members of Christ's race, we left Adam's race. Adam's race was dominated by **sin.** As members of that race, we were dominated by sin and were instruments of **sin.** This is the meaning of **body of sin** (v.6), just as "body of humiliation" (literal translation) in Php 3:21 means the body that is characterized by humiliation. The parallel structure of vv.12–13 indicates that **your body** (v.12) and **yourselves** (v.13) are synonymous. When our old self is crucified with Christ, the self that is dominated by sin is **done away with** (katargeō, v.6). Katargeō (done away

with) can also mean "abolish" or "release from association." The result of abolishing the **body of sin** is that we are **no longer slaves to sin** (v.6). Greathouse writes, "It is not the body as such that is to be destroyed, but *the body as sin's tool*" (p. 134).

Therefore, if we have experienced the grace of God, it is inconsistent for us to **go on sinning** (v.1). As members of Christ's race, we participate in the destiny of Christ. In this section, when Paul mentions our participation in Christ's **death,** he uses the past tense (vv.2, 3, 4, 5, 6, 7, 8). When, however, he talks about our participation in Christ's **resurrection,** he uses the future tense (vv.5, 8). Our full participation in Christ's **resurrection,** namely, our bodily resurrection, is in the future (cf. 8:23). We are no longer members of Adam's race. However, some effect of that race still remains with us. Therefore v.12 calls our body a **mortal body,** a body destined to death. Now, however, we have partially participated in the effect of Christ's resurrection. This is manifested in our living a new life (v.4).

Since Christ died **to sin** and lives **to God,** v.11 commands believers to **count** themselves **dead to sin but alive to God in Christ Jesus.** To **count** (*logizomai*) means to make it operative in one's live. This command is in the present tense. One has to keep on doing it. Vv.12–13 spell this out in concrete terms: **Do not let sin reign in your mortal body.** Since we have been united with Christ in his death, we have been freed from sin and are no longer slaves to sin. Now it is possible to obey this commandment. When we were members of Adam's race, we were enslaved to sin. We could not dethrone sin. But now the situation has changed. Christ has dethroned sin from our lives. We are to keep sin dethroned. Otherwise sin may reign again in us. This freedom from the bondage to sin is normative for the Christian.

There are, however, some subnormative Christians over whom sin still rules (see the discussion on 7:14–25). Paul commands them to dethrone sin. Evidently, sin is not automatically dethroned or kept dethroned in Christian life. Christians have to play their part. **Do not offer the parts of your body to sin, as instruments of wickedness, but rather offer yourselves to God . . . and offer the parts of your body to him as instruments of righteousness** (v.13). The commands in vv.12–13 are in the present tense. "If it is going on, it must be stopped. If it is not going on, we must not allow ourselves to be involved in it. For sin's method is seldom a big, decisive dedication. It is generally an accumulation of concessions, compromises, and indulgences that enthrones sin" (Dayton, 45).

V.14 provides the foundation for the commandment in vv.12–13. Grace communicates power to resist sin, which the law could not do (cf. 8:3–4). Under grace, sin lost the power to be our master. Therefore it becomes possible for us **not** to **let sin reign in our body** and to **offer** ourselves **to God.**

2. Freedom from sin, slavery to righteousness (6:15–23)

The preceding section concludes with the statement, **You are not under law, but under grace** (6:14). This naturally raises the question, **Shall we sin because we are not under law but under grace?** (v.15). This question is different from that in 6:1. The former question is "Shall we go on sinning?" (or lit., "Shall we remain in sin?"). Now the question is, "Shall we sin [in any given circumstance, or sin at all]?"

Paul answers from the perspective of slavery. A human being is enslaved either to sin or to righteousness. There is no third alternative. Formerly, you were enslaved to sin. But you became Christians and **wholeheartedly obeyed** the moral **teachings** of the Christian life. In the early church there was a standard teaching regarding the Christian life (cf. Ac 2:42). **The form of teaching to which you were entrusted** (v.17) refers to this. You were entrusted to that teaching like slaves were transferred from one master to another. By obeying this teaching, **you have been set free from sin.** This means you **have become slaves to righteousness.** Freedom from sin and slavery to righteousness are two sides of the same event. Christian freedom is not autonomy but change of lordship. If you commit sin, you offer yourselves to obey sin and will become enslaved to sin again (Greathouse, 143).

Then Paul writes, **When you were slaves to sin, you were free from the control of righteousness** (v.20). There are only two masters; one is **sin**, the other **righteousness.** No one can serve two masters. He has to choose one or the other. The same idea is expressed in v.22, **But now that you have been set free from sin and have become slaves to God.**

Vv.19–23 compare the consequences of serving one or the other. Serving sin leads to **wickedness** (v.19), and the result is **death** (vv.21, 23). Serving righteousness **leads to holiness** (*hagiasmos*), **and the result is eternal life** (vv.19, 22). Therefore, Paul calls upon Christians to present themselves to God, to **righteousness** (v.19).

Some people think that *hagiasmos* (NIV "holiness," RSV "sanctification") is a process, not a state. However, *hagiasmos* here refers to a religious and moral state. V.19 sets serving sin and serving righteousness in contrast. A literal translation of v.19 reads, **Just as you presented your members as slaves to impurity and to lawlessness unto lawlessness, so now present your members as slaves to righteousness unto holiness** [hagiasmos]. **Holiness** structurally parallels and is the opposite of lawlessness. Since lawlessness is not a process but a state, so is **holiness.** Paul is not talking about gradually being separated from sin, but a decisive separation from sin once for all. In 1Th 4:3–4 "holiness" (*hagiasmos*) is joined with "honor" and refers to a state of moral purity. In 1Th 4:7 holiness (*hagiasmos*) is the opposite of uncleanness. Evidently it is a state of moral purity. 1Ti 2:15 declares, "Women will be saved through childbearing—if they continue [*meno,* lit. 'remain'] in faith, love and holiness [*hagiasmos*] with propriety." Like faith, love, and propriety, holiness (*hagiasmos*) is a state one can remain in.

Christian holiness is not merely a process. It is a religious and moral state that Christians can attain in this life by the grace of God. This is a result of presenting ourselves to God to serve him. It is our part to present ourselves to God and God's part to sanctify us and make us holy (Greathouse, 139). **Holiness** is a fruit of enslavement to God and will issue in **eternal life** (v.22).

3. Impotence of the law (7:1–25)

a. Dead to the law (7:1–6)

In 6:14 Paul declares, "For sin shall not be your master [*kurieuō*], because you are not under law, but under grace." And in 6:15–23 Paul answers a question that can be easily raised by this statement. "Shall we sin because we are not under law but under grace?" (6:15). The paragraph before us now explain the declaration of 6:14. V.1

states, **The law has authority over** [kurieuō] **a man.** Here Paul intentionally uses the same Greek word occurring in 6:14 (*kurieuō*) to indicate the parallel thoughts. There are several parallels between 6:15–23 and 7:1–6. The former deals with freedom from **sin,** the latter, freedom from the **law.** Ro 7:1–4 corresponds to 6:16–19, and 7:5–6 to 6:21–23.

In 7:1 Paul appeals to knowledge of the law. (In the early church, even gentile Christians had a good knowledge of the OT [cf. Gal 4:21].) It is true that only Jews had the law. So only they could die to the law. However, the death of Jews to the law does affect Gentiles. Christ redeemed Jews from the law so that in Christ Jesus the blessing of Abraham might come upon Gentiles (Gal 3:13–14). Therefore, Paul includes all Christians when he talks about death to the law.

Paul uses the analogy of marriage to demonstrate our freedom from the law. In marriage, when there is a death, the surviving partner is no longer bound to the marriage and is free to marry another. So Paul says, the death of believers sets them free from the law, to be married to Christ.

Christ Jesus was born under the law (Gal 4:4). When he died on the cross, he died to the law as well. The law lost jurisdiction over him. By his death he abolished the law (Eph 2:15; Col 2:14). **Through the body of Christ,** that is, being united with Christ in his death (*Notes,* 378), we died to the law, so that we might be married to Christ in order to **bear fruit to God.** Here Paul designates Christ Jesus as the one **who was raised from the dead** (v.4) to emphasize his death and resurrection. This signifies the coming of the new age. So we have been redeemed from under the law (Gal 4:4–5). Our redemption from under the law and our union with Christ are two sides of the same event. Our marriage to Christ is to **bear fruit to God** (v.4).

In contrast v.5 describes how we used to bear fruit to death. When we were living in the flesh (*en tē sarki*; NIV **controlled by the sinful nature**; NIV note "the flesh"; RSV, NASB "in the flesh"), **the sinful passions aroused by the law were at work in our bodies** to bear **fruit for death.** The past tense **were** indicates that we are no longer living in this condition. This condition is not normative for the Christian.

In 7:7–13 Paul describes in greater detail how sin takes the opportunity afforded by the commandment to produce in us the desires that lead to sin. Paul describes a person's moral struggle in 7:14–23. He or she wants to follow the law and does not want to do evil. But the action inevitably is the opposite of this desire. Finally, he or she cries out, "Who will rescue me from this body of death?" (7:24). Paul summarizes this condition by saying "*tē sarki* [NIV 'in the sinful nature'; RSV, NASB 'with my flesh'] [I am] a slave to the law of sin" (7:25). The same Greek word, *sarx*, is used both in 7:5 and 7:25 to describe the condition of 7:5 and 7:7–25. This is another evidence that 7:5 is further elaborated in 7:7–25.

V.6 reports our emancipation from the law. **Dying to what once bound us** refers back to 7:2–3. We died to and are released from our first husband, **the law.** Now **we serve in the new way of the Spirit, and not in the old way of the written code** (*gramma*, lit. "letter"). This concept occurs also in 2Co 3:6. There the **Spirit** has to do with the new covenant, which came by Christ Jesus, and the **letter** (*gramma*) refers to the old covenant represented by the Mosaic Law. The expression **written code** (*gramma*, or "letter")

emphasizes the powerlessness of the Mosaic Law. This is elaborated on in 8:1–17. **The law** is weak and powerless (8:3), but the new covenant is empowered by the **Spirit** and is powerful and productive.

b. The law, the sin, and the flesh (7:7–25)

Several points made by Paul in the course of his argument, particularly in 5:20; 6:14; and 7:1–6, may give the impression that the law is evil and is identical to sin. So here in v.7 he raises the question, **Is the law sin?** and proceeds to answer it. In this section Paul uses **I** as the subject. Is this his autobiographical experience? Even if this is autobiographical, it is not merely Paul's own experience. It has universal application (*Notes*, 379). As discussed earlier, this section is a further elaboration of 7:5. There Paul uses "we" as the subject. In 8:4 he describes the opposite of the condition of 7:7–25 and uses "us" as the object of God's enabling work. Moreover, on the level of practical life, everyone can identify with this experience. Whether autobiographical or not, this **I** is inclusive and represents all men and women.

From this analysis of general human experience, Paul demonstrates that **the law is not sin. The law** itself is not evil. **Sin** is the cause of the evil effects of **the law. Sin** in this context is not merely an evil act but the power that causes men and women to commit sin. Wesley calls it "inbred corruption" (*Notes*, 379; cf. Murray "sinful principle" (1:250). Black gives the title "The Problem of Indwelling Sin" to 7:7–12 (p. 96). The **law** itself is **holy, righteous, and good** (v.12). The **law** is to bring life. But **sin** perverts it and actually brings death through it. By this, **sin** is shown to be **utterly sinful** (v.13).

In vv.14–25 Paul describes a familiar

moral struggle. **I delight in God's law and want to do it. But the law** (principle, or power) **of sin** within me prevents me from doing it and compels me to do **the evil I do not want.** So in desperation I cry out, **What a wretched man I am! Who will rescue me from this body of death?** "This body of death" means the body dominated by death in the sense of vv.10–11, or by "the law of sin and death" (8:2). The deliverance comes **through Jesus Christ** (v.25a).

Some commentators understand v.25b to be the result of the deliverance. They maintain that after the deliverance we will still be living in the same way as before. So, in this view, vv.7–25 describe the normal condition of the Christian life (Morris, *Romans,* 288).

If this were true, why would **I** be excited about the deliverance? In order to bring the contrast to a sharp focus, Paul summarizes the condition before the deliverance in v.25b and treats the condition after the deliverance in 8:1–17. This is confirmed by **so then** in v.25b. So the same condition is described in v.5, vv.7–25a, and v.25b. The opposite condition is described in 7:6 and 8:1–17. After the deliverance through Christ Jesus, **I** no longer lives in the former condition.

The verbs in 7:1–13 are in the past tense, but the verbs in vv.14–25 are in the present tense. This leads some commentators to think that the condition described in vv.14–25 is the normative Christian experience (Nygren, 285–97). However, the "I" in vv.14–25 is **sold as a slave to sin** (v.14), and **sin** lives in him (vv.17, 20). He is **a prisoner of the law** (power, or principle) **of sin,** which is **at work within** his **members** (v.23). This is radically different from the Christian experience described in 6:1–7:6. Christians have

died to sin (6:2). They are no longer enslaved to sin (6:6), but are freed from it (6:7), and have become slaves of righteousness (6:18, 22). They have been released from the law, dead to what once bound them (7:6).

Other commentators think that vv.14–25 describe non-Christian experience (Dodd, 107–8). However, the "I" knows **that the law of God is good** (v.16) and wants **to do what is good** (v.18). He delights **in God's law** (v.22). This is not the picture Paul paints of non-Christians in 1:18–3:20.

Who, then, is this **"I"** whom Paul is describing in vv.14–25, if it is not a normative Christian nor a non-Christian? Paul is describing the condition of the worldly person (*sarkinos, sarkikos*), any person living in the flesh (*en tē sarki*). This is supported by the following evidences. (1) As mentioned earlier, 7:5 is a summary of vv.7–25; v.5 explicitly states that the condition pertains to when "we were in the flesh" (*en tē sarki*). (2) This section repeatedly emphasizes the condition of the flesh (*sarx*). V.14 says, **I am** *sarkinos* (NIV **unspiritual;** RSV "fleshly"; NASB "of flesh"); v.18 "in my flesh" (*en tē sarki*). (3) V.25b summarizes the condition of "I" in vv.14–25. Here Paul writes *"tē sarki* [NIV **in the sinful nature;** RSV, NASB **with my flesh**] [I am] **a slave to the law of sin.** (4) The "I" in this section cannot do the requirements of the law because of sin. God, however, condemned sin so that the condition is reversed (8:3–4). In 8:3 Paul intimates that the condition exists because the law "was weakened by *sarx*" (NIV "the sinful nature"; NIV note, RSV, NASB "the flesh"). So the problem in vv.14–25 is due to the flesh (*sarx*). (5) The condition in 8:1–17 is the opposite of that in 7:14–25. The condition of 8:1–17 is that of those who live according to the Spirit (8:4). The opposite of this is living according to the flesh (*sarx,* 8:4, 5, 6, 7, 8, 9, 12, 13, NIV "the sinful nature"; NIV note, RSV, NASB "the flesh"). (6) The destiny of **I** in vv.14–25 is **death** (v.24), and the destiny of the flesh (*sarx*) is **death** also (7:5; 8:6). (7) The "**I**" in vv.14–25 cannot do good (vv.18, 21), that is, the demands of **the law** (v.16). The mind of the flesh (*sarx,* NIV "sinful mind"; RSV, NASB "the mind that is set on the flesh") does not and cannot submit to God's law (8:7).

The key concept is that of *sarx* and its derivatives. *Sarx,* usually translated as "**sinful nature,**" "**unspiritual,**" or "worldly" in NIV and as "flesh" in NIV notes, RSV, and NASB, has a wide range of meanings. The most important, however, is the theological meaning, which is the key to the understanding of this discussion.

According to 1Co 3:3, fleshly believers (*sarkikos;* NIV "worldly"; RSV "of the flesh"; NASB "fleshly") behave like mere human beings. Ro 7:4 mentions our marriage to Christ Jesus to bear fruit to God. In contrast, 7:5 says that we were in the flesh (*sarx*) bearing **fruit to death.** Being in the flesh is the opposite of being married to Christ and drawing upon his resources. V.25b summarizes the condition of the fleshly person. **So then, I myself [***autos egō***] in my mind am a slave to God's law, but in** *tē sarki* **[**NIV **the sinful nature;** RSV, NASB 'flesh'] a slave to the law of sin.** In Greek *autos egō* is an emphatic way of saying, "I, myself." The meaning is "I, independent of any outside influence, and thus completely on my own."

Thus *sarx* (flesh) is human nature independent of God's grace. In such condition, it is invaded, enslaved, and corrupted by **sin** (v.14). Therefore, even though **sin** and the flesh are not identical, they produce the same effects. In 8:1–17 walking according to *sarx*

(NIV **sinful nature**; RSV, NASB "flesh") is contrasted to walking according to the Spirit. To walk according to the flesh is to function without God's grace, but only on the resources of this corrupted human nature.

Surely non-Christians are of the flesh. 1Co 3:1–3 clearly indicates that some Christians, "infants in Christ," are still fleshly (*sarkinos;* NIV **worldly**; RSV, NASB "of the flesh"). This is subnormative for Christians. They should be spiritual, not fleshly. Ro 7:5 says, "When we were *en tē sarki* (NASB "in the flesh"; RSV "living in the flesh"; NIV "controlled by the sinful nature"). This means that we are no longer in the flesh. We are no longer living in the condition of vv.14–25.

Thus we come to this conclusion. Non-Christians and some Christians are living in the condition of vv.7–25. Greathouse writes:

> To the extent, therefore, that a believer has not met the conditions of 6:11–13, to that extent sin still remains to trouble his new-found peace. To the extent that he is depending upon his own self-effort for sanctification, to that extent he is yet under the law. . . . Something of this divided condition and occasional defeat is therefore present experience for the believer until he is cleansed from remaining sin by the sanctifying power of the Spirit. (Greathouse, 160)

Gal 3:3 mentions that the Galatian Christians have begun with the Spirit but are trying to be made complete by *sarx* ("flesh"). Since the danger of living in the condition of vv.14–25 is ever present with Christians (cf. Wesley, *Plain Account,* 39, 45), the verbs in this section are in the present tense. But this is subnormative for Christians. They should be living in the state of 8:1–17. If Christians are living in the condition of vv.7–25, they should present themselves to God, and God will sanctify them (6:19–22) and enable them to live in the condition of 8:1–17. This is the "second work of grace" of Wesleyan theology.

4. Life in the Spirit (8:1–17)

In 7:24 the "I" calls for help to be rescued from the miserable condition. This rescue is mentioned in 7:24b–25a and explained in 8:1–17. **There is now no condemnation [*katakrima*] for those who are in Christ Jesus** (v.1). Usually **condemnation** means pronouncement of guilt. This meaning, however, is not appropriate here. The preceding section, 7:17–25, deals with the issue of the power of sin, not that of guilt. V.2, **Because through Christ Jesus the law of the Spirit of life set me free from the law of sin and death,** also indicates that the **condemnation** in v.1 is more than a pronouncement of guilt.

In fact, *katakrima* means more than a pronouncement of guilt. In 5:12–17, the condemnation (*katakrima*) brought about by Adam's sin is death. Death surely is not a mere pronouncement of guilt, but punishment. According to v.3, God **condemned** (*katakrinō*) sin, which **the law** cannot do. Surely **the law** can pronounce guilt. So **condemnation** is more than pronouncing guilt.

God broke the power of **sin** (Murray, 1:275) **for those who are in Christ** so that they no longer live in the condition of 7:7–25. In vv.3–4 Paul explains what God did to effect this. According to 7:7–25, **sin** corrupted the human nature so that man and woman cannot do what **the law** requires. **The law** is not powerful enough to deal with this condition. It cannot cope with sin to enable man and woman to obey the law. So **God** sent **his own Son in the likeness of** *sarkos hamartias* (NIV **sinful man**; RSV NASB "sinful flesh,") and for sin, condemned

sin in the flesh. The human nature is controlled by sin, so it is called sinful flesh. The place to attack and conquer sin is the very fortress where sin has established its seat. God's Son took up the human nature, yet without sin. This is the meaning of **in the likeness of sinful man** (v.3) (Murray, 1:280). In the human nature of his own Son, God broke the power of **sin.**

Now **the righteous requirements of the law** can be fulfilled in us **who do not live according to** *sarka* (NIV "the sinful nature"; RSV, NASB "the flesh") but according to the Spirit. This reverses the situation of 7:7–25.

The law as a system ended when Christ Jesus came (Gal 3:25). **The righteous requirements of the law,** however, are still valid as expressions of God's will for human conduct. **Those who live according to the Spirit** will fulfill these requirements, such as, "Do not steal," "Do not murder," etc. (cf. 13:8–10). The fruit of the Spirit is in harmony with the law (Gal 5:23).

V.5 begins with "for" in Greek and places vv.4 and 5 in the causal relationship. **To live according to the Spirit** (v.4) is the result of having **their minds set [*phroneō*] on what the Spirit desires** (v.5). Vv.5–8 contrast the mind of the flesh and the mind of **the Spirit.** To **have their minds set** (*phroneō*) includes the elements of thinking, willing, pursuing, and doing (cf. Php 2:5). The mind of the flesh is **hostile to God** and consequently cannot **submit to God's law.** This leads to **death.** To have their minds set on the things of **the Spirit** is to pursue what pleases God, which leads to doing the **requirements of the law** as expressions of God's will. This results in **life and peace.**

Vv.9–11 treat the effects of **the Spirit** in our lives. In this section Paul uses "the Spirit," "the Spirit of God," "the Spirit of Christ," and "Christ" interchangeably (Black, 111), since **Christ** lives in us through the Holy Spirit. **The Spirit of God lives in you** (v.9) means that he has a settled permanent penetrative influence upon you (Cranfield, 1:388). If (or since) this is true, you are not in the flesh, but in the **Spirit.**

Some commentators understand the "spirit" (*to pneuma,* NIV **your spirit**) in v.10 to be the human spirit. Death, however, is the separation of body and spirit. Since the human spirit is involved in death, it would be strange to make human spirit and death antithetical (Murray, 1:290). Moreover, in vv.1–11 **the Spirit** in all other instances refers to the Holy Spirit. It is unlikely that Paul would switch the meaning of the word in this verse without any indication. Therefore, it should refer here to the Holy Spirit as well.

Vv.10–11 indicate that at present we have received only partial blessings of **Christ in you.** We will receive its full blessings in the future. At present, the negative effects of sin have not yet been completely removed. Our bodies are still destined to death and are called **"mortal bodies"** in v.11. This is the meaning of the declaration, **"Your body is dead,"** in v.10. **The [Holy] Spirit is life** (v.6). He makes us spiritually alive now (vv.1–9) and will make our bodies alive in the future as he resurrected Christ Jesus. This will happen to us because we have the good standing of right relationship with God.

V.12 begins with **therefore**, indicating that vv.12–17 spell out the ethical implications of vv.1–11. In view of the truths presented, one should live according to **the Spirit,** not according to the flesh. To do this one has to put to death the deeds of the body (cf. 1Co 9:27). One should sacrifice the natural for the sake of the spiritual (Greathouse, 174). "Moral and spiritual life thrives on self-discipline and self-denial. Without them, it fades away" (Dayton, 55). This is possible only if one is led by the Spirit. **Led by the Spirit of God** emphasizes the activity of the Spirit. **Put to death the misdeeds of the body** emphasizes the activity of the believer. These are complementary. The latter is the evidence of the former, and the former is the cause of the latter (Murray, 1:295). Persons so **led by the Spirit** are **sons of God, co-heirs with Christ.** If we **share in his sufferings** now, we will **share in his glory** in the future.

D. Future Glory (8:18–27)

Our future glory is such that **our present sufferings are not worth comparing** with it. At present, the whole **creation** is subject to the **bondage to decay** and eagerly awaits the future deliverance. Even we, **who have the firstfruits of the Spirit, groan inwardly** awaiting **the redemption of our bodies.** Now we have the Holy Spirit as the **firstfruits,** which are a part of the gift as well as a pledge of the future fuller gift. Our salvation will be completed when we receive the resurrected body. Then **our adoption as** God's **sons** will be fully realized. Since we have experienced the work of the Holy Spirit in us now, we can be sure of the future bodily resurrection (cf. 8:11).

Before the final completion of our redemption, the creation groans and so do we (vv.22–23). Due to **our weakness, we do not know what we ought to pray.** But the Holy **Spirit,** who knows the will of God, **helps us** by praying **for us with groans,** which God understands.

E. Assurance (8:28–39)

This brings the presentation of God's provision of salvation to the climax. This salvation was planned by God before the foundation of the world (cf. Eph 1:4). He has a specific purpose and design that he will follow through. Therefore, we know and are confident that the ultimate goal of salvation, our final glorification, will be achieved (vv.28–30).

The word *predestined* (*prohorizō*) occurs in vv.29–30. This has been misinterpreted to mean that God arbitrarily determined in advance certain individuals to be saved. This, however, is not the meaning of the word. This word occurs six times in the NT: Ac 4:28; Ro 8:29, 30; 1Co 2:7; and Eph 1:5, 11. In all other occurrences, the context indicates clearly that it has to do with the plan, the design, the condition of some event, or salvation. It is also so used here (Murray, 1:318). Those who participate in salvation are **those who love** God. They are called according to God's **purpose** (*prothesis*, v.28). In the entire NT when **purpose** (*prothesis*) is used of God, it has to do with the plan, the design, or the condition of some event, never with certain persons. God's purpose regarding salvation is that all be saved and none be lost (1Ti 2:4; Tit 2:11; 2Pe 3:9). The call is the invitation addressed by God to all human beings. It is inclusive, not exclusive.

In v.29 the object of **predestine** is **to be conformed to the likeness of his Son.** In v.30 the object seems to be certain persons. These persons, however, are **those** whom **God foreknew,** not those arbitrarily chosen by God. Foreknowledge does not cause them to have faith, but rather their faith causes God to foreknow. My knowing does not cause you to do something. But your doing causes me to know. In the same way, God's knowledge does not cause us to do something, but our doing causes God to know. Since, however, God is not bound by time, he can know before we do it.

The central thought of vv.31–39 is this: Since **God is for us, who can be against us** (v.31)? God has done the harder thing—giving his own Son for us; surely he will do the easier thing— give us all the blessings he has promised. He is the only one who can justify, and he has already justified us; **who** can **bring any charge against us?** The judge himself, **Christ Jesus, died,** was resurrected, and now is **interceding for us.** Surely no one will condemn us. God loves us so much. Surely nothing can **separate us from the love** God has for us in **Christ.**

IV. GOD'S RIGHTEOUSNESS AND ISRAEL (9:1–11:36)

Faithfulness promotes right relationship. God's righteousness includes his faithfulness. The OT bears witness to the Gospel. God promised salvation to Abraham and his descendants. Yet the Israelites have not accepted it. Is God, then, not faithful?

A. Paul's Sorrow for Israel (9:1–5)

The Israelites have many spiritual privileges. Yet they have not accepted the salvation that is provided through them. Paul has great **anguish** and desire for their salvation.

B. God's Sovereignty (9:6–29)

The Israelites have not yet received the salvation God promised Abraham and his descendants. It seems that God's promise has failed. But this is not the case. Not all of Abraham's descendants are the heirs of promise. His heirs do receive salvation (11:1–10). How do we, then, determine who are his heirs? God is sovereign. He decides what kind of people are Abraham's heirs. Paul appeals to the OT to demonstrate this. This section has been misinterpreted to mean that God arbitrarily determines the destiny of people, regardless of their action and behavior (Murray, 2:20, 24). Paul's thought development and the context of the OT quotations and allusions demonstrate the opposite.

The sovereignty of God, emphasized in this section, can be understood in two different ways. (1) God arbitrarily decides who are and who are not Abraham's heirs. The unsaved Jews are not saved because God arbitrarily decides that they are not Abraham's heirs. In this case, they are not responsible since they cannot do anything about it. (2) God is free to lay down the condition of heirship and thus determine what kind of people will be Abraham's heirs (Wesley, *Notes*, 388). The Jews are not saved because they do not comply with God's condition. Therefore they are responsible for their condition and are guilty.

If the first interpretation were true, the quotations from Hosea and Isaiah in 9:25–29 are meaningless. Why would God first arbitrarily reject them and later change his mind to accept them? The entire section following 9:30 indicates and 11:20–23 explicitly states that these Jews are unsaved precisely **because of** their **unbelief,** not because of God's arbitrary decision to count them out. **If they do not persist in** their **unbelief,** they also will be saved. This surely contradicts the first and supports the second interpretation. The statement in 10:21 that God has **held out** his **hands to a disobedient people** (Israel) has the same effect. So does Paul's **anguish** for the Israelites (9:1–5). All these lead to this conclusion: God's sovereignty consists in his freedom to lay down the condition of salvation, not in his arbitrary consignment of some to salvation, others to damnation.

In the OT not all the descendants of Isaac are Abraham's heirs. Even before Jacob and Esau were born, God had already laid down the condition of heirship. God did not wait until after they were born and then pick a condition favorable to Jacob (vv.10–13). God proclaimed before Moses, **"I will have mercy on whom I have mercy"** (cf. Ex 33:19). The meaning, again, is that I decide what kind of people I will show mercy to (cf. Ex 32:33). God showed mercy to Moses because, while the Israelites worshiped idols, Moses did not (Ex 32:1–33:23). God shows **mercy** to those who are faithful (vv.14–15) and **hardens the heart** of those who oppose him. In Ex 5:1–12:51 Pharaoh first hardened his own heart. Only after that did God harden his heart (vv.16–18).

The potter has **the right to make out of the same lump of clay, some pottery for noble purposes and some for common use** (v.21). This is an allusion to Jer 18:5–12. The true meaning is clearly spelled out in Jer 18:6–10:

> "Like clay in the hand of the potter, so are you in my hand, O house of Israel. If at any time I announce that a nation or a kingdom is to be uprooted, torn down and destroyed, and if that nation I warned repents of its evil, then I will relent and not inflict on it the disaster I had planned. And if at another time I announce that a nation or kingdom is to be built up and planted, and if it does evil in my sight and does not obey me, then I will reconsider the good I had intended for it."

The sovereignty of the potter over the clay means that the Lord is completely free to lay down the conditions under which he will bless or punish. It is not his arbitrary decision to consign some to salvation and others to damnation (vv.19–21).

This truth is illustrated in vv.22–29. Originally Gentiles were **not** God's **people,** but God will accept them as his own because of their faith. The Israelites were God's people, but because of their unbelief, they will be judged.

C. Israel's Unbelief (9:30–10:21)

Israel pursued the **law of righteousness** but missed it (v.31). It is called **law of righteousness** because it showed the Israelites how to maintain the right relationship with God that was previously granted to them. Why did they miss it? **Because they pursued it not by faith but as if it were by works.** The phrase **"as if it were"** indicates their misunderstanding. They observed **the law** in order to put God under obligation to them. By insisting on their own way, **they stumbled over** Christ.

In 10:1–21 Paul explains the summary statement of 9:30–33. The zeal of Israel was **not based on knowledge. They did not know** God's way of granting the good standing of right relationship with him. They sought to achieve it in their own way and **did not submit to God's** way (10:2–3). Paul explains this in v.4. Christ is the goal, the intention, and the real meaning (*telos*, NIV **end**) of the law. Since the law points to Christ, righteousness is available to everyone who believes in him.

In 10:5–13 Paul explains v.4. The law says, **"The man who does these things will live by them"** (10:5; cf. Lev 18:5). Christ did fulfill the law, and he earned the status of righteousness and eternal life for himself and those who will believe in him (vv.6–13). Vv.6–13 demonstrate that the Gospel of righteousness by faith is included in the law. The quotation,

"Do not say in your heart" (v.6), is from Dt 8:17 and 9:4, which warn against presumptuous boasting in one's own achievement, merit, and which exhort trust in the Lord. This is completely in harmony with the righteousness by faith.

The rest of the quotation in 10:6–8 is from Dt 30:12–14, which states that the Israelites do not have to go to heaven or cross the sea to get the law. It has been given to them. Paul identifies this law with the message of righteousness by faith (v.8). Vv.9–10 give the content of this word of faith. Believing and confessing Jesus the Lord leads to salvation. Vv.11 and 13 quote Isa 28:16 and Joel 2:32 to substantiate this.

To call **upon the name of the Lord** (10:13), four conditions must be met: (1) Someone is sent, (2) someone preaches, (3) they hear, and (4) they believe (10:14–15a). The first condition has been met. There are those who bring good news (v.15b). The second has been met. The message has been proclaimed **through the word of Christ** (v.17). The third has been met (v.18b). Israel has heard and understood the message (vv.19b–20). The point of these OT quotations is this: If Gentiles, who are spiritually underprivileged, have come to know, surely Israel must have come to know the message. The fourth condition is not met. Israel has not believed (v.16). Therefore, Israel is clearly without excuse! V.21 concludes by quoting Isa 65:2 to bring Israel's rebellion into sharp focus, and at the same time, it sounds a note of hope.

D. Israel's Remnant (11:1–10)

God has not rejected Israel. Paul, himself an Israelite, is saved and is engaged in God's work. Just as in the days of Elijah, God has a **remnant** who are faithful to him. Israel sought righteous standing before God, but they did not obtain it. Only **the elect** obtain that righteousness.

Some understand **the elect** as those arbitrarily chosen by God for salvation (Murray, 2:71–72). The rest of the Israelites are rejected. This interpretation, however, contradicts 9:1–4; 10:21; and 11:20, where Paul explicitly states their unbelief as the reason for their rejection. The correct understanding of election is this: God collectively elected Israel. This was God's act of pure grace, not because of their works. However, the majority of them became unfaithful and missed out on God's blessings. Those who remained faithful received the blessings and became **the elect.** The hearts of **the others were hardened** in the same sense that Pharaoh's heart was hardened (see comment on 9:18).

E. Israel's Future Salvation (11:11–32)

Israel has stumbled, yet only temporarily. Her stumbling has become the occasion of the Gentiles' salvation. And this, in turn, will make Israel envious and ultimately will bring about her salvation. The remnant guarantees this (vv.11–16).

The **olive** tree represents God's people. Because of unbelief, **some branches are broken off.** Some Jews are not saved. Because of faith, some Gentiles are **grafted into** the **olive tree** to receive the blessings of salvation. However, if the Jews do not persist in unbelief, God can and will **graft them** back in. If the Gentiles do not remain in faith, God will **cut** them off. God will do this, but not because he is capricious. He has established the condition of salvation. Different human responses call forth God's different actions (vv.17–24).

Vv.25–32 disclose a mystery. Israel is hardened in part until the Gentiles as a whole are saved. This means there will be "a vast harvest among the heathens" (Wesley, *Notes,* 395). After that there will be a vast harvest among Israel. God's ultimate goal is to **have mercy on them all.** Through allowing human beings to exercise their freedom and his judicial act (1:24, 26, 28; 11:7), God brings this about. All human beings, both Jews and Gentiles, are imprisoned in their disobedience. They cannot escape, except through God's mercy, which releases them.

F. Concluding Doxology (11:33–36)

God uses even human rebellion to achieve his ultimate purpose in salvation. May God's wisdom be praised.

V. GOD'S RIGHTEOUSNESS IN DAILY CHRISTIAN LIFE (12:1–15:13)

Paul brings the doctrine to bear upon Christian daily life. The two sections are connected with **"therefore"** (12:1). They are causally related.

A. General Principle (12:1–2)

Vv.1–2 state the general principle of Christian conduct. On the basis of **God's mercy,** as presented in chs. 1–11, Paul urges Christians to **offer** their **bodies** to God as a sacrifice. Here Paul elaborates on 6:12–13, where **"body"** means "self," or "total person." Here **"bodies"** has the same meaning. When the principle of vv.1–2 is applied to the various circumstances in 12:3–15:13, it touches many aspects of our total person. The self we offer to God is to be **living, holy,** and **pleasing to God.**

"Living" means spiritually alive to God (cf. 6:13). That means to be responding to God, having active fellowship with him.

God is **holy** and anything or any

person related to him is holy (Nu 16:5). For moral beings, holiness also has ethical significance. "But just as he who called you is holy, so be holy in all you do; for it is written: 'Be holy, because I am holy'" (1Pe 1:15–16). Paul often uses "holiness" in the moral sense (cf. 1Co 6:9–11; 1Th 4:3; et al.), which means the absence of moral defilement.

V.2 spells out, in terms of daily living, the meaning of offering ourselves as sacrifices to God. We should **not conform** ourselves **to the pattern of this world** but be continually **transformed by the renewing of** our **minds.** Once our thoughts were filled with the points of view, the value scales of this world. These need to be replaced by those of the Bible. Then, and only after then, will we be able to discern (*dokimazō,* "to find out and then accept") what is the will of God, namely, what is good, acceptable (or pleasing to God), and perfect (RSV).

"**Good**," "**pleasing to God**," and "**perfect**" are the guidelines for discerning the will of God. In 12:3–15:13 Paul applies these guidelines to discern the will of God in different circumstances. He instructs us to take certain action because it is good (12:9, 21; 13:4; 14:16; 15:2), perfect (highest possibility), cf. 12:18), acceptable or pleasing to God (14:18).

What is "**good**" is helpful to people (12:20–21) and conforms to the moral standard revealed by God (2:10; 7:12, 19). "**Perfect**" means to use our gifts, resources, and opportunities for maximum effect in God's kingdom. (Cf. 12:18. Do your best, make the best effort to bring about the kingdom value.) What is **pleasing to God** can be found from the Bible.

B. Application to Particular Cases (12:3–15:13)

1. Ministries in the church (12:3–8)

In the church each member belongs to and needs all the others. Different members have different gifts. Paul writes, "**Do not think** [*phroneō*] **of yourself more highly than you ought, but rather think of yourself with sober judgment** [*sōphroneō*), in accordance with the measure of faith God has given you" (v.3). The verb *phroneō* ("think") occurs also in 8:5, "have their minds set on." It involves thinking, desiring, and acting. To **think with sober judgment** (*sōphroneō*) means to recognize our limits and respect them in desiring and acting. Do this with reference to **the measure of faith God has given you,** which means the gift assigned to you in the domain of **faith.**

Confine activity within the limits of your gift. If you have the gift of **prophesying,** prophesy. In prophesying, however, do it in the analogy (*analogia;* NIV **proportion**) of the **faith.** The prophet is not free to say whatever he wants. The message should be in harmony with the **faith,** that objective body of truth, the teachings of the Lord through the apostles (Wesley, *Notes,* 397). For this reason, the congregation needs to evaluate the message of the one prophesying (1Co 14:29).

If you have the gift of **serving, serve;** if the gift of **teaching, teach.** Use your gift to bring the maximum help to others, and do not go beyond your gift.

2. Love as the standard of Christian conduct (12:9–21)

All Christians should have love, manifested in **brotherly love** and in respecting one another (v.10). Vv.11–12 deal with the inner life of love; vv.13–21 with practical instructions on how to love brethren, strangers, and enemies.

3. Christian civil duties (13:1–10)

In 12:19–21 Paul advises not to take revenge but to leave matters with God, who will avenge. He does it through government. The rulers are God's **servants** to execute judgment (vv.4, 6). The government is established by God for the good of all. Therefore Christians should support it with **taxes** and submission.

Here Paul speaks in terms of the normative, assuming that the government is fulfilling the duty assigned by God (Morris, *Romans,* 459–61). He does not specifically deal with abnormal conditions, such as when the government usurps the absolute authority of God. However, if Paul's directive is carefully observed, his intent is clear. Paul exhorts submission (*hupotassō*), not absolute obedience. In Eph 5:21 Paul calls for Christians to submit (*hupotassō*) to one another. Constantly taking the lowly place over against one another is possible, but obeying one another constantly is not. Therefore, if the government no longer serves God and does what is contrary to God's will, we should, like the apostles in Ac 4:19, follow God rather than blindly obey the government (Bruce, 237).

Vv.8–10 deal with the issue of justice, though **love** is mentioned first. Yet here Paul does not mention the positive things **love** does, only the wrongs **love** does not do. Paul is not treating **love** per se, which has been treated already in 12:9–21. Here he is treating the Christian duty of justice. This is evident from v.8, **Let no debt remain outstanding**. Paul sees and treats **love** as the means of fulfilling justice. Since **love** does no harm to one's neighbor, **love** fulfills those negative commandments of the law. These commands have to do with justice in the society.

4. Christ's return and purity of life (13:11–14)

Our salvation (v.11) is the future salvation that will take place at the second coming of Christ. That day is near, at least nearer today **than when we first believed.** We should live in anticipation of that day and ethically live in such a way as though Christ had already come and were present with us.

5. Christian conscience (14:1–15:13)

Christians do not always agree on some issues in life that are not essential to the Christian faith. Paul instructs us in ways to handle this.

a. Not to judge one another (14:1–12)

The overscrupulous are **weak** in **faith.** Their **faith** is not strong enough to enable them to perceive the full liberty in Christ to partake of certain food. Since this is not an important issue in the kingdom of God (14:17), when opinions differ, neither side should criticize nor condemn the other. It is the Lord, not we, who judges. Each one is individually responsible to the Lord. Each of us has to give account of himself, not others, before the Lord.

b. Love as well as knowledge (14:13–23)

We know that all foods are clean; therefore, we may eat them. If, however, eating should cause the weaker Christian to stumble, we should abstain from eating in public. This is the principle of love. Those who have the knowledge and are strong in faith are blessed. They may enjoy their freedom in privacy (v.22). But the weak in the faith will experience self-condemnation if they eat (v.23).

c. Unity of the strong and the weak (15:1–13)

We should bear the failings of the weak. We should not please ourselves, but seek to **please** our neighbors **for** their **good.** Jesus set a good example for us in this regard. He did **not please himself** but sought to do God's will, even though that would incur the anger of his contemporaries (15:3). This is written in the Scripture to teach us and to serve as a means through which God gives us **endurance** and **encouragement** (vv.1–6).

We should **accept one another, just as Christ accepted** both Jews and Gentiles, according to the purpose of God. The OT quotations in vv.9–12 demonstrate that it was God's plan from the beginning to include both Jews and Gentiles in the plan of salvation (vv.7–13).

VI. Conclusion (15:14–16:27)

A. Paul's Ministry to the Gentiles (15:14–22)

Paul received God's **grace** to be a **minister to the Gentiles.** In stating the objectives of his mission, Paul indicates that sanctification, or holiness, is the central emphasis of his Gospel. He has fully proclaimed the Gospel **from Jerusalem to Illyricum,** the eastern region of the Roman Empire. Because he has been occupied with evangelizing the East, Paul has not come to Rome.

B. Paul's Plan to Visit Rome (15:23–33)

Since he has fully covered the East with the Gospel, Paul now looks toward the West and wants to go to **Spain** to minister. He hopes that before he goes to **Spain,** he can spend some time in Rome to establish a closer relationship with the Roman Christians. He also hopes that the Roman church can become his home base for his missionary work in the West, as Antioch was in the East.

During his missionary work, Paul urged gentile Christians to contribute to a fund to assist the saints in **Jerusalem.** This fund is now ready. Paul is about to start the journey to **Jerusalem** to deliver it. On the eve of his departure, Paul has two apprehensions. He is concerned that this fund be received in the right spirit. This represents the love of gentile believers for **the saints in Jerusalem.** Through this Paul wants to promote unity between gentile and Jewish Christians. But the Jewish Christians, particularly the Judaizers, may misinterpret Paul's intention and use it to promote their own cause. Second, he is concerned about his personal safety in Jerusalem. The Judaizers misunderstand and misinterpret his teaching on the law. They accuse him of desecrating the Mosaic Law. They may want to destroy him. Therefore, Paul requests the prayers of the Roman Christians. After he completes this mission, he will then come to Rome.

C. Personal Greetings (16:1–27)

Ro 16:1–2 commends **Phoebe** to the Romans. **Phoebe,** from nearby **Cenchrea,** is going to Rome. Paul takes this opportunity to send this epistle with her.

In 16:3–16 Paul sends greetings to certain people who probably had been with him in the East and later moved to Rome.

Toward the end of the letter, Paul probably took the pen from **Tertius** (v.22), his secretary, and wrote the words in 16:17–20. He cautions the Romans about heretics. One way to resist heretics is to understand and hold fast to the accepted doctrine. Another important step is to stay **away from them,** giving them no chance to spread their heresy (v.17). In this conflict with Satan, the victory will come from two sides: the one, divine (**God . . . will . . . crush**) and the other, human (**under your feet,** v.20). God gives strength, but we have to appropriate and use it. Paul concludes his own writing with a benediction (v.20).

In 16:21–24 those who are with Paul send greetings to the Roman Christians.

The entire epistle ends with the benediction and doxology of 16:25–27. Like the opening section of the epistle, this closing benediction and doxology include a statement about the Gospel.

BIBLIOGRAPHY

Barrett, C. K. *A Commentary on the Epistle to the Romans.* HNTC. New York: Harper, 1957. Reprint, Peabody, Mass.: Hendrickson, 1987.

Black, Matthew. *Romans.* NCBC. 2d ed. Grand Rapids: Eerdmans, 1989.

Bruce, F. F. *The Epistle of Paul to the Romans.* TNTC. Grand Rapids: Eerdmans, 1963.

Clarke, Adam. *The Holy Bible, Containing the Old and New Testaments, With a Commentary and Critical Notes.* 6 vols. Vol. 5. Romans. A New Edition. London: Ward, Lock & Co. Syracuse: Wesleyan Methodist Publishing Association, n.d.

Cranfield, C. E. B. *The Epistle to the Romans.* ICC. 2 vols. Edinburgh: T. & T. Clark, vol. 1, 1975; vol. 2, 1979.

Dayton, Wilbur. "Entire Sanctification as Taught in the Book of Romans." *Wesleyan Theological Journal,* vol. 1, no. 1 (Spring 1966), 7–10.

Dayton, Wilbur. *Romans.* WBC. Vol. 5. Grand Rapids: Baker, 1965–69.

Dodd, C. H., *The Epistle of Paul to the Romans.* MNTC. New York and London: Harper, 1932.

Greathouse, William M. *The Epistle to the Romans.* BBC. Vol. 8. Kansas City: Beacon Hill, 1968.

Guthrie, Donald. *New Testament Introduction.* Downers Grove, Ill.: InterVarsity Press, 1970.

Morris, Leon. *The Apostolic Preaching of the Cross.* Grand Rapids: Eerdmans, 1955.

_____. *The Epistle to the Romans.* Grand Rapids: Eerdmans, 1988.

Murray, John. *The Epistle to the Romans.* NICNT. 2 vols. Grand Rapids: Eerdmans, vol. 1, 1959; vol. 2, 1965.

Noth, Martin. *The Laws in the Pentateuch and Other Studies.* Translated by D. R. Ap-Thomas. Philadelphia: Fortress, 1967.

Nygren, Anders. *Commentary on Romans.* Translated by Carl C. Rasmussen. Philadelphia: Muhlenberg, 1949.

Wesley, John. *Explanatory Notes Upon the New Testament.* 16th ed. New York: Phillips & Hunt. Cincinnati: Cranston & Stowe, n.d.

_____. *A Plain Account of Christian Perfection.* Louisville: Pentecostal Publishing, n.d.

1 CORINTHIANS
George Lyons

INTRODUCTION

I. THE CITY AND ITS PEOPLE

A. Location

Corinth is strategically located on the narrow isthmus connecting the Peloponnesus and the Greek mainland.

B. History

New Corinth was founded in 44 B.C. as a Roman colony to serve as a residence for freedmen from Rome. During the first century A.D., Corinth was the third largest city in the Roman Empire and was probably no more depraved than any other city of its time. Archaeologists have identified twenty-six sacred places devoted to various "gods" and "lords" in the remains of first-century Corinth.

C. Demographics

Corinth was a virtual salad bowl of diverse influences from East and West: Roman laws, culture, and religion; Greek religion, philosophy, and art; mystery cults from Egypt and Asia; some Jews and their religion. Corinth's wealthy citizens lived alongside the poor majority, consisting of artisans, freedmen, and slaves. Sincere itinerant philosophers and unscrupulous charlatans proclaimed their messages side by side in the streets of the city.

II. THE CHURCH AND ITS PROBLEMS

The evidence of Ac 18:1–8 and 1 Corinthians suggests that "the church was in many ways a mirror of the city" (Fee, 3). The majority of its members were Gentiles, former idolaters, largely of lower socioeconomic status. The heterogeneous mix of Jew, Greek, slave, free, rich, and poor inevitably led to tensions and internal rivalries. We cannot reconstruct the specific Corinthian situation with precision. First Corinthians, an ad hoc response to serious problems in the church, was probably written in the spring of A.D. 54–57. Paul's knowledge of the situation depended on oral reports and a letter from the church.

III. LITERARY UNITY OF 1 AND 2 CORINTHIANS

By ancient standards both 1 and 2 Corinthians are unusually long letters. The diversity of subjects treated and the abrupt transitions from one subject to another have lead some scholars to propose that both are composite editorial compilations of several Pauline letters. Although most scholars today consider 1 Corinthians to be a unified composition, perhaps the majority of serious scholars today doubt the literary integrity of 2 Corinthians. In this commentary both letters are treated as unified compositions.

IV. OCCASION AND PURPOSE

First Corinthians is Paul's third contact with this church. The first was his founding visit. The second, an earlier letter, dealt with serious moral problems among community members. The third, 1 Corinthians, was occasioned by disturbing news from Corinth: oral reports from believers of Chloe's household; a letter from the church; and the visit of Stephanas, Fortunatus, and Achaicus.

The most serious problem was division within the church. Paul first asserts his apostolic leadership in order to convince the Corinthians to end their divisions and change their theology and behavior to conform with his. Then he responds to the questions raised in their letter to him. Paul repeatedly challenges the Corinthians' arrogant understanding of themselves and of Christian spirituality, which were expressed in various theological aberrations.

V. THEOLOGICAL RELEVANCE OF 1 AND 2 CORINTHIANS

Paul's letters to the Corinthians retain a remarkable degree of contemporary relevance. The cosmopolitan setting of the church, the individualism of its members and their behavioral aberrations, its arrogant spirituality, and its accommodation to culture strikingly mirror today's church. Paul's guidance is still up to date, particularly the call for discipleship modeled after the weakness of Christ, love, edification in worship, and permanent marriages. Though nearly two millennia have passed, Paul's call for eschatological urgency is still timely. Even if we are not persuaded that the end of the world is at hand, our lives are too short to be lived for lesser values. Paul spells out the paradoxical implications of the good news of a crucified Messiah, who brings reconciliation to God by means of suffering and death. Paul's personal mode of ministry, marked by weakness, and his Gospel of the Crucified One are totally consistent. Just as God raised Christ from the dead, Paul expected God to vindicate his own Christlike ministry. His opposition to the gospel of success and to its superministers arises from their proclamation of "another Jesus." As we eavesdrop on these ancient letters, we do so with the expectation that we may learn how to translate our theological commitments into a style of ministry that is consistent with, not a compromise of, the Gospel we proclaim.

VI. OUTLINE

COMMENTARY

I. LETTER OPENING (1:1–9)

A. Prescript (1:1–3)

That the Corinthians were **sanctified in Christ Jesus and called to be holy** (v.2) implies only that their calling had set them apart from the world to be numbered among the people of the Holy One.

B. Thanksgiving (1:4–9)

Paul's guarded thanks prepares us for his subsequent discussions of the Corinthians' spiritual gifts in the areas of speech, knowledge, and power. His emphasis on the future hope anticipates his attention to eschatology.

II. ABANDON YOUR ARROGANCE (1:10–4:21)

The opening appeal in 1Co 1:10 comes earlier than in any other Pauline letter. Here Paul begs his hearers to turn from division to unity. In subsequent appeals he urges them to imitate his example of humility as modeled by Timothy (4:16–17) and to follow the servant leadership of Stephanas, a Corinthian believer (16:15–16). At the root of their division is the problem of arrogance (see 4:18–19; 5:2), evidenced in their tolerance of immorality.

A. Appeal for Unity (1:10–17)

Paul does not explicitly say that the Corinthians are divided, only that there are quarrels among them. Their need for restoration to unity implies its absence. Apparently the Corinthians gave special allegiance to the leader who baptized them (1:14–17), as in the mystery religions. Paul's goal was less to destroy all factions than to end factionalism. Furthermore, the contrast between baptism and preaching should not be overemphasized; the real contrast is between the humbling message of the Cross and the arrogance of wisdom.

B. The Gospel (1:18–2:5)

The Gospel of Christ in its three major facets is the subject of 1:18–2:5: (1) the essential content of its message (vv.18–25), (2) the character of its recipients (vv.26–31), and (3) the conduct of the messenger (2:1–5). In each aspect, the logic of the Gospel defies human wisdom and conventional expectations.

C. The Problem (2:6–3:4)

Paul's diagnosis of the Corinthians' problem challenges their arrogant self-estimate by means of irony. They are not as mature or spiritual as they imagine. Paul should not be taken to imply that there are two orders of Christians: the **mature** (2:6) or **spiritual** (3:1), and the **worldly** or **infants** (3:1). He apparently adopts Corinthian language here to challenge their arrogant self-image. In the mystery religions the word **mature** (*teleios*, "perfect") referred to the fully initiated as opposed to merely casual adherents (see Php 3:12–15). The claim to be **spiritual** may have involved an inflated notion of one's status and security as a Christian, like the one who mistakenly "thinks he knows something" (1Co 8:2) or who thinks he is standing firm (10:12; see Gal 6:1–5).

D. The Solution (3:5–4:17)

It is to the arrogant attitude of partisanship that Paul next turns. He proposes partnership as the solution to the Corinthians' problem. Paul offers them an alternative way to understand themselves and their leaders—as servants of God. Cooperation is to replace competition. Suffering servanthood, not success, is to be their aim.

E. Transition: Preparation for Paul's Visit (4:18–21)

This section is a crucial transition from Paul's discussion in chs. 1–4 to that in chs. 5–16. The behavioral issues he addresses in the subsequent chapters seem to be specific manifestations of the Corinthian arrogance he attacks and warns them to forsake in the preceding chapters. Paul expects them to resolve these issues before he visits Corinth again. Their response to his warnings will determine whether he comes with severity or with gentleness. In 2 Corinthians we learn that their continuing arrogance made this visit extremely unpleasant for both Paul and them.

Timothy was not only to remind the Corinthians of Paul's positive example, but to embody his warning to them to forsake their arrogant lifestyle in favor of his humble example. They not only have Paul's representative and this letter to reckon with, but the apostle himself. His visit will verify whether their high claims conform with reality or are merely empty boasts. Are they only talk or also power (4:19)? Paul's visit will determine whether **the kingdom of God** is already here or not (4:20; see Ro 5:17).

III. ATTENTION TO PROBLEMS (5:1–16:12)

Corinthian arrogance is manifested in paradoxical ways. They are at once reluctant to judge serious wrongdoers within the congregation (ch. 5) and anxious to take Christians guilty of petty grievances before pagan courts (6:1–8). Some visit prostitutes (vv.9–20), while others consider marital intercourse a sin (7:1–40). Some are so strong as to disdain idols as nothing, others so weak as to have scruples

about eating meat once offered to idols (chs. 8–10). They are zealous for some traditions and flaunt others; they celebrate the Lord's Supper, but not really (ch. 11). They are infatuated with spiritual gifts, yet they have no understanding of their purpose (chs. 12–14). They deny the future resurrection of the dead while practicing baptism in behalf of the dead (ch. 15). Not surprisingly, Paul urges them to mend their ways before his next visit (ch. 16).

A. Immorality: Incest (5:1–13)

The Corinthians' toleration of intolerable immorality in their midst threatens the church's existence as a community. Thus Paul calls for drastic, immediate, and thorough response: Get rid of the evildoer.

B. Lawsuits (6:1–8)

The issue here as in ch. 5 is the Corinthians' failure to exercise proper judgment. Both passages insist upon the competence of Christians to judge wrongdoing. In ch. 5 judgment implies the necessary condemnation of sinning believers; in ch. 6 judgment implies the unfortunate necessity of deciding between competing claims of believers. Paul apparently shares the Jewish apocalyptic view that believers at the eschaton will judge the world (Da 7:22; Wis. 3:8; Mt 19:28; Lk 22:30). Thus they must be more than competent to judge misdemeanors.

Legal disputes between members of the Christian community were being taken into the civil courts. Paul is distressed that they paraded their disharmonies before the ungodly public instead of arbitrating them internally, which was the normal practice in Jewish communities (Héring, 39). No matter who wins the case, the very existence of public lawsuits among Christians is a moral defeat for the church. In the interests of the Christian community, Paul urges them to put aside their personal grievances, to forgive, and to surrender their rights rather than fight for them. To accept being wronged is better than to wrong, particularly fellow Christians.

C. Transition: The Unrighteous (6:9–11)

In both 6:1 and 6:9 Paul mentions the *adikoi*, the "ungodly," or **wicked** (NIV). Those to whom the Corinthians have appealed for judgment are doomed; they will not inherit **the kingdom of God** (6:9–10). Paul's list of unrighteous people emphasizes sexual and social vices. He reminds his readers that they were once just such ungodly people, but God completely changed them. Paul describes their thorough regeneration as being washed, sanctified, and justified. This sequence presents no problem to the Wesleyan order of salvation (Clarke, 6:217–18; Wesley, *Notes* on 6:11). "The three verbs do not seem to denote three stages but three aspects of the Holy Spirit's action" (Héring, 42). The Corinthians were forgiven of their sins, set apart as God's people, and put into a right relationship with him. These are three concomitant, redemptive, divine acts—conceived as the work of God the Father, the Lord Jesus Christ, and the Spirit. Thus here sanctification denotes, not entire, but initial sanctification.

D. Immorality: Prostitution (6:12–20)

Paul's quotation of the same slogan in 6:12 and 10:23, **Everything is permissible,** suggests that there is some kind of inner connection within chs. 6–10 (Conzelmann, 109). Paul accepts and modifies what must have

been a Corinthian motto. He concedes, "That's true, but. . . ."

Paul urges his hearers to continue to **flee from sexual immorality** (v.18), and provides several reasons for sexual purity. Sexual sins are especially sinful because they are inherently self-destructive (see Pr 6:23–35; Sir 23:16). Paul rejects the notion, held by sophisticated pagans in his day and ours, that what one does with one's body is one's own business. On the contrary, he reminds his readers that their bodies are temples of the Holy Spirit. Unlike 3:16, here Paul refers to the individual bodies of his hearers as dwelling places of the Holy Spirit, whose holy presence demands individual lives of sexual purity (see 1Th 4:3–8).

God's gift to believers places a claim on their lives: **You were bought at a price** (6:20; see 7:23). The mercantile imagery of the transfer of slaves underlies this claim. Paul's anthropology leaves no room for the notion of absolute freedom. Human beings always live under the influence of one lordship or another. We are not free to be free but to choose our master. Sinners are helpless slaves to sin. As believers, we are not our own property; we belong to God. Since he is our Lord, we are to honor him with our bodies.

In the Wesleyan tradition this passage has a long history of application to personal vices beyond the sexual realm. And rightly so; fornication is not the only sin we may commit against our own bodies. The lordship of Christ requires us to put aside every "right" that threatens to compromise our exclusive bodily allegiance to him. It is not enough simply to abstain from evil; we are to praise God by the active giving of ourselves to his service in daily life.

E. Sex, Marriage, and Celibacy (7:1–40)

Paul's total rejection of sexual immorality is the necessary preparation for his treatment of the appropriate place of sex within marriage. It is unnecessary to assume that either sexual indulgence or asceticism was widely practiced within the Corinthian community. Paul's customary approach to ethical instruction is moderation, the middle course between legalism and license. The crucial issue here is not marriage per se but the place of sex within marriage. Some Corinthians concluded that sex itself, even within the bond of marriage, was sinful. Paul's goal is to exclude this misunderstanding without opening the door to another. His pastoral counsel on the subject of sexuality is both grounded on clearly articulated principles and realistically adapted to various groups within the church.

Paul's own singleness and his rigorous rejection of sexual immorality perhaps led some Corinthians to assume that he was sympathetic with the slogan, **It is good for a man not to marry** (v.1). But his mention of their letter at this point makes it likely that they, not he, were responsible for the slogan.

It is striking that nowhere in Paul's discussion does he mention a major consideration in modern discussions of marriage and sex—mutual love. Equally striking, however, is the prominence he assigns the mutuality of marriage, balancing his advice to men with similar advice to women. This egalitarian stance resists both conventional first-century practice and contemporary ultraconservative Christian assumptions.

Paul opens ch. 7 with a discussion of the power and propriety of sex (vv.1–7). Throughout the chapter he applies the principle of the status quo (vv.17–24) to each of the groups within the church. By this principle Paul urges his hearers not to seek to change their marital status. Because believers belong to God regardless of their social status, they must not allow dissatisfaction with their lot in life to become an enslaving preoccupation (vv.23–24). His advice is also predicated upon the assumption that the time is short (vv.25–31). In light of the hastening end of history, all worldly relationships are relativized. Paul recommends not ascetic retreat from earthly life, but paradoxical detachment from even legitimate earthly preoccupations.

Paul addresses his advice to the single (vv.8–9), to the married (vv.10–11), to those married to non-Christians (vv.12–16), and to the virgins (vv.25–35). Paul's lengthy counsel to this last group suggests that their situation was in need of particular attention. If these virgins are engaged people (v.36), the status quo principle would seem to trap them in a kind of limbo between single and married life. Paul summarizes his concerns in the conclusion of the chapter (vv.36–40), explaining the circumstances under which men and women should or should not marry.

The status quo principle arises from early Christian apocalyptic convictions, not from any fundamental commitment to social conservatism. Paul believed that by the intervention of God the world was about to end (see 7:26, 29a, 31b; 10:11). The continuation of the world for nearly two millennia may explain why few Christians today feel bound by Paul's preference for celibacy. But even if we admit that he was shortsighted in his imminent eschatology, his more basic conviction that life is too short for trivial pursuits stands. We can agree that **many troubles in this life** are avoidable, without concluding that marriage is the occasion of such troubles (7:28b). Those who lack the gift of celibacy can still appreciate Paul's pastoral concern to spare his converts needless grief (vv.32–35). The "as if not" existence Paul recommends in 7:29–31, not the single state, is his prescription for freedom from concerns (v.32). Engaged people need not be anxious about whether to marry or remain single. Both states are equally good.

F. Food Sacrificed to Idols (8:1–11:1)

The shift from sexual issues in chs. 5–7 to food sacrificed to idols in chs. 8–10 appears abrupt at first glance. But in ancient practice idolatry and immorality were inevitably linked (see 5:9–11; 6:9–10). The introductory formula (**now about**) in 8:1 and 7:1 seems to indicate that both topics were raised in the Corinthians' letter to Paul.

Despite the new topic, Paul's approach is thoroughly consistent with the tone and argumentative approach of the rest of the letter. He quotes the slogan **We all possess knowledge** (8:1), and, like earlier slogans, immediately relativizes it by appealing to superior principles. The opening chapters of the letter prepare us to expect Paul's devaluation of alleged human knowledge. The presumptuous claim of knowledge makes people arrogant (**puffs up**, NIV; cf. 4:19; 5:2). **Love is not arrogant** (13:4); on the contrary, **love builds up** (8:1). A commitment to building up other people challenges the slogan that **everything is permissible** (10:23; see 6:12; 8:9). Similarly, "building up" is a significant criterion in Paul's assessment of spiritual gifts in ch. 14 (seven times; see also 3:9–16).

In 1Co 8–10 Paul addresses three distinct issues related to the general subject of food sacrificed to idols: eating sacrificial food at pagan temples (8:9–13; 10:14–22); purchasing for home consumption the same food sold in the marketplace (10:25–26); eating this food in the home of an unbeliever (vv.27–30).

Paul's lengthy discussions of his surrendered apostolic rights in ch. 9 is not intended to defend his challenged apostolic status. His positive example illustrates and substantiates his reasoning in chs. 8–10, which significantly, concludes with an appeal for the Corinthians to imitate his example (11:1). Israel's negative example in ch. 10 challenges the Corinthians' false sense of security and impresses on them the serious consequences of irresponsible behavior—the risk of forfeiting their salvation.

Paul's insistence on the centrality of the love ethic historically has found a sympathetic hearing among Wesleyans. Orthodox knowledge cannot displace the priority of love. This stance is not antiintellectual; it is prorelational. Communal responsibilities take precedence over individual rights. Traditionally, Wesleyans have been more likely to err on the side of legalism than of license. Thus we should note Paul's intention not to put anyone in bondage to another's overly scrupulous conscience. Today some Christians seem to have become so "enlightened" that, like the Corinthians, they take offense at Paul's insistence that there are absolutes. We all need to be reminded that love may call us to surrender our personal rights in the interests of communal needs.

Paul's shift to the first person singular in 8:13 provides the necessary transition from his critique of the Corinthians' insistence on their rights to the presentation of his personal example of not exercising his apostolic rights. The key issue is not apostleship (see 9:1, 2, 5), but freedom/rights (9:1, 4, 5, 6, 12 [twice], 18, 19). Although in this section the issue of food sacrificed to idols moves into the background, it is never out of sight. The function of ch. 9 is to substantiate and illustrate Paul's argument as to the proper approach to eating food offered to idols in ch. 8 on other, presumably less sensitive, grounds. His example of foregoing personal rights as a concession to the needs of others urges the Corinthians to put aside their alleged right to continue to frequent pagan cultic meals in the interests of their fellow believers.

Paul rehearses Israel's disobedience in the wilderness as an example of behavior the Corinthians are not to imitate. This serves as a typological warning that even the "knowledgeable" Corinthians might fail to obtain eschatological salvation. Christian liberty unchecked may deteriorate into license and endanger not only the weak but the strong Christian as well. Repeatedly Paul challenges the imagined security of his enlightened hearers.

Paul concludes his arguments against idolatry begun in 8:1 with this final exhortation. He repeats the slogan quoted earlier (10:23; cf. 6:12) before amending it in 10:24. The correction (**but not everything is constructive**) connects this passage closely with Paul's repeated concern for building up others (8:1, 10; 14:3, 4, 5, 10, 17, 26).

Although Paul agrees in principle with "the knowledgeable," he spells out conditions under which meat possibly offered to idols may be eaten or should be refused (10:25–30). He urges his hearers to eat to the glory of God and, like him, to take care not to cause fellow Christians to sin (vv.31–32; cf. 8:13). He recommends his personal example of pleasing everyone in every way by not seeking his own advantage (10:33; cf. v.24) and concludes his exhortation in 11:1 with a call to

imitate his Christlike model (cf. Ro 15:1–3, 7–8).

Paul urges readers to renounce their personal rights in the interests of what is **beneficial** (10:23; cf. 6:12; 12:7) or **constructive** (10:23; cf. 3:9–14; 8:1, 10; 14:3, 4, 5, 10, 17, 26). **Love** and "building up" are more crucial than **knowledge** and **rights.** Their insistence upon their right to eat **food sacrificed to idols** is only one expression of their fundamental misunderstanding of the Christian life. The issue is not with specific terms or issues, but the difference between a self- and other-centered approach to life. **Nobody should seek his own good, but the good of others** (10:24; see v.33; 13:5; 14:12).

Paul is not prepared to sacrifice personal freedom for petty reasons. Nevertheless, he is more than willing freely to surrender it for the good of others. His concern here is to distinguish between situations when freedom may operate and when it must be relinquished. In 10:25–27 Paul explains when one is free to eat; in 10:28–30 he explains when one is free to refrain.

Much of the food available in meat markets throughout the Greco-Roman world had once been offered in pagan sacrifices to idols. Paul considers the prior history of the food one eats totally irrelevant. He rejects the Jewish requirement to investigate the source of the meat. Freedom prevails since God is its ultimate source (10:26; citing Ps 24:1). In 10:25–27 two issues are held together by their shared advice, in effect, "Don't ask whether the food was previously offered in a sacrifice to an idol. It is not a moral issue." Although Paul forbids eating at pagan temples (10:1–22), here he insists that the issue is not food itself but the situation in which it is eaten. In religiously neutral situations, the source of the food is a matter of indifference.

Paul cites two examples of such situations: the public meat market where food is purchased for home consumption and private meals in a nonbeliever's home. Because the origin of meat market food is irrelevant, and because the sanctity of Christians is not threatened by association with unbelievers (see 7:12–16; 9:20–22), the same advice applies at a private meal in the home of an unbeliever: **Eat . . . without raising questions of conscience** (10:27; cf. v.25). If, however, an unbeliever tells Christians in either situation, **This has been offered in sacrifice,** they must not eat it (v.28). The pagan world was fully aware of Jewish scruples over such food. If the unbeliever felt compelled to warn Christians of the origin of the food, they were not to offend his expectations of them (Fee, 485).

In 10:29b–30 Paul turns from the second person plural imperative (vv.25–29a) to the first person singular. He defends not his past conduct, but Christian freedom. Christian freedom is not restricted by the conscience of another person. What is a moral issue to one person is not necessarily so to another. Christians refrain from eating in certain situations, not because the information someone supplies changes the character of the food, but because it changes the character of the situation. I am free to eat anything because I give thanks to God for the food. But I am free to refuse to eat out of concern for my informants because I put their interests ahead of mine (v.24).

In 10:31–11:1 Paul concludes and summarizes his discussion of food sacrificed to idols (chs. 8–10), expanding the implications of the issue to include not only eating and drinking but **whatever you do** (10:31). Ultimately, his concern is not to restrict his hearers' freedom, but to turn them from preoccupation with their rights to two decisive principles. First, everything must be done "for the glory of God" (v.31). Second, nothing must be done to cause another to sin (v.32; cf. 8:9). His restriction of his personal rights in the interests of others is the basis for his concluding appeal: "Follow my example, as I follow the example of Christ" (11:1; see Ro 15:1–3).

G. Worship (11:2–14:40)

Paul addresses three issues related to Corinthian worship practices: the role of women (11:2–16), the celebration of the Lord's Supper (vv.17–34), and the understanding and exercise of spiritual gifts (chs. 12–14). Although he begins by commending the Corinthians' observance of his instructions (11:2), he soon moves to condemnation (vv.17, 22).

1. Men and women in church (11:2–16)

Every translation of this passage assumes answers to questions whose answers are widely disputed. What is the metaphorical sense of the term *head* in 11:3–5? Is a **covered** head (11:4, 5, 6, 7, 13, 15) one partially wrapped by a cloth shawl, concealed by long as opposed to short hair, or with hair arranged on top of the head or braided as opposed to loosed? What were the customary hairstyles of Greeks, Romans, and Jews; rich and poor; men and women; in public, private, and religious settings; and in different geographical areas? What is the precise cultural significance in Paul's day of a woman's covered head?

Paul assumes that culturally appropriate modes of dress are not to be lightly flaunted by Christians. But since customs differ significantly historically and geographically, the specific contemporary relevance of this passage may be debated.

2. Abuse of the Lord's Supper (11:17–34)

For all the strangeness of the previous section, this one suffers for the opposite reason. Our familiarity with the words of institution of the Lord's Supper may let us miss the reason Paul cites them here. The Corinthian observance of the sacrament was so far removed from the reality it symbolized that their **meetings do more harm than good** (v.17) and their communal meals do not deserve the name *Lord's* Supper (v.20).

Paul tells the Corinthians that obvious social divisions **when you come together** destroy the unity the Lord's Supper celebrates so that it ceases to be **the Lord's** (v.20) and is merely your own supper (v.21). The Greek word for supper identifies "the main meal in the Hellenistic world, usually eaten toward or in the evening" (Fee, 539, n. 43) or a cultic meal held in honor of a deity (Conzelmann, 195, n. 21). Early Christians apparently observed the Lord's Supper either as or in connection with a full regular meal.

When Paul objects to the Corinthian observance of the Lord's Supper, his goal is not to separate the sacrament from meals designed to satisfy hunger nor to urge them to use grape juice instead of real wine. His concern in 11:21b is not to attack the problem of starvation or drunkenness, but Corinthian excesses. Some do not have enough to eat and drink while others overdo both. Paul's concern is not with Corinthian table etiquette but with their practice, which, by humiliating **those who have nothing,** abuses **the church of God** (v.22).

Paul does not directly address the structural problem of the inequitable distribution of wealth (see v.22). But neither does he get lost in petty symptomatic issues (vv.22, 34). He does not lecture the rich on the sin of gluttony, nor the poor on the virtues of frugality and industry. But he will not countenance the parading in church of the social and economic distinctions his class-conscious hearers took for granted. When the classes came together, it was customary for those of the higher classes to eat from a better menu, with larger portions, and in an inner dining room while the lower classes ate inferior and inadequate fare in an outdoor courtyard (Fee, 534–45). Corinthian toleration of such class distinctions within the church indicates that they misunderstand the unity the Lord's Supper celebrates. Indirectly Paul's call for self-emptying, not self-exaltation, attacks the class system in a way that few Christians have fully appropriated.

Paul takes for granted that the church is a heterogeneous entity. His solution is not one church for the rich, another for the poor; one for Jews, another for Gentiles. Unity in Christ counts for nothing if it merely accommodates existing distinctions as the Corinthians are doing. His challenge to their abuse would seem to reject the homogeneous unit principle of the modern Church-Growth Movement as a mission strategy. This is not to say that it does not work; it may work simply because it allows the church to be conformed to the world's patterns. The question is not, Does it grow a *church*? but, Is the *church* it grows Christian? Do we celebrate the *Lord's* Supper or our own?

"The verbs 'received' and 'passed on' . . . are technical terms from Paul's Jewish heritage for the transmission of religious instruction" (Fee, 548). In 11:23–26 Paul appeals to tradition to explain why he is displeased with the Corinthian observance of the Supper (see vv.2, 17, 22). Their abuse is not in the frequency of their celebration. The term *whenever* (vv.25, 26) assumes that the Supper should be perpetually observed but does not prescribe how often. We can only guess what Paul might say about the typical infrequency of the Supper's celebration in churches of the Wesleyan tradition.

Paul's formation of the Lord's Supper tradition is not exactly like any of the other three versions in the NT (note esp. 1Co 11:26). Only Luke and Paul mention Jesus' command for repetition of the Supper, **Do this in remembrance of me** (Lk 22:19; 1Co 11:24–25). These distinctive features may explain why Paul reminds his hearers of familiar tradition (11:23). His reference to the historical setting for the first Lord's Supper **on the night he was betrayed** (v.23) recalls that it was "one of us" who handed Jesus over to his enemies. What a poignant reminder of our continuing need for the gift of new life and forgiveness the Supper celebrates (Fee, 549)!

The Corinthians seem to have forgotten why they observed the Supper. Because it was intended as a reminder of Jesus' self-sacrificing death in their behalf, their self-centered observance unworthily memorialized the Lord's body and blood (see v.27). Their arrogance (4:8–10) exposed their forgetfulness of its intention to point them beyond the salvation begun in **the Lord's death** to its future culmination in his second coming (11:26). Their social elitism abused one another, the sacrament, the church, and the Lord. It neglected the very point of Christ's death—to create one new people, in which distinctions based on human fallenness no longer mattered (Fee, 557–58). Thus it was not the Lord's

Supper they celebrated (v.20) but their "own supper" (v.21 NRSV).

The Corinthians observed the Supper **in an unworthy manner** (11:27). "Worthiness" is not concerned with one's spiritual status but with one's attitude in observing the sacrament (Conzelmann, 202, n. 108). Paul calls for self-examination (v.28), not morbid introspection, as the means of worthily observing the Lord's Supper. We examine ourselves that our observance of the sacrament may be consistent with its intention. Though unworthy, we may observe the Supper in a manner that worthily reflects our grasp of its significance, **for us** (see v.24). The question is not Are we worthy? but Does our celebration proclaim Christian faith and unity?

Failure to judge ourselves will result in divine judgment (11:29–34). Paul does not imply that sickness and death come as God's judgment on especially unworthy observers of the Supper. Rather he calls his hearers to consider these sicknesses as divine discipline, intended to spare the church as a whole from the coming condemnation of the world (Fee, 565–66).

3. Other directions (11:34b)

We can only guess what **further directions** Paul has in mind. Further instructions concerning the Lord's Supper? rich-poor relations? the proper conduct of worship in church assemblies? other traditions? Such passages should give us a greater sense of modesty in asserting with overconfidence our interpretations of the rest of the letter. We are, after all, reading someone else's mail.

4. Spiritual gifts (12:1–14:40)

Paul continues his treatment of problems related to Corinthian corporate worship practices (see 14:19, 23, 26)

begun in 8:1. It is generally assumed that the crucial issue here is glossolalia, the phenomenon of speaking in tongues. If so, Paul's approach is indirect, for he discusses spiritual gifts in general (ch. 12) and theologically assesses their significance (ch. 13) before addressing the use of **tongues** (ch. 14).

a. Spiritual gifts (12:1–31)

Paul seems to use synonymously the terms *pneumatika,* literally "spiritual things," and *charismata,* "gifts" (see 1:7; 12:31; 14:1), to refer to special endowments or manifestations of the Holy Spirit. Assuming that the repeated expression, **Now about . . .** (12:1; see 7:1, 25; 8:1; 16:1), refers to the Corinthians' letter to him, it was they who raised the issue.

"Inspired" speech was a normal feature of pagan worship and probably a part of the Corinthians' pre-Christian experience. As pagans they were once **somehow or other . . . led astray to mute idols** (v.2), perhaps even "inspired" to curse Jesus (v.3). The fact of inspiration, being **influenced and led** (v.2), is no evidence that one is either spiritual or Christian. The content of inspiration is the crucial criterion, specifically the confession that Jesus is Lord (v.3; see Ro 10:9).

Paul emphasizes the need for diversity in the Christian assembly. Although God is one, he gives different gifts to the church (vv.4–11). Although the human body is one, its parts are many and varied (vv.12–26). Although the church is to be united, it should be characterized not by uniformity but by a diversity of gifts (vv.27–31).

Paul challenges the mind-set of the self-preoccupied, self-important, and self-sufficient, who stand aloof from and unconcerned for others in the community (v.25). Every member of the body is indispensable (vv.21–24a). Paul calls for **equal concern** (v.25)— that is, a mutuality in which every member shares the weakness and the strength, the honor and the shame of the others (v.26; see vv.22–24; see 7:32–34). Here it is probably the perception of unequally distributed spiritual gifts rather than unequally distributed wealth and social status (11:17–34) that Paul addresses.

Paul probably would take issue with modern charismatics who overly emphasize tongues. But what would he say to Wesleyans, who seem all too ready to tell their theological cousins, **I don't need you!** (see 12:21). Clearly he would disapprove of the divisive tactics of tongues-speakers in noncharismatic churches who destroy church unity. But he also reminds those inclined to amputate other body parts of God's intention **that there should be no division in the body** (v.25).

The point of Paul's rhetorical questions in 12:29–30 is more obvious than that of his ordered list in v.28. The grammatical form of each question implies a negative answer. Not everyone is an apostle, prophet, teacher, miracle worker, healer, tongues-speaker, or tongues-interpreter. The diversity of the Spirit's gifts implies that not all possess the same gift. Thus tongues cannot be considered evidence of the infilling with the Holy Spirit, nor can any other gift. Paul's point is to deny the uniformity of the Spirit's operation and to affirm the diversity of his gifts.

b. Love: The more excellent way (13:1–13)

Ch. 13 presents in three parts the excellence of Christian love personified by comparison to every gift and all other human values. The first (13:1–3) explains love's necessity; the second (vv.4–7) describes its activity; the third (vv.8–13) affirms its eternity and superiority to all other values. The conclusion to ch. 12 and the introduction to ch. 14 suggest that ch. 13 is something of a parenthesis within the apostle's argument. But it is neither irrelevant nor independent of its context. It refers both forward and backward in the logic of Paul's treatment of spiritual gifts and has numerous points of contact with the earlier chapters as well. Parts one and three are intelligible only in their present context, and part two, which is a self-contained unit, is most appropriate in the Corinthian setting (Fee, 626, n. 2; and 627, n. 9; contra Conzelmann, 218).

(1) The necessity of love (13:1–3)

The singular point of this paragraph is that no spiritual gift nor any other human achievement, for that matter, is evidence of the Spirit-filled life; Christian love is. These achievements refer back to four gifts mentioned in ch. 12: tongues, prophecy, knowledge, and faith. The form of each construction is nearly identical.

(2) The activity of love (13:4–7)

With a series of fifteen verbs Paul describes what love **is** and **is not,** and **does** and **does not** do. The vices contrary to love mentioned here appear elsewhere in the letter as characteristics of the Corinthians, whereas the virtues never describe them. Paul employs the literary device of personification to suggest that a person who loves demonstrates it by selfless actions, marked by patience, kindness, etc. That is, if I have love, I am not proud or arrogant. If, on the contrary, I am easily angered and keep a record of wrongs, I do not have love. Love is not one of many virtues; it embodies them all. Love is not merely the doing of some heroic or

virtuous action or refraining from vices or evil deeds. It is a "way" of life (12:31b).

(3) The eternity of love (13:8–13)

Love is superior to all other attributes or achievements because it **never fails** (13:8a). Of the familiar Christian triad—faith, hope, and love—which comprehends Christian existence as a whole for the present, love is **the greatest** (v.13), for it lasts forever. When the future age comes in its fullness, faith and hope will give way to sight (see Ro 4:14–22; 8:24–25). Then will remain only love, intimate, personal relationship with God (v.12). All that is partial and imperfect will disappear when the age to come dawns in perfection (vv.9–10). Just as the speech, the thoughts, and the reasoning of childhood are abandoned when one reaches adulthood, so the partial and indirect knowledge of the present will give way to full and intimate knowledge of God in the coming age (vv.11–12). Spiritual gifts, which now mediate the life of God to the community, will no longer be necessary when **I shall know fully, even as I am fully known** (v.12).

Paul's lengthy "digression" on love prepares for ch. 14, providing the rationale for Paul's preference for prophecy over tongues. Spiritual gifts are meaningful only within a community in which love for others, not self-interest, dominates. Love is not an end in itself. Its excellence resides in its ability to build up others (see 8:1). The effectiveness of prophecy as an instrument of love upbuilding the church is the basis for Paul's preference of it to tongues (14:3, 4, 5, 12, 17, 26).

Ch. 13 is a forceful critique of arrogant Corinthian spirituality. Paul does not deny the genuineness of spiritual gifts, but he dismisses their value as evidence of spiritual superiority. Submission to the lordship of Christ, not inspiration, is the hallmark of spiritual people (12:1–3). Holy love, not gifts, is the one essential evidence of the Spirit-filled life (Ch. 13; 8:1; 16:14). Ch. 13 prepares for the central emphasis of ch. 14: Clear, intelligible communication, not confusion and chaos, is to characterize everything that is said and done when Christians gather together. Edification, not enthusiasm, is the criterion by which spiritual gifts should be measured. Others, not self, are to be the focus of Christian existence. In a word, the pursuit of love succinctly describes the Christian way of life (14:1).

In recognizing love as the highest goal of the Christian life, Wesleyans have correctly caught the emphasis of 1 Co 13. Nevertheless, our emphasis on perfect love makes us especially vulnerable to ridicule when we fail to demonstrate it. Have we lived out our profession in dealing with tongues-speakers in our churches? Have we shown them patience and kindness (13:4)? Have we kept **no record of wrongs** (v.5)? Have we given them the advantage of the doubt (v.7)?

c. Comparison of tongues and prophecy (14:1–40)

Ch. 14 explains Paul's preference for the gift of prophecy over tongues, based on his concern for love, defined here as edification ("building up"). His discussion of the two criteria essential for edification, intelligibility and order, decides the two major divisions of the chapter: 14:1–25 and 26–40.

(1) The criterion of intelligibility (14:1–25)

According to Paul the goal of everything that takes place when Christians gather together is edification (14:1–5;

see vv.12, 17, 26). Essential to assure the achievement of this goal is intelligibility; everyone, believers (14:6–19) and unbelievers (vv.20–25) alike, must be able to understand clearly what is being said if they are to be built up by it. The burden to be intelligible rests on the shoulders of the speakers, not the listeners. Nevertheless, it is the Spirit, who grants the gift of prophecy and/or interpretation, who enables those with the gift to speak in such a way as to be understood.

Paul's preference for prophecy over tongues expresses three essential concerns (14:2–5). He prefers speech that addresses man rather than God, is intelligible rather than esoteric, and builds up the church rather than the speaker. His concern for relevance and helpfulness to all those who gather for worship determines his emphases here. Edifying oneself is not wrong, it is simply not the reason Christians gather for corporate worship (see Heb 10:23–25).

In 14:18 Paul claims to **speak in tongues;** in fact, he claims to **speak in tongues more than all of** the Corinthians. Precisely what he means by this and why he feels compelled to boast of this is debated by interpreters. Some assume that he refers to his multilingual gifts, suggesting that Paul "speaks more languages" than the Corinthians (Carter, 220; Clarke, 6:276). But this view is impossibly flawed by the fact that *mallon,* **more,** is an adverb modifying **speak** rather than an adjective modifying **tongues.** Paul's preference for prophecy and his depreciation of uninterpreted tongues-speaking is not due to any personal deficiency. Did the Corinthians doubt that he possessed this or other spiritual gifts (see 2Co 10–13)?

Whatever boastfulness Paul may be guilty of in 14:18, he retracts in v.19.

Tongues are useless **in the church.** The contrast between his preference in church for **five intelligible words** to **ten thousand words in a tongue** is striking—all the more so because **ten thousand** was the largest word for a number available in Greek. **Intelligible** (14:19 NIV) is literally "with my mind" (NRSV; see 14:14–15; **intelligible** in 14:9 is literally "easily understood"). The purpose of Paul's intelligible words is **to instruct others,** to make himself understood (from *katexeo,* as in the English "catechism"). Only intelligible communication is capable of edifying others.

Paul's solution to the problem of the negative response of unbelievers and these others to tongues-speaking is not to exclude them from Christian gatherings. It is instead to exclude uninterpreted tongues from these assemblies and to limit severely even interpreted tongues (14:27–28). In light of the strikingly different responses of unbelievers to tongues (v.23) and prophecy (vv.24–25) as Paul envisions them, it is surprising that he does not totally exclude tongues from church. But he does not (see vv.27–28, 39).

Paul assumes that church meetings might be effective for of evangelism if everyone prophesies (14:24–25). He envisions a succession of four responses by unbelievers or inquirers to this, moving them from conviction for sin to a confession of faith and, presumably, to their conversion. Would that God's presence were so overwhelmingly real in our churches that the unconverted might be compelled to turn to faith! Intelligibility must be a concern not only in churches of the charismatic movement. Wesleyan churches at times use clichés and shibboleths that are unintelligible to unbelievers and nearly meaningless to the younger generation.

Our message must be communicated in common language.

(2) The criterion of order (14:26–40)

If edification and intelligibility are to be achieved when Christians gather, **everything should be done in a fitting and orderly way** (14:40). This arises from the character of God (v.33a).

The unifying concern of 14:26–38 is orderly worship. The solution to the problems with spiritual gifts in Corinth is not the exclusion of one of the gifts or of those who practice it, but regulation of its use by means of the criteria of order and intelligibility in worship. The five components of Corinthian worship that Paul mentions in 14:26 include the singing of hymns (see 14:15), giving words of instruction (see 12:28–29; 14:6), sharing revelations (14:6), tongues, and the interpretation of tongues. Is it significant or purely coincidental that he does not mention prophecy in the list (see v.37)? Paul offers no correction for the Corinthians' broadly based participation in one component or another of worship. He merely reminds them that everything done when they gather is to be directed toward the building up of the church.

Since Paul's instructions presume that tongues-speakers may choose to speak or be silent at their discretion, he must assume that **tongues** are not spoken in a state of ecstasy, overcome by the Spirit. Rather, it seems to be a gift granting its recipients the ability subsequently to speak in tongues at will (Wesley, *Notes* on 14:27). Here, as in 12:10 and 14:28–30 (unlike 14:6, 13), Paul assumes that the interpreter is a different person from the tongues-speaker. The gift of **interpretation** must similarly enable its recipients to interpret at will. If it were an endowment given only for a particular occasion, compliance with Paul's instructions in 14:28 would be impossible. A tongues-speaker could never know whether an interpreter was present.

As with tongues-speakers, Paul presumes that the prophet is not in an ecstatic state when he/she speaks (v.32). A prophet is one already known to possess the gift of prophecy and who, as such, requires no immediate revelation to speak. Thus, for someone (whether known to be a prophet or not) to receive some kind of special revelation, determining the content of his/her prophecy (v.30) may be the exception rather than the rule. When this does take place, the prophet who has the floor is to control himself and defer to the other speaker.

The operative theological principle throughout 14:26–40 is that **God is not a God of disorder but of peace** (v.33a; see v.40). Paul assumes that the character of the Christian God (see Ro 15:33; 1Th 5:23) should determine the character of Christian worship. God's people are to worship in this peaceful way so as to win the favor of others (see 7:15; 14:22–25; 1Th 4:11–12). This is what he expects of all of his churches.

Paul urges the Corinthians to demonstrate their spiritual insight by recognizing the divine authority of his instructions ordering corporate worship in 14:26–35. His opening rhetorical questions confront them with the reality that they are not the source or sole beneficiaries of **the word of God.** Paul's questions seem intended to challenge Corinthian arrogance (cf. 4:7, 18).

What is speaking in tongues? It seems certain that it was the problem gift in Corinth. But contrary to the opinion of many interpreters, we cannot be certain that it was a problem

because it was overvalued and abused. We should be cautious about assuming that the modern practice of tongues in charismatic circles and in Corinth are essentially similar—or different. The two nearly contemporary phenomena by the same name in Ac 2 and 1Co 12–14 appear to be quite different.

The evidence of 1Co 12–14 allows several safe conclusions about the phenomenon of **tongues.** It appears to have been some sort of noncognitive communion/communication with God, which neither the speakers nor their hearers could understand. The gift seems to have involved an endowment by the Spirit, which gave its recipients the ability subsequently to pray in this audible and inarticulate/unintelligible manner at will. Those who possessed the gift were benefited by using it, but those who heard it in a congregational setting not only received no benefit but were repulsed by it. Those with the gift of interpretation were able to transform the apparent cacophony of tongues into a meaningful and helpful message.

Yet a number of uncertainties remain concerning the phenomenon. What are we to make of the apparent contradiction between Paul's call for diversity of gifts and his wish that all the Corinthians might have the same gifts—the ability to speak in tongues and to prophesy? Or of his refusal to exclude tongues from corporate worship settings despite his obvious reservations about its appropriateness there? Did one faction in Corinth reject the gift while another was preoccupied with it?

Such uncertainties should make us less dogmatic about taking sides in the contemporary debate. Because Scripture nowhere presents tongues as the necessary evidence of the Spirit-filled life, it is wrong for charismatics to pressure those who already enjoy the experience of the Spirit to seek the gift of tongues. Those who are dissatisfied with their experience of the Spirit should seek the Giver, not any one of his gifts. When he is with us, we excel in building up the church, not only ourselves. But if the sovereign Spirit allegedly endows another with the gift of tongues, who are we to dictate to the Spirit what he may or may not do? Who are we to forbid another from speaking in tongues when Scripture plainly teaches we must not? Who are we to exclude from the body of Christ one whose gift we do not possess (or understand) as if we have no need of him when Scripture plainly teaches that we must not?

H. The Future Resurrection of the Dead (15:1–58)

Nothing prepares for the abrupt transition from the problems of corporate worship in chs. 11–14 to that of the Resurrection in ch. 15. Nevertheless, the reminder concerning **the gospel** in 15:1 returns the letter to its point of departure before chs. 11–14 (see 9:12, 14, 16, 18, 23), which, in turn, resumes the concern of the early part of the letter (see 1:17, 18, 23; 2:2; 4:14–15).

Although some interpreters set Paul's preaching of the death and resurrection of Christ in tension, Paul himself did not. The Gospel message of the saving death of Christ is powerful precisely because God raised him from the dead. Paul's repeated references to God's power (1:17, 18, 24; 2:4, 5) anticipate his treatment of the Resurrection as the supreme manifestation of that power in ch. 15. Apart from the Resurrection, **preaching is useless** (v.14) and the Gospel is a lie (v.15).

Paul emphasizes not only the centrality of the Resurrection to the Gospel in ch. 15, but its essential futurity. By contrast, Corinthian eschatology seems to have been collapsed, overrealized, spiritualized. What Paul literally expected only in the future they considered present spiritual realities. But he takes issue not merely with their calculation of the timing of the eschaton but with their misunderstanding of its character, manifested in their arrogance (4:18–19; 5:2; 8:1). They are not mature, as they imagine (2:6), but childish (3:1–2; see 14:20); not spiritual, but fleshly (3:1–4); not kings (4:8); not tolerant (5:1–8); not knowledgeable (8:1). They are not powerful but only talk (4:20).

Paul stresses also the corporeal character of the Resurrection. It is not immortality of the soul he proclaims, but *bodily* resurrection. Did the Corinthians despise bodily existence as did many people in the Hellenistic world (see 6:13–14)? Did they conceive of death not as an enemy to be conquered but as an ally who would liberate them from the limitations of bodily existence? Did they imagine that their spiritual status exempted them from the mortality of the rest of humanity? Did they conceive of the Resurrection in a spiritualized sense only?

Ch. 15 has three major divisions and a conclusion. Vv.1–11 introduce the first division and present the resurrection of Christ as the heart of the Gospel message. Both second and third parts conclude with exhortations to proper behavior. Part two (vv.12–34) makes the case for the *fact* of the Resurrection as essential for the achievement of God's redemptive purposes, and calls for the Corinthians to stop sinning (vv.33–34). Part three (vv.35–58) concerns the *mode* of the Resurrection and calls them to positive Christian activity in the light of Christ's victory over death (v.58).

1. The message of the Resurrection (15:1–11)

Paul's purpose here is not to prove that the resurrection of Christ occurred. Both he and his hearers take that for granted. His purpose is to remind them of the centrality of Christ's resurrection in **the gospel.** On this, despite their other differences, all Christians agree (v.11). As frequently in the letter, Paul stresses their common ground with Christians in all the churches (see 4:17; 7:17; 11:16; 14:33b, 36).

2. The fact of the Resurrection (15:12–34)

It is only at this point in Paul's discussion of the Resurrection that we learn what occasioned it. **Some** Corinthians were saying, **There is no resurrection** (v.12). His approach to this denial is first to detail the consequences **if** this were true (vv.12–19). Second, he considers the consequences of the fact that Christ has been resurrected (vv.20–28). Third, he notes the personal contradictions that are suggested by the Corinthians' and his own practice **if** there is no Resurrection (vv.29–32). He concludes with three exhortations (vv.33–34).

Although the Corinthians take for granted the universal Christian faith in Christ's resurrection, **some** of them deny the **resurrection of the dead** (v.12). Paul challenges the logic of their belief with a series of seven hypothetical constructions, stating the awful consequences that would follow **if** there actually were no Resurrection.

Paul reasons from the general to the specific. If there is no general resurrection, then there can have been none in the specific instance of Christ (vv.13, 15b, 16). If the Corinthians are right, then he and the other apostles are wrong. Then Paul's preaching is not

only futile, it is false, and he is a liar (vv.13–15). Their faith is not only worthless and empty; they are still hopeless sinners (vv.14, 17). To deny their future deliverance from death is to deny their own present experience of deliverance from sin. If there is no Resurrection, Christian believers who have died are **lost** (v.18). Their fate is no different from that of unbelievers. To deny the resurrection of the dead is not merely to nitpick about indifferent, esoteric theological opinions. It is to undermine the very basis of the Christian faith. Christ's death is without saving significance if God did not raise him the from the dead (vv.17–19).

Denial of the Resurrection undermines moral urgency, but not because Christians do good in order to be rewarded and avoid evil so as not to be punished. Nevertheless, **if the dead are not raised,** there is no moral accountability (see Ro 14:9–12), in which case the tranquilizing pursuit of pleasure in the face of despair—**Let us eat and drink, for tomorrow we die** (15:32; citing Isa 22:13)—becomes attractive. Only a fool would pursue a painful mission in the cause of a **gospel** predicated on a fraud and possessing neither help in the present nor hope for the future (see vv.12–19).

3. The mode of the Resurrection (15:35–58)

Having established the fact of the Resurrection in 15:12–34, Paul here discusses its mode, drawing upon botanical, zoological, and astronomical analogies (vv.35–41). He insists that the Resurrection is both spiritual and bodily (vv.42–44a), and he rehearses the Adam-Christ contrast (vv.44b–49; see vv.21–22) to bolster his arguments. But he finally concedes that the nature of the Resurrection existence remains an impenetrable **mystery** (vv.50–57). Paul concludes his discussion of the Resurrection from the dead with three exhortations (v.58; cf. vv.33–34).

Paul's hypothetical question, **But someone may ask,** anticipates a potential objection arising from the preceding discussion and prepares for the mutually clarifying questions, **How are the dead raised? With what kind of body will they come?** (v.35). The first asks, "By what means or power are dead people raised?" The second question makes it clear that his concern is with the *mode,* not the means of Resurrection existence. Paul obviously can conceive of no other Resurrection mode than some kind of bodily existence. To demonstrate the folly of anyone who would ask such questions (v.36), Paul appeals to analogies. Paul denies that resurrection involves the mere resuscitation of corpses (v.50), insisting rather that it involves a thorough transformation of the physical body into a **spiritual body** (v.44), the precise nature of which remains a **mystery** (v.51).

Normally the NT uses the word *mystery* (v.51) to identify revelations of what once were secrets, now disclosed by God to believers. But here the undisclosed circumstances of the Resurrection retain their mysterious character. The **mystery** does not seem to be a rational explanation for the Resurrection. It is instead information concerning the fate of living believers at the time of the Second Coming. They will experience a transformation as radical as the resurrection of those who died before Christ's return. It is not simply death, but **flesh and blood** that must be overcome, or transformed. Although **the perishable** cannot enter resurrection existence directly, when Christ returns, **the dead will be raised imperishable** and the living **will be changed** (v.52). When mortal existence gives way to immortality, God will eliminate death from human experience (vv.54–55).

The metamorphosis of the living and the resurrection of the dead will occur instantly and simultaneously when Christ returns (15:52; see Mt 24:31; 1Th 4:16–17; Rev 11:15). Just as trumpets announced the dawning of the new year in Israel's ancient festival cycle (see Lev 23:23–25; Nu 29:1–6), so they will announce the dawning of the new age. At the Second Coming God will raise the dead "never to die again" and change the dead into "what cannot die" (15:52–53 TEV). It is apparently in this sense that we shall become like the Risen Christ (see 15:49; Ro 6:9; 8:11; 1Jn 3:2).

Although God will only in the future deprive death of its victory, he is now giving **us the victory** (v.57). Our present victory consists in our participation in the triumph Christ is now winning by defeating God's enemies (vv.20–28). Christ's resurrection from the dead in the past, his ongoing defeat of God's enemies in the present, and the future certainty of his final conquest of death provide the basis for the conclusion of 1Co 15. Paul's **therefore** reaches back to the consequences of Christ's resurrection described in vv.20–57. On the basis of his victory, which is ours as well, Paul makes three appeals. The first and second are essentially synonymous—**Stand firm** and **Let nothing move you** (cf. vv.1–2). Faithfulness is an essential condition for final salvation. The formulation of these appeals presumes that Paul takes for granted the Christian status of his hearers. His third appeal exhorts them to give themselves **fully to the work of the Lord,** motivated by the knowledge that their **labor in the Lord is not in vain.** The effectiveness of Christian activity is based on the certain victory of Christ. Empowered by the Spirit of the risen Christ and motivated by the privilege of participation in his winning cause, Christians may invest their energies fully in **work** that is assured of ultimate success.

I. Travel Plans (16:1–12)

This section consists of two parts, each beginning with the formula **Now about** (16:1, 12: cf. 7:1, 25; 8:1; 12:1). In response to Corinthian questions, Paul announces his travel plans and those of his associates. His goal is to guide and inform them in preparation for his visit.

Paul's initial instructions (16:1–4) concern **the collection for God's people**—that is, the offering he undertook among his Gentile churches in behalf of impoverished Jewish Christians in Jerusalem (see Ac 24:17; Ro 15:24–33; 2Co 8–9; Gal 2:10). He commends to the Corinthians the same procedure he suggested to his Galatian churches— systematic, proportional, free-will offerings (v.1) collected on Sunday, which already seems to be the customary Christian day of worship (v.2). Paul plans to deliver the collection to Jerusalem accompanied by their representatives (vv.3–4). We know from 2Co 8–9 that he had considerably more difficulty completing the collection arrangements in Corinth than he envisioned at this writing.

Paul details his personal travel plans (vv.5–9) and Timothy's (vv.10–11). Since Timothy is to deliver the letter we know as 1 Corinthians (v.10; 4:17), Paul urges the Corinthians to extend him hospitality and to finance his return journey (v.11). Paul writes from Ephesus, where he plans to stay until late spring (v.8). From there he plans to go through Macedonia on his way to Corinth, where he hopes to stay, perhaps through winter (vv.5–6). Apparently his itinerary calls for him to pass near Corinth on his way to Macedonia, since he explains his reluctance to pay them only a **passing visit** and his preference for spending more time than his present schedule permits (v.7). We know from 2 Corinthians that Paul subsequently changed his mind and did, in fact, stop in Corinth, to both his and their sorrow (see 2Co 1:15–2:4).

IV. CLOSING (16:13–24)

Paul brings this lengthy letter to a conclusion in his typical fashion. He repeats crucial concerns of the letter and bids his hearers farewell. The letter concludes with two groups of exhortations. Paul's five closing moral exhortations (vv.13–14) recapitulate concerns expressed earlier in the letter. His second group of exhortations urges the Corinthians to recognize and submit to the leadership of Stephanas (cf. 1Th 5:12–14). Paul greets the Corinthians in behalf of Ephesian believers (v.20a), particularly Aquila and Priscilla (v.19), important early, Jewish-Christian leaders in Corinth, currently residing in Ephesus (Ac 18:1–3, 18, 24–26). Paul's compact parting personal remarks (vv.20b–24) succinctly convey several significant messages.

BIBLIOGRAPHY

Barrett, C. K. *A Commentary on the First Epistle to the Corinthians*. HNTC. New York: Harper & Row, 1968.

Carter, Charles W. "First Corinthians." WBC. Grand Rapids: Eerdmans, 1965.

Clarke, Adam. *Romans to the Revelation, The New Testament of Our Lord and Saviour Jesus Christ With a Commentary and Critical Notes*. Vol. 6. New ed. New York: Abingdon, n.d.

Conzelmann, Hans. *1 Corinthians: A Commentary on the First Epistle to the Corinthians*. Trans. by James W. Leitch. Bibliography and references by James W. Dunkly. Ed. George W. MacRae. Hermenia. Philadelphia: Fortress, 1975.

Fee, Gordon D. *The First Epistle to the Corinthians*. NICNT. Grand Rapids: Eerdmans, 1987.

Héring, Jean. *The First Epistle of Saint Paul to the Corinthians*. Trans. A. W. Heathcote and P. J. Allcock from 2d ed. in the Commentaire du Nouveau Testament. London: Epworth, 1962.

Wesley, John. *Explanatory Notes Upon the New Testament*. Naperville, Ill.: Allenson, 1950 (reprint of 1754 ed.).

2 CORINTHIANS
George Lyons

INTRODUCTION

I. THE CITY AND ITS PEOPLE
See Introduction to 1 Corinthians

II. THE CHURCH AND ITS PROBLEMS

While 1 Corinthians reflects problems between the apostle and the community, 2 Corinthians indicates that these differences escalated into open hostility. The tensions that developed between Paul and the Christian community in Corinth seem to have come to a head in his unexpected visit there between the writing of the two canonical letters. Paul addressed this problem in a "sorrowful letter," now apparently lost, which partially resolved the friction. Second Corinthians celebrates the restored congenial relations between him and his converts.

III. THE LITERARY UNITY OF 1 AND 2 CORINTHIANS
See Introduction to 1 Corinthians.

IV. THE OCCASION AND PURPOSE

Assuming the integrity of 2 Corinthians, its occasion may be described as follows. When Paul wrote 1 Corinthians he planned to go directly to Macedonia, foregoing a necessarily brief stop in Corinth on the way in favor of an extended visit there upon his return. Subsequently, he changed his mind and decided to visit the Corinthians on both legs of his journey. When the first of these visits turned out to be a fiasco, Paul left hastily and did not make the previously announced return visit. Instead, he sent Titus with a "sorrowful letter," which succeeded in bringing them to repentance and renewed loyalty. Paul wrote 2 Corinthians to celebrate his joy and renewed confidence in his converts. Second Corinthians 1–9 was also written to inform the Corinthians of Paul's distress as he anxiously awaited news of Titus's mission and to explain why he had failed to make his promised third visit to Corinth.

The last four chapters of 2 Corinthians suggest that, sometime after the writing of 1 Corinthians, some Jewish-Christian missionaries invaded Corinth and denigrated Paul, his message, and authority. They took advantage of the Corinthians' gullibility and claimed to be "super-apostles," although Paul calls them "false apostles," even agents of Satan. Once the Corinthians were reconciled to the apostle, he could call them again to the completion of the collection for the poor saints in Jerusalem, which had been interrupted by the interference of the invading missionaries and the problems they created. Chs. 10–13 refute the view of ministry advanced by these false missionaries.

V. THEOLOGICAL RELEVANCE OF 1 AND 2 CORINTHIANS

See Introduction to 1 Corinthians.

VI. OUTLINE

I. The Letter Opening (1:1–7)
    A. Prescript (1:1–2)
    B. Thanksgiving (1:3–7)

II. Reconciliation With Friends and Refutation of Enemies (1:8–13:10)
    A. Celebration of Reconciliation (1:8–9:15)
        1. Autobiographical notices (1:8–2:13)
        2. Paul's ministry (2:14–7:4)
            a. The nature of Paul's ministry (2:14–4:1)
            b. The basis for Paul's hope (4:2–16a)
                (1) The power of Paul's message (4:2–6)
                (2) The weakness of Paul's person (4:7–16a)
            c. The Resurrection hope (4:16b–5:10)
            d. Responsibility and reconciliation (5:11–6:2)
            e. Reconciliation: Paul and the Corinthians (6:3–7:4)
                (1) Assertions (6:3–12)
                (2) Appeals (6:13–7:4)
        3. Autobiographical notices continued (7:5–16)
        4. The collection (8:1–9:15)
            a. Complete the collection (8:1–15)
            b. The delegation (8:16–9:5)
            c. Benefits of generosity (9:6–15)
    B. Refutation of Alien Ministry (10:1–13:10)
        1. Introduction: Paul's unimpressive presence (10:1–11)
        2. Proper and foolish boasting (10:12–12:13)
            a. Competition and commendation (10:12–18)
            b. Foolish boasting (11:1–12:13)
        3. Conclusion: Paul's imminent presence (12:14–13:10)

III. Letter Closing (13:11–13)

COMMENTARY

I. THE LETTER OPENING (1:1–7)

A. Prescript (1:1–2)

If in 2 Corinthians Paul vigorously defends his divine office in the face of doubts and rejection by his readers, as most interpreters assume, it seems strange that elsewhere only in 12:12 does he explicitly identify himself as an "apostle." His intended readers include Christians in the province of Achaia (see 9:2) as well as the church in Corinth. Within the letter Paul gives no indication that a given commendation or condemnation is addressed to a more specific audience. This makes it difficult to sustain theories that presume chs. 1–9 address a loyal majority and chs. 10–13 address a dissenting minority. Never explicitly named, but never far in the background, are "some people" whose views and behavior Paul opposes and who perhaps oppose him.

B. Thanksgiving (1:3–7)

Instead of his standard thanksgiving form, Paul offers a eulogy blessing God. Clearly the most prominent idea in 1:3–7 is **comfort,** referring to God's deliverance of Paul from some unspecified suffering and troubles. His experience of suffering and deliverance points to his participation (*koinonia*, 1:7) in the death and resurrection of Christ. His suffering in the fulfillment of his mission vicariously benefits the Corinthians as did Christ's suffering, bringing them comfort and salvation (v.6). Paul's hopes for them remain undiminished (v.7); but God, not they, is the source of his comfort (vv.3–5).

II. RECONCILIATION WITH FRIENDS AND REFUTATION OF ENEMIES (1:8–13:10)

The letter's body consists of two major sections. Whether and how the two sections relate to one another continue to be subjects of heated scholarly debate. The first, 1:8–9:15, seems to have been occasioned by the end of strained relations between Paul and his readers. The second, 10:1–13:10, saturated with biting irony and sarcasm, seems difficult to reconcile with an exuberant celebration of reconciliation in chs. 1–9.

Certainly Paul did not write this or any of his longer letters in one sitting; this could account for some internal inconsistencies. But in this case, all historical or psychological explanations seem inadequate to preserve the presumption of a unified letter. Perhaps it is simplest to presume that it was the collector-editor of the Pauline letter corpus who brought the two sections together. Nevertheless, for the purposes of this commentary, 2 Corinthians is treated as a rhetorical unity.

A. Celebration of Reconciliation (1:8–9:15)

Paul celebrates his recent reconciliation with his readers, effected by an earlier letter delivered by Titus (see 2:4, 9; 7:8–12). What Paul says about this letter makes it unlikely that it is to be identified with either 1 Corinthians or 2 Corinthians 10–13. This presumably lost letter was itself occasioned by the unpleasant circumstances of an unannounced visit Paul made to Corinth between the two canonical letters. The painful memories of this surprise visit led him to alter his travel plans again and not come to Corinth as previously announced (see 1Co 16:5–9; 2Co 2:1–11).

In an autobiographical notice, Paul first turns to an explanation of his unfulfilled visit (1:8–2:13). He returns again to a discussion of the historical circumstances underlying the letter in 7:5–16, following a lengthy and, at first glance, almost parenthetical discussion of the character of his **ministry** in 2:14–7:4. Within this section, 6:14–7:1 is an appeal for moral separation from unbelievers, which seems to interrupt Paul's appeal for his readers' unreserved acceptance. Chs. 1–9 conclude with appeals for the Corinthians to fulfill their promised participation in the **ministry** of the collection for impoverished Judean Christians (chs. 8–9). The diverse concerns of chs. 1–9 and the abrupt shifts within them have led many scholars to presume that the unity of even these chapters may be the work of the redactor.

1. Autobiographical notices (1:8–2:13)

At the outset, as he often does, Paul narrates certain events from his own experience that serve as a background for the major concerns of the letter (cf. Ro 1:13–15; Gal 1:11–2:21; Php 1:12–26; 1Th 2:1–12). Whatever the introductory formula, these autobiographical notices remind his readers of events with which they are familiar. Such reminders, used illustratively in support of other points, generally offer insufficient detail to reconstruct historically the precise events they report.

Paul's first notice refers to his deliverance by God from **hardships** experienced in the province of Asia Minor. We cannot tell whether this hardship involved physical illness, unjust persecution, imprisonment, the threat of death, misunderstanding, anguish concerning the failure of his work in Corinth, or anxiety over his inability to find Titus as previously arranged. This "affliction" (NRSV) was probably not actually life-threatening, despite the arguments of most interpreters. It was more likely psychological distress that led him to despair of life (see 1:8, 9), for Paul implies that God delivered him from despair, not by releasing him from prison, but by teaching him to rely on the **God who raises the dead** (1:9). Deliverance came when Paul accepted his mortality, acknowledged his humanity, and quit rebelling against the idea that he too would die.

Paul had previously announced that he would not stop in Corinth on his way from Ephesus to Macedonia, but only on his return journey to his next destination (1Co 16:5–9). Subsequently he changed his mind and decided to favor them with a visit on both legs of his journey before going on to Judea (2Co 1:15–16). The unannounced visit to Corinth was so unpleasant that Paul again changed his plans. He did not stop in Corinth after leaving Macedonia, nor did he go on to Judea. Instead, he proceeded (apparently) to Ephesus, from where he wrote the Corinthians an anguished letter rather than paying them another painful visit (1:23–2:4). In 2:12–13 Paul mentions yet another instance in which he changed his travel plans.

Paul's rehearsal of his itinerary is not intended simply to satisfy the Corinthians', or our, curiosity. It is motivated by a concern that they understand his behavior (1:12–14) as neither arbitrary nor fickle. On the contrary, he behaves in a manner consistent with the character of God's redemptive activity in Christ (vv.15–22) and determined by love for them and their best interests (1:23–2:4). Further, Paul urges them to pursue a redemptive course of action in dealing with the one responsible for their mutual pain during his unfortunate, surprise visit (2:5–11).

In 2:5–11 Paul refers to a person largely responsible for the pain of his second visit, but he does not name him or identify his offense. Paul insists that actually it was they, not he, who were injured by the wrongdoer (2:5; see 1Co 5:2, 5–6). Many interpreters assume that this is simply rhetoric; Paul was, in fact, personally attacked and only reinterprets the circumstances as a source of grief for them. But perhaps Paul means what he says and implies only that his failed visit should not be construed as further discipline.

Paul's explanation of the intention of his anguished letter—as a test of their obedience (2:9; see vv.3–4)—probably implies that in it he had ordered the punishment of the wrongdoer. Now he insists that their discipline of the man has been sufficient, having accomplished its redemptive purpose of bringing him to his senses (v.6), and he urges them to **forgive and comfort** the man with their love (vv.7–8). Paul assures them that if he has suffered any wrong needing forgiveness, he has forgiven it for their sakes (v.10). Further discipline of the man would serve Satan's, not God's purposes (v.11). Paul's insight into the necessity and limits of remedial discipline within the Christian community might well serve the contemporary church, too prone to forget one or the other.

It is not immediately obvious why Paul describes the trauma he experienced when he failed to find Titus in Troas. He presumes upon the Corinthians' awareness of events that do not become clear to us until he refers to them again in 7:5–16. There we learn that Titus was Paul's representative in delivering the anguished letter. Apparently, after his return from Corinth, Paul had arranged to meet Titus in Troas. In this port city of Asia Minor they planned to evangelize. Although Paul's preaching was favorably received there, his anxious concern for Titus so distracted him that he again changed his plans and departed for Macedonia in search of his colleague.

2. Paul's ministry (2:14–7:4)

The rehearsal of Paul's specific missionary itinerary in 1:8–2:13 paves the way for his generalized thanksgiving for what God accomplishes through his ministry **always . . . and . . . everywhere** (2:14). Paul discusses the multifaceted character of his ministry in 2:14–7:4, before concluding the narrative, begun in 2:12–13, about his anxious search for Titus in 7:5–16. Despite the changed plans and difficult circumstances of Paul's itinerant ministry, God used him as a means of making Christ known. Four times in 2:14–7:16 Paul commends his ministry as the manifestation of the work of God (3:1; 4:2; 5:12; 6:4). This explains why he does not **lose heart** (4:1, 16) despite his afflictions.

a. The nature of Paul's ministry (2:14–4:1)

Paul illustrates the nature of his ministry by appealing to the imagery of the Roman triumph (2:14–16a) and of Moses' mediation of the law (3:7–4:1). Between these two images (in 2:16b–3:6) Paul identifies God as the sole basis for his confidence in and competence for ministry.

b. The basis for Paul's hope (4:2–16a)

Paul explains the paradoxical basis for his hope and the nature of his ministry. In 4:2–6 he comments on the power of his message, while in 4:7–16a he concedes the weakness of his person.

(1) The power of Paul's message (4:2–6)

Although Paul commends himself in contrast with dishonest teachers (4:2; cf. 2:17–3:1), he insists that Christ, not he, is the content of his proclamation (4:5; see 10:12–18). He tries not to get in the way of his message or ministry. Those who reject the Gospel of Christ he preaches do so because they refuse to believe. They have made this world their god and so are blind to the splendor of Christ, who makes the true God known. They **are perishing,** but their situation is not hopeless. They are not incapable of believing, nor are they already lost. Perhaps they will yet turn from unbelief and be saved through the ministry of the Gospel. God's light may yet break through their darkness as it did for Paul (4:3–4, 6). The implied parallel here between the creation of the world (Ge 1:3) and Paul's encounter with Christ (see also 1Co 9:1; 15:8; Gal 1:16) accounts for his description of conversion as a new creation in 2Co 5:17.

(2) The weakness of Paul's person (4:7–16a)

Paul concedes that despite the extraordinarily powerful message he proclaims, he does so as a vulnerable human being. The OT is the origin of this use of the metaphor **jars of clay** with reference to human weakness (Job 10:9; Isa 29:16; 30:14; 45:9; 64:8; Jer 18:6; 22:28; Lam 4:2; see Talbert, 156). The contrast between the fragile container and its precious contents has a purpose. It is **to show that this all-surpassing power is from God and not from us** (4:7). The tribulations Paul lists in 4:8–10 demonstrate that despite the oppressive forces he faces, paradoxically God's power sustains him (cf. 6:4–10; 11:23–29). Though threatened with death, his survival reveals in his person the resurrection life of Jesus, which in turn enables him to minister life to the Corinthians (4:10–12). Hardships reveal the Christlike character of his ministry.

c. The Resurrection hope (4:16b–5:10)

Paul characterizes the Resurrection hope, which sustains him despite his present suffering (see 4:14), by appeal to the metaphors of a tent and clothing (5:1–5). His present afflictions are slight and temporary in contrast to the future, substantial, eternal glory that will be his. This hope provides the basis for his personal confidence (4:16b–18) and motivates his circumspect conduct (5:6–10). Both 5:1–5 and 5:6–10 have an almost confessional character (**we know,** 5:1, 6).

d. Responsibility and reconciliation (5:11–6:2)

This resurrection hope (4:16b–5:10) accounts for Paul's "therefore" (NRSV) in 5:11. He does not take lightly his appointment **before the judgment seat of Christ** (5:10). He knows **what it is to fear the Lord** (v.11a); his future reward or punishment is based on the faithful performance of his ministry of persuading people to become and remain believers. Effective ministry demands transparent integrity; he stands open for inspection by God and the Corinthians (v.11b). The appeals in 5:20 and 6:1 reflect Paul's concern to be persuasive.

As he does in previous (2:14–4:1; 4:2–16a) and subsequent (6:3–7:4) sections, Paul commends himself in 5:11b–12a. His goal is not to gloat in his accomplishments but to give the Corinthians suitable grounds for assessing his ministry and for answering those whose basis for assessment is style rather than substance (5:12). This is what he proceeds to do in the balance of this section, explicating the motives and nature of his ministry.

Paul refuses to make his private religious experiences, whatever they may be, a basis for public inspection;

they are between him and God (5:13a; see 1Co 14:1, 19). Christ's love for him and his love for Christ compel him to minister to those for whom Christ died. Christ's self-giving, other-directed love motivates, preoccupies, and dominates Paul's life and ministry (vv.13–15). His pre-Christian, merely "human" (NRSV), **worldly** (NIV) evaluation of Christ, based on outward appearances (v.12), is no longer viable. In the same way Christ enables him to see other people from an entirely new perspective (v.16). Living for Christ and as Christ lived has revolutionized his world— there is, as it were, **a new creation.** This radical change is not only his experience as an apostle, but that of **anyone [who] is in Christ** (v.17; see Gal 6:15). This is Paul's **answer [for] those who take pride in what is seen rather than in what is in the heart** (v.12).

Paul insists that all this newness comes from God. He is the one who reconciled Paul to himself through the death of Christ and who gave Paul the ministry of reconciliation. That is, by making Paul his friend, God gave Paul the opportunity to serve him and people by also making them his friends (5:18). Here the apostle uses the language of diplomacy to explicate the nature of salvation (see Ro 5:10). In 5:21 Paul appeals to the more traditional Septuagint language of sacrifice to do the same. God made the sinless Christ (Jn 7:18; 8:46; Heb 4:15; 7:26; 1Pe 2:22; 1Jn 3:5) to be a sin offering for us sinners so that we might be made right with God through Christ. Clearly Paul insists that Christ's death is the divine means of salvation for the world (5:18, **through Christ;** 5:19, **in Christ**). Interpreters are divided on precisely how Christ's death provides salvation (translations and commentar-

ies tend to defend particular theories of the Atonement).

According to 5:19, in the Christ-event God accomplished three things: (1) he provided the means by which all people might be reconciled to himself; (2) he demonstrated his decision not to hold the sins of humanity against them; and (3) he entrusted to reconciled people the task of sharing this reconciling message. As an ambassador on behalf of Christ, Paul represents God's interests, appealing for peace on his behalf (5:20).

e. Reconciliation: Paul and the Corinthians (6:3–7:4)

Reconciliation continues to concern Paul, but here it is between himself and the Corinthians, not between God and sinful humankind. Just as God took the initiative to make reconciliation possible, Paul puts **no stumbling block in anyone's path** that might discredit his ministry (6:3). He has **wronged no one, . . . corrupted no one, . . . exploited no one** (7:2b). On the contrary, the conduct of his ministry commends him as a servant of God (6:4a; see 3:1; 4:2; 5:12).

(1) Assertions (6:3–12)

Paul makes three claims. The first describes what he does not do in the pursuit of his ministry (v.3). The second enumerates the ways in which his ministerial conduct recommends him as a servant of God (vv.4–10). Paul lists ten hardships (vv.4b–5) and eight virtues (vv.6–7a), each introduced with the Greek preposition *en* (**in**). Then he lists three twofold circumstances, each introduced with the Greek preposition *dia* (**with/through**—vv.7b–8a). He concludes with a list of seven paradoxes contrasting outward experiences and essential reality, each introduced with the Greek particle *hos* (**as**—vv.8b–10).

(2) Appeals (6:13–7:4)

Three appeals arise from the preceding assertions. The first and third appeals identify reciprocity (**a fair exchange,** 6:13) as the necessary requirement for reconciliation between Paul and his hearers, and genuine friendship, for that matter. Their lives are so intertwined that they live together and die together (7:3). Since he has not withheld his affection from them, they should not withhold theirs from him (6:11–12; 7:2a). Since he takes such pride in them, he implies that they should take similar pride in him (5:12; 7:4). The second appeal calls for the Corinthians to make a complete break with idolatrous and immoral influences. Paul insists that separation from pagan influences is the essential prerequisite for the effective operation of God's reconciling work in their lives and for remaining on good terms with Paul.

Once a classic text in churches of the Wesleyan tradition, the message of sanctification as separation in 2Co 6:14–7:1 is no longer sounded forth as frequently or forcefully from our pulpits. Have we outgrown our legalistic roots, or have we simply grown so much like the world that we fail to appreciate the threat it presents? Will feeble human strategies for church growth ever adequately compensate for the absence of the powerful presence of God in our midst? Has the appeal of the prosperity gospel and upward mobility diverted us from the urgency of **perfecting holiness** (7:1)?

3. Autobiographical notices continued (7:5–16)

Here Paul resumes and concludes the autobiographical notices begun in 1:8–2:13 concerning the intense anxiety he experienced in Asia. The Corinthians must have known most of the events he reported in the earlier notices. The new information Paul provides consists only of his emotional reaction to these events. The present section contains mostly new information, offering four reasons why Paul was overjoyed (7:4): (1) Titus's successful mission to Corinth (vv.5–7); (2) the Corinthians' repentance (vv.8–13a); (3) Titus's response (vv.13b–15); and (4) Paul's confidence (v.16).

4. The collection (8:1–9:15)

In chs. 1–7 Paul explains his failure to visit the Corinthians as promised earlier, clarifies the nature of his ministry, urges them to remedy lingering problems in the community, and expresses his unequivocal confidence in their loyalty to him. This prepares the way for the most urgent concern of the letter: the collection for the poor saints in Jerusalem, to which he turns in chs. 8 and 9. Paul's problems in Corinth had delayed the completion of his plans for the collection for the poor Jewish Christians in Jerusalem. He seems to have intended to deliver the offering to Judea after his delayed third visit (see 1Co 16:5–9; 2Co 1:15–16).

Paul obviously attaches great theological significance to the collection. He considers the Corinthians' participation with his other churches in this effort a tangible demonstration of their *spoude,* "earnestness" (eight times in chs. 7 and 8); their *diakonia,* "ministry" (six times in chs. 8–9); and an act of *charis,* "grace" (ten times in chs. 8–9). The collection was not only an act of Christian love, providing financial relief for needy fellow believers (Ro 15:25; 2Co 8:14; 9:12; Gal 2:10), it was a demonstration of solidarity between Paul's Gentile converts and the Jewish mother church (Ro 15:27; 2Co 9:13–14). Perhaps it even anticipated the fulfillment of the apocalyptic vision in which the wealth of the Gentiles would pour into Jerusalem (Ro 9–11).

Apparently Paul's plans for the collection were already in place when he advised the Corinthians concerning the procedure for collecting the necessary funds in 1Co 16:1–4. Now, a year later (see 8:10; 9:2), he hopes to bring the plan to completion (8:6). We know from Paul's letter to the Romans, probably written from Corinth, that he succeeded in doing so (see Ro 15:25–27). But we also know from Acts that the results were not as he had hoped (see Ac 20–28). Thus 2Co 8–9 provides us with an inside look at Paul, the fund-raiser.

a. Complete the collection (8:1–15)

Here Paul explains why and how the Corinthians should complete the collection. Although he will give more reasons for generosity in 9:6–14, the reasons he offers in vv.1–9 are as follows. Paul mentions the extraordinary generosity of the Macedonian contribution to the project (vv.1–5), praising their self-sacrificing giving as granted them by the **grace** of God (v.1; see v.7; Ro 12:6–8). Beyond and behind their financial support, he highlights their gift of themselves **to the Lord and then to [Paul]** as especially **in keeping with God's will** (v.5). It is on this basis that Paul announces that he has urged Titus to return to Corinth to allow the Corinthians to pay their pledges to the financial campaign (v.6). The apostle exploits the ancient technique of comparisons between rivals to challenge the Corinthians not only to emulate, but to surpass, the Macedonians (vv.7–8; Talbert, 183). He appeals to the model of self-giving of Jesus Christ as a reminder to the Corinthians of their indebtedness (v.9). Not only competition, but gratitude

and reciprocity, should motivate their giving. Generosity to others would demonstrate **the sincerity of [their] love** (v.8) for the Lord and for Paul (see 6:11–13; 7:2; 8:5, 8).

Paul appeals again to the principle of reciprocity or mutuality (**equality,** NIV; 8:13, 14) to motivate the Corinthians to finish what they began a year earlier. Their actions should match their willingness to give; their gift should match their ability to give and their indebtedness to the recipients (vv.11–12). The spiritual generosity of Jewish Christians of Jerusalem had enriched the Gentile Christians of Corinth (vv.13–15; see 9:12–14; Ro 15:27). Thus their gift is a just and only partial repayment of their indebtedness to these materially impoverished saints.

b. The delegation (8:16–9:5)

Paul has already mentioned his intention to send Titus back to Corinth to complete the arrangements for the collection (8:6). Here he elaborates, commending the men who will carry out his plans and explaining his motives for them.

c. Benefits of generosity (9:6–15)

Paul offers additional reasons why the Corinthians should give generously (cf. 8:1–9). He mentions only in passing the most obvious and direct result of the collection: **supplying the needs of God's people** (9:12a), the poor in Jerusalem. Instead he stresses how Corinth's generosity will benefit the Corinthians and God (vv.11b–14). Despite Paul's mention of the self-serving benefits of generosity, he makes it clear that people are not to give in order to get, but because they have already received. **Thanks be to God for his indescribable gift (v.15).**

B. Refutation of Alien Ministry (10:1–13:10)

The relationship between 2Co 1–9 and 10–13 is difficult regardless of one's decision as to the unity of the letter. On the one hand, defenders of the letter's literary integrity must explain what motivates Paul's move from the exultant tone of thanksgiving at the close of ch. 9 to the mood of irony and defensiveness in chs. 10–13. On the other hand, those who presume that 2 Corinthians is a compilation of two or more letters are obliged to explain the logic that led an editor to do the same. It is impossible to prove or disprove either the traditional assumption of the letter's unity or one of the modern scholarly challenges to it. Thus it seems reasonable to try to make sense of the present canonical form of the letter.

Paradoxically, Paul's weakness validates the Christlike character of his cruciform ministry and demonstrates Christ's resurrection power within it (see 1:5; 4:8–12; 10:1, 4, 7, 8, 11; 12:9–10; 13:3–4, 10). His weakness is like the weakness of Christ, which is not weakness at all, but a demonstration of God's power (1Co 1:18–2:5). Paul insists throughout the letter that his message and his character as the messenger are fully congruent (1:17–22; 4:13–14; 10:11). He praises his ministry in order to praise Christ and ultimately to urge his readers to comply with his requests.

Paul insists that his God-given authority is intended to edify his converts, not destroy them (10:8; 13:10). Nevertheless, his demeanor upon his return to Corinth will depend on them (12:14; 13:10). He warns them of his readiness to punish the disobedient among them (10:6; 13:1–2), despite his reluctance to do so. He urges them to test themselves, and he expresses his hope that they will not fail (13:5–7). Paul's words are at once a threat and an expression of concern. Should the Corinthians fail the test, his ministry among them will likewise prove to be a failure. Thus he prays that they will be fully restored so that when he comes he will not be forced to exercise toward them the severity he has in mind only for his opponents (vv.9b–10).

A precise identification of these opponents is beyond the scope of the present brief commentary (see Barrett). Paul never names his detractors; the Corinthians knew well enough. Nevertheless, he does distinguish them from his readers (see 10:10–16). He warns the Corinthians that external appearances are deceptive (4:7–12, 16–18; 5:7, 12; 6:8–10; 11:23–28; 12:10), for despite the opponents' appearance as **super-apostles,** they are agents of Satan (11:5, 12–15, 22–23; 12:11). As such, these self-propagandists and perverters of the Gospel in Corinth threaten the Christian status of Paul's converts and undermine his ministry (2:17; 3:1; 4:2, 5; 6:14–7:1; 10:7–12; 11:1–5, 12–15, 19–20; 12:11, 21; 13:2). They must be removed from the scene if Paul is to win the support and participation of all Achaia in the collection for Jerusalem, something Ro 15:26 suggests he succeeded in doing.

At both the beginning and end of 2Co 10:1–13:10, Paul anticipates his delayed third visit to Corinth (10:1–11; 12:14–13:10). Between those sections he contrasts proper and improper boasting (10:12–12:13). In both the introduction (10:1–11) and conclusion (12:14–13:10) he appeals to the Corinthians to be prepared for his visit so that he will not need to take severe disciplinary action against the unrepentant when he comes.

1. Introduction: Paul's unimpressive presence (10:1–11)

Paul discusses five features of his personal presence. These perhaps represent "accusations" raised against Paul by a "Corinthian challenger and his sympathizers" and Paul's "response to each" (Talbert, 111). In any case, these features obviously echo the assertions of others: **some people ... think** (v.2); **anyone is confident** (v.7); **some say** (v.10); and **such people should realize** (v.11).

We can only conjecture as to what occasioned such assessments of Paul. His stated purpose in 2Co 10:1–11 is not to inform his first readers of opinions about him that they knew well. Nor is it to defend himself against their accusations. At the outset of the section he insists that his goal is hortatory: **I appeal to you** (10:1). Although he notes the basis for his appeal in **the meekness and gentleness of Christ** (v.1), Paul never formally completes the appeal he begins (note the punctuation of the NIV). Nevertheless, its burden appears to be expressed implicitly in the verses following the verb *deomai,* **I beg,** in 10:2. They should put their house in order so as not to force him to display his boldness in opposition to the disobedient in Corinth on his next visit (explicit in 13:10). They are to conform to the pattern of Christ modeled in the example of Paul's despised personal presence.

2. Proper and foolish boasting (10:12–12:13)

The contrast between proper and improper boasting is introduced in 10:12–18, where Paul distinguishes those who **commend themselves** and those **whom the Lord commends** (10:12, 18). In 11:1–12:13 Paul engages in ironic self-commendation, at once parodying the **super-apostles** and demonstrating the folly of their boasting.

a. Competition and commendation (10:12–18)

Paul rejects comparison as a means of commending himself (10:12; see Gal 6:3–4). It was standard practice in the rhetoric of his day to compare and contrast oneself with others as a basis for self-advertisement. Itinerant preachers and teachers especially abused the practice as a means of advancing themselves at the expense of their competitors. Accordingly, many serious philosophers disavowed such pretentious boasting as inappropriate (see Talbert, 114). For similar reasons Paul refuses to boast **beyond proper limits** (v.13).

b. Foolish boasting (11:1–12:13)

Paul attempts to demonstrate the folly of improper human boasting by engaging in it. His ironic self-commendation parodied the **super-apostles** (11:5; 12:11) in order to show that their boasting was foolish (11:1, 16, 17, 19, 21; 12:6, 11). His object was apparently to discredit these alleged **apostles** and diminish their influence with the Corinthians. His name for them, **super-apostles,** ridicules their vaunted superiority in contrast to his weakness, for, in fact, he considers them **false apostles** (11:13). He questions the adequacy of their gospel (11:4) and the propriety of their practice of living at community expense (12:11–13).

The excessive boasting of the **super-apostles** stands in stark contrast to Paul's reluctant boasting in 2 Corinthians, which appears to fall within the culturally accepted bounds of self-praise. Nevertheless, his obvious discomfort with self-praise appears in his characterization of the practice as folly

(11:1, 16, 17, 19, 21; 12:6, 11), even insanity (11:23). Driven to boasting unwillingly, Paul conforms to existing customs for inoffensive self-praise. Thus, for example, he concedes his failures while commending his successes (11:30–33; 12:8–9). He boasts not in his own interests but out of concern for others (11:1–4, 28–29; 12:19). He mixes his boasting with relevant moral exhortations (10:2, 6; 13:5, 11). And he contrasts the moral failures of others with his own practice (10:13–18; 11:12–15, 23–29).

Although Paul introduces his foolish boasting in 11:1, he does not really begin to boast until 11:16. In 11:2–15 he explains the desperate circumstances that compel him to resort to boasting, the satanic deception of the false apostles (vv.3, 13–14). Why must Paul boast? (1) Because of the Corinthians (vv.2–4): Paul must preserve the Corinthian church's fidelity to Christ. (2) Because of the opponents (vv.5–15): The Corinthians' infidelity involves a departure specifically from Paul's proclamation of the Gospel to that of the super-apostles. Paul demonstrates why he rejects his opponents and their message.

Having explained in 11:1–15 why the tactic was called for, only now does Paul begin to engage in the foolish boasting he announced in 11:1. Following an introduction explaining why he considers this boasting folly (11:16–21), he presents his boast in four parts: He compares himself with his opponents in terms of heritage (v.22), credentials (vv.23–33), mystical experiences (12:1–10), and miraculous accomplishments (vv.11–13). Paradoxically, the section conveys a tone of sarcasm, irony, and parody in an atmosphere of utter seriousness.

Before closing this section, Paul returns in 12:13 to the issue of his financial relationship with the Corinthians, broached earlier in 11:7–11 and about to be resumed in 12:14–18. That money was a sensitive issue should not be surprising in light of the central role the collection for the poor in Jerusalem plays in 2 Corinthians. Paul had vigorously insisted in 1 Corinthians 9 upon his right to refuse their financial support, claiming there that he would rather die than be deprived of this boast (1Co 9:15; cf. 2Co 11:9–10). With obvious sarcasm he insists that if this refusal to **burden** them made them **inferior to the other churches, "Forgive me this wrong!"** (12:13; see v.14).

3. Conclusion: Paul's imminent presence (12:14–13:10)

Paul concludes his refutation of his opponents (10:1–13:10) as he began it (see 10:1–11), announcing his impending third visit to Corinth in 12:14a and 13:1a. These announcements mark the beginning of the two major subsections of this unit, 12:14–21 and 13:1–10, both urging the Corinthians to be prepared for his visit.

2Co 12:14–21 consists of two subunits. The first (12:14–18) continues the topic of the previous section—finances. The second (12:19–21) raises again Paul's concern that there should be no unrepentant sinners in the community when he comes to Corinth. He expects them to be prepared for his approaching visit financially by having the collection ready as per his instructions in chs. 8–9. And he expects them to be prepared ethically so that there will be no repetition of the unfortunate scene that marred his second visit (see 2:1–11; 7:5–16).

In 13:1–10 Paul mentions again his coming third visit to Corinth (13:1a; see 12:14a), warning the Corinthians to be prepared or risk facing severe discipline. Paul's demeanor upon his return to Corinth depends entirely upon the Corinthians (13:10; see 1Co 4:21). He is ready to punish the unrepentant, despite his reluctance to do so (13:10, 1–2; 10:6; 12:21). They seem to have seen the problems in their relationship with him as entirely his. Paul turns the table, urging them to consider their own failures in the light of divine judgment. **Examine your-selves** . . . ; **test yourselves** (13:5; see Gal 6:4). He hopes and prays that they will not only pass the test of faithful obedience (13:5–7; see 1:24; 2:9), but that they will be fully prepared for his visit, sparing him the necessity of severely disciplining them (13:7–10). He is less concerned that he should pass their examination than that they should do what is right (13:7; see 1Co 11:19).

III. LETTER CLOSING (13:11–13)

Paul closes with a series of brief exhortations that recapitulate the major concerns of the entire letter (v.11). The first can be translated in several plaus-ible ways: **Aim for perfection** (NIV); "Mend your ways" (RSV, NEB); "Pull yourselves together" (Barrett, 342); "Be restored" (Furnish, 581); or "Put things in order" (NRSV). The same Greek root in 13:9 seems to remind the Corinthians to be prepared for his visit by having their moral house in order and the collection in hand. The second exhortation, **Listen to my appeal** probably identifies the rhetorical goal of the letter as deliberative (cf. 10:1; Heb. 13:22). That is, he hopes to persuade them to heed his advice. The third and fourth appeals, to **be of one mind** and **live in peace** remind Paul's readers of the theme of reconciliation prominent in the early chapters of the letter and his advice for them to resolve their internal community problems (see 12:20). The appeal to **greet one another with a holy kiss** (v.12) calls for a visible symbol of reconciliation; in the ancient world to greet fellow community members with a kiss signified mutual acceptance and respect. The letter concludes with a trinitarian prayer-wish (13:14).

BIBLIOGRAPHY

Barrett, C. K. *A Commentary on the Second Epistle to the Corinthians*. HNTC. New York: Harper & Row, 1973.

Furnish, Victor Paul. *II Corinthians*. AB. Vol. 32A. Garden City, N.Y.: Doubleday, 1984.

Héring, Jean. *The Second Epistle of Saint Paul to the Corinthians*. Trans. A. W. Heathcote and P. J. Allcock from the 1st ed. in the Commentaire du Nouveau Testament. London: Epworth, 1967.

Martin, Ralph P. *2 Corinthians*. WdBC. Vol. 40. Waco: Word, 1986.

GALATIANS
E. Herbert Nygren

INTRODUCTION

I. AUTHORSHIP

Virtually no NT scholar has challenged the traditional claim that Paul was the author of this epistle. Hans Deiter Betz, a recognized authority, well summarizes the consensus that "the theological argument ... is characteristically Pauline both in method and content," further noting that there was unquestioned acceptance "of authorship even in the earliest period of historical study" (Betz, 1; see also Tenney, 216).

II. READERS

The name *Galatia* was used in two different ways in the ancient world. It originally referred to the geographic region in northcentral Asia Minor occupied by the Gauls since 279 B.C. Later the political region was extended southward by Rome to Lycia, Pamphilia, and Antioch. For this reason biblical scholars have disagreed on the region to which the letter was originally sent (Cole, 16ff.; see also Ramsey, 1–234).

Some scholars including Calvin, Lightfoot, and Kümmel argue for the northern, or Celtic, designation of Galatia. F. F. Bruce, Ramsey, Ridderbos, and Burton argue for the southern, or provincial, designation of Galatia (Lightfoot, 1–21; Burton, 1–21; BBC, 9:22; WBC 5:322).

The South Galatian theory seems to be more acceptable for several reasons.

1. There is evidence in the NT that Paul founded the churches in South Galatia (Ac 13). There is only a passing comment suggesting that he might have traversed North Galatia (Ac 16).

2. There is a better probability of interrelating Gal 2 and Ac 15, which seem to be concerned with a similar issue. Burton writes strongly that the similarity of the narrative in these two passages "makes it necessary to suppose that these ... refer to the same event" (115–17; also Ridderbos, 78–79; Bruce, 43ff.).

3. There is more likelihood that Judaizers would have been in the southern area. Tenney suggests that the southern cities "lay on the direct routes of travel between Palestine and the Aegean ports, and a Jewish population is specifically mentioned in ... Acts 13:14, 14:1" (p. 54).

III. DATE

The date of the writing of the epistle is related to the identification of the recipients. The North Galatian theory would mandate a date after Ac 16, following Paul's travels in the region of Phrygia and Galatia on his way to Troas, not before the late 50s. On the other hand, the South Galatian theory would allow for an early date, anytime after the first journey of Paul, described in Ac 13–14, possibly as early as A.D. 47 or 48. To hold to the later date does not mandate the North Galatian theory, but it does allow for the letter to have been written at nearly the same time as Romans and 1 and 2 Corinthians, which have similarities of style and content.

IV. OCCASION

Paul had received word that in Galatia, where he had preached the Gospel, there were some who were preaching "another gospel," which was unsettling the believers. These other preachers were responsible for "bewitching" (3:1; cf. 1:6–9) them. These perceived troublemakers apparently were not only casting aspersions on Paul's preaching, but also on his person. The issues seem to center on (1) whether non-Jewish believers must enter into Christian fellowship via Judaism and its covenantal mark, circumcision, and (2) whether Paul had legitimate apostolic authority to teach and preach.

V. OUTLINE

    I. Salutation (1:1–5)

    II. The Character of the Gospel (1:6–2:21)
        A. Without a Rival (1:6–10)
        B. Revealed by God (1:11–24)
        C. Supported by Jerusalem Council (2:1–10)
        D. Based on Faith for All People (2:11–21)

    III. The Demonstration of the Gospel to the Galatians (chs. 3–4)
        A. The Experience of the Galatians (3:1–5)
        B. The Principle of Faith Illustrated in the Abraham Narrative (3:6–4:7)
        C. The Readers and Their Relationship to Paul (4:8–20)
        D. An Allegory From History (4:21–31)

    IV. The Effects of the Gospel (5:1–6:10)
        A. Stand in Freedom (5:1–12)
        B. Freedom As a Basis for Service (5:13–26)
        C. Warning To Be Careful in Judging (6:1–5)
        D. Closing Metaphor on Sowing (6:6–10)

    V. Concluding Remarks and Benediction (6:11–18)

COMMENTARY

I. SALUTATION (1:1–5)

This is actually a one-sentence salutation including the usual elements of a letter: the writer's name and names of his companions, the intended readers, and a note of divine authority. As most commentators have observed, Paul generally included as well a prayer on behalf of his readers and a commendation for their witness. This salutation is different in that respect, and in omitting the commendation, it seems to reflect Paul's disturbance at the word he has received concerning the churches of Galatia.

To prepare for a strong defense of his own preaching, the opening paragraph includes a clear affirmation of Paul's commission as an apostle from Jesus Christ and from God the Father. Perhaps the readers had been told that Paul's apostolic claim lacked authenticity since it did not come from the original apostles in Jerusalem. Paul implies, however, that he holds ministerial equality with the Twelve, as he too was commissioned by God just as they had been commissioned by Christ (Burton, 363).

The salutation closes with a doxology of praise to God whose redemptive plan was revealed in Jesus Christ. It is the only epistle with such a designation of Christ in the introduction. This may indicate, as the *Wesleyan Bible Commentary* suggests, that the Galatians had "ignored the atoning death of Jesus in their emphasis on fulfillment through works" (p. 386).

II. THE CHARACTER OF THE GOSPEL (1:6–2:21)

A. Without a Rival (1:6–10)

Paul uses the present tense in this paragraph. The churches are shifting their allegiance from Paul's preaching to other preachers with another "gospel." **"I am astonished,"** writes Paul. The verb *thaumazo* implies an "indignant rebuttal and attack on the things the opposition . . . has done," Betz suggests (p. 47). Arichea and Nida suggest that Paul is expressing an "element of intense unbelief in what has happened" (p. 11).

Paul sees his readers as having turned away from the Gospel of grace that he had preached to them and turning to a different, or another gospel, which is no gospel at all. Paul declares that any gospel other than the one he preached is a "travesty" (Phillips) of the Gospel. The one who proclaims such a travesty is placed under *anathema,* a curse. Arichea and Nida have suggested that the best literal translation of v.8 is, "May he be condemned to hell" (p. 14).

Luther wrote forcefully: "The doctrine of grace can by no means stand with the doctrine of the Law. The one must simply be refused and abolished, and the other confirmed and established" (p. 69). F. F. Bruce has stated: "The logic of the 'gospel according to Paul' was implicit in his Damascus-road experience. . . . The bankruptcy of the Law and the all-sufficiency of Christ came to him at once. Knowledge of the Law was the prerogative of the Jews, but if salvation was bestowed by grace (as it was bestowed on Paul) and not on the ground of law-keeping, then it was accessible to Gentiles equally with Jews" (pp. 93–94). John Wesley said that whatever good one does, "faith does not *find* but *brings*" (*Works,* 1:194).

In the present age there is no tendency for believers to adopt Jewish legalism as a supplement to grace, yet there always seems to be the temptation to relegate God's grace to second place. It is the human tendency to put our own achievements on a pedestal. "See what we have accomplished," we want to say to God. To mingle grace with anything is to make a travesty of the Gospel.

It is probably justified to maintain the distinction between the two terms **an other** (*heteros*), and **another** (*allos*) in vv.6–9. The classic writer Trench wonders, if there is no difference, why Paul would change the word (pp. 357ff.)? *International Critical Commentary* states that there is "no room for doubt that for Paul *heteros* suggested difference of kind more distinctly than did *allos*, and that the latter, in contrast with *heteros*, signified simply numerical non-identity" (p. 427). What the readers are accepting as just a different gospel is so totally contrary as to be no gospel at all.

B. Revealed by God (1:11–24)

This paragraph gives support to Paul's claim that his gospel did not originate in his own wisdom but in the grace of God. A connecting conjunction "for" is omitted in the NIV. This omission seems to be in error, for it ties v.11 to the previous paragraph. V.11 gives the supportive argument for Paul's statement above. The reason for his claim of singular truth is that "his" gospel is not his own gospel at all, but was revealed to him by Jesus Christ. It is Christ's Gospel that is being distorted by those who have come into Galatia and are upsetting the believers. Whenever human tradition and divine revelation come into opposition, it cannot be divine revelation that is in error.

Paul reminds the readers that they have heard of his past when he violently persecuted the church and tried to destroy it, but God revealed his Son to him and turned his life around. A strong devotee of Judaism and zealous for its cause, Paul had no predisposition toward the Gospel, and yet God called him to preach to the Gentiles. This radical change from a violent persecutor to an ardent proclaimer of the Gospel can be explained only by divine intervention. "An encounter with the living, risen Lord is the indispensable beginning of every transformed life—the miracle of the new birth," writes R. E. Howard (BBC, 18:37).

Paul was so sure of his divine commission that he felt no need for getting authority from any person. In v.17 he makes the point that he did not even consult with the apostles in Jerusalem; rather, he went into seclusion where he could ponder what had occurred in his life. Paul makes it clear that he believed his call by Christ to be an apostle to the Gentiles was as legitimate as the call of Christ given to the Eleven. (In a similar way, John Wesley, late in life, considered himself to be a legitimate "missionary bishop" with the right to ordain elders for the people called Methodists, first in the new nation of America and later in Britain. He believed that it was God's hand and not man's hand that had put him into the apostolic succession of the ministry [*Letters,* 7:238–39]).

Paul emphasizes in this paragraph that he did not receive from the apostles in Jerusalem the authority to preach to the non-Jews, including or excluding circumcision. On the contrary, he had, under God, pursued an independent mission without insisting upon circumcision. The visit to Jerusalem recorded in v.18 did nothing to alter Paul's assertion that "his" gospel was in actuality "God's" Gospel received by direct revelation.

Between Paul's visit to Peter in 1:18 and the visit mentioned in 2:1, he had no contact with Jerusalem, but instead he had used his time in Syria and Cilicia, in the same area as Tarsus. This seems to be in agreement with Acts, which described Paul's living in Tarsus for a number of years following his conversion experience. Paul's purpose was not to present a precise chronology of his itinerary, but to emphasize that he had been authorized by God, not by the Jerusalem apostles.

C. Supported by Jerusalem Council (2:1–10)

Paul substantiates his claim of divine revelation by citing the early support he received from the church leadership in Jerusalem. The chronology here is in dispute. Commentators are about equally divided as to whether this meeting is the same as that recorded in Ac 15, or occurred prior to Ac 15 but subsequent to Ac 11, the "famine visit" (Ridderbos, 78–80; Lightfoot, 123–28; Betz, 81–83; Burton, 64–68). If Gal 2 is to be associated with the "famine visit," the problem cited in the epistle could not have risen from the Galatian preaching in Ac 13–14, which would have been later. If, on the other hand, it is associated with the incident in Ac 15, the meeting would be after Paul's preaching mission in South Galatia.

That Paul went by **revelation** (v.2) is not incompatible with the incident recorded in Ac 15. Revelation could mean by direct divine inspiration or indirectly through the suggestions of the church. In any event, "Paul did not go as a humble petitioner" (Betz, 86), but sought to avoid what Bruce calls a "cleavage between the gentile mission and the mother church [which] would

be disastrous" to the work of the gospel (Bruce, 111).

When the traditionalists insisted on the circumcision of the Gentiles, Paul and Barnabas came to Jerusalem to secure recognition of the Gospel that Paul had preached. They brought with them Titus, a Gentile. The essence of Paul's conviction was that provision for the salvation of the Gentiles was complete and could not be ensured further by subjection to circumcision. Since a theological issue of real import was involved, Paul refused to allow himself to be adversely influenced by the status of those in Jerusalem. Paul's words are not to be construed as casting aspersions on the leaders in Jerusalem. They do emphasize, however, that Paul did not see himself as having gone to Jerusalem to accept their decision, whatever it might have been. In his opinion, to make an advance commitment to the authority of Jerusalem would be failing to be obedient to God's call.

There were, it seems, three parties at the Jerusalem Council: (Ac 15): Paul and Barnabas, who wanted to recognize Gentile believers without circumcision; the "pillars," including James the brother of the Lord; and the "false brethren," who wanted to have the Gentile Christians circumcised. The latter disapproved of the decision not to require circumcision, as supported by James in a letter given to Paul for transmission to the Galatian churches. The "false brethren" continued to cause more disturbance by denouncing Paul and his ministry.

D. Based on Faith for All People (2:11–21)

Having concluded his reference to the approval given in Jerusalem, Paul brings up a confrontation he had with Peter. This is designed to emphasize the universality of faith as the heart of the Gospel, not only to the Gentiles, but to the Jews as well.

When Peter went to the home of Cornelius, it was in violation of a Jewish tradition. But it had been revealed to him in his vision that God showed no favoritism. After that experience, Peter had even eaten with Gentile believers in Antioch. Then, for an unexplained reason, Peter changed his attitude when traditionalists came from Jerusalem, and he began to separate himself from the Gentiles.

Paul was greatly disturbed at what he perceived to be inconsistency in Peter's actions. There are no details in the text in regard to fellowship at meals, but it appears that the separation of Jews and Gentiles was based on legalist grounds. Evidently, in the presence of the traditionalists, Peter did not want to be looked upon as a violator of the Law. As a result he pulled back from what had been his practice.

Paul, in his public rebuke, appealed to Peter's original relationship to Christ. (It cannot be determined from the text whether or not the confrontation was in the presence of the congregation or a smaller group.) Peter himself had originally turned from legalism to salvation in Christ by faith. Returning to legalism or showing hypocrisy is wrong. More than just meal fellowship was involved. At stake was the basic principle of justification by faith as opposed to justification by obedience to the law. Paul says, **"We who are Jews by birth and not 'Gentile sinners' know that a man is not justified by observing the law, but by faith in Jesus Christ"** (vv.15–16a). In Ro 8:3 he writes, "What the law was powerless to do in that it was weakened by the sinful nature, God did by sending his own Son in the likeness of sinful man to be a sin offering." "Justification,"

wrote John Wesley, "is that act of God the Father whereby, for the sake of the propitiation made by the blood of his Son, he . . . will not condemn. . ." (*Sermons,* 1:189).

If . . . we seek to be justified in Christ, it becomes evident that we ourselves are sinners" (v.17). Both Jews and Gentiles are in need of God's forgiving grace. Paul further declares that he **died to the law so that [he] might live for God** (v.19); **[He had] been crucified with Christ** (v.20). John Wesley, in his *Explanatory Notes Upon the New Testament,* wrote, "The apostle describes how he is freed from sin, how far he is from continuing therein." His old life of sin has passed away, and he is living a new life in Christ by faith. The verb is in the perfect tense, implying a past event making for a present reality: "I am now in the condition of having been crucified!"

III. THE DEMONSTRATION OF THE GOSPEL TO THE GALATIANS (CHS. 3–4)

A. The Experience of the Galatians (3:1–5)

Paul reminds his readers of their spiritual experience as he preached the Gospel to them. He opens with a vocative, **"You foolish Galatians,"** translated by Phillips as "You dear little idiots." Arichea and Nida translate it: "You Galatians are not thinking right" (p. 53). **"Who has bewitched you?"** Paul asks. The use of the rhetorical question here means that the evidence is incontrovertible, that Paul believes the false teachers have brainwashed them. "Who knows better," Dayton asks, "than a backslider what he has fallen from. . . ? In moments of honesty he knows how wretched he is" (WBC, 5:345).

Implied in this question (v.3) is that it is an expected part of Christian experience for believers to receive the Holy Spirit. He asks them to reflect on their experience: Had the Spirit come upon them as the result of their faith in Christ or as the result of following the law? If it was by faith in Christ, then why would they even consider returning to legalism?

How can that which was begun by the Spirit be nurtured by the flesh? (Burton, 486). Paul, once and for all, rejects the notion that the law and efforts under the law can release God's power or Spirit. Nor can they promote God's gracious dealing with humankind, as the "false teachers" had been suggesting. To be captivated by the Jewish ritual of circumcision was to reject the legitimacy of a spiritual experience by faith.

B. The Principle of Faith Illustrated in the Abraham Narrative (3:6–4:7)

Gal 3:6 is a quotation of Scripture that is followed by the apostle's exegesis and application. Paul reminds the readers that it was because of Abraham's faith that God blessed the nations through him. It was not good works but his faith that God counted as righteousness. He then declares that all who have faith are children of Abraham, not those who would attempt to do good works, including circumcision. Ridderbos says that to have faith meant "to surrender unreservedly to the word of the Lord, regardless of how incredible it seemed" (p. 118).

Paul insists that the covenant of faith was never set aside by the law. In his *Notes* on 3:11, Wesley wrote: "The man who is accounted just or righteous before God, shall continue in a state of acceptance, life, and salvation, by faith. This is the way God hath chosen."

Wesley, in his sermon "Justification by Faith," wrote: "Faith . . . is the necessary condition of justification; yea, and the only necessary condition thereof. . . . On the other hand, though a man should have everything else without faith. . . . He cannot be justified" (*Sermons,* 58–59).

Paul also saw in Ge 12:3 a prediction of God's acceptance of the Gentiles when they too have faith in God. A sharp contrast with the Abraham illustration is introduced in 3:10. Those who live under the law (Burton, 443–74; Bruce, 158–61), depending upon obedience to it rather than being reconciled to God, are living under a curse. Arichea and Nida point out a specific contrast between the blessing in vv.8 and 9 and the curse in v.10 (p. 62). Instead of the joy of salvation by faith, there comes the threat of condemnation. Dt 27:26 is quoted to support Paul's position that *total* obedience to the law had value, but such total obedience was not possible. Paul has been variously interpreted here. Some scholars maintain that "Breaking one law" equals "breaking the Law." Others hold that Paul should be understood as saying that the very notion of trying to be justified by the law is liable to a curse.

V.11 is a quotation from Habakkuk. In its original context, the OT prophet's complaint was that Babylonian cruelty as an agent of divine judgment was far more oppressive than any earlier injustices inflicted on Judah. As the prophet cries to God, God responds by telling him that ultimate vindication will come, but he must wait and have faith. (The point of Paul's utilization of the verse here seems to be, not that the prophet was justified by faith, but that Habakkuk illustrates what it meant to put one's complete trust in God.) Paul believed and preached that we must trust the way in which God had revealed himself in Christ Jesus. The opposite is to live by legalism. In support, he cites Lev 18:5.

In vv.13–14, referring to the OT tradition that the exposure of a corpse was the sign of a curse, Paul sees that tradition as an illustration of the experience of Christ on the cross. The whole OT sacrificial ceremony was an anticipation of Christ. This being true, now that Christ had died, the OT had been fulfilled. If indeed the OT had been fulfilled in Christ, then what was the need to revert to former practices? To do so would mean not only the rejection of Christ as the fulfillment of the OT but also, in actuality, a rejection of the hope of the OT.

Paul makes reference to other OT Scriptures in the paragraph beginning with v.15. He uses the illustration of adoption. The argument utilizes Paul's understanding of what is entailed by a promise or agreement or covenant between two parties, which is unalterable when once ratified. Just so, Paul writes, God gave a spoken promise of a blessing to Abraham and his descendants. This promise extended to Paul's day unaltered by the giving of the law to Moses. "The promise, with its method of faith was never changed or abrogated. It is Judaism, not Christianity, that has deviated from Old Testament revelation" (WBC, 5:347). It is not as though there is anything wrong with the law given to Moses. It did come from God. That law was given, however, not as a part of the redemptive plan, but to point out sin so that it could be recognized as such. The law was given as a *paidagogos* (v.24), a guardian or a teacher. The law, then, had a limited period of time in which to be in effect—only until the promise itself was fulfilled. Living under the law was like living under a tutor who keeps

one from full freedom until maturity is reached.

Paul's intriguing exegesis forms the core of the argument. God promised Abraham and his **seed,** a singular noun, his blessing (v.16). This reign true, it obviously could not possibly refer to all the descendants of Abraham, but only to Christ. The term translated **"transgressions"** in v.19 is also crucial here. The Greek word means "wrongdoing as a result of willfully violating an existing law." Thus there could not have been transgressions before the giving of the law.

The law, then, was to be in effect only until Christ came. As Paul continues his argument, he points out the weakness of the law in that it did not come directly from God, but through angelic and human mediators. On the other hand, God himself gave the promises to Abraham and his descendants. This indicates that the New Covenant—the redemptive plan—came from God to be accepted by humanity without negotiations.

V.21 shows that in no way does this interpretation negate the value of the law, insofar as one does not forget that the law's real purpose was to show wrongdoing. It was not the function of the law to bring life, i.e., eternal life. Even though the law was given, the world was still under the power of sin, thus revealing the need for Christ's redemptive work. What the law has done is to keep us restricted till, recognizing the pressures of our sin, we would accept the freedom and forgiveness offered by Christ. Having served its purpose, the law can now be put aside, as the time for faith has come.

In the first paragraph in ch. 4 Paul compares the children of God under the law to a child who, though an heir, is no better than a slave until he comes of age. The child is cared for by others who look out for his needs until such a time as established by the father. So it is with a Christian who had been enslaved by forces of the world and then set free.

In baptism believers have borne witness to being reclothed in Christ. God himself has borne witness to their faith by sending the Holy Spirit into their hearts (Gal 4:6). They are now designated as the spiritual seed of Abraham and the heirs of God's promises. Thus, since Jews and Gentiles, male and female, slave and master, all have the same experience, those distinctions are forever eliminated (BBC, 18:68).

It is God's own Spirit in us that gives evidence of our adoption. This may reflect on what was intimated earlier: repentance, baptism, and receiving the Spirit are all aspects of one experience. Thus it is that by means of this multifaceted experience God bears witness to our deliverance from the law. It is the presence of the Spirit of God in our lives that makes it possible to call God our Father. John Wesley preached that "the testimony of the Spirit is an inward impression of the soul, whereby the Spirit of God directly 'witnesses to my spirit that I am a child of God'; that Jesus Christ hath loved me, and given himself for me; that all my sins are blotted out, and I, even I, am reconciled to God" (*Sermons,* 1:229).

C. The Readers and Their Relationship to Paul (4:8–20)

Paul reminds his readers of their former state when they did not know God. It has been interpreted to mean pagan ignorance of God or Jewish dependence on the law, which was tantamount to being ignorant of the God of grace. Paul compares that state to their current state of knowing God, having had a personal experience with God initiated by grace. To him it is unthinkable that they would even consider a return to what was once their lot of subservience, in adhering to **those weak and miserable principles.** By giving heed to the false prophets' travesty of the Gospel, the Galatians are allowing themselves to fall into slavery again. This slavery may be to religious celebrations designed to win favor with God, or to pagan magical observations and astrological charts. (The notion of "lucky" and "unlucky" days is a remnant of pagan practices.)

Paul expresses, in v.11, a fear that his preaching to them will have come to naught. Consequently in v.12 he begins a passionate appeal to the Galatians to follow him in accepting his persuasion that the law has no value whatsoever in gaining righteousness before God.

He reminds them of the circumstances under which he found his way to Galatia: an illness had caused considerable anxiety and concern on their part. It is probably foolish even to speculate as to the nature of his illness. Whether it was eye trouble, malaria, or epileptic seizures matters little. Paul reminds them that whereas they once welcomed him graciously as if he were Christ himself, they are now ready to reject him because of the Judaizers. They had accepted him in his frailty; why do they now reject him as a messenger of God?

Paul expresses his concern that false prophets are striving to win them over, but not for the good of the believers. These Judaizers want to separate them from Paul and his teachings and recruit them for their cause (4:17). He uses the metaphor of childbirth as once again he depicts himself as the mother going through pangs of childbirth on their behalf. Cole likens it to the "agony of the pastor watching for signs of Christian growth in his flock" (p. 127). Paul sees them reverting to a state of immaturity in which their faith in Christ is not strong enough to enable them to reject the false gospel that has been preached to them.

D. An Allegory From History (4:21–31)

The next paragraph concludes this section with Paul using the OT account of Abraham, Hagar, and Sarah allegorically to contrast slavery under the law with freedom in the promises of God. The allegory builds on the thought of two groups claiming descent from Abraham. Hagar was the slave girl who gave birth in a normal, physical way, without any divine intervention. Sarah was the wife who gave birth in an extraordinary way—through a conception that occurred when she was well beyond the age of childbearing. This happened because God had promised a son to Abraham and Sarah. Paul's point is that a follower of Christ is a child of promise and a true heir, but the child of the slave is not an heir; he is another slave. The allegory is pushed to an extreme. Hagar represents the old covenant as seen in Jerusalem and its temple and its laws, which equals slavery. Sarah represents the new covenant as seen in the new or heavenly Jerusalem and its promise, which equals freedom in Christ (Bruce, 158–61).

In v.27 is a quotation from Isa 54, from the context of the Babylonian captivity. Jerusalem before the Exile is portrayed as a woman living with her husband and capable of producing children. During the time of the Exile, however, Jerusalem is pictured as a woman thought incapable of having children, who suddenly becomes joyful as she realizes that she is again capable of bearing children. This word of Isaiah is meant to provide hope for a return from exile with its concomitant restoration. A double metaphor is employed. The barren woman is the heavenly Jerusalem, which in turn is the joy of becoming the people of God. The woman with the husband, on the other hand, is taken to be the earthly Jerusalem, which is inferior to the heavenly Jerusalem.

The chapter ends with one final comparison between Abraham's two sons—the one who receives the inheritance and the other who is dismissed to fend for himself. Even as Isaac is the child of promise, so are those who have become God's children through trusting in him. As Ishmael, the naturally conceived child, is the child of the flesh, so are those who through trusting in their own ability to secure God's blessing have been dismissed by God as though they were slaves. "Have nothing to do with the servile Mosaic dispensation, . . . being free from the curse and the bond of that Law," wrote Wesley (*Notes*, 4:31).

IV. THE EFFECTS OF THE GOSPEL (5:1–6:10)

A. Stand in Freedom (5:1–12)

This chapter, the beginning of the third major division of the letter, opens with a direct exhortation. The RSV correctly includes a **"therefore,"** tying chs. 5–6 to chs. 3–4 in a causal relationship. If indeed the readers are not the children of slavery but children of promise, they are to stand firm in freedom, not allowing themselves to become enslaved. The epitome of slavery was the ritual of circumcision by means of which a proselyte was accepted into Judaism with the understanding that he was then expected to observe all of its laws and ceremonies. The argument of Paul is direct: One need not, in fact, must not, become a Jew in order to become a Christian. To do so would imply the legitimacy of the law as a means of attaining righteousness with God. In addition, to do so would deny implicitly salvation through faith in Christ, to hold that the death and resurrection of Christ were inadequate for salvation. Those who do this "cut themselves off from Christ" (Arichea and Nida, 74). They have "fallen from grace." Wesley noted, "You hereby disclaim Christ, and all the blessings which are through faith in him" (*Notes,* 5:1; BBC, 18:84). Arichea and Nida emphasize that it is not that "grace has been taken away from them, but . . . that they have turned their backs on it" (p. 108).

V.5 shows how Paul can use the idea of salvation in different ways: Salvation is something that was realized in the past in the death and resurrection of Jesus Christ in the present—in one's own personal acknowledgment of its efficacy for oneself and, finally, in the future—the realization of the final consummation. The word *hope* is here used in the true sense of the anticipation of a certainty so that one can live in the present with that anticipation. It is the glory of this relationship to Christ that makes circumcision and uncircumcision equally irrelevant. Neither the ceremony nor the lack of it has any value in God's sight.

In vv.7ff. Paul expresses shock and disappointment at his readers' being so easily persuaded by an influence that did not come from God. He refers to this influence as **a little yeast** that is working through the whole batch and having its effect on the churches. Nevertheless, Paul expresses his confidence that they will heed his warning and turn from the one(s) turning them from Christ. He declares that whoever is confusing them will receive the punishment due from God himself.

In v.12 Paul strongly denounces the Judaizers. He goes so far as to say that he wishes the agitators who advocate

ceremonial circumcision would totally castrate themselves. Jewish tradition held that an emasculated male was no longer a part of the covenant. Paul seems to be saying that those who insist on Gentiles becoming Jews in order to become Christians are totally in error. To be obsessed with circumcision is to put oneself in danger of losing one's own place in God's kingdom!

B. Freedom As a Basis for Service (5:13–26)

Freedom in Christ is not to lead into any form of antinomianism, the view that the law has no relevance for Christians. They are not free to do as they wish but are free to serve one another in love, free to live responsibly (BBC, 18:90–91). Paul says that the entire law is summed up in a single quotation from the sacred writings of the Law (probably Lev 19:18), "Love your neighbor as yourself" (v.14).

Following the law is not required to become a disciple of Christ, but fulfilling the law is expected of the disciples of Christ (Betz, 275). Living by the Spirit is contrasted to living according to sinful nature in vv.16–20. Humankind is a virtual battleground where sinful nature and divine Spirit are set against each other; no compromise is possible. Paul tells his followers that if they live by the Spirit they will not gratify the desires of the sinful nature. He also says that if they are led by the Spirit they are not under law.

Even as the law without the Gospel becomes legalism—righteousness depends on good works—the Gospel without concomitant responsibility can easily become libertinism—the belief that one can behave without restrictions. The Gospel contains an imperative! Redemption through Christ and the witness of God's Spirit are to be made evident by a new lifestyle. To have the Spirit is to live by the Spirit.

Vv.19–21 are a list of the typical acts of sinful human nature. At first glance these appear to be random, but after a further study, there does seem to be an order: sensual passions, spiritual sin, social evils, lack of temperance. A comparison of several translations will help in interpreting Paul.

Following immediately, in sharp contrast, is a list of virtues that are to be evident in the character of those who are directed by the Spirit of God (vv.22–25). It may be possible to list them as characterizing habits of the mind, relationships to others, and conduct in general. It should be noted that **"fruit"** is singular. The list is a unity. It should not be confused with the gifts of the Spirit discussed by the apostle in 1Co 12–13. "The fruit of the Spirit is the witness of the Spirit," said Wesley (*Sermons*, 1:294). These are not natural traits of the human personality but are the results of the Spirit's coming upon those who acknowledge Christ as Lord and Savior. The Spirit testifies to them that they are the children of God. "The immediate result of this testimony is "The fruit of the Spirit . . . and without these the testimony itself cannot continue" (*Sermons*, 1:296).

In using the metaphor, perhaps Paul was reminded of Isaiah's "Song of the Vineyard" (ch. 5), in which the prophet speaks of God's preparing a vineyard. When the vineyard did not produce the expected good fruit, it was abandoned by God and returned to nature, a wasteland. The issue is not salvation by good works but instead the expectation of good works from those whom God had dealt with lovingly.

John Wesley's three distinctions of God's grace fit Pauline theology at this point. Wesley believed that humankind, as a result of the Adamic fall, was totally depraved, spiritually corrupt. Had it not been for God's universal prevenient grace, no one could have responded to the offer of saving grace in the atoning death and resurrection of Jesus Christ. When that saving grace is accepted by the sinner, God's sanctifying grace begins its work of bringing that redeemed sinner to holy living.

The chapter concludes with a summary statement that those who are Christ's have **crucified** their sinful human nature, with its passions and desires, and have received God's Spirit. That being true, it is totally inconsistent to live according to the flesh. The Spirit makes it possible for the fruit of the Spirit to be evident in our lives (BBC, 18:96–110).

C. Warning To Be Careful in Judging (6:1–5)

The last chapter begins with a plea to the Galatians to deal kindly with an individual who is **caught in a sin.** Those who are spiritual should not condemn but guide that one into a state of renewal and restoration, being mindful that they too can be tempted to sin. One should not imply that he is better than the sinful brother. Paul said that one should take a close look at oneself and not compare oneself with others.

D. Closing Metaphor on Sowing (6:6–10)

Paul has now come to the end of a letter that could not have been easy to write. The proverbial thought of reaping what one sows gives the basis for his last exhortation. Paul writes that the way one lives will undoubtedly be recognized by God as a true indication of what one is. In fact, to sow to please one's sinful nature may very well be related to Paul's early discussion on circumcision—to be circumcised is to sow that which is of the flesh, which then results in death, for it misses the fullness of the gift of grace. To allow natural desires to bring forth their fruit results in a judgment of death, while to allow the spiritual presence to bring forth its fruit results in eternal life. V.9 suggests that eschatological judgment may be what Paul had in mind. Until the very end one should not be weary in doing good to all people, especially to **the family of believers,** for that is the norm for the disciples of Jesus (v.10). In this final metaphor Paul uses the imagery of the greater family of the redeemed of God.

V. CONCLUDING REMARKS AND BENEDICTION (6:11-18)

Finally, Paul calls attention to the fact that he himself is writing, possibly the entire letter. But in view of his practice of utilizing a scribe, as noted in other letters, it is more likely that he takes the pen from the hand of his scribe and adds his own concluding comment. Once again he denounces false teachers as he accuses them of trying to force circumcision on the Galatians, only that they may boast in the number of converts they have won rather than glorying in the cross of Christ. By making converts their way, they avoid persecution at the hand of others of like mind. The Judaizers saw the Galatian Gentile believers as potential proselytes, whereas Paul sees these same Galatian Gentiles as brothers and sisters in Christ, by God's grace. Therefore, to become a Jewish proselyte meant to turn away from grace.

In conclusion Paul says that, for the believer, circumcision or uncircumcision is of no importance. What does being a Jew or a Gentile matter, as long as one is a new creature in Christ? In v.17 Paul seems to contrast the mark of circumcision on the body with **the marks of Jesus,** possibly scars on his back from the beatings at the hands of the Jews. (If the South Galatian theory is accepted, some of the readers could well have been among the apostle's early converts who witnessed the stoning at Lystra, Ac 14.)

Peace, mercy, and grace are bestowed on all who are of the new creation, as Paul brings his explosive letter to an end. These blessings are directed to the "Israel of God"—the new Israel, which is the church. In spite of all he has said, Paul still calls them **brothers.**

BIBLIOGRAPHY

Arichea, Daniel C. and Nida, Eugene A. *A Translator's Handbook on Paul's Letter to the Galatians.* London: United Bible Societies, 1976.

Beacon Bible Commentary. Vol. 18. Kansas City: Beacon Hill, 1965.

Betz, Hans Dieter. *Galatians.* Philadelphia: Fortress, 1979.

Bruce, F. F. *The Epistle to the Galatians.* Grand Rapids: Eerdmans, 1982.

Burton, Edgar Dewitt. *Epistle to the Galatians.* ICC. Edinburgh: T. & T. Clark, 1921. Rep. 1962.

Cole, R. A. *Galatians.* Grand Rapids: Eerdmans, 1965.

Dayton, Wilbur T. "Galatians." WBC. Vol. 5. Grand Rapids: Eerdmans, 1965.

Lightfoot, J. B. *The Epistle of Paul to the Galatians.* Grand Rapids: Zondervan, 1865, reprint.

Luther, Martin. *A Commentary on St. Paul's Epistle to the Galatians*. New York: Robert Carter, 1845.

Ramsey, W. M. *A Historical Commentary on St. Paul's Epistle to the Galatians*. Grand Rapids: Baker, 1900, reprint.

Ridderbos, Herman N. *The Epistle of Paul to the Churches of Galatia*. Grand Rapids: Eerdmans, 1971.

Tenney, Merrill C. *Galatians*. Grand Rapids: Eerdmans, 1971.

Trench, Richard Chenevix. *Synonyms of the New Testament*. Grand Rapids: Eerdmans, 1948.

Wesley, John. *Explanatory Notes Upon the New Testament*. New York: Carlton, n.d.

_____. *Letters*. London: Epworth, 1924.

_____. *Forty-Four Sermons*. London: Epworth, 1952.

_____. *Works*. Nashville, Abingdon, 1984.

EPHESIANS
Wesley E. Vanderhoof

INTRODUCTION

I. THE AUTHOR

The content of Ephesians indicates that it is one of Paul's Prison Epistles (3:1, 13; 4:1; 6:20), along with Colossians, Philippians, and Philemon. For many scholars, however, Paul's authorship of the epistle is problematic. *Wesleyan Bible Commentary,* aware of the difficulties and in spite of some internal evidence to the contrary, nevertheless accepts the traditional viewpoint that the apostle wrote the letter from prison (Carter, 370–72). Because the epistle bears a great deal of similarity to Colossians—nearly half of the verses of Ephesians have verbal parallels in Colossians; about one-third of the words of Colossians are found in Ephesians; and the role of Tychicus is virtually the same in both letters (Eph 6:21–22; Col 4:7)—it appears that the two letters belong together, written at nearly the same time by Paul. Carter maintains that the differences between Ephesians and Colossians "serve only to make their relationship more evident" (Carter, 370). Furthermore, the greeting is typically Pauline, and the author identifies himself as Paul.

II. THE OCCASION

Unlike the typical Pauline letter, Ephesians does not address any particular local conflict or issue. Also, no personal greetings appear at the end, as one would expect if Paul wrote this letter to people with whom he had spent three difficult years (Ac 19; 20:13–31).

Because the phrase "in Ephesus" is missing in some of the early copies of this epistle, scholars have proposed a different destination. That Ephesians is "the letter [to] Laodicea" was first proposed by Marcion in the second century, but the idea has little support today. It is more likely that the author intended this as a circulating letter. The contents are appropriate to a number of churches in Asia Minor, of which the church at Ephesus was typical. That an encyclical could not easily contain personal greetings might explain their absence.

At Ephesus, the center of Paul's Asian ministry on his third journey (Ac 19:10), the Christian faith had come face to face with black magic, cult religion, and the power of demons. There, too, it had been maligned by

Jews (Ac 19:9), and later it was infiltrated with new doctrine offered through the "cunning and craftiness of men" (4:14) and was stripped of its ethical principles (4:17–5:20). Therefore, having seen how the "devil's schemes" (6:11) had affected his ministry in Ephesus, and having already encountered the "new religion" sweeping through the province of Asia, Paul wrote Ephesians and Colossians to believers in Asia to remind them that no religion offered more than the Gospel, because in Christ every spiritual blessing had already become theirs.

III. THE DATE

If Paul was the author of Ephesians, during which of the recorded imprisonments was it written? The overnight jailing in Philippi (Ac 16:23–26) hardly qualifies. The second recorded imprisonment in Jerusalem and Caesarea (Ac 21:27–22:29) seems too early (A.D. 57–59). At the end of Acts, Paul was in Rome under guard "in his own rented house" for "two whole years." If Bruce (*Letters,* 160–61) and others are right that there was also an imprisonment in Ephesus, the date (A.D. 53–55) is too early. Therefore, the traditional view that Rome was the place of imprisonment common to Philippians, Philemon, Colossians, and Ephesians remains popular among evangelical scholars in spite of the problem of distance between Rome and Ephesus.

Those who deny Paul's authorship of Ephesians date the letter near the end of the first century. By then Gnosticism had made serious inroads into areas previously evangelized by Paul. If one sees the advanced system of thought as the false doctrine against which both Colossians and Ephesians were directed, then one must accept the later date. If, however, one sees emerging doctrine as the false wisdom attacked in both of these epistles, then one can move Ephesians into Paul's own lifetime. After all, the apostle had warned the elders of Ephesus with strong words: "I know that after I leave, savage wolves will come in among you and will not spare the flock. Even from your own number men will arise and distort the truth in order to draw away disciples after them. So be on your guard!" (Ac 20:29–31a). Does this premonition connect Paul to Ephesians?

The date A.D. 61–66 seems likely, but to fit the epistle into the chronology of Acts may not be possible. The view that Paul was released after two years in Rome, resuming travels before being rearrested, lacks textual support. However, such a hypothesis, if true, might resolve some of the problems associated with assigning to Paul both the Prison and the Pastoral Epistles.

IV. OUTLINE

    I. Salutation (1:1–2)

    II. Formation of the New Community (1:3–3:21)
        A. The Role of Jesus Christ in the Formation of God's New Community (1:4–14)

COMMENTARY

I. SALUTATION (1:1–2)

The author identifies himself as **Paul, an apostle of Christ Jesus.** Paul defends his use of the title on the basis of his call on the Damascus road (Ac 9:1–16), arguing in Gal 1:11–17 that he possesses apostolic authority, not by the vote of men, but **by the will of God.** In 3:1–8 and elsewhere (Ac 22:21; Gal 2:7), Paul notes that his calling is primarily to Gentiles, who make up a large portion of the group to whom this letter is directed.

The epistle was penned to instruct, edify, and encourage **the saints . . . the faithful in Christ Jesus.** Touched by the Holy Spirit, they are among God's new people, part of the new community formed by the Lord himself. Saints are not "holier-than-thou" people. They are those who have entered into a covenant with God through belief in Jesus as Messiah and Lord. In that relationship they continue to be beset by every human problem and trouble, but they are **faithful in Christ Jesus.** Having faith in Jesus as God's condition for their salvation, they remain committed to their faith in spite of earthly problems and struggles. In the biblical sense of the word, saints are holy ones (*hagioi*) because they belong to the God who is holy (*hagios*) and are sealed by God's Holy Spirit.

"Grace" and **"peace"** are fairly uniform elements of early Christian greetings. To **"peace"** (*shalom*), the typical Jewish greeting, believers in Jesus added **"grace"** (*charis*), aware of the unmerited favor bestowed on them through Jesus, the Father's gracious gift. Grace suggests that God has made himself and his unlimited resources available. Therefore, believers can be at peace, free from anxiety, secure in the knowledge that by grace they can and will endure.

II. FORMATION OF THE NEW COMMUNITY (1:3–3:21)

This epistle sets forth the fundamental facts of Christian experience. At the same time, these facts are highlighted with special attention to the Gentiles, new to the covenant community. Paul had come to believe, along with the apostles (Ac 15:13–18), that God had planned to include non-Jews among his people. This newly constituted family he describes as a new community. Although its roots are in the Judaism of the past, its constitution is new and unique in human history. The new community is both a new Israel and the true Israel. In these three chapters, the doctrinal section of the epistle, Paul describes the formation of this new community.

A. The Role of Jesus Christ in the Formation of God's New Community (1:4–14)

The church is God's new community. It is founded on Jesus Christ, the Mediator of every spiritual blessing. To offer **praise** to the God who conceived and implemented this new community is, therefore, appropriate. So Paul glorifies the God and Father of the Lord Jesus Christ. The wording of the phrase suggests that Jesus acknowledged the God of the Hebrews as both the God he worshiped and the Father he loved and obeyed. The phrase joins sovereignty and intimacy. Jesus was both subject to God and Son of God.

Why is praise to God appropriate? It is fitting because the Father of Jesus the

Messiah has given the Gospel and the "gifts and graces of the Holy Ghost . . . to prepare them for heavenly places" (Clarke, 431). The "mysteries" of the ancient world offered nothing that God has not already provided. In fact, every spiritual need has been supplied, every spiritual blessing has been provided, every grace has been given to those "in this heavenly state" (ibid.). In effect, God has poured out the blessings of heaven upon all those who have put their trust in Jesus, thus unlocking the channels of spiritual grace. Those who await an additional revelation, hope for a deeper insight into the nature of God, or anticipate fuller participation in the Godhead will be disappointed.

The phrase **"in the heavenly realms"** demands attention here. Although for Paul it often seems to mean heaven, sometimes it refers not to God's abode, but to the space between heaven and earth in which principalities and powers hold sway, and from which they disburse both bane and blessing. Thus the phrase may and perhaps should be translated "in the realm of spiritual activity." Gnosticism, a heresy that may have been emerging at this time, built a theology around this "space between." Gnostics taught that Jesus lived in this realm, subject to the whim of the fallen angels who ruled it. In using the phrase, then, the writer intends to show not only that spiritual blessings are administered in Christ, but also that Jesus has conquered the principalities and powers alleged to rule this world beyond earth (cf. 1:20–22).

Beginning with 1:4, Paul enumerates the blessings that have come through Jesus. First, God chose the saints **in him before the creation of the world** [lit. "cosmos"] **to be holy and blameless in his sight.** The work of Christ was determined prior to creation. Through the Son, the salvation of

God's people was to be accomplished; through Jesus, God would constitute his people, choosing as his those who accepted Jesus as his Son and their Savior. More important, however, is the goal God had in mind for those chosen through Christ. The plan of the Father was that they should be holy and blameless in his sight, not only absolved of guilt, but sharing in the nature of the Trinity. For Wesleyan scholars, then, the emphasis here is not on the choosing so much as on the condition of the choosing. Simply put, God made the choice that those who were to be his would be his through Christ. Therefore, the true people of God in the OT were those who anticipated the Messiah, who were "waiting for the consolation of Israel" (Lk 2:25), who "fled to take hold of the hope offered" (Heb 6:18). "Living by faith when they died" without seeing the promise fulfilled, "they admitted that they were aliens and strangers on earth . . . longing for a better country" (Heb 11:13–16).

Moreover, **in love he predestined** those who would believe **to be adopted as his sons through Jesus Christ.** The destiny of believers was preestablished. They would be sons of God by adoption through faith in Christ. The new life believers have is none other than the indwelling Son of God. Through Christ, they are made children of God, having both a new relationship and a new position. The relationship gives right and title to the Father's riches; the position grants privileges associated with belonging to the Father's family.

God was not forced by either logic or social pressure to adopt believers as children. He took **pleasure** in willing their adoption and in planning and executing the action. This is to the praise of his grace, freely given in

Christ, **the One he loves.** Paul saw, in other words, that God the Father had not provided minimally for believers. Rather, God had gone beyond forgiving their sins. From the beginning, God had established a plan by which sinners might be not only pardoned but parented, not only absolved but adopted. Such a plan can be attributed only to grace. In the divine plan, acquittal has been followed by adoption, and believers, as God's children, have become "heirs with Christ" (Ro 8:17).

Paul moves now from the conception of the plan to its execution (1:7–15). What God intended for believers he accomplished successfully at Calvary. There, through the blood of Christ, he redeemed from bondage those who await their release from sin's grip. The eternal plan was executed in time. In Gal 4:3–5 Paul wrote, "When the time had fully come, God sent his Son, born of a woman, born under law, to redeem those under law, that we might receive the full rights of sons." In the Incarnation, the preestablished purposes of God moved into the arena of history. The grand plan, conceived in the mind of God and anticipated in the shadows of the Old Covenant, was expressed in Jesus Christ.

To establish the new community, God provided forgiveness of sin and redemption from the powers of bondage. If the divine scheme can be attributed to grace, then certainly the actual act of redemption is accomplished as a result of God's grace lavishly poured out. Although grace cannot be measured, Paul says that God was extravagant in dispensing it. In effect, God gave more than anyone knew how to ask for in order to bring to fruition the divine plan for his people. Paul believed that he, and every believer, had benefited from God's decision to pour out abundant grace.

The NIV rendering of v.8, unlike the RSV and slightly different from the KJV, includes the phrase **with all wisdom and understanding** as a part of the display of grace. This rendering suggests that God, fully aware of both human need and the divine plan, wisely extended grace beyond human measure. The initiative was divine, not human. God did not act in response to a human call for help, but in line with his own design, when he graciously put the plan into action.

In addition, in Jesus, God revealed the **mystery** of his will according to his good pleasure. In the Son, God showed the grand plan for the formation of the new Israel. In Galatians and Romans Paul wrote of his revelation that faith was the most justifiable means of salvation because it was fair to all, Jews and Gentiles alike. That God had anticipated the salvation of Gentiles was only hinted at in the OT. The full vision did not come until after Pentecost, when the significance of the work of Jesus was slowly but finally grasped. Since the life, death, and resurrection of Jesus and his sending of the Holy Spirit, the plan of God has been totally revealed. The **mystery,** hidden through the ages, has been uncovered, not by human effort or intelligence, but by divine pleasure. God chose to reveal to all the magnificent panorama of human salvation conceived prior to creation, that through Christ he would adopt into sonship these fallen creatures who, by free choice, separated themselves from God. If the plan to bring together sinful Jews and Gentiles into a new community was wonderful, how much more wonderful is the revelation of the plan.

God intended to accomplish this plan in Christ **when the times will have reached their fulfillment.** The phrase is reminiscent of Gal 4:4, although use of the future tense here suggests that the consummation of the eternal plan awaits some final historical condition. On the other hand, had not the divine idea already been enacted? Is not the point of this epistle to show that God has already seated Christ **at his right hand in the heavenly realms, far above all rule and authority, power and dominion, and every title that can be given, not only in the present age but also in the one to come** (vv.20–21)? And has not God already **placed all things under his feet and appointed him to be head over everything** (vv.22–23)? Fulfillment of God's plan is not postponed to some future time.

On the other hand, it is true that there remains a yet unfulfilled dimension of the marvelous divine plan, a universal worship of Jesus and a universal recognition of his lordship (Php 2:10). That Jesus is Head of all things is a current fact; that his lordship will be universally acknowledged remains a promise in the divine agenda of grace.

Returning to the facts of grace previously noted, summarizing as a literary transition, Paul reminds his readers that they have been **chosen, having been predestined according to the plan** of God. This he has already mentioned to them. Why does he repeat himself here? The answer may be in the single word **also** (*kai*). Here the emphasis turns not toward the great plan of redemption, but toward its purpose. That is, believers have been predestined not only as an act of divine grace, but as a living testimony to that grace. The salvation of Jewish believers, the first to hope in Christ, brings praise to God's glory.

Up to this point the apostle has spoken primarily about Jewish believers. After all, the history of redemption is, up to the time of the apostle himself, a story of God's dealings with Israel. Observe, therefore, the use of the pronoun *we,* by which Paul means those Jews who, as he, have believed the Gospel and have accepted Jesus as Savior.

In v.13, however, the mystery begins to unfold as Paul calls attention to the true significance of the work of God in Christ: **"And you [Gentiles] also were included in Christ."** The work of Jesus the Christ was not for the Jews alone but for Gentiles as well. Why this is so astonishing is demonstrated in ch. 2. For now, though, Paul simply reminds those persons whose roots are in gentile paganism that they, along with the remnant of faith of the old community of Israel, have been included in God's new community. Once excluded because of blood line, they have now been included because of faith.

Having believed, they have been marked **with a seal, the promised Holy Spirit.** Having met the condition for their salvation, they have been marked by God, who now lays claim to them. The presence of the Holy Spirit serves to identify them as God's people. Several times in Acts the Holy Spirit came upon a group of people as a way of convincing the apostolic community that God accepted those who did not meet Jewish standards for inclusion (Ac 8:14–17; 10:44–46; 15:8; 19:6). That they belong to God has been established by a formal seal certifying the legality of the adoption. As one would file in a county courthouse a wedding certificate or a deed, so God has recorded the adoption of Gentiles, not by noting the date of their circumcision, but by sending the Holy Spirit into their hearts. To exercise the rights of adoption rests with them, but God has already marked them as his own.

For Jew and Gentile alike, the Holy Spirit, by way of analogy, is a **deposit guaranteeing [their] inheritance** until God redeems his **possession.** At a time in the future when the full benefits of belonging to God are realized, when the inheritance of the saints is actualized, the seal of the resident Holy Spirit will be the condition by which the inheritance is effected. Until that day, believers are kept by the Spirit, **to the praise of [God's] glory.**

B. A Prayer for Spiritual Insight Within the New Community (1:15–23)

That the Gentiles of Asia have received the Gospel by faith, have been received by God through Christ, and have been sealed for the day of redemption has brought joy to Paul's heart. Because of their **faith in the Lord Jesus,** the apostle has continually given **thanks** for them. Since he first learned of their becoming part of God's new community and of their love for all the saints (the demonstration of their full participation in this new community), he has been praying for them.

For what has he prayed? He has been asking God to give them the **Spirit of wisdom and revelation.** Why? He wants them to know God better. Paul hopes that they will know God not only as the Father who legally adopted them but also as the Father who loves them. More than legal heirs, they are also children; not only granted citizenship (see 2:12–19), they are members of God's household. It is his prayer that these who belong to the family will get to know God more intimately. If Paul's prayer is answered, God will show himself to the Gentiles in particular and give them insight to understand the divine mystery of grace.

Furthermore, Paul prays for the Ephesians' spiritual enlightenment that they **may know the hope to which he** has called them, the extent of their inheritance, and the **incomparably great power** available to them. It would be wonderful if God showed these believing Jews and Gentiles the glorious provision already made for them! If they could envision God's dreams for them, they would not want to miss their realization. If they could see their inheritance, they would certainly not want to lose it. If they could realize the power available to them, they would not need to fail. That power, like the working of his mighty strength in creation and the miracles of the OT, was most powerfully demonstrated when God raised Jesus and exalted him to **his right hand in the heavenly realms.** Surely that same power is available to keep believers until their inheritance is fully realized. In Ro 8:31–39, Paul spoke of that power: If God could spare his Son from defeat by death, he can spare us from defeat by life. That is what he wants these citizens to see: **the hope** to which God has called them, the **inheritance** he has for them, and the **power** at their disposal. Who, then, would want or need to turn away from God by abandoning faith in Christ as Savior and Lord? Obviously, Paul is trying to convince readers not to defect and return to alien status.

Vv.20b–22a are creedal in regard to the present role of the risen Son, although they also demonstrate the scope of divine power. Not only did the Father raise the Son from death, but he made him co-regent, with authority **far above all** [human] **rule and authority, power and dominion, and every title that can be given** on earth. Jesus has authority and dominion both now and in the age to come. Furthermore, God gave Jesus supremacy over all creation (cf. 1Co 15:28) and gave

him to the church, **his body,** as its supreme Head.

Here, then, is the new community, the called-out ones (*ekklesia*), from both Judaism and paganism that now constitute the church. By divine power and appointment Christ now presides over the church **the fullness** [or complement] **of him who fills everything** and provides all spiritual vitality. The fulfillment of the Father's purpose for the Son is his lordship over the church. Jesus, who fills the whole universe with his presence and governs the entire creation with his given authority, finds his completion as Head of the body, the church. A head without a body is incomplete. As the body renders the head complete, so the church fulfills God's purpose for Christ.

C. The Unique Nature of God's New Community (2:1–22)

Speaking primarily to the gentile component ("you" as opposed to "we"), Paul now begins to unfold the divine mystery. Reared on Hebrew interpretations, he shared the typical Jewish perspective on Gentiles, the people outside the covenant with Israel. He reminds them that they were previously dead in **transgressions and sins.** Before coming to Christ they **followed the ways of this world,** under the influence of the spirit now working in those who disobey God. In fact, all, even believing Jews, once lived in trespasses and sins, **gratifying the cravings** of the **sinful nature** [NIV fn. "our flesh"] **and following its desires and thoughts** (cf. Ro 7:14–20). Before accepting the Gospel by faith, all persons are **by nature objects of wrath** (cf. Ro 3:9, 23). Whatever advantages there were to being a Jew (cf. Ro 3:1–2; 9:1–5) were lost amid the reality of universal sinfulness.

However, in spite of their transgressions, God brought the dead to life (cf. Ro 6:3–4). Not only was righteousness imputed, but spiritual life was imparted. Surely this was an act of grace. (Notice Paul's emphasis on grace in this entire paragraph.) Moreover, in Christ's exaltation, believers were seated **in the heavenly realms in Christ Jesus.** Whereas in 1:20–21 this exaltation to universal authority is bestowed upon Jesus, here Paul includes believers in the granting of authority even as he includes them in the Resurrection. If Christ's resurrection is theirs, then Christ's exaltation must also be theirs. The purpose: **that in the coming ages he might show the incomparable riches of his grace.** A king who buys a beggar a new coat demonstrates altruism; making him coruler shows grace. Christians have a rags-to-riches story: though born spiritually depraved, they now reside in a throne room. How magnificent God's grace is, as shown us in Christ Jesus! In the denouement of salvation history, Paul suggests, those who rule with Christ will uniformly testify: "I was once a sinner, but I came, pardon to receive from my Lord." And for emphasis, Paul repeats himself: **"For it is by grace you have been saved, through faith"** (in Jesus as God's condition for your salvation). The power to believe is God-given, but one must use the God-given power (Clarke, 6:430) or it is of no effect.

If salvation were by works, by effort, or by obeying the law, there would be justification for human boasting, since some would be more obedient, more industrious, and more precise than others. Those born with an advantage could utilize, even flaunt, that advantage. The truth is, however, that human redemption is **not** brought about by **works,** so there is no room for boasting.

At the same time, all believers must realize that they are designed **in Christ Jesus to do good works.** Wesley emphasized that predestination relates to outcome: to be children of God, to rule with Christ, to attain to the measure of the fullness of Christ, to do good works (Wesley, *Notes,* 489, 492). Even before creation **God prepared in advance** for believers to follow after good works as an expression of their love of God and their appreciation for divine grace.

Now returning to the theme of the chapter, the unique nature of the new community, Paul resumes his discussion of the Gentiles' condition prior to their faith in Christ. He asks them to remember that **formerly** they were **Gentiles by birth and called "uncircumcised"** by Jews who practiced circumcision **by the hands of men.** How could Gentiles ever forget that they stood outside the covenant made with Israel? Only on rare occasions could Gentiles participate in covenant observances. Had they wanted to join with Israel, the barriers were indeed great. In that condition, before the Gospel, they were separate from Christ, **excluded from citizenship in Israel and foreigners to the covenants of the promise.** How desperate the Gentiles' condition, according to the Jews. Gentiles were aliens, unable to apply for citizenship, excluded, and thus without spiritual rights. They were, therefore, **without hope.** Even worse, they were **without God in the world,** alone, bereft, drifting. Without access to the rituals of the Hebrew faith, what prospect for salvation did they have?

Surely the Gentiles needed a miracle if they were to be saved. Who could remove the obstacles to God for them? Who could offer them access to grace and salvation? Was there any possibility that they, too, might assume the throne, or were they always to be without hope?

In God's plan and in God's time, provision was made. **Through the blood of Christ** those who **once were far away have been brought near.** Access has been provided through Christ, the believer's **peace.** The *shalom* of the ancient covenant finds its fulfillment in God's designated Messiah, who has broken down the wall that separated them, a **wall of hostility** greater than the actual barrier in the Jerusalem temple that divided it into gentile and Jewish sections.

How did Christ destroy the barrier? He did so **by abolishing** the **commandments and regulations** that even Jews had not "been able to bear" (Ac 15:10). In doing so, Jesus created **in himself one new** humanity **out of the two** peoples, one circumcised and the other not. In creating this new humanity he established **peace,** reconciling to **God through the cross** both those who thought of themselves as citizens and those considered aliens. Therefore, through Jesus the Christ, Gentiles and Jews alike **have access** to God **by one Spirit.** This is, indeed, a unique community. Nonexclusive, it encompasses the entire race.

Consequently, Gentiles **are no longer foreigners and aliens.** Now they are **fellow citizens with God's** earlier **people,** spiritual Israel (cf. Ro 9:6), **and members of God's household** in the kind of relationship that only family can know. This conjoined community is established on the teachings of the **apostles and prophets,** and built around Jesus, **the chief cornerstone.** Once rejected by human kingdom builders (Ps 118:22; Lk 20:17), Jesus now has joined together the **whole building,** like a holy temple in which God lives. In Christ, believing Jew and believing Gentile are **being built together** into the magnificent structure over which Christ rules as Head. Where, Paul must have wondered, is there such a human institution? Apart from Christ, how can the church be explained?

D. How Paul Came to the Knowledge of the Mystery (3:1–13)

In 3:1, Paul begins a prayer. **"For this reason I, Paul, the prisoner of Christ Jesus for the sake of you Gentiles. . . ."** But before proceeding he wonders if these Gentiles might need interpretation of the divine mystery he has been trying to explain to them. So he leaves off the prayer and begins a discussion of how and why God's grace was given to him on their behalf. He does not resume the prayer until v.14.

He hopes that they will gain insight **into the mystery of Christ.** Such knowledge was not previously possible because the full truth about God's eternal plan had not been revealed. What, in short, is the mystery now revealed? It is that **the Gentiles are heirs together with Israel,** as one body sharing in **the promise of Christ Jesus.**

Paul believed he was selected to declare the mystery as the result of **God's grace and** sovereign **power.** Undeserving of the responsibility placed upon him, he modestly accepted both the **grace** and the challenge to tell the Gentiles about the **riches of Christ,** and to make clear **to everyone** the mystery of grace, **hidden** for ages in the councils of God.

What purpose did God have in bringing Jews and Gentiles into unity through Christ? His plan was to make known, in the environment of world empire, the **manifold wisdom of God,** seen in God's new community. To whom is this divine plan to be revealed? Demonic **rulers and authorities,** principalities and powers, and those in high places need to know that God's **eternal purpose** has been **accomplished in Christ.**

There are now no barriers, either divine or human, to God. Through faith in Christ all have "free birthright and [the] right of access, with full confidence to exercise it" (Bruce, *Letters*, 275). The rights they now enjoy, Paul has been pleased to announce to them. His sufferings have been for their **glory** and benefit. Therefore they must not be discouraged because of his sufferings, but should, instead, think of the privileges they now enjoy because of him.

E. A Prayer for the Ephesians (3:14–21)

Paul now resumes the prayer begun in 3:1. Invoking the image of God as Father, from whom fatherhood (*patria*) derives both name and meaning, Paul asks largely. If earthly fathers give good gifts to their children, certainly God, the archetypal Father, gives his children what they need (cf. Mt 7:11; Lk 11:13).

What does Paul ask of God for these believers? There are two requests. First, he asks God to strengthen them with the power of the Spirit. Paul hopes that as the reality of spiritual power grips them, their resolve to maintain faith in Christ will grow, for they will realize that Christ is all they need for salvation. Second, he prays that they will be empowered to grasp the extent of that love by which they have been saved and made secure. If they can personally approve or acknowledge the love that they cannot comprehend (Clarke, 418), if they can experience the fullness of Christ's love for them, they will be **filled to the measure of all the full-**

ness of God. The fullness of love brings with it "all those gifts and graces which [God] has promised to bestow on man, and which he dispenses to the church" (ibid.). Here is further support for the Wesleyan doctrine of the fullness of love as the overarching goal of Christian living. To experience fully divine love is to enjoy fully the divine plan for human redemption in the present world.

To those who feel that Paul's estimate of God's purpose for citizens of the new community is unrealistic, the apostle offers the benediction of 3:20–21. God can **do immeasurably more than** anything and everything one can ask or even imagine. Divine power is at work in God's people to bring them to divine fullness. Thus God is glorified in the community of redeemed persons in whom the Spirit is at work.

III. FUNCTIONS WITHIN THE NEW COMMUNITY (4:1–6:20)

Paul now moves from theory to practice. Having made believers aware of the hope to which God has called them (1:18), he admonishes them to **live a life worthy of the calling.** Paul's ethics are of motivation, not of prohibition; instead of legislating behavior, he sets ideals (cf. Php 4:8–9). That he is a prisoner adds urgency to his appeal.

A. General Exhortation (4:1–3)

By way of general exhortation, Paul notes that humility and gentleness are characteristic attitudes for believers, as are patience and forbearance. (For a longer list, see Gal 5:22.) Love makes one less apt to judge others (cf. 1Co 13:4–7). Each of these characteristics, when practiced within the community of faith, aids in maintaining harmony, **the unity of the Spirit through the bond of peace.**

B. Living in the New Community (4:4–6:9)

1. Unity of the new community (4:4–6)

Unity is not automatic. It is maintained by diligent effort. Yet the basis for unity is clearly evident because the new community has been established on common ground. The church is vitalized by **one Spirit;** there is **one hope** to which all believers are called; there is **one Lord** and, therefore, only **one** saving **faith** and **one baptism.** There is only one access to the new community, even though God is the Father of all persons. The word "one" serves as a reminder of the equality of the citizens who all are sinners saved by grace.

2. Gifts for the new community (4:7–12)

Within the community of believers joined by common grace is diversity of function. Individuals have been gifted for certain offices. This, too, is the result of grace, **as Christ apportioned it,** to serve the community. If one is saved by grace, then it must be true also that one is prepared to serve by grace. Paul cites Ps 68:18 as proof that the conqueror distributed gifts. It is worthy of note that Paul does not use either the MT or the LXX, both of which indicate that the Messiah received gifts from persons who had been delivered. Reaching back into Jewish antiquity, Paul gives an alternate reading that replaces the idea of tribute received with that of favor bestowed. The alternate reading, found in both the Peshitta (the Syriac version of the OT) and the Aramaic paraphrase of the Psalms, is more in keeping with Paul's point that gifts of function are gifts of grace given *to* liberated persons rather than *by* them.

Vv.9–10 are parenthetical. As an aside, Paul gives a Gospel interpretation of the rest of the verse just cited. If Christ **ascended,** leading the freed **captives in his train,** then, by implication, he previously had **descended.** Paul is stretching a bit to make his point, but he wants to say more about Jesus' victory. While more than one interpretation is possible, the most likely is that Paul saw death and the grave (the lower, earthly regions) as the ultimate phase of the descent from heaven (cf. Php 2:6–8). The one who **descended** beneath the earth (to hades or sheol, the region of the dead) is the same one who **ascended higher than all the heavens,** the realms above the earth, thus having filled "the whole universe with His presence, from the lowest depths to the highest heights" (Bruce, *Ephesians,* 84). Because Christ fills the entire universe, his ascension has not made him inaccessible (cf. Mt 18:20; 28:20).

V.11 returns to the theme of v.7. It was Jesus who gave the church its leaders (apostles, prophets, evangelists, and pastor/teachers). This is confirmed in other passages, notably 1Co 12:4–11; 12:28. Here, however, the emphasis is altered slightly to suggest that Spirit-endowed persons are God's gift to the church. Apostles are those commissioned to preach the Gospel. Accordingly, in 1Th 2:6 Timothy and Silas are counted among the "apostles of Christ," as is Barnabas in Ac 14:4. Prophets speak in the churches under the direct prompting of the Spirit; evangelists lead people to knowledge of the Gospel; pastor/teachers ("shepherds") help converts to understand and apply the Gospel.

Why are they given to the church? Their purpose is **to prepare God's people for works of service.** To what end? These offices are of first importance because those who have these gifts/offices direct others to perform their respective ministries for the common good. As persons perform better their particular ministries, the entire body is strengthened. The body builder knows that each muscle must be strengthened if the whole body is to be developed properly. Some persons in the community fill the vital role of assisting others to exercise their gifts that the whole **body of Christ** might be built up.

3. Challenge for the new community (4:13–16)

The spiritual development of believers in Asia was essential. New systems of thought, the "New Age" movements of the day, lured Christians with the prospects of higher knowledge. Paul calls upon the church to function as it ought until all reach unity of faith, knowledge of Jesus, and maturity, i.e., the full potential of grace.

While it is true that each believer needs to attain spiritual maturity, there must be corporate spiritual maturation as well. Why? Because a community that is growing spiritually fosters individual spiritual growth, even as an individual who matures in spiritual thinking and living inspires similar development in the community. The higher reaches of Christian living are realized in relationship, not in isolation. The fullness of the body is attained in the spiritual growth of the members who constitute it.

As the church matures and fosters individual spiritual growth, its members are grounded in faith. Once mature, they are no longer susceptible to the winds and waves of false doctrine. Therefore, to preserve the faith of its members and to prevent their falling into error and heresy, the church must lead them to spiritual maturity. Com-

mitted to the truth, and speaking and doing the truth in love—the contrast with "cunning," "craftiness," and "deceitful scheming" is obvious—the church will **grow up into him who is the Head.** Unlike the cults, the church does not need to redesign the message for the modern mind; it needs to speak and do the truth, matching it with love. The verb here (*aletheuo*) may be rendered "be true in word and conduct." By accepting the truth, one becomes a person of truth.

Paul may have had in mind the image of the body of the infant that literally grows to the head. It is an analogy appropriate for the spiritual body, the church. From **the Head,** the body **grows and builds itself up in love,** each part doing its work. Therefore, leaders must help others exercise their gifts for service in the church. As each part works, the body grows, functioning harmoniously under Christ.

4. Moral standards for members of the new community (4:17–5:20)

Paul now spells out what it means to "walk worthy of the calling" (4:1) by citing some examples. Obviously, believers must no longer follow gentile patterns of living that are the result of the failure to acknowledge God (Ro 1:21). Vv.18–19 summarize Romans 1:21–32, in which Paul pointed out the logical consequences of turning away from God.

Paul has shown earlier that Gentiles were outside the covenant and thus aliens to the promise. Here he focuses on their wickedness that, because of **the hardening of their hearts,** separates them from the life of God and leaves them spiritually dead. **"Having lost all sensitivity"** means "having lost the fear of consequences." The Bible teaches that God often uses the consequences of sin as judgment, letting men and women reap what they sow. Those who live wickedly have brought themselves under both the judgment and the control of sin's consequences.

So Paul reminds these believers of the preaching and teaching to which they responded. They were taught **the truth that is in Jesus,** who embodied what he taught. Apostolic preaching included the admonition to follow Jesus' ethical teachings and example. Converts were told to put aside the vices of their former lives, to accept the transformation of their attitudes (Ro 12:2), and to take on Christlike character. The natural image derived from Adam has been superseded by the restored divine image. Therefore, Paul calls upon them to be in practice what they are in principle, to be righteous and holy in deed as well as by declaration. The power of sin over the believer was destroyed when the "old man" was crucified (cf. Ro 13:14). The old nature is inherited by birth; the new nature is imparted in new birth. The Adamic nature, though conquered, must be set aside; the new nature, though imparted, must be appropriated.

What does that mean? Paul now gives examples of how the new lifestyle works out in practice (4:25–5:7). **Falsehood,** characteristic of the Devil (Jn 8:44), must be replaced by truth, characteristic of God (cf. Col 3:9). The allusion is to Zec 8:16. No body can function harmoniously if its members do not interact sincerely and openly with one another. In addition, anger must be checked. Quoting the opening clause of Ps 4:4, Paul reminds believers that they must not let anger run out of control. He interprets Jesus (Mt 5:22) to mean that anger itself is not sin, but because anger is the first step to murder, "anyone who is angry with his brother will be subject to judgment."

Anger can be controlled. One must not let the sun go down while one is still angry, for in doing so one gives the Devil (*diabolos,* "the adversary") **a foothold** from which he can tempt one to sin.

Moreover, **stealing** must cease. Some scholars believe that this admonition is addressed especially to Christian slaves who did not consider it inappropriate to steal from their masters. The admonition is applicable to all, however. One who earns a living through gainful employment becomes no longer a taker but a giver. Also, **unwholesome talk** must be renounced, replaced by wholesome, uplifting conversation, **helpful for building others up** and beneficial to **those who listen.** Harmful talk grieves the Spirit because it divides the church, whereas helpful words assist the Spirit to maintain the unity of the body until **the day of redemption,** when the sons of God shall be revealed (Ro 8:19). In short, they must abandon every practice that threatens the church's unity and, thereby, grieves the Spirit. Believers are to be kind and compassionate as Christ was, and forgiving (Lk 6:35–36), always remembering that **in Christ God forgave** them.

As children imitate their fathers, so they must imitate God, who is love (1Jn 4:8) and has **dearly loved** them (cf. 1Jn 4:9–11). Like Jesus, they must live a life of sacrificial love. Thus Paul understood love to be the supreme evidence of the believer's relatedness to God. In that sense 5:1–2 is a positive statement of Christian behavior, the "royal law" (Jas 2:8), the "fulfillment of the whole law" (Gal 5:14), the "law within" (Jer 31:33). These verses both summarize 4:17–32 and, by contrast, anticipate 5:3–5. Both the apostle and John Wesley saw love as the characteristic of **God's holy people.** To both, any form of **impurity,** including greed, was **out of place,** not appropriate to the Christian's walk. Although wanting to stress the positive call to holiness, Paul here simply reminds his readers that worldly behavior has no place in the kingdom of God.

Finally, they must guard against being deceived **with empty words.** Purveyors of vain words have brought God's wrath on humankind ever since the serpent misrepresented the truth of God to Eve. Therefore, partnership or cooperation with those deceivers who make false claims is denounced. On the basis of later Gnostic writings, we know that there were those who distinguished between actions in the body and aspirations of the soul. They taught that one could be spiritual in spite of actions deemed immoral, because the realm of the spirit and the realm of the body are distinct. Paul considered such teaching **empty words,** and so he urges believers to reject this or any deceptive heresy that poses as enlightenment. Those who cooperate with heretics share the judgment such unenlightened nonsense deserves.

Children of light have been rescued "from the dominion of darkness" (Col 1:13), not by having received special spiritual knowledge granted to a few, but by having been brought into the kingdom of the Son. Now delivered, they must **live as children of light,** practicing **goodness, righteousness, and truth,** in order to learn **what pleases the Lord** or, perhaps, to discover God's pleasure for them as his children. They must totally abandon the immoral **deeds of darkness** permitted by deceivers. Instead, as the Lord himself, they should turn the light of God's truth upon the secret deeds practiced by false teachers and be quick to point them out for what they are: sins against God (see Jn 3:20). Even as

light expelled darkness at Creation, so the light of the Gospel expels moral darkness.

The second part of v.14 appears to be a ritualistic hymn, possibly used in early Christian baptisms. Paul uses it here to remind the believers that they have risen from the sleep of spiritual death and that, as a result, the light of Christ has shone upon them. What are the implications of that light having shone upon them? They must **be very careful** how they live as reflectors of that light, **not as unwise but as wise.** In the hostile environment of western Asia Minor, where slanderous rumors of Christian behavior circulate, Paul urges prudence, perhaps reflecting the words of Jesus in Mt 10:16, "Be as shrewd as snakes and as innocent as doves."

If Paul's readers are to seize every opportunity to give a true witness, they will need to **understand what the Lord's will is.** That will is not discovered by consuming wine to excess as the mysteries, particularly the cult of Dionysius, taught. In fact, drunkenness "makes it impossible to exercise the prudent recognition and exploitation of fleeting opportunity" (Bruce, *Ephesians,* 110). To **be filled with the Spirit** one does not overindulge in wine. Instead, one lets the Holy Spirit rule the heart. A person so filled is a living testimony to friends and neighbors. Such a person, furthermore, has no difficulty making music in the heart and knows no barrier to thanking **God the Father for everything.** Filled with the Spirit, the believer gives an undistorted reflection of the light.

5. Submission as the standard for human relationships (5:21–6:9)

To close the section on life within the new community, Paul takes up the volatile question of human relationships. If Christianity delivers from bondage to the law, how are interpersonal relationships to be conducted? Is there a principle that can be applied to all Christian relationships? Yes, there is. The principle is submission **out of reverence for Christ.** It was taught with general uniformity in the early church (e.g., 1Pe 2:13–3:7; 5:5). Probably the instruction "does not so much mean that every Christian must be subject to every other Christian, but rather that among Christians there should be willingness to accept the Christian conventions about the deference one group should pay to another" (Mitton, 195–96), subordinating their own interests to the interests of others. Paul said much the same thing in 1Co 8:12–13 in regard to his right to eat meat. Of course, such submission is not to replace reverence for Christ or run counter to obedience to God.

The apostle now applies the principle in representative situations: husband-wife, parent-child, and master-slave. In every permanent relationship, someone has to assume responsibility. Parents exercise authority over their children; masters over their servants; and, in the culture of that day, husbands over their wives. In each of the cases mentioned here, however, the one who has authority is cautioned against abusing it. This may well have been a unique concept in the Roman world.

While wives are instructed to **submit** to husbands, they are told to do so **as to the Lord** (cf. Col 3:18). As v.29 indicates, however, wives' submission must be earned by the husbands, who are to **love** their **wives, just as Christ loved the church** and gave himself **to make her holy.** While **submit** is a stronger word than the "obey" of 6:1 and 6:5, both carry much the same idea. The rationale is as follows: **the husband** has authority over **the wife as**

Christ has authority over the church, of which he is the Savior. In v.33 the author softens the command, instructing wives **to respect** their husbands.

Paul, in 1 Co 11:8–12, offered a Christian perspective on husband-wife relationships. Both that passage and this show signs that he was a product of his culture even while advancing a loftier, Christian position. Because in relation to faith men and women are the same (Gal 3:28), the new freedom and status given women in Christianity must be practiced in such a way that onlookers will not misconstrue the Christian wives' relationship to their husbands.

Moreover, the author complements the word to the wives by offering a word to husbands: as a wife, who has been freed from second-class citizenship by Christ, submits in order to maintain both harmony in the home and a Christian witness among her neighbors, her husband must reciprocate. He must **love . . . just as Christ loved.**

Certainly there is more here. Paul believed that submission by wives to husbands was proper. In fact, only in relatively modern times has this idea been questioned. Someone had to be head of the home and take responsibility for discipline and decision-making if chaos was to be avoided. Christian leaders wanted strong homes and model families. To turn society upside down would not have helped their cause in either the Roman or the Jewish world. So the kind of hierarchy about which Paul spoke in 1 Co 11:3 is implied here, and **as the church submits to Christ** its Head, **so also wives should submit to their husbands in everything.** However, whereas the emphasis in 1 Corinthians is on the hierarchy, the language here suggests something more profound, using two ideas to illustrate each other. The idea of the husband's authority over his wife helps Christians to understand Christ's authority over his church; the relationship of Christ to the church illuminates the relationship between husband and wife in Christian marriages. Against those who taught that subjection of wives to husbands was a natural duty, Paul argues that submission is a Christian duty.

Moreover, Christ, as Head of the church, does not *demand* obedience, but, as the **Savior** who gives the church its life, he *deserves* obedience. Therefore, the subjection of wives to husbands is governed by several principles: **out of reverence for Christ** (v.21), **as to the Lord** (v.22), **as Christ is head of the church** (v.23), and **as the church submits to Christ** (v.24).

Similarly, the husband's obligation to his wife is illustrated by the author in two ways. First, it is patterned after Christ's love for his church (vv.25–27). How much did Christ love the church? He loved so much that **he gave himself** to make the church **holy** and **radiant.** Also, husbands ought to love their wives as their own bodies. After all, persons do not despise or neglect their own bodies, but feed and care for them. Therefore, as Christ gave himself to nurture his body, the bride-church, so the husband must give himself to nurture his bride. In quoting from Ge 2:24, Paul illustrates the unity that characterizes marriages within the Christian community. Therefore, each husband **must love his wife as he loves himself,** for in the marriage the two are one, and in Christ they are equally a part of the church. (See also 1Pe 3:1–7.)

Next, the author applies the principle to the parent-child relationship (6:1–4). In doing so, of course, he has on his side the fifth commandment (a slightly edited LXX reading of Dt 5:16). Furthermore, disrespect for and disobedience to parents were seen as signs of disintegration of society (Ro 1:30; 2Ti 3:2), and the early Christians hoped that believers might check the disintegrating tendencies of their time. But notice that again Paul does not allow parents to abuse their authority. To obey is to accept authority; but in exercising authority, parents must not **exasperate** their children. Instead, they should use their God-given position of authority to provide Christian **training and instruction,** telling about Jesus and his teachings, and teaching, as Jesus did, by example.

Similarly, the principle can be applied in master-slave relationships (6:5–9). Slaves should obey their **earthly masters** in the same way as they **obey Christ.** Such obedience is essential not only when they are under the watchful eye of the master, but even more when they are not. They must remember that they serve another master, that they are **slaves of Christ** and full of love. Therefore, they are to **serve wholeheartedly,** for by doing so they demonstrate that they **serve the Lord,** not merely men in authority over them.

Masters, too, are under the authority of Christ and must demonstrate that fact in the treatment of their slaves. They are exhorted not to **threaten them,** since Christ, who is Lord of both the master and the slave, makes no distinction between slaves and free men (cf. Gal 3:28) and shows **no favoritism** (cf. Ro 2:11). To threaten another person unfairly uses one's authority over that person, provoking resentment and destroying the unity that the Christian is to maintain (4:3). (See 1Pe 2:13–25.)

Thus, Paul, through these three examples, illustrates how all Christian relationships are to be conducted.

There is always, for the Christian, a third party involved. Not only is Christ the "unseen guest" in every conversation, but he is the Model for all conduct. Every relationship, therefore, must be conducted in the light of Christ's Spirit.

6. Provisions for triumphant living (6:10–20)

The antecedent of the word *finally* is not clear. Does it suggest merely a final word of exhortation, or should the reader go back to 5:1? If the latter was Paul's intention here, then one must understand the exhortation to **be strong in the Lord and in his mighty power** as one of the appropriate consequences of being **imitators** [KJV "followers"] of God. In other words, while Christians must be submissive to one another, they must be **strong** in resisting the evil forces that surround them. Claiming the Lord's strength, they can **stand against the devil's schemes** (cf. 1Pe 5:1–9). After all, the real enemy of Christians is not physical torment, but spiritual treachery. Christians do not struggle **against flesh and blood,** but against rulers, authorities, and powers that are merely representative of **the spiritual forces of evil** in "the 'unseen universe,' which lies behind the world of sense . . . [where] great forces are at work" that oppose and wrestle against God's people (Robinson, 21).

These forces, of course, have already been conquered (1:19–23). The **mighty strength** that God exerted when he raised Jesus from the dead and exalted him above all authorities (1:19) is the same **mighty power** available to believers (6:10) in their struggle against evil spiritual forces. God is a great defender, a mighty fortress, "a bulwark never failing." He has provided **the full armor** for his followers. With this armor, **when the day of evil comes,** whether it be future (as in 1Th 2:1–10a) or present (as in Eph 5:16), they **may be able to stand** their ground. At such a time as this, human strength will not suffice.

So Paul urges, as he did in 1Th 5:8, that believers put on **the full armor of God.** The description can almost certainly be traced to Roman soldiers with whom Paul was all too familiar. We might imagine that as he wrote he glanced from time to time at the soldier who guarded him, giving each piece of armor a spiritual function. Only by the armor provided by God can the Christian hope to overcome "the strategems by which the supreme enemy endeavors to gain an advantage over the people of God" (Bruce, *Ephesians,* 127). According to tradition, the fallen angels, unable to overcome God in heaven, turned upon God's Son in his human weakness, only to find themselves once again defeated (Col 2:15). Thus, in union with Christ, believers also are able to overcome those forces that stand between them and their eternal salvation (cf. Ro 8:35–39).

The pieces of armor require minimal comment. The **belt of truth** represents loyalty and faithfulness. Isa 11:5 says that faithfulness (the LXX has "truth") is the sash around the waist of the Messiah. The **breastplate of righteousness** represents the Christian's character, which models that of God (cf. Isa 59:17). Being faithful to God and being righteous in conduct as God is, are essential elements in the believer's strategy for survival. Also, the true disciple of Jesus will have his **feet fitted with the readiness that comes from the gospel of peace.** The allusion here is most likely to Isa 52:7, and the implication is that bearing good news to others helps Christians keep their own souls from spiritual lethargy and thus less vulnerable to the Devil.

The shield of faith is necessary to ward off (NIV "extinguish") the Devil's evil assaults. The word used for shield is the large whole-body shield, rather then the small shield used for deflecting sword thrusts in hand-to-hand combat. This larger shield provided comprehensive protection for the Roman soldier, so use of that image is appropriate to Paul's purpose. Jesus met the most subtle of Satan's temptations with a faith that did not depend on any special display of divine power. The **helmet of salvation** (cf. Isa 59:17) had also been urged upon the Thessalonian believers (1Th 5:8) as a basis of hope. The helmet protects the head, essential to the proper functioning of all other parts. Thus, the apostle suggests that the hope of salvation is a most important weapon at the disposal of all Christians, aiding them as they struggle toward "the prize for which God has called [them] heavenward" (Php 4:14).

The sword of the spirit is **the word of God** that is "sharper than any two-edged sword" (Heb 4:12; cf. also Hos 6:5; Isa 11:4). Paul may very well have intended to mean by the term **word** (*rhema*) **of God** the sacred Scriptures of Judaism that Jesus had used so effectively at the time of his own temptation, particularly Dt 8:3 ("Man does not live on bread alone but on every word that comes from the mouth of the Lord"). The same word is used in Eph 5:26, however, to connote words spoken at the time of baptism. If the latter is the intended sense, then the **word of God** is any helpful word from God in the moment of need (as is suggested in Lk 12:12; 21:15; and possibly Eph 6:19). One other resource is available: prayer. It, too, is part of the equipment accessible whenever believers are tempted or on the verge of surrendering to the enemy.

Having thus called their attention to the power of prayer, the author now encourages his readers in Asia to **keep on praying for all the saints.** By praying for one another, Christians everywhere help fellow believers overcome the evil influences bent on destroying those whom God has called. Moreover, he includes himself among those who need the prayers of the saints. He requests his readers to pray that, whenever he speaks, the right words will come to him so that he will declare **the mystery of the gospel,** even though and because of which, he is **in chains.** In those chains, he remains, nonetheless, **an ambassador,** intent on carrying out his mission **fearlessly** (lit. "boldly"). (Luke uses the same root word in Ac 28:20 to describe Paul's two-year ministry under guard in Rome, perhaps answering the question of the epistle's origin.)

IV. FINAL WORDS (6:21–24)

A. Tychicus, the Messenger (6:21–22)

Tychicus, the bearer of the letter, had a relationship with Paul traceable as far back as Ac 20:4. There, along with Trophimus, he is one of the representatives from Asia (the Western text says Ephesus) with Paul at the time of his departure from Corinth near the end of the third journey. Evidently Tychicus was a Gentile, and in accompanying Paul to Jerusalem he represented the gentile churches that had collected funds for the Judean believers. Whether Tychicus stayed with the Ephesian elders following Paul's speech at Miletus (Ac 20:17–35) or accompanied him to Jerusalem as Trophimus did, is not clear from the text, but probably Tychicus witnessed Paul's arrest in Judea (Ac 21:29). He appears as "a fellow servant" (*syndoulos*) in Col 4:7, in phrasing nearly identical to that here, and is named again in the Pastorals (2Ti 4:12; Tit 3:12) as a messenger of the writer. As envoy to the Asian churches, he will not only carry this letter and others, but he will tell about Paul. Perhaps his appearance in Ephesus is calculated to head off the revolt against Paul's authority and Gospel.

B. Benediction (6:23–24)

The closing words of the epistle are typically Pauline. The benediction includes three elements: **peace to the brothers, love with faith,** and **grace to all who love our Lord Jesus Christ with an undying love.** The word here translated **"undying"** perhaps literally means uncorrupted or incorruptible and communicates the idea of "immortal." The generic phrase **"to the brothers"** may indicate that the letter is for more than one congregation. The proposal that Ro 16 belongs at the end of Ephesians has little support among scholars today, even though Aquila and Priscilla, who are greeted there, had been in Ephesus since the end of the second journey (Ac 18:19).

BIBLIOGRAPHY

Bruce, F. F. *The Epistle to the Ephesians*. London: Pickering & Inglis, 1961.

_____. *The Letters of Paul: An Expanded Paraphrase*. Exeter: Paternoster, 1965.

Carter, Charles. "Ephesians." WBC. Vol. 5. Grand Rapids: Eerdmans, 1965.

Clarke, Adam. "Ephesians." *A Commentary and Critical Notes*. Vol. 6. New York: Abingdon n.d.

Mitton, C. Leslie. *Ephesians*. NCBC. London: Marshall, Morgan & Scott, 1973.

Robinson, J. Armitage. *Commentary on Ephesians*. Grand Rapids: Kregel, 1979.

Wesley, John. *Explanatory Notes Upon the New Testament*. New York: Lane & Sandford, 1844.

PHILIPPIANS
Vern A. Hannah

INTRODUCTION

I. PHILIPPI—THE CITY

The letter is addressed "to all the saints . . . at Philippi." Philippi was the site of the first Christian mission in Europe. It resulted from Paul's response to "the Macedonian call" (Ac 16).

The city, named after Philip of Macedon, father of Alexander the Great, was located eight miles north of Neapolis, the port city. Philippi became a Roman colony in 42 B.C. It was a strategic city for the launching of Western Christianity.

II. AUTHORSHIP

With rare exceptions, scholars consistently support Philippians as a genuine production of the apostle Paul. While the unity of the letter has been questioned, there can be little doubt that Paul is the author. Both the external evidence from the church fathers and the internal evidence of the letter itself strongly support its Pauline character.

III. DATE AND ORIGIN

The date of the letter is uncertain. Paul was writing from prison (1:7, 12–16), expecting possible release (v.19) or death (v.20). But *which* imprisonment? Acts records three: Philippi, Caesarea, and Rome. Obviously Philippi must be ruled out; Caesarea is a possibility; the traditional view supports Rome.

Another possibility is an Ephesian imprisonment. Paul spent well over two years in Ephesus. If the letter originated there, the date would be approximately A.D. 55; if written from Caesarea, about A.D. 58; and if from Rome, about A.D. 61. The question remains open.

IV. THE UNITY OF THE LETTER

The question of unity is the major critical issue. Some scholars say the letter is fragmented into distinct sections that originally may have been as many as three separate letters later joined together. Specifically, 1:1–3:1; 3:2–4:1; and 4:10–20 have been questioned (see Beare, 1–5).

Most scholars, while noting the fact of some lack of coherence, hold to the unity of the letter. Lightfoot suggests that Paul may have been interrupted while writing. Others point out that the lack of unity is not inconsistent with the letter's intense personal nature. It is best to let the letter stand as is.

V. CHARACTERISTICS

Philippians has been cited as the most personal of Paul's writings. A strong note of mutual affection and warmth is sounded here. A mostly joyous confidence fills the letter. The note of "joy" appears in verb or noun form sixteen times. This is remarkable given the fact that Paul writes from the confines of prison.

There appears to be no major doctrinal focus such as we have in Galatians or Romans. This does not mean, however, that the epistle lacks theological content. On the contrary, several crucial doctrines of the church are raised or implied: Christology; resurrection-life; faith-righteousness; the Second Advent; Christian perfection; and the Cross. Furthermore, the epistle contains vital moral and practical admonitions basic to Christian holiness. Oneness in Christ is affirmed in various ways. A strong corporate note is sounded by the frequent use of "you all."

In this intensely *pastoral* letter, Paul, who had more than once received their material support, expresses his deep gratitude and love to the Philippians.

One feature much discussed among scholars is the question of the identity of the "opponents" mentioned in 1:28 and possibly referred to again in 3:2–19. They may have been Jews (Judaizers) seeking to impose the Mosaic Law (esp. circumcision), or some group advocating a blend of Jewish-Greek ideas that undercut the significance of the Cross and the true meaning of Christian perfection and resurrection. Whoever they were, they prompted a strong response from Paul.

VI. OUTLINE

I. Introduction (1:1–11)
   A. Salutation (1:1–2)
   B. Paul's Grateful, Affectionate Prayer (1:3–11)

II. Paul's Imprisonment: Results and Prospects (1:12–26)
   A. His Confinement Has Advanced the Gospel (1:12–18)
   B. Living Means Christ; Dying Is Gain (1:19–26)

III. Exhortations and Encouragement (1:27–2:18)
   A. Appeal for Unity, Faithfulness, and Perseverance (1:27–30)
   B. The Challenge of the Christlike Mind (2:1–11)
      1. Living and loving for others (2:1–4)
      2. The humility and exaltation of the Servant-Christ: our example and pattern (2:5–11)
   C. Cooperating With God (2:12–13)

COMMENTARY

I. INTRODUCTION (1:1–11)

A. Salutation (1:1–2)

This typical Pauline greeting follows a form common to the Greek world. Note the absence of reference to apostleship. Instead Paul and Timothy are identified as **servants of Christ Jesus.** "The saints" means the holy covenant people of God. The phrase **"in Christ Jesus,"** frequent in Paul's writings, means the sphere of God's saving activity. The terms **grace** and **peace** combine the typical Greek and Jewish greetings respectively.

B. Paul's Grateful, Affectionate Prayer (1:3–11)

A note of joyous and optimistic realism fills this letter. Paul was **confident** (v.6) that God, having **[begun] a good work** (of saving grace) in them, would tend to its "completion" (its final perfection) until **the day of Christ Jesus** (either the day Christ returns, or the day the believer meets him in death). Wesley comments, "He who, having justified, hath begun to sanctify you, will carry on this work, till it issue in glory." The emphasis here is on *inaugurated holiness*, with the hope of final perfection based on confidence in God's ability and faithfulness.

Paul prays for his readers' abounding holiness in 1:9–11. This is not only typically Pauline, it is a very Wesleyan prayer focusing on the key aspect of Christian holiness: love. **Love** (*agapē*) is "the distinctive feature of the Christian character" (Beet, 39). Love is the supreme commandment of God, the highest excellence of biblical religion, and the core of holiness. This love, which originates with the Spirit, is to **abound** (progressively) in experiential **knowledge** and **insight** so that the **best** of spiritual truth may be tested and proved. This progressive aspect of holiness (**"abound"** is present tense) is fully as crucial as the instantaneous work. Paul further prays that this abounding love will result in his readers' being found **pure** and **blameless** for the **day of Christ.** Wesley says this means "having a single eye to the very best things, and a pure heart. . . . Holy, unblameable in all things."

The Greek term translated **"pure"** means unmixed, having no foreign element. The term *blameless* (not *faultless*) means not blameworthy. One is **blameless** who has pure motives, even though performance may be flawed.

V.11 completes Paul's prayer, stressing the fact, the means, and the goal of holiness. The fact: having been **filled with the fruit of righteousness** (righteousness = right relationship); the means: **through Jesus Christ;** the goal: **the glory and praise of God.**

II. PAUL'S IMPRISONMENT: RESULTS AND PROSPECTS (1:12–26)

A. His Confinement Has Advanced the Gospel (1:12–18)

What matters most to Paul is the **advance** of the **gospel** of God's saving work in Christ. The messenger is imprisoned, but the message is not. Indeed, his imprisonment **for Christ** has impacted **the whole palace** (Roman Praetorium). All know why he is there. This public awareness had the effect of encouraging other Christians to preach even more **fearlessly.** God often uses adversity to advance the good.

Paul reminds us in 1:15–18 that motives in preaching are not always noble. Some **preach Christ** only for **selfish ambition,** having the right message but the wrong motives. This is always a peril in the church. Paul's response to this (v.18) was neither resigned nor naïve. He was magnanimous: **Christ is preached.**

B. Living Means Christ, Dying Is Gain (1:19–26)

This section expresses confidence in God's providence. We are reminded of two crucial resources of Christian life: **prayers** and the **help** (supply) of the Spirit. This help of the Spirit may mean either the Spirit who *is* the resource or the resources that the Spirit supplies. No matter, for he is "both Giver and Gift" (Beet, 48). Because of these resources, Paul is confident of **deliverance** (*sōtērian*), whether that means release from prison or final salvation. In light of 1:24–26 he hopes for the former, but he expresses uncertainty at two attractive alternatives (v.23). To be released from prison means more service for **Christ; to die** is to be with him. Either way the center of life for Paul is Christ. Whether Paul is released or executed, Christ **will be exalted** in Paul's **body** (v.20).

Two especially significant aspects of Paul's thought arise from this passage and are elaborated further in this and in some of his other letters: (1) A prominent theme of glory through suffering, pointing to a theology of the Cross (see comments under 1:29); and (2) the importance of bodily existence, pointing to the significance of resurrection (cf. 3:10–21).

III. EXHORTATIONS AND ENCOURAGEMENT (1:27–2:18)

A. Appeal for Unity, Faithfulness, and Perseverance (1:27–30)

The one particular church problem the Philippians faced was the threat of disunity (cf. 2:1–3; 4:2–3). Paul urges them to **stand firm** united **in one spirit** (*pneumati*), and **as one man** (lit. with one *psyche*) in their battle of **the faith** (i.e., the truth) of the Gospel. This united front will enable them to resist the influence of those who oppose them (possibly those mentioned in 3:2; see comment there), and faithfully to preserve the true faith of Christ. Their faithful, united preservation of the truth will prove to be their salvation while it will signal the opposers' destruction in God's judgment.

As already indicated, 1:29–30 emphasizes a key concept in Paul and in NT Christianity generally, i.e., suffering as a Christian. Note that Paul describes it as a privilege. Not only is belief a privilege, but **to suffer** for Christ is also a privilege. For **it has been granted to you,** he says (cf. 2:17, 30; 3:10, 18; 4:11–14). Paul does not have a martyr complex nor feel victimized by the gospel; he is a realist. He knows "how the nature of the Christian calling gets its model from the incarnate Lord himself (2:6–11). . . . The life of the church is thus cruciform since it derives from him who exemplified the 'dying to live' pattern" (Martin, 81).

Those who advocate a "success theology," which in essence makes it obligatory upon God to make a believer "healthy, wealthy, and happy" in this world, profoundly misunderstand the Cross and the whole scope of biblical religion generally. Paul was an advocate of triumph to be sure. But it was triumph *through* suffering, not through exemption from it.

B. The Challenge of the Christlike Mind (2:1–11)

1. Living and loving for others (2:1–4)

The theme of unity continues here with particular emphasis on the importance of "unison of thought" (Lightfoot, 108) or quality of mind. Right thinking is crucial to right living (cf. 4:8). The controlling factor is a humble **love** that enables one to consider **the interests of others** (v.4). The thrust of the passage is "the concord . . . of a common love" (Lightfoot, 108).

2. The humility and exaltation of the Servant-Christ: our example and pattern (2:5–11)

While this famous section is not simply a call to imitate Christ, it clearly is presented by Paul as a challenge to conform to Christ's example of humble, self-giving service.

This classic Christological expression, whether written originally by Paul or borrowed from the community before him (a pre-Pauline hymn to Christ?) illustrates like nothing else the essence of Paul's words elsewhere: "For you know the grace of our Lord Jesus Christ, that though he was rich, yet for your sake he became poor, so that you through his poverty might become rich" (2Co 8:9).

This segment falls naturally into two parts (Hawthorne): (1) Jesus' humiliation by his own act (vv.5–8); (2) Jesus' exaltation by God's act (vv.9–11). The literature on this famous segment is enormous. The issues are critical and complex (see Hawthorne and Martin for sources for further study). In modern times the focus of debate is on whether the reference is to the preexistent Son who became the human Jesus, or whether the human Jesus only (as second Adam) is described in these verses. In other words, is this Christology from "above" or from "below" or both? Surely it is both.

The key motif is struck in 2:4–5 where the **attitude** of servanthood is stressed. Here we see the mind behind the manger, the service, and the cross of Christ. This Christlike attitude should mark **each of you,** says Paul. For (the preexistent) Christ, this self-giving attitude meant that even though he was **in very nature God** (*en morphē theou,* v.6), he **did not consider equality with God** (and all the benefits involved) a thing **to be grasped** (*harpagmon,* i.e., held on to or exploited for his own advantage). Rather, **he poured himself out** (*ekenōsen,* v.7) by becoming in very fact a **servant,** and a human one at that! (The NIV rendering **made himself nothing** is weak; it fails to capture the strength of Christ's decisive action in becoming both human and servant; cf. Isa 53:12; Mk 10:45.) Scholars have debated the term *ekenōsen* (v.7) asking, "Of what did Christ empty or divest himself?" We must not consider it as an emptying of something essential to his nature. Rather, he "poured out himself, putting himself totally at the disposal of people" (Hawthorne, 86).

The attitude that first prompted the preexistent Son to "pour himself out" through incarnation and servanthood is carried through every step of his earthly human life until it ends on the cross. "As a man" he **humbled himself,** becoming **obedient to death,** and not just an ordinary death, but **even death on a cross** (v.8)! In costly self-sacrifice and humility, the God-man demon-strated the meaning of love in a fallen world.

But note the turning point. The descent turns to ascent. **Therefore** (v.9), because he was faithful, **God exalted him to the highest place** and **gave him the name . . . above every name,** even the name **Lord.** The serv-ant who poured himself out for human-ity is now Lord! This high exaltation, however, is not to be understood as a reward, but rather as God's act of vindicating the Servant-Christ accord-ing to the kingdom principle that Jesus himself had often taught: "Whoever wants to become great among you must be your servant, and whoever wants to be first must be slave of all" (Mk 10:43–44).

The victory of Christ has cosmic implications (2:10–11). The phrases **every knee** and **every tongue** do not support unconditional universal salva-tion; they do indicate universal *recogni-tion* that the Servant-Christ is indeed Lord of all.

C. Cooperating With God (2:12–13)

Therefore (v.12), in light of the humble, self-sacrificing service called for, **continue to work out your salva-tion** with "awe inspired by . . . the divine presence" (Beare, 91). This is a call to perseverance, which requires human cooperation. "Here is our duty," says Wesley. This is to be done because **"it is God who works in you,"** to which Wesley responds, "Here is our encouragement." That there is paradox in perseverance is obvious. Salvation is ultimately the work of God's grace; but his grace is effective in salvation only as we "trust and obey."

D. Shining as Examples of Holy Living (2:14–18)

V.14 again touches the need for unity, this time through the absence of

complaining or arguing. Beet (p. 77) says that the goal of becoming **blameless and pure** (v.15) is "a designed result of laying aside" complaining and arguing. He further suggests "that these defects are the last to cling to the Christian."

The terms **blameless, pure** (Wesley: unmixed, "aiming at God alone"), and **without fault** (without shame) are dynamic moral terms descriptive of Christian perfection (cf. comments on 1:10). Such qualities enable the Christian to display "light" and **life** to a dark and fallen world. The phrase **"word of life"** (v.16) is the Gospel, which brings life.

V.17 is difficult (see standard commentaries for full treatment). Both Jewish and pagan religions practiced **drink offerings** (libations). The Jews **poured out** theirs *around* the altar, while in pagan practice the offering was poured *upon* the sacrifice. The predominantly Gentile membership of the Philippian church suggests the latter meaning here. In a context of adversity and suffering, Paul urges them to persevere and triumph. In such a context, Paul views their Christian living as a sacrificial offering. They are as priests offering sacrifices, i.e., their own costly faith and service (cf. Ro 12:1). Paul sees his own costly ministry, which may include imminent martyrdom, as a crowning offering being poured out on top of their sacrificial living. The language is metaphorical but has deep spiritual meaning.

IV. ABOUT TIMOTHY AND EPAPHRODITUS (2:19–30)

A. Timothy To Be Sent Soon (2:19–24)

Timothy will be sent, for Paul wants to know his readers' state, and he wants them to know his. Note the phrases: **"I hope"** (vv.19, 23); **"I am confident,"** v.24); and **"in the Lord"** (vv.19, 24). Paul was no cocksure religionist. His expressions reveal his reverent commitment to God's will in the matter.

B. Epaphroditus, Now Well, Is Returning (2:25–30)

Epaphroditus, the bearer of the letter, had been sent to Paul with the Philippian believers' gifts, but had fallen ill and **almost died** (vv.27, 30) on his mission of mercy. What is noteworthy about this episode is the fact that God uses people to be his hands, feet, and voice in ministering in the community of believers. However, God does not exempt his servants from adversity, even when they are engaged in missions of mercy. We see again a hint of the realism of (and confidence in) Paul's theology of the Cross.

V. ASPECTS OF TRUE RELIGION (3:1–4:9)

A. Christ: The Source of True Righteousness (3:1–9)

1. Rejoice in the Lord: beware of law-righteousness (3:1–2)

Here are words of encouragement (**"rejoice in the Lord"**), and of warning (**"watch out"**). It is unlikely that Paul refers to three separate classes of troublemakers in v.2. He probably refers to certain Jewish Christians (Judaizers) who insisted on Gentiles keeping the Mosaic Law, especially circumcision; or they may have been "gnosticizing Jews" (Martin) who stressed secret knowledge, initiations, and rituals as necessary for salvation. Whoever they were, Paul refers to them as **those dogs,** no doubt likening them to "half-savage dogs who prowl about a camp and steal any food left unguarded" (Beare, 103). Paul saw their actions in the church in this manner.

The term **mutilators** (*katatomein*) or "concision" is a sarcastic substitute for the real thing: (*peritomē*), true circumcision (cf. Gal 5:12).

2. True righteousness by faith in Christ (3:3–9)

a. Real "circumcision" is in Christ (3:3)

Those are the true covenant people **who worship by the Spirit of God** and **who glory in Christ Jesus.** This is a spiritual circumcision of the heart, constituting the "Israel of God" (Gal 6:16). Some versions and commentators translate **Spirit** (*pneumati*) to mean the worship of God by the human spirit (RSV; Wesley; Beare). It does not matter since we cannot worship in our own spirits without the help of the Holy Spirit. As Hawthorne (p. 127) puts it, "the Spirit of God is the divine initiator at work in the depths of human nature." Of this worship Wesley comments, "Not barely in the letter, but with the spiritual worship of inward holiness."

b. Paul's former impressive standing means nothing (3:4–7)

It would be a serious mistake to think that Paul castigates the whole of Judaism in this section. Paul had great respect for the Law as such. His purpose is not to ridicule his background, but to show its insufficiency compared to Christ. What were once considered assets are now counted as liabilities compared to Christ (v.7).

c. The surpassing excellence of Christ (3:8–9)

Christ is now Paul's "magnificent obsession." Note the "intensely personal" (Beare) expression: **"Christ Jesus my Lord." Knowing** [him] is **the surpassing greatness.** This knowledge (3:8, 10) is not merely theoretical

or theological; it is experiential. Paul yearns to **be found in him,** having God's **righteousness.** Again we see a key concept of Paul: **in him.** To be **in Christ** by faith is to be in the sphere of God's redemptive actions. The emphasis on **righteousness** (rightness with God) through faith—union with Christ is the core of Paul's religion and the evangelical Protestant principle.

B. Resurrection the Goal (3:10–4:1)

1. Sharing the power of life through death (3:10–11)

Resurrection is crucial to Paul's hope. The Greek construction here indicates that Paul wants to come finally and completely to **know** Christ, both in the **power of his resurrection** and the **fellowship of . . . his sufferings. Resurrection** refers to the whole range of life-power, i.e., the presence of new life in Christ now, but primarily the hope of bodily resurrection to come. The term used here (v.11) is *exanastasin,* literally "out-resurrection" from the dead. Paul nowhere refers to a general resurrection. His focus is on believers.

2. Pressing toward final (resurrection) perfection (3:12–4:1)

V.12 in the context of pressing to perfection by the way of the Cross may be the crux of the issue between Paul and his opponents (cf. 3:2, 18–19 and comments). Some groups (e.g., Gnostics) so spiritualized resurrection as to deny a future (bodily) resurrection or the need for daily discipline. Hence Paul's urgency, **"I press on."** He had not yet **taken hold** of or reached perfection. Again, note the need for final perseverance. It is obvious from Paul's emphasis that he did not believe either that salvation could never be lost or that full perfection is possible in this life.

This element of paradox in "perfection" is evident in the context overall, especially in v.15 where the Greek *teleioi,* rendered "mature" by NIV, is used. Paul disclaims final perfection either spiritual or bodily (v.12), but he does teach a proper present Christian "perfection" in this world (v.15). Here the meaning is fitness. Christian perfection is wholeheartedness in process toward the final goal. Wesley distinguishes between the two kinds of perfection in that v.15 means fitness for the race, while v.12 means receiving **the prize** (v.14).

The reference to the **enemies of the cross of Christ** (v.18) is significant and may refer to certain "gnosticizing Christians" (Martin, 144). They imagined they had *already* attained a spiritual perfection that made ethical/bodily discipline unnecessary. How they lived in the body was irrelevant to spiritual perfection. Therefore they denied the costly self-denial and discipline that is the way of the Cross. They were advocates of easy religiosity and "cheap grace." Paul says their **destiny is destruction** (v.19). They will not attain the resurrection unto life.

By contrast, true believers live in faith and discipline as they **eagerly await** their heavenly **Savior** (v.20). Only then will they realize full perfection through the power of the resurrection transforming their present **lowly bodies** (v.21). Resurrection is not resuscitation; it is a transforming re-creation, the defeat of death, the capstone of God's saving work, the way to eternal life. Of this hope Christ's own resurrection is both the pledge and pattern.

C. A Plea for Unity and Cooperation (4:2–3)

Again the need for unity surfaces. The identities of the persons named here, along with the "loyal yokefellow," are unknown (see major commentaries). They were no doubt influential persons. Paul stresses the need for *mutual* cooperation toward reconciliation and unity. Disunity in the church is everyone's business.

The phrase **"book of life"** refers to the record of all who experience the blessedness of eternal life through resurrection.

D. Rejoice—Be Patient—Pray (4:4–7)

Once again a keynote is sounded: **Rejoice in the Lord!** Here is an appeal for the optimism of faith since being **in the Lord** is assurance of victory. **Gentleness** (v.5) means a gracious patience with a spirit of magnanimity. These virtues can be practiced because **the Lord is near;** i.e., "the Lord who will come again is presently very near in his Spirit" (Hawthorne, 192). There is no need to be fretfully **anxious about anything.** Rather, thankful **prayer and petition** is the antidote to anxiety and the way to **the peace of God.** The **peace of God** is the sense of well-being that results from being **in Christ. This peace,** which **transcends all understanding,** is the guardian of both **heart** and **mind.** The **heart** is primary; it is the center of the deepest feelings and motivations.

E. Think Christianly (4:8–9)

The focus of this segment is on quality of thinking or the Christian mind-set. The admonition is to **think** ("take account") of the great and positive facts and virtues of God's ways. The mind is a vital factor in the shaping of human character. Right thinking results in right living, which results in the presence of **the God of peace** (v.9).

VI. GRATITUDE FOR THEIR SUPPORT (4:10–20)

A. Paul's Contentment and Sufficiency in Christ (4:10–13)

The words **at last you have renewed your concern** (v.10) should not be interpreted to imply ingratitude on Paul's part, or that they should have acted sooner with their support. Some circumstance probably hindered their uninterrupted service. Paul is grateful, and in spite of periods of difficulty, he has **learned to be content** (v.11). Note that he *learned* this! He did not rely on favorable circumstances for his joy and strength. He found these in a higher source: in Christ (v.13).

B. God Will Honor Their Generosity (4:14–20)

Paul warns them to see that their sharing in his troubles (v.14) is of mutual benefit. He was indeed helped by their gifts (v.18), but he reminds them that their sharing can be **credited to** their own **account** as well. Such loving service is actually laying up treasures in heaven.

V.19 poses an interesting difficulty. As it stands in the NIV, it reads as a promise: **"My God will meet [supply] all your needs."** However, some an-cient texts read it as a wish/prayer: "*May* God supply. . . ." Hawthorne (p. 194) prefers the latter, "a reading which better reflects the apostle's own reverent attitude. He . . . prayerfully asks God to come to their aid." This view certainly is not unfitting to Paul's thought generally. Whether promise or prayer, v.19 is not to be viewed as a mechanical compensation of their char-ity, but as the gracious care of God. These **glorious riches** are **in Christ Jesus,** the sphere of all God's resources.

VIII. FINAL GREETINGS— BENEDICTION (4:21–22)

Each and all of the **saints** in Philippi are greeted from the **brothers** who are with Paul, i.e., his colleagues and friends; and from the **saints** who are connected with **Caesar's household.** Where this is located depends on the city of origin (see introduction).

Paul's closing benediction (v.23) sounds a central note in his theology and experience: **the grace of the Lord Jesus Christ.** This is the Gospel in a nutshell! The phrase **your spirit** (*pneuma*) is used frequently in the NT to mean the whole person and simply means "with you."

BIBLIOGRAPHY

Beare, F. W. *A Commentary on the Epistle to the Philippians*. BNTC. 3d ed. London: Adam and Charles Black, 1973.

Beet, J. A. *A Commentary on St. Paul's Epistles to the Ephesians, Philippians, Colossians, and to Philemon*. Salem, Ohio: Schmul, n.d.

Hawthorne, G. F. *Philippians*. WBC. Vol. 43. Waco, Tex.: Word, 1983.

Lightfoot, J. B. *St. Paul's Epistle to the Philippians*. London: Macmillan, 1913. Reprint: Zondervan, 1956.

Martin, R. P. *Philippians*. NCBC. London: Marshall, Morgan & Scott, 1976.

Wesley, John. *Explanatory Notes Upon the New Testament*. London: Epworth, 1941.

COLOSSIANS
Wayne McCown

INTRODUCTION

I. THE QUESTION OF AUTHENTICITY

Most Christians regard Colossians as Pauline. The letter purports to have been written by "Paul, an apostle . . . and Timothy, our brother" (1:1). A few biblical critics contest this ascription. For example, Lohse has recently stated, "There are strong reasons to doubt the Pauline authorship of Colossians" (p. 176).

The majority of scholars, however, remain convinced that the author was Paul. Kümmel argues that Colossians is "doubtless Pauline" (p. 155). F. F. Bruce concludes, "There seems, in short, to be no sound argument against the genuineness of this epistle" (p. 83). The *Wesleyan Bible Commentary* states, "All things considered, . . . there seems to be no adequate basis for doubting that the letter before us is from the hand of the Apostle" (p. 488).

II. THE CITY OF COLOSSE

Colosse lay inland of Ephesus about one hundred miles. At one time the main road from Ephesus to the Euphrates ran through this region, following the Lycus Valley. Today the site of Colosse lies deserted, as does the neighboring site (about eight miles east) of Laodicea. Across the river valley twelve miles to the north, Hierapolis, with its famous mineral pools and springs, is the scene of a small resort; its ruins are impressive.

Colosse is the most isolated and unimpressive of the three ancient sites. It can be reached only by a dirt road, at the end of which lies a small Turkish village called Honaz. A couple of miles distant, in farming fields accessible only on foot or by tractor, lie the remains of ancient Colosse. While plowing their fields, local farmers have turned up some ruins of the Roman era. The site has never been systematically excavated.

Historical records tell us that while Colosse was a populous city, wealthy and large in the classical period (fourth–fifth century B.C.), during the Christian era it was only a small town. In the Byzantine era (third century A.D.), Colosse served as an archbishop's see. The only visible evidence of Christianity dates back to this era: Honaz is located near the ruins of a moderately sized Byzantine church.

III. THE OCCASION OF THE LETTER

Though the first-century town was small and relatively insignificant, the "brothers in Christ at Colosse" (1:2) and the issues at stake were vitally important to Paul. His co-worker Epaphras had brought report of God's gracious work at Colosse (vv.6–8); it is also evident that Epaphras had shared with the apostle his concerns about the Colossian church (2:1–5; 4:12–13).

A strange teaching was being promulgated at Colosse. No exposition of this heresy is extant; its features must be inferred from what Paul says in argument against it (see ch. 2). A syncretistic form of human philosophy, the heresy seemed to promise its adherents protection from evil powers through ascetic legalism. The apostle's antidote to these claims is a strong doctrine of Christ's sovereignty.

At the time of writing, Paul is in prison (4:18). The location of his imprisonment, however, is uncertain. "But," as F. F. Bruce argues, "in the case of Colossians and Ephesians (with which Philemon necessarily goes) the arguments for a Roman origin are stronger [than for Philippians]" (p. 87). References in the three prison epistles suggest that all were dispatched at the same time (see Col 4:7–9; Phm 10; Eph 6:21–22). Phm 22 seems to indicate that the apostle's appeal to Caesar was yet forthcoming and he expected to be released shortly. Based on such data, the traditional view dates the writing of this epistle to Paul's first Roman imprisonment, c. A.D. 62. The letter was to be delivered by Tychicus, accompanied by Philemon's slave, Onesimus (4:7–9).

IV. THE DEVELOPMENT OF THE ARGUMENT

For a letter, Colossians exhibits remarkable coherence. The major argument develops a singular theme: the *sovereignty of Jesus Christ*. The first half of the letter (chs. 1–2) proclaims the universality of Christ's dominion, while the second half (chs. 3–4) applies his lordship to daily living.

At the outset of the letter (1:3), the apostle refers to Jesus Christ as "Lord." This choice of title calls to remembrance one of the earliest confessions of the Christian church: "Jesus is Lord." In 1:15–20, a hymn of praise to Christ develops this theme of Jesus' lordship with great majesty and power.

In 2:6–23 Paul combats the false teaching at Colosse by using this touchstone. He exhorts his readers, "So then, just as you received Christ Jesus as Lord, continue to live in him" (v.6). He appeals to them on the basis of their initial confession of faith. They had received instruction in the Gospel and had personally acknowledged the lordship of Christ. That is now the foundation on which they ought to build and thereby grow in their faith (see v.7).

The apostle argues his case against the heresy on the basis of the absolute sovereignty of Jesus Christ, in whom "all the fullness of the Deity lives" (2:9). Jesus has disarmed the rulers and authorities. The false teaching has its own mandates, but they do not accord with Christian doctrine. To follow them is to deny Christ's sovereignty, because it is to submit to lesser authorities. Why should believers submit to these lesser rulers when they "have been given fullness in Christ, who is the head over every power and authority" (v.10)?

Paul then applies this theme to specific areas of daily living. He begins with a general exhortation for every Christian: "Since, then, you have been raised with Christ, set your heart on things above, where Christ is seated at the right hand of God" (3:1). This description of Christ's supremacy is derived from Ps 110:1, a text frequently used in the NT to acclaim Christ's conquest over death and his present dominion.

The exhortations that follow flesh out the meaning of Christ's sovereignty for those who seek to live in his kingdom. The general principle is stated in 3:17: "And whatever you do, whether in word or deed, do it all in the name of the Lord Jesus." A believer's whole life, both in thought and conduct, is to be subordinated to the lordship of Jesus.

Christ's sovereignty is to be the reference point for all personal relationships. Thus wives are exhorted to be subject to their husbands, "as is fitting in the Lord" (v.18). Children are to be obedient to their parents in everything, "for this pleases the Lord" (v.20). Likewise, slaves are to be obedient to their earthly masters, in "reverence for the Lord" (v.22). The exhortations to slaves have a general applicability to all Christian workers: "Whatever you do, work at it with all your heart, as working for the Lord, not for men. . . . It is the Lord Christ you are serving" (vv.23–24).

It is evident that Paul extensively argues and applies the theme of Christ's sovereignty. However, Colossians is not a doctrinal essay; it is a letter. As such, it contains some personal comments (1:1–2, 3–14, 24–2:5; 4:2–18) that do not fit easily into the thematic outline. The common feature of these personal comments is their description of *servant ministry*. Thus they represent a logical counterpoint to the epistle's major theme of sovereign lordship.

In the first of Paul's personal comments, he opens the letter by introducing himself as "an apostle of Christ Jesus by the will of God" (1:1). He then describes his ministry on the Colossians' behalf. He prays for them with this goal in view, "that you may live a life worthy of the Lord" (v.10).

The universality of Christ's kingdom represents for Paul the scope of his commission as a minister. His task as "a servant" is to proclaim the Gospel of Jesus Christ "to every creature under heaven" (1:23).

The extent and nature of Paul's servant ministry are well illustrated in his relationship with the Colossians. He states that he has endured a great struggle "for you and those at Laodicea, and for all who have not met me personally" (2:1).

At the end of the letter, the apostle speaks not only of his own ministry but of the ministries of others as well. Here, too, the themes of sovereignty and servanthood are evoked. Tychicus is commended as "a dear brother, a faithful minister and fellow servant in the Lord" (4:7). Epaphras is called "a servant of Christ Jesus" (v.12). Aristarchus, Mark, and Justus are also named as "my fellow workers for the kingdom of God" (vv.10–11). Finally, there is a word of exhortation for Archippus: "See to it that you complete the work you have received in the Lord" (v.17).

V. INFLUENCE ON WESLEYAN THOUGHT

Wesleyan biblical commentators have often focused on Paul's doctrine of the person and work of Christ in this epistle. Adam Clarke, for example, launches into a full-page excursus on the deity of Christ in his commentary on 1:16–17. The apostle Paul, he argues, "must have considered Jesus Christ as being truly and properly God" (6:516). The epistle's emphases on the sufficiency of Christ and the efficacy of his work (through death and resurrection) have also attracted considerable Wesleyan comment.

The Wesleyan emphasis on personal sanctification and practical holiness reflects those texts that speak of living "worthy of the Lord" (1:10), living "holy in his sight, without blemish and free from accusation" (v.22), and living "perfect in Christ" (v.28). Special attention is accorded such passages in Wesleyan circles.

Paul teaches that the "word of Christ" (3:16) and "spiritual wisdom and understanding" (1:9; cf. 2:3) are vital to the Christian's growth and maturity. He underscores the importance of prayer and evangelism for the Christian community, especially in 4:2–6. These themes have guided the emerging shape of Wesleyan church life.

However, at some points Wesleyans have been reluctant to apply the full force of Paul's teachings in Colossians. For example, Calvinists generally reflect a greater appreciation and affirmation of the doctrine of Christ's sovereignty; Wesleyans fear too great an emphasis on divine sovereignty. Further, there is a need among evangelical Wesleyans to take what Paul says about legalism more seriously, to reexamine their understandings of God's grace in relation to human responsibility.

VI. OUTLINE

    I. Proclaiming His Lordship (chs. 1–2)
        A. Paul's Ministry as an Apostle (1:1–2:5)
        B. The False Teaching at Colosse (2:6–23)
    II. Living His Lordship (chs. 3–4)
        A. Moral Exhortations for Christian Living (3:1–11)
        B. Social Duties Within Christian Community (3:12–4:1)
        C. Personal Examples of Servanthood (4:2–15)
        D. Instructions to Area Churches (4:16)
        E. Exhortation for Archippus's Ministry (4:17)
        F. Closing Salutation (4:18)

COMMENTARY

I. PROCLAIMING HIS LORDSHIP (CHS. 1–2)

The predominant feature of chs. 1–2 is Paul's proclamation of the sovereignty of Christ. He declares that Christ holds **in everything ... the supremacy** (1:18). Christ is **head over every power and authority** (2:10). Paul describes his own ministry in relation to this truth (1:1–2:5); he also applies it against the false teaching at Colosse (2:6–23).

A. Paul's Ministry as an Apostle (1:1–2:5)

Paul introduces himself as Christ's **apostle** (1:1). His apostolic commission is to **proclaim him** among the Gentiles (vv.27–28). Paul aligns himself with others as a **fellow servant in the Lord** (see 4:7), as a minister of the Gospel **proclaimed to every creature under heaven** (1:23).

Paul broadly defines the task of ministry. It is fulfilled in preaching, teaching, and admonishing people about Christ (1:25, 28). It includes prayer and suffering on behalf of the church (vv.3–4, 9, 24; 2:1). It entails warning God's people against error (2:4, 8) and challenging the claims of those who oppose the Gospel (vv.16–23).

With this letter, as with Romans, Paul is writing to a congregation he has not met (1:1). Nevertheless, he is with them **in spirit** (2:5) and continually ministers on their behalf in prayer (vv.3, 9). The report he has received about them occasions thanksgiving and concern (vv.3–4, 9–10; 2:1–4).

The introduction (1:1–2) follows the epistolary formula used in all of the Pauline letters. First the writer is identified (v.1); then the recipients are named (v.2a); finally, greetings are extended (v.2b).

The title *apostle,* to which Paul lays claim, has about it a ring of authority. Elsewhere in this letter he describes himself as a **servant** (1:23, 25) and **fellow servant** (v.7; 4:7). He invokes his apostolic authority only at the outset of the letter, to establish his right to challenge the false teachings at Colosse.

Paul's apostolic authority is derived from his appointment by God. Because it is **by the will of God** (1:1), the identification of himself as an apostle is no idle claim. Paul addresses the congregation at Colosse as a divinely commissioned leader of the church. He is Christ's apostle, in accord with God's will. He is an emissary under orders. He speaks, not on his own authority, but as a divine messenger like the prophets of old.

The readers are addressed as Christian believers. They are described as **holy** ones or "saints," in a slight variation on Paul's typical usage (cf. 1:2; Php 1:1; Eph 1:1). Other Pauline letters are generally addressed "to the church" (1 and 2Co, 1 and 2Th, and Gal). The two forms of address—"to the saints" and "to the churches"—appear synonymous.

At the beginning of the letter proper, Paul describes his ministry of prayer on behalf of the church at Colosse. The description naturally divides into two paragraphs. In the first (1:3–8), Paul tells his readers that he thanks God for the evidences of spiritual vitality at Colosse. In the second (vv.9–14), he affirms his ongoing prayer of concern for them, asking that God will complete the work begun among them. The first paragraph identifies the evidences of Christian experience in its initial stages; the second lists the attributes of Christian maturity.

According to Paul, *thanksgiving* is one of the hallmarks of Christian experience (see 1:12; 2:7; 3:15, 17). It is one of the attributes that the apostle exemplified personally. In all of his letters to the churches (except Galatians, where special circumstances prevailed), Paul began with expressions of thanksgiving. Reflecting his awareness of the fact that the basic root (*charis*) of the Greek word for thanks (*eucharistia*) means "grace," Paul expresses his thanksgiving as a natural response for the gifts of God's love.

In the case of the Colossians, there is good cause for thanksgiving. Paul is grateful (1:3–4) because of the evidences that (1) God's Spirit is at work in their hearts and that (2) God's Word is at work in their fellowship.

The familiar triad of faith, hope, and love emerges in this prayer of thanksgiving. **Faith in Christ Jesus** (1:4) is fundamental to all of Christian experience. Elsewhere Paul clearly articulates what faith is. Faith consists of putting our trust in the person of Jesus Christ, and receiving the saving benefits of his death for our sins.

But, as James says (2:17), faith without works is futile and vain. Genuine faith expresses itself in love. So **the love [they] have for all the saints** (1:4) is another significant evidence of the Colossians' saving relationship with Christ. This love God pours into our hearts by the Holy Spirit, whom he has given us (Ro 5:5).

At this point the apostle theologizes while praying. Faith and love, he says, **spring from** the hope of the Gospel, the "living hope" of which 1 Peter 1:3 speaks. Faith and love are inspired by the hope set before us—and all of these are evidences of initial Christian experi-

ence. But they are subjective evidences that must be anchored in the **word of truth, the gospel** (1:5).

So, in the course of his prayer of thanksgiving, the apostle acknowledges the working of God's Word among believers. He describes that Word as **bearing fruit** and working to produce growth, not only at Colosse, but **all over the world** (1:6). It is the working of God's Word in the midst of believers that produces real growth in the church. The Gospel provides the objective basis for our subjective experience in Christ.

This portrayal of Christian experience is reflected in the traditional Wesleyan understanding. The new birth is grounded in God's Word. A transforming experience, it expresses itself in tangible evidences of spiritual growth.

The next prayer paragraph (1:9–14) touches on things central to Christian growth: (1) knowing and doing God's will, (2) cultivating the attributes of Christian maturity, and (3) responding gratefully to God's gracious work in our lives.

The attributes of faith, love, and hope constitute only the foundation stones of Christian living. So Paul pleads that the Colossians may be filled with the knowledge of God's will: **"And we pray this in order that you may live a life worthy of the Lord and may please him in every way"** (1:10). The apostle then highlights four attributes of such a life: (1) fruitbearing, (2) growth, (3) empowerment, and (4) gratitude. This is how Paul characterizes a Christian life that is perfect and fulfilled, made complete in the will of God. The goal is to live a life worthy of the Lord, to please him in every way. The attainment of this goal requires not only spiritual enlightenment but also spiritual enduement. Here Paul portrays the life of Christian perfection as dynamic and characterized by continuing growth.

Christians need to be reminded that **joyfully giving thanks** (1:11–12) is an attribute worthy of the Lord and is pleasing to him. We have much for which to be grateful, as Paul suggests in these verses. The focal point of our thanksgiving is the salvation that God has wrought on our behalf. He has adopted, rescued, and redeemed us from our fallenness. He has forgiven our sins and made us his own.

The final verses of this passage (1:12–14) lead into a hymn of praise to Christ. The movement in Paul's prayer is exemplary: Beginning with thanksgiving, he proceeds to intercession, then follows with joyful praise. This is a positive model of prayer. We should further note that Paul is not praying for himself so much as he is praying for others. He expresses appreciation for what God is doing in the lives of the Colossians. He intercedes for them, asking that they might achieve full maturity in their Christian experience. His thanksgiving to the Father and praise to the Son follow naturally. This is the kind of praying that modern Christians should emulate and practice.

The following passage (1:15–20) is hymnic in structure and seems to preserve a primitive Christian hymn of praise to Christ. Paul appears to quote the hymn verbatim; his application of it follows in 1:21–23.

The hymn consists of two stanzas (1:15–16 and 1:18b–20) separated by a refrain (vv.17–18a). The two stanzas reflect a similar structure, as do the two lines of the refrain. This is more evident in the Greek text than in English translation (see chart below).

The theme of the hymn is the sovereignty of Christ. The first stanza expounds his sovereignty over the natural order of creation, as the Creator of the world. The second stanza extols him as the Savior of the world and the Head of the church.

The passage is rich in Christology. It declares Christ's divine essence, preexistence, creative agency, and absolute lordship. As noted earlier, Adam Clarke was particularly impressed with its affirmation of Christ's deity.

With regard to Christ's relation to creation, the text affirms that **all things were created by him and for him** (1:16) and **in him all things hold together** (v.17). Paul finds in Christ "the key to creation, declaring that it is all there with Christ in view" (Hunter, 60). He is the one through whom all things exist, by whom they hold together, and for whom they have their being. Not only does he reflect the very image of the One who created all things, but as the **firstborn,** he is the heir of all creation.

A HYMN OF PRAISE TO CHRIST
Colossians 1:15–20

Verse	Greek Text	Literal Translation
15	*hos estin* (1), (2)	who is (1) *title*, (2) *title*
16	*hoti en auto* ...	because in him ...
17	*kai autos estin* ...	and he himself is ...
18a	*kai autos estin* ...	and he himself is ...
18b	*hos estin* (1), (2)	who is (1) *title*, (2) *title*
	hoti en auto ...	because in him ...

The title *firstborn* is particularly significant in this passage, where it occurs twice (1:15, 18). This title derives from the messianic promise of Ps 89:27, where God says, "I will also appoint him my firstborn, the most exalted of the kings of the earth." These words are applied directly to Jesus Christ in Rev 1:5 and 19:16, as King of kings and Lord of lords.

The second stanza of the hymn declares that Christ is Lord of the new creation brought into being through his saving work. He is not only Creator of all things but Savior as well. Through his death on the cross, God accomplished the reconciliation of **all things** to himself. This is a daring proclamation that often seems foolish to those who are educated, and it proves offensive to those of other religious persuasions (see 1Co 1:23).

The Christology of 1:15–20 is so exalted as to be breathtaking. The position of Christ in the mind of the primitive church challenges our own understandings, which often seem paltry by comparison. Jesus Christ is Lord of all, by reason of his role in both Creation and redemption.

Paul immediately proceeds to make an application of this Christological vision to everyday life. The paragraph that follows (1:21–23) exemplifies the applied theology of the NT. It describes the transformation that God has wrought in the believer through Christ's death, defining it in terms of a change of heart and conduct. It speaks of God's purpose for the believer in terms of personal holiness. It specifies that faith is the sole and necessary condition of such a relationship with God. And, finally, it portrays the urgent need to carry the evangelistic proclamation of the Gospel worldwide.

First, the declared truth about Christ's reconciling death is applied to the Colossians. Paul says that the Colossians, like all sinners, were **once** in need of reconciliation to God. They were estranged from God and at enmity with him. This situation found its expression in **evil behavior** (1:21). **But now** they have been reconciled to God through Christ's death. Just as their former alienation from God found expression in rebellious behavior, so now their reconciliation will be reflected in an obedient life. God's redemptive purpose, the apostle declares, is **"to present you holy in his sight without blemish and free from accusation"** (v.22). This is the purpose for which Christ died—that his people might be holy, blameless, and irreproachable. This is the kind of conduct that accords with God's will and pleases him (see v.10).

The holiness of life depicted here can and should be a present reality for every Christian. It is a work of God, contingent on faith. As **you continue in your faith** (1:23), you will progress in holiness. Thus sanctification as well as justification is produced by God's grace.

Second, Paul uses the affirmation of Christ's sovereignty over all creation to define the scope of the Christian mission. Because Christ's lordship is cosmic in scope, the Gospel of salvation through his name ought to be **proclaimed to every creature under heaven** (1:23). These words echo the Great Commission of Mt 28:19–20. Characterizing himself as a **servant** of the Gospel of Christ, Paul perceives his personal commission as encompassing the whole world. John Wesley similarly declared, "The world is my parish."

Having identified himself as a servant/minister in 1:23, Paul speaks personally in the next section concerning his ministry. He testifies to his sense of divine commission. He articulates his evangelistic purpose and concerns. He reaffirms his commitment to proclaim the Gospel of Christ, despite the costs.

Paul's reference to suffering (v.24) may reflect his present circumstances as a prisoner. Such personal hardship he interprets as a part of his ministry to Christ's body, the church. All of his life experiences are dedicated to the end of serving Christ's church. Paul declares that this is his divine **commission.** More particularly, his special calling is to serve as an apostle to the **Gentiles,** to proclaim the Word of God, and to disclose Christ to them.

Paul says that his purpose is to **"proclaim him ... so that we may present everyone perfect in Christ"** (1:28). Alongside proclamation (preaching), he mentions **admonishing and teaching** as means of propagating the Gospel. All of Paul's energies are directed to this end, as he is empowered by God. Paul's statement of purpose reaches beyond evangelism, implying that he is involved in the processes of discipleship and nurture that are essential to Christian perfection. This succinct statement describes well the prevailing philosophy of ministry in the evangelical Wesleyan movement.

In the next paragraph (2:1–5) the apostle speaks not only of himself as a "servant," but also of his "brothers" at Colosse. His mention of **"struggling for you"** probably refers to his ministry of prayer on their behalf (cf. 1:3–14; 4:12). His purpose is that they might grow to maturity, **firm** in the faith (cf. 1:23) and "perfect in Christ" (v.28). The parallelism with statements in the preceding chapter indicates that Paul is making specific application of the general principles he enunciated there. Paul believes the antidote to the Colossian's deception **by fine-sounding arguments** (2:4) is a **complete understanding** of the **full riches** hidden in Christ (v.2).

B. The False Teaching at Colosse (2:6–23)

The next portion of the letter relates particularly to the situation at Colosse. The apostle addresses straightforwardly and combatively the false teaching being promulgated there. The two major claims of fulfillment and freedom are addressed. The apostle wrests both from his opponents, claiming them for Christ.

The little we know about the so-called Colossian heresy lies buried in this text. Scholars differ in their reconstructions of this heresy from the available data. Some attribute it to so-called Judaizers; others, to gnostic influences. Almost all agree that it was syncretistic, philosophical, astrological, and ascetic.

Paul contends aggressively with the false teaching at Colosse. In doing so, we assume that he draws on much of the vocabulary peculiar to the heresy, thereby stripping its claims of their power. He countermands them by setting forth the claims of Christ. Thus his previous declaration of Christ's sovereignty here finds further application.

The organization of Paul's argument is hard to discern, but the attack of 2:6–15 clearly rests on the lordship of Christ. The readers are reminded of the benefits they derive from his person and work.

The apostle begins by reminding his readers of their initial confession of faith: "Jesus is Lord!" Jesus' lordship constitutes the theological and experiential grounds of Paul's argument. On this basis, he exhorts the Colossians: **"So then, just as you received Christ Jesus as Lord, continue to live in him"** (v.6). They must keep their focus on Christ in order to continue in the way of salvation they have entered.

Their attention is being diverted by the false teaching; they are being tempted to leave the Christian way in pursuit of other things.

A mixing of metaphors occurs in 2:7, but the effect is only to emphasize Paul's essential point: There is room to grow in Christ, and that is what every believer ought to do! We find several connections between this exhortation and the preceding texts of 1:9–11, 22–23, and 1:28–2:5. Paul's assertions of God's purpose in Christ's death, his own goals as a minister, and his prayer desires for the Colossians are now brought to focus on the problem at hand.

The warning of 2:8 is clear and stern. False teaching poses a dangerous threat to the church. **Captive** is a rare Greek verb that refers to the carrying off of booty. The Colossians have much to lose if they are beguiled by heresy. The false teaching is characterized as a **hollow and deceptive philosophy.** It has the appearance of wisdom (see 1:23), but lacks substance. It builds on the foundation of **human tradition and the basic principles of this world** (2:8). Paul disavows that it has any connection with Christ. Thus it is set in opposition to Christian doctrine. Its basis, content, and purpose are not only non-Christian; they are anti-Christian.

Paul has put his readers on alert, forewarning them of the personal threat posed by this philosophy. He proceeds, however, not by arguing against it tenet by tenet. Rather, he reminds his readers (vv.9–12) of a more important matter: namely, the nature of their identification with Christ as forgiven sinners. Presumably, in doing so, he also counters certain claims of the false teaching at Colosse.

Paul's declaration of **fullness** in Christ (2:9) is based on the doctrine of Christ's sovereignty (1:18–19). Lohse

suggests that "since the words 'fulness' and 'to be filled' . . . are stressed so emphatically, they must have been key concepts in the 'philosophy' " Paul was refuting (p. 100). The apostle contradicts the claims of his opponents with this polemical assertion: The entire fullness of deity dwells in Christ; therefore the experience of fullness is to be found in him, and in him alone.

Christian experience is indeed filled with significance and power. Through conversion, symbolized by baptism, the believer has been united with the sovereign Christ. In a unique and interesting way, Paul speaks of Christian baptism under the figure of circumcision. (Possibly, the Colossian philosophy taught and/or mandated circumcision of the flesh.) Christian baptism is likened to fleshly circumcision but is characterized as a **circumcision done by Christ** (v.11).

Wesley interpreted this passage as referring to the "circumcision of the heart" (Ro 2:29), symbolizing entire sanctification (*Sermons,* no. 13). The hermeneutical tradition of Wesleyanism still reflects that linkage. But the passage clearly refers to conversion.

Paul's discourse on the believer's identification with Christ is extended in 2:13–15, where he gives special attention to the meaning of God's forgiveness. In a profound declaration of the benefits accruing to the believer from Christ's death, the apostle declares: **"He forgave us all our sins"** (v.13). In the Greek, the following verbs are formally linked to this basic affirmation: "having forgiven" (*charisamenos*), "having canceled" (*exaleipsas*), "having nailed" (*proselosas*), "having disarmed" (*apekdusamenos*), and "having triumphed" (*triambeusas*). Most of these words are uncommon in the NT and are strikingly dramatic. Together they present a metaphor of Christ's conquest over **the powers and author-ities** (v.15). This metaphor highlights the essential connection between Christ's forgiveness of sins and his victory over the principalities of this world.

Evangelical Wesleyans view the Cross as a symbol of Christ's triumph over death, sin, and Satan. Through the power of the Cross, Christians may live a life of holiness and victory over sinning. The tyranny of sin and the power of the world's temptations have been broken through Christ's death and resurrection. Through their identification with him Christians experience a death to sin, self, and the world; in him they are quickened to new life, holiness, and power.

This affirmation is followed by exhortation (vv.16–23), as the apostle specifically addresses the Colossian situation. At issue is the freedom of Christian believers from the legalistic mandates of the false teaching.

Some of the regulations that Paul mentions possibly were derived from Judaism. See, for example, the reference to **a Sabbath day** (v.16). On the other hand, some elements of these heretical rules may have been derived from non-Jewish sources. **"What he has seen"** (v.18) is a technical term found in the mystery religions. The references to **the worship of angels** (v.18) and to **harsh treatment of the body** (v.23), moreover, suggest practices that are, if not non-Jewish, at least nonbiblical in origin. All in all, it appears that the false Colossian philosophy drew its teachings from a number of different religious sources.

As suggested earlier, 2:16–23 poses a challenge to contemporary Wesleyans who have a tendency to overdiscipline the Christian life and favor various forms of legalism. These well-intentioned and zealous believers should review the basis for and value of their regulations in the light of what Paul says here.

The passage poses another challenge to us: modern Christians often lack a systematic theology, thus leaving themselves open to "every wind of teaching" (Eph 4:14). Many—including Wesleyan pastors and laypersons alike—operate with a personal theology drawn from a variety of incompatible elements. This theological syncretism is a serious threat to the modern church.

The **deceptive philosophy** (v.8) at Colosse demanded the observance of sacred taboos and hallowed times. The apostle warns his Christian brothers and sisters not to allow anyone to rob them of their prize, their **fullness in Christ** (v.10), on the basis of such man-made religious standards (v.18). Spiritual growth comes only by holding fast to Christ and by continuing to participate in his body, the church.

Not infrequently, those who claim to have attained higher spiritual insights are unspiritual and simply puffed up with **idle notions** (v.18). Preoccupied with their own exalted experience, such persons have **lost connection with the Head** (v.19), so all of their religiosity is for naught. A religion based on man-made rules rather than Christ is misdirected and illusory. It leads, not to spiritual growth, but to religious presumption. **Since you have died with Christ to the basic principles of this world** (v.20), human commands have no value in promoting true spirituality.

II. LIVING HIS LORDSHIP (CHS. 3–4)

The theme of Christ's sovereignty is continued throughout Colossians. Chs. 1–2 contain a rich exposition of the theme, while chs. 3–4 specifically apply it to everyday living. The latter half of the epistle stresses that all of life must be encompassed under Christ's lordship.

A. Moral Exhortations for Christian Living (3:1–11)

This section sets the stage for all that follows. The believer's identification with Christ becomes the basis for Paul's moral exhortations to godly living. Christ has become the center of focus for the Christian's life. **Earthly things** (v.2) are now viewed from a new perspective, and this change in perspective results in a change of behavior. The Christian exchanges old sinful practices for new ones, striving to reflect the character of Christ himself.

Christ's name is written over the whole of a Christian's life. Thus the apostle exhorts us to look to Christ to receive direction for our conduct. Our thoughts and affections are to be focused on him, who is the source and goal of our lives.

This kind of devotion requires our dying to certain things that belong to the old life. Impure thoughts, filthy language, and immoral deeds have no place in the kingdom of God. The old self must be taken off, **with its practices** (v.9). In its place, we must **put on the new self** (v.10), which reflects the image of God as Christ is made **all** in our lives (v.11). As we reflected the old way of life in sinful conduct, so we are now to reflect Christ's sovereignty in our **walk** (v.7). A radical transformation of life is required. Wesleyans understand this moral transformation to be real, actual, and effectual. They believe God expects a genuine change in the inner person of the believer— not simply a change in the believer's status or relationship with God. It is a real change of character, experienced as God makes the believer holy in his sight (see 1:21–23).

Does this transformation occur in a moment or is it progressive? The Wesleyan typically responds that both statements are true. Commenting on 3:5, John Wesley said that **"put to death"** means to "slay with a continued stroke" (*Notes,* 334). In other words, while God's transforming work is decisive, it is also perpetual. We are being renewed day by day, transformed from one degree of God's glory to another. So we must die to self daily, and constantly put away evil. This is both our privilege and responsibility as those who bear the image of Christ.

B. Social Duties Within Christian Community (3:12–4:1)

There is a natural break in the text at 3:12 (clearly marked by **"Therefore"**), a shift from negative to positive exhortation. There also is a subtle shift in contents: from exhortations respecting personal morality to a depiction of social duties within Christian community.

The first arena of application is the church. As head of his body, Christ is Lord of the church. Members of the church thus are to reflect his lordship in their relationships with one another and in their corporate witness before the world. If indeed **Christ is all, and is in all** (v.11), then Christians ought to reflect his image. **"Clothe yourselves,"** the apostle exhorts (v.12), with the virtues Christ manifested. As **the Lord** (v.13), Christ sets the standard for interpersonal relationships. The Greek makes a direct comparison at this point: **"As the Lord . . . so also you."**

Paul identifies several virtues of Christian behavior. The crowning virtue is **love,** which binds all the rest together **in perfect unity** (v.14). In Japanese ceremonial dress, layers of expensively decorated cloth are draped over a person, each beautiful in its own right. But the costume is incomplete until the belt (*obj*) is placed around the waist, holding the costume together. In a similar way, love functions as the *obj* of the virtues with which a Christian is to be clothed.

Paul then illustrates the application of these virtues to everyday life. Patience finds its application in bearing with each other (vv.12–13). Forgiveness becomes especially pertinent when there arise **grievances . . . against one another** (v.13). In the church we are to exercise patience and forgiveness in order to reflect God's calling upon and Christ's sovereignty over our lives.

Also in our corporate activities as the church in the world, we are to reflect Christ's rule. Chief among the attributes characterizing Christ's body are **peace,** to which **you were called** (v.15), and **giving thanks** (v.17). A climactic verse exhorts: **"And whatever you do, whether in word or deed, do it all in the name of the Lord Jesus"** (v.17). This places the Christian's entire life under obedience to Christ. Everything we say and do bears witness to our confession of faith that "Jesus is Lord!"

In practice, churches do not always live up to this ideal. They do not always practice **perfect unity** (v.14), Christ's forgiveness and peace, nor abundant thanksgiving. So this exhortation is a pertinent contemporary challenge. This is our calling as Christ's church today.

A series of brief exhortations (vv.18–21) are addressed to specific members of the Christian household. In their relations with one another, **wives,** and **husbands, children** and **parents** have opportunity to witness by their lives that Jesus is Lord. His lordship is evoked twice in this passage (vv.22, 23) as the rationale undergirding the prescribed behavior.

Wives are exhorted: **"Submit to your husbands, as is fitting in the Lord"** (v.18). This directive does not imply the downgrading of a woman's dignity. Rather, it specifies that she is to place herself under the headship of her own husband.

There is a corresponding admonition to husbands: **"Love your wives and do not be harsh with them"** (v.19). The husband is to serve as head of the household, but his exercise of authority is to be tempered by responsible love. A parallel passage (Eph 5:25) declares that husbands are to love their wives "as Christ loved the church." Again, Paul points out that Christ's example is our standard.

Next, children are instructed to **obey [their] parents in everything, for this pleases the Lord** (v.20). The goal of a Christian, whether young or old, is to please the Lord (see 1:10). Again, there is a counterpart to the exhortation: Fathers, representing parental authority, are admonished to behave properly in relation to their children. They are to exercise authority and apply discipline, but not in an overbearing or harsh manner. The goal, as stated in Eph 6:4, is to "bring them up in the training and instruction of the Lord."

A third pair of household members—slaves and masters—are addressed in 3:22–4:1. Bo Reicke, in his commentary on a parallel passage in 1 Peter suggests that the Greek word translated "slaves" may be rendered "employees" (see p. 98). Thus, these exhortations to slaves and masters might today be applied to employees and employers.

Broadly speaking, this passage describes the relationship between the believer and Jesus Christ, using the relation of slave-master as an analogy. The exhortations to wives, husbands, children, fathers, and masters are terse; the exhortation to slaves is considerably longer—in fact, longer than all the others combined. (The same is true in the parallel passages of Eph 5–6 and 1Pe 3–4.) The exhortations to slaves seem to be accorded special prominence because the early church found in the servant-master relationship a model of our relation to Christ.

Slaves are exhorted to **obey [their] earthly masters in everything.** They are to work, not merely for personal gain or for the favor of their earthly masters, but with **sincerity of heart and reverence for the Lord** (v.22). The same principles are reiterated in the verses that follow, as the readers are reminded: **"It is the Lord Christ you are serving"** (v.24).

The principles of this passage apply to all workers. (1) You are working, not merely for your employer but for the Lord. (2) Your employment is an opportunity to bear witness to the sovereignty of Christ in your life. (3) Your inner attitude (the **heart**) is expressed in the quality of your work. (4) The Lord will recompense you fairly and generously for your work, even if your employer does not. (5) There is no excuse for wrongdoing (e.g., thievery) in the workplace, even if you are ill-treated and underpaid. (6) Remember that you are serving the Lord Christ, so your work should reflect your reverence for him—wherever you are, whatever your circumstances, whatever kind of work you do.

Masters are exhorted: **"Provide your slaves [employees] with what is right and fair, because you know that you also have a Master in heaven"** (4:1). The same principles apply to both sides of the slave-master relationship: They are the principles by which our Lord judges all persons. He is the Master above every other, the King of kings and Lord of lords. All people—even those who are over other people—must bow the knee to his lordship.

Thus all persons and their activities are brought under the sovereignty of Jesus Christ. His lordship is the standard by which every relationship—in the church, at home, and on the job—must be measured. Mature Christians in pursuit of holiness need to appreciate this fact as much as new converts who are trying to find their way. The overarching lordship of Christ is continually relevant and constantly challenging.

C. Personal Examples of Servanthood (4:2–15)

The materials at the close of Colossians reflect its origins as a letter. After final exhortations of a personal nature, the apostle greets his fellow servants in Christ, then concludes with a handwritten salutation. This section has the appearance of a miscellaneous medley; but it does have coherence when viewed in light of the letter's theme. It illustrates in practical ways the nature of Christian servanthood, which is a counterpart to Christ's sovereignty. The theme of ministry/servanthood is evoked by the apostle's own example of Christian concern and by the actions of other persons named.

The apostle requests the prayers of his readers, to the end that **"God may open a door for our message"** (4:3). Here we find prayer coupled with evangelistic concern. Both the apostle and his readers, in different circumstances, are joined in a common endeavor. Christianity is a missionary faith, and we define our mission in terms of evangelism. However, unless we witness in the power of the Holy Spirit, little can be accomplished for God. Thus we are aware of our need for personal and corporate prayer as we undertake the work of evangelism.

There is a dearth of prayer and

evangelism in the modern church. This is not true worldwide, but it is true within American and European Christianity. A revival of prayer is desperately needed if the Gospel is to flourish and new converts are to be ushered into the kingdom of God. This is the challenge of God's Word.

The personal exchanges that follow (vv.7–17) reflect Paul's close relations with his fellow workers. His strong personal support of them is evident in his words of commendation. He accords each of them respect as **a dear brother** (v.7), **a servant of Christ Jesus** (v.12), or **dear friend** (v.14).

The apostle makes arrangements for a personal emissary (who presumably will carry his epistle to Colosse); presents greetings from other Christians who are with him or who are known to the readers; gives instructions regarding an exchange of letters with the church at Laodicea; and directs a personal word of encouragement to Archippus, who seems to be serving as pastor at Colosse.

Since Paul is in chains (vv.3, 18) and unable to come to Colosse, he makes arrangements for Tychicus to serve as his personal emissary. Tychicus is to be accompanied by Onesimus, the runaway slave of Philemon. Both of them are described as Christian brothers, and Tychicus as a **minister and fellow servant in the Lord** (v.7). Their mission is to bring to the Colossian church news about Paul. Paul expects that this news will **encourage [their] hearts** (v.8).

The apostle mentions several coworkers who wish to extend greetings to the church at Colosse (vv.10–15). He also asks that his personal greetings be extended to congregations near Colosse (v.15).

Epaphras is the only person mentioned in Paul's final comments who is also named elsewhere in this letter. Both in 1:7 and 4:12, Paul identifies him as a Christian servant/minister. It seems clear that Epaphras has ministered at Colosse (see vv.9, 12, which describe him and Onesimus as **one of you**). The context also suggests that he is not one of the **Jews among [his] fellow workers** (v.11); therefore, he may have been a Gentile.

More important is the description of Epaphras's ministry on behalf of the Colossians and **those at Laodicea and Hierapolis** (v.13). Though absent from them, he still is concerned for them. He is **working hard** (v.13) in praying for them. The Greek word translated **wrestling** (*agonizomenos*) is the same verb Paul uses to describe his own ministry (1:29; 2:1).

Epaphras's ministry to these congregations was twofold. While present with them, he offered "God's grace in all its truth" (1:6–7). Now absent from them, he wrestles in prayer on their behalf. Having received Epaphras's report concerning them, Paul shares his prayer burden for them. He also writes this letter as a ministry of teaching and exhortation.

D. Instructions to Area Churches (4:16)

The neighboring church of Laodicea has been mentioned twice previously in this letter (2:1; 4:13). Obviously, Paul's concern extends beyond the Colossians. This verse suggests that Paul had written the Laodiceans a letter that is no longer extant. He proposes an exchange of letters for the mutual edification of Laodicea and Colosse and calls for a public reading of these.

E. Exhortation for Archippus's Ministry (4:17)

As mentioned earlier, Archippus seems to have been the pastor of the

Colossian church. Perhaps the church met in his home. Paul speaks of a **work** or ministry that Archippus had **received in the Lord** (v.17). The reference may be to a specific task, or it may be a general description of his vocation. Whatever the case, the apostle exhorts his fellow soldier (Phm 1:2) to give attention to his work and see it to completion.

F. Closing Salutation (4:18)

Colossians appears to have been dictated by the apostle to an amanuensis (secretary). For the final line, however, Paul takes the pen to verify the authenticity of the letter and to give it a personal touch. He pens both a petition and a blessing. The petition is, **"Remember my chains,"** a reminder of Paul's present circumstances as a prisoner (see 4:3, 10; 1:24). The blessing is a simple benediction that points the readers to God's grace. Paul wishes them well and prays that God's blessing may be with them. In this way, he signs off the letter in his own handwriting.

A remarkable letter it has been: brief but potent. Even today we sense Paul's concern for those who read it. The epistle calls us to consider the person and work of Christ and his authority within the church. It juxtaposes our servanthood and his sovereignty, two realities that are central in the life of every Christian believer.

BIBLIOGRAPHY

Clarke, Adam. *Commentary and Critical Notes on the NT.* New York: Bangs and Emory, 1826.

Hunter, A. M. *Interpreting Paul's Gospel.* London: Collier, 1954.

Kümmel, Werner Georg. *Introduction to the NT.* New York: Abingdon, 1966.

Lohse, Edward. *Colossians and Philemon.* HCS. Philadelphia: Fortress, 1971.

Martin, Ralph P. *Colossians and Philemon.* Grand Rapids: Eerdmans, 1973.

McCown, Wayne. "The Hymnic Structure of Colossians 1:15–20," *The Evangelical Quarterly* (July–August, 1979), 156–62.

Reicke, Bo. *The Epistles of James, Peter and Jude.* AB. Vol. 37. New York: Doubleday, 1964.

Simpson, E. K., *Ephesians;* and Bruce, F. F., *Colossians.* NICNT. Grand Rapids: Eerdmans, 1957.

Wesley, John. *Explanatory Notes Upon the New Testament.* London: Epworth, 1754.

Wesleyan Bible Commentary. Grand Rapids: Eerdmans, 1965.

1 THESSALONIANS
K E Brower

INTRODUCTION

I. THE SETTING
Most scholars assign 1Th to the Pauline corpus, although some note that most of 2Th could have been written jointly by Paul, Silas, and Timothy (see Bruce, xxxii–xxxiv). The epistle reflects Paul's thought, however, and would have been sent only with his contribution and approval.

II. THESSALONICA
Founded around 300 B.C., Thessalonica was the cosmopolitan capital of the Roman province of Macedonia. As a "free city," it was governed by its own politarchs (see Ac 17:6). Situated on a fine harbour and the Via Egnatia, 150 kilometers west of Philippi, this market centre differed little from Corinth in its social structure, pagan rites, and cultural mores. The orgiastic Cabirus cult had been absorbed into the imperial cult, leaving a vacuum in the religious life of the ordinary people (see Jewett, 127–32). Frame calls Thessalonica "important, populous and wicked" (2).

III. THE PAULINE MISSION IN THESSALONICA
During Paul's first stay (see Ac 17:1–9), he preached in the synagogue with some Jews and a large number of God-fearing Greeks becoming Christians. First Thessalonians suggests that the Jewish converts were in a minority (see 1:9; 2:7–16). Jewish opponents wished to lynch Paul and Silas (no mention is made of Timothy) but failed to find them. So they dragged Jason and other converts before the city officials. However, the politarchs released them on bail, perhaps barring Paul and Silas from Thessalonica for as long as they were in office.

IV. DATE AND OCCASION
According to the Delphi inscription, Gallio was proconsul in Achaia sometime between late summer 50 and spring A.D. 53. While Paul was in Corinth, he was arraigned before Gallio (Ac 18:12–17). If Paul wrote 1Th shortly after arriving in Corinth, then it was written between A.D. 50 and 51 (see Best, 7–13; Bruce, xxxv).

First Thessalonians responds to Timothy's report on his visit. Best suggests two other reasons: Paul's knowledge of the needs of young Christians in general and the specific conditions in Thessalonica (p. 15). The latter point dominates.

Three practical issues can be detected: the legitimacy of Paul's apostleship, persecution of the believers, and sexual ethics. Two theological issues also emerged: the fate of "the dead in Christ" at the Second Coming (Parousia) and its timing, and the indissoluble link between high standards of ethical behaviour and the Spirit-filled life.

V. OUTLINE

COMMENTARY

I. GREETING (1:1)

Letter openings in the Hellenistic world followed the formula: "A to B, greeting." Paul often elaborates on this form. Here "A" is more than one person: Paul, Silas, and Timothy. Any contribution of Silas ("Silvanus," see Ac 17:1–9; 18:5) and Timothy, one of Paul's co-workers (see 1Co 4:17; Php 2:19–20), cannot be identified.

The epistle is addressed to the **church** (Gk. *ecclesia,* "assembly"), the people called into being by God in Christ. The linking of God and Christ shows Paul's high Christology (see 3:11–13).

Into the words **grace and peace** Paul packs a wealth of theology. **Grace** is God's love, active in redeeming an undeserved humanity. **Peace** (Heb. *shalom*) describes the condition of wholeness that comes from being reconciled to God and therefore with oneself and one's fellows.

II. RECALLING THE PAST (1:2–3:10)

The first half of the epistle recalls the planting of the church.

A. Thanksgiving (1:2–10)

1. Thanksgiving Prayer (1:2–3)

The thanksgiving contains commendations that indicate the condition of the church, matched by Paul's deep concern (see 2Co 11:28–29). Paul thanks God for their model behaviour: faith, love, and hope producing work, labour, and endurance. **Faith** includes acceptance of, and trust in, the message of salvation and obedience to Christ. **Love** is at the centre of all Christian relationships. **Hope** is the conviction that God will bring salvation to completion (see Php 1:6).

Work, labour, and steadfastness "confirm the reality of the spiritual attitudes which inspire them" (Marshall, 51). Salvation is not earned by works, but it produces a grateful response in action. Labour issues from deep devotion to God. Endurance comes from the confidence that God's purposes for his creation will triumph despite present circumstances.

2. Thanksgiving for the Effectiveness of the Gospel (1:4–10)

The Thessalonians are among the elect (**chosen**) of God. Paul's view of election has several undergirding themes. First, the stress is on God's initiative: God elects. Second, Jesus is the Elect One, par excellence. Those who are in Christ are the elect, and believers are corporately elect only in Christ (see Eph 1). Third, election does not imply that God has withheld salvation from anyone. Finally, the elect are those whose lives demonstrate election. The Thessalonians are living exemplary lives. Hence, they are demonstrably elect. The Wesleyan understanding of the doctrine of election follows Paul closely.

Paul proclaims the Gospel in the power of the Spirit. Miraculous deeds sometimes accompanied this proclamation (see, e.g., Gal 3:5). But attention here is entirely upon the impeccable behaviour of the missionaries. Their public image is consistent with private reality.

Paul urges his converts to imitate him (see 1Co 11:1), even in suffering (2:14). They are prepared to do so. In turn, with characteristic hyperbole (see Ro 1:8; 2Co 2:14; Col 1:6), Paul notes that their **"faith in God has become known everywhere"** (v.8).

In the NT, **"suffering"** (Gk. *thlipsis,* "tribulation") is the normal experience of the Christian (see Jn 16:33; Ac 14:22; Ro 8:17). Joy given by the Spirit characterizes the Christian response to tribulation.

The Thessalonians **turned to God from idols,** an OT phrase that suggests they had been pagans. Now they are to live holy lives in response to their salvation and in expectation of deliverance from the coming wrath (see Jer 10:10).

Wrath is the just reaction of a holy God to wickedness. It is seen in the mess that humanity has created in its rebellion against God (see Ro 1:18–32). Within the consequences of human choice, God's judgment is evident. But the wrath of God also will be experienced when God brings final judgment on all ungodliness. Here Paul refers to that future judgment.

B. The Apostles' Behaviour (2:1–2)

Despite opposition, the missionaries received courage from God to continue proclamation of the Gospel (2:2). The success of their visit was evident from the long-term results, for which Paul is thankful.

1. Motives and Conduct (2:1–6)

Success came because the Gospel is not based on error. It is the truth of God, from God (see Gal 1:11–12). This message of God's love was proclaimed from pure motives, which excluded any sexual impropriety, ambition, pride, greed, or trickery. The cultural background made these claims important. Rather, the missionaries were approved by God and were subject to a continuing "quality control" (Marshall, p. 66). Their sole aim was to please God. Their mindset was completely focused on God and his purposes for them.

Conduct matched motives. They did not seek to manipulate through flattery. They "did not use the apparently good action of preaching the gospel as a means of covering up (and so achieving) their real aim . . . [of] material gain" (Marshall, 67). They did not seek praise ("glory" in Gk.) from men. Rather the only glory went to God.

2. Examples (2:7–12)

Paul had the right of financial support (see 1Co 9:14; Mk 6:7–13) but never exercised it. Rather, he desired to proclaim the Gospel without even the hint of offense. Instead of using their authority and status, the missionaries were gentle, sharing the Gospel and their very lives (v.8). Their lives were holy, righteous, and blameless examples. A holy life is patterned after the holiness of God. As Airhart observes, "The Christian ethic is related to the nature of God" (p. 457). Righteous actions do not exploit others.

The present and future dimensions of God's kingdom and our salvation are evident throughout 1Th. Christians are called into his kingdom now and are to walk worthy of it now. But the call has a future dimension as well. Paul here draws attention to the goal of salvation: God's kingdom and glory.

The missionaries acted as mother (v.7) and father (v.8), two similes that describe God's relationship to his people (see Ps 103:13; Isa 66:13). The proper care of a leader for his people combines the nourishment and tenderness of a mother with the example and instruction of a father. This care produces lives that are a worthy response to God's present call into acceptance of that future kingdom.

C. Further Thanksgiving (2:13–16)

Despite suffering, the Thessalonians readily accepted the Gospel as the Word of God (see Gal 1:11–12), a fact confirmed by its effect.

In words echoing 2Ch 36:16 and Mt 23:29–36, Paul denounces his opponents (see 1Co 2:8). In their zeal for God, they really were opposing God and were hostile to humanity because the Gentiles were prevented from hearing the Gospel. Hence, his opponents experienced God's wrath now.

Paul's opponents did not wish to exclude the Gentiles. But neither could they accept Paul's view that Gentiles could enter the covenant without first becoming Jews. In Paul's view, they were simply obstructing the Gentile mission.

Paul was a Jew, a man of his time, and a Christian. If these are his words (but see Bruce, 49), they need to be understood on his terms. Paul held that judgment comes upon all who reject God's salvation in Christ. To impede the progress of the Gospel is to resist God. To reject Christ is to incur God's wrath.

Despite these disclaimers, the seemingly anti-Semitic tone of this passage remains. It "sounds like an echo of slanders current in the Greco-Roman world" (Bruce, 46). It is small comfort to note that Christians themselves are similarly slandered. More disturbing is the way in which generations of Christians have misused passages like this as warrant for unspeakable atrocities against Jews. May God forgive us.

D. A Desired Visit (2:17–3:10)

1. Desire To See Spiritual Children (2:17–20)

Paul emphasizes that he, personally, had planned repeatedly to visit them, but his way had been blocked by Satan, perhaps through bail conditions (Bruce, 55) or personal circumstances (Marshall, 86). It was not a check by the Spirit, because it worked against the furtherance of the Gospel (see Ac 16:9–10).

Paul rejoices in the fruit of his labours. If the converts held steadfast to the end, his missionary activity would be judged a victory. Timothy's report confirmed the genuineness of their faith. At the Lord's coming, they could be presented as trophies.

In contemporary usage "coming" (*parousia*, v.19) connoted an official state visit with attendant pomp and circumstance. These images prompted its use to denote the Lord's coming. The idea, however, was derived from the OT.

2. Timothy's Mission (3:1–5)

Because Paul fears that they might succumb to temptation, he sends Timothy from Athens to strengthen them. Perhaps persecution was threatening anew. Certainly distorted views about the Parousia and the Christian life were causing doubts. If they yielded to temptation, all Paul's efforts would have proved useless.

3. Timothy's Report (3:6–10)

Timothy's report confirmed their steadfastness. Paul responds immediately, recalling happy memories and noting his genuine longing to see them again. He also wants to remedy any deficiencies in their faith. All Christians need to grow, but Paul deals with potential problems before they become serious.

III. FIRST PRAYER (3:11–13)

Here Paul introduces the themes of holiness, love, and the Lord's return. He addresses his prayer both to God and Christ. The worship of the early church, including instances like this when prayer is offered to Jesus, laid the foundations for the later Trinitarian doctrine.

The focus comes in the second petition: that love would increase and overflow. Love must be expressed within and without the community of believers. Once again Paul cites the missionaries' example.

The intimate tie between love and holy living is central both to Pauline and Wesleyan thought. Love, the source of holy living, prevents a legalistic holiness that is impervious to the situations of others. Equally, a settled holiness of heart is necessary if the Christian is to demonstrate love in action. Christian holiness is both freedom from sin and the presence of love (see McCown, 27; Bruce, 72).

Paul prays that they would be found blameless and holy at Jesus' coming. But this does not mean holiness must await the final judgment. Because Paul expected the Lord's return in the immediate future, he urges them to prepare themselves now. Holiness could not wait. It also has a future consummation, at the Lord's coming. Holiness is both present reality and future hope.

IV. EXHORTATIONS (4:1–5:22)

A. On Spiritual Growth (4:1–12)

Holiness must issue in a changed lifestyle. For Paul, the present reality of holiness is intimately connected with ethical living. Here he concentrates on sexual ethics and work habits.

Paul supports his call to holiness by drawing attention to the will of God, the judgment of God, the call of God, and the Spirit of God (McCown, 28–29).

1. General Exhortations to Growth (4:1–2)

Ethical instruction is given by the authority of the Lord through the apostles. The Thessalonians were already leading exemplary lives, but Paul urges them to continue on. The desire to please God is the natural expression of inward holiness (see 3:13).

2. Holiness and Sexuality (4:3–8)

Paul flatly states, **"It is God's will that you should be sanctified"** (4:3). Careful attention to its literary and theological context is essential for understanding this verse.

First, the term *sanctified* always has ethical content in Christianity (see McCown, 29). Sexual purity is a specific manifestation of the general holiness of life demanded of God's people.

Second, just as God's purposes of salvation for his creation are dynamic and ongoing, so sanctification here refers to the active and dynamic process of making holy (see McCown, 28). Paul's ethical commands point to this continuing expression of holiness in life.

Third, sanctification is both the path and the goal of the Christian walk. The essential contribution of Wesleyan theology to the wider church is to remind it of the present, realized dimension of God's eschatological work of sanctification. To see holiness only as a goal is to deprive the present Christian life of true significance. On the other hand, overconcentration on the realized aspect, the present state of holiness, is to empty salvation of its future hope and purpose.

Fourth, the whole will of God can be summed up in this one statement: "Be holy, as I am holy." Holiness is the normal condition of the Christian, not an option available only to superlative Christians. *Sanctification* thus becomes one of many terms used in the NT to express God's saving purpose for his creation.

Problems of sexual immorality in the young church reflect the complex situation in Thessalonica. As new converts from paganism, some may not have broken completely with their former pattern of life. Given the prominence of phallic symbolism in the Cabiri cults and Paul's exhortation to sexual self-control, the NIV translation **"his own body"** (lit. "vessel") is appropriate in v.4. (See 1Sa 21:5 where in NRSV "vessel" is a euphemism for the male genitalia.) Holiness is incompatible with sexual promiscuity.

But holiness is not asceticism. Human sexuality can be expressed legitimately and honourably within the bounds of marriage. Sexual immorality, by contrast, is essentially selfish and dishonourable. Such actions will not go unpunished, because God did not call his people *for* uncleanness but *in* holiness (see RSV, which captures Paul's meaning in v.7 better than NIV). "The change in preposition from *epi* [for] to *en* [in] implies that sanctification is part of the Christian calling" (Bruce, 86).

Few things have contributed more to the downfall of believers than sexuality. However mature one might be, the constant bombardment from a society that does not know God (v.5), coupled with the nature of sexual desires, provide ready ammunition for the Tempter (see 3:5). Paul's implied remedy is the continuing presence of the Spirit in the believer's life.

Implicit here and throughout the epistle (see esp. 2:12; 3:13; 4:3; 5:23) is the conviction that the holy life is not just a future possibility but must be a present reality. As Marshall observes, "What God calls his people to be, he will do for them, and sanctification in

particular is his work in the believer (1Co 1:30; 6:11)" (p. 113).

3. Love in Action (4:9–12)

Paul really does not need to write to the Thessalonians about love. They were taught by God to love each other. Their growth in love is attributable to the sanctifying power of the Spirit.

Even so, Paul urges them to continue their daily occupations. Some men have quit working to wait for the Lord's return. This group created a needless burden on the church, brought the church into disrepute, and demonstrated a lack of love.

B. On the Coming of the Lord (4:13–5:11)

Two questions trouble the Thessalonians. What would be the fate of the **dead in Christ** at his coming? And when would Christ return?

Paul's answers are couched in apocalyptic language. Apocalyptic came to prominence about 200 B.C. to A.D. 100. The NT ideas of resurrection, final judgment, the wrath of God, and the return of Christ are all realities variously expressed in apocalyptic language.

Apocalyptic language has suffered two fates. Because it is so strange, it has been rejected or ignored in both form and content. But this tack dismisses a prominent feature of the Scripture. Equally wrong has been the failure to recognize that it was understood as parable rather than interpreted in prosaic literalness by the first readers. We must think in the same pictorial fashion as Paul did. Otherwise we will miss the intended meaning of the passage just as surely as those who ignore or reject it.

The Parousia of Christ, described in apocalyptic language, is a real event. But we need to distinguish between the reality of Christ's return in power and great glory, and the imagery used to express that reality. If we succeed in making that distinction, we will avoid both extremes noted above.

1. The Dead in Christ
(4:13–15)

Paul does not want the Thessalonians to be anxious about the fate of the **dead in Christ.** Nor does he want them to grieve as those who do not know God, and are therefore without hope (see Eph 2:12).

In fact, Christians, like all persons, do grieve over death. Grief is a normal and essential part of coping with death. But Christian grief is tempered by hope. For Christians, death is not the end.

Without doubt, the Thessalonians knew and believed that the dead in Christ would rise. The question seems to be whether they would share in his coming. Paul emphatically states that they shall suffer no disadvantage.

2. The Coming of the Lord
(4:16–18)

Using OT imagery, Paul describes the Parousia as a coming with authority and power, heralding the resurrection of the **dead in Christ.** After this, the **dead in Christ** will join the living and together join the Lord. Christians will share in the coming of Christ to earth. The stress is upon the eternal unity between Christ and his body, the church.

Paul is not contrasting the dead in Christ with those who are dead but not in Christ. He says nothing about the resurrection of the latter anywhere. There is therefore no support whatsoever in this passage for any idea of a "first resurrection." As Bruce astutely observes, "It is precarious to draw inferences from Paul's silence about his views on the nature and timing of the resurrection of those who are not in

Christ" (p. 105). Equally slender is the biblical support for the doctrine of the "rapture." Since the mid-nineteenth century, this single verse has been the cornerstone of the dispensationalist view of the Lord's return.

The pastoral intent of the teaching is summed up in v.18. Bruce (p. 103) cites a pagan writer who ends a letter of condolence with the words, "So comfort one another." No word of hope is included. Could one find a more poignant reminder of the contrast between the lostness and hopelessness of those outside of Christ and the hope of the Christian?

3. The Day of the Lord (5:1–5)

The term *day of the Lord* has a rich OT background as the day of Yahweh's righteous judgment and vindication of his holiness. In the NT this imagery describes the coming of Christ.

The issue concerning the "dead in Christ" may have led to the question of times and dates for Jesus' coming. In Paul's view, they already were adequately instructed about this.

Unlike some modern students of prophecy, Paul refuses to speculate. Instead, he reminds them that the Day of the Lord will come unannounced. For those who are not in Christ, it will be completely unexpected and not particularly welcome.

For Christians, however, that day will not come as a surprise because they will be watchful and alert. For them, it is the day of salvation, not judgment. Paul's careful language stresses both the present reality of salvation and the anticipation of its future consummation. It is ours now but also awaits the coming of the kingdom in fulness. As Marshall states, "God's salvation is still to come in all its fullness and replace the present age of sin; but it already has come and God's people can enjoy its benefits through faith. The age to come overlaps the present evil age for the believer. The Christ who will come has already come" (p. 136). The NT tension between the "already" and the "not yet" of salvation must be maintained.

4. Watchfulness and Armor (5:6–10)

Vigilance is not a zealous attempt to read "the signs of the times." Rather, it is a life lived in faithfulness (see 3:13). The children of light are already children of (future) salvation and are ready for the consummation of salvation. The alert Christian will be fully armed with faith, love, and the hope of salvation.

God's purpose is salvation, not wrath. The choice of verbs in v.9 is significant. In using **"appoint,"** Paul indicates that God did not intend wrath for his creation. **"To receive"** implies that humans must accept God's salvation. His purpose will be fulfilled, but humans have the choice to accept the free and undeserved gift or to maintain their arrogant independence from God.

There is a paradox between God's purposes and human choice. But two things are clear. First, God does not force persons to follow him. Second, "a predestination to wrath that operated independently of the responsible action of mankind in sinning and rejecting the gospel is as unthinkable as a predestination to salvation that overrules human responsibility or makes it ultimately of no account by operating through it" (Marshall, 140).

Paul notes that Jesus died for us so that we might live together with him (5:10). Salvation is wholly based on the death of Jesus Christ. It is his death for our life.

5. Pastoral Summary (5:11)

Mutual encouragement is essential to growth. Paul commends this practice among the Thessalonians. His focus on the blessed hope is for the same purpose: upbuilding and a spur to action.

C. On Life in the Church (5:12–22)

1. Respect for Leaders (5:12–15)

The local leaders may have been under pressure from those with flawed views on the Parousia. Paul reminds them that their leaders have authority from the Lord. Honour and respect is to be given in love to them.

Paul singles out three groups: the idle, the timid, and the weak. Patience is to be shown to all, even towards those who actually deserve far worse.

"Getting even" is not to be tolerated in the church (see Mt 5:44–48; Lk 6:27–36). Rather the Christian response to wrong, whatever the source, is to try to bring good out of evil. This challenges the spirit of our age in which retaliation is seen as strength and any attempt to return good for evil is seen as weakness.

2. Principles for Life in the Spirit (5:16–22)

Life lived in the power of the Spirit produces "a stable and deep-rooted joy" (Marshall, 155), which is not a worked-up, human emotion of "feeling good." In circumstances of suffering, persecution and distress (2:14; 3:7–8), the Spirit keeps the believer's eyes firmly fixed on Jesus (see Heb 12:2). External circumstances neither create nor prevent this joy.

Prayer is the constant attitude of the believer (see Ro 12:12; Eph 6:18; Col 4:2). To **pray continually** means that every activity must be carried on with a sense of God's presence (see Bruce, 127).

Paul commands his readers to give thanks *in the midst of* all circumstances, not to give thanks *for* all circumstances.

There is a world of difference between these two views. The latter denies evil and suffering. The former believes that in every circumstance one can give thanks for hope in Christ that cannot be vanquished (see Ro 8:39).

Life in the Spirit consists of the positive joy, communion, and thanksgiving made possible by his presence. God's commands are not met in one's own strength.

Paul warns against putting out the Spirit's fire (v.19). The specific issue is prophecy. Paul is unequivocal: **"Do not treat prophecies with contempt"** (v.20). Equally, they ought to test everything, hold on to the good and reject any "evil type of phenomenon allegedly inspired by the Spirit" (Marshall, 159).

Prophecy was important to the early church for the task of explaining the meaning of the OT in light of Jesus and for building up the church through correction and instruction.

Paul strikes a balance between a gullible acceptance of any claim to prophetic utterance and a cynical disdain that denies its possibility. He does not give the criteria for discernment here, but other texts may help (see especially 1Co 12–14). Prophetic utterance must be consistent with the oral tradition. It does not announce revelation direct from God independent of the tradition. It draws attention to the lordship of Jesus who is God's final and complete revelation (see Heb 1:1–2). Finally, it builds the church.

V. SECOND PRAYER (5:23–24)

God's full purpose of salvation may be described as peace. This peace is the wholeness and completeness of the individual centred on God. It contrasts with the disorder, disintegration, and chaos that characterizes all of humanity's relationships since the Fall. Peace and sanctification are intimately connected (see McCown, 30).

Persons who are sanctified **through and through** (v.23) live lives with every aspect conforming to God's purposes of salvation. "Wholly" (KJV), according to Wesley, "signifies *wholly and perfectly;* every part and all that concerns you; all that is of or about you" (p. 763).

Here again, Paul implies a tension between the present reality of the believer's sanctification and its future consummation. But, as McCown observes, "the petition is for the consummation of God's saving work in the life of the believer" (p. 30).

Christians cannot present themselves blameless (v.24). God's call to sanctification is based on his faithfulness to accomplish it. He will bring his purposes to pass in those who have responded to his call and who follow him.

VI. CLOSING REMARKS (5:25–28)

Finally, Paul requests prayer and gives some instructions. First, he urges his readers to **greet all the brothers with a holy kiss.** Although a holy kiss may be less acceptable in some cultures today, Christians still need a way to express concretely their mutual love (see Marshall, 165).

The second command is emphatic: **"I charge you before the Lord to have this letter read to all the brothers"** (v.27). Clearly, Paul wishes to ensure that all who need these exhortations should hear them.

The epistle closes with a brief benediction: **"The grace of our Lord Jesus Christ be with you"** (v.28).

BIBLIOGRAPHY

Airhart, Arnold E. *I and II Thessalonians*. BBC. Vol. 9. Kansas City: Beacon Hill, 1965.

Best, Ernest. *A Commentary on the First and Second Epistles to the Thessalonians*. HNTC. New York: Harper & Row, 1972.

Bruce, F. F. *1 and 2Th*. WdBC. Waco: Word, 1982.

Frame, J. E. *A Critical and Exegetical Commentary on the Epistles of St. Paul to the Thessalonians*. ICC. Edinburgh: T. & T. Clark, 1912.

Jewett, Robert. *The Thessalonian Correspondence: Pauline Rhetoric and Millenarian Piety*. Philadelphia: Fortress, 1986.

Klopfenstine, W. O. *The First and Second Epistles of Paul to the Thessalonians*. WBC. Vol. 5. Grand Rapids: Eerdmans, 1965.

McCown, Wayne. " 'God's Will . . . For You': Sanctification in the Thessalonian Epistles," *Wesleyan Theological Journal* 12 (1977): 26–33.

Marshall, I. H. *1 and 2Th*. NCB. Grand Rapids: Eerdmans, 1983.

Wesley, John. *Explanatory Notes Upon the New Testament*. London: Epworth, 1754.

2 THESSALONIANS
K E Brower

INTRODUCTION

I. THE SETTING

The mission to Thessalonica was a success. Thessalonica's importance (see introduction to 1Th) meant that the church encountered many of the problems of a cosmopolitan city. The pagan cults were prominent. Sexual license was rampant. The temptation to divorce religion from ethics and holiness from life was coupled with anxiety over the timing of the Lord's return.

Paul had addressed these problems in 1Th. But the issues remained alive. Paul soon received further information about developing problems, which he addressed in 2Th (see Jewett, 60). The church continued to misunderstand the Parousia. In particular, some seemed to believe that the Parousia had already occurred. Others failed to heed Paul's injunctions about idleness.

Recently, many scholars have argued that 2Th is a post-Pauline imitation of 1Th designed to teach a different lesson. The arguments are substantial but not compelling. Marshall concludes, "That 2 Th. contains some unusual features in style and theology is not to be denied, but that these features point to pseudonymous authorship is quite another matter. Moreover, the early church had no doubts about the Pauline authorship of 2 Th." (p. 45).

II. OUTLINE

I. Greetings (1:1–2)

II. Thanksgiving and Prayer (1:3–12)
 A. Thanksgiving (1:3–4)
 B. God's Righteous Judgment (1:5–10)
 C. Prayer (1:11–12)

III. The Day of the Lord and the Man of Lawlessness (2:1–12)
 A. The Rise of the Man of Lawlessness (2:1–4)
 B. The Fall of the Man of Lawlessness (2:5–12)

IV. Thanksgiving and Prayers (2:13–3:5)
 A. Thanksgiving (2:13–15)

COMMENTARY

I. GREETING (1:1–2)

This greeting is similar to 1Th with two modifications. First, the word *our* in reference to God the Father indicates that God is the Father of Christians. Second, the source of grace and peace is God the Father and the Lord Jesus Christ, a theologically significant combination (see 1Th 3:11). Jesus is the coequal source of peace (see 3:16; Jn 14:27).

II. THANKSGIVING AND PRAYER (1:3–12)

A. Thanksgiving (1:3–4)

The opening thanksgiving seems formal. Some suggest liturgical overtones (see Bruce, 143); others, a trace of coolness. Nonetheless, it is a genuine thanksgiving for their continuing growth in grace, evoked by further good news about their steadfastness.

Their circumstances have not improved, however. Nor have their problems been resolved. Pressure continues, both from within and without. So does growth in grace. Interestingly enough, Paul does not give thanks for their love and faith; it is their perseverance in the face of trials that brings thanksgiving.

B. God's Righteous Judgment (1:5–10)

For the persecuted, hope of vindication sustains. This has always been so, from the OT to the modern experience of slaves in America, blacks in South Africa, and oppressed Christians in totalitarian regimes. The Thessalonians endure persecution because they have confidence in God's righteous judgment. Present circumstances are not God's final word.

Their perseverance is evidence that God's judgment is just. It demonstrates the genuineness of their faith. Since they suffer for God's kingdom, they will be judged worthy. Their good works are evidence of their salvation.

Paul believes in the *lex talionis* (see the wordplay in 1:6). But two points bear noting: First, God avenges, not Christians (see Ro 12:17–21); second, God's judgment is the consequence of rejecting salvation. Persecutors suffer the consequences of their choices (see 1Th 2:13–16).

God's righteous judgment at the Parousia is described in apocalyptic language connoting authority, judgment, and power. Judgment affects all those who do not know God and who reject the Gospel, including all who reject God's freely offered love (see Bruce, 151).

Their punishment will be **everlasting destruction** and exclusion from the presence of the Lord. Paul's understanding of the future depends on his belief in resurrection. Resurrection to life is the destiny of the "dead in Christ." Those not in Christ will be raised to judgment, but Paul never speculates on the details of their fate. For him, the worst imaginable fate would be separation from the Lord. To be separated from God is to be without hope (see Eph 2:12). As Marshall observes, "This is the reality for which the other pictures used are merely symbols" (p. 180).

The contrast is striking. "If eternal life is the life of the age to come, the resurrection age, 'eternal destruction' is the destruction of the age to some [*sic*, read "come"] with a strong implication of finality. . . . Here the 'eternal destruction' consists in exclusion from the presence of him with whom is 'the fountain of life'" (Bruce, 152).

The precise sense of "eternal" is uncertain. Best states, "so long as existence continues in the age to come persecutors will be separated from God. . . . The sense 'everlasting, of infinite duration' is to be rejected but the meaning 'characteristic of the age to come' may well be present; the punishment of persecutors belongs to the next and not to this age" (pp. 262–63).

Although the wicked will be excluded, Christians do not gloat. The Day of the Lord is the day of Christ's vindication. By their redemption, Christians bring glory to the Lord and in turn share in his glory. When he comes, his majesty, power, and authority will be clearly seen by those who are his. For believers, the occasion will be marvellous because they have believed and remained steadfast despite persecution.

C. Prayer (1:11–12)

Paul prays that they may be worthy of God's election. Although NIV translates **"count you worthy,"** Paul means that God will make them worthy. Paul does not postulate a pious fiction.

Paul also prays that God will bring that election to completion. Both past election and present growth are crucial. They are already children of God; they are to live lives governed by this reality. Thereby, Jesus' name will be glorified and they in turn will be glorified in him. All of this is accomplished through grace.

III. THE DAY OF THE LORD AND THE MAN OF LAWLESSNESS (2:1–12)

1Th did not dispel the flawed beliefs about the Parousia. On the contrary, they gained in strength. Some were even saying **that the Day of the Lord [had] already come** (v.2).

The source of the deception (2:3) is unclear. Perhaps something had happened (so Bruce, 164). Perhaps it was a prophetic message, a nonecstatic spoken word, or a misreading of 1Th which fanned this "radical millenarianism" (see Jewett, passim). Paul finds such a misinterpretation so incredible that he wonders whether the source may be a forgery. At the end of this letter he takes deliberate steps to preclude that possibility; at this point he sets the record straight about the timing of the Parousia.

A. The Rise of the Man of Lawlessness (2:1–4)

First, **the rebellion** will occur and **the man of lawlessness** will appear before the Parousia. Paul thinks of one complex event that seems to be a general abandonment of the basis of civil order (Bruce, 167; Marshall, 188) and is hence a revolt against God. Opposition to God has an inevitable fate: it is **doomed to destruction** (v.3).

Although modern interpreters have difficulty identifying the persons or events to which Paul alludes, his first readers would not. Among several plausible identifications is Gaius' (Caligula's) attempt to have his statue erected in the Jerusalem temple. Fortunately, assassination thwarted his plan, but the attempt would live in infamy. Paul's point is clear, however: this person or principle usurps the rightful place of God.

B. The Fall of the Man of Lawlessness (2:5–12)

Now, the Man of Lawlessness is being restrained so **that he may be revealed at the proper time** (v.6) and not before (Marshall, 194). Lawlessness is now present but restrained (v.7).

But what is the restraining power? Several suggestions have been made: a supernatural power, either God or Satan; the principle of law and order; the Jewish state; the Gospel; or the emperor himself. Given Paul's benign view of the Roman Empire (see Ro 13:1–7), the most likely identity is the empire (Bruce, 171).

Paul could conceive of a time when the empire would not exercise such a restraining influence. At that time, the lawless one will become manifest. His counterfeit signs and wonders will delude those who have refused to accept the truth, making them the victims of their own folly (see Ro 1:18–32).

VI. THANKSGIVING AND PRAYERS (2:13–3:5)

A. Thanksgiving (2:13–15)

In 1:3 Paul had expressed thanksgiving for the Thessalonians' steadfastness;

now he offers thanks for their election. Because they are **loved by the Lord** (v.13), they ought not to be anxious about their destiny.

The NIV translation **"from the beginning"** (v.13) reflects one textual tradition (Gk. *ap' archas*). On this reading, Paul reassures the readers on the basis of God's longstanding purpose. But a slightly stronger textual tradition reads "firstfruits" (Gk. *aparchan*). On this reading, Paul refers to the Thessalonians as the firstfruits of God's salvation. Their assurance rests on this evidence of God's saving purpose. On either reading, the Thessalonians can be confident in God's purposes of salvation.

Salvation is theirs **through the sanctifying work of the Spirit and through belief in the truth** (v.13). Wesleyans point to the necessary response by persons to the salvation offered in Christ. Sanctification, God's transforming work in man (see Airhart, 523), also requires their belief (see 1:10). Belief itself is a gift of God's prevenient grace and is not any human achievement. Sanctification is wrought by the Spirit because they believe the truth. Unlike those who refused to believe (v.12), they will share in the **glory of our Lord Jesus Christ** (v.14) at his parousia.

After this summary of his theology, Paul draws pastoral conclusions. Instead of being deceived (see 2:2–3), they should hold fast to the teachings (Gk. "traditions") the missionaries had delivered. Paul believed that his gospel captured the grand purpose of God. It could not accommodate the aberrations that were being advanced by the alarmists and idlers in Thessalonica.

B. First Prayer (2:16–17)

Paul knows that the Thessalonians cannot stand firm on their own, so he follows his exhortation with a prayer that God would help them.

As in 1Th 3:11, Paul addresses his prayer both to the **Lord Jesus Christ** and to God. When coupled with the singular number of the verbs *loved* and *gave,* indicating a collective subject (Marshall, 211), the verse gives further evidence of Paul's high Christology. The verb tenses suggest that Paul has a past, completed event in mind, Christ's death, as the supreme demonstration of God's love.

The gift of God is **eternal encouragement,** the long-term hope of the Christian (Best, 321). **Every good deed and word** is the present issue of the past gift of salvation and the future hope.

C. Prayer Request (3:1–4)

Paul also needs prayer. The prayer is that the Gospel may be spread rapidly and effectively and that the missionaries would not be hindered in their mission.

Opposition comes from **wicked and evil men** (v.2), either a general reference to opposition to the Gospel (see Bruce, 194; Best, 325) or the opposition noted in 1Th 2:13–16 (Marshall, 214). They are wicked because they do not have faith (see 2:12).

Not everyone has faith, **but the Lord is faithful** (v.3, see 1Th 5:24). Paul is confident that the Lord would **strengthen and protect [them] from the evil one.** "Evil one" may also be translated "wickedness," but the context, in which Satan and eschatological conflict figure so prominently, makes **evil one** the preferred translation (see Best, 328).

Paul has confidence that the Thessalonians will obey his past instructions and the exhortations he gives in this letter. But his confidence is based, not on their ability to obey, but on God's

ability to strengthen and preserve them (vv.3–4).

D. Second Prayer (3:5)

Paul knows that they will require the help of God to do the things he commands (3:4). His prayer is that the Lord himself will direct them into **God's love and Christ's perseverance,** that is, taking Christ's example of perseverance, or, perhaps, receiving the steadfastness that Christ imparts.

V. EXHORTATIONS (3:6–15)

A. On Idleness (3:6–13)

Evidently the problem of idleness had worsened. Using language associated with church discipline (see, e.g., 1Co 5:4–5), Paul becomes more pointed: idleness and unruliness are not acceptable in the church.

Paul addresses the whole congregation, warning the majority to remain aloof from those who had quit working. They are not to support the idle by feeding them, and they are to avoid following their example.

Instead, they are to follow Paul's example (see 1Th 2:3–12). Paul urges both the problematic minority and the tempted majority to remember both his model and teaching: **If a man will not work, he shall not eat** (v.10). A refusal to work disrupts the fellowship, especially in a poor economic setting. (It is worth noting that this statement has no bearing on current conditions of unemployment where work is simply not available.)

As if to reinforce the teaching, Paul refers to the report he has received: **We hear that some among you are idle. They are not busy; they are busybodies** (v.11; NIV brings out the play on words in the Greek very well). In what sense they are busybodies is unclear, but, as Bruce wryly observes, "the vice to which they were prone is familiar enough for us to be thankful that it is so severely condemned in the apostolic teaching" (p. 209).

Paul commands these people **to settle down and earn the bread they eat** (v.12). They must use their time usefully rather than in a disruptive and disreputable manner. Equally, the majority is to be unflagging in its desire to do right.

B. On Discipline (3:14–15)

Although Paul expects to be obeyed, he is aware of the possibility that someone (probably an individual rather than a group) might not heed his commands. If this occurs, the church is to **take special note of him,** perhaps some official censure (see Best, 343) or, more likely, a more informal procedure. Association is to be stopped, possibly exclusion from communal meals but not exclusion from worship.

The purpose of this dissociation is redemptive. It is not from the community: he remains **a brother** (v.15). In this sense, the situation is clearly differ-ent from the problem Paul encountered at Corinth (1Co 5).

VI. FINAL GREETINGS (3:16–18)

A. Third Prayer (3:16)

In 1Th 5:23, Paul refers to the God of peace. Now, with characteristic interchangeableness, he ascribes peace to Jesus, **the Lord of peace.** Paul means much more than absence of strife. Peace is God's purpose of wholeness or salvation for his people. That is Paul's wish. The prayer concludes with a benediction.

B. Closing Greetings (3:17–18)

In light of the possibility of a forgery circulating in Paul's name or of any doubt that this letter came from him, Paul writes the final greetings in his own handwriting and apparently appends his characteristic mark (v.17). This authentication underlines the authority of what is written. This letter must not be ignored.

The letter concludes with a standard greeting almost identical to 1Th 5:28.

BIBLIOGRAPHY

See the bibliography following the commentary on 1 Thessalonians.

1 TIMOTHY
William H. Vermillion

INTRODUCTION

I. AUTHORSHIP AND DATING

Until the nineteenth century, scholars assumed that Paul wrote 1 Timothy. Since then, Pauline authorship has been challenged in four areas: history/chronology; ecclesiastical structure; theological distinctives; and language, vocabulary, and style issues (see Guthrie, 11–52, and appendix A).

A. History/Chronology

First Timothy mentions Paul leaving Timothy in Ephesus, then going on to Macedonia (1:3); he is now planning to visit Timothy. These events are not found in Acts, nor do they fit in the chronology of Acts; it is possible, however, that Paul was released from the house arrest of Acts 28 and then rearrested. After all, Acts does not propose to give the conclusion of Paul's ministry. The period following Acts allows for the events of 1 and 2 Timothy and Titus.

B. Ecclesiastical Structure

Non-Pauline critics argue that the discussion regarding overseers, deacons, and deaconesses in ch. 3 reflects a greater complexity of leadership in the early church than Acts and the other Pauline Epistles support. Such a claim appears to be an overreading of 1Ti 3, which really focuses on qualifications rather than duties. The early church needed structure and had it: Acts 6 tells of the selection of men to take care of the daily distribution of food, and Php 1:1 addresses "overseers and deacons." The synagogue had similar offices and may have served as a model. Based on Tit 1:5–7, "overseer" and "elder" are synonymous. Hence an argument that overseer means bishop does not appear to have merit.

C. Theological Distinctives

First, 1 Timothy does not present Paul's customary discussion of justification by faith and the empowerment of the Holy Spirit. Using this to argue non-Pauline authorship does not allow for the differences in nature between these epistles and the other Pauline letters. After all, 1 and

2 Timothy and Titus are addressed to individuals, not churches. Second, Timothy and Titus, Paul's chosen representatives, were already discipled by Paul. Hence, Paul makes frequent reference to "sound teaching" or "sound doctrine" (1Ti 1:10; 4:6; 6:3; 2Ti 1:13; 4:3; Tit 1:9; 2:1, 8), of which they are recipients and in which they are to instruct others (2Ti 2:2). Third, Paul's purpose is not to enunciate the basic elements of the faith to his pastoral colleagues, but to encourage them to persevere in the faith, combat heresies, and establish the church.

D. Language, Vocabulary, and Style Issues

The Pastorals have many words (175) that occur only once in the NT as well as words that are not typically Pauline. Again, such a critique does not take into account the different nature of the Pastorals. In addition, it does not allow for any change in style or vocabulary reflecting Paul's new experiences and maturation following his imprisonment (see Guthrie, appendix A).

There is no compelling reason to deny Pauline authorship. The teachings and tones are consistent with Paul's other writings. Paul, as always, is concerned with believers conducting themselves as befits the faith. First Timothy was probably written between A.D. 62 and 66 from some place in Greece, possibly Corinth.

II. AUDIENCE

The first mention of Timothy in Ac 16:1 identifies him as having a Jewish mother and Greek father. From his grandmother and mother he received a rich faith heritage (2Ti 1:5). He was circumcised (Ac 16:3) and accompanied Paul on his second and third missionary journeys (see Acts, introduction). Paul mentions Timothy by name in eight of his non-Pastoral letters—Ro 16:21; 1Co 4:17; 16:10; 2Co 1:1, 19; Php 1:1; 2:19ff; Col 1:1; 1Th 1:1; 3:2, 6; 2Th 1:1; and Phm 1. In Php 2:19–20 Paul recommends Timothy as one who will take a genuine interest in the welfare of the Philippians. Timothy is frequently referred to as Paul's child in the faith (1Ti 1:2, 18; 2Ti 1:2; 2:1; and Php 2:22) and was placed in Ephesus as Paul's representative (1Ti 1:3).

III. HISTORICAL BACKGROUND AND PURPOSE

Paul seems to have three major purposes:

1. To encourage Timothy to guard/preserve the truth, the body of teachings about Christ (1:10, 18–19).

2. To exhort Timothy to instruct others in how to live as part of God's household (3:15).

3. To command Timothy to combat heresies that were attacking the faith. The false teaching cannot be identified with any one sect. Its characteristics include: (1) a preoccupation with tales and genealogies (1:4, 4:7); (2) a desire to teach the law, reflecting a Jewish influence (1:7); and (3) an overemphasis on asceticism (a deprivation of the body

for purity) (4:1–4). Some, on the basis of 6:20, have identified the heresy with Gnosticism, but that would necessitate a later date, since Gnosticism per se did not exist until the second century.

IV. LITERARY CHARACTERISTICS

Paul's tone is warm—"my dear son" (1:2)—but forceful, as illustrated by his frequent use of "command." He often uses the word *godliness* to describe behavior that reflects well on being a member of God's household (2:2; 3:16; 4:8; 6:5, 6). Twice (2:5–6; 3:16) Paul provides hymns that focus on Christ.

V. OUTLINE

COMMENTARY

I. REMEMBER THE COMMAND (1:1–20)

In this opening chapter, Paul reminds Timothy of his important role in managing God's household (vv.3–4), defines the goal of God's command (v.5), explains the role of the Law (vv.8–11), testifies to the Lord's grace in saving **the worst of sinners** (vv.12–17), and challenges Timothy to fight the good fight (v.18).

A. Greetings of Paul to Timothy (1:1–2)

Paul introduces himself as Christ's **apostle,** which establishes his position and authority. Rather than saying "by the will of God," which is his usual pattern, Paul states more strongly **by the command** [epitagē] **of God.** This introduces the command structure so important in the Pastoral Epistles. Paul's description of God as **our Savior** draws from the OT witness to God's saving acts. Christ Jesus, **our hope,** stresses the strength and courage available to the believer through Christ.

In 1:2 Paul describes Timothy as a **true son** (Gk., "child") **in the faith,** placing importance on the quality and character of the relationship. He continues the relational concept by describing God as **Father** and Christ Jesus as **Lord.** The expansion of Paul's normal greeting of **grace and peace** by interjecting **mercy** reflects the mercy Paul has received (cf. v.16).

B. Errors of False Teachers Versus the Truth of God's Command (1:3–7)

Command shows that Timothy, like Paul, has authority. The **false doctrines** disrupted the management of God's household by undermining faith and promoting controversies instead of love. This love results from a **pure heart,** a **good conscience,** and a **sincere** (Gk., "non-hypocritical") **faith** (v.5). These qualities describe an inner character that is in contrast with the hypocrisy of the false believer. Internal qualities are reflected in external action. This is a major emphasis in the Wesleyan doctrine of holiness.

C. Purpose of the Law (1:8–11)

These actions, contrary to sound/healthy doctrine are identified by the proper use of the law (v.8). This list of fourteen activities ranges from general to specific and from lawbreaking to perjury. V.11 defines sound doctrine as that which is according to the **glorious gospel,** the good news that was **entrusted** to Paul. **Entrusted** continues the idea of the importance of faith (v.4) and further identifies Paul as a lawful and genuine recipient of God's apostleship.

D. Salvation of Paul (1:12–17)

Faith is central to salvation (v.12). Describing himself (v.13), Paul asserts that his actions were a result of **ignorance and unbelief,** and he **was shown mercy.** This seems to suggest that willful disobedience will not receive God's mercy. Paul asserts that his own life is a pattern of God's patient mercy for those who would believe in Christ and receive eternal life. Christ **considered** him faithful; strengthened him; appointed him to service; showed mercy to him (vv.13, 16); poured out grace, faith, and love on him; saved him; and displayed unlimited patience toward him. Reflecting on this, Paul breaks out in a doxology to the eternal, sovereign God.

E. Challenge to Timothy (1:18–20)

The use of **son** returns the reader to the earlier section and reminds Timothy of his resources in God; his relationship with God, Christ, and Paul; and his responsibility to promote love not controversy. **Instruction** is translated "command" in 1:5. The unspecified prophecies were to give encouragement to Timothy in the fight (v.18). Timothy must possess faith and a good conscience. This warfare is serious business as illustrated by Hymenaeus (2Ti 2:17) and Alexander (2Ti 4:14), who refused to listen to their conscience and wrecked their faith. **Handed over to Satan** probably indicates that they were cast out of the church (see Mt 18:17) as part of church discipline. **To be taught** is better translated "to be disciplined or corrected," in keeping with church discipline, which seeks to redeem the sinner, not merely to punish (see 1Co 5:5). Note that Paul had been a blasphemer (1:13).

II. CONDUCT YOURSELVES AS GOD'S HOUSEHOLD (2:1–6:21)

In the remainder of 1 Timothy, Paul discusses the characteristics of God's household. Servants of God must understand and practice prayer (2:1–10), and live responsibly in Christ's freedom (vv.11–15). Next comes the qualifications for leadership of God's household (3:1–13), followed by a discussion of godliness (3:14–4:16). No program in godliness or life in God's household is complete without a discussion of interpersonal relationships, which occupies 5:1–6:2. The letter closes with Paul writing about the relationship between riches and godliness (6:3–19). In the last two verses (vv.20–21), Paul reiterates his earlier commands to Timothy in 1:18–20 and 6:11–12, that one must actively guard the faith while opposing false knowledge.

A. Primacy of Prayer (2:1–10)

Paul gives a brief theology of prayer, showing its importance by his entreaty that prayer be made **first of all** (v.1). Prayer is given four descriptive elements: **requests** (*deēseis*)—specific askings of God; **prayers** (*proseuchas*)—general talk with God; **intercessions** (*enteuxeis*)—seeking something from God on someone else's behalf; and **thanksgiving** (*eucharistias*)—adoration, praise, and thanks to God. V.1 concludes that prayer is for **everyone.** This inclusiveness fits well the inclusiveness of the Gospel. The words **all/every** are used seven times in this section. V.2 particularizes prayer for kings and those in authority. The purpose and result of such praying is a quiet, restful lifestyle characterized by all godliness and dignity. (The NIV translation of *semnotēti* as **holiness** is unfortunate. See 3:4, where the same word is translated "respect.") This pleases God because he wants all men to be saved and to come to a knowledge of truth. Prayer enables us to practice lifestyle evangelism, which fulfills God's purpose.

1Ti 2:5–6 provides the corresponding theological hymn. **One God** is the traditional Jewish affirmation (cf. Dt 6); **one mediator** means that Jesus brings people to God and is not meant in the modern sense of peacemaker (see Gal 3:19–20; Heb 8:6; 9:15; 12:24); **the man Christ Jesus** focuses on Christ's humanity; **gave himself** stresses Christ's freewill; **ransom** is a payment to set another free (see also Mt 20:28; Mk 10:45); **for all men** depicts the inclusiveness of salvation; and **the testimony given in its proper** time means that Christ's coming was at exactly the right point in history.

Now Paul affirms his own appointment (v.7) as **a herald,** one who announces the message; **an apostle,** one sent forth with the message; and as **a teacher,** one who presents the message. Paul's special appointment, characterized by faith and truth, is to the Gentiles. His assertion that he is telling the truth may indicate that Paul's apostleship is still under attack (see Gal 2:7–8; 2Ti 1:11–12).

Based on the efficacy of prayer, Paul provides directions on how to pray. **Holy hands** is a posture of praise and worship. **Without anger and disputing** is essential, for wrath and dissension blunt and block prayer. In 2:9–10, **also** (better translated "likewise") tells us that, like the men, women everywhere are to pray. However, Paul's specific directives focus on outward adornment. Women who profess to worship God should be "dressed" in good deeds, not in fancy clothing or jewelry.

B. Special Instructions for Women (2:11–15)

1Ti 2:11 is concerned with women being orderly in the worship services. Like Jewish synagogues, early Christian churches separated men and women for worship, so questions by women of men during the service were disruptive at best. Evidently the women in Ephesus were overzealous in their new status as freed in Christ. Consequently, Paul firmly asserts that on the basis of God's creation of man first and the subsequent deception of woman (vv.13–14), he does not permit women (v.12) to teach or to exercise authority over men. Rather, they are to "learn in quietness" (the same word is translated "silent" in v.11). Representative of traditional rabbinic teaching, this is not

congruent with Paul's earlier affirmation in Gal 3:28 or with the general tenor of Scripture.

This section, with 1Co 11:2–16 and 14:33–40, represents directions given to a city dominated by a female deity. In Ephesus she was known as Artemis or Diana, an earth mother goddess (not the Diana of classical Greek mythology); her counterpart in Corinth was Aphrodite or Venus, the goddess of love. It seems clear that in these cultures Christian women felt so liberated that they needed stricter boundaries to guide their new freedom than did their counterparts of Galatia, Rome, or Philippi (Mickelsen, 197–212). Consequently, it is questionable whether the prohibitions in 1Ti 2 and 1Co 11 and 14 are of a universal nature. This interpretation is one of the reasons why Wesleyans ordain women.

1Ti 2:15 presents several possibilities of interpretation: (1) Women are **saved through childbearing** (NIV); (2) the woman will be saved through the childbearing—a reference to Mary giving birth to Jesus (NIV footnote); or (3) women are preserved through the bearing of children (NASB), which refers not to salvation but to the preservation of the race in fulfillment of Ge 3:16.

All the options of interpretation are fraught with difficulties. If women are saved through childbearing as the NIV suggests, what about single women and women who are unable to have children? The NIV note forces the Greek text but does have the advantage of alleviating the difficulties of options 1 and 3. The NASB seems to do a disservice to *sōzō*, usually translated "save," as well as raises questions regarding option 1. The best approach is to say that Paul's meaning is unclear.

This text does not appear to follow the teaching of salvation by faith, which is found elsewhere in Scripture and even in this very letter (2:4). V.15 closes with a triad prefaced by a condition of probability, implying that they can remain in **faith, love and holiness** with good sense (NIV **propriety**). V.15 presents a high view of the lifestyle to which a woman can attain.

C. Qualifications for Leadership (3:1–13)

1. The Elder (3:1–7)

Overseer (*episkopēs*) may be translated guardian or bishop. Aspire and desire are used positively and indicate that one may seek leadership. To aid in that personal assessment, Paul lists qualifications (vv.2–7). The first group, 3:2–3, lists desirable qualities. Of these, **husband of but one wife** raises the most questions. Polygamy did occur in the first century but was not widespread. Remarriage is commended for widows later in this epistle so it is assumed that widowers could also remarry (5:11–15; see also 1Co 7:39). Remarriage following divorce is still controversial, although many interpret Mt 19:9 and 1Co 7:15 as providing grounds for divorce and remarriage. In keeping with the other qualities listed, the interpretation should fit in with a lifestyle that reflects well on the church of God.

Paul's emphasis on male elders is consistent with Jewish customs regarding the position of an elder in the synagogue. Such a gender-specific reference may also reflect the culture of Ephesus (see notes on 2:11–15). 1Ti 3:4–5 shows that the care and management of one's own home is an important priority if there is to be involvement in God's house. Immaturity in the faith and a poor reputation can set a person up to fall and thus bring success to the Devil (vv.6–7). **The same judgment as the devil** indicates that the

Devil's rebellion was a result of conceit (pride). One's **reputation** (Gk., "witness") with outsiders is crucial to the lifestyle that evangelizes (2:2–4). The references to the Devil are in harmony with Paul's view that we are involved in a war (1:18–20).

2. Deacon (3:8–13)

Deacon literally means "server" or "waiter" (see Ac 6:1–7). **Likewise, as** the overseer, the deacon should be of good character. **The deep truths of the faith** indicate the fundamentals of the faith, which have been revealed by God, as in 2:5–6. **With a clear conscience** reminds one of 1:5 and again attests to the sound character of the deacons. V.10, like 3:6–7, affirms the truth: Do not place people in leadership until they have served well first. Starting in v.11, Paul gets gender-specific and addresses women. The phrase **in the same way** indicates that qualifications follow. Hence the footnote "deaconesses" is to be preferred to the NIV translation **their wives** (**their** does not occur in the Greek text). In v.12 Paul turns to the male deacon and presents the same criteria as found in vv.2–4 for the overseer. Service as a deacon or deaconess will result in an increased sense of one's security and significance in Christ and promote a bold witness (v.13).

For both the overseer and the deacon, Paul outlines the qualifications, not a job description. Character and reputation are most important in overseers and deacons.

D. Call to Godliness (3:15–4:10)

1. Mystery of Godliness (3:14–16)

The instructions in vv.14–15 tell people how to conduct themselves in God's household. The importance of God's house is emphasized by its description as **the church of the living**

God and **the pillar and foundation of truth.** These terms could be used to describe a literal, physical temple, but here the focus is on the function served by the church rather than a physical description.

The hymn in 3:16 defines the **mystery of godliness.** "Mystery" applies to truth we could not apprehend unless God revealed it to us. **"He"** refers to Christ, making the whole hymn a song of praise to Jesus. **Body** is better translated flesh (*sarx*). **Vindicated** (Gk., "justified") recognizes that Jesus' claims about himself and his ministry are proved by the Spirit. In the Greek all the verbs are aorist passives and all but one phrase uses the preposition **in,** which creates a rhythmic quality. The aorist passive indicates that these are accomplished actions.

2. Truth Versus Deception (4:1–5)

Contrary to the truths of the faith presented in 3:14–16 are the lies encountered in 4:1–3. We are not surprised because we are forewarned by the Spirit (v.1). These false teachers' consciences have been branded (NIV **seared as with a hot iron**). Either their consciences are burnt with evil or they bear the Devil's own brand. In either case, they lack the good conscience commended in 1:5 for the believer.

1Ti 4:3 refers to two specific false teachings of which abstinence from certain foods receives the major focus. Drawing on Ge 1:29–31, and possibly Ac 10:15, Paul offers an apologetic for the goodness of creation. The twice-mentioned **thanksgiving** emphasizes its importance for our attitude and action. **Consecrated** (Gk., "sanctified") demonstrates that the food may be set apart/made holy. The sanctifying agents are (1) **the word of God,** referring to either God's pronouncement at cre-

ation that all was very good (Ge 1:31) or the blessing by the believer or both, and (2) **prayer,** which would include thanksgiving.

3. Life of Godliness (4:6–10)

If should be omitted since it does not occur in the text and implies a condition. The idea is, rather, that as Timothy points these things out, he **will be a good minister. Brought up,** used in a continuous sense, indicates a constant nourishing on the **truths of the faith** and sound doctrine. **Old wives' tales** is an idiom meaning silly or made-up stories and is better translated as such (e.g., RSV). **Train** stresses the believer's personal responsibility for godly spiritual exercise. In 4:8 Paul does not condemn physical exercise but points out its limitations in comparison with spiritual exercise. V.9 may refer back to v.8 or ahead to v.10. When this formula is used in 3:1 it refers to the next thought, hence the NIV's choice. **Labor and strive** are continuous action, indicating ongoing determination and volition. The focus of all their work is on hope in a living God. In the phrase **Savior of all men,** Paul clearly is not endorsing universal salvation. God can save everyone; however, God's salvation is actualized only by personal belief/faith.

E. Commands for Believers (4:11–5:24)

1. Conduct of Timothy (4:11–16)

Paul's exhortation in v.12 shows an obvious awareness that some may not respect Timothy's youth and that Timothy might even use his youth as an excuse for immature belief. **Example** is a pattern or copy from which other patterns or copies are made. The trio of **love, faith,** and **purity** conforms nicely to the admonition of 1:5.

V.13 refers to Paul's plans shortly to

be with Timothy and directs attention to three elements of the worship service—the reading of Scripture, preaching, and teaching, which parallel synagogue worship.

Paul then turns (v.14) to the topic he had raised previously in 1:18. **Gift** is a gracious bestowment of God on Timothy. **Body of elders** (*presbyteriou,* a different Greek word from that used in 3:1) seems to indicate a group of older religious leaders. (The singular form of the same word is used in 5:1, where it is translated "older man.") The laying on of hands is also used for the passing on and/or bestowal of authority such as in Ac 6:6. V.15 says that by Timothy's practice of these commands, he will make obvious progress in his Christian walk. **Progress,** a military term, signifies advance. By continuous attention to his life and the doctrine and persevering in them, Timothy will insure his salvation and that of his hearers (v.16).

2. Relationship Between Older and Younger (5:1–2)

Using the illustration of a family, Paul commands Timothy to treat older men as fathers, **younger men as brothers, older women as mothers, and younger women as sisters.** Harsh rebuke creates resistance, especially when done to an elder by a younger person (v.1). V.2 reminds us that purity in relationships with the opposite sex is essential for the believer.

3. Care for Widows (5:3–16)

This lengthy treatment of widows reflects the importance to the church of their care (see Ac 6). Paul sets guidelines for honoring widows who **are really in need** (literal Greek shows emphasis).

In 5:4–8 Paul says that a widow who has children and grandchildren should be cared for by her own family since this is pleasing to God (see Jas 1:27). Such responsibilities are commanded (v.7); in fact, if not followed, the offender has **denied the faith and is worse than an unbeliever** (v.8). Clearly, God considers provision for one's family to be an essential aspect of living the faith.

1Ti 5:9–10 sets criteria for listing widows. **On the list** (Gk., "enrolled") indicates that the early church kept a roll of those who qualified to receive help. For **faithful to her husband** see notes on 3:2–3. The NIV correctly identifies most of 5:10 as illustrations of good works that should characterize an enrolled widow. Note that these are service-oriented actions involving hospitality and may have included a ministry of prayer (v.5).

1Ti 5:11–15 discusses younger widows, who are to be encouraged to marry. **Broken their first pledge** seems to indicate that the listed widow took a vow of dedication to Christ (v.12). Vv.13–15 are a vivid reminder of Paul's concern that Christians live above reproach (see ch. 3).

In 5:16 Paul returns to the subject of vv.3–4. Paul's primary concern is that the church care for widows who have no one else to care for them. This social concern is still important to us. Wesley saw this text as one more illustration of the church's duty to care for the less fortunate in an organized and systematic way (*Works,* 8:265).

4. Care of the Elders (5:17–20)

Now Paul turns his attention to ruling elders and their provisions and discipline. Honor is more than just a recognition of position; it also involves physical provision as illustrated by Paul's supporting OT quotations. Both Scriptural illustrations are service-oriented. Using OT guidelines (Dt 17:6; 19:15 [Mt 18:16]), Paul counsels Timothy not to receive or even allow an accusation against an elder unless two witnesses support the charge (v.19). Leaders often hear accusations and must be careful not to give credence to unfounded attacks. On the other hand, if discipline is needed (v.20), it is to be done publicly as a corrective warning.

5. Care of Timothy (5:21–23)

Timothy is to show no partiality or favoritism (v.21) nor elevate people too quickly to positions of authority (v.22); moreover, he is to keep himself pure (v.22), and take care of himself physically (v.23). **God and Christ Jesus and the elect angels** is an unusual triad but one signifying the solemnity of the charge Paul is giving Timothy. **A little wine** indicates moderation and probably is a comment on the local water. Perhaps Timothy may be interpreting purity more physically/ascetically than Paul intended.

6. Discernment of Conduct (5:24–25)

Using comparison and contrast, Paul maintains that sins and good deeds are obvious. Some are more easily seen, but in the end all human works will be apparent, bad or good.

F. Relationship Between Slaves and Masters (6:1–2)

Slaves who are Christians are still to render their masters all honor even when their masters are believers. This is a good testimony in the community. **Under the yoke** graphically describes the slave. **Full respect** (honor) is the same word used concerning widows (5:3) and elders (5:17). **Serve them even better** illustrates how Christians are to relate to one another (see Gal 6:10).

G. Conflict Between Love of Money and Godliness (6:3–10)

In 6:3–5 Paul discusses the controversies and quarrels characterizing the opponents of the Gospel and the confusion of godliness with financial gain. **Sound instructions,** better translated "healthful," sets up the contrast in 6:4 with **unhealthy** [unhealthful] **interest in controversies.** The lifestyle of 6:4–5 is diametrically opposed to that of the Christian community in 2:2. **Have been robbed** seems to indicate that they had the truth and it was stolen from them. However, another possibility is that the robbery results from their constant friction. This would fit with the concept of seared consciences (4:2) and place the responsibility on the false teachers.

1Ti 6:6–8 is an insight into Paul's understanding of the relationship between godliness and money. **Contentment** is really the great gain/profit. If our daily need for food and clothing is met, we should be contented.

This attitude of v.8 contrasts with that of v.9. Here the one who wants riches is pictured in ruin and destruction. In v.10 **the love of money** is pictured as **a root of all kinds of evil. Some people, eager for money** had **wandered from the faith and pierced,** or wounded, **themselves with many griefs.**

H. Fight of Faith (6:11–16)

Unlike those who wander from the faith (6:10), Timothy is to flee the desire for riches, pursue godliness, and run the race of faith. **Fight the good fight** misses the athletic imagery of the games used here. This is in contrast to the military imagery of 1:18. **"Take hold of"** conveys the idea of a prize for which the athlete reaches. **To which you were called when"** is in keeping with Timothy's public testimony to serve Christ. Thus Paul charges Timothy before God to maintain a consistent lifestyle that will bring no reproach on Christ or his church.

At the mention of Christ's return, Paul breaks into a doxology full of biblical doctrine (vv.15–16). God controls the time of Jesus' return; God is ultimate Ruler, King, and Lord (Dt 10:17); God is immortal; God lives in unapproachable light (Ps 104:2); and no one has seen or can see God (Ex 33:20). Little wonder that God is to receive **honor and might forever.**

I. Teaching for the Rich (6:17–19)

This is the God in whom the rich are humbly to **hope.** Why? First, God is the ultimate provider. Second, God provides **richly.** By using the word **richly,** Paul reminds them that God is the rich One and that it is he to whom they should give thanks and look as a model. Third, God gives us **everything** to enjoy and share. Consequently, with God as their model, the **rich** are to be **rich** (note pun) in good works and to be generous and willing to share. In this way, they will lay up treasures as a firm foundation for the coming age (contrast with 6:17). Then they may take hold of real life, which is more than the physical and material (cf. 4:8; Mt 6:25–34).

While these commands are directed to the rich, they apply to all of us. Even the one who has little can be selfish and miserly. God help us to use and enjoy all we have for him, remembering that he is our gracious Provider and our Hope. Hence John Wesley's emphasis on caring for the needy.

J. Importance of These Commands and Teachings (6:20–21)

Paul closes by commanding Timothy to be vigilant for the truth. **Knowledge** suggests that an early form of gnosticism may have existed in Ephesus (see Introduction: Purpose). However, Paul may be ridiculing a system that exalts the human mind and claims special knowledge but that is antithetical to the clear teachings of Christ. Staying true to Christ's teachings requires grace; thus Paul's benediction. **You** is plural, including more than Timothy. Only with God's grace can we conduct ourselves as God's household.

BIBLIOGRAPHY

Bratcher, Robert G. *A Translator's Guide to Paul's Letters to Timothy and to Titus.* New York: UBS, 1983. An excellent translating and interpretive tool from the dynamic equivalent perspective.

Guthrie, Donald. *The Pastoral Epistles.* TNTC. Ed. R. V. G. Tasker. Grand Rapids: Eerdmans, 1957. Dated, but the best and most concise critique of the arguments on Pauline authorship.

Mickelsen, Alvera, ed. *Women, Authority and the Bible.* Downers Grove, Ill.: InterVarsity Press, 1986. A superbly balanced approach to the controversial passages regarding women in the Scriptures.

The Works of John Wesley, 3d ed. Peabody, Mass.: Hendrickson, 1986. Vol. 8, p. 265. Wesley's classic comment on the church's mandate for care of widows (see 1Ti 5:16).

2 TIMOTHY
William H. Vermillion

INTRODUCTION

I. AUTHORSHIP AND DATING

Until the nineteenth century it was commonly assumed that 2 Timothy was written by the apostle Paul. Since that time some scholars have questioned the chronology, theology, ecclesiology, and vocabulary of the letter. For a brief discussion of these areas, see introduction to Pastoral Epistles and 1 Timothy—Introduction: Authorship and Dating. No compelling reason forces us to accept the notion of non-Pauline authorship. The teachings and tone are consistent with Paul's other writings. It was written from Rome about A.D. 67–68.

II. AUDIENCE

See 1 Timothy—Introduction: Audience.

III. HISTORICAL BACKGROUND AND PURPOSE

A. Ephesus

See 1 Timothy—Introduction: Historical Background and Purpose.

B. Purpose

Paul's major purpose is to command Timothy to come to him before winter (4:9, 21). However, Paul also wants Timothy to keep himself approved before God (2:15), so he encourages Timothy to utilize his gift of God with power (1:6–7), to suffer with Paul for the sake of the Gospel (v.8), to guard the faith (v.14), to handle the word of truth correctly (2:15), to flee evil desires (v.22), to stay true to the faith (3:14–16), and to preach the Word (4:2).

IV. LITERARY CHARACTERISTICS

Paul continues his frequent use of triads (1:2, 7, 11, et al.) and hymnic structure (2:11–13). Of all Paul's letters, this one has a tone of pathos because of Paul's imprisonment (1:8, 16; 2:9), his awareness of impending death (4:6), and his twice-repeated desire for Timothy to join him (vv.9, 21). Poignancy is heightened by some of Paul's companions who were ashamed of his imprisonment (1:8) and deserted him (4:10). Because of his sense of impending death, Paul repeatedly commands Timothy to stay with and promote the faith (4:2–5), and he frequently refers to "that day" (1:12, 18; 4:8).

V. OUTLINE

COMMENTARY

I. INTRODUCTION (1:1–2)

The letter opens with Paul affirming his apostleship as a result of God's will, not his own. For comments on the triadic blessing—**grace, mercy, and peace**—see 1Ti 1:2. **Our Lord** states clearly that Paul and Timothy are his servants.

II. A SINCERE FAITH (1:3–18)

To maintain the heritage of sincere faith requires diligent action without fear (vv.5–7). Timothy is then prepared to suffer for the Gospel even as Paul has (vv.8–12). This section is further unified by the use of the phrase

Do not be ashamed (v.8, cf. vv.12, 16). Confidence in God's Spirit enables us to overcome fear and embarrassment.

A. Fan into Flames God's Gift (1:3–7)

Serve (v.3) may also mean worship and describes an act of service performed for God. **As** [Gk., "from"] **my forefathers** (v.3) suggests the continuity of faith in God from Judaism to the full revelation of God in Christ in Christianity. **Remember** (v.3), or a similar concept, occurs three other times in this paragraph—**recalling**

(v.4), **reminded** (v.5), and **remind** (v.6). The repetition underscores the importance of using our minds and memories for spiritual purposes. **Your tears** (v.4) is a reference to Timothy's sadness when they parted. **Sincere** [Gk., non-hypocritical] **faith** (v.5) links with 1Ti 1:5. For more on Eunice see Ac 16:1. **Persuaded** (v.5) means to become convinced by reason (see v.12). **Now lives** is not in the Greek; Paul simply asserts that such faith *is* in Timothy.

Fan into flame (v.6) is Paul's metaphor to suggest Timothy's tendency to neglect or depreciate his grace gift from God (see 1Ti 4:14). For **when the body of elders laid their hands on you,** see 1Ti 4:14. V.7 gives us a commanding triad. The placement of the verse indicates that Timothy had difficulty being bold (see v.6 and 1Ti 4:12–14). **Timidity** (Gk., *deilias*) is a very good translation since this is not the usual word for fear (*phobos*). *Deilias* means cowardly and is never used positively in the Bible. This fear is not from God. **Spirit** has been interpreted as either human spirit or the Holy Spirit, but given the context of God's gift (v.6) and God's giving this spirit, Holy Spirit is preferred. Like Timothy, we must affirm and activate the Spirit's resources to be God's workers. This is a main tenet of Wesleyan doctrine.

B. Suffer for the Gospel (1:8–12a)

Fear and/or ridicule are not to cause Timothy to be ashamed of the Gospel or of those who suffer for its sake. The negative command, **Do not be ashamed,** is rapidly followed by the positive command, **Join with me in suffering for the gospel** (v.8). This is possible only through God's saving us and calling us to a holy life; the Greek is emphatic, "called with a holy calling" (v.9). **Purpose and grace** (v.9) clearly shows that God's purpose is joined with grace and has nothing to do with our works (see Eph. 2:8). **The beginning of time** (v.9) refers to that which God planned even before creation, but which was revealed only when Christ came in the flesh (v.10).

V.10 succinctly presents the main tenets of the Gospel. **To light** indicates the spiritual darkness and, metaphorically, the ignorance that characterized humankind before the revealing of Christ. On v.11 see 1Ti 2:7. Because of this appointment, Paul suffers (v.12).

C. Guard the Deposit (1:12b–14)

Suffering for the Gospel does not cause fear or embarrassment for Paul because he has confidence in the keeping ability of the One in whom he has trusted (v.12). We can have the same confidence. **Know, believed, convinced** (v.12) emphatically show Paul's confidence and faith in God. **Entrusted** indicates that Paul has given God something of worth. The phrase also may refer to what has been entrusted to Paul (see RSV, TEV), in which case it refers to the Gospel and indicates that God will keep it safe. **Guard** is military imagery to show God's strong keeping power. **For that day** refers to the Lord's return and/or judgment. **Sound teaching** (Gk., "healthful words") must be held with love and faith in Christ, otherwise it becomes merely good words (see 1Co 13:1). V.14 reaffirms Paul's command in 1Ti 6:20. **The good deposit** refers either to the commands Paul gave Timothy when placing him at Ephesus, the **sound teaching** (v.13), the **gift** he received from God (v.6), or all three. Timothy can do this only through the Holy Spirit. The Holy Spirit is the believer's main empowering agent.

D. Know the Deserters and the Refreshers (1:15–18)

Not all guard the deposits with which they have been entrusted, as Paul crisply reminds Timothy (v.15). **Every-one,** is hyperbole, probably reflecting the anguish and loneliness Paul is experiencing. The **province of Asia** was the Roman province with Ephesus as its capital; it is located in modern western Turkey. Phygelus and Hermogenes perhaps were leaders of the group that deserted Paul. Paul, however, has been encouraged by a faithful guard of the deposit, Onesiphorus, who is mentioned only here. He had helped Paul in Ephesus (v.18) and searched diligently in Rome for Paul (v.17). He was not ashamed of Paul's prisoner status and refreshed (Gk., "make cool") him (v.16).

III. A PURE HEART (2:1–26)

A pure heart requires strength, faithfulness, and God's approval. Timothy will demonstrate these by imparting to others what he has received (v.2) and by reflecting on Paul's illustrations of the committed soldier, disciplined athlete, and hard-working farmer (vv.3–7). Finally, Timothy is to use God's Word correctly (v.15), avoid wickedness (vv.16–19), pursue righteousness (vv.20–23), and rescue those captured by the Devil (vv.24–26).

A. Be Strong in Christ (2:1–7)

In the grace that is in Christ Jesus clearly identifies whose grace it is as well as indicating the position that every believer has in Christ, that of being in grace. V.2 commands Timothy to pass on Paul's teaching. These reliable/faithful people are to be qualified and competent in teaching others. The result is an ever-widening group of informed and informing believers.

Paul now presents in rapid succession three illustrations—the soldier (vv.3–4), the athlete (v.5), and the farmer (v.6). For **endure hardship with us,** see 1:8. Hardships/sufferings are part of being in Christ's army, and

believers suffer together. We serve Christ, the one who enlisted us (NIV **commanding officer**). Since Christ has enlisted (KJV "chosen") us, we owe him our loyalty and are not involved in civilian affairs. The illustration of the athlete focuses on obeying the rules in order to win. The **victor's crown** is a wreath of laurel leaves. The farmer imagery stresses hard work. The crops (Gk., "fruits") go to the laborer, not the lazy. V.7 explains that these illustrations are designed to give us better insight into the Lord's desire for us as servants. God's workers must be committed, willing to suffer hardships, obedient, and hardworking.

B. Be Faithful to Christ (2:8–13)

These illustrations are followed by a capsule definition of the Gospel, which emphasizes Christ's resurrection and Davidic lineage (v.8). The Resurrection is a central doctrine of the faith (see 1Co 15) without which there is no hope of eternal life, no power over sin, and, most distressingly, only a dead Jesus. The Davidic lineage affirms Jesus as Messiah, the Christ, and thus the fulfillment of the law and the prophets. **My gospel** means the message that Paul supports and proclaims, not that it is his exclusive property or his created Gospel. Paul's chains are strongly contrasted with God's lack of chains (v.9). Messengers may be imprisoned but God's Word transcends chains. This encourages Paul's faithfulness (v.10).

Faithfulness is also the theme of the hymn (vv.11–13). **"A trustworthy saying"** (Gk., "faithful word") is frequently used in the Pastorals (1Ti 1:15; 3:1; 4:9; 2Ti 2:11; Tit 3:8) to designate something noteworthy. The hymn is composed of four conditional causes concerning our actions toward Christ followed by corresponding results. The first two results represent what we shall receive while the last two results are what Christ will do. **He will remain faithful** emphasizes Christ's covenantal faithfulness in meting out judgment and/or in being true to his nature as Savior.

C. Present Yourself to God (2:14–26)

Faithfulness calls for continual reminding, especially concerning speech and conduct. The solemnity of the warning in 2:14 is indicated by the phrase **before God. Do your best** conveys accurately the intent of the command in v.15 and implies diligence and eagerness. Paul then compares Timothy to a master craftsman who **correctly handles** [Gk., cut straight] **the word of truth.** Then he can stand unashamed and approved before God. The command is still the same for interpreters of God's Word.

In contrast with 2:15 is the v.16 discussion of ungodly chatter (Gk., "empty or foolish talk"; see 1Ti 4:7). Such speech only leads to further ungodliness and spreads like gangrene, a rotten, flesh-eating canker. What a vivid picture of the subtle destructive power of ungodly chatter! Unfortunately, two men already have incorrectly handled the word of truth (2Ti 2:17). **Resurrection** refers not to Jesus' resurrection but to the resurrection of the dead that will occur at the Lord's appearing (1Th 4:13–18). **Destroy the faith,** is a solemn reminder that false doctrine can deceive and destroy.

The encouragement in 2:19 is that God's foundation is solid and stays firm. **Sealed** is a sign of God's ownership, security, and significance. God is not fooled—he knows his own; they confess him and turn from wickedness. In considering the believer's responsibility, Paul uses a metaphor of household articles made of different materials. What is really important is their purpose, honor (NIV **noble**) or disho-

nor (NIV **ignoble**). Cleansing makes us an article (NIV **instrument**) for honorable purposes.

We are then characterized as holy, useful, and prepared to do any good work. The perfect passive participle—**made holy**—indicates that we have been made holy at a point in time and are to continue in it. This is a major Wesleyan doctrine. We make ourselves available to receive God's holiness by choosing not to be involved in dishonorable purposes. **Prepared** is also a perfect passive participle that indicates we have been prepared for good works at a point in time and are to continue in them.

Having affirmed the believer's responsibility to be an article of honor for God, Paul swiftly commands Timothy to **flee the evil desires of youth and pursue righteousness, faith, love and peace** (v.22; see 1Ti 6:11). **Call on the Lord** is similar to 2:19, **who confesses the name of the Lord.** In 2:23–26 Paul points out that the Lord's servant is characterized as a shepherd of words, not a gladiator of words. The Lord's servants focus on the opponent—not resentfully, but hopefully. These opponents are actually senseless captives of the Devil. The Lord's servant = shepherd is on a rescue mission that requires the correct handling of the word of truth (v.15).

IV. A GODLY LIFE (3:1–4:8)

This section contrasts the empty, godless living that will characterize the last days (3:1–9), with the faithfulness of Timothy who continues in God's Word (vv.10–17), preaching the Word so that, like Paul, all can finish the race, having kept the faith (4:1–8).

A. Be Aware of the Last Days (3:1–9)

This whole section parallels 1Ti 4. **Last days** refers to the time preceding the Lord's return and is characterized as terrible times. The particularizations given in 3:2–4 are a misuse and abuse of love (1Co 13:4–7). The dark situation is intensified in 3:5 with the characterization of people as having a form of godliness but denying its power. They are hypocrites. Consequently, Timothy is to **have nothing to do with them.** In keeping with 2:24–26, this means that we are not to endorse or follow their teachings but to seek to lead them to repentance.

In 3:6–9 Paul describes the actions of these hypocrites. **Worm** is an apt verb for their techniques, and is perhaps suggestive of their master. Their targets lack assurance of freedom from sin and power over temptations, and they are easy prey for false teaching. This would support the cultural situation where the Ephesian women have received a new freedom and status in Christ, but at least some have not yet fully appropriated the sound teaching and lifestyle required of a Christian. The hypocrites are like Jannes and Jambres, who in Jewish tradition were the Egyptian magicians who opposed Moses (see Ex 7:22; 9:11). **Oppose** (v.8) is to stand against. **Depraved** (v.8) means "corrupt" (see 1Ti 6:5). **Rejected** (v.8) indicates that they did not pass muster so far as the faith is concerned. **Those men** refers to Jannes and Jambres, whose folly was clear to everyone.

B. Continue in Faithfulness (3:10–17)

Paul now contrasts himself with these false teachers of 3:1–9. **Know all about** (v.10) means "have closely followed or accompanied," which was exactly what Timothy had done (see Ac 16:1–5). **Antioch, Iconium and Lystra** probably refers to Paul's first missionary journey (Ac 13:13–14:25). Paul's declaration in 3:12 would hardly

be encouraging if not for his own testimony of the Lord's deliverance (v.11). This is in sharp contrast with 3:13, where the **evil men and impostors** continue to worsen. Note the irony of the deceiver being the deceived.

In contrast, Timothy is to **continue** in the truth and faith. Paul reminds Timothy of his heritage. He identifies Timothy's training in Scriptures, referring to the OT, which provides wisdom for salvation through faith in Christ Jesus. V.16 tells us why the Scriptures can do this: They are **God-breathed,** which supports God's direct involvement in the giving of the Scriptures but is inadequate in providing a definitive theory of inspiration by itself. This in no way affects the authority of the Scriptures as Paul quickly goes on to show their usefulness and the ultimate goal (vv.16–17). The result of properly using the Scriptures is a person of God fully qualified and equipped (NIV **thoroughly equipped** combines the two concepts). This result helps to explain **wise for salvation** (v.15). Salvation here, as elsewhere in Paul (e.g., Php 3:12), encompasses one's total relationship with Christ.

C. Receive the Charge (4:1–8)

Now Paul issues nine commands, stressing their importance by using a formal court scene (cf. 1Ti 5:21). He calls on the ultimate authority, God, and the ultimate Judge and King, Christ, as his witnesses (v.1). Five imperatives are presented in 4:2: **Preach the Word**—proclaim the Gospel; **be prepared**—stand ready at all times, continually alert; **correct**—reprove, rebuke as NIV does in 3:16; **rebuke**—admonish, command; and **encourage**—from the same word family as *paraklēte.* All are to be practiced with **great patience** (Gk., "all longsuffering") and **careful instruction**

(Gk., "all teaching"). Patience addresses the manner, teaching, and method that Timothy is to practice (Guthrie, 166).

The rationale and urgency of Timothy doing this is given in 4:3–4. In 4:3 Paul uses a superbly ironic metaphor to illustrate the way these unsound people want a teacher who only itches/tickles their ears. The teachings hit the outer ear but never go any deeper. V.4 speaks of the tragic consequence and gives a succinct definition of heresy: to turn from *the* **truth** to *the* **myths.**

Paul, as in 3:10, 14, employs the emphatic **you** as he shifts to Timothy and the remaining commands. **Keep your head** is a good translation emphasizing the idea of vigilance (see 1Th 5:6, 8). **Endure hardship** has been a frequent theme of 2 Timothy (1:8; 2:3, 9). **The work of an evangelist** is to preach/proclaim the Gospel (Gk., "evangel"). **Discharge . . . ministry** conceptualizes the fulfillment of his task.

Fulfilling one's ministry causes Paul to reflect on his imprisonment and ministry. Using the emphatic **I,** Paul describes himself as a drink offering that is being poured out. This progressive idea contrasts with an earlier description of himself in Php 2:17, which is conditional. **Drink offering** was designed as a completion of the burnt offering ceremony (Nu 15:10, 28). He then asserts, using a series of three perfects (I have **fought, finished,** and **kept**), that there is a completion of his ministry (4:7). In 4:8 Paul affirms the confidence that he and any believer can have when they have fulfilled 4:7. **The crown of righteousness** is a victor's crown (see 2Ti 2:5). **The Lord, the righteous judge** correctly identifies Christ (v.1). **Award** is in keeping with having fought, finished, and kept. **On that day** refers to the Day of Judgment (see 1:12). This crown is not just for

Paul, but for *all* who long for Christ's appearance.

V. A FAITHFUL MESSAGE (4:9–18)

Aware of his approaching death, Paul reflects on his few remaining companions and his need of Timothy. Paul then warns Timothy to be on guard concerning Alexander (vv.14–15). This solemn note quickly changes to praise as Paul reflects on the Lord's faithful presence and deliverance (vv.16–18).

A. Come Quickly (4:9–13)

Paul's opening command reflects a note of urgency concerning his need for Timothy. On **do your best,** see 2:15. The remaining verses add to the mood of pathos and somberness as we see Paul's companions involved elsewhere. Some, like Demas, have deserted because they loved **this world** (Gk., "the now age"), while others like Crescens and Titus and Tychicus have been assigned elsewhere (vv.10–12). Demas is one of Paul's companions in Col 4:14. Crescens is not found elsewhere in the NT. Galatia is in Asia Minor. For more on the introduction to Titus see Titus: Introduction. Dalmatia is in modern-day Albania. Tychicus was a carrier of letters (see Eph 6:21; Col 4:7–8) and may have carried this letter. Perhaps he is to relieve Timothy so he can come to Paul. Only Luke (Col 4:14) is still with Paul. Mark is probably the same man over whom Paul and Barnabas quarreled (Ac 15:37–40; Col 4:10). If so, there has been reconciliation.

When you come is not conditional, but rather, "as you come" (4:13). The reference to **cloak, scrolls,** and **parchments** lends a very personal authentic tone. A **cloak** is a durable, heavy woolen outer garment. **Scrolls** are rolled papyri, a reedlike plant that is split, layered, and pressed to form writing material. **Parchments** are animal hides, tanned for writing. They were expensive and hence infrequently used at this time. Whatever was on the parchments (suggestions range from Paul's citizenship to the Gospels), this reference, along with the scrolls, indicates Paul's literary interests and the importance of these materials to him. Troas was a major port in Asia Minor (see Ac 16:8).

B. Guard the Faith (4:14–15)

This Alexander cannot be identified clearly with any other NT reference (see Mk 15:21; Ac 19:33–34; 1Ti 1:20). Regardless, Paul's attitude toward him is instructive: evil is not to be repaid with evil; the Lord will avenge (see Ps 62:12; Ro 12:17). This is not license for passivity or foolishness, since Timothy is to be on guard.

C. Glorify God (4:16–18)

The desertion and opposition cause Paul to remember his first trial and his faithful companion, **the Lord. "At my first defense"** refers to something like a pretrial hearing where friends would be expected to render testimony. **May it not be held against them** indicates a business term for keeping an account. The result of the Lord's faithfulness is that the Gentiles hear the Gospel; Paul is delivered from the lion's mouth; and Paul is encouraged so that he proclaims glory to God (vv.17–18). **The lion's mouth** refers to either the real lions of the arena or of a metaphor for danger. The Lord stands with us to empower us, rescue us, and preserve us. Truly he deserves **glory forever and ever.**

VI. FAREWELL (4:19–22)

The letter closes with more personal greetings and another reminder to Timothy to arrive before winter. Priscilla and Aquila were tentmakers and Jewish believers (see Ac 18:1–26). The positioning of Priscilla's name before Aquila's is an indication of Paul's respect for her. For **household of Onesiphorus** see 1:16. With Timothy, Erastus is a fellow helper of Paul (Ac 19:22). Trophimus is Paul's companion in Macedonia (Ac 20:4) and in Jerusalem (Ac 21:29). Miletus is a seaport in Asia Minor (Ac 20:15). **Do your best** is a repetition of 4:9. **Before winter** is a reminder of the hazards of winter sea travel (see Ac 27). Eubulus, Pudens, Linus, and Claudia are all Latin names and unknown. They may have been new converts, since they are not mentioned in Ro 16.

A double benediction ends the letter. The first is for Timothy—**your,** singular—and recalls 1:7. The second is addressed to **you,** plural, and affirms the theme of grace. **Grace** is a gift from Christ (2Ti 1:9); it is strength from God (2:1; see 1Ti 6:21).

BIBLIOGRAPHY

See the bibliography at the end of 1 Timothy.

TITUS

William H. Vermillion

INTRODUCTION

I. AUTHORSHIP AND DATING

Until the nineteenth century it was commonly assumed that Titus was written by the apostle Paul. Since that time some scholars have questioned the chronology, theology, ecclesiology, and vocabulary. For a brief discussion of these areas, see Pastoral Epistles: Introduction and 1 Timothy—Introduction: Authorship and Dating.

There is no compelling reason to accept non-Pauline authorship. The teaching and tone are consistent with Paul's other writings. Titus was probably written between A.D. 62–66 from some place in Greece, possibly Corinth.

II. AUDIENCE

Titus was Paul's child in the faith (1:4), who according to Tit 1:5 had been left as Paul's representative in Crete to straighten out what was unfinished and to appoint elders in every town.

Titus is unmentioned in Acts. In Gal 2:1–3 he is identified as an uncircumcised Gentile who accompanied Paul and Barnabas to Jerusalem and helped prove that Gentiles could receive the Gospel. Titus is mentioned again in 2Co 2:13; 7:6–14; 8:6, 16, 17, and 23, where he is commended for his character and ministry and designated as one of those to receive the love-gift offering. In 2Ti 4:10 Titus is in Dalmatia (modern-day Albania).

III. HISTORICAL BACKGROUND AND PURPOSE

A. Crete

Located southeast of Greece, Crete is the fourth largest island in the Mediterranean and home of the famous Minoan civilization. However, by Paul's time, the Cretans had a poor reputation so that even one of their own countryman said, "Cretans are always liars, evil brutes, lazy gluttons" (1:12). Paul's ship stopped at Crete en route to Rome (Ac 27:7–13), and a possible reference to Cretans may be found in 1Sa 30:14.

B. Purpose

Paul's major purpose is to make sure the church is continuing in sound/healthful doctrine. Consequently, Paul reminds Titus of the criteria for an elder (1:6–9), the relationships that should exist in the church (2:1–10), and the importance of doing good (2:7, 14; 3:1, 8, 14). On the negative side, Paul tells Titus to rebuke those who are unsound in faith (1:10–16), to avoid foolish controversies (3:9), and to reject unrepentant divisive people (3:10–11). The letter also introduces Zenas and Apollos (3:13), while alerting Titus to Paul's need for him at Nicopolis (3:12).

IV. LITERARY CHARACTERISTICS

The tone of the epistle is personal and warm as illustrated by the use of pronouns: "my" (1:4), "us" (2:8), "we" (3:3), "me" (3:12), and "our" (3:14). As observed in other Pauline writings, Paul uses repetition, such as soundness (1:9, 13; 2:1, 2, 8) and good works (2:7, 14; 3:1, 8, 14); triads such as in 1:16; and emphatic summaries such as in 2:1, 15, and 3:8. When discussing deceivers (1:10–16) and divisive people (3:9–11), Paul's tone is stern and demanding. As in the epistles to Timothy, Titus also has clear, succinct sections of Christian doctrine (2:11–14; 3:3–7), but Titus contains no poetry.

V. OUTLINE

Major Theme: Sound Doctrine and God's Household

I. Introducing Sound Doctrine (1:1–4)
   A. Promised by God (1:1–2)
   B. Entrusted to Paul (1:3)
   C. Illustrated in Titus (1:4)

II. Promoting Sound Doctrine (1:5–16)
   A. Choosing Elders (1:5–9)
   B. Identifying the Rebellious (1:10–16)

III. Practicing Sound Doctrine (2:1–3:2)
   A. Applied to Relationships (2:1–10)
   B. Designed to Redeem and Purify (2:11–15)
   C. Applied in lifestyle (3:1–2)

IV. Defining Sound Doctrine (3:3–11)
   A. Saved and Justified by God (3:3–7)
   B. Devoted to Doing Good (3:8) and Warned to Avoid the Unprofitable (3:9–11)

V. Furthering Sound Doctrine (3:12–15)

COMMENTARY

I. INTRODUCING SOUND DOCTRINE (1:1–4)

In this opening section Paul identifies himself as a proclaimer of the truth that was promised by God for godliness and hope. This truth is illustrated in Titus who, like Timothy, is a **true child in the faith.**

A. Promised by God (1:1–2)

Paul introduces himself both as a **servant** and **apostle.** The term **apostle** (in keeping with 1Ti 1:1 and 2Ti 1:1) shows the authority that Paul has. By placing **servant** before **apostle,** Paul clearly demonstrates humility and obedience: he is a servant leader. The **elect** are chosen or called out ones, those who respond to God. It does not imply limited atonement, that only the chosen will be saved.

Paul sees his servant apostleship as promoting the faith of the elect and the full knowledge (*epignōsis*) of the truth. The definite article with **truth** identifies truth as a specific body of absolute teaching. This **faith and knowledge** of the truth leads to godliness and rests on the hope of eternal life, which is assured by God's faithful nature and promise.

B. Entrusted to Paul (1:3)

God's promise has now been made plain at the right time through preaching, which was entrusted to Paul. For **entrusted** see 1Ti 1:11. **Command** reminds us that Paul is an obedient servant. For **God our Savior** see 1Ti 1:1.

C. Illustrated in Titus (1:4)

Titus, like Timothy, is a true child (NIV **son**) in the faith. For more on Titus, see the introduction above. **Grace and peace,** Paul's common greeting, combines both Greek (**grace**) and Jewish (**peace**) ideas while linking the working of the two together,

reflecting beautifully the Gospel message itself.

II. PROMOTING SOUND DOCTRINE (1:5–16)

To make sure that the truth is proclaimed correctly, Titus must choose elders for God's household (vv.5–9) and identify the rebellious (vv.10–16). Elders are to be recognized as blameless and observed as encouragers of the faithful and refuters of false doctrine. The rebellious are to be recognized as deceivers and observed as corrupters of the faithful and deniers of the truth.

A. Choosing Elders (1:5–9)

In 1:5 Paul clearly states why he left Titus in Crete. **Straighten out** means to set in order or proper array. Titus is to **appoint elders** from those who are leaders in each town. The criteria for being a church leader, or elder, parallel those found in 1Ti 3:1–7 (which see for detailed discussion). Tit 1:7 clearly indicates that an **overseer** (*episkopos*) and an **elder** (*presbuteros*) are interchangeable titles for the same office. Twice, in 1:6 and 7, the elder is identified as **blameless,** above reproach. A good witness to the outside world is essential for a church leader. **Holy** (Gk. *hosios*) means "devout" and "pure."

Tit 1:9 summarizes the criteria for an elder. To hold firmly to the trustworthy message, the elder must fully comprehend it. In practical application, this means the elder is both an encourager and a refuter. He **encourages** some just by presenting **sound** (Gk., "healthful") **doctrine.** At the same time, he **refutes** others who are opposing, or contradicting the doctrine. Thus, **sound doctrine** is a two-edged sword.

B. Identifying the Rebellious (1:10–16)

In sharp contrast to those who are to be leaders in the church are those who are in rebellion and need refuting. Like the elders, the criteria for identifying these rebels are found in their lifestyle. Their speech—vain, or empty, talking, and their actions—deception and greed, are sinful and require decisive action—a sharp rebuke (1:13). They must be silenced—that is, their mouths must be bridled—since whole households are being ruined. The devastating hyperbole in 1:12 is from Epimenides, a Cretan philosopher of the sixth century B.C. who was venerated by his countrymen and called a prophet (Guthrie, 188). Rebuke is to help people stay sound in the faith. Evidently part of the unsound faith was due to the influence of Jewish legalism as seen in 1:10, 14.

Tit 1:15–16 declares forcefully that what is inside people corrupts people and will be evident in their actions (see Lk 11:39–41 and Mt 15:17–20). These disobedient disbelievers find nothing pure, since they are themselves unclean in their minds and consciences. Thus they are **detestable** —objects of disgust, the same word family used to describe the image set up by the Antichrist (Mt 24:15); **disobedient** —not open to persuasion; and **unfit for doing anything good** —not able to stand or pass the test (KJV "reprobate").

III. PRACTICING SOUND DOCTRINE (2:1–3:2)

Having given guidelines for ensuring that **sound doctrine** will be promoted, Paul turns his attention to the practice of sound doctrine within the community of faith. First, relationships are examined by age and gender classifications and then between slaves and masters (2:1–10). Reflecting on these relationships, Paul exclaims that God's purpose in Jesus was to redeem and purify people for himself (2:11–14). This is sound doctrine which is to be taught and practiced in a lifestyle of obedience, peace, and humility (2:15–3:2).

A. Applied to Relationships (2:1–10)

Tit 2:1 is an emphatic command that introduces nine verses of relational teaching. **Sound doctrine** is concerned with sound relationships.

The first area of relationships concern the church family and is based on age and gender: first, older men and women; then, younger women and men (3:2–8). Notice how Paul establishes a structural symmetry—older to younger, with men on the outside framing the women. This structure of balance, harmony, and interdependence mirrors perfectly what Paul wants their relationships in the church to be.

Temperate refers first to moderation in the use of alcohol and second to a paced, measured character. There is a consistent interrelationship between the different groups as illustrated by **likewise** (v.3), **then** (v.4), and **similarly** (v.6). The picture is one where older and younger are vitally involved with one another, and especially where older women are involved in training younger women. In discussing younger men (v.6), Paul expands the section to include remarks directed to Titus (vv.7–8) that parallel 1Ti 4:12. Titus is to encourage the young men by living an exemplary life. As he does this, he fulfills one criterion of an elder (1:9).

Paul wants no one to **malign** [Gk. *blasphēmeō*] **the word of God** (v.5), or to be able to say anything bad about us (v.8). The use of **us** includes Paul and means that the lifestyle witness of one Christian has a direct effect on the way other Christians are viewed. By being obedient and pleasing, not argumentative nor stealing, slaves show that they can be fully trusted. Then **they will** make the teaching about God our Savior more attractive (Gk., *cosmosis*; Eng. cosmetic) (2:10). We make the Gospel more appealing by our lifestyle, a central tenent of the Wesleyan doctrine of holiness.

B. Designed to Redeem and Purify (2:11–15)

Sound doctrine is simply and clearly defined in these vv.11–14. **Has appeared** is a reference to the ministry, death, and resurrection of Christ. **To all men** is the universal appeal of the Good News (see also 1Ti 2:4). This means that God's grace in Christ is available for everyone and that it has appeared. John Wesley called this prevenient grace, which enables people to respond to God. This grace impacts our present lifestyle (v.12). We desire to live godly lives because we await the return of Jesus Christ—this is **the blessed hope** (v.13). V.14 reinforces v.12 by affirming the purpose of Christ's ministry. **Redeem** means to buy back, to free from the bondage of sin. **Purify** means to cleanse, to free from impurity. Sound doctrine teaches redemption and purification.

Since all that Paul has presented in 2:2–14 is sound doctrine, he now gives Titus a threefold command to **teach, encourage, and rebuke with all authority.** To **encourage** and **rebuke** are tasks of an elder (1:9). By doing these things, Titus will prevent others from disregarding or overlooking him. (Either translation is preferable to NIV **despise.**) Thus, if they fail to act soundly on Titus's teaching, they bear the responsibility and consequences.

C. Applied in Lifestyle (3:1–2)

As in the discussion on slaves in 2:9–10, Paul stresses subjection and obedience regardless of who the ruler is. Our highest allegiance is to God (cf. Ac 4:18–20), but we must remember that the Bible teaches us to pray for our rulers and not overthrow them. The kingdom of God is internal but is reflected externally in doing whatever is good, such as refraining from **slander,** promoting peace, and showing **humility. Humility** is a mindset that results from acknowledging God's grace to me, which enables me to see myself and others with gentle understanding.

III. DEFINING SOUND DOCTRINE (3:3–11)

In this section Paul expands on his earlier definition of sound doctrine in 2:11–14. We are **saved** and **justified** by God (vv.3–7). As a result, we are to be devoted to doing good (v.8) and are warned to avoid the unprofitable (vv.9–11).

A. Saved and Justified by God (3:3–7)

As if the phrase **true humility toward everyone** were in his mind, Paul reflects on the time prior to God's salvation. The use of **we**'clearly shows that Paul includes himself. The description in 3:3 of the person without Christ vividly demonstrates why we need a Savior. Note how God's kindness and love for all people (NIV **love** is an inadequate translation of *philanthrōpia*) are exactly the right remedy. **Appeared** is simple past action; it has already taken place (see 2:11).

God's appearance brought salvation on the basis of his mercy, not our righteousness. In the Greek text, "not by works of righteousness" appears first in the clause and thus receives the emphasis. **Washing of rebirth** may refer to baptism, but since this phrase is linked grammatically with **renewal by the Holy Spirit,** the figurative cleansing by the Spirit in the believer's life is intended. Vv.5–6 clearly show the triune God in operation, God generously pouring out the Holy Spirit through Jesus Christ. The result is justification—made as if we had never sinned—and inheritance of the hope of eternal life. How beautifully this hope corresponds with "the blessed hope" of 2:13. When comparing 2:11–14 with 3:3–7, we see 2:11–14 stressing the lifestyle that God desires and 3:3–7 providing the theology that backs up that lifestyle.

B. Devoted to Doing Good (3:8) and Warned to Avoid the Unprofitable (3:9–11)

This is the fourth occurrence of **doing good,** the earlier ones being in 2:7, 14, and 3:1, with one further occurrence in 3:8. Sound doctrine promotes a lifestyle that is excellent (Gk., "good") and profitable for all.

This sharply contrasts with the behavior described in 3:9, which is unprofitable and useless and which the believer is to avoid. The references to genealogies and quarrels about the law in 3:9 may reflect the influence of Jewish legalism (see 1:10, 14; 1Ti 4:1–7; 6:3–5).

Vv.10–11 lay out guidelines for dealing with a divisive person, one who creates factions. Warning/refuting according to sound doctrine is a responsibility of the church leader. A divisive person is **warped** (Gk., "turned inside out") and **sinful. Warped** is past tense while **sinful** is present tense. Past attitudes determine present actions. Divisive people have made their own judgment: They stand self-condemned.

V. FURTHERING SOUND DOCTRINE (3:12–15)

Paul closes with a potpourri of concerns. Artemas is unknown except for this reference. Tychicus, the carrier of the Ephesian/Colossian letters (Eph 6:21; Col 4:7–8), is also mentioned in Ac 20:4 and 2Ti 4:12. Evidently Artemas or Tychicus will relieve Titus. Two cities were named Nicopolis: one inland and north of Philippi; the other a seaport on the Adriatic, northwest of Corinth. The seaport city is preferred here, although we have no record of Paul being in either. **Winter** was always a difficult time for sea travel (see 2Ti 4:21). Zenas is unknown except for this reference. **Lawyer** may be used of an expert in Jewish or Roman law. Given the Greek name, Zenas was probably an expert in Roman law. Apollos was a powerful Jewish preacher who was born in Alexandria and fully instructed in the Gospel at Ephesus by Priscilla and Aquila (Ac 18:24–26; 1Co 3:5–6; 16:12). Zenas and Apollos were coming to Crete, perhaps even carrying this letter, and were to receive Titus's hospitality.

In 3:14 Paul reminds Titus that the people must devote themselves to doing good (see v.8) in order to meet daily necessities and thus not be unfruitful.

Those with Paul send greetings to Titus. **You** is singular. Titus is then requested to greet **those who love us in the faith.** The qualification of love clearly shows that this is a love springing from and residing in faith in Christ. This love is possible only because of God's grace (2:11; 3:7). Thus Paul writes **grace** be with all of you, the whole community of faith.

BIBLIOGRAPHY

See the bibliography at the end of 1 Timothy.

PHILEMON
Wayne McCown

INTRODUCTION

Philemon was a lay leader in the church at Colossae. This letter concerns a slave he owned named Onesimus (v.10). Onesimus had run away but, coming into the company of Paul, had become converted.

Paul is now sending Onesimus back, along with this letter. It is a personal appeal to Philemon, to treat his slave as a Christian brother. The social influence of the Gospel is evident, in both the example of Paul and his entreaty.

Unlike many NT epistles, few modern scholars doubt the authenticity of Philemon: "No serious objection stands in the way of receiving this letter as genuine" (Martin, 153).

Philemon has close connections with Colossians. Both letters include greetings from Epaphras, Mark, Aristarchus, Demas, and Luke (see vv.23–24). Archippus, who is given a special word of instruction in Col 4:17, is one of the persons addressed in Philemon (v.2). Onesimus likewise is named in both letters, as being sent back by Paul to Colossae (vv.11–12; cf. Col 4:9). Most probably, Philemon was written and sent at the same time as Colossians—while Paul was a prisoner in Rome, ca. A.D. 62.

OUTLINE

COMMENTARY

I. INTRODUCTION (VV.1–7)

The opening reflects Paul's customary format: the salutation is followed by a thanksgiving and prayers on behalf of those addressed.

A. Salutation (vv.1–3)

Paul identifies Timothy as coauthor, as he does in Colossians. Philemon is named as the principal recipient and is warmly commended as **"our dear friend and fellow worker."** Also mentioned along with Philemon are Apphia and Archippus, presumably his wife and their son, and **"the church that meets in your home."** Archippus may have been the minister (see Col 4:17), but it was a family ministry.

B. Thanksgiving (vv.4–7)

This description of Paul's prayer ministry follows Col 1:3–12 but is foreshortened and personalized. Philemon is especially commended for his **love for all the saints,** which has been a source of **great joy and encouragement** to Paul (vv.4, 7).

II. APPEAL (VV.8–21)

The heart of the letter consists of Paul's appeal to Philemon on behalf of Onesimus.

A. A Commendation of Onesimus (vv.8–14)

Paul uses personal influence but refrains from the exercise of apostolic authority. Rather, he appeals to Philemon on the basis of Christian love (v.8).

A special relationship had developed between Paul and Onesimus whom he affectionately calls **"my son"** (v.10). Philemon's erstwhile slave, **formerly . . . useless,** had ministered to Paul in his chains and had proved himself true

to his name, **"useful"** (v.11). Says the imprisoned apostle, **"I would have liked to keep him with me. . . . But I did not want to do anything without your consent"** (vv.13–14).

B. A Request of Philemon (vv.15–21)

In sending Onesimus back, Paul requests Philemon not to treat him as a vagrant slave, but to receive him as a Christian brother. The apostle puts himself on the line personally in behalf of Onesimus: **"Welcome him as you would welcome me"** (v.17). **"If he has done you any wrong or owes you anything . . . I will pay it back"** (vv.18–20).

Obviously, Paul's appeal is strong, undergirded by his own affection for Onesimus and his personal identification with him. The apostle is confident that Philemon, if he considers him a partner (v.17), will do even more than Paul asks (v.21). So he sends the slave, now a converted Christian believer, back to his Christian master, appealing for treatment that will accord with Christian love.

The appeal to love (*agape*) as the principal motive and norm of Christian conduct is, of course, central to Wesleyan theology. Its transforming effect, not only on persons but also on society, is exemplified in this letter. Wesleyans find in Paul's attitude and action a model for Christian faith, "expressing itself through love" (Gal 5:6).

III. CONCLUSION (VV.22–25)

This brief letter, personal in tone throughout, closes with a request and greetings from friends.

A. Proposed Visit (v.22).

Paul expresses his hope for a release from prison, **in answer to [their] prayers,** to be followed by a visit; he requests the privilege of staying in Philemon's home.

B. Personal Greetings (vv.23–25).

Epaphras is mentioned in Col 4:12 as "one of you and a servant of Christ Jesus." He was with the apostle at the time these letters were written, presumably imprisoned with him (v.23). Paul also extends greetings from other **fellow workers** who were known to both Philemon and the church at Colossae. The apostle closes as he had begun, with a benedictory prayer for divine grace.

BIBLIOGRAPHY

Clarke, Adam. *Commentary and Critical Notes on the NT*. New York: Bangs and Emory, 1826.

Hunter, A. M. *Interpreting Paul's Gospel*. London: Collier, 1954.

Kümmel, Werner Georg. *Introduction to the NT*. New York: Abingdon, 1966.

Lohse, Edward. *Colossians and Philemon*. HCS. Philadelphia: Fortress, 1971.

Martin, Ralph P. *Colossians and Philemon*. Grand Rapids: Eerdmans, 1973.

McCown, Wayne. "The Hymnic Structure of Colossians 1:15–20," *The Evangelical Quarterly* (July–August, 1979), 156–62.

Reicke, Bo. *The Epistles of James, Peter and Jude*. AB. Vol. 37. New York: Doubleday, 1964.

Simpson, E. K., *Ephesians;* and Bruce, F. F., *Colossians*. NICNT. Grand Rapids: Eerdmans, 1957.

Wesley, John. *Explanatory Notes Upon the New Testament*. London: Epworth, 1754.

Wesleyan Bible Commentary. Grand Rapids: Eerdmans, 1965.

HEBREWS
John Walters

INTRODUCTION

Hebrews is unfamiliar to many readers. It is an elegant piece, full of import and authority, but obscure. Its fine argumentation, particularly about Melchizedek and the ritual of the tabernacle, is difficult to grasp twenty centuries later. The vigorous challenge of this book is understood only as we reacquaint ourselves with the author's religious perspective and the historical setting.

I. OCCASION

The title "To the Hebrews" (NIV "Hebrews") is traditional and dates from the second century. The epistle clearly was addressed to people who were well acquainted with the covenant of Moses, the Jewish Scriptures, and the worship rituals they specified. The epistle bases its argumentation, however, in the OT rather than in the Judaism of the first century. This curiosity, coupled with the author's employment of philosophical language, leads some commentators to conclude that the epistle's first readers were Gentiles rather than Jews. More likely, they were Greek-speaking Jewish Christians living outside Palestine. These Diaspora Jews had heard the Gospel and received Jesus as their awaited Messiah. Their Bible was the LXX, a Greek translation of the Jewish Scriptures, and it is the LXX rather than the Hebrew Bible the author quotes. "Those from Italy send you their greetings" (13:24) may indicate an Italian destination for the document. The earliest extant citation of Hebrews is found in a letter from Clement of Rome to Corinth dated about A.D. 96, suggesting this epistle was first known in Rome and received there as authoritative.

The document itself informs us that the addressees had learned of Jesus by way of apostolic testimony (2:3). Their own religious background had instilled in them a reverence for the covenant of Moses as mediated by angels (2:2; cf. Ac 7:53), an awareness of the Day of Atonement ritual (9:7), a concern for ceremonial washing (6:2; 9:10), and a hope in the coming Day of God's visitation (10:25). These elements point to a Jewish faith not entirely unlike that of the separatists at Qumran—very conservative, with a heightened regard for purification rituals, perfection of life, and an eschatological (end-times) focus (see Bruce, " 'To the Hebrews' or 'To the Essenes'?"). Soon after coming to Christ the addressees had suffered persecution, public abuse, confiscation of property, and perhaps even imprisonment; they accepted these torments joyfully for the sake of Christ (10:32–34). Now, however, the threat upon them was sufficient to make them neglect church fellowship (10:25) and shrink from Christian espousals (10:35–39).

Accepting the arguments of William Manson, I suppose the readers were living in Rome and had come to Christ from a conservative wing of the Jewish community. The perceived desertion of their ancestral religious traditions had resulted in persecution from their fellow Jews at the time of their initial conversion (10:32–34). The present threat, though, appears to have been a Roman one and much more severe. These believers were about to drop their profession of Christ to escape the shedding of their blood (3:12–14; 10:29; 12:4).

Under Roman law the Jewish religion was a legal cult, but Christianity, when once the Romans learned of the distinction between the two, was not. In Rome in A.D. 49 a minor Jewish persecution of Christians occurred, causing some to flee (cf. Ac 18:2). Fifteen years later, the emperor Nero actually took the lives of many Christians by feeding them to wild animals in the Colosseum, by crucifixion, and even by covering them with pitch and setting them alight on roadside poles. Caught in such circumstances, Jewish Christians understandably though improperly were tempted to retreat again into the protective orbit of Judaism, their ancestral religion. The author of Hebrews viewed such retreat as trampling the Son of God under foot and insulting the Spirit of grace (10:29).

The document leaves some clues that suggest a date before the fall of Jerusalem in A.D. 70. Some points are argued that would make little sense were the temple already destroyed. The author states that the priestly ministry inaugurated by Moses has been superseded by Christ's ministry, saying in 8:13, "What is obsolete and aging will soon disappear." It sounds here as though the old temple sacrificial system were yet functioning at the time of writing. In 9:6–9 the author explains the layout and furnishings of the tabernacle under the Mosaic covenant and also the ongoing activities of the Levitical priesthood, especially of the high priest on the Day of Atonement. In the Greek this passage is in the present tense. The NIV regards it as an historic present, describing past occurrences as happening presently. However, the author may intend the reader to take this description of the ancient tabernacle and its functions as an antiquated depiction of the current temple system. He actually comments, "This is an illustration for the present time" (9:9). In 10:2 the author asks why the offerings should continue year after year if indeed they were able to perfect the worshiper for the presence of God. In 13:10–11 tabernacle ministrations and atonement rituals are mentioned in the present tense. Taken together, these clues suggest a date before the fall of Jerusalem and the destruction of the temple. The letter appears best to fit the traumatic days before the outbreak of Roman persecution in A.D. 64, since the author says, "You have not yet resisted to the point of shedding your blood" (12:4). That prospect was before them.

II. AUTHOR

It is not known who wrote Hebrews. The ancient church was divided on this point until the late fourth century. At that time it was received as from Paul, mainly to justify its place in the canon. Martin Luther was the first to suggest Apollos as author on the grounds that he was from Alexandria. The epistle exhibits certain characteristics in vocabulary and thought matter typical of Alexandrian literary production. Curiously, the Alexandrian church never claimed the letter as its own.

Although Wesley accepted the traditional ascription of the letter to Paul, few would be prepared to do so today. The author was a second-generation Christian, having first heard the Gospel from one or more of the apostolic witnesses (2:3). A native Greek speaker, he was well educated and at points reflected thought modes of Alexandrian philosophy (see Williamson, "Platonism and Hebrews," 423). On the other hand, he reflects a thoroughly Jewish frame of mind steeped in the LXX. He subscribed to current eschatological expectation and shared much of the theological perspective of Stephen and the Hellenists in Acts 6–8 (Manson, 167–71).

This, of course, is not so descriptive of Paul as someone else in the early apostolic circle. The style and vocabulary of the Greek in this epistle shows more classical refinement than any of Paul's letters. Was the author Apollos? Perhaps. But in Rome where the epistle early circulated, Tertullian (ca. A.D. 160–240) regarded Barnabas as the author. Acts 4:36 calls Barnabas a "Son of Encouragement," well suiting him for this self-described "word of exhortation" (13:22). He was a Levite well acquainted with temple ritual and the Bible, a Greek Cypriot by birth, and an estate owner of means. Likely, he would have been educated and versed in Alexandrian thought. Other names have also been suggested, but no definitive pronouncement can be made as to who wrote Hebrews.

III. CONTENTS

This epistle is not strictly in letter form. Actually a "word of exhortation," it is a sermonic discourse recorded and sent as written communication. It was composed to move its addressees beyond the wall of protection afforded by Judaism and toward Christ who "suffered outside the city gate" (13:12). It attempts to redirect their gaze from a backward fixation on the provisional wilderness tabernacle to the enduring "city that is to come" (v.14).

The key, therefore, to the epistle is its eschatological movement (Barrett, 366). It charts a course from former times through this final age to the promised everlasting inheritance, and it exhorts the reader to run this race with perseverance. It redirects the Jewish Christian from what is provisional and fading to what is enduring, from what is fragmentary to what is complete, from what is imperfect to what is perfect, from a sacrificial system based on separation and repeated mediation to direct access to the very throne of God once for all.

Older scholarship, citing parallels to Philo of Alexandria and the philosophical school that developed there, sees two levels of reality reflected in this epistle. The corrupt material existence of the present world order is contrasted with the perfect eternal world order. However, the contrast in Hebrews is not philosophical but historical. The movement is not from the temporal plane to the eternal plane, but from an age of incomplete revelation granted Moses to the age of perfect revelation in the Son (see Barrett, Hurst, Williamson).

The writer employs material from the OT to show divine sanction and purpose in moving beyond the pale of Judaism to Christ. The six major biblical passages cited by the writer point beyond themselves to something greater. In effect, they divinely argue their own self-obsolescence (Caird, 49). This proves God's age-long intention to replace the temporary tabernacle with an everlasting one, to replace the line of mortal high priests with One after the order of Melchizedek who has no beginning or end. The old covenant must give way to the new covenant; God has spoken.

In the fullness of time, through sufferings, Jesus pioneered the way into the presence of God. Access now has been gained to the very throne of grace. The course we are running has a finish line; faith has as its goal the promised entrance into God's own glory and Sabbath rest. To lay hold of such an inheritance, then to surrender it up again in the interest of self-preservation, is to trample the Son of God under foot and insult the Spirit of grace (10:29). Such shrinking back (v.39) does not reflect the faith that will receive the better and lasting promise Christ offers (8:6; 11:39–40). This is reserved for those who "go to him outside the camp, bearing the disgrace he bore" (13:13).

IV. OUTLINE

This epistle is well structured and orderly. It begins in ch. 1 with a series of seven biblical quotes presented in chained fashion. This *catena* leads to the first of six principal biblical passages around which the entire sermon is arranged.* Each of the six passages occurs near the beginning of its respective section. Each is given an eschatological interpretation that manifests a tension between old and new, promise and fulfillment, present realities and future hope. The hortatory portions of this discourse fall mainly at the junctures of the respective sections, and the sermon closes with a final extended exhortation.

    I. Introduction: "My Son" (1:1–2:4)

    II. First Point: "You Crowned Him" (2:5–18)
        OT Text Ps 8:4–6

---

*G. B. Caird, "Exegetical Method," was first to suggest the structure of the epistle through ch. 10 as being based on four principal biblical passages. The present analysis is based on his observation.

COMMENTARY

I. INTRODUCTION: "MY SON" (1:1–2:4)

The opening sentence sets the entire discourse within the time line of Jewish sacred history. That history now reveals a dividing line separating all the past revelatory activity of God from what has happened **in these last days** (1:2). That line is drawn at the appearing of Christ, **appointed heir of all things** and presently seated **at the right hand of the Majesty** (v.3). Whatever God said previously through the prophets must give way to what now has been spoken by the Son, the living presentation of God's own being (v.3). Whatever God said in the past through angels (cf. 2:2) must now be subordinated to what has been communicated by Jesus of Nazareth. Thus, sacred history is divided into two epochs: the former times and these last days. Jewish theology commonly looked ahead to a coming age of glory in contrast to the present. This author begins by announcing the dawning of the new age in God's Son and the end of the former epoch thereby.

The people to whom this letter was sent apparently shared the perspective of Jews elsewhere who regarded the covenant of Moses as imparted through angels. Paul in Gal 3:19 accepts this belief. Stephen in Ac 7:53 accuses the Jews of not obeying the law **put into effect through angels.** The Septuagint, the Hebrew Scriptures translated for Greek-speaking Jews, in its account of the Sinai theophany, mentions angels at God's right hand at the giving of the Law (Dt 33:2, LXX). Acknowledging this, the author still argues the superiority of Christ to angels. Thus, the Gospel has precedence over the law of Moses.

The Scriptures themselves prove the Son's exalted position over all things, angels included. At the moment of his exaltation to the right hand of Majesty, the position of Christ as only Son was made manifest to all creation (1:3, 5). Jewish tradition held that at Creation God invited angels to worship man, but the author sees the invitation coming when Christ, the **Firstborn,** is introduced to the world (v.6). As servants the angels are bidden by God to become wind and fire accomplishing his will (v.7). The Son, however, is called **"God"** by God himself and is enthroned on high in everlasting dominion (v.8). Likewise, God calls him "Lord" who laid earth's foundations and fashioned the heavens in the beginning (v.10; cf. v.2). The writer is clearly propounding here the creative activity of the preexistent Christ. His final proof-text is Ps 110:1, a text commonly understood to apply to the enthronement of the Messiah (v.13). The conclusion to be drawn is that the angels are ministering agents, subordinates sent in service to the true heirs of salvation (v.14), precisely because of the man Jesus who reigns at God's right hand. This opening *catena* of biblical texts in 1:5–13 signals that the entire discourse to follow will flow from several principal Scripture passages (see Introduction: Outline).

Having proved the superiority of the Son, the application follows. The Law of Moses (2:2) carried with it the force of just punishment, and certainly the greater salvation offered in Christ carries greater penalties if ignored. The danger is one of loss by way of lapse. The benefits of the Gospel message announced by the Lord include the miraculous attentions of God, the several **gifts of the Holy Spirit** (v.4), and ultimately **the world to come** (v.5). All these could be lost in one's wayward drift toward an unnamed oblivion. The only sure ground is the Gospel itself; the only safety is heeding Christ's Word (v.1). The addressees are in danger of slipping away from the essentials of Christian faith. They are casting a backward glance again to the perceived safety of the Sinai covenant and placing at risk a far greater security offered in the Son (Westcott, xxxvi–viii).

II. FIRST POINT: "YOU CROWNED HIM" (2:5–18)

In the author's perspective, religion serves the sole purpose of providing access to God. The goal of the devout is to find a place in **the world to come,** to enjoy eternally the perfect bliss of God's presence. This is precisely what God has achieved for all in Christ. To understand this one point about access is to unlock the entire theology of Hebrews and explain its great central image of Christ the High Priest.

The salvation **announced by the Lord** (2:3) is the offer of a place in **the world to come** (v.5). That offer is the sole prerogative of the One to whom that world and we too have been subjected; no angel can fill that role. Human destiny has been fashioned and fulfilled by the divine Creator. Ps 8 sets forth God's plan for humanity. It gives God's solemn assurance that humanity's ultimate destiny is to exercise lordship over all creation, and this eventually includes even the angels (vv.7–8). Of course, it is an incomplete prophecy at present. More is yet in store for humanity, but even now this destiny stands fulfilled. Jesus has fulfilled the destiny fashioned by God for humankind. Moreover, Jesus stands in our place and on our behalf by God's gracious will (v.9). Therefore, our destiny is assured as well.

How is this so? The author goes on to explain the workings of Christ's priestly atonement. God's intention is to bring the **many** to divine **glory** through the One (v.10). Humanity gains access to God's eternal presence through the consecrating work of Jesus, our High Priest. This involves two processes: God must consecrate the priest, and the priest must consecrate the people (v.11).

Christ, though perfect, nevertheless was perfected by God through suffering. To lead a perfect life, one must begin it in perfection and continue in perfection to the end. This Jesus did, but not without great suffering and unimaginable testing of his will to obey God at every point (2:13a; cf. 4:15). This process of maintaining perfect obedience through utter hardship and sacrifice sealed Christ's consecration as humanity's Priest before God. He **loved righteousness and hated wickedness** (1:9a), thus resulting in his exaltation at death (1:9b, 13), fulfilling the divine intention for humanity expressed in Ps 8:5–6. His untimely death completed his perfection through sufferings, a perfect life culminating in a perfect sacrifice.

The benefit to us is that Christ accomplished this not for his own sake, but with each of us in mind (vv.11–13). In sharing our nature and lot, in embracing us, and in submitting to death, Christ consecrated us to God. In being exalted and enthroned, he liberated us from bondage to death and servitude to Satan (vv.14–15). Only a perfect life ended undeservedly could put the wielder of death, Satan, in the wrong. By resurrecting Christ from the grave, God judged Satan as having stepped beyond his rightful bounds. Satan's regency and power were broken forever, and broken by One who shared all the frailties of the human constitution (vv.14, 17) and yet prevailed against the Tempter's wiles. Jesus was not superhuman, but fully human; he showed us what humanity in God's design is intended to be. Only a high priest perfectly faithful to God, and thus perfectly human, could offer himself mercifully for the sins of the people (v.17). Only a high priest who mastered the Tempter can aid us in our own struggle against temptation (v.18). Crowned now with glory and honor, Christ is all the help we need.

III. SECOND POINT: "TODAY" (3:1–4:13)

We have already been made holy by the consecrating work of Christ who claimed us for God. Moreover, we too are called to be holy, as befits our heavenly destiny (3:1). That means even now we are to be as God is (cf. Lev 19:2). To that end we have Christ's help; only he who has gone before us can guide our steps along the same perilous way (see 2:18). That is why he is given the title **apostle,** one sent as God's emissary entrusted with a divine mission on our behalf. Moses too was God's emissary to the household of faith; but Jesus is the greater of the two. Moses served God's interests and God's elect faithfully, being one of the elect himself. Yet God in Christ instituted that election long before it came about (3:2–4), and Christ in God now oversees its full implementation (3:6; cf. 1:2–3).

Moses faithfully bore witness to things God in Christ would later speak (3:5; cf. 1:2). Here the author reveals the underlying point of his argument: Moses brought God's Ten Commandments through the mediation of angels (2:2; see Dt 33:1–4), but Jesus himself has brought the everlasting Word (cf. 1:3). The OT bears witness to things beyond its own compass, things only finally revealed in Christ (Caird, 49). The principal OT passages by which the author frames his argument clearly point out the provisional nature of the former covenant concluded under Moses. For example, Ps 8 proclaims the destiny of humanity as crowned with glory and honor (2:7–8), a destiny yet unfulfilled and beyond the capacity of the former covenant to bring about. Only now in Jesus is this destiny realized.

This hope is now within grasp for all who do not lose courage and surrender their faith in Jesus for more immediate gain. The household of faith is comprised of those who do not let circumstances rob them of their hope (3:6).

The Holy Spirit brings a timely warning in the words of Ps 95 to the recipients of Christ's benefits who are now wavering under opposition (3:7–11). The entire sermon is an exhortation to hold fast to what is promised in Christ. Today, as never before, the hope of entering God's own rest is ours, provided we keep our trust fixed on Christ. Ps 95, like Ps 8, speaks of a human destiny yet unfulfilled. Here again the OT points beyond itself to the full and final revelation in Jesus Christ. The promise reserved for us is the hope of entering God's own rest (3:11; cf. Ge 2:2–3). The warning is to those who would forfeit that which Christ has won.

Hebrews contains five so-called severe passages (2:1–4; 3:7–4:13; 5:11–6:12; 10:19–31; 12:14–29). In each the danger warned against is apostasy. A severe fate awaits those who drift away from Christ (2:1) or ignore such a great salvation . . . first announced by the Lord (2:3), or turn away from the living God who has spoken now by his Son (3:12; cf. 1:2). Movement away from Christ means forfeiting our only sure hope. The recipients of this epistle possibly were contemplating a return to Judaism, which Rome sanctioned because of the safety from persecution it offered to Hebrew Christians facing Jewish intolerance and Roman disfavor. Today the danger of forfeiting one's heavenly reward is present for any who takes his or her Christian affiliation lightly. As Wesley put it (Notes, 570), "The day of life will end soon, and perhaps the day of grace yet sooner." We only have Today. Our destined reward is in Christ, but we share in it only as we maintain our initial assurance of salvation through life's final day (3:14). Backward glances and backward steps

heed the siren call of sin, not the upward call of God (vv.13, 15).

The very people whom Moses led out of Egypt by God's saving grace were those who later tried and tested God in repeated stubbornness. They died in the desert because for forty years they resisted their Savior in unbelief (3:19). Becoming a Christian offers no guarantee of reaching the Promised Land, should one not remain a follower of the Lord all the way there. To fall from grace is one thing; to forfeit it is quite another.

The Holy Spirit still speaks Today (3:7). The promise of entering God's rest was given to the Exodus sojourners, but they all fell by the wayside. Therefore, the promise yet stands Today for any who will grasp the opportunity (4:1). God's Word of grace has come to us (by the Son) just as to them (by Moses). Indeed, even now believers are entering God's promised rest, says the author (v.3), because they are responding to the divine offer with hearts open in faith.

What is the rest of God promised to us? First, consider that after six days of activity, God rested on the seventh day of Creation (see Ge 2:2). Ps 95 clearly states God's intention to extend that rest to others, but the invitation has been delayed by disobedience (4:6). When the psalmist uttered the word today, it was long after the time when Joshua brought the people into the Promised Land (4:8). Therefore, the author concludes, the psalm speaks not of rest from wilderness wanderings but of God's own Sabbath-rest. The psalmist uttered words pointing beyond his own day to a day when the rest God enjoys should be extended to his people (4:9). Since Christ has come, the day God has fixed is Today. The point, of course, is that we do our utmost to follow Christ and enter that divine rest while the promise remains.

The voice speaking in Christ's Gospel (4:12; cf. 1:2–3; 3:15; 4:2) is God's Word alive and effective **Today.** When it comes, who can claim not to hear it? As it comes, it convinces or it convicts, the judgment depending on the heart's response (cf. Jn 12:47–50). Just as the priest with deft cuts laid open the sacrifices brought before the Lord, every inward thought and motive is exposed by the Word's penetrating edge. If our acts seem godly but our intentions are not, God sees right through our folly. Though one day we shall all give account for ourselves, the eyes from which nothing can remain hidden see the genuineness or falsity of our lives **Today** (4:13). The Word of God comes to convince us in belief or to convict us in unbelief. As the Gospel meets us, so too does the sifting judgment of God.

IV. THIRD POINT: "A PRIEST FOREVER" (4:14–7:28)

The purpose of religion is to provide communion with God. While it is our sure hope to enter the **Sabbath-rest** of God some day, even **Today** through Christ we may approach God's throne (4:16). Moses approached with great fear and trembling (Ex 3:6; cf. Ac 7:32), but we may approach with confidence because Jesus has passed from earth to heaven to assume humanity's destiny in the presence of God.

Our **High Priest** sees our blemishes and our weaknesses. He knows our mixed responses to his Word. He knows our limitations and our adverse circumstances; he shared them and proved himself victorious over them (4:15). That is, he faced what we face, and much more, without ever taking the easy way out. In fact, that is precisely what temptation and sin offer

us—the path of least resistance. The High Priest most sympathetic to the human condition is the One who has himself experienced, more than anyone else, the unremitting onslaught of temptation. **We have** such a **high priest,** and he remains at the altar of God to offer mercy and grace now. His mercy covers our nakedness and shortcomings; his grace sustains and supports us in adversity (4:16). With this in mind, again the plea is given to hold fast to professed faith in Christ.

The high priest represents the people and their concerns before God while sharing their unhappy lot. To the author of Hebrews, the human condition is marked not so much by "original sin" as "original **weakness**" (5:2; cf. 4:15), that finite creatureliness that leaves humanity defenseless before sin's deceit (see 3:13). Were the human constitution equipped to fend off the Tempter's wiles in its own strength, Christ's passion would be superfluous. Under the covenant of Moses, the only remedy for the human plight was repeated sacrifices for sin (5:3), since the weakness inherent in humanity remained unchanged. High priests served to meet the ongoing need for atonement.

In quoting Ps 110:4, the high priesthood of Jesus is now presented for consideration (5:6), though already introduced in 2:17; 3:1; 4:14. The author approaches this theme from a singular given: the glorification of Christ is his heavenly enthronement. The indisputable fact is that the Resurrection proclaims his entitlement at the hand of God. Jesus never claimed high priestly honor for himself in his earthly life (5:5). God conferred upon Christ, once for all, the glory and title of eternal High Priest in exalting him to the heavenly throne (5:6; cf. 1:3, 8–9, 13; 2:9). Here the author equates the Son's investiture to high priesthood with his glorification, because he adjoins Ps 2:7 to Ps 110:4.

Jesus is the great High Priest. God called him to a special position of unique sonship (5:5), a divine appointment Jesus would have forfeited had he relied on his own strength. For he too shared our weaknesses (see also 2:14, 17; 4:15), but he relied on God to grant him the strength he lacked, just as we must do. This is the reason mention is made of his **prayers and petitions with loud cries and tears** (5:7). The all-knowing and all-powerful has no need of petition and no reason to cry. But Jesus fully shared our limitations. Ever reliant upon God, he was able to resist sin and submit to the divine will. The Gethsemane experience echoed in 5:7 was only the final and greatest of the tests Jesus endured. Had he failed God at any point after receiving his call, however early or late in life, he could not have become the eternal High Priest. His unwavering submission to the will of God won him vindication against the wrongful death he suffered. God delivered him **from death** rather than merely from dying (5:7). That greater victory was for us (see 2:14–15).

Jesus comprehended the Father's will through prayer, but **he learned** the utter challenge of **obedience** through **what he suffered** (5:8). Son by appointment though he was (see 1:2), obedience did not come naturally to him thereby. Appointment to high office offers no security against failure. Still, it is wrong to conclude that, in learning obedience, he must have progressed from initial disobedience. The author cannot allow that, since Jesus was sinless (see 4:15; 7:26). Likewise, it is wrong to conclude that, in being perfected, initially at least he must have been imperfect. These facile antitheses are the hollow constructs of shallow reasoning.

To understand what Jesus underwent in life, we must begin with two equivalent statements. In 2:10 the author declares that God made Jesus **perfect through suffering.** In 5:8–9 he says Jesus **learned obedience** through suffering and was perfected. Both passages state that Jesus underwent a process of perfecting by clinging to God through adversity. In other words, the call of God drew him forward, and the grace of God sustained him in the face of mounting odds and growing opposition. In the process, he learned to respond more exactingly to the will of God. Jesus' perfection was his unflagging willingness to obey God as the difficulties and demands increased. His was, so to speak, a perfection in process.

Modern thought typically views perfection as an unattainable ideal, following ancient Platonism. Jesus' perfection is thereby attributed to his divinity. He is viewed as a special case, and we do not share his advantages. Our perfection must be awaited until the life to come.

Neither the author of Hebrews nor Wesley follows this line of thought, however. A Jewish Christian, the writer of Hebrews viewed perfection much as did the Qumran community and the prophets before his time. Perfection comes by God's grace in faithfulness to his covenant (see Ps 51; Jer 31:33–34; Eze 36:23–27). Jesus is precisely a case in point. The obedience necessary to covenant faithfulness was possible only by the operation of God's grace, even for him. Life had to be lived in unwavering trust (see 2:13; 3:2), not in himself but in God. By trusting and obeying God at every point, Jesus learned more and more fully the perfect response to the divine will. God taught him what obedience entailed. He had no advantage over us; in fact, he shared all our human limitations (cf. 2:14, 17; 4:15). But the grace and power of God were upon him as never before in human experience. When his life was taken, the perfecting process was ended. Ever having remained faithful, he became the perfect offering of humanity to God, once for all. In receiving Jesus, God received all those with whom he identified (see 2:9–10, 17), who thereafter have come to heed his call (5:9). In resurrecting him, God bestowed on him the everlasting title of **high priest in the order of Melchizedek** (v.10).

The author's intention is to explain more fully this priestly entitlement. However, he is writing to people whose spiritual faculties have been stunted (5:11). Unlike Jesus, they are responding to adversity by shrinking from the sterner challenges of faith (cf. 10:35–39; 12:3–13, 25). By now, the leading of God's grace should have taught them deep insight and moral fortitude; instead, they are failing to grasp the basic pronouncements delivered by the prophets (see 1:1), let alone those imparted by the Son (see 1:2). The author himself is compelled to teach them these elementary points again (5:12) in the epistle's six major points. He accuses them of being infantile, literally, inexperienced and untried (*apeiros*) in God's program of righteousness (5:13). Jesus, though, was tried (*pepeirasmenos*) in all respects (see 4:15). The Word illumines the proper path; the faithful learn its landmarks, turns, and ascents. Seasoned travelers (*teleioi*) on the righteous road have trained faculties and fine moral discrimination, long tried and true (5:14; cf. 12:11). The addressees have not used the faculties God gave them to perceive and do what is right. Now they must

be admonished, since they have not properly digested the prophetic pronouncements and the words of Christ.

What is the wrong these people are contemplating? It amounts to a forfeiture of the grace of God offered in Christ Jesus (see 12:15), a refusal to hear the word God speaks today (see 12:25). Judaism, their ancestral religion, is sanctioned by Rome, and the attractive option in the present dilemma is to return to the safety it offers. When faced with exposure and persecution for being Christians, some would back away from Christ to save themselves.

The author will have none of their expedient. God has provided only one way to safety, and that way lies forward through adversity (see 12:1–13). There can be no looking back now. He calls his audience to leave the first step and scale the heights (6:1). They have had problems embracing the teaching originally delivered by Christ (not **"about Christ"**; see 2:3), and it is long past the time when they should have allowed God to bear them on to his own perfection.

Notoriously misunderstood is 6:1 because perfection (*teleiotēs*; not mere **maturity** here) is commonly viewed in terms of an unattainable ideal rather than relational dynamics. Consequently, two important clues are commonly passed over. First, the verb (*pherō*) is in the present tense (denoting continuous action, not momentary crisis) in the middle/passive voice, and here it means "to be borne along" by a power outside and greater than self. Westcott (p. 145) conveys the sense in remarking, "The thought is not primarily of personal effort, 'let us go on,' 'let us press' . . . , but of personal surrender to an active influence." Second, the goal is the state of perfection (*teleiotēs*) God alone enjoys, not to be confused with the process of perfection (*teleiōsis*) by which God brings us to the attainment of that goal. By God's grace, this is much more than moral maturity; it is relational dynamics directed in terms of purposed divinity.

Christ underwent the same process. He attained the goal only by remaining obedient through sufferings even unto death (see 2:10; 5:8). God also will bear us through the adversities of life to the ultimate attainment of his own perfection, provided we allow him continuously to work his will in our lives. This perfective process is impeded by any unwillingness to surrender one's heart and mind, will and understanding to God's leading. To move beyond spiritual infancy, we must accept not only the original teaching of Jesus, but also the prompting of the Spirit, and that might unsettle us and pull us beyond our familiar moorings. Perfection is the relational dynamics of Spirit-led living; Jesus called it the kingdom of God. As such, it is itself the goal, having no predefined end to its movement, no exhaustion of its forward momentum.

Wiley represents many proponents of Wesleyan theology in commenting on this passage. His first point is that "the redemptive process is twofold because sin is twofold. (1) It is an act which requires forgiveness, and (2) it is a state or condition of the heart known as inbred sin or inherited depravity, which can be removed only by cleansing. . . . It is for this reason that we speak of Christian perfection as 'a second blessing, properly so-called'" (p. 206). Contrary to Wiley, the author of Hebrews knows nothing of inherited depravity nor of perfection as the removal of such. Wiley makes a sharp distinction between sin and infirmity: "This distinction is based upon a difference between sin and its consequences.

Sin, whether in act or in state, is removed in this present life by the all-atoning blood of Jesus; but the consequences of sin manifest in weakness and infirmity will be removed only at the time of the resurrection" (p. 209). The author of Hebrews would disagree, viewing weakness as an element of the created human condition, mere creatureliness vulnerable to sin's greater power (without divine assistance).

The Jewish Christians to whom this epistle was sent were having difficulty accepting tribulation as part of the path ordained by God for their perfecting. They were in retreat. They questioned Christ's teachings on fundamental points: repentance and faith (see Mk 1:15), the futility of rites of cleansing (see Mk 7:1–8; cf. Heb 9:10), the laying on of hands (see Mk 7:31–37), the resurrection from the dead (see Mk 12:18–27); and eternal judgment (see Mk 8:34–38). These were the familiar moorings of Jewish religious practice and theological debate. The author interestingly qualifies repentance in terms of dead works (*ergoi nekroi*, 6:1). These are not **acts that lead to death** (contrary to the NIV) but acts that *perpetuate* death. The author understands death to be perpetuated by the former covenant in the repeated demand for blood sacrifices (see 9:13–14). Jesus' call for repentance and faith in God, then, is a call to leave the deadness of the former covenant and believe the Gospel. In believing Christ's Gospel and surrendering to his leading, we are thus borne along to God's perfection. This, indeed, is God's good pleasure to accomplish for us (6:3).

The third of five severe passages in this epistle, 6:4–8 flows from the rejection of God's good pleasure. God desires to bear us along to his own perfection and to the enjoyment of his own Sabbath-rest. What more can God do for us than he has already done in Jesus Christ? He freely offers us the light of his glory, his indwelling Spirit, and his victorious power. To reject this **heavenly gift** (v.4) is to strike one's own path to salvation (even if through Moses). This falling away (v.6) is more than a mere lapse into sin; it is ultimately self-destructive. The impossibility of God renewing their repentance is due to their willful independence. God, by sovereign self-limitation, forces no one to keep his heavenly gift. If Christ is rejected, no alternative remains. The former covenant has been superseded (see 8:13).

The Calvinist doctrine of eternal security questions the possibility posed here that one who receives the Holy Spirit can commit apostasy. Arminian-Wesleyan theology acknowledges that possibility, if God's grace is refused. Disillusionment with Christ sealed his crucifixion; it is no different when his own abandon him.

In the divine scheme, blessing produces further blessing (6:7). Rain enables parched soil to yield produce. But blessings do not flow unabated to those who abandon the divine plan. At some point it becomes useless to cultivate ground that steadfastly bears noxious weeds (cf. 12:15). God eventually must honor one's steadfast decision to reject Christ. Without his salvation, the end for that one is the consuming fire (6:8; cf. 10:27; 12:29). In the case of the recipients of the letter, God's blessing is yet evident in their continuing service (6:10). The danger is that some should begin to lag in their demonstrated concern for other Christians, since that would readily identify them as Christians too. Sluggards (*nōthroi*) shrink from the hope set before them in Christ (6:12; cf. 10:39), but faith shows patient endurance (cf. 10:36). The promised inheritance of faith is the corporate enjoyment of God's perfection (see 11:39–40).

Abraham is the biblical example of patient faith. In Ge 13 God promised childless Abram that he would be blessed with many descendants. Only many years later, in old age, did Sarah give birth to Isaac. The story shows that Abraham's faith consisted in patience and endurance; persevering, he received what God had promised (6:15). Later still, God commanded Abraham to sacrifice Isaac on Mount Moriah, and Abraham obeyed. As the knife was raised to slay the child of promise, God intervened and provided a ram instead. Again Abraham proved his obedience in faith. In staying his hand, God reaffirmed the promise by swearing an oath which the author quotes in 6:14. God did this **to make the unchanging nature of his purpose very clear** (v.17) to Abraham, Isaac, and their descendants. The promise and the oath are unchangeable; God cannot go back on them (v.18).

They find their fulfillment in the hope offered to us, a sure hope resting on the unchanging nature of his purpose to bless us. Nor is that hope a mere longing for future blessing. Even now we may take hold of it and enter the heavenly Holy of Holies. In prayer and supplication we may go behind the veil to receive strength and encouragement from Jesus our High Priest, eternally ministering on our behalf (6:19–20). This hope is much better for the people of promise than the momentary access of their earthly representative once each year (see 9:7).

Now the author begins the topic he set out to address in 5:8–11, the priesthood of Christ in the succession of Melchizedek. **King of Salem and priest of God Most High,** in Ge 14 Melchizedek appears in the narrative suddenly and disappears two verses later as the story line moves on. Bringing bread and wine, he blesses Abraham and receives a tithe of his battle spoils. The author finds meaning in Melchizedek's name, translated **"king of righteousness."** Moreover, as **"king of Salem"** (from *šālôm*, which means "peace"), he is declared to be **"king of peace"** (7:2). The implication is that Melchizedek prefigures Christ.

The silence of Genesis concerning Melchizedek's genealogy and life is also meaningful to the author. It is as though this priest of God enters salvation history from beyond. The man serves God yet does so outside the covenant relationship God inaugurated with Abraham in Ge 12. No mention is made concerning the beginning or end of Melchizedek's walk with God. It is as though he comes to Abraham through the veil of eternity, only to leave through it again. That is why the author says, **Like the Son of God he remains a priest forever** (7:3).

Is the author constructing a fanciful argument that can bear no weight, finding meaning as he does in the silence of the Genesis narrative? Actually, he is on solid ground. Long before his time, an earlier Jewish theologian had declared Melchizedek to be alive eternally: "You are a priest forever, in the order of Melchizedek" (Ps 110:4). The author of Hebrews is only reiterating the psalmist's claim concerning the Messiah, now applying it specifically to Jesus.

Of course, Melchizedek is greater than the patriarch of the people of faith, for the greater receives tribute from the lesser (7:4, 7). Since all high priests trace their succession from Levi, Abraham's descendant, in no way can the priesthood of Melchizedek be construed to derive from the Levitical line. Furthermore, because Melchizedek receives the tithe from Abraham, he receives it from the promised seed of Abraham as well, and this includes Levi (vv.9–10). Thus, the author argues that a priestly succession functions above and apart from the Levitical succession.

The law was given to the people to delineate the way of perfection. It provided bounds for proper relationship to God and the enjoyment of his blessings. Every Jew understood this, from the clergy in exile at Qumran to the housewives across the land who prepared for the Day of Atonement by removing every last vestige of leaven from the home. The author does not argue the point but merely presents it as a fact understood by all with no need of support (7:11). He argues that perfection could not be maintained (not **attained,** as in the NIV) through the offices of the Levitical priesthood. God in his grace provided perfection through covenant relationship. Obedience to the law and the prescribed sacrifices were the means for its maintenance. Why then did God send another priest in the succession of Melchizedek? The only possible conclusion is that it was necessary because the Aaronic priesthood and the covenant of Moses were powerless to change disobedient humanity. The law prescribed holiness (see Lev 19:2); it did not produce it (7:19). The Aaronic sacrificial system temporarily filled the gap, but a better expedient was needed, one which would fulfill the law's demand rather than abide human failings. That expedient would change both the law's priestly provisions (vv.12, 18) and the human capacity to meet its demands.

Under Mosaic Law Jesus had no claim to priestly office (7:13–14). But like Melchizedek he suddenly appeared, and he is declared to be alive (cf. v.8). He became a priest, **not on the basis of . . . ancestry but on the basis of the** power of an indestructible life (v.16). The display of God's power that raised and exalted Christ to the right hand of Majesty on high (see 1:3) can only mean that another priest like Melchizedek has entered into his appointed office. God's oracular declaration is now shown to be true: "**You are a priest forever, in the order of Melchizedek**" (7:17; Ps 110:4). The Mosaic legislation has been set aside, with it the Aaronic priesthood, because it shares humanity's weakness and inability to maintain perfection (7:18–19). Our perfection is assured only because of the **better hope** that is ours in Christ, the one High Priest who makes it possible for *us* to approach God.

In accordance with his declared purpose, God has done it all himself. He swore an oath (see Ps 110:4) that could apply to no priest in the succession of Aaron (7:20). That oath can apply only to One who comes in the succession of Melchizedek. Now it is plain why so much was made of the divine oath to Abraham in 6:13–20. Just as God could not go back on his promise to provide Abraham many descendants, so much the more he cannot go back on his oath to himself to make Jesus the eternal High Priest in the order of Melchizedek (7:21). The divine oath is what assures us that **a better covenant** is in place (v.22), one providing us the perfection God requires.

The new covenant is better because of the better High Priest. All Aaronic priests saw limited tenure (7:23); Christ's priesthood and intercession on our behalf are unending. They offered atonement perpetually; Jesus offered atonement in perpetuity. They served in human weakness; Jesus serves in God's absolute power. Jesus saves to the uttermost (v.25). We have a better High Priest: **who is holy,** hence substantively one with God; who is **blameless,** yet intentionally one with humanity; who is **pure,** thus purifying us (cf. 2:11; 10:10); who is **set apart from sinners,** thus able to remove our sin (7:26; cf. 10:1–2). Unholy, blameworthy, defiled by sin, we have no hope of bettering ourselves to the point of being acceptable to a holy God. Even the Aaronic high priest offered sacrifices on the Day of Atonement for his own sins as well as those of the people (7:27). Sinless himself, Jesus' self-offering was entirely for the sins of others, all-embracing and perfect; thus no subsequent sacrifice is required.

Like every human being, every high priest is beset with weakness (7:28; cf. 4:15; 5:2). In comparison with divine standards, all flesh and blood is weak and dependent. Not inbred depravity, it simply is not possible to live divinely within human capacity. We share Adam's original weakness, not as a consequence of the Fall but as a condition of creatureliness. Weakness is the inability to maintain perfection without divine assistance. The Aaronic priesthood offered no remedy for this.

The Mosaic covenant, in appointing men to the office of high priest, made no adequate provision for their weaknesses. The divine oath subsequently uttered through the psalmist has appointed to this office the Son, who has been perfected forever (7:28). Christ shared our weaknesses (see 2:14, 17; 4:15; 5:7), but through the oath of God, divine power sustained him in living out his divine appointment. No one else could accomplish precisely what Jesus did on our behalf. His calling was unique as the Pioneer (cf. 2:10; 6:20; 10:20) and Perfecter (cf. 5:7–9; 10:14; 12:2) of humanity in faith. Now Jesus has entered into his office as High Priest forever, having been perfected in the sense that God has brought him to his divine destiny without his once becoming entangled in sin and without his leaving any aspect of his divinely appointed work unfinished. The proof for human observance is to be found in his resurrection and exaltation in accordance with Pss 8 and 110.

V. FOURTH POINT: "A NEW COVENANT" (8:1–10:31)

The high priesthood of Jesus is founded upon a new and better covenant. What greater priest could there be than One who took his seat next to the throne of Majesty, appointed minister of **the true,** heavenly **tabernacle** that he himself has pitched (8:2)? If God has done this, who would dare attend the services of any lesser functionary?

The author understands the earthly tabernacle (even the Jerusalem temple present in his own day) to be **a copy** foreshadowing the real, heavenly sanctuary (8:5). Citing Ex 25:40 as proof, he states that God showed Moses **the pattern** by which **to build the tabernacle.** Therefore, **the true tabernacle,** which Jesus would later build (see 3:3), was already in God's mind from the beginning. That is why the author says Moses' tabernacle foreshadowed Christ's heavenly one.

The function of the priest was to serve his divine appointment by offering the **gifts and sacrifices** mandated by the law. Jesus, as God's High Priest, also had to offer something (8:3), but it had to be offered outside the existing sacrificial framework since others were already appointed to that task. Thus, **a new covenant** was required upon which his sacrifice could be based.

The **better promises** contained in the new covenant provide Jesus with a ministry superior to the Levitical priesthood (8:6). The former covenant under Moses proved inadequate due to the weakness of the people (vv.7–8; cf.

5:2; 7:18, 28). God had more in mind even from the beginning, and through the prophet Jeremiah he presented better promises. The new covenant would deal with the problem of human weakness and inconstancy. To overcome the problem of faithlessness, God promised to put his laws directly into the human mind and write them upon the heart (v.10) so that consent to the divine will would spring readily from within the human soul. To overcome the problem of human waywardness, God promised not merely to take his people by the hand and lead them (as formerly), but to make himself known to them in the most intimate way possible—inwardly (v.11). To overcome the problem of human sin, God promised to forgive and remember their sin no more, removing it once for all (v.12). These are the better promises which make the new covenant superior to the old one. In announcing a new covenant, God has made the former one obsolete. Therefore, the covenant of Moses is outworn and aged, soon to disappear (v.13).

The earthly sanctuary and its offices are described next, providing the proper background (9:1–5). The details are mentioned in the past tense because the author is describing the tabernacle as it is depicted in the biblical record. The NIV does not reflect it, but the author switches to the present tense in describing the current, ongoing priestly offices (vv.6–10). The point here must not be lost: though the tabernacle is depicted in ancient biblical terms, the author clearly has in mind the current temple system and its ongoing activities as the evolutionary culmination of the biblical model. He is making the distinct point that, though the temple has every appearance of being the most modern and up-to-date of religious institutions, it is in fact exceedingly old-fashioned and time-worn. The ongoing priestly ministrations are as obsolete as the ancient tabernacle itself. Whether made of great carved stones or sewn canvas and poles, the earthly tabernacle is a thing of the past.

The Aaronic high priest entered the Holy of Holies each year on the Day of Atonement and sprinkled the room with the blood of sacrifices. Access to God's presence was thus limited to one individual on only one day of the year for one brief moment (9:7). The obvious conclusion is that so long as the present temple stood, the people had no access to God. The way to the Father remained unrevealed (v.8). The perpetual offering of **gifts and sacrifices** signified a people perpetually caught in sin, whose hearts and minds and consciences remained weak and imperfect. Temple sacrifices could not perfect the worshiper inwardly (v.9). The covenant of Moses focused on outward observances, says the author, on matters of proscribed **food and drink** (see Lev 11) and prescribed baths (see Lev 16:20–28). Only the imposition of religious reforms could remedy this, and the time was long overdue (9:10). Who then would wish to entrust one's soul again to such antiquated means?

Christ has entered the heavenly Holy of Holies once for all, securing eternal redemption! He is High Priest of the good things already in place for everyone wishing to approach God (9:11). He came before God **through the greater and more perfect tabernacle that is not man-made,** and this was in keeping with his prophecy, as restated by false witnesses in Mark 14:58 and recorded in John 2:19–21. Jesus built the more perfect tabernacle himself by virtue of what he accomplished in his death and resurrection, by virtue not of the blood of animals but **his own blood** (9:11–12). What the earthly tabernacle foreshadowed has become the heavenly reality! Jesus embraced us all through what he suffered, and by clinging in faith to him we are become the very house of God in which his presence abides (see 3:6).

The intent of religion is to **serve the living God** (9:14). Purity is demanded of one who would do so. God had commanded the people, "Consecrate yourselves and be holy, because I am the Lord your God. Keep my decrees and follow them. I am the Lord, who makes you holy" (Lev 20:7–8). The Levitical code is full of regulations regarding the clean and the unclean, defilement and purification, ceremonial purity and impurity. **The blood of goats and bulls** slain as sin-offerings was efficacious in God's sight for the removal of sin's offense (see Lev 4). **The ashes of** the red **heifer** when mixed with water (see Nu 19) also removed sin's offense and restored ceremonial purity. To be thus sanctified was to be purified and restored to proper fellowship with God and his holy people (9:13). Yet, sin is more than ceremonial uncleanness and even more than moral defilement. The rites and regulations provided only temporary benefit; the problem would return again and require yet another sin-offering so long as the inward weakness of the worshiper remained unaddressed. But Christ's self-offering is perfect, not as an unblemished animal substituting for sinful humanity but as unblemished humanity for sinful humanity. Once and for all, the blood of Jesus is applied to our need. Concern for the ceremonial purity of the body has given way to the purification of the conscience or inner being. Covenant-keeping rites and regulations that required repeated slaying and that could not bring the worshiper out of repeated sin have given way to edifying and glorifying ministry in service to **the living God** (v.14). All this has been accomplished **through the eternal Spirit** of God at work, both in Jesus during his days on earth and now in us who believe.

Christ, then, in keeping with his words at the Last Supper (see Mk 14:22–25) has instituted **a new covenant.** He alone could mediate the covenant for two reasons: He came appointed as God's heir and spokesman (see 1:2), and he served obediently as man embracing all humankind (see 2:11–17), thus representing both parties of the covenant in his own person. His death has brought about our redemption (9:15). By his own unmerited death, he has overcome Satan, who wields the power of death (see 2:14) and who exercised that power wrongly in this case, taking the life of the world's only innocent man. For death can rightly claim only those who have sinned against God. In overcoming death and thus nullifying Satan's power, Christ effectively emancipated a powerless humanity enslaved to sin and subject to death (see 2:15). We are now free to follow God's call (see 3:1) and receive the **eternal inheritance** he has promised to everyone in Christ, the **Sabbath rest** awaiting the people of God (see 4:1, 9).

The author now provides an explanation for the necessity of Jesus' death. *Diathēkē* in the Greek can mean "covenant," "testament," or "will." A last will and testament becomes operative only at death. Likewise, the divine covenant required a death in order to become operative. **In the case of a will,** the person who made it must die for it to take effect. In the case of the covenant of Moses, provision was made for death to claim a substitute instead. The author describes the ritual of atonement

based on Ex 24:3–8, but its details here in 9:19–22 probably are derived from his knowledge of contemporary temple practice. The point is that Jesus brought a new will and final testament, and its provisions could not become operative until his own death as testator had occurred.

The earthly sanctuary must be cleansed of sin by the sprinkling of blood. The penalty of sin is death, and a death is required for the sin to be covered. But must the heavenly sanctuary also be cleansed? Yes, claims the author (9:23). Why? For the very reason that Christ has taken upon himself our sin and has entered the heavenly sanctuary (v.24). Without the covering blood, it too would be defiled. Because it is heaven's own sanctuary, the blood of earth's bulls and goats will not suffice. The better sacrifice can be only the blood of heaven's Firstborn who is also earth's last Adam. He has entered heaven's sanctuary to stand for us and plead our cause (see 7:25). Through Jesus alone may we approach God.

His sacrifice is the better one because it is efficacious once for all time and for all humankind. The Aaronic high priest offered the atoning blood every year for the Jews alone, but Jesus appeared in the fullness of time to nullify sin forever (9:26). How so? God himself promised through Jeremiah, **"I will forgive their wickedness and will remember their sins no more"** (Heb. 8:12; cf. Jer 31:31–34). The author follows in conclusion, **"And where these have been forgiven, there is no longer any sacrifice for sin"** (10:18). Death remains with us, and judgment still follows death, but the burden of our sin has already been borne by Jesus (9:27–28). All that remains now is for our Lord to return and manifest to us the benefits he has already won on our behalf. Let those who belong to Christ eagerly await him, and let those who do not yet belong to Christ earnestly seek him.

Contrary to Jewish belief, the law of Moses is not the full and final revelation of God's will. It is merely provisional, since it cannot bring humanity beyond the perpetuated requirement of atoning sacrifices for sin (10:1). It simply foreshadows **the good things that are coming.** The ambiguity of the Greek here allows two renderings: "The good things which were to come," or "the good things which are to come." On the basis of what was just stated by the author at the end of ch. 9 regarding the return of our Lord, the NIV has opted for the futuristic rendering, **the good things that are coming.** But to which good things is the author referring? He is referring to the things that constitute the perfection of those who would approach God (10:1). If perfection is understood as an endowment of the next life, then the NIV translation is appropriate. But the author clearly states, **"He has made perfect forever those who are being made holy"** (10:14; cf. v.10). It is already accomplished! Clearly, as the NIV rightly states elsewhere, Christ is **high priest of the good things that are already here** (9:11). We already enjoy perfection by virtue of our High Priest who has nullified our sin (cf. 9:26). And he is even now making us holy (see 2:11; 10:10, 14). For, in fact, sanctification is progressive; so too is glorification (cf. 2Co 3:18). So too, then, is perfection.

If it were at all possible for the law to have brought perfection, at some point the sacrifices for sin should have ceased (10:2). The blood of animals cannot abolish human sin; it can serve only as a reminder of sin's penalty (vv.3–4). By God's design, the law was never intended as the means of perfecting weak humanity. In its limited function, though, it did foreshadow the perfect sacrifice to come.

Christ came into the world to take away sins (cf. Jn 1:29). Christ came to put an end to the sacrifices; God took no delight in them anyway. The proof is found in God's own Word spoken in the Son: Ps 40 (LXX) quoted as though from the mouth of Jesus himself (10:5–7). To the author's mind, the Scriptures are not only the oracles of God but can also be the very words of Christ or of the Holy Spirit (see 3:7). The law may prescribe sacrifices for sin, but God is not thereby pleased in accepting them (10:8). Most pleasing to God is the One who says, **"Here I am, I have come to do your will"** (v.9). Christ came to do God's will. Christ came to set aside the former covenant by establishing a new one. Christ came to make us holy, and we are now sanctified through his complete offering of himself in the will of God (v.10; cf. 2:11). Christ came into the world to bring about the perfection of humanity in accordance with the destiny already ordained by God in Ps 8 (see 2:6–11).

The author's understanding of holiness is instructive. The Pioneer of our salvation makes us holy by bringing us to God's glory (see 2:10–11). To enter the Holy of Holies (10:19), to stand before the Holy One, is to be made holy. Holiness is the gift and garb of approach to God, an endowment bestowed in blessed relationship. Perfection is exactly the same thing (v.14). So too is salvation or glorification (2:10). These terms all describe, from different theological perspectives, the one outcome of Jesus' sacrifice as it pertains to us: Access to the Father in intimate relationship. As such, it affords opportunity for the dynamics of growth and depth in bonding. Holiness, perfection, and glorification are not plateaus of attainment but dynamics of limitless life enjoyed in boundless exploration.

In one act of sacrifice we have been perfected (10:14). Yet God continues his sanctifying work in us. Growth in holiness knows no bounds. Perfection is not an endowment of the next life; it is an already completed work now begun in us. Growth in perfection likewise knows no bounds, because it is a relationship rather than a state of being. God's design for humanity, God's plan for our perfection, is to bring many to glory (see 2:9–10), God's glory. It is to enter into the Sabbath-rest (see 4:9–10), God's own Sabbath-rest. It is to have access to God's own throne, access the law could never provide (see 7:18–19). It is absolute and uttermost salvation (see 7:25). It is to have even now the good things God promised through the prophets (see 8:10–12; cf. 9:11). Perfection, through the blood of Christ, is power applied to our sanctification, applied to our weakness, applied to cleanse and purify our inward souls and enable us truly to serve God in pleasing ways (see 9:14–15). Perfection is so to have God's law in our hearts and minds that his will is our will (10:14–17). Perfection is the living of this life in such union with Christ that we are borne along to God's own perfectness by God's own hand (see 6: 1, 3). These things are already ours, and yet they continue to be worked out in our lives in ever greater fashion. Perfection in this epistle, then, is at once both being and becoming.

The author makes three bold statements in this chapter that lead him to a grand conclusion. First, by the will of God **we have been made holy** (10:10). Second, **by one sacrifice he has perfected** eternally those **being made holy** (v.14). Third, **there is no longer any**

sacrifice for sin to be made where forgiveness has already been applied (v.18). His conclusion is that **the blood of Jesus** gives us the **confidence** we need **to enter** boldly into **the Most Holy Place** and to stand before our God (v.19). That is true perfection, our destiny in Christ.

Wesleyan theology as articulated by some within the so-called "holiness tradition" depicts the Christian life in the following manner. It is entered at the moment of conversion with justification and regeneration occurring concomitantly. Thereupon the believer enters into a process of sanctification or purification. At some subsequent point the process yields to a momentary experience of entire sanctification at which time both "the guilt and power of sin," as Wesley put it, are eradicated and the Holy Spirit comes to dwell within in fullness. This "second blessing" is the rest of faith, perfection in love. Unhappy with any notion of perfection that involves an incomplete process, Wiley (p. 325) interprets **"those who are being made holy"** (10:14) iteratively, i.e., the one definite act of entire sanctification repeating itself from individual to individual over time.

The author of Hebrews looks at it differently. Perfection provides full access to God (10:1, 19–22). Nothing is left incomplete; no sacrifice for sins remains (9:26; 10:18). Christ has accomplished everything necessary for us to draw near to God (cf. 4:3; 7:19; 10:22). To be brought near to God is to be brought into the sphere of divine holiness (see 2:10–11). The nearer one approaches to God, the more holy one becomes. Contrary to the view of many that the process of sanctification leads to eventual perfection, the author of Hebrews regards perfection as the initial introduction of the Christian to the divine presence, whereupon holiness is obtained. Perfection initiates sanctification. Salvation and perfection are one and the same, and the process of sanctification proceeds therefrom. The author finds support for this in the testimony of the Holy Spirit (10:15–17). The forgiveness of sins, ostensibly integral to justification, is equated with the eradication of atoning sacrifices, i.e., perfection (10:18; cf. v.14). Proceeding therefrom is the dynamic internalization of the divine will, i.e., sanctification (10:16; cf. v.14). What some call the "second blessing" is in fact the one dynamic blessing which initiates and perpetuates one's eternal life with God.

A totally new situation obtains for those who would approach God (10:19). **Today** (see 3:12–14) **we have confidence to enter the Most Holy Place** and approach the very throne of grace (cf. 4:16). In direct contrast to the situation depicted in 9:25 wherein one approaches on behalf of many, now the many may approach. The way of entrance is a fresh and **living way** (10:20) providing immediacy of access. A new covenant has been inaugurated; a new sanctuary has been dedicated. The way to the presence of God is the ever-living Christ (cf. Jn 14:6). The curtain, or veil, divided the Holy Place from the Most Holy Place, preventing access to the mercy seat of God (see 9:2–5). The curtain is now no longer a barrier; the entrance is ever open, and the High Priest is ever interceding there, and we are welcome now that we too have been perfected (see v.14).

Christ's very physicality is the curtain rent asunder. Human inability to abide by divine standards proved a problem the law was able to handle only remedially, not overcome entirely. As the curtain hung between the Holy Place

where men served and the Most Holy Place where God dwelt, so on the cross heaven's Firstborn hung between humankind and God. When Christ died, the curtain in the temple was torn in two from top to bottom (see Mk 15:38). The way to God was unveiled; the problem of human inability was overcome.

Christ is our great High Priest (10:21). We are the perfected and sanctified **house of God** (see 3:6). That means we are able now to approach the mercy seat with true and sincere hearts, without even a shadow of falsity or duplicity (v.22). It means an inward work of God cleansing us by the blood of Christ sprinkled on the altar of our hearts, thereby removing our guilt and washing away our defilement so that we are fit to enter his presence. Every priest had to bathe before entering the Most Holy Place (see Lev 16:3–4); in our case, this cleansing work of God takes place in the waters of baptism administered at the time of our own entrance into the household of God. We cannot draw near to God if any unseemliness remains as a barrier. At the same time, our High Priest stands ready to remove all such hindrances so that we may indeed gain access. Faith is fully assured of this, giving the heart confidence to draw near (v.19).

God is faithful to his promise, and therein lies our hope (10:23; cf. 6:13–20). To waver in our confession that Jesus has opened the only living way to God, to lose sight of the firm and secure hope offered us in Christ, is to find ourselves outside the curtain again looking for some other way in. Apparently some of the original recipients of this letter were in just such a predicament, even to the point of giving up meeting together (10:25). The true worshiper of God, however, is mindful of every inducement to love and do good to others, providing encouragement and support as required. Christ is faithful, and the same faithfulness and commitment mark those who await his promised return.

The greatest danger of all is to lose one's grip on Christ and to seek an alternative way through the curtain to God. The deadly sin, for which **no sacrifice for sins is left,** is apostasy, here the return to the former covenant after having gained the full truth of Christ's more perfect sacrifice (10:26; cf. 6:4–6). The author equates sin with unbelief (3:12) and the refusal to obey God's voice (3:16; 12:25). When some discover that obedience to Christ brings unexpected adversity, they return to a prior understanding they had with God, an easier pact involving less hardship and difficulty. Unfortunately, God cannot honor it any longer. The new covenant is in place now, and no alternative compact can carry any weight. No other sacrifice for sins remains. Outside of the offer of God's new covenant, the only prospect left is the fire intended for his enemies, namely, those who reject his plan and provision in seeking their own terms of access (10:27).

Even the former covenant had its severe provisions. In the case of an imperfect animal offered for sacrifice or the worship of false gods, Dt 17:1–6 calls for death by stoning of the perpetrator on the evidence of two witnesses. Either of these actions constitutes an affront to the grace of God in flagrant disregard of his covenant (10:28). How much greater the effrontery of one who, after accepting the benefits of Christ's perfect sacrifice, subsequently rejects his lordship! Whether by denial of his name outright or by refusal to hear him speaking from heaven, one tramples Christ underfoot and profanes the very blood that graciously binds us

to God (v.29). Certainly, the Spirit of God cannot remain upon one who would ignore and reject so great a love. Willfully and persistently turning from what we clearly know to be the Spirit's leading and God's will in Christ, we place ourselves once again beyond the curtain. Unless we turn back and reenter through the way opened for us by our High Priest, we remain outside his benefits and liable to destruction. God will have the last word, and it has already been spoken (see 1:2)!

VI. FIFTH POINT: "BY FAITH" (10:32–12:2)

When the original recipients of this epistle received Christ, they came into persecution (10:32–33). Some were even imprisoned (v.34). They endured these sufferings joyfully because they recognized the far greater inheritance that was reserved for them in heaven (cf. 6:12; 9:15; see also Jesus' teaching in Lk 6:22–23). The character of the present threat must have been more ominous to bring them to contemplate rejecting for themselves the benefits of Christ's passion.

The former persecution arose in earlier days when they **had received the light** of Christ (10:32). The Jewish persecution of Christian converts became a widespread problem (see Ac 17:5–7). However, the persecution that fell upon the recipients of this epistle at the time of their conversion was milder, since 12:4 says that they had not yet shed their blood. The Roman historian Suetonius (*Claudius* 25) mentions that in A.D. 49 riots overtook the Jewish quarter in Rome "at the instigation of Chrestus" and that Emperor Claudius expelled them all from the city (cf. Ac 18:2). This could be the incident the author recalls in mentioning **those earlier days,** especially if the clue in 13:24 means the letter was sent to Italy.

Now, however, the threat was more terrifying. The possibility existed that blood would be shed. This was enough, apparently, for some to question Christ's actual teaching (see 6:1) and for others to fall away (see 6:6) and no longer meet with other Christians (see 10:25). The author clearly regards this as falling away from Christ himself.

Only those who lack faith would **throw away** their **confidence** (10:35) and be destroyed. Sustained by the light of truth in the hour of trial, faith calls for courage and carries a rich reward. Receiving what God has promised is contingent upon doing his will, and to do that one must persevere in the doing until all is done (10:36; cf. 3:13–14). Christ is soon to come, and he shall bring the reward he has promised (10:37; cf. 4:1–11; 9:15).

Here again at the head of this section a primary text is quoted, Hab 2:3–4 as found in the LXX; it is the foundation for all that follows in ch. 11. The author does an interesting thing, though. He places a definite article before *erchomenos,* and the Greek participle, which normally would be translated *coming,* must now be understood as "the coming One." The LXX itself long before had already adopted the messianic sense the author is clarifying, and common Jewish understanding in his day interpreted the verse the same way. The novelty in the author's use of the passage is in understanding it with reference to the Second Coming. With Christ's return so imminent, now is not the time to forsake him and forfeit the reward he is bringing.

The day of Christ's coming will bring the reward of life to the righteous who have kept faith (10:38). Faith alone will stand on the day of salvation; the faithless will not be rewarded with life

(v.39). Even now, to **shrink back** from the confession of Christ is to court destruction.

Faith embraces the reality of one's hope in God. Faith embraces with conviction things not yet seen on earth, for faith even now sees Jesus as having tasted death for all by the grace of God (11:1). Faith sees him seated at the right hand of Majesty in heaven, crowned now with glory and honor (cf. 1:3; 2:9). Hope is the certitude that one day, perhaps soon, the entire universe will be subjected to humankind in Christ, just as in Ps 8 God ordained it to be. Hope is the certitude that we shall be brought to glory and the enjoyment of God's own Sabbath-rest (cf. 2:10; 4:9). The promise of God on oath guarantees the reality of our hope (see 6:17–19).

The starting point of faith is God and his all-powerful Word (11:3). The universe is not an accident of chance. Faith knows it was spoken into being from nothingness. Faith knows it remains only by the Word of his power (see 1:3). Faith knows the Word of God is alive and energetic (see 4:12) and accomplishes everything it purposes. Faith knows the powers of the coming age have been brought by the goodness of God's own Word to us (see 6:5). Faith hears God speaking; faith responds to God's call (see 12:25).

Time and again, the heroes of faith in former days looked forward and embraced God's promises from afar (11:13). Abel is the first example of faith; God accepted his offering (11:4; cf. Ge 4:3–10). As the author later states, **Without faith it is impossible to please God** (11:6). Since Abel's offering **pleased God,** therefore Abel's faith must be exemplary. What makes him an example worthy of note is that he was killed for being righteous and having God's approval, a fate also distinctly possible for those in Rome during Nero's declining reign. After Abel's death the voice of his blood cried to God from the ground. It spoke urgently and compellingly because of Abel's righteousness (cf. 12:24). He did not shrink back but died in faith, and God vindicated him.

Enoch is an even greater hero of faith (11:5). He never experienced death at all. Enoch walked with God and **pleased God** (see Ge 5:24). Because of his faithfulness God took him. The principle to be observed here again is that **without faith it is impossible to please God** and gain life (11:6). God rewards faith, as the story of Enoch demonstrates. The one who would approach God and walk with God must grasp in faith not merely that God exists but that God is a rewarder of the faithful. Faith trusts that he comes as rewarder to those **who earnestly seek him.**

Noah exhibited faith in allowing God to instruct him about unforeseen realities (11:7; cf. 11:1). In reverent attention to God's command, he did something with absolutely no apparent rationale behind it. In building the ark in faithful submission to the command of God, he saved his family from a dire fate. In remaining faithful to God, he stood alone against the tide of wickedness engulfing the world; the floods proved him right and everyone else wrong. He thereupon joined the ranks of those whose right responses accord with their vision of the unseen and whose rewards come only thereby.

Abraham showed his faith in stepping into the unknown on God's call (11:8). He left behind all that afforded him security in life. He trusted God to provide him a better inheritance, a land to call his own (see Ge 12:1–7). The faith that inherits what God has prom-

ised must be able to proceed without specific knowledge of the ultimate outcome, trusting instead for signposts along the way. For Abraham Canaan was not the ultimate destination, but a signpost or way station where the wayfarer sojourned for a time. He ever remained a nomad tent dweller even after he arrived there, as did Isaac and Jacob; for by faith the patriarchs looked forward to the new Jerusalem of God's own building (11:10; see 12:22; cf. 3:3–4).

Abraham regarded God as faithful to his promise (11:11). This enabled him to entertain even the impossible and to trust God for it, even though he himself was virtually given over to death at the age of ninety-nine (v.12). Isaac, the child of God's promise, was born to elderly and barren Sarah (see Ge 21:2). God proved faithful and rewarded the couple who trusted his promise.

The ultimate reward for heroes of faith is the heavenly city of God. Abraham, Isaac, and Jacob sojourned in the land of promise in advance of the time when God gave it to Israel under Joshua's leadership. They did not possess it themselves. They dwelt upon it and were sustained by it, but they could only look ahead to the day when God would place it in their hands. Abraham at the end of his life confessed himself to be an alien and stranger among the Hittites in the land (see Ge 23:4). Jacob stood before Pharaoh and confessed himself to have been a sojourner for 130 years, as his father and grandfather had been throughout their lives (see Ge 47:9). The patriarchs still sought a homeland for themselves (11:14). They could have returned to the land of their ancestors, but they longed for a better homeland wherein they might dwell before the Lord (v.16). Because of their forward-looking faith, God accepted them and prepared a heavenly city to be their inheritance and their reward when Christ should open the way.

Abraham offered Isaac back to God in faith (11:17; see Ge 22:9–10). The God who promised an heir and provided one in old age could provide yet again, even if by way of raising the dead (11:19). Instead, God provided a ram caught in a thicket, and Abraham's only son was returned to him from the very altar of death. Thereupon God on oath blessed Abraham anew.

Isaac, Jacob, and Joseph also looked forward in faith. With spiritual insight, Isaac foresaw Esau's eventual emergence from the shadow of Jacob (11:20; see Ge 27:40). Jacob foresaw the preeminence of Ephraim over his older brother, Manasseh, and blessed the younger with the greater blessing (v.21; see Ge 48:19). This turnabout by divine sanction was plain to Jacob only because, as the LXX states, he worshiped God and in faith accepted the divine leading given him. Joseph foresaw the day when God would bring his people from Egypt and instructed them in advance to take his remains with them to the Promised Land (v.22; see Ge 50:24–25). These men by faith were certain of realities not yet seen in their times.

Moses, too, lived by faith. By the faith of his parents who trusted God to preserve their son, Moses lived through Pharaoh's purge of the Hebrew male children (11:23; see Ex 2:3). By the faith that he himself had gained, Moses chose to surrender all the privileges and benefits bestowed upon Pharaoh's court in favor of the privations and brutalities laid upon God's people. In Moses' case, the sin would not have been in the enjoyment of such favors as are reserved for the elite but in the denial of his proper allegiances (11:25). All the **treasures of Egypt** cannot

begin to compare with the rewards reserved for those who identify themselves with Christ and then bear the stigma attached thereto (v.26). Moses, in looking to the promised reward (cf. 10:36), was actually looking to what God would eventually accomplish through Christ. He was steadfast in faith. He left Egypt, not because he feared the wrath of Pharaoh, but because he recognized the time for confrontation had not yet come (v.27). When the time came, God spoke to Moses from a burning bush, and Moses beheld God (see Ex 3:3–6). The interesting thing about the author's comment here is that Moses' steadfastness in faith was due to his unwavering vision of the invisible God (*horōn*, present continuous participle). That unwavering vision guided him in instituting the Passover observances (v.28; see Ex 12:21–30). It guided him in opening a channel through the Red Sea and escaping the Egyptians (v.29; see Ex 14:19–29). It guided him all the way through the desert wanderings for forty years until at last it brought him to Mount Nebo, where his eyes could behold the Promised Land.

Faith is rewarded. In faithful obedience to the command of Joshua, for seven days **the people** did a thing that seemed most foolish, and the wall fell as God had promised (11:30; see Jos 6:12–21). Faith made their hope certain. In faithful recognition that the Lord of heaven and earth was giving Jericho into Israelite hands, Rahab assisted the spies (v.31; see Jos 2:9–11). Faith had made her sure of what would be. Her allegiance was rewarded (see Jos 6:21–25).

The annals of faith hold many more heroic stories. Gideon with but three hundred men routed the host of Midian (11:32; see Jdg 7:19–22). From Mount Tabor Barak led ten thousand against the chariots and army of Sisera (see Jdg 4:14–16). Samson prayed, then removed the pillars and brought the roof down on the Philistine lords (see Jdg 16:28–30). Jephthah looked to God for victory over the Ammonites (see Jdg 11:29–33). The shepherd boy David slew Goliath, the Philistine champion (see 1Sa 17:37-51). At Mizpah Samuel made offering to God as the Philistines approached, and the men of Israel overcame them at God's hand (see 1Sa 7:5–12). These conquered, rendered justice, and saw divine promises fulfilled (11:33).

In times of persecution the faithful persevered. When Daniel was thrown into the lions' den for worshiping God, the angel of the Lord shut the animals' mouths (see Da 6:22). The angel of the Lord kept Shadrach, Meshach, and Abednego safe in the midst of the fiery furnace (see Dan 3:23–28). Elijah prayed and brought the son of the widow of Zarephath back to life (11:35; see 1Ki 17:22). Elisha prayed and restored the Shunammite son to his mother (see 2Ki 4:35). The apocryphal books of the Maccabees tell of the valor of Jews in gruesome torture martyred for their faith, all the while holding to the hope of resurrection (2Mc 6–7; 4Mc 8–12). Another nonbiblical book, The Martyrdom of Isaiah, states that the prophet named in the title died a martyr's death by being sawn in half (11:37). By faith some persevered out of harm's way and others through it. Because of their unflagging devotion to God, they proved themselves of greater worthiness than this world could bear (11:38).

Their reward is an eternal inheritance (cf. 6:12; 9:15; 10:36). Yet their faith did not bring them to enter into it directly (11:39). God's provision is for the faithful of every age of human existence to enter the sanctuary through the new, living way opened by Christ, our great High Priest (11:40; cf. 10:19–22). This is the promise par excellence. This too is the key to understanding perfection in this epistle: it is bestowed corporately. It is Christ's endowment enabling all the faithful together to gain access to God forever. And it is ours even now by faith. This corporate understanding enables the author to conclude that we have already been sanctified (10:10) and perfected (v.14). Even now, with Christ as our High Priest, we have attained the destiny God had in mind for us. That said, it still remains for us to progress in faith and obedience in order to secure what we have already gained.

The challenge is ours now to do as the faithful of previous times did (12:1). The point of this whole section has been to lift up the necessity of persevering in faith especially when adversity comes. The promised reward is reserved for those who hold firm in faith through all of life's challenges (cf. 10:35–39). We are in the arena now. Watching on all sides from above are those who met the challenge before us. Whatever encumbers us and holds us back from winning the reward, whatever sin weighs upon us and causes us to drag our feet, whatever slows our progress in following Christ, must be shaken off. Like it or not, we are in a race for the ultimate prize, and the reward goes to the one who perseveres against fatigue, the elements, and hurdles placed in the way, and who carries the torch of faith to the finish line.

The race of faith begins and ends with Jesus (12:2). Jesus pioneered the way to begin with. As God's *archēgos* ("pioneer"; NIV **"author"**), he blazed the path of the perfection of faith through the sufferings of this life (cf. 2:10; 5:8). He defined the way; he set the pace. The challenge is ours now to follow and not to shrink back. Jesus perfected the way once for all. As God's *teleiōtes* (**"perfecter"**), he persevered in perfect faith, and he endured to the end without once shrinking back in sin, enduring even the cross. In faith he fixed his gaze on **the joy** of glory **set before him.** As God's *teleiōtēs,* he was brought to heaven's throne to enjoy at God's right hand the perfectness that is forever beyond the reach of corruption, and this eternal salvation he avails to all who follow and obey him (cf. 5:9). God will bring us to enjoy that divine perfectness as well (cf. 6:1), provided we do not shrink back when the test comes. From start to finish, our eyes must remain fixed on Jesus lest we get off track and lose out (cf. 10:39).

VII. SIXTH POINT: "DO NOT LOSE HEART" (12:3–13:19)

In times of trial we are reminded to consider the opposition Christ faced (12:3). Faith requires the same endurance Jesus showed in going to the cross. In adversity faith looks to him for strength. Opposition comes from the foes of God against those who heed his Word. The letter's addressees had **endured such opposition from sinful men** in their espousal of Christ. This **struggle against sin** had not yet resulted in loss of life (v.4); still they had not resisted apostasy so fully as they could and might yet be required to do. Jesus demands no more of anyone than he has endured himself. As with the cross, good comes of it when we remain steadfast in following his will.

Any child worthy of God's name must be willing to endure opposition for the sake of God's reign. Sonship (12:5) is the reward of perseverance, and it offers encouragement against losing heart in the hour of trial. The entire epistle is a "word of exhortation" (see 13:22) offering encouragement to those facing dire opposition (cf. 2:1, 18; 3:12–13; 4:1, 11, 14; 6:11–12, 18; 10:23–25, 35; 12:1, 3, 12, 15, 25; 13:7–8, 13). It is no surprise, then, that the sixth and final principal passage from Scripture is a **word of encouragement** (12:5) from God himself to his children. Pr 3:11–12 summarizes the entire thrust of the author's previous as well as subsequent admonitions, **"Do not lose heart"** (12:5). The entire epistle culminates with this call to see the hardships of the life of faith as God's loving discipline fitting us to be his children (v.7).

This passage reveals the hardships of Christian living from which none of us is free to turn aside. Struggling against sin is the same as enduring the opposition of sinful men, and enduring opposition and hardship is the same as submitting to God's disciplining love (12:7, 9). Only by submitting to God's disciplining love are we made partakers of that holiness which is God's by nature (v.10). Any Christianity that promises peace and prosperity now as rewards for faith is an aberration of our true calling. Without painful adversity disciplining us, we cannot bring forth for God the harvest fruit of true righteousness tested and verified (v.11). Only by coming through adversity and seeing it as God's discipline do we become trained to distinguish good from evil (see 5:14). Such experience provides us with genuine peace because we are all the more sure of God's will and of our own standing before him. Any turning aside for any religious posture that does not recognize adversity as a factor in God's providence cannot benefit us in the end. Fortitude and courage are required of any who would become God's children; he will provide those qualities as we remain fixed on the course of faith (12:12–13).

God's grace proves sufficient for all our needs in every situation. It enables us to pursue peace with all, even the most contrary (12:14). It furthers us in the process of holy growth (*hagiasmos*), leading ultimately to the endowment of divine holiness (*hagiotēs*; 12:10). The former is the necessary precondition to seeing the Lord, the latter the reward. Both are the benefits of ongoing grace. Those who construe this verse merely as a call to the crisis experience of entire sanctification miss the richness of the offer. To seek a dousing is to overlook the onrushing flood. God's grace comes with the power of flood water to carry us. To shrink back from our confession in the face of adverse circumstances, not momentarily but as a settled posture, is to forfeit **the grace of God** given to carry us through our trials and bring us victorious into his presence. Esau is the biblical example of a profane person who forfeited the grace and blessing of God, an attitude common to hedonic humanity even today (see Ge 25:29–34). Isaac without regret later rejected Esau's tearful plea to reverse circumstances and regain the blessing. Grace offered now cannot be called upon later to undo what its forfeiture has done in the meantime.

The grace offered now is not like the giving of the Law with its attendant terrifying spectacle (12:18; see Ex 19:16–22; 20:18–21; Dt 5:22–27). The oracle that spoke to the Israelites was the voice of God, and all who heard it were struck with fear. When God's wrath was kindled, even Moses became afraid (12:21; see Dt 9:19). And yet that was only an earthly visitation in which the overwhelming holiness of God was veiled in smoke and thunder. How much greater the import of the present moment for those who have given their allegiance to Christ! For we have come and now stand before God's *unveiled* presence in **the heavenly Jerusalem** itself. Everything the biblical heroes of faith longed to receive is already ours. Dare we forget even for a moment where we stand? Dare we forget where grace has brought us?

Our perfection consists in a rightful place among the heavenly host. Because of the sacrifice of Jesus our High Priest, we now have standing before God Almighty and his myriads of angels in full assembly. We are in the vast congregation of those whose names have been enrolled in heaven, firstborn children of God by virtue of Christ's self-identification with them and theirs with him (12:23). We have come before the one Judge whom none can avoid, who separates the just from the unjust in accordance with his own pronouncements. We have come to stand with those who have been pronounced just and have been given standing before God (i.e., perfected) because they lived and departed in the forward-looking faith that anticipated Christ's arrival (see 11:39–40). By grace we now stand before Christ who mediated on our behalf a new covenant in his own blood (12:24), blood that ever speaks more insistently for mercy than Abel's blood did for vindication (see Ge 4:10). Dare we forget where that blood has brought us?

Dare we disregard the Spirit's voice, which now speaks so insistently and so plainly (12:25)? Dare we turn away from Christ merely because allegiance to him might cost us dearly? Is not his blood more dear than life itself? Is not eternal standing before God more desirous than temporary avoidance of the persecutor's fire? Disregard of the Law brought unavoidable judgment upon the Israelites in their wilderness sojourn. What more severe judgment, then, will disregard of the Gospel bring to those who have the benefit of the Spirit's inward counsel? The voice that imparted the Law shook all the earth, but the voice that imparts grace and mercy now will soon shake both heaven and earth like a sieve (12:26; see Hag 2:6). The entire universe will shudder at the call to judgment on that final day. Only by heeding the voice of him now speaking can we stand the sifting judgment of God that will remove the entire created order (v.27). In its place, we are being given an eternal and therefore unshakable kingdom in which to abide in his presence forever (v.28). To receive it, we dare not disregard Christ. Rather, the proper attitude is gratefulness for the opportunity now given us through our High Priest to **worship God acceptably.** Nor should this opportunity be taken for granted or exercised half-heartedly, for God is ever the God who shook the mountain in thunder and smoke, lightning and quake. **Reverence and awe** are due him. In the white-hot purity of his holiness every lesser thing shall be consumed as dross is devoured by fire, whether it be spiritless worship or listless service or staunchless faith. Dare we flee his refining grace?

This life is for us a time of training and growth through testing. The Lord is disciplining those he loves. And discipline calls for certain behavior: unceasing love, hospitality, supportive outreach, fidelity in marriage, simplicity of life-style, and deference to those in leadership (13:1–7). Elders in faith have demonstrated their increasing maturity throughout their lives and are to be emulated. The important criterion here is not chronological maturity but spiritual maturity gained by way of long experience in ascertaining the will of God in the welter of human existence. One who has attained that deserves to be heard, for that one knows

and trusts the manifold workings of God's grace.

Jesus is ever true to his Word (13:8). What he spoke on earth, he affirms in heaven. Teaching that has a novel twist or strange application must be verified against the message brought by Christ (v.9). Some would dilute or modify his spoken Word to fit their own schemes. This adulteration of the Gospel can carry the feeble away. The Word is a message of grace; without that the Gospel is weakened. Our hearts are to be sustained by divine ministrations of grace, not restrictions on foods and their preparation. Returning to the covenantal confines of the Jewish law removes one from the operative sphere of God's grace in Christ Jesus (cf. 9:10).

Only those who belong to him may partake of the priestly fare on the altar that Christ has made ready for them. He is our sacrifice; the benefits of his passion grant us eternal access to the throne of grace (13:10). In the ongoing temple ritual, when the yearly sacrifice of a bullock and goat for the sins of the priest and the people was carried out, the victims' bodies were to be burned **outside the camp** (v.11; see Ex 29:14; Lev 16:27). From the author's perspective, this was still current practice; the temple was yet in operation. What we are to note is that Christ, likewise offered in sacrifice, suffered death and was buried **outside the city gate** (v.12). In so doing, his blood has sanctified the people in perpetuity (cf. 10:10). Those who claim the benefits of his passion must go **outside the [Jewish covenantal] camp** to join his company, fully prepared themselves to bear the same disgrace now as was borne by Christ at the hands of sinners then (v.13; cf. 11:25–26; 12:3). To enjoy the good things provided at Christ's altar, to find **the city that is to** come, we must embrace the stigma attached to his name (v.14).

In closing his final exhortation, the author outlines again what faithful people do. They continue to confess Christ's name; they do not lose heart. The sacrifice acceptable to God now is praise for the grace offered through Jesus our High Priest and the public confession of allegiance to him, which is sure to bring reproach (v.15). Having stood by his name, one must not bring reproach upon him through neglecting the opportunity to assist others sacrificially (v.16). Nor may one disregard the leaders he has placed in positions of responsibility and pastoral care; the best course is one of prayerful support of them in their endeavors to do well for God (vv.17–18).

VIII. CLOSING: "THE GOD OF PEACE" (13:20–25)

The full tale of life's keeping can be summed up in one word: God! Throughout all of life, both this and the next, God has moved toward us in his grace to lift us up and bear us home. He lifted Christ, our great Shepherd, from death and bore him to the heights of glory. By the blood of Christ, efficacious in perpetuity, God has lifted us from death and borne us home as well. In his covenant love we have true and lasting peace, the peace God enjoys and bestows on those who love him. It comes to us in the midst of our struggles and our pain. It sustains us in the onslaught of evil brought against those who confess Jesus' name. In the end, all of life must be seen through the operation of God's grace. Whatever goodness comes to us, rests upon us, and finds expression through us is God's doing. God makes us perfectly fit with every good endowment necessary for the doing of his will (v.21). As we submit to him, God accomplishes in and through us that which he pleases to do for his name's sake and for the glory of Christ. No higher calling is available than to be the instrument of his good purpose. Faith is yielded to that purpose, and perfection is merely its outworking in the grace and power of God.

This entire letter was meant to be admonitory and encouraging, a sermonic discourse (v.22) delivered to Christians facing adversity. It came at a time when Christian leaders were being imprisoned; Timothy, apparently recently released (v.23), is the individual known to us in the circle of Paul's friends. The note of urgency in the epistle reflects the situation facing those to whom it was sent. This personal postscript (vv.22–25) was added as the letter was dispatched.

Regardless of the circumstances in which Christians, ancient or modern, have found themselves, God's grace is present and more than sufficient for the need. The faithful of every age will find that grace and persevere.

BIBLIOGRAPHY

Barrett, C.K. "The Eschatology of the Epistle to the Hebrews." In *The Background of the New Testament and Its Eschatology*. Edited by W.D. Davies and D. Daube. Cambridge: University Press, 1956.

Bruce, F.F. "'To the Hebrews' or 'To the Essenes'?" *New Testament Studies,* 9 (1962–63): 217–32.

Caird, G.B. "The Exegetical Method of the Epistle to the Hebrews," *Canadian Journal of Theology* 5 (1959): 44–51.

Hurst, Lincoln D. "Eschatology and 'Platonism' in the Epistle to the Hebrews." *Society of Biblical Literature 1984 Seminar Papers*. Edited by Kent Harold Richards. Chico, Calif.: Scholars Press, 1984.

_____. *The Epistle to the Hebrews: Its Background of Thought*. Cambridge: Cambridge Univ. Press, 1990.

Lane, William L. *Hebrews: A Call to Commitment*. Peabody, Mass.: Hendrickson, 1985.

McCullough, J.C. "Some Recent Developments in Research on the Epistle to the Hebrews," *Irish Biblical Studies* 2 (1980): 141–65.

_____. "Some Recent Developments in Research on the Epistle to the Hebrews, Part 2," *Irish Biblical Studies* 3 (1981): 28–45.

Manson, William. *The Epistle to the Hebrews*. London: Hodder & Stoughton, 1951.

Peterson, David. *Hebrews and Perfection*. Cambridge: Cambridge University Press, 1982.

Wesley, John. *Explanatory Notes Upon the New Testament*. Salem, Ohio: Schmul, reprint (1754).

Westcott, Brooke Foss. *The Epistle to the Hebrews*. London: Macmillan, 1903.

Wiley, H. Orton. *The Epistle to the Hebrews*. Kansas City: Beacon Hill Press, 1959.

Williamson, Ronald. *Philo and the Epistle to the Hebrews*. Leiden: Brill, 1970.

_____. "The Background of the Epistle to the Hebrews," *Expository Times* 87 (1976): 232–36.

_____. "Platonism and Hebrews," *Scottish Journal of Theology* 16 (1963): 415–24.

JAMES

James D. Yoder

INTRODUCTION

I. CHARACTER

James is unique as a NT epistle. It is a book of admonitions. Proverbial sayings are intermingled with prescriptions of conduct, strongly reminiscent of Proverbs. It represents the Wisdom Literature in NT form.

Although introduced as a letter, no features of a letter are evident elsewhere. M. Dibelius identifies its literary genre as paraenesis. "By this," he explains, "we mean a text which strings together admonitions of general ethical content." He compares James with the admonitory sections of Paul's letters and characterizes both as "sayings and groups of sayings very diverse in content, lacking any particular order, and containing no emphasis upon a special thought of pressing importance for a particular situation" (p. 3).

For this reason, Dibelius and others have discouraged attempts at outlining the epistle. It is apparent, indeed, that certain subjects surface repeatedly. Nevertheless, R. V. G. Tasker affirms a description of the epistle that he heard in school chapel in his early years: "The Epistle of James is a collection of sermon notes" (TNTC, 9). The propriety of this characterization is demonstrated in the outline below.

II. AUDIENCE

To address the readers as "the twelve tribes scattered among the nations" immediately identifies them as people for whom the OT has meaning. Scholars are agreed that the epistle exhibits a Jewish milieu. Probably the accustomed meeting place for the readers was the synagogue. (The NIV leaves this matter open by translating the Greek word *synagōgē* as "meeting" in 2:2.)

Most striking about the epistle, furthermore, is the want of distinctively Christian features. "Except for two or three references to Christ, it would fit rather well in the OT. The life to which the epistle exhorts is that of a profoundly pious Jew who is fulfilling the law in every regard. Gospel, redemption, incarnation and resurrection are not mentioned" (Dayton, ZPEB, 3:396). By the same token, large segments of OT Wisdom literature lack evidence of Israelite tradition.

III. AUTHOR

The author, whether out of modesty or simplicity, qualifies his name in the most general of terms: "a servant of God and of the Lord Jesus Christ" (1:1). Since the letter is not addressed to a particular locality, it is impossible to declare categorically which James of the primitive church is the author. Indeed, the testimony of the church fathers reflects this uncertainty. Not until the third century was this epistle mentioned with other NT books and then with qualifications. Accordingly, over the years assignment of authorship has been made to James the son of Zebedee, James the brother of Jesus, and to an unknown writer who "wrote in the name of James of Jerusalem, now a revered figure of a relatively remote past, in whose spirit he intended to speak" (Barnett, 795).

The following summary statement of Tasker represents the conservative position on authorship:

> The homiletic character of the work, its Jewish-Christian flavor, its echoes of the later Wisdom literature of Judaism . . . and of the sayings of Jesus which became embodied in the Sermon on the Mount, . . . and the note of authority with which the author speaks, are all consonant with the tradition that he was the first bishop of the Jerusalem church who presided at the conference described in Acts 15. Moreover, its Hebraic features, coupled with the frequent use of rhetorical questions, vivid similes, imaginary dialogues, telling aphorisms, and picturesque illustrations, make it not unreasonable to suppose that we are listening to the bilingual Palestinian Christian . . . who by virtue of his commanding position was brought into contact with Jews and Christians from all parts of the world (NBD, 597).

Strong exception has been taken to this position on the basis of the stylistic elegance of the epistle. Is it reasonable to expect a Galilean fisherman to write Greek, moreover a literary Greek? J. N. Sevenster has effectively demonstrated that Greek was the vernacular language in Galilee in the first century. He mentions a Greek inscription ordered by Antiochus III (200 B.C.) that was found near the Sea of Galilee south of Tiberius, issuing the directive to duplicate the orders inscribed thereon in other villages. Sevenster reasons, "Apparently it was taken for granted that all who lived there, including the Jews, could read them" (p. 109).

IV. DATE

Assuming the author was James, the brother of Jesus, the epistle cannot be dated later than A.D. 62, the year of his martyrdom. As a brother of Jesus, James experienced exposure to him to a far greater degree than any person outside the home of Mary and Joseph. We may reasonably assume that Jesus shared his understanding of Scripture with other members of the family in years prior to his public ministry. As he ordered his life in keeping with his sense of God as Father, he explained to them the guiding principles of his life. These insights were brought to maturity as he embarked on his teaching ministry. In reality, Jesus' family, James included, were his first listeners for more than a decade.

A fair number of the sayings of Jesus, notably those included in the Sermon on the Mount, are echoed in this epistle. "The parallels between the ethical precepts of the Epistle and the dominical sayings," observes Tasker, "are not so close as to suggest direct quotation from any document. Rather does it seem that James is giving fresh expression to truths he had often heard from the life of Jesus himself, before they became treasured documentary possessions of the Christian Church" (TNTC, 28).

It would not be unreasonable, therefore, to suggest a date for the epistle within a few years after the resurrection appearance to James. With the thoughts of Jesus indelibly impressed upon his mind, brother James, now convinced of Jesus' lordship by his resurrection, became a protagonist in the synagogue for a revitalized expression of the Hebrew faith, invigorated by the teaching of Jesus. The homiletical character of the epistle suggests a setting like that of a synagogue. This "unofficial" setting may account for the fact that the letter was not known in wider circles in the Christian church until the third century.

V. THEOLOGY

The epistle is not intended to be a primer on Christian theology but a mosaic of admonitions on how to order one's life in keeping with a professed faith in God. Belief in the existence of a God who enters into the experiences of people according to his wisdom and grace is assumed. God demands recognition and requires accountability on the part of humankind. He makes himself available and responds to the sincere appeals of the believer offered in prayer. He hallows the adverse experiences of life and ensures peace and goodwill among people who walk before him in humble faith.

The Messiah has come in the person of Jesus. Through him a believer is enabled to relate to the law with new power and unaccustomed freedom. Although man was created in the image of God, he has fallen into sin and permits the incubation of sin when he yields to his lower impulses despite his understanding of God's will. God, however, provides a new quality of life for those who conquer sin.

This epistle lends itself to the Wesleyan focus on holiness of life because of its preoccupation with conduct. Adam Clarke sees this perspective where he comments, "Be then, to the Lord, what He required His sacrifices to be; let your whole heart, your body, soul and spirit, be sanctified to the Lord of Hosts, that He may fill you with all His fulness" (Clarke, 6:760).

The Wesleyan emphasis on conversion is found in "the word planted in you" (1:21). Clarke interprets James' definition of pure religion in this light: "Religion is of such a nature that no man can learn it but by experience; he who does not feel the doctrine of God to be the power of God to the salvation of his soul, can neither teach religion, nor act according to its dictates, because he is an unconverted, unrenewed man" (Clarke, 6:765).

VI. OUTLINE

I. Salutation (1:1)

II. Cultivation of Personal Religious Experience (1:2–27)
   A. Making Tests Work for You (1:2–4)
   B. Making Prayer Work for You (1:5–8)
   C. Managing Change (1:9–11)
   D. When Testing Is Misused (1:12–16)
   E. God's Creative Role (1:17–19a)
   F. Attending the Implanted Word (1:19b–21)
   G. The Fruit of Gracious Deeds (1:22–27)

III. Cultivation of Corporate Religious Experience (2:1–3:18)
   A. Recognition of Social Discrimination as Sin (2:1–9)
   B. Operation of the Law of Liberty (2:10–13)
   C. Faith Reaching Out in Acts of Mercy (2:14–26)
   D. Critical Selection of Teachers (3:1–12)
   E. Crucial Exercise of Wisdom (3:13–18)

IV. Converting the Wider Community (4:1–5:6)
   A. Summons to Surrender to God (4:1–10)
   B. Warning Against Playing God (4:11–12)
   C. Caution Against Ignoring God (4:13–17)
   D. Alerting to God's Judgment (5:1–6)

V. Christian Culture: Facets of the Fellowship (5:7–20)
   A. The Quality of Patience (5:7–11)
   B. The Exigence of Integrity (5:12)
   C. Drawing on Resources (5:13–18)
   D. Renewing the Bonds (5:19–20)

COMMENTARY

I. SALUTATION (1:1)

The salutation conforms to contemporary epistolary style and is notable for its brevity. This brevity suggests that James is anxious to get on with counsel for his Jewish compatriots.

The OT milieu is evident, both in James's self-qualification and the designation of the addressees as **the twelve tribes scattered among the nations.**

When he calls himself **"a servant** [lit. "slave"] **of God and of the Lord Jesus Christ,"** James is reflecting the role of spokesman for God associated with Moses and the prophets. Significantly, however, he presents himself as the spokesman for Jesus also. His Christian calling, therefore, is set forth in terms of God's historical way of addressing his people.

In identifying his readers as **the twelve tribes,** James places himself and them wholly in the mainstream of the Jewish faith as the people of God were originally constituted. Unexpected, however, is the qualification of the twelve tribes as **scattered among the nations.** Does he intend this to be understood in the classic sense of the Jews living outside of Palestine? Many scholars disagree and interpret it in a metaphorical sense: "Unlike the twelve tribes who have Palestine for their native land, Jerusalem for their capital, and the temple as the center of their religious worship, the twelve tribes addressed in the letter have no earthly fatherland, nor any capital upon earth, but always, no matter where they may be settled, live scattered in a strange world, like the Jewish exiles in Mesopotamia or Egypt" (Zahn, 1:76).

On the other hand, the scattered ones are potentially the gathered ones. James may be thinking of his people, to whom he had an evangelistic commitment, and anticipating a new gathering. God has performed a miracle in the Resurrection to bring the people of all nations together to reconstitute the people of God. Jesus of Nazareth was raised from death!

II. CULTIVATION OF PERSONAL RELIGIOUS EXPERIENCE (1:2–27)

Although the paraenetic nature of this document allows sentences and paragraphs to be loosely connected, at places only by catchwords, a sequence is still observable in ch. 1 in this manner. Occasions of testing should be used as instruments for developing strong Christian character. To make them serve in this way requires extraordinary wisdom that is accessible through prayer. One difficult area of testing surfaces when one's socioeco-nomic status changes upwards as well as downwards. But blessing awaits its successful management.

Conversely, a person may invite testing to flaunt his spiritual maturity. The motivation for this is evil, and the end is death. One must never forget that the new birth is a gift from God and is sustained by him. The implanted word, therefore, requires cultivation, both in ridding the surrounding area of objectionable growth—to pursue the metaphor—and in producing deeds that express the meaning of faith. This section of the letter opens with a call to develop inner fortitude and closes with a summons to a vigorous demonstration of faith. At the center stands the birthing act of God **through the word of truth** (v.18).

A. Making Tests Work for You (1:2–4)

Most scholars feel that the last word of the salutation (*chairein,* **"greetings"**) suggested the second word (*charan,* **"joy"**) at the opening of the initial homily. But the connection may lie deeper than this. In constituting the people of God, after the miracle of the Exodus, God subjected them to testings in the wilderness. Numbers bristles with trials confronted and too often failed. It would be no different for the new people of God, given identity through the resurrection miracle.

There is wide agreement that the trials in mind rise out of deliberate persecution of Christians. But the modifying adjective (**many kinds**) and the later discussion of the subject (1:13–15) suggest a much broader setting. Many experiences come in the guise of testings. It may be in the home (sickness), in the workplace (competition), or even in the Christian community (jealousy). They come in many sizes and shapes, often irritating, always unplanned (Adamson, 54), and always demanding a response. We prefer not to have to contend with them, hoping to be spared the strain and stress.

The stark realities of opposition, discrimination, and resentment, however, become the rule rather than the exception. James charges the reader to turn these difficult, trying experiences into spiritual profit. When he commands them to **consider it pure joy**, he challenges them to take a definite positive stance in the midst of trials. "Take charge!" he shouts, "Welcome the challenge!" This testing of their faith will begin to generate endurance, which serves as a basic ingredient in the development of Christian character.

James challenges the readers to be open to the ultimate effect of endurance—a mature and complete Christian life. The word *perfect*, a favorite of James, describes "a fullblown character of stable righteousness" (Davids, 69). It comes by making trials work to the advantage of the believer. It sounds great, but it is not easy to do. Each situation requires perception, evaluation, and an informed response. Who has that kind of resourcefulness? It is within reach through prayer.

B. Making Prayer Work for You (1:5–8)

James directs the readers: Ask God for wisdom; ask in steady faith. The wisdom James has in mind must surely be the kind found in the Proverbs. It is sound judgment, proceeding from a reverence for God (Pr 1:7). To ask in faith is to embrace the way of righteousness and to be committed to it. Admission of need is not reprehensible, but equivocation is intolerable to the Lord. Doubt creates uncertainty and prevents clear thinking. James is graphic in portraying indecision as

erratic waves that dictate the outcome—emptiness.

C. Managing Change (1:9–11)

It takes reverential wisdom to manage fundamental changes in life. How easy it is to lose control when stations in life are suddenly reversed! Those suddenly rich can go off the deep end; those suddenly poor can precipitate a sure end to their lives. It is not clear whether James has in mind material changes or spiritual changes due to Christian conversion. Christian faith obliterates class and social distinctions. It takes wisdom to make the adjustment and to understand the Christian perspective of life.

D. When Testing Is Misused (1:12–16)

James underscores the positive role of testing in v.12. Using the metaphor of the games, he holds forth the victor's crown to the Christian who demonstrates endurance. **The crown of life** is generally viewed as eschatological life after death, but the Greek expression may also be construed as referring to this life. It is life as God intended in creation: an intimate, personal relationship with God in love, the development of fortitude through repeated victory in every test. It is the complete life (1:4), having "every grace which constitutes the mind that was in Christ, so that your knowledge and holiness may be complete" (Clarke, 6:760).

The Greek word translated **"trial"** also means "temptation." Many interpreters feel that James suddenly changes the meaning of the word to that of tempting in vv.13–14. (He now uses the verb form.) OT theology clearly affirms that God subjects people to tests to confirm their faith. (Recall God's directive to Abraham to make Isaac a human sacrifice, Ge 22). So it would be incorrect to say that "God himself tests nobody." It is altogether proper, however, to retain the meaning of testing and to render the passage as follows: "When a person is testing himself, he must not say, 'I am being tested by God,' for God is not liable to testing with reference to evil, and he himself does not cause testing in anyone. But each man, in testing himself, allows himself to be hooked and dragged away by his own deep desires." An individual may intentionally create a situation in order to invoke special help from God or to demonstrate spiritual superiority. But there is no need for a person to engage in self-testing. This is born of unwholesome desire. Its true nature will become evident in consequent sin (1:15). James understandably hastens to warn such persons: **"Don't be deceived, my dear brothers!"** (v.16). V.16 fittingly concludes the paragraph.

E. God's Creative Role (1:17–19a)

It must be reaffirmed that God's movements toward humankind can be only good and right. This was evident at Creation when God overpowered the darkness of the abyss with light through his creative word. It is evident also in the firstfruits among his creation, through the new birth, that proceeds from the word of the Gospel. Although the celestial lights fluctuate in brightness, the Creator-Father is unwavering in his benevolence. He is unrelenting in his determination to achieve his purpose in creation. So his design, recently revealed, involved him in birthing a new creation. This is his firstfruits—Exhibit A—in the whole realm of creation. Adamson (p. 77) reflects Liddell and Scott in pointing out "that 'firstfruits' was used not merely of that which was first in order,

but of that which was first in honor." James underscores this amazing truth with the exhortation, **"My dear brothers, take note of this."** Again a change in paragraph division is warranted.

F. Attending the Implanted Word (1:19b–21)

The **word planted in you** suggests a metaphor from horticulture. Consonant with this is the fact that the words translated **"the evil that is so prevalent"** may refer to tangled undergrowth. James is painting a picture of the Lord's garden which the husbandman must keep. He must clear away the tangled undergrowth and a variety of noxious plants (**moral filth**). The robust growth that follows will exhibit **the righteous life that God desires** and will issue in salvation.

The word translated **"humbly"** has within it a certain nuance that suggests submissive restraint, "that self-subduing gentleness which is among the fruits of the Spirit" (Adamson, 81). In applying the metaphor, James directs that restraint be used in the area of speech and anger. How strong the impulse is to react to provocations with hurting words and fiery anger. On the other hand, listening and sorting out what one hears provides ingredients for cultivating the implanted word.

G. The Fruit of Gracious Deeds (1:22–27)

Attentive hearing is not an end in itself. **"Do not merely listen to the word, and so deceive yourselves. Do what it says"** (v.22).

The Gospel is like a mirror. It creates awareness and reveals need. As the mirror prompts the viewer to action (to remove blemishes or enhance beauty), so the Gospel prompts a persistent application of self in pursuit of gracious acts.

The hearing of the Gospel introduces a new perspective in a person's religious experience. It is the **perfect law that gives freedom** (v.25). Compared with the OT law as it was practiced, the Gospel offers a feeling of fulfillment by way of release from an enslaving law. It takes the spotlight off oneself alone and draws others into the circle of interest. The older law was reduced to ceremony (the facet of **religion** in v.27), but the newer one is not realized unless it issues in deeds of service, especially to the most needy.

III. CULTIVATION OF THE CORPORATE RELIGIOUS EXPERIENCE (2:1–3:18)

Christian faith is radically personal but also inescapably corporate. This section of the homily focuses on the gathered community, for it opens with a consideration of conduct in the **meeting** and continues with a concern for the consequence of teaching. The former may have in view leaders or the membership in general and has to do with maintaining the true spirit in the community. The latter cautions individuals who aspire to be leaders and has to do with sustaining the community with wisdom from above.

A. Recognition of Social Discrimination as Sin (2:1–9)

James continues to challenge: "Stop condoning favoritism as though it is consistent with Christian faith" (my paraphrase). Jesus, in his exemplary life ("**our glorious Lord**"), refused to curry the favor of the powerful and rich. Although the courting of the wealthy might enhance the economic and social status of the community, it is nothing less than sin, as evaluated by the **royal law** (v.8). It may be smart,

but it is sin, as adultery and murder are sin.

In his description of their conduct, James makes the rich person so attractive and the poor person so objectionable as to heighten the reasonableness and propriety of "discriminating" conduct. But the response of the members must be considered evil because the motivation is wrong (v.4). Moreover, they are acting contrary to God's design. God bestows on the poor true riches because they have learned to love him (v.5). Furthermore, favoring the wealthy only condones their exploitation and defamation of the poverty-stricken believers (v.6).

The criterion for such conduct is an ancient law: "Love your neighbor as yourself" (Lev 19:18), which Jesus elevated to a dominating position by his own exemplary life. He demonstrated how one should be as solicitous of the welfare of other persons as he is attentive to his own needs. The life of faith is the way of selflessness.

B. Operation of the Law of Liberty (2:10–13)

By heightening the ancient law, Jesus placed the observance of the Jewish law in a new light. He would have his followers live in responsible freedom. James calls it **the law that gives freedom** (v.12). It is the spirit with which one approaches the observance of the law that makes the difference between fulfillment and failure. Many of James' contemporaries had adopted an attitude toward the law that allowed them to ignore or violate certain points that did not suit them. They considered themselves approved of God as long as their credits exceeded their debits in observance of the law. But this is contrary to the basic purpose of the law, namely, to make the gathered ones truly the people of God. Excluding just one regulation makes God's goal impossible of attainment. A change in attitude toward the law shifts attention from self and its merits to others and their needs.

C. Faith Reaching Out in Acts of Mercy (2:14–26)

If the spirit of mercy is a basic element in Christian faith, then the expression of mercy is an integral part of faith. This expression of mercy constitutes faith in action. Devoid of this energy faith is dead (v.17). Faith is alive in self-forgetting deeds. This removes the tendency to make good works the instrument of salvation. Failure to put faith into practice promotes a selfishness that protects self and withholds material help from those in need. Its heartlessness hides behind the façade of politeness. Even the demons are more honest about their understanding of God: they shudder for their very existence.

James illustrates full-orbed faith with reference to two OT personalities, one the father of the Hebrew race and the other a pagan harlot. For both, knowledge of and about God informed their faith. Rahab declared, "When we heard of it [what the Lord had done to the Egyptians and the two kings, Sihon and Og], our hearts sank . . . because of you, for the LORD your God is God in heaven above and on the earth below" (Jos 2:11). For both, self-abnegation was operating. Abraham would wipe out his future with the sacrifice of Isaac; Rahab would wipe out her family if her deception were discovered. Faith that is self-centered is only a corpse; it has the appearance of the real, but not the life.

D. Critical Selection of Teachers (3:1–12)

James now turns his attention to the critical role of the teacher in the spiritual formation of the congregation. He may be introducing the subject with a negative command: "Many of you, do not aspire to be teachers, because we know that we shall come under heavy criticism [judgment]" (my paraphrase). It may be, also, that he is opening with a question: "Surely not many of you are aspiring to be teachers, are you?"

The teaching ministry of the church was especially critical in those pioneering days of the new faith. James wants the aspirants to be aware of it. He does this with a series of vivid pictures: a (chariot) rider racing his horses; a pilot steering his ship; a fire ravaging a forest. The first two pictures focus attention upon the requirement to exercise control in the face of enormous power. The third dramatizes the consequence of power that has escaped control. Another feature has to do with the contrasting of entities: the small bit in the mouth of a sizable horse; a rudder and a wind-driven ship; a spark and a forest fire.

James is trying to give the readers proper perspective on the role of the teacher, especially his grave responsibility. The aspirant may see it simply as a local congregational setting in which he repeats the facts of Jesus and truths of the faith that he was taught. But the demand is far greater than this. What he teaches issues in conduct, and conduct determines the character of the community. All of this is made more acute by the pernicious fallibility that dogs every effort (v.2).

James employs two figures of speech. The first is metonymy. The substance of teaching (**"what he says,"** v.2) is represented by the tongue, the instrument of speech. So he says **"the tongue . . . makes great boasts"** (v.5). The second figure used is metaphor: **"The tongue also is a fire"** (v.6). The first two metaphor pictures (the horse and the ship) illustrate the deftness of the diminutive: how small the bit and the rudder, but how effective in guiding. Although the teacher is merely talking (as compared with physical activity), his words powerfully influence personal conduct and community complexion. How critical is the need to control the tongue—to say the right thing and only the right.

The next two pictures (the forest fire and the world of evil) are negative and illustrate the danger of the undeterred. Barclay suggests that *kosmos* ("world") be treated in its active sense: "adornment" of evil. So he explains, "The tongue is the organ which can fatally and fascinatingly make evil attractive" (p. 101). When control is not exercised, the consequences may be disastrous. Only the truth and the sincere application of the truth may be taught. But the hard fact is that the tongue **is itself set on fire by hell** (v.6). Moreover, **no man can tame the tongue** (v.7). Here is the doctrine of human depravity.

Many people thus live under the delusion of doubleness, sanctioning both praise of God and cursing of others from the same lips. James exposes the capricious paradox when he asks, **"Can a fig tree bear olives, or a grapevine bear figs?"** (v.12). The nature of a thing determines its product. If a teacher is going to exercise proper control and secure salutary results, he must be sure to possess that nature that enables him to receive wisdom from above. Here is the doctrine of regeneration, a central focus in the Wesleyan tradition.

E. Crucial Exercise of Wisdom (3:13–18)

After issuing a warning and probing the heart of the teacher, James addresses the subject that ordinarily attends a teacher—knowledge. Immediately, however, he places it in the larger context. Both the possession and the product of wisdom must be kept in view. So he exhorts that the wise person must utilize his resources to fashion a beautiful life (v.13). This will happen through enlightened self-restraint (**the humility that comes from wisdom**, v.13). The wisdom of Christian faith always has something to do with the ordering of an exemplary life.

James calls attention to the presence of wrong attitudes among would-be teachers. **"If [since] you harbor bitter envy and selfish ambition in your hearts, do not boast [stop boasting] about it or deny [stop denying] the truth"** (v.14). These attitudes proceed from a depraved, this-worldly, unholy spirit. They are self-centered and will ultimately create disorder in the community. But when the divine Spirit invades a person, he cleanses the heart and enables him to subordinate the natural drives and to choose that course of action that will promote peace.

This table of virtues given here describes the person who resists the temptation to exalt himself and to exult over the failures of others. When this kind of wisdom is operative, God is in process of fashioning a harmonious, holy community that manifests his perfect design.

IV. CONVERTING THE WIDER COMMUNITY (4:1–5:6)

The subject of the preceding section is peace; the subject of this new section is **fights**. The mood becomes more intense; the style becomes staccatolike through a series of verbs that characterize and condemn the readers for their strife-ridden society. The crescendo reaches its peak with a quotation from Scripture: "God opposes the proud, but gives grace to the humble" (4:6).

Then follows a series of commands to surrender and to allow the Lord to lift up the person emptied of sin.

As an evangelist, James addresses the hearts of both the believer and the unbeliever in the same message. Adam Clarke (p. 781) insists that James has outsiders in mind, for he writes, "What a strange view must he have of the nature of primitive Christianity, who can suppose that these words can possibly have been addressed to people professing the Gospel of Jesus Christ, who . . . were persecuted and opposed both by their brethren the Jews, and by the Romans!" It may be more proper, however, to place the letter in the context of a wider community.

A. Summons to Surrender to God (4:1–10)

This whole section has in view an acquisitive society, the competition for material things and the pleasure they bring. It begins with the manifold desires of individuals that need to be satisfied; so individuals mobilize, each one, to seize the desired object. When they step outside the self, they engage in competition with other persons, even to the point of fierce conflict. So intense is the desire for possessions that they are ready to commit murder (Barclay). At the same time they use from their arsenal the instrument of prayer; but this proves ineffective, for "you ask with wrong motives, that you may spend what you get on your pleasures" (3:3). (JB says, **"You have not prayed properly; you prayed for something to indulge your own desires."**) Inappropriate prayer proceeds from a tenuous relationship with God.

To address the people as **adulterous** (v.4) sounds unduly harsh. The word, however, is intended to strike at the very heart of the problem—unfaithfulness in covenant privileges. It is appli-cable to both Jew and Christian. James follows with the accusation: **"Don't you know that friendship with the world is hatred toward God? Anyone who chooses to be a friend of the world becomes an enemy of God"** (v.4). (The way he asks the question implies that they do know.) Jesus expressed the contradiction succinctly: "You cannot serve both God and Money" (Mt 6:24).

James continues with a paraphrase from Scripture, which, he insinuates, they have been ignoring. Translators are divided as to which of the two contrasting meanings is intended. Barclay gives priority to the following sense: **"God yearns jealously for the loving devotion of the spirit he implanted within us."** The NEB understands it conversely: **"The spirit which God implanted in man turns toward envious desires."**

The latter rendering, which is followed by the NIV, treats the scriptural allusion as a climactic confirmation of spiritual infidelity. James follows immediately, then, with the evangelical assurance, **"But he gives us more grace."** The former rendering, on the other hand, makes the quotation the turning point in the appeal. The choice of meaning may rest upon the function of the phrase **"That is why,"** which introduces the reference to Scripture. James is pointing out two counts in which they are wrong in tolerating avaricious materialism: suspending reason and ignoring Scripture.

God fights on the side of the humble person who has surrendered to him. This surrender has a number of facets. James displays these in a series of ten commands directed toward a fundamental change in life. He bids them to meet God, rid themselves of polluting attitudes, and allow God to renew their spirits. By this a person claims victory over the flesh and the Devil. This is the Wesleyan understanding of conversion.

Adam Clarke (6:781) elaborates the summons to purify oneself as follows:

> Separate yourselves from the world, and consecrate yourselves to God; this is the true notion of sanctification. . . . Two things are implied in a man's sanctification: 1. That he separate himself from evil ways and evil companions, and devote himself to God. 2. That God separates guilt from his conscience, and sin from his soul, and thus makes him internally and externally holy.

B. Warning Against Playing God (4:11–12)

The paragraph beginning at 4:13 does not share in the central theme of the section, but it may be regarded as a sequel to the positive injunction that precedes. Addressing the readers again as **brothers**, James senses the temptation toward censoriousness on the part of those who attain to holiness. They may think it is their prerogative to expose the sins of others through disparaging criticism, but in reality they want to arrogate to themselves the right to establish criteria for sanctified conduct. In this they may be presuming to act in place of God. Intolerant persons often claim they are representing God by strictness, but actually they are usurping his throne. Usually the persons who pull each other to pieces (see PHILLIPS) aim more to destroy than to save.

C. Caution Against Ignoring God (4:13–17)

Accumulating goods may not always engender strife, but it may precipitate another sinful attitude that is counter to the spirit of Jesus, hyper-self-confidence with a total disregard of God. Phillips translates 4:16: **"You take a certain pride in planning with such confidence."**

James paints a picture of businessmen who are programming their business activities for the next year. When they say, **"We will go to this or that city,"** they use the indicative mood of the verb. The nuance is that of an undaunted determination that will not possibly be thwarted. They are in full control of the future as they plot their destination and profits. Their fault, however, is that they are forgetful of the frailty of life. The opening word of the Greek text of v.14 (**"Why"**), which is generally not expressed by translators, suggests that James is insinuating, "Who do you think you are?" He likens their life to visible smoke or water vapor, which can disappear suddenly by a change in wind or temperature. These traders not only disregard God, they also flaunt his will. This kind of arrogance is not only disgusting; it is sinful, too.

D. Alerting to God's Judgment (5:1–6)

In this larger group of strife-prone business people, James singles out the wealthy. He laments for them because he sees what they do not see. He looks at their accumulated treasures, whether food, cloth, or metal, stored up as security against an unpredictable future. On the outside all looks good, but on the inside there is taking place the slow processes of decay, larva-feasting, and rust. When the day of need arrives, they will thrust their hands into worthless powder.

The rottenness of the fruit is matched by the rottenness of the human heart. Like an OT prophet, James lashes out at the injustice of the rich. Sadistically they have withheld pay from their workers, leaving them hungry and in want. But they have revelled and caroused in disgusting self-indulgence. The terminology James uses suggests sheep frisking about in rich pastures, well-fed and fattening. Unknown to them, the day is approaching when they will be slaughtered. So also is the destiny of these sensate, insensitive, successful businessmen.

James's concluding statement in the description surprises the reader: **"You have condemned and murdered innocent men who were not opposing you."** Translators generally agree in using the plural, but the Greek word is singular—innocent man. Is it simply a coincidence that the same word was on the lips of the centurion who was in charge of the crucifixion of Jesus? "Beyond all doubt," he said, "this man was innocent" (Lk 23:47, NEB). Then, curiously, James shifts from the past tense (**"condemned," "murdered"**) to the present tense: "He does not resist you." James does not say that these oppressed workers are Christians, but they may well be, since he is pleading their cause. Their spirit of surrender, their refusal to fight (4:1) portrays them in the image of Jesus Christ.

V. CHRISTIAN CULTURE: FACETS OF THE FELLOWSHIP (5:7–20)

Another change in atmosphere takes place. The focus is now upon the community of faith. Most striking is the fivefold mention of **the Lord** in the opening paragraph. (Up to this point in the epistle the Lord has been named only three times.) In a sense, James presents here a description of a living church: the Lord in the midst of Christian brothers. That is the very heart of the church. His numinous presence and the channeling of his power by means of prayer characterize this section.

A. The Quality of Patience (5:7–11)

The Lord Jesus, after his resurrection, appeared personally to five hundred persons on one occasion (1Co 15:6). This nucleus must surely have alerted thousands to anticipate daily the sudden appearance of Jesus. When James writes, **"The Lord's coming is near"** (v.8), he is using the same verb that John the Baptist and Jesus used in announcing the approach of the kingdom of God (Mt 3:1; 4:17). The perfect tense indicates that the arrival of the kingdom is an imminent reality; surely the kingdom was present in power in the ministry of Jesus.

James may be suggesting that, although Jesus is not visibly present, his imminent presence was a reality in their midst. Did not Jesus say, "Where two or three come together in my name, there am I with them" (Mt 18:20)? They must practice the presence of the Lord, as they anticipate his visible presence. If they do, they must know that he is present both to encourage and to judge, for **the Judge is standing at the door!** (v.9).

The distinctive attitude of the Christian community is patience. The Greek word suggests "great-heartedness." Irritating and disconcerting things do not change the settled condition of the heart. Anxieties cannot disturb, for the heart is at peace; but vigilance is still required (**"stand firm,"** v.8). The farmer cannot make it rain, but he rests on the "promise" of nature with "confident expectancy" (Tasker, NBD or TNTC, 119).

James would have them identify with the prophets, OT men of the highest order. Men like Jeremiah were subject to unpredictable experiences, but they maintained a remarkable equanimity, for God's presence was assured them. If they are considered **blessed**, then the Christian who knows the presence of the Lord in varied circumstances may also know blessedness. Job, too, is used as an example, but his patience involved the exercise of endurance. His last words testify to an unusual sense of God's presence: "My ears had heard of you, but now my eyes have seen you" (42:5). Assuredly the Lord is working in the community out of compassion as they cultivate uncommon patience.

B. The Exigence of Integrity (5:12)

The new thought of 5:12 is heralded with the words **"Above all"** and leaves the reader to provide the connection with what precedes. Briefly, James takes up the necessity for integrity. The habit of affirming with an oath was deeply ingrained in Palestinian society. It served various purposes, one of which was the exhibition of piety. This became a subtle form of hypocrisy, trading with counterfeits. The words translated **"be condemned"** contain the notion of hypocrisy. The readers accordingly are warned about falling into hypocrisy. James summons them to integrity when he orders: **"Do not swear."** Integrity is best served by simplicity and straightforward conversation.

C. Drawing on Resources (5:13–18)

The paragraph beginning at 5:13 offers a cross section of circumstances in which people of the church find themselves: trouble, prosperity, sickness, and sin. These and all experiences may and should be addressed with an awareness of the presence of the Lord. The focus is upon the agency of prayer. That is what prayer is: activating the presence of the Lord by consciously seeking his involvement. The practice of prayer pervades the passage; but it is **the prayer offered in faith** and **the prayer of a righteous man**, not just a recitation of liturgy. James uses three words for prayer; together they suggest a vital relationship with the Lord, entailing personal commitment, that may provide the energy (Gk. *energoumenē*) effectuating the prayer of the righteous man.

Particularly significant is the emphasis on mutuality in prayer. The meaning of fellowship is dramatized when the elders are present with the sick person. Here is prayer plus comfort. The anointing oil ministers through touch. Here is prayer plus an act. But fundamental to the total operation is confidence in the Lord's presence and power. Moreover, whatever sin is present must be dealt with, too, for a prayer of faith is impossible if sin is allowed to remain. This is not to be regarded as a formula for healing but as a prescription as to how **brothers** can express their mutual concern and offer assistance.

Unexpectedly, James shifts his commands to the second person at 5:16 as he writes, **"Confess your sins to each other."** He is now looking at the needs shared by all members of the fellowship. The word translated **"confess"** means to declare openly, to deal frankly with a matter. When Christians have spiritual needs, this openness makes it possible to pray for each other with specific petitions and thus expect wholeness in every way.

D. Renewing the Bonds (5:19–20)

The final sentence of the homily expresses concern for those who tend toward breaking the bond of fellowship. The message is "Don't minimize the possibility of apostasy." The bonds of fellowship should be so sensitive that a brother cannot wander from the gospel without someone seeking him and restoring him to a vital relationship. Apostasy is depicted in its extreme status by the term **"multitude of sins."**

The homily closes on this seemingly negative note, but it summons the whole congregation to mutual respon-sibility for sustaining and renewing the fellowship of faith in Jesus Christ.

BIBLIOGRAPHY

Adamson, J. B. *The Epistle of James*. NICNT. Grand Rapids: Eerdmans, 1976.

Barclay, William. *The Letters of James and Peter*. DSBS. Philadelphia: Westminster, 1960.

Barnett, A. E. "James, Letter of." IDB. New York: Abingdon, 1962.

Blackman, E. C. *The Epistle of James*. TBC. Naperville: Allenson, 1958.

Clarke, Adam. *Commentary and Critical Notes on the New Testament*. Vol. 6. New York: Bangs and Emory, 1826.

Davids, P. H. *The Epistle of James*. NIGTC. Grand Rapids: Eerdmans, 1982.

Dayton, W. T. "James, Epistle of." ZPEB. Edited by M. C. Tenney. Vol. 3. Grand Rapids: Zondervan, 1975.

Dibelius, Martin. *James*. Hermeneia. Philadelphia: Fortress, 1976.

Harper, A. F. "James." BBC. Kansas City: Beacon Hill, 1967.

Mayor, J. B. *The Epistles of James*. New York: Macmillan, 1897.

Reicke, Bo. *The Epistles of James, Peter and Jude*. AB. Garden City, New York: Doubleday, 1964.

Ropes, J. H. *A Critical and Exegetical Commentary on the Epistle of James*. ICC. Edinburgh: T. & T. Clark, 1916.

Scaer, D. P. *James the Apostle of Faith*. St. Louis: Concordia, 1983.

Sevenster, J. N. *Do You Know Greek?* Leiden: Brill, 1968.

Tasker, R. V. G. *The General Epistle of James*. TNTC. Grand Rapids: Eerdmans, 1960.

————. "James, Epistle of." NBD. London: InterVarsity, 1962.

Thompson, R. D. "James and Jude." WBC. Grand Rapids: Eerdmans, 1966.

Wesley, John. *Explanatory Notes Upon the New Testament*. Naperville: Allenson, 1966.

Zahn, Theodor. *Introduction to the New Testament*. Vol. 1. Grand Rapids: Kregel, 1953.

1 PETER
David W. Kendall

INTRODUCTION

I. OVERVIEW

The balance with which 1 Peter describes Christian grace offers a rich theological and practical resource for the church in general and the Wesleyan tradition in particular. God's grace changes people and distinguishes them as holy. This holiness is both "spiritual" and "social." That is, holiness embraces both personal integrity before God and public responsibility. Grace creates and then sustains an earnest Christianity that models Christlike love in the real world. Grace equips believers for facing the rigors of following Jesus in a hostile world with confidence and joy as they anticipate the final revelation of Christ's glory. In such terms as these 1 Peter describes (for Wesleyans and non-Wesleyans alike) the sort of holiness without which "no one will see the Lord" (Heb 12:14).

II. AUTHOR

The author identifies himself as Peter, an apostle of Jesus Christ (1:1). Undoubtedly this is a reference to Simon Peter, spokesman for Jesus' disciples in all of the Gospels. Two other specific references have a bearing on the question of authorship. In 5:1 the author makes his appeal to the elders as a "fellow elder." Significantly Peter establishes his partnership with them as the basis for his exhortations. The second reference is found in 5:12 where the author indicates he has written "with the help of Silas" (5:12). That is, Silas is identified as the secretary who actually formulated the letter at the direction of the author. Consequently 1 Peter claims the apostle Peter as its author with the secretarial help of Silas (a variant of the Gk. "Silvanus").

Several considerations make the Petrine authorship plausible though not certain. One of the earliest creedal statements in the NT (1Co 15:1–5) shows that Peter was recognized widely as an apostolic witness to the Christ event. Peter could well have written to and gained a hearing from Christians anywhere in the world. Moreover, "Peter" claims to have written from "Babylon," a cryptic reference to Rome, and there is clear evidence from early Christian traditions (c. A.D. 150–200) that he ended his apostolic career in Rome and was executed in the Neronian persecution

(c. A.D. 64). These traditions establish not only the possibility that Peter wrote this epistle from Rome but also suggest an upper limit for dating the document. If he wrote 1 Peter, he must have done so no later than A.D. 64. On the face of it, the claim of Peter's authorship is credible.

With the rise of the modern critical investigation of Scripture, however, a number of scholars have raised serious questions about this claim. But we do not find that these questions compel a rejection of this claim and conclude that 1 Peter most probably was written by Peter from Rome sometime before A.D. 64. (For detailed discussions of this question see especially the commentaries by Selwyn, Kelly, and Best).

III. RECIPIENTS

Peter addresses believers who make up several Christian communities scattered throughout Asia Minor. That these believers were predominantly Gentile in background seems clear from his description of their former lifestyle (1:14, 18; 4:3).

He uses several special terms to describe his readers. In the opening greeting he addresses them as "strangers" (1:1, *parepidemoi*), and throughout the letter he uses similar terms (e.g., 1:17, "live your lives as strangers here," *paroikoi kai parepidemoi*). In modern parlance, the readers are addressed as "exiles and refugees."

These terms illumine Peter's understanding of the Christian life. Within the Roman Empire, these terms indicated sociopolitical status. "Resident aliens" designated persons who had been transplanted from their native land to a foreign locality where they did not belong and could not enjoy the privileges of citizenship. "Visiting strangers" designated persons who moved from place to place without ever establishing permanent ties with any of the communities they visited. The first-century world was full of such resident aliens and visiting strangers. Peter's use of this terminology implies that Christians do not "belong" in the world.

To call Christians aliens and strangers, however, is to imply more than "This world is not my home; I'm just apassin' through." The concrete sociopolitical realities implied describe well what it means to be a Christian in the world. In short, aliens and strangers suffer by the very nature of their existence, and so do Christians. Thus Peter's description of his readers as exiles and refugees underscores a fundamental theme of his letter. The impact of grace upon the readers' lives has brought them into situations of conflict with the expectations and norms of their society. (For further reading on the exile terminology, see Elliott.)

IV. OCCASION

Strange as it may seem, it is the character of grace itself that provides the occasion for this letter (see 5:12). The readers had found that their life in grace involved a basic conflict with the prevailing norms and customs of their society. That conflict had expressed itself in a variety of ways that together comprise the readers' suffering. We should not understand this suffering as a state-organized campaign of persecution against Christians. Rather, the suffering of the readers resulted from the social tensions created by their distinctive lifestyle. Their way of life inspired discrimination, slander, ostracism, and reproach from the non-Christians around them (1:6; 2:12, 19–20; 3:9, 13–17; 4:3–4; 5:8–10).

If Peter understood such suffering to be part and parcel of Christian life, clearly his readers did not. To them the sufferings seemed strange (4:12) and called into question the reality and vitality of their faith. Therefore, Peter writes in order to explain the nature of grace and to urge them to submit to the way of grace, which leads to glory (see the purpose in 5:12, summarized in 5:10). While grace accounts for the readers' suffering, grace also casts that very suffering into an entirely new light. Grace stimulates confidence, faithfulness, and joy as the readers anticipate glory when Christ returns.

V. OUTLINE

I. Epistolary Greeting (1:1–2)

II. God's Saving Grace: Rebirth to a New Way of Life (1:3–12)

III. The Implications of Saving Grace (1:13–5:11)
  A. Be True to Your Calling as God's People (1:14–2:10)
   1. Holiness (1:14–21)
   2. Love (1:22–2:3)
   3. Election (2:4–10)
  B. Act as God's People (2:11–4:11)
   1. Good conduct in situations of conflict (2:11–12)
   2. Christians in society (2:13–17)
   3. Servants and cruel masters (2:18–25)
   4. Wives and non-Christian husbands (3:1–6)
   5. Husbands and their Christian wives (3:7)
   6. The community's conduct when facing abuse (3:8–4:11)
    a. The community's internal relations (3:8; 4:7–11)
    b. The community's external relations with a hostile world (3:9–4:6)
  C. Depend On God's Future (4:12–5:11)
   1. In responding to hostilities (4:12–19)
   2. In structuring community life (5:1–7)
   3. In resisting evil (5:8-11)

IV. Final Greeting (5:12–14)

COMMENTARY

I. EPISTOLARY GREETING (1:1–2)

Peter identifies himself as an **apostle,** as one who carries authority under the commission of Jesus Christ. Immediately he indicates his primary concerns in writing by the way he describes his readers (cf. 5:12). They are God's unique people (elect strangers) by virtue of God's initiatives in Christ (his foreknowledge and sprinkling by Christ's blood) who live distinctive lives in the world (sanctified for obedience). In all that Peter writes he intends to clarify the unique character and conduct of God's holy, elect people.

II. GOD'S SAVING GRACE: REBIRTH TO A NEW WAY OF LIFE (1:3–12)

Peter begins by praising God for the mercy of his saving grace. God has given his people an entirely new life through Jesus Christ. So new is this life that Peter employs the notion of rebirth, a notion used infrequently in Scripture despite its widespread use today. What sort of life does God give his people in their rebirth?

It is a life oriented toward the future. Those who are reborn have a hope that animates their present lives (1:3–5; cf. 1:13, 21; 3:5, 15). Accordingly, joy and exultation characterize the daily lives of Christians (1:6, 8, 9). Peter does not say that rebirth makes people happy, at least not in the way that word is commonly used. Peter does say that rebirth equips Christians with ability to see all of life in the light of the glory to be revealed when Christ returns.

The new life God gives in Christ is also a life of fulfillment, the fulfillment of all God's promises to Israel. What the prophets announced beforehand,

what they anticipated in the sufferings and glories of the Messiah, is precisely that saving grace that has enlivened believers (1:10–12).

Peter does not, however, promise a life of ease. If God gives his people a life of hope, joy, certainty, and fulfillment, it is also a life subject to testing and trial. Saving grace comes through the Christ who suffered and then received glory (1:10–11). That same pattern, from present suffering to future glory, characterizes the life of those reborn. For that reason, just as he describes the joy and hope, he also describes the suffering that attends Christian life (1:6). Such suffering, however, serves as an aid to grace and becomes a basis for even greater joy and praise to God. In light of God's redemptive purposes, the sufferings of his people, like the fiery testing of gold, will prepare them for the glory that awaits them at Christ's return (1:7).

If Christians' sufferings are to serve this purpose, they must be true to their calling as God's people. Peter addresses the implications of that calling in the exhortations that comprise the bulk of his letter.

III. THE IMPLICATIONS OF SAVING GRACE (1:13–5:11)

Peter exhorts his readers to fulfill their unique calling in the world. In 1:3–12 he expresses the content of saving grace; in 1:13–5:11 he exhorts his readers to conduct in keeping with saving grace.

A. Be True to Your Calling as God's People (1:14–2:10)

Christians, who are God's children through rebirth, are called to be uniquely his people. Peter elaborates that call in terms of holiness, love, and election.

1. Holiness (1:14–21)

Being God's people means being holy. In the Bible, holiness implies the setting aside of something or someone for God's work and will. The holy people of God are the people who have been distinguished by God's gracious calling for doing God's will in the world. Thus Peter urges the readers, as God's obedient children (by virtue of rebirth), not to be conformed to their prior way of life (1:14). Rather, they are to be holy as God is holy (1:15). In other words, who Christians are and what they do must be determined by that One to whom they belong, that is, by God who claims them as his children. Quite simply, as the holy people of God, Christians base their conduct in the world exclusively on God's revealed will. If they claim God as the Father, who desires only their best, they do not forget that he is also the Judge who demands their best. Accordingly, the holy life of God's people proceeds from reverential fear of God (1:17).

Peter makes it clear, however, that Christians do not simply try to be different. In fact, Christians *can* be holy only because of the historic manifestation of Christ. His death provided redeeming power to free Christians from **the empty way of life handed down to you from your forefathers** (1:18). It is only because they *have been* freed through Christ's death (1:18–19) that they *can be* free from their former way of life (1:14). Additionally, it is only because they have been established in a life of faithfulness and hope toward God through Christ's resurrection (1:21) that they can live consistently as obedient children of God. In short, through Christ all that hinders people

from being wholly faithful and obedient to God has been dealt with decisively. To be reborn is to be set free from former futile ways of life to a life of faithfulness to God. Peter's call to holiness is a call to appropriate fully all that Christ has done for his people so that the whole of their lives may be integrated and coordinated by God's will. In this sense, Wesleyans in particular have understood that Christians who *are* holy because they are reborn (1:2) are also summoned to a holiness that extends to the whole of their conduct (1:14–15).

2. Love (1:22–2:3)

Being God's people means governing relationships by love. Close attention to Peter's language will clarify what he has in mind when he calls his readers to love.

That he *commands* them to love one another already implies that **love** has essentially to do with one's will and disposition rather than one's emotions. Love is active goodwill or acting for the highest good of another person. Of course, "the highest good" must be understood in light of the good revealed by God in Christ. It is in this sense that Peter commands Christians to love one another.

As with holiness, however, the capacity to love is not natural. Rather, love is a capacity that Christians acquire when they receive life through the Gospel (1:23–25). Peter reminds them that when they were obedient to the truth of the Gospel they were purified so that they could genuinely love one another (1:22). Therefore, because they now have the capacity, they must love one another sincerely.

Of course, the love that governs relations among God's people will preclude all unloving attitudes and actions. Every sort of evil, deceit, insincerity, and slander must be rejected (2:1). The love that works for another's highest good in Christ cannot be invalidated by these typical and all too common features of human relationships.

Finally, love will order relations among God's people consistently only as they are nurtured continuously by the life-giving and sustaining Word of God. The Word that purifies Christians for a life of love must be to them as milk is to the nursing infant (2:2). By constantly feeding upon God's Word they will receive what they need to sustain mature relationships of love as they grow toward final salvation.

Wesleyans have described the capacity for and ascendancy of love in the Christian life with such expressions as "perfect love" and "Christian perfection." The biblical content of these expressions comes into clear focus in the light of Peter's remarks. Believers are called to love God wholly and their neighbors as themselves (see 1:8, 22; Mk 12:30–31). The capacity for such love comes as God's gracious gift through the Word (2:22–25). As Christians exercise that capacity, love reigns supremely over their relationships.

3. Election (2:4–10)

Being God's people means fulfilling their function as the **elect** of God. Some find the doctrine of election difficult to understand. For Peter, however, it is simply a fact that Christians are the elect people of God (1:1–2; 2:9; 5:13). Several observations will clarify what he means.

Election must be seen in relation to Jesus Christ. Christ is the Elect One of God who was "chosen before the creation of the world, but was revealed in these last times for your sake" (1:20). Christ's function as the Elect One of God serves as a basis for the Christian's election. Thus Christians, in coming to the Living Stone who is elect and honored by God, become living stones themselves and together comprise the elect and honored people of God (2:4–5, 9–10)—that is, as they come to Christ they become identified with his vocation as the elect of God. Christians are elect as they are in Christ.

If election is in Christ, then clearly election does not preclude personal faith. To use a Pauline expression, election is "by grace through faith" (Eph 2:8–9). Hence, the manifestation of Christ, the Elect One of God, occurred so that "our faith and hope might be in God" (1:21). Peter leaves no doubt that one's inclusion among the elect is dependent on one's trust in Christ (2:6–8; cf. 1:3–5; 5:9).

What does it mean to be the elect of God? Quite simply, the elect of God identify with the vocation of Christ and are a holy people who manifest God's glory in the world. As Christ bore the rejection of humanity, so will his followers. Yet as Christ fulfilled his calling as the Elect of God and was honored, so it will be for his followers. God's elect people identify with God's elect Son and assume his vocation in the world.

For this very reason, Peter concludes this section by ascribing to Christians the titles of honor enjoyed by Israel (2:9–10). Like the redeemed of old, those who have been redeemed through Christ are God's chosen, holy people who make known the wonderful deeds of God in the world. As the elect people of God they are the unique people through whose Christlike conduct God reveals his mercy and power to the world.

B. Act as God's People (2:11–4:11)

Peter now turns to address the conduct of Christians as God's people in the world (2:11–4:11). If they are God's people (1:3–12; 1:13–2:10), they must act as God's people.

1. Good conduct in situations of conflict (2:11–12)

Two guiding principles must govern the conduct of God's people. Negatively, they must abstain from **sinful desires.** These desires are characteristic of the pagan society from which they have been redeemed and to which they must no longer conform (1:14, 18). Since such desires would involve a rejection of redeeming grace (and militate against their souls), Christians must reject them.

Positively, however, there can be no withdrawal from the world. Rather, Peter calls his readers to maintain good conduct as they interact with non-Christians. Significantly, Peter calls them to do good and to demonstrate Christian grace to those who abuse them. In so doing, at least some non-Christians eventually will be able to glorify God on the final day.

In the sections that follow (2:13–4:11), Peter addresses several situations faced by his readers. In each of them he applies these general principles as he urges his readers to act as God's people.

2. Christians in society (2:13–17)

Peter draws on early and pre-Christian ethical traditions and shapes them for application to his readers' situation. These traditions stress the theme of submission to constituted authority as the fundamental way of ordering life (cf. Eph 5:22–6:9; Col 3:18–4:1; 1Ti 2–6; Tit 2–3). Christians will do good, says Peter, *by means of* their submission to the authority structures and social realities around them (2:13, 18; 3:1, 5; 5:5). It is important to observe, however, that the primary call of Christians is to good conduct, which

is shaped always by reference to God's will and the impact of grace on their lives. Therefore, the call to submit is a strategy for implementing good conduct in the world but is not an absolute call. If instances arise (as they did for Peter's readers) where doing good conflicts with submission, the former takes precedence over the latter.

As agents of good in the world, Christians should be subordinate to the worldly structures of authority. They are subordinate out of supreme respect for the Lord, who stands above all authority and whose interests all authority is meant to serve. In addition, through their submission they will be doing what is good as well as silencing the slanderous and ignorant charges of people against them. Such submission, Peter asserts, is the will of God for his readers (2:15).

If Christian submission expresses obedience to God, then Christians submit not as servants of Caesar but of God. In reality, they are *free* with respect to Caesar and *slaves* with respect to God (2:16). It is Christians' appropriate service to God that should compel them to reject all forms of evil and to do what is good by submitting to civil authority. Peter concludes by summarizing the unique relationships that shape all Christian conduct. While they hold all persons in honor, including the king (Caesar), they hold each other in love as they serve God in reverential fear (2:17).

3. Servants and cruel masters (2:18–25)

Peter next addresses household servants who likewise must maintain good conduct even in their difficult situations. The general rule for servants is this: **"Submit yourselves to your masters with all respect"** (2:18). "Fear," KJV, is not fear of the masters, but reverence of God, a fear basic to Christian life (1:17).

Peter's particular interest is the difficult situation of servants whose masters are **harsh** or "cruel." Christian servants must submit even to the harsh master. Of course, Peter assumes that the masters in question are simply mean men who ill-treat others without provocation. Thus he observes that when a servant provokes his master by disobedience or misconduct and receives a beating, that servant has not acted in a Christian way. But, when a servant, mindful of God, bears unjust treatment without retaliating, he demonstrates God's grace at work (2:19–20). More importantly, to bear unjust suffering in this way is to fulfill the Christian servant's calling (2:21–23). In beautiful and poetic words Peter lifts up Christ as the exemplar in whose footsteps these servants are called to walk. When Christ suffered he refrained from sin, deceit, retaliation, and threatening, and he committed himself to God who judges justly (2:22–23). Christian servants must do the same when they suffer.

On what basis can servants follow the example of Christ? They *can* because Christ's sufferings are redemptive as well as exemplary. In his suffering, Christ "bore our sins in his body on the tree" (2:24). Christ provided a full remedy for the problem of human sin, which otherwise would preclude the possibility of following his example in suffering. Through Christ's suffering we may be through with sins and live for righteousness (2:24). Moreover, in the wounds of Christ there is healing for these servants who sustain wounds from unjust suffering (2:24). Finally, by appropriating Christ's work for them, they have come under the protective care of Christ who acts as the

Shepherd and Overseer of their souls (2:25).

Peter urges Christian servants who suffer unjustly to meet suffering as Christ did. Yet he is not raising before them an impossible ideal. What these servants are urged to do, they are enabled to do as they appropriate the benefits of Christ's suffering.

4. Wives and non-Christian husbands (3:1–6)

In the situation of conflict and uncertainty that can arise from a marriage of a Christian and a non-Christian (note the mention of **fear** in 3:6), Christian wives must do good. That is, they are called to submit to their husbands even if husbands persist in rejecting the Gospel (3:1). It is, in fact, precisely through their submissive conduct that their husbands may be brought to faith without verbal argument or coaxing (literally, "without a word").

Peter assumes that authentic Christian conduct (here submission) flows from God's grace and has the power to attract and win non-Christians. He describes the wives' submissive life-style as pure and carried out in fear (3:2), recalling their purification at conversion (cf. 1:22 with 1:15–16) and the reverence that qualifies Christian life in general (1:17; 2:17). Such a lifestyle has a powerful missionary impact on non-Christians (cf. 2:12; 3:1–2). This fact provides us with the key for understanding Peter's instructions on the wives' adornment (3:3–4). Peter is not commenting on matters of fashion, as has been often assumed in some Wesleyan circles. Rather, he urges that a Christian wife's adornment, that upon which she depends for attracting and winning her husband to faith, should not be external but internal. The hidden person of the heart, not the fleshly outward appearance, will render the most effective witness to the Gospel.

Peter concludes by assuring these wives that in so relating to their husbands they are following the venerable example of the holy women of old who, like them, set their hope in God. In particular, the behavior outlined for Christian wives will demonstrate their kinship to Sarah and confirm their belonging to the people of God.

5. Husbands and their Christian wives (3:7)

Peter finishes his exhortations to specific groups by addressing Christian husbands. Because husbands and wives both share a new life by God's grace (1:3–4), they stand in a new relationship to each other. They must now live in partnership. That wives generally are acknowledged to be physically weaker should prompt the Christian husband to show her all the more consideration and honor.

It is important to note the basis and purpose for Peter's exhortation. Christian husbands and wives are fellow **heirs of the gracious gift of life.** Both share a common experience of grace and a common destiny of salvation. A husband must honor his wife since she, as much as he, has access to God's grace in Christ. In addition, since husbands and wives are partners together in grace, a husband's relationship with God will be affected for good or ill by his relationship with his wife. When husbands treat their wives with consideration and honor, they are true to the nature of grace. They are acting as God's people, and thus their relationship with God may be deepened through prayer.

6. The community's conduct when facing abuse (3:8–4:11)

Since all of the readers face situations of conflict, Peter now calls the whole community of Christians to maintain good conduct as they face abuse. Peter's concerns run in two directions: the community's internal relations, first sounded in 3:8 and taken up in 4:7–11, and the community's external relations with a hostile world (3:9–4:6).

a. The community's internal relations (3:8; 4:7–11)

Because Christians are reborn into God's loving family (1:3, 22–23), harmony, familial love, and mutual humility must shape all relationships (3:8). These qualities are not natural. They are manifested only when Christians appropriate God's grace in their relationships with each other.

If loving relationships depend on grace in times of calm, how much more in times of turmoil. Especially when Christians are abused and pressured because of their faith, *nothing* is more important than holding each other in fervent love (4:8). In the face of hostility, mutual love will help the community remain free from sin (4:8) and will provide the support that is needed to glorify God through Jesus Christ (4:9–11).

b. The community's external relations with a hostile world (3:9–4:6)

Peter's concern is that his readers respond appropriately to the hostility directed against them. Remarkably, in 3:9–4:6 we find Peter urging the same good conduct for the whole community as he did for servants and wives. Clearly the latter become examples to the former of appropriate response to suffering.

Christians are to face abuse as agents of peace. They must not repay evil with evil, but with blessing. They *must* because God calls them to such a response. Besides, their own ultimate blessing depends on this response (3:9). Peter explains why this is so by citing Scripture (3:10–12 quotes Ps 34:12–16).

The psalmist indicated that God's people must avoid all evil and do good because **"the eyes of the Lord are on the righteous and his ears are attentive to their prayer"** (3:12a). At the same time, the **"Lord is against those who do evil"** (3:12b). Accordingly, Christians who act as God's people must not retaliate but do good (as Christ did) because God promises blessing upon those who do good in the face of evil. For this reason, no one can *really* harm the Christian who takes the call to do good seriously (3:17). In light of God's promise, Christians know they ultimately *will* be kept safe.

Christians may, however, still suffer for righteousness. But that fact does not cancel out God's promise of blessing (3:14). Rather, when they suffer for doing good they must respond as agents of God's blessing (recall 3:9). Peter outlines three such responses (3:14b–16). First, they must not be intimidated by the threats of their adversaries. Second, they must recognize that Christ is the Master of the situation. Third, they must be prepared to share the reason for their hope (for their Christian lives) to anyone who asks. Peter assures them that by explaining their hope appropriately they will vindicate themselves in the face of their accusers (3:16). Each of these responses finds its roots in a principle that was illustrated and vindicated by Jesus Christ. The principle is this: If it comes to a choice between suffering for doing good or not suffering by doing evil it is always better (and pleasing to God) to suffer (3:17).

Peter argues that Christians who fight back will lose; if they do good, as Jesus did, God will bless them and make them victorious. This argument, however, is much more than mere assertion. As earlier, Peter recounts the sufferings of Jesus as the basis for a Christian response to suffering. In 3:18–22 we learn that Jesus' victory guarantees victory for all his followers.

This passage, one of the most difficult in the Bible, recounts a series of events in Christ's redemptive ministry: death, resurrection, proclamation to imprisoned spirits, exaltation, and lordship over all powers. This ministry, Peter insists, assures victory for Christians who suffer as Christ did. The fundamental statement comes first: Christ's suffering is wholly sufficient to bring suffering Christians safely to God. That fact is certain because Christ's suffering signaled two victories of crucial significance for Christians who suffer. The first victory is over sin and death, its chief consequence. Christians who suffer as Christ did have victory over sin (see 4:1), which indicates that even physical death cannot harm them ultimately. Therefore, they need not fear even in the presence of mortal danger; the tyranny of death has ended.

The second victory signaled by Christ's suffering is victory over the demonic spirits that inspire the evil adversaries of suffering Christians. This victory is the theme of 3:19–21. In the first century, Jews and Christians liked to speculate on obscure portions of Scripture and little-known biblical characters. One such passage was the story of the "sons of God" who married "the daughters of men" (see Ge 6:1–3), and one such character was Enoch (see Ge 5:21–24). It was widely believed that the disobedient spirits of Ge 6 had led to the corruption of the world and eventually to the Flood. According to this belief, God punished these spirits who continue to inspire evil on earth by imprisoning them until Judgment Day (see 2Pe 2:4–5; Jude 6). It was also widely believed that Enoch was a prophet of God who had been sent to these disobedient spirits to announce their condemnation. Peter draws on these widely held beliefs in order to say that *Christ* did, in fact, what had been ascribed to Enoch.

Christ's death and resurrection signal an absolute victory over these disobedient spirits and all the hostility they inspire against God's people. As it was in the time of Noah, so it is for Peter's readers. Just as God saved a few persons through flood waters despite the activity of demonic spirits, so now their new life signaled by baptismal waters also signals the final salvation of Peter's readers, despite the activity of those same spirits. Christ's death assures absolute victory over all evil spirits for Christians who suffer as Christ did. By virtue of Christ's victories over sin, death, and the demonic, Christians may follow his example and be confident of future victory.

Since Christ's suffering has proved to be the way to absolute victory, Christians must align themselves fully with that way. Peter exhorts: Adopt the same attitude that Christ displayed in his suffering (v.1a). In so doing, he implies, they will find that suffering confirms their decisive break with a life of sin and their distinctive Christian behavior. Because of their good behavior, their former companions may respond with surprise and slanderous abuse (4:2–4). Despite their abuse, however, the slanderous detractors will not have the final word. God will judge them (1:17) and will vindicate his people (4:5). Such assurance extends even to Christians who have died. The Gospel was proclaimed to them so that even if they were condemned by others in their earthly lives, they will be vindicated by God and someday, like Christ (3:18), be made alive in the Spirit (4:6). Therefore, Christians who remain faithful in their sufferings have assurance of final victory.

C. Depend on God's Future (4:12–5:11)

In this final section Peter sharpens and summarizes his exhortations. Christians who *are* God's people and who *act* as God's people recognize that their lives are shaped entirely by God's grace. Since that grace will issue in future victory for God's people, they must face their suffering in the light of the future God plans for them.

1. In response to hostilities (4:12–19)

Christians should not be surprised when they suffer. It is the nature of Christian life that it leads to conflict with the non-Christian world (1:6). The suffering that ensues, however, has redemptive value (see 1:6–7) and for that reason becomes a cause for joy. Such suffering confirms that Christians are in the succession of Christ and will receive glory as Christ did (4:13–14).

Peter does, however, caution his readers. They must be certain that their sufferings are *unjust* sufferings, that is, on account of their commitments to God (4:15–16). The God they serve is also the God who judges, and his judgment begins with his own people. Suffering, then, must motivate God's people to greater faithfulness and to supreme reliance upon God as their faithful Creator (4:17–19).

2. In structuring community life (5:1–7)

If Christ is the model for all Christians who face suffering, the leaders among them must be the best representatives of that model. Thus Peter addresses the elders not as a weighty apostle, but as a fellow elder in whose life the model of Christ may be seen. It is as one who presently suffers and who anticipates future glory that he addresses the elders (5:1).

As a leader who models the Christlike life, he urges his fellow elders to do the same. They must not lead by coercion or domination or for selfish gain. Rather, they must shepherd the flock of God, principally by way of example, so that when **the Chief Shepherd** (Christ) appears they may receive glory (5:3–4). That is, as Christ the Shepherd cared for his people by providing an example (2:21–24), so these elders must do for those in their charge.

If such a leadership style seems rather meek and unassuming, it does so by design. Peter concludes this section by exhorting all members of the community to relate to each other in a spirit of humility (5:5). He does this for good reason: Ultimately all things lie in the mighty hand of God who opposes the arrogant but gives grace to the humble. Consequently, Christians (both leaders and followers) must be submissive to God's mighty hand and await the grace that is sure to come. In the meantime, they commit all their cares to him who cares for them (5:6–7).

3. In resisting evil (5:8–11)

Peter ends his exhortations by placing his readers' situation in a broader, cosmic perspective. Christians must understand who the *real* enemy is: the Devil who assaults God indirectly by assaulting his people wherever they are found in the world. Further, they must understand that God has already won the battle in Christ. He is the God of all grace who calls them to a life of temporary suffering but whose grace *is* sufficient to bring them to glory (5:10).

That God has already won the victory must not, however, obscure the important role Christians play in the victory. Having recognized the true enemy, they must alertly, steadfastly, and unitedly resist that enemy by their faith. As they resist, they will depend on the call of their gracious God who in Christ *will* restore, strengthen, and establish them (5:10).

IV. FINAL GREETING (5:12–14)

The letter concludes with a summary of Peter's purpose for writing. He has declared the nature of God's saving grace that makes the readers God's people, and he has exhorted the readers to live by that grace.

Grace has made them the unique people of God, honored and blessed by God but suspected and abused by non-Christians. The same grace, however, provides them with all they need to be true to their calling as God's people and to conduct their lives in ways becoming to that call.

BIBLIOGRAPHY

Best, Ernest. *1 Peter*. NCBC. London: Oliphants, 1971.

Dalton, William Joseph. *Christ's Proclamation to the Spirits: A Study of 1 Peter 3:18–4:6*. Rome: Pontifical Biblical Institute, 1965.

Elliott, John H. *A Home for the Homeless: A Sociological Exegesis of 1 Peter, Its Situation and Strategy*. Philadelphia: Fortress, 1981.

Kelly, J. N. D. *A Commentary on the Epistles of Peter and of Jude.* HNTC. New York: Harper & Row, 1969.

Reicke, Bo. *The Epistles of James, Peter, and Jude. A New Translation With Introduction and Commentary.* AB. Garden City, N.Y.: Doubleday, 1980.

Selwyn, Edward Gordon. *The First Epistle of St. Peter: The Greek Text With Introduction, Notes and Essays.* 2d ed. Grand Rapids: Baker, 1981.

Senior, Donald P. *1 and 2 Peter.* New Testament Message. Vol. 20. Wilmington, Del.: Glazier, 1989.

Stibbs, Alan M. *The First Epistle General of Peter.* London: Tyndale, 1959.

2 PETER
David W. Kendall

INTRODUCTION

I. OVERVIEW
Second Peter urges its readers to a fuller understanding of Christian grace and to a deeper acquaintance with God and the Lord Jesus Christ. The primary concern is the Christian's growth in grace. Accordingly, the author sets forth an exposition of the resources God gives for the growing Christian, grounding these resources in the sure prophetic Word of God, now fulfilled in Jesus, and calling his readers to reject false teaching in order to grow in the grace and knowledge of Jesus (3:18).

II. AUTHOR
The writer of 2 Peter identifies himself as Simon Peter, a servant and apostle of Jesus Christ (1:1). That this is a reference to the apostle Peter of the Gospels finds confirmation when the writer claims to have been an eyewitness to the transfiguration of Jesus (1:16–18). In addition, the writer alludes to a previous letter to his readers, most probably 1 Peter.

Scripture scholars, however, have raised serious questions about the Petrine authorship of 2 Peter. Indeed, a comparison of the differing contents of 1 and 2 Peter, the differing occasion each letter seems to presuppose, and certain indications of the time period in which each letter was written have caused most modern scholars to deny Petrine authorship. It should be observed, however, that the evidence by no means precludes its possibility. Some scholars have suggested that, at the least, there is an indirect connection between our epistle and the apostle Peter so that the teachings and memoirs of the great apostle were taken up by a follower and fashioned into a second letter in order to deal with a situation of crisis within these early Christian communities.

III. RECIPIENTS
Peter writes to members of several Christian communities who have received and been grounded in the Gospel. They have received and are established in a "precious" faith (1:1) as members of the eternal kingdom (1:10–11), and they are acquainted with the writings of Paul (3:15). In addition, the readers are threatened by certain false teachers who have

perverted God's grace and who would lead them into theological and ethical error.

IV. OCCASION

Peter intends to remind his readers of the truth so that they may remember it and live by it after he dies (1:12–15). This reminder comes in response to a critical situation confronting the readers. Certain false teachers were troubling the churches by promoting destructive heresies that denied the lordship of Christ (2:1). Peter acknowledges the success of these false teachers—the way of truth was being reviled (2:2), the spiritually unstable were being enticed (2:14, 18), and some had already abandoned their faith (2:20).

Unfortunately, Peter does not elaborate on these heresies, and we are left to infer what they may have involved. Most likely the false teachers had misunderstood or misrepresented the teachings of Paul, particularly his understanding of Christian grace and freedom (see 3:16). Clearly these teachers believed they had a corner on the truth and boldly claimed divine authority for their teachings (2:10–11, 18). Evidently they believed grace made them "free" to do whatever they pleased (2:19). Accordingly, they exercised their "freedom" in immoral behavior and ridiculed those who did not follow their example (perhaps labeling them prudish or legalistic).

These false teachers, like others in the first century, could hold such teachings because they subscribed to a view of reality that understood matter as evil and spirit as good. Consequently, "salvation" involved a spiritual deliverance from the constraints of this evil material world. Since they were spiritually delivered, they were immune to contamination from the physical world, so they thought. In their view, "salvation" was all but complete, awaiting only the final liberation of the spirit from the body at death. In the meantime, since they had been "saved" they were "free," if they wished, to indulge the flesh.

Under the sway of such a worldview, these false teachers denied the essential character of Christian life and Christ's work of redemption, as it was understood by the apostles. Furthermore, they scoffed at the notion of Jesus' second coming, which seemed doubtful because of the temporal delay and, moreover, irrelevant because their "salvation" was already (so they thought) complete (see 3:1–10). Peter responds to this distorted theology. He reminds his readers of the truth of the Gospel which will lead them to a godly life (1:3) and a place in Christ's eternal kingdom (1:11).

V. OUTLINE

I. Epistolary Greeting (1:1–2)

II. The Resources for Growth in Grace (1:3–11)

III. The Basis for Growth in Grace (1:12–2:22)
   A. The Prophetic Word Fulfilled by Jesus (1:12–21)
   B. The Perverted Word Condemned by God (2:1–22)

COMMENTARY

I. EPISTOLARY GREETING (1:1–2)

Peter, writing as an apostle and servant of Christ, addresses Christians who have received the same faith he has received. This faith, made effective by the gracious work of Christ (**the righteousness of our God**), has brought Christians into a vital relationship with God (**the knowledge of God and of Jesus**). Peter writes with the prayer that his readers may deepen their relationship with God by growing in grace.

II. THE RESOURCES FOR GROWTH IN GRACE (1:3–11)

Peter makes an important assumption about the Christian life: it is a relationship with God that moves toward a future climax. Thus Christians continue to grow in anticipation of their future goal (see 1:3, **life;** 1:11, **the eternal kingdom**). At least two important aspects of Christian life follow from this assumption. First, Christians must grow in the grace and knowledge of God. Therefore, second, they must realize that life in grace never reaches a point (or a level) where growth is no longer necessary. For this reason, and especially in view of the circumstances of his readers, Peter writes to encourage growth in grace. In this passage he offers both a word of confirmation and correction for tradi-

tional Wesleyan understandings of grace. By way of confirmation, Peter indicates the transforming character of grace. Christian life can never be merely a change in one's status or position before God. Wesleyans have rightly insisted that grace effects a change in the whole of one's life before God. By way of correction, Peter indicates the dynamic character of grace. Christian life never reaches a state of grace where growth is arrested. As he asserts, the very character of grace demands an ever deepening, constantly growing, relationship to Christ.

In a real sense, to grow in grace is simply to take advantage of what God has already done for us. Peter declares that God, in divine power, has bestowed upon us all the resources we need to reflect his own glory and excellence (1:3), to escape from the impact of a corrupt world, and to participate in God's divine nature (1:4). These resources assume the form of promise, indeed very precious promises (1:4). God promises through his divine power all the resources needed for a growing and deepening Christian life.

Sincere Christians, then, will make every effort to trust God's promise, rely on God's power, and grow. Peter insists that genuine faith should express itself in decisive ways. Faith must shape what we are (character), what we know or think (knowledge), what we do (self-control), and how we do it (steadfastness, godliness, brotherly kindness, and love). A growing faith that is decisive in these ways will help Christians to live productive lives. Peter's chief concern is that his readers take full advantage of the resources God gives them in Christ. As they do, they will confirm the reality of God's call on their lives, and they will receive a rich welcome in Christ's eternal kingdom.

III. THE BASIS FOR GROWTH IN GRACE (1:12–2:22)

The circumstances that both Peter and his readers face make growth in grace urgent. The Lord had shown Peter that he soon would die (1:14). In light of that fact, Peter writes to remind his readers of the nature of Christian life and of the necessity for their continuing growth.

In addition, he has learned of certain false teachers who have infiltrated the churches and have promoted another understanding of Christian life. These heretical teachers (2:1) denied the lordship of Christ, led many into theological error (especially the weak in faith and newly converted), and promoted an undisciplined and immoral lifestyle. Their destructive teachings (see introduction), which presumed an authority above that of the highest angels, had led some to abandon the way of truth.

Such circumstances compelled Peter to remind his readers of the truth about grace. In this section he offers solid grounds for his urgent exhortation to grow in that grace.

A. The Prophetic Word Fulfilled by Jesus (1:12–21)

The issue of authority has always been of concern to the Christian community. How do we attest the claims of

those who would speak for God? From the very beginning Christians have understood that God's final revelation of truth came in his Son, Jesus, whose life and teachings were interpreted by the earliest apostolic followers (see, e.g., Lk 1:1–4). This apostolic interpretation and application of the truth revealed in Jesus became the rule against which all other teachings were measured. Peter reminds his readers of this rule and uses it as a basis for encouraging their growth in grace.

The apostolic teaching about Christ and the Christian life is not a human fabrication but a divine revelation that fulfills the prophetic Scriptures (the OT). Peter was among those who heard God's affirmation of Jesus as his unique Son. That initial affirmation, later validated by Christ's resurrection, verifies that the prophetic promises of Scripture find their fulfillment in Christ. Thus all of God's promises become effective and actual in the life of those who follow Christ. Conversely, none of God's promises come to fulfillment for those who do not follow Christ. Therefore, Peter urges, pay attention to (and live in) the way of life God has revealed in Christ. That way provides the only light there is in a dark world, and they must heed that light diligently until the dawn of Christ's final coming.

In this way, Peter affirms that the prophetic word of Scripture finds its fulfillment in Christ. Only through their continuing life in Christ can Christians find the fulfillment God's Word promises and thus grow in grace. Their eventual entrance into the eternal kingdom (1:14), therefore, depends on their adherence to the apostolic understanding of Christian life.

B. The Perverted Word Condemned by God (2:1–22)

Just as false prophets arose in opposition to the true prophetic Word of God in the past, so false teachers will arise in opposition to the word of Jesus, the One who fulfills that prophetic word. In fact, it is to meet the challenge of such false teachers and their perverted word that Peter writes.

If it is difficult to determine the content, the consequences of this perverted word are clear. The false teachers promoted **destructive heresies** that led to a denial of **the Sovereign Lord who bought them.** Whatever their specific tenets of faith, the practical outcome of their teaching involved a rejection of Christ as Lord and therefore a repudiation of Christ's saving work. This outcome, however, was far from obvious. Evidently the false teachers presented their theology in an attractive and persuasive manner. In fact, so many became followers of the "new" teaching that the integrity of the Gospel itself was in jeopardy (2:2). These confident and bold teachers preyed especially upon immature and new Christians (2:14, 18). Peter says that their acceptance of these heresies placed them in so great a danger that it would have been better for them never to have become Christians (2:20–22).

Two crucial issues were at stake in these heresies. First, and most fundamentally, was the issue of authority— who or what provides the norms for our lives as Christians? Second was the issue of Christian freedom—in what ways are Christians to express their freedom in Christ? Clearly the false teachers set up their ideas as normative for Christians, and that led to a distorted understanding of freedom. Just as clearly, Peter asserts that such teaching is a perversion of the Gospel, a denial of the lordship of Christ, and a way not to freedom and life but to bondage and death.

Peter responds to these false teachers with a scathing denunciation that demonstrates God's condemnation on this perverted word and its proponents. He cites examples from sacred traditions and Scripture to indicate how God deals with those who teach and act as these false teachers do. In each case, certain condemnation followed (2:4– 10). These examples show that the false teachers and all their adherents are headed for judgment. Peter concludes his denunciation by describing the corrupt behavior endorsed and practiced by these false teachers (2:11–16). By this means he exposes the moral impotence and ethical emptiness of their lives, only to demonstrate again the condemnation that awaits them.

Christians *must* reject such teachings and the lifestyle they endorse. Continued growth in grace and final entry into the eternal kingdom requires such rejection. Peter encourages his readers to make the proper response by assuring them that the Lord is fully able to rescue his people when they are tested by the slick and appealing arguments of false teachers (2:9).

The basis, then, for growth in grace is twofold. First, the prophetic word of Scripture has been fulfilled in Jesus whose person and teachings have become normative for living in grace. Second, the perverted word of the false teachers has met (and always will meet) with God's condemnation. By rejecting the false perverted word and by embracing the true prophetic word in Jesus, Christians find a solid basis for growing in grace.

IV. THE NECESSITY OF GROWTH IN GRACE (3:1–17)

Peter explains why it is necessary for Christians to continue their growth in grace. In so doing, he declares the error of the false teachers and why their teaching must be rejected.

God's triumphant work of grace

awaits its climax at the second coming of Christ. While Christians have come to a saving knowledge of God through Jesus, they have yet to reach their final destiny in the eternal kingdom. As they await their destiny, they are called to live as God's holy people in the world. Such a life necessarily involves a rejection of destructive heresies and continued growth in grace.

A. The Certainty of the Lord's Coming (3:1–7)

Many early Christians were disappointed when Jesus did not return immediately to bring final salvation and judgment to the world. The false teachers, in turn, denied the reality (and no doubt the necessity) of the Second Coming. That Jesus *had* not come meant that he *would* not come. This logic, in turn, suggested that he did not need to come. The false teachers who used this logic promised full and final redemption here and now and consequently mocked the notion of a Second Coming.

Peter's response is helpful in dealing with the modern as well as ancient scoffing at the idea of Christ's second coming. He reminds us that the holy prophets predicted not only the Second Coming but also the appearance of scoffers in the last times who would deny the Lord's coming. Therefore the appearance of these scoffers suggests that the readers are living in the time just before the coming of Christ. Ironically, despite themselves, these scoffers actually confirm the Second Coming!

Peter meets the challenge of the scoffers by affirming that God's word of promise is always effective. God created and sustains the world by the authority of his word. If his word has always vindicated itself in the past, at Creation and in the Flood, it will vindicate itself in the future. In other

words, when God speaks, it happens. Peter's first answer to the scoffers is that God can stand on his record—when he promises a final coming of Christ to judge and save the world, he can be trusted to keep his word. Peter declares the certainty of the Lord's coming.

B. The "Timing" of the Lord's Coming (3:8–10)

The Lord will keep his word, however, on his own terms. God's work is not calculated by the clock; he does not work in ways that are predictable in terms of hours and minutes (hence the folly of every attempt to predict the time).

Rather, God's work is calculated according to his purposes for his people and the world. The Lord is not slow, nor has he forgotten the promise of his return. In fact, the Lord is exercising mercy and patience. What seems like a delay must be understood as grace and love. The Lord continues to give time and opportunity to people because he does not want anyone to perish. He wants everyone to repent and to accept saving grace.

God's Word is sure, but God's Word is redemptive in its purpose. The so-called delay in the second coming of Christ is God's continuing gift of time and opportunity so that as many as possible may be reached for the kingdom.

C. The Responsibilities in View of the Lord's Coming (3:11–17)

If God's Word can be trusted and Christ will return for judgment and salvation, then Christians must be ready at all times for his coming. They will express their readiness by holy living as they anticipate the new heavens and new earth God will create. Peter understands the holy life in terms of loving relationships with others and with God. In such relationships, which are ultimately rooted in God's grace, Christians will seize every opportunity to cooperate with God's desire that all persons come to know him through Jesus.

That the Lord will come is precisely why Christians must grow in grace. Only as they continue to shape their lives by God's grace will they avoid the snare of false teaching and embrace God's saving work in the world (see the purpose statement in 1:4) in anticipation of their final triumph in the eternal kingdom (1:11).

V. THE FINAL EXHORTATION: GROW IN GRACE (3:18)

Peter concludes his letter with the exhortation to which all his remarks have led. If life in grace works as he has indicated and awaits its necessary climax at Christ's coming, then all Christians must grow in the grace and knowledge of the Lord Jesus Christ. To fail to grow is to fail to confirm one's call and election (1:10), which, in turn, is to fail finally to enter the kingdom. If, however, there is no hope for those who refuse to grow, there is abundant help for those who trust the very great promises of God's Word (1:3). The Lord who makes the promises knows how to deliver the godly (2:9) and to preserve them for the new world in which righteousness will dwell (3:13).

BIBLIOGRAPHY

See Bibliography for 1 Peter.

1, 2, AND 3 JOHN

H. Ray Dunning

INTRODUCTION

These epistles have a place of special interest in the Wesleyan tradition. Of the thirty texts upon which John Wesley is reputed to have based his teaching on Christian perfection, ten come from 1 John. But, strangely enough, this epistle also seems to offer powerful support for the opposite view (e.g., 1:8; 1:10), and those who argue against the possibility of present cleansing from sin are quick to take advantage of it (see Conner, 22–23). This anomaly whets one's appetite to explore the theological message of these letters.

I. AUTHOR

The first epistle is anonymous, but as early as the late second century it was attributed to John the apostle. This tradition has significant support; it stands today as a solid attribution, even if not universally accepted. The second and third Johannine letters have been less clearly identified with this John. The author of the two shorter letters refers to himself as "the presbyter" or "the elder" and many, both ancient and modern, have thought this suggests a different person from the apostle.

But 1 John and 2 John appear to address the same set of problems and thus to originate at about the same time.

II. DESTINATION

Although 1 John was the first of the General Epistles to be classified as a catholic epistle (Brown, 3), its nature and contents indicate that it was directed to a specific church or group of churches (Brooke, xxx), although these are unnamed.

III. THE SITUATION

The first epistle was written to a group of Christian believers who had experienced a division within their community. The seceders were making claims of superior spirituality, thus creating a sense of uncertainty in the minds of those who were left (2:19).

John is writing to those who have remained faithful to assure them that they are of the true faith. His intention is clearly stated in 5:13, "I write these things to you who believe in the name of the Son of God so that you may know that you have eternal life."

At the same time, he is speaking against the false character of the deserters. Tradition has identified the false teaching with a gnostic teacher named Cerinthus, known to be an opponent of John. However, contemporary scholarship has questioned this identification. We can identify the characteristic ideas opposed in the epistle. They involve a threefold perversion of the Gospel: (1) theological—denying the reality of the Incarnation; (2) ethical—being antinomian in regard to sin; (3) attitudinal—manifesting a lovelessness inconsistent with authentic Christian faith.

IV. THEOLOGICAL PERSPECTIVE

The central theological motif of the first epistle is *eternal life*, which is defined as *fellowship with God*. The presupposition that informs the message is that fellowship with God (eternal life) is possible only on the basis of the divine nature. That is, God's nature defines the conditions of fellowship. Three aspects of the divine nature (also emphasized in the fourth gospel) are identified: God is light; God is righteous; God is love. The whole letter revolves around these three themes, and they give us the basis for an outline of the contents.

V. OUTLINE

1 John

COMMENTARY

I. THE PREFACE (1:1–4)

This prologue parallels the prologue to the fourth gospel. But whereas the Gospel emphasizes the deity and eternality of the Word (*logos*), the epistle lays its stress on the full humanity of the Word that became flesh and thus is the **Word of life**. Hence the Word both embodies and conveys the eternal life that is the basis of **fellowship** (*koinonia*) with the apostles (**us"**) and with God (v.3).

The key theme of 1 John is **eternal life**. As in the fourth gospel eternal life does not primarily refer to unending existence as a future hope, but to the "life of the age to come" that has become a reality in the present. The NT writers all declare that the age to come has broken into the present age in the person and work of Jesus Christ (see Ladd, 45ff.). Thus to be united with him is to experience this life here and now.

The paragraph opens with a series of relative clauses, piled up to emphasize the reality of the Word become flesh. He was no mere appearance, as false teachers apparently insisted, but was subject to the empirical senses. He could be heard, seen, and touched: "to have *handled* was the conclusive proof of material reality" (Stott, 59).

That which was from the beginning here refers to the beginning of the Gospel, not the beginning of the universe (as Jn 1:1). John proclaims his own knowledge of it from personal contact with Jesus Christ.

II. GOD IS LIGHT— FELLOWSHIP AS WALKING IN THE LIGHT (1:5–2:28)

The key verse to this section is 1:5, identifying God as light. It is a summary of the whole discussion to follow. In Jn 1:9 the eternal Word is referred to as "the true light that gives light to every man" and in Jn 8:12 Jesus refers to himself as the "light of the world." Thus the epistle says, **We have heard from him** [Christ] this truth, clearly affirming that God's nature as light has been most fully revealed to the world through the Son. This is a logical corollary of the prologue, which speaks about a sensory revelation to those with whom John identifies himself (**us**). As in the Gospel, the antithesis of light is darkness, typical religious symbols for good and evil.

While **light** conveys multiple meanings, in this affirmation it declares that God is "the source and essence of holiness and righteousness, goodness and truth; in Him there is nothing that is unholy or unrighteous, evil or false" (Bruce, 41). This quality, then, becomes the first test of life. Those who know God (i.e., have eternal life) are those who walk in the light.

A. False Teachings (1:6–2:2)

The principle of fellowship by walking in the light is used to refute three false claims made by the teachers who are the opponents of the Gospel. These are addressed in 1:6–2:2, each one introduced by the phrase **If we claim** and then refuted.

False claim one (1:6): The claim to have fellowship while continuing in darkness (sin). Theologically this is known as antinomianism, a perversion to which the Christian Gospel is always susceptible (cf. Ro 6:1ff.). In this particular situation, it may have resulted from gnostic presuppositions that the spirit remains pure, even though the body, which is evil by nature, engages in immorality.

We lie is not falsehood in the sense of telling something contrary to fact, but "active hostility to the truth" (Brown, 199). As in the Dead Sea Scrolls, it refers to those who do not keep the law. Notice the distinctive designations, "doing a lie" and "doing the truth." This is why it can be said in 2:21, **No lie comes from the truth**. One cannot be "doing" both at the same time.

False claim two (1:8): The denial of the principle of sin in our nature. The meaning here goes beyond the guilt of transgression and refers to the inherited principle of sin, best defined as self-centeredness. The biblical writers, both OT and NT, recognized the human predicament as twofold, involving both acts of transgression and inward defilement. There is consequently a recognition that a twofold remedy is needed. It is hoped for in the OT (e.g., Ps 51:2; Zec 13:1) and proclaimed in the NT as presently available.

False claim three (1:10): The denial that one has sinned. This entails the denial of any need for atonement. Such a claim runs counter to both revelation and experience and could be made only on faulty presuppositions about either sin or human nature.

John counters each of these claims of the false teachers with a declaration of the true Gospel as revealed in Jesus Christ.

B. The Truth of the Gospel (1:7–10)

Truth number one: Walking in the light results in fellowship and cleansing (1:7), the antithesis of walking in darkness. "Walking" is an idiom for pursuing a certain way (cf. Ps 1); walking in the light implies actively living in conformity to God's will, as well as complete transparency.

Fellowship in this context apparently has a dual reference, including both God and fellow believers. The Bible consistently emphasizes the inseparability of vertical and horizontal relations; both are essential to true religion.

Purifies connotes sanctification, as distinct from justification. It refers to the divine provision to purify the "defilement of our fallen nature" (Stott, 76). It is appropriate to attribute this cleansing to the **blood of Jesus,** since the shedding of blood in the cultic sacrifices refers to sanctification (see notes on 2:1–2). It is used in the same ceremonial sense as in Hebrews but— as there—with ethical overtones.

It is important to note that **purifies** is in the present progressive tense and implies an ongoing provision for a moment-by-moment relationship.

Truth number two: Confession of sins results in forgiveness (1:9). John is not laying out the order of salvation but simply responding to the gnostic claim not to have sinned. (The issues are addressed in reverse to the traditional understanding of the order of salvation. Forgiveness of sins precedes cleansing from sin, both in experience and in theology.)

Faithful and just means dependableness or being true to promises given. God's promise is the basis of faith, confession is the human condition that becomes the occasion for claiming God's promise of forgiveness (cf. Dt 7:9; 1Co 1:9; 2Ti 2:13).

Truth number three: All have sinned and are in need of forgiveness (1:10). God's judgment is that the human race is universally in need of redemption (Ro 3:23). To claim otherwise is to **make him out to be a liar**. This is even more heinous than lying to ourselves (1:6).

Taken out of context, 1:10 appears to affirm the impossibility of freedom from sin in this life. But it ought to be interpreted in light of the larger context, including 3:6–10. The author is speaking against a position that claims never to have sinned, affirming the ongoing necessity of sinning after conversion.

C. The Ongoing Provision of the Atonement (2:1–2)

In the light of the forgoing provisions for forgiveness and cleansing, John says, **You will not sin.** Sin breaks fellowship, and the substance of John's message is that we may live in unbroken fellowship with God. However, in the light of human frailty and the constant liability to falling, he says provision is made in case something arises to disrupt fellowship. Jesus Christ comes to our rescue and pleads our cause. He is our Advocate, or Lawyer. This is a theological way of saying that God is always for us and never against us.

The NIV wisely renders *hilasmos* as **atoning sacrifice,** thus avoiding the controversy over whether it should be translated "propitiation" (appeasing God) or "expiation" (removal of sin). The clue to its meaning is found in the fact that this imagery appropriates the sacrificial theology of the OT. Some sacrifices function to establish covenant relations (see Ge 15). But the cultic sacrifices (cf. Lev 1–6), especially the sin offering, are for the purpose of maintaining covenant relations through the covering of inadvertent sins. The sin offering speaks of the need for ongoing purification, such as referred to in 1:7. In sum, *hilasmos* speaks of the continuous, sanctifying significance of the atonement (see Dunning, 359).

D. Knowledge of God Evidenced by Keeping His Commandments (2:3–11)

The thesis of this section is that walking in the light involves obedience to the commandments.

1. The commandments are summarized as "walking as Christ walked" (2:6). Here is one of John Wesley's favorite phrases to describe the essence of the sanctified life. The exciting implication is that the commandments are not arbitrary impositions designed to limit a believer but expressions of the nature of God as embodied in Jesus Christ. Thus they lead to the fulfillment of human personhood.

2. The commandments are embodied in love for the brothers (2:9–11). There is a dual purpose in the mind of the writer. Negatively, he is speaking against the loveless attitude of those who had seceded from this community of faith. Positively, he is emphasizing the centrality of love as the focus of the commandments.

John Wesley found in v.5 the possibility of perfection in terms of love: "'Made complete' means that the Christian's love is entire and mature" (Marshall, 125). In no sense can this mean a state of perfection that excludes the possibility of sin (2:1).

The command to love is **old** since it has been the ideal of divine-human and human-human relations from the beginning. The OT summarizes the commandments in terms of love, demonstrating that love always has been the essence of biblical faith (Dt 6:4–5; Lev 19:18). The commandment is **new** in the sense that a new enablement is available to those who are in Christ. This meaning is implicit in the last half of v.8, **because the darkness is passing and the true light is already shining.** This is a graphic way of speaking about the eschatological dualism that informs all NT theology. In Jesus, the age to come has broken into the present age so that the power of the age of salvation may be experienced in the here and now (see Heb 6:5). The choice of language is precise. The old is **passing** while the new is **already shining.** Thus the idiom of the two ages is portrayed here by the symbolism of light and darkness. Unlike apocalyptic theology, there is not a radical separation between the two ages but an overlapping so that we now are living in the time between the times. The new commandment belongs to the new age "which has been ushered in by the shining of the true light" (Stott, 94).

E. Exhortation to Various Groups of Believers (2:12–14)

Addressing his readers directly, John appeals to the believers at all stages of their spiritual development, warning them about the dangers that lurk in the shadows of the world of darkness.

Wesley used this passage to illustrate various stages of Christian experience. He identified **fathers** as those who were entirely sanctified, the spiritually adult in the congregation (see *Works,* 7:236–38). However he definitely did not consider the **children** and **young men** as second-class citizens, to be condemned for their level of maturation. They were simply pilgrims on the path toward their divinely intended destiny of being renewed in the image of God.

F. Exhortation to Avoid Worldliness (2:15–17)

John now speaks of the relation of light-dwellers to the world of darkness and warns against being influenced by it. Perhaps he is recalling Jesus' prayer that his disciples be in the world but not of it (Jn 17:15).

World is a Johannine idiom refer-ring to those who are part of the present age, the world system apart from Christ, humankind organized in rebellion against God. This world lies in darkness (see Jn 1:5; 12:46) and sin.

Do not love carries the idea of attraction to something in order to enjoy it. Why are love of the world and love of God contradictory? The answer is in 2:16 where John refers to the three avenues by which the **world** satisfies its desires: the unlawful pleasures of sense; the unlawful sights to be seen; the pride (vainglory) that comes from the possession of goods.

The transitory character of this age leads to a third digression in 2:18–27.

G. Warning Against Antichrists (2:18–27)

Based on their teaching, the seceders are condemned as **antichrist.** Certain key ideas emerge in this section.

The last hour may simply be a synonym for "the last days," a NT idiom referring to the time between Christ's first and second advents. Some, however, think it is more specific than that and suggest the climactic **hour** of the last days, hence the closing moments of history. The basic principle is the same in either case: That which is to appear in the end already appears in the penultimate period, though perhaps in paler form. This conceptual model justifies John's declaration that antichrist is to be embodied in a single person at the end of the age but is also a present fact. The spirit of antichrist will come to climactic expression in "the lawless one" (2Th 2:3–12) in the Day of the Lord, but that spirit is already at work in the world.

For John, seceders who deny the reality of the Incarnation embody the spirit of antichrist (4:3); here it expresses itself in denial that Jesus is the Christ. Those with gnostic tendencies who regard the material world as evil would have intellectual difficulty believing that the eternal Christ could be embodied in the human Jesus. Cerinthus, who many think is the main teacher rebuked here, taught that the Christ took temporary possession of the man Jesus at his baptism but departed before the Passion. Yet our redemption depends on a real Incarnation. Otherwise there is no salvation. Since this denial is at the same time a denial that the Father was really involved in our redemption, it denies the Father as well as the Son (2:22).

A second heresy of the seceders is also condemned: The claim to have esoteric knowledge not available to the general body of believers. In response, John declares the knowledge of truth to be universal among believers: **All of you know the truth.** This knowledge is the result of **an anointing from the Holy One** (lit. "the Anointed One," i.e., Christ).

What is the meaning of this anointing? Two major interpretations have been offered. First, based on the OT use of the term, most interpreters think it refers to the Holy Spirit. This has the added strength of being the natural interpretation of the work of the Paraclete referred to in John 14:17; 15:26; and 16:13. However, this position is open to the same criticism as the claim of the heretics. It can be accused of being a private illumination susceptible to subjective fantasizing.

The second proposal avoids this weakness by referring the **anointing** to the Word of God. There is a parallel to this idea in 2:14 and 2 John 2 where the Word of God or truth remains in them (this would be the preached word). This view has an objective point of reference that avoids the latent subjectivism of the first position.

Following I. de la Potterie, I. H. Marshall attempts to combine the two by defining the anointing as "the Word taught to converts before their baptism and apprehended by them through the work of the Spirit in their hearts (cf. 1 Thess. 1:5f)." In summary, this interpretation says that "the antidote to false teaching is the inward reception of the Word of God, administered and confirmed by the work of the Spirit" (Marshall, 155).

The reference to the **anointing from the Holy One** is clearly a reference to Jesus and is another evidence of the writer's commitment to the incarnational truth of the Gospel with which he opened his epistle.

H. Summary (2:28)

The one who came as Bethlehem's Babe will be the same one who will return as conquering Judge. The same truth that he brought at his first appearing will be the basis of judgment at the second. Those who remain in him may therefore live without fear or shame in anticipation of that final event. (Some commentators think this verse introduces a new section; here it is treated as a closing exhortation to the preceding section.)

III. GOD IS RIGHTEOUS— FELLOWSHIP AS DOING RIGHTEOUSNESS (2:29–4:6)

In 2:29 John declares his thesis; the subsequent verses serve as an exposition of its implications. A new metaphor is introduced here in the words **born of him.** It is not new, however, to the Johannine world of thought, since it is a major motif in Jesus' conversation with Nicodemus (Jn 3). Here it appears to be used primarily to introduce the concept of sonship since the following passages emphasize the necessity of children bearing the family likeness. This is a truth that runs throughout

Scripture. God's people are to manifest his character in their daily lives; here that character is defined as **righteousness**.

A. Likeness to God to Be Perfected at the Second Coming (3:1–3)

Just as the Word who became flesh was not welcomed when he appeared in human history because the world did not know who he was (Jn 1:10–11), those who share his character likewise will go unrecognized. They travel incognito, as he did. Nonetheless, God's intention to have a creation in his own likeness is now being fulfilled. The perfected replica, however, must await the Consummation.

Yet this goal provides a powerful magnetic force that even now draws those who have been born into the family of God toward ever closer conformity to the divine likeness. This truth is one of the major emphases of Wesleyan theology as it speaks of the image of God as the *telos* toward which the lifelong process of sanctification is moving the faithful believer.

While the point is not explicitly made, it seems clear from the repeated incarnational emphasis that John is thinking of the Father's image being most fully present in the Son as the paradigm of full maturity. "Being like him when he appears" has this connotation. Subtly, John has moved from speaking about the Father to speaking about the Son. In a word, this implies that holiness is Christlikeness.

B. Righteousness the Antithesis of Sin (3:4–6)

Pursuing righteousness, i.e., conformity to the Father in the Son, cannot coexist with sin, defined here as lawlessness. The KJV has obscured the real meaning of this definition by giving it a legalistic flavor. Sin is an attitude before it is a behavior, the latter being an expression of the former. This is the truth that informs Wesley's classic definition of sin as "a voluntary transgression of a known law of God." There is no superficial Pelagianism in this but a profound recognition that, at its roots, sin is essentially antagonism to God that refuses to acknowledge his sovereignty.

The real point of the argument here is to emphasize that the purpose of Christ's coming is to do away with sin. The Sinless One cannot cover for "sinning saints." No doubt the antinomian seceders lurk in the background. John wants his readers to know that their claims to spirituality—while living immoral lives—can withstand neither the test of logic nor of truth. The Atonement covers sin by destroying it, not by hiding it from God's view.

C. Children of God Contrasted with Children of the Devil (3:7–10)

The idea of family likeness continues: As God's children, we bear his likeness. Conversely, the children of the Devil bear his. But once again John focuses on the positive purpose of the Incarnation, to **destroy the devil's work.** The Devil's work is sin; Christ's work is to put an end to sin (the practice of sinning) and this result occurs with those who have truly experienced the new birth.

God's seed remains in him; he cannot go on sinning has been a troublesome phrase. The NIV properly captures the meaning and avoids the problem posed by the KJV, "cannot sin." It does not describe moral inability. It describes the incompatibility of sin and the new birth. One cannot continue sinning and have **God's seed** (RSV "God's nature"; NEB "the divine seed") remain in him. This is one of the strongest passages in Scripture on "sinless perfection," but such a term is dangerous and should be balanced with 2:1. John Wesley consistently rejected such terminology.

D. Righteousness Manifested in Love of the Brothers (3:11–24)

This lengthy section focuses on righteousness in terms of love, a theme to which the writer returns again and again. He elaborates the theme first by emphasizing a contrast between love and hate, illustrating the latter with a hate-motivated fratricide, Cain's murder of Abel. As Jesus taught, the attitude of the heart is as heinous and guilty before God as the act.

Then he illustrates the reverse by the model of Christ as self-giving love. Just as the Incarnation is the criterion of truth, so it is the paradigm of love. Here we learn that God's kind of love is more than an emotion but is defined by self-giving action. The most graphic expression of such love is to lay down our life for **our brothers.** Although few face this necessity, most believers have occasion to show this love by sharing. Love is "the willingness to surrender that which has value for our own life, to enrich the life of another" (Dodd, 86).

Loving behavior is now described as the basis of confidence before God (3:19–24). Knowledge that one has eternal life is the major concern of this epistle. John now addresses an important issue in connection with this matter—confidence before God: If love (*agape*) were merely an emotion and not a lifestyle, it would be a tenuous basis for certainty since the ebb and flow of emotions would make for vacillating certainty. The confidence that one has love, and thus that he knows God (has eternal life), is evi-

denced by this self-sacrificing way of life.

Whenever our hearts condemn us may refer to a guilty conscience or perhaps to an uncertainty about our acceptance by God. **God is greater than our hearts** may be interpreted as suggesting that God condemns us the more. However, this is no consolation. The context makes it clear that John is suggesting that God's knowledge of us and the life of love lived out is more significant than our own feelings about acceptance. As Barclay says, "The perfect knowledge which belongs to God, and to God alone, is not our terror, but our hope" (Barclay, 103).

Wesley's mature understanding of the witness of the Spirit is informed by this truth. He spoke of those who, in the early days of the revival "made sad those whom God had not made sad." They would ask, "Do you know that you are a child of God?" If the answer was not a clear affirmative they would respond, "Then we know you are not." Wesley came to see that the "witness" was not essential to acceptance with God. It was, on the other hand, the privilege of ordinary believers, and one they should seek diligently (see *Letters,* 5:235, 359; *Works,* 7:199; and Dunning, 441–48).

The relationship of a sense of acceptance (does **not condemn us**) and confidence gives a boldness in God's presence that Wesley would call the "faith of a son." Such a confidence has a twofold result: (1) the freedom to ask largely with expectation that the Father's love will respond, and (2) not merely keeping commandments, which might be mere legalism, but doing that which pleases the Father, even going beyond the letter of the law.

The commandment we are to keep calls for faith and love. Their relation is one of the most important considerations in a proper theology of the Christian life. "Here the faith is the initial act of believing which leads to the life of faith. . . . Faith in Christ, then is the first step of life in the family of God, and this life is a life of love as well as a life of faith" (Bruce, 100).

E. Exhortation to Test the Spirits (4:1–6)

Once again John turns his attention to the false teachers. Two spirits are in the world: the spirit of Christ and the spirit of antichrist. One should test the spirits to see which he shares. Appeal to spirit (enthusiasm) or even to the Spirit is not an adequate guarantee of truth. The NT writers consistently insist that the person of Jesus Christ as the incarnation of God's truth is the only valid test of truth.

In one sense, this brief passage could be considered the focal point of the whole epistle since the Incarnation and its reality is the basis of every claim made against the perverse teachings, behavior, and attitudes of the secessionists. John's doctrine of the Holy Spirit is Christological through and through.

IV. GOD IS LOVE— FELLOWSHIP AS ACTING IN LOVE (4:7–21)

This section does little more than bring together themes that have been introduced throughout the previous passages. They have been used there more or less as illustrations of the motifs of light and righteousness, aspects of God's nature defining the basis of fellowship. But here they are derived directly from the proclamation that **God is love.** For that reason we have a third major movement in the symphony of this great letter.

It is important to recognize that the declaration **God is love** must be heard in tandem with the other two motifs of

this letter. Many have failed to do this and the result is a sentimentality that loses touch with the holiness of God (reflected in the idioms of "light" and "righteousness"). Neither is love alone to be considered the test of life. "John makes it plain enough elsewhere that the true child of God *both* believes *and* loves ([3Jn] 3:23)" (Marshall, 211).

John addresses three major truths in this section, and they are interwoven throughout, which is a characteristic of his literary style.

A. God as the Source of Love

The implication of this point is theologically crucial: Our love is a response to God's love and not the basis of his love for us. A further truth is that our love is enabled by God's love and not independently produced. God's gift of his Son for our salvation is that which defines the meaning of love, as John has stated before. This thought is the occasion for a further emphasis on the relation of love and sound doctrine. If God's gift of his Son was a charade (as the false teachings would imply) and the Son was not a real human being fully involved in our history, God's love is called into question. Hence, belief that the human Jesus was the Son of God is essential to the validity of the claim that God is love. There is no artificial connection between love and sound doctrine and no tension between them (Bruce, 110–11).

B. Living the Life of Love

Interestingly, John does not draw the conclusion that because God loved us, we ought to love him; rather he declares that we **ought to love one another** (v.11). This in no way suggests that love for God is an illegitimate concept. The first commandment enjoins it. It does imply that a mysticism that could result from an exclusive preoccupation with love for God is misguided. Love for God must show itself in love for a tangible human being. This shift not only recognizes the finite difficulty of loving a reality **not seen,** but the importance of showing love toward those who *need* love. In a word, love for God will show itself in self-sacrificing love for others. They are inseparable truths.

C. Love Can Be Perfect

Here in 4:17–18 is another central Wesleyan text, providing reinforcement to the claim for the present possibility of **perfect love.** Such love produces boldness, a distinctive emphasis of this letter (see 2:28; 3:21; 22; 5:14, 15). Here it is future oriented and refers to the Day of Judgment. Absence of fear (boldness) derives not from a sense of self-sufficiency but from the relation of child to Father. Love and fear of punishment are incompatible. This does not imply flawless behavior on the part of the child; any claim to perfection at this level can result only in bigotry. Rather it is God's full and free acceptance and the believer's trust in his love that elicits a full confidence that excludes fear and uncertainty.

V. SUMMATION—LIFE IN THE SON (5:1–21)

All the themes from the previous arguments are now woven into a lovely tapestry of truth regarding eternal life, which is **life in** the **Son** (v.11). Like an intricate tapestry, it is difficult to structure and present in outline form. The following may be helpful if not completely adequate.

A. Results of Life in the Son (5:1–5)

A whole series of relations are summarized in this paragraph: the relation between faith and love, belief and the new birth, the new birth and victorious living, faith and triumph over evil, faith and enabling grace (from the Son). Each of these could be the subject of a major theological dissertation. Nonetheless, all are necessary to a full-orbed presentation of truth about the Christian life. We focus on the one really new element: Overcoming the world.

There is a play on words in the clause **This is the victory that has overcome the world** that cannot be reproduced in English. In the Greek a different form of the same root is used for both **victory** and **overcome.** The first refers to an individual experience in the past, a victory won. It is this conquest that enables ongoing victory over the world. **The world** is the world of darkness, antagonistic to the children of God (see notes on 3:11–15). In his death on the cross, Jesus entered into mortal combat with the powers of darkness and overcame them in his death. When by faith we appropriate the benefits of his atoning work, we enter into the power by which he gained this victory and thus in him we have (and do) overcome the world (v.4). It is the finished victory at the cross (past tense) that is the source of the present victory available to persons of faith: "To believe that Jesus has been victorious is to have the power that enables us to win the battle, for we know that our foe is already defeated and therefore powerless" (Marshall, 229). This focus on the victory of the Son as the source of the believer's life leads to a comment on the Son and the witnesses to his validity.

B. Witnesses to the Son (5:6–12)

The previous section has emphasized the importance of faith in the Son and, as in his gospel, John holds that faith depends on testimony, thus "the reasonableness of believing in Jesus is grounded upon the validity of the testimony which is borne to Him" (Stott, 176).

1. The water and the blood

Water probably refers to Jesus' baptism and **blood** to his death. It emphasizes the unity of his life, in contrast to the false teaching that joined the eternal Christ with the human Jesus at his baptism but separated them before his death. This emphasis is at one with the early preachers in Acts who insisted that the glorified Christ was this same Jesus whom their audience had put to death (Acts 2:32). He was fully human and fully divine throughout his whole career; thus there is life in the Son.

2. The Spirit

This refers to the Spirit speaking through the Word, convincing the hearer of the truth of Jesus to which the Word bears witness (see note on 2:20–23).

3. The Spirit, the water, and the blood

(Persons familiar with the KJV will recognize that the witness of the heavenly Trinity is omitted. See any contemporary commentary for a full explanation of this exclusion. It has no valid manuscript support.) Here John collates the earthly witnesses (**water and blood**) with the witness of God (cf. Jn 5:36–37). The Spirit bore witness to the historical Jesus and continues to bear witness to his authenticity. No doubt the phrase here refers to the internal witness of God to the truth of the objective witness of the **water and the blood.** The result of accepting God's testimony is **life in the Son.**

C. Concluding Notes (5:13–21)

1. Confidence in prayer (5:13–15)

This is a good summary of the whole epistle in terms of its purpose. The members of the church to whom John wrote were in a state of uncertainty about their own status. He has now built his case: They are true believers; those who had separated from them were false. This awareness should give them confidence (a distinctive emphasis of 1 John) in the presence of the heavenly Father. They can **ask anything according to his will** and expect to receive it. This is not an invitation to "name and claim" anything their carnal desires may want. The stipulation **according to his will** elevates it to moral, truly spiritual commitment to God's knowledge of what is best.

2. Responsibility to the fallen brother (5:16–17)

The redemptive attitude represented here presents us with no difficulty of understanding. The distinction between a sin unto death and one that is not does. As Bruce puts it, "It is difficult to see how they could recognize the distinction except by the result" (p. 124). Various theories have been offered. Perhaps the safest course is to assume that any fallen (or falling) brother is redeemable and to seek to be the divine instrument in his restoration.

3. Security in the Son (5:18–20)

The key word of the epistle, **know,** comes to the forefront as John rehearses the certainties he has described in his letter. It is a recapitulation of the basic themes. While the gnostic teachers claimed superior knowledge, the believer in Christ "knows" certain practical and existential truths because he has known the **true** Representative of the **true** God and thus is saved (has eternal life).

The first thing we **know** is that the new birth results in new behavior. Second, we **know** we belong to God and have been delivered from the dominion of Satan. Third, we **know** that we have found the source of life in Jesus Christ, the incarnate Son of God.

4. The final word (5:21)

This brief and somewhat abrupt closing exhortation may be a simple, straightforward warning against idolatry. But nothing in the letter anticipates it. In the light of the struggle throughout the letter between the false teaching about the Incarnation and the truth of it, Blaiklock's suggestion may be correct. He says it means, "Do not abandon the real for the illusory" (quoted in Stott, 196). At the least, it warns us to avoid faulty conceptions of God. The true God is, as the whole letter insists, to be found in Jesus Christ, the Son of God, incarnate in human history.

2 JOHN

This epistle is the shortest in the NT. It is closely akin to 1 John and emphasizes the same themes. The author identifies himself as **the elder** (v.1). This is not necessarily an official ecclesiastical title; it probably refers to one who is known and respected in the community, being of venerable age and a bearer of tradition. In this case, he would seem to be one who provided the link between this community and the origin of the Gospel. (See Introduction for fuller discussion of authorship.)

I. THE DESTINATION (VV.1–2)

The letter is addressed to **the chosen lady.** This may refer to an individual, or it may be a euphemism for a local congregation. The nature of the contents leads most contemporary interpreters to identify the **lady** as a church. **Her children** would then refer to members of the church who are known to the author. These somewhat veiled references may reflect a period of persecution when it was prudent to avoid speaking too openly.

The word of address is given with deep affection. The phrase **love in the truth** may mean "in all Christian sincerity" (Stott, 202), since the definite article is absent in the Greek. There could also be a suggestion that some are outside the truth, reminiscent of the situation addressed in 1 John.

II. THE GREETING (V.3)

John adopts the threefold greeting used in the Pastoral Epistles. These blessings flow from the Father and the Son of the Father. "Grace and mercy are both expressions of God's love, grace to the guilty and undeserving, mercy to the needy and helpless. Peace is that restoration of harmony with God, others and self which we call 'salvation.' Put together, peace indicates the character of salvation, mercy our need of it and grace God's free provision of it in Christ" (Stott, 204). The wording of this statement about Jesus Christ indicates that John has in mind the false teachings that he discounts in vv.7–11.

Both truth and love are keynotes of this short letter, the former being used five times and the latter four times. These two are important correlatives in Johannine theology. Love without truth is sentimentality, and truth without love is harshness (see Eph 4:15).

III. THE OCCASION FOR THE LETTER (V.4)

The writer has encountered some of the **children** of the "elect lady," probably members of the church who were in the vicinity where he lived. He writes to express his joy that they are walking in the truth according to the commandment (this terminology is characteristic of the Johannine literature). But he also takes this opportunity to warn the church against false teachers.

IV. THE WARNING (VV.5–11)

The exhortation to **walk** in love and obedience merely reiterates one of the major emphases of 1 John and possibly suggests that the author is seeking to guard against antinomianism in behavior and lovelessness in attitude, both characteristic of the false teachers referred to in 1 John.

Many deceivers suggests that there is a danger this congregation may be contaminated by the false teaching. The theological dimension of it is Christological, denying that the Incarnation is real (see notes on 1 John). **The teaching of Christ** is regarded as the test of truth and the **deceivers** have run ahead of this. One of the major tests of aberrant teaching is the claim to have gone beyond the revelation in Jesus Christ to new or better "truth." But for John and the NT as a whole, God's final revelation has occurred in and through his Son (see Heb 1:1–3).

John's words against extending hospitality to such teachers must be read against the background of the situation. Many traveling teachers and prophets were in the early church. Usually they were welcomed into the churches to teach and/or preach. This congregation is being advised to test such a person's doctrine and not allow perversive instruction in the **house.** One of the early Christian documents, the Didache, gives similar instruction: "Let every apostle who comes to you be received as the Lord. . . . But not everyone who speaks in the spirit is a prophet; he is only a prophet if he has the ways of the Lord. The false and the genuine prophet will be known therefore by their ways" (Bettenson, 51).

V. CONCLUSION (VV.12–13)

John hopes for a personal visit in the near future. Some have suggested that the words reflect the failing strength of an old man to whom writing is a burden. He sends greetings from the members (**children**) of a sister church, no doubt the congregation where he lives.

3 JOHN

I. SALUTATION (VV.1–4)

As in 1 John the author identifies himself as **the elder** (see notes on 2Jn 1). This personal note is addressed to an individual named Gaius, possibly a leading member of this church. It is impossible to determine precisely which Gaius is intended, since this was one of the most common names in the Roman Empire. He is held in high esteem by the writer who has utmost confidence in his religion. Once more, the central concern about walking in the truth appears.

The greeting is somewhat unusual. Instead of the common form normally used, there is a more personal wish for Gaius's physical and spiritual well-being.

II. THE ISSUE OF THE LETTER (VV.5–8)

This exhortation addresses a reverse issue from that in 2 John, which forbids hospitality to the false teachers (see notes on 2 John); in 3 John the author urges that hospitality be extended to traveling teachers of the truth. Evidently, there had been some trouble in the church caused by a member named Diotrephes (see v.9) who had been instrumental in keeping such traveling preachers from exercising their ministry to the congregation. John wanted Gaius to set an example of hospitality to the rest of the people.

III. THE TROUBLEMAKER (VV.9–11)

Whatever position this **Diotrephes** held in the church, he had prevented one of John's letters from being read and had spoken maliciously against him. Possibly he was a sympathizer with the false teachers whom John opposed. He prohibited others from preaching (preferring to do it himself evidently, according to v.9) and excommunicated those who were favorable to the traveling preachers. Here is a "church boss" par excellence! We can only guess how this man attained such a place of power, but John's condemnation of him is severe. To Gaius he says, "**Do not imitate** [him]."

IV. THE GOOD DEMETRIUS (V.12)

Demetrius is probably the bearer of the letter to Gaius. He stands in stark contrast to Diotrephes. He has a threefold witness to his goodness: his brethren all give him a good report, the Spirit of truth (the Holy Spirit) approves him, and John testifies on his behalf. He was surely a godly man.

V. CONCLUSION (VV.13–14)

The closing is almost identical to 2 John. The use of the term **friends** implies a close relation among members of the early church.

BIBLIOGRAPHY

Barclay, William. *The Letters of John and Jude* in *DSBS*. Philadelphia: Westminster, 1960.

Bettenson, Henry, ed. *The Early Christian Fathers*. Oxford: Oxford University Press, 1978.

Brooke, A.E. "The Johannine Epistles." ICC. Edinburgh: T. & T. Clark, 1964.

Brown, Raymond. *The Epistles of John*. AB. Garden City, N.Y.: Doubleday, 1982.

Bruce, F.F. *The Epistles of John*. Grand Rapids: Eerdmans, 1970.

Conner, W.T. *The Epistles of John*. Nashville: Broadman, 1957.

Dodd, C.H. "The Johannine Epistles." *MNTC*. London: Hodder & Stoughton, 1946.

Dunning, H. Ray. *Grace, Faith and Holiness*. Kansas City: Beacon Hill, 1988.

Ladd, George Eldon. *A Theology of the New Testament*. Grand Rapids: Eerdmans, 1975.

Marshall, I. Howard. "The Epistles of John." ICC. Grand Rapids: Eerdmans, 1978.

Stott, J.R.W. "The Epistles of John." TNTC. Grand Rapids: Eerdmans, 1978.

Wesley, John. *Explanatory Notes Upon the New Testament*. London: Epworth, 1954.

———. *Letters to the Reverend John Wesley*. Edited by John Telford. 8 vols. London: Epworth, 1931.

———. *Works of John Wesley*. 3d ed. 14 vols. London: Wesleyan Methodist Book Room, 1872. Reprint, Kansas City: Beacon Hill, 1978.

JUDE

John E. Stanley

INTRODUCTION

Four introductory issues relate to the interpretation of Jude: authorship, date, the relationship of Jude and 2 Peter, and the literary form.

I. AUTHOR AND DATE

Dating Jude depends on identifying the author. Richard Bauckham, Duane Thompson, and Delbert Rose have argued that Jude was the brother of James and Jesus (Mk 6:3). J.N.D. Kelly disputes that claim. The opponents of Jude, however, are similar to the incipient gnostics Paul addressed in the A.D. 50s in 1 Corinthians, as Thompson and Rose acknowledge. Jude can be dated early enough to allow authorship by the brother of James and Jesus.

II. RELATIONSHIP OF JUDE AND 2 PETER

The contents of Jude and 2 Peter, especially 2Pe 2, are similar, as indicated by the following chart.

Jude	2 Peter	Jude	2 Peter
4	2:1–3	11–12	2:13–14
5	2:5	12–13	2:12
6–7	2:4, 6	16	2:18
8–9	2:10–11	18	3:3

III. LITERARY FORM

Jude uses six OT illustrations. They include the wilderness rebellion, the giants on earth (Ge 6:1–4), Sodom and Gomorrah, Cain, Balaam, and the rebellion of Korah. Jude did not follow the order in which these incidents appear in the Hebrew Bible. Second Peter, on the other hand, uses three of these references (2:4, 5–6, 15) and arranges them in the order they appear in the Hebrew Bible. Jude 9 seems based on the pseudepigraphal Assumption of Moses. Jude 14–15 explicitly quotes 1En 1:9. Second Peter omits the Enoch citation and discreetly disguises the allusion to the Assumption of Moses. It appears that 2 Peter has a tighter concept of what constitutes Scripture than does Jude. Jude is earlier than 2 Peter, contrary to John Wesley's view. Second Peter probably is dependent on Jude.

Jude is a general letter, not addressed to a specific church. That a specific controversy occasioned its writing, however, may be seen in the fact that it attacks a specific group of opponents. Jude's polemic alternates descriptions of the opponents (vv.4, 8, 10, 12–13, 16, 19) with judgments against them based on authoritative traditions (vv.5, 7, 9, 11, 14–15, 18).

IV. JUDE AND THE WESLEYAN QUADRILATERAL

Sometimes tensions exist between those who emphasize faith as a creed and those who stress faith as the relational means of Christian experience. At first glance Jude seems to give faith priority to tradition, even as that tradition was becoming Scripture. Jude functions as an apologist who used reason. Yet "loved" and "saints" are relational words denoting Christian experience. Thus Jude appeals to tradition, Scripture, reason, and experience—the same four avenues to truth valued by Wesleyans.

V. OUTLINE

I. Greeting (vv.1–2)

II. Polemic (vv.3–19)

III. Exhortation to Edification and Evangelism (vv.20–23)

IV. Doxology (vv.24–25)

COMMENTARY

I. GREETING (VV.1–2)

Jude identifies himself as **a servant of Jesus Christ and a brother of James.** Jude does not call himself an apostle.

The author addresses the readers generally as **loved, called,** and **kept.** Two features imply Jude was sent to a specific people. **"Loved"** and **"dear"** (vv.1, 3, 17, 20) denote a close, even affectionate, relationship. **"Kept"** and the imperative **"keep"** in v.21 signify a desire to preserve the readers from the doctrinal and moral threats Jude graphically describes.

II. THE POLEMIC (VV.3–19)

While preparing to write in general about **the salvation we share,** a crisis motivated Jude to exhort saints **to contend for the faith that was once for all entrusted** to them. *Pistis* ("faith") has several possible meanings. Faith is trust in Christ (Ro 5:1), an assured attitude toward the future (Heb 11:1), or a spiritual gift (1Co 12:9; 13:2). In Jude 3 faith is that which is believed, a system of belief. Like Paul in 1Co 11:3 and 15:3, Jude's language evokes images of a reliable tradition delivered and received. V.20, when translated objectively rather than as an instrumental dative, reinforces Jude's concept of "the faith" as authoritative doctrine linked to the apostolic era (v.17). Jude's appeal to a belief system sets doctrinal boundaries for his offensive against false teachers. Ironically, Jude does not spell out the content of the opponents' creed, except for charging them with denying Christ (v.4).

In v.4 Jude attacks the opponents' practices. He accuses them of being subversive, of being impious (also in v.15), and of using Christian liberty as a license for disregarding accepted norms and behavior. Not content merely to pronounce judgment, Jude emphasizes their condemnation by citing three OT examples of persons whom God judged because they rebelled after having known God's grace: (1) The rebellion in the wilderness was complaining against God's grace (Nu 14). (2) The angels of Ge 6:1–4 abandoned their heavenly order and became sexually involved with women. Ge 6:1–4 does not mention God's judging and binding the angels, although the commentary on Ge 6 in 1En 12–13 does. Evidently Jude was familiar with and valued 1 Enoch. (3) The men of Sodom desired to transcend their natural order and have sexual relationships with the two angels visiting Lot.

The last two examples from v.7 set the stage for three more accusations. **"Dreamers"** (v.8) refers to the opponents' ecstatic visions, which led to the defilement of their flesh. Two other charges dealt with the rejection of spiritual authority. Such charges are similar to Paul's accusations against the incipient Gnostics of 1 Corinthians.

V.9 requires knowledge of the apocryphal Assumption of Moses. That text speaks of a dispute between the Devil and the archangel Michael. Rather than revile or judge the Devil, Michael left it to the Lord to rebuke the Devil. But Jude's opponents discredit the reputations of spiritual beings. Jude blames them for rejecting basic spiritual realities for which they have no experiential basis for understanding because they are devoid of the Spirit (v.19).

Three more comparisons to OT malefactors appear in v.12: Cain (Ge 4), Balaam (Nu 22–24), and Korah (Nu 16). The Balaam incident seems puzzling because in Numbers Balaam is a faithful prophet. However, some later Jewish interpreters depicted Balaam as an unprincipled prophet who caved in to Balak's offer of money (see Philo, *Vitae Moses* 1.268; Josephus, *Antiquities* 4.118).

Five analogies depict the opponents as selfish intruders, spiritually empty, and errant waves and stars. vv.4 and 12 imply that the rivals were within the church, even participating in love feasts.

Although v.6 hinted at Jude's knowledge of 1 Enoch, in v.14 Jude explicitly uses a prophecy from 1En 1:9 to pronounce judgment on the antagonists. First Enoch was a Jewish apocalypse from the Maccabean era. Jerome reports that some leaders did not consider Jude worthy of canonization because it cited 1 Enoch.

In his final polemical sketch (vv.18–19) Jude chastizes the rivals as arrogant complainers and faultfinders who flatter people to gain an advantage.

The false teachers claim that their experience in grace elevates them above the necessity of moral discipline. They lack sexual restraint. They parade as leaders while lacking the fruit and discipline characteristic of leaders. They are faultfinders and manipulators who use the church to their own advantage.

III. EXHORTATION TO EDIFICATION AND EVANGELISM (VV.20–23)

Jude calls the church to edification. The beloved were to strengthen themselves and to pray in the Holy Spirit, in contrast to the Spirit-void troublemakers. While remaining in God's love, they face the future, waiting for the full flowering of eternal life when Christ will show mercy to the faithful.

References to the Holy Spirit, God, and the Lord Jesus Christ are not a Trinitarian formula, especially in light of the order in which the names are mentioned. But these three titles show that later Trinitarian theologies are implicit in Jude.

Despite his vigorous exposure of the opponents' errors, in vv.22–23 Jude calls the church to evangelize them. Jude holds out the evangelistic hope for renewal, even to selfish schismatics who upset congregational fellowship and mission. Jude's prescription of edification for the saints and evangelism of the schismatics is an effective antidote for contemporary church fights as well.

IV. DOXOLOGY (VV.24–25)

Jude reminds his readers of God's power to preserve the faithful from falling. Jude ends, as does Revelation, by emphasizing that believers will meet Christ in heaven.

BIBLIOGRAPHY

Bauckham, Richard J. *Jude, 2 Peter.* Waco: Word, 1983.

Kelly, J.D.N. *A Commentary on the Epistles of Peter and Jude.* London: A. & C. Black, 1969.

Rose, Delbert. "The Epistle of Jude." Vol. 10 BBC. Kansas City: Beacon Hill, 1967. Pp. 419–51.

Thompson, R. Duane. "Jude." Vol. 6 WBC. Grand Rapids: Eerdmans, 1966. Pp. 381–98.

REVELATION
John E. Stanley

INTRODUCTION

I. AUTHORSHIP, DATE AND CULTURAL SITUATION

John wrote Revelation while a political prisoner of Domitian, the Roman emperor, on the island of Patmos around A.D. 92–96 (see 1:1, 9; 22:8).

The persecutions mentioned in Revelation suggest a date in Domitian's time (1:9; 2:10, 13; 6:9–11; 12:11; 13:7; 17:6). These references to persecutions should not be spiritualized by calling them exaggerated stress. They are historical references to local occasional persecutions that arose in Domitian's tenure.

Roman religion centered in the state. Other institutions (including the family, trade unions, cities, and churches) were ordered to support the state. Texts such as Ro 13:1–7 and 1Ti 2:1–2 reflect the importance to the Romans of that support. Roman citizens considered Christians to be atheists when they either claimed that pagan gods did not exist or that pagan deities were evil demons. When misfortune struck a community, citizens could blame the failure of Christians to honor local gods as the cause of the disaster. These neighbors believed their well-being required them to observe civil religious duties, including praying for the emperor. Persecution arose, not from the emperor, but at the grass-roots level when local citizens accused Christians of neglecting the ritual duties of Roman state religion. The emperor acted against Christians when citizens brought charges against them.

II. REVELATION AS A CHRISTIAN APOCALYPSE

Revelation is an apocalypse (*apokalypsis*, 1:1). It contains the sociological and literary features typical of apocalyptic literature as a literary form and the theological worldview of an apocalypse. An apocalypse is a narrative that conveys a disclosure of salvation coming from heaven to earth, usually through an angelic mediator. The salvation involves a new era and a new world.

An apocalypse usually arises in a situation of social stress when a dominant religious majority pressures a religious minority to accept religious and social change. Rather than accept a new form of religion or internal reforms, the minority affirms its traditions, values, and communal life and rejects accommodation with, or assimilation into, the dominant group. Revelation was written during the conflict between early Christians and Roman state religion. John challenged the church to intensify the value clash with Roman society, demonstrating the basic schism between the church as a religious minority and the dominant pagan society. Revelation is a chapter in the ongoing critique of Roman culture.

Literary characteristics of apocalyptic literature include visions (1:12–20), auditions (1:10–11), and journeys to heaven (4:1–2). Apocalyptic writers use symbols with special meanings including colors (6:2, 4, 5, 8), animals (13:1–15), and numbers (11:2–3; 13:18). A catalog of cosmic woes signaling the end of the old order and the dawn of a new age includes earthquakes (6:12–17), famines (6:5–6), rampant diseases (6:8), and insect invasions (9:3–11). Revelation departs from the general norm at one point: it is an apocalypse with a named author rather than using a pseudonym.

Theological motifs characteristic of the apocalyptic message include dualism and pessimism about the current age. The writer believes this world is winding down. Signs of spiritual decline include false prophets (2:20) and backsliding (2:4–5; 3:15–16). The declining current age contrasts with a coming blessed age. A moral and spatial dualism accompanies the temporal opposition as war wages between good and evil, light and darkness, God and Satan (12:9; 19:19; 20:2). Salvation comes through a Savior who brings victory and judgment (5:6–14; 19:11–21) prior to the dawn of the new creation (21:1–8).

III. WESLEYAN/HOLINESS METHODS OF INTERPRETING REVELATION

John Wesley wrote of Revelation, "Oh how little do we know of this deep book! At least how little do I know!" (*Journal*, 4:540). Elsewhere he confessed, "I by no means pretend to understand, or explain all that is contained in this mysterious book" (*Notes*, 650). Likewise, Adam Clarke "resolved for a considerable time, not to meddle with this book, because I foresaw that I could produce nothing satisfactory on it" (Clarke, 966).

Wesley and Clarke sought to explain the book literally. They both included summaries that applied the symbols of Revelation to historical events after the first century. Their interpretations succumbed to anti-Catholicism, however, when they identified the leopard beast of 13:1–10 as the Roman Catholic church (Wesley, *Notes*, 696–98; Clarke, 1020).

Varied interpretations of Revelation emerged from nineteenth-century holiness revivals. Charles Dillman notes that "no single eschatological view can be baptized exclusively Wesleyan" (Dillman, 534). Premillennial approaches have characterized the Christian and Missionary Alliance, Pillar of Fire, and the former Pilgrim Holiness Church. The Church of God (Anderson, Indiana) has followed an amillennial position: D.S. Warner and F.G. Smith articulated an elaborate church historical approach that depicted the birth of the Church of God in 1880–81 as the fulfillment of the 1,260 days of Rev 12:6. Otto F. Linn, in 1942, published the first historical-critical exposition of Revelation among twentieth-century holiness writers, followed by Harvey Blaney in *The Wesleyan Bible Commentary* (1966). Ralph Earle, *Beacon Bible Commentary* (1967), combined the historical-critical, the church-historical, and the futurist views.

I assume that Revelation has a contemporary and future message as well as a first-century meaning. Then, now, and the future—these are the inescapable time frames for readers of Revelation. To understand its message, we must begin by trying to state what John meant when he originally wrote. But the Bible's message should not be locked into its first-century setting. The themes of Revelation continue to have an abiding value. Moreover, the book continually speaks of the future coming of Jesus Christ. That second coming of Christ cannot be ignored. The text points us toward the future.

The symbols function with several layers of meaning. For instance, Babylon refers to the city of Rome whose armies burned Jerusalem in A.D. 70. The Roman Empire is the first-century version of the Neo-Babylonian Empire that destroyed Jerusalem in 587 B.C. Also, Babylon refers to any city in history that becomes a center of idolatry and power used against the church. The leopard beast (13:1–10) has three meanings. It recalls Antiochus IV of Dan 7; it refers to Domitian in John's day; and it applies to any political ruler who persecutes the church in any age.

This amillennial stance occasionally will be contrasted with the futurist/millennial approach of J.B. Smith.

IV. REVELATION AND WESLEYAN/HOLINESS THEMES

1. John begins and ends his book with an emphasis on urgency. The phrase "that must soon take place" (1:1; 22:6) speaks of closing the curtain of history. Likewise, "the time is near" (1:3; 22:10) highlights the significance of the pregnant present that soon will give birth to God's new creation. Repeatedly John announces that Jesus is coming soon (1:7, 8; 2:25; 3:3, 11; 4:8; 14:7; 19:7; 22:7). The emphasis on urgency encourages the persecuted church to stand faithful just a little longer and dramatizes the call to decision.

2. The Spirit empowers and speaks to Christians. Wesley writes that John on Patmos was "overwhelmed with the power and filled with the light of the Holy Spirit" (*Notes,* 654). Phoebe Palmer preached that "holiness is power." The Spirit gave John the audacity to challenge the Roman Empire. Periodically the Spirit refilled John at critical intervals in ministry (4:2; 17:3; 21:10). And the Spirit spoke to each of the seven churches (2:7, 11, 17, 29; 3:6, 13, 22).

3. Holiness requires purity. John calls God's people "saints." Saints persevere and keep the commandments (14:12). Saints are overcomers. Life's conflicts can climax in victorious living because of the conquest of Christ. The seven promises related to conquering in chs. 2–3 and the

declaration that Christ "has triumphed" (5:5) anticipate the final conquest of sin in 19:11–21. The image of life as a conquest translates into the imperative to remember that Christian growth requires overcoming adversity and sin. Sanctification involves the decision to do good though evil seduces. This is the path to the purity required for the contemporary church.

4. Holiness involves social justice. The conflict in Revelation is not merely a struggle among individuals. The conflict is institutionalized. John's portrait of the church as a people oppressed by the state reminds us that institutions often clash. Some institutions liberate, and others victimize. William Booth's *In Darkest England* outlined a vision of ministry for the Salvation Army that understood the need for institutional justice.

John depicts the struggle in terms of the kingdom of God versus the state. The application to contemporary situations can be identified by asking, "Where is justice being denied? Who are the underdogs being trampled by oppressors? Where do the claims of Christ conflict with the claims of the state? Where do the forces of evil and Satan challenge Christ?" Revelation speaks to the corporate nature of modern life through the images of conflict and conquest.

John pits Roman rules against the rule of Christ the Lamb. The word *throne* appears in seventeen of the twenty-two chapters. Using political terms like "authority," "power," "war," "worship its throne," "kingdom," "the ruler of the kings of the earth," "the kingdom of the world," and "the kingdom of our Lord, and of his Christ," John protested Rome's supposed supremacy. He posits the throne of God and the church as the religious and political alternative to the secular state.

5. Revelation reinterprets the OT through the Christ event. John especially drew upon Daniel, Ezekiel, and Isaiah 40–66. John never directly quotes the OT. Instead he reinterprets its sacred tradition through his new experience in Christ.

6. Revelation is full of hope. The ultimate symbol of the Christian hope is the vision of the new heaven and new earth (21:1ff.). The heavenly hope provides a reason to withstand the conflicts that strike the church. We live by hope.

7. Music celebrates holiness, hope, and victory. Whether it be "Holy, Holy, Holy" (4:8), Handel's "Messiah" (11:15), or gospel songs of heaven and victory, Revelation has furnished lyrics for vibrant Christian music. Fifteen percent of the hymns and songs in the 1989 edition of the United Methodist hymnal are derived from Revelation.

V. OUTLINE

COMMENTARY

I. INTRODUCTION AND SEVEN LETTERS (1:1–3:22)

A. Prologue to an Authoritative Apocalypse (1:1–8)

The **revelation** [*apokalypsis*] **of Jesus Christ** came to John from God through an angel. This heavenly chain of reception imparts authority to John's message. An apocalypse is a disclosure sent from heaven to earth in story form that transmits a vision of salvation to a besieged church and pronounces judgment upon the oppressor. Repetition, a literary trait of apocalyptic literature, appears in John's emphasis on the lateness of the hour (1:1, 3, 7). Repetition signals significance. The beatitude in v.3 is the first of seven beatitudes in Revelation (1:3; 14:13; 16:15; 19:9; 20:6; 22:7, 14). It indicates that Revelation was to be read aloud and accents the imminent end of time.

Vv.4–8 introduce key words and themes and greet the churches. The number *seven* appears fifty-one times in Revelation. **Seven** symbolizes completion because it combines the heavenly number three with the earthly number four. John's seven churches represent all churches; we know there were more than seven churches in Asia Minor (Col 4:13). Yet John addresses specific situations in seven local churches (chs. 2–3).

John defines God temporally in terms of present, past, and future existence (1:4; 4:8). Later on, this contrasts with the Beast whose life will end on a day (17:8–11).

Revelation is a tale of two thrones dueling for the allegiance of humanity. The word *throne* appears forty-six times. John pits the throne of the Roman Empire against the throne of

Christ, who is the true Ruler of the kings of the earth. Revelation presents the kingdom of God as the alternative to human political dominions. John had given up on human political institutions. Thus Revelation contains strong political overtones.

B. John's Call (1:9–11)

The Roman emperor Domitian banished John as a political prisoner to the penal colony on the island of Patmos. Domitian's reign forced Christians to choose between following Christ or Caesar. Revelation raises the question: "What does the rule of Christ mean in a political situation of persecution and social stress?"

John's audacity to send a book to churches on the mainland emerged from his empowering experience in the Spirit. His call came from heaven. Yet three bonds linked John's call to his readers' experience: their common suffering, the sovereignty of Jesus over their lives, and their steadfast endurance. John endured distress brought about by external circumstances because the Spirit empowered him. The Spirit imparted the courage to obey God rather than a fallen human sovereign. John's emphasis on the church and the kingdom of God as alternatives to Roman society parallels John Wesley's concern to revitalize society through religious revival.

C. Christ at the Center of the Church (1:12–20)

Drawing upon images of authority from Daniel and Ezekiel, John presents Christ standing at the center of the church. The vision announces Christ as the eternal Victor who has conquered death and Hades. Thus, as God is eternal (1:4, 8), so is Christ. Because

	Ephesus	Smyrna	Pergamum	Thyatira	Sardis	Philadelphia	Laodicea
"Say to"	2:1	2:8	2:12	2:18	3:1	3:7	3:14
Christ's title	2:1	2:8	2:12	2:18	3:1	3:7	3:14
Praise	2:2–3, 6?	2:9	2:13	2:19	3:2, 4	3:8, 10	none
Criticism	2:4	none	2:14–15	2:20	3:2	none	3:15–17
Prescription	2:5	2:9	2:16	2:22, 25	3:3	none	3:18
Warning	2:5	none	2:16	2:21–23	3:3	none	3:19
Conquering promise	2:7	2:11	2:17	2:26–28	3:5	3:12	3:21

the One at the center of the church has conquered sin and death and is alive forever, readers and listeners are prepared for the victorious conquest of sin and Satan in 19:11–21. This introductory vision alerts readers to the way the conflict between God and Satan, Christ and Caesar, and church and state will come to its climax.

D. Letters to the Seven Churches (2:1–3:22)

John organized the seven letters around a literary pattern. See chart above.

"Say to" is an introductory address in the decrees of Persian kings and OT prophetic utterances. Except for 3:14, the Christ titles recall symbols from 1:12–20. The conquering promises relate to the contents of the letters to Smyrna, Pergamum, and Sardis. They correspond with later rewards as follows:

2:7 / 22:2, 14	2:11 / 21:7–8
2:17 / 19:12–13	2:26–28 / 19:15
3:5 / 21:27	3:12 / 21:2, 22
3:21 / 20:4	

The tight organization of Revelation undoubtedly imparted a sense of order to the chaotic lives of its listeners and readers.

Five conflicts challenged the seven churches. First, defining true and false apostles and teachers spawned doctrinal tensions (2:2, 14–15, 20). Second, a crisis of self-definition arose after the Jerusalem War as the emergence of rabbinic Judaism forced Christians to distinguish themselves from Jews (2:9; 3:9). Third, differences existed between rich and poor (2:9; 3:8, 17–18). Fourth, Roman society required assimilation into Roman ways. But John called Christians to abstain from food sacrificed to Roman idols. Avoidance of sacrificial meat set the church at odds with Roman society and fostered social stress. Fifth, occasionally social stress resulted in political strife as symbolized by the martyred Antipas (2:13). John depicted Pergamum as the site of Satan's throne because it was the center of emperor worship in Asia Minor.

These tensions provide a context for appreciating the motif of conflict. The verb *nikao* ("to conquer") and its derivatives occur seventeen times in the book. John promised eventual citizenship in the New Jerusalem to those faithful conquerors who hold fast to Christ. The saints are to persevere until the demise of Rome and the return of Christ bring ultimate victory. The seven conquering promises generate resistance to pagan society and inspire willingness for martyrdom if necessary. Wesley's insistence that "the gospel of Christ knows of no religion but social; no holiness but social holiness" pertained to the seven churches. Christ calls the church to be a social alternative to pagan society. For the Christian, life is a process of overcoming sin and conflict.

II. ADORATION OF GOD AND THE LAMB (4:1–5:14)

A. Adoration of God as Creator (4:1–11)

An apocalypse contains a message sent from heaven to earth. John indicates his reception of communication from heaven through the literary form of a vision. In the vision, John enters heaven and stands before the throne of God. Twenty-four elders surrounding the throne probably symbolize completion representing the twelve tribes of Israel and twelve apostles. God, the One on the throne, is honored by all of creation (4:4, 10). Two songs (4:8, 11) proclaim God as holy and worthy of worship because God is Creator.

B. Adoration of the Lamb as Conqueror (5:1–14)

Ch. 5 stands between the heavenly harmony of the chorus of creation (ch. 4) and the havoc unleashed by opening the sealed scroll (ch. 6). Ch. 5 is the key to Revelation.

John saw a sealed scroll. The scroll was a first-century symbol for a news bulletin from heaven announcing God's purpose for history. But because the scroll was sealed, John wept. No one was found worthy to open the scroll. John wept because as long as the scroll remained sealed, no word of hope would come from heaven to the troubled churches in Asia Minor. For all John knew, perhaps the Roman Empire would have the last word in the struggle between church and state. John wept because if he could not find clarity in heaven, how could the churches find direction amid their stress on earth?

The adoration given to the Lamb (5:5–14) contrasts with the agony of John's tears. As all of creation worshiped God as Creator in ch. 4, now all of creation worships the Lamb as Conqueror (5:5, 8, 12, 13). The announcement of the Lamb's conquest (5:5) recalls the conquering promises of chs. 2–3 and anticipates the vision of Christ as the final Conqueror in 19:11–21. Because the Lamb has conquered sin and death, John anticipates the church's final victory over sin and death. Charles Naylor's "Be An Overcomer" captures the now-but-not-yet aspect of ch. 5:

> Be an overcomer, you are
>   heaven's heir
>   And a crown of life you may
>   ever wear;
> So with courage press the battle
>   to the gates,
>   Till you gain the prize which in
>   heaven waits.

Christ has won the victory, but our final claiming of the prize remains an anticipation.

The language of Christian adoration contrasts with the actions of the beasts in ch. 13, where the beasts must force persons to adore them. What Caesar and the Beast claim blasphemously belongs by right to God and Christ.

In the figure of Conqueror, the Lion and the Lamb converge. Royal and suffering traditions merge in the slain Lamb. Although the Lamb receives the seven virtues ascribed to God (5:12) and is worthy of worship (vv.13–14), the Lamb became the Conqueror through suffering and death (v.9). The hope for a royal Messiah who will rule on earth has always existed in the church. But John's Lamb is a crucified God. The way to victory for the church lies in following the Lamb in sacrificial living. God's kingdom is a dominion of servants.

Ch. 5 announces the conquest of the Lamb. Therefore, the rest of Revelation can be read anticipating the victorious ending.

III. THE SEVEN SEALS AND SEVEN TRUMPETS (6:1–11:19)

A. The First Six Seals (6:1–17)

By opening the sealed scroll, the Lamb unleashes judgment upon the church's antagonists. Judgment continues in the parallel visions of seven trumpets (8:6–11:19) and seven bowls (16:1–21).

A literary pattern exists in the first six seals. The phrase, "As the Lamb/he opened the seal," appears in 6:1, 3, 5, 7, 9, and 12. In the first four seals one of the four living creatures commands, **Come,** calling forth colored horses representing conquest, war, famine, and death. These first four judgments, probably based on Zec 1:8; 6:1–8, depict the traumas of an empire built on conquest.

The fifth seal breaks the sequence and departs from the pattern of the first four. A martyrs' lament asking, **How long, Sovereign Lord?** (6:10) foreshadows 7:9–17 and reminds us of the persecution experienced by the faithful church at the hands of the pagan conqueror (2:13 and 6:2).

The sixth seal brings judgment on seven classes of people who refuse to repent (6:15).

B. Two Interludes (7:1–17)

Ch. 7 is a pause amid the intensity of the judgments unleashed from the scroll. John's audience needed a break.

1. Interlude of sealing the saints (7:1–8)

The sealing of the saints identifies God's people and protects them from judgment (also, 9:4; 14:1; 22:4). In contrast, the followers of the Beast are marked with a seal classifying them as opponents of God (13:16; 14:9; 16:2;

19:20; 20:4). The 144,000 symbolize a faithful spiritual Israel as in 14:1–5. The number is a sign of completeness.

2. Interlude of the martyrs' chorus (7:9–17)

The martyrs sing a song of salvation (7:10). The ministry of the pastoral Lamb foreshadows the promises eventually available to all saints (21:4–6). As H.B. Swete stated, the purpose of ch. 7 is "to contrast the preparedness of the church for the coming end with the panic of the unprepared world" (p. 95).

C. The Seventh Seal (8:1–5)

In contrast to the judgments let loose on earth by the blowing of the first six trumpets (8:6–9:21), 8:1–5 affirms the stability and security of heaven. To a church tormented by tribulation, John accents the value of prayer as an offering to God, thus the symbol of the altar (see Wesley, *Notes,* 679).

Opening the seventh seal leads into the sounding of the seven trumpets.

D. First Four Trumpets (8:6–12)

The first four trumpets dispatch cosmic plagues, reminiscent of Ex 7:1–10:29. These limited judgments destroy one-third of the earth's trees and grass; poison the sea and fresh water; and darken the sun, moon, and stars.

E. First Two Woes/Fifth and Sixth Trumpets (8:13–9:21)

The first two woes, which are the fifth and sixth trumpets, inflict torture on persons for five months and kill one-third of humanity through plagues of fire, smoke, and brimstone. At first glance, these judgments may seem capricious. However, a consistent moral discipline pervades Revelation. Their purpose is to move persons to repentance (9:20–21). Idolatry, materialism, murder, sorcery, immorality, and thefts are the sins the text lists. In ch. 18, John will apply this general list to the specific misdeeds of Babylon/Rome. The saints are spared these judgments, and the judgments are limited in time and number.

Although it often has been fashionable to sneer at the idea of one-third of the earth, waters, and light being destroyed, the moral relevance of Revelation is obvious to those who live with the greenhouse effect and the nuclear arms race. The very materialism John described in 9:20 may destroy God's creation.

F. Two Interludes (10:1–11:3)

1. Interlude of angel and little scroll (10:1–11)

Just as John placed two visions (7:1–8, 9–17) between opening the sixth and seventh seals, likewise chs. 10 and 11:1–14 are two interludes before the blowing of the seventh trumpet.

Applying Jer 15:15ff.; Eze 2:8–3:11; and Dan 12 to his situation of persecution, John provides two affirmations for the ancient and modern church. To those upset by stress and cosmic judgments, God announces through the mighty angel that the last woe is at hand. **There will be no more delay!** The text imparts authority to this declaration with the reminder that God **lives for ever and ever** as is stated throughout the book (1:8, 17; 4:9–10; 15:7; 21:6). John recalls God's authority and the imminence of Christ's return.

Vv.8–11 constitute a second commissioning for John. God sensed John's need of encouragement. The ministry of proclaiming judgment to the world and calling the saints to persevere was wearing John down. Then John remembered that he stood in the prophetic tradition of Jeremiah, Ezekiel,

and Daniel, who previously provided God's people with hope amid despair. When the burden is heavy and hearts are weary, the study of Scripture can rekindle one's calling. Renewal of the call to minister is as critical as receiving the initial call to ministry.

Because of this renewal, John did not dilute his message. Any doubt John had about his mission should have been erased with the commission of v.11 that he must prophesy to peoples, nations, languages, and kings—a political emphasis similar to 1:5–7 and 14:6. The Greek *dei* ("it is necessary"; NIV "you must") denotes a compulsion of divine destiny and duty. When God calls and renews, the minister is enabled to continue even under stress.

2. Interlude of the two witnesses (11:1–13)

Ch. 11 concludes the first half of Revelation and previews the second half. Chs. 12–22 begin with an assault on the church and end with a reward for the faithful. So does 11:1–13 where John describes an attack on the temple, symbolizing the church, for three and one-half years by a warring beast. References to Daniel imply that John perceived the crisis under Domitian as a replay of the suffering of the saints under the Syrian king Antiochus IV Epiphanes. Daniel depicted Antiochus IV as the terrible fourth beast who assaulted the saints for three and one-half years (Dan 7:7–8, 19–25; 12:7). Three times John refers to Daniel's three and one-half years (11:2, 3, 11) and to the Beast making war and conquering the saints (11:7). Like Daniel, John envisions a last limited era when evil will run wild prior to the inauguration of the final kingdom of God.

Interpretations abound of what the temple and the two witnesses symbolize, but most probably they represent the church. Measurement of the temple denotes protection, as sealing symbolized protection in 7:1–8.

G. Third Woe and Seventh Trumpet (11:14–19)

As in Daniel when the fourth world kingdom was followed by an everlasting kingdom from God (2:44–45; 7:27), so in Revelation the final time of stress climaxes in the advent of the kingdom of God after the judgment of the world. God's reign is more enduring than any human rule. The final trumpet crescendos in a note of glorious proclamation of victory for the church and a woe for the earth dwellers. A persecuting kingdom gives way to the kingdom of our Lord.

IV. THE CONFLICT IN HEAVEN AND ON EARTH (12:1–15:4)

A. The Woman and the Dragon (12:1–17)

Ch. 12 begins the second half of Revelation. It is the first of seven visions in 12:1–15:4 and underscores the theme of persecution that appeared throughout chs. 1–11 and anticipates the intensified persecutions of ch. 13. It recalls the conquering promises of chs. 2–3 as well as the Lamb's conquest in 5:5. It anticipates victory for the faithful saints in Rev 20–22.

Scholars debate whether the woman represents Mary, the church, Israel, or Jerusalem (Beasley-Murray, 191–97; Mounce, 235). Regarding the woman, Collins correctly concludes, "Her importance for the Apocalypse lies not so much in her identity as her destiny" (Collins, *Apocalypse*, 88). The pregnant woman prepares to give birth to a messianic child. However, a cosmic antagonist depicted by the four names

of "dragon," "serpent," "devil," and "Satan" attempts to kill the child. But God protects and nourishes the mother and child. Again, the Dragon pursues the woman. When salvific eagle's wings, reminiscent of Ex 19:4, preserve the woman, the frustrated, enraged Dragon makes war with the woman's faithful offspring. The offspring overcome the antagonist through the blood of the Lamb, their testimony, and their fidelity (v.11).

Although the identity of the woman is unclear, four names identify the antagonist as the one **who leads the whole world astray** (v.9). John knew the church was engaged in a conflict between truth and falsehood, a contest between faithful Christian conquerors and faltering compromisers, and, ultimately, a contest between Satan and the Lamb. The antagonist was and is a clever deceiver who tried, and tries, to get Christians to accommodate their standards to those of pagan society. John designated the enemy's mission as spiritual deception. Ch. 12 inspires resistance to moral compromise, even if resistance to the morality of pagan society results in martyrdom. Also, ch. 12 depicts a pouting Dragon/Satan going off to make war against the faithful. While John envisions the angry dragon stomping off to wage war, faithful saints conquer the cosmic deceiver by their consistent moral lives and by clinging to the testimony of Jesus. The world's greatest battles are won behind the closed doors of human hearts. God enables saints to withstand the pressures of Satan, even when Satan is allied with the state as in ch. 13.

B. The Leopard Beast (13:1–10)

Whereas ch. 12 described the Dragon as God's enemy, ch. 13 identifies two beasts as enemies of the church who ally themselves with the state against the saints. Ch. 13 lifts up the theme of conflict and demonstrates John's application of the OT to the first-century crisis.

John condensed the four beasts of Dan 7 into this leopard beast. Daniel's lion, bear, leopard, and terrible fourth beast furnish the physical features for John's leopard beast (13:1–2). J.B. Smith observes that Revelation "is a supplement to that of Daniel" (Smith, 4). It seems that John believed that the historical crises of the Jews during the persecutions of Antiochus IV of Syria were being repeated and fulfilled during Domitian's reign. Thus John turned to Daniel as a scriptural basis for understanding what was happening. His visions update Daniel for the first Christian century.

The leopard beast commits blasphemy, has dominion over the earth, is worshiped, and makes war on the saints (13:1, 5, 6). These evil deeds recall the misdeeds of Antiochus IV as recorded in Dan 7:21–25. John mentions the leopard beast's authority (13:2, 4, 5, 7) and power. These words, the actions of the beast, and the revision of Dan 7 suggest, as Beasley-Murray concludes, that the beast represents "the deification of secular authority" (Beasley-Murray, 251). The leopard beast represents the Roman emperor Domitian.

John Wesley, Adam Clarke, Alma White, and F.G. Smith erred in interpreting the first beast as Roman Catholicism. They read back into Revelation the tensions related to the Protestant Reformation. Ralph Earle regards the beast as Domitian, while allowing it to represent possibly a forthcoming antichrist at the end of time (Earle, 578).

C. The Lamblike Beast (13:11–18)

Here John went beyond Daniel. No parallel in Scripture or antiquity seems to exist for the account of the second beast. Two verbs explain the meaning of the lamblike beast. John employs forms of the verb *poeio* ("to do, make") four times (13:12a, 12b, 13, 16). The lamblike beast is a doer. He **deceived** (Gk. *planao*). John introduces the second beast from the earth as the implementing accomplice of the beast from the sea. The first beast acts against God and believers, but the second beast deceives humans. It functions as the deceptive cohort of the first beast. Thus, if the first beast represents the Roman emperor, then the second beast symbolizes the priests of the imperial cult religion. Later John will speak of a false prophet (16:13; 19:20; 20:10) who should be understood as the priest of the imperial state religion. Earle agrees with this approach.

The mark of the Beast parodies the sealing of the saints (7:1–8). The sealing protects the saints from the tribulations, and the mark of the Beast grants economic privilege to those who follow the Beast. Sealing brings eternal spiritual protection while the mark brings ephemeral material prosperity.

Diverse, and sometimes bizarre, interpretations of the number 666 exist (see Mounce, 262–65; Earle, 577–78). However, 13:15–18 and the literary device of gematria explain the number. In 13:15–17 the number denotes a power who can divide humanity into supporters and opponents. The authority can even kill resisting opponents. The number appears to refer to a civil authority who makes war on the saints as in 13:1–10. Gematria is the practice of applying numerical values to letters. The Greek letters that spell "Nero Caesar," when transliterated into Hebrew and added together, equal 666. So 666 could be a symbolic way of speaking of the Roman emperor.

The first beast was Domitian, the Caesar when John wrote. Today the first beast refers to any political ruler who calls Christians to acknowledge the state's claims to be more authoritative than the claims of Jesus Christ. For instance, when Hitler claimed to be lord of both the church and state in Germany, he was acting as the leopard beast. Any civil religion can produce a political ruler parallel to the first beast. Such rulers have emerged throughout history and will continue to appear.

The lamblike beast represented the priests of Roman state religion. Modern parallels exist in religious leaders who unite the separate kingdoms of the state and God into a civil religion that places one's allegiance to the flag alongside or above one's allegiance to the Cross.

D. Song of the 144,000 (14:1–5)

After the conflicts in heaven (ch. 12) and on earth (ch. 13), this section alternates between assurances for the faithful saints and anticipated judgments for followers of the Beast.

The 144,000 with the Lamb on Mount Zion recall the sealed saints of 7:1–8. They are faithful, pure victors who probably are martyrs. Vv.2–3 show their blessed attainment of victory in Christ.

E. Anticipations of Judgment (14:6–13)

Three angels proclaim judgment, the fall of Babylon/Rome, and judgment on the followers of the Beast. V.8 anticipates 17:5 and 18:2. 2Ba 11:1 and 1Pe 5:13 attest that other writers referred to Rome as Babylon in the first century. Rome inherited the infamous name of Babylon because both Babylon and Rome destroyed Jerusalem and the temple.

Amid the chorus of judgment, John affirms faithful saints who persevere.

F. Judgment at God's Winepress (14:14–20)

This scene foreshadows the eventful judgment of Rome detailed in chs. 17–18.

G. Martyrs' Song of Moses (15:1–4)

Whereas the leopard beast emerged from the sea as the enemy of God, here victorious martyrs stand on a firm sea of glass. The song of Moses contains OT texts acknowledging God as Lord, King of the nations, holy and true. God's moral traits stand in contrast with the deceitful ways of the beasts. Again John applied the OT to his situation.

V. THE SEVEN BOWLS AND THE JUDGMENT OF ROME (15:5–19:10)

A. The Seven Bowls (15:5–16:21)

With the pouring out of God's wrath from the seven bowls, the final judgment of the beasts and Dragon begins (16:1). In one sense the seven vials are a third heptad reemphasizing the judgments announced in the seven seals and trumpets. Beasley-Murray and Mounce compare these three sets of judgments. The bowls culminate against Babylon/Rome as the persecutor of the church (16:19) so that chs. 17–18 are expansions of 15:5–16:21. Ch. 17 identifies Babylon as the Roman Empire and 18:3 accuses Babylon of making **nations** drink **the maddening wine of her adulteries.** Now, in retribution, Rome must drink the cup of God's wrath. Ironically, Rome's golden cup is filthy (17:4).

The parallels to the plagues against Pharaoh in Egypt are another way John establishes the significance of these judgments. However, Pharaoh had the chance to change his course of action because of the divine power he witnessed. John does not give Rome the opportunity to repent. The last call to repentance was in 9:20.

Remembering that Revelation often sets up contrasts, it seems that the evil trinity of 16:13 might be a parody on God, Christ, and the Holy Spirit. The Dragon, Beast, and False Prophet frequently appear as deceptive antagonists in chs. 12–20.

How does one interpret 16:16? The original intention of vv.12–14 probably reflects the Roman fear that kings from Parthia would invade and defeat Rome. Evidently John knew of this Roman phobia, because he pictured the eastern kings and the evil trinity gathering the world for a war at *Har Magedon*. But the war did not occur! Instead, an earthquake symbolizing judgment split Rome into three parts. Even though a final battle does not occur at *Har Magedon* in Revelation some futurist interpreters, such as J.B. Smith, still anticipate a final battle near Mount Megiddo that "will be the great decision as to whether Satan or God Almighty will be the final and sole ruler of the earth" (Smith, 236). Adam Clarke listed options for translating and interpreting *har meggido* or *har magedon*. He complained of the ridiculous conjectures that have been made regarding this passage and did not give an opinion on its meaning. Because no place in biblical history accurately corresponds to this place name, it seems best to interpret *har magedon* as a symbol for the final clash between God and Satan. It is not a future place located in the physical land of Israel. Rev 5:5 announced the Lamb as victorious, thus the battle has already been won in the death and resurrection of Christ. We know who will be the final

ruler. God has already triumphed over Satan. The return of Christ in the final judgment will be a gathering of the saints and damning of sinners (20:11–22:21).

B. Identification of Babylon/Rome (17:1–18)

The judgment of the great harlot in Rev 17–18 elaborates on the judgment emanating from the seventh bowl. Ch. 17 identifies the great city of 16:19 and provides reasons for the judgments of ch. 18.

John ties together chs. 17 and 18 through seven common references. They are the designation of Babylon as a city (17:5, 18; 18:2, 4, 10, 16); Babylon as a woman/prostitute (17:1–7, 9, 15–16; 18:3, 7, 16); the claim that kings prostitute themselves with the woman (17:2; 18:3, 9); earth dwellers drunk with the wine of adulteries (17:2; 18:3, 9); the burning of Babylon with fire (17:16; 18:8–9, 18); the judgment of the harlot (17:1; 18:20); and the mention of the blood of the saints (17:6; 18:24). These common phrases and designations join the chapters together as a literary unit.

Using **"prostitute"** as a symbol continues the prophetic pattern of Isaiah, Jeremiah, Ezekiel, and Hosea. Again John forces his readers to recall OT precedents for their experience. The harlot image is another instance of John's use of contrast; elsewhere he uses the positive feminine images of a mother (12:1–6) and bride (21:2) to depict the faithful people of God.

In the Spirit (17:3) signals the significance of Babylon's judgment. The phrase appears four times at critical junctures in Revelation—when John receives his call to write (1:10), when he begins his heavenly vision (4:2), when he describes the judgment of the evil earthly city (17:3), and when he surveys the New Jerusalem (21:10). Three of these experiences are blissful, positive times. One, the judgment of Rome, is a time of terrible judgment.

In the Spirit reminds readers of the divine elements in John's visions even as he reworked OT traditions for the church. John's experience **in the Spirit** illumined his study of Scripture. **In the Spirit** reminds readers and listeners that God undergirded John and prepared John to tell of the tragedy descending on the great city of Babylon/Rome. As John experienced renewal in the Spirit at these four significant intervals in his ministry of writing Revelation, Christians today are called to experience spiritual renewal during their ministries. Continual renewal of the call is as important as the reception of the original call.

Two symbols need identification: Babylon and the Beast. After Nebuchadnezzar's destruction of Jerusalem in 587 B.C., Jews and Christians depicted their political antagonists as successors to Babylon. Jeremiah referred to Babylon as dwelling by many waters and making "the whole earth drunk" (51:7). Although Rome did not sit on many waters, it sat on seven hills (17:9). References to persecution (vv.6, 14) recall the persecutions of Nero and Domitian. Rome's civil religion challenged the church with a counterfeit religion culminating in idolatry. Rome was a universal empire (v.18). Rome stands for international oppression, the misuse of affluence, and pride. In John's symbol system, Rome as Babylon is the opposite of the future New Jerusalem.

The Beast, as stated in comments on ch. 13, symbolizes Emperor Domitian in John's day. In a larger sense, the Beast represents a political ruler in any age who persecutes the church. In the largest eternal sense, the Beast represents the final antagonist of God and the Lamb.

John judges Rome because of her idolatrous nationalism. A Roman rule based on Roman religion tried to make Christ subservient to Caesar. John called the saints to choose allegiance to Rome or to the church. Like the Barmen Confession of the twentieth century, Revelation calls Christians to give priority to Christ rather than to a political ruler who tries to unite the church and state, or who, as in the case of Hitler, claims to be lord of both the church and the state. Revelation judges an unjust state and calls Christians to withdraw their support from the state when perverted nationalism functions as an idolatrous religion. The Cross must always stand higher than the flag. Ch. 17 shows why Rome as God's antagonist must be judged. Those reasons will be elaborated on in ch. 18.

C. Judgment of Babylon/Rome (18:1–24)

In *The Aeneid* Virgil voiced the Roman dream of an everlasting empire (1.272–90; 12.828–23). Contrary to Virgil's assumptions of an eternal destiny, John composed ch. 18 as a dirge lauding the demise of the supposedly eternal city. The chapter contains three laments (vv.10, 16, 19) and three pronouncements (vv.1–3, 4–8, 21–24). Each lament contains a double woe, a remembrance, and a statement citing the swiftness of Babylon's fall. The three laments use the words **"weep," "mourn"** or **"mourning,"** and **"cry"** (vv.9, 19, 15, 16, 19). Kings, merchants, and sailors voice the laments. Irony tinges John's use of repetition as he announces that the **great city** (vv.10, 16, 18, 19, 21) fell **in one hour** (vv.10, 17, 19). Anyone who has marveled at the beauty and grandeur of the Forum, Palatine Hill, and the Colosseum should appreciate John's gall in describing Rome as a foul prison (v.2). Evil so encases Rome that John calls his people to withdraw from Roman society so that they **will not share in her sins** (v.4). John so disagreed with Roman beliefs, norms, and behavior that he sought to separate the saints from ethical compromise with and assimilation into pagan society. The church in Revelation is to be a people of God who are a holy, consecrated alternative to the inferior values of the dominant pagan society—a church against culture. The church is to be a holy people. The church's ethic emerges from her essence as God's people. As Leon Hynson proclaims, "The church is called to help heal the world and this is carried on through the spiritual renewal of persons and the improvement of societies" (Hynson, 45). The contemporary church cannot withdraw from society as John advocated.

Any institution that misuses wealth, power, and pleasure resembles Babylon. Not only does John judge Babylon, but he implores his people to avoid being enticed and then entrapped by the illusion that prosperity and power protect persons and institutions from the ultimate demands of God's justice. That message has contemporary relevance. The seductive powers of wealth, social status, and culture threaten the church because they are subtle deceivers that blur the distinction between the values of God and the values of the world.

D. Fourfold Hallelujah Chorus (19:1–6)

In contrast to the previous dirge and three laments announcing Babylon's judgment, 19:1–6 contains four hallelujahs rejoicing over the judgment. The final praise anthem affirms the reign of God as was anticipated in 11:15 and 12:10.

E. Invitation to the Marriage Supper (19:7–10)

John leans into the imminent future as he invites faithful conquerors to the marriage feast of the Lamb. John combines the image of the coming of Christ as a feast (cf. Mk 14:25; Lk 14:15) with the symbol of the church as a bride (cf. Eph 5:23–32). He contrasts the clean, bright, linen-clothed bride of the Lamb (19:7–8) with the corrupt harlot, Babylon (v.2). This literary contrast between the harlot and the bride also is a moral distinction between faltering compromises with Babylon/Rome and faithful saints who **hold to the testimony of Jesus.** Revelation calls for holiness in Christians. The morality of the church is to exceed that of the world.

VI. FINAL JUDGMENT (19:11–20:15)

A. Coming of the True Conqueror (19:11–16)

Since chs. 12–13, the evil trinity of the Dragon, the Beast, and the False Prophet have waged war on the church (12:17; 13:7). In 17:14 John anticipated that the Lord will "overcome" these antagonists. Anticipated conquest now becomes victorious achievement. By using five names **Faithful," "True," "the Word of God," "King of kings," and "Lord of lords"**—and three symbols of judgment in 19:15, John's imagery announces that the One sitting on the white horse of victory will conquer the evil trinity. However, back in the song of redemption (5:9–10), the Savior was a slain Lamb. Now this conqueror **is dressed in a robe dipped in blood.** Some commentators interpret the blood in 19:13 as a reference to the blood of enemies, martyrs, or of the wine press of judgment. Another understanding links the Lamb of ch. 5 and the Conqueror of 19:11–16: the Conqueror is the crucified Lamb first identified in 5:9–10. The blood in 19:13 recalls the saving blood of Christ shed for our sins as in 1:5; 5:9; 7:14; and 12:11. The robe dipped in blood shows that just as John was a fellow sufferer with the saints (1:9), so the Lamb has walked the lonesome valley of suffering and death. The red robe recalls the historical death of Jesus. Just as Jesus was crucified by a Roman ruler and rose triumphant on Easter, so in his second coming he will defeat the evil powers that persecute the church. And he will gather up the faithful saints. The returning Christ will be the crucified Christ. Suffering can be a vehicle to victory. The death of Christ began God's victory over sin, death, and Satan. The return of Christ will consummate God's victory. The Christology of Revelation is rooted in the death, resurrection, and return of Jesus Christ. It resonates with suffering and anticipates a final victory over death and the evil trinity.

B. Capture of the Evil Trinity (19:17–21)

After the glorious announcement of the *parousia* of Christ, the capture of the evil trinity is almost anticlimactic. Rather than a battle, the Beast and False Prophet are seized. The text withholds from readers the details of this final denouement. When one compares John's sketch of this event with the Gospels' detailed descriptions of the death of Jesus, one can conclude that Christians should say far more about the saving death of Jesus and his victorious return than about the mechanics of how the enemy finally will be

defeated. Preach the truth of victory and leave the details to God.

C. Binding of Satan (20:1–10)

John gives four names to the ultimate spiritual antagonist and accuses it of a ministry of deception (also in 12:9). These titles appear throughout Scripture. Their order in 20:2 is of increasing abstraction even though the mission of deception is constant.

Six times the text mentions a **thousand years** in terms of the binding of Satan and the reign of the martyrs and saints. Wesley mused over these verses asking, "How far these expressions are to be taken literally, how far figuratively only, who can tell?" (Wesley, *Notes,* 723). Bence's conclusion that "in no place does Wesley introduce a millennial concept into his doctrine of the coming kingdom" is shared by David Cubie and Charles Dillman (Bence, 53). Five basic interpretations of these verses exist. A postmillennialist believes the return of Christ will not take place until the church has set up the kingdom of God on earth. Premillenialists, such as J. B. Smith, understand these verses to say that Christ's return (19:11–16) will be followed by the binding of Satan and a thousand-year reign of saints before the final judgment (20:11–15). Dispensationalists, disciples of a specific form of premillennialism based on the teachings of John Nelson Darby, divide history into seven eras or dispensations, with the final era culminating in a kingdom centered in a renewed Jerusalem with a rebuilt temple. Charles Ryrie, Hal Lindsey, and John F. Walvoord articulate dispensational theologies. Amillennialists do not look for a thousand-year reign on earth, because they interpret the thousand-year reign symbolically. Harvey Blaney in *The Wesleyan Bible Commentary* accepts such a view (Blaney, 508), as do I. Adam Clarke agrees: "I am satisfied that this period should not be taken literally" (Clarke, 1055). The fifth position, realized eschatology, as taught by Mathias Rissi, contends that the reign of Christ began with the Resurrection and that any talk of a second return of Christ is metaphorical.

In spite of these genuine differences, at least two truths can be affirmed. First, as noted by David Cubie, "The last word in any true Christian millennialism or amillennialism is God's victory" (Cubie, 404). The capture and defeat of the evil trinity ends the struggle between God and Satan, the church and the world, good and evil. Second, the faithful saints of John's day and thereafter will reign eventually with Christ in heaven.

D. Judgment (20:11–15)

The return of Christ culminates in judgment. At this cosmic judgment, individuals (19:20; 20:11–15) receive the reward or punishment that enables the justice of God to be realized.

VII. RENEWAL AND EPILOGUE (21:1–22:21)

A. "I Am Doing a New Thing!" (21:1–8)

This section throbs with the theme of newness. *Kainos,* new, appears in 21:1, 2, and 5. John envisions a new heaven, a new earth, and a New Jerusalem. God announces a new existence free from tears, death, mourning, crying, and pain because the **old order of things has passed away** (vv.3–4). John drives home the emphasis on newness by defining God as the one **making everything new,** which is similar to Isa 43:19, where God announced, "See, I am doing a new thing!" John draws upon Isa 40–66 at least five times in these verses. As Isaiah

promised a new creation and restoration of Israel after the judgment of the Babylonian exile, John speaks of a new creation for the church after the final judgment.

John ties the content of Christian hope to the previous twenty chapters through the repetition of eight key themes, summarizing Revelation.

1. The sentence skeletons, **I saw** and **I heard,** refer to the inspiration guiding John's writing. They denote the divine and human elements in John's writing of Scripture. What he saw and heard from God passed through his human personality.

2. The end time equals a return to the beginning of time. After the judgment, a new era will dawn, which will be a return to the harmony of Eden.

3. **The Holy City, the New Jerusalem** sets up a contrast between Babylon the harlot (ch. 18) and Jerusalem the bride (21:10ff.) By picturing heaven as a holy city, John establishes an ideal for human society. Revelation is not an antiurban book. John's answer to the pagan city of Babylon is a city of God.

4. The word *throne* (22:3) appears in seventeen of the twenty-two chapters. **Throne** denotes the political message of this dramatic contest between the rule of God and the rule of Caesar/Satan. Also, **throne** recalls the scenes before the throne of God in the visions of creation and redemption in chs. 4–5.

5. The parallelism of *skana/skanosei,* **dwelling/he will live** establishes a relationship between God and God's people in 21:3. That corporate relationship has a parallel in the promise of a personal relationship for faithful overcomers (21:7). In opposition to this relationship between God and the church, John contrasts Pergamum as the place where Satan's throne dwells

(2:13). Faithful saints enter into a saving relationship with God.

6. The new era is a time of healing for a church battered by persecution, social stress, and sin. In heaven God acts as an eternal pastor. Heaven is a place of healing for Christians who do not experience physical or emotional wholeness on earth. Revelation relegates tears, death, mourning, crying, and pain to the banished first heaven and first earth. Heaven is a place of healing, not as a mental escape from suffering as Karl Marx accused, but as God's eternal response to earthly suffering. John's church endured sufferings on earth because they believed God would soon act on their behalf to end their stress and bring eternal victory. The human spirit can encounter and endure tremendous tension if the mind believes its capacity for survival will not be stretched *ad infinitum*. Sometimes we live not by what we have but by that for which we hope. Heaven is our ultimate hope. That hope supplies stamina during stress.

7. Designating God as **the Alpha and the Omega, the Beginning and the End** continues the tendency to speak of God in terms of time (1:8; 4:8). Revelation abounds with temporal contrasts. As John nears the end of the book, he returns to an initial announcement that punctuates Revelation with a contrast between what is and what is to come.

8. In 22:7–8 a moral contrast is set up between faithful conquerors and faltering compromisers. *Nikon* ("conquering, overcoming") recollects the seven conquering promises in chs. 2–3. The Lamb "has triumphed" (5:5). Martyrs conquer and attain eternal life (12:11; 15:2–3). Yet the leopard beast conquered saints and the evil trinity waged war against the church. Built into the structure of Revelation is a

dualism that creates a moral contrast. Faithful conquerors including God, the Lamb, martyrs, and saints oppose antagonists including the beasts, the serpent, the Dragon, the harlot, and faltering compromisers. These verses contrast the faithful overcomers who received a halo of victory with those who do not enter heaven. Heaven serves an ethical and moral purpose.

With these eight verses, John affirms truths he has taught throughout Revelation.

B. The Holy City (21:9–22:5)

The almost identical language of 17:1 and 21:9 implies that the vision of the heavenly bride is an inversion of the earthly harlot of chs. 17–18. Also, whereas the Spirit transported John into a wilderness because the vision of the harlot's judgment was so gruesome, here the Spirit transports John to a mountain because the vision of **the Holy City** is so grand. God's answer to the polluted city of Babylon/Rome is a holy city.

Does the New Jerusalem symbolize an actual city or the perfected church? Most likely, **the Holy City** symbolizes the sanctified church gathered in heaven, the holy completed church. Symbols of completion saturate the passage. **The glory of God** is a term for God's completion and fullness. John's numbers represent completion. Twelve is a product of the divine number three multiplied by the earthly number four. The **144 cubits** and **12,000 stadia** are products of twelve times twelve, and one thousand times twelve. The twelve names of the tribes of Israel and the twelve apostles represent a fulfillment of Israel within the church. The coming of kings from the nations symbolizes the universal outreach of the church and a fulfillment of the hopes of Ezekiel and Isaiah.

Cities on earth need light from the sun and moon, but in the heavenly city God's presence supplies constant light so that there will be no darkness (21:23; 22:5). Such light contrasts with the absence of light in the evil Babylon (18:23). Being in the presence of God and the Lamb constitutes eternal life for all faithful saints. Just as John stood before God and the Lamb (chs. 4–5), so faithful saints will be in the presence of God and the Lamb. At that time all of life's contradictions will be overcome and understood.

Symbols of purity include the twelve precious stones, the pure gold streets, the twelve pearls, and the fact that no pollutants or perverse persons shall enter the pure city. Whereas Babylon was a dwelling place of demons, unclean spirits, and immoral passions (18:2–3), John depicts the Holy City as a pure place. Although John criticized Babylon/Rome's misuse of wealth in ch. 18, he employs symbols of wealth to signify the value of the Holy City in ch. 21. Wealth is neutral. The worship and misuse of wealth is sinful. Because heaven will be a pure place, Christians aiming for heaven are to overcome sins on earth and to live pure and holy lives.

The Spirit's inspiration enabled John to challenge Jewish and pagan belief systems. The vision contains allusions to OT symbols such as the trees and river of life (Eze 47:1–12), and the demise of the sun because God is light and glory (Eze 39:21; Isa 60:19–20). Obviously John knew Ezekiel's vision for rebuilding Jerusalem and the temple (Eze 40–48). But whereas Ezekiel spent eight chapters diagramming the New Jerusalem, John radically changes Ezekiel's blueprint. John's Holy City does not have a temple. Revelation continues the antitemple tradition found in Jesus, Paul, Luke, and the Gospel of John. For Jesus, destruction of the Jerusalem temple needed to occur before the return of the Son of man (Mk 11:12–21; 13:1–2). According to Luke, Stephen was stoned because he spoke against the temple and announced that God does not dwell in houses made by human hands (Ac 6:13–14; 7:48). Paul defined the bodies of Christians as temples of the Holy Spirit (1Co 3:16; 6:19). In John, Jesus affirmed the universal nature of Christianity by defining worship as occurring in the Spirit rather than limiting worship to a sacred space in Jerusalem (4:21–24). Throughout Revelation John has announced Jesus as the transcendent Lord of all nations (1:7; 11:15). Here he continues to proclaim a universal message by changing the OT traditions, which imparted special significance to the temple in Jerusalem.

John challenged the worldview of paganism. The twelve foundation stones of the city wall are the twelve stones of the ancient zodiac. Pagans looked to the zodiac to guide their destiny because, supposedly, it reflects the order and purpose of life. Because John listed the twelve stones of the zodiac, he evidently knew of the zodiac and the meaning pagans attached to it. But John turned the tables on the pagan search for purpose and order. He listed the stones in the reverse order of their appearance in the zodiac. This reversal suggests that it is the church as the people of God who truly are in touch with the purpose and order of life. Throughout Revelation martyrs and faithful saints experience victory. But the final victory, earlier anticipated in ch. 7, is being in the presence of God forever (22:3–5).

C. Epilogue (22:6–21)

The final fifteen verses make many literary and theological connections to the prologue (1:1–8) and the seven letters (see comments on chs. 2–3). These ties document the interrelatedness of Revelation and are a literary means of affirming a theological truth of apocalyptic literature that the end time will be a return to the beginning time. Beyond these signs of unity, two truths dominate the epilogue.

The text accentuates the authenticity of Revelation. Readers are implored to honor the words in the book (vv.7, 9, 18, 19) because they are **trustworthy and true** and they came to John from God (vv.8, 16). Revelation is to be read and heeded. It is not to be sealed up and stored away (v.10), in contrast to Daniel's visions (Dan 12:4).

John confidently commends the coming of the Lord. The plea **Come, Lord Jesus** invokes as a pregnant prayer, the expectancy emphasized with phrases such as **must soon take place** and **I am coming soon.** If repetition indicates significance, the threefold repetition of **I am coming soon** (vv.7, 12, 20) signals the fervent hope that stands at the center of NT faith. We await the coming of our Lord.

Some circles of Christianity in the late first century were moving away from a belief in the imminent coming of Christ. They were settling in for the long haul and were comparing a day to a thousand years (2Pe 3:8). They were building institutions and adjusting to living alongside the Roman Empire. In contrast, as the final book in the Christian canon, Revelation concludes the NT with the same apocalyptic thrust that characterized Paul as the earliest NT writer (Ro 8:18–25; 13:12; 1Co 15; 1Th 4:13–5:11) and Mark as the first gospel writer. The presence of Revelation in the canon attests the value of apocalyptic theology. Centuries later we still await the second coming of our Lord. Reading Revelation imparts an urgency to our mission and message. It reminds us that history will have a final purpose and meaning in the return of Christ. Until the Lord comes again, Revelation calls the church to follow him rather than any Caesar, to be a holy people, and to attain the promises reserved for faithful overcomers who do not falter in the struggle against sin. **Amen. Come Lord Jesus!**

BIBLIOGRAPHY

Beasley-Murray, George B. *The Book of Revelation.* Grand Rapids: Eerdmans, 1978.

Bence, Clarence. "Processive Eschatology: A Wesleyan Alternative." *Wesleyan Theological Journal* 14, no. 1 (Spring 1979): 45–59.

Blaney, Harvey J.S. "Revelation." WBC. Vol. 6. Grand Rapids: Eerdmans, 1966, 403–523.

Clarke, Adam. *The New Testament of Our Lord and Saviour Jesus Christ.* Vol. 2, Romans to the Revelation. New York: Abingdon-Cokesbury, 1832.

Collins, Adela Yarbro. *The Apocalypse.* Wilmington, Del.: Michael Glazier, 1979.
_____. *Crisis and Catharsis.* Philadelphia: Westminster, 1984.

Dillman, Charles, "In Newness of Life: A Wesleyan Theology of the Kingdom of God." In *The Spirit And The New Age.* Wesleyan Theological Perspectives. Vol. 5. Edited by Alex Deasley and R. Larry Shelton, 513–40. Anderson, Ind.: Warner, 1986.

Earle, Ralph. "Revelation." BBC. Kansas City: Beacon Hill, 1967, 453–629.

Fiorenza, Elisabeth Schüssler. *Justice and Mercy*. Philadelphia: Fortress, 1985.

Hynson, Leon. *To Reform the Nation*. Grand Rapids: Zondervan, 1984.

Mounce, Robert. *The Book of Revelation*. Grand Rapids: Eerdmans, 1977.

Smith, J.B. *A Revelation of Jesus Christ*. Edited by J. Otis Yoder. Scottdale, Pa.: Herald, 1961.

Swete, Henry Barclay. *Commentary on Revelation*. London: Macmillan, 1913. Reprint. Grand Rapids: Kregel, 1977.

Wesley, John. *Explanatory Notes Upon the New Testament*. 18th edition. New York: Eaton and Mains, n.d.

———. *The Journals of John Wesley*. Edited by Nehemiah Curnock. London: Epworth, 1938.